N
E
SHAH
SHIGATSÉ
NGOR
GYANTSÉ
APURNA
TINGRI
HARA
MT. EVEREST
KATHMANDU
PARPING
A
SIKKIM
THIMPHU
GANGTOK
L
BHUTAN

NYOSHUL KHENPO JAMYANG DORJÉ

A MARVELOUS GARLAND OF RARE GEMS

A MARVELOUS GARLAND OF RARE GEMS

Biographies of Masters of Awareness in the Dzogchen Lineage

A Spiritual History of the Teachings of Natural Great Perfection

NYOSHUL KHENPO JAMYANG DORJÉ
Translated by Richard Barron (Chökyi Nyima)

PADMA PUBLISHING
2005

Published by
Padma Publishing
P.O. Box 279
Junction City, CA 96048

Frontispiece photo courtesy of Tertön Sogyal Trust
Endpaper illustrations by Mike Reagan

ISBN 1-881847-41-1

First Printing
Printed in the United States of America

LIBRARY OF CONGRESS CIP DATA

'Jam-dbyaṅs-rdo-rje, Smyo-sul Mkhan-po.
[Rang-bzhin rdzogs-pa chen-po'i chos-'byung rig-'dzin brgyud-pa'i rnam-thar
Ngo-mtshar nor-bu bai-du-rya'i phreng-ba. English.]
A marvelous garland of rare gems: biographies of masters of awareness
in the Dzogchen lineage: a spiritual history of the teachings of
natural great perfection / by Nyoshul Khenpo Jamyang Dorjé;
translated from the Tibetan by Richard Barron (Chökyi Nyima).—1st ed.
p. cm.
Includes index.
ISBN 1-881847-41-1 (9781881847410 : alk. paper)
1. Rñiṅ-ma-pa lamas—China—Tibet—Biography.
2. Tibet (China)—Biography. 3. Rdzogs-chen—History.
I. Barron, Richard, 1952- II. Title.
BQ7662.9.A2J3613 2005
294.3'923'0922—dc22

Contents

Introduction by Sogyal Rinpoché xv

Translator's Preface xliii

The Precious Lamp: Author's Introduction 1

The Precious Mirror: Preliminary Remarks 11

The Precious Lattice: A Synopsis of the Oral Lineage of Dzogchen 16

The Precious Garland: A Supplication to the Lineage of the Secret Nyingtik Teachings of Utter Lucidity 21

Introductory Verses 26

I. THE LINEAGE

1. The Mind-to-Mind Transmission by Victorious Ones 31
   - Samantabhadra 31
   - The Buddhas of the Five Families 31
   - The Twelve Teachers 32
2. The Transmission Through Symbols by Masters of Awareness 37
   - Garab Dorjé 37
   - Mañjushrimitra 38
   - Shri Simha 39
   - Vimalamitra and Jñanasutra 40
   - Padmakara 41
3. The Oral Transmission by Human Individuals 49
   - Kama, the Historical Transmissions: The Categories of Mind and Expanse 49
   - Bairotsana 49
   - Pang Sang-gyé Gönpo (Pang Mipam Gönpo) 51
   - Ngenlam Jangchub Gyaltsen 51

Zadam Rinchenyik 51
Khugyur Salwaichok 52
Katokpa Dampa Deshek and His Students 52

Terma, the Hidden Treasure Transmissions: The Category of Direct Transmission 55
Early History and Guru Padma 55
King Trisong Detsen 57
Other Students of Guru Padma 60
Yeshé Tsogyal 61
Pema Ledrel Tsal 70
Gyalsé Lekpa Gyaltsen 73
Longchen Rabjampa Drimé Özer 75
Other Teachers of the Lineage 76

4. The Lineage of Vimalamitra 78

The More Extensive Lineage: The Category of Direct Transmission 78
Vimalamitra 78
Nyang Tingdzin Zangpo 82
Bé Lodrö Wangchuk 83
Drom Rinchen Bar 84
Dangma Lhundrup Gyaltsen 84
Chetsün Seng-gé Wangchuk 85
Gyalwa Zhangtön Tashi Dorjé 86
Drupchen Khepa Nyima Bum 88
Guru Jober 89
Trulzhik Seng-gé Gyappa 90
Drupchen Melong Dorjé 91
Rigdzin Chenpo Kumaradza 93

5. Longchen Rabjampa Drimé Özer 98

Longchenpa's Outer Biography: Enlightened Form 98
Longchenpa's Inner Biography: Enlightened Speech 131
Longchenpa's Secret Biography: Enlightened Mind 156

6. The Combined Lineages from Longchenpa to Jigmé Gyalwai Nyugu 162
Khenchen Chabdal Lhundrub 162
Gyalsé Tulku Drakpa Özer 163
Trulzhik Sang-gyé Önpo Sherab Gyatso 165
Gyalsé Dawa Drakpa 168
Drupchen Kunzang Dorjé 170

Chöjé Kunga Gyaltsen Palzang 171
Tulku Natsok Rangdrol 172
Tulku Tendzin Drakpa 174
Khedrup Do-ngak Tendzin 176
Rigdzin Chenpo Trinlé Lhundrup 178
Terchen Gyurmé Dorjé (Terdak Lingpa) 181
Gyalsé Rinchen Namgyal 191
Ngak Rabjampa Orgyen Chödrak 194
Ngakyi Rabjampa Orgyen Palgön (Drupwang Shrinatha) 196
Rigdzin Jigmé Lingpa 198
Jigmé Gyalwai Nyugu 216

7. The Lineages of Jigmé Gyalwai Nyugu: Paltrul Rinpoché 223
Paltrul Orgyen Jigmé Chökyi Wangpo 223
Nyoshul Lungtok Tenpai Nyima Gyaltsen Palzangpo (Gyalsé Jangchub Dorjé) 238
Khenchen Ngawang Palzangpo (Khenpo Ngaga, Khenpo Ngakchung, Khenpo Ngagi Wangpo) 247
Lungtrul Shedrup Tenpai Nyima 256
The Second Palyul Drupwang Pema Norbu, Rigdzin Palchen Düpa 260
Dartang Choktrul Chökyi Dawa Rinpoché 263
The Third Palyul Drupwang Pema Norbu, Jigmé Tupten Shedrub Chökyi Drayang (Kyabjé Penor Rinpoché) 265

8. The Lineages of Jigmé Gyalwai Nyugu: Jamyang Khyentsei Wangpo 270
Jamyang Khyentsei Wangpo 270
Dza Pukhung Gyurmé Ngedön Wangpo 280
Dudjom Rinpoché Jigdral Yeshé Dorjé 283
Adzom Drukpa Rinpoché Drodul Pawo Dorjé 290
Jamyang Khyentsé Chökyi Lodrö 296
Dilgo Khyentsé Rinpoché Rabsel Dawa 306
Yukhok Jadralwa Chöying Rangdrol 316

9. The Lineage of Rigdzin Jigmé Lingpa: The Dodrupchen Line of Incarnations 319
The First Dodrupchen, Jigmé Trinlé Özer 319

The Lineage of Dodrupchen's Incarnations 322
The Second Dodrupchen, Jigmé Puntsok Jungné 322
The Third Dodrupchen, Jigmé Tenpai Nyima 323
The Fourth Dodrupchen, Jigmé Trinlé Palbar 326

THE LINEAGE OF THE FIRST DODRUPCHEN'S STUDENTS 338
Chögyal Ngagi Wangpo 338
Zhabkar Tsokdruk Rangdrol 339
Kyabgön Pema Gyatso 342
Dakki Chönyi Zangmo (Shuksep Jetsünma Mani Lochen) 343
Trehorpa Kyabgön Yeshé Gyaltsen 350
Chönyön Dharma Seng-gé 351
Zhadeu Trulzhik Chenpo Ngawang Chökyi Lodrö 352

10. The Students of Longchen Rabjampa 354
THE LINEAGE OF LONGCHENPA'S TEACHINGS 354
Orgyen Chöjé of Drok Valley 354
Guru Ösel Rangdrol 355
Tulku Paljor Gyaltsen 357
Dokhampa Dengom Chödrak Zangpo 357
Khedrup Delek Gyatso 359
Takok Jadral Chöjé Tashi Jungné 360
Guru Zhenpen 360
Namkha Dorjé 361
Ösel Longyang 361
Dzogchenpa Sönam Rigdzin 362
Kunchen Ngawang Pema 362
Dzogchenpa Sönam Wangpo 363
Lhatsün Namkha Jigmé 364
Dzogchenpa Longdzok Tadral 366
THE LINEAGE OF LONGCHENPA'S INCARNATIONS 367
Rigdzin Pema Lingpa 367
The Second Pema Lingpa, Tendzin Chökyi Drakpa (Yenpa Lodé) 368
The Third Pema Lingpa, Kunchen Tsultrim Dorjé 370
The Fourth Pema Lingpa, Dorjé Mikyö Tsal (Ngawang Kunzang Rolpai Dorjé) 371
The Fifth Pema Lingpa, Kunzang Tsewang (Pema Tendzin Drupchok Dorjé) 372
The Sixth Pema Lingpa, Kunzang Tenpai Gyaltsen Palzangpo 373
The Seventh Pema Lingpa, Pema Tendzin (Kunzang Ngawang Chökyi Lodrö) 374
The Eighth Pema Lingpa, Kunzang Dechen Dorjé (Ngedön Tenpai Nyima Palzangpo) 375
The Ninth Pema Lingpa, Tendzin Chökyi Gyaltsen 376

The Tenth Pema Lingpa, Pema Ösel Gyurmé Dorjé (Tupten Chökyi Dorjé) 376
The Eleventh Pema Lingpa, Kunzang Pema Rinchen Namgyal Ngedön Tenpai Nyima 377
Rigdzin Pema Trinlé and the Family Lineages of the Pema Lingpa Tradition 378

11. The Students of Rigdzin Terdak Lingpa 380
The Lineage of Rigdzin Terdak Lingpa's Main Seat 380
Kunzang Mingyur Paldrön 380
Khenchen Oddiyana (Orgyen Tendzin Dorjé) 381
Trichen Gyurmé Trinlé Namgyal 382
Jetsünma Trinlé Chödrön 382
Other Students of Rigdzin Terdak Lingpa 384
Lotsawa Chöpal Gyatso 384
Riksé Choktrul Pema Gyurmé Gyatso 384
Minling Trichen Kunzang Pema Wangyal 385
Katokpa Gyalsé Rinpoché Sönam Detsen 387
The Second Dzogchen Rinpoché, Gyurmé Tekchok Tendzin 388
Barchung Lama Tashi Gyatso 390

12. The Students of Rigdzin Jigmé Lingpa and the First Dodrupchen, Jigmé Trinlé Özer 392
The Students of Rigdzin Jigmé Lingpa 392
Jigmé Kundrol Namgyal 392
Getsé Jigmé Ngotsar Tendzin 393
Other Students of Jigmé Lingpa 395
The Students of the First Dodrupchen, Jigmé Trinlé Özer 395
Do Khyentsé Yeshé Dorjé (Ngakchang Jalü Dorjé) 395
The Fourth Dzogchen Rinpoché, Mingyur Namkhai Dorjé 400
Gemang Gyalsé Rigpai Dorjé (Gyalsé Zhenpen Tayé Özer) 404
Chöying Tobden Dorjé 407
Choklung Repa Damtsik Dorjé 408

13. The Students of Jamyang Khyentsei Wangpo 410
Jamgön Kongtrul Yönten Gyatso Lodrö Tayé 410
Chungtrul Pema Wangchen 415

Mipam Jamyang Namgyal Gyatso 415
Khenchen Jampal Dewai Nyima 425
The Fourth Zhechen Gyaltsap, Gyurmé Pema Namgyal 426
The Fifth Dzogchen Rinpoché, Tupten Chökyi Dorjé 428
Terchen Orgyen Chokgyur Lingpa 431
Urgyen Tulku Rinpoché 435
Negang Chokling, Orgyen Tobgyal, and the Second Dzigar Kongtrul 436
The Third Katok Situ, Kunchen Orgyen Chökyi Gyatso 436
Gyakor Tulku Kunzang Tekchok Tenpai Gyaltsen 440
Drugu Tokden Shakya Shri 442
Lopön Rinpoché Lama Sönam Zangpo 443
Ritrul Rigdzin Chögyal and Namkha Drimé Rabjam 445
Jedrung Jampa Jungné 446
Kangyur Rinpoché Longchen Yeshé Dorjé 447

14. The Students of Adzom Drukpa Rinpoché and Yukhok Jadralwa Chöying Rangdrol 450

The Students of Adzom Drukpa Rinpoché 450
Gyalsé Gyurmé Dorjé 450
Druktrul Rinpoché 454
Khen Rinpoché Karma Dorjé 454
Tarthang Tulku Kunga and Zurmang Trungpa Rinpoché 455
Tsö Paltrul Rinpoché 456
Sertar Rinpoché 457
Golok Lama Kunzang 458

The Students of Yukhok Jadralwa Chöying Rangdrol 459
Rakor Khen Drimé Özer 459
Gyarong Tsöndrü 460

15. The Students of Jamyang Khyentsé Chökyi Lodrö and Other Masters 462

The Students of Jamyang Khyentsé Chökyi Lodrö 462
Lakar Sögyal Choktrul Rinpoché 462
Sakya Khen Rinpoché Appey 463
Other Living Masters 463
Katok Öntrul Rinpoché 464

The Students of Dudjom Rinpoché, Dilgo Khyentsé Rinpoché, and Others 464

16. The Students of Paltrul Rinpoché 465
Tendzin Drakpa 465
The Second Katok Situ, Chökyi Lodrö 465
Minyak Kunzang Sönam 466
Dzogchen Khenchen Pema Dorjé 467
Golok Lang Lama Tupten Chökyi Jorpa 468

Khenchen Yönten Gyatso and His Students 469
Khenchen Yönten Gyatso 469
Changma Khenchen Tupten Chöpel 471
Washul Mewai Khenchen Tsewang Rigdzin 472
Khenchen Jigmé Puntsok 475

Khenchen Kunzang Palden Chödrak and His Students 476
Khenchen Kunzang Palden Chödrak 476
Bötrul Do-ngak Tenpai Nyima 479
Mewa Khenchen Tupten 480
Rahor Khenchen Tupten 481
Khen Rinpoché Pema Tsewang Lhundrup (Khenpo Petsé) 481
Khen Chöchap 482
Orgyen Tendzin Norbu 482

17. The Students of Orgyen Tendzin Norbu 487
The Personal Transmission for Spiritual Practice 487
Dergé Lama Kunga Palden 487
Apang Terchen Orgyen Trinlé Lingpa 488
Jangchub Dorjé 491

The Personal Transmission for the Explanatory Teachings 492
Zhenga Dorjé Chang (Zhenpen Chökyi Nangwa) 492
Palpung Tai Situ Rinpoché Pema Wangchok Gyalpo 500
Zurmang Khenchen Pema Namgyal 500
Zurmang Tenga Rinpoché 501
The First Dzigar Kongtrul Rinpoché 501
Bo Gangkar Rinpoché (Karma Shedrup Chökyi Seng-gé) 501
Nyarong Guru Tulku 501
Drukpa Geshé Tenpa Rinchen 502
Other Students 502
Khenchen Tsöndrü 503
Nyoshul Khenchen Ngawang Palzang Rinpoché 504

Tuksé Serkha Chödrak 504
Rahor Palden Chökyi Drakpa 504
Khunu Rinpoché Tendzin Gyaltsen 506
Tuksé Doring Choktrul Rinpoché 507

18. The Students of Nyoshul Lungtok Tenpai Nyima 508
Khen Rinpoché Dorjé Dzinpa Tobden (Tupten Gyaltsen Özer) 508
Naktar Tulku Sönam Chokdrup 509
Lhazang Lama Rigdzin 510
Sa-ngen Lama Wangchen 510
Lama Ngakchen (Orgyen Tutop Lingpa) 511
Terchen Lerab Lingpa (Tertön Sögyal) 513
Pema Gyaltsen 514
Dretsé Tulku 515
Sungtrul Kunzang Nyima 515

19. The Students of Khenchen Ngawang Palzang 517
Katok Chaktsa Rinpoché 517
Tromgé Choktrul Arik Rinpoché 519
Khen Lama Rinpoché Achuk (Drupwang Lungtok Gyatso) 521
Khen Rinpoché Lekshé Jorden (Khenchen Dulwai Dé) 522
Khenchen Nüden Khyentsei Lodrö 523
Khenchen Yizhin Norbu Tupten Gyaltsen Özer 523
Golok Khenchen Munsel 524
Choktrul Garwang Nyima Rinpoché 526
Pema Tumpo (Orgyen Kusum Lingpa) 527
Golok Lama Garchö 527
Choktrul Orgyen Chemchok 527
Choktrul Sang-ngak Tendzin (Tulku Sang-ngak) 528
Trakya Lama Rinpoché Palden 528
Polu Khen Rinpoché Dorjé 530
Taklung Tsetrul Rinpoché 532
Chatral Rinpoche Sanjé Dorjé 533
Tersé Chimé Rinpoché 534
Bairo Rinpoché 536
Lama Rinpoché Orgyen Rigdzin 536

20. The Students of Lungtrul Shedrup Tenpai Nyima 539
Khen Ngawang Palzang Yangsi Rinpoché (Tekchok Tenpai Gyaltsen) 539

Choktrul Nyima Gyaltsen Rinpoché 540
Dragyab Lama Chöden Rinpoché 541
Jokhang Choktrul Rinpoché 541

21. A Summary of the Nyingtik Lineage 544

22. The Transmission of the Teachings of the Early Translation School 547

THE FOUNDING OF NYINGMA CENTERS 549

THE SIX MAJOR MONASTERIES 550
Tupten Dorjé Drak 550
Ogmin Orgyen Mindroling 550
Palri Tekchok Ling 551
Dzogchen Rudam Orgyen Samten Chöling 551
Zhechen Tennyi Dargyé Ling 552
Pal Katok Dorjéden 553
Palyul Namgyal Jangchub Chöling 554

II. THE INSTRUCTIONS

23. The Tantras That Concern the Supreme Secret 559

THE CATEGORY OF MIND (SEM DÉ) 559
THE CATEGORY OF EXPANSE (LONG DÉ) 560
THE CATEGORY OF DIRECT TRANSMISSION (MEN-NGAK DÉ) 560

24. The Three Phases of Ground, Path, and Fruition 566

GROUND 566
PATH 570
FRUITION 577

III. CONCLUSION

Prayers of Dedication, Aspiration, and Auspicious Wishes 593

Colophon 598

Afterword 601

Appendix: Lineage Diagrams 603

Notes 615

Index 671

Introduction
by Sogyal Rinpoché

It is an honor, and a blessing, to introduce this extraordinary work, Nyoshul Khenpo Jamyang Dorjé's definitive history of the teachings of Dzogpachenpo, the "Natural Great Perfection." For me, this is a moving and yet a daunting task, because Nyoshul Khenpo was one of my most beloved teachers. Long before I ever received teachings from him, I had heard of his reputation; what I learned was that, after the very greatest Dzogchen masters of our time, such as Kyabjé Dudjom Rinpoché and Kyabjé Dilgo Khyentsé Rinpoché, Nyoshul Khenpo was the most outstanding and knowledgeable exponent of Dzogpachenpo, the summit and heart of the teachings of the ancient Nyingma tradition of Tibetan Buddhism brought to Tibet in the eighth or ninth century by the great Guru Padmasambhava.

I came to discover that everything they had said about Nyoshul Khenpo was accurate. He was indeed someone who had about him the unmistakable air of the great masters of the past I had been fortunate to know closely: Jamyang Khyentsé Chökyi Lodrö, Dudjom Rinpoché, and Dilgo Khyentsé Rinpoché. Like them, he had actually made real within his experience the truth of the teaching of Dzogpachenpo. This must have been the reason for his amazing presence—that spaciousness and lightness that everyone remarked on, that fathomless depth that seemed to go on forever and to know no kind of end or limit. When you were with Nyoshul Khenpo, you felt yourself irresistibly gathered into the well of total relaxation and peace that existed at the core of his being. A great aura of warmth, tenderness, and humor surrounded him, and all of his students knew his intense kindness. I will always remember the meticulous care, the profound love that he showed us, each and every one.

As Nyoshul Khenpo revealed himself to me more and more over the years, I was astounded to find that there were simply no bounds to the depth of his understanding or the expanse of his knowledge of the teachings. On the one hand, he had an unparalleled grasp of the teachings of Dzogchen, their systematic structure and unique vocabulary, and on the other, he had all the experience and unshakable certainty of a great Dzogchen yogi. At the same time, he possessed such a complete command of all the schools of Tibetan Buddhism, and of both sutras and tantras, that I was tempted to think of him alongside those towering figures who inspired the Rimé, "nonpartisan," renaissance of Buddhadharma in nineteenth-century Tibet.

In paying homage to Nyoshul Khenpo, I will quote some brief excerpts from the oral teachings he gave to me or the Rigpa sangha over the years. But first, it seems fitting that in this book, which comprises a collection of biographies of the vidyadhara masters of the Dzogchen lineage, some glimpses should be included of Khenpo's own remarkable life story. After all, he too was a vidyadhara—"a holder of pure awareness, or *rigpa*"—and a figure of vital importance in the transmission of this lineage to the masters of the present day.[1]

I remember an evening in the French Alps in 1989, during one of the annual retreats that I hold with my students, when Khenpo told me the story of his life. The parts of it that I had come across before in his commentaries on his poetic songs of realization had not really prepared me for the impact of the entire story. After I left his house, I wandered home under the August moon, stunned by the sheer drama and range of his experiences, which outdid any movie screenplay you could ever imagine. He had been born into a poor family in the Nyarong district of eastern Tibet. According to the Tibetan calendar, it was on the tenth day of the Monkey month in the year of the Water Monkey, a day held particularly sacred and celebrated as the anniversary of the birth of Guru Padmasambhava. This was in July 1932. His was a large family. The father and two elder sons made their living as herders, and as a child, Khenpo was sent out into the hills to look after the animals. Yet he had an instinctive yearning to practice dharma, which was encouraged by his mother and his grandmother. In fact, his grandmother had been a disciple of Nyoshul Lungtok Tenpai Nyima, the great holder of Paltrul Rinpoché's transmission of the oral lineage of Dzogchen pith instructions, and it was from her that Khenpo first heard Nyoshul Lungtok's name. When she was young, she had also been a disciple of the famous Dzogchen masters Adzom Drukpa and Nyala Pema Duddul. She used to sit her little grandson in her lap and pull her warm fur wrap around him while she prayed and practiced and talked to him about taking refuge or about the great Nyoshul Lungtok. Khenpo said that meeting the dharma like this so early in life was as if the famous prayer of aspiration by the peerless Dzogchen master Longchen Rabjam were coming true:

> In all my lives, wherever I am born,
> May I obtain the seven qualities of birth in higher realms.
> As soon as I am born, may I come across the dharma
> And have the freedom to practice it correctly.

[1] I am grateful to Tulku Pema Wangyal Rinpoché for clarifying a number of historical details, and also to Drupwang Tsoknyi Rinpoché and Mingyur Rinpoché for contributing some of their own memories about Nyoshul Khenpo.

Then, may I please the sacred lama
And put the dharma into action day and night.
May I realize the dharma, actualize its innermost meaning,
And so cross the ocean of existence in this very life.
May I teach the sacred dharma to beings wandering in samsara
And never tire or grow weary of working to help others.
Through my vast and impartial service to others,
May all beings attain buddhahood together, as one!

When Khenpo was small, he actually saw Khenpo Ngakchung (Khenpo Ngawang Palzang, 1879–1941), who was Nyoshul Lungtok's principal disciple and an emanation of Vimalamitra, when he came to the area to give the empowerments of *Nyingtik Yabzhi (The Four Higher Collections of the Heart Drop)*. As a young boy, Khenpo loved to dress up in the robes of a dharma practitioner, no matter how much people made fun of him. At the age of five, he took refuge with the incarnation of Katok Getsé Mahapandita, and three years later enrolled in the local Sakya monastery. He began to learn to read with the head lama, Jamyang Tapké, a distant relative who had been a disciple of the legendary teachers Jamgön Loter Wangpo and Khenpo Zhenga. Once more, he took care of the livestock and tended the sheep out in the open on the slopes, beneath the vast sky of Kham. He used to go out begging for alms, fending off the ferocious guard dogs with a stout staff he carried with him.

Khenpo then went to study with an outstanding master of Mahamudra and Dzogchen, Rigdzin Jampal Dorjé. He practiced *ngöndro,* and *shamatha* and *vipashyana* meditation, with a special emphasis on bodhichitta. So poor was he at this time that when he came to the practice of mandala offering, he had to make do with a flat piece of stone from the riverbed, and as he could not afford a single grain of rice, he used river sand. He then began to study texts and to follow the twelve-year training of a khenpo. He committed to memory the thirteen great scriptures, studied hundreds of required texts by Indian and Tibetan scholars, and was appointed a khenpo at the age of twenty-four. He became very learned in both sutras and tantras. By this time, he was receiving empowerments, transmissions, and instructions from many renowned lamas, especially at Katok Monastery. They included Katok Getsé Tulku, Katok Chaktsa Tulku, Choktrul Pema Gyaltsen, Adzom Gyalsé Rinpoché, Gemang Drungpa Tulku, Tromgé Kundun Tulku, Dza Ling Ru Khachö Tulku, Tromgé Khachö Tulku, Tromgé Arik Tulku, and Jamyang Khyentsé Chökyi Lodrö.

Nyoshul Khenpo counted twenty-five great masters as his principal teachers, among whom the most central to his life was Lungtok Shedrup Tenpai Nyima (1920–?), the reincarnation of Nyoshul Lungtok and dharma heir of Khenpo Ngakchung. Khenpo served as his attendant for three years, and at the age of seventeen or eighteen, he began to receive from him the teachings of *Longchen Nyingtik (The*

Heart Drop of Longchenpa), and particularly "the great oral lineage of pith instructions" of Dzogpachenpo. This became Khenpo's special lineage, a lineage that stretched back to the primordial buddha Samantabhadra in an unbroken line of extraordinary masters. He received this rare and precious teaching from Shedrup Tenpai Nyima some thirteen or fourteen times, absorbing everything in great detail—meditation instructions, explanatory teachings, investigation, and pith instructions—while practicing intensively in retreat.

Khenpo was well known for his determination when it came to practice. However arduous the conditions, he would never slacken or give up. In the experience-oriented training (*nyong tri*) of the oral lineage and the approach of Paltrul Rinpoché, the master gives the student an instruction and then sends him or her away to practice and master it; only then does the student return for clarification or for the next phase of the teaching. In the case of Khenpo, it was he who set the time frame, reappearing only when he had thoroughly experienced and accomplished the master's instruction. Shedrup Tenpai Nyima would joke, "With Jamdor [as Khenpo was known], we don't have to worry. He sets the pace of the schedule himself." Khenpo received the entire transmission of this lineage from his master, who then told him he had given him everything that he knew. Khenpo was regarded by many as Shedrup Tenpai Nyima's main lineage holder in the great oral lineage of pith instructions. He spent years practicing in the mountains, in caves or forests, and even in a depression in the snow under a tree, and came to a complete experiential realization of the teachings.

Khenpo was also to master the teachings of Lamdré, the Six Yogas of Naropa, *Kalachakra,* and Chö. He trained in all the eight great traditions, or "chariots," of Buddhadharma prevalent in Tibet, and by the age of twenty-five he had completed his study and practice. In Tibet he was revered, so much so that people looked upon him as a *mahasiddha*. As many people knew, Khenpo had been recognized by a number of lamas as an emanation of Katok Situ, Orgyen Chökyi Gyatso (1880–1923?), who was a nephew and disciple of Jamyang Khyentsei Wangpo and the teacher of Jamyang Khyentsé Chökyi Lodrö.

When tragedy overtook Tibet in 1959, Khenpo made a narrow escape. As the southern border was closed, the party he was with headed from Kham toward the north and then west through Changgyu. For months they hurried on in terror, desperate for food, evading attacks by land and air, and witnessing destruction and carnage everywhere. Khenpo carried a scar where he had been grazed by a bullet. Instead of continuing westward into Kashmir and Ladakh, they turned south and crossed into western Nepal, near Mustang. Of the nine hundred people in the group that had set off from Nyarong, fewer than thirty eventually struggled alive into Nepal. This experience made a lasting impression on Khenpo, heightening the profound sense of impermanence that haunted him all of his life. He always used to wonder if in a year's time he would still be alive, and it seemed to him a constant source of surprise that he had lived so long.

From Nepal, Khenpo went quickly to the Himalayan region of west Bengal and the hill town of Kalimpong. Because of his connections with Katok Monastery, he was appointed tutor to the young Katok Zhingkyong Rinpoché. This was early in 1960. Later, Khenpo would marvel at the fantastic extremes he had known in his life, sometimes presiding on a golden throne giving teachings and empowerments to incarnate lamas (*tulkus*) and huge assemblies, sometimes living in great simplicity, sometimes mingling with the *sadhu* renunciants in Rishikesh on the banks of the River Ganges, and once finding himself washing the dishes in a hotel in Calcutta. And yet whatever happened, he would say, it only reinforced his trust in the unfailing wisdom, compassion, and power of the Buddha, dharma, and sangha.

One thing you noticed about Khenpo was that he treated everybody with kindness, no matter who they were. He was known for his pure perception, for seeing the good in people, whoever they might be, and for showing love and compassion to absolutely everyone he met. Though his learning and realization set him apart from others, he never acted proud in the slightest way or ignored anyone. If he was with members of a royal family, he never appeared to be in awe of them or intimidated at all. If an important official came to see him, looking very impressive, Khenpo seemed to grow in stature and outshone everyone with his presence. Yet if a poor beggar came to see him, or someone so destitute he had hardly anything to eat or drink, Khenpo would treat that person with such sympathy that anyone watching would think he was talking to one of his oldest friends. He would not allow anyone to be overlooked or turned away because he or she was deemed to be unimportant. I noticed that even when my humblest students would send him personal letters, he unfailingly took the time to write a reply.

In exile, Khenpo received teachings from Kyabjé Dudjom Rinpoché and Kyabjé Dilgo Khyentsé Rinpoché, whom he called in his poems "the two incomparably great tertöns" and who both urged him to write this history of the Dzogchen lineage. From Kyabjé Dudjom Rinpoché, for example, he received the transmission of the Nyingma kama and most of the Nyingma tantra teachings, especially the *Guhyagarbha Tantra* (*The Heart Essence of Secrets*), with Longchenpa's commentary the *Chok Chui Munsel* (*Dispelling Darkness in the Ten Directions*), Lochen Dharma Shri's two commentaries the *Sangdak Gong Gyen* (*The Ornament of the Lord of Secrets' Enlightened Intent*) and *Sangdak Zhal Lung* (*The Oral Transmission of the Lord of Secrets*), and a commentary by a khenpo from Nyarong that Dudjom Rinpoché had requested and of which he was the only holder. He also received Khenpo Yönga's two commentaries on Rigdzin Jigmé Lingpa's *Yönten Dzöd* (*The Treasury of Enlightened Qualities*). These transmissions took place over about three years beginning in 1960, and then from 1967 to 1969, when Khenpo would go every summer to study with Dudjom Rinpoché.

From 1967 until the early 1970s, Khenpo served as the head of the Katok community in Dehra Dun. Gradually, masters such as the sixteenth Gyalwang Karmapa, Kyabjé Dudjom Rinpoché, H.H. Sakya Trizin, Kyabjé Tai Situ Rinpoché, and Kyabjé Penor Rinpoché invited him to serve as khenpo in their monasteries. In the 1970s, he spent three years at Penor Rinpoché's monastery in Mysore, South India. At the time, the Ngagyur Nyingma Institute, the college for higher Buddhist studies that is now so famous, was just beginning, and he was instrumental in its development. Thousands of people would attend his teachings, and he became a central figure in the community that was gathering around Penor Rinpoché.

Then Kyabjé Dudjom Rinpoché invited him to give the oral transmission of the Kangyur—"The Words of the Buddha"—in Kalimpong. At the time, he was well known there for the beauty of his voice, his charisma, and his eloquence when he taught. Unfortunately, while he was in Kalimpong, he fell very seriously ill. For three years, from 1975 to 1977, he was incapacitated and was cared for by the family of the late Kyabjé Kangyur Rinpoché at their monastery in Darjeeling. The distress of these years comes through in a few of his poems of the time. For Khenpo, the paramount source of inspiration and refuge was always the great Dzogchen master Longchenpa (Longchen Rabjam, 1308–1364), to whom he called out constantly during these harrowing years. He told me later, "Only one thing—the blessings and the power of the dharma—has kept me alive. Otherwise I would have gone long ago." During this period, however, he was able to continue compiling his history.

Deeply concerned about Khenpo's health, Kyabjé Dudjom Rinpoché requested the late Queen Mother of Bhutan to take care of him. In 1977 and 1978, he spent quite a long time at the retreat center above the Queen Mother's palace, Dechen Chöling. At the suggestion of the great Bhutanese yogi Lopön Sönam Zangpo, Khenpo married one of his disciples, Damchö Zangmo, a lady who was perfectly suited to him in every way and whose amazing and devoted care without any doubt prolonged his life. All of us who were Khenpo's students came to appreciate her for the simply remarkable way in which she served him.

With the help of the wife of the Home Minister of Bhutan, Kyiduk Lönpo, Khenpo managed to raise the funds for a flight to Switzerland, where a doctor he had met had promised him treatment. He stayed in Switzerland for some time with Tibetan families, before being invited to France and the Dordogne area, where Tulku Pema Wangyal Rinpoché, Kyabjé Kangyur Rinpoché's son, had established the retreat center of Chanteloube. There, in the depths of the French countryside, he stayed once more as a guest of Kyabjé Kangyur Rinpoché's family. With his own hands, he helped the retreatants build the retreat center, and then he visited them and gave them instructions. Yet often he would walk alone in the forest practicing, meeting only deer, rabbits, and wild boar. A close friend at this time was Lama Gendun, the outstanding yogi and teacher who was head of the neighboring Karma Kagyü center. Khenpo was taken to visit Paris and other parts of France, and it was then that he began to form his impressions of life in the West. He was struck by the haste and pressure and emptiness of modern life, and by its countless distractions. In his "Mirror of Essential Points," a letter in praise of *shunyata*[2] written at the time, he said:

> There's an endless variety of spectacles,
> Like patterns all the colors of a rainbow,
> Yet when examined, they're simply the mistaken perceptions of the mind,
> Amounting to no more than a dream.

Khenpo stayed in France for eight years, during which time he was joined by his wife, Damchö. Then, as his health improved slightly, invitations to teach came from many quarters, and Khenpo traveled to India, Nepal, Taiwan, France, Britain, Switzerland, Germany, and the United States. It was during this period that he began to be present and teach at the retreats I was leading for my students in Europe and America. Beginning in the Dordogne in 1984, when both Kyabjé Dudjom Rinpoché and Kyabjé Dilgo Khyentse Rinpoché gave teachings, he visited us regularly during all our retreats in France, the United States, Great Britain, and Germany. To me it seemed he was always there to give his support during many of the most important moments as I endeavored to teach the dharma in the West—for example, when His Holiness the Dalai Lama accepted our request to give Dzogchen teachings in Paris in 1982; when he gave Dzogchen teachings in San Jose, California, in 1989; when Kyabjé Dilgo Khyentsé Rinpoché gave some of the most important Dzogchen empowerments and transmissions at Prapoutel near Grenoble, France, in 1990; and during the Dalai Lama's inauguration of Dzogchen Monastery in South India in 1992.

On two occasions, Khenpo returned to Tibet: with Kyabjé Dilgo Khyentsé Rinpoché in 1990 and with Kyabjé Penor Rinpoché in 1992. By that time, he had taken up residence in Thimphu in Bhutan, where he had many disciples and where he could be near the sites sacred to Longchenpa, such as Tarpa Ling, the monastery he founded in Bumthang in the fourteenth century during his ten-year exile in Bhutan.

In 1987 it was my supreme good fortune to begin to receive personal teachings formally from Nyoshul Khenpo. It was when he taught that he took on the most extraordinary presence. His voice, affected by a throat condition, was reduced to a whisper, which gave his words an unforgettable air of intimacy. Without any effort, he would create an almost tangible atmosphere of sacredness and enchantment. Many are the lamas I have spoken to who have said that in his presence they experienced a sudden

[2] [Translated in this volume as "emptiness."—R.B.]

clarity of mind, a freedom from conceptual thoughts. Or else they felt he read their minds, and found themselves uncomfortably aware of what they were thinking and naturally inclined to be particularly mindful when they were with him. Many times it would happen that if they were puzzled and uncertain about a particular point in the teachings, the very next day Khenpo would immediately clarify it, without their having to ask. If they were on the point of telling him about their meditation experience, before the words could come out of their mouths, he would have anticipated what they were going to say, and Khenpo's confirmation at that instant would give them more conviction than anything on earth.

Receiving teachings from him used to conjure up images of the legendary khenpos of the past, like those who gathered around Dzogchen Monastery from the time of Paltrul Rinpoché onward, the kind who taught Khunu Lama Tendzin Gyaltsen and Khenpo Jigmé Puntsok Rinpoché. I used to imagine that they must have been just like him. I felt convinced that once you had received the teachings from him, you did not need to seek them anywhere else.

When he taught from the pith instructions of Dzogchen, Khenpo would quote the sutras—the Buddha's own words—and the tantras, and then bring in the crucial points of the *upadesha*s (pith instructions), and finally speak from his own experience. Each quotation would be clear and exact, and he would never pause or hesitate. He would direct his gaze into space, and then the teaching would flow from his wisdom mind with tremendous clarity and precision, as if he were reading from some beautifully written invisible scripture. It seemed so well constructed and poured out of him like a waterfall. The teaching was so lucid and so complete, it sounded as if he had never forgotten a single word of his masters. He was totally authentic, and he insisted on the unique vocabulary of Dzogpachenpo and the specific nuances of its terminology. Yet he also brought out the meaning of each experience. And when you listened, you had no other thought in your mind, as if all grasping had dissolved.

Whenever he meditated, Khenpo would sit in the perfect seven-point posture of Vairochana, and his eyes would never close, even if he sat for an hour. His gaze did not waver at all. Some said that this must have been a sign that his wisdom mind was never separate from the *dharmata,* the intrinsic nature of reality.

In the case of the Dzogchen teachings, Khenpo would always take enormous care at the outset to establish the correct attitude and frame of mind, for as he used to say, "In the past, during the time of the great masters, never did a teacher give the teaching of Dzogpachenpo, nor did a student receive it, in an ordinary frame of mind." He once explained to me:

> With the great masters of the past, this approach resulted in some really extraordinary situations. For example, when Jigmé Gyalwai Nyugu was teaching Dzogchen, all the beings living in the same valley, even the animals, fell

into a natural state of meditation, quite spontaneously. When Dzogchen Paltrul Rinpoché was teaching the *The Three Cycles of Being at Ease* (*Ngalso Korsum*), he and all those who were listening experienced their minds merging as one, so that everyone enjoyed the same state of mind. When Nyoshul Lungtok Tenpai Nyima was teaching in a certain region, granting the transmission for all the Dzogchen tantras, it is said that the people present, master and students, all arrived at an experience of the primordial state. And when Khenpo Ngawang Palzang (Khenpo Ngakchung) was teaching Dzogchen in his private room, teacher and disciples all experienced a merging of their minds, so that they were of one indivisible realization—which is to say that they all arrived at the experience of the fundamentally unconditioned nature that is Dzogpachenpo, the Great Perfection.

In every one of these instances, the reason this took place was that the individuals concerned were not entertaining any kind of ordinary thoughts or concepts. Their ordinary grasping at mundane perceptions had ceased entirely, allowing them to arrive at the immediate experience of Dzogchen, the fundamentally uncontrived nature of mind. It was while they remained without wavering from that recognition that the teaching took place.

In fact, one of my very own root gurus, Lama Orgyen Rigdzin, told me that when he requested these teachings from his master, he asked him about such occurrences. The lama replied, "Well, that does happen in our case from time to time. But when a really great master, a truly compassionate master like Nyoshul Lungtok, teaches Dzogchen, what occurs every single time is that the master and students experience their minds blending, so that they are all of one mind, with no separation. This is because the actual meaning of Dzogpachenpo has been directly introduced, and people are able to arrive at the very experience of the unconditioned natural state, or 'way of abiding,' as it is called. From that point on, any doubts or speculations that they have in their minds are cut through."

Khenpo always placed enormous emphasis on the purity of motivation and the attitude of bodhichitta, and he would teach on it again and again. His whole character and life in fact embodied the spirit of compassion and altruism. What struck everyone, and especially the lamas, was his complete freedom from the eight worldly concerns: the hope for happiness, gain, praise, and fame, and the fear of sorrow, loss, criticism, and obscurity. There was nothing frivolous about him, absolutely no pretense, and what he taught was pure dharma. Often he would stop a teaching in the middle and ask his students to recheck their motivation. He would recount how Paltrul Rinpoché gave his students three chances to frame the correct motivation before he taught. First, a gong would wake them up at about 3 a.m.; this was called "the motivation gong." Next, as they came to Paltrul Rinpoché's tent, they had to squeeze through a deliberately narrow gap devised between the entrance to the enclosure and a stupa; this was the second chance. Finally, at the beginning of the teaching, Paltrul Rinpoché would invite his students to change their motivation. This was the third chance, and if they missed this, they were asked to leave.

Khenpo would quote the buddha Maitreya's famous definition of bodhichitta in the *Abhisamayalankara (The Ornament of Higher Realization)*—"Arousing bodhichitta is: for the sake of others, longing to attain complete enlightenment"—and observe:

> These days, people don't have much grasp or understanding of what bodhichitta really is. With lay people, this is understandable, but even lamas and monks who claim to be learned and adept at practice don't have a thorough understanding. If you ask them what "arousing bodhichitta" means, they will simply reply, "May all sentient beings have happiness and be free of suffering," which is actually only a prayer of aspiration. Others who are slightly better informed will begin, "For the sake of all sentient beings, as limitless as space, . . ." which indicates limitless compassion and love, but *not* bodhichitta. However much merit it may generate, if it is not focused on complete enlightenment, then it is not complete bodhichitta. Whatever your practice or its merit, it will not be the cause for enlightenment. . . . That is why you need to train again and again in the correct way of arousing bodhichitta.

Khenpo would explain the specifically Dzogchen understanding of bodhichitta motivation:

> What is arousing bodhichitta according to the uncommon approach of Dzogchen? This is something that is not even mentioned in the other vehicles. It is "summoning forth or evoking mind as wisdom." There is a difference between "generating bodhichitta using the mind" and "summoning forth or evoking mind as wisdom." What is the uniqueness of generating the heart of the enlightened mind "as wisdom"? It begins from the same premise as the motivation of the sutra vehicle, from the realization that "all sentient beings who do not realize shunyata and who are deluded wander endlessly in the ocean of samsara." But the key point here is that all these sentient beings are recognized as having within themselves inherent wisdom, self-abiding dharmakaya—the self-knowing rigpa, the unity of space and wisdom, that is the actual lama who is the all-pervasive sovereign, the glorious primordial buddha Samantabhadra. That actually resides within us all, and so we wish: "May I be able to bring all sentient beings to the level where they realize this."
>
> You could also call this intrinsic wisdom "self-arising rigpa" or "buddha

> nature," but whatever term you use, according to Dzogchen it exists spontaneously within all sentient beings, without ever wavering or fluctuating. It is because they fail to see or realize this that beings are deluded and cling dualistically to concepts of "self" and "others." So our aspiration is to bring them to the primordially pure level of Samantabhadra. However, this is not the attainment of enlightenment as something separate, or some buddhahood to be achieved, as it were, from outside, since it already exists within them. Rather, it is a question of actualizing the wisdom that they already possess within themselves.

Once I asked Khenpo exactly how he had become so realized, and he replied with his usual humility, "I don't have any deep understanding; I just prayed to the lama." He would often speak of the power of devotion and prayer to evoke the realization of the innermost, essential nature of the mind. It was in this context that he told me a story that I shall never forget. It concerns Polu Khenpo Dorjé, a truly great Dzogchen master, whose life is described in this book. He was born near Dergé and received teachings from many masters, including Jamyang Khyentsé Chökyi Lodrö. But his main teacher was Khenpo Ngakchung, who granted him the teachings of the oral lineage of Dzogchen and empowered him as a holder of "the ultimate lineage of realization." After Polu Khenpo went into exile, he spent a lot of time in Bhutan. Shortly after Nyoshul Khenpo had arrived from Tibet, Polu Khenpo was talking to him about the different masters they had known. He mentioned one particular yogi, whom everyone thought was completely mad, and explained that this yogi had been one of his root masters. Nyoshul Khenpo was surprised, as he knew of the yogi but did not know that he was a master. Then Polu Khenpo told this story.

It took place not long after Polu Khenpo had received the complete transmission of the instructions of the oral lineage directly from Khenpo Ngakchung. He was still a young man, and because he had been introduced to the nature of mind and felt he had received all the instructions, he was almost overconfident. It was then that he met this mad yogi and straightaway sensed an uncanny connection with him. No one else took the yogi seriously, but Polu Khenpo knew there was something special about him. He decided that here lay an opportunity for him to clarify his meditation.

He began by trying to coax the yogi into teaching him, but he could not seem to engage him in any way, and the yogi was so unresponsive it was as if he was not even there. Finally, in frustration Polu Khenpo grabbed him and blurted out, "Look, even if you are not going to tell me in words, at least give me a sign by nodding your head. I am going to sit in the nature of my mind. Just tell me, please, I implore you, whether I have got it right or not." The yogi gave some indication that he had registered his request, at which point Polu Khenpo tried to sit in his best state of rigpa, which had just been freshly introduced to him by Khenpo Ngakchung. He sat there. A few minutes went by, and the yogi shook his head. Polu Khenpo gathered himself together and tried to sit once more. But again the yogi shook his head wistfully from side to side.

Once this had happened two or three times, Polu Khenpo was overtaken by a tremendous feeling of sadness. All his confidence seemed to seep away, and as his spirits sank lower and lower, he began, with all his heart, to pray to Khenpo Ngakchung and the masters of the lineage, begging for their inspiration and for some confirmation that all his study and practice had not been fruitless and that his realization was genuine.

A tremendous wave of devotion erupted inside him, and tears began to run down his face. He was so immersed in that rapture of devotion that he forgot everything. He forgot his mind; he even forgot about the yogi. He lost track of time altogether, until suddenly he became aware of someone tugging at his sleeve. He opened his eyes and saw the yogi, leaning toward him, with a broad smile on his face. His head was nodding vigorously up and down.

What Nyoshul Khenpo showed through this story was that guru yoga and devotion are the most direct and powerful ways to evoke the view of Dzogpachenpo. He said once in a teaching he gave us:

> According to Dzogchen, and the special approach of the great Dzogchen master Shri Singha, there is a way of recognizing the nature of mind solely through devotion. There are cases of practitioners who simply through their heartfelt devotion attained realization, even though their teacher had already passed away or was nowhere near them physically. Because of their prayers and devotion, the nature of mind was introduced. The classic example is that of Jigmé Lingpa and his consuming devotion for Longchen Rabjam.

On another occasion, he explained:

> This wisdom mind of Samantabhadra, the primordial buddha, can be received only through the medium of pure faith and devotion. The blessing of Samantabhadra must enter the core of our being, the innermost depths of our heart. According to the causal vehicle of the Sutrayana, you attain realization through purification and the accumulation of merit and wisdom. In the resultant vehicle of the secret mantra Vajrayana, it is through the twin paths of the generation and completion phases of *kyérim* and *dzogrim* that you attain realization. In the path of Dzogchen, true realization can be awakened only through the blessing of the vidyadhara masters of the lineage, and so through the practice of heartfelt devotion and guru yoga. You do not need anything else. If you possess that heartfelt devotion to the lama and the lineage, then you can, and will, receive the blessing of Dzogpachenpo. For when you are able to pray in this way with unwavering devotion, the wisdom

> of realization can arise in your mind, without your having to rely on any other factor as a path.

This extraordinary lineage of Dzogchen, of which Khenpo was such a perfect representative, was what was closest to his heart. His foremost, and constant, concern was that it flourish long into the future, and in his teachings he placed enormous emphasis on its uniqueness as the supreme path to liberation. He once quoted the omniscient Longchenpa's analysis of its special qualities:

> As regards this precious lineage of the unsurpassed secret teaching, because its river of powerful blessings has never ceased flowing, the direct transmission of the profound secret mantra remains unbroken. Because the golden chain of its lineage of pure samaya vows has never been tarnished by breakages, it fulfills every imaginable wish. Because the introduction is by way of direct experience, it is unspoiled by the language of intellectual theory. Because it is verified by scriptures, oral transmissions, and pith instructions, it commands the deepest confidence. And because this lineage of attaining the *siddhi* of realization is uninterrupted, it brings a tremendous infusion of blessings. This, then, is why the lineage of this profound path of the Natural Great Perfection, which leads those of the greatest diligence to awakening in this very life, those of middling diligence to awakening in the bardos, and those of average diligence to awakening in a naturally manifest paradise, is known as "a garland of light, strung with precious wish-fulfilling jewels."

Khenpo would always make a point of drawing out the specific shades of understanding that were particular to Dzogchen. One of these was its explanation of the nature of the Buddha and of the origin of the teachings from the point of view of the three kayas.

> Let us consider all the teachings of the buddhas—all that the buddhas of the past have ever given, all that the buddhas of the future will give, and all that the buddhas of the present are giving. All of this sublime speech of the buddhas can be divided into two kinds of approach. There is the approach in which the path is based on the ordinary mind, which refers to the eight graded vehicles, and there is the single approach that transcends ordinary mind, which is the path of Dzogchen. Gyalwa Longchen Rabjam stated that the teachings of the buddhas fall into these two categories: those conferred by the dharmakaya, in which the path is forged with primordial wisdom, and those conferred by the rupakaya, in which the path is forged with the ordinary mind. To sum up, the teachings given by the dharmakaya teacher comprise the approach that creates the path out of primordial wisdom; those

given by the two kinds of rupakaya constitute the approach that creates the path with the ordinary mind, which in fact is a reference to the eight vehicles. Now, the rupakaya is twofold. The teachings bestowed by the nirmanakaya buddhas constitute the three levels of the dialectical approach, which is based on causes. The teachings bestowed by the sambhogakaya buddhas are the classes of tantra in the secret mantra approach, the path based on the state of fruition or result. This is a general classification of the teachings of the buddhas.

Now, the Dzogchen classification of the teachings differs from that of other approaches. The difference lies in its view that the three kayas—dharmakaya, sambhogakaya, and nirmanakaya—are *identical* in essence. This means that the nirmanakaya Shakyamuni and the dharmakaya Samantabhadra are not two separate buddhas but manifestations of a single state of buddhahood.

Let us look at one explanation that incorporates them both. Our teacher, the lord Buddha, Shakyamuni, awakened into complete buddhahood many eons ago as the dharmakaya Samantabhadra and taught the 6,400,000 Dzogchen tantras. Now, in the case of those disciples who have attained the first level of bodhisattva realization, while they are not able to encounter the dharmakaya Samantabhadra, they can, however, encounter the sambhogakaya. So it was because of their particular circumstances that the tantras of the Vajrayana were presented by the sambhogakaya buddhas. Then, for beginners, who on account of the obscurations imposed by their negative karma and negative emotions are not even able to encounter the sambhogakaya, the Buddha manifested in the form of the nirmanakaya Shakyamuni and taught the approach based on causes, or the dialectical approach.

Nevertheless, Samantabhadra and Shakyamuni are both aspects of a single state of buddhahood. This buddhahood in the context of dharmakaya is Samantabhadra; in the context of sambhogakaya, it is Vajradhara; and in the context of nirmanakaya, it is Shakyamuni. And so we need to understand the three kayas as inseparable. Otherwise we could reach some kind of erroneous conclusion, such as, "Dzogchen is not the teaching of the Buddha Shakyamuni." Misconceptions such as this develop out of ignorance of this inseparability of the three kayas.

We also need to understand that it is in response to individual beings to be guided, and their various levels of understanding, that buddhas manifest as they do. But from the point of view of the actual way in which things are, Samantabhadra, Vajradhara, and Shakyamuni are not three buddhas; they are aspects of a single state of buddhahood.

Let's explain a bit further. If we take the wisdom mind of buddhahood

> itself, we can give it the name "Samantabhadra." However, in the perception of disciples, this dharmakaya of the wisdom mind has no way of manifesting, because Samantabhadra is the wisdom mind itself, not some form manifestation or rupakaya. In other words, because Samantabhadra represents the actual wisdom mind of buddhahood—the very essence, the true nature, of reality—whether we call it "Dzogpachenpo" or "the wisdom mind that is the true nature of reality" or "the primordial lord Samantabhadra," what we are talking about is something that has absolutely no way of manifesting itself in the perceptions of others who are to be guided. Rather, as we saw, it is the wisdom mind of buddhahood itself, the utterly pure essence, what we call "Samantabhadra" or often "the original buddha."
>
> You could say that this original buddha's emanations are the forms that manifest when the splendid merit of those to be guided meets the emanating force of Samantabhadra, resulting in the sambhogakaya manifestations of the buddhas of the five families. But without the total purity of dharmakaya, these sambhogakaya emanations could not come about in the first place, so we can say that *these two* are, in essence, one.
>
> "Well, yes," you might say, "but aren't they separate, really?" Only from the point of view of manifestation is there an apparent separateness; from the point of view of their ultimate essence, there is no separateness at all. On account of the converging of the power of the students' merit with the power of Samantabhadra's aspirations, an auspicious interdependence takes place. It is like leaving a bowl of water out at night beneath the moonlit sky; a reflection of the moon will appear in the water. Without these circumstances coming together, this interdependence cannot happen, but when they do, the reflection of the moon shines on the surface of the water. In the very same way, because of the force of Samantabhadra's aspiration, motivation, and miraculous powers, and because of the merit of beings on both bodhisattva and beginner levels, the two kinds of rupakaya—sambhogakaya and nirmanakaya—can and do manifest and present the teachings.

Of all the amazing qualities of the Dzogchen tradition, Nyoshul Khenpo used to highlight the purity and authenticity of this "ultimate lineage of realization," which has been its hallmark and kept it alive, in its full strength, down to the present day:

> In the case of the Dzogchen teachings and the great oral lineage of pith instructions, from the time of the primordial buddha until today, the lineage has continued unbroken and unimpaired. If we trace the lineage back to the primordial buddha Samantabhadra, or even simply to the omniscient Longchenpa, we have tangible signs of this lineage in this world—for example, the Ngadrama ("Looks Like Me") statue of Longchenpa and the paintings

and other representations of him that exist. In the case of Guru Rinpoché, there are the five major *kutsap,* or "representative" images, the "twenty-five *kutsap*" images, and others. In the case of Samantabhadra, there are various paintings, statues, and so on. All of these constitute representations of enlightened form.

As for representations of enlightened speech, we have such treatises by Longchenpa as *The Seven Treasuries* and *The Three Cycles of Being at Ease.* Originally there were the 6,400,000 stanzas of the Dzogchen tantras, which came into this human world and are found in tantras such as the seventeen Dzogchen tantras. These have not disappeared or diminished, but still exist in this world; they are to be found in *The Collected Tantras of the Nyingma School.*

As for enlightened mind, there is a well-known saying in the teachings: "Confer the enlightened intention on the fortunate child." What this refers to is the transmission of the realization of this ultimate wisdom mind by the master to the student. But this does not happen for just any ordinary person. A number of circumstances have to come together, in terms of how the master and the student interact: there are the *authentic* teachings, or pith instructions; there is the master, who has the *authentic* blessing of the lineage; and there is the student, who has *authentic* faith and devotion. When these three "authentics" come together, the realization of Dzogpachenpo, the Great Perfection, can awaken in the student's mindstream.

When it does so, it means that the person who has received the transmission has had this wisdom mind conferred on him or her. For example, some seven hundred years ago, when the omniscient Longchenpa passed on this transmission to his students, he actually transmitted this enlightened realization to his disciple Chabdal Lhundrub, to his own son Drakpa Özer, and to other masters, such as Dokhampa Dengom Chökyi Drakpa. Yet it was not just Longchenpa who did this. It has *always* been like this, from the primordial buddha, Samantabhadra, down to our own root guru, with the previous generations passing on this enlightened realization and transmitting it to the succeeding generation in an uninterrupted line that has lasted until the present day. And this is why the Dzogchen lineage has not waned or disappeared, but is still alive in this world of ours.

In every case, from Samantabhadra down to our own root guru, all of these masters have transmitted this to their disciples, one after another, generation after generation. Whether we think of the dimensions of form, speech, or the enlightened wisdom mind, none of them have disappeared; they are all still present. So we can truly have conviction in the authenticity of this lineage.

In particular, Khenpo underlined the importance of studying the complete teaching of Dzogpachenpo, along with its history and its classifications, since he saw with tremendous clarity the danger of merely partial or piecemeal knowledge. This is why he insisted on its unique features: its terms, its vocabulary, its spirit and history, and its understandings and meanings in practice. Especially for the lineage holders, he would say, it is vital nowadays that they have as complete an understanding as they can of the Dzogchen teachings and their background. They need to be aware of exactly where these teachings have come from and through whom these teachings have passed.

> If we fail to understand this kind of historical background, then what we find these days is that there are many people who don't comprehend the roots of these teachings at all. They may, for example, have studied only one teaching, like the instruction manual *Yeshé Lama* (*Timeless Awareness as the Guiding Principle*), and they conclude, "Well, *Yeshé Lama* is Dzogchen." Yes, *Yeshé Lama* certainly is Dzogchen, but it is only one teaching manual on Dzogchen, one of many. It is not the whole of Dzogchen. For one thing, *Yeshé Lama* has been around for only two hundred years or more; since Jigmé Lingpa came into this world and wrote this text, not very much time has elapsed, compared to the fact that the teachings of the Dzogchen lineage have been going on since the time of Garab Dorjé. What we need to ask ourselves is, what has happened in the meantime? Since the first appearance of these teachings, millennia ago, what kind of practice has been done, what kind of transmission has taken place—where has Dzogchen "been" in all that time between its beginnings and the writing of *Yeshé Lama?* But if you ask people nowadays, many of them will say, "Well, I don't know. Other than *Yeshé Lama*, I don't know anything. That's all I know. That's Dzogchen." Things have reached such a pass.
>
> It is almost as if we were children who had lost their mother. Or, to take another example, imagine we have an exquisite vase made of gold, encrusted with gems, and to the handle of this vase we attach a string that goes to another vase, one made of clay. From that clay vase, another string is attached that goes to yet another vase, and so on, until we have five, six, seven, eight vases down the line. At a certain point, the person who holds the last one in the succession may have no idea where the original golden vase is. That person has forgotten it or does not know how to find it, simply thinking, "Well, I've got this vase that I'm holding in my hands; there's nothing other than this." In order to avoid such a predicament, we need to understand everything that has gone before. But if you ask people today, "Tell me, is this a tantra? Is it an explanatory commentary, an *agama?* Or is it a pith instruc-

> tion, an *upadesha?*" they simply do not know what to say. They just blurt out something vague like, "Well, I just take teachings on mind. I get mind teachings . . . mind teachings. . . ." They repeat this over and over again, but they do not have the faintest idea of what is constituted by the entirety of Dzogchen.

On account of his remarkable qualities, Nyoshul Khenpo was held in the highest esteem by all the masters. Once, His Holiness the Dalai Lama asked him a number of questions about the difficult crucial points in Dzogchen. Khenpo replied to him essentially on the spot, but then later he wrote what amounted to a moderate-sized book with complete answers and sent it to His Holiness. Some time afterward, they met by coincidence at Jammu Airport in India. The Dalai Lama told Khenpo that the explanations he had written were quite exceptional.

Nyoshul Khenpo was such an authority on Longchenpa and his works that many of his students regarded him as Longchenpa in the flesh. Often he would speak of the ultimate significance of this great master and the power of his blessing:

> Longchenpa embodies all the buddhas and bodhisattvas of the three times and ten directions, all gurus, devas, and dakinis. What we need to realize is the actual meaning of "Longchenpa," which is the essence of what is meant by "being at ease in the nature of mind" (*semnyi ngalso*). It was in order to exemplify and demonstrate that absolute Longchenpa that the omniscient Longchenpa manifested in our world, nearly seven hundred years ago. So by seeing his representation in form, by hearing his speech, and by remembering him, we can receive the blessing that will bring about the realization of the ultimate meaning of Dzogpachenpo. He embodies the intrinsic nature and essence of Dzogpachenpo, which pervades all beings in samsara and nirvana, and so he is never separate from us. All we need to do is to open our hearts in genuine devotion, and his blessing is immediate and utterly within our reach. By praying to Longchenpa, we can awaken the intrinsic, or absolute, Longchenpa within us, the wisdom of our own rigpa, present within the nature of our mind.

Khenpo would pray constantly to Longchenpa and always encouraged practitioners to recite this verse:

> O Longchenpa, in the depth of your compassion, your learning and realization,
> You are the equal of the great sages of India, the six ornaments and two supreme ones who beautify our world.
> Yet you lived as a hidden yogi, practicing in forest retreats,

> And perfected both samsara and nirvana as dharmakaya.
> Immaculate Radiance, Drimé Özer, at your feet I pray:
> Fill me with your blessing, so that I may realize the natural state, the essence of my mind!

In one of his teachings, Khenpo summed up the unique place that Longchenpa holds at the heart of the Dzogchen lineage and gave a key to his extraordinary writings, placing them within the context of the entire Nyingma tradition. He began by outlining the two great currents of Dzogchen teachings in Tibet that would be brought together so conclusively by Longchenpa: the *Vima Sangwa Nyingtik* (*The Secret Heart Drop of Vimalamitra*) transmitted by Vimalamitra in the kama lineage and the *Pema Khandro Nyingtik* (*Padma's Heart Drop of the Dakini*), the terma transmission taught in Tibet by Guru Rinpoché:

> In Tibet there were two mainstream forms of transmission, kama and terma. From Vimalamitra, the teachings passed as the kama lineage to Nyang Tingdzin Zangpo, Bé Lodrö Wangchuk, Drom Rinchen Barwa, Dangma Lhundrup Gyaltsen, Chetsün Sengé Wangchuk, Tulku Gyalwa Zhangtön, Drupchen Khepa Nyibum, Guru Jober, Trulzhik Sengé Gyappa, Drupchen Melong Dorjé, and Lama Kumaradza. There are these twelve masters, from Vimalamitra to Lama Kumaradza, that constitute the kama lineage that was passed on to Longchenpa, who was the disciple of Kumaradza.
>
> In the case of the terma transmission that was transmitted to Longchenpa, it was Longchenpa's previous rebirth, known as Pema Ledrel Tsal, who rediscovered the *Khandro Nyingtik* (*The Heart Drop of the Dakini*) cycle and then passed on the entire transmission to a student of his named Shuk Gyalsé Lekpa. Pema Ledrel Tsal then told him, "Soon I shall pass away, and some eight or ten years afterward I will return and become your student. Until that time, practice these teachings and take care of them, and then return them to me."
>
> Pema Ledrel Tsal died fairly young, and some years later, as predicted, Longchenpa was born. When Longchenpa grew up, he went to Gyalsé Lekpa to ask for teachings, and the two of them began to talk and share information. It became obvious to Gyalsé Lekpa that this was his root guru in a new body and that all of the qualities that he had perceived in Pema Ledrel Tsal were present in Longchenpa. Just like someone moving from one building to another, his consciousness had moved from one body into another one. He said to Longchenpa, "Truly, you are my root guru, and I need to offer these teachings back to you. Here are the texts you left with me." With that, he merely handed the texts back to Longchenpa. But Longchenpa

said, "That won't do." It was not that he was denying that he was Gyalsé Lekpa's root guru, the reincarnation of Pema Ledrel Tsal. But because his form had changed, it was important for the maintenance of the lineage that Longchenpa receive the teachings in a formal transmission from Gyalsé Lekpa, even though Gyalsé Lekpa did not feel worthy of offering them to his master. Because of this need to uphold the transmission, Longchenpa received the entire body of teachings of the *Khandro Nyingtik* cycle from Gyalsé Lekpa. And this is how the terma transmission was passed on to Longchenpa.

In fact, before Longchenpa was born, there had been a number of early tertöns, such as Sangyé Lama, Nyang-ral Nyima Özer, Rigdzin Gödem, and Guru Chöwang, who had already appeared and revealed Dzogchen teachings in their termas. Longchenpa received all of the termas that had been revealed by these tertöns prior to his coming. So he truly combined the kama and terma lineages.

Concerning the teachings of the master Vairochana on the categories of Mind and Space (Sem Dé and Long Dé), it is clear from Longchenpa's biography that he received these as well—for example, the Aro tradition of Sem Dé that had been established by Aro Yeshé Jungné. So Longchenpa received all of the existing teachings on Dzogchen. Furthermore, from Rigdzin Kumaradza he received teachings on the *Guhyagarbha Tantra* and on *The Oral Lineage of Pith Instructions*, and studied all of the treatises and commentaries on Dzogchen. After this long period of study and practice, Longchenpa received permission to compose his own works.

The works of Longchenpa, at least the ones that concern Dzogchen, can be divided roughly into three groups. First are those that represent the extensive, scholarly or pandita's approach, principally *The Seven Treasuries* and the trilogy known as *The Three Cycles of Natural Freedom* (*Rangdrol Korsum*). This group also contains commentaries such as Longchenpa's overview of the tantra *Kunjé Gyalpo* (*The All-Creating Monarch*), which constitute the Sem Dé portion of his writings. The Long Dé portion of his writings in this extensive scholarly mode includes a short text known as *Namkha Rabjam* (*The Vast Array of Space*) and his commentary on that.

The second group of Longchenpa's writings is that of the profound, *kusuli*'s approach, that is, the streamlined approach of a Dzogchen yogi. This group consists of the three Yangtik cycles that Longchenpa revealed: the *Lama Yangtik* (*Innermost Heart Drop of the Guru*), the *Khandro Yangtik* (*Innermost Heart Drop of the Dakini*), and the *Zabmo Yangtik* (*Innermost Heart Drop of Profundity*). These teachings are designed for the very unelaborate lifestyle of a wandering yogi or someone in retreat.

The third group consists of the teachings that are the underpinnings of both the extensive, scholar's approach and the profound, yogi's approach. These are Longchenpa's teachings on the graduated path (*lamrim*). The most well known is *The Three Cycles of Being at Ease* (*Ngalso Korsum*): *Being at Ease in the Nature of Mind* (*Semnyi Ngalso*), *Being at Ease in Meditative Stability* (*Samten Ngalso*), and *Being at Ease in the Illusoriness of Things* (*Gyuma Ngalso*). This whole group of *The Three Cycles of Being at Ease* consists of three root texts, three commentaries, three structural analyses, three teaching manuals, an overview, and a number of smaller, related texts.

Similarly, in the *Lama Yangtik* cycle there is a collection of some fifty-four teachings and methods. In the *Zabmo Yangtik* cycle, there are texts that concern *trekchö, tögal,* what is called "dark retreat," and *tsalung* practice—some thirty-five teachings and texts in all. In the *Khandro Yangtik* cycle, there are teachings of quite an incredible nature on trekchö, tögal, the key points of Dzogchen practice, tsalung, the path of skillful means, and *chülen* (extracting the vital essence)—some fifty-five titles. So the three Yangtik collections contain nearly two hundred texts dealing with various practices—trekchö, tögal, union practice, dispelling hindrances, enriching one's practice, and more. A truly incredible range of topics is covered in these treatises. Taken as a whole, these three collections are like a treasury of jewels. Added to these, just as there are the seventeen tantras of Dzogchen, there are the 119 pith instructions, which are all ways in which the key points of Dzogchen are distilled. These pith instructions are found throughout the three Yangtik collections.

Now, as far as the trilogy *The Three Cycles of Being at Ease* is concerned, as we saw, this falls within the category of lamrim, or the graduated path, beginning with meditation upon the precious human life and taking refuge in the Three Jewels, through the basic vehicle (the yana of shravakas and pratyekabuddhas), all the way up to and including the Dzogchen path, with complete teachings and instructions on all of these aspects of the path. The basic text is known as *Being at Ease in the Nature of Mind*, which is like the root or source of the whole cycle. There is a second text called *Being at Ease in Meditative Stability,* which deals primarily with meditation, being an instruction on how to practice meditation. And third in the trilogy is *Being at Ease in the Illusoriness of Things,* which deals primarily with conduct or action.

This is why Longchenpa's writings are considered so important. From the point of view of the Dzogchen teachings, and both kama and terma traditions, they are like the mother; you can find everything that you need to know about Dzogchen in Longchenpa's writings. If you have a command of

> this material, then you can understand all of the terma cycles, because it is like having understood the body of the mother from which they are all born.
>
> As far as both the kama and terma traditions are concerned, the root lies in Longchenpa and his writings. There is a saying: "The kama lineage upholds the mainstream, while the termas provide additional adornment." The primary, or mainstream, transmission of Dzogchen lies in the kama lineage, and the termas provide it with embellishment. Each of the termas contains quite extraordinary pith instructions, according to the specific needs of the times in which they were revealed, such as advice on how to "meditate," in the Dzogchen sense of the word. In each of these termas, there is a teaching associated with Dzogchen. So when we talk about the Nyingma school, the real mother is found in the kama tradition, and the additional adornment is provided by the terma tradition. That is really what the Nyingma school boils down to.

In my mind, I feel that Nyoshul Khenpo made two great contributions to the teachings of the dharma and the ultimate welfare of living beings. First was his perfect realization and transmission of the Dzogchen teaching and this precious lineage. He was a master who held the blessing of "the great oral lineage of pith instructions." If he discerned an improvement in the practice of a particular disciple, he would often attribute it directly to the power of this blessing. He continued, right up until the end of his life, with the utmost care, to pass on this lineage, and he gave it to some of the greatest lamas of our time—to Kyabjé Penor Rinpoché, Kyabjé Tulku Urgyen Rinpoché, and Kyabjé Taklung Tsetrul Rinpoché—as well as to many of the younger generation of lamas, such as Dzongsar Khyentsé Rinpoché, Dzigar Kongtrul Rinpoché, Chokling Rinpoché, Chökyi Nyima Rinpoché, Tsoknyi Rinpoché, Mingyur Rinpoché, and Pakchok Rinpoché. He safeguarded this lineage, and in so doing he continued the momentum of everything described in this book.

Among Khenpo's Western students were a number of Buddhist teachers, who became very devoted to him and included prominent members of the Insight Meditation community. Sharon Salzberg, for example, wrote movingly in her book *Faith:*

> Khenpo was the most spacious person I'd ever met. It seemed as though the wind passed right through him and translucency was the major component in his makeup. Many times in his company I had the strange sense that we were standing in a wide open field, great empty expanses spreading out in all directions. Even if we were in a crowded little room, the walls closing us in seemed to evaporate. Perhaps this effect was a reflection of Khenpo's wide-open consciousness and huge unbounded heart. Being with Khenpo was the

> closest I'd come to experiencing transformation through just being in the presence of a realized person. Yet he was entirely unself-conscious, like a magician unattached to his own magic.[3]

Many of the lamas to whom Nyoshul Khenpo transmitted his lineage teach in the West, and I remember he would talk with great enthusiasm and interest about the spread of the dharma and the Dzogchen teachings in the developed world. Speaking to an audience of five and a half thousand after one of His Holiness the Dalai Lama's teachings on Dzogchen in San Jose in 1989, he said, "The entire body of Buddhist teachings that was developed in Tibet remains intact to the present day. Its foundation has not been undermined, nor has its pinnacle been destroyed. We think of our tradition of Buddhism as a gift we have to offer the world. And all that we, the teachers of the Tibetan Buddhist tradition, would ask is that you accept our offering, enjoy it, make use of it, and benefit from it."

One of the intriguing features of what Khenpo used to say when he taught was that it was completely up to date and completely relevant. It seemed there was no question, about anything at all, that you could not ask him. You did not even have to be a follower of the dharma to benefit from his wisdom. Somehow he had a truly remarkable understanding of other religions, and tremendous respect for them all. And although he did not speak English fluently, he evidently had a profound understanding of the Western mind, for his answers and examples were always so very incisive and apt.

Khenpo had his own insights and predictions about the future of the dharma, many of which I now see coming to pass. He would often speak of Khenpo Ngakchung's dream. On the day that Nyoshul Lungtok completed his transmission of the teachings on the main body of the practice to Khenpo Ngakchung, he told him to examine his dreams that night. As Khenpo recounted it: "In the later part of the night, he dreamed he saw a monument erected long ago by Ashoka, the Buddhist king of India. It crumbled from the spire downward and fell into the western ocean, as though carried on a great flood. The color of the ocean turned a murky red. From the sky sounded a voice saying, 'Millions of beings living in the ocean have seen the truth.'" Khenpo added that "this dream would seem to have been an omen foretelling the destruction of the teachings in Tibet and their spread to countries in the Western Hemisphere." And the fact that the Dzogchen teachings *are* now spreading in these countries is in no small way owing to Nyoshul Khenpo himself.

His second great achievement must be this history, in which his deep concern for the future of the lineage was crystallized. "There could come a time in the future," he

[3] Sharon Salzberg, *Faith: Trusting Your Own Deepest Experience* (New York: Riverhead Books, 2002), pp. 158–159.

wrote, "when holders of the lineage would profess to transmit the lineage without being able to recall even the names of its masters." This is why he considered this history to be "as indispensable as our eyes or our life force," providing all the grounds and inspiration ever needed for total conviction. He compared the life stories of the vidyadhara masters in this lineage to a fine chain of gold or a garland of rare gems. What are the special features of this book? With immense attention to detail, Nyoshul Khenpo maps out the "ultimate lineage of direct transmission," the heart of all the lines of transmission of Dzogpachenpo from the primordial buddha to the present day, showing the connection between masters and students in an unbroken line of succession. His work stands out because of its completeness, for it includes all of the distinct lineages, along with the lives of the students of the great masters, stories from the oral tradition, and the different teaching styles. Anyone who matters is represented here, every link in the chain, including masters of our time. Khenpo suggested that it was right that this history be held in the highest regard. In my humble estimation, it serves as a companion to Kyabjé Dudjom Rinpoché's *History of the Nyingma School;* indeed, what Dudjom Rinpoché did for the Nyingma school and the overall Dzogchen tradition with his great work Nyoshul Khenpo has achieved for the Dzogchen lineage, and especially the *Longchen Nyingtik* lineage, with this history. It is a milestone, and I do not feel it will ever be equaled.

Above all, Nyoshul Khenpo was a teacher of the dharma, and not a master who was known for building many great temples or monasteries, gathering patrons, or overseeing grand projects. Where he existed, and where he exists now, is in everyone's minds and hearts, and the only material thing he left us in fact is this book, his history. He said that his temple would be this book. It is his great legacy. It took him many years to complete. He told me that if anything were ever written about it, this is all it should say: "This old lama regarded the Dzogchen teachings as immensely precious, and he wrote a two-volume history, with biographies of the lineage masters, entitled *A Marvelous Garland of Rare Gems,* which will be of tremendous benefit to students in the future. It is neither too high nor too low. In the future, when these things are explained, you need to know the original history. It is neither exaggerated nor self-promoting. It simply tells what happened."

Nyoshul Khenpo enjoyed a close friendship with the late Chagdud Rinpoché, who was one of the "heart sons" of a direct disciple of Khenpo Ngakchung, Tromgé Choktrul Arik Rinpoché, from whom Khenpo also received teachings. One of Chagdud Rinpoché's great achievements was to have inspired the translation into English of Longchenpa's masterworks, *The Seven Treasuries,* and it is, I feel, both appropriate and auspicious that Khenpo's great history has been translated by the same translator, Richard Barron, Lama Chökyi Nyima, an extremely experienced and conscientious *lotsawa.* In the vision of Chagdud Rinpoché, let us dedicate this great work to the masters of this lineage, of the present and the future, and to their students, so that this chain of purest gold, this garland of jewels, continues for all time. May all those who received teachings from Nyoshul Khenpo be able to uphold his vision, and practice and realize these teachings of Dzogpachenpo, and may all the great masters of today live long, to pass on these teachings and fulfill everything that Khenpo had wished for and foreseen. In Nyoshul Khenpo's own words:

> Through the merit of this,
> May the light of the buddhas' precious teaching remain for ages to come—
> The ground for every single kind of benefit and happiness.
> May all the supreme holders of the teachings, who uphold its living truth,
> Accept to live for eons, and their lotus feet stand firm;
> And so may the sun of altruism and well-being, in all its blazing splendor,
> Shine the brilliant light of the study and practice of Buddhadharma
> Throughout every corner of the universe.

Khenpo's last visit to Lerab Ling, the international center of my work in France, was in 1996, when Khandro Tsering Chödrön, the spiritual wife of my master Jamyang Khyentsé Chökyi Lodrö, was present, along with his reincarnation, Dzongsar Jamyang Khyentsé Rinpoché. During the final few years of his life, Khenpo continued to live in Bhutan, until he was obliged by poor health to return to France in the spring of 1999 for medical treatment. Cared for once more by the family of Kyabjé Kangyur Rinpoché at their home in the Dordogne region, he passed away on August 27, 1999. Even near the end, when he was very seriously ill and his disciples flocked to see him, he was totally present, as if untouched by the pain and depredations of the illness. Kyabjé Penor Rinpoché conducted all the necessary ritual practices, as Khenpo's body was preserved and eventually returned to Bhutan, where it is now enshrined as an object of devotion and merit in a golden stupa, fittingly enough, at Tarpa Ling, the seat of Longchen Rabjam in Bhutan.

Toward the end of his life, Khenpo would ask his close attendants to chant a prayer to Longchenpa that Khenpo Ngakchung had adapted for his own personal practice, a song of yearning that invokes his blessing, as if calling out to him from afar:

> Beloved master, precious one, father of mine,
> You are forever one with all the buddhas.
> Now show your kindness and love to your devoted child,
> You who took birth intentionally
> In the form of a supreme bodhisattva—
> Lord of all victorious buddhas, Longchenpa,
> Father of mine—your blessings are not lacking in power,
> Yet my mind is gripped by tempestuous, disturbing emotions,
> And as our negative actions and karma grow ever stronger,

All that awaits the sentient beings of this degenerate age
Is to fall into the depths of the lower realms:
Longchenpa, father of mine, look on me with all your compassion!

Whatever I've done in the past has been devoid of any meaning,
The dharma I have practiced 'til now has been riddled with the eight
worldly preoccupations.
Never did it occur to me, even once, to follow the genuine path.
Now there is no one I can rely on, save you:
Longchenpa, father of mine, look on me with all your compassion!

While the Lord of Death hounds me from behind,
Days, months, years—time draws me onward from in front,
And in between, I'm seduced and enthralled by distraction.
There's a danger—that, without ever realizing it, I'll be completely
deceived:
Longchenpa, father of mine, look on me with all your compassion!

In the prime of youth, the mind is immature.
When we come of age, we're distracted by busyness.
Once old age and infirmity set in,
We may think about the real dharma, but then it's far too late:
Longchenpa, father of mine, look on me with all your compassion!

I wish to stay on here, but it's out of my control;
I wish to bring my possessions, but I cannot take a thing;
I wish for the comfort of companions, but I have to go alone.
Sooner or later I will go on to the next world, that's for sure:
Longchenpa, father of mine, look on me with all your compassion!

Propelled by the habitual patterns of this life,
What will it be like, my journey through the bardo realm?
It will be as hard for me to control
As the dreams I had in my sleep last night:
Longchenpa, father of mine, look on me with all your compassion!

All things in samsara and nirvana are devoid of any substance.
This body will not last and has no reality of its own.
Like the rainbow that arches across the sky,
It is taken as real, but fades into thin air:
Longchenpa, father of mine, look on me with all your compassion!

Toward the buddhas, I have not the slightest devotion,
For sentient beings, only the most meager compassion,

The red robes I wear are only a show,
And my shaven head means next to nothing:
Longchenpa, father of mine, look on me with all your compassion!

So many teachings I've heard, but I've not yet got the crucial point;
However artful at talking, my basic being is still untamed;
I put myself into retreat, but I'm craving for home and family;
I've got my eyes in the right gaze, but lack any real experience:
Longchenpa, father of mine, look on me with all your compassion!

By marking even the smallest failing in others,
But failing ever to notice how rotten I am inside,
By constantly fooling and misleading other people,
Aren't I just purchasing my own misery?
Longchenpa, father of mine, look on me with all your compassion!

How can ignoring that the teachings of all the buddhas
Are there to benefit my mind,
And studying instead for the sake of profit or renown,
Ever lead me along the path to liberation?
Longchenpa, father of mine, look on me with all your compassion!

Passing for a practitioner, though my practice is mere worldly
achievement,
Taking offerings from all and sundry,
Careless and easygoing, I watch my life go by.
Yet when I breathe out for the very last time, what'll happen to me then?
Longchenpa, father of mine, look on me with all your compassion!

Because of all this, I feel my heart breaking in sorrow,
And I pray now to all the buddhas,
For the beings of this degenerate age, and
Especially those like me, who just bear the likeness of practitioners:
Longchenpa, father of ours, look on us with all your compassion!

This child has no one to rely on now but you.
Idling my time away—happy, suffering—
Whatever happens to me, I am in your hands.
Lord, in the palace of the space of immaculate great bliss,
May I remain one with you, always and forever!

Looking back, when I think about those of us who received teachings together from Nyoshul Khenpo, our good fortune seems almost unbelievable: to have met and loved a teacher who had such profound wisdom and such an infinitely generous heart.

Khenpo adored nature, and if I close my eyes now, I can picture him so easily, dressed in his favorite yellow and sitting in perfect posture on an island in a lake in the Pyrenees or on the cliffs above Lerab Ling. Somehow he revealed the primordial in everything. To see him was to realize how amazing the teaching of Dzogpachenpo is. To be with him gave us a joy unlike any other. As long as I live, I shall always be grateful for the hours I spent with him, and I still marvel at his extraordinary power to clarify even the subtlest detail of the Dzogchen teachings, the priceless advice he would give on how to teach, his uncanny gift for communicating the view and the very heart essence of the teachings, and his ability to gather every shade of understanding on any particular topic, so that everything clicked and fell into place. How could we ever measure his realization? It went through his life like a thread through a needle. Everything he did was stitched with its colors.

Khenpo was one of the last of the generation of great masters who trained and attained realization while in Tibet. There was no one like him. He was what legends are made of. And the way he would teach Dzogchen was quite out of this world. Nobody who ever met him could forget his extraordinary presence or the spirit in which he taught, which embodied so perfectly the fathomless ease and vastness of Dzogpachenpo. For in every way, he himself was the greatest statement of Dzogchen, in simply how he was and how he incarnated that natural ease of the innermost nature of mind, *semnyi ngalso,* the "natural great peace" he wrote of so beautifully:

> Rest in natural great peace.
> This exhausted mind,
> Beaten helpless by karma and neurotic thoughts
> Like the relentless fury of the pounding waves
> In the infinite ocean of samsara.
> Rest in natural great peace.

Translator's Preface

History in the Tibetan world is not a chronological record of events, a backdrop against which individuals serve as players; rather, it focuses on the lives of remarkable individuals who themselves define the course of history. This is particularly the case in the spiritual realm. *A Marvelous Garland of Rare Gems* is an account of how a system of teachings and methods—the Dzogchen tradition known as the Nyingtik, or "Heart Drop"—has been passed down through generations of masters to the present day.

When there is so much material about the teachings themselves and the means of putting them into practice, why read biographies? The traditional answer is that the inspiring lives of great practitioners arouse our faith and devotion; however, there is something more. As Chögyam Trungpa Rinpoché once told me, "You must make the dharma your own. It's as though Milarepa were your old granddaddy." By learning about those from whom we have received the great legacy of teachings, we come to feel more connected to them—even a part of their family. At the same time that Nyoshul Khen taught his students the Dzogchen manual *Timeless Awareness as the Guiding Principle* (*Yeshé Lama*), he taught them this history. Clearly he felt that this was not just a reference book, but an integral element of the living transmission of the teachings.

The structure of the book may prove challenging to many readers, as Nyoshul Khenpo does not order his material in a strictly linear way. Although it is crucial to demonstrate that a lineage is an uninterrupted line of transmission, the tracing of that lineage does not always proceed in a straight line. In every generation, there are any number of authentic masters of the tradition who are capable of handing it down to any number of qualified students, who in turn become masters in their own right. Indeed, a careful reading of the book, aided by the lineage diagrams in the Appendix, will show that a certain degree of backtracking is required, as parallel lineages or those branching off the main trunk come under discussion. We have taken the liberty of inserting chapter divisions that, in conjunction with the diagrams, will help to clarify the organization of the book.

In his introduction, "The Precious Lamp," Nyoshul Khenpo points out that today's students can trace their lineages back in a number of ways through their primary teachers to the very origin of all the lineages—the primordial buddha Samantabhadra—without the integrity of any one lineage being compromised. "This history," he tells us, "shows how the individual lineages can be traced back to Samantabhadra in a straightforward way, without any error. The distinct lineages will not be blurred." Still, in shaping this book, he had to make certain choices about which lineages to emphasize. As he explains in his summary (Chapter 21):

> Likewise, in discussing what I refer to as the primary and secondary lineages, I have regarded as primary the particular lineage I myself have received, for, as is said, it is "the deity on whom my flower has fallen." It should be understood that it is on this basis alone, and not on the basis of any assumption of superiority or inferiority, that other lineages have been considered "secondary." Those who are small-minded or prejudiced might think that the distinction I have made between primary and secondary Dzogchen lineages is somehow fixed in stone. I humbly request that people respect my attempt to portray the realization that masters of awareness in the lineage have attained in the past due to their skillful practice in following the example of our Teacher, the Buddha.

Thus Nyoshul Khen underscores his sense of personal connection to the lineage and the teachings.

Integral to the Nyingma understanding of transmission is the "threefold lineage," comprising the "mind-to-mind transmission by victorious ones" (*gyal-wa gong-gyü*), the "transmission through symbols by masters of awareness" (*rig-dzin da-gyü*), and the "oral transmission by human individuals" (*gang-zak nyen-gyü*). It is through this threefold lineage that the Dzogchen teachings came into our human world. Nyoshul Khen discusses the components in Chapters 1 through 3, respectively; and, in fact, everything from Chapter 3 onward pertains to the third, oral transmission by human individuals.

A further development in the third transmission (and extremely important for the Tibetan tradition) is explored in Chapters 3 and 4. It was Mañjushrimitra who originally divided the Dzogchen tantras received by Garab Dorjé into three categories: the Category of Mind (*sem dé*), the Category of Expanse (*long dé*), and the Category of Direct Transmission (*men-ngak dé*). But it was three of Shri Simha's students—Bairotsana, Padmakara, and Vimalamitra—who brought distinct lineages of these categories of teachings, called the "three wellsprings" of the Dzogchen teachings, to Tibet. The kama transmissions of teachings from the Categories of Mind and Expanse were passed down primarily by Bairotsana (Chapter 3). The teachings of the Category of Direct Transmission came from both Padmakara (Guru Rinpoché) (Chapter 3) and Vimalamitra (Chapter 4). Those from Padmakara were terma transmissions, whereas those from Vimalamitra contained elements of both kama and terma; Nyoshul Khen refers to the latter as the "more extensive lineage" (*ring-gyü*). He traces each of these parallel lineages down to the fourteenth-century master Longchenpa (Chapter 5), who is arguably the most significant figure in the book and in whom all three lineages converged.

In Chapter 6, Nyoshul Khen follows the mainstream lineage from Longchenpa down to Jigmé Gyalwai Nyugu in the late eighteenth and early nineteenth centuries. At this point, there are two parallel lineages to consider, deriving from the two principal students of Jigmé Gyalwai Nyugu.

The lineage from the famous Paltrul Rinpoché is discussed in Chapter 7. It is with this lineage—from Paltrul Orgyen Jigmé Chökyi Wangpo, to Nyoshul Lungtok Tenpai Nyima, to Khenchen Ngawang Palzang, to Lungtrul—that Nyoshul Khen was most closely associated. In addition, he examines the lineage of the second Penor Rinpoché, who also studied (as did Nyoshul Khenpo's teacher) with Khenchen Ngawang Palzang; this lineage brings us to the present day and the present Penor Rinpoché, the third in this series of incarnations.

In Chapter 8, Nyoshul Khenpo returns to the early nineteenth century and traces the second lineage from Jigmé Gyalwai Nyugu. This begins with another of his students, the great Jamyang Khyentsei Wangpo, and consists of several branching lines: through Khyentsei Wangpo's student Gyurmé Ngedön Wangpo down to the late Dudjom Rinpoché (another of Nyoshul Khenpo's Dzogchen teachers), and through his student Adzom Drukpa Rinpoché down to Jamyang Khyentsé Chökyi Lodrö and Dilgo Khyentsé Rinpoché (yet another master from whom Nyoshul Khenpo received Dzogchen transmissions).

With Chapter 9, Nyoshul Khenpo returns to the time of Jigmé Lingpa and the lineage of the Dodrupchen incarnations (the first Dodrupchen and Jigmé Gyalwai Nyugu had been fellow students of Jigmé Lingpa). Here, as elsewhere in the book, Nyoshul Khenpo discusses both the line of the original master's incarnations and that of his or her students and their students in turn. Historically, one of the roles played by students was to recognize and train successive incarnations in order to provide the living link that is essential to a viable lineage. The line of students in this chapter brings us to the present day with Trulzhik Rinpoché, who also had a close connection to Dilgo Khyentsé Rinpoché, reminding us that, while they remain uninterrupted, lineages are often anything but linear.

Beginning with Chapter 10, Nyoshul Khenpo looks back to consider the major figures in the mainstream lineages that he has covered to this point, taking them as "nodes" from which lineages comprising students other than the primary ones already discussed branch out. Thus other students of Longchenpa (and their students in turn), including the Pema Lingpa line of Longchenpa's incarnations, are examined in Chapter 10. Other students of Terdak Lingpa Gyurmé Dorjé are discussed in Chapter 11; those of Jigmé Lingpa and his student, the first Dodrupchen, in Chapter 12; those of Jamyang Khyenstei Wangpo, in Chapter 13; and so on. As Nyoshul Khenpo moves into more recent times, these branch lineages become rather complex, especially as he does not always follow a chronological line within a chapter, sometimes going back to discuss a parallel line. Inevitably, the records of more recent masters contain greater detail than those of masters of past centuries, and so there are further instances of crossover, in which a given master received transmission not only from the teacher under whose lineage he or she is discussed, but from other contemporary teachers. Nyoshul Khenpo's listings, as he states, are not "fixed in stone."

A complication facing Western readers unfamiliar with Tibetan names and titles is the casual way in which Tibetan authors refer to a single figure by multiple names or variations of a single name. Thus Longchenpa is referred to as Longchen Rabjam, Drimé Özer, the Omniscient King of the Dharma, the Omniscient Guru, or simply the Omniscient One. Jamyang Khyentsé Chökyi Lodrö is occasionally referred to as Khyentsé Chökyi Lodrö (and several times as Jamgön Chökyi Lodrö). Indeed, the author of this book is known variously as Nyoshul Khenpo and Nyoshul Khen Rinpoché (titles) and as Jamyang Dorjé (his personal name). Nonetheless, rather than standardize the names, we have for the most part retained those that Nyoshul Khenpo recorded. The variation of names is only one issue among many raised by numerous references in the text that may be unfamiliar to Western readers but that would be clear to an educated Tibetan reader. This book is filled with a wealth of biographical, bibliographical, geographical, and political references; a companion volume that will provide background information for these references is in preparation.

It was more than ten years ago that Nyoshul Khenpo did me the great honor of asking that I translate into English what turned out to be the first volume of his work (making up the first part of the present book, through Chapter 9). I received the second volume several years later, and on several occasions Nyoshul Khenpo sent me whole passages that he had rewritten in his meticulous efforts to ensure the accuracy and thoroughness of his work. It was not until shortly before his untimely passing that I was able to send Khen Rinpoché a draft of my completed translation. I know that he would have wanted to see the publication of his monumental work in English before his death, and I can only hope that the painstaking effort that has gone into refining this translation has justified the delay in publication.

After the completion of my draft, based on a copy of the manuscript given to me by Nyoshul Khenpo, the publication of his work in Tibetan made it possible to compare the two versions and thus ensure that my translation reflected the version that Nyoshul Khen approved as the definitive edition. Completing this work has been a poignant, even painful, process, an ongoing reminder of the force of impermanence. In a number of cases, a master was still alive when Nyoshul Khenpo wrote his text, but in the intervening time it became necessary to alter the translation to account for that master's demise. Indeed, it is entirely possible that some of the information in this book is no longer current. For me, this reflects what Khen Rinpoché felt very keenly when he undertook to write this history: that without constant effort and care, looking to the past for guidance and toward the future with inspiration, even a lineage as precious as this one is always in danger of disappearing from our world.

First and foremost, I offer my deepest gratitude and thanks to Nyoshul Khen Rinpoché Jamyang Dorjé for allowing me to translate his text. The late Chagdud Tulku Rinpoché Pema Gargyi Wangchuk urged me to undertake the translation, and I can never repay him for opening the door to the Dzogchen teachings. More recently, Sogyal Rinpoché has been instrumental in guiding the project and graciously agreed to write the Introduction, which does so much to enhance the book. In the true spirit of humility, Nyoshul Khenpo wrote nothing in *A Marvelous Garland of Rare Gems* about his own life; Sogyal Rinpoché's account provides a moving glimpse into the humanity and profound realization that Khen Rinpoché exemplified, in addition to the important role he played as one of the principal modern-day holders of this lineage. My thanks go also to Chagdud Tulku Rinpoché, Yongé Mingyur Rinpoché, Khentrul Lodrö Tayé, and Khenpo Orgyen Trinlay for their insightful answers to some of the questions that arose during the translation.

I wish to express my appreciation to all who contributed to the publication of this book. In particular, my thanks go to the Tsadra Foundation, which provided support during several crucial phases of the editing; I am deeply grateful to the directors of the Foundation for their commitment to the process of translation. My editor at Padma Publishing, Mary Racine, continues to show me how much better a writer I could be and that no translator can ever stand on his or her own. To those at Padma Publishing—Linda Baer, Gina Phelan, and Dan Tesser—as well as Brad Cottel, Edna Adler, Marc Schneider, and Jane Bye, go my profound thanks for rising to the challenge of long days and nights to bring this book to completion. I am also grateful to Patrick Gaffney for his encouragement and advice, and to Daniel Goleman and Tara Bennett-Goleman for their support. And finally, my heartfelt thanks go to my wife, Jeanne McSloy, who was constant in her insistence about the importance of this book and the necessity that it see the light of day. If this translation *could* not have been finished without the support and guidance of my teachers and friends, it is fair to say that it *would* not have been finished without her.

The Precious Lamp

Author's Introduction

Imbued with the vajra of space, permeating space without ever being
characterized by conceptual elaborations,
you are the splendor of perfect youth endowed with the major and minor
marks of perfection—spontaneously present and timeless awareness
with its vast range of enlightened qualities.
You are constantly at play in the realms of those to be guided, dancing the
vajra dance of manifold and magical display.
My guru, glorious protector and sovereign lord of the hundred buddha
families, watch over me; never be separate from me until my
enlightenment!

The following is my introduction, "The Precious Lamp," which
illuminates
this treasure house of gems—biographies of masters of the three lineages.[1]

The quintessence of the enlightened minds of the entire array of victorious
ones
is found in the teachings concerning the heart essence of utter lucidity,
the most secret of secrets.
In order for these to endure until the end of time, without vanishing,
I present this wealth—biographies of past masters of awareness who
make up these lineages.

This treasure house of marvelous rare gems,
which will provide such excellent nourishment to future generations of
those to be guided,
is a collection of teachings in sections whose number equals that of the
garland of auspicious emblems.
I now set forth the banquet of this introduction to illuminate my work.

To begin with, let me explain my reasons for writing this spiritual history. The abbot, the master, and the king,[2] as well as the hundred or more translators and scholars,[3] were beings who consciously took rebirth in order to usher in the teachings and illuminate the Land of Snows. It is because of their kindness that the extensive lineages of the mainstream kama traditions formed a bridge of direct transmission between India and Tibet. These mainstream traditions are as follows:

1. The general explanations of source texts, including commentaries on and synopses of these
2. The instructions transmitted orally, including the manuals on key points and expository teaching
3. The empowerments that confer blessings, including the means of bestowing these and the techniques of directly introducing the nature of mind
4. The practical methods for carrying out enlightened activities, including the practices focusing on the guardian deities of the teachings and the use of wrathful mantras

What we identify as the Early Translation school of the Nyingma[4] embodies these four mainstream traditions. According to holy masters of the past, "The *kama* traditions maintained the mainstream transmission, while the *terma* traditions provided further adornment."[5] Thus the integration of the kama and terma traditions led to the activities of explanation and practice extending like the rays of the sun and moon throughout the central and outlying regions of the Land of Snows.

It was due to the aspirations and unparalleled activities of the sublime Minling Terchen[6] that the source texts of the extensive kama traditions were collected, further clarified in great detail, and supplemented with practice texts, activity rituals, mandala ceremonies, pith instructions, and so forth. In conjunction with this collection, a number of biographies were part of the great legacy left by this master, whose realization was that of the ultimate transmission of the secret Nyingtik, or Heart Drop, teachings of utter lucidity—the extensive lineages of the mainstream kama traditions. These biographies include those of the dharmakaya Samantabhadra down to the great Omniscient One,[7] written by the Omniscient One himself and found in his *Four Higher Collections of the Heart Drop,* as well as the supplementary biographies (including Terdak Lingpa's autobiography) that were written by Terchen himself.

However, from Terdak Lingpa's time until the present—a matter of some centuries—there has been no extensive history dealing with the successive figures in the Nyingtik lineage in an orderly fashion. What if we continue to let things slide in this way? Just as we know only the names of such masters of ancient India as Rikpai Kujuk, Dhanashila, and Jinamitra, but have no actual histories of them, there could come a time in the future when holders of the lineage would profess to transmit the lineage without being able to recall even the names of those involved! I couldn't bear the thought of that happening.

True, there are the incredible terma teachings—the legacy of the Guru's aspirations maturing in a timely way—and each of these terma cycles contains an account of the terma's origins, an account in which the *tertön* establishes the authenticity of the cycle. But suppose we lacked an account of the extensive lineages through which the teachings were transmitted? During the centuries between the time of Guru Rinpoché and that of Sang-gyé Lama,[8] the first of all the tertöns, the terma teachings remained in their places of concealment, such as cliff faces or even the sky. During that entire time, the lineage that brings attainment of the sublime goal was made up of accomplished masters of awareness whose numbers equal the motes of dust on the earth, but there exists no extensive record. So, as I see it, this history of the successive generations of the lineages will prove to be something as indispensable as our eyes or our life force, for—much like a royal genealogy or a record of the provenance of a gemstone—it will provide a basis for conviction and chronicle the venerable origins of the lineage for future generations of those to be guided by these teachings.

My introduction to this spiritual history has two parts: an overview and a detailed treatment. As for the first part, this collection consists of eight major sections:

1. This introduction and table of contents, in eighteen folios
2. My preliminary remarks, in five folios
3. The synopsis, in four folios
4. The prayer to the lineage, in four folios
5. The guru yoga, in eleven folios[9]
6. The ritual of fulfilling the sacred bond with the lineage, in nine folios[10]
7. The spiritual history itself, the great collection of biographies, in 570 folios
8. My letter of advice and songs, in thirty-six folios[11]

There are thus eight sections, matching the number of auspicious emblems.

Second, as for the detailed table of contents, I have divided the major work in this collection—my spiritual history of the approach of natural great perfection—into two volumes, *E* and *VAM*.[12]

The pith instructions of the Dzogchen approach, which derive from such a lineage as this, bring anyone who comes into contact with them to the level of primordial being. It is fitting that all those who wish the very best for themselves hold these instructions dear, as vital to them as their heart or their life force, and make whatever effort they can to put them into practice. In his *Treasury of the Way of Abiding*, the great Omniscient One states:

> Natural great perfection is vajra basic space.
> Whoever encounters it receives the most excellent and definitive
> transmission.

> Effortless and totally free, the nature of phenomena is a spacious expanse.
> This is truly the precious samaya that brings conditioned existence to an end.
> Therefore, fortunate people who have embarked on this approach,
> rejoice and rest in the uncontrived, genuine nature.
> Renounce worldly confusion and the phenomena that result from conceptual elaboration.
> In a solitary place, look to the heart essence, in which nothing need be done.
> This is, in truth, my profound and heartfelt advice.[13]

And in his *Treasury of Words and Their Underlying Meaning:*

> The one in attendance upon a hundred deities, on whose head their lotus hands were placed,
> was honored by those who were foremost among a vast host of seers
> and, in the middle of a great lake of the enlightened qualities of complete freedom, was paid homage by the original victorious one.
> Therefore, those who see or hear this treasury, the teachings of natural great perfection, which surpasses any metaphor,
> are the most sublimely fortunate of all, for they will reach the far shore of the river that is the three realms of conditioned existence.
> With diligent practice, they can ensure that the elements will vanish of their own accord. What other approach can ensure that?
> In the natural state, effortless and unforced, negative emotions are naturally pure—a vast expanse—
> and so are completely beyond the duality of being flaws to be removed or needing antidotes, beyond the process of causality; this is the pinnacle of everything.
> Holy people, you who pursue enlightenment to the highest degree,
> make this your path—this sublime spiritual teaching that is found nowhere else!
> In the intensely delightful garden of the swift attainment of peace,
> the groves of the kayas and timeless awareness will burst into bloom.

And in his *Treasury of Pith Instructions:*

> These days, worry and anxiety are on the rise.
> Life offers us no leisure, and we waste our time on the "path" of distraction.
> There is no end to things we can know, no end to conceptual elaborations.
> Therefore, day and night, practice the teachings of the heart essence.

We are about to die and have no time to finish all the things we have to do
in this life.
One follows after another, like ripples on water.
To ensure that when you die you feel supported or content,
from today on, practice to gain the enlightenment that brings liberation.

We haven't a clue where we are going or what will happen.
Who has any confidence about who is an ally, about where happiness lies,
about how to be fearless?
So now, while you have some free will,
it is fitting that you strive for something of lasting value, the state of
liberation.

Think of it: you must go alone, with no ally,
casting off all the experiences of this life without exception—
body, possessions, spouse, friends, and the rest.
It is fitting that you now seek a refuge and supportive friends.

Since the way things are now cannot be guaranteed forever,
when the Lord of Death comes, and heaven and earth change places,
whatever will you do then? On whom will you rely?
Therefore, practice the sacred teachings now.

Whether or not you are prudent, whether or not you are wise,
the moment of your death is all-important, so marshal the forces
of virtue as your allies.
Meditate on the meaning of what is genuine, mind itself as the heart
essence.
Then the joy of higher states of rebirth will automatically be yours.

Into the jeweled palace, the noble state of liberation,
you will be ushered by victorious ones and enjoy the boundless wealth
of sublime and self-cognizing timeless awareness,
experiencing the meaning of supreme bliss that is ever unchanging.

With such words I, the beggar bereft of spirituality, encourage you.
This is useful heart advice, so keep it in mind!

And in his *Innermost Heart Drop of the Dakini:*

Ah, my friends! Once you have beheld the meaning of the heart essence,
as you use this precious body to free yourself to the far shore of
conditioned existence,

you will have no time to indulge in things of this world,
so please, practice the teachings diligently, day and night!

Among the six classes of being, it is the human existence that is rare to find.
Rarer still is the chance to meet with spiritual teachings and practice them.
And rarer than either of these is the opportunity to encounter this, the heart essence.
Please cultivate meditative stability in solitary places!

Things are such that although we gather them they disperse, and although we meet we part.
Possessions, friends, family, and so on—
look at the painful nature of samsara.
Please cultivate meditative stability in peaceful groves!

However things appear, they are mere reflections.
Empty of truth, they are like melodies heard as echoes.
Having come to understand that they are like illusions or dream images,
please meditate in the forest on what has profound meaning!

Beings' lives pass like water cascading down a rock face.
Like the encroaching shadows of twilight, the Lord of Death is relentless.
Things are such that those who are born must die, and those who meet must part.
Please reflect on this from today on and meditate!

Now that you have gained this human existence,
if you do not set out on the path to the Isle of Liberation,
how will you know where you are going in the future?
Please hold firmly to the path of supreme bliss!

Such words as these are my way of speaking what is useful.
They are from my heart—all of you, please exert yourselves.
Do not return from the Isle of Jewels empty-handed,
but please obtain the wish-fulfilling gem, the heart essence that has profound meaning!

. . . .

These days, decrepitude sets in when we are fifty years old.[14]
Even if we live out a full life, we spend about half of it in the torpor of sleep

and two-thirds of the other half in distraction and busyness.
During the remaining third, our senses are like so many thieves and robbers.
Even though, seeing things in this light, I have long meditated and practiced,
thinking, "I will definitely train in the dharma," still I'm depressed;
what need, then, to speak of other beings?
Throughout time without beginning, our negative emotions
have become engrained in our minds, our habit patterns uninterrupted.
We wander under their influence, subject to our confused perception of samsara.
In such straits, there is no way to fathom what "liberation" is.
At the hour of our death, there is so much to think about, but it's far too late.
What medicine could help someone whose head has been cut off?
All beings are helpless in the city of samsara.
Like people imprisoned in a ruler's dungeon,
they never know happiness, but suffer for such a long time.
Please strive at the means of liberating them from conditioned existence!

Look to the most majestic view—naturally occurring timeless awareness.
Cultivate the most majestic meditation—utterly lucid and spontaneous presence.
Engage in the most majestic conduct—seeing the world of appearances and possibilities as an illusion.
Let yourself be led to the most majestic fruition—the primordial state in which all is resolved.
Become Samantabhadra in the state of spontaneous presence.
This is the significance of your genuine nature, perfect as the ground of being.
This is useful advice, so keep it in your heart!

And in his *Innermost Heart Drop: The Wish-Fulfilling Gem:*

> Henceforth, you who follow in my footsteps, turn your back on things that pertain to this life. Pursue things that pertain to future lifetimes. Rely on authentic spiritual mentors. Receive the instructions on the heart essence of utter lucidity and practice in solitude, implementing the secret advice of the Nyingtik teachings. If you reach a final decision about samsara and nirvana in this lifetime and so experience a prophetic sense of your impending enlightenment, act in any way you can to benefit others, forbear all perversity and fatigue, and ensure that this advice flourishes and spreads.

I ask that you heed the Omniscient One's words, exerting yourselves and putting these teachings into practice, and add the following aspiration:

> May this spiritual approach, like the light of the sun and moon, permeate everywhere, dispelling the darkness of ignorance.
> Like a gem, may it be the source of what has ultimate meaning, fulfilling the hopes of all beings.
> Like a river, may it flow without interruption, an ever-present and powerful force.
> Like a ruler, may it enact limitless activities, serving as an adornment of this world.

In conclusion:

> With the original victorious one's discovery of utter lucidity,
> there rose the sun of this treasury of spiritual teachings;
> masters of awareness still follow these methods in the present day.
> Cherish these biographies as you would the nectar of your heart.
>
> In order to arouse your conviction,
> I compiled this history of how the teachings were transmitted.
> By the merit so created, may all beings embark on this, the heart essence of all spiritual approaches,
> and become free on the level of the great perfection of utter lucidity.

May these comments written by the author serve as a cause for the earth to be covered with carefree yogins of the Dzogchen approach of utter lucidity, who, having shattered the bonds of samsara and nirvana, are free. *Sarva mangalam!*

Let me again summarize the contents of this work for those like myself, an old dodderer who is as stupid as a yak. This spiritual history includes some 230 biographies of successive generations of masters, mentions more than 2,500 by name, and has 111 line drawings of deities and masters.[15] Let me discuss the significance of what is presented in the text: the spiritual history, the table of contents, and the biographies and stories. These masters have ensured enormous benefit for beings and for the teachings, both the teachings of the victorious ones in general and those of their own traditions in particular. I have summarized the vast, oceanlike range of their accomplishments—their study, contemplation, and meditation; their teachings, practice, and activity; and their erudition, purity, and nobility—and the result is as though the wish-fulfilling gems in a universal monarch's treasury were piled together.

The special feature of this spiritual history of the secret Nyingtik teachings of utter lucidity is the fact that it discusses the ultimate lineage of direct transmission, which is the fundamental element of all the lines of transmission of the Dzogchen approach—the mind-to-mind transmission, the transmission through symbols, and the oral transmission—from the victorious one Samantabhadra, the original teacher of great perfection, down to the holy masters of the present day. This history documents the connections between masters and students in this unbroken line of succession, showing just how the transmission occurred, and from whom to whom. As such, it is an indispensable synopsis, imparting new vitality to previous histories, like a fine chain of gold or a garland of rare gems strung on a fine cord.

Furthermore, the fundamental lineage can be traced directly from the original victorious one in succession down to the masters of recent times and the present: Khenchen[16] Ngawang Palzang, Jamyang Chökyi Lodrö, Yukhok Chöying Rangdrol, Gyalsé Gyurmé Dorjé, Kyabjé[17] Dudjom Drodul Lingpa, Kyabjé Dilgo Khyentsé, Drupwang[18] Penor, Dodrup Trinlé Palbar, Zhadeu Trulzhik, and others. Alternatively, the current students of Khenchen Jigmé Puntsok of Sertar can trace the lineage back through Khenchen Jigpun's master, who was Batar Khenchen Tupten Chöpel; Batar Khenchen's master, who was Yönten Gyatso; and Yönten Gyatso's master, who was Paltrul Rinpoché, from whom the lineage can be traced back to Samantabhadra. Similarly, the students of Khenchen Chöchap can trace the lineage back through his master, Bötrul; Bötrul's master, Khenchen Kunpal; and Khenchen Kunpal's master, Paltrul Rinpoché; and so on. The students of both Khenchen Munsel of Golok and Chatral Sanjé Dorjé can trace the lineage back through their master, Khenchen Ngawang Palzang, and so on. The students of Drupwang Lungtok Gyatso, who is also known as Khen Achuk of Tromtar, can trace the lineage back through his master, Arik Rinpoché of Tromtar; Arik Rinpoché's master, Khenchen Ngawang Palzang; and so on. The students of both Adzom Gyalsé and Jamgön Chökyi Lodrö can trace the lineage back through their master, Adzom Drukpa, and so on, while the students of Lungtrul Rinpoché can trace the lineage back through his master, Khenchen Ngawang Palzang, and so on.

Thus, for all those who explain, promulgate, and confer the Dzogchen teachings throughout the world today, this history shows how the individual lineages can be traced back to Samantabhadra in a straightforward way, without any error. The distinct lineages will not be blurred. Future lineage holders will find that their vast spiritual vision is improved by this history, as though a precious wand of gold had removed cataracts from their eyes. And this will ensure that the teachings of this most sublime spiritual approach endure.

For these and many other specific reasons, it is perfectly clear how fitting it is that this work be held in high regard. So it is my fervent prayer, which I repeat a hundred times, that masters who have yet to appear in the future will hold to their basic lineages—relying on their gurus, who are like the deities on whom their flowers have fallen[19]—and so come to a definitive conclusion, without error, concerning the significance of the enlightened intent of this most secret unsurpassable cycle; and that they will continue to act in noble ways, ensuring benefit and happiness that fill all of space, bringing to beings the splendor of their gracious efforts to teach, practice, and enact the teachings of the Dzogchen approach of utter lucidity, the heart essence of all the victorious ones' teachings.

> The majestic pinnacle of all spiritual approaches is Dzogchen, the approach of utter lucidity,
> illuminated by the three lineages of masters of awareness.
> May it be ushered into the skylike minds of beings whose good fortune is equal to mine
> and, by its power, tear to shreds the net of our complete bewilderment in conditioned existence.
>
> May all the cycles of spiritual teachings that exist, whether they concern the way things abide or the way they manifest,
> and all the outward expressions of the kayas and the radiant display of timeless awareness
> be free within the primordial ground of original purity—
> inner basic space, the profoundly lucid embrace of the youthful vase body.[20]
>
> Beings in the present degenerating times have many prejudices.
> Although I have no certainty that this work will be of benefit,
> I leave it as a legacy for those with spiritual vision in the future—
> a precious wand of gold to open their eyes.
>
> Although I have not achieved any degree of erudition or accomplishment,
> I have spent my life hearing, contemplating, and meditating
> on the oceans of sutras and tantras.
> As a mark of this, I, the old Tibetan Jamyang Dorjé, have written this.

Such are my words. May they prove auspicious! Good fortune!

The Precious Mirror

Preliminary Remarks

Completely and timelessly pure, the unity of awareness and emptiness is
the genuine, fundamentally unconditioned nature of reality.
The splendor of this manifests as a youthful and invincible form adorned
with the major and minor marks of perfection,
Longchenpa, the spiritual guide to the heart essence of utter lucidity.
Merge with me in the indestructible sphere in the center of my heart.

What is it that this text discusses? With respect to the origins of these teachings—the three categories of Dzogchen in general—the principal concern is to present a clear exposition of the mainstream transmission, that is, the extensive lineages of the secret Nyingtik teachings of utter lucidity. These constitute the most secret unsurpassable cycles of teachings deriving from the three great masters who were their main codifiers. From the time of Garab Dorjé to that of Longchenpa, some 2,019 years, the Dzogchen lineage in India and Tibet consisted of countless masters whose lives serve as models of complete liberation. Since it would be impossible to describe them all, in this work I focus on Padmakara,[1] Vimalamitra, and Bairotsana,[2] the three great masters from each of whom came a lineage of succession. These primary lineages all converged in Longchenpa, who thus became, as it were, the second Teacher of this tradition.[3]

Following him, the lineages proliferated throughout upper, middle, and lower Tibet,[4] like a hundred thousand streams flowing in all directions. The most famous and enduring of these were the two passed on by Khedrup[5] Delek Gyatso and Drok Khenchen Chabdal Lhundrup. Of the two, I have focused on the lineage of Drok Khenchen as the primary line of transmission. Thus, up to the time of Terdak Lingpa, the eleventh successive master following Longchenpa, not only did the lineages multiply in all directions, beyond counting, but Terdak Lingpa himself—through the lineages of his students and those who maintained his monastic seat—left a legacy that covered the earth. In this work, I have focused primarily on two lineages—that of the students down to the time of Jigmé Lingpa and that of the throne holders down to lord Khyentsei Wangpo—which blended into a single mainstream transmission.

Jigmé Lingpa's heart sons[6]—principally the four named Jigmé and others—ensured that countless lineages would extend throughout the East and West in this world, to the far shores of distant oceans. But in modern times, the most enduring and self-sustaining of these have been the three lineages in the ultimate sense, which derived from Dodrup Trinlé Özer and Jigmé Gyalwai Nyugu's two students, Paltrul and Khyentsei Wangpo. Among those of us to be guided, these lineages have proved to be the most glorious expression of our merit, and so I have considered all three of them to be mainstream transmissions.

Next, I have supplemented the foregoing with general biographies of those who do not figure in the mainstream transmissions—biographies of heart children and students and their students, of tulkus[7] and teachers, of throne holders and those who maintained monastic seats, and so forth, from the time of Longchenpa onward. In addition, I have given an account of the founding of the major monasteries of the Early Translation school.

What lies at the very heart of these accounts, that which is as indispensable and dear to us as our eyes, is the treatment of the ground, path, and fruition in the Dzogchen approach. I have concluded with this.

The preceding discussion provides an overview of this work. There may be some who feel that this is merely a history of *The Heart Drop of Longchenpa*. That cycle, however, constitutes a single terma of enlightened intent, a cycle of teachings also entitled *The Treasury of Space,* which was codified by Rigdzin[8] Jigmé Lingpa under the guidance of Guru Rinpoché's and Longchenpa's embodiments of timeless awareness.[9] From that time on, these teachings have been known by their common name, *The Heart Drop of Longchenpa*. Similarly, in other terma cycles, each terma teaching includes a specific, often extensive history related to that particular cycle. If you wonder what this present work consists of, it is a discussion of the great system of definitive personal transformation—the pith instructions passed down by the Omniscient One Longchenpa, which convey the enlightened intent underlying the secret Nyingtik approach of utter lucidity. This discussion covers such themes as all of the topics that were taught, the ways in which the teachings were passed down, and the successive masters who upheld the teachings in the general Dzogchen tradition (with emphasis on the extensive lineages of kama teachings), *The Four Higher Collections of the Heart Drop,* the extensive treatments in the scholars' cycles,[10] the profound treatments in the *kusulus*'[11] pith instructions, and such sources as the fundamental tantra—*The Reverberation of Sound*—and *The Supreme System of Ati.* Please understand that I have composed this work to emphasize the lineage of the Dzogchen approach in general—or, to put it another way, the ultimate lineage of pith instructions—which unites the kama, terma, and *daknang*[12] lines in a single mainstream transmission.

I acknowledge that in undertaking the task of writing this spiritual history and the accompanying biographies, I lacked discerning intelligence and other qualifications of an erudite person. But I could see that there might come a time when the noble deeds of masters of awareness in the Nyingtik lineage would no longer be recounted with any certainty, so that people would be like the blind, groping about with staffs. This inspired me to take up the challenge of composition, solely out of a sincere sense of altruism. For any flaws in this work—deriving, for example, from my lack of understanding or my misunderstanding—I ask from my heart for the forbearance of the entire assembly of the victorious ones of the Three Roots and their attendant oath-bound guardians, as well as the sublime masters with the sacred outlook of the dharma, who uphold the teachings.

And that is not all. In the Dzogchen lineages of the Categories of Mind and Expanse, the lineages of Mahayoga and Anuyoga, and the lineage of the bodhisattva vow, there are lineage prayers from the past that include both Indian and Tibetan masters, as well as records of empowerments and oral transmissions received by various masters. These sources contain unambiguous lists of the names of successive masters. Though these masters actually lived, there exist no lengthy biographies recounting their individual deeds and exemplary lives. The same is true even of modern-day masters who are still living. I simply could not let the situation stand at that.

Similarly, as far as the mainstream sutra sources are concerned, there were such great figures as the Indian abbot, the master, and the Buddhist king; the three masters Nyak, Nup, and Zur;[13] the three victorious ones Rongzom,[14] Longchenpa, and Shakya Jungné; the three Katok masters Dampa Deshek, Tsangtön, and Jampa Bum; Ngari Panchen;[15] the brothers of Mindroling;[16] the three masters Khyentsé,[17] Kongtrul, and Chokgyur Lingpa; Gyalsé Zhenpen Tayé; Khenchen Zhenpen Chökyi Nangwa; the two masters Paltrul and Khyentsé; and Jamgön Mipam. By the power of the aspirations and activities of these sublimely learned and accomplished masters, the study and practice of the Early Translation school, which is said to consist of four mainstream transmissions,[18] have illuminated the world like the sun and moon; moreover, this self-sustaining system has never had to rely on an external source.

With respect to mainstream sutra sources, Mipam Rinpoché's intention to compose extensive commentaries on such texts as *The Source Verses on Sublime Knowing, The Entrance into the Middle Way,* and *The Highest Continuum* (as well as a detailed overview of Madhyamaka)[19] has ensured that these are currently taken as standard works to be consulted. But although Mipam Rinpoché composed numerous smaller works on such sources, he did not actually complete a comprehensive collection of extensive commentaries.

With respect to the tantra sources, there exists a large array of extensive commentaries and pith instructions on both the Mahayoga and Anuyoga approaches. As for the Dzogchen Categories of Mind and Expanse, there are the cycles of Aro and Nyang, which are specific to the Category of Mind, and the cycle *The Vajra Bridge,* which is specific to the Category of Expanse. Teachings concerning these two categories are also contained in such works as *The Seven Treasuries, The Four Higher Collections of the Heart Drop,* and the cycles *Natural Freedom* and *Being at Ease.* However, as for extensive commentaries dealing with these categories, in the past there were two by the great Omniscient One: *Rays of Sunlight* (an extensive commentary on the tantra *The All-Creating Monarch*) and *Loosening the Seal into the Freedom from Any Fixed Dimension* (an extensive commentary on *The Entire Array of Space*).[20] Although these two important commentaries, along with their auxiliary texts, constituted the most extensive treatments of the Categories of Mind and Expanse, due to the changing times[21] they no longer exist.

Furthermore, there are many important source texts of both the sutra and tantra traditions that merit commentaries and other explanations. But in such cases, holders of the teachings whose sublime vision of the dharma should be truly vast, and who have an abundance of all the qualities necessary to compose such treatises, seem interested only in belittling other schools. Like people viewing an entertaining spectacle, they feel satisfied with studying a few instruction manuals and terma teachings. Engaging in conduct like that of pratyekabuddhas, they boast, "We don't look to anyone else!" Turning their backs on the great source texts—the tantras, explanatory commentaries, and pith instructions—they plug their ears and cover their eyes, or peer as though through the eye of a needle, arrogantly presuming their cleverness as they close the door on their own intelligence. This reminds one of the saying, "People in the land of Chitta beat the victory drums when their fathers are slain."[22]

Therefore, I would point out that the Omniscient One said, "These teachings are the province of those of finely tuned acumen, who have reinforced their positive qualities to the greatest extent and have studied and contemplated on a vast scale." By this, he meant that true practitioners of the vast expanse of being, in all its spaciousness, are unfettered by any restriction due to partiality or bias. They are demolishers who destroy confusion. They are free in the equal taste[23] of samsara and nirvana. They have come to a decisive experience within the expanse of the great perfection, in which everything is equal in space. Through the naturally occurring lamp of sublime knowing[24]—the dynamic energy of awareness—they are able to distinguish, without perceiving any conflation or conflict, all the individual systems of spiritual approaches and philosophical schools. It is my plea that holders of the teachings pay attention to the meaning of the foregoing comments and write countless treatises, whether spiritual histories, biographies, or commentaries and explanations, on the topics found in the sutras and tantras. With this, I fold the petals of my ten fingers into the mandala of a lotus in bloom and place it at the chakra of supreme bliss,[25] offering this heartfelt prayer to the sublime masters who hold the teachings:

May this work exemplify everything positive that has been accomplished,
whether in conditioned existence or the peace of nirvana.
By the power of all this being dedicated within basic space, endowed with
the most sublime of all attributes,
may every being become a majestic ruler of dharmakaya,
mastering the empire of primordial being, the timeless ground of being!

Concerning the empowerments, oral transmissions, and instructions of this approach, the extensive lineages of the kama transmissions are of primary concern. The sources for the Category of Mind are *The Detailed Instructions on the Category of Mind,* the Nyang tradition, and the Aro tradition. The source for the Category of Expanse is *The Vajra Bridge* cycle. The sources for the Category of Direct Transmission are *The Four Higher Collections of the Heart Drop, The Seven Treasuries, The Three Cycles of Being at Ease, Timeless Awareness as the Guiding Principle,* and the great oral Dzogchen tradition. Taking these as one's foundation, one should in addition receive any or all kama and terma transmissions associated with the three categories of Dzogchen.

This was written down by Jamyang Dorjé. Good fortune!

The Precious Lattice

A Synopsis of the Oral Lineage of Dzogchen

I pay homage at the feet of the holy gurus!

What is discussed in this work is the oral lineage of teachings on the natural and utterly lucid state of great perfection. Any extensive explanation of the topics covered in the pith instructions of this lineage would have two parts: one concerning the successive gurus in the lineage and one concerning the pith instructions transmitted by the lineage.

In keeping with all great histories of the Dzogchen tradition, the first part would include the holy gurus of the mind-to-mind transmission, of the transmission through symbols, and of the oral transmission, from the transcendent and accomplished conqueror, the primordial protector, Samantabhadra, down to one's primary gurus. Where appropriate, certain figures—Longchenpa, Terdak Lingpa, Khenchen Ngawang Palzang, Shedrup Tenpai Nyima, and others—would be discussed in more detail.

The second part would consist of detailed elaborations of the topics found in the instructions transmitted by the lineage. This would include three aspects of the "precious embrace of spontaneous presence"—that is, the three aspects of ground, path, and fruition.

GROUND

First, a detailed explanation of the ground of being would involve discussions of such topics as the following:

> the way of abiding that is the universal ground of being, supreme and primordial;
> the arising and resolving of the spontaneously manifest aspect of that ground;
> the way in which Samantabhadra is free; and
> the way in which ordinary beings, with their erroneous ways of thinking, are confused.

PATH

Second, a detailed explanation of the secret topic of the path that is the precious embrace of spontaneous presence would involve lengthy discussions of the following topics:

> the essence of basic space as the underlying basis of the path;
> the way in which the vajra body forms the support for the path; and
> what is supported within that body—both the subtle channels, energies, and bindu that are causal on the relative level, and the subtle channels, energies, and bindu of timeless awareness on the ultimate level.

The actual path involves two stages: empowerment, which brings the practitioner maturity, and instruction, which brings liberation. The first stage has two further steps: the maturing empowerment itself and the accompanying samaya that acts as a support. The second stage, that of the liberating instructions, also has two further steps: the preliminaries and the main body of practice. The latter of these, the main body of practice, involves any of three approaches, depending on whether the acumen of the practitioner is of the highest, average, or lesser kind.

In the first case, whereas a more ordinary student (one whose mind inclines toward objects as a frame of reference) is instructed through the four topics of view, meditation, conduct, and fruition, for a more extraordinary student (one whose mind inclines toward pure awareness and its natural manifestations), there are the topics covered in two major approaches: original purity, or *trekchö,* and spontaneous presence, or *tögal.*[1]

First, the trekchö approach involves several phases, including the preliminaries, known as "tearing down the hut of ordinary mind"; the main body of practice, direct introduction to the awareness that is the very essence of being; and the conclusion, the way in which meditative experiences are maintained. These are explained at length by means of such teachings as those concerning coming to a final decision ("the monarch-like cycle"), making clear distinctions ("the brahmin-like cycle"), and demonstrating natural freedom in one's direct experience ("the cycle of pith instructions").

Second, the tögal approach is explained at length by means of teachings concerning the themes that are crucial to this approach in general; those concerning the path that demonstrates three key points in one's direct experience; those concerning the way in which the four visions[2] arise as signs of progress; and those concerning the pith instructions that provide ongoing support.

In the second case, students of average acumen are instructed through the teachings on the bardo states, while in the third case, students of lesser acumen are instructed through the teachings on gaining freedom in a naturally occurring nirmanakaya pure realm.

FRUITION

Third, a detailed explanation of the secret topic of the fruition—the completion of the path—which is the precious embrace of spontaneous presence, would include lengthy discussions of the following topics:

- the nature of the kayas—the three kayas, the five kayas, and so forth—as supports;
- the nature of timeless awareness as what is supported, including:
  - the three aspects of timeless awareness as it abides as dharmakaya, the ground of being,
  - the five aspects of timeless awareness as it exhibits attributes as sambhogakaya,
  - the two aspects of timeless awareness as it applies to nirmanakaya, perceiving the real nature of things, as well as things in all their multiplicity;
- the nature of enlightened actions and activity, demonstrating, for example, how enlightened actions (which are marked by the three characteristics of being ongoing, pervasive, and spontaneously accomplished) are carried out for as long as space itself endures, embodying the three enlightened qualities of wisdom, love, and spiritual power.

Furthermore, according to the tradition of this most majestic and sublime spiritual approach, the fruition is referred to by such phrases as the following: "inward lucidity," "the youthful vase body," "lucidity without engaging in concepts," "inward direction without oblivion," "being what it is without having identity as such," "precision without thinking in terms of details," "sublime knowing hanging in space," "timeless awareness resolving in basic space," "the elements subsiding into a quiescent state," and "utter lucidity merging with basic space." Accordingly, the explanation would emphasize the teachings that are specific to the Dzogchen approach.

If one were to explain these teachings in the foregoing way, one would be able to present the teachings specific to the Dzogchen approach in either an extensive or a concise manner according to the power of one's intellect. If the preceding topics were analyzed in detail, in conjunction with those topics as found in the tantras, explanatory commentaries, and pith instructions, the material would fill a thousand folios; if they were analyzed to a moderate extent, about three hundred folios; if in a very concise way, several dozen folios. Until one's doubts concerning these spiritual methods have been resolved, as my kind guru used to say, "You can wait for nine years sucking your thumb, but still have no chance of understanding the great perfection."

How wondrous!
The secret Nyingtik teachings, like one's very heart,
are found in the seventeen tantras concerning the quintessence of lucidity—utter lucidity.
Their practical application lies in 119 pith instructions.
The heart essence of all of these is found in the four "mother and child" Nyingtik cycles.[3]
Most profound of all are the great *Treasuries* and the cycles of *Being at Ease*.
Such teachings as these are the treasury that lies at the very heart of this oral lineage.
"These are the key points of unerring enlightened intent—
the supreme spiritual approach that is the path of the vajra heart essence of utter lucidity,
the precious lineage of the Omniscient Ones, father and son."[4]
Such statements do not come from the mouths of foolish meditators who cast stones in the dark.[5]
How could a pedant, whose mind is never made up, know of these teachings?
They are the milk of the white snow lioness;
the vessel that holds them must be the finest, a ewer of precious gold,
for their essence cannot be held in any ordinary, inferior vessel.[6]
The profound basic space of phenomena is a realm so difficult to fathom
that those who lead one along paths strewn with nearsighted concepts
are like blind birds trying to find the limits of the sky.
The nearsighted ordinary mind cannot reach the domain of advanced spiritual practitioners.
It is said that it is ridiculous to rely on any means
other than the blessings transmitted through the ultimate lineage of enlightened intent.
In writing this work, like someone trying to get a dog to look up at the stars,
I wondered how people in these degenerating times could gain understanding.
My mind was filled with trepidation.
So I composed this synopsis of the instructions found in the oral lineage
as a key to open a hundred doorways to their profound meaning.
In accordance with the teachings transmitted by my guru, the lord of the dharma,

and drawing on the treasury of teachings from the masters of awareness,
the gurus of the three lineages,
this was written by me, Jamyang Dorjé, a Tibetan without a home
(for although the seedling of my body grew in the Land of Snows,
the soles of my feet have taken me around the world).
Whatever faults there are in this work, due to my lack of understanding or
to my misunderstanding,
I confess in the presence of my guru, my glorious protector and sovereign
master of the hundred buddha families,
as well as the deities of the Three Roots, the vast assemblies of oath-
bound guardian deities,
and those who are the custodians of these teachings.[7]
Through the virtue of this undertaking, like the root of a lotus and as
completely pure as a conch shell,
may all beings reach the level of primordial being,
may the oral lineage endure as a source of instruction,
and may the blazing glory of all that is auspicious adorn this world
of ours.
Good fortune! *Mangalam!*

In accordance with the directive I received from my sublime refuge lord, the precious Vajradhara,[8] *I, Jamyang Dorjé, who is under his protection, make this humble offering with countless prostrations. I ask that he look upon me with loving compassion until I attain the very heart of enlightenment.*

The Precious Garland

A Supplication to the Lineage of the Secret Nyingtik Teachings of Utter Lucidity

I pray to the dharmakaya Samantabhadra.
Grant me your blessings that I may realize the nature of mind itself
as the way of abiding.
I pray to the sambhogakaya Vajrasattva.
Grant me your blessings that I may realize the nature of mind itself
as the way of abiding.
I pray to the nirmanakaya Garab Dorjé.
Grant me your blessings that I may realize the nature of mind itself
as the way of abiding.
I pray to the master Mañjushrimitra.
Grant me your blessings that I may realize the nature of mind itself
as the way of abiding.
I pray to Rigdzin Shri Simha.
Grant me your blessings that I may realize the nature of mind itself
as the way of abiding.
I pray to the learned one Jñanasutra.
Grant me your blessings that I may realize the nature of mind itself
as the way of abiding.
I pray to Panchen[1] Vimalamitra.
Grant me your blessings that I may realize the nature of mind itself
as the way of abiding.
I pray to Padmakara of Oddiyana.[2]
Grant me your blessings that I may realize the nature of mind itself
as the way of abiding.
I pray to the Buddhist king Trisong Detsen.
Grant me your blessings that I may realize the nature of mind itself
as the way of abiding.
I pray to the dakini Yeshé Tsogyal.

Grant me your blessings that I may realize the nature of mind itself
as the way of abiding.
I pray to Lochen[3] Bairotsana.
Grant me your blessings that I may realize the nature of mind itself
as the way of abiding.
I pray to Tingdzin Zangpo, priest of the Nyang clan.
Grant me your blessings that I may realize the nature of mind itself
as the way of abiding.
I pray to Lodrö Wangchuk, teacher of the Bé clan.
Grant me your blessings that I may realize the nature of mind itself
as the way of abiding.
I pray to Rinchen Barwa, teacher of the Drom clan.
Grant me your blessings that I may realize the nature of mind itself
as the way of abiding.
I pray to the spiritual elder Dangma Lhungyal.
Grant me your blessings that I may realize the nature of mind itself
as the way of abiding.
I pray to Seng-gé Wangchuk, venerable one of the Ché clan.
Grant me your blessings that I may realize the nature of mind itself
as the way of abiding.
I pray to Tulku Gyalwa Zhangtön.
Grant me your blessings that I may realize the nature of mind itself
as the way of abiding.
I pray to his sublime son, Khepa[4] Nyibum.
Grant me your blessings that I may realize the nature of mind itself
as the way of abiding.
I pray to Guru Jober, custodian of the teachings.
Grant me your blessings that I may realize the nature of mind itself
as the way of abiding.
I pray to Trulzhik Seng-gé Gyappa.
Grant me your blessings that I may realize the nature of mind itself
as the way of abiding.
I pray to Drupchen[5] Melong Dorjé.
Grant me your blessings that I may realize the nature of mind itself
as the way of abiding.
I pray to Rigdzin Kumaradza.
Grant me your blessings that I may realize the nature of mind itself
as the way of abiding.
I pray to the Omniscient One Longchen Rabjam.

Grant me your blessings that I may realize the nature of mind itself
as the way of abiding.
I pray to Khedrup Chabdal Lhundrup.
Grant me your blessings that I may realize the nature of mind itself
as the way of abiding.
I pray to Tulku Drakpa Özer.
Grant me your blessings that I may realize the nature of mind itself
as the way of abiding.
I pray to Trulzhik Sang-gyé Önpo.
Grant me your blessings that I may realize the nature of mind itself
as the way of abiding.
I pray to Kunchen Dawa Drakpa.
Grant me your blessings that I may realize the nature of mind itself
as the way of abiding.
I pray to Drupchen Kunzang Dorjé.
Grant me your blessings that I may realize the nature of mind itself
as the way of abiding.
I pray to Khedrup Gyaltsen Palzang.
Grant me your blessings that I may realize the nature of mind itself
as the way of abiding.
I pray to Tulku Natsok Rangdrol.
Grant me your blessings that I may realize the nature of mind itself
as the way of abiding.
I pray to Gyalwang Tendzin Drakpa.
Grant me your blessings that I may realize the nature of mind itself
as the way of abiding.
I pray to Khedrup Do-ngak Tendzin.
Grant me your blessings that I may realize the nature of mind itself
as the way of abiding.
I pray to Sangdak Trinlé Lhundrup.
Grant me your blessings that I may realize the nature of mind itself
as the way of abiding.
I pray to Rigdzin Terdak Lingpa.
Grant me your blessings that I may realize the nature of mind itself
as the way of abiding.
I pray to Gyalsé Rinchen Namgyal.
Grant me your blessings that I may realize the nature of mind itself
as the way of abiding.
I pray to Rabjam Orgyen Chödrak.

Grant me your blessings that I may realize the nature of mind itself
as the way of abiding.
I pray to Drupwang Shrinatha.
Grant me your blessings that I may realize the nature of mind itself
as the way of abiding.
I pray to Rigdzin Jigmé Lingpa.
Grant me your blessings that I may realize the nature of mind itself
as the way of abiding.
I pray to Jigmé Gyalwai Nyugu.
Grant me your blessings that I may realize the nature of mind itself
as the way of abiding.
I pray to Orgyen Chökyi Wangpo.[6]
Grant me your blessings that I may realize the nature of mind itself
as the way of abiding.
I pray to Lungtok Tenpai Nyima.
Grant me your blessings that I may realize the nature of mind itself
as the way of abiding.
I pray to Khenchen Ngagi Wangpo.
Grant me your blessings that I may realize the nature of mind itself
as the way of abiding.
I pray to Shedrup Tenpai Nyima.
Grant me your blessings that I may realize the nature of mind itself
as the way of abiding.

The foregoing is the primary lineage of the Nyingtik teachings. In addition:

I pray to Rigdzin Dudjom Dorjé.
Grant me your blessings that I may realize the nature of mind itself
as the way of abiding.
I pray to Jamyang Khyentsé Özer.
Grant me your blessings that I may realize the nature of mind itself
as the way of abiding.
I pray to Drupwang Pema Norbu.
Grant me your blessings that I may realize the nature of mind itself
as the way of abiding.
I pray to my twenty-five tutors and mentors.[7]
Grant me your blessings that I may realize the nature of mind itself
as the way of abiding.
I pray to the lineage that is the mainstay of spiritual practice.
Grant me your blessings that I may realize the nature of mind itself
as the way of abiding.

I pray to the gracious root guru.
Grant me your blessings that I may realize the nature of mind itself
as the way of abiding.

I pray to the glorious and holy guru, who is the essence of all buddhas of
the three times and the embodiment of the four kayas.
I pray that you grant your blessings of empowerment.
I pray that you grant your blessings that the special realization found
through this profound path may awaken in me.
I pray that you grant your blessings that I may realize the view of the
originally pure way of abiding.
I pray that you grant your blessings that I may fully experience the
timeless awareness of the four visions of spontaneous presence.

Moreover:

On the slopes of Rinchen Nyingpo in Gang-ri Tökar,[8]
in the pleasant grove of Yönten Kunjung,
you, the hidden yogin,[9] beheld the ultimate quintessential meaning.
I pray to you, noble Longchen Rabjam.
Grant your blessings that I may recognize my true nature as the nature of
mind itself.

After many repetitions of this prayer, blend your mind with the guru's enlightened mind, without allowing your attention to drift into the past, anticipate the future, or indulge in contrived thoughts in the present. Make whatever effort you can to maintain an ongoing experience of this uncontrived way of abiding.

Glorious and precious root guru,
you dwell on a lotus seat in the center of my heart.
I pray that you care for me with supreme kindness
and grant me the siddhis of enlightened form, speech, and mind.

In all rebirths, may I not be separated from the true guru,
and may I enjoy the bounty of the dharma.
Totally perfecting the qualities of the spiritual paths and levels,
may I swiftly attain the state of Vajradhara.

Formulate these and other such prayers of aspiration.

The old priest Jamyang Dorjé, who received the title of khenpo in the valley known as Jangchub Jönpalung, offered this method of prayer as an aid to spiritual practice for His Excellency Gyagar Tapshé, chief minister to His Majesty the King of Bhutan. May it ensure that His Excellency's mind is filled with the blessings of enlightened intent, the ultimate lineage of natural great perfection. The scribe was Sönam Tobgyé.

Introductory Verses

I pay homage to and take refuge in the holy guru, [1.1b][1] who is none other than a transcendent and accomplished conqueror, a *sugata*,[2] Rirap Marmei Gyaltsen.[3] I pray that you grant me your blessings.

> Samantabhadra is uncontrived and unborn dharmakaya;
> the unceasing natural radiance of being is the splendor of sambhogakaya;
> guiding beings in myriad ways, the Lord of Sages[4] is nirmanakaya.
> I bow to Vajradhara, the three kayas as teacher. [1.2a]
>
> Within the state of suchness, in as many realms as there are atoms in the universe,
> appear countless manifestations of the five buddha families—Vairochana and others—
> their forms radiant and perfect, with all the major and minor qualities.
> I bow to the lineage of mind-to-mind transmission, embracing the basic space of phenomena.
>
> Simply through symbolic means that indicate the key point, you thoroughly mastered
> the ultimate meaning of the six million verses of tantra, without exception.
> You are sublime masters of awareness, whose vajra form is rainbow body.[5]
> I pay homage to the gurus of the lineage of transmission through symbols.
>
> The meaning of the direct transmission of the supremely secret Nyingtik teachings [1.2b]
> has been transmitted orally as the direct perception of the true nature of phenomena.
> In ordinary human form, you possess the enlightened intent of victorious ones.
> I pay homage to the gurus of the oral lineage.

For you, the vast expanse (*longchen*)[6]—the enlightened intent of dharmakaya—became evident,
and the entire array (*rabjam*) of purity arose as the display of spontaneous presence.
You are the great vehicle of the teachings, the three categories of Dzogchen.
You are a perfect buddha, O majestic Drimé Özer.

Terdak Lingpa, champion of the kama and terma traditions of the Early Translation school;
Namkha Jigmé, glorious heruka;
and Jigmé Lingpa, the second Omniscient One,[7] who controls the quintessential life force
of the sublime and superb spiritual approach: grant me your protection.

The theme is the natural great perfection of utter lucidity,
discussed in the 6,400,000 verses of tantra.
I bow to Khenchen Ngagi Wangpo, who in these later times
elucidated the teachings of Samantabhadra, wholly positive enlightened mind.

Utter lucidity is the subtle essence that embraces all of conditioned existence and the peace of nirvana.
Your vajra form is that of coemergent supreme bliss, without transition.
O protector of the teachings concerning the uncompounded state of primordial unity,
majestic Shedrup Tenpai Nyima, you are the master of my buddha family.[8]

True regents of Padma in this final period of five hundred years,[9] [1.3a]
universal monarchs among all of the siddhas who bring forth termas,
sublime leaders who liberate all beings without exception in these degenerating times:
I carry these two great, peerless tertöns[10] on the crown of my head.

You bear the marks of Vajradhara's command as your emblems.
Yours are the wrathful faces of fierce masters over the life force of those who break samaya.
One-Eyed Ekajati, Thousand-Eyed Maheshvara, and others,
be my allies on the path until my enlightenment.

The river of spiritual injunctions has flowed as a successive transmission
from the primordial protector down to my root gurus.

To ensure that it endures [1.3b]
and to show future generations the venerable origins of these spiritual teachings,
I am publishing this collection of biographies, *A Marvelous Garland of Rare Gems.*
Deities of the Three Roots, vast hosts of oath-bound ones,
and custodians of these teachings, grant me your permission.

This crowning jewel of the ocean of profound and extensive spiritual approaches[11]
is borne as an adornment on the heads of the many faithful,
so I honor it as the tip of the brocade victory banner of my belief
and publish this splendid source of all the virtue and excellence one could wish for.

The great tantras *The Conjunction of Sun and Moon* and *The Blazing Clear Expanse* both state, "In order to arouse students' faith, explain the lineage, beginning with Samantabhadra." Accordingly, I will describe the exemplary lives of the masters of awareness in the lineage, emphasizing the great transmission of the secret Nyingtik teachings—the river of spiritual injunctions that constitute the extensive transmissions of the approach of natural great perfection.

This book has three sections: the lineage from which these teachings derive, the instructions that derive from the lineage, and the conclusion that completes the text. To begin with, the Nyingtik lineage is threefold, comprising the mind-to-mind transmission by victorious ones, the transmission through symbols by masters of awareness, and the oral transmission by human individuals.

PART I

The Lineage

1

The Mind-to-Mind Transmission by Victorious Ones

Samantabhadra

In the first case—the mind-to-mind transmission by victorious ones— [1.4a] our teacher, the glorious Samantabhadra,[1] awakened to true enlightenment in primordial basic space, the ground of being. Samantabhadra's mode is that of abiding without wavering from the enlightened intent that constitutes the kayas and timeless awareness, which never come together and then separate. Within the scope of inner lucidity, or dharmakaya, omniscient timeless awareness is itself utterly lucid, because its three aspects—essence, nature, and responsiveness—are indwelling as the three kayas of basic space, not engaged with any objects. Within that context, the excellent environment [1.4b] is the pure realm of dharmakaya, where the excellent teacher is Samantabhadra; the excellent retinue is a vast assembly of aspects of timeless awareness; the excellent occasion is the duration of the nature of phenomena, the nature that is without transition or change; and the excellent teaching is that of utter lucidity within the realm of natural spontaneous presence.

The Buddhas of the Five Families

Without wavering from that sphere, manifestation occurs naturally as sambhogakaya. Due to this aspect of natural manifestation, the blissful pure realm is the dense array of total purity, in which everything comes about from the natural inner glow of the five aspects of timeless awareness, without any of the ordinary spatial dimensions of up or down, of primary or secondary directions. The buddhas of the five families manifest within an elegant array of precious mansions of light, surrounded by hosts of their respective mandalas, hundreds of thousands in number and beyond description. There is no duality of someone to be guided and someone else who guides, but rather a naturally occurring quality of mastery over the spontaneous presence of naturally manifest appearances. It is from this manifest aspect that an inconceivable number of buddhas of the five families emanate. All apparent phenomena, moreover, are elegantly arrayed like a field of fine silk brocade and radiate light of five colors; [1.5a] this takes place naturally as rays of light emanating without limit from six syllables within the mandalas of the buddhas' mouths and tongues. Within this context, the excellent environment is the dense array of total purity, where the excellent teachers are the buddhas of the five families; the excellent retinue is that of the immeasurable mandalas of buddhas that surround them; the excellent teaching is that of the enlightened intent of utterly lucid timeless awareness; and the excellent occasion is the duration of the inconceivable nature of phenomena. As a natural attribute of being, the enlightened intent of utter lucidity [1.5b] is revealed in a way that defies description.

Under the foregoing circumstances, nirmanakaya forms then become apparent. Appearing according to the acumen of those to be guided, these forms are radiant and naturally manifest, like a reflection of the moon in water. Due to the force of confusion present in the six distinct classes of beings—above, below, in different directions—ordinary beings fixate on the confusing appearances in their minds and therefore perceive their individual environments and the manifold appearances of joy and sorrow. Within that sphere, individual buddhas of the five families manifest as naturally occurring emanations in realms throughout the ten directions, ensuring benefit for bodhisattvas who have attained the first to the tenth levels of realization. And countless transcendent and accomplished conquerors turn the wheel of spiritual teachings among the six classes of beings, ensuring benefit for those in such states.

The Twelve Teachers

One example of such manifestation is the way in which emanations appeared in this world of sorrow. From the naturally manifest realm of the dense array of spontaneous presence appeared the two main kinds of emanations just mentioned. With regard to the latter, there were three ways in which sublime emanations came about through blessings: (1) From some 101 types of precious jewels appeared naturally manifest forms that were equal in physical appearance and life span to given groups of beings, liberating them by performing many miracles. [1.6a] (2) From these jewels, a great text, *The Tantra of the Teachings: The Single Child,* manifested naturally, ensuring benefit for beings through the inherent proclamation of countless variations of teachings. (3) The true nature of phenomena ensured freedom for beings in the first years of vajra time, with a rain of teachings and material objects falling to guide them in whatever way was necessary. The texts, moreover, were proclaimed in whatever languages were appropriate.[2]

These emanations caused rays of light to shine forth in all ten directions of the six worlds,[3] carrying out enlightened activities that freed countless beings in a completely natural way, without effort. [1.6b] They are referred to as "sublime emanations appearing naturally through the principles of enlightened form, speech, and mind." So-called holy emanations of timeless awareness manifested as leaders and others who ensured benefit by guiding beings in whatever way was necessary.

In this regard, the nirmanakaya emanations of the great Vajradhara appeared naturally from the ongoing mandala of inexhaustible adornment—the enlightened form, speech, and mind of all victorious ones in the naturally manifest pure realm of the dense array of spontaneous presence. In the first eon (known as the "Age of Manifold Joy") of this universe, Vajradhara had appeared naturally in sambhogakaya form atop a lotus. This emanation gave Vajrasattva and Vajrapani all the teachings of natural great perfection—teachings beyond words and letters—ensuring that understanding occurred naturally through enlightened intent. At that point, this perfect buddha, the great Vajradhara, emanated in nirmanakaya forms to guide beings—in as many as there were countless beings to be guided. To ensure the purification of the five mind-body aggregates that constituted their retinues, these emanations were endowed with the five aspects of excellence.

VAJRASATTVA

VAJRAPANI

That is to say, the excellent teacher, the great Vajradhara, in the realm of Ganden Tsekpa, in the excellent environment atop a lotus flower, [1.7a] appeared first as the incredible teacher Cheu Nangwa, expounding the earliest of all tantras, the source of all teachings—*The Reverberation of Sound*—to a retinue of 1,002 buddhas. The compiler of the tantra was a child of the gods named Gajé Wangchuk; his companions were other children of the gods, such as Nyima Raptu Nangjé. This took place when the human life span was immeasurably long. Although the teacher and the retinue were not separate from one another, their enlightened intent to guide beings was such that they seemed to be so. [1.7b] And during this current eon, by virtue of the same enlightened intent to guide, buddhas appear in a distinct succession, at separate times and with individual names and teachings.

CHEU NANGWA

Nirmanakaya emanations then emerged in succession. The second manifested in the environment of our world of sorrow as the teacher Cheu Ö Mitrukpa, who gave a retinue of two hundred thousand dakinis the teachings of the five tantras (enlightened form, speech, mind, qualities, and

CHEU Ö MITRUKPA

JAMPAL JIGPA KYOPA

ZHÖNNU ROLPA

VAJRADHARA

ZHÖNNU PAWO TOBDEN CHENPO

activities). He spoke in the language of Vishnu—known as "the god with five locks of hair"—a language that arose from the natural sound of the elements interacting due to heat and cold. This took place when humans enjoyed a life span of ten million years.

The third emanation manifested in the environment of a mass of light resulting from the combination of warmth and moisture. The teacher Jampal Jigpa Kyopa addressed a retinue of six hundred thousand bodhisattvas. The teachings of several tantras—*Dredging the Pit of Cyclic Existence, Peacocks with Entwined Necks,* and *The Glorious Resolution of the Four Elements*—carried on the gentle murmuring of the wind, fell from the sky and were given after having been translated into the language of the three-tufted garudas. This took place when the life span of humans was one hundred thousand years.

The fourth emanation manifested in the environment of a womb, the source of desire and attachment. [1.8a] The teacher Zhönnu Rolpa Nampar Tsewa addressed a retinue of five thousand *yaksha* spirits and rock demons, giving them the teachings of eleven tantras: five basic tantras of the Category of Mind and six auxiliary tantras. This took place when the life span of humans was eighty thousand years.

The fifth emanation manifested in the environment of the garden of the physician Kumara. The teacher of the sixth buddha family, Vajradhara, addressed a retinue that consisted of the "seven successive buddhas,"[4] giving them an immeasurable number of teachings, including those concerning the six transcendent perfections. This took place when the life span of humans was seventy thousand years. [1.8b]

The sixth emanation manifested in the environment of Meri Barwa, the charnel ground of the display of the supreme secret. The teacher Zhönnu Pawo Tobden Chenpo addressed a retinue of seven bodhisattvas, who were described as "having the strength of clouds," giving them the teachings of many classes of tantra—father tantras, mother tantras, and so forth.[5] This took place when the life span of humans was sixty thousand years.

The seventh emanation manifested in the environment known as Sinpo Rului Dradang Denpa. The teacher Drangsong Tröpai Gyalpo gave a retinue of ten million

DRANGSONG TRÖPAI GYALPO

SER-Ö DAMPA

TSEWAI ROLPAI LODRÖ

KASHYAPA THE ELDER (ÖSUNG DRÉPO)

bloodthirsty demons the teachings of such texts as the ten tantras for guiding wild beings. This took place when the life span of humans was ten thousand years.

The eighth emanation manifested in the environment of Vulture Peak,[6] in the region of Rajgir in India. The teacher, the arhat Ser-ö Dampa, addressed a retinue consisting of countless spiritually advanced shravakas who were endowed with miraculous powers, giving them tens of thousands of teachings concerning the Vinaya of the sacred dharma. This took place when the life span of humans was five thousand years.

The ninth emanation manifested in the environment of the victorious mansion of the bodhi tree known as Sokpo Yuyi Minmachen. The teacher Tsewai Rolpai Lodrö addressed a retinue of bodhisattvas who had attained the eighth level of realization, [1.9a] giving them teachings on texts such as the seven tantras concerning subtle teachings. This took place when the life span of humans was one thousand years.

The tenth emanation manifested on Vulture Peak. The teacher Kashyapa the Elder addressed a retinue of seven fully ordained arhats, giving them such sacred teachings as the sutras, the Kriya tantras, and the seventy-five thousand sections of the Anuyoga approach (which is based on explanatory commentaries). This took place when the life span of humans was five hundred years.

The eleventh emanation manifested in the environment of the vajra seat of Bodh Gaya,[7] the source of enlightenment. The teacher Ngöndzok Gyalpo addressed a retinue of the lords of the three families,[8] transmitting to them only the definitive meaning of the teachings. This occurred when the life span of humans was three hundred years.

The twelfth emanation manifested in the excellent environment of the garden of Anathapindika.[9] The excellent teacher Shakyamuni taught the excellent dharma to the four groups in his retinue,[10] turning the wheel of the teachings concerning the Four Noble Truths sixteen times. The sixteen topics were impermanence, suffering, emptiness, the nonexistence of the self, causal factors, the origin of suffering, the process of origination, conditionality, the spiritual path, correct reasoning, [1.9b] spiritual at-

NGÖNDZOK GYALPO

SHAKYAMUNI

tainment, renunciation, the cessation of suffering, the state of peace, the state of perfection, and disengagement from the world. This took place when the life span of humans was one hundred years.

These emanations appeared in these twelve environments, presenting teachings through the five aspects of excellence, resulting in a total of sixty aspects of spiritual teachings, the underlying intent of which was to purify the sixty cycles of evolution and devolution of this eon.

Furthermore, some ninety-six aspects of the dharma must come together in one who is a foremost holder of the teachings, or a manifest nirmanakaya emanation; such a one is referred to as a "master of spiritual teachings." (If a buddha lacking some of these aspects were to appear in the world, that buddha's teachings would be said to be fragmentary.) Emanations like this come about by having perfected the altruistic motivation they previously aroused. Only in this way could they have appeared as holy leaders of beings from the time the human life span was immeasurable until it was one hundred years. Similarly, in the future, from the advent of Maitreya[11] until Adhimuktika, the last buddha of this eon, emanations will appear successively as guides for beings.

In general, the phrase "threefold lineage" is unique to the Early Translation school of secret mantra. [1.10a] The mind-to-mind transmission of enlightened intent is the root of all three lineages. The ultimate significance of this enlightened intent can be described metaphorically: Because the moon in the sky is marked by the shape of a rabbit, however many of its reflections appear in water, all are adorned with that shape. In an analogous way, the entire range of collections of teachings—both scriptural and experiential—are complete within the enlightened intent of the teacher (the union of the masculine and feminine aspects, Samantabhadra and Samantabhadr›), which constitutes the attainment of the consummate vision of omniscient timeless awareness. Because victorious ones, including the two kinds of emanations mentioned above, appear naturally as this or that buddha within the essence of Samantabhadra alone, they do not waver from this single enlightened intent. Nevertheless, they appear in succession, all of them definitely and solely buddhas who have discovered timeless awareness that entails knowledge of all phenomena. Thus this succession is referred to as the "mind-to-mind transmission of victorious ones." To gain a greater understanding of the nature of these victorious ones, the reader can consult the cycle *The Heart Drop of Vimalamitra, The Precious Treasury of the Sublime Spiritual Approach,* and other works.

2

The Transmission Through Symbols by Masters of Awareness

Garab Dorjé

In the region of Dhanakosha in the country of Oddiyana, [1.10b] the king Uparaja (also known as Dharma Ashva) and his queen, Nangsel Ödenma, were renowned because their daughter, a fully ordained nun, was said to be superhuman. While she was meditating by a vast body of water whose banks were strewn with gold dust, she dreamed that a being made of crystal bestowed an empowerment on her with a crystal vase marked with the five syllables of the dakas. When the nun related this to her maidservant (whose name was that of a dakini), she replied that this foretold the coming of a nirmanakaya emanation. Before long, the nun gave birth to an emanation of Vajrasattva,[1] a child of the gods named Semlhak-chen, [1.11a] who had spread the Dzogchen teachings in the realm of the gods. Ashamed because the child had no father, she cast him into a pit of ashes, from which came sounds, lights, and showers of blossoms. Three days later, she went to look for him and, finding him unharmed, bathed him. Gods and dakinis appeared in the sky to make offerings to him.

When he reached seven years of age, the boy asked his mother if she would permit him to discuss spiritual issues with scholars. She refused, saying, "A child whose baby teeth have not yet fallen out can hardly discuss spiritual matters." But he insisted, and when he debated with the five hundred scholars who were the pride of Uparaja's court, no one could best him. He was acknowledged by the scholars as a nirmanakaya emanation and shown all befitting honors. The king was extremely delighted and so named the boy Garab Dorjé.[2]

Garab Dorjé went to live on the mountain of Nyima Nangjé to the north, where fierce preta spirits lived, and there cultivated meditative absorption for thirty-two years. At the end of that period, earthquakes shook the land and a voice was heard saying, "Those who uphold extreme views have been defeated." A cowherd related this to the king of these extremists, who dispatched assassins to kill the yogin. They could not harm Garab Dorjé, however, for his body had become diaphanous, like a ray of sunlight. He then rose into the sky, [1.11b] whereupon faith was instantly aroused in the assassins, and they converted to Buddhism.

A vast number of teachings of the Three Repositories[3] and the 6,400,000 verses of the Dzogchen tantras were primordially present in Garab Dorjé's mind. Vajrasattva, showing himself directly to Garab Dorjé, bestowed empowerment on him through intense rays of light and revealed to him the timeless awareness that requires no learning. Vajrasattva granted him permission to commit the tantras to writing, and these were arranged in volumes of scripture by the dakini of immutable basic space, the dakini of limitless enlightened qualities, and others. These volumes were placed under the care of the dakini Semdenma and venerated by her. Meanwhile, the master Garab Dorjé rode on the back of the naked daughter of Vishnu, journeying to the charnel ground of Shitavana, where he taught the dharma to dakinis, many hundreds of thousands of whom attained rainbow body.

It was from Garab Dorjé that the master Mañjushrimitra heard the teachings.

Mañjushrimitra

At that time, west of the vajra seat at Bodh Gaya in central India, a son was born in the city of Rimpa Nyipa to the brahmin Lekden Tönpa and his wife, Nangwa Drönma. The son was known as both the brahmin Nyingpo Druppa and the master Mañjushrimitra, [1.12a] proficient in the five fields of knowledge.[4] The deity Mañjushri advised him, "Ah, child of spiritual heritage! If you wish to attain buddhahood in a single lifetime, go to the charnel ground of Shitavana." Immediately upon hearing this, Mañjushrimitra set out for the charnel ground and there met the master Garab Dorjé, who bestowed empowerments and teachings on him. He remained for seventy-five years, thoroughly mastering all of the tantras, explanatory commentaries, and pith instructions. When Mañjushrimitra had finished listening to the teachings, Garab Dorjé dissolved into a mass of light at the source of the Dantik River. Mañjushrimitra cried out in distress:

> Alas! Oh, woe! Oh, immeasurable woe! [1.12b]
> If the teacher's illuminating light is extinguished,
> how will the darkness in this world be dispelled?

Thereupon out of the light fell a jeweled locket the size of a fingernail, which contained the testament of Garab Dorjé, *Three Verses Hitting upon the Key Points*. By merely glancing at this, Mañjushrimitra became his master's equal in realization. He divided the 6,400,000 verses of the Dzogchen tantras into three categories: the Category of Mind, which concerns the abiding state; the Category of Expanse, which concerns the state free of anything needing to be done; and the Category of Direct Transmission, which concerns the significance of key points. He also divided the cycle of the profound Nyingtik teachings, which further summarize the most crucial key points, into two sections: the explanatory tantras and the tantras transmitted orally. He wrote down annotated versions of the orally transmitted tantras. Failing to find anyone suitable to receive the explanatory tantras, he concealed them as termas in a boulder marked with crossed vajras northeast of the vajra seat at Bodh Gaya. He dwelled for 109 years in the charnel ground of Sosadvipa, west of Bodh Gaya.

It was from Mañjushrimitra that Shri Simha heard the teachings.

Shri Simha

During those times, in a Chinese city called Shocham Nakpo, a son was born to the householder Gewadang Denpai Yidchen and his wife, Nangsel Raptu Chenden. This boy became known as the great master Shri Simha.

Beginning at the age of fifteen, [1.13a] he studied the five fields of knowledge—Sanskrit grammar, valid cognition, astrology, and so on—with the master Hastibhala and became very proficient. One day, while he was traveling on the road to the city of Serling, the exalted Avalokiteshvara appeared in the sky and advised him, "Ah, fortunate one! If you definitely seek the goal in this single lifetime, go to the charnel ground of Sosadvipa to the west of the vajra seat in India." Having said this, the deity vanished.

Shri Simha thought, "In order to realize the goal of the secret mantra approach, I shall spend seven years studying the outer and inner meanings of the tantric approach." [1.13b] He thus studied with the outcaste master Bhelakirti in the east, on the five-peaked mountain of Wu Tai Shan, thoroughly mastering the tantras, explanatory commentaries, and pith instructions according to the outer and inner levels of the tantric path.

One morning, as Shri Simha was bathing in a pond, the supremely compassionate Avalokiteshvara appeared again and gave him similar advice, then vanished. Shri Simha thought, "It is difficult to travel to India. I shall therefore go after I have achieved the yogic ability to move swiftly." With this intention, he practiced for three years and, after having gained accomplishment, made the journey to India using the miraculous power to move swiftly, his body a yard above the ground. In nine days, he reached the great charnel ground of Sosadvipa, where he encountered the eminent master Mañjushrimitra. He prostrated to and circumambulated him with the request, "Please take me under your care!" The master agreed to do so and granted him instructions, prophesying as well that Shri Simha would recover the texts that Mañjushrimitra had concealed.

When Mañjushrimitra passed away, dissolving into a mass of light in the sky above the charnel ground, Shri Simha cried out in distress, "Alas! Oh, woe!" Thereupon out of the sky fell a jeweled locket containing the testament of Mañjushrimitra, *The Six Meditative Experiences.*

Then the master Shri Simha retrieved the texts that Mañjushrimitra had concealed in the boulder at Bodh Gaya and returned with them to the vicinity of the bodhi tree growing in China. [1.14a] He divided these texts concerning the most sublime secret into four cycles: the outer, inner, secret, and most secret unsurpassable cycles. He concealed the first three cycles in the capital of a pillar in the temple of Tashi Trigo. He kept the final cycle but, in keeping with a dakini's prophecy, later concealed it in the same place and so caused it to disappear. He then went to the great charnel ground of Siljin.

It was from Shri Simha that Vimalamitra and Jñanasutra heard the teachings.

Vimalamitra and Jñanasutra

JÑANASUTRA

At that time, in the city of Langpo Gang in western India, the great master Vimalamitra was born, son of the householder Deden Korlo and his wife, Daknyi Selma. [1.14b] In the city of Kamaru in eastern India,[5] Jñanasutra was born as the son of a low-caste man named Shinta Lakpa and his wife, Gewai Semden. Both Vimalamitra and Mañjushrimitra became learned in the five fields of knowledge.

Once, while they were staying at Bodh Gaya, in order to relax they hiked to a place several miles to the west, a lush marshy area in which flowers grew. Vajrasattva appeared in the sky and exhorted them, "Ah, you two children of spiritual heritage! For five hundred lifetimes, you have taken rebirth as scholars but have yet to attain your goal; [1.15a] so if you wish to become free in this single lifetime, go to the charnel ground of Siljin in China!"

Immediately upon hearing this, Vimalamitra went to Siljin and met Shri Simha, who bestowed on him the complete transmission of the instructions of the oral lineage, as well as the outer, inner, and secret cycles of teachings. When Vimalamitra returned to India, he met Jñanasutra near the city of Gajé. Recalling their time together in Bodh Gaya, Jñanasutra asked, "Did you meet a holy being in Siljin?"

He replied, "I met an emanation of a buddha."

Vimalamitra then proceeded to the charnel ground of Tachung to pursue tantric activities, while Jñanasutra went to the great master Shri Simha at the charnel ground of Siljin. "Please take me under your care," he requested, and Shri Simha agreed to do so. He first bestowed on Jñanasutra the oral lineage and the outer, inner, and secret cycles concerning the sphere of being; he then bestowed the teachings of the most secret unsurpassable cycle. He also prophesied that Jñanasutra would reveal termas.

At that point, Shri Simha passed away, dissolving into a mass of light, whereupon Jñanasutra cried out in distress, "Alas! Oh, woe!" From the sky fell a jeweled locket containing the testament of Shri Simha, *The Seven Linking Principles.* Jñanasutra then retrieved the texts concealed by his master in the pillar at the temple of Tashi Trigo [1.15b] and went to live in the charnel ground of Bhasing in India.

About the same time, Vimalamitra received advice from the dakini Palgyi Lodröma, who said to him, "O fortunate one, if you wish to receive instructions even more profound than those you were given previously, go to the great charnel ground of Bhasing." Upon hearing this, he journeyed there and met again with Jñanasutra, whom he asked to be his guide. Jñanasutra granted him the complete transmission of the instructions and then passed away, dissolving into a mass of light, whereupon Vimalamitra cried out in distress, "Alas! Oh, woe!" At that, from the sky fell a jeweled locket containing the testament of Jñanasutra, *The Four Means of Resting.*

Vimalamitra then went to live in eastern India. By day he served as royal priest to Simhabhadra, the king of Kamaru; by night he taught the dharma to dakinis in charnel grounds. Furthermore, an emanation of his dwelled in the city of Bhirya in western India, acting as royal priest to King Dharmapala. By night this emanation would travel five hundred leagues to the north to teach the dharma to dakinis in the charnel ground of Raptu Nangjé and would serve as royal priest to King Indrabodhi the Younger in the city of Kapila.[6] [1.16a]

The foregoing biographies of the masters of the lineage of transmission through symbols were written primarily from a conventional perspective. The accounts of their extraordinary secret deeds can be found in the cycle *The Heart Drop of Vimalamitra.*

Padmakara

The following is an account of how the master Padma heard the teachings from Shri Simha. Generally speaking, there are an inconceivable number of spiritual biographies of this great being, which are found in the accounts of both the kama and terma transmissions. Here I shall relate the most well known version, that of the terma tradition. According to a prophetic prayer of praise in *Mañjushri: Web of Magical Display:*

> The glorious buddha Padma will be born,
> endowed with a treasury of omniscient timeless awareness.
> This ruler, possessing an array of myriad magical powers, [1.16b]
> will be great, a holder of the awareness mantras of buddhahood.

In keeping with this passage, Padmakara was an emanation of the buddha Amitabha and the very embodiment of the enlightened speech of all tathagatas.[7]

In the land of Oddiyana, west of India, there were three great lakes in the eastern, southern, and northern regions. On an island in the southern lake (which was, more accurately, to the southwest), close to an area inhabited by bloodthirsty *rakshasa* demons, there grew, by the blessings of the buddhas, a long-stemmed lotus of many colors. In the center of the lotus appeared a golden vajra, marked with the syllable *Hrih,* which had emanated from the heart of the protector of the pure realm of Sukhavati.[8] From this vajra appeared a small boy, eight years of age, sitting in the lotus, his form adorned with the major and minor marks of physical perfection, holding a vajra and a lotus and giving teachings to gods and to the dakinis of the island.

In the meantime, because Indrabodhi, king of the region, did not yet have an heir, he made offerings to the Three Jewels and distributed wealth from his treasury as alms.[9] Having exhausted his reserves, he and his advisers journeyed to an island in the ocean to retrieve a wish-fulfilling gem. On their way home, the king's spiritual adviser, Krishnadhara, encountered the boy, whose destiny it was to be the king's heir, and brought him before the king. Indrabodhi invited the boy to return with them to the palace. [1.17a] The king named him Padmakara and Saroruhavajra[10] and placed him on a jeweled throne that had appeared by the power of the wish-fulfilling gem. With the gem, moreover, he brought joy to the entire populace by manifesting an abundance of food, clothing, and precious jewels.

Padmakara brought countless beings to spiritual maturity through his youthful play and games. He made the dakini Bhasadhara his queen and ruled the empire of Oddiyana according to the dharma, becoming famed as King Torchokchen. At one point, however, he realized that if he continued to rule his kingdom, he could not accomplish great benefit for others. He therefore asked his father for permission to abdicate, but was refused. This led him to perform a playful dance during which he pretended to lose his grip on a trident, killing the son of a wicked minister and sending the boy's consciousness into basic space.[11] According to the laws governing murder, Padmakara was banished to the charnel grounds, so he pursued his tantric activities in Shitavana, Nandanavana, and Sosadvipa. There he was empowered and blessed by two dakinis, Marajita[12] and Shantarakshita. When he had brought the dakinis of the charnel grounds under his power, he too became known as Shantarakshita (Guardian of Peace).

He journeyed to the island in Lake Dhanakosha, where he practiced the secret mantra approach using the symbolic language of the dakinis, [1.17b] thus bringing the dakinis of that lake under his power. He pursued tantric conduct in Parushakavana, where the goddess Vajravarahi revealed herself and granted him blessings. He bound the *nagas*[13] of the oceans and the planetary demons of the heavens[14] to obedience. The dakas and dakinis of the three places granted him *siddhis*,[15] and he became known by the name Dorjé Drakpo Tsal (Vajra Dynamic Wrath).

Then he journeyed to the vajra seat at Bodh Gaya, where he demonstrated various miracles, causing people to ask who he was. He avowed that he was a naturally occurring buddha, but they did not believe him and instead reviled him. Seeing many reasons for doing so, he went to the country of Sahora, took monastic ordination under the master Prabhahasti, and became known as Shakya Seng-gé (Lion of the Shakyas). He heard teachings on the Yoga tantras some eighteen times, whereupon he had visions of the deities. He requested empowerments from Anandi, the dakini Guhyajñana manifesting in the form of a Buddhist nun. She transformed him into a *Hum* syllable and swallowed him; while he was inside her, she bestowed on him the outer, inner, and secret empowerments in their entirety and then expelled him through her vagina, in this way refining away the three levels of obscuration. He received the Eight Commands of Sadhana Practice from the eight great masters of awareness. With Buddhaguhya, he studied *The Web of Magical Display,* [1.18a] and from many other learned and accomplished Indian masters, he received teachings on all of the sutras, tantras, and other fields of knowledge. In undergoing this training, he became learned in all of these with only a single exposure to them. He had visions of deities without having to practice deliberately to do so. He became known as Loden Choksé (Intelligent Seeker of the Sublime) and so provided the world with a model of a master of awareness who is still experiencing the consequences of karma.[16]

Then he captured the heart of the princess of Sahora, the daughter of King Arshadhara, who bore the dakini name Mandarava. He took her away to be his consort and to support his spiritual attainment, and they spent three months in Maratika Cave[17] pursuing practice to attain longevity. The protector and buddha of infinite life, Amitayus, actually appeared to them and bestowed empowerment, granting them blessings so that they were united with him. He bestowed on them a billion tantras of longevity, and they attained the siddhi of a master of awareness with power over longevity. Having achieved birthless and deathless vajra forms, they went forth to guide the kingdom of Sahora. When the king and his ministers tried to burn them alive, they miraculously manifested on top of a long-stemmed lotus in a swirling lake of sesame oil, and so aroused faith in everyone. All the people converted to Buddhism and were brought to levels of realization from which they would not fall back. [1.18b]

In addition, the master and his consort went seeking alms in order to guide those they encountered in the kingdom of Oddiyana. The inhabitants recognized Padmakara, and an evil minister and others tried to burn him and Mandarava alive in a fire of sandalwood. The two consorts once again appeared atop a long-stemmed lotus in the center of a lake. Because he wore a miraculous garland of skulls symbolizing the liberation of beings from samsara, Padmakara came to be known as Pema Tötreng Tsal (Lotus Dynamic Garland of Skulls).

He acted as the king's spiritual adviser for thirteen years, bringing the entire kingdom to the dharma. He conferred the maturing empowerments and liberating instructions of vast collections of teachings. The king, queen, and everyone else with the appropriate karma accomplished the state of a sublime master of awareness. Padmakara became known as Pema Gyalpo (Lotus King).

As prophesied in the sutra *The Magical Emanation's Sphere of Activity*, he then emanated as a Buddhist monk named Indrasena to guide King Ashoka. He inspired the king with incontrovertible faith to erect, throughout the known world and in a single night, ten million stupas containing relics of tathagatas. There were several rulers with extreme views, powerful enemies out to harm the Buddhist teachings, whom Padmakara released from this realm or guided by skillful means. When one king tried to have Padmakara poisoned, [1.19a] the master was not harmed; when he was cast into the Ganges River, the water rose up in the air and he danced in the sky. He became known as Cheu-chung Khading Tsal (Dynamic Youth Soaring in Space).

Furthermore, he manifested under many names and in many embodiments, such as the master Saroruha (who revealed the outer tantra of Hevajra), the brahmin Saraha, Dombi Heruka, Virupa, and Krishnacharin the Elder.[18] He went to great charnel grounds such as Kuladzokpa, where he gave dakinis teachings on the secret mantra approach. He captured the life essence of all arrogant gods and demons,[19] both outer and inner, and enjoined them to serve as guardians of the teachings.[20] When performing such deeds, he was known as Nyima Özer (Rays of the Sun).

When some five hundred teachers of extreme views were preparing to refute the Buddhist teachings at Bodh Gaya, the master matched his debating skill and spiritual powers with theirs and emerged victorious. When they then began practicing black magic, he turned back the power of their evil mantras with a wrathful one that had been offered to him by the dakini Marajita, liberating these teachers by causing great bolts of lightning to strike them. Their town was consumed by fire, and those who remained alive converted to Buddhism. While thus raising high the victory banner of the dharma, he was known as Seng-gé Dradrok (Roaring Lion). [1.19b]

Up to this point, Padmakara manifested in the manner of a master of awareness with power over longevity—one who has exhausted the three kinds of unstable degeneration[21] and has perfected the most sublime spiritual path. Then, in Yangleshö Cave on the border of India and Nepal, the princess Shakyadevi, daughter of the Nepalese king Kushaladhara, became his consort and supported his spiritual attainment. While they were pursuing the sublime siddhi through practice on the deity Samyak, three powerful demons tried to obstruct them. For three years, drought, disease, and famine fell on the land. Padmakara sent emissaries to India to secure teachings from gurus that would enable him to quell these obstacles. The tantras and explanatory commentaries concerning the deity Vajrakila were therefore dispatched from India, two men being required to carry the texts. Upon the arrival of these texts in Nepal, the obstacles were immediately pacified, rain fell, and the sickness and famine came to an end. The two consorts attained the sublime siddhi and manifested as masters of mahamudra awareness. Padmakara saw that the practice of Samyak, although bringing great siddhis, was prey to as many dangers as a traveling merchant, while the practice of Vajrakila was as indispensable as an armed escort, so he composed many sadhanas combining the practices of Samyak and Vajrakila. He bound to oaths the sixteen guardians of Vajrakila and all the other male and female lineages of worldly protectors, enjoining them to guard the teachings.

Furthermore, in the regions of Hurmaju, Sikodhara, [1.20a] Dhanakosha, and Rukma in Oddiyana, in the kingdom of Tirahuti and other remote regions, in Kamaru—in these and other places and at various appropriate times, Padmakara taught the dharma in accordance with people's good fortune, benefiting many beings through his more common siddhis. Where there was no water, he caused water to flow; in other cases, he caused great floods to drain into the earth. In eastern, southern, and central India, three monuments to gods worshiped by upholders of extreme views appeared spontaneously, severely threatening the Buddhist teachings; through the power of Vajrakila, Padmakara annihilated all three of these. When Buddhism flourished in the land of Kanja, a barbaric king mounted an army and camped by the Nila River. The master made a threatening gesture, whereupon five hundred of the king's ships capsized. Any further threat from these border tribes was halted.

It is not certain just when Padmakara traveled to the land of Dramila, but he gradually guided the humans and nonhumans—dakinis and so forth—of that region and had them build Buddhist temples. After his departure, the traditions associated with the master—a threefold transmission of study, explanation, and meditation based on all four classes of tantras, principally *The Hevajra Tantra,* the tantra *The Secret Sphere of the Moon,* and the tantras of Samyak, Hayagriva, Vajrakila, and the wrathful *mamo* goddesses—continued to flourish and spread in Dramila. [1.20b] The historical accounts of these traditions state that Padmakara went from that region to the land of bloodthirsty demons in the southwest.

This narrative of Padmakara's time in India is the most widely known, appearing in authentic Indian Buddhist histories. It is generally said that he remained there for some 3,600 years, bringing benefit to the teachings and to beings; however, it may be that scholars either used half-years as a unit of measure or were simply indicating a long period of time.

In addition, Padmakara emanated variously as prescient rulers and powerful yogins to guide the people of Mongolia and China. He also appeared as a naturally manifest youth named Vihricha in the land of Zhang Zhung,[22] leading many fortunate people to the "body of light"[23] through the orally transmitted instructions of Dzogchen.

Together, these accounts illustrate the unlimited breadth and scope of Padmakara's enlightened activities, which brought many kinds of beings to the path of liberation through a variety of means to guide them in any way necessary, in different lands and in different languages.

The foregoing biographical treatment focuses on some of the representative forms and names of Padmakara's manifestations. Some of his emanations may be more obvious than others, [1.21a] but there is not a single realm that has not been influenced by this one nirmanakaya. No one can possibly describe with any accuracy how those abiding in the state of primordial unity demonstrate their complete liberation.

Those of great spiritual attainment may not be directly perceptible at all times to ordinary beings who are to be guided, but may be seen to manifest again physically only after a long time has passed, so that it seems they have lived for long periods of time. As well, they may sometimes be invisible in certain regions but visible in others, or they may at one point seem to pass away and at another point manifest by taking rebirth. In the past, Virupa disappeared three times, only to reappear in his actual physical form. Jalandharipa disappeared and returned five times. It was said that Krishnacharin the Elder seemed to die at Devikota and that his students finished cremating his remains, only to find that he was living in another country, benefiting beings, in the very same form that he had had before; he is also reputed to have taken rebirth anew in several countries, seeming to attain the sublime siddhi there. Because such manifestations are beyond limit, they cannot be neatly arranged or reconciled in the perceptions of ordinary mortals with respect to time span and physical location (just as the circumstances of commoners can never be reconciled with those of a ruler), [1.21b] for these are deeds performed by powerful masters of miracles, who have free rein to manifest them in response to the devoted interest and mental acuity of beings. As the exalted sutra *The True Summation of All Phenomena* states:

> If they will the eon of destruction to be the eon of creation, the eon of destruction will become the eon of creation, and beings will know it to be the eon of creation. If they will the eon of creation to be the eon of destruction, the eon of creation will become the eon of destruction, and beings will know it to be the eon of destruction. Destruction and creation do not become anything else. It is through their intention that such change seems to occur. Similarly, if they will an eon to be a single morning, then beings will know an eon to be a single morning. If they will a single morning to be a whole eon, there will be just such a change, so beings will know just that to be so. This is what is meant by "miracles coming about through the will of a bodhisattva." [1.22a]

The following account relates how the great being Padmakara heard teachings concerning the great perfection of utter lucidity from the master Shri Simha. The deity Vajravarahi prophesied to him:

> O fortunate one, the transmission that ensures the goal in a single lifetime
> is not like anything else and is not realized by just anyone.
> It resides in the vajra mind of Shri Simha.
> You will find enlightened intent in Parushakavana.

When she had thus spoken, Padmakara journeyed instantly by his miraculous powers to the great charnel ground of Parushakavana. He offered prostrations to and circumambulated the master Shri Simha, asked for guidance, and was accepted as a student. Shri Simha taught him the entire range of cycles in the Categories of Mind, Expanse, and Direct Transmission, including the tantra *Great Perfection Equal to Space* and other texts. In particular, after Padmakara had listened to all of these outer, inner, and secret cycles concerning the sphere of being, he supplicated Shri Simha, "O great master, I humbly ask you to grant me an instruction that will cause this physical body—subject to decay—to vanish in this very lifetime, while allowing me to behold pure sambhogakaya realms and to awaken to buddhahood in the pure realm of dharmakaya."

Shri Simha replied, "O child of spiritual heritage, this is excellent! The very pinnacle of all teachings, the furthest reach of all views, the transcendence of all spiritual approaches, [1.22b] the heart drop of all dakinis, the ultimate significance that is the most secret of all—this is the supreme approach of the vajra heart essence of utter lucidity. It transcends ordinary mind, is free of speculation, does not fall within the province of any state of ordinary consciousness, does not fall within the limit of 'is' or 'is not,' and is beyond being an object to view or meditate upon, to develop or complete. It is the mother of all victorious ones of the three times, the short path of great masters of awareness, the unsurpassable, consummate direct transmission. I have these instructions, which bring the enlightenment of buddhahood in three years, and I shall grant them to you."

He then entrusted the teachings to Padmakara, conferring the empowerment into the most secret unsurpassable Dzogchen cycle *The Heart Drop of the Dakini*, as well as an enormous number of texts of pith instructions concerning the practical application of this transmission. As supportive teachings, Shri Simha taught him the following eighteen tantras in their entirety:

The Reverberation of Sound, the primary tantra
The Tantra Without Words, the tantra concerning the ground of being
The Blazing Remains, the tantra concerning signs of successful practice
Naturally Occurring Perfection, the tantra concerning empowerment
Adornment Through Direct Introduction
The Blazing Lamp
Naturally Arising Awareness
Vajrasattva: Mirror of the Heart
The Heaped Jewels
The Conjunction of Sun and Moon [1.23a]
The Array of Inlaid Gems
The Natural Freedom of Awareness
The Pearl Garland

Samantabhadra: Mirror of Enlightened Mind
Auspicious Beauty
The Perfect Dynamic Energy of the Lion
The Six Expanses
The Sun of the Clear Expanse of Samantabhadrā

Padmakara remained for twenty-five years, listening to and contemplating Shri Simha's instructions. He then went to the great charnel ground of Sosadvipa and practiced for three years, achieving an enlightened form that was like the moon's reflection in water, not subject to birth or death. Using his miraculous powers and appearing in various forms, he then benefited untold numbers of human and nonhuman beings in various places. In particular, by day he served as the spiritual adviser to the Indian king Dharmapala, while at night he traveled to such great charnel grounds as Shitavana, Sosadvipa, Prabhaseti, Nandana, Bhasing, Tachung, and Bhairava. There he stayed, engaging in tantric activities, together with hosts of radiant dakinis.

The foregoing constitutes the lineage transmitted through symbols by masters of awareness. [1.23b] This was not a transmission between individuals with separate minds, for it arose entirely from the natural dynamic energy of awareness, the timeless awareness that is the enlightened mind of the teacher. It was solely a matter of realization and freedom occurring simultaneously upon the mere demonstration of some symbolic means, and so the Early Translation school refers to this as the "lineage transmitted through symbols," a term unique to this school.

3

The Oral Transmission by Human Individuals

In the case of the third lineage, that of oral transmission by human individuals, there developed three great wellsprings in Tibet, from which lineages flowed to spread the traditional teachings of the three categories of Dzogchen. From Bairotsana came the kama transmissions of the Categories of Mind and Expanse. As for the Category of Direct Transmission, from Guru Padmakara came terma transmissions [1.24a], and from Vimalamitra, a more extensive lineage. These constitute the extensive transmissions of the great Nyingtik teachings, a virtual river of spiritual instructions.

KAMA, THE HISTORICAL TRANSMISSIONS: THE CATEGORIES OF MIND AND EXPANSE

Bairotsana (8th–9th Centuries)

The master Bairotsana was born in the region of Nyemo Jekar. Following the urgings of the Tibetan king Trisong Detsen,[1] he underwent some 507 terrible hardships—eight great terrors and so forth—which eventually brought him to the land of India. In a cool forest of sandalwood trees in Dhanakosha, he came upon a nine-storied pagoda that had been created by the miraculous powers of the master Shri Simha. Bairotsana asked a yogini who had come to fetch water to deliver a message to the master, but she would not answer him, so he used his gaze to cause her bucket to stick to the ground. The yogini bared her breast, revealing the mandala of immutable basic space, and then helped him meet the master Shri Simha. He made a mandala offering of gold to the master with a request for teachings on the effortless spiritual approach, to which the master assented.

The next morning, Shri Simha said, "I can demonstrate to you the profound key points under a seal of secrecy,[2] but your life will be in danger under the king's punitive laws if you do not keep this very secret. [1.24b] So by day you will listen to the teachings on cause and effect from other great scholars; by night I will reveal to you the spiritual teachings of direct transmission." In this way, Shri Simha ensured that others would remain ignorant of the situation and set auspicious circumstances in motion.

By night the master wrote down the eighteen pith instructions of the Category of Mind. He inscribed them on white silk with the milk of a white goat, and when the silk was held over a smoking fire, the letters became visible. He formed a pact with the guardians of the teachings, applying a seal of extreme secrecy. Even then, Bairotsana was not satisfied, so he remained with Shri Simha, who bestowed on him all of the empowerments and pith instructions of some sixty classes of tantra, as well as the three cycles of the Category of Expanse: the White, Black, and Varicolored cycles.[3] Bairotsana plumbed the depths of all these teachings, and still he seemed dissatisfied, so the master said to him:

> Although the basic space of phenomena is endless,
> if you understand one thing, suchness itself,
> you will find that everything else without exception is complete in that.
> I swear to you there is nothing other than that!

He then described the three ways in which the instructions are put to use,[4] the four criteria for imparting them, and the four criteria for not imparting them.[5]

Bairotsana next journeyed to the great charnel ground of Dhumagata, where he met the master Garab Dorjé[6] [1.25a] and received from him the ultimate lineage of the 6,400,000 verses of the Dzogchen tantras. At that point, he truly attained the supreme siddhi of the freedom that occurs simultaneously with realization. From this transmission came a cycle known as *The Heart Drop of Bairotsana,* variations of which are found in termas.

Bairotsana then returned to Tibet, relying on his yogic ability to move swiftly. By day he gave the king of Tibet ordinary teachings on cause and effect, while by night he expounded to him alone the Dzogchen teachings as a private transmission. He produced the "five early translations" of tantras of the Category of Mind.[7]

At that time, envious of Bairotsana for having taken such teachings back to Tibet, some Indians slandered him in order to arouse suspicion in the Tibetans' minds. As well, one of the Tibetan queens and some of the ministers were hostile to the dharma and, at a certain point, caused the master Bairotsana to be exiled to Tsawa Rong.[8] In the wilderness of the local god of Gyalrong, Draklha Gonpo, he accepted Yudra Nyingpo[9] as his student and in other ways led beings to spiritual maturity and liberation. Bairotsana also taught the Dzogchen cycles to Sangtön Yeshé Lama at Taktsekhar in Tsawa Rong, to the old man Sang-gyé Gönpo of Pang at Drakar Göndzong in Tongkung Rong,[10] to Nyak

YUDRA NYINGPO

Jñanakumara in central Tibet, and to the princess Sherab Drönma of Khotan.[11] He is thus said to have expounded these cycles of teaching on five occasions. The princess also invited Bairotsana to her region of Li. [1.25b] Finally, in the place called Bhasing in Nepal, Bairotsana became an embodiment of the state of primordial unity and passed into rainbow body.

One lineage was passed down successively from Bairotsana through Nyak Jñanakumara to Sokpo Palgyi Yeshé, Dra Palgyi Nyingpo, Lhalung Palgyi Dorjé,[12] Odren Palgyi Zhönnu, and so on. Another tradition was passed down from Sokpo to Nupchen,[13] while yet another was passed down from Bairotsana, through Shakya Dorjé of the Tsang region, to Pang Rakshita, Latri Darma Sherab, the monk Zermo Gelong, Marpa Sherab Ö, and so to Zur Dropukpa. All of the students who received the lineage from Pang Sang-gyé Gönpo, Bairotsana's student, attained rainbow body.

Pang Sang-gyé Gönpo (Pang Mipam Gönpo) (8th–9th Centuries)

Pang Gönpo reached the age of eighty-five without ever having practiced the dharma. When he became elderly, his attendants and relatives cast him out. He began practicing, but because of his advanced age, his body was very decrepit, so he used a meditation belt and support and, to keep his attention focused on the instructions, propped his chin up with a stick. He applied himself according to the oral transmissions of his master, Bairotsana, and was directly introduced to naked perception of the true nature of phenomena. His realization grew by leaps and bounds. Overjoyed, the old man threw his arms around his master's neck, [1.26a] refusing to let him go for a whole day and night. He attained siddhis and lived to be more than a hundred years old.

Ngenlam Jangchub Gyaltsen (9th–10th Centuries)

Ngenlam Jangchub Gyaltsen was Pang Gönpo's student. Known as Ralsumpa of Ngenlam in the region of Uru, he was a monk and sixty-seven years old when he came to Gyalmo Taktsekhar. He requested and received instructions from Pang Mipam Gönpo, who then said to him, "Do not return to your country now, but meditate at the cliff known as Wa Seng-gé Drak."[14] Heeding his master's injunction, he went to the cliff and meditated, and when he reached the age of 172, [1.26b] he passed away without leaving any physical remains.

Zadam Rinchenyik (9th–10th Centuries)

Zadam Rinchenyik, Ngenlam's student, came from the high steppes of eastern Tibet. After requesting and receiving instructions from Ngenlam, he stayed at the same cliffside cave, meditating without ever being separate from his guru. When he reached the age of 144, he passed away without leaving any physical remains.

Khugyur Salwaichok (9th–10th Centuries)

Zadam had a student named Khugyur Salwaichok, who came from Chongyé in the valley known as Yarlung.[15] He was a fully ordained monk and fifty-seven years old when Zadam Rinchenyik gave him instructions, whereupon he abandoned any idea of returning to his homeland. Khugyur Salwaichok stayed at Wa Seng-gé Drak meditating and at 117 years of age passed away without leaving any physical remains.

ARO YESHÉ JUNGNÉ

These three students in the direct line thus passed away together, like mist or rainbows vanishing, in the later part of a Serpent year, at Wa Seng-gé Drak. The transmission was then passed in succession to the master Yudra Nyingpo, Aro Yeshé Jungné of Longtang in eastern Tibet, the great lord Setsün, the lord Jangtön Namdak, and down to Dampa Deshek of Katok. [1.27a]

Katokpa Dampa Deshek (1122–1192) and His Students

Katokpa Dampa Deshek studied at the feet of many hundreds of spiritual mentors in all corners of Tibet and as far away as Nepal, becoming a great repository of the canon of Buddhist teachings. In accordance with a prophecy by Drowai Gonpo of Dzam, he founded the great monastic center of Katok Dorjéden at the cliff known as Seng-gé Drak in Hor, an important holy site blessed by Guru Padmakara, close to the ridge of Drida Zalmo Gang in eastern Tibet.

His view was based on three cycles: *The Discourse on United Intent*, *The Web of Magical Display*, and the mind teachings.[16] His explanatory teachings were based on three fields of study: Madhyamaka, Prajñaparamita,[17] and Vinaya. [1.27b] His guardian deities were known as the "three black ones."[18] He thus established a mainstream tradition specific to the Early Translation school.

This tradition comprised countless sublime individuals, including the thirteen successive Katok gurus (foremost among them Tsangtön Dorjé Gyaltsen and the "three named Bumpa"—the lord Jampa Bum, U-ö Yeshé Bumpa, and so forth),[19] the thirteen successive regents who maintained the monastic seat,[20] the thirteen successive *khenpos*[21] who explained the teachings,[22] and the thirteen successive siddhas of the Mok clan.[23]

MANI RINCHEN

This lineage of the students of Dampa Deshek, lord of the dharma, spread throughout the region, from Chungpo Karu Nakru in western Tibet to eastern Tibet and Gyalrong. The monastic communities comprised some 180,000 monks, and it was said that when they gathered to participate in the ceremony for restoring and purifying their vows, the light reflecting from their robes changed the color of the sky. Many hundreds of thousands of people attained rainbow body, among them the "three named Töchok" from the Gyalrong region and Druptop[24] Mani Rinchen. One of the early progenitors of Katok, Khawa Karpowa Namkha Gyatso, alone founded 108 major monastic centers (including the three of Bu, Bor, and Zhak), some as far away as the region of Jang,[25] so that the whole area of eastern Tibet was illuminated by the precious kama transmissions of the Early Translation school, spreading in all directions like the light of the sun. Countless individuals attained rainbow body through the detailed teachings of the Category of Mind and the path of *The Vajra Bridge* cycle of the Category of Expanse. [1.28a]

Parallel Lineages: The Spread of the Early Translation School

In addition, a lineage developed in central Tibet starting with a student of Khugyur named Nyang Jangchub Drak and his students, including Nyang Sherab Jungné and the master Bagom, also known as Nyang Shawachen.[26] From Tsang Lama Drakarwa and others, there developed a lineage that spread throughout the entire region of Tsang. Over time, it came to be said that "the third mainstream transmission of the teachings of the Early Translation school fell to Zur." This refers to the principal transmission that was passed on by the three major figures of the Zur clan.[27] [1.28b]
In western Tibet, there were three majestic masters of the Vajrayana: So Yeshé Wangchuk, Zurchen Shakya Jungné, and Nupchen Sang-gyé Yeshé. In eastern Tibet, the three principal figures were the spiritual lords of Katok: Dampa Deshek, Tsangtön Dorjé Gyaltsen, and Jampa Bum. In central Tibet, two omniscient spiritual lords were famed like the sun and moon: Rongzom Chökyi Zangpo and Longchen Rabjampa. In this way, countless sublime beings caused the illumination of the precious kama transmissions of the Early Translation school to permeate the spiritual kingdom of the Land of Snows, thus spreading these teachings on a vast scale.

RONGZOM CHÖKYI ZANGPO

The Lineage of the Categories of Mind and Expanse Down to Longchenpa

The extensive lineages of the kama transmissions of the Categories of Mind and Expanse were passed down to the Omniscient King of the Dharma, Longchenpa.[28] The initial teacher was the "all-creating monarch," awakened mind. The transmission was passed successively to the buddhas of the five families, the Lord of Secrets Vajrapani, Garab Dorjé, Mañjushrimitra, Dhahena Telo, his son Rajahasti, his daughter Varahi, the naga king Takshasa, the female yaksha spirit Bodhi, the courtesan Arali, the master Akshobhya, Kukkuraja, Sarani, Buddhasamanta, Maharaja, Gomadevi, the master Aloke, Kukkuraja the Younger, the "great king of Kashmir," the seer Bhashita, the courtesan Atmaka, the master Nagarjuna, Devaraja, Mañjushrimitra the Younger, Buddhaguhya, Lochen Bairotsana, Yudra Nyingpo, [1.29a] Drimé Dashar, the Mongolian Jñanashri, Nupchen Sang-gyé Yeshé, the great minister Pak of Bagor, Yöntenchok of Den, Salwaichok of Dri, Lodrö Zhönnu of Gya, Tsultrim Zangpo of Gar, Panchen Rongzom Chökyi Zangpo, Yewang of Tsur, Chökyi Wangchuk of Den, Chokla of Zhang, Yönjung of Kyé, the exalted Zhönnu Döndrup of Den, and the Omniscient One Longchen Rabjam.

In earlier times, many textual sources were used in this approach, including *Awakened Mind: Refining Gold from Ore, The Great Transmission of the Category of Mind* by Bairotsana, *The Turquoise Record of Direct Transmission, The Great Teaching Manual of Aro, The Detailed Instructions on the Category of Mind,* [1.29b] and *The Vajra Bridge* cycle of the Category of Expanse.

The Written Works of Longchenpa

On the basis of these, the great Omniscient One Longchenpa composed *Rays of Sunlight: A Commentary on the Category of Mind,* an important commentary on the tantra *The All-Creating Monarch;* a structural analysis entitled *The Net of Sun and Moon;* and the teaching manual *The Clear Expanse of Space.*

He wrote what are known as *The Three Cycles of Natural Freedom,* which include one of the source texts, *Great Perfection: The Natural Freedom of the Nature of Mind;* a teaching manual that deals with the essential points of this graduated path; a supplication based on *The Natural Freedom of the Nature of Mind; Great Perfection: The Natural Freedom of the Nature of Phenomena; The Wish-Fulfilling Essence,* a teaching manual dealing with the ultimate significance of this text; *Great Perfection: The Natural Freedom of Equalness;* and *The Jewel Essence,* a teaching manual dealing with the ultimate significance of this text.

He also wrote *The Jeweled Ship,* a teaching manual dealing with the ultimate significance of the tantra *Awakened Mind: The All-Creating Monarch,* as well as a commentary, *The Wheel of Light;* a teaching manual, *Naturally Arising Dharmakaya;* a commentary, *The Frond of Light;* a teaching manual, *Utter Relaxation in Dharmakaya;* a commentary, *The Web of Light;* and a teaching manual, *The Spontaneous Presence of Dharmakaya.* These are his works concerning the Category of Mind.

Concerning the Category of Expanse, Longchenpa wrote such texts as *Loosening the Seal into the Freedom from Any Fixed Dimension,* which is a commentary on *The Entire Array of Space,* and *The Precious Treasury of the Basic Space of Phenomena,* a commentary on the ultimate significance of pith instructions concerning the so-called nine expanses,[29] as well as a further commentary, *Illuminating the Basic Space of Phenomena,* and a teaching manual, *The Spacious Expanse of Infinite Extension.* [1.30a]

He also wrote the source text *The Precious Treasury of the Way of Abiding,* which is a commentary on the quintessential significance of all three categories, as well as a further commentary, *The Commentary on "The Precious Treasury of the Way of Abiding"; The Heart Essence of Spontaneous Presence,* an extensive treatment of the kayas and timeless awareness, as well as its commentary, *The Victory Banner That Never Falls; Major and Minor Marks of Perfection,* which deals with practical instructions concerning the three kayas; *The Crucial Juncture of All-Encompassing Awareness,* a commentary on the meaning of the pith instructions; a commentary on the quintessential meaning of *The All-Illuminating Sphere of Being;* and *Frond of Light Concerning the Intermediate State.*

In composing these and other texts, Longchenpa caused the Dzogchen teachings to shine like the sun.

TERMA, THE HIDDEN TREASURE TRANSMISSIONS: THE CATEGORY OF DIRECT TRANSMISSION

Early History and Guru Padma

Termas, or hidden treasure teachings, that were revealed successively comprise a second style of transmission, one directly from Guru Padmakara. [1.30b] In general, those principally responsible for bringing the dharma to Tibet, the Land of Snows—those whose kindness to beings there was greatest—were the "three ancestral Buddhist kings,"[30] in particular Songtsen Gampo and Trisong Detsen. Among the scholars, the greatest in terms of their kindness and amazing qualities were Guru Rinpoché, Shantarakshita, Vimalamitra, and the three translators Kawa Paltsek, Chokro Luyi Gyaltsen, and Zhang Yeshé Dé.[31] It is truly because of their motivation and aspirations that the Nyingma

SHANTARAKSHITA

tradition—established by the abbot Shantarakshita, the master Padmakara, and the Buddhist king Trisong Detsen—continues to flourish in this world, so that we have access to these teachings. [1.31a]

It was King Trisong Detsen who invited Guru Padmakara to Tibet, where he bound all of the gods and demons to oaths and built the temple of Mingyur Lhungyi Druppai Tsuklak Khang[32] at Samyé. While the abbot and the master together cast flowers in benediction, countless amazing signs manifested. As repositories of enlightened form, this and other temples—both the supporting structures and the images within them—were erected. As repositories of enlightened speech, sacred Buddhist teachings were translated. One hundred and eight great scholars of the Indian Buddhist tradition were invited to Tibet, as were many groups of scholars from such regions as Khotan, China, and Zhang Zhung. The Tibetan translators were led by the aforementioned three: Ka, Chok, and Zhang. All the sublime teachings of the Teacher existing at that time in India—sutras, tantras, and the commentaries on their intent by other masters—as well as the sutras *The Amassing of the Rare and Sublime* from Khotan and *The Garland of Buddhas* from China were translated. Hence all the texts of the sacred Buddhist teachings, the repositories of enlightened speech in this world, were translated without omission into the Tibetan language.

For ordinary students, Guru Padma taught many outer and inner tantras and pith instructions of the secret mantra approach, such as *Pith Instructions: A Garland of Views* and *The Great Graduated Path of Secret Mantra*. [1.31b] In so doing, he established the community of white-robed, long-haired lay practitioners who maintained the tantric tradition. The abbot ordained the first monks of Tibet, known as the "seven chosen men,"[33] thus establishing the community of saffron-robed monastics.[34] And so the chapters of the exalted sangha were founded as repositories of enlightened mind.

Together, the abbot, the master, and the Buddhist king cast over the entire Land of Snows a unique, positive influence, the illumination provided by the precious teachings of victorious ones.

The Guru convened three great gatherings of those with pure karma, extraordinary students such as the twenty-five who were his intimate disciples, among them the king of Tibet and his subjects. At the first gathering, he bestowed *The Gathering of Sugatas* (a cycle focusing on the Eight Commands); at the second, *The United Intent of the Gurus;* and at the third, *The Gathered Commands: An Ocean of Spiritual Teachings*. In these and other ways, he bestowed countless empowerments, sadhanas, tantras, explanatory commentaries, and pith instructions. It was during these gatherings that King Trisong Detsen composed the liturgy of the seven-point mandala offering that begins, "The earth is anointed with perfumed water. . . . "[35] In gratitude for the empowerments, he offered the Guru a consort, the dakini Yeshé Tsogyal; he also offered his empire, subjects, and retinue. On these occasions, foremost among the twenty-five intimate disciples (that is, the king and his subjects, who were greatly accomplished and gained realization during the empowerments) [1.32a] were the Guru's nine heart children: the Buddhist king Trisong Detsen, Sang-gyé Yeshé of the Nup clan, Gyalwa Chokyang, Namkhai Nyingpo, Jñanakumara, Yeshé Tsogyal, Palgyi Yeshé, Palgyi Seng-gé, and Bairotsana. Among these heart children, three are referred to as the ruler, the subject, and the consort,[36] of whom the ruler was King Trisong Detsen.

King Trisong Detsen (Middle to Late 8th Century)

The king received the pith instructions of the lineage of the secret Nyingtik teachings of utter lucidity from three masters. In the middle story of the temple,[37] which had turquoise facades, five individuals—the king, Kawa Paltsek, Jñanakumara of the Nyak clan, the monk Nyang Tingdzin Zangpo, and Prince Mutik Tsenpo[38]—received the instructions of the secret Nyingtik teachings of utter lucidity from Vimalamitra, each of them like one vase being filled from another. Then, at the glorious center of Samyé, the king received the instructions that were transmitted by the Guru. During an empowerment, the flower cast by the king fell into the center of the mandala, whereupon the king had a vision of the deity Mahottara and realization awakened in him. Finally, the king received many transmissions from Bairotsana, including those of the five early translations of the Category of Mind and *The Vajra Bridge* cycle of the Category of Expanse. He also received transmissions of the thirteen later translations of the Category of Mind from both Vimalamitra and Bairotsana. [1.32b]

In brief, the king received complete transmissions of profound teachings from three masters who were mainstays of the Dzogchen tradition: Vimalamitra, Guru Rinpoché, and Bairotsana. Putting these teachings into practice, he was directly introduced to the naked perception of the true nature of phenomena. He became the primary custodian of the teachings, gaining an ongoing state of authentic being, the spacious sky of the vast expanse of enlightened intent. For him, the dynamic energy of awareness welled up as an expansive state of sublime knowing, resulting in an extremely precise analysis of phenomena, and he wrote numerous works, including *The Authentic Standards of the True Words of the Buddha*. Furthermore, among all the sacred teachings translated in the land of Tibet by more than a hundred scholars and translators, there was not a single transmission that Tsogyal and the king did not receive.

Today, more than a thousand years later, the precious teachings of the Victorious One, especially those of the Dzogchen approach of utter lucidity, have spread to all corners of the earth and are being implemented as they were intended to be, through explanation, study, meditation, and spiritual practice. This is an expression of the influence of this great Buddhist king, whose benevolence and motivation were superb. As Mipam Rinpoché wrote:[39]

In order to skillfully guide all in Tibet,
the venerable Mañjushri, foremost of the Victorious One's children,
manifested magnificently as the king of Tibet.
I offer homage and praise at the feet of Trisong Detsen. [1.33a]

The abbot and the master, like the paired sun and moon,
the scholars and siddhas of India, the translators of Tibet,
and the nirmanakayas who brought benefit and happiness to the Land of Snows:
I offer homage and praise to you who manifested in such variety.

You had secular works, sutras, tantras, and commentaries
translated without error and established as standard sources,
planting the victory banner of the study and practice of the teachings.
I offer homage and praise to you, great ruler.

You exerted your might over the kingdoms along your four borders,
erected temples and repositories of enlightened form, speech, and mind,
and established the twofold transmission of sutra and tantra.
I offer homage and praise to you, protector of the realm of Tibet.

You ruled your kingdom by integrating spirituality and politics through various means,
governing strictly and guarding tradition to bring happiness to your empire.
Your fame as the ruler Tsangpa Lhayi Metok[40] spread across the land.
I offer homage and praise to you.

You made evident your accomplishment of the "nectar practice"[41] of Mahottara,
perfecting the supreme dynamic energy of your enlightened intent in unwavering meditative absorption
and promulgating the excellent commentaries on subjects such as valid cognition.
I offer homage and praise to you, O spiritual king.

The transmissions of the secret mantra approach are rarer even than the Buddha. [1.33b]
With these and the instructions they contain,

you made the land of Bhota[42] like that of Oddiyana.
I offer homage and praise to you.

With the seals applied by the dakinis of basic space, the profound and secret teachings—
the three classes of inner tantra—are difficult for anyone to gain access to,
a treasure trove of gems gathered by the most sublime siddhas.
I offer homage and praise to you who brought these to this land.

In this region, surrounded by a ring of cooling snow mountains,
however many communities uphold the Victorious One's teachings,
that is due to your kindness, O protector.
I offer homage and praise to you whose kindness is unrivaled.

The Buddhist teachings have endured to the present,
for various nirmanakayas have caused the teachings of the Victorious One,
as well as the benefit and happiness these bring, to flourish in the Land of Snows.
I offer homage and praise to you whose incomparable motivation led to this.

For us, the people living in this land of snowy mountain ranges,
that we can even hear the name of the dharma, the precious teachings of the Victorious One,
is due to your kindness.
Why wouldn't any intelligent person have respect for you?

And so, if with one-pointed faith and devotion
I offer praise and homage to you, O protector, [1.34a]
through your great motivation and commitment in the past,
please grant us your blessings and take us under your care.

May the victorious ones of the ten directions confer empowerments and prophecies on us.
Through the force of Avalokiteshvara's motivation
and in accordance with your intentions, O king, emanation of Mañjushri,
may the Victorious One's teachings endure.

May you lovingly take all countless beings under your care
and carry out enlightened activities to benefit others as long as space itself exists.
May I become like you, our protector—
a crown jewel among the heroic children of the victorious ones!

Other Students of Guru Padma

There were other students of the Guru who, in that lifetime, gained the immutable form of rainbow body—the state of primordial unity—as well as such individuals as the twenty-five mahasiddhas of Chimpu, the twenty-five realized ones of Yangdzong, the groups of 108 in both Yerpa and Chuwori who attained the body of light, the thirty tantric practitioners of Sheldrak, the three noblewomen who showed authentic signs of attainment, the seven siddhas of Tsang, and the twenty-five dakinis who passed away into bodies of light. Countless other men and women became siddhas.

The Guru instructed the king and his subjects according to their individual needs, [1.34b] giving them the entire range of tantras, methods of accomplishment, and pith instructions of the Dzogchen approach, primarily those dealing with the deities of the Three Roots and the practices of guru yoga, Avalokiteshvara, and Dzogchen.

Thinking of future generations, the Guru intended that teachings for later times be concealed as termas. So, accompanied by Tsogyal and others with pure karma, he traveled to all parts of Tibet, leaving not even a square foot of ground uncovered. He consecrated all of the mountains, lakes, glaciers, and cliffs as primary or secondary holy sites—the glaciers of western Tibet, the twenty-one principal holy sites of central and southern Tibet, the twenty-five principal holy sites of eastern Tibet,[43] the three foremost of the so-called hidden valleys, the "five valleys," the "three districts," and the "one region." He planned for every future generation, unwavering in bestowing his blessings so that the secret mantra teachings would not wane or be subjected to the corrupt and contrived influence of pedants and ensuring that those of his students with the proper karma to reveal these termas would appear in succession. To these ends, he concealed countless caches of termas—named and unnamed works of the dharma, objects of wealth, and sacred samaya substances—foremost among these such teachings as the "hundred majestic termas of the gurus," the "five major termas of enlightened mind," and the "twenty-five major profound termas." He left prophecies foretelling such details as the occasions on which these would be revealed, the individuals who would reveal them, those whose karma it would be to act as custodians of these teachings, [1.35a] and the secret consorts who would accompany those revealing the termas.[44] The Guru and his consort then sealed these termas with their injunctions. They were entrusted to the eight classes of terma guardians, among them the triad of the mamo goddess Ekajati, the planetary *mara*[45] Rahula, and the oath-bound one Vajrasadhu;[46] the triad of maras, *tsen* spirits,[47] and nagas; and the three masters of life force.

In thirteen places described as "tiger's lairs," such as Nereng Seng-gé Dzong in Bhutan, the Guru manifested in the form of the great and glorious Dorjé Drolö, binding all arrogant ones—gods and demons, both great and small—to oaths of allegiance. In order to inspire faith in future generations, he left impressions of his body in rocks at Dorjé Tsekpa in the Bumthang region of central Bhutan and other places;

handprints in four famous lakes, including Namtso Chukmo; and footprints in the cliff known as Drakarpo at Paro in Bhutan. He made marks at Dorjé Drak as easily as if stamping forms into fresh butter, leaving immutable signs that have inspired his devoted followers to this day and that serve as a focus for the gathering of merit by his students.

Notably, in keeping with prophecies by gurus and dakinis, he bestowed the most secret unsurpassable Nyingtik cycles, which he had received from Shri Simha, as an intimate personal transmission to a single person—his consort, Tsogyal, master of the entire range of tantra classes in the secret mantra approach. The following is the story of Tsogyal's life. [1.35b]

Yeshé Tsogyal (8th–9th Centuries)

Tsogyal was born in the Chokdro Dri area in the great region of the Kharchen clan.[48] There a chieftain named Tökarlek married Gyalmotso, a woman of the Nup clan. Following their union, Gyalmotso dreamed that a blue woman appeared in the sky emitting light, which sent a star shooting into Gyalmotso's womb. Between nine and ten months later, she gave birth to an exceedingly lovely baby girl whose forehead bore the mark of crossed vajras and whose body gave off the fragrance of a lily. They named her Tsogyal, and when she grew up she was chosen to be the queen of Tibet. She came to have great faith in the master Padmakara and such disenchantment with samsara [1.36a] that she begged the king for permission to practice the dharma. He assented and offered her to the master, who took her as his consort. She accompanied him wherever he went, honoring and serving him, and pursuing her practice so one-pointedly that she became accomplished, attaining the sublime and more common siddhis. Her biography is contained in a terma revealed by Taksham,[49] as summarized in verse by Jamgön Kongtrul:[50]

> *Namo guru jñana dakini ye!*[51]
>
> All-noble Samantabhadrā, the perfection of sublime knowing;
> powerful goddess of basic space, mother of victorious ones, Vajrayogini;
> goddess Sarasvati, venerable Yeshé Tsogyal:
> To the guru, the dakini of the three kayas, I pray.
>
> Before Dharma Arya, you formulated your vast aspirations.
> In the presence of the Sage, you emanated as the goddess of the Ganges.
> In a pure realm, you revealed yourself in the form
> of the exalted goddess Sarasvati. To you, I pray.

When the time came to guide those to be tamed in the Land of Snows,
you entered the womb of one of the Kharchen clan in the region of Drak
in the form of the syllables of skillful means and sublime knowing falling from the sky.
To you who caused immeasurable positive signs to manifest, I pray.

When you took birth at sunrise on the tenth day of the Monkey month of a Bird year,
the earth shook, thunder roared, [1.36b]
showers of blossoms fell, the sacred lake overflowed,
and huge pavilions of rainbow light appeared. To you, I pray.

As soon as you were born, you uttered the Sanskrit vowels and consonants and verses of poetry
while many goddesses in the sky gave benedictions,
and in a single month, you grew to the size of an eight-year-old.
To you whose fame spread throughout the land, I pray.

Exceedingly disenchanted with the prison of samsara,
you fled far from the suitors who came from minor kingdoms,
and in accordance with the wishes of the sovereign Trisong,
you came to be a holy presence at his court. To you, I pray.

Reading, writing, the five fields of knowledge, and so forth—
you mastered these in your heart with the merest instruction from scholars.
Your karmic tendencies from prior training awakened you to the dharma,
and you were entrusted with it. To you, I pray.

The master Padmakara, dwelling at Chimpu,[52]
was invited by the king, who presented him his empire as a mandala offering.
Once he had been asked to confer the effortless spiritual approach,
the master demonstrated the rarity of the secret mantra path. To him, I pray.

Furthermore, you, Tsogyal, offered him a *ganachakra*[53]
of appropriate samaya substances, and he gladly agreed to accept you. [1.37a]
He invested you as a noble lady and caused your mind to mature through empowerment.
To you who accompanied him to Chimpu for secret practice, I pray.

Having trained your mind in the Three Repositories and other teachings on cause and effect—

the provisional truth of the lesser and greater spiritual approaches—
you had a vision of Sarasvati and gained the sublime power of complete recall.
To you who attained prescience and miraculous powers, I pray.

Able to carry out what was to be accomplished, mastering what was explained,
fully understanding what was to be known, you defined the nine spiritual approaches.[54]
The ability to differentiate between what is valid and what is not welled up from the depths of your being.
To you who saw the hidden flaw inherent in karmic causality,[55] I pray.

Seeking the profound secret that lies beyond cause and effect,
you received the samaya concerning death from the lord Guru.
In Yarlung, your mind was first brought to spiritual maturity
through *The Gathered Commands: An Ocean of Spiritual Teachings*. To you, I pray.

You accompanied the lord to Tidro in upper Zho,
where you offered the mandala of supreme bliss in the great assembly hall.
Through the four secret empowerments, you matured into enlightened form, speech, and mind.
To you who trained in the sacred outlook of the Guru, I pray.

Having trained for six months to experience the significance of these empowerments,
on an auspicious occasion you stopped your subtle energy, purified the twelve links of causality,
and refined your appreciation of the four states of experience,[56] gaining the sublime twelfth level of realization.
To you who possessed unimaginable qualities, I pray. [1.37b]

In keeping with the Guru's prophecy, you went to Nepal.
For resurrecting the corpse of a slain man, you were rewarded with gold
and ransomed Atsara Salé, hero of skillful means.
To you who guided many beings difficult to guide, I pray.

With Vasudhara, Shakyadema, and others,
you exchanged teachings and then returned to Tidro.
Training in the four degrees of joy,[57] you attained the siddhi of the vital essence.
To you who gained mastery over the five elements, I pray.

At the Buddhist king's request, you and your consort went to Chimpu,
where some 120 mandalas of the unsurpassable tantras were revealed
and 300 fortunate people were brought to spiritual maturity.
To you who received the supreme transmission, the sadhana of
enlightened mind, I pray.

At Tidro you accomplished the state of the guru and received great
blessings;
all appearances arose as the guru's display.
You journeyed to Oddiyana, land of dakinis, and other sublime realms.
To you who beheld marvelous signs, I pray.

Food, clothing, body, speech, mind, the Buddha's teachings,
the welfare of others, and compassion—you met these eight challenges
fully
according to the Guru's injunction.
To you who showed signs of success in each instance, I pray. [1.38a]

On the edge of Ya Glacier, you attained the bliss and warmth of *tummo;*[58]
you needed no ordinary garments, for the six bone ornaments were your
adornments.[59]
Nourishing yourself with medicinal herbs at Seng-gé Dzong,
you were venerated by seers and deities of healing. To you, I pray.

Your physical body fell away as you discovered rainbow body, the
enjoyment of space;
your speech, with sixty melodious qualities, was perfect;
your mind was absorbed in vajra-like meditation.
To you who attained the sublime and more common siddhis, I pray.

At Nereng Dzong, you subdued hordes
of humans and nonhumans, instilling in them the basis of faith.
Powerful gods and demons offered you their life essence.
To you who appointed them guardians of the teachings, I pray.

At Paro Taktsang, you practiced the tantric discipline of the profound
path;
the three avenues of your being became the three vajras of supreme bliss.
You shone with the charming radiance of a sixteen-year-old maiden.
To you, courageous heruka goddess, I pray.

From Amitayus you received empowerments and prophecies.
You became a master of awareness with power over longevity, not subject
to aging or decrepitude,

and the principal goddess of all mandalas without limit.
To you, radiant dark blue master of longevity, I pray.

Practicing Vajrakila at Önpu Taktsang,
you took the Bhutanese woman Tashi Cheu Dren under your care [1.38b]
and captured the life essence of all gods and demons in the three-thousand-fold universe.
To you, foremost goddess of the hosts of the richness of basic space, I pray.

You vanquished wicked shamans with your miraculous powers,
blocked the malicious actions of many evil ministers,
and resolved dissension within the sangha, extending guidance with skillful means and compassion.
To you who caused the teachings of the Victorious One[60] to shine like the sun, I pray.

At Karak Glacier, at Jomonang in Tsang,
and in the valley known as Ukpalung, you spread the lineage of oral transmission,
bringing spiritual maturity and liberation to the seven men with fortunate karma,
the five hundred siddhas, and countless others. To you, I pray.

At Shampo Glacier, you gave seven bandits direct introduction,
so that they attained siddhis, and sent them to Oddiyana.
You took the Nepalese dakini Kalasiddhi under your care
and freed her through your instructions. To you, I pray.

In Chimpu you dwelled for eleven years
with the lord Guru, receiving the treasury of his enlightened mind
with nothing omitted, like one vase being filled from another.
To you who spread the teachings of theory and practice, I pray.

One million methods for accomplishing enlightened mind, tens of thousands of cycles of Nyingtik teachings,
vast and profound teachings of tantras, explanatory commentaries, and pith instructions—
you codified these on yellow scrolls in a variety of scripts.
To you who made the preparations for profound termas, I pray. [1.39a]

You and your consort journeyed to central, southern, and eastern Tibet with other siddhas,
covering these areas with your footprints, consecrating them with your practice,

filling them with termas concealed in the earth, and leaving accounts of these.
To you who made prophecies concerning those with appropriate karma, I pray.

At Tsashö Rong, as you escorted the Guru upon his departure for the land of bloodthirsty demons,
he revealed in full the instructions
of the supreme, extensive Ati approach,
and you received his final prophecies and three testaments. To you, I pray.

You dwelled at Shang and Zambu, where you brought fortunate people
to spiritual maturity and freedom.
Resting evenly in the enlightened intent of Ati, you experienced the full expression of awareness.
To you who journeyed to sixty pure realms, I pray.

You rescued the wicked minister Shanti from hell.
Giving food, clothing, medicine, wealth, and protection to others' bodies and life force,
honored by the leaders of gods and nagas,
you performed amazing feats of exchanging yourself for others. To you, I pray.

In Chimpu you acted as spiritual adviser to the divine king.
Your spiritual lineage spreading throughout the world,
you became the source of instruction for all those in Tibet who were and are followers of the Guru.
To you who brought beings benefit as extensive as space, I pray. [1.39b]

You practiced everywhere in central Tibet and the surrounding regions.
You left handprints, footprints, syllables, and images of deities.
You ensured purpose and meaning for all those beings who
would be connected to you in the future through faith and devotion. To you, I pray.

You journeyed to more than one hundred primary and seven million secondary holy sites,
to twenty-five great glaciers, eighteen great fortresses,
twelve hidden valleys, seven sublime places of marvels,
and five secret regions. To you, I pray.

In those places, you concealed countless terma caches
of teachings, objects of wealth, and sacred samaya substances, covering up the traces.
Uttering prayers of aspiration and benediction,
you ensured the increase of what is positive and excellent. To you, I pray.

At the temple of Karchung Dorjéying,
to fortunate spiritual brothers and sisters—the princes[61] foremost among them—
you brought maturity and liberation through your profound and extensive teachings
of *The Three Gatherings* and other cycles. To you, I pray.

While you practiced *The Gathering of Secrets,* the Guru actually appeared to you
and remained for seven days, bringing the princes to spiritual maturity and liberation.
Through his compassion, he bestowed profound instructions
never encountered before, such as *The Natural Freedom of Enlightened Intent.* To him, I pray.

You went to Kharchu and rested in the equipoise of enlightened intent,
directly experiencing the vision of phenomena resolving into their true nature. [1.40a]
Emanating to guide others in any way necessary within the six classes of beings,
you dredged the pit of samsara. To you, I pray.

Mandarava came from the holy land of India.
You discussed the dharma, comparing instructions
and exchanging teachings; you heaped garlands of praise on each other.
To you who sang sweet melodies of auspicious wishes, I pray.

Once again, you went to Zambu Valley in Shang
and offered a great ganachakra.
To your eleven main students, you imparted more than a hundred pith instructions,
which were like the beating heart of the oral lineage. To you, I pray.

Responding to the supplications of those with the appropriate karma,
you bestowed personal instructions, prophecies, and words of advice.
For fully 211 years,
you protected those to be guided in the land of Tibet. To you, I pray.

On the eighth day of the Bird month, dakinis of the three places
and the eight classes of bloodthirsty demons from Chamara arrived to escort you.
You granted requests nine times to the gods and humans of Tibet
and prophesied nine great events. To you, I pray.

You drew the two dakinis from Bhutan and Nepal[62] into the right and left sides of your heart center.
On the tenth day, borne by dakinis of the four families [1.40b]
on a palanquin of light, you abided in a sphere of light.
To you who left your loving testament, I pray.

In essence, although you seemed to journey to the palace of Pema Ö[63] in the realm of Chamara,
in truth you attained enlightenment within the youthful vase body.
In the form of the dakini Ting-ö Barma, the radiant dark blue goddess,
you are the consort of the one who rules over bloodthirsty demons. To you, I pray.

Your form, speech, mind, qualities, and activities
are equal to those of the Guru himself,
and these five inexhaustible adornments of your being
extend wherever space extends, benefiting beings. To you, I pray.

In particular, your love for those in the land of Tibet
led to twenty-five primary manifestations, and at all times
your emanations and secondary emanations, which occur without interruption,
appear in whatever way is necessary to guide beings. To you, I pray.

Bestowing prophetic guidance on those with the appropriate karma,
dispelling obstacles, and granting siddhis, you act as our ally.
In this and in other ways, you always protect Tibet.
To you, only mother of great kindness, I pray.

Your profound enlightened intent extends equally throughout space.
The greatness of your mind shines more brightly than the sun.
A sweet rain of siddhis falls from the clouds of your blessings.
To you, O supreme mother whose activity is swift, I pray. [1.41a]

By the power of the prayers we offer to you with faith and devotion,
gaze upon us fully with your stainless eye of timeless awareness,
swiftly seize us with the hook of your great compassion,
and draw us to the realm of Khechara.[64]

Guide us with your great compassion in all our rebirths and throughout
all our lifetimes.
Grant us your blessings at all times and in all ways.
Now and forever, be our guru.
Grant us the sublime and more common siddhis without exception.

Whatever the all-noble Padmakara and his consorts are like,
may we swiftly become just as they are.
Through an exemplary life indistinguishable from those of all victorious
ones,
may we bring all beings, as extensive as space, to buddhahood!

While the master and his consort were practicing in Tidro Cave in upper Zho, dakinis of timeless awareness exhorted the noble Tsogyal, saying, "This great master, this nirmanakaya emanation, holds in his mind the profound transmission of the Nyingtik teachings of direct experience, through which one awakens to buddhahood in three years and which causes the physical body to vanish in this very lifetime. You should therefore pray that he give you these instructions." She thus offered a large ganachakra and made her request: [1.41b] "Great master, I humbly ask that you bestow on me the sacred transmission of the Nyingtik teachings of direct experience, which brings about awakening to buddhahood while causing the body to vanish in this very lifetime." With this supplication, she made numerous prostrations and circumambulations.

The great master replied, "Tsogyal, your request is an excellent one. This advice is quite unlike any other you have received previously. It represents the pinnacle of all the developmental stages of the nine spiritual approaches. Perceiving its key point nullifies view and meditation that involve intellectual speculation. The paths and levels of realization are perfected without any need for effort. Negative emotions are freed in their own place without the need for contrivance, transformation, or antidotes. Without being created by causes, the fruition is perfect in itself. Spontaneously present enlightened intent arises in an instant. In this very lifetime, the flesh and blood body is freed as sambhogakaya, a state of utter lucidity. Within three years, one can journey to Akanishtha, the pinnacle realm, and reach the ongoing state of genuine being in the pure realm of precious spontaneous presence, dharmakaya. Such advice is to be found in *The Heart Drop of the Dakini*, and I will impart it to you."

In the great hall of dakinis at Tidro Cave in upper Zho, he revealed the ultimate mandala of peaceful and wrathful deities, [1.42a] bestowed empowerment on a hundred thousand dakinis of timeless awareness, the bride of the Kharchen clan foremost among them, and conferred the complete teachings. He taught the seventeen tantras as well as the eighteenth, *The Sun of the Clear Expanse of Samantabhadrā*, and gave many pith instructions based on these tantras. Of these, the pith instructions that greatly expanded on the themes of the tantras were grouped into one category, while the cycles for mendicant yogins, written by the master himself, made up another. These were recorded and classified by both the Guru and Tsogyal. The teachings having been classified, Guru Padmakara conferred the empowerment for them, along with the seal of his aspirations and entrustment,[65] on Princess Pemasel, the daughter of King Trisong Detsen.[66] Thinking of future generations, he concealed the teachings as a terma. Later, when the time came for Padmakara's prophecy to be fulfilled, Pema Ledrel Tsal, the rebirth of Pemasel, revealed the terma at the cliff known as Tramo Drak in Dang Valley. Thus the lineage was transmitted from the Guru and his consort to Pema Ledrel.

Pema Ledrel Tsal (Mid-13th to Early 14th Centuries)

In a place called Rizhing, near the cliff of Koro Drak on the plateau known as Drintang in the lower region of Nyaldang Loro, the great Pema Ledrel Tsal was born in a Female Iron Hare year,[67] the son of a couple who were venerable lay tantric practitioners from the Nyang clan.[68] [1.42b] Since both parents' circumstances were difficult, the boy grew up amid great poverty and suffering. One day, when all those close to him had forsaken him and he was sad at heart, he left Koro on the plateau of Drintang. He met a middle-aged monk, whom he asked, "Learned sir, where are you going?"

The monk replied, "I am not going anywhere. I have come to see you." He immediately drew a scroll from the folds of his robes and gave it to Pema Ledrel Tsal, [1.43a] enjoining him, "My son, examine this well. Make no mistake about the meaning of the words and take them to heart. You will have the good fortune to attain siddhis." With that he vanished, and after a brief moment of disorientation, Pema Ledrel Tsal realized that he had no way of searching for him. He decided to return to his home.

One day, he examined the scroll and found the following passage: "One year from now, in the Female Water Ox year,[69] it will be time for you to receive your share of wealth.[70] Go forth on the tenth day of the first month of autumn. On the face of the cliff of Tramo Drak in Dang Valley in the region of Dakpo is a swastika[71] drawn in red, an indication of a terma. Search to the northeast of this, where you will see a cube-shaped stone about the size of a quart measure. Remove the stone to find the profound termas within."

So Pema Ledrel Tsal went to Dang Valley and spent three days in a cave at Tramo Drak, unearthing the profound termas from their place of concealment. He then set out on the road back home and reached upper Nyal. Traveling through Shotserma Valley, he stayed the night with a lay tantric practitioner and his wife. They served him well with food and beer, and they passed much of the evening in conversation.

[1.43b] The tantrika asked him, "Where did you come from yesterday? Why did you go there?"

Pema Ledrel Tsal replied, "On the basis of a prophecy I once received, I went to the region of Dakpo."

The tantrika asked, "Well, did you find any termas?"

"I did," he answered.

"What were they?"

He replied, "*The Heart Drop of the Dakini,* pith instructions concerning three supportive deity practices, and the cycle for accomplishing the practice of the planetary mara Rahula, as well as tantras."

"In that case, you must give us an empowerment with the casket[72] in which the texts were found." So Pema Ledrel Tsal picked up the casket of texts and blessed the tantrika and his wife, as well as their son. The next morning, as he prepared to leave, the tantrika's son, Gyalsé Lekpa Gyaltsen, came to offer prostrations to him with great faith. Pema Ledrel Tsal took the youth under his care, granting him all of the spiritual injunctions of the secret Nyingtik teachings.

He returned home to Drintang, whereupon news of his travels spread among the inhabitants. They said, "Ledrel Tsal is incapable of carrying out any of the duties of one from a tantric lineage, and now he is trying to perpetrate some fraud. Termas? What termas could he possibly have?" [1.44a] Thus the local people spread rumors.

Disappointed with his countryfolk, Pema Ledrel Tsal decided to become a wandering mendicant. He set off with a retinue of four: Lekpa Gyaltsen, Namkha Wangchuk, Rinchen Dorjé, and Palgyi Seng-gé. Passing through the areas of Jar and El, they arrived in Yarlung. They spent three days at the cliff known as Sheldrak, establishing a connection with that holy site. They then went on to Samyé Monastery and visited the temples there. Continuing on to Chimpu, they spent seven days at the shrine of Gegong, establishing a connection with that site. After about five days, a red woman appeared in the middle of the night, saying that she was Vajravarahi. She instructed Pema Ledrel Tsal, "Do not remain here! Go to Lhasa, where there is a student with a karmic connection to you whom you should meet." And so the five of them, teacher and students, traveled to Lhasa.

They spent about five days circumambulating the city. At the same time, the Karmapa, the lord Rangjung Dorjé,[73] was encamped on Kubum Plain near Lhasa. He summoned them, saying, "Let the tertön from the southern ravines and his students come to see me!" [1.44b] Pema Ledrel Tsal and his students thus went, made prostrations, and offered the Karmapa a pill of a brahmin's flesh,[74] a bolt of silk, and a small pouch of musk. Rangjung Dorjé said to the five men, teacher and students, "Do you have the termas that you withdrew from concealment? If so, you must reveal them to me."

Pema Ledrel Tsal replied, "Only five days have passed since the five of us, teacher and students, came here to perform circumambulations. Since we have not had the time to make copies of the texts of these termas, we have only the yellow scrolls that I brought forth."

The lord Rangjung Dorjé said, "How wonderful that you retrieved these yellow scrolls! Show them to me!" They presented him the scrolls for inspection; he examined them in detail, touched them to the crown of his head, and handed them back.

The group of five then returned to Lhasa and spent the night at the foot of an obelisk. That night, a red woman wearing bone ornaments appeared in Rangjung Dorjé's dreams. She told him, "Request the profound spiritual injunctions of the secret mantra approach from Pema Ledrel Tsal, who is a heart son of Orgyen. Offer him some of your hair. If you do this, the teachings will flourish in the future." [1.45a]

The next morning, an emissary sent by Rangjung Dorjé told the teacher and his students, "You are summoned to the holy presence." When they returned for an audience, the lord Rangjung Dorjé said, "You must give me the oral transmission for the scrolls you had yesterday."

Pema Ledrel Tsal replied, "I cannot presume to give transmission to such a high personage as you."

"But you must," the Karmapa insisted. Unable to refuse his request, Pema Ledrel Tsal gave him all of the oral transmissions for *The Heart Drop of the Dakini,* which was written on yellow scrolls. Pema Ledrel Tsal thus acted as a guru to Karmapa Rangjung Dorjé. The lord gave the group of five some of his hair, saying, "Divide these clippings equally among you."

Pema Ledrel Tsal then returned to the cliff of Koro Drak on the plateau of Drintang and spent seven months in meditation practice. He actually met the Guru and his consort, who bestowed their blessings by granting him the realization of the lineage of enlightened intent. During that time, he conferred on Lekpa Gyaltsen all of the oral transmissions for his spiritual injunctions.

Pema Ledrel Tsal then went on to a site in front of the cliff of Chöten Drak and spent three months practicing, while Lekpa Gyaltsen stayed below the cliff. [1.45b] When the king of the dharma Rinchen Lingpa[75] came to see Pema Ledrel Tsal, Lekpa Gyaltsen responded, "Since the precious tertön is currently in retreat, there is no chance of having an audience with him."

"In that case," Rinchen Lingpa replied, "you must transmit to me all of the oral transmissions you have received from him." Thus Gyalsé Lekpa Gyaltsen gave the entire body of oral transmissions for *The Heart Drop of the Dakini* to Rinchen Lingpa.

Once Tulku Ledrel Tsal had finished his retreat at Chöten Drak, he journeyed to lower Nyal. Lekpa Gyaltsen and Rinchen Lingpa both followed to seek an audience with him and encountered him near Sechen Bumpa. Tulku Ledrel Tsal asked, "Where are you two headed?"

"We have come to meet with you, lord of the dharma," they replied.

"Well, then, come with me. I'm going to Drintang." Teacher and students then journeyed toward the plateau. On the way, they stayed at Chöling Monastery, where Pema Ledrel Tsal gave Rinchen Lingpa the key to termas concealed within a black boulder shaped like a tortoise on a mountain pass on the route to China. [1.46a] He said, "My son, take this key and retrieve the termas concealed in that boulder. Use them to ensure benefit for beings."

Having carried out such activities for the sake of the teachings and of beings, Pema Ledrel Tsal spent the rest of his life practicing *The Heart Drop of the Dakini*, so that he found little opportunity to disseminate these teachings, spreading them to only a slight extent. He was unable to make contact with his consort as prophesied by the Guru, because a witch created obstacles for him. Due to external conditions imposed by this and other circumstances, he entrusted Gyalsé Lekpa with the profound termas, and the display of his emanated form then resolved back into the primordial being of inner basic space.[76]

It was from this guru that Gyalsé Lekpa heard the teachings. [1.46b]

Gyalsé Lekpa Gyaltsen (1290–1366)

This glorious and holy guru, also known as Tulku Lekden, was born in Chödro Sewa Valley in lower Nyal. He was the son of the master Wangchuk Gyal of a noteworthy line of tantric practitioners and his wife, Dorjé Gö of the Dru clan. From a very early age, Lekpa Gyaltsen could recall many of his previous lifetimes, knew how to read and write without having to be taught, and possessed great wisdom. About him Druptop Orgyenpa[77] and Tokden[78] Gönpo Yeshé prophesied, "He will be a person who benefits beings." When he reached the age of eight, he received prophecies directly from dakinis of timeless awareness, who blessed him as the hereditary master of the teachings of his ancestral line.

He then learned and contemplated the topics found in the excellent teachings of the Buddha. With his father, he studied *Reading Literature* (a treatise on Sanskrit grammar), a detailed analysis entitled *Flow of the Ganges*, as well as the source text *The Drops for Healing People* and its commentary. He also received from his father, and became learned in, the tantras of Hayagriva, Avalokiteshvara, and Tara, as well as methods for accomplishing the practices of these deities, and the tantras and pith instructions of the lord and lady protectors. [1.47a] From Lama Tamché Chenpa, he received the empowerments and instructions of the later lineage of the Zhijé[79] school.

He went to study with his paternal uncle, Lama Gyalsé Tsönwang, who told him, "There have been very good omens in my dreams. You will be of enormous benefit to beings. You should take Gyalsé Lekden as your name." During that time, he studied the glorious tantra *The Heart Essence of Secrets* and *The Two Chapters* and devoted himself to learning these. He began teaching and studied widely, receiving instructions in such works as the *Katun Tantra of Mañjushri,* the cycle of Mañjushri known as *The Lord of Longevity, The Gathering of Wrathful Deities, The Chakrasamvara Tantra* and related pith instructions, the cycles of teachings passed down from Tropu Lotsawa,[80] and the teaching cycles of Jigten Gonpo, spiritual lord of the Drigung school.[81]

From Sang-gyé Önzhön, he received *Sixfold Equal Taste* and other cycles of teachings from the Drukpa school. With Lama Chögyal Dzompa, he studied *The Lamp of the Perfection of Sublime Knowing,* the glorious *Guhyasamaja Tantra,* [1.47b] the Ngok clan's tradition of Hevajra, *The Union of All Buddhas in Equalness,* the six doctrines of the Chyal tradition of Vajravarahi, and other works. From Böngom Nangwa Gyayen, he requested Saraha's[82] *Three Doha Cycles* and their commentaries according to the Nepalese tradition. From the master Len, he received the oral transmissions for the termas of the lord Nyang-ral: the cycle entitled *The Gathering of Sugatas,* the five tantras of Hayagriva and related methods of accomplishment, the teaching cycle of Avalokiteshvara, the cycle for accomplishment of *The Dakini: The Wish-Fulfilling Gem,* and other teachings. From Nyima Özer, who upheld the Guru's lineage, Gyalsé Lekpa Gyaltsen requested the transmissions for *The Guru, the Gathering of Secrets; The Union of All Buddhas in Equalness; The Condensed Quintessence* cycle of Mahakarunika; and other cycles. With Ritrö Repa, he studied the cycles of instructions of Zhang Tsalpa, such as *The Five Linking Principles* and *The Consummation of the Sublime Path.* From Zhikpo Jigmé Bepa, he received the so-called four volumes of profound teachings—the empowerments and teachings of Vimalamitra—as well as the seventeen tantras connected to these. From the yogin Ah-Hum Dorjé, he requested the terma cycles of Yangdzongma of Drak. With Jamyang Sherab Rinchen, he studied and became learned in many kinds of beneficial activity, [1.48a] such as the Ngadü system of astrology and the medical system, including herbal medicines and diagnosis.

Notably, he met Tertön Pema Ledrel Tsal, the guru with whom he had had a karmic connection for lifetimes. Wherever the guru went, he took Lekpa Gyaltsen along. The latter received the entire range of empowerments, teachings, tantras, explanatory commentaries, and secret pith instructions for *The Heart Drop of the Dakini* and examined these spiritual instructions in depth. When the tertön was preparing to leave his body, he gave Lekpa Gyaltsen the yellow scrolls, saying, "Practice this profound terma cycle correctly, applying it in a profound way. You are the prophesied custodian of these teachings." He then left his final instructions: "Do not waste these termas! Five years from now, I will be reborn at Drapu in central Tibet as the son of a man named Tenpa and a woman named Sönamkyi. At that time, we will meet again."

In accordance with his guru's last wishes, Gyalsé Lekpa Gyaltsen spent twelve years applying himself to practice, and the enlightened intent of great perfection—the perception of awareness's naturally manifest appearances without bias[83]—was born in his heart. He felt an authentic degree of confidence in his view and meditation. Lekpa Gyaltsen had many marvelous experiences, such as encountering Guru Padma face-to-face in the pure realm of Zangdok Palri[84] and being given a drum of sandalwood by Nup Namkhai Nyingpo, who declared that Lekpa Gyaltsen was karmically connected to him as a student. [1.48b]

The lord of the dharma Karmapa Rangjung Dorjé invited him to the region of Kongpo and requested the complete transmission of the teachings and instructions for the profound terma *The Heart Drop of the Dakini*. With great delight, Lekpa Gyaltsen assented and revealed these spiritual injunctions, causing the teachings to flourish widely. In turn, Lekpa Gyaltsen received many teachings from the lord Karmapa, including the commentary on *The Kalachakra Tantra* entitled *Stainless Light*, the oral transmission for the Jataka stories chronicling the Buddha's previous births, the Six Techniques of Union from the Kalachakra cycle, the Six Yogas of Naropa, the three cycles of teachings for mountain retreats, and other works.

It was the holy Lekpa Gyaltsen, whose life was graced by such sublime marvels, who the great Orgyen had prophesied would be the one with karma equal to the task of spreading this profound terma cycle in an appropriate way. He was extremely capable of carrying out the activities of pacification, enrichment, power, and wrath. In keeping with prophecies in the termas, he completed his life's work and brought those students who had the appropriate karma to spiritual maturity and liberation. When he was seventy-eight, on the tenth day of the twelfth month of Gyal in a Serpent year,[85] he passed away, his physical remains producing many images of deities, relics, and so forth. There were innumerable marvelous signs, such as rainbows filling the valley, so that fortunate people were inspired to faith.

It was from this holy guru that the Omniscient King of the Dharma, Drimé Özer, heard the teachings. [1.49a]

Longchen Rabjampa Drimé Özer (1308–1364)

In keeping with Tertön Ledrel's final prophecy, in due time Longchenpa met Gyalsé Lekden and recounted his former lifetime. Lekpa Gyaltsen remarked, "You have merely changed your body; other than that, you are truly my guru who has come back to me, so there is no need for me to give you empowerments or oral transmissions."

Longchenpa responded, "It is precisely because the change from my former lifetime to the present one has taken place that this will not do. The lineage must be an unbroken one." Thus he received from Gyalsé Lekpa Gyaltsen the complete transmission of the tantras, explanatory commentaries, empowerments, teachings, and instructions for the secret cycle *The Heart Drop of the Dakini*. This is how the succession of terma transmissions, the short lineage from the Guru, came down to the Omniscient King of the Dharma.[86]

Other Teachers of the Lineage

In addition, there appeared individual emanations of the king and his subjects, such masters as the five sublime ones titled Lingpa, the two named Drimé, and the three teachers Nyang-ral Nyima Özer, Guru Chöwang, and Rigdzin Gödem.[87] Up to the present day, like the innumerable stars and planets in the vast heavens, emanations of the Guru have appeared as masters of termas, foremost among them more than a hundred major and a thousand minor tertöns. They have revealed teachings that combine practices on the deities of the Three Roots, guru yoga, Dzogchen, and Avalokiteshvara—such cycles as *Great Perfection: The Black Innermost Heart Drop; The Oral Lineage of Enlightened Mind* from the *Namchö* cycle; [1.49b] the termas of Longsel Dorjé Nyingpo;[88] *The Primordial Drop of the Heart Essence of Profound Significance;* and the Dzogchen cycle *Unobstructed Enlightened Intent.* The phrase "short lineage of successive termas" refers to all such termas, cycles that unerringly reveal the key points of the tantras, explanatory commentaries, and pith instructions of natural great perfection in a complete yet concise way.

Even in such unbearable circumstances as our current time of spiritual degeneration, there have appeared such masters as Kyabjé Dudjom Rinpoché Jigdral Yeshé Dorjé, sovereign lord of the hundred buddha families; Kyabjé Dilgo Khyentrul Rinpoché Rabsel Dawa, whose kindness to us can never be repaid; and Kyabjé Dokhampa Chenpo Khamtrul Dongyü Nyima.[89] The Guru himself appeared to them, made prophecies, and empowered them as regents of his three secret aspects,[90] transmitting to them innumerable precious termas of profound enlightened intent. I quote from the lord of yogins Buddhavajra, better known as Chatral Rinpoché Sanjé Dorjé:

> I supplicate those who lead us to the palace of Pema Ö
> through any association made by seeing, hearing, thinking of, touching,
> or even speaking of them.

I myself encourage everyone to make some connection with these great beings who have actually lived and continue to live among us as the glorious, unbiased lord protectors of all those to be guided throughout the world, bringing great purpose to all who are associated with them. [1.50a] If you do so, you will have made your human existence truly meaningful.

The foregoing describes the second of the three major traditions: the profound short lineage of successive termas transmitted from the Guru. There are a number of classification systems within this tradition. In addition to the four cycles—outer, inner, and so forth—mentioned previously as divisions within the Category of Direct Transmission, there are classes such as the General Yoga and the Innermost Yoga of the Dzogchen approach that have their own extraordinary vocabulary and methods of transmission. There are other remarkable systems of classification that refer to a sixfold lineage—three in addition to the threefold lineage of kama transmissions previously discussed—or a ninefold lineage, and so forth. These classification systems are discussed in the individual teaching cycles of the major tertöns, *The Biographies of One Hundred Tertöns* by Jamgön Kongtrul, and the great spiritual history of the Nyingma, the Early Translation school.[91]

4

The Lineage of Vimalamitra

THE MORE EXTENSIVE LINEAGE: THE CATEGORY OF DIRECT TRANSMISSION

Vimalamitra

The following account of the third wellspring of the oral lineage demonstrates how the tradition of Vimalamitra was transmitted. In the city of Kapila in India lived a king named Indrabhuti the Younger.[1] A patron of the dharma and an emanation of the bodhisattva Maitreya (who will manifest as the buddha after Shakyamuni), he retained five hundred Buddhist scholars as honored members of his court. Among them was one both learned and spiritually accomplished—Vimalamitra, [1.50b] whose form was the result of a process of transference[2] and who for sixty years served as the royal priest.

Meanwhile, in Tibet, King Trisong Detsen, an emanation of the bodhisattva Mañjushri, was building the temple of Lhungyi Druppai Zhalyé Khang[3] at the glorious site of Samyé, thus ensuring that the sacred dharma would spread and flourish. His royal priest, Tingdzin Zangpo of the Nyang clan, could see all four continents at once, having completely purified his faculty of vision by maintaining a one-pointed state of calm abiding for seven years and seven months. This great priest of Nyang [1.51a] advised his king, "Your Majesty, in the city of Kapila in India there is a king named Indrabhuti, who retains some five hundred Buddhist scholars at his court. From among them, let Your Majesty invite one who is learned in the result-oriented approach of secret mantra, so that the teachings of this path may spread and flourish in the realm of Tibet." The king was extremely pleased with this counsel and said, "Let it be done!"

At that time, there lived in Tibet two men of very keen intelligence. One, Kawa Paltsek, was from Kawapa in Pen Valley of central Tibet, the son of Loten of the Kawa clan and his wife, Dorjécham of the Dro clan. The other, Chokro Luyi Gyaltsen, was from Dargong in Shang Valley, in the region of Rulak, the son of Gyaljung of the Chokro clan and his wife, Dzema of the Dro clan. The king summoned both of these men with all honors. He donned his jeweled ceremonial crown and issued a command: "You two sons of good family, who have acquired power through your miraculous command of language—so that the utterly profound teachings of the result-oriented secret mantra approach may spread in our realm of Tibet, it is my wish that you go to the city of Kapila in India, where there dwells a king named Indrabhuti, who has five hundred scholars at his court. [1.51b] In his royal presence, offer seven plaques with designs worked in gold and nine measures of powdered gold. I command that, having made these offerings, you relate humbly to His Majesty, 'These are gifts from the king of Tibet. In return, he asks that you send with us a highly trained scholar who is especially learned in the result-oriented secret mantra approach.' Now go!"

Thus ordered by their king, the two translators obeyed and went to India. Having paid homage to King Indrabhuti, they presented the gold plaques and powdered gold from their king and conveyed his message. Extremely pleased, King Indrabhuti said, "You two bodhisattvas from Tibet, rest here in my guesthouse." When his scholars, including Vimalamitra, assembled in the dining hall for their midday meal, the king addressed them: "Great learned ones, the king of Tibet has sent me a most excellent gift. In return, he has humbly urged me to send him a highly trained scholar especially learned in the result-oriented secret mantra approach. I intend to send someone."

The master Buddhaguhya asked, "Where are the envoys who conveyed this message? Bring them to us!" The king had the two translators brought in, [1.52a] and upon seeing certain marks and signs on Vimalamitra's body, they instantly felt deep devotion for him. All of those seated higher than Vimalamitra and all of those seated below directed their gaze as one toward him. Aware of this, Vimalamitra rose and uttered, "Kakapari." The two translators understood this in two different ways. Chokro Luyi Gyaltsen took it to mean:

> With arrows nocked in their bows,
> if the archers' fingers can but make the effort,
> the arrows will be sent afar.

Kawa Paltsek took it to mean:

> If they can but exert themselves with the ferryman's oars,
> people riding in boats
> will reach freedom on the ocean's far shore.

They thus inferred the same meaning, though they expressed it in different words, and offered their interpretations to Vimalamitra, who said:

> O king who relies on me, Vimala,
> if you are able to let me go,
> I will be of benefit to Tibet.

Taking with him texts of the extremely profound and secret Nyingtik teachings, Vimalamitra set out, a master named Kshitigarbha accompanying him as his attendant. That night, everyone had very disturbing dreams of all the flowers, fruits, forests, and crops of India being taken to Tibet and of the sun and moon moving in the same direction. [1.52b] On that night, too, the dakinis of the charnel ground of Shitavana were heard wailing and lamenting. The king's clocks and standard measures were all thrown off. The following morning, the king's subjects gathered in front of his palace and compared their dreams, finding them identical. They discussed among themselves what to make of this. Finally, one woman said, "Invite the king to join us. Ask whether His Majesty has lost his royal priest to Tibet. The omens last night indicated that a scholar has taken all of the spiritual teachings of the result-oriented secret mantra approach, leaving no texts behind."

When the king came before them, he replied, "Yesterday, we lost Vimalamitra to Tibet." At this, the Indians sent swift runners to post notices on all the passes and roads leading to Tibet. The notices read, "Two Tibetan priests, accompanied by someone versed in the evil mantras of shape-shifting demons from the border regions, are going to Tibet to bring ruin on the country."

Around this time, the Tibetan king invited Vimalamitra to Samyé. [1.53a] When he arrived, the two translators arranged for him to be received with every honor. They told the king, "This scholar is spiritually accomplished and has taken his current form for the sake of beings through a process of transference. In general, he is learned in all the categories of the teachings without exception, and his mind is especially well versed in the result-oriented secret mantra approach. He has brought all of his texts to Tibet, without leaving a single one in India."

The king told them, "Have him spend the night at the Golden Hall of Butsal. In the morning, he will be served whatever meal is most pleasing to him." So they stayed at Butsal Hall.

Meanwhile, some malicious government ministers in Tibet had read the notices posted at the borders and heard reports that an Indian scholar had arrived at Samyé. They gathered for an audience with the king and petitioned him, saying, "Someone has brought many kinds of evil mantras associated with shape-shifting demons from the border regions into Your Majesty's realm. We humbly ask Your Majesty to punish him. Do not let him remain!"

The next morning, the two translators came to the king, saying, "We humbly ask Your Majesty to grant Vimalamitra an audience."

The king replied, "It appears that this scholar of yours is not genuine. He has brought with him all manner of evil caused by shape-shifting demons, [1.53b] so I will examine him for signs over the next few days." He refused to grant the audience, which upset the two translators.

After staying at Butsal Hall for three days and nights, Vimalamitra arose one morning and performed prostrations, saying, "Vairochana is the deity in material form. The deity of timeless awareness pays homage to the deity in material form." Thereupon the statues in the hall crumbled to a pile of dust. Awestruck, the two translators related what had happened to the king, who replied, "What the ministers said must be true. All of that is the evil work of a shape-shifting demon."

At this, the two translators were crestfallen. With great sadness, they thought, "We have undergone such hardship, traveling all the way to India and escorting back such an amazingly learned person, yet what does His Majesty think?"

Another three days passed, and when Vimalamitra arose in the morning, he said, "Vairochana is the deity in material form. The deity of timeless awareness confers empowerment on the deity in material form." Taking off his hat, he placed it on the pile of dust, whereupon the statues were restored to a form more excellent than before, done in the Indian manner and with a lustrous sheen. [1.54a] Again the two translators related this to the king, who thus became convinced of Vimalamitra's authenticity and commanded, "Let swift runners be dispatched throughout the country of Tibet with this message: 'Assemble in a month's time on the third day.'"

On that morning a month later, outside the gate of Utsé Riksum,[4] an impressively high throne inlaid with turquoise was erected on the right for the king; a similarly high throne covered in gold leaf was built on the left. All of the Tibetans congregated, and the king paid homage to the scholar. On the king's shirt of fine silk, at the level of his heart, appeared the deities known as the lords of the three families. These were brilliant and clearly visible to all present. Vimalamitra snapped his fingers over the jeweled crown on the king's head while saying, "Om Ah Hum," and the buddhas of the five families appeared on it, brilliantly apparent to everyone there. With this, the people of Tibet praised Vimalamitra.

By this time, Vimalamitra had lived for 300 years. When he met the king, who was an emanation of a bodhisattva,[5] and the ministers of Tibet, exactly 1,080 years had elapsed since the Buddha had passed into nirvana.

From then on, Vimalamitra was honored as the holy spiritual adviser to the king. He taught the dharma of the transcendent perfections and Madhyamaka. [1.54b] Once, while Vimalamitra had gone to eat a meal, a beggar approached the throne from which Vimalamitra had been teaching *The Compendium of the Perfection of Sublime Knowing* and, unknown to others, left a note with two lines of verse:

> Buddhahood cannot come about from the immature teachings of shravakas.
> A raven cannot cover the earth's surface with a vajra gait.

When Vimalamitra returned to the throne and opened the stand holding his texts, he saw the note. He asked, "Who was here?" The monks who were attending the teachings replied, "No one at all," but a young boy told him, "A while ago an old beggar was wandering around."

"Seek out that beggar!" ordered Vimala. Leading the search, his retinue found the man in the house of a woman who served alcohol and brought him back. When questioned by Vimalamitra, the beggar said, "I am a student of Bairotsana of the Bagor clan. I am called Yudra Nyingpo." He proved to be learned in the five earlier tantras of the Category of Mind, so Vimalamitra subsequently taught him the thirteen later tantras. He and Yudra were like a mother bird and her chick, equal in status with respect to view, meditation, and conduct. [1.55a] It was during this period that a distinction began to be made between the earlier and later translations of tantras—the earlier ones of Bairotsana and the later ones of Vimalamitra.

At one point, the king and his ministers offered Vimalamitra a magic goblet filled with an oblation of medicinal potion, as well as a blue horse called Turquoise Bird with a golden bridle, a brocade saddle blanket, a bit studded with turquoise, and a golden saddle inset with turquoise. With these offerings, they requested that he translate the Buddhist teachings. Vimalamitra replied, "I have no need of horses and gold. If the Buddhist teachings are to be translated for the sake of beings, I will translate whatever is appropriate."

In Dragyur Gyagar,[6] located on the southwest side of Utsé Riksum, Jñanakumara of the Nyak clan translated from Indian languages literature on the transcendent perfections, the tantra *Vajrasattva: The Web of Magical Display*, and most of the tantras of the glorious deity Samyak, Vajrakila, Mamo, and Yamantaka. He also translated some of the pith instructions of the Categories of Mind and Expanse, as well as the five source tantras of three cycles of the Category of Direct Transmission.

By night in the inner sanctum of Utsé Riksum, without anyone else's knowledge, Vimalamitra taught the tantras, explanatory commentaries, and pith instructions of the sublime secret to five people: the king, Nyang Tingdzin Zangpo, the prince Muné Tsepo,[7] [1.55b] and the two translators Kawa Paltsek and Chokro Luyi Gyaltsen. (Ma Rinchen Chok had passed away, and so was not present on these occasions. Whoever claims that no more than two people were present—the king and Nyang—is an ignorant fool.)

Vimalamitra later combined these instructions in a single collection of the so-called four profound volumes and concealed them as a cache of termas in Gegong at the cliff known as Drakmar in Chimpu. He then proceeded to the five-peaked mountain of Wu Tai Shan in China. He will remain there until this eon has come to an end. Since this supreme scholar and siddha attained the rainbow body of supreme transference, he will remain in the form of a human being for as long as the Buddha's teachings endure; an emanation of his will appear every century in Tibet.

It was from this holy guru that Nyang Tingdzin Zangpo heard the teachings.

Nyang Tingdzin Zangpo (8th–9th Centuries)

Once Nyang Tingdzin Zangpo had received the complete transmission of the tantras, explanatory commentaries, and pith instructions of the sublime secret from

Vimalamitra (as explained above), the latter departed for China. For fifty-five years, Nyang practiced as he had been instructed, totally purifying his mind and experiencing his body on a very subtle level.

The guardian Vajrasadhu made hail fall in a region in eastern Tibet and obtained a harvest of five hundred camel loads of barley as a result. Nyang threw a nine-pronged golden vajra [1.56a] into the sky, inciting Vajrasadhu to recall his former samaya commitments. The guardian then offered the grain to Nyang, who accepted it to finance the temple of Zhai Lhakhang and enjoined Vajrasadhu to be its protective deity. It was within this temple, thus erected with nonhuman sources of material and wealth, that Nyang placed the explanatory tantras associated with the lineage of the Nyingtik teachings, concealing three cycles within three layers of crypts. A clay urn filled with scrolls, the manuscripts of the oral lineage, was concealed above the lintel of the gatehouse. Nyang concealed *The Golden Heart Essence: The Intensely Illuminating Sun,* a text from the most secret unsurpassable cycle, [1.56b] in the three-tiered capital of the central pillar. For the benefit of future generations of fortunate people, he applied seals to these, rendering them invisible. He recorded the annotated texts of the oral lineage and entrusted them to Lodrö Wangchuk of the Bé clan, thus ensuring that the transmission of the lineage was intact. When he passed away, he dissolved into a mass of light in the sky above Draklha Cave near Lhasa, leaving no physical remains.

It was from this holy guru that Lodrö Wangchuk of the Bé clan heard the teachings of natural great perfection.

Bé Lodrö Wangchuk (9th Century)

Lodrö Wangchuk was born into the Bé clan in Pen Valley, central Tibet. [1.57a] He was placed under the care of Nyang Tingdzin Zangpo, with whom he studied all the pith instructions of the oral lineage of the secret Nyingtik teachings, the Dzogchen approach of utter lucidity, receiving the complete transmission with nothing omitted, like one vase being filled from another.

At the cave known as Zongpuk in the district of Yoru, at Tanak in the region of Tsang, and at other holy sites in central Tibet, he pursued practice focusing on the ultimate heart essence. He achieved a very high level of spiritual attainment, the immutable form of rainbow body that leaves no physical residue. After this, he entrusted the instructions to Drom Rinchen Bar and then passed away, dissolving into a mass of light in the sky.

The great Omniscient One Longchenpa refers to him in the verse, “I pray to the teacher of the Bé clan, Lodrö Wangchuk, at Zongpuk in Yoru." Adzom Drukpa spoke of him as "Venerable Lodrö Wangchuk, who attained the body of light."

It was from this holy guru that Drom Rinchen Bar heard the teachings.

Drom Rinchen Bar (9th–10th Centuries)

Drom Rinchen Bar was born into the Drom clan in central Tibet. He was placed under the care of the teacher of the Bé clan, Lodrö Wangchuk, from whom he received the oral lineage of the secret Nyingtik teachings, the Dzogchen approach of utter lucidity. [1.57b] He was granted the complete, uninterrupted transmission of authentic pith instructions from India and Tibet, with nothing left out, like one vase being filled from another. He pursued practice focusing on the ultimate heart essence at the holy site of the cliff known as Drakar Taso[8] and other places, as well as at holy sites throughout the mountains, lakes, and cliffs of western Tibet.

He attained the sublime siddhi through the secret path of natural great perfection, reaching a very high level of accomplishment. He passed the instructions on to Dangma Lhundrup Gyaltsen in a one-to-one transmission. At a certain point, his enlightened intent resolved into the primordial expanse of inner basic space. It is this master to whom the great Omniscient One refers in the verse, "I pray to the teacher of the Drom clan, Rinchen Bar, [1.58a] in the wilderness of Drakar Taso." (In historical accounts, "Drom" and "Dro" both appear as variant spellings of his clan name; here I have followed *The Great Account of Transmission* and the Omniscient One Longchenpa's *Supplication to the Oral Lineage*.)

It was from this holy guru, Drom, that Dangma Lhundrup Gyaltsen received the complete transmission of the tantras, explanatory commentaries, and pith instructions of the sublime secret.

Dangma Lhundrup Gyaltsen (10th–11th Centuries)

One hundred years after Nyang Tingdzin Zangpo had faded into a mass of light, the spiritual elder Dangma Lhundrup Gyaltsen, son of Gechok of the Dangma clan, [1.58b] received a prophecy from the deity Vajrasadhu and so revealed the manuscripts hidden in the temple of Zhai Lhakhang in central Tibet. He also received from Drom Rinchen Bar the complete transmission of the oral lineage, the uninterrupted lines of pith instructions from India and Tibet that concern the secret Nyingtik teachings, the Dzogchen approach of utter lucidity. Not content to remain at the level of intellectual speculation, he pursued his spiritual practice in order to experience the true nature of phenomena.

Having discovered the cache of termas, he spent some fifteen years searching for someone suitable to receive the explanatory tantras. This proved to be one he met in Rizar Göpo Valley, Chetsün Seng-gé Wangchuk, son of Tuppai Wangpo of the Ché clan, from the lake known as Nyangtso in the region of Nyang-ro. Seeing that Seng-gé Wangchuk was the suitable recipient he had been seeking, Dangma Lhun-gyal seized the opportunity to teach Chetsün at Kharak and took him under his care, granting him the complete transmission of the teachings.

As Dangma passed away, the entire sky was filled with rainbow light, and after his passing, countless marvelous remains and relics appeared.

It was from this master that Chetsün heard the teachings.

Chetsün Seng-gé Wangchuk (11th–12th Centuries)

It was Chetsün who copied the manuscripts that had been hidden as termas. As related in the preceding account, he met Dangma and received all of his spiritual instructions. Chetsün wrote out all of the terma texts and then concealed the original manuscripts from the terma cache near Takdra Spring [1.59a] in Langdro Chepa. While staying there, he dreamed one night that a mendicant yogin from India came to him and said:

> I am the learned Vimalamitra.
> Fortunate one, if you wish to extract the innermost heart essence,
> in the recesses of Gegong at the cliff of Drakmar in Chimpu
> are the secret Nyingtik teachings, which are truly like one's heart.
> Take these texts to Oyuk Chigong[9]
> and meditate for seven years without being seen by anyone.
> Your corruptible physical form will cease to be visible.

Having heard these words, Chetsün went to Chimpu, where he met a woman with straight, even teeth made of conch shell and eyebrows of turquoise, who revealed the manuscripts [1.59b] and gave them to him. He took them to Dzayi Rawa in Oyuk Chigong. There Vimalamitra actually came to him and stayed for a fortnight, granting him the complete transmission of empowerments, teachings, and instructions and then returning to China.

Chetsün then meditated for seven years, attaining a form that would leave no physical remains upon death. It was at that point that Tulku Gyalwa Zhangtön met him. Knowing that he was a suitable recipient, Chetsün bestowed all of the instructions on him. At the age of 125, Chetsün passed away, dissolving into a mass of light rays in the sky.

It was from this great lord of yogins that Gyalwa Zhangtön Rinpoché [1.60a] heard the cycles of the vajra heart essence of utter lucidity.

Gyalwa Zhangtön Tashi Dorjé (1097–1167)

Zhangtön was born in a place called Lado near Nuptso Lingu in the region of Yardrok Gang.[10] His father was Zhangtön Ngödrup, and his mother was Zhumo Nyarcham. They named their son Tashi Dorjé. When he was eleven, he met Chegom Nakpo, a guru from southern Tibet, who took him under his care. From him Tashi Dorjé received the complete transmission of instructions in a single year. From then until he was twenty-one, Tashi Dorjé relied on numerous learned and accomplished gurus, thus allowing his wisdom to blossom. His general range of studies included Vinaya, the Sutras, and Abhidharma, as well as many classes of tantras from the Nyingma and Sarma schools of the mantra approach.

While staying in the region of Nangkhu in upper Nyang,[11] one morning at dawn Zhangtön beheld all the gurus of the past, as well as dakas and dakinis, Avalokiteshvara, and Tara, in the center of a pulsating mass of light in the sky. They prophesied to him, "Ah! Ah! How marvelous! The direct transmission that brings buddhahood in a single lifetime, the most secret unsurpassable cycle of the Dzogchen approach, can be found in a cliff that resembles a lion. Reveal these teachings and so benefit innumerable beings!" [1.60b] Having said this, they disappeared.

Then a man wearing a white hat came to him and said, "I will grant you a siddhi, so go forth!" Thereupon Zhangtön set off, and on the evening that he arrived in the Patsap Nyima Lowlands in lower Nyang Valley, he met many priests clad in yellow robes, who served him food and drink. It occurred to him that this was the siddhi, but at dawn the same man in the white hat appeared to him and said, "That was not the siddhi, so keep going." The man showed Zhangtön the way, and he set off once again. On the evening that he arrived at Taktap, he slept in an empty house. The same man warned him, "Don't stay here! Keep going!" At that, he ran out of the house, which immediately collapsed. That night there was a great downpour of rain, so he spent the time resting beneath the overhang of a cliff. His mysterious companion—in fact his own projection—came to him, bringing much food and drink.

The next morning, Zhangtön traveled through Ralaktsuk and continued down into the lowlands of Oyuk. Although the region was plagued by unrest, his phantom emanation pressed on fearlessly to Oyuk Valley; the phantom gathered and split firewood during the day, then brought back food and drink. When Zhangtön reached the foot of a cliff that looked like a lion, he wondered if he had gotten lost and considered turning back. He looked around in all directions, but there seemed no way to go.

He saw some fine grass growing at the mouth of a cave that faced north, hiding it from view. [1.61a] He threw a sharp spear, which landed inside with a clatter. When he entered the cave, he found on the walls a mandala that had been effaced by many snakes and frogs slithering and scurrying about. Looking further, he found more than a hundred plaques indicating the presence of termas. While he dug into the earth, the man in the white hat came, bringing food, drink, and a lamp.

A little later, he heard a frightening voice outside the cave. Zhangtön asked, "Is that the emanation that the prophecy hinted I would meet?" The man in the white hat said, "I'll go and bring back my elder sister." In a short time, a terrifying presence appeared outside the cave with a staring, bloodshot eye about the size of a large pan and a single bared fang. Again Zhangtön called out, "Is that the emanation that was prophesied to me?" The presence answered:

> I am Ekajati.
> Offer 108 ganachakras!
> Do not speak of this for three years!

Having said this, the presence went away. The man in the white hat was Vajrasadhu, while the wrathful feminine presence was in fact the guardian goddess of mantra, Ekajati.

Then Gyalwa Zhangtön used one of two pieces of turquoise left by Ekajati at the mouth of the cave [1.61b] to buy a sack of meat, and the other to buy three pack loads of barley. With these he offered 108 ganachakras. He brought forth the terma caches in succession and copied the manuscripts completely at Takdzong in Nyang, with Shakmo Kartso acting as his patron. He said that he would be unable to keep these a secret for more than three years.

Then, when he was twenty-five years old, he journeyed to the central regions, where he built a small house on the ridge of Chilgang. On the road back to Tanak in Shang, he encountered the lord of the dharma, the great siddha Seng-gé Wangchuk, who bestowed on him the empowerments, teachings, and instructions of the secret Nyingtik cycles of the Dzogchen approach of utter lucidity in their entirety. After granting him permission to teach with the words, "Ensure the welfare of others!" the teacher vanished.

Gyalwa Zhangtön then returned to central Tibet, where he was invited to Tsurkung by Nyergom. There, one morning at dawn, he met Vimalamitra, who gave him permission to teach and then vanished.

When he reached the age of sixty-one, he married Gyalmoyang and lived in a meditation cabin, bringing benefit to beings. The couple had at least three children. The guru said, [1.62a] "Had I not maintained a center, I would have attained the level of leaving no physical remains upon my death." Even so, his body cast no shadow, and on occasion he was clearly seen as the mandala of the buddhas of the five families. When he gave Dzogchen teachings, everyone saw canopies of rainbow light, and he was responsible for many other amazing phenomena.

In his seventy-first year, at midnight on the twenty-second day of the Pig month, he manifested his passing from his physical body. A loud sound was heard seven times in the eastern direction, and three large earthquakes were felt. The sky was filled with pulsating rainbow lights, the naturally occurring sweet sounds of cymbals, and the fragrant odors of perfumes, and shimmered with spheres of five colors, like many small shields of light. Everyone witnessed these events and was moved to faith.

Later that evening, when the guru's remains were cremated, five marvelous relics representing the five kayas were found, as were relics of five colors. Blossoms rained from the sky, and all the people gathered there rested quite naturally in a state of meditative stability.

It was from this amazing, superb guru that Drupchen Khepa Nyibum received the tantras, explanatory commentaries, and pith instructions [1.62b] of the unsurpassable secret, the vajra essence of utter lucidity, without any omission.

Drupchen Khepa Nyima Bum (1158–1213)

Nyima Bum was born to the great Gyalwa Zhangtön and his wife, Gyalmoyang. While he was in the womb, his mother dreamed of many suns rising at once. She related the dream to her husband, who said, "This is a sign that the child will serve the teachings of the unsurpassable secret and dispel the darkness of ignorance for countless beings." He named the child Nyima Bum.[12]

Between the ages of five and nine, the boy was taught by his father, who gave him all of the empowerments, teachings, and instructions [1.63a] of the secret Nyingtik cycles, like one vase filling another. At the age of twenty, after his father had passed away, Nyima Bum went to study with Gyaltsa of the Ngok clan[13] and became learned in many tantras of the Sarma schools and the instructions associated with these.

At twenty-two he married, and at twenty-seven he went to study with the Sakya master Drakpa Gyaltsen[14] of the Khon clan, as well as with Lama Taksopa. He became learned in *The Three Continua*[15] and related instructions and the Malgyo tradition of Chakrasamvara.[16]

When he was twenty-nine, he took a woman named Pang-gyen as his second wife. At thirty he studied with Kyitön Drakpa of Öndruk in Karak, receiving the teaching cycles of the Tsalpa Kagyüpa school,[17] such as the Achi tradition of Chakrasamvara, the Ra tradition of the venerable goddess Tara, and the protective deity of timeless awareness. From a number of learned and accomplished masters, Nyima Bum received teachings on all of the sutras and tantras and became learned in them.

Most important, he became a master of the Nyingtik teachings. According to a prophecy in the tantra *The Reverberation of Sound*, he was considered an emanation of Vajrapani. At a ceremony of investiture when he was ten, he astonished all of the students present by giving a discourse on the seventeen tantras, [1.63b] the principles of which he practiced assiduously and exclusively until he was twenty.

At the age of fifty-six, on the eighth day of the first month, that commemorating the Buddha's miracles, he passed away at sunrise. When his remains were cremated, canopies of rainbow light covered the sky, the earth was strewn with relics, and small alpine flowers bloomed around the site of the funeral pyre (which was on a cold ridge in the wintertime). The five kinds of marvelous remains, *sharira*[18] and others, manifested spontaneously in the ashes, arousing wonder in those who saw them.

It was from this sacred guru that the custodian of the teachings Guru Jober received the instructions in their entirety.

Guru Jober (1196–1255)

Guru Jober was born the son of Dawa Bum [1.64a] (the younger brother of Khepa Nyima Bum) and Gyamo Ulu. Until he was seven, he seemed mentally handicapped, but from the age of eight onward, his knowledge blazed like wildfire. He studied with his uncle, Nyima Bum, until he was eighteen, receiving all of the empowerments, teachings, and instructions of the unsurpassable secret without exception and spending his time explaining the tantras and pursuing his practice with diligence.

From nineteen to twenty years of age, he received from Sakya Lotsawa *The Three Continua* and related pith instructions, as well as the Malgyo tradition of Chakrasamvara, and became learned in these. He also mastered the Madhyamaka teachings, valid cognition, and other fields of study.

At twenty-two he received from Tropu Lotsawa *The Three Cycles of Tropu* and the rest of the instructions deriving from Mitra the Yogin. With the Nepalese master Drakpa Bummé, he studied the *dohas*[19] and various transmissions of the Mahamudra instructions.[20] In addition, he received many teachings on the Three Repositories and many tantras, explanatory commentaries, and pith instructions from a number of learned and accomplished masters. He completed his studies at the age of thirty-six, having mastered the various subjects.

His practice gave rise to visions of his meditation deities. Once, in Lhasa, [1.64b] he beheld the face of the Jowo statue[21] in the main temple wreathed in five-colored rainbow light. From the mouth issued five spheres of light, in the center of which he saw the masculine and feminine aspects of Vajrasattva in union, Vajrapani, and Avalokiteshvara. At dawn he perceived the protector Amitayus in the midst of a field of rainbow light. Of this vision he said, "This must have arisen from enlightened qualities that ensure longevity. Although I do not hail from a long-lived family, things will turn out well for me."

Having acted as a leader of beings, guiding them with his immeasurable wisdom and innate compassion, he passed away during the full moon in the first month of autumn of a Hare year.[22]

It was from this supreme lord of yogins that the great Trulzhik Seng-gé Gyappa received the instructions of the vajra heart essence of utter lucidity in their entirety.

Trulzhik Seng-gé Gyappa (13th Century)

Seng-gé Gyappa was born in the village of Sogétreng in the Dra Uplands of the Yoru region of central Tibet. His father was Trashi Ngödrup and his mother was Pal-lek. At sunrise, when he was born, everyone saw a canopy of rainbows over the house. When he was nine, he experienced an awakening of his spiritual heritage.[23] [1.65a] He had innumerable pure visions, and immeasurable devotion arose in him, turning his mind away from the ordinary. At the age of ten, he felt, "All that I perceive is illusory; how could anything like this be real or permanent?" He perceived the world of all appearances and possibilities to be his teacher. At the age of twelve, he became disenchanted with the things of samsara and felt determined to find release from it.

At dawn one morning when he was thirteen, he dreamed that, among other wondrous events, the sun and moon rose at the same time. When he awoke, Avalokiteshvara appeared and said to him, "How marvelous! Fortunate one, meditate on the meaning of the most secret unsurpassable Nyingtik teachings; this will bring freedom in a single lifetime." With that, the deity vanished. [1.65b] Seng-gé Gyappa later said that, from that time forward, his compassion for all beings increased impartially and he always thought of every single being as his only child.

When he was eighteen, he realized that neither appearances nor mind ultimately have true existence as such, and by following the free and all-encompassing conduct of an inspired madman,[24] he trained in the ultimate meaning of naturally occurring timeless awareness. During this period of his life, his parents would gather the things normally offered to deities and dedicate them with the words, "We offer these to the *gyalpo* demons; we offer them to the *senmo* demonesses."[25] They would say, "How unfortunate that a son like you has been born to us!"

At the age of twenty, Seng-gé Gyappa took monastic ordination from the abbot Deu Gangpa and the preceptor Trashi Gangpa, and studied and contemplated Vinaya. At twenty-five he went to Seng-gé Gyap in Sizhal and received the entire cycle of empowerments, teachings, and instructions of Zhang Tsalpa from the master Seng-gé Gyappa the Second.[26] He then practiced these teachings. He requested from Lama Tsaripa teachings on texts such as *The Intertwined Necks of the Lions,* which concerns the unity of mind and subtle energy. He also studied with the masters Repa Drimé Ö, Lharipal, Zhönnu Bum, Tönchar Jangchub Yönten, and Loppön Chösé, among others. He studied the teachings of Chö and Zhijé,[27] Mahamudra, and the complete range of the sadhana classes of the Nyingma and Sarma schools of the secret mantra path, [1.66a] together with their associated pith instructions.

In particular, from the custodian of the teachings Guru Jober, he received the empowerments, teachings, and instructions of the secret Dzogchen approach in their entirety. He spent many years at mountain retreats and solitary places like Drowo Valley, devoting himself assiduously to these teachings as the very heart of his practice. He then brought many fortunate students to spiritual maturity and liberation.

At the age of sixty-four, he passed into the primordial basic space that is the true nature of phenomena. When his remains were cremated, the sky was filled with rainbow light, and many relics and images of deities were found in the ashes, moving beings to an unsurpassable state of wonderment.

It was from this holy and sublimely marvelous guru that Drupchen Melong Dorjé received the tantras and pith instructions of the sublime secret in their entirety.

Drupchen Melong Dorjé (1243–1303)

Melong Dorjé was born in the lowlands of Drak Valley. His father was the yogin Samyé, and his mother was Barma. At the age of nine, he took monastic ordination from Druptop Zalungpa and Khenchen Selungpa. He practiced meditation at the lakeside cliff of Zang-ri and his experiences developed, [1.66b] so that he gained a degree of supernormal perception.

At sixteen he stayed at Zhok in the Drak Uplands, reading the sutra *The Perfection of Sublime Knowing in Eight Thousand Verses* about a hundred times, so that he realized the ultimate meaning of the way of abiding. His conduct thereafter was that of supreme, naturally arising freedom, without any fixed reference point.

By the time he was seventeen, Melong Dorjé had traveled to various places to study at the feet of many learned and accomplished masters, training in the authentic instructions he received from them. He practiced at many important holy sites, like Sha-uk Takgo and Kharchu[28] in the southern reaches, sustaining himself for three weeks or a month on a few handfuls of barley and undergoing many other privations.

At eighteen [1.67a] he went to see the great Trulzhik Seng-gé Gyappa. From him he requested in their entirety the tantras, explanatory commentaries, and pith instructions of the secret Nyingtik teachings of utter lucidity. While engaged in the preliminary practices of these teachings, he saw Vajrasattva in the sky before him, a vision that lasted six days. He said that while he was undertaking the main body of practice, he met with the gurus of the lineage in his dreams and received their blessings.

When he was twenty-three, Melong Dorjé received many terma teachings from Sang-gyé Repa,[29] including some related to the goddess Vajravarahi. His ensuing diligent practice led to an actual encounter with Vajravarahi when he was twenty-four. On that same occasion, in the midst of a mass of light in the sky, he beheld the masculine and feminine aspects of Chakrasamvara in union, as well as the deities Hayagriva, Tara, the supremely compassionate Avalokiteshvara, Samantabhadra, Vajrasattva, and the gurus Vimalamitra, Orgyen, Zalungpa, Sang-gyé Repa, and Drogön Rinpoché.

Later, he spent time in Dang Valley, where he awoke one morning at dawn to hear the extremely sweet, natural song of the dakinis:

> How marvelous! In your comfortable bed, as you gaze at the ultimate meaning of the true nature of phenomena,
> cut through the ongoing flow of rebirth, O yogin.
> During the stages of practice, continually repeat the essence mantras that control our life force. [1.67b]
> We will be your allies, never separate from you, dear son.

In Kawachen, one morning on the twelfth day of the lunar month, Melong Dorjé saw Red Varahi and Druptop Zalungpa in the center of the sky. In a dream at the cave known as Ngarpuk, he beheld a mandala of five deities: Varahi and her four attendants. An earthquake woke him, and he actually saw the form of Varahi made of light. When he was residing at Kyapné Dzong, he dreamed that his five gurus and Vajrasattva bestowed on him all four empowerments of the Dzogchen approach, directly introducing him to the ultimate meaning.

Beginning in his twenty-sixth year, Melong Dorjé studied with many teachers, such as Trulzhik Darma and Tulku Gyatso, requesting from them many empowerments, teachings, and instructions of the secret mantra approach. In all, he relied on thirteen especially exalted gurus and three who were peerless: Druptop Zalungpa of the Dra Uplands, Dowo Repa of the Tsurpu Uplands, and Trulzhik Seng-gé Gyappa of Götsé. He mastered a vast body of instructions on the essential meaning of the teachings.

Through his uncontrived conduct, eschewing ordinary acceptance or rejection, Melong Dorjé was able to authentically maintain the samaya of the secret mantra approach. [1.68a] Once, he saw a young vulture soaring in the sky, and this experience honed his awareness and ability to manifest uncontrived conduct with such intensity that he flew into the sky himself. Solid rock was as soft as clay to him. In such ways, Melong Dorjé demonstrated various kinds of conduct worthy of a siddha. At many important holy sites in the southern reaches, such as Khenpa Jong, Khenpa Ling, Seng-gé Dzong, Kunzang Ling, and Kharchu, he planted the victory banner of practice and brought numerous fortunate students to spiritual maturity and liberation.

Although it was predicted that Melong Dorjé would die at thirty-seven, the prayers of one of his fortunate students, Loppön Kunga, extended his life. In his sixty-first year, at a charnel ground on a mountain pass, his enlightened intent merged with the basic space of all phenomena. This took place at dawn on the twenty-fifth day of the last month of autumn in a Hare year.[30] Everyone present saw a great light and heard sounds, all of which faded away to the west. When his remains were cremated, the sky was extremely clear, and there were countless marvelous signs—the crematory was bathed in rainbows and swathed in lattices of light, his bones were marked with white *A* syllables, [1.68b] and the five kinds of sharira were found in the ashes—moving all present to states of awe.

To Melong Dorjé fell the transmission of an extraordinary terma cache entitled *The Heart Drop of Melong;* currently, however, there remains only a lineage of the oral transmissions for the texts in Bhutan.

It was with this holy guru that the great Rigdzin Kumaradza[31] studied, receiving the cycles of the vajra heart essence of utter lucidity in their entirety, like one vase being filled from another, with nothing left out.

Rigdzin Chenpo Kumaradza (1266–1343)

Kumaradza was born in Barsar Dzingka, a village in Ön, in Yoru, central Tibet. His father, Jo-sé Sönam, and his mother, Chertsa Bummé, named him Tarpagyen. [1.69a] From an early age, he demonstrated faith and compassion and was highly intelligent; he knew how to read and write without having to be taught.

At the age of seven, Kumaradza received the empowerments for Hevajra and Chakrasamvara from Lama Gyedorpa of Tuteng Monastery in Öshö, in the southeastern Tibetan region of Kongpo, and so began his spiritual development. At nine he took full lay ordination[32] from the abbot Tsangpa and trained in the cycle of teachings related to the form of Mahakarunika known as Khorwa Dongtruk. At twelve he took monastic ordination from the abbot Yerpa and the preceptor Ngaripa of the Pakmodrupa Kagyü school; he received the name Zhönnu Gyalpo and studied Vinaya.

He spent five years studying with Drakpa Yerpa Rinpoché, receiving many instructions, such as the Six Yogas of Naropa. He also studied with Lama Tsartengpa and became learned in *The Two Chapters*. From Önpo Sangshé, he learned the ritual art of painting deities. Once, while reciting the six-syllable mantra, he had a vision of the supremely compassionate Avalokiteshvara appearing, smiling, within a small building made of crystal. Then, from Shakdar of the Chungnak clan, he received the oral transmissions for *The Collected Tantras of the Nyingma School,* as well as many explanatory commentaries and pith instructions.

At the cave known as Ngarpuk, [1.69b] he met Drupchen Melong Dorjé, who taught him Mahamudra; he was introduced to the true nature of mind, and realization dawned in him. He then accompanied Melong Dorjé as his attendant when the mahasiddha went to Khandroi Ling in Bhutan. There he received from him many teachings, such as a cycle focusing on Vajravarahi. On the night of the tenth day of the lunar month, while he was in an intensive retreat practicing these teachings, he dreamed that Orgyen Pema came to him, red, dancing gracefully, wearing the six bone ornaments, and saying, "How marvelous! O child of good family, always follow the dharma!"

He then traveled to the uplands of Tsurpu, where he spent several years receiving the teaching cycles of the Karmapas from Lama Nyenré and Lama Darmagön. At Lakor, Purang, and other places in the Ding-ri region of upper La, he met with Drupchen Orgyenpa and the Karmapa Rangjung Dorjé, recently ordained at the age of seventeen. He requested this mahasiddha's instructions in their entirety. Several years later, when Orgyenpa requested the Nyingtik teachings from Nyenré, Kumaradza was also present and received the full range of instructions. He thereafter received many of the secret cycles of the Dzogchen approach, such as *The Direct Introduction: Mirror of the Key Point,* from a guru of Gyamen named Namkha Dorjé, [1.70a] and *The Mirror of the Key Points of Secrecy,* from Kalden Chökyi Seng-gé.

Returning to Kharchu, he again met that great and powerful lord of yogins who are masters of awareness, Drupchen Melong Dorjé. He unerringly conferred on Kumaradza the key points of the tantras, explanatory commentaries, and pith instructions of the secret Nyingtik teachings of the Dzogchen approach of utter lucidity and transmitted to him fully his seal of entrustment together with the maturing empowerments and liberating instructions. Having nothing else to offer, Kumaradza served his teacher with body and speech. He spent two whole summers painting murals on the interior walls of a small building called the Bumchung, built by Dowo Repa. His guru had given him four measures of barley, but he used two of these to purchase paper so that he could spend his nights copying texts, and the other two to buy lamps to copy by, as well as food. He became violently ill due to his austere existence, but also experienced extraordinary states of realization, so that his guru was extremely delighted and gave him permission to teach others.

At that time, while sitting in an empowerment, he beheld the four-armed Mahakala in the sky above the guru's head. On another occasion, the black goddess Ekajati appeared to him at the door of the guru's chambers, holding in one hand a club made of a human corpse and in the other a wolf bitch. [1.70b] She was equal in height to a two-story building; in front of her was one of her minions, a wrathful mamo goddess, scooping blood from a small lake with her two hands and drinking it.

Kumaradza then spent the next eight years steadfastly attending his guru, never leaving his side. The two passed a winter in the thatched hut that Orgyen had inhabited. There Kumaradza had a vision of Vajravarahi, and his wisdom and intelligence in all areas expanded. Later, just before his gracious guru passed away, Kumaradza traveled to Yarlung, where he founded the hermitage of Tsading Ritrö, and stayed there for a short time. When he learned that Melong Dorjé had passed away, he returned to Kharchu and met his guru's two sons at Chak. After returning to Yarlung, he began performing a memorial ceremony on the twenty-fifth day of the month.

He then went to Tsari on a pilgrimage, during which he witnessed many marvelous signs. Five-colored rainbow light emanated from the naturally manifesting stone image at Neuring in Trikmo Lha. One morning, while skirting the lower tip of the glacier on the glorious Crystal Mountain, he arrived at a round, turquoise tarn; a five-colored rainbow rose straight up between the absolutely limpid lake and the equally limpid sky.

The lord of the dharma Karmapa invited Kumaradza to the uplands of Tsurpu. [1.71a] There Kumaradza bestowed on him the explanatory commentaries of the tantras and instructions of the Nyingtik teachings. Kumaradza next went to Shang, where he requested the oral lineage of the secret cycles and *The Lamp of the Eye of Meditative Stability* from the teacher Chegompa, holder of the lineage of Chegom Nakpo.

In Namar, in the area of Ding-ri in upper La, he requested from Önpo Jangdruppa *The Spiritual Teachings for Mountain Retreat* of Yang-gönpa. Returning from his meeting with that mahasiddha, he met one Lama Tralungpa on the road and received from him the cycle of the deity Black Yamari and many other cycles of the Sarma schools of tantra. With the teacher Yeshé Gönpo and others, he studied in great detail all of the pith instructions concerning the stage of completion that were then renowned in Tibet, including the secret cycles, the instructions of Götsangpa, *The Great Teaching Manual of Aro,* the cycles of concise teaching manuals, and other works. With this, he brought his oceanic study of the teachings to full expression.

Then, having circumambulated the mountain of Tsari, sacred to the Sarma schools, he spent eight months alone by the shore of the turquoise lake sacred to the Nyingma school. During this time, he witnessed impressive evidence of the machinations of gods and demons, but he accepted it with equanimity, resting in the immediate experience of his true nature. Jambhala[33] gave him gems, the local god Ghayadhara invited him to his dwelling [1.71b] and accorded him much honor, and in the middle of the lake he saw lights of five colors, with yellow bubbles the size of large plates dissolving into each other. He related that he witnessed many such miraculous signs.

Kumaradza spent his time entirely in glacial retreats and mountain hermitages, assiduously pursuing his practice, the essence of his life. He transmitted the teachings of the unsurpassable secret to many great spiritual beings, like the precious Karmapa Rangjung Dorjé, and fortunate students. He also sowed the seeds of liberation in the inhabitants of towns and rural areas. He benefited his companions, and even the wild animals and fish he saw on his travels; from Kongpo to É, for those afflicted by fear, he sealed the mountains, rivers, and dangerous paths.[34] He thus brought happiness and ease to beings on the face of the earth. In every valley and town in which he stayed, he pacified all the injuries and illnesses arising from hail and frost, epidemics, and other calamitous events. His powerful enlightened activity was such that all who saw, heard, or thought of him were brought closer to enlightenment.

This holy guru bore all the signs and marks characterizing an emanation of Vimalamitra [1.72a] (one such emanation, it had been prophesied, would appear in each century). On his nose was a mole in the shape of the syllable *A*, which never changed. The three protective deities—the guardian goddess of mantra Ekajati, Rahula, and the oath-bound one Vajrasadhu—bowed to and praised him, communicating with him as one person to another. He guided beings with his immeasurable qualities of wisdom and innate compassion. His mind was blessed with supernormal powers of perception.

At that time, the definitive points of the Nyingtik teachings had been diluted by the intellectual faults of various teachers. Kumaradza clearly distinguished himself from those who behaved erroneously by blurring the distinction between these points and the view and meditation of the Mahamudra approach, the Zhijé school, the Six Techniques of Union of the Kalachakra cycle, and so forth. He elucidated the philosophical tenets of the most secret unsurpassable approach, and all those fortunate people who came under his compassionate care manifested rainbow light and relics upon passing away, so that those around them gained conviction. These events showed that he was indeed an actual emanation of Vimalamitra.

Acting thus to benefit beings while in his physical body, Kumaradza lived to the age of seventy-eight. Then, at sunrise on the twenty-fifth day of the middle month of autumn in a Female Water Sheep year,[35] he passed away at the hermitage of Dang Valley in Dakpo. [1.72b] The occasion was marked by countless amazing marvels, such as sounds coming out of nowhere and networks and pavilions of five-colored light. His faithful students sat before him, his attendant, Gomdar, foremost among them. Responding to their supplications with his innate compassion, Kumaradza awoke in an instant as though from sleep. Sitting up cross-legged, he smiled and said to them, "None of you should grieve, for I have not died." Later, with no sign of illness or pain, he granted audiences and gave appropriate advice for the benefit of all.

One morning seven days later, the teacher Loden, the attendant Gomdar, and others asked him, "After you have passed away, what should we do? What changes should take place? Should we invite the Omniscient Guru?"[36]

He replied, "What are you saying, all you fools? Don't cause him so much trouble! If by now you have not studied my teachings in enough detail, go to him. Loden and the rest of you, I have already discussed things with you at great length and have given you much good advice. Don't chatter so much; use your ears instead!" He never spoke again, but sat smiling in the posture of a crouching sage [1.73a] with his eyes in the gaze of dharmakaya.[37] At dawn on the eighth day, he passed on to his destination, the supreme primordial place where phenomena fall away.

Kumaradza sat in that state until the twenty-fifth, when his remains were cremated.

The sky was extremely clear, and countless interlacing light rays appeared. His skull remained whole among the ashes, and inside it was a mandala of the five buddha families. Above the right and left ear cavities were dark blue forms of the venerable goddess[38] several inches long. The surroundings were filled with networks of five-colored rainbows, and shafts of light shone upward to form a pavilion. There were relics from the fragments of his bones, as well as the five kinds of marvelous physical remains. These great, amazing events moved many beings to faith and devotion.

Then, in the wake of Kumaradza's passing, a stupa was built, and during the monthlong memorial services that followed, the sky remained clear, with countless light rays appearing in the west.

> Alas, alas, gracious lord protector!
> Gaze directly on us from primordial basic space with your innate compassion.
> I pray, lead all of us in conditioned existence without exception [1.73b]
> to the basic space of peace!

It was from this holy guru that Longchenpa received the teachings.

5

Longchen Rabjampa Drimé Özer

Although you possessed a power equal in innate compassion, scriptural learning, and realization
to that of the "six ornaments" and the "two excellent ones" who adorned the world,[1]
you maintained a hidden discipline in holy forest hermitages.
Longchenpa, of the vast expanse of being in which samsara and nirvana are perfect and complete as dharmakaya,
venerable Drimé Özer, I supplicate you.

LONGCHENPA'S OUTER BIOGRAPHY: ENLIGHTENED FORM[2]

Birth and Early Life

The Omniscient King of the Dharma, Longchen Rabjam, appeared in Tibet, the Land of Snows, as the second Teacher[3] of the three categories of the Dzogchen teachings. He was born in a village called Entsa in upper Dra Valley in Yoru, the eastern part of central Tibet. [1.74a] His paternal grandfather, the teacher Loppön Lhasung, belonged to the twenty-fifth generation of a clan descended from Gyalwa Chokyang of Ngenlam. The latter had been an accomplished master of the practice of the deity Hayagriva and one of the first seven Tibetans chosen to receive monastic ordination. An accomplished master of the practice of the healing deity Dütsimen, Loppön Lhasung lived to the age of 105. His son, the teacher Loppön Tenpasung, became in turn an accomplished master, continuing the family tradition.

Longchenpa's mother was Sönamgyen of the Dro clan. When her son was conceived, Sönamgyen dreamed of a great lion, the sun and moon rising together on its brow and forming a swirling mass of light, which was absorbed into her body. Many other amazing signs manifested during her pregnancy, and her son was born on the tenth day of the second month of the lunar calendar in a Male Earth Monkey year,[4] in the lunar mansion of Gyalwa. He was named Dorjé Gyaltsen. The moment he was born, the wrathful goddess of the lunar mansion, Revati, appeared, a black woman with bared fangs and frowning brow, wielding a sword. Taking him in her lap, she said, "I shall guard him!" Then, returning him to his mother, she vanished.

Once, Sönamgyen put her son down on the ground and was weeding the garden, when it began to hail. She ran inside without him, but immediately remembered her child and went to fetch him. Unable to find him, she went back into the house weeping. [1.74b] Again the goddess Revati appeared, emerging from the storeroom carrying the child. She admonished Sönamgyen, saying, "You have mistreated this tulku!" and brandished her sword as if to strike the woman before placing the child in her arms. Throughout Dorjé Gyaltsen's childhood, the goddess manifested in this distinct form and watched over him.

As soon as he could speak, he would describe things with great clarity as though recalling previous lifetimes. When he was quite young, his family moved to a place close to Khamsum Metokdrol in the area of Samyé Monastery. Blessed as he was with very powerful faith, compassion, and intelligence, by the age of five Dorjé Gyaltsen knew how to read and write without difficulty, merely having been shown the letters. At the age of seven, he began studying with his father, receiving the empowerments, explanatory commentaries, pith instructions, and traditional practice methods for the Eight Commands cycle entitled *The Gathering of Sugatas* and cycles focusing on Hayagriva, Vajrakila, and peaceful and wrathful forms of Guru Rinpoché. In addition, he studied and mastered medicine, astrology, and other fields of learning. At Tsongdü in Drachi Valley, when he was nine, he learned the meaning of the sutras *The Perfection of Sublime Knowing in Twenty Thousand Verses* and *The Perfection of Sublime Knowing in Eight Thousand Verses* by reciting these texts aloud a hundred times each.

Later Studies

At twelve he was ordained as a novice monk at Samyé Monastery by the abbot Samdrup Rinchen and the preceptor Kunga Özer. He was given the name Tsultrim Lodrö. Studying Vinaya, he wrote a commentary on this subject at fourteen and gained fame as a scholar.

At sixteen years of age, [1.75a] Tsultrim Lodrö studied with the teacher Rinchen Trashi, receiving from him the empowerments and instructions of the Lamdré cycle, the Six Yogas of Naropa, the deity Vajravarahi, Ghantapada's lineage of the deity Chakrasamvara, and Mahachakra Vajrapani. With the teacher Wangchuk Yeshé, he studied *The Kalachakra Tantra* and most of the other tantric cycles of the Sarma schools. From Zaplung Rinpoché, he received the teaching cycles of the Tsalpa school;

Götsangpa's[5] teachings on the path; the early, middle, and later transmissions of the Zhijé school of Padampa Sang-gyé; and the teachings of the Chö school of Machik.

At nineteen Tsultrim Lodrö went to Neutok in the Sangpu Uplands, where he studied principally with the great teacher Tsengönpa, the administrator Chöpal Gyaltsen, and Zhönnu Rinchen, who was renowned as a second Dharmakirti.[6] With these three masters, he studied *The Five Treatises of Maitreya, The Detailed Commentary on the Compendium of Valid Cognition, The Compendium of Valid Cognition,* as well as all of the main texts and commentaries concerning Prajñaparamita and valid cognition. Learning both the words and the underlying meaning of these texts, he became quite erudite.

With the teacher Zhönnu Gyalpo, he studied Nagarjuna's *Six Collections of Reasoning—The Collected Aphorisms* (a commentary on the Four Noble Truths), *The Source Verses on Sublime Knowing, The Sixty Verses on Reasoning, The Seventy Verses on Emptiness, The Minute Scrutiny,* and *The Refutation of Arguments*—as well as his *Commentary on the Definitive Collection of the Ultimate* and *Praise of the Basic Space of Phenomena.* [1.75b]

With Loten Panglo Chenpo, he studied detailed explanations of *The Seven Treatises on Valid Cognition* and explanations of the class of profound sutras such as *The Most Majestic State of Meditative Absorption,* as well as all of the sources for the fields of secular knowledge, like the source text *The Mirror of Poetics* and the commentary on it.

Studying these in their entirety, he came to master thoroughly all of the words and their underlying meaning in three years. He traveled to the *shedras*[7] in centers where scriptures and correct reasoning were taught and encountered no impediment in mastering the full range of source texts, developing the dynamic energy of his wisdom and perfecting all the expressions of his intelligence. He gained universal fame as a great scholar, undisputed and unparalleled, and was known as Samyé Lungmangpa.[8]

While studying at Sangpu, he practiced the phases of approach and accomplishment for deities associated with the development of sublime knowing, such as Achala, Sarasvati, and Vajravarahi, and was graced with visions of them. In particular, the goddess Sarasvati placed him in the palm of her hand and spent seven days showing him the four continents and Sumeru, so that he developed the force of his untrammeled intellect. In *Playful Delight of Youthfulness,* his prayer of praise to her, he writes:

> Ah! Goddess of good fortune,
> my longtime aspiration has been realized today!

From that time on, he was never separate from Sarasvati, who manifested in various distinct forms for him. [1.76a] As he said:

> Your embodiments, in a mass of light,
> are white, yellow, red, and green . . .
> Sometimes, within canopies of clouds,
> your form is varicolored—brilliant white, crimson, dark blue.
> You appear in forms that play or move or stand.

In addition, with Zhönnu Döndrup of Denbak, he studied *The Collected Tantras of the Nyingma School* and many pith instructions from *The Discourse on United Intent, The Web of Magical Display,* and the mind teachings. With Zhönnu Dorjé, he studied Shantideva's *Engaging in the Conduct of a Bodhisattva* and *A Compendium of the Training,* as well as the cycles of teaching from the Kadampa school. From several khenpos, he received teachings on *The Ocean of Sadhanas, The Ocean of Dakinis, The Ocean of Dakas, One Hundred Religious Histories, The Scriptural Transmission of the Vinaya,* the extensive, middle-length, and abridged classes of sutras, the sutra *The Vajra Cutter, The Condensed Verses on the Perfection of Sublime Knowing, The Heart of Sublime Knowing,* the sutra *The Perfection of Sublime Knowing in Ten Thousand Verses, The Methods in One Hundred and Fifty Verses,* and other texts.

With the lord of the dharma Karmapa Rangjung Dorjé, Longchenpa studied such teachings as the Six Techniques of Union from the Kalachakra cycle, including the auxiliary methods for dispelling hindrances; the Six Yogas of Naropa; *The Direct Introduction to the Three Kayas;* "The Tradition of the King" for the form of the supremely compassionate Avalokiteshvara called Jinasagara; and the tantras of Guhyasamaja, Samputa, Mahamaya, and the red and black forms of Yamantaka.

From the teacher Loppön Wang-gyé, he received detailed teachings on meditation deities, as well as many sadhanas and pith instructions concerning the tantra *The Buddha Skull Cup,* [1.76b] the tantra *The Dakini Pavilion,* the tradition of Ra Lotsawa[9] for the deity Vajrabhairava, the cycle concerning subtle energy for the deity Jambhala, the deity Kurukulle, the six consorts of the sages, Maitreya, the sixteen arhats, Bhaishajyaguru, and so forth.

With Shukseppa, he studied Saraha's *Three Doha Cycles, The Three Cycles of Spiritual Teachings for Mountain Retreat, The One Hundred Points of Interdependent Connection,* and other works.

The teacher Loppön Töntsul taught him the process of refining mercury[10] according to the methods of the sage Zhungkyé. Lama Jamyangpa imparted to him the full range of instructions concerning the astrological charts of *The Kalachakra Tantra,* as well as *The Two Chapters,* the tantra *The Vajra Pinnacle, The Source Tantra of Mañjushri, The Vajra Source, The Compendium of Suchness,* the tantra *The Compendium of Suchness for Refining Lower Realms,* the tantra *Immutable Basic Space,* the tantra *The All-Knowing One,* and *The Clear Meaning of Consecration.*

With the great Sakya master Lama Dampa,[11] Longchenpa studied *The Great Awakening of Motivation* as well as all of the instructions of *The Three Continua*. From the precious master Tropupa, he received *The Vajra Garland* and the cycles of the protective deity of the tantra *The Vajra Pavilion*.

With Lama Tsongdüpa, he studied the Eight Commands cycle of Guru Chöwang entitled *The Complete Secret; The Condensed Quintessence* cycle of Mahakarunika; the Dzogchen cycle *The Union of All Buddhas in Equalness;* the practice of Khorwa Dongtruk; *The Guru, the Gathering of Secrets;* the practice of the protective deity Ma-ning Nakpo; [1.77a] and such secular texts as *The Hundred Teachings on Extracting the Vital Essence, The Patra* (a technical manual for defensive measures against invasion), *The Catapult of Fire and Water,* and *The Means of Ensuring Great Power.* From Kangmarwa he received teachings on the protective deities Tsedak Palapatra, Tsatsa Nyönpa, Tsitta Marpo, the wrathful mamo goddess Dugi Pudri, and Duwa Lungzhon; *The Black Stupa* (concerning seven non-Buddhist deities); and the pith instructions for preventing or bringing down hailstorms. Tingma Sang-gyé Drakö transmitted to him such teachings as *The Great Gathering of Sugatas* (a cycle focusing on the Eight Commands that was a terma teaching of Nyang), Namchak Umro, Vajrakila, the dakini Guhyajñana, the protective deity Lekden, and the guardian deities Takshön and Sengshön.

Thus Longchenpa completed his study and training in the entire range of fields of inquiry. He mastered the empowerments and permission blessings[12] of the Nyingma and Sarma schools of secret mantra, explanations of many major and minor source texts of the sutra and tantra traditions, explanatory commentaries and profound teachings, and such secular subjects as grammar, poetics, and astrology.

Training under Rigdzin Kumaradza

During his time at Sangpu, some monks from eastern Tibet evicted him from his rooms seven times. [1.77b] Longchenpa wrote enough tracts on the faults of these eastern Tibetans to fill a basket, which he carried to the teaching throne in his dormitory. As he was leaving, he encountered a friend in front of the hall housing the statues known as Lotsawai Kubum.[13]

"Where are you going?" his friend asked.

"Since there is no place for me to stay among those eastern Tibetans, I am leaving," he replied. "Here, I want you to have this." And Longchenpa gave him a copy of a poem he had composed entitled "Saddened by My Circumstances," a work based on the Tibetan alphabet.[14]

Wearing only the bare necessities of clothing—the skirt and vest that all Tibetan children wear in monastic schools—he traveled toward the higher elevations of upper Uru in central Tibet, begging along the road. Resting in a meadow in lower Cha

Valley, he met a scholar named Geshé[15] Töntsul from Gyama. Longchenpa asked him whether there was a cave associated with Druptop Chokla in Gyama.

The scholar replied, "I know that Master Chokla stayed in an excellent cliffside cave."

Longchenpa said, "I gathered a full bag of barley while begging, so I feel I should stay there for the winter."

"Please do so! I will stay as well and serve you," Töntsul suggested.

In the village, Longchenpa performed a ritual for the stillborn child of a lay tantric practitioner. Taking the small payment that he received in exchange, he spent the next eight months in the cave of Chokla in complete, continual darkness, day and night.[16] At dawn, between his meditation sessions, he would confer the teachings of the transcendent perfections to the scholar. [1.78a] Otherwise, he remained in the equipoise of one-pointed meditative absorption.

After five months had passed in this way, Longchenpa had a meditative experience one morning at dawn. He found himself in a low valley, with sandy dunes and a waterfall. Above him he saw a horse caparisoned with a leather saddle and small bells; its rider was a sixteen-year-old girl of unparalleled loveliness, richly dressed in a brocade robe, a jeweled tiara, and a golden veil. He seized the hem of the girl's robe and pleaded with her, "Exalted lady, take me under your compassionate care!"

She removed her crown and placed it on his head, saying, "Henceforth, I shall bless you and grant you siddhis." She also prophesied that he would meet Rigdzin Kumaradza. Thereafter, he spent a month deeply absorbed in a state of bliss, clarity, and nonconceptual awareness.

Having finished his retreat, Longchenpa performed one hundred repetitions of the ritual of Sarvavid Vairochana to benefit his parents. Töntsul thought to himself, "Such a ritual would definitely bring me blessings," and he formally requested the empowerment from Longchenpa, who agreed to give it. In a small clearing next to a spring, Longchenpa drew the complete mandala in colored sand and bestowed the empowerment on Töntsul and a lay tantric practitioner, as well as about thirty other men and women. [1.78b]

In fulfillment of the girl's prophecy, when Longchenpa was twenty-seven, he set out to meet Rigdzin Kumaradza in the Yartökyam Uplands, where the latter and some of his students were living in felt tents. As soon as he saw Kumaradza, Longchenpa knew with certainty that before him was Vimalamitra in person. The guru himself was extremely delighted and said, "Last night I dreamed of an amazing bird, which I was told was of divine origin, surrounded by a flock of a thousand smaller birds. They took my texts and flew away in all directions. When I saw you, I immediately knew that you would become a holder of my lineage of spiritual teachings."

That spring and summer, while Longchenpa waited to receive teachings from Kumaradza, the camp moved nine times, from one empty valley to another. So exhausted was Longchenpa's body and so worn his clothing that even the young monks and watchdogs spurned him. On the evening before the teachings were to begin, two administrators came to him carrying a large basket and asked, "O scholar of Samyé, where is your contribution to the cost of the teachings? They begin tomorrow, and we are taking up a collection of seven loads of barley."

He replied, "I haven't even a single measure of barley, but since the guru told me I would receive the teachings from him, I have stayed on." [1.79a]

They left, admonishing, "If you cannot be responsible for your contribution to these teachings, who will cover your share?"

He thought to himself, "Since in previous lifetimes I did not gather sufficient merit, even though I have waited with such hardship I am now to be denied the teachings for lack of a material contribution. I must leave, but am so embarrassed to be around the other people here that I will make sure I reach the lower end of the valley before anyone awakens tomorrow morning."

Having made this plan, he went to sleep and arose before dawn. Just then, someone came to summon him, saying, "O scholar of Samyé, come right now into the guru's presence!"

He thought, "I am all ready to leave, but it would not do to ignore the guru's command," and so he went to Kumaradza. Smiling, the guru said to him, "Don't be so concerned! Sit down and have some tea." He then sent for the administrators and told them, "I will cover the cost of the teachings for this scholar, so don't bother him about it. I would rather he attend than all of the others who intend to listen to my teachings."

Later the guru told him, "In a dream, I met a scholar who I was told was Vimalamitra, wearing a scholar's cap and carrying a text. He said to me, 'This fellow Drimé Özer is a holy person who has prayed and aspired to safeguard my teachings. You, Zhönnu Gyalpo, will give him the pith instructions in their entirety. He will become the custodian of your teachings [1.79b] and a protector of the Dzogchen teachings.'"

The following year, teacher and student journeyed together to Shampo Glacier. There the teacher bestowed many empowerments and instructions on Longchenpa, especially the teachings of the unsurpassable secret: the outer, inner, and secret cycles of the Dzogchen approach of utter lucidity; the four volumes of profound pith instructions; and the seventeen tantras, such as *The Reverberation of Sound,* the most majestic of all tantras, together with the 119 pith instructions. He conferred the sadhana cycles, empowerments, and permission blessings, secondary activity rituals, and traditional methods for Ekajati, the great guardian of conditioned existence; the lord Lekden and his lady; the planetary spirit Rahula; Vajrasadhu; and others. Kumaradza empowered Longchenpa as his main regent, and the guardian deities of the teachings actually manifested and presented their sadhanas, pith instructions, and essence mantras of life force. In particular, Rahula promised him that none of his lineage holders would be harmed by poisons and offered him his own emblem as an amulet against contamination and poisoning. It was a red seal renowned as the "seal of the planet Rahu," marked with designs of the ten syllables of power from the Kalachakra cycle and inscribed with Rahula's own name; it could make a sharp impression through hundreds of sheets of paper all at once. Rahula also promised to serve Longchenpa in whatever way he enjoined him to do so. [1.80a]

Accordingly, over time the great Omniscient One performed seven ceremonies for summoning the presence of this wild planetary deity. While Longchenpa was staying in Bhutan, the goat that had been chosen as the symbolic representation of Rahula's spirit during the ritual got caught in a thorny thicket somewhere nearby, where it died and could not be retrieved. Longchenpa enjoined the deity, "Bring the slayer of this goat here quickly!" A great dust storm arose, uprooting the thicket and carrying the thorny bushes close to Longchenpa's quarters. This and many other such events that occurred were perceived by all present.

All this time, Longchenpa had very few provisions. He sustained himself on several pounds of flour and about twenty-one pills of mercury. When snow fell, he would wrap himself in a sack and use it as both a bed and a sitting mat. While undergoing such great privations, he heard all of Kumaradza's spiritual instructions.

Then he went to the Chimpu Uplands, where he made a firm vow not to waver from his purpose in thought, word, or deed for several years. Initially, while he was staying at the ridge known as Lundrup Gang, he beheld the form of Black Vajravarahi for seven days, and from time to time he had visions of Guru Drakpo[17] and the twenty-one-headed form of the deity Mahottara surrounded by the 724 deities of the Eight Commands. Dorjé Yudrönma[18] offered him her own outer, inner, and secret sadhana practices, and Jambhala presented him with a gem.

While he stayed at Gegong, he had a vision of a peaceful form of Guru Rinpoché. [1.80b] He also journeyed to the pure realm of Khechara, where he experienced numerous marvels. In one instance, he taught the dharma to the dakinis there. They cast flowers of auspicious benediction on him and escorted him for a short distance when he left, offering him the permission blessings of the Nyingtik teachings. He was continually immersed in such pure visions.

At Ge-ur he had visions of bodies of light—standing forms of Red Varahi, Vajrasattva, Hayagriva, Tara, and Amitayus. Then, as he practiced in a charnel ground, deities revealed their forms to him and undertook to carry out his enlightened activities. Among these were the dark blue form of Ekajati, bearing a club and riding a wolf bitch; Rahula, the planetary mara; Vajrasadhu, the four-armed protective deity; Zhanglön Dorjé Duddul; and the guardians known as the twenty-one lay practitioners.[19] He discussed the dharma with dakinis as one would speak to another person.

During this period, whenever the need arose, he would immediately go to his gurus to clarify his understanding, then meditate one-pointedly, delighting them to the highest degree with his dynamic realization and fortitude in meditation.

He once went to Lhasa to make offerings to the Jowo statue in the main temple. He saw rays of light shining from the statue's midbrow and dissolving into his own. He had visions of Vulture Peak in India [1.81a] and the country of Khotan and clearly recalled his former lives as scholars in those places, as well as the vast range of topics of the dharma that he had mastered. Powerful experiences of bliss and clarity arose in his mind.

At Kani Gozhi, the timeless awareness embodiment of Machik Lapkyi Drönma took him under her care, giving him the transmission of her teachings on Chö.

Teaching Activities

When he first gave the Nyingtik teachings to many fortunate candidates at Shuksep in the Nyepu Uplands, Özer Gocha offered him a volume of the Nyingtik teachings for his inspection. Longchenpa realized that this volume had been given to him once before by the protective goddess Sokdrupma. At that time, he had been speaking with one Lama Remawa when a black woman approached, placed a volume in his hands, and vanished without a trace. Remawa saw that the volume was a text entitled *The Heart Drop of the Dakini*. Amazed, he brought this to Longchenpa's attention. Knowing that the visitation had been an exhortation by the goddess Sokdrupma, the master made a commitment to teach *The Heart Drop of the Dakini* at the Chimpu Uplands.

During the middle month of autumn in a Hare year,[20] when he was thirty-two, he taught the cycle to eight fortunate men and women at Rimochen in the Chimpu Uplands. At some point during the empowerment, the glorious guardian goddess of mantra, Ekajati, took possession of a yogini. When the other students expressed doubts about the authenticity of what had taken place, [1.81b] Longchenpa replied, "This woman has truly been possessed by a dakini. Since I am a yogin who has realized that mind and the sensory appearances it perceives are of one taste, this will present no obstacle."

Thereupon the yogini prostrated to her guru and, looking toward the mandala, said, "Why is there no peacock feather?"[21]

Longchenpa replied, "I have visualized it in my mind."

She retorted, "How could such a spiritual symbol simply be imagined?"

Longchenpa then removed the tripods supporting three vases on the shrine and placed these vases in a row. He proceeded to perform the ritual in a very precise manner, whereupon the yogini folded her hands and exclaimed, "This is wonderful!"

However, when he pronounced the word *rigs* as *rig*, dropping the final letter, she cried out, "No, no! It's pronounced *rigs!*"[22] And when Longchenpa recited the mantra, the yogini said to him, "Imitate my way of doing it!" Then, in the language of the dakinis, she chanted the mantra slowly to a haunting melody. During the main part of the empowerment, she sang a song about the view and meditation that are free of conceptual speculation:

> Though the mind that is free of meditation may be enjoyable,
> oh, how happy is the meditation that is free of the mind!

She stated, "These meager offerings will never do," and offered a sweet song instead. During the ganachakra, when the consecrated alcohol was served to the guru, the yogini said, "This is the samaya substance of the dakinis, so by all means partake." And she served it to him until there was none left. Inspired, the gathered students danced and sang, [1.82a] experiencing a one-pointed and utterly lucid state of mind, far beyond the ordinary experience of deep sleep.

They actually saw the phantomlike forms of dakas, dakinis, and protective deities. A black woman appeared and said, "The first portion of the flour you offered is stale," while the oath-bound protector Vajrasadhu took the form of a white man who said, "You neglected to put an ornament of red meat on my torma offering." The protector Jomo Dangla came as a white man seeking a torma offering, but refused the torma of meat that was given to him. Hosts of dakas and dakinis raised a ceremonial parasol over Longchenpa's head and circumambulated him; they shouted syllables like "Hum" and "Phat," making a terrific din. Many such miraculous events took place. One of the yogins present was terrified and said, "Tonight heaven and earth have changed places. These beings must be bent on having our flesh and blood!" Likewise, other protective deities such as Odé Gungyal, Nyenchen Tanglha, and the seven Menmo sisters came to receive their torma offerings.

Vajravarahi actually appeared to them, her form blue-black and ornamented with jewels and bones. She conversed with Longchenpa, saying, "Tonight is an occasion of great significance. I have come to observe your worthy students. [1.82b] How is your holy guru's health?"

Longchenpa replied, "This year his health has been failing. What will happen?"

The dakini responded, "How could an emanation of a buddha experience obstacles? He is thinking only of those he is to guide. Don't you realize that he is Vimalamitra appearing in Tibet?"

"How much longer will he live?" asked Longchenpa.

"He will live at least until the next year of the Sheep.[23] After that, it is not certain that those he guides will be sufficiently worthy for him to live any longer."[24]

"Hasn't my guru Kumaradza enjoined me to help others?"

"Indeed, he has."

"If I practice intensively, will I attain the body of light? Or, if I work to serve others, of how much benefit will that be? How many years will I live?"

She replied, "Even if you attain the body of light, you must benefit other beings. Definitely serve others. You will live another thirty years."

Longchenpa asked, "Which are the guardian deities of my teachings?"

"There are so many. All of your guru's guardians are also yours. In particular, your guardian is Dorjé Yudrönma. Thus your ability to help others is associated with her direction, the southwest, and there your ability to help others in a future lifetime will be even greater than it is now."[25]

Longchenpa pressed her further. "Well, is that due to my teaching of *The Heart Drop of the Dakini?* Is it appropriate for me to confer the empowerment and instructions?"

"Yes, of course! No fault in that, no fault at all. You are without question the custodian of these teachings." [1.83a]

"So people won't think me a charlatan?" he asked.

"What's the point of paying attention to gossip? I will make sure that fortunate people meet you. Anyway, those who are unfortunate would slander even the Buddha."

Longchenpa asked, "Should I confer the Nyingtik teachings only at sites holy to Dorjé Yudrönma?"

She replied, "Since dakas and dakinis gather here naturally, you should confer them here." She also prophesied clearly that there were terma caches hidden in Bumthang.[26]

Longchenpa pursued his questions. "Will I meet the Great Master?"[27]

"You will meet him where three upland regions converge and the slopes of three mountains meet, on the right side of a small cliff facing west."

"And will I meet Vimalamitra?"

She retorted, "You have already met him!"[28]

"This view that I have realized, is it the ultimate intent underlying the Nyingtik teachings?"

"There is no error or confusion concerning what is ultimate," she responded.

Someone present, a master named Rinchen Dorjé, asked her, "Where is Panggangpa Rinchen Dorjé?"

Pointing her finger at the guru Longchenpa, she said, "There he sits."[29]

But the guru Longchenpa protested, "He was to be reborn in Bumthang in his next lifetime, so how could I be he?"

"He was not born there, as it happens. [1.83b] For a time, it was necessary for him to explore some sambhogakaya pure realms. After having revealed his termas, this master Rinchen Dorjé was to have practiced in secrecy for several years. If he had done so, he would have mastered the training on the sambhogakaya level and experienced the utter lucidity of being for his own benefit, and so would have been of enormous benefit to others. But he did not preserve this secrecy, and so did not live out his full life span. Now he has been reborn as you, and these visions of utter lucidity that you have experienced in your spiritual practice are the result of his temporary exploration of those sambhogakaya realms."

Longchenpa continued, "Will I achieve a state such that my body will vanish without a trace upon my death?"

The dakini answered, "If you simply meditate, you will achieve that state in this life, but if you serve others, you will gain freedom in the bardo. Your incarnation will take rebirth in Bumthang and help others. He will also journey to the land of Oddiyana and there manifest as one who awakens to buddhahood."

He persisted, "Which cycle of the Nyingtik teachings will allow me to be of the most benefit, that of Vimalamitra or that of the dakini?"

"Both will be of benefit," she said. "The teachings of Vimalamitra will last for one hundred years, those of the dakini for five hundred years, beginning now."[30]

Longchenpa felt greatly inspired and rose from his seat, singing a vajra song[31] that ended with the following lines:

> This life is fine, and my next lifetime will be a happy one.
> What bliss there will be in recognizing the true nature of the bardo.
> Now I shall go from bliss to even greater bliss.
> I make this song my offering, O Three Jewels. [1.84a]
> Please rejoice, you hosts of dakas and dakinis!

The people present saw incredible manifestations of dakinis, all of which dissolved into their guru. They then witnessed other marvels, such as the guru transforming himself into the forms of sambhogakaya deities.

One day during that time, people saw the Great Master coming from the southwest, his form white, wearing a brocade cloak and a cap of soft deerskin, surrounded by an enormous retinue. He dissolved into the guru Longchenpa. That evening, dakinis wearing bone ornaments approached, flying to and fro through space and making offerings to the guru. Three women with dark brown skin danced and sang the following song:

> We have come, we have come, we have come from the realm of supreme
> bliss.
> We have come to observe your worthy students.
> We have come to witness the purity of their samaya.
> O child of spiritual heritage, please help beings!

As well, when Longchenpa was performing the inner stage of an offering ceremony, the Great Master appeared. To his right was Vimalamitra, to his left was Varahi, and in front of him were many dakas and dakinis blowing *kanglings*.[32] Behind him were many tantric yogins dancing and surrounding him were a multitude of dakinis wearing gold armor, dancing, and singing. In the midst of all this, the guru Longchenpa rose from his seat and sang vajra songs:

> How joyful, how happy, all you yogins! [1.84b]
> Tonight, in the pure realm of Akanishtha,
> my body is the palace of the peaceful and wrathful deities.
> Within it unfolds the mandala of the victorious ones, the unity of emptiness and lucidity.
> Buddhahood does not lie outside, but within us!

And:

> O meditator who abides in mind alone,
> don't focus your attention on any one thing, but let it go where it will.
> Your mind is empty though it stirs, empty though it rests.
> Everything you experience is the display of timeless awareness.

DORJÉ YUDRÖNMA

At that point, the white goddess Dorjé Yudrönma, together with the six sisters in her retinue, approached him and said, "We ask that you come to our realm."

The guru Longchenpa replied, "I should always remain in your realm," to which the goddess answered, "I would be delighted if you were to stay there always, but it seems you won't remain beyond the middle of winter."

"Why have you come to see me?"

The goddess responded, "Since I am under oath to the Guru, I have followed after his terma teachings."

"But the teachings were revealed elsewhere, and the one who revealed them has died.[33] What are you doing here?"

"Although the teachings were revealed elsewhere, their meaning is right here. Although your former incarnation passed away, we the guardians have not, and so we have come."

The guardian deities then uttered prophecies, saying, "Because these teachings are so sacred, their weightiness could present obstacles to your longevity; it would be best if you taught them sparingly."[34] [1.85a]

Longchenpa asked, "Will I receive the scrolls on which these terma teachings are written?"

"Of course, of course! We are surely keeping that in mind," said Dorjé Yudrönma. "Don't you recall that I granted you siddhis in Uru?"

"I recall what happened in the cave of Chokla. Was that you, Dorjé Yudrönma?"

"No, no! Then I was Varahi. Didn't you recognize me? I need to take two distinct forms: a mundane one for carrying out enlightened activities and a transcendent one for conferring the most sublime siddhi."

Longchenpa then asked, "In certain teaching cycles, the explanations focus on the bindu energies. Why is the third empowerment conferred employing an actual consort?"

"This method is intended to bring those with much desire to the spiritual path. For those who have renounced desire, it is sufficient for the consort to be visualized."[35]

"When I am introducing students to their true nature, do I explain that one rests in the unborn nature of thought or that one rests the mind without making any evaluation?"

She answered, "What is the point of stabilizing one's thought processes? Introduce them to the enormous expanse of timeless freedom!"

"Well, since there seem to be so many who are explaining these Nyingtik teachings, why should I teach? There are, for instance, teachers such as Karmapa and Rinchen Lingpa who simply confer the oral transmissions to 'give people a handle' on the teachings, so to speak."

"I do not like those means of transmission," she replied. "Even a clay cup has a handle, so how could that be enough? [1.85b] There absolutely have to be a few who truly take possession of that cup."

"What about the termas of Rinchen Lingpa?" asked Longchenpa.

"They exist, it is true, but they are not the pure Nyingtik teachings," said Dorjé Yudrönma.

"Why is it that I have gained your accomplishments without meditating on you?"

"Am I a deity on whom you must meditate? Have I a mantra you must recite? Am I an object of worship? Don't you realize that I am constantly in attendance on those yogins who uphold their samaya and gain realization? Throughout all of your lifetimes, our connection has been beyond our coming together and separating in the ordinary sense."

"The wealth of the princess[36] that is in Chimpu, where is it located?" Longchenpa queried.

"It can be found in a rock face shaped like a food offering torma with its top cut off. But the time is not yet ripe for it to be discovered."

He asked her, "How long will it be before the termas of Vimalamitra are revealed?"

She replied, "Five years from now, a tantric practitioner dressed in white will reveal these teachings and disseminate them. The four volumes of these profound teachings will come into your possession."

During all of this, the key points of these teachings arose in Longchenpa's awareness, and when Tsogyal herself appeared in her timeless awareness embodiment, he offered her an explanation of his direct understanding of these points. It was also during this vision that Guru Padmakara conferred the name Drimé Özer (Stainless Ray of Light) on Longchenpa, while Yeshé Tsogyal named him Dorjé Ziji Tsal (Vajra of Dynamic Brilliance).

Then, when Longchenpa was preparing to confer the elaborate empowerment, a red woman appeared and held the measuring thread,[37] [1.86a] while another woman appeared and helped him draw the mandala. On the same occasion, someone was taken over by the guardian goddess Namdru Remati, who in a boastful manner made a great fuss about being the guardian of many terma caches. Longchenpa responded:

> As I have opened the doorway to the inner terma of utter lucidity,
> I have no need of termas hidden in holes in rock faces.
> If I have termas, it's all right; if not, it's all right.
> If I am one with such good fortune, it's all right; if not, it's all right.
> For a yogin such as I, phenomena and ordinary mind have fallen away,
> so you need not try to buy me off with your arrogant boasts of guarding termas.

Longchenpa directly introduced his students to the path of tögal without having to use metaphors—the light of a great, dark blue expanse and the so-called lamps of totally pure basic space and of empty spheres[38]—to illustrate the process.

On another occasion, a dakini took possession of someone and told Longchenpa, "The Guru and Tsogyal say of you, 'Is there another like him? He is marvelous!'" Then Vajrasadhu took possession of someone else; he instructed Longchenpa to go to Orgyen Dzong and made prophecies concerning his students. The goddess Revati then possessed yet another person and implored Longchenpa not to leave, but showed her appreciation when he said things like, "Joy and sorrow are simply the machinations of ordinary mind." [1.86b] Guru Rinpoché also instructed him to restore such places as the cliff of Lharing Drak, Orgyen Dzong, and the temple of Zhai Lhakhang and gave him permission to write treatises.

Terma Revelations and Other Activities

In the past, the Guru and his consort had made two terma caches from the cycle *The Complete Distillation of Samantabhadra's Intent.* They had concealed these in a stupa and in the capital of a pillar in the Chimpu Uplands. In keeping with a prophecy Longchenpa received from the goddess Sarasvati and her four sisters, he revealed the second of these two cycles during his stay at Chimpu. On his journey down from the uplands, he was escorted by Dorjé Yudrönma, the twelve Tenma goddesses, and the gods known as the "nine Lharap brothers." He reached Gang-ri Tökar, where he established his hermitage, naming it Orgyen Dzong, and there he turned the wheel of the dharma on a vast scale, teaching, for example, *The Heart Drop of the Dakini* to twenty-one fortunate students. At night, the dakinis introduced him to the direct experience of his true nature—of how the visions of utter lucidity are embraced within the basic space of original purity (the enlightened intent of dharmakaya) and how these visions manifest as the dynamic expression of being (the arising of the sambhogakaya). Encouraged by the yogin Özer Gocha, he composed the texts of *The Innermost Heart Drop of the Dakini,* during which marvelous events occurred; rainbow light appeared and hosts of dakinis gathered. [1.87a]

Longchenpa wrote many of his major works, most notably *The Seven Treasuries,* at Orgyen Dzong. At dawn on several mornings, he dreamed that Rigdzin Kumaradza pointed directly at him without saying a word; he interpreted this as a sign that he had received an empowerment.

Although there had been indications that Longchenpa's death was imminent, he averted it during a single session of meditative absorption. Once, just as the first rays of the sun had broken over the horizon, Longchenpa heard a sound coming from the east. He looked up to see a mass of light, in the center of which was Samantabhadra surrounded by many mandalas of peaceful and wrathful deities, filling the sky in all directions, above and below. He also saw Vimalamitra, whose form was yellow-green,[39] four gurus who had ascended to the pure dakini realm of Khechara, Kumaradza in sambhogakaya garb, and Orgyen Pema Gyalpo. As he gazed at these figures, the deities and gurus graced him with visions and uttered prophecies. Henceforth, the experience of "awareness reaching full measure,"[40] a vision of the spontaneous presence of utter lucidity, arose continuously for him. The true measure of this experience became obvious: his body could pass unimpeded through solid rock as though it were space, the slightest sound of his speech captivated the minds of discriminating individuals, and as repeatedly demonstrated by his vajra speech, his mind was imbued with the deep, indwelling confidence of realization.

While Longchenpa was performing a fulfillment ritual of the peaceful and wrathful deities at Lharing Drak, he saw the mandala of these deities in the sky, [1.87b] complete with secondary circles within the main mandala configuration. When this had faded away, Vimalamitra appeared in the sky to the southwest, pointed his finger to the southeast, and exhorted Longchenpa to restore Zhai Lhakhang in Uru. At that time, Longchenpa dreamed that Vimalamitra came to him, saying:

> I am Kumaradza.
> I have gone to the pure realm of Padmakuta.
> Disseminate the teachings of the Buddha!

From this he knew that his guru, Kumaradza, had passed away. In an effort to finish carrying out the enlightened intent of his guru, Longchenpa performed the dedication of total threefold purity[41] three times. In addition, in order to guarantee that the teachings of the vajra essence of utter lucidity would not wane, he completed the treatise entitled *The Treasury of the Sublime Spiritual Approach* in a very short time, using his miraculous powers to emanate numerous bodies and to bind the planetary mara Rahula to his service.

At Gyamané he gave the Nyingtik teachings to a gathering of many academics, including Sönam Seng-gé and the master Loppön Palchok. When the time for questions came, he was asked if it was appropriate to engage in debate. He replied, "I will remain here for a month, debating with you over any sutras and tantras that you present to me." And so Longchenpa took on the scholars, and with the lightning bolts of scriptural authority and logical reasoning flashing, he crumbled the mountains of their arrogant pedantry. [1.88a]

Later, Longchenpa was invited to Drigung by Gompa Kunrin, who served him with devotion and showed him every honor, offering him both the funds necessary to restore Zhai Lhakhang and the actual monastery of Orgyen Gön. The master took Kunrin under his care, giving him profound spiritual instructions and leading him on the path to liberation.

When Longchenpa journeyed to Tidro, an escort of dakinis greeted him along the way and offered him that holy place. He arrived at Zhai Lhakhang, where a white man wearing a white hat prostrated to him and pointed emphatically toward the temple; from this Longchenpa knew that Vajrasadhu was encouraging him and that the time was ripe to begin the restoration. From among the numerous termas concealed within the cupola of the temple, he brought forth a small amount of gold and many sadhanas of the twelve Tenma goddesses, Vajrasadhu, and other deities.

When the earth was cleared away from the foundations, many skulls of different kinds were discovered that had previously been placed there during a suppression ritual. Longchenpa reburied these, but as he began the suppression ritual, demonic manifestations arose. Earth and stones hailed down violently, a fierce wind blew, and a gloomy darkness fell like nightfall. His retinue was upset and dumbfounded, but Longchenpa himself chanted mantras wrathfully and assumed a menacing posture. The skulls, which had been leaping about and clattering together, he crushed underfoot, and immediately the manifestations disappeared. [1.88b] Some of those present actually perceived Longchenpa as Guru Drakpo.

Many marvels manifested during the restoration of the temple. But there was one particularly remarkable phenomenon: Every day a youth with a turquoise earring helped the artisans working on the reconstruction, though no one could tell where he went at night. Concerned, all of the artisans surrounded the youth; he then dissolved into a crack in the wall and was never seen again. The oath-bound guardian deities plainly discussed the entire project—its successes and problems—with Longchenpa, just like people speaking aloud. Two pillars had previously toppled, and there were no means of any kind to raise them. Longchenpa recited a liturgy invoking the power of truth and with his robe fanned the pillars, which the artisans, to their amazement, were then able to raise to their original positions.

During the consecration ceremony, numerous fortunate students saw Longchenpa manifest in the form of Samantabhadra, from whose heart rays of light shone; on the tip of each ray were buddhas surrounded by innumerable bodhisattvas, all casting down flowers. To Longchenpa himself, the Lord of Sages Shakyamuni and the future buddha Maitreya appeared, surrounded by the sixteen elders of early Buddhism. Maitreya pointed at him and encouraged him, prophesying, "Two lifetimes from now, in the pure realm of Padmakuta, you will become the victorious one Sumerudipadhvaja."

On the tenth day of the Monkey month, Longchenpa beheld Orgyen Rinpoché amid a mass of light in the sky, [1.89a] surrounded by the luminous forms of dakinis of the five classes. When he had called together an assembly of some four thousand, the dakinis of Tidro converged and took possession of many people. Through them they foretold many events, both positive and negative—for example, that at some point Longchenpa would have to go into exile in the Bumthang region of Bhutan.

He journeyed on in the area of Tidro and restored another holy site, which had recently fallen into disrepair, practicing a fulfillment ritual of the peaceful and wrathful deities for three weeks. Using his miraculous powers, he went to places inaccessible to ordinary beings, where he planted victory banners and flags.

Once, when Longchenpa was staying at Shuksep, he had a significant meditative experience. From behind the mountain Jomo Karak appeared the enormous head of a wrathful deity without a body, its eyes rolling and lightning shooting from its mouth. Then another deity, Zadong Gongpo Rani, appeared, even more enormous than the first, with a black head, rolling eyes, and light shining from its mouth. These figures reached the summit of Jomo Karak and then vanished into an ascending stream of light. Longchenpa saw all of central and eastern Tibet covered by hail and a rain of rocks, with fork and sheet lightning flashing everywhere. He understood that this signified the problems in central and southern Tibet caused by political infighting between the Sakya and Pakmodrupa factions. He saw that a time of widespread social unrest was imminent, and despite his plans to restore a site at Yerpa and to build a *mani* temple[42] in Lhasa, [1.89b] he told his followers, "For the time being, these projects cannot be completed. All of us, teacher and students, are going to Bumthang."

On the way, Longchenpa passed through Lhasa, where (due to connections he had forged previously with the Drigung faction) the armies of Yarlung surrounded and attempted to kill him. He used his miraculous power to vanish, thwarting his aggressors' attempt to harm him. They exclaimed, "Now where is he who was just here? Has he fled? He isn't here!"

That night, as Longchenpa was sleeping in an inner room, he dreamed he was seated before the Jowo statue in Lhasa's main temple. Rays of golden light streamed from Jowo's form, and within a mass of radiant light above the statue's head, he saw the seven generations of buddhas, Bhaishajyaguru, the white and blue forms of Tara, Chakrasamvara, Hevajra, Avalokiteshvara (the form promulgated by King Songtsen Gampo), the thousand-armed, thousand-eyed form of Avalokiteshvara, and the deity Jinasagara. In their midst stood the glorious protective deity Bernakchen, the great guardian kings of the four directions, the Lion-Headed Dakini who protects against maras, and the glorious protector goddess Shridevi. He beheld all of these in the space before him.

On the day he went to the Naga Cave in Drakra, Longchenpa had a vivid vision of a huge mountain of crystal. [1.90a] That night, he dreamed that he traveled to Mount Kailash, Tsaritra, and other holy mountains and saw for himself what they were like. Next, when he arrived at the plain known as Poma Jangtang, he was met by an escort of the local spirits called the "twenty-one lay practitioners" and the god Muri, who kept him constantly supplied with provisions. On the plain of Layak Mentang, many fortunate students, headed by Khenchen Chabdal Lhundrup, served Longchenpa with devotion, and he brought them to spiritual maturity with the Nyingtik teachings and other instructions of the profound path.

Exile and Return

Eventually, Longchenpa reached the Bumthang region of Bhutan in the south.[43] There he founded a number of hermitages, which became known as his "eight centers": Tarpa Ling in Bapnön, Dechen Ling in Shingkar, Orgyen Ling in Tang, Kunzang Ling in upper Kuré, Drechak Ling in Ngen Valley, Pema Ling in Menlok, and Samten Ling in Paro. Due to his spiritual attainment, he brought forth springs of water and left many hand- and footprints in the rock near these sites. When he was to be received with honors in Menlok by Sönam Rinchen, a descendant of Drukgom Zhikpo, Longchenpa flew from one mountainside to another to get there and back.

In these and other ways, displaying numerous unhindered miraculous powers, he tamed border regions [1.90b] where even rumor of the dharma had never been heard. He introduced the practice of observing the ten kinds of virtuous behavior and brought people to spiritual maturity and liberation through the dharma according to each person's character. He subjugated malevolent nonhuman spirits—Chungdü, Dongzur Menmo, and others—and bound them to his service. Even today, the amazing deeds of the one remembered as Lama-la Ngawang Drimé Özer are recounted and held in the highest regard.

At Tarpa Ling, Longchenpa concealed numerous pith instructions as termas, among these the cycle *The Complete Distillation of Samantabhadra's Intent*. He was invited to Lhodrak by its influential people, and in such places as Layak, Lhalung, and Dang-né, he transmitted the empowerments and teachings of the secret Nyingtik to gatherings of thousands, which included such figures as Khenchen Chabdal Lhundrup. In Yardrok he taught the dharma and was honored by the throne holder Tripön Dorjé Gyaltsen. On that occasion, Gyalsé Zöpa was explaining *The Heart Drop of the Dakini* to Tripön Dorjé Gyaltsen. Longchenpa told him, "It is excellent that you have received *The Heart Drop of the Dakini* from both Rinchen Lingpa in Kongpo and Lekdenpa in the region of Dakpo. But since I am the ultimate custodian of these teachings, [1.91a] if you have no pressing business elsewhere, stay a while and listen to my teachings. As the saying goes, 'If one sings the song one knows best on stage, it only becomes clearer.'" He then taught *The Heart Drop of the Dakini* to the throne holder and some fifteen students and conferred teachings on a vast scale to many others gathered there.

Due to the power wielded by the Drigung faction, the Tai Situ who ruled the Pakmodrupa government had little respect for Longchenpa. Nevertheless, he came to admire Longchenpa's wisdom, realization, and activities. At his seat in Yorpo, a reconciled Tai Situ hosted him for a long time, showing him great honor, and Longchenpa transmitted the Nyingtik empowerments and teachings to a gathering of about two thousand people. Tai Situ was awed by the superior wisdom of this lord of the dharma and gave him the title Longchen Rabjampa (Master of the Vast Array of the Supreme Expanse). Henceforth, he was known by that title.

At Gongkar he cared for his students, Tai Situ foremost among them, by bestowing many empowerments and instructions. In the eastern part of central Tibet, he founded the monasteries of Kalden Jampading, Yuding, and Pangding, staying at these places for as long as was appropriate; they became known as the "three Dings" of the Dra region.

In response to questions from the Sakya Lama Dampa concerning his methods of explaining the ground, path, and fruition, Longchenpa wrote a text entitled *A Petition: The Lamp of Gold*. In turn, Lama Dampa offered the following verse to Longchenpa to please and honor him:

> This pleasant and totally illuminating speech [1.91b]
> is that of one who engages in explaining, debating, and composing
> without confusion
> and who has the inner vision of scripture, reasoning, and numerous pith
> instructions.
> To the yogin who has realized suchness, the essence of being,
> this verse is offered in this place of heaped jewels.

Furthermore, Longchenpa wrote many treatises on key points of the sutras and tantras in general, and on the Dzogchen approach in particular. For Drakpa Zangpo of Sangpu and other scholars, he answered questions, illuminating the subjects that their mundane minds could not comprehend, both directly in the form of advice and indirectly in his eminently well reasoned essays and letters. He thereby inspired conviction in others, who came to have faith in him and his teachings; thus he was given the highly apt title Kunchen Chöjé (Omniscient King of the Dharma). Longchenpa was truly endowed with the qualities extolled by Dengom Chödrak Zangpo[44] in the following verses of praise offered to the master:

> When I beheld how Ngagi Wangpo explained the teachings,
> the methods of the "three brothers"[45] seemed clumsy and halting.
> When I beheld the ordered reasoning of Longchen Rabjam,
> the teachings of Cha, Tsang, and Den[46] seemed like nothing but
> squabbling.
> When I beheld the works composed by the great Omniscient One,
> the works of Bu, Dol, and Shak[47] seemed lackluster.
> When I beheld the view and enlightened intent of Natsok Rangdrol,[48]
> the tenets of the "three great systems"[49] seemed superficial. [1.92a]

An invitation came from Tai Situ, but before Longchenpa could depart in response to it, one of his students in retreat came to ask him a question. He was so occupied throughout the day that he was unable to reply, but that evening someone named Lama Zöpa wrote a letter answering the question and sent it off to the student.

During his journey, Longchenpa was honored by Kyishö Sangdar, Yönten Gyatso (the master of Sangpu), and others. While they offered him tea, each of them asked a short question, to which Longchenpa gave a terse reply. They were humbled by this and offered him presents, such as ten measures of gold. When he reached Lhasa, Longchenpa was received by a procession of many monks. For a fortnight, seated on a throne erected between the city and the temple of Ramoché,[50] he gave extensive teachings on cultivating altruistic motivation and other topics.

At Sangtsu, Longchenpa used his knowledge of scriptures and his powers of reasoning to humble many arrogant scholars learned in the Three Repositories. Reduced to confusion, they came to have faith in him. He made offerings in holy places and gathered the accumulations on a great scale at many centers of study and practice, dedicating all of these to the benefit of the teachings and the happiness of all beings. [1.92b] Journeying to Nyepu Shuksep, he brought more than a thousand fortunate people gathered there to spiritual maturity by teaching the profound approach of Dzogchen.

He predicted to a monk named Öndrakpa that the journey along the road to upper Ur would take a long time, but that if the monk were to take a shortcut, his horse would throw him and he would be injured. It was with such unerring prescience that Longchenpa would speak of many things as obvious to him as they were hidden to others. Many of his students also received prophecies from dakinis.

At Khawari he was honored by Situ Shakya Zangpo,[51] whom he blessed with many empowerments and instructions. Situ offered enough provisions for him to stay through the summer and then accompanied him on his travels, receiving teachings as they journeyed from the upland regions of Orgyen Monastery down to the lowlands. Longchenpa conferred the empowerments, teachings, and background material of the vajra heart essence of utter lucidity on more than three thousand people, including some forty masters who were teachers of the dharma in their own right—the scholars and students of Drigung among them—as well as many other important lay people and monastics. He distributed many gifts and, on each tenth day of the lunar cycle, made offerings to all of the monastic communities from Penyul to Tsemogyal.

In his earlier years, whenever Longchenpa went into solitary retreat, before very long he would begin to teach, showing his clear understanding of all the source texts [1.93a] concerning Prajñaparamita, valid cognition, and so forth. Later, when his activities to benefit beings became more evident, he continued to teach in this vein. He tended not to stay in monasteries, but even when living in solitary hermitages—in caves or under overhanging rocks or in huts made of grass and leaves, free of all the entanglements of retinue and personal wealth, spending his time entirely in practice—Longchenpa would still teach those fortunate people who were pursuing liberation. To groups ranging in size from a hundred to three thousand people, he gave unflaggingly, and without sectarian bias, explanations of sutra and tantra texts, empowerments, and teachings commensurate with each individual's level of comprehension. He was unstinting in his efforts to serve the teachings.

On the tenth day of each month, Longchenpa would offer two-thirds of whatever donations had come into his hands from the faithful and use only the remaining portion for his immediate needs. When important or impressive people came expecting to give him something, indifferent to their status he would refuse their offerings, saying, "I couldn't possibly accept this." When passing out offerings, he would say, "Those of high status need never fear being overlooked," and would then proceed to distribute things starting with those of lower status. He would say, "The sangha—not wicked people—deserve honors," [1.93b] and he would never accord any honor, not even spreading out a sitting mat, to ordinary people who wanted some high station. No matter how fine the things his patrons offered him, he would simply comment, "This possession would only be wasted if they were to sell it," and he would never give a gift in return. But when poor and humble people offered him whatever they could, however meager, he would be delighted and offer prayers of dedication on their behalf. He was unwavering in his resolve.

Later Life and Passing

On one occasion, he conferred higher empowerments and special advice, as well as pith instructions and explanations of the tantras, on more than a hundred people who were capable of benefiting others with such teachings. Later he said to Gyalsé Zöpa, "Close the door to the stairway and let no one enter while you take down this letter," and then dictated his last testament, *Stainless Light,* as follows:

> Homage to all those exalted ones endowed with supreme
> compassion!
>
> I pay homage to the one immersed in the experience of basic space,
> the primordial ground,
> who cares for all beings through the proliferation and resolution of
> activities,
> revealing a display in all its variety by the power of his innate
> compassion—
> a sublime sun, exceedingly and superbly radiant. [1.94a]
>
> I pay homage to the one who, having completed his task in full,
> went to a most superb and holy site,
> the town of Kushinagar,
> to tame those fixated on the permanence of things.[52]
>
> I have come to understand the nature of samsara,
> and because things of this world lack any true essence,
> I now cast off this impermanent, illusory body,
> so listen as I give this singularly beneficial advice.
>
> We are, as it were, seduced by our belief that this life is real.
> Things are by nature impermanent and without any real meaning,
> so, having realized with certainty that nothing is reliable,
> please practice the sacred dharma from now on.
>
> Friends and companions are like guests, in no way permanent.
> Although they gather around you for a time, all too soon you are parted
> from them,
> so let go of emotional ties to your friends, who are like magical
> apparitions.
> Please practice the sacred dharma, a lasting source of benefit.
>
> Wealth and possessions that you gather and hoard are like honey—
> things that you amass but others enjoy—
> so while you can, gain merit by increasing your generosity.
> Please make preparations now for your future journey.
>
> Your dwellings, well built yet subject to destruction, are like something
> on loan.
> You have no power to stay when it is time to move on. [1.94b]

Give up completely your fascination with busy places,
and rely on a place of solitude from now on.

Liking or disliking is akin to a child's game.
Pointless attachments and aversions are a burning mass of flames.
Give up completely your quarrels and the malice you bear one another,
and tame your own minds from now on.

Actions, without true essence, are like magical illusions.
Although you strive at present, there is no final outcome.
Let go of the activities of this life and things of this world,
and seek the path to liberation from now on.

This body of freedom and opportunity that you have attained is like a precious ship,
granting you the power to free yourself from the ocean of suffering,
so give up laziness, lethargy, and procrastination
and arouse the strength of your diligence from now on.

The holy guru is like an escort accompanying you through a fearsome land.
To this guide who protects you from the enemy, samsara,
please show great honor, respect, and trust unflaggingly
with body, speech, and mind from now on.

Profound spiritual advice, like healing nectar,
is the most excellent cure for the disease of negative emotions,
so please rely on it in your life and cultivate it thoroughly,
gaining mastery from now on. [1.95a]

The three higher trainings,[53] totally pure, are like a wish-fulfilling gem.
They are the path that brings happiness in this and future lives and leads to the most sublime goal.
Since they ensure enlightenment, the holy state of peace,
please apply them to your life from now on.

Teachings in all their variety are like a precious lamp,
banishing the darkness of ignorance and illuminating the path to liberation.
Since listening to them opens the eye of timeless awareness and sheds the light of benefit and happiness,
please be impartial and nonsectarian from now on.

Thorough contemplation is like the skill of a goldsmith,
cutting through all hesitation or speculation about what is or is not true,

so with the sublime knowing that comes from contemplating the nature of what you have heard,
please gain complete mastery from now on.

Meditation, by nature, is like tasting nectar.
To meditate on the meaning of what you have heard and contemplated pacifies all the illnesses of negative emotions.
You will cross the ocean of conditioned existence and arrive at the far shore—the heart essence.
Please meditate in the forest from now on.

View, by nature, is like clear open space,
free of all distinctions of high and low, all restrictions or extremes.
With no fixed dimension, it is beyond expression, imagination, or description.
Please use methods for realizing it from now on.

Meditation, by nature, is like a mountain or an ocean,
without transition or change, limpid and unsullied.
It pacifies all that characterizes distraction and conceptual elaboration.
Please meditate on reality just as it is from now on. [1.95b]

Conduct, by nature, is like a wise person,
aware of what is timely or beneficial in any situation.
Attachment and obsession, acceptance and rejection, repression and indulgence—these are of the realm of illusion,
so please be free of dualistic fixations from now on.

Fruition, by nature, is like the wealth a good leader takes possession of:
you yourself become wealthy and benefit for others is spontaneously ensured.
There is no hope or fear, only a mind that is automatically at ease.
Please endeavor to attain the fruition from now on.

Mind, by nature, is the basic space of phenomena, which is like the sky.
Space, by nature, is the ultimate meaning of the genuine nature of mind.
The supreme state is perfectly uniform, ultimately nondual,
so please realize it with certainty from now on.

Phenomena in all their variety are like reflections in a mirror.
They are apparent yet empty, with "emptiness" not to be found elsewhere.

In a cheerful frame of mind, without labeling phenomena as identical or separate,
please know this with certainty from now on.

Grasping at the objects you reify is like being in a dream.
Truth is nondual, for dualistic perceptions are caused by habit patterns
and are only labels applied by ordinary consciousness, empty by virtue of their very essence.
Please be aware of nonduality from now on.

Samsara and nirvana are, by nature, like the play of illusion. [1.96a]
Although things may appear to be good or bad, they are in essence equal.
Everything is unborn as the nature of space,
so please know this with certainty from now on.

Pleasant and painful perceptions based on confusion are, by nature, like phantoms.
Even as positive and negative causes and effects arise individually,
by nature they are unborn, their essence without transition or change.
Please know this with certainty from now on.

Phenomena labeled by ordinary consciousness are like children's games.
In actuality, they do not abide in a fixed way,
but through conceptual analysis, people cling to particular philosophies about good and bad.
Please be aware of the equalness of phenomena from now on.

Generosity, moreover, is like a treasure trove of jewels,
the cause of inexhaustible and ever-increasing wealth.
To all who provide an opportunity for you to gain merit—be they humble, great, or in between—
please be generous, in whatever way is appropriate, from now on.

Discipline is like a noble, flawless vehicle,
transporting you to higher states of rebirth and the true excellence of enlightenment.
Whether avoiding what is negative, consolidating what is positive, or ensuring benefit for beings,
please apply discipline to your life from now on.

Patience is like a vast ocean, sublimely serene. [1.96b]
To remain undisturbed by challenges is the best of all spiritual qualities.
Accepting suffering, developing compassion, and so forth—
please become well acquainted with these virtues from now on.

Exertion is like a huge blazing bonfire,
incinerating what is unsuitable and feeding on what is positive.
Without succumbing to procrastination, apathy, or laziness,
please pursue the path to liberation from now on.

Unwavering meditative stability is like the most majestic mountain,
unruffled by any conceptual framework, undistracted by sense objects,
a state of equipoise, resting with whatever is the focus, not disturbed by anything.
Please cultivate meditative stability from now on.

Sublime knowing, vast in scope, is like the sun,
dispelling the darkness of ignorance, illuminating the sacred dharma,
nurturing the garden of liberation, and drying up the reservoir of flaws.
Please see that it flourishes from now on.

Skillful means is like one who guides those seeking gems,
leading beings across the ocean of suffering to the Isle of Happiness.
All attain the three sublime kayas, and the two kinds of benefit are spontaneously ensured.
Please benefit others with skillful means from now on.

Fortitude is like a champion who defeats opponents,
vanquishing the hordes of negative emotions and bringing them to the path of enlightenment.
Since it perfects the accumulation of virtue and ensures freedom from obstacles,
please apply it to your life from now on. [1.97a]

Aspiration is like a great wish-fulfilling gem.
All wishes are spontaneously fulfilled, and supreme bliss flourishes as a matter of course.
To apply your mind to the state of peace is to have your hopes fulfilled.
Please develop aspiration to the highest degree from now on.

Timeless awareness is like the massing of clouds in the sky.
From the clouds of meditative absorption and complete recall fall the rains of benefit and happiness,
completely ripening the crops of amassed virtue for all beings.
Please endeavor to gain the experience of timeless awareness from now on.

Skillful means and sublime knowing are like a noble mount.
They prevent you from falling into conditioned existence or the peace of nirvana, and your own and others' benefit is certain.

You bring the five paths[54] to consummation, and the three kayas are spontaneously present.
Please strive to accomplish skillful means and sublime knowing from now on.

Things that lead to enlightenment, left in the wake of exalted ones throughout the three times,
are like a great, fine road.
There are thirty-seven of these—the four bases of mindfulness and the rest.
Please endeavor to nurture them from now on.

Love, moreover, is like fine parents
who have unceasing sympathy for their children throughout the six classes of beings,
serving them with affection and always being of benefit.
Please cultivate love in your life from now on.

Compassion is like a bodhisattva, a child of victorious ones, [1.97b]
for whom the suffering of others is like his own
and who wears the armor of exertion in the quest to free them from this suffering.
Please apply compassion to your life from now on.

Joy is like the elder of a family,
who delights in the virtues of others
and rejoices in being able to provide for them.
Please become thoroughly familiar with joy from now on.

Impartiality, by nature like the level ground,
is free of affliction and of attachment or aversion to near or far,
supremely blissful, abiding invariably in the equalness of everything.
Please become naturally familiar with impartiality from now on.

The two aspects of bodhichitta are like a trusted guide,
leading all who are virtuous to the Isle of Liberation,
undaunted by conditioned existence and ensuring abundant benefit for others.
Please arouse them repeatedly from now on.

Devotion is like the huge reservoir of the ocean,
filled with what is virtuous yet of a single taste from beginning to end,
swelling with the waves of faith that never fails.
Please rely on devotion from now on.

Dedication is like the inexhaustible treasury of space.
By dedicating something within the basic space of phenomena, you guarantee that it will never wane but always increase.
Dharmakaya is the single taste within which the rupakayas are spontaneously present.
Please purify subject, object, and their interrelation from now on. [1.98a]

Rejoicing is like the realm of space,
embracing unlimited merit, without a fixed frame of reference, free of arrogance,
unwavering, and utterly limpid.
Please rejoice again and again from now on.

Mindfulness, moreover, is like an excellent hook,
holding the rampaging, untamed elephant of the mind,
drawing it completely away from what is flawed and bringing it naturally toward what is virtuous.
Please apply mindfulness to your life from now on.

Alertness is like a fine, undistracted watchman
who does not provide the thief, nonvirtue, any opportunity
but undertakes to guard the wealth of virtue.
Please rely on alertness with certainty from now on.

Heedfulness is like a surrounding wall and moat,
preventing the marauding hordes of negative emotions from invading
and marshaling the forces that emerge victorious over the enemy, karma.
Please strive to guard your mind from now on.

Faith, moreover, is like a fertile field
from which comes all that is wished for, where the harvest of enlightenment ripens,
and which ensures happiness in this and future lives, and benefit forever.
Please make certain that your faith flourishes from now on.

Benevolence is like a lovely pond of lotuses,
attracting what is sacred and delighting beings; [1.98b]
it is the very essence of the enjoyment of wealth and its rewards.
Please bring others happiness from now on.

Pleasant speech is like the sonorous drum of the gods,
never inappropriate, appealing to the minds of beings,
resonating for those to be guided and arousing joy in them.
Please engender happiness by praising others from now on.

Calm deportment is like a holy sage,
inhibiting nonvirtue and arousing faith in others,
rejecting hypocrisy and ensuring a state of natural quietude.
Please adopt impeccable conduct from now on.

The sacred dharma is like the powerful Sugata,[55]
appropriate for everyone, yet far greater than anyone,
in harmony with everything, yet unlike anything else.
Please rely on the sacred dharma from now on.

This body with its freedoms and opportunities is like an illusory mansion.
It is temporarily apparent, but will collapse with no warning.
There is no time to waste in this life, for phenomena are composite and
will disappoint you.
Please bring this to mind again and again from now on.

Wealth is unreliable, like clouds in the autumn.
Good fortune will, by nature, decline;
there is no true essence at its very core.
Please realize this truth with certainty from now on.

All beings are impermanent, like guests who come and go.
The preceding generation has passed on, [1.99a] as will the younger
in time.
Those alive today will be gone in a hundred years.
Please realize this with certainty from now on.

The experiences of this life are like those of a single day,
while the experiences of the bardo are like a nighttime dream.
The experiences of the next lifetime will come as soon as does the morrow.
Please practice the sacred dharma from now on.

Having thus described all aspects of the dharma metaphorically,
I have one more admonition for those with faith.
The end of all coming together is parting,
so I will not remain, but will go to the Isle of Liberation.
Since nothing in samsara is trustworthy,
please reach the continual state of authentic being, unborn dharmakaya.

The sensory appearances of this world are like cunning sorcerers,
by nature false, like a flirtatious coquette.
Since they rob the mind of its virtue and reinforce negative emotional
patterns,
please cast them aside and practice the sacred dharma.

If you have no contentment, you are poor though you may be wealthy,
for the mind of a miser is never satisfied.
Those who are content are truly the richest.
Even if they have little, their minds are filled with happiness.

Wine and women are sources of emotional affliction, [1.99b]
so cast off thoughts of desire, craving, and obsession.
Emulating the conduct of the sages,
cultivate the meaning of peace in solitary places.

It has been said, "Without tarrying day or night, your mind focused on what is virtuous,
give up all that is injurious and bring about benefit."
So please practice the sacred dharma without being distracted for a moment;
you will face death without regret and will benefit in the future.

One more thing, my students: we are connected through the dharma and through samaya,
thanks to our shared karma and pure aspirations over a very long time.
Although we have met, we must separate; master and disciples must part company.
Please understand that we are like travelers meeting in a marketplace.

I give this advice from my heart entirely to benefit you.
Homeland, wealth, dear friends, loving relations—
let go of all such distractions and complications of this life,
and please cultivate meditative stability in peaceful places.

When it is time for you to go, nothing will prevent it;
you need the sacred dharma to meet death fearlessly.
From now on, please exert yourselves in becoming familiar
with the guru's pith instructions, the teachings on what lies at the very heart of profound meaning.

Among all the teachings, those on the heart essence of utter lucidity—
the secret meaning of the Nyingtik teachings—lie at the core of everything.
They are the most sublime of all, [1.100a] the path to buddhahood in a single lifetime.
Please endeavor to accomplish this wholly positive state of supreme bliss.

Furthermore, seek teachings from the holy ones of the lineages
who hold the quintessential nectar of profound meaning.

Use the strength of your diligence to practice these in solitude.
Then you will swiftly attain the state of a victorious one.

The sacred dharma ensures complete, sublime bliss from now on
and benefit into the future.
Not all of its qualities may be immediately apparent,
so please exert yourselves from now on in order to realize the meaning of the heart essence.

The lord of the stars, the moon unobscured by clouds,
replete with all the qualities of fullness, is on the point of rising.
Canopies, parasols, victory banners, the sound of music,
and the gathering of hosts of dakas and dakinis make everything so beautiful.
The lotus visage of the protector,[56] the embodiment of compassion who takes me under his care, inspires me.
Now it is time to depart, like a traveler journeying on the open road.
The joy I feel at dying is my finest accomplishment,
greater by far than that of any merchant who has gained an entire ocean of wealth,
or that of Indra, lord of the gods, who has emerged victorious in battle,
or that of anyone who experiences bliss by achieving meditative stability.

Now I, Pema Ledrel Tsal, will not linger, [1.100b]
for I go to assume the throne of immortality and supreme bliss.
This life, my karma, the momentum of my aspiration,
my worldly concerns, the perceptions of this lifetime—all have come to an end.
When the panoramic visions of pure realms arise in the bardo,
I will be aware, instantly and spontaneously, that in essence these are awareness's own manifestations
and that I am therefore close to attaining the ongoing and authentic being of the primordial state.

Because I am truly blessed, you and others should be happy.
Use this illusory lifetime to attain the goal, the Isle of Liberation.
It is my aspiration that we will then meet again, my holy disciples,
and that we will be gladdened, rejoicing in the dharma.

But for now, our connection in this life has ended.
Do not lament the passing of this wandering beggar who is happy with his lot.
Instead, pray to him constantly.

These are my words of advice, offered for your benefit,
like a multitude of lotus flowers delighting the bees—you, my faithful ones.
May the virtue of these well-chosen words ensure that those in the three realms
pass into nirvana on the level of primordial being!

This concludes my testament, *Stainless Light,* advice from Drimé Özer.

Longchenpa thus composed both this testament, *Stainless Light,* and one entitled *The Mirror of Key Points* and included them in the collection *The Innermost Heart Drop of the Dakini.* When he was celebrating a ganachakra with his students, he encouraged them repeatedly, [1.101a] saying, "All of us, master and students alike, have only this evening to share teachings and celebrate this ganachakra. Those of you capable of benefiting others should care for fortunate students, bestowing empowerments, explaining the tantras, and transmitting pith instructions, without any thought of your own vested interests. Those of you who are pursuing personal practice, rest in equipoise according to the approaches of trekchö and tögal without becoming caught up in mundane activities. If at certain times there are things you do not understand, consult my collection *The Innermost Heart Drop: The Wish-Fulfilling Gem.* It truly is like a gem that fulfills wishes and provides all that is desired. Examine it carefully and extract the very essence of lasting bliss in meditation."

Having given this advice, Longchenpa left for the temple of Zhai Lhakhang, where he made offerings and prayed. As he was teaching to a crowd, a marvelous rain of flowers fell. He continued in stages to the monastery of Orgyen Gön, where he remained for a brief time. Upon departing, he said to those present, "I will not bother you any longer," and continued on to Chimpu. Along the way, he was met by an escort of students and patrons from Gyama. He chided them, saying, "All of you, go back! Don't come to me out of worry. None of you will see me after this. [1.101b] You should instead exert yourselves in practicing the dharma."

When he arrived at Chimpu, he observed, "This holy site is so like the charnel ground of Shitavana in India that it is considered better to die here than to be born anywhere else. I have come because I intend to leave my illusory body at this charnel ground." Nevertheless, he went to Samyé upon the invitation of its six stewards and taught the unsurpassable secret to a large gathering. Because there were so many people, the unelaborate empowerment took a number of days, during which Longchenpa, who had fallen ill, grew progressively sicker. Then, on the sixteenth day of the month, he said, "Set out offerings for a ganachakra. I shall perform an empowerment."

"But you are ill; that would be tiring," his attendants protested. "You should rest for a few days."

He replied, "It is not necessary for me to rest. I will finish these empowerments."

They were insistent, however, so he said with resignation, "It is my desire to complete these empowerments, but none of you will listen."

At the age of fifty-six, at midday on the eighteenth day of the month of Gyal in a Female Water Hare year,[57] Longchenpa instructed Ösel Rangdrol, Kunpal, and the others who were attending him [1.102a] to set out offerings and leave him alone. They prepared and arranged the offerings but then asked permission to stay.

"Since I am getting ready to cast off this broken-down, illusory body, don't make a fuss. Stay if you will, but rest in meditative equipoise!" He adopted the dharmakaya posture and passed into the primordial state of resolution. At that time, the clear sky was filled with canopies of rainbow light and a rain of flowers fell. Wild roses and other flowers began to bloom. Some people experienced the stable realization of utter lucidity.

These and other marvelous signs continued to manifest throughout the month of funeral ceremonies. While Longchenpa's remains were kept in state for twenty-five days and venerated, an odor more fragrant than sandalwood or camphor was perceptible everywhere. As his remains were taken to the pyre, the earth shook three times. His heart, tongue, and eyes were unscathed by the fire. In addition, his skull survived intact, yellowish white and as hard as stone, by nature a holy relic. As well, relics representing the five buddha families and countless smaller relics, [1.102b] along with many images of Amitayus and other deities, formed in the ashes. A statue of Longchenpa (as an inner support), a stupa of complete enlightenment (as an outer one),[58] and other structures were later erected on that very spot.

The preceding account describes how Longchenpa guided others with the enormous merit of his physical embodiment.

LONGCHENPA'S INNER BIOGRAPHY: ENLIGHTENED SPEECH

Longchenpa's Written Works

The following is an account of how Longchenpa guided others through the spiritual vision that imbued his written works. These works are not simply compositions—thoughts recorded by an ordinary person indulging in his own opinions. They came spontaneously and at appropriate times from the mandala of timeless awareness, the spacious and supreme expanse of his enlightened intent, and were written down by the three guardians of mantra—Ekajati, Rahula, and the oath-bound Vajrasadhu—to revivify the teachings.

Generally speaking, Longchenpa studied every single one of the countless traditions of teachings extant in Tibet at the time. His collected works are famous in that he wrote a teaching manual for each of these traditions; the majority of these works, however, were reclaimed by the dakas and dakinis. His own index, *The Treasure Chamber,* lists the works that remained in the human realm as follows: [1.103a]

> The sacred dharma—the teachings of the Buddha, the transcendent and accomplished conqueror—comprises an incredible array of spiritual approaches that are based on either causes or results. Those that my generation has received through the kindness of holy mentors have been interpreted in the following treatises so that future generations can understand them more easily. The topics of these treatises fall into three categories: outer, inner, and secret.
>
> The first category consists of my treatises that are of a more common nature, serving as a staircase for those new to the holy words of the Buddha. The most important of these, comparable to a body, are the following:
>
> *The Jeweled Frond,* an introductory manual on metrics, in two editions, full and abridged
> *A Summary of the Art of Reading Literature*
> *Rules of Word Formation in Sanskrit Grammar*
> *The Illuminating Moon,* a treatise on reading[59]
> *The Chariot of the Sun,* an introduction to metrics
> *The Jeweled Key,* a discussion of weights and measures
> *The Flowering Vine,* an introduction to semantics
> *A Grove of Flowers in Full Bloom,* a treatise on poetics
> *The Flowers of the Naga's Tree,* a manual on standard writing style
> *The Melodious Speech of Brahma,* an introduction to literary composition
>
> The following are minor treatises, comparable to the body's limbs, dealing with secondary topics: [1.103b]
>
> *The Kinnara's Delight,* a play
> *A Bouquet of Flowers: The Legend of Shanti the Youthful*
> *The Legend of the Clever Hare*
> *Excellent Advice: Speech Like the Drum of the Gods*
> *Joyful News from Potala*
> *The Most Excellent Moonlit Vine,* a well-crafted poem
> *A Garden of Flowers*
> *White Lotus: An Account of Life in the Forest*
> *Ornament of the Snow Mountains: An Account of Life in the Forest*

Wholly Positive: An Account of Life in the Forest
The Vine of Lilies: An Account of Life in the Forest
An Account of Life in the Delightful Forest
Flawless Speech: A Fourfold Summation of the Dharma
The Precious Garland: A Fourfold Summation of the Dharma
Determining the Qualities of an Authentic Spiritual Master
A Detailed Analysis of Monastic Life
A Detailed Analysis of Lay Life
A Detailed Analysis of Wisdom and Folly
A Detailed Analysis of Companions
A Detailed Analysis of What Is or Is Not Spiritual
A Record of Traditional Treatments of Difficult Topics
An Ornament for Defining Styles of Ritual Chanting
Tales to Arouse Renunciation in Our Time
Tales to Instruct Myself
Tales to Inspire One to Liberation [1.104a]
Tales to Invoke the Compassion of the Sugatas
Tales to Advise Those with Sectarian Views
The Jeweled Golden Stupa, a letter to my holy guru
The Thousand-Petaled Lotus: An Epistle
A Web of Gems: An Epistle
The Peacock's Cry: An Epistle
The Drumbeat of the Gods: A Prayer in Praise of Students
The Treasure Chamber of Jewels: A Prayer in Praise of Patrons
A Detailed Answer to Twenty Questions
Detailed Answers Concerning Timeless Awareness and Ordinary Mind
The Greater or Lesser Degrees to Which Learned and Accomplished People Attain Nirvana
Sorrowful Contemplations on the Degeneration of the Teachings
Garlands of Flowers: Saddened by Underlying Causes[60]
The Thirty Letters of the Alphabet: Saddened by My Circumstances
The Mirror of Memory: Saddened by Both Causes and Circumstances
The Play of Song and Dance: Arousing Joy in People
The Monkey, a play to amuse children
The Hero's Magic Scroll: Embarking on the Ways of the World
The Melody of the Great Drum, a prayer of praise to the Sugata

The Wish-Fulfilling Gem, a prayer of praise to the Mother
In Praise of Immeasurable Qualities
In Praise of the Inconceivable [1.104b]
In Praise of the Incomparable
The Cymbals of the Gods, a prayer of praise to Avalokiteshvara
Garlands of Lightning Bolts, a prayer of praise to Hayagriva
The Pearl Garland, a prayer of praise to White Mañjushri
The Melody of the Kinnaras, a prayer of praise to Red Mañjushri
The Lute of the Gandharvas, a prayer of praise to Yellow Mañjushri
The Thunder of the Clouds, a prayer of praise to Blue Mañjushri
The Maiden's Joyous Song, *The Garland of Lilies*, and *The Web of Lotuses*, prayers of praise to the exalted Sarasvati
Golden Banks of Clouds, a prayer of praise to the exalted Vasudhara
The Lute of Power, a prayer of praise to Kurukulle
The Crown Jewel of the Nagas, a prayer of praise to Janguli
Dispelling All Fears, a prayer of praise to Marichi
The Blossoms of Power, a prayer of praise to Lakshmi
Holder of the Garland of Glory, a prayer of praise to White Varahi
The Garland of the Maras, a prayer of praise to Red Varahi
The Source of All Spiritual Attainment, a prayer of praise to Black Varahi
The Garland of Jasmine Flowers, a prayer of praise to White Achala
Clouds at Twilight, a prayer of praise to Red Achala
Tamer of All Harmful Spirits, a prayer of praise to Blue Achala
The Call of Springtime, a prayer of praise to Tara
The Treasure Chamber of Gems, a prayer of praise to Ganapati
The Flowers of the Gods, a prayer of praise to Ishvara [1.105a]
The Roar of the Nagas, a prayer of praise to Vishnu
The Lily's Companion, a prayer of praise to Uma
The Waves on the Ocean, a prayer of praise to Brahma
The Quintessential Drop of Springtime, a prayer of praise to the god of time
The Roar of the Directions, a prayer in praise of mountains and oceans
The Flowers of the Four Seasons, a prayer in praise of the holy site of Chimpu

The Garland of Lotuses, a prayer in praise of the holy site of Yerpa
The Sweet Melody of Music, a prayer in praise of the holy site of Gang-ri Tökar
The Waves on the Ocean, a prayer in praise of the temple of Yumbu Tsuklak Khang[61]
The Ornament of the Glaciers, a clear description of the area around Samyé
The Gathered Garlands of Qualities, a prayer in praise of the shedra at Sangpu
The Massing Clouds of Music, a prayer of praise to Pema Wangchen Lhakhang
The Detailed Letter, an extensive listing of these works
The Marvelous Mnemonic, an abridged listing

As well, I have composed countless prayers and minor works, such as *The Adorning Flower,* to help people who are just becoming involved in the dharma.

Poetry is a large lake in which the lotus groves of metrics are found,
while semantics provides the stamens and thousands of fully opened petals.
Words and their underlying meaning are elegantly arrayed in all their vividness. [1.105b]
May the honeybees—those of clear intelligence—rejoice in this!

This has been the first part, a list of treatises dealing with topics on an outer level.

Next, the treatises giving an extensive treatment of topics on an inner level are divided into two categories: those related to the dialectical approach, which concerns causes, and those related to the mantra approach, which concerns results. The following are the works related to the dialectical approach:

The Jeweled Staircase, source verses and a commentary that present a structural analysis of the spiritual paths and levels and discuss the general meaning of *The Five Treatises of Maitreya*
The Vision of "The Ornament," a clear analysis of the main body of *The Ornament of Higher Realization*
A Frond of Light, a clear analysis of the source verses of the monastic code

An Introduction to the Realm of Suchness, a summary of three basic works of the Svatantrika branch of Madhyamaka
A Summary of Utter Nonabiding, a clear discussion of the topics of the Prasangika branch of Madhyamaka
An Introduction to Delineating the Two Levels of Truth and the instructions that accompany it, *Clarifying the Graduated Spiritual Path*
The Ultimate Heart Essence of Mental Training and a listing of its scriptural sources, *The Garland of Jewels*
The Precious Golden Flower, a discussion of arousing motivation
The Noble Path for the Children of Victorious Ones, a work on guidelines for spiritual training
An Explanation of the Meaning of Five Profound Sutras
The Heart Essence of the Ocean, a prayer of aspiration
Carrying Purity on the Spiritual Path, a manual for the practice of trekchö
The Practical Application of the "Three Aggregates"
The Means of Meditating on Timeless Awareness at the Time of Death [1.106a]

I carefully composed these and other works on numerous topics related to the sutras and to the training of a bodhisattva for those who wish to gain liberation by relying on the profound path of cause and effect.

The sublime speech of the buddhas, vast and profound, is a glacial lake,
a place of power for the nagas—victorious ones and their heirs—
a source of all qualities one might wish for, which I have illuminated.
May those of faith who seek liberation rejoice in this!

The second major division comprises treatises on the Vajrayana approach of secret mantra:

The Pure Melody of Thunder, an overview of the mantra approach, which demonstrates the vast and profound topics of the four classes of tantra
The Precious Wish-Fulfilling Treasury, source verses that clarify topics discussed in the tantras, as well as its commentary, *The White Lotus,* and the teaching manual, *The Vajra Heart Essence*
Dispelling Darkness in the Ten Directions, a major commentary

on *The Heart Essence of Secrets* (also known as *Defining Suchness Itself,* one of the tantras of the cycle *The Great Web of Magical Display*), as well as its overview, *Dispelling Darkness in the Mind,* and a structural analysis, *Dispelling the Darkness of Ignorance*

The Verdant Tree of Enlightenment, [1.106b] a commentary on the tantra *The Manifest Realization of All Spiritual Activities, The Five Stages,* and *The Vision of Timeless Awareness*

The Vajra Rising, an explanatory overview of the four classes of tantra

Rays of Sunlight, a detailed explanation of *The Threefold Array of Samaya*

As for the sadhana-based rituals that I have composed, these include the following:

An extensive ritual of fulfillment and confession focusing on the mandala of peaceful and wrathful deities, as well as an abridged version

The Precious Lamp, a sadhana ritual of guru yoga

The Lotus Coronet, a ritual of the form of Avalokiteshvara called Khorwa Dongtruk

A ritual for conferring the empowerment of and introducing students to the fundamental mandala of Sarvavid Vairochana

An Extensive Treatment of the Duties of a Vajra Master

A Summary of a Student's Duties

Wholly Positive, a ritual of consecration

A Frond of Light, an extensive, three-part ceremony, and *Jewel Heart Essence,* an abridged version

A Thorough Elucidation of the Meaning of Fire Rituals

The Garland of Light, a manual about proportions in painting

The Source of Bliss and Excellence, a four-mandala ritual of Tara

The Wish-Fulfilling Gem, a ritual to effect release from prison

The Web of Lotuses, a ritual for protection from the eight sources of fear

The Verdant Tree of Nectar, a ritual of the exalted goddess Janguli

The Precious Gem, an ablution ritual of the exalted goddess Sarasvati

The Wish-Fulfilling Garland, a ritual of Vijaya

Gathered Garlands of Qualities, a ritual of the healing buddha, Bhaishajyaguru [1.107a]

The Gem That Benefits Others, a ritual of the sixteen arhats
Dispelling All Obstacles, an extensive torma offering ritual of Jvalamukhi
The Wheel of Meteoric Iron, a ritual of the ten wrathful deities for protection and averting
Pacifying the Hordes of Hindrances, a ritual of Ushnisha
The Source of All Spiritual Attainments, a ritual of fulfillment and renewal focusing on the arrogant gods and demons
An extensive offering ritual of the protective deities
The Extensive Offering of Fine Substances
The Great Record of Remuneration
The Boiling Lake of Blood, a specific ritual of fulfillment and renewal focusing on the mamo Ekajati
Complete Victory over Enemies, a ritual of fulfillment and renewal focusing on Rahula
The Tiers of Sumeru, a ritual of fulfillment and renewal focusing on the reddish black form of Yaksha
The Spontaneous Accomplishment of the Four Kinds of Activity, a ritual of fulfillment and renewal focusing on Vajrasadhu
The Spontaneous Accomplishment of Wish Fulfillment, a general ritual of fulfillment and renewal focusing on the masculine and feminine protective deities

The sadhanas that I have composed emphasizing the stage of development include the following:

A Treasure Trove of Spiritual Attainment, a general sadhana of the guru
A Shower of Spiritual Attainment, a specific sadhana of Vimalamitra
The Precious Storied Mansion, a sadhana of a peaceful form of Guru Padmakara
Blazing Meteoric Iron, a sadhana of the wrathful form of Guru Padmakara
The Ultimate Heart Essence of Truth, a general sadhana of the peaceful and wrathful meditation deities
Hayagriva, Who Annihilates Arrogant Ones
Vajrakila, in Whom the Three Kayas Unite
Chakrasamvara: The Wish-Fulfilling Wheel
Mañjushri, the Source of Nectar [1.107b]
The Web of Gold, a general sadhana of the dakinis

The Wheel of Skillful Means, a specific sadhana of a single form of the dakini
The Wheel of Sublime Knowing, a sadhana of a single form of the daka
The Wheel of Supreme Bliss, a sadhana of combining the single forms of the daka and dakini
The Garland of Key Points, a sadhana of the secret heart essence of being
The Drop of Life Force, a sadhana of the most secret practice of tögal

In the category of minor sadhanas are the following:

The Vase of Nectar, a longevity sadhana
The Powerful Garland of Immortality
The Moon Gem, a sadhana of five deities to purify beings in lower realms
Purifying All Lower Realms, a sadhana of Vairochana
Dispelling Obscurations Completely, a sadhana of Vajrasattva
The Total Purification of Lower Realms, a sadhana of Akshobhya
The Source of Light Rays, a sadhana of Shakyamuni
Heaped Lotuses, a sadhana of Maitreya
Illuminating Sublime Knowing, a sadhana of White Mañjushri
Dispelling Darkness in the Mind, a sadhana of White Mañjushri Vadisimha
The Wheel of Sublime Knowing, a sadhana of White Mañjushri Arapachana
The Vision of Light, a sadhana of Yellow Mañjushri Arapachana
Dispelling Darkness in the Heart, a sadhana of White Achala
The Heart Essence of Light, a sadhana of White Varahi
The Arousal of Joy, a sadhana of White Ekajati [1.108a]
The Moon That Grants All Wishes, a sadhana of White Sarasvati
The Sun That Grants All Wishes, a sadhana of Red Sarasvati
The Precious Flower, a sadhana of Kurukulle
The Treasure Chamber of Gems, a sadhana of Red Ganapati
The Pinnacle of the Victory Banner, a sadhana of Vaishravana
The Golden Storied House, a sadhana of Yellow Jambhala
The Ocean of Wealth, a sadhana of Black Jambhala
The Treasure Vase, a sadhana of Vasudhara
The Sphere of the Sun, a sadhana of Angula
The Sphere of the Moon, a sadhana of Marichi

The White Garland, a sadhana of the goddess Dharani-mañjari
Illuminating the Three Worlds, a sadhana of Ishvara
The Three-Tiered City, a sadhana of Vishnu

Furthermore, I have composed rituals such as the following for carrying out the four kinds of activity to ensure that the teachings endure:

Massive Black Mountains, a general sadhana of the arrogant gods and demons
The Timely Weapon, a specific sadhana of the masculine and feminine protective deities
The Razor of Life Force, a sadhana of the fearsome mamo Ekajati
Destroying the World, a sadhana of the wrathful Rahula
The Zombie's Shooting Star, a sadhana of Shenpa Nöjin
The Great Blazing Ging Warrior, a sadhana of Vajrasadhu
The Magical Treasure Chamber of Evil Omens, a sadhana of Chötrul Namchak [1.108b]
Suppressing the Vast Hordes of Invaders, a ritual to contain adverse circumstances

The following works, concerning the definitive meaning of the stage of completion—the ultimate significance of the heart essence—present the key point of the most secret sphere of being, the stages associated with the cycle *Magical Display:*

The Wheel of Timeless Awareness, the stage of completion of Samyak, the Heart Essence of Enlightenment
The Refined Extract of the Heart Essence, the profound meaning of the five stages of Chakrasamvara
The Wheel of Utter Lucidity, the profound meaning of the five stages of Guhyasamaja
A Summary of Suchness, a synopsis of the Six Techniques of Union
The Wheel of the Two Stages for the "Path and Fruition" Cycle
The Total Refinement of Utter Lucidity, a condensation of the heart essence of the Six Yogas of Naropa
The Suchness of Secrecy, a summary of the profound path of skillful means
Demonstrating the Heart Essence of the Instructions on Mind, the graduated path of sublime knowing
The Heart Essence of the Four Yogas, the profound meaning of the graduated path of Mahamudra

The Immediate Experience of Profound Meaning for Those of Instantaneous Realization
The Three Cycles of Space: The Ultimate Instructions on the Three Kayas, an auxiliary text to the two manuals of thorough instructions
The Way of Abiding of the Four Mirrors
The Vajra Song of Mind
The Integration of Samsara and Nirvana: Carrying Perceptions on the Path [1.109a]
A Summary of Profound Meaning: The Natural Freedom of Apparent Circumstances
The Quintessential Meaning of Zhijé
Chöyul: The Utter Relaxation of the Way of Abiding

I composed the preceding works on the basis of teachings I received from my gurus on the stage of completion, the profound meaning of all the systems known in this land of Tibet. Having applied the three kinds of sublime knowing[62] in order to gain certainty about them, I condensed their meaning to the essential points.

The most profound fruition is the wish-fulfilling pinnacle pure realm.
Universal supreme bliss is the immeasurable mansion of the three kayas.
With the beauty of utter lucidity accompanied by the drum beat of timeless awareness,
may hosts of fortunate people rejoice in this!

This has been the second part of the listing of my treatises, those dealing with topics on an inner level.

Next, I have written works that offer an extensive examination of suchness itself. These fall into two categories: general discussions of this secret topic and specific explanations of topics concerning the unsurpassable approach of the supreme secret. To begin with my general discussions, these serve to show how the Dzogchen path, together with its fruition, is in accord with, and incorporates, all other spiritual approaches, so that one can understand the ultimate point of these approaches: that they are simply skillful preliminary paths leading to the Dzogchen path. The following treatises clarify this fundamental point: [1.109b]

Great Perfection: Being at Ease in the Nature of Mind
Its structural analysis, *The White Lotus*

Its commentary, *The Supreme Chariot*
The structural analysis of that commentary, *The Garland of White Lotuses*
The Noble Path to Enlightenment, an instruction manual on the meaning of the three topics and three aspects of virtue
Great Perfection: Being at Ease in Illusoriness
Its commentary, *The Noble Chariot*
Its structural analysis, *The Garland of Mandarava Flowers*
An instruction manual on its meaning, *The Wish-Fulfilling Gem*
Great Perfection: Being at Ease in Meditative Stability
Its commentary, *The Totally Pure Chariot*
Its structural analysis, *The Garland of White Lilies*
An instruction manual on its meaning, *The Distillation of the Heart Essence*
The Ocean of Excellent Explanations, an overview of *The Three Cycles of Being at Ease*
The Thousand-Petaled Lotus, an index to *The Three Cycles of Being at Ease*

I wrote the following explanations of the general principles of the Category of Mind:

Rays of Sunlight, a major commentary on the tantra *Awakened Mind: The All-Creating Monarch*
The Net of Sun and Moon, a structural analysis of *The All-Creating Monarch*
The Clear Expanse of Space, a teaching manual for *The All-Creating Monarch*
The Jeweled Ship, an instruction manual on the meaning of *The All-Creating Monarch*

I also composed *The Three Cycles of Natural Freedom* as commentaries on the meaning of the pith instructions:

Great Perfection: The Natural Freedom of the Nature of Mind
Its commentary, *The Wheel of Light*
Its teaching manual, *Naturally Arising Dharmakaya*
Great Perfection: The Natural Freedom of the Nature of Phenomena [1.110a]
Its commentary, *A Frond of Light*
Its teaching manual, *Utter Relaxation in Dharmakaya*
Great Perfection: The Natural Freedom of Equalness

Its commentary, *The Web of Light*
Its teaching manual, *The Spontaneous Presence of Dharmakaya*

The following works concern the Category of Expanse:

The Entire Array of Space: A Thematic Explanation of the General Principles of the Three Expanses
Its commentary, *Loosening the Seal into the Freedom from Any Fixed Dimension*
The Precious Treasury of the Basic Space of Phenomena, a commentary on the meaning of the pith instructions
Its commentary, *Illuminating the Basic Space of Phenomena*
Its teaching manual, *The Spacious Expanse of Infinite Extension*
The Precious Treasury of the Way of Abiding and its commentary, *The Exposition of the Quintessential Meaning of the Three Categories*

The following works constitute my explanations of the Category of Direct Transmission:

The Precious Treasury of Pith Instructions, a developmental treatment of the key points one should carry on the spiritual path
The Heart Essence of Spontaneous Presence, an extensive treatment of the kayas and timeless awareness
Its commentary, *The Victory Banner That Never Falls*
Major and Minor Marks of Perfection, practical instructions concerning the three kayas
The Crucial Juncture of Awareness, a commentary on the meaning of the pith instructions
A commentary on the meaning of *The All-Illuminating Heart Essence*
The Frond of Light Concerning the Intermediate State

The preceding works treat their subject matter in profound and extensive ways.

In the sky of the most profound spiritual teachings, the heart essence of definitive meaning,
shines the sunlight of the kayas and timeless awareness.
May it cause the lotus beds of the unsurpassable teachings to blossom [1.110b]
and at the same time gladden the flocks of birds, those to be guided.

The second major category concerns my explanations of general and specific principles of the unsurpassable approach of the supreme secret. The first group of works explains the general principles in detail, while the second summarizes the heart essence of profound meaning.

The Precious Treasury of Philosophical Systems is a systematic presentation of the most majestic spiritual approach, that of the definitive supreme secret, and delineates the topics requiring a definitive conclusion concerning the ultimate meaning of the Ati approach.
The Precious Treasury of the Sublime Spiritual Approach is a commentary on the meaning of the seventeen tantras and the 119 pith instructions.
The Precious Treasury of Words and Their Underlying Meaning is a commentary on the meaning of the key points to be carried on the path.
The Golden Casket of Precious Pith Instructions defines the major themes of spiritual practice.

In the following works, I summarize the heart essence of profound meaning:

The Sevenfold Training of the Mind, an instruction manual
The Union of All Buddhas in Equalness
The Garuda with Fully Grown Wings
The Innermost Heart Drop of the Guru: The Wish-Fulfilling Gem, which sets forth the complete transmission of pith instructions in fifty-one chapters
The Innermost Heart Drop of Profundity, a summary of even more profound topics in forty-eight chapters

The preceding five works make up the cycle of sacred practical instructions connected with *The Heart Drop of Vimalamitra.*

In particular, I should mention the texts found in *The Innermost Heart Drop of the Dakini,* which definitively codify in seventy-three chapters the three sections of timely pith instructions from *The Heart Drop of the Dakini;* these three are: the essence of the transmission based on the dakini's prophecies, set forth as practical instructions; the ways in which the empowerments and teachings are to be imparted; [1.111a] and advice on the heart essence of definitive meaning, which causes blessings to arise in one's mind.

My incidental works include a manual of common liturgies, including six supplication prayers and about thirty vajra songs concerning the ultimate heart essence. I wrote these as auxiliary supports to the preceding texts.

The lord Longchenpa himself arranged this listing of the works included in the amazing, marvelous cycles of his teachings on the most profound topics of all. He did so at Tarpa Ling in Bumthang, Bhutan, for the benefit of fortunate people of future generations. The listing is included in this biography to illustrate the superior qualities of Longchenpa's body, speech, and mind.

The lord Longchenpa signed the 307 foregoing works by a variety of names, including Tsultrim Lodrö (Discipline and Intelligence), Kunchen Chöjé (Omniscient King of the Dharma), Longchen Rabjam (Vast Array of the Supreme Expanse), Samyépa Ngagi Wangpo (Lord of Speech from Samyé), Penpa Zangpo (Noble Benefactor), Pema Ledrel Tsal (Lotus of Dynamic Karmic Connection), Namkhai Naljor (Yogin of Space), Natsok Rangdrol (Natural Freedom of the Myriad Display), Guyang Lodé (Spacious Mind of Bliss), Lodrö Chokden (Possessed of Sublime Intelligence), and Longsel Drimé (Immaculate Lucid Expanse). His works on the dialectical approach [1.111b] are generally no longer extant due to circumstances of time and place;[63] however, those concerning the mantra approach and Dzogchen remain, like the sun and the moon, the very heart of the Victorious One's teachings, which have endured for so long in this world. Longchenpa's works are indistinguishable from the words of the Victorious One and constitute an inconceivable body of secrets. Simply to read them causes realization of the enlightened intent that is the true nature of phenomena to arise in one's mind, for these are great models of realization, vajra dohas that concern genuine being.

Paltrul Rinpoché's Prayer of Praise

The lord of the dharma Paltrul Rinpoché composed the following prayer of praise to Longchenpa:

> *Namo sarva jñaya guruve!*[64]
>
> I pay homage to one endowed with the mandala of true perfection—
> the limitless qualities of victorious ones without exception—
> the Omniscient Guru who serves as the courageous regent
> of all victorious ones.
>
> The primordial ground of being as basic space is the expanse (*long*) of perfect qualities.
> For you, phenomena have resolved into their true nature within the womb of supreme (*chen*) emptiness.
> With the vast array (*rabjam*) of your wisdom, you know with precision all that can be known.
> Omniscient Guru, you are one who knows all.

Hearing even a fragment of a single word of the excellent explanatory teachings of this lord of refuge
causes the fabric of conditioned existence to be truly rent asunder.
What need, then, to speak of one who listens to and contemplates his works
in their entirety, the complete range of his teachings? [1.112a]

Through the power of their meditative stability, which confers courage and other qualities,
victorious ones and their great spiritual heirs
enact all manner of noble and worthy deeds
through their various emanated forms, both spiritually advanced and quite ordinary beings.

This sublime nirmanakaya, this omniscient master,
thus protected beings in degenerating times using the means of a victorious one
and ensured that the teachings of the vajra heart essence were illuminated
by cycles of instruction concerning the pinnacle approach that brings freedom upon being heard.

The utterly pure nectar of the excellent explanatory teachings
of this perfect buddha, the Omniscient Guru,
is such that only a cow with upper teeth[65] would not understand this sublime transmission of the dharma,
words spoken from the Buddha's lips.

All who have good fortune, rejoice!
See with certainty that this master is a buddha.
Studying the excellent explanatory teachings of the Omniscient Guru
is not different in the slightest from meeting the Buddha.

The major and minor marks of the Sage's[66] physical perfection are nectar to the eyes,
arousing the three aspects of faith[67] in the minds of the fortunate.
But the words of these excellent explanatory teachings are also the nirmanakaya manifesting as an art form.
There is nothing better than this to nurture one's faith.

The melodious tones of the Teacher are nectar to the ears, [1.112b]
arousing sublime knowing in the minds of the fortunate.
But the sentences of these excellent explanatory teachings are also nectar to the ears.
There is nothing equal to them in nurturing one's knowledge.

The blessings of the Victorious One are nectar to the heart,
revealing the truth in the minds of the fortunate.
But the noble meanings of these excellent explanatory teachings are also nectar to the heart.
There is nothing greater than they for nurturing one's experience of timeless awareness.

Blessed with the power of his completely liberated mind of meditative absorption,
these works, upon being studied, unfailingly awaken the experience of the true nature of phenomena in one's mind.
They can instantly reveal the enlightened intent of original purity,
and so are peerless in breaking down one's ordinary perceptions.

The play of these words is the very manifestation of the Lion of the Shakyas.[68]
The sentences they form are the speech of the Omniscient Guru.
The meanings they convey are the mind of all victorious ones.
To behold these excellent works is to behold all sugatas.

Now that we are in the final period of the five-hundred-year cycle of teachings,
the Buddha himself attested to the fact that
the forms this master's words take—the manifest play of his excellent speech—
embody the actual presence of the Teacher.

These excellent explanations of noble meaning—*The Seven Treasuries* and other works—
represent the entire body of the teachings, the dharma that leads to buddhahood in a single lifetime.
Who would deny that these drops of nectar, this profound path, [1.113a]
are the words of an omniscient guru?

Spontaneous presence is imbued with qualities that are extremely vast in scope,
while original purity is imbued with the profundity of basic space.
The primordial unity of these is the pinnacle approach, the teachings of the vajra heart essence.
What could there be besides this secret, the enlightened mind of victorious ones?

The form of the Sage is beautiful, like a mountain of gold.
Although to behold the rupakaya is extraordinary,

the pinnacle approach reveals the indescribable nature of phenomena;
surely this is the good fortune of beholding dharmakaya.

All that the Protector[69] came to understand while under the bodhi tree
and all the truth seen by heirs of victorious ones—
the inexpressible, ultimate meaning—is revealed through skillful means
with a single word from the excellent explanatory teachings of the Omniscient Guru.

Dzogchen is the complete perfection of all things that contribute to enlightenment,
which, without exception, are positive by nature.
It is the monument to the dharmakaya of all victorious ones.
There is no better focus for merit than this.

Dzogchen reveals what is both vast and profound, all of the inconceivably sublime qualities
referred to in every one of the Sage's discourses.
Such are the qualities of this approach, which reveals in all its nakedness
the vast and profound nature of phenomena. [1.113b]

Therefore, the fortune of those who hear even a single word of these texts,
and those who remember them, read them, and put them into practice,
is equal to that of anyone who hears, remembers, reads, and practices
all of the Victorious One's teachings; the resulting merit is the same.

The ultimate meaning of the eighty-four thousand collections of the teachings
is surely subsumed within the expanse of awareness.
Why, then, would this meaning not be contained in a single verse of these profound teachings,
for they are the excellent explanatory teachings of the Omniscient Guru, which give expression to it?

Encountering them even for an instant with a mind filled with faith
arouses a deep yearning in one's heart,
which clears the murkiness of negative emotions as a matter of course.
The excellent explanatory teachings of the Omniscient Guru bring liberation upon sight.

Hearing a single word causes a peaceful state of meditative absorption
to arise effortlessly in anyone's mind,
completely removing the dust of conceptual thought.

The excellent explanatory teachings of the Omniscient Guru bring liberation upon hearing.

They have a peaceful, soothing, and gentle texture
that removes the flawed roughness of intellectual pedantry.
They are the deathless approach that dispels the pain of samsara.
The excellent explanatory teachings of the Omniscient Guru bring liberation upon touch.

They have the delicious flavor of the nectar of noble and profound meaning.
The smallest taste nourishes one's "body"—listening to, contemplating, and meditating on the teachings—
so that it soars in basic space, the true nature of phenomena, like a bird in flight. [1.114a]
The excellent explanatory teachings of the Omniscient Guru bring liberation upon taste.

Thus did the Omniscient Guru reveal in excellent works
the entire range of the Victorious One's teachings.
Never before had any of the wise masters of India and Tibet
left such a legacy to the world.

The advice of the Omniscient Guru
opens the doorway to the spiritual approaches based on causality
and leads to the decisive experience of the uniformity of basic space, which involves no causality.
There has never been another learned and accomplished master who has given such advice.

These noble works are like the fully developed form of a lovely deity,
whose every limb is graced with ornaments.
Compared with these, the treatises of other learned masters
are like mere fragments of those limbs strewn about.

The Omniscient Guru's works are beautified by the holy embellishments of noble words and poetic expressions.
Their great meaning is the youthful, vigorous body of all the Victorious One's teachings.
They wear a crown topped with a sublime gem—the pinnacle of spiritual approaches.
These noble works are truly like the lord of the gods.

The staircases of the developmental path of spiritual approaches based on causality are laid out.
The dome of the path of the supreme secret is majestic and imposing.
The blazing pinnacle is the arrival at the four kayas of spontaneous presence. [1.114b]
These noble works are truly like a palace of complete victory.

The realm of desire results from the ten virtuous actions—the imposing lord of mountains.
The realm of formlessness results from meditative absorption—gathering clouds of peace.
The realm of form results from the noble path—the perfect pinnacle realm.
These noble works are truly like the three realms.

They guide any who are to be guided according to their interests.
They distinctly explain things that are to be known in all their variety.
They do not stray from the expanse of ultimate equalness.
These noble works are truly like a perfect buddha.

They reveal all of the unlimited variations of spiritual paths.
They delineate the nine approaches according to the intellectual examination of the paths based on causality.
Renunciation and acceptance resolve within the expanse of the direct experience of utter lucidity.
These noble works are truly like both conditioned existence and the peace of nirvana.

To understand their meaning is the path of the vajra heart essence,
the profound key point of the secret Nyingtik, like one's heart.
Other treatises by learned masters that do not reveal this point,
though seemingly like lovely bodies, are corpses that lack this heart.

The very likeness of realization, the song of the vajra heart essence,
is the speech that reveals the true nature of phenomena, directly perceptible in all its nakedness.
To listen to this upwelling advice even for an instant [1.115a]
unfailingly arouses the timeless awareness of utter lucidity in one's mind.

More profound than the profound is the precious basic space of phenomena.
It is a unique treasury of realization, the timeless awareness realized by the lineage of blessings.

These works are like the advent of one's experience of the true
dharmakaya.
For those who put them into practice, there will be no more rebirth in
conditioned existence.

Such pith instructions as these—revealing the Omniscient Guru's
enlightened mind,
unobstructed awareness in all its nakedness—
are actual buddhahood, the actual dharma,
and spiritual mentors, if one feels devotion for them.

They are what is known as the fourth empowerment,[70]
the consummation of the profound key points of all classes of tantra.
The totality of the four levels of empowerment is embodied in the
empowerment into the dynamic energy of awareness.[71]
This is apparent in noble works like these, but not in others.

The illusory form of the Omniscient Guru's rainbow body
is not something that existed in the past but is now gone.
It is right before you, if you could only see it,
but if your perception is obscured by concepts, what would be the point
even if it actually appeared?

These key points of enlightened speech are the likeness of realization.
The words and their underlying meaning are infused with the blessings of
supreme timeless awareness.
They were entrusted as words of truth to those with devotion.
If one relies on them with certainty, they are the guru himself.

Having aroused devotion, when one examines and understands the words
and their underlying meaning,
for as long as one studies noble works like these,
how could one's mind possibly stray [1.115b]
from the sublime experience of the direct perception of utter lucidity?

Other treatises are pedantic, at best, with too many concepts;
looking at them only increases one's confused thinking.
But to hear even a single word from the works of the Omniscient Guru,
which reveal what is beyond ordinary consciousness, is to effortlessly
experience meditative absorption.

One gets lost in many ordinary works involving convoluted pedantry;
such dalliance is meaningless and wearying.

But the works of the Omniscient Guru lend one ease
on the jeweled staircase of excellent words and their underlying meaning.

Partial knowledge is like a winged bee
whose fantasy of circling the world can never come true.
But upon reaching the summit of Sumeru, the vajra heart essence,
one soars like the most majestic of the great garudas, with the nine spiritual approaches clearly laid out beneath.

The treatises of the immature are filled with childish arguments,
their authors obsessed with their own opinions of what is or is not so.
But the straightforward, excellent explanatory teachings of the Omniscient Guru
reflect a mature intelligence that has experienced the uniform nature of phenomena.

When you feel confused or ignorant or in doubt,
consult these noble works,
and the sword of sublime knowing found in the Omniscient One's excellent explanatory teachings
will cut through the web of confusion.

When the fog of excessive conceptualization enshrouds you,
consult these noble works,
and the vajra of timeless awareness [1.116a] found in the Omniscient One's excellent explanatory teachings
will knock down the walls of concepts based on confusion.

When the pain of emotionality based on confusion afflicts you,
consult these noble works,
and the bonfire of realization found in the Omniscient One's excellent explanatory teachings
will instantly consume the fuel of negative emotions.

When you are distracted by circumstances and filled with regret,
consult these noble works,
and the sublime healing nectar found in the Omniscient One's excellent explanatory teachings
will soothe and restore your mind with renunciation.

When you are dwelling in a solitary place,
consult these noble works,

and the comforting ally of awareness found in the Omniscient One's
excellent explanatory teachings
will allow you to pass your time, day and night, in spiritual practice.

When you feel attachment and aversion in the midst of too many people,
consult these noble works,
and the jeweled staircase found in the Omniscient One's excellent
explanatory teachings
will bring you ease of mind within the uniform expanse of being.

When you are obsessed with the concepts of intellectual speculation,
consult these noble works,
and the key of skillful means [1.116b] found in the Omniscient One's
excellent explanatory teachings
will release you from the chains of belief in the seeming truth of things.

When your meditation is hindered by laxity, agitation, or dullness,
consult these noble works,
and the pith instructions on key points found in the Omniscient One's
excellent explanatory teachings
will arouse an excellent, flawless state of peaceful meditative absorption
within you.

When you are threatened by illness or suffering,
consult these noble works,
and the philosopher's stone (which turns base metal into gold) found in
the Omniscient One's excellent explanatory teachings
will transform negative circumstances into supportive ones.

When your realization—the dynamic energy of awareness—intensifies,
consult these noble works,
and the enriching key points found in the Omniscient One's excellent
explanatory teachings
will directly introduce you to equalness within the expanse of
dharmakaya.

When random meditative experiences arise,
consult these noble works,
and the spontaneous vajra song found in the Omniscient One's excellent
explanatory teachings
will cause uncontrived conduct to flourish in a state without fixation.

When you feel uncontrollably concerned with sense pleasures and personal wealth,
consult these noble works,
and the peacock (which delights in poison) found in the Omniscient One's excellent explanatory teachings
will allow you to enjoy whatever you desire as an adornment, in a state without fixation.

When you feel self-important, [1.117a] caught on the dualistic horns of hope and fear,
consult these noble works,
and the means of cutting through the maras found in the Omniscient One's excellent explanatory teachings
will grant you the confidence to enjoy uncontrived conduct.

When, in an entrenched state of confusion, you reify things,
consult these noble works,
and the magician's advice found in the Omniscient One's excellent explanatory teachings
will eliminate the turmoil of taking things to be so solid and real.

The Omniscient One's excellent explanatory teachings, like a treasure trove of gems,
are truly a necklace of qualities whose value is inestimable.
I lack the confidence to do them justice,
so how could I convey all there is to say about them?

In countless realms, these praiseworthy works
serve as the basis for the holy spiritual advice
of victorious ones and their learned heirs.
They are truly the province of the most precise, sagacious insight.

In the playful realm of the learned, like the vault of space,
I, a person of ordinary intelligence, am a winged bee,
whose buzzing is this song of praise, [1.117b]
intoned with joy in the garden of these excellent explanatory teachings.
Feel this joy also, you fortunate ones who share my purpose.
Sip sweet nectar from these blossoms again and again.
Join me in hymns of praise,
and inexhaustible certainty will be yours.

The virtue of this noble undertaking
is like a cloud of what is truly praiseworthy.

I dedicate it, not so that we remain within two extremes—trying to gain
peace in samsara or to find some worldly purpose in nirvana—
but so that we may fulfill the enlightened intent of the victorious ones and
their heirs.

When I think of the wisdom of the hero Mañjushri,
whose color is like twilight's glow and who blazes with the splendor of the
major and minor marks of perfection,
I aspire to follow his example, without false hope, dedicating the merit
completely
by letting go of the ordinary mind that invests all things with seeming
truth.

Moreover, I pray that henceforth I might reach the threshold
to the wealth of skillful means for bringing beings to spiritual maturity
and liberation, conferred by the Omniscient One and the lineage,
and that my begging bowl of threefold faith might never be empty,
so that I have the good fortune to look upon the guru and lineage as the
most humble one among them.

Whenever conditioned existence and the peace of nirvana blend in a state
of equalness,
the pit of samsara is dredged from its depths, and one arises in the vase
body.
All samsara and nirvana without exception is the expanse of the single
sphere of being.
May we merge with the enlightened intent of the Omniscient Guru!

Dzogchen Commentaries

As the foregoing prayer of praise implies, [1.118a] Longchenpa appeared in this world as a second Samantabhadra, transmitting teachings with the lion's roar of the three categories of the Dzogchen approach. Regarding the Category of Mind, Longchenpa wrote treatises like *Rays of Sunlight,* his major commentary on *The All-Creating Monarch.* Regarding the Category of Expanse, his works include *The Entire Array of Space: A Thematic Explanation of the General Principles of the Three Expanses* and its commentary, *Loosening the Seal into the Freedom from Any Fixed Dimension.* As for the Category of Direct Transmission, Longchenpa produced extremely clear manuals based on the teachings that had been transmitted orally until the time of Kumaradza. Over a six-day period, Longchenpa received from the Guru and his consort the cycle *The Heart Drop of the Dakini*—the very heart of the terma teachings—including a direct introduction to the nature of mind and their seal of entrustment. Thus Longchenpa became one who had received the transmission of all three categories of Dzogchen. This great master's works contain countless points that either were not discussed in previous teaching manuals or were unclear; these welled up quite naturally in the expanse of his enlightened intent. Because of their appreciation of the innumerable special features of these texts, masters of awareness in the past all received these great Nyingtik cycles many times. Given the importance of Longchenpa's written works, I have chosen to include a listing of them, without concern for its length. [1.118b] It is my heartfelt prayer that those of future generations will understand that these works, especially those of the fourth section and onward, are the very core of the most sublime spiritual approach and will take great care to cherish them, as is fitting.

LONGCHENPA'S SECRET BIOGRAPHY: ENLIGHTENED MIND

The third main section of this chapter is Longchenpa's biography on the secret level, that of his enlightened mind. This is, in fact, the unique state of perfect buddhahood, the state of a victorious one, far beyond even the province of masters on the tenth bodhisattva level, and so a realm that we cannot hope to perceive accurately. Longchenpa actually brought the four visions to consummation in a single lifetime through the path of natural great perfection. He fully experienced the enlightened intent of perceiving awareness's naturally manifest appearances without bias. He reached the empire of the primordial protector, the point at which phenomena resolve. The development of his inner realization is expressed in his vajra songs of genuine being, which are spontaneous outpourings of his realization. In *The Precious Treasury of the Basic Space of Phenomena,* Longchenpa writes:

> Within the spacious expanse, the spacious expanse, the spacious vast expanse,
> I, Longchen Rabjam, for whom the lucid expanse of being is infinite,
> experience everything as embraced within a blissful expanse, a single nondual expanse.
> I, Natsok Rangdrol, have reached the point of natural freedom where phenomena resolve. [1.119a]
> Unchanging spontaneous presence is the pinnacle of my excellent counsel.

Outwardly, the expanse of sensory appearances is spacious as a supreme and timelessly empty state without any underlying basis. Inwardly, the ex-

> panse of mental activity is spacious as a supreme and naturally pristine state in which thoughts leave no trace. Secretly, the expanse of awakened mind is spacious as a naked, unobstructed state. These three abide as an uncreated spontaneous presence. I, Longchen Rabjam, a yogin of the sublime spiritual approach, have realized this in all its nakedness and natural lucidity. With the arising of a supreme state of infinite spaciousness—the expanse of samsara, originally pure without having to be abandoned, and nirvana, spontaneously present without having to be accomplished—everything is embraced within the blissful expanse of my realization that samsara and nirvana are nondual within the single expanse of awareness. I, Natsok Rangdrol, a yogin for whom myriad phenomena are inherently free in their true nature, have reached dharmakaya, enlightened intent beyond ordinary consciousness. And so my realization has reached full expression at the point where phenomena resolve in their true nature. Thus, since I have gained the ongoing state of authentic being, the most majestic state of dharmakaya, in this present life, I would say that I have reached the summit of the most excellent endeavor.[72]

And in his work *The Precious Treasury of the Sublime Spiritual Approach,* he states:

> If I look at my experience—this unique state in which my ordinary consciousness has fallen away—I, for whom phenomena have resolved, burst out laughing. Since I have already gained the ongoing state that is the true nature of phenomena, about which nothing need be done, [1.119b] I am free of the narrow confines of dualistic perceptions, of hope and fear. It is all right if I meditate, but it is all right if I just leave things as they are. It is all right if I undertake something, but all right if I just let it go. For me there is no fixed reference point, no "It is this!" This utterly relaxed enlightened intent of spontaneous presence does not require that anything be done. There is nothing I must do. I have not achieved this state by doing anything. It is beyond anything needing to be done. I make no judgment about what is or is not to be done. There is no need to meditate, for there is nothing to meditate on. This is beyond meditation; to meditate would spoil it. There is no need to exercise view, for there is nothing to view. This is beyond being anything to view—what would I view? There is no need to seek anything, for there is nothing to seek. It is beyond seeking; there is nothing to find. Thus everything has an unobstructed quality. However I look at it, I am content, for enlightened intent arises as the supreme expanse of pure space. Having been led to this level of resolution, I am forever a yogin for whom it can be said that there is no division between samsara and nirvana.

> In putting such an experience of enlightened intent into words, I have left you fortunate people of the future with a likeness you can encounter as though actually meeting me. Therefore, please use it as a focus for your devotion so that realization arises for you as well!

We can gain some understanding of Longchenpa's realization as it is illustrated throughout his extensive writings by passages like these. [1.120a]

In conclusion, I will mention this master's heart sons, the foremost among his students nurtured by the nectar of his speech. Three of the most famous were called "learned and accomplished ones": Khedrup Chabdal Lhundrup, Zhoktar Lingpa Khedrup Delek Gyatso, and Khedrup Chökyi Drakpa. As well, his students included his "five heart sons": Dengom Chödrak Zangpo, Gyalsé Zangpo Drakpa, Lama Palchok, Guru Yeshé Rabjam, and Zhönnu Sang-gyé. Four were known as the "four mentors who spread the teachings": Tulku Paljor Gyatso, Loppön Sang-gyé Kunga, Loppön Lodrö Zangpo, and Jadral Chöjé Tashi Jungné of Takgo. Four were referred to as "spiritually accomplished yogins": Pagö Tokden Gyalpo, Naljor Özer Gocha, Guru Ösel Rangdrol, and Jatang Sönam Özer. In addition, Longchenpa taught such masters as Trulzhik Sang-gyé Önpo, Orgyen Chöjé of Drok, Khenpo Sönam Seng-gé of Lu, Drakpa Pal, and Sang-gyé Palrin, as well as many thousands of others who received the complete transmission of empowerments, explanatory commentaries, and pith instructions. Those who received at least some empowerments or instructions [1.120b] are beyond counting, and many of them gained an authentic measure of meditative experience. In this way, Longchenpa caused the hills and valleys of Tibet to be filled with practitioners meditating on the great perfection.

In the generations after Longchenpa, the majority of those who upheld this lineage—such masters as the lord of realized ones Lhatsün Chenpo, the great Rigdzin Terdak Lingpa, Chögyal Rinchen Puntsok, Rigdzin Jigmé Lingpa, and Khenchen Ngawang Palzang (an emanation of Vimalamitra)—were nurtured by his embodiment of timeless awareness. The ultimate lineage, the direct realization of enlightened intent, was passed from his mind to theirs, and they were authorized as masters of these teachings. In particular, there has been an unbroken lineage from the time of Jigmé Lingpa, based on his visionary experiences. The fact that the Dzogchen tradition has not waned, but has continued to flourish throughout the world up to the present day is due entirely to the powerful force of kindness shown by this king of the dharma.

> Your timeless awareness is an ocean on which billow the waves of the two accumulations.
> The foaming whitecaps of your wisdom and love surge against the sides of the most majestic mountain.

The rivers of the four empowerments cleanse the flaws of all the many beings.
I praise with devotion you who rest so comfortably in the two levels of truth. [1.121a]

The naga king, your innate compassion, is beautified by the hood of your wisdom and love.
The timely rain of your spiritual energy and power nurtures the fields of the many beings.
The call of your love resounds in all directions.
I praise with devotion you who are the great refuge, the god of water.

Your study and contemplation of the dharma are a tiered mountain,
a sublime and holy place where the hosts of gods, spiritual mentors, gather.
Imposing and majestic is your realization of the unchanging way of abiding.
I praise with devotion you who are this great mountain of the dharma.

The sun of your enlightened activity shines with the thousandfold radiance of your deeds,
bathing in its glow the lotus beds of the fortunate,
causing them to blossom fully and release the pollen of the three higher trainings.
I praise with devotion you who nourish your followers as though bestowing nectar on bees.

You gratify others with the four kinds of generosity,
while your own is replete with the three kinds of discipline.
With the three kinds of patience, you met your spiritual challenges and triumphed over them.
I praise with devotion you who perfected the enlightened intent of the three lineages.

With the three kinds of exertion, you ensured the very best of the two kinds of benefit.
With the three kinds of meditative stability, you gained insight and supernormal cognition.
With the three kinds of sublime knowing, you reached the pinnacle of Ati.
I praise with deep faith you who are Samantabhadra, lord of the dharma.

Through the skillful means of the two stages, [1.121b] you gained the power of timeless awareness.
You dedicated virtue throughout the three times in a state of threefold purity.
You know your true nature, the way of abiding, and you understand the full range of the knowable.
I praise with devotion you who are the actual presence of Mañjushri.

The superb pinnacle of spiritual approaches is Dzogchen, the approach of utter lucidity.
Its most profound key points are contained in 119 pith instructions.
I praise you who are the actual manifestation of Vimalamitra, clarifying these points
in your *Seven Treasuries,* three Yangtik—Innermost Heart Drop—cycles, and other works.

You gaze constantly on beings with loving eyes.
With compassion, you constantly protect those who are wanting or in pain.
With joy and delight, you liberate beings from the ocean of conditioned existence.
You are unwavering in your efforts to benefit beings; enemy and child are alike to you.
I praise with devotion you who are endowed with the four immeasurable attitudes.

You summon beings with the call of spiritual and material generosity.
With your pleasant speech, you bring them into contact with definitive truth.
Acting harmoniously, you conscientiously bring them to the path of Ati.
I praise you who ensure benefit for beings with the four means of influencing others.

By listening to teachings, you became learned in the meaning of the sutra and tantra approaches.
By contemplating them, you realized that profound meaning is found in the Nyingtik teachings.
By meditating, you arrived at the level of Samantabhadra.
I praise you who are the Buddha emanating in the form of a spiritual mentor.

You journeyed to the Dra Uplands, Samyé, the uplands of Sangpu and of Kyam,
Lharing Drak, Shuksep, Orgyen Dzong, [1.122a]
Gyama Drong, Yarpo Zhung,
Lhodrak, and Bhutan,
planting seeds of liberation in fortunate people.
You turned the wheel of the dharma, bringing students to spiritual maturity and liberation on a vast scale.
Your final deed was passing into nirvana at the Chimpu Uplands.
I pay homage to all those places where you resided, O great being.

Thus this great Omniscient One appeared in the world as the headwater of the river of teachings concerning natural great perfection, the source of a hundred thousand springs. The eastern Tibetan tradition of the Nyingtik cycles was carried on by his students Katokpa Dorjé Bum, Dengom Chödrak, and others. The Lhalung lineage was carried on by Jadral Chöjé of Takgo. Countless such lineages developed, each engendering in turn a host of learned and accomplished masters, so that the lineages of Longchenpa's students have spread throughout the world. I could not begin to describe them all; a description of the lineage that passed through Khenchen Chabdal Lhundrup will have to suffice for now.

6

The Combined Lineages from Longchenpa to Jigmé Gyalwai Nyugu

Khenchen Chabdal Lhundrup (14th Century)

Chabdal Lhundrup was born in Dangtro, in the southern border region of Lhodrak. His father was Paldren, [1.122b] and his mother was Samdrupkyi. At an early age, he clearly experienced the forceful awakening of his spiritual heritage as someone holy. He learned how to read and write at the age of five, mastering these skills without difficulty. At thirteen he was ordained as a novice monk at the center of Densa[1] Tenchikpa in Lha Valley.[2] At twenty he took full monastic ordination from Khenchen Sönam Drakpa,[3] the abbot of Chölung Monastery, where he received training, practical instruction, and scriptural transmissions related to monastic discipline.

He trained with numerous spiritual mentors, becoming learned in Prajñaparamita, valid cognition, Vinaya, and Abhidharma. He then taught at many shedras specializing in the teachings of the dialectical approach and thus became widely renowned. [1.123a] He was an elder who was like a mountain of gold[4]—the very embodiment of erudition, venerability, and nobility.

He studied the systems of Lojong[5] and arousing bodhichitta with Gyalsé Tokmé.[6] From Jamyang Lekdenpa, he received the Lamdré cycle and other instructions of the Sakya school; from Lama Kunrin, *The One Hundred Transmissions of Mitra* and other transmissions; from the great tertöns Dorjé Lingpa and Rinchen Lingpa, their respective terma cycles; and from Yeshé Gyalpo, the transmission for the form of Mañjushri known as Ayushpati. In short, from numerous spiritual mentors, he received many teachings on the sutras and on the tantras of the Nyingma and Sarma schools, and mastered all of them. By order of Khenchen Jangsem Sönam Drakpa of Chölung, Chabdal Lhundrup was appointed the head abbot of Jodendé Monastery in Lha Valley, where he cared for his monastic community both spiritually and materially; thus this monastery became an excellent center.

During this period, the great Omniscient One was traveling to Bhutan in the south.

Chabdal Lhundrup invited him to Mentang, where he remained for an entire summer. Chabdal Lhundrup became convinced that Longchenpa had been his guru in previous lifetimes and served him devotedly, demonstrating the three kinds of faith. He was brought to spiritual maturity by numerous empowerments and teachings concerning the unsurpassable secret.

After the Omniscient One continued on to Bhutan, [1.123b] Chabdal Lhundrup built a retreat hut at Zekhar, the hermitage in Lha Valley, where he spent five years without interruption practicing the yoga of the Dzogchen approach of utter lucidity, cutting off all distracting complications. He reached a consummate realization of the great perfection, perceiving awareness's naturally manifest appearances without bias. He had visions of numerous meditation deities; and many oath-bound protective deities, such as Vaishravana and those of the five classes, listened to his commands and carried out their enlightened activities. With his untrammeled powers of higher perception, he was able to foresee things hidden from ordinary perception, things that turned out just as he foretold.

He was foremost among those who invited the Omniscient One Longchenpa to return from Bhutan. All of the people of Lhodrak honored the Omniscient Guru with devotion and requested that he turn the wheel of the dharma on a vast scale. In particular, Chabdal Lhundrup received instructions on *The Heart Drop of the Dakini* and wrote commentaries based on his questions about the transmissions he had previously received. The lord of the dharma Longchenpa was extremely pleased and accepted him as his heart son, entrusting him with the lineage. He instructed him, "Pass this on to Drakpa Özer."

Though he gained mastery over the entire array of teachings of the Nyingma and Sarma schools in general, Chabdal Lhundrup focused specifically on the theory and practice of the lord of the dharma's Dzogchen tradition of the supreme secret. He brought countless fortunate students to spiritual maturity and liberation, among them such excellent holders of the teachings as Tulku Drakpa Özer, Terchen Dorjé Lingpa, [1.124a] Guru Donyöpa, Jatang Gyaltsendrak, Tokden Yepalwa, and Tsultrim Tsen.

He lived to the age of ninety-seven, when, on the twenty-second day of the fourth month, Saga, his emanated form resolved back into the basic space of phenomena. His remains were kept in state for one month. Upon their cremation, numerous relics were found, just one of the many amazing miracles that took place, moving everyone to faith.

Gyalsé Tulku Drakpa Özer (1356–1409)

Chabdal Lhundrup's principal student was Gyalsé Tulku Drakpa Özer. [1.124b] A portion of *The Golden Garland of Questions and Answers* from the cycle *The Heart Drop of the Dakini* reads:

The next incarnation of Ledrel Tsal
will remain for a short time in a sambhogakaya pure realm
and then take birth at Tarpa Ling in Bumthang.
From the age of fifteen, he will benefit beings.
Then the son, Dawa Drakpa, an emanation of Hayagriva, will appear;
he, too, will benefit beings.

In fulfillment of this and other prophecies, the great Omniscient King of the Dharma, Longchenpa, attained a sambhogakaya pure realm, for he experienced the full expression of awareness as a vision of the spontaneous presence of utter lucidity. From that state, he manifested as his own son,[7] a tulku to guide beings; the child's mother was named Kyipala.[8]

At an early age, Drakpa Özer felt the attributes of someone holy awaken within. He would sing songs of advice to his mother and explain the meaning of the dharma to anyone who came near him. During that period, many people saw the guardian goddess of mantra Ekajati holding him in her lap and the Seer[9] guarding him.

When the child was five, Khedrup Chabdal Lhundrup invited him to Zekhar in Lha Valley, in keeping with the prophecy uttered by the lord of the dharma Longchenpa. There he was well looked after, being accorded both spiritual honors and material support.

At the age of eight, he took the vows of a novice monk and was given the name Drakpa Özer. [1.125a] He studied and contemplated many avenues of the dharma. Like one vase being filled from another, he received from Chabdal Lhundrup the full range of empowerments, teachings, and oral transmissions concerning the unsurpassable secret that this great khenpo had himself received from the great Omniscient One. Drakpa Özer mastered all of them.

When he was nine, he was invited to central Tibet by students of his former incarnation. He was honored by many of the faithful at such centers as Jamding in Dra Valley, Riwo in the Drak region, Shuksep in the Nyepu Uplands, and Drigung in Gyama. He bestowed the nectar of the dharma on them according to their individual fortunes. The great scholar Yakdé Panchen respectfully sought an audience with him, during which he praised Drakpa Özer with the following words of admiration:

You have achieved this rebirth, and with the sublime knowing of someone
spiritually advanced,
you have mastered the meaning of the essence of being.
Bodhisattva, mahasattva,
Drakpa Özer, may you be victorious!

On his way back to southern Tibet, Drakpa Özer was welcomed at Yardrok with honors by the glorious Sakya Dakchen Lodrö Gyaltsen and the throne holder Dorjé Gyaltsen, both of whom received his kind teachings. Passing through Lhodrak, Lhalung, and other areas, he traveled to Bhutan, where he founded a retreat center at Langmatil. In such border regions as Bumthang, Ngenlong, and Menlok, [1.125b] he illuminated the path to liberation for many fortunate people with the torch of the dharma, including the teachings of the vajra heart essence of utter lucidity.

He returned to Tibet, where he carried out activities at the principal spiritual centers in order to create benefit and happiness on a vast scale. He especially worked to spread the traditions of the vajra heart essence of utter lucidity. He gathered many learned and accomplished students, among them Trulzhik Sang-gyé Önpo; his own son, Dawa Drakpa; Jatang Drakpa Gyatso; Sherab Palden of lower Ling; and Zhönnu Lodrö of Kyang Valley. He received whatever he could of the nectar of the dharma from all those who had been students of the great Omniscient One Longchenpa. In this way, he held the extensive lineage of the teachings and spread it everywhere.

At the age of fifty-four, on the twenty-fourth day of the fourth month in an Ox year,[10] he passed into a state of peace at Kalden Jampading. When his remains were cremated, all those present were moved to faith by amazing signs, such as the many relics and images of deities that were found in the ashes and the canopies of rainbows that arched over the site. This great master blessed all of the places in which he stayed, his positive influence pacifying illness, famine, warfare, social unrest, and other problems. He ensured that the teachings of the heart essence would endure. [1.126a] From this master came Kunchen Dawa Drakpa and many other great teachers whose activities filled all of space, spreading the teachings and bringing beings to spiritual maturity. Today descendants of Drakpa Özer can still be found in the Bumthang region of Bhutan.

Trulzhik Sang-gyé Önpo Sherab Gyatso (14th–15th Centuries)

Drakpa Özer's main student was Sherab Gyatso, also known as Trulzhik Sang-gyé Önpo. He was born in the vicinity of Samyé Semkyé Ling, son of the Buddhist layman Pema-kyap and his wife, Önpo Kyipa. From an early age, the boy experienced an awakening of his noble predisposition. Upon hearing groups of monks chanting, he felt certain of the need to seek release from samsara [1.126b] and longed to enter the religious life. But because he was their only son, his parents prevented him from doing so until, at the age of seven, he was bitten by a rabid dog. Only then was he allowed to take monastic ordination from the abbot Sherinpa and the preceptor Shegyalwa and to enroll in the monastic community of Samyé.[11]

At first, while he was learning the daily liturgies and other texts, he did not do well, having been exposed to leprosy while attending to someone afflicted with the disease.[12] From Lama Shakrinpa in the Chimpu Uplands, he requested the transmission for White Mañjushri. Having engaged in this practice intensely, he dreamed one night that a person, completely white, gave him a crystal mala and that he picked white flowers the size of plates. With this, his intelligence increased greatly.

At various stages of his life, he received a vast range of teachings on the sutras and on the tantras of the Nyingma and Sarma schools, studying with more than fifty holy mentors, including four successive abbots of Chölung Monastery. Among his teachers were the lord of the dharma Karmapa Rangjung Dorjé, Butön, Gyalsepa, Lama Sönam Gyaltsen, Jonang Chokgyalwa, and Khenchen Sönam Drakpa.[13] Later, at the age of eighteen, he was given full monastic ordination by Lama Sönam Gyaltsen and the master Mandzuwa as abbot and preceptor, respectively. [1.127a] In a Bird year,[14] Lama Sönam Gyaltsen led the gathered leaders of many chapters of the sangha in the consecration ceremonies for the restored monastery of Samyé. To all those assembled, Sherab Gyatso gave an original explanation of Prajñaparamita, for which he was highly honored.

He later attended the shedra of Tsetang,[15] where he studied with Goshri Shakya Gyaltsen, the master Palgyalwa, and other scholars. He trained in Prajñaparamita, valid cognition, Vinaya, and Abhidharma, gaining stature as a scholar. When the lord of the dharma, the great Omniscient One Longchenpa, was returning from Bhutan in the south and staying at Zhung Mountain, Sherab Gyatso met with him. He offered him gifts and distributed alms to the three hundred people in Longchenpa's retinue. He received many empowerments, teachings, and pith instructions of the secret Dzogchen cycles, as well as kama and terma transmissions, including the tantra *The All-Creating Monarch.*

Longchenpa's attendants encouraged him, saying, "You surely are the lineage successor. You should stay and be the guru's personal secretary." But with real affection, the lord of the dharma advised him, "When one is young, it may be profitable to study; but this dialectical approach is for those of little faith, so do not waste your time on it." [1.127b] He gave Sherab Gyatso symbols of enlightened form, speech, and mind, as well as his hat, robes, and sitting mat, and authorized him to pass on the lineage of ultimate meaning.

Although Trulzhik continued to undertake appropriate study and contemplation, he came to feel that no external events or pursuits had any ultimate point, so he went into solitary retreat at the hermitage of Gyalnang. Thus a dynamic and sublime knowing born of meditation blossomed in him.

Once, when the great Omniscient One was staying in Drigung, Trulzhik invited him to the Chimpu Uplands, where Longchenpa bestowed the empowerments and gave teachings from the Nyingtik cycles. After he had finished teaching the path of trekchö, Longchenpa passed away into a state of peace. Trulzhik made offerings and honored his guru's remains, and erected outer and inner supports, each of which included a shrine.

His parents then died, one after the other, and he decided to spend the rest of his life meditating in solitude. So he went to the central region of Uru, where he sought a spiritual connection with the great scholar Panchenpa at Ewam.[16] Most notably, he met with Lama Orgyenpa at the mountain hermitage of Lhundrup Ling, pleasing him greatly. He undertook an intensive retreat on the deity Vajravarahi and perceived signs of having received the deity's blessings. The same teacher conferred on him many transmissions of the dharma from the Nyingma and Sarma schools, foremost among them the tradition of the lord of the dharma Longchenpa, [1.128a] as embodied in the empowerments, teachings, oral transmissions, and background material for the Dzogchen approach of the secret Nyingtik cycles.[17]

He then decided to improve his meditation in places where he was unknown, but just as he was setting out for the area around Mount Kailash, his guru ordered him not to go; he therefore spent time meditating in the mountain hermitages of lower central Tibet, Penyul, and other regions. He also established connections with several other holy teachers before returning to Chimpu. There he received from Tsungmé Ösel Rangdrol, also known as Guru Wadrakpa, the entire range of empowerments, teachings, and pith instructions of the secret Nyingtik teachings. He alternated periods during which he received these teachings with periods of intensive practice, relying on this teacher for six years without interruption.

When Gyalsé Tulku was returning from the southern region of Lhodrak, Trulzhik and his students went to meet him and made extensive offerings. On several occasions, Trulzhik received the entire range of teaching cycles from the tradition of the great Omniscient One, such as the two Nyingtik cycles, and trained in the practices of these cycles. The guru was extremely delighted, and their minds merged, becoming one. Drawing from prophecy, Gyalsé confirmed that Trulzhik was the custodian of his teachings, and Trulzhik considered the transmissions he received from this teacher to be the primary source of his lineage.

When his precious teacher Guruwa passed away in the Chimpu Uplands, Trulzhik completed the memorial services following his guru's final wishes. [1.128b] He then devoted himself one-pointedly to practice at numerous isolated places in the mountains, making do with meager food and shabby clothing and cutting off all complicating entanglements in his life. Although he had mastered the avenues of the dharma without making sectarian distinctions, he taught only the tradition of the great Omniscient King of the Dharma. And he taught only to those with faith, commensurate with their individual fortunes. He had countless learned and accomplished students who gained meditative experience on the profound path of practice, among them Shakya Shri of Gyangchen and Sherab Palden of lower Ling. In particular, he entrusted his students, great masters such as Gyalsé Dawa Drakpa and Jatang Drakpa Gyatso, with the task of carrying out his instructions.

He spent the last years of his life at the forest hermitage of Palgyi Naktrö located near a spring on the mountain called Riwoché in the region of Drak. He never wavered in his practice or his teaching of the dharma. Finally, he passed away amid amazing signs. For about two generations afterward, a practice center focusing on this profound path existed on that very spot.

Gyalsé Dawa Drakpa (14th–15th Centuries)

Trulzhik Sherab Gyatso's principal student was Gyalsé Dawa Drakpa. Tulku Drakpa Özer had taken Machik Gyaltsen Bum as his spiritual consort, and she bore two sons. The elder, Nyima Özer, was invited to become the guardian of his father's students in the northern reaches of Uru in central Tibet, [1.129a] and he created great benefit there, both by continuing the family line and by teaching the dharma. The birth of the younger son, Dawa Drakpa, which had been prophesied, took place at Kalden Jampading in Dra. From a very early age, the boy had the obvious attributes of someone holy. At five he knew how to read and write and recite liturgies without any difficulty. From his father, he received the empowerments and teachings of the Dzogchen approach of utter lucidity, as well as other transmissions of the dharma.

At twelve he was ordained as a novice monk at the shedra of Tsetang. Relying on the master Gyalsangpa, he mastered valid cognition, Prajñaparamita, Vinaya, Abhidharma, [1.129b] and the text *Engaging in the Conduct of a Bodhisattva.* At eighteen he took full monastic ordination at Tsalmin from the great abbot Sönam Zangpo and was given the name Lodrö Zangpo.

He studied *The Scriptural Transmission of the Vinaya,* the Lojong teachings, the Six Techniques of Union from the Kalachakra cycle, and the most secret, wrathful form of Hayagriva, as well as many other empowerments, teachings, and oral transmissions. He also received and trained in a vast range of approaches of the dharma from many learned and accomplished masters, including Lozang Drakpa of the Tsang region, Jamyang Kaché, and Khenchen Seng-gé Pal. Through study and contemplation, he cut through his imprecise speculation and gained in stature as an omniscient scholar.

In particular, from Trulzhik Sang-gyé Önpo he received and mastered, like one vase being filled from another, all the empowerments, teachings, and pith instructions of the tradition of the Omniscient King of the Dharma, as exemplified by the mother and child cycles of the Nyingtik teachings. During that time, Trulzhik invested him as his heart son and regent of the ultimate transmission of realization and entrusted him with the responsibility of continuing the lineage. Dawa Drakpa also received the lineage of the terma revealed by Yeshé Rabjam of Shuksep that had been passed down through Gyalsé Lekdenpa.

He cut through his erroneous assumptions with study and contemplation until the age of eighteen, [1.130a] by which time he had opened the doorway to the teachings of *The Heart Drop of the Dakini* for more than two hundred men and women. For many years afterward, he taught the two Nyingtik cycles annually without fail, bringing countless students to spiritual maturity and liberation in the Yoru area of central Tibet. Later on, traveling south to Bhutan, Gyalsé Dawa Drakpa went to the center founded by Tulku Dorjé Seng-gé at Kawachen in the region of Lhodrak. There he taught many of the faithful according to their capacities, among them nine important teachers of that area, satisfying their wish to receive the teachings of the dharma. He spent a year in retreat, meditating at the holy lake of Pema Ling.

He then continued on to Bumthang, Ngenlong, Paro, and other places in Bhutan, where he gave the faithful a great sense of purpose through the activities he undertook to bring benefit and happiness. He spent three years in retreat in the wilderness of Chöjé Drak and founded the meditation center Samten Ling in Bumthang. His students invited him to Kuré Valley and Dung-rang in the east, where he provided an opportunity for them to gather merit. He taught the development of bodhichitta and gave empowerments and teachings according to their wishes. There he was also honored by two rulers from India. [1.130b]

Gyalsé Dawa Drakpa spent long periods practicing intensively in such places as Dza Rinchen Pungpa and Sha-uk Domtsang, focusing assiduously on experiencing the heart essence of being. He had visions of the entire array of his personal meditation deities and experienced the enlightened intent of great perfection—the perception of awareness's naturally manifest appearances without bias—so that he attained a high level of accomplishment.

He journeyed to Zangyak, Drushul, and other places, where he was received with respect by Terchen Ratna Lingpa,[18] Gönrinpa, and other teachers. He bestowed the empowerments, teachings, and pith instructions of the Dzogchen approach on a vast scale. He gradually traveled as far as Mao Chokpo in Tamshul, benefiting many students, before returning to Bumthang.

Gyalsé Dawa Drakpa was extremely learned in all of the sacred dharma in general. He gained a high level of realization through meditation practice and personal experience and was constantly graced with visions of meditation deities. On a number of occasions, many people with the appropriate karma perceived him in the form of Hayagriva. Using his untrammeled psychic power, he foretold events hidden from normal perception, and whenever he taught the dharma, rainbows and many other amazing signs appeared. All of the regions he traveled through or stayed in enjoyed good harvests, [1.131a] an absence of illnesses, and so forth. His activities, bringing benefit and happiness to an enormous number of students, were truly boundless.

In addition to those already mentioned, the students who received the nectar of the sacred dharma from Gyalsé Dawa Drakpa included many famous teachers, such as Panchen Sönam Namgyal of Jamling and the throne holder Sherab Palden of lower Ling. He also brought countless other students to spiritual maturity and liberation, among them those of vast learning, such as Drupchen Kunzang Dorjé (who passed on his personal style of exegesis), Tsungmé Sherab Zangpo, and Lama Tuchenpa. He thus spent forty years working for the welfare of beings, then passed into nirvana on the day of the new moon of the Pig month in a Rat year[19] at Samten Ling. After his remains were cremated, many relics, as well as images of deities such as Vajrayogini, were found in the ashes. Throughout Bhutan and the central region of Tibet, memorial services were held to fulfill his last wishes, and outer and inner supports were erected.

Drupchen Kunzang Dorjé (14th–15th Centuries)

Drupchen Kunzang Dorjé was the main student of the sacred guru Gyalsé Dawa Drakpa. He was born in Menlok, Bhutan, south of Tibet. From an early age, he experienced an uncontrived sense of disenchantment, certain of the falsity of all happiness within conditioned existence. [1.131b] In his moral conduct, he instinctively considered the ineluctable cause and effect of karma when weighing his options. From several holy masters, he received all of the appropriate transmissions of the dharma, including detailed discussions of the results of karma, the vow of refuge, empowerments and permission blessings for meditation deities, and oral transmissions of mantras for recitation. He diligently applied himself to the practice of these, inspiring faith and praise in all who met him.

Kunzang Dorjé first met Gyalsé Dawa Drakpa when the latter came to Bhutan. At that moment, Kunzang Dorjé felt an unshakable, irresistible respect and devotion awaken, and he relied on this teacher for seven years. [1.132a] Like one vase being filled from another, he received from Dawa Drakpa the empowerments, teachings, oral transmissions, and background material for the two Nyingtik cycles of the Dzogchen teachings concerning the unsurpassable secret. He also received the empowerments, teachings, oral transmissions, pith instructions, activity rituals, and practical methods for the tradition of the great Omniscient King of the Dharma, such as the three Yangtik cycles.[20] With great diligence, he gained mastery through contemplation, meditation, and training and became Dawa Drakpa's great regent in the ultimate sense.[21] Encouraged by his guru's instructions, he also spread these teachings to others whenever appropriate.

When the lord of the dharma, the great Gyalsé, passed away, Kunzang Dorjé oversaw the memorial ceremonies and completed all of the activities necessary to fulfill his guru's last wishes. Then, cutting himself off from all distractions—material possessions and ordinary activities—he frequented solitary mountain sites, such as Tarpa Ling and Kujédrak in Bumthang, Taktsang in Paro, and the forest retreat of Khotang. Relying on meager food and simple clothing, he one-pointedly practiced the heart essence of the profound path. To those fortunate seekers of liberation who gathered around him, he bestowed empowerments, teachings, and pith instructions. He never lapsed in these pursuits and so reached the consummate level of meditative experience and realization of the profound way of abiding, thus ensuring his own welfare; by mastering the activity that brought benefit and happiness to his students, he ensured the welfare of others. [1.132b]

Once, Kunzang Dorjé went to central Tibet, visiting the principal holy sites—Lhasa, Samyé, and so forth—and making offerings and prayers of aspiration. In Lhasa he was honored by a large number of his students and patrons from the Yo area, among them the lord of the dharma Kunga Gyaltsen Palzang, Dzogchenpa Sönam Rinchen, and Zhönnu Lodrö of Chang Valley. According to their wishes, he bestowed on them the nectar of the sacred dharma. He ensured enormous benefit for beings, as illustrated by the fact that numerous great teachers such as the lord of the Drigung tradition, Rinchen Puntsok, bowed at his feet and listened to his teachings.

Eventually, he spent most of his time in strict solitary retreat in the wilderness of Bumthang, occasionally bestowing the appropriate empowerments and teachings of this profound path, so that he was continually bringing about the two kinds of benefit. He did this unfailingly for a long time, until he passed away into the peaceful basic space of dharmakaya amid amazing signs. Drupchen Kunzang Dorjé was a contemporary of Tsewang Drakpa, the son of Ratna Lingpa.

Chöjé Kunga Gyaltsen Palzang (1497–1568)

Kunzang Dorjé's main student was the lord of the dharma Kunga Gyaltsen Palzang. He was born in a Female Fire Snake year[22] in Tenchar in the border country of Bhutan, [1.133a] into the clan of the eight brothers of Masang Arwa. At the time of his birth, a spring burst forth from the ground. He later said that his habitual tendencies from previous lifetimes were quite evident. He clearly exhibited the attributes of someone holy—for example, tracing the six-syllable *mani* mantra in rock faces as though they were soft clay.

At the age of fourteen, he went to central Tibet, encouraged by Zhönnu Tsewang of Sordrang, a guru of Lhundrup Chödé Monastery. He was ordained as a novice monk by Chen-nga Chödrak, who gave him the name Kunga Gyaltsen Palzang and cared for him well, both materially and spiritually. [1.133b]

Taking a nonsectarian approach, Kunga Gyaltsen Palzang studied and trained in the various avenues of the dharma, listening to and mastering the teachings of the sutras and tantras as well as secular subjects. He received these teachings from a number of spiritual mentors, such as Lotsawa Rinchen Chögyal of Chag, Rinchen Chöwang of Bumrap, Lochen Chökyong Zangpo, Tulku Dorjé Seng-gé, Chökyi Sherab of Yulgyal, and Chökyi Palwa of Kunzang Ling.

Tashi Gepel, the lord of the dharma from Yulgyal, appointed Kunga Gyaltsen Palzang holder of the seat of Nyidé; later, he also became the head of Lhundrup Chödé Monastery. While engaged in these duties for the sake of beings, he came to feel that his previous accomplishments in studying, meditating, and teaching the dharma had brought him to an experience of the mere shadow of the truth and that he still had not touched the ultimate heart essence. Although discouraged, he felt a powerful resolve to acquire an indwelling confidence concerning the ultimate way of abiding. To that end, he received instructions from Drupchen Kunzang Dorjé, who Kunga Gyaltsen Palzang felt was unrivaled at the time in all the ways of knowing, realizing, and practicing this profound path. From Kunzang Dorjé, he received the empowerments, teachings, and pith instructions of the unsurpassable secret and practiced diligently to gain an abundance of meditative experiences and realization. [1.134a] His respect and devotion for the guru and his instructions matured, and later he received the instructions and auxiliary transmissions for the tradition of the great Omniscient King of the Dharma, Longchenpa, such as the mother and child cycles of *The Heart Drop of the Dakini*. These formed the core of his practice, and his meditative experiences and realization flourished. He became his guru's regent in the ultimate sense, making the explanation and dissemination of the teachings his life's work.

In addition, in ways consistent with the individual interests and intelligence of his students, he taught all avenues of the sacred dharma, as exemplified by the Kangyur.[23] Among his students and spiritual children were his heir, Rinchen Puntsok of the Drigung school; Khenpo Kunlo of Chölung Monastery; Sherab Gyaltsen of Kyitsal; and countless other venerable and learned mentors, major figures in their own right. He also taught many who upheld the teachings of the heart essence, such as Tulku Natsok Rangdrol and Dzogchenpa Sönam Rinchen. Later in his life, Kunga Gyaltsen Palzang made Nenang and Yangpachen his seats. In this and other ways, he spent his seventy-two years engaged in an abundance of enlightened activity to benefit others. He passed into a state of peace in a Male Earth Dragon year.[24] [1.134b]

Tulku Natsok Rangdrol (1494–1571)

Chöjé Kunga Gyaltsen Palzang's main student was Tulku Natsok Rangdrol, the immediate rebirth of Terchen Ratna Lingpa. He was born in a Wood Tiger year[25] at Mentangzhol in the southern Tibetan region of Lhodrak. His father was Tsewang Samdrup and his mother was Orgyen Kyi. As a small child, he demonstrated great faith and compassion, and the attributes of someone holy awakened in him. At the age of seven or eight, he learned to read and write, mastering these skills without difficulty.

At fifteen he was ordained as a novice monk at Lhalung Monastery by Khenchen Tsulpalwa and the preceptor Lhuntrepa. He studied a succession of subjects, including rituals and sadhana practices, sacred dance, and the laying out and drawing of mandalas, and before long he was able to teach others. [1.135a] Following this he asked Kunga Lodrö of Pökhang and Tsulpal of Chölung to act as his abbot and preceptor, respectively, and took full monastic ordination, thoroughly studying and training in the practical methods of monastic discipline.

Over the years, he studied with some sixty holy mentors, among them his abbot and his preceptor; Khedrup Rinchen Zangpo; Terchen Pema Lingpa; Tulku Jangchub Lingpa; and Kunpang Lekpai Sherab. He received the empowerments, teachings, oral transmissions, explanations, and pith instructions of many lineages of the dharma, such as the Kadam, Sakya, Nyingma, Dakpo Kagyü, Shangpa Kagyü, Zhijé, Chö, Jonang, Zhalu, and Bodongpa.[26] It would be difficult to even enumerate the transmissions he received. In particular, with such masters as the peerless Kunga Gyaltsen, Dzogchenpa Kunga Tashi, Lodrö Gyaltsen of Mentsé, Khedrup Mati Dhvaja, and the Jé-ön[27] of Jamding, he studied the tradition of the great Omniscient King of the Dharma with real determination. Through contemplation and meditation, he mastered the entire range of Longchenpa's teachings, including *The Four Higher Collections of the Heart Drop, The Seven Treasuries,* [1.135b] and *The Three Cycles of Being at Ease,* as well as the transmissions for the activity rituals and guardian deities.

He undertook many retreats, spending months and even years at a time one-pointedly practicing the profound yoga of the stages of development and completion, frequenting such solitary retreat places as Sheldrak, Chimpu, Kharchu, and Yangdzong. He reached a level of consummate attainment, gaining an authentic measure of the view, meditation, and fruition of natural great perfection. He was graced with visions of many meditation deities and received their prophecies. Untainted by the bonds of the eight worldly concerns,[28] his enlightened activities arose spontaneously to benefit beings.

In his forty-second year (a Wood Sheep year),[29] Natsok Rangdrol founded the mountain hermitage of Dargyé Chöding. A community grew—more than five hundred people seeking liberation—and he inspired them all to lead their lives according to the dharma. He had a yearly schedule of intensive teaching sessions in the summer and winter, and at all times gave empowerments and teachings in response to individuals' interests. Because of this, many came to have meditative experiences and realization.

He traveled to the central and southwestern regions of Ü and Tsang, to Bhutan in the south, and elsewhere as the guest of those with faith in him, passing on the various avenues of the dharma—sadhana practices, empowerments, teachings, oral transmissions, and pith instructions—to people commensurate with their fortune, so that everyone who made contact with him found the connection meaningful. [1.136a] Among his students in the sacred dharma were many great masters, such as Zhamarpa Könchok Bang[30] and the Drigung Zurpa; holders of personal transmissions of profound termas, including Tulku Jangchub Lingpa, Gargyi Wangpo of Nangtsé,[31] and Dechen Lingpa; many scholars, such as Palding Rabjampa and Palkhang Lotsawa; and many accomplished yogins, including the great master Longyangpa and Kunzang Palbar. In particular, he taught Tendzin Chökyi Gyalpo, his heart son Kunga Drakpa, Paljor Gyaltsen of Shami, and many others who maintained the very essence of his tradition, as well as many secular rulers such as the governors of Yardrok and Chongyé.[32] As well, he benefited many men and women, including monastics, lay tantric practitioners, hermits, and householders. Many of his students, and their students in turn, came to maintain his lineage in the central, southwestern, western, and eastern areas of Tibet, in the southeastern region of Kongpo, and in Bhutan. In this and other ways, this single holder of the Nyingma lineage accomplished tangible results through his widespread activities.

Natsok Rangdrol lived for seventy-seven years in this world, passing away on the twenty-fourth day of the eleventh month in an Iron Horse year[33] [1.136b] near the temple of Tradruk[34] in Yoru, central Tibet. His remains were brought in state to his monastic seat to be venerated and committed to the flames of the funeral pyre. An inner monument containing his death mask and a casket of precious substances, as well as other memorials, were erected on a vast scale in fulfillment of his last wishes, and throughout this time amazing signs manifested.

Tulku Tendzin Drakpa (1536–1597)

Tulku Natsok Rangdrol's main student was Tulku Tendzin Drakpa.[35] He was born in a Fire Monkey year[36] in Ngenlung Genlar, Bhutan, the son of Tashi and his wife, Samten Zangmo. In keeping with prophecies concerning his birth, he was recognized as the tulku of Tertön Pema Lingpa. As soon as he could speak, he clearly described residual memories of his previous lifetimes. [1.137a] At the age of four, he was invited to Bumthang by Pema Lingpa's sons, who paid him great honors at their respective seats. He remained at Pema Ling as heir to one of the sons, Könchok Zangpo, and was ordained there as a novice monk. He spent his time receiving the empowerments, oral transmissions, sadhana practices, and activity rituals of the terma cycles of his former incarnation and training in these practices. Before long, however, the lord of the dharma Könchok Zangpo passed away, so Tendzin Drakpa went to stay for a time at Dechen Ling, the center of Pema Lingpa's son Dawa. There he studied all transmissions of the dharma relevant to his needs.

At fourteen he was invited to Tibet by Tulku Natsok Rangdrol. He visited the principal centers of southern and central Tibet, where he was accorded great honors. He received the entire range of teachings of the dharma, both the sutras and tantras. In particular, Natsok Rangdrol gave him, in the manner of one vase filling another, all of the empowerments, teachings, oral transmissions, pith instructions, and practical methods in the teaching cycles of both the great Omniscient King of the Dharma and the tertön Pema Lingpa. While studying with his guru, Tendzin Drakpa practiced the profound yoga of the stages of development and completion. On the basis of the transmissions he received, he was able to cut through imprecise thinking concerning the meditation, practice, and training he had already carried out. Thus he became a true Dzogchen master, upholding the ultimate lineage. [1.137b]

At twenty Tendzin Drakpa traveled to the southern region of Lhodrak, where all of the students and patrons of his former incarnation bowed to and venerated him. In one case, Drakarwa of Tsoyul offered him his monastery. There he also received appropriate empowerments and oral transmissions from and studied sacred dance with Lama Umdzepa. In Bumthang he requested several empowerments and oral transmissions from Dawa, including an empowerment for a sadhana focusing on the Eight Commands. He was honored by everyone in that region, high and low, and made a meaningful connection with them by teaching the dharma according to their interests.

He then returned to Tibet, where he studied the entire range of Buddhist approaches with many tutors, among them the lord of his buddha family, the great tulku Natsok Rangdrol himself, as well as the great Sakya master Ngakchang Chenpo, Jetsün Drolchok, and Nangtsé Rigdzin. He diligently practiced the profound path in the Chimpu Uplands and other places, and so realized the ultimate meaning of the equally profound way of abiding. He had many visions of his personal meditation deities and received their prophecies.

Then the lord of the dharma Natsok Rangdrol empowered Tendzin Drakpa to succeed him, bequeathing to him his monastery and all of its representations of enlightened form, speech, and mind.[37] After the guru had passed away, [1.138a] Tendzin Drakpa dutifully carried out his guru's last wishes, which included building monuments. In later years, he continued his guru's activities, erecting a number of memorials (such as gold life-sized statues of Guru Rinpoché and his retinue), caring for his students and patrons, leading group retreats, bestowing empowerments, and teaching every summer and winter.

He traveled to the various regions where his students lived—the southern regions, Bhutan, Tsang, and Rong—where he was honored by such figures as Gyalsé Pema

Chögyal and Jangdak Wangpoi Dé, bringing benefit while fulfilling their wishes. He cared for Riksé Pema Trinlé, the second hereditary successor of Pema Lingpa, both spiritually and materially. Following his guru's order to found a monastery on a mountainside near his home valley, Pema Trinlé established the monastic center of Gangteng Sang-ngak Chöling and maintained the teachings there as a continuation of Tendzin Drakpa's enlightened activities.

Tendzin Drakpa invited Do-ngak Tendzin, the rebirth of Tulku Natsok Rangdrol, to his seat in central Tibet. He bestowed on him the entire range of empowerments, oral transmissions, and pith instructions and invested him as a master of the teachings. Not long afterward, at the age of sixty-two, on the twenty-eighth day of the third month in a Female Fire Bird year,[38] Tulku Tendzin Drakpa passed away amid amazing signs at the hermitage of Dargyé Chöding. [1.138b] His immediate rebirth, Sungtrul[39] Tsultrim Dorjé, was appointed to the seat of Lhalung Monastery in Lhodrak by the great fifth Dalai Lama.[40] From that time until the present, there has been an uninterrupted succession of tulkus, all of whom have resided at Lhalung, spreading the teachings of the heart essence throughout the region of Lhodrak in southern Tibet.

Khedrup Do-ngak Tendzin (1576–1628)

Tulku Tendzin Drakpa's principal student was Khedrup Do-ngak Tendzin. He was born in a Male Fire Rat year[41] in the Dol area of Yoru in central Tibet. His father was Dorjé Tsewang of Nyö, and his mother was Sönam Butri. As a young child, he exhibited the attributes of someone holy; [1.139a] for example, he spoke clearly of his past lifetime as the lord Natsok Rangdrol. At the age of six, he was invited to his former incarnation's seat. He mastered the skills of reading, writing, rituals, and spiritual practice without difficulty. When he was eight, he received lay ordination from Zhamar Könchok Bang and was given the name Könchok Özer.

At thirteen he was ordained as a novice monk by the lord of victorious ones Tendzin Drakpa and received the name Do-ngak Tendzin Zangpo. Tendzin Drakpa bestowed on him the entire range of empowerments, oral transmissions, teachings, pith instructions, and practical methods from the collection of teaching cycles given by the great Omniscient King of the Dharma, Longchenpa, and Terchen Pema Lingpa. Thus, due to his realization, he was empowered as Tendzin Drakpa's true regent.

In addition, at various stages in his training, he received a great variety of transmissions of both the Nyingma and Sarma schools from many mentors. These included such masters of the Nyingma school as Kunga Drakpa (the heart son of Natsok Rangdrol), Drupchen Kunga Dorjé, the tantric practitioner Kunga Paljor, Gyalsé

Norbu Wangyal, and Jangdak Wangpoi Dé, as well as the great throne holder of Sakya, the Karmapa,[42] and the Zhamar tulku.[43]

At eighteen Do-ngak Tendzin went to Kyitsal in Sikkim, where with the consummate scholar Bumrampa Tarpa Gyaltsen [1.139b] he studied the main traditions of logic and debate, valid cognition, Madhyamaka, Prajñaparamita, Vinaya, Abhidharma, the three levels of ordination,[44] and fields of secular knowledge. He trained with great perseverance, gaining unanimous recognition at that shedra as one unparalleled in the knowledge of scripture and the powers of reasoning. He also studied such subjects as grammar, poetics, metrics, medicine, and manual arts, mastering these under the tutelage of several siddhas. He thus achieved the status of a scholar.

When he was twenty-five, the ninth Karmapa, who was very impressed with him, summoned him to an audience at his encampment. Do-ngak Tendzin ended up spending three years there, teaching the approaches of sutra and tantra, as well as history and other fields of secular knowledge. He demonstrated unlimited intelligence in his explanations and skill in debate, and so inspired the praise of many wise people.

On various occasions, he traveled between major centers and spent months and years at a time in numerous solitary retreats at places like the Chimpu Uplands, Yama Valley, and Kharchu in Lhodrak, carrying out intensive practice on his meditation deities or one-pointedly pursuing the yoga of natural great perfection. In these and other ways and, through the profound stages of development and completion, [1.140a] he reached a consummate level of meditative experience and realization. He was inspired by visions of Guru Rinpoché, the venerable Tara, and many other meditation deities. He also benefited beings through the samaya substances he consecrated during *drupchen* rituals[45] focusing on guru yoga, the supremely compassionate Avalokiteshvara, the peaceful and wrathful deities, and the Eight Commands. He organized these rituals at principal centers in the southern and central regions of Tibet, as well as at many other places inhabited by the faithful. He gave many empowerments and teachings, both scheduled and extemporaneous.

Many carried on his tradition, including his natural son, Sangdak Chenpo Trinlé Lhundrup;[46] Dzogchen Namkha Drukdra; the ruler Tendzin Chöwang; Chöwang Lhundrup of Paro; Powo Bakha Rigdzin Gyatso; and Mangtö Damchö Zangpo. Those who gathered for his teachings were great teachers of scripture and reasoning, scholars learned in fields of secular knowledge, and yogis and yoginis with meditative experience, who populated every region throughout Ü, Tsang, and Lhodrak, as well as Bhutan. In addition, the hereditary governors of Tibet, the throne holder of Jasa Monastery, Taktsewa of Chongyé, Podrangwa of Yarlung, and others of high family status and great wealth [1.140b] were among the many patrons who honored him with faith. Wherever he chose to bestow empowerments and teachings or to exercise the four kinds of enlightened activity, he fulfilled people's hopes in ways that bore fruit and were meaningful to them.

He increased people's understanding of the moral consequences of their actions by accurately predicting events hidden from ordinary perception. He founded the monastic center of Tsukchen at Tashi Gang in Lhodrak, and at Jangchub Ling, he commissioned some truly marvelous statues of the gurus of the Dzogchen lineage, as well as many paintings of the Buddha and the sixteen elders, the deities of the Nine Classes of Sadhana, the eight manifestations of Guru Rinpoché, and so on. He arranged for the publication of many volumes from the Kangyur and Tengyur, such as *The Scriptural Transmission of the Vinaya.* At the monastic center of Samyé, in Lhasa, and in other places, he made offerings of votive lamps and prayers of aspiration on a number of occasions throughout his life. At many centers for the study and practice of the dharma, he generously offered numerous articles to increase his own merit and deepen his experience of timeless awareness. In these and other ways, he unhesitatingly benefited the teachings and beings to an enormous extent through every kind of appropriate physical, verbal, and mental activity.

In his autobiography, which recounts his life up to his fifty-third and final year, the year of the Male Earth Dragon,[47] he states: [1.141a]

> Especially to the children who hold my lineage,
> I constantly gave many empowerments, oral transmissions, pith instructions, and teachings.
> I established circumstances so that the teachings of the supreme secret would be upheld.
> Now that my tasks are finished, I have no regrets.
> I am Do-ngak Tendzin, who is happy to die.
> I go to dwell forever on the level of primordial being.

At Dargyé Chöding, on the fourth day of the month of Chu, three months after he had left this and other pithy words of advice, the mandala of his emanated form resolved amid amazing signs back into its ultimate nature. His son, the great Sangdak, oversaw the memorial rites of making offerings and erecting outer and inner supports to carry out his last wishes and ensure the continuation of his activity.

Rigdzin Chenpo Trinlé Lhundrup (1611–1662)

Khedrup Do-ngak Tendzin's main student was Rigdzin Chenpo Trinlé Lhundrup. He was born at Jangchub Ling in Lhodrak in a Female Iron Pig year.[48] His father was Dongak Tendzin, a greatly learned and accomplished teacher of the Nyö clan, and his mother was Gödzom Dzema of the Gyal clan. From the moment he could speak, the boy inspired awe in all intelligent people by his entirely spiritual demeanor. At the age of five, he knew how to read and write. [1.141b] At eight he received lay ordination from his lord guru and was given the name Orgyen Tsepel. He studied a series of rituals and sadhanas, and progressed to a study of the root texts and commentaries of Longchenpa's *The Wish-Fulfilling Treasury* and the cycle *Being at Ease in the Nature of Mind,* as well as such subjects as grammar and astrology. He was highly intelligent, and his wisdom deepened.

Notably, from his noble father, he received the entire range of empowerments, teachings, explanations, oral transmissions, and pith instructions of many kama and terma lineages of the supreme secret, including the three practices of guru yoga, Dzogchen, and the supremely compassionate Avalokiteshvara; *The Four Higher Collections of the Heart Drop;* the peaceful and wrathful deities; and the Eight Commands. Through contemplation and meditation, [1.142a] he came to a definitive understanding of these teachings, and absorbed and mastered them thoroughly.

Then, with the passing of the lord of the southern reaches, Trinlé Lhundrup went to live for a time in the monastic community in Lha Valley. He was ordained as a novice monk by Pawo Tsuklak Gyatso. He also received from him the empowerments and oral transmissions for such deity practices as Sarvavid Vairochana, Vajravarahi, and Kalachakra. In addition, he readily learned the sadhanas, the drawing and painting of mandalas, and the ritual dances connected with these deities. He became especially proficient in a vast range of profound subjects pertaining to the sutras and tantras, studying *The Highest Continuum* and *The Profound Inner Meaning.*

He returned home and studied diligently under his father, receiving the empowerments and teachings of the Nyingtik cycles. Thus he thoroughly assimilated a whole range of many profound subjects and proved worthy of having been entrusted with the teachings. Before long, his father passed away into a state of peace at Dargyé Chöding. Trinlé Lhundrup oversaw the final rites in fulfillment of his father's last wishes, such as arranging his funeral and erecting outer and inner supports.

His gurus from the Nyingma school—his noble father foremost among them—included Sungtrul Tsultrim Dorjé, Lochen Zhenpen Dorjé, Lhatsün Namkha Jigmé, [1.142b] the Dzogchen master Namkha Drukdra, Tsultrim Gyaltsen of Bon Valley, and the great Chöying Rangdrol of the Zur clan. His teachers from the Sarma schools included Pawo Tsuklak Gyatso,[49] Gushri Drakpa Chokyang, Naysar Kangyurwa, and Tulku Karma Tensung. He studied the entire range of teachings of sutra and tantra with more than thirty holy mentors, and spent months and years at a time practicing their essential traditions as they were intended, through the key points of the profound stages of development and completion. He was never distracted from ongoing, rigorous practice, and he came to experience directly the enlightened intent of great perfection: the perception of awareness's naturally manifest appearances without bias. He experienced samsara and nirvana as the display of timeless awareness and gained such spiritual mastery that he was graced with visions of numerous meditation deities.

All of his tutors, with the exception of his father, Sungtrul Rinpoché,[50] and the Pawo regent, eventually became his students, partaking of the nectar of his teachings of the dharma and bowing to him with reverence. He also counted among his fortunate students many teachers in their own right, as well as monastics, lay tantric practitioners, great meditators, and householders. Foremost among them were those of high station, whether by birth, by being part of an incarnation lineage, or by learning, such as Palri Tulku Trinlé Namgyal, Lochen Chögyal Tendzin, [1.143a] Dampa Longyang Ösel, and Tripön Ngakchang Chenpo.

Trinlé Lhundrup conferred empowerments, teachings, oral transmissions, and pith instructions on all of his students. In some cases, he was able to bestow without hindrance the teachings of varied and distinct approaches of the dharma on students commensurate with their individual fortunes. In this way, he carried out unparalleled activities as one equal to the highest holders of the teachings of the Early Translation school. Without wavering from the true nature of phenomena—the very essence of being, the way of abiding as a supreme state of equalness—he functioned as a vajra master who had mastered the ten definitive topics[51] and instilled confidence in them in others. When he summoned the blessings of timeless awareness during empowerments, people would have an immediate, direct experience of the ultimate meaning of the empowerment. When he gave lectures, he skillfully guided people on the basis of their individual experiences, introducing them directly to unerring states of realization through this profound path. In this way, many attained a significant degree of meditative experience.

In the perceptions of ordinary people, Trinlé Lhundrup unfailingly brought meaning to and successfully completed all of the four kinds of enlightened activity that he undertook, such as rituals to guard against obstacles and avert calamities. He influenced others in a positive way through, among other things, his rituals of exorcism and blessing, [1.143b] immediately curing those sick from demonic possession, those near death due to paralysis, and those suffering from having been struck dumb, from insanity, or from psychotic episodes. He cured many lepers. There were numerous instances in which, when he performed the transference of consciousness[52] for a person at the moment of death and provided guidance after death, he caused the crown of the corpse's skull to bulge and could predict the circumstances of the subsequent rebirth. Merely by focusing his attention, he could avert frost and hail and prevent epidemics that affected either people or animals. In these and other ways, his mastery answered the needs of individual beings. He did not care about the social status of those supplicating him, making no distinctions based on mundane concerns, but satisfied their expectations just as they wished. Never hoarding his wealth for personal reasons, he used whatever came into his hands for building monuments and creating images of the Three Jewels. Notably, he published hundreds of new editions of teachings from both the kama and terma lineages. He ensured that his offerings and generosity would bring about for those who received them the gathering of the two accumulations of merit and timeless awareness.

In brief, he remained unsullied by the eight worldly concerns, considering dearer than his own life whatever served the teachings and brought happiness to others. With this motivation, he spent his exemplary life involved in the three pursuits of study and teaching, meditation, and spiritual activities [1.144a] in the central and southeastern regions of Tibet and in Bhutan to the south, as well as in the home areas of his students. By carrying out his activities for the benefit of beings impartially, he never wavered from ensuring the spontaneous accomplishment of the two kinds of benefit.

Having thus lived for fifty-two years, on the twenty-second day of the second month in a Water Tiger year,[53] he transferred his consciousness. The crown of his head swelled, and vapor issued forth like incense smoke as the mandala of his emanated form resolved back into the basic space of dharmakaya, utter lucidity. At that time, there were countless amazing signs and occurrences. The regent of his three secrets, Rigdzin Terdak Lingpa, carried out the memorial services and the preservation of his remains.

Terchen Gyurmé Dorjé (Terdak Lingpa) (1646–1714)

Rigdzin Chenpo Trinlé Lhundrup bestowed on Terchen Gyurmé Dorjé the complete range of the tantras, explanatory commentaries, and pith instructions of the sublime secret. Gyurmé Dorjé's father was, in fact, Sangdak Trinlé Lhundrup, and his mother was Lhadzin Yangchen Drolma. He was born on the tenth day of the second month in a Fire Dog year.[54] His birth was marked by inconceivable marvels. In his later life, he could vividly recall that, until the age of three, he was constantly attended by two people: a dark-complexioned yogin with a topknot [1.144b] and a beautiful woman. Even while he was in his mother's lap or playing, as his sacred birthright awakened within him his virtuous nature moved intelligent people to faith.

At the age of four, he received from his noble father the empowerment for *The Complete Secret* (a cycle focusing on the Eight Commands). In all his perceptions and conduct, he applied the principle of the mandala, seeing the central deity as inseparable from his guru and planting the seeds of the four empowerments in his mind. At ten, while receiving the empowerment for *The Gathering of Sugatas,* he had an experience of utter lucidity [1.145a] in which the great Orgyen bestowed empowerment and blessings on him, on the strength of which his spiritual energy waxed. During the vase empowerment, he came to a definitive understanding of the illusory nature of sensory appearances. From that point on, he acted as his noble father's regent and carried out the latter's activities.

As soon as he turned eleven, he received the initial monastic vow from the fifth Dalai Lama, who cut his hair and gave him the name Ngawang Pema Tendzin. The ordination coincided with the arrival of the Kyirong Rangjung Pakpa,[55] which delighted the Dalai Lama. He gave Gyurmé Dorjé much encouragement, observing that the circumstances were highly auspicious. On that occasion, the image was peaceful and smiling, with a charming expression, and Gyurmé Dorjé beheld rays of light emanating from the image's heart, which were absorbed into his own body. At seventeen, when he met the Lord of Victorious Ones[56] at Samyé, he beheld him in the form of Avalokiteshvara. Gyurmé Dorjé not only was treated with the greatest kindness by the fifth Dalai Lama, the sovereign lord of all buddha families, and by his own noble father during their lifetimes, but in later years was also blessed by their embodiments of timeless awareness. He regarded them as the two gurus whose kindness to him had been truly incomparable.

He further relied on sixteen mentors who bestowed profound maturing empowerments and liberating instructions, and thirty-five tutors with whom he studied a wide variety of profound teachings, [1.145b] including the Three Repositories, the four classes of tantra, and fields of secular knowledge. In addition to these general subjects, he studied all of the kama transmissions of the Early Translation school that existed in his day, foremost among these *The Discourse on United Intent*, *The Web of Magical Display*, and the mind teachings. He also studied all of the most well known terma cycles of the three sections of guru yoga, Dzogchen, and the supremely compassionate Avalokiteshvara, as well as the general and specific classes of sadhana practices. Moreover, he received the majority of extant lineages of the maturing empowerments and liberating instructions of the Nyingma and Sarma schools of Vajrayana Buddhism, as well as the oral transmissions for the Kangyur and other sources of these teachings.

Beginning at about the age of thirteen, he memorized the fundamental tantra *The Heart Essence of Secrets*, *The Highest Continuum*, the cycle *Being at Ease in the Nature of Mind*, and the root text of and commentary on *The Wish-Fulfilling Treasury*. He then studied their explanations with his excellent noble father. In particular, he mastered the works of the great Omniscient One Longchenpa, so that the force of his intellect knew no impediment. He thus put to rest all of his speculation regarding the whole range of the teachings of the dharma. Extremely delighted, his noble father entrusted him with the entire collection of tantras and instructions, like one vase filling another, empowering him as the regent of his three secrets and investing him as a master of the ultimate lineage of realization. [1.146a]

Through his meditation, Gyurmé Dorjé gained a direct experience of the yoga of the four visions of spontaneous presence. He supplicated the Omniscient King of the Dharma, Longchenpa, whereupon that great being revealed himself as a monk in the garb of a scholar. At that point, the enlightened intent of great perfection—the perception of awareness's naturally manifest appearances without bias—became evident to Gyurmé Dorjé, and the realization of the ultimate lineage was passed to his mind. A mural on the wall of the meeting hall at Mindroling Monastery depicts this: Gyurmé Dorjé, with the gaze of the dharmakaya and in the garb of a scholar-monk, is smiling and holding a crystal in his hands. On that occasion, he composed *Waves on the Ocean of Enlightened Qualities,* a prayer of praise to the Omniscient One Ngagi Wangpo, Longchenpa:

> Within the expanse (*long*) of the youthful vase body, all-pervasive timeless awareness,
> you reached enlightenment in the supreme (*chen*) and extensive basic space of phenomena,
> for you are a magician who manifests the entire array (*rabjam*) of phenomena in all their variety.
> I supplicate you, sublime and powerful lord of the four kayas.
>
> Because you mastered the realm of omniscience, knowledge of all phenomena,
> there is by nature no limit to your speech (*ngagi*), the enlightened speech of a victorious one.
> O ornament of the human world, powerful lord (*wangpo*) who speaks in boundless ways, [1.146b]
> I supplicate you who see all knowable phenomena.
>
> From the lofty mansion in which the chariot of the sun of the five fields of knowledge displays itself,
> stainless (*drimé*) awareness shines forth as a thousand rays of light (*özer*),
> an illuminating treasure trove that banishes the darkness of opposing opinions.
> I supplicate you, the sun, friend of the lotus of the Sage's teachings.
>
> In the watercourse of the Ganges, flowing from the feet of Vishnu and purifying evil conduct,
> runs the water of discipline (*tsultrim*) endowed with eight qualities,[57]
> rippling with a million waves of amazing intelligence (*lodrö*).
> I supplicate you who embody this uninterrupted flow of enlightened activity.

Treasure house of the gem of stainless intelligence (*lodrö*),
gateway to the freedom that is the wealth of the sublime (*chok*) spiritual approach, endowed (*den*) with richness like that of the golden age,
utterly generous one who bestows excellent explanatory teachings unstintingly—
I supplicate you, treasure trove of lucid intellect that fulfills all wishes.

From the basic space of original purity, the dynamic energy of spontaneously present awareness
emerges as the clouds of samsara and nirvana—the unceasing display in all its variety—
naturally free in the basic space of the sky of self-knowing awareness.
I supplicate you who discovered wholly positive enlightened intent.

From the vajra pinnacle of a hundred suns coalescing
comes the splendor of a massing radiance that has no limit,
leading us into the sky of the Sage's teachings through the power of discriminating analysis.
I supplicate you who lead us to the heart essence of utter clarity. [1.147a]

In the mirror of basic space—the tantra classes of the Categories of Mind, Expanse, and Direct Transmission—
is reflected the visage of the master of the ten powers,[58]
whose lion's roar of stainless scriptural transmission resounds.
I supplicate you, master of the teachings of the sublime spiritual approach.

Through your karma and aspirations, you have a connection
with the victorious one who emerged spontaneously from the bud of a lotus.
You are a lord of the dharma with untrammeled, dynamic power to reveal profound termas.
I supplicate you, sublime guide of those with good fortune.

The thousand-spoked wheel of learning and accomplishment
has given you mastery over the realm of the four continents of the Sage's teachings,
so that inconceivable enlightened activities are spontaneously accomplished.
I supplicate you, vast treasure trove of marvels.

The thick, tangled forest of impure distortions
is incinerated by your insightful awareness, beside which even the fearsome inferno

of apocalyptic fire is reduced to the glow of a firefly.
I supplicate you, venerable and powerful lord of speech.

The lightning bolts of your direct experience and deduction
are evoked by the force of heaven's wrath—the path of awareness—
which completely shatters the rock face of wrong opinions, Buddhist
or not.
I supplicate you, sublime and powerful lord of awareness. [1.147b]

Your special intellect dwells within the heart of the gentle protector
Mañjushri,
casting rays of all possibility on everything knowable without exception,
a perfect mandala of amazing benefit and happiness.
I supplicate you, dancer in the web of magical display.

The illness of the three poisons, compounded by the stains of
nonrecognition of awareness,
is annihilated by the life-giving flow endowed with eight qualities—
Agasta[59] arising in the throat of the three higher trainings.
I supplicate you, great venerable seer.

Surrounded by the wall of a variety of spiritual approaches
are the mountains, continents, and oceans that are the perfection of the
sutras and tantras,
of which you are the universal god, master over the golden wheel of
discriminating intelligence.
I supplicate you, venerable king of the dharma.

A song resonates in the reservoir of your throat,
a strain that becomes an ocean of melodious notes
as lovely as a garland of the jasmine flowers of profound meaning.
I supplicate you, the second Vira[60] who enhances our experience of the
meaning.

The sapphires of your captivating verses
are set in the golden chain of your prosodic expertise,
skillfully crafted as an adornment of the charming maiden of your
discriminating mind.
I supplicate you, venerable one of incomparable intelligence.

The terms applicable to all knowable phenomena [1.148a]
are a garden of the sweet young lilies of definitions,
peerless because the moon of your intelligence causes them to bloom.
I supplicate you, venerable and powerful lord of consummate knowledge.

In the dance of a variety of languages and powers,
you have the amazing radiance of the full bloom of youth,
a glory that captivates the minds of beings throughout the three planes of existence.
I supplicate you, venerable one who brings happiness to all.

The mirror of polished sapphire—your discerning awareness—
reflects a hundred thousand lovely images of what to accept and reject,
so that your speech is unhindered in explaining the outer, inner, and transcendent levels of experience.
I supplicate you, hero who belongs to the family of siddhas.

Issuing from the lake of the nine spiritual approaches,
the four great rivers of the uninterrupted course of excellent explanations[61]
constantly flow to the ocean of the faithful.
I supplicate you, precious treasure of excellent explanations.

The meaning of the final, profound turning of the wheel, the excellent speech of the Buddha,
is that of utter lucidity as the nature of mind, buddha nature.
I supplicate you, who reveal the heart essence of definitive truth
found in the Victorious One's teachings, free of the flaws of affirmation and denial.

In harmony with the enlightened intent of Samantabhadra,
you realized without confusion [1.148b]
the profound definitive truth found in *The Discourse on United Intent* and the Categories of Mind, Expanse, and Direct Transmission.
I supplicate you who completely free the three realms with a fearless lion's roar.

Mounting the stone lion of scriptural transmission and logical reasoning
and wielding the wheel of your fearless confidence,
you annihilate the hordes of barbarians who attack the teachings of Samantabhadra.
I supplicate you, venerable one victorious in all directions.

The wish-fulfilling gem of awareness of the structure of the sutras and tantras
is placed at the pinnacle of the victory banner of the three kinds of pure investigation.

I supplicate the one who beautifies the world
with millions of excellent explanations in his superb compositions.

The bowed heads of arrogant rulers,
proud of their knowledge and influence in this world,
are crushed under the heels of the hero who feels no terror for them.
I supplicate you, venerable and fearless hero.

On the glacier of original purity roams the snow lion of self-knowing
awareness,
in whom the three aspects of dynamic energy are perfect at the point at
which the four visions resolve
and whose roar dredges the pit of the three realms from its depths.
I supplicate you, lion among humans.

Embodying the deeds and teachings of the Sage,
and prophesied by him to be a lord of his teachings,
you are foremost among all who hold his teachings. [1.149a]
I supplicate you, second Lord of Sages.

By the power of these praises, may I and other beings
in all lifetimes enjoy the splendor
of the inexhaustible ocean of your enlightened qualities.
May these praises delight you, so that you take us under your care.

May we understand that your tradition, the unerring, noble path
of victorious ones,
is itself the heart essence of the Sage's teachings,
and with the courage to forsake our bodies and lives,
may we uphold these teachings in theory and in practice.

Let those who uphold them—groups in centers of study and practice,
renunciants,
whoever they are—be engaged in the two areas of spiritual endeavor,[62]
and let the kama lineage, edified by the splendor of conditioned existence
and the peace of nirvana, spread in all directions and times.

Grant your blessings that our buddha nature, obscured by distortions,
may be completely revealed through the Dzogchen path of profound
meaning
and that beings in the three realms may be swiftly freed
within the ground of supreme bliss—dharmakaya, the fruition free of
all flaws.

In addition, from both Chögyal Tendzin, the teacher of Dakpo, and Pema Trinlé of Dodrak, [1.149b] he received the great empowerment for *The Discourse on United Intent*. These two masters gave him the secret name Gyurmé Dorjé.

The following describes how, because of his previous aspirations, Gyurmé Dorjé revealed profound termas that were transmitted to him personally. In Yama Valley of the Samyé region, on the tenth day of the fifth month in a Water Hare year,[63] when he was eighteen years old, he revealed the profound teachings of *The Heart Drop of Masters of Awareness*. On the twenty-second day, in a display of miraculous power, he discovered the cycle *Yamantaka: Vanquisher of the Arrogant* at Sheldrak in Yarlung. When he was thirty-one, in a Fire Dragon year,[64] he revealed a cycle concerning Guru Drakpo and the Vajrasattva Ati cycle at Kardark in O. In his thirty-fifth year, an Iron Monkey year,[65] on the twenty-ninth day of the sixth month, he revealed a terma of enlightened intent[66]—the cycle *The Gathering of Sugatas*—at Dechen Yeshé Kyi Khorlo in Sha-uk Takgo. He revealed these publicly to a crowd of hundreds of Bhutanese and Tibetans.

Throughout his life, Gyurmé Dorjé applied himself to the very essence of spiritual practice at many important hermitages and eventually completed the phases of approach and accomplishment for thirty-five principal mandalas of both the Nyingma and Sarma schools. By focusing on the key points of the stages of development and completion, and due to his subsequent achievement of stability in the development stage, he carried out his enlightened activities without hindrance. [1.150a] Once he had purified the patterns of the subtle channels, subtle energy, and bindu in his central channel, the bliss of timeless awareness blazed constantly for him. He directly experienced the enlightened intent of great perfection—the perception of awareness's naturally manifest appearances without bias—and was immersed in an ongoing state of utter lucidity.

He experienced his perceptions and conduct as a display of timeless awareness, and he was taken under the care of many learned and accomplished masters of India and Tibet, such as Padmakara, Vimalamitra, Humkara, Bairotsana, and Yeshé Tsogyal. He conferred empowerments for many kama and terma teachings, exemplified by his own terma cycles, and widely and freely taught the key points of advice on the spiritual path. He was graced with visions of the entire array of his personal meditation deities, including Vajrakumara, Samyak, and the peaceful and wrathful deities, and received prophecies from them. He had countless pure visions in which he journeyed to pure realms, such as Zangdok Palri in the realm of Chamara, and in which dakinis and protective deities carried out activities for him without impediment. With insight that was free of attachment or hindrance, Gyurmé Dorjé had unobstructed knowledge of the three times, past, present, and future.

From the age of thirty-one, he continually experienced the ultimate meaning of the vase empowerment. This was a time during which he benefited beings primarily through his physical presence, for he traveled to many different regions, [1.150b] planting the seeds of liberation and freedom in the minds of an incredible number of students.

At the age of thirty-two, the ultimate meaning of the secret empowerment arose for him as self-knowing awareness, empty yet lucid. This was a time during which he guided beings primarily with his speech, turning the wheel of the profound and vast dharma without pause.

Starting in the eighth month of a Water Pig year,[67] when he was thirty-eight, Gyurmé Dorjé experienced the four successive degrees of joy intensifying in his experience—the state of ultimate timeless awareness, as exemplified by the bliss of melting found through the "path of the messenger,"[68] the innate unity of awareness and emptiness, supremely blissful, coemergent with being itself, and unchanging. This initiated a time during which he guided beings primarily with his mind, giving whatever profound instructions and advice would bring them to spiritual maturity on the basis of their own experience and leading fortunate ones directly to an encounter with their own true face, naturally occurring timeless awareness.

In these and other ways, he became an embodiment identical to the three vajras of buddhahood. During this time, he carried out his activities on a vast scale, benefiting beings in a balanced, spacious, pervasive, and extensive manner; everything he did was free of the mental distortions of vested interest. With the excellent motivation of ensuring enormous benefit for the teachings and happiness for beings, Gyurmé Dorjé spent his time in completely noble activities, explaining the teachings, practicing, and undertaking spiritual projects. [1.151a] Greater detail can be found in his extensive biographies.[69]

He was particularly concerned with ensuring that the Victorious One's teachings would endure. To this end, he brought together the essential points of the entire range of tantras, explanatory commentaries, and pith instructions, collecting those that were scattered, standardizing those that had been corrupted over time, and clarifying those that were obscure. He thus left a legacy of teachings consisting primarily of empowerment manuals, sadhanas, mandala rituals, and teaching manuals for both the kama and terma transmissions of the unsurpassable approach of the Early Translation school—a great many works that have stood as a tradition to introduce his followers to the path. These works are outlined in an index compiled by his son, Gyalsé Pema Gyurmé Gyatso.

In addition, Gyurmé Dorjé founded Mindroling Monastery, which housed as many as three hundred monks. He commissioned more than five hundred volumes of texts, including the Kangyur written in gold and silver ink, and the hundred thousand main images of the monastery, which brought about liberation upon sight, as well as an untold number of other representations of enlightened form, speech, and mind. He pursued the three cycles of spiritual activity[70] on an enormous scale, ensuring that the victory banner of the precious teachings concerning the definitive secret of the heart essence would remain firmly planted, triumphant in every direction.

Finally, in his sixty-ninth year, during the first month of a Wood Horse year,[71] Gyurmé Dorjé showed slight signs of illness [1.151b] and bestowed advice on his relatives. Henceforth, the melodious sound of *gyalings*[72] came continuously from the west, and a fragrant scent like camphor permeated his entire residence. He rose, saying, "Now I must take seven steps to the east." Having done so, he sat cross-legged and gave what amounted to his last testament:

> Appearances, sounds, and awareness are the spheres of deity, mantra, and dharmakaya,
> the infinite display of the kayas and timeless awareness;
> in the practice of the profound secret of Mahayoga,
> may they be experienced as inseparable, of one taste within the sphere of enlightened mind.

Then, one morning in the following month, he said, "An escort of dakinis has now arrived." Ringing a bell, playing a hand drum, and with a particular gaze, he instantly left for the pure realm of Khechara. Upon his departure, canopies of light, showers of blossoms, earth tremors, and many other amazing signs arose. When his remains were cremated, his heart and skull emerged unscathed. There were numerous relics, as well as hardened droplets of bodily fluids in the form of the guide Amitabha, resplendent and shining. [1.152a] Thus the signs were complete that Gyurmé Dorjé had gained realization through the most sublime spiritual approach, so that his students were moved to faith.

Of the students who tasted the nectar of this lord's teachings, foremost were the fifth Dalai Lama and his regent, Sang-gyé Gyatso[73]—these two, teacher and patron, being like the sun and moon.[74] Gyurmé Dorjé also taught Dodrak Rigdzin Pema Trinlé; the throne holder of Sakya, Kunga Tashi; the Tsedong regents, uncle and nephew; and other great masters, holders of principal and secondary seats. He taught the Gyaltsap of Tsurpu Monastery and Trehor Choktrul, both of the Kamtsang Kagyü school; Könchok Trinlé Zangpo of the Drigung Kagyü; Tendzin Sizhi Namgyal of the Taklung Kagyü; Kunchen Paksam Wangpo of the Drukpa Kagyü; Gampo Choktrul Zangpo Dorjé and his family members; Gyalwa Pakpa Lha of Chamdo; Ngawang Chogi Tulku; Ngawang Kunga Tendzin of Dokham, the elder and younger Tala tulkus; Gyalsé of Katok Monastery; and the second Dzogchen, Gyurmé Tekchok Tendzin. These were some of the great renowned gurus of his time, the majority of whom bowed at his feet. [1.152b] On the inner level, the only heart son of Gyurmé Dorjé was his younger brother, Lochen Dharma Shri. Gyurmé Dorjé's children included Pema Gyurmé Gyatso; his regent, Yizhin Lekdrup; the supremely kind Rinchen Namgyal; and his daughter, Jetsün Mingyur Paldrön. His attendants were Ge-jong Losel Gyatso, Ngak Rabjampa Orgyen Chödrak, Bumrampa Orgyen Kalzang, and others, all of them capable of acting as great pillars of the teachings.

Gyurmé Dorjé's activities in spreading the theory and practice of the teachings were enhanced by the great gatherings of those who studied with him. Not only was this great tertön enormously kind, directly and indirectly, in serving both the Nyingma and Sarma schools, but he also, through his own efforts and his encouragement of others, revivified endangered lineages, such as the Jonang, Shangpa Kagyü, Zhijé, Chö, and Bodong. Most notably, he maintained the theory and practice of the kama transmissions of the Early Translation school of the Nyingma, the legacy left by King Trisong Detsen and his ministers, particularly that of *The Discourse on United Intent, The Web of Magical Display,* and the mind teachings.

From Gyurmé Dorjé came a great many lines of transmission through which the secret Nyingtik teachings spread all over eastern Tibet—through Gyalsé Sönam Detsen of Katok Monastery, Dzogchen Tulku Gyurmé Tekchok Tendzin, and others — [1.153a] but this account describes only the mainstream lineage.

It was from this holy guru that the son of victorious ones Rinchen Namgyal heard the teachings.

Gyalsé Rinchen Namgyal (1694–1758)

In the scriptural transmissions of terma cycles, we find the following statement: "An emanation of Vimalamitra, Ratna Vijaya[75] by name, will appear in the region of Yuru." Fulfilling this prophecy, Rinchen Namgyal was born in a Wood Dog year,[76] the youngest of all the sons and daughters of the great Rigdzin Terdak Lingpa. It was evident that he was the immediate rebirth of a master named Rechen Rigdzin Namgyal. [1.153b] Terdak Lingpa bestowed on him, along with other relatives, his own terma cycles as well as the tantras, explanatory commentaries, and pith instructions of the Dzogchen approach of utter lucidity, transmitting these to him like one vase filling another.

With his uncle, Lotsawa Chöpal Gyatso, Gyalsé Rinchen Namgyal completed his studies of *The Heart Essence of Secrets* and the entire range of sutras, tantras, and other fields of knowledge. He was ordained as a novice monk by Gyurmé Gyatso.[77] He also served Khenchen Tennyi, as well as many other sublime masters such as Dodrak Choktrul Rinpoché.

When the Mongol armies posed an imminent threat to the teachings,[78] his sister, Kunzang Mingyur Paldrön, fled to Khachö Dechen Ling in Sikkim. This noble teacher, Rinchen Namgyal, remained in hiding for a time on the border between Bhutan and Tibet; then, joining a party of monks from eastern Tibet, he traveled east through Tsari and stayed at the monastery of Gojo Khochim. There he engaged in intensive retreat, practicing the sadhanas of peaceful and wrathful aspects of Guru Rinpoché and many of his meditation deities. He received authentic signs of accomplishment and was graced with visions of the entire array of these deities. On occasion, he would exhort them to carry out the wrathful activities [1.154a] of direct, powerful intervention, and they would comply with his wishes. He remained thus for two years, during which time all of the leaders and great gurus of eastern Tibet bowed to and honored him, and his activities increased greatly, on both a spiritual and secular level.

Later, he journeyed to Drakmar Monastery in the Tak Uplands, to other places in the lower elevations of eastern Tibet, and to Rudam Dzogchen Monastery. His activities flourished as he taught and spread the teachings of the dharma extensively. He had many groups of students in such regions as Goser, Nyarong, and Dergé.

It was during this period that the seventh Dalai Lama, Kalzang Gyatso,[79] was installed at the Potala, the great palace of the Lord of the World who guides beings. He issued an emphatic proclamation directing the various peoples of Tibet to continue observing spiritual and secular activities according to their respective customs, as they had in the past. This calmed the great unrest that had occurred in central Tibet.[80] The excellent scholar Rabjam Orgyen Chödrak and others came to Gyalsé Rinchen Namgyal from the latter's monastic seat with the commission to invite him to return. He thus came back to central Tibet and was granted an audience with the Lord of Victorious Ones, Kalzang Gyatso, who confirmed that Rinchen Namgyal would assume the throne formerly occupied by Rinchen Namgyal's father, the king of the dharma Terchen Gyurmé Dorjé. [1.154b] The Dalai Lama made the enthronement official by issuing an edict permitting Gyalsé Rinchen Namgyal to bestow empowerments. Rinchen Namgyal then returned to Mindroling Monastery, where he was established with all honors on the golden throne,[81] and so once again was the rightful lord of the Mindroling tradition of teachings.

In fact, this holy master had already been established as the true throne holder when his father, the great tertön, knew that he himself was close to death. During the year in which Terchen Gyurmé Dorjé was approaching his passage into nirvana,[82] his younger brother, Kunga Tsultrim, had accepted the important task of commissioning both the Kangyur to be written out in gold and an impressive golden cupola to crown the main teaching hall of Mindroling. The latter was built and adorned the hall with beauty; it was duly consecrated, and both projects were brought to a successful completion. At that point, Gyurmé Dorjé had planned an elaborate ceremony investing his youngest son, Rinchen Namgyal, instead of his oldest, as the heir to his lineage. He had said, "Though I have sown a small grain of barley, the portents are great."

At that time, Rinchen Namgyal had beseeched his father, "For the time being, while you are still alive, only you should sit on this throne. Do not let anyone else do so." He had thus tried to refuse the honor, but Gyurmé Dorjé had said to his son,

"You must definitely attend tomorrow's gathering, which will be a celebration to consecrate the improvements to the monastery. I have done well enough until now, but none of you are heeding my wishes. It will be difficult for us, father and son, [1.155a] to be together much longer, so tomorrow, Rinchen Namgyal, you must attend the gathering." The steward, who had already arranged the seating, had asked where he should seat Rinchen Namgyal. Gyurmé Dorjé replied, "Set up a throne with a high seat at the very head of the assembly on the left side of the hall, and there he shall sit." Thus Rinchen Namgyal had been seated and invested with great ceremony as regent of the ultimate lineage of realization, holder of both the family and spiritual lineages of Gyurmé Dorjé.

In keeping with these prophetic events of the past, Rinchen Namgyal now returned and made Mindroling his seat. He repaired the damage inflicted on the meeting hall[83] and both reinstituted the regular rituals that had taken place in the past and inaugurated many new ones. He ensured that the monastic population, which again grew to more than three hundred, was engaged in the three higher trainings and the three cycles of spiritual activity. In addition to reinstating traditions that had waned, he maintained those instituted by his paternal ancestors—sadhana rituals of the kama and terma teachings observed on the tenth day of the lunar month—as well as the monastery's own traditions of chanting, ritual music, sacred dance, and so forth. He was thus extremely effective in serving the teachings.

The powerful ruler [1.155b] Mawang Sönam Tobgyal, who served Rinchen Namgyal with faith and devotion, appointed him royal tutor. At Mindroling, Rinchen Namgyal followed the examples set by his noble father and the former throne holders, spreading the teachings and passing on all the lineages of empowerments, oral transmissions, and teaching methods, with emphasis on the exegeses of the tantra *The Heart Essence of Secrets.*

At appropriate intervals, he devoted himself to the very essence of spiritual practice and was guided by the entire array of his personal meditation deities. He directly experienced the enlightened intent of the great perfection of utter lucidity: the perception of awareness's naturally manifest appearances without bias. He took a spiritual consort, who bore him two sons—one of whom was Khenchen Oddiyana—and became a pivotal figure in spreading the teachings. By preserving tradition and in other extensive ways, Rinchen Namgyal benefited beings greatly. He also installed his sister, Kunzang Mingyur Paldrön, at the monastic seat. Moreover, he wrote a number of teaching manuals and other works, such as instruction manuals for the mother and child cycles of the Nyingtik teachings, and bestowed empowerments, teachings, and spiritual advice. Under his guidance, Chung-ré Pema Longyang and many of his other students, both local and from afar, developed their ability to benefit others. In these and other ways, he caused the monastic seat to flourish.

In brief, there were no lineages of empowerments, oral transmissions, or instructions in the Mindroling tradition that were not entrusted to this great throne holder Vijaya. [1.156a] From the highlands of the central and southern regions to the lower steppes of eastern Tibet, China, and Mongolia, he transmitted the dharma to all of the monasteries and centers associated with the Mindroling tradition. His service to the teachings was thus extensive. The fact that all of the kama and terma transmissions of the Mindroling tradition are extant today is due to the enlightened activities of this sublime being. This accounts for his fame as the "supremely kind Rinchen Namgyal, who maintained the tradition of Mindroling."

Having accomplished these activities to ensure the two kinds of benefit in many excellent ways, Rinchen Namgyal, at the age of sixty-five, in a Male Earth Tiger year,[84] made the decision to journey to Olka in the east. He performed ceremonies for the longevity of his descendants and composed his last will and testament. On the twentieth day of the third month of Nak, in the midst of an inconceivable array of miraculous events, his emanated form resolved back into the utterly lucid basic space of dharmakaya. His remains were brought back in state to his monastic seat and cremated. His skull and heart were not consumed by the flames and were recovered by onlookers as objects of faith. There were marvelous relics, and a stupa of enlightenment formed of quicksilver was found inside the cranium. [1.156b] The stupa was preserved at Sang-ngak Podrang, the central meeting hall of Mindroling Monastery.

It was from this holy guru, Rinchen Namgyal, that Ngak Rabjampa Orgyen Chödrak heard the teachings.

Ngak Rabjampa Orgyen Chödrak (1676–?)

Orgyen Chödrak was born into a wealthy Buddhist family in the region of Dra. When Terchen Rinpoché founded Mindroling Monastery, in accordance with the edict of the great fifth Dalai Lama this noble child was chosen from among the conscripts from Dra to enter monastic life. He began with lessons in reading and writing, and passed his examinations up to the third level. In addition, in due time, he learned ritual dance, painting, chanting, music, [1.157a] the sculpting of torma offerings, and so forth. Among the many youths from Dra, he became foremost in learning.

From about the age of ten, with a large group of boys his own age, he was ordained as a novice monk by Lochen Dharma Shri. Terchen Rinpoché Gyurmé Dorjé, who had the ability to make prophecies, told his two younger brothers, Gyalsé Tennyi and Lochen, "This boy Chödrak will someday benefit our teachings. You should do your best to teach and train him in the ordinary and extraordinary fields of knowledge."

Thus Orgyen Chödrak assiduously pursued his studies and contemplations, primarily with Terchen Rinpoché, Lochen, and Mingyur Paldrön, but also with the great Dodrak Rigdzin and many other learned and accomplished masters. In his twenty-first year, with Lochen Rinpoché acting as his abbot, Orgyen Chödrak received final monastic ordination. Becoming both venerable and learned, he figured significantly in the lineage of transmission of the monastic vows of Mindroling Monastery. He received insightful explanations of and teachings on Vinaya, Prajñaparamita, *The Treasury of Abhidharma,* and other works. [1.157b] Most notably, Terchen Rinpoché brought him to spiritual maturity through the empowerments for the cycles of kama teachings in general and that of the peaceful and wrathful deities of the tantra *The Web of Magical Display* in particular.

Under Lochen he resolved his doubts by studying and contemplating the explanations of the tantra *The Heart Essence of Secrets, The Garland of Views* of the great master Padmakara, Indian commentaries like Buddhaguhya's *Graduated Path,* and the many Tibetan commentaries, such as those by Drol, Yung, Rongzom, and Longchenpa. During his examination on *The Heart Essence of Secrets* before the great assembly of Mindroling, he thoroughly impressed the holy elders with his superb explanation of both the words of the text and their underlying meaning, unsullied by any fault or distortion. This greatly delighted both Terchen and his brother. The title Ngakyi Rabjampa[85] was conferred on him, and he was elevated to the position of both vajra master and head abbot of the monastery. He thus became an exemplary lineage holder.

Given that Gyalsé Rinchen Namgyal was truly Terchen Rinpoché's regent, heir to both his family and spiritual lines, Orgyen Chödrak studied with him, receiving once more all of the empowerments, teachings, and instructions he had previously received, [1.158a] in particular, the tantras, explanatory commentaries, and pith instructions of the Nyingtik cycles of the Dzogchen approach of utter lucidity. Whenever appropriate, he gave himself entirely to the practice of meditation, including the phases of approach and accomplishment for the Three Roots. His level of spiritual attainment was thus very high, so that he directly experienced the enlightened intent of the ultimate lineage. For fifteen years, he concentrated on the detailed teachings of *The Heart Essence of Secrets* in the company of Lochen, while also teaching the dharma to others in the monastery. He wrote *Notes on the Lectures of Chödrak,* an amazing general commentary on *The Heart Essence of Secrets.*

In that Orgyen Chödrak bore primary responsibility for protecting Mindroling from ruin during the period of the Dzungar Mongol desecration, his service to the teachings was exceedingly great. In the upper and lower regions of far eastern Tibet, the central region, and other areas, there was not one shedra or center of his tradition that he did not visit, and as the archives of these places clearly attest, he turned the wheel of the dharma of both sutra and tantra traditions on a vast scale, extending benefit to beings throughout space. At a certain point after Orgyen Chödrak had ensured the spontaneous accomplishment of the two kinds of benefit, the display of his emanated form resolved back into the inner basic space of primordial being. [1.158b]

Many sublime individuals who were among his heart sons and students, and who held the realization of the ultimate lineage, such as Rabjam Gyurmé Chöden and Drupwang Shrinatha, appeared everywhere in eastern and central Tibet. Although Orgyen Chödrak had studied with the brothers Terchen and Lochen, he also studied with Rinchen Namgyal, from whom he is considered to have received the transmission of the lineage. This is similar to the fact that Trulzhik Sang-gyé Önpo considered Guru Drakpa Özer to be the one prophesied to carry on the lineage. Some archival records have erroneously omitted Orgyen Chödrak's name; however, we must take as the authority *The Earrings of Sun and Moon,* the record of teachings Jigmé Lingpa received, which is found in the Dergé edition[86] of that master's collected works.

It was from this holy guru, Orgyen Chödrak, that Ngakyi Rabjampa Orgyen Palgön, also known as Drupwang Shrinatha, received in their entirety the tantras, explanatory commentaries, and pith instructions of the sublime secret, like one vase being filled from another.

Ngakyi Rabjampa Orgyen Palgön (Drupwang Shrinatha) (18th Century)

Orgyen Palgön was born amid amazing signs in central Tibet. He was related to Rigdzin Jigmé Lingpa and, from an early age, effortlessly exhibited the attributes of someone holy. [1.159a] He learned to read and write without any difficulty and possessed the wisdom of one who has consciously taken rebirth. In time, he was accepted at the great monastic center of Mindroling, where he studied at the feet of both the throne holder and the head abbot,[87] as well as Rabjam Gyurmé Chöden and the many other great masters then in residence.

He studied the cycles of recently discovered termas of the Mindroling tradition, the kama transmissions of the Early Translation school, the explanatory treatises concerning *The Heart Essence of Secrets,* the commentary on the three levels of ordination entitled *The Wish-Fulfilling Frond, The Oral Transmission of the Lord of Secrets, The Ornament of Enlightened Intent,* [1.159b] and other texts. After he took his examinations, he was given the title Ngakyi Rabjampa and became known as Rabjam Orgyen Palgön. He chose to maintain the discipline of a fully ordained monk in that lifetime, a "vajra holder in saffron robes."[88]

He spent many years studying with Ngak-rampa Orgyen Chödrak, receiving in their entirety all of the lineages handed down by Terdak Lingpa and his sons: tantras, explanatory commentaries, and pith instructions concerning the secret Nyingtik cycles of the Dzogchen approach. Practicing the key points of these, he attained remarkable realization. He was impeccable in his conduct, erudite, venerable, and noble. He left a great legacy through his teaching of the dharma in the shedras and centers throughout upper, middle, and lower Tibet. After Rabjam Orgyen Chödrak, this master was the most accomplished scholar of Mindroling.

In retreat he applied himself to intensive practice on the phases of approach and accomplishment for Yamantaka, *The Gathering of Sugatas* (a cycle focusing on the Eight Commands), and other cycles, training in the key points, so that signs of accomplishment became evident. He had visions of his meditation deities and became a great lord of siddhas, [1.160a] easily attaining the two kinds of siddhis.

Orgyen Palgön traveled throughout central Tibet to Drachi, Dranang, Samyé, and other places. He benefited beings extensively by turning the wheel of the dharma, emphasizing the glorious *Heart Essence of Secrets*. He remained under the care of his gurus and personal meditation deities, and was a great lord of siddhas, attaining the level of a master of awareness. Jigmé Lingpa said of him, "I recognized that he was an accomplished master of Yamantaka and the Eight Commands cycle *The Gathering of Sugatas,* and so received profound teachings from him: the empowerments, oral transmissions, and pith instructions of the secret Nyingtik teachings."

The most significant of this teacher's enlightened activities was offering the great Rigdzin Jigmé Lingpa the profound and secret Nyingtik teachings of utter lucidity, an uninterrupted transmission of the definitive pith instructions of India and Tibet. As the guru Pema Duddul of Nyarong pointed out:

> From a single snow lioness came a single cub, unsullied by the slightest flaw.
> From a single watchdog came nine puppies, but I have not seen many enlightened qualities in them.

This meant that rather than gathering tens of thousands of shallow students, [1.160b] Orgyen Palgön ensured great benefit for beings by serving, in this one definitive way, the very life force of the special teachings concerning the heart essence of utter lucidity. His consummate deeds and activities moved countless fortunate students to wonder and faith.

At a certain point, Orgyen Palgön's enlightened intent resolved back into the supreme, inner basic space of primordial being, just as it is. An extensive biography of this guru has never existed. This account is derived from the biography of Jigmé Lingpa and the records of teachings he received, as well as from the supplications to the lineage by those who transmitted the monastic vows of individual liberation according to the Mindroling tradition. In addition, I have embellished this rendition with facts gleaned from the oral tradition, making it a supplement to the accounts of the lineage. If a reliable biography is ever found, I ask those who hold the dharma in their esteem to make it available.

It was from this holy guru that Rigdzin Jigmé Lingpa heard the teachings.

Rigdzin Jigmé Lingpa (1730–1798)

By this time,[89] the teachings of the Dzogchen approach of utter lucidity had become somewhat adulterated by intellectual speculation. So once again there appeared an illusory display of the timeless awareness of the Indian mahasiddha Mañjushrimitra, the Tibetan king Tsangpa Lhai Metok, the Omniscient One Drimé Özer, and others. [1.161a] That is to say, the great Rigdzin Jigmé Lingpa consciously took rebirth in this world of conditioned existence as the universal monarch of all the siddhas and tertöns in Tibet. This great being was born at a sacred place in Yoru, with amazing portents attending his birth, fulfilling the vajra prophecies of the great and glorious Orgyen, who repeatedly foretold his coming in glowing terms in many termas. One of these, *The United Intent of the Gurus,* states:

> Knower of all that can be known, treasure trove of affectionate concern
> for beings,
> emanation of Drimé Özer, treasury of the termas of enlightened mind,
> yogin of space, the vast expanse of utter lucidity:
> I supplicate the venerable Jigmé Lingpa. [1.161b]

Before he was twenty, Jigmé Lingpa entered the shedra at Palri Tekchok Ling. He lived as an ordinary monk, studying basic grammar and poetics. Then he began to follow the Vajrayana path of maturing empowerments and liberating instructions with his lord guru—Tukchok Tsal—and others, receiving cycles such as *The Heart Drop of Freedom: The Natural Freedom of Enlightened Intent,* a teaching of Trengpo Terchen Sherab Özer. In all, he spent twelve years devoting himself entirely to practice.

In particular, he studied the works of the Omniscient One Longchenpa, the second Buddha, laying the foundations of a firm devotion for and faith in one he considered to be an awakened buddha. Jigmé Lingpa then spent three years practicing at the cave of Sangchen Metok Puk in Palgyi Naktrö in the Chimpu Uplands, where he was taken under the care of the timeless awareness embodiments of both the great master Longchenpa and the great and glorious master of Oddiyana. He received their legacy, that of superhuman teachers demonstrating the natural manifestation of sensory appearances, and the blockages were freed in the subtle energy channels within the *sambhoga chakra* in his throat. The intent underlying the vast reservoir of termas of enlightened mind welled up in him, such that he gave voice to genuine vajra songs. These and other events are clearly set forth in detail in his extensive biography.

To supplement the present history, the following narrative is adapted from Jigmé Lingpa's two personal accounts of his visionary experiences, *Secret Conversations with the Dakini* [1.162a] and *The Moon Dancing on Water:*

Once, while pursuing my spiritual practice at Shri Parvatai Ling, I had a pure vision of utter lucidity in which I beheld the Indian masters Mañjushrimitra and Humkara. They granted me the realization that is the ultimate lineage, so that I experienced the infiniteness of indestructible basic space, the unity of awareness and emptiness. At another time, I had a vision of a deity, who predicted, "With the Guru inseparable from the meditation deity, there is no doubt that the son will inherit the father's wealth." This was a premonition of the profound termas I would later reveal.

In a dream one evening, again a visionary state of utter lucidity, I mounted a white snow lioness and journeyed to the stupa of Boudhanath in Nepal. There a dharmakaya dakini of timeless awareness came to me and entrusted me with a flattened urn made of wood, shaped like a locket, its edges sealed with resin. She said:

> In the perceptions of your pure retinue, you are Trisong Detsen.
> In the perceptions of impure students, you are Seng-gé Repa.
> The treasury of Samantabhadra's enlightened mind—
> symbol of the vast expanse of Padma, master of awareness—
> is the great secret treasury of the dakinis. [1.162b]
> The sign dissolves.

Then she vanished into nothingness, and my perceptions became vague and indistinct. Thereupon I felt an upsurge of great enthusiasm.

I broke open the wooden urn, out of which rolled five scrolls of yellow paper and seven clear crystals the size of peas, clattering as they fell. I eagerly seized the largest scroll and opened it. An incredible fragrance of fine medicinal plants like camphor wafted forth, and my head and body tingled all over. I had the sudden fleeting thought, "The lord of this terma is Rahula, so the command is a very strict one," and my mind whirled at the thought. Unrolling the scroll further, I realized that what looked on the surface like plans for a stupa was actually the secret symbolic script of the dakinis filling the scroll from top to bottom, unfathomable to the ordinary, rational mind. Unable to decipher this, I began to roll the scroll back up, whereupon the drawing of the stupa vanished like an optical illusion. The symbolic script changed completely into Tibetan and proved to be a cycle of sadhana practice of Avalokiteshvara, the deity of supreme compassion. I put off reading it further, but questions arose in my mind: "Who is to receive this transmission? [1.163a] On whom has the seal of entrustment been conferred? Whose tulku am I?" Examining the end of the document, I could clearly see the line, "This advice is given as a personal gift to the Buddhist king and his son.༔" I also read the additional comments, and in the next instant, all the words and their underlying meaning were as clear in my mind as images reflected in a mirror. Finally, I experienced an ineffable state, as though I no longer knew how to read.

With immeasurable joy and enthusiasm, I placed one of the clear crystals in my mouth, picked up the scrolls, and prepared to go home. Suddenly a monk with a smiling countenance appeared and said, "For a long time, I have thought that something like this would befall you." With this, he caused me to have an incomparable vision, and I recognized that he was the great seer Rahula, the guardian deity of these teachings.

Then I came to the northern portion of the path encircling the stupa. I opened another scroll and found the text *The Casket of Enlightened Mind: A Record of Key Points*. My mind became extremely lucid, and irresistible supreme bliss blazed in me. As I thought to myself, "This is none other than that which brings liberation upon sight; I must show it to my mother," [1.163b] a woman graced with ornaments, whom I took to be my mother, suddenly appeared in the sky. (It was she who later came to me at the Chimpu Uplands in the region of Samyé and unraveled the mystery of these teachings.)

I showed her the text and said, "Gaze on that which brings liberation upon sight."

She replied, "In showing me this, which is to be kept secret, there is a real danger that you are being impetuous. There is no need of liberation upon sight. Eat these, for they also bring liberation upon taste." She made me eat all of the crystals and scrolls, and as I swallowed them, I felt an immeasurable sense of amazement, as though all the words and their underlying meaning were stamped on my mind. At that very moment, I awakened from the visionary experience, my awareness completely immersed in the supreme unity of bliss and emptiness.

In *The Moon Dancing on Water,* I have clearly recorded the instances during which I experienced pure visions on a vast scale—for example, while asleep I remained completely immersed in a continual state of utter lucidity—as well as stories of my other lifetimes. I showed this account to my lord guru, Tukchok Tsal, seeking his opinion. The guru said, "There is no doubt that you have received a personal transmission from the lineage of accomplished masters of self-knowing awareness, and regardless of whether this is a terma text received in a personal transmission or a terma of enlightened intent, incalculable doorways to the dharma have been opened. [1.164a] However, it is crucial that you keep this secret from others." For the time being, I applied a seal of secrecy to this transmission.

Later, I spent three years at the cave of Sangchen Metok Puk pursuing the very essence of spiritual practice. At a certain point, I had a pure vision of utter lucidity. I beheld the one known as the "glorious man of Samyé Monastery"—the Omniscient One Ngagi Wangpo, Longchenpa, an emanation, in deceptively ordinary human form, of the sugata Rirap Marmei Gyaltsen. He was adorned with the three robes of a monk[90] and seemed somewhat middle-aged, but I felt it entirely appropriate to regard him as a tathagata. Beholding his form was like seeing an optical illusion.

I clearly heard him chant aloud, "May the mind of enlightenment—the ultimate reality that the teachings describe—be passed to you. May it be passed to you. May the lineage of words that describe that ultimate reality be perfected. May it be perfected."

Such irresistible faith and devotion arose in me that I felt I would faint. Without taking the time to prostrate, I suddenly seized the Omniscient Guru's hands and placed them like a crown on the chakra of supreme bliss at the top of my head. [1.164b] I cried out, praying until I thought I would swoon with devotion, "Omniscient King of the Dharma, you know all! Omniscient King of the Dharma, you know all! Omniscient King of the Dharma, you know all!"

I heard the guru say, "Only after my lifetime would someone say such words to me." He seemed to be lamenting the situation that he described in his *Flower Garland: An Open Letter to the Community from Eastern Tibet* and other works; he had found it disheartening that, while he was physically present in this world, people of little merit who had neither faith in nor devotion for him attempted to thwart him.

I humbly responded, "Recalling the grace with which you have benefited the teachings and beings solely through works such as your *Seven Treasuries* and the termas of enlightened intent of the Nyingtik cycles, I feel a firm and enduring devotion for you, whose greatness equals that of an actual buddha."

He turned his steady gaze on me and said, "O child of spiritual heritage, due to the aspirations that you have just formulated, I have applied the seal of entrustment and passed the enlightened intent of the ultimate lineage to you. Make a firm fortress of your practice, and teach fortunate people on a vast scale. Your song has been most excellent." [1.165a]

At that moment, it occurred to me to ask for a teaching, but my vision of the three kayas resolved into basic space like an optical illusion. I retained an unbearably powerful memory of the Omniscient Guru.

> I, the mendicant, this venerable beggar who frequents caves among
> the rocks,

have not grown old dwelling in solitude,
so one would think it impossible for me to have experienced the awakening of such realization.
Although arrogant, self-important people may mock me,
I have beheld the face of Longsel Drimé,
who is Padma, son of victorious ones, in the guise of a spiritual mentor.
Simply having seen him has eradicated habit patterns, the effects of harmful actions, and obscurations.
Merely having heard him has caused the vast expanse of realization to well forth.
Although I have not trained in conventional spiritual teachings,
by merely looking at texts I am aware of the secret key points of advice.
I think of the guru, aware of his grace, which transformed an ordinary being into a buddha in a single day.
On the outer level, he is the lord Humchen, the flawless tamer of beings;
on the inner level, he is the Singhalese master Mañjushri;
on the secret level, he is Longchenpa, an embodiment of timeless awareness.
He granted me the ultimate lineage through the interdependence of many skillful symbols.
Ephemeral visions are fleeting, like lightning in the sky. [1.165b]
Even evil people who uphold extreme views can leave their footprints in rocks.
Since meditative experiences and realization do not appear to our ordinary senses,
what would be the point of speaking to others of something permanent, stable, and unchanging?
This was the first blessing I received, that of his enlightened form.

In older accounts of sacred places, the site where I had this vision was called "Nyang's upper cave," referring to the fact that it was the cave—actually a cavity with an overhanging ledge—in which Nyang Tingdzin Zangpo practiced. Nowadays, to the right of the mouth of the cave, white willows grow out of crevices in the rock face, and on the rock are three carvings of stupas. The foregoing events took place while I was staying there, with only a curtain of woven thatch to protect me from the wind. Because this site had come to be conventionally designated "Nyang's lower cave," writers in the past attributed the name "Nyang's cave" to a cave south of this one, used in later times. But the authenticity of the clear vision I have described gave me the certainty to identify my cave—the one known as "Nyang's lower cave"—as the cave used for spiritual practice, first by the Buddhist king Tsangpa Lhai Metok and later by his minister, Nyang. It was in this place, which I call Sangchen Metok Puk, that I undertook this very strict retreat.

During that time, my mind was filled with the firm resolve to find release from samsara. My subjective experience of phenomena as seemingly solid objects was undermined, [1.166a] and in the face of that, at a certain point I encountered the Omniscient One Longchenpa, the second Buddha. He handed me a text, saying, "This clarifies all of the most obscure topics presented in my work *The Supreme Chariot*." In addition, he explained the symbols of the supreme treasury of secrets.[91]

Then he handed me a scroll, saying, "This is a record of your successive rebirths." When I opened it, there seemed to be two lines of writing. The upper line read, "In a previous lifetime, you were the Omniscient King of the Dharma." As I began to read the lower line, the clear vision passed like a cloud fading in the sky. All the while, I had no conscious impression that Longchenpa's body had a particular shape. This was my second vision, in which I received the blessings of his enlightened speech and permission to write treatises.

Then, after several months had passed, I once again beheld the Omniscient Guru, dressed as a scholar, with a smiling countenance, his form youthful, like that of someone in his twenties. He wore a scholar's cap with long ear flaps, which were like silken banners hanging from the two pediments of a mansion— [1.166b] his superb body mandala with its vajra mind-body aggregates. He used the flaps to empower me with the symbolic signs of spontaneous presence, the primordial union of masculine and feminine buddhas of the five families. He bestowed on me the empowerment into utter lucidity as a vast array of purity.

Without saying a word, he smiled at me with great delight, whereupon this manifestation of supremely pure timeless awareness dissolved into basic space. This was my third vision, in which I received the blessings of his enlightened mind and permission to be a master who had realized the ultimate lineage.

Jigmé Lingpa then composed the following prayer of praise, *The Queen of Spring's Far-Reaching Song*, using the conventions of formal poetry to praise Longchenpa in reference to the five great fields of knowledge:[92]

Homage to Mañjushrighosha!

O Longchenpa, primordial protector, yours is the vajra realm—the thorough pacification of all elaboration, sublimely unchanging and imbued with six special attributes.
Emptiness, endowed with the four modes of complete liberation, was profoundly aroused for the sake of those to be guided, by the charming goddess of supremely blissful compassion.
Many fortunate eons in the past, in the pure realm of the supreme manifestation
of the ground of being, endowed with the five aspects of excellence,
you awakened to buddhahood as Rirap Marmei Gyalsten, you, king of the dharma, Longchenpa.

O protector, although in times past, beyond any finite time frame,
you perfected all aspects of renunciation and realization, [1.167a]
with your supremely compassionate concern you cannot bear the suffering of those to be guided,
and so, in their perceptions, you have come and gone in all of your successive lifetimes.

O Longchenpa, you are a dancer who emanated like a lotus, newly formed, from the fresh shoot of compassion
that was the lord Trisong, who dispelled the darkness of the three realms with his spiritual and temporal power, like the light of the sun and moon.
When the cycle of your allotted time came to a close and your dance was ending,
you were empowered and extolled as a master of the Nyingtik teachings by the naturally occurring master Padma.

O Longchenpa, with the beating of the secret drum of summer thunder, truly proclaiming that you were a master of awareness with power over longevity,
you were a dancer who emanated from the basic space of emptiness, falling like a gentle rain as Rinchen Tsultrim Dorjé.
At that time, you were Pema Ledrel Tsal, master of the ultimate lineage of ground, path, and fruition, who could cause the bud of a terma—*The Heart Drop of the Dakini*—to blossom.

O Longchenpa, from the hatching of the egg of the fivefold transmission
issuing from the womb of the peahen—the tantra *The Reverberation of Sound*—came four divisions.

You were reborn in the region of Yorpo, nurtured in the bosom of the family of Dromtön and Chokyang.[93]
When the power of the harbinger of death was exhausted, [1.167b] on the tenth day of the second lunar month of the year of Jupiter in the fifth sexagesimal cycle,[94]
you took rebirth, spreading your wings, the signs of your virtuous nature rivaling those of the Sage, the sublime nirmanakaya.

O Longchenpa, on that occasion, Remati, powerful mistress of the desire realm,
stretched out her hand and vanquished the petty forces of evil.
You were unrivaled in your consummate wisdom
and powerful compassion gained throughout lifetimes.

O Longchenpa, from your youth, familiar with the Vajrayana approach and proficient in upholding, defining, and translating its teachings,
you focused your mind by training in the discipline of the Three Repositories, which are the very foundation of the teachings.
With the passage of the sun and moon—the two levels of truth united—through the twelve mansions of the enlightened qualities that you developed,
you directly experienced the renunciation and realization of the five paths and ten levels, which transformed you for all time.

O Longchenpa, you studied Kapala, Chandragomin, Panini, Sarasvata, and the rest,[95]
imbibing the distilled essence of their exhaustive treatises of grammar, thorough explanations of Sanskrit,
singing your far-reaching song of syntax—the root words and case endings—
in the science of grammar.

O Longchenpa, with the principles of debate—direct perception and deductive reasoning, contradictions and connections, argumentation and examination—
you used the lion's adroitness
to shatter the preconceptions of the elephants who speak falsely,
for you are one who demonstrates correct reasoning. [1.168a]

O Longchenpa, you are the powerful lord of the earth, skilled in the arts of painting deities, building temples, and so forth.
Your thousand eyes are open with the inner knowledge of the Three Repositories and the profound meaning of the secret mantra approach.

You play in the pleasure grove of the eight sciences of examining the qualities
of men, women, wood, bodies of water, cloth, jewels, horses, and elephants.[96]

O Longchenpa, when the seeds of ignorance, which is the source of the twelve links of interdependence,
sprout into the young seedlings of the three poisons, and the branches and leaves of illnesses grow,
the nectar of your skillful diagnosis and application of medicine cut through the pain,
for you are the second Yutok.[97]

O Longchenpa, while you were studying the ten fields of knowledge,
you engaged in the yoga of illusion, the unity of lucidity and emptiness,
and Achala, Sarasvati, Mañjushri, and others appeared to you in visions
and made prophecies.

O Longchenpa, in the basic space of *E*,[98] the forest grove of sublime knowing, is the syllable *Vam,* the new pavilion of the unity of bliss and lucidity.
Within this, total purity is ensured as the dance of a thousand patterns, a transforming array that waxes and wanes. [1.168b]
You behold the passage of the four seasons through the play of the seers embodying the twelve mansions of the sun, spread out across the vault of the heavens.
The three dimensions of *The Kalachakra Tantra*—outer, inner, and transcendent[99]—merged in one taste within the sphere of your enlightened mind.

O Longchenpa, in the past you reached the summit of the snow mountain—the pinnacle system of spiritual teachings—and the blockages of the sambhoga chakra in your throat
were freed simultaneously, so that your intellect embraced a vast range of teachings and you shook your turquoise mane of scriptural knowledge and realization.
A lion among men, you shattered the preconceptions of the elephants—those whose theories are erroneous—with the might of your claws of brilliant argumentation and analysis
and proved yourself unparalleled among all logicians with the thundering roar of your logic.

O Longchenpa, you hatched out of the confining shell of biased views and philosophies that are based on the arrogant assumption that one's own opinions reign supreme.
You spread your wings of omniscient awareness, having thoroughly examined your own experience
in light of all the spiritual traditions, Buddhist and otherwise, that spread in the Land of Snows,
and perfected your mastery of flight, soaring in the sky so that your own and others' benefit was spontaneously accomplished.[100]

O Longchenpa, with your understanding of things in all their variety, you crossed the ocean of study and contemplation to its far shore on the ship of meditation.
With your realization of the very nature of reality, you found the wish-granting gem on the Jeweled Isle of the three kayas. [1.169a]
To do so, you followed the path of the yoga of darkness, focusing intently on the illumination of basic space in the cliffside cave of Chokla Drak.
Thereupon you beheld the face of the exalted goddess Chintamanichakra Tara, mother of the victorious ones and embodiment of the five expanses, and heard her prophecies.

O Longchenpa, though not attached to even the finest this world has to offer, you gaze with your four faces of wisdom, love, energy, and might.[101]
Without rushing, without a mere partial grasp of spiritual teachings, you examined all that is knowable through the eight modes of the sublime guiding force of wisdom.
In the supreme empire of the Sage's teachings—the theory and practice of the sutras and tantras—on a vast throne in this world of sorrow,
your sublime nirmanakaya manifested, acclaimed by all who are endowed with the ten powers speaking in a single voice.

O Longchenpa, how lovely! You are like the Kinsman of the Sun,[102] foremost among those endowed with the ten powers,
like the powerful crystal gem that adorns the locks of Shambhu's hair,[103]
like the azure garuda that hatched by the banks of the river of Vasudhara,
for you are foremost among the learned ones in the Land of Snows.

O Longchenpa, in the Kyam Uplands, a wilderness guarded by Yarlha Shampo, a powerful spirit of the region,
your guru Rigdzin Kumaradza—Vimalamitra appearing magically in human form—

served you a feast of the nectar of the Dzogchen teachings. [1.169b]
You imbibed the quintessence of the three categories and nine expanses,
becoming drunk with your realization and shattering the contrived philosophies of the eight lower approaches.

O Longchenpa, your elegant mansion is that of original purity, like a flawless crystal—the inwardly lucid vase body of basic space, the ground of being.
Your throne is the genuine state of utter lucidity, free of the eight extremes and endowed with six special attributes.[104]
There you gained an ongoing state of authentic being, as a majestic master of enlightened intent within the infinite expanse of timelessness beyond the three times.
Within the confines of the rupakaya, you are the primordial protector, for whom phenomena and ordinary mind have fallen away.

O Longchenpa, in the great charnel ground of the Chimpu Uplands, which resembles Oddiyana or Shitavana,
on the slope of the holy site known as Gang-ri Tökar, a place that confers blessings on those who stay there, you focused intently on the key point of the direct experience of awareness.
Within the expanse of the spheres and rays of light of the six lamps,
you brought the dynamic process of the four visions to completion and playfully enjoyed sambhogakaya pure realms.

O Longchenpa, for you the treasure trove of enlightened intent welled up within the lucid expanse of being, so that you experienced forms and sounds
as symbolic teachings and scriptures, and wore the crown of a vast range of termas of enlightened mind.
Inspired by the authentic prophecies of Padmakara, you brought forth the profound teachings that are the quintessence of the earth and were the foremost of the 108 principal tertöns. [1.170a]
Your treatises, those on the general topics of the mainstream teachings, as well as your *Three Cycles of Being at Ease* and your great *Seven Treasuries*, are an elegant array of steps leading to the shrine,
while the brilliant force of your knowledge, like a majestic dome,[105] can cause the great earth, that of the "six ornaments" and "two sublime ones," to quake.

O Longchenpa, you were graced with visions of the vast range of the Three Roots, who empowered you into the direct experience of the dynamic energy of awareness.

The oath-bound guardians pledged to be your subjects, and you mastered the enactment of enlightened activity to annihilate and nurture.[106]
Learned and accomplished master of the Land of Snows, the powerful Jambhala was inseparable from you, guarding you as one worthy of others' faith.
You were skilled in churning the quintessence of your three Nyingtik collections[107] from the expanse of enlightened intent.

O Longchenpa, you are omniscient and all-seeing, the ruler of the dharma, the universal monarch of the nine progressive approaches.
Without the thousand-spoked wheel preceding you,[108] you brought those in the three worlds who were to be guided under your control through the force of your innate compassion.
Without marshaling the four divisions of a great army,[109] you emerged victorious in your battle with the all-consuming thought and habit patterns that are the foes of liberation.
Without it being due to the force of mere karma and merit, you led all beings along the path to omniscience through the four means of positively influencing others.[110]

O Longchenpa, [1.170b] in the center of the palace of the Sage's teachings—the city of immortality, lovely to behold—
you are the powerful ruler of Dzogchen, sitting on the throne of the Atiyoga approach.
When you gaze with your thousand eyes,[111] the eyes of the four visions, and exert your majesty,
you give meaning to your renown as one who overwhelms with splendor the forces of the demigods—the all-consuming thought patterns of the ordinary mind.

O Longchenpa, you are not like the lovely maidens who fascinate the world, their brows adorned with strands of pearls,
nor like a peacock whose rainbow-hued feathers are aglow with vivid eyes.
Rather, you are like a sublime lady—the embodiment of the qualities of scriptural knowledge and realization—
whose visage, upon being seen, instantly captivates the minds of elders in this world, bringing them a peace free of passion.

O Longchenpa, your extensive study of the mainstream Buddhist and non-Buddhist traditions brought you immeasurable spiritual knowledge, knowledge like the purest gold from the world's rivers.

Your determined contemplation, entailing the completely pure process of threefold validation,[112] was like the blacksmith's skill in refining, cutting, and polishing gold to fashion a monument to the three mainstream traditions.[113]
The warmth of direct experience, gained through your outstanding practice of meditation on the slopes of snow mountains, adorned that monument with the inset gems of your attainment of the level of twofold purity.[114]
With the cunning of your legacy, you eclipsed the treatises on logic by Sakya Pandita,[115] that skilled proclaimer, which cater to those who are concerned with words.

O Longchenpa, [1.171a] even an old seer who is absorbed in meditation can be roused by the sound of a *gandharva*'s[116] flute.
Even a universal monarch who is full of arrogance can become lost in the spectacle of the landscapes he beholds on his royal progress.
The unvacillating meditative equipoise of advanced spiritual practitioners cannot be disturbed by such things,
but you have robbed such people, captivating their minds with your great *Seven Treasuries*.

O Longchenpa, in our human world, the six ornaments and two sublime ones were truly amazing.
In the Land of Snows, the "three ancestors"[117] were truly courageous.
But with the supreme and uncontrived conduct of a master of awareness, you embodied the enlightened activity of them all,
you who illuminated the teachings in the last of the five-hundred-year periods.

O Longchenpa, when a frog whose belly is filled with water from the well of biased views and philosophies
tries to fathom the ocean of the secret tantras, he pokes a toe in and comes to erroneous conclusions.
But you are famed for your critique of logic that comes from argumentation and analysis based on a mere gulp from the reservoir of the sutras and tantras,
pointing out, "This is a caricature of the teachings."

O Longchenpa, you experienced original purity as the boundless view, in which the elaborations of the eight extremes have resolved into basic space.

You gained freedom in meditation as the naturally expansive state of spontaneous presence, in which antidotal methods of focused attention faded into openness.
Conduct became second nature to you as the naturally free state with no fixed reference point, [1.171b] overwhelming the bandits of hope and fear with its brilliance.
You embraced this Land of Snows with the fame of your erudition and accomplishment.

O Longchenpa, even though you were not the lord Nagarjuna, who established the mainstream tradition of the path,[118] you were certainly like him, O Omniscient One of Samyé.
Nor were you the lord Garab, who distilled the enlightened intent of the secret tantras, for you appeared due to the motivation of Gangchentso.[119]
You were Bairotsana, of marvelous repute, your renunciation and realization extending farther than the reaches of space.
Adorning the goddess of wealth Vasudhara with earrings formed from the sun and moon, which together illuminate our world,
you were the lord Saraha, or Danun,[120] forefather of hundreds of siddhas, skilled at singing haunting spiritual songs concerning the state free of elaboration.
If you were not he, I am left in a web of doubt that you could have been anyone else.[121]

Who could be so marvelous in speaking about the five fields of knowledge
that he could silence the six ornaments and two sublime ones?
Wouldn't it be one who had taken a firm stance within the expanse of enlightened intent
of the primordial protector, endowed with six special attributes?

How wondrous! O Omniscient One, on the surface of the mirror of your supreme expanse,[122]
there is not an atom of the vast range of phenomena in the universe, animate or inanimate, that does not appear—
no reflection of anything that can be known, of which those endowed with the ten powers could say, "Here is something overlooked!" [1.172a]

O Longchenpa, the nature of composite things is not permanence; the great winds of time cause things to amass and then scatter.
When the "Lovely Cloud Mansion," the temple of Zhai Lhakhang in central Tibet, was reduced to ruins,

Vimalamitra pointed dramatically at the rubble and predicted that what had been destroyed would be rebuilt.
When you carried out the restoration fulfilling this prophecy, you showed your mastery over phenomena and overwhelmed the universe with the adornment of your uncontrived conduct.

The seven-horsed sun[123]—the tradition of the commands of victorious masters of awareness—
causes hundredfold rays of light—the teachings of the sutras and tantras—to shine.
These arose in the form of a human being
who, with his brilliance, banished the darkness of those who speak falsely and in vain.

For those who have attained levels of realization, birth and death do not exist as such.
Yet, in order to inspire renunciation in those to be guided, who cling to things as permanent,
the monument of your rupakaya manifestation in the Chimpu Uplands served as a source of relics representing the five buddha families as well as smaller relics.
You sat upright in the dharmakaya posture and slept in the state of peace, but your three secrets—the culmination of a vast range of scriptural knowledge and realization—
were left, in the form of texts, as the massed relics of the dharmakaya; thinking of your kindness, I fold my hands.

With these words, *The Queen of Spring's Far-Reaching Song,* I have directed my praise toward this knower of the three times. [1.172b]
May it ensure that, in all my successive lifetimes, I will pass to the far shore of the three worlds.
During that entire time, may I follow in the footsteps of the Omniscient Guru and be capable of walking the path of renunciation and realization of which he wrote so elegantly.
My only wish is that the crops of enormous benefit for the teachings and for beings may ripen to fullness.
This praise is not without ultimate purpose or logic,
like that found in non-Buddhist works or the Vedas of the brahmins.
Since this master is the mainstay of the teachings of the sutras and tantras,
O victorious ones and your heirs, join with me in honoring him!

Thus, in an instantaneous transmission from the Omniscient One Longchenpa himself, Jigmé Lingpa received, unerringly and in their entirety, the key points of all the tantras, explanatory commentaries, and pith instructions of the secret Nyingtik teachings of utter lucidity. He received the inheritance of his spiritual father's enlightened intent, which accounts for his bold statement:

> Therefore, what is my lineage, you ask?
> On the crown of my head sits Drimé Özer.
> I do not rely on lineages that are like frayed cords or fragile strands.

Nevertheless, Jigmé Lingpa avoided treating the secret mantra teachings casually and ensured that the mainstream transmission of the oral lineage, the lineage of definitive pith instructions from India and Tibet, would not be broken. [1.173a] To this end, he requested and received the cycles of Dzogchen teachings from various teachers. From Orgyen Palgön, the great scholar of Mindroling Monastery, who was also known as Drupwang Shrinatha, he received *The Four Higher Collections of the Heart Drop,* the glorious *Heart Essence of Secrets,* and other transmissions. With Mönla Kunzang, he studied collections like *The Three Cycles of Being at Ease.* From the nomad of the steppes, Pema Rigdzin, and his brother, Jigmé Lingpa received the extensive transmission of Longchenpa's great *Seven Treasuries* and other works. His account *The Earrings of Sun and Moon* describes how he received an enormous number of the profound teachings available to him.

Exhorted by the great Omniscient One, the foremost goddess of basic space[124] revealed to Jigmé Lingpa the meaning of the symbols he was shown in a vision. This took place when Jigmé Lingpa was offering a large ganachakra on the tenth day of the Monkey month in a Male Earth Monkey year.[125] During the liturgy of invitation, he beheld with his own eyes the glorious king of the dharma Orgyen and his consort in the midst of a swirling mass of dakas and dakinis, like sesame seeds overflowing from a pod, all of them moving in a vajra dance. Almost fainting with devotion, he felt himself expand into the realm of indestructible basic space, the unity of awareness and emptiness.

Jigmé Lingpa perceived that three tulkus from the southern reaches and others [1.173b] were intent on his codifying a great terma of enlightened mind, though they didn't specifically request that he do so. Seeing that conditions were favorable and the time was ripe, he decided to present the teachings known as *The Heart Drop of Longchenpa.* Initially, he codified the outer sadhana practice of guru yoga, and many people came to him promising to repeat its *siddhi* mantra[126] a hundred million times. This established the auspicious circumstances whereby all who came into contact with these teachings would find meaning in them. He then gradually codified the cycles for the deities of the Three Roots and the three cycles, concerning guru yoga,

Dzogchen, and the supremely compassionate Avalokiteshvara. These made up two volumes of the basic Nyingtik teachings. More specifically, he composed both the root text of and commentary on his *Treasury of Enlightened Qualities* as a clarification of the enlightened intent of the Omniscient One Longchenpa; *Timeless Awareness as the Guiding Principle* with its background material; *Answers to Questions on Topics Concerning Meditation;* the treatise *Answers to Questions: A Treasury of Scripture and Reasoning;* his collected prayers of praise and words of advice; his extensive commentary on the cycle *The United Intent of the Gurus;* and other works. These are included in the nine volumes of his collected works, which brought about a renaissance of the teachings on the heart essence.

During this time, as Jigmé Lingpa attests in his vajra speech,[127] "My small tent of white cloth sheltered me from the fears of samsara, [1.174a] and my seat of solid rock gave me great, unwavering confidence." In *Spiritual Teachings for Mountain Retreat,* he says, "Having given up possessiveness within and without, I had no storehouse of wealth other than a single pack on my back." As these quotations show, he adopted the ways of a carefree mendicant, maintaining the uncontrived conduct of a master of awareness while appearing as an ordinary lay practitioner in white clothing. Surrounded by hosts of dakas and dakinis who gathered like clouds, he wandered around just as he pleased, frequenting mountains, cliffside caves, glaciers, and lakes in every direction.

Eventually, he established his seat at Tsering Jong in Dönkhar, overseeing the building of a new temple, as well as the statues and decorations inside. Then, like a bee going from one flower to another, he traveled from western and southern Tibet and Bhutan to eastern Tibet, as far away as Doser, gathering about him innumerable people with the karma to be his students. For them he turned the wheel of the dharma, imparting primarily his own Nyingtik termas[128] and the excellent works of the great Omniscient One Longchenpa. He taught so that his students came to a decisive realization of these most secret unsurpassable teachings on the basis of their personal experiences, and he captivated the attention of all who were lords among scholars and leaders among siddhas. [1.174b] They flocked to him from all directions, as numerous as stars gathered in the night sky, so that he caused the vision of the teachings concerning the heart essence of utter lucidity to extend effortlessly to the far reaches of space.

Having received the blessings and instructions of Lang Palgyi Seng-gé, Jigmé Lingpa codified a cycle of Vajrakila teachings. In addition, at the center of Palri, he instituted a new custom of drupchen practice based on *The Discourse on United Intent.* Among other things, he inaugurated the practice of the peaceful and wrathful deities at Jang Tekchen Ling, made offerings to the throne holders of the three centers of the dharma,[129] commissioned the gilding of the spire of the stupa of supreme enlightenment at Samyé, and oversaw the printing of the precious *Collected Tantras of the Nyingma School* in gold and silver ink. In addition, he ransomed the lives of many beings from certain death. Thus using conventional means, he cultivated the roots of virtue on a grand scale. With his powers, he put an end to border wars that threatened Tibet with destruction, and in these and other ways, he served the teachings and brought about enormous benefit and well-being for others.

Under his direction, the king and queen of Dergé and their heirs financed the publication of his collected works, as well as a collection that he compiled, the precious *Collected Tantras of the Nyingma School.* That alone exemplified kindness beyond all measure. Due to their great support of this lineage, Longchenpa and Jigmé Lingpa became as renowned as the sun and moon and were referred to as the "omniscient father and son."

Jigmé Lingpa thus came to the end of his life, having ensured the spontaneous accomplishment of the two kinds of benefit as a glorious protector of all the teachings and all beings, [1.175a] moving fortunate ones to faith. Sometime after he reached his seventieth year, amid marvelous signs his emanated form resolved back into the palace of Pema Ö in the realm of Chamara.

Five sublime tulkus appeared: that of his enlightened form was Jamyang Khyentsei Wangpo, that of his enlightened speech was the great bodhisattva Paltrul, that of his enlightened mind was Khyentsé Yeshé Dorjé, that of his enlightened qualities was Mingyur Namkhai Dorjé, and that of his enlightened activity was Gyalsé Zhenpen Tayé. Each of these tulkus, whose qualities were so great as to defy description, spread the teachings of the Early Translation school in the ten directions.

As for those nurtured by the nectar of Jigmé Lingpa's enlightened speech, there was no one of consequence those days in eastern and central Tibet who did not sit at his feet. He was honored by an incredible number of students, foremost among them Dakchen Rinpoché of the Sakya school, the leaders of the Shartsé and Jangtsé colleges of Ganden Monastery,[130] Getsé Mahapandita of Katok Monastery, Dzogchen Ngedön Tendzin Zangpo, and the great Buddhist king of Dergé and his queen and heirs. [1.175b] Among his main students were "the four named Jigmé," heart sons who held the teachings of the ultimate lineage of inner realization: Dodrup Jigmé Trinlé Özer, Dza Trama Lama Jigmé Gyalwai Nyugu, Lama Jigmé Kundröl Namgyal of Bhutan, and Lama Jigmé Ngotsar Tendzin of Getsé Monastery. In turn, each of these had countless students who were lineage holders, spreading the teachings of the heart essence of utter lucidity over the face of the earth.

Three main lines of transmission—the extensive lineage, the direct lineage, and the pure visionary transmission[131]—converged in the sublime being Jigmé Lingpa. While the traditional lineages of these are without limit, the oral lineages of the instructions concerning the three personal transmissions of Dzogchen—kama, terma, and daknang—exist today entirely due to the kindness of this teacher.

One of Jigmé Lingpa's students, Dodrup Jigmé Trinlé Özer, passed on a lineage of transmission that will be discussed later.[132] Here I will speak of Gyalwai Nyugu, for it was from the holy guru Jigmé Lingpa that Jigmé Gyalwai Nyugu heard the teachings of the great perfection of utter lucidity. [1.176a]

Jigmé Gyalwai Nyugu (1765–1843)

Jigmé Gyalwai Nyugu, truly the embodiment of the exalted Avalokiteshvara, was from the highlands populated by nomads north of Dergé in the eastern Tibetan region of Dokham, where the Dzachu River[133] gently flows. It is a region guarded by a renowned protective deity, Dorjé Penchuk Karpo, known as "the king of Dza," an attendant[134] sworn to uphold the teachings of Padmakara. Amid amazing signs and portents, Jigmé Gyalwai Nyugu was born in a place where the waters of an auspicious milky lake swirl and the alpine meadows are like pleasant parks dotted with flowers, to a wealthy family among the hundreds who inhabited that area. Of the four sons born to the family, the younger two died at birth [1.176b] and the eldest died at a very young age. When this lord himself was still quite young, his father passed away. Although everyone in the region had great hope that he would take charge of the family's affairs, he felt an unwavering desire to find a qualified guru and practice the dharma in a pure way.

His mother, who exhibited the signs of a dakini, once asked, "My son, what do you wish to do with your life?" When he spoke of his heart's desire honestly, his mother replied, "That is my opinion, too, but if others hear of this, it won't rest well in their minds. So you must definitely go off to central or southern Tibet and there practice the dharma purely." With this, she secretly gave him a lump of Chinese silver the size of a horse's hoof, and he set off in pursuit of teachings.

He gradually journeyed through Lhasa and points south, arriving at last at Sheldrak in Yarlung, where he had an audience with Dodrupchen Rinpoché Jigmé Trinlé Özer, who was there in retreat. He described his circumstances to the guru, who said, "How extremely fine! Now you must go to see my guru, Kunchen Jigmé Lingpa. It will be excellent if you request spiritual advice from him and practice according to whatever instructions he gives you." And Dodrupchen Rinpoché sent him off with a letter of introduction. [1.177a]

It was at the hermitage of Tsering Jong that Jigmé Gyalwai Nyugu first beheld the omniscient guru Rigdzin Jigmé Lingpa's mandala of enlightened embodiment. He was wearing the simple white robes of a lay tantric practitioner and was endowed with the major and minor marks of physical perfection. There was nothing disagreeable about his form; in fact, Jigmé Gyalwai Nyugu couldn't stop looking at him. The devotion he felt upon merely meeting the guru caused realization to dawn in his heart.

He presented the letter of introduction along with a mandala offering to support his request for advice. With delight, Jigmé Lingpa took him under his care and granted him the complete transmission of the tantras, explanatory commentaries, and pith instructions of the secret Nyingtik teachings of the Dzogchen approach of utter lucidity, like one vase filling another. He empowered Jigmé Gyalwai Nyugu as his regent of the ultimate lineage of realization.

Jigmé Gyalwai Nyugu spent the next three years at Tsari Chikchar, devoting himself to the very essence of spiritual practice, and through the secret path of the great perfection of utter lucidity, he reached the level at which phenomena resolve into their true nature. The local gods, the male and female protectors of the region, appeared as a Bhutanese man and woman and offered him sustenance. At Taktsang, Domtsang, and other places of solitude in the southern land of Bhutan, he practiced assiduously, similar to the venerable Milarepa in his immeasurable courage, ascetic discipline, and meager sustenance.[135] He walked barefoot to most places, [1.177b] and because, among other things, the soles of his feet were frozen by the snow, they became as hard as stone. His feet were so big—almost a cubit in length—that while he was staying at the holy site of Tsari, someone who saw his footprints in the snow mistook them for those of a yeti.

During this time, he had countless meditative experiences and dreams. Once, he was staying at a site in the Chimpu Uplands to circumambulate a temple there. One evening, as the sun was close to sinking behind the mountains, he saw coming from a far hillside a tall, barefoot man dressed in red serge and wearing a red hat. Merely upon beholding this person, he felt an unshakable faith dawn in him, and he bowed with devotion. They circumambulated together several times, and Jigmé Gyalwai Nyugu, feeling great trust in the man, asked him some questions. He suggested that they spend the night at a retreat cave on the side of the mountain. The man agreed to this, and so they went to the cave. That night, Jigmé Gyalwai Nyugu questioned him closely about how meditative experience and realization come about and became certain that his companion was in no way separate from the Buddha. [1.178a]

Later, the man exhaled several times and then spent the rest of the night in a squatting posture, holding his breath as though using the technique known as the "intermediate breath." The next morning, preparing to go out and circumambulate the temple at sunrise, Jigmé Gyalwai Nyugu served him tea and offered him a full bag of roasted barley flour. The man seized the bag in his right hand and waved it in the air, exclaiming, "I offer this to the Three Jewels!" When Jigmé Gyalwai Nyugu offered him a new pair of shoes, the man refused, saying, "I don't need to wear shoes."

As he was leaving, Jigmé Gyalwai Nyugu asked for a prophecy. The man responded by predicting how long and where he would live, adding, "Later in your life, return to your native region. There is a valley, the head of which is to the north and the mouth of which is to the southwest. In this valley is a cliff laid out like the plan of Zangdok Palri.[136] You should pursue your spiritual practice there." After he left,

Jigmé Gyalwai Nyugu thought to himself, "I have no idea who that was, but if I were to meet the Omniscient One Longchen Rabjam in person, he would be no different than this one." His realization then became vast, his mind like space.

At another time, in a place near Tsari, he was in very strict retreat, for the snow had cut him off from human contact. During this retreat, a number of circumstances [1.178b] contributed to the enrichment of his realization. Later on, when he encountered Kunchen Jigmé Lingpa, he related these events to him. The guru said, "The one you encountered at Chimpu was Guru Rinpoché himself, actually come to see you." He also said, "In general, as far as realizing timeless awareness is concerned, anything that occurs, whether the blessings of the guru or the machinations of gods and demons, illnesses, and so forth, should enrich your realization. Now that excellent meditative experiences and realization have dawned in your mind, you have reached the point at which phenomena resolve."

Jigmé Gyalwai Nyugu then spent a long time practicing with Dodrupchen. They traveled to a place in the Tsang region, but by the time they arrived, their provisions were almost exhausted. Jigmé Gyalwai Nyugu thought to himself, "What if there were some obstacle to the long life of Dodrupchen? He is the heart son holding the teachings of our Omniscient Guru's ultimate lineage, so we must find food somewhere." But because they hadn't eaten anything solid in some time, Dodrupchen Rinpoché was completely unable to move. The lord Jigmé Gyalwai Nyugu carried their baggage a long distance ahead, then returned to carry Dodrupchen Rinpoché on his back; they thus proceeded in stages. At one point, as they rested in the middle of a large plain, boiling some water at midday, [1.179a] they heard a crow cawing from the top of a distant boulder. Dodrupchen Rinpoché said, "I dreamed last night that we got some help. Can you find out where that crow is?"

"I will," Jigmé Gyalwai Nyugu replied, and went off. At the spot where he had seen the crow was the leg of a musk deer with a little meat left on it. He returned with it and added it to the water to make a broth, which they both drank. Dodrupchen Rinpoché ate the meat and regained some strength, so that he was just able to continue walking.

Jigmé Gyalwai Nyugu alternated periods of time listening to spiritual advice from his guru with periods of solitary practice. Returning to his home area as his guru had instructed, he devoted himself solely to practice in places such as the cave of Drelkar Puk in Dzagyü. When Sang-gyé Nyenpa went to central Tibet, Jigmé Gyalwai Nyugu accompanied the caravan. There he received much advice on Mahamudra and Dzogchen from Kunchen Jigmé Lingpa, as well as from numerous gurus living in Daklha Gampo and other areas, and put this advice into practice. In the presence of his guru, he cut through any misunderstanding concerning the profound teachings so that none remained. [1.179b]

As he prepared to return to his home area, his omniscient guru said to him, "You were born in a border region not unlike the island of bloodthirsty demons. My teachings are intended primarily for taming such savage, unruly beings; so in keeping with the prophecy of Guru Rinpoché, you must devote yourself principally to practice and so benefit others. This will be very useful to many beings." With this, Jigmé Lingpa gave him *The Application of Mindfulness* (the preliminary practices for the Nyingtik cycle),[137] the methods for the practical implementation of these teachings, and most notably, his teaching manual *Timeless Awareness as the Guiding Principle*, marked with his thumbprint in which a *Hya* syllable could be clearly seen. He honored him as his inner heart son, holder of the ultimate lineage, and gave him the name Jigmé Gyalwai Nyugu. His compassionate love flowed uninterruptedly, and he cared for Jigmé Gyalwai Nyugu as a father would care for his son. For his part, as the foundation of his practice, Jigmé Gyalwai Nyugu maintained the discipline of a vajra master who was also a fully ordained monk.

At last Jigmé Gyalwai Nyugu set off on his return journey, going by way of the lake known as Namtso. There he developed edema in his feet, and so was not able to travel much. One midday he came to a large valley, where he rested in the shade of a great boulder. He had to crawl on all fours as he drew water, boiled tea, [1.180a] and prepared food. He stayed for a day and a night. In the evening, he did his usual meditation practice and performed the ritual of Chö extensively, using his drum and bell. At daybreak he found himself unable to resume his journey, and so boiled water for his morning tea. He thought, "I can't go anywhere, so I must stay here as long as my provisions last." He did so, exerting himself in his meditation practice. In the distance curled the smoke of a nomadic camp, and from that direction a man approached. The man asked Jigmé Gyalwai Nyugu about himself, and he answered at length.

The man then said, "In this valley, the only local spirit is an extremely malevolent one associated with this boulder. Last night we saw that an older man was staying next to it. We didn't know who you were, and this morning we thought you were dead. We were amazed to see your fire, so my patron sent me to investigate. Did anything disturbing happen?"

Jigmé Gyalwai Nyugu replied, "Whether or not it was because I was so exhausted, I fell asleep before daybreak and nothing at all disturbing occurred."

"Since you are a great guru, my patron asked me to offer you an invitation." [1.180b] With that the man had him mount a horse, and they rode to the nomad camp. A doctor was summoned, Jigmé Gyalwai Nyugu's illness was treated, and he was well cared for. His patrons, man and wife, came to have faith in him and said, "Because you are a man of such good character, it is fitting that you take possession of all the wealth of this household. Choose a wife who is agreeable to you. If that is impossible, spend the rest of your life in some mountain retreat. We will provide whatever support you require." But despite their assurances and although they urged him to stay for at least three years, he left as soon as he was cured. Taking nothing but the provisions he needed to satisfy his immediate needs, he returned to his home region.

He became renowned as Lama Tsampa, the "retreat lama," for he spent his time primarily in spiritual practice. He was also known as Dza Trama Lama because he had spent twenty-one years practicing in a solitary hermitage prophesied by Guru Rinpoché—Trama Valley, in which rock faces and meadows come together in a pattern resembling Zangdok Palri. Turning the wheel of the dharma uninterruptedly for students who had faith in him, Jigmé Gyalwai Nyugu carried out activities on a vast scale, giving a sense of purpose to all who came into contact with him. [1.181a] Every year without fail, he extensively taught *The Heart Drop of Longchenpa* of the Dzogchen approach of utter lucidity, usually conferring the maturing empowerments and liberating instructions of this cycle in the summer and winter. All of those holding the teachings of the Early Translation school of the Nyingma in eastern Tibet came to study at his feet.

Dodrupchen Rinpoché Jigmé Trinlé Özer once dreamed that he was driving a sizable herd of cattle out of a large valley, moving southwest. Looking back, he saw Jigmé Gyalwai Nyugu in the lower part of the valley, driving before him a huge bull that cast its shadow over the entire area. Because of this dream, Dodrupchen Rinpoché predicted, "Of the benefit you and I will bring beings, yours will be the greater," and this is in fact how it came to be.

Among those of the northern region of Dzagyü, even the humblest men and women, there was no one who did not receive teachings on the preliminary practices from this lord teacher or who did not then perform these practices five hundred thousand times or train in the transference of consciousness. It was also widely reported that every one of them, at the point of death, actually saw this guru's face. In terms of activities carried out in this lifetime, the benefit Dodrupchen brought to beings was the greater. However, we think of Jigmé Gyalwai Nyugu's as ultimately being the greater in that his activities produced lineages that passed through both Paltrul and Khyentsé to fill the entire world. [1.181b]

Once, a large flock of sheep had been driven to a hillside near the Dzachu River. From a facing distant hillside, this precious lord guru cast amulets to protect the animals from slaughter, and they grazed the backs of the sheep so far away. Nonhuman beings presented to him a mongoose made of stone, the "spirit stone" of the yaksha spirits. In these and many other ways, he demonstrated signs of his accomplishment.

After the passing of Dodrupchen Rinpoché, this lord guru dreamed that he journeyed to Zangdok Palri. Seated in the presence of Guru Rinpoché were the figures of Kunchen Jigmé Lingpa and his spiritual son Dodrupchen Rinpoché. The lord guru Jigmé Gyalwai Nyugu found himself seated among the masters of awareness, between the father and son. He thought to himself, "How fortunate I am to have joined such a gathering of masters!" He felt immeasurable faith, devotion, and joy. At a certain point, both the omniscient guru[138] and Dodrupchen touched their foreheads to that of Tsampa Rinpoché, saying, "Son, go back, for your mission to benefit beings is not yet finished. There certainly will come a time when we shall meet here again." Jigmé Gyalwai Nyugu then awoke, despondent, from his dream. He spoke often of such pure visions that occurred.

During the later part of his life, [1.182a] he traveled to Terlung in the Dergé region, where he met Jamyang Khyentsei Wangpo, whom he recognized as the tulku of Kunchen Jigmé Lingpa. Jigmé Gyalwai Nyugu turned the wheel of the dharma, transmitting in their entirety the empowerments and teachings of the Dzogchen cycle *The Heart Drop of Longchenpa.* Throughout the teachings, until the transmission was completed, everyone saw amazing signs, such as rainbow light shimmering above the tent in which he was staying. He thus bestowed the teachings of the ultimate lineage of realization upon Jamyang Khyentsei Wangpo. As well, Paltrul Jigmé Chökyi Wangpo, the crown jewel of all learned and accomplished masters in the Land of Snows, became his principal heart son. These two lord gurus caused the teachings on the heart essence of utter lucidity to spread in later times to the shores of distant oceans, serving as lifelines for the teachings so that "Pal and Khyen" have become as famous in this world as the paired sun and moon.

In addition, Jigmé Gyalwai Nyugu taught the heart son of Dodrupchen Rinpoché, Drupwang Heruka Khyentsé Yeshé Dorjé; the fourth Drupwang Dzogchen, Mingyur Namkhai Dorjé; Gyalsé Zhenpen Tayé; Khenchen Pema Badzra; and others. As this indicates, [1.182b] he trained truly incredible holy masters who maintained the vitality of the Nyingtik teachings concerning definitive truth. Thus he caused this sublime spiritual approach to flourish and spread. His activities extended to all schools of Buddhism everywhere without bias; for example, he once gave the Nyingtik empowerments and teachings to Khamtrul Chökyi Nyima, the great upholder of the Drukpa Kagyü teachings.

This lord guru's oral instructions were recorded by the great bodhisattva Paltrul Rinpoché in *The Oral Transmission of the Guru Samantabhadra,*[139] a teaching manual on the preliminary practices of *The Heart Drop of Longchenpa.* The influence of this text has been felt everywhere throughout China, Tibet, India, Nepal, and Bhutan. Anyone can appreciate the fact that it is the essential nectar of the spiritual practice of all practitioners in all schools—Sakya, Geluk, Kagyü, and Nyingma. In the final days of his life, Jigmé Gyalwai Nyugu founded a monastery in Dzagyal called Puntsok Norbu Ling, dedicated to maintaining the lineage of the *The Heart Drop of Longchenpa.*

Once, when he was in the company of Kunchen Jigmé Lingpa, the latter had given him a fingernail clipping, saying, "As an inner support, you should build a statue of me containing this clipping and it will be just like me." In keeping with the promise he had made on that occasion, Jigmé Gyalwai Nyugu erected a statue of Kunchen Jigmé Lingpa, one cubit in height, fashioned of copper and gold. [1.183a]

He thus brought his life and activities to consummation, having fulfilled his mission to bring about the two kinds of benefit. At a certain point, his form resolved back into the youthful vase body—supreme, primordial inner basic space. His remains, like a wish-fulfilling gem, were preserved in a statue of Padmakara in the form of Guru Nangsi Zilnön, which still exists, a great image that brings purpose to the lives of all who come in contact with it, fulfilling all their aspirations.

Although Jigmé Gyalwai Nyugu received the empowerments and oral transmissions of the Nyingtik teachings of the Dzogchen approach from Dodrup Jigmé Trinlé Özer, that teacher's biography will be presented later.[140]

Jigmé Gyalwai Nyugu's immediate rebirth was recognized by the fourth Drupwang Dzogchen, Mingyur Namkhai Dorjé, through the latter's flawless vision born of timeless awareness. This tulku was Kunzang Dechen Dorjé, who was enthroned as the successor to the lord guru's former incarnation.

At one point during the lord guru Jigmé Gyalwai Nyugu's later life, he heard of many sheep being slaughtered for the wedding feast of a bride from the Seshul clan. Of this he was heard to say over and over, "Alas! If I were a bodhisattva with sufficient power to do so, I would take rebirth as this woman's son. Otherwise, who could save her from lower states of rebirth?" [1.183b] It was therefore widely held that this lord guru took rebirth as her child.[141]

When he was conceived in her womb, the family's felt tents were bathed in white light that all the neighbors could see. Other signs were perceived as well. When the time came to enthrone the child, the fourth Dzogchen wore a white shawl,[142] prophesying, "This noble being will act as a lay tantric master in the future." This tulku came to be a practitioner who brought the four visions to consummation just as they are described. Another incarnation of Jigmé Gyalwai Nyugu was born in the encampment of Khamgar and was enthroned with the title "Khamtrul."

7

The Lineages of Jigmé Gyalwai Nyugu: Paltrul Rinpoché

Paltrul Orgyen Jigmé Chökyi Wangpo (1808–1887)

The foremost students of Gyalwai Nyugu were Paltrul and Khyentsé. Of these two, the first, Paltrul Chökyi Wangpo, was compared to the moon. This chapter gives an account of how the lineage passed through him.

Khyentsé Rinpoché spoke of Paltrul in the following way:

> On the outer level,[1] you are Shantideva, child of victorious ones;
> on the inner level, you are Shavari, lord of siddhas;
> on the secret level, you are truly the exalted and sublime Avalokiteshvara,
> Duk-ngal Rangdrol.[2]
> I supplicate you, Jigmé Chökyi Wangpo.

Similarly, it is widely held that references in the prophecies of the Avalokiteshvara cycle *Being at Ease in the Nature of Mind,* an earth terma revealed by Khyentsei Wangpo, [1.184a] confirm that Paltrul was on the outer level an embodiment of the bodhisattva Shantideva of India and teachers such as Aro Yeshé Jungné of Tibet. It is said that a long biographical poem, a prayer of praise to Paltrul found in Khyentsei Wangpo's collected works, is the extensive version of Paltrul's biography in the ultimate sense.

The most widely accepted opinion is that the first Paltrul incarnation was Palgé Lama Samten Puntsok, declared to be an emanation of Avalokiteshvara by Mokdrup Namkha Chöwang of Katok Monastery. The second incarnation did not live very long. The third was Orgyen Jigmé Chökyi Wangpo, [1.184b] who was born in a Dragon year[3] at Getsé Gong, into the Gyaltok branch of the Mukpodong clan.[4] Dola Jigmé Kalzang[5] recognized him as the rebirth of Palgé Samten Puntsok. Dodrupchen Rinpoché Trinlé Özer named him Orgyen Jigmé Chökyi Wangpo and prophesied that he would become a master of the Nyingtik teachings, conferring on him the seal of entrustment and investing him as a tulku.

From Jigmé Gyalwai Nyugu, who was the exalted and sublime Avalokiteshvara in person, Paltrul Rinpoché received teachings on *The Heart Drop of Longchenpa.* He heard the teachings on the preliminary practices alone some twenty-five times. He carried out the practice of the teachings with similar perseverance. He was certain that this holy man had been his guru in previous lifetimes and spent a long time serving him. Like one vase filling another, Jigmé Gyalwai Nyugu conferred on Paltrul the cycles of the vajra heart essence of utter lucidity in their entirety, as well as the seal of entrustment, and empowered him as a holder of the ultimate lineage of the heart essence. Jamyang Khyentsei Wangpo and Paltrul were united as Jigmé Gyalwai Nyugu's inner heart sons, forming the foundation of his lineage; they became known as "Pal and Khyen, the paired sun and moon." Through them came the lineage of the extensive tradition of the heart essence of utter lucidity [1.185a] that has spread across the oceans, east and west. Some holy teachers say that there were five tulkus of Kunchen Jigmé Lingpa, those of his enlightened form, speech, mind, qualities, and activity, and that among these Paltrul Rinpoché was the incarnation of his speech.

He studied extensively with Dola Jigmé Kalzang, Jigmé Ngotsar of Ki Valley, Gyalsé Zhenpen Tayé, and Öntrul Tutop Namgyal[6] of Zhechen Monastery, mastering the sutras, tantras, and other fields of knowledge. He received many empowerments and teachings from the fourth Dzogchen Rinpoché—Mingyur Namkhai Dorjé—and others.

Once Könchok, Palgé Lama's brother, had passed away, the monastic estate was transferred to Paltrul Rinpoché in order to fulfill his former incarnation's intentions. He practiced assiduously at random sites, including the caves for the sadhana practice of Vajrakila and Yamantaka at Dzogchen Monastery in Rudam, Drelkar Pukpa in Dzagyü, and Pema Rito in Den. Together with Sönam Palgé of Rogza, he spent a long time training in the advanced yogic practices of *The Heart Drop of Longchenpa.*

On his way to meet Zhabkar of Amdo, he learned of the latter's passing. So he stayed at Pemaköpa in Sertal Yarlung, [1.185b] where Gyalsé Zhenpen Tayé was giving an extensive explanation of the tantra *The Heart Essence of Secrets* to an assembly. During each of the next two years, the lord Paltrul Rinpoché conducted a forty-five-day course of extensive explanations of this tantra and so fulfilled the prophecy that the teachings of the heart essence would spread in the region of upper Ser. He also received instructions on the Six Techniques of Union (from the Kalachakra cycle) from Ngawang Chöjor, a monk of the Tsang region.

One of Dodrupchen's four students who were named Dorjé, Khyentsé Yeshé Dorjé, demonstrated uncontrived tantric conduct based on his recognition of awareness, thus greatly enhancing Paltrul Rinpoché's meditation practice.[7] As well, when Paltrul came to Yeshé Dorjé's encampment[8] at Yutsé in Nyenpo specifically to meet him, Yeshé Dorjé bestowed on him the profound empowerment for the dakini Dechen Gyalmo and the extraordinary empowerment into the dynamic energy of awareness.

He also gave many prophecies on outer, inner, and secret levels, such as the assurance that Paltrul would live to be eighty. Paltrul Rinpoché said that while the direct introduction to the great perfection that he had previously received from Jigmé Gyalwai Nyugu was like daybreak, what happened on this occasion was like the sun actually rising. From then on, he held Yeshé Dorjé to be the extraordinary lord of his buddha family. This affirms several accounts of the lineage in which Paltrul is described as Khyentsé Yeshé Dorjé's student. [1.186a]

Paltrul Rinpoché was ordained as a monk by Sengtruk Pema Tashi, also known as Sherab Zangpo, a khenpo of Dzogchen Monastery. He received the name Jigmé Gewai Jungné. He spent time at Dzogchen Monastery, Shri Simha Shedra, Pema Tang, the hermitage of Nakchung, and other places. In the later part of his life, he stayed in the area around Dzagyal Monastery, the seat of Jigmé Gyalwai Nyugu, where he continually gave explanatory teachings on such texts as *Engaging in the Conduct of a Bodhisattva, The Ornament of Higher Realization, The Source Verses on Sublime Knowing, The Ornament of the Sutras, The Treasury of Abhidharma, The Heart Essence of Secrets, Ascertaining the Three Levels of Ordination,* and *The Treasury of Enlightened Qualities*. In all of the surrounding regions, he bestowed the oral transmission for and taught *The Collected Teachings on the Mani Mantra*. At Dzamtang he taught *The Highest Continuum* based on Dolpopa's commentary and composed his own structural analysis of the text. He regularly bestowed the sadhana practice focusing on the pure realm of Sukhavati as well as other practices, so that his enlightened activities were felt throughout such regions as the northern steppes[9] of Dzachukha and the upper, middle, and lower parts of Golok. Their effects were incalculable in that people stopped taking the lives of animals and hundreds were inspired to repeat the six-syllable *mani* mantra a hundred million times. Paltrul Rinpoché restored a wall made up of stones engraved with the six-syllable mantra, which had been erected by his former incarnation, Palgé. [1.186b] He directed all of the gifts he received from the faithful toward the cost of engraving a hundred thousand large stones. This site became known as the "long pillars of Paltrul," and it was said that Khyentsé Rinpoché Yeshé Dorjé miraculously consecrated it from afar.

Paltrul Rinpoché bestowed the empowerments, teachings, explanations, and oral transmissions for the *The Heart Drop of Longchenpa* on Gemang Ön Rinpoché, also named Orgyen Tendzin, at Trama Valley in Dza and on other teachers—primarily his heart son, the precious guru Lungtok Tenpai Nyima—in other places.

While practicing in the cave of Shinjé Drubpuk, he was afflicted with leprosy. He did an intensive retreat on the black form of Hayagriva revealed by Ratna Lingpa, completely curing the disease. At Dzogchen Gangtrö, Paltrul received from Terchen Chokgyur Dechen Lingpa the transmission of the cycle of the deity Samyak called *The Union of All Buddhas in Equalness*. Chokgyur Lingpa declared Paltrul the custodian of his cycle *The Heart Drop of the Three Families*, and so with great reverence,

Paltrul received the empowerments, teachings, and oral transmissions for this cycle. He did intensive retreat on the form of Mañjushri called Jampal Dzogchen from *The Heart Drop of the Three Families,* and all the signs of successful practice clearly manifested for him just as described in the manuals.

Paltrul Rinpoché convinced Chokgyur Lingpa to pass on the sadhana and oral transmissions for the cycle *The United Intent of the Gurus* to the monks of Dzogchen Monastery. [1.187a] Upon the completion of this transmission, Paltrul said, "Today we have had the good fortune to receive the empowerment for *The United Intent of the Gurus* in the presence of Tertön Sang-gyé Lingpa. Everyone should complete the phases of approach and accomplishment for this practice." When he encountered *The Heart Drop of Chetsün,* a cycle revealed by Jamyang Khyentsei Wangpo, Paltrul praised the latter, exclaiming, "He measures up to the standards of the mahasiddhas of India. He is truly the Omniscient One Longchenpa in person."

Paltrul Rinpoché could recall instances from many of his previous lifetimes, such as the time when, eighty incarnations earlier, he had offered a precious gold ring to Krishnacharin, an Indian mahasiddha. Since then, he said, he had not taken an ignoble rebirth. Due to his supernormal powers of perception, he could see things without impediment. He was under the care of Mañjushri. A great number of such facts were substantiated by his own words.

He went to Gemang Monastery, where he did a year's retreat in the quarters of Khenpo Yönten Gyatso, assiduously practicing the cycle of peaceful and wrathful deities, *Dredging the Pit of the Hells,* from the kama transmissions of the Nyingma school. In the breaks between practice sessions, he gave a detailed, lengthy transmission of all the explanatory teachings on that most majestic tantra *The Heart Essence of Secrets* and *The Treasury of Enlightened Qualities.* [1.187b] Khenchen Yönten Gyatso himself thoroughly studied, contemplated, and meditated on these teachings. Patrul Rinpoché also began work on his paired "Sun" and "Moon" commentaries on *The Treasury of Enlightened Qualities,* as well as many other treatises that made a unique contribution to the benefit of future generations.

Paltrul Rinpoché memorized *Dispelling Darkness in the Ten Directions,* a commentary on *The Heart Essence of Secrets* by the Omniscient One Longchenpa, and gave a detailed, extensive teaching on it—what became known as "the oral transmission of Paltrul"—every year thereafter. Many of his students who were learned and accomplished, including the elder Sang-gyé Nyenpa tulku, Lushul Tulku, and the khenpo of Changma, named Tupten Chöpel, attended these teachings. It was from Changma Khenpo that Kyabjé Dilgo Khyentsé Rinpoché received this transmission, and many of us in turn have received it as a result of Khyentsé Rinpoché's kindness; thus this tradition of explanatory teachings has spread widely and has been passed down to the present day. This transmission from Changma Khenpo was also received by Khenchen Jigmé Puntsok of Serta, who disseminated the tradition throughout the eastern and northeastern regions of Tibet. In brief, it is clear that the traditions of the Early Translation school, including explanations of the noble source texts of the sutras and tantras—traditions that have continued without interruption—have come down to us through the kindness of two masters, Gyalsé Zhenpen Tayé and Paltrul Rinpoché, [1.188a] and the lineages they transmitted to their students, which were passed on to their students' students and so on.

Paltrul Rinpoché extensively taught *Engaging in the Conduct of a Bodhisattva* in the main hall of Katok Monastery, as requested by Katok Situ Chökyi Lodrö;[10] there Drimé Zhingkyong Rinpoché[11] also established a spiritual connection with him. Paltrul Rinpoché taught all of the learned and accomplished Nyingma masters of his day, including the fifth Drupwang Dzogchen, the second Kuzhap Gemang, Gyarong Namtrul Kunzang Tekchok Dorjé, Lingtrul Tupten Gyaltsen, Khenchen Pema Badzra, Khenpo Könchok Özer, Khenpo Kunzang Palden Chödrak, the fifth Zhechen Rabjam,[12] the third Zechen Gyaltsap, and Zhichen Tulku. His students of the Kagyü school included Pawo Rinpoché, Khenchen Rinchen Dargyé of the Karma Kagyü school, and Khenchen Tashi Özer. Also among those who studied with him were all of the major and minor geshés, including Hor Khangsar Kyabgön[13] of Ganden Monastery and Geshé Lharampa Tupten, the throne holder of Seshul Monastery in Dzagyü.

As this illustrates, of all the gurus renowned throughout eastern Tibet, [1.188b] there was none who did not directly or indirectly bow at the feet of Paltrul Rinpoché. In particular, four of his students outshone him (just as the students of the Indian Buddhist master Vasubandhu outshone their master): Lungtok Tenpai Nyima of Nyoshul was even greater than Paltrul in his view, Orgyen Tendzin Norbu was even greater in explaining the teachings, Tendzin Drakpa of Gyarong was even greater in his logical reasoning, and Kunzang Sönam of Minyak was even greater in his conduct. Patrul Rinpoché also taught Jamgön Mipam Rinpoché; Pema Dechen Zangpo of Mura; Khenchen Yönten Gyatso; Dodrup Puntsok Jungné; Drimé Drakpa; the son of Khyentsé, Rigpai Raldri; Choktrul Kunzang Dechen Dorjé; Adzom Drukpa Rinpoché; and others. These were his special heart sons, upholders of the vitality of the Early Translation school's teachings. His students also included the governor of the Dergé region, Palden Chimé Takpai Dorjé, as well as his brother, spouse, and children, and Chipung Lungpa of Do, the great general of the Tibetan government forces. The human and nonhuman beings who established spiritual connections with Paltrul were beyond number. Even among the peasantry, it seemed that everyone either understood the laudable greatness of bodhichitta (having attended his teachings on *Engaging in the Conduct of a Bodhisattva*) [1.189a] or knew the four causes of rebirth in the pure realm of Sukhavati. Paltrul Rinpoché thus exerted a positive influence over all of eastern Tibet.

In brief, he was in no way different from the bodhisattva Shantideva, for his way of life was such that he always practiced the dharma purely and was never involved with the eight worldly concerns. He was renowned for this, and it was evident to all. Kunchen Jamyang Khyentsei Wangpo, Jamgön Mipam, and others praised him as one who had attained the level of a great master of speech, for his written works, imbued with a sense of harmony, give the reader easy access to profound topics. Many of the finest scholars of the Gedenpa[14] school, moreover, have consistently praised all of this lord's works explaining the sutras and tantras, noting that they are unique, based as they are on his own spiritual practice; they were written from the experience of one who has heard, contemplated, and meditated on the teachings. *Ketaka,* a commentary on the chapter concerning sublime knowing in *Engaging in the Conduct of a Bodhisattva,* is a fundamental work by the omniscient, all-seeing Mipam Rinpoché that eloquently explains the profound view and meditation of the Early Translation school. [1.189b] It is clear from the colophon that the text is based on the oral transmission that Mipam received from Paltrul Rinpoché.

Later in life, extending his activities to other schools of Buddhism without sectarian bias, Paltrul Rinpoché taught constantly, focusing on *Engaging in the Conduct of a Bodhisattva* according to the interests of his audiences; for example, he used Darma Rinchen's commentary for Gandenpa[15] students, Jetsün Sönam Tsemo's for Sakyapa students, and Pawo Tsuklak Trengwa's and Sazang's for Kagyü students. He gave the transmission of the maturing empowerments and liberating instructions for *Great Perfection: Being at Ease in the Nature of Mind* to his foremost heart son, Lungtok Tenpai Nyima of Nyoshul, over a period of more than three years. In this and other ways, Paltrul Rinpoché ensured that Lungtok Tenpai Nyima was invested as the regent of his ultimate lineage, conferring on him the entire range of maturing empowerments and liberating instructions of the earlier and later Nyingtik cycles.[16]

To Ön Rinpoché Orgyen Tendzin Norbu[17] of Gemang Monastery in Trama Valley, he taught the preliminary and main practices of *The Heart Drop of Longchenpa* over a long period of time. He confirmed that Ön Rinpoché had attained consummate realization of the meaning of great perfection through his training in these teachings, and that his realization had become equal to space as a result of his training in the oral lineage of maturing empowerments and liberating instructions from the cycle *The Innermost Heart Drop of the Guru: The Wish-Fulfilling Gem.* [1.190a] What these two holy masters accomplished through their enlightened activity was incredible, for they ensured that the transmission of the experiential teaching methods[18] of *The Heart Drop of Longchenpa* would continue until the present day.

Later, Paltrul Rinpoché spent five years near the precious, enshrined remains of Jigmé Gyalwai Nyugu, continually performing an intensive sadhana ritual of the deity Khorwa Dongtruk, which derives from the kama transmissions. He thus lived for eighty years as a glorious protector of all the teachings and all beings, bringing his deeds and activities to completion.

During the Monkey month of a Monkey year,[19] he offered a large ganachakra. At some point, he seemed to fall slightly ill and began speaking at length of the qualities of the eastern pure realm of Abhirati. He said that he heard a voice saying, "Those to be guided by you are to the east." But he also said things like, "It would seem that my emanation must return once more to this world." He passed away on the eighteenth day of Saga, the fourth month of a Fire Pig year.[20] The lord Ön Tendzin Norbu and Sönam Tsering presided over the memorial ceremonies and the construction of his tomb. As well, the lord Ön Rinpoché completed a vast array of projects, among them overseeing the publication of Paltrul Rinpoché's collected works at Rudam Dzogchen Monastery [1.190b] and instituting the ritual of Khorwa Dongtruk as a commemorative annual event at Dzogchen Monastery and its affiliates.

The fifth Drupwang Dzogchen declared Changma Khen Rinpoché Tupten Chöpel to be the sublime tulku of this lord. As well, many other extraordinary holy beings were incarnations of Patrul Rinpoché, including Tsö Paltrul of Repkong; Khedrup Namkha Jimgé, son of Dudjom the elder; and Jigmé Wangpo, son of the second Tsamtrul.

The preceding is Paltrul Rinpoché's outer biography; there is not much to recount in terms of his inner and secret biographies, his enlightened mind having been so profound that he did not divulge those facts to anyone. He did, however, say to his heart son, Lungtok Tenpai Nyima, "My dear Lung, at this point, I am completely unable to bear contemplating the suffering of beings in the three lower states of existence. When I train my mind, I can only contemplate the suffering of those in higher states." What his words actually indicated was that he had fully trained his mind through renunciation. [1.191a]

He also said, "In the brief time that it takes to dismount and remount a horse, in a single instant of complete recall, I can visualize the 725 deities of the Eight Commands cycle *The Gathering of Sugatas,*[21] but I have no thought of this constituting the stage of development. While holding a single breath, I can perform a complete cycle of the higher yogic exercises of *The Heart Drop of Longchenpa,* including the exercises of the masters of awareness,[22] but I have no thought of this constituting the full measure of practice involving subtle energy. And while I was pursuing meditation using the Six Techniques of Union from the Kalachakra cycle on the plateau of Dzamtang to the east, I brought the ten signs of empty forms to full measure, until I could inhale goddesses of empty form through my nostrils,[23] but I have no thought of this constituting the stage of completion. All of you, make sure you achieve consummate mastery of these stages of development and completion."

Paltrul Rinpoché remarked on another occasion, "While frequenting haunted places in Menyak, Lau Tang, and so forth, I experienced countless disturbances and upheavals due to all kinds of machinations.[24] I then prayed to the entire lineage of the masters of awareness of the Nyingtik teachings, and especially to the Omniscient King of the Dharma, whereupon the disturbances and upheavals subsided of their own accord, and I perceived signs that I had received blessings. I related this to Khyentsé Yeshé Dorjé, who said, 'You have cut through the four maras[25] all at once [1.191b] and attained the most sublime siddhi.' Since then, I have not entertained many concepts about what is or is not virtuous." In fact, he meant that he had trained his mind in bodhichitta by refining his experience through all of the graduated paths, both ordinary and extraordinary; that he had brought his indwelling confidence to full measure through the stages of development and completion in the secret mantra approach of Vajrayana; and that by directly experiencing the enlightened intent of great perfection—the perception of awareness's naturally manifest appearances without bias—he had reached the level of primordial being at which phenomena resolve into their true nature.

Most notably, Paltrul Rinpoché had a vision of the Omniscient King of the Dharma, Longchenpa, in which he received from him the transmission of the enlightened intent of the ultimate lineage. He made *The Precious Treasury of the Basic Space of Phenomena* the very quintessence of his own spiritual practice. He gave extraordinary explanations of this text to his heart sons—Lungtok, Gyarong Namtrul, and others—and developed a great tradition of studying and explaining *The Seven Treasuries* and other works of Longchenpa. Paltrul Rinpoché composed the following poem urging others to study these works:

> *Namah sarva jñaya!*[26]
>
> The extensive realm of genuine being is one of primordial, utter peace.
> Timeless awareness, the expanse of dharmakaya, is forever unmoving.
> Yet you manifest the perfection of the supreme dynamic energy of enlightened intent. [1.192a]
> I pay homage to the Omniscient Guru.
>
> Ah! The nature of sublime enlightened qualities
> is such that one cannot come by them without relying on sacred scriptures.
> If priceless gems can be found only in the vast ocean,
> why should one look in a lesser place?
>
> Since the illumination of the sun—the realization of timeless awareness—
> assuredly comes from the unbroken lineage of blessings and the guru's pith instructions,
> few reach the state of genuine being through this excellent path
> if their meditation on emptiness consists of plunging themselves into darkness.

It is a great flaw in this world not to study,
but an even greater evil to study the wrong things!
While one has this time to examine the works written by the learned,
why would one not refine one's vision by listening to these teachings?

The precious tradition based on the written works of the Omniscient Guru
is a unique, wish-fulfilling gem in this world.
Since buddhahood cannot be found elsewhere,
who would not find great joy in reading them?

These precious treasuries contain the meaning of the enlightened intent underlying the hundreds of thousands of tantras
of the pinnacle spiritual approach, the sublime vajra heart essence.
Their treatment is so vast, their subject matter so profound in meaning,
that to encounter them is to encounter the very face of Samantabhadra.

They bring mastery of the meaning found in the sixty-four thousand verses of tantra, [1.192b]
knowledge of the way of abiding of all samsara and nirvana,
and realization of the special features of enlightened intent on the profound path of the pinnacle approach.
Therefore, please read these source texts diligently!

The way of abiding, dharmakaya, which cannot be maintained,
is the treasury of Samantabhadra's enlightened intent, beyond causality.
If a treatise as noble as *The Treasury of the Way of Abiding* cannot cut through concepts,
how could an inferior approach based on intellectual speculation do so?

The heart essence of all pith instructions
is thoroughly summarized in the treasury of the sacred dharma that is arranged in groups of six.
To meet a path as noble as *The Treasury of Pith Instructions* is to meet the Victorious One face-to-face,
but is it not difficult to study this even once?

The Precious Treasury of Philosophical Systems is a detailed commentary
summarizing the entire body of teachings in a single work.
A treatise as noble as this has never appeared before,
either in India or in Tibet, and I truly doubt that one ever will.

The treasury of study, contemplation, and meditation on the entire dharma,
like a wish-fulfilling gem, thoroughly reveals all that is to be accepted or rejected.
To encounter *The Wish-Fulfilling Treasury* is to understand the point of all the teachings
and to train with one work in what a hundred have to say.

The words and underlying meaning of the enlightened intent of the pinnacle approach [1.193a]
are beautifully subsumed under eleven headings in *The Treasury of Words and Their Underlying Meaning*,
which presents the key points for practicing the pith instructions in a complete but concise way.
This text is singularly powerful in cutting through the root of conditioned existence.

In particular, the genuine nature of mind, the ultimate significance of dharmakaya,
is revealed precisely as naked timeless awareness, free of anything to be added or removed.
This lies at the very core of the Omniscient Guru's enlightened intent.
Most profound of all is *The Treasury of the Basic Space of Phenomena*.

It is a work that truly ushers in the authentic dharmakaya.
A work as noble as this is an actual buddha;
it accomplishes the task of victorious ones in this world.
It is a work that directly reveals the enlightened intent of the victorious ones.
Even if you were to meet the Buddha, I truly doubt that there would be more than this.

A work as noble as this is a treasury of the entire sacred dharma.
It is the ultimate focus of all the teachings.
It reveals the timeless awareness of dharmakaya in all it nakedness.
Even if you were to compare it to all the other teachings, I truly doubt that there would be anything more than this.

A work as noble as this is the enlightened mind of the entire exalted assembly.
The timeless awareness realized by exalted victorious ones and their heirs
in the past, present, and future derives from it.
I truly doubt that the awareness of these exalted ones is anything more than this. [1.193b]

It is the totality of the Three Jewels, the stupa that enshrines the relics of dharmakaya,
and the unsurpassable legacy left by all victorious ones.
It is the portrait of the Omniscient Guru's realization.
For whoever meets with it, the end of conditioned existence is in sight.

If hearing even a single word of a work as noble as this
can tear asunder the veil of one's ordinary perceptions and reactions,
how could it make any sense at all to reject it
once you have the good fortune to study it in its entirety?

Ah! The Three Repositories and the teachings of the nine stages
are, for the most part, intended for those with diligence.
"Meditate, practice, strive, and you will become free!" it is said,
but what is not seen is timeless awareness, free of anything to be added or removed.

This vajra pinnacle—effortless, beyond ordinary consciousness—
is the expanse that is the naked unity of awareness and emptiness, buddhahood without meditation.
It is introduced as dharmakaya even to lazy people.
It involves none of the striving mind's meditation or spiritual practice.

In this world and that of the gods, the one who reveals this path
is the unique dharmakaya, the Omniscient Guru.
For as long as the teachings of the dharmakaya last,
this *Treasury of the Basic Space of Phenomena* will remain the quintessence of those teachings.

Therefore, in this world of ours, a work as noble as this
brings liberation upon being seen, [1.194a] being heard, being recalled.
Those who forge a connection with it are the buddhas of the future.
If you discover its intent, you are a buddha of the present.

It has the sharp edge of the lineage's blessings, which has not become dull.
It directs to you the flow of enlightened intent—timeless awareness, the ultimate transmission.
Secured with the seal of entrustment for future generations,
it is like the Omniscient Guru's actual presence.

Even if you do not unravel the words and their underlying meaning exactly as intended,
if you feel devotion toward it, blessings and timeless awareness will flow to you.

Encountering this work is nothing other than receiving the precious word empowerment,
the perfect empowerment into the dynamic energy of awareness.

When you are afflicted by sadness, depression, fear, or revulsion,
if you study this work, you will experience the supreme delight of timeless awareness.
You will feel cheerful and delighted, your mind lucid and clear.
The confused way in which you perceive sense objects will collapse.

When delight increases and great happiness blazes within you,
if you study this work, your fixation on frivilous states of ebullience will collapse.
This work reveals the enlightened intent of the Omniscient Guru,
the far-reaching expanse of genuine being, free of the distinctions of acceptance and rejection.

When you are afflicted by the fixations and stresses of this life,
if you study this work, the seeming solidity of your conceits will collapse.
Such a spacious outlook is fine under any and all circumstances. [1.194b]
Meditative equipoise unfolds in a relaxed way, without the strictures of hope and fear.

This work is Madhyamaka, it is Prajñaparamita,
it is Dükyi Chöyul,[27] it is Duk-ngal Zhijé,
it is Mahamudra, it is truly Dzogchen.
All teachings are contained in it, and it is far greater than them all.

If you are an heir and follower of the Omniscient Guru,
never be separate from this noble work,
and it will be enough if you rely on it as the constant ally of your awareness.
I truly doubt that there could be any other such enduring support for your mind.

For now, it supports your mind, but eventually you will attain buddhahood.
Unhampered by effort, you will feel the mind's bonds dissolve.
When you are ebullient, it will sober you; when you are sad, it will be a companion to you in your sorrow.
A work as noble as this is the one thing that will never let you down.

Therefore, lift up your voice and sing it aloud!
Study it as you recite its verses and read its prose.

If you are never separate from it,
your confused perceptions of samsara will crumble to pieces.

At a certain point, once the transmission of blessings—the key to realization—has flowed to you,
ineffable timeless awareness will well up within you.
You will behold the true face [1.195a] of the omniscient dharmakaya guru.
Relying on the blissful ground of being, the mind will be uninterruptedly blissful.

There is no spiritual practice other than studying this work.
This itself lies at the very heart of meditation and spiritual practice.
As long as you study noble works like this,
the enlightened intent of dharmakaya will arise as a matter of course.

So without increasing the inner turmoil of mental striving,
examine this work in a spacious frame of mind.
Its profound meaning is not far away at all;
come to this decision and rest in a natural state of relaxation.

You need not be tense and seek out the words and their underlying meaning,
as is the case with the treatises of pedants, so difficult to penetrate.
In this state of natural relaxation, blend your mind with this work.
The naked, spacious state is disclosed without obstruction.

This is direct introduction, this is the genuine state of timeless awareness,
this itself is the advice of the Omniscient Guru.
This is the topic under discussion, this is the actual empowerment,
this alone is sufficient as the quintessential practice.

Whether or not you unravel the derivations of the words and their underlying meaning,
whether or not you understand the profound significance being discussed,
whether or not you discover the true depths of enlightened intent,
cut through your hope and fear, and look into the undistracted state.

Look again, look again, look while blending this state with your meditative experience. [1.195b]
Blend your mind with this work, and apply its seal to your mind.
Chant the words to a joyful melody, feeling yourself inseparable from them.

The dynamic energy of your devotion will blaze, and timeless awareness will be aroused as realization.

Ah! This is what lies at the very heart of things,
the most profound of the profound; there is nothing more than this.
It is a treasure trove of blessings, it is the quintessential teaching,
it is the actual teacher, it is buddhahood in the palm of your hand.

Even if I were to speak of its virtues for an eon,
an intellect as small as mine could not exhaust the possibilities;
how much more could those confident ones of greater intellect have to say?
There is no noble path like this to delight the exalted ones.

Ah! At this point, when you have found the good fortune
to meet freely with a gem as precious as this,
even if you remain in conditioned existence, why be so sad?
Why not just arouse your devotion and be spacious?

My heart friends, let your minds light on this master's works.
Focus your attention on them in a spacious way.
The plans and designs of your turbulent, striving mind will fall away in them.
The complicated instructions of so many other works will be resolved in them.

What is the point of many written works, however elegantly composed?
What is the point of many pith instructions, [1.196a] however profound?
What is the point of many practices, however elaborate?
What is the point of many glib explanations of how things are?

For this work alone leads to carefree meditation, sufficient for the mind to rest.
This work alone leads to a spacious and happy frame of mind, naturally free.
This work alone is the noble work that shows how knowing one thing liberates all.
This alone is the single bridge under which a hundred pith instructions flow.

Aha! Don't leave this work at home to seek it elsewhere.
Aha! Don't discard the kernel to keep the husk.
Aha! Don't reject effortlessness to strive at making effort.

Aha! Don't dismiss freedom from anything needing to be done and
instead become involved in all kinds of projects.

Given that it was born of the experience of the Omniscient Guru,
a work as noble as this is the legacy of our forefathers.
A path as noble as this was forged by our ancestors.
If ever anything could bring us ease of mind, surely it is this.

Ah! Ah! How great is the compassion of the three lineages.
How fortunate are we that we can still study this noble work.
How privileged are we that we can still practice this noble path.
How true it is that buddhahood is within us.

Therefore, my dear friends, blend your minds with the dharma
on this noble path that delights the victorious ones.
This is my heartfelt advice, so let it penetrate to the depths of your hearts.
If you hold it in your hearts, [1.196b] it is possible that it will become your
essential purpose.

I, a ragged old guy, careless and stumbling about,
have no wish to prattle on about teachings that I myself have not realized,
but there is one thing I have gained,
and that is confidence in the works of the Omniscient One's lineage.

The five emotional poisons blazed in me like fire, and I wandered about
burdened with distractions.
Yet when I, whose negative karma makes it hard for me to deal with my
confused perceptions,
encountered and studied such a noble work as this,
my ordinary perceptions and reactions just collapsed.

Therefore, for you and those like you, whose minds are firm and little
troubled with thoughts based on the five poisons,
whose fortune is good and whose samaya is pure, to encounter and study
this work
means that you will assuredly receive the transmission of blessings and
attain the sublime experience of timeless awareness,
so remind yourselves of this over and over again with certainty.

For whoever is touched by the radiant blessings
of the Omniscient Guru, the perfect buddha,
it is evident that realization is simultaneous with freedom.
The Omniscient Guru is the common ancestor of hundreds of siddhas.

The great Lhatsün, powerful lord of realization,
Rigdzin Jigmé Lingpa, for whom an expanse of enlightened intent welled forth,
and Terchen Lama,[28] master of the teachings—
they all received the transmission of blessings from the works of the Omniscient One.

My dear friends, think of what they did.
Like them, hold the excellent explanatory teachings of the Omniscient One in high regard
and receive the ultimate transmission, that of timeless awareness.
May you gain freedom in the expanse of enlightened intent, the basic space of suchness! [1.197a]

Such were Paltrul Rinpoché's words. It was from this holy guru that Nyoshul Lungtok Tenpai Nyima Gyaltsen Palzangpo, also known as Gyalsé Jangchub Dorjé, heard all of these spiritual teachings without omission, like one vase being filled from another.

Nyoshul Lungtok Tenpai Nyima Gyaltsen Palzangpo (Gyalsé Jangchub Dorjé) (1829/30–1901/2)

This great being was one of the lord of the dharma Paltrul Rinpoché's previously mentioned four students who outshone him; Paltrul Rinpoché once said, "With respect to the view, [1.197b] Nyoshul Lungtok Tenpai Nyima surpasses me." He stood out like the clear, white moon among the constellations of Paltrul's students, a master of the ultimate lineage of realization, one endowed with the nine qualities of someone holy: he was wise, benevolent, powerful, erudite, venerable, noble, and so forth. In the oral histories of the Juwa region of upper Dza, it was said, "If there had been no Lungtok of Nyoshul, Palgé's[29] line would have died out." Palchen Dorjé gave us the ultimate biography of this sublime master when he wrote:

The knots of the eight worldly concerns have come untied in the state of equal taste.
The designs of ordinary consciousness have faded in the basic space of original purity.
You have directly experienced the way of abiding that is the great perfection.
Lungtok Tenpai Nyima, I pray to you.

Lungtok Tenpai Nyima was born during the fourteenth sexagesimal cycle of the Tibetan calendar within the jurisdiction of the great Buddhist ruler of Dergé in eastern Tibet, into the same line as Vajradhara Ngagi Wangpo—that is, the Nyoshul family, a nomadic branch of the Mukpodong clan. From an early age, Lungtok effortlessly manifested the signs of someone naturally holy, demonstrating an inherent grasp of love, compassion, and bodhichitta. [1.198a] He mastered these qualities by repeating the mantra of Avalokiteshvara, the exalted bodhisattva of supreme compassion, as his personal spiritual practice.

He studied the Dzogchen teachings with Gyalwa Jangchub of upper La, who gave him the instructions of direct introduction for one with instantaneous understanding and proclaimed him to be an emanation of the supremely compassionate Avalokiteshvara. Lungtok then offered his realization for approval[30] to Lama Garab of Yilhung, who said to him, "We two are a matched pair."

Later, Lungtok Tenpai Nyima went to Dzogchen Monastery, where he met Gyalsé Zhenpen Tayé.

"Have some yogurt," said the master.

"I have no bowl," he replied.

"Can't you hold out the 'naturally occurring skull cup'?" asked the master.

Lungtok held out his cupped hands, whereupon the master murmured with great delight, "Such a fine intellect!"

From both this master and Khenpo Pema Dorjé, Lungtok received the entire range of empowerments and teachings, such as the precious kama transmissions of the Early Translation school. He was also fully ordained as a monk by Gyalsé Zhenpen Tayé. It was then that he received the name Lungtok Tenpai Nyima. Paltrul Rinpoché commented, "That's a little too short for an ordination name, so you should end it with 'Gyaltsen Palzangpo.'" The newly named Lungtok Tenpai Nyima Gyaltsen Palzangpo, [1.198b] as a vajra holder who was also a fully ordained monk, was as solid as a mountain of gold, unsullied by even the slightest flaw of impairing or falling short of his vows. Terchen Lerab Lingpa praised him, proclaiming him an incarnation of the great Indian master Shantarakshita.

Lungtok received the oral transmissions for the Kangyur from Lingtrul. With Mingyur Namkhai Dorjé, he studied many profound teachings, such as *The Positive Path to Liberation: The Definitive Meaning, The Heart Drop of the Dakini's Secret,* and *The Demonstration of the Vajra Path,* a text concerning secret conduct from the cycle *The Innermost Heart Drop of the Dakini.*

To Lungtok, Paltrul Rinpoché was the outstanding lord of his buddha family, the guru with whom he had shared a karmic connection for lifetimes. When Lungtok first met him, Paltrul was reading *Reciting the Names of Mañjushri* aloud and had reached the line that states, "The most excellent guru, worthy of being shown homage...." Paltrul remarked, "This is a very auspicious coincidence," and repeated the line aloud, showing his delight. Like a father being reunited with his son, Paltrul Rinpoché cared for Lungtok with loving affection. From that point, for the next twenty-eight years of his life, Lungtok Tenpai Nyima acted as Paltrul's attendant, [1.199a] inseparable from his master. There was not a single word of anything the guru said about the sutras, tantras, or any secular subject that Lungtok did not hear. He and Kunsö of Minyak were both reputed to have received Paltrul's teachings on *Engaging in the Conduct of a Bodhisattva* eighty times. It was Kunsö who composed, according to standard methods of exegesis, a major commentary of more than seven hundred folios on *Engaging in the Conduct of a Bodhisattva,* which is of a kind rarely found in either the Indian or Tibetan Buddhist tradition.

The sublime master Lungtok based his own spiritual practice on *Engaging in the Conduct of a Bodhisattva* and on bodhichitta. He memorized such texts as *The Highest Continuum, The Ornament of the Sutras,* and the root text *The Heart Essence of Secrets* and its commentary. In these and other ways, he mastered the entire array of the mainstream traditions of sutra and tantra.

When the master Paltrul and the student Lungtok were staying in the region of Arik in Do, Lungtok received the transmission of *The Three Cycles of Being at Ease.* When they came to the cycle *Being at Ease in Illusoriness,* he noted, "The seeming truth with which I have invested my perceptions now arises in my experience as the unreal phantasmagoria of illusion."

At this point, both master and student were short of provisions, so for a long time they lived on a poor diet, digging up the roots of a shrub called *surkar.*[31] [1.199b] They would make this into a tea every morning, resteeping the roots throughout the day, so that the tea got progressively weaker, until by evening it was only clear water. As a joke, dear old Abu[32] would say, "This is the Dzogchen tea of the three kayas."[33]

Once, while they were staying at the hermitage of Changma, Paltrul Rinpoché asked, "My dear Lung, do you ever think of your old mother?"

"I don't think of her all that much," Lungtok replied.

"Meditate for seven days on the understanding that she is your mother, being aware of her kindness to you," said Paltrul.

Lungtok did so, and that insight arose in his heart in an uncontrived way. He told his guru that he had a strong desire to visit his old mother.

Paltrul Rinpoché responded, "I have told you not to rely on tainted food offerings, which are morally compromising, but this one time, take whatever provisions you can acquire."[34]

Accordingly, Lungtok traveled from the Dzachu River to Yilhung, where he met his old mother. He later said, "When I deliberately chase after such tainted offerings, I find nothing; but when I don't need them, they seem to keep piling up."

While student and teacher were together again, staying in a small thicket near Dzogchen Monastery, every evening dear old Abu would practice the exercise known as "threefold space," which involves stretching out one's body. Every night, Lungtok dreamed of a skein of black yarn [1.200a] that he was saving. Then one night he dreamed that dear old Abu had unraveled the skein by pulling on one end, revealing a golden statue of Vajrasattva hidden within. In the dream, Lungtok thought to himself, "If I had known earlier that it was there, I wouldn't have gone to so much trouble!"

Another night, dear old Abu asked, "Tell me, my dear Lung, would you say that you know how to meditate?"

"No, I don't know how," he replied.

"Well, just stretch out as I do, and there is nothing you won't understand," Paltrul said. "Do you see the vault of the sky? Do you hear the dogs barking at Dzogchen Monastery? Do you understand what we say when we speak? What we call 'meditation' is nothing more than that."

Upon hearing this, Lungtok was freed from the bonds of things having to be this or that. Conviction arose in him, and he realized timeless awareness, the naked unity of awareness and emptiness. Were one to try to analyze such an experience after the fact, it would seem to simply be something like, "Both visual consciousness and auditory consciousness are awareness." But Lungtok noted, "It is said, 'For those in whose heart the guru's pith instructions are planted, it is as though a treasure lies in the palm of their hand.' This signifies that I have met a guru who is a siddha and that the enlightened intent of the ultimate lineage has been passed to my heart. It also shows that the crucial point in this lineage is that of gaining freedom through devotion." [1.200b]

While Lungtok was training with the syllable *Hum* (as explained in *Timeless Awareness as the Guiding Principle*) in the cave of Shinjé Drubpuk, he perceived the world of appearances and possibilities in an unobstructed way. He said, "Palchen Dorjé came to me pretending to be a calf, carrying in its mouth the peg to which its tether was tied; this gave me real insight."[35]

It was here that Lungtok received from Paltrul Rinpoché the transmission of *The Treasury of the Basic Space of Phenomena, The Heart Essence of Secrets,* and many other profound teachings on the entire range of pith instructions concerning the ultimate meaning of the tantras—the key points of the development and completion stages in the Vajrayana approach. He received these not as a mere plethora of words, but as truly meaningful pith instructions, which he applied in the immediacy of his own experience.

In brief, Paltrul empowered Lungtok as his regent in the ultimate sense, that of realization, bestowing on him in their entirety the tantras, explanatory commentaries, and pith instructions of the secret Nyingtik teachings of utter lucidity, as well as all the written works of the Omniscient One Longchenpa and his spiritual heir, Jigmé Lingpa, including the great *Seven Treasuries, The Four Higher Collections of the Heart Drop, The Three Cycles of Being at Ease,* and *Timeless Awareness as the*

Guiding Principle. Dear old Abu bequeathed to his student his own copies of *The Seven Treasuries* and *Timeless Awareness as the Guiding Principle,* with annotations in red ink in the margins. Today these books are on display at the library of Shugushar.

One day, dear old Abu said, "Go to the hermitage on the glacier of Dzogchen and meditate!" Following his guru's instructions, Lungtok spent three years on the upper glacier above Dzogchen Monastery, [1.201a] practicing the heart essence, relying on nonconceptual space as his sustenance. He was graced with visions of a vast array of his personal meditation deities. He directly experienced the great perfection of utter lucidity, the enlightened intent of dharmakaya—the perception of awareness's naturally manifest appearances without bias—and he brought the four visions of spontaneous presence to consummation.

After three years, Lungtok met with his guru, who asked him, "Did you have a hard time of it?"

He replied, "Although I had absolutely nothing to sustain me, I was happy just thinking that I was there both by your wish and for the sake of Mingyur Namkhai Dorjé's longevity."[36] Extremely delighted, Paltrul Rinpoché remarked, "Whoever said, 'If a practitioner does not impair samaya, the gods and demons of the world provide sustenance,' had someone like you in mind."

One day during Lungtok Tenpai Nyima's fortieth year, Paltrul said to him, "My dear Lung, the time is ripe for an emanation of the master Vimalamitra to appear, but it seems I won't meet him. You, however, will. Now go home, live in a hermitage, and look after your retinue." Lungtok thus returned to his homeland in Nyoshul Valley. In cliffside and forest retreats such as Dzong Karnak and the hermitage of Gyaduk, with only birds and wild animals for companions, [1.201b] relying on nonconceptual space for sustenance, and wearing mist and rain clouds as his garments, he lived in caves, hollow trees, and so forth. He moved about randomly and frequented lonely, unpopulated places, where he planted the victory banner of his spiritual practice. Following the example of the venerable Milarepa, he practiced by focusing on the heart essence of the teachings.

He then went to meet Jamyang Khyentsei Wangpo, from whom he received many profound teachings, such as *The Four Higher Collections of the Heart Drop*. Following this, Khyentsei Wangpo gave him a *tangka* of the great Omniscient One Longchenpa, a piece of that master's skull, and some of Jigmé Lingpa's hair, appointing him a master of the secret Nyingtik teachings. He recognized Lungtok as the tulku of both the hidden yogin known as the "madman of Kongpo"[37] and Jé-ön Kundrol Namgyal.[38] Later, while using this tangka in his spiritual practice, Lungtok had a vision of the Omniscient One, and the realization that is the ultimate lineage of enlightened intent was passed to him. At Jamyang Khyentsei Wangpo's monastic seat, to such teachers as Gotsa Lama Tenpel, Jamyang Loter Wangpo,[39] and Jamgön

Mipam Rinpoché, Lungtok offered instructions on *Timeless Awareness as the Guiding Principle,* embellishing it with oral commentaries that had been transmitted to him by dear old Abu. Loter Wangpo subsequently gave the transmission to Jamyang Chökyi Lodrö, [1.202a] who held this "great experiential transmission of pith instructions" in the highest esteem. This explains the following reference in the account of Chökyi Lodrö's spiritual development:

> From Jamyang Loter Wangpo,
> you requested the experiential transmission of the Nyingtik teachings,
> the pith instructions of Lungtok Tenpai Nyima.

Loter Wangpo himself pursued this practice and compiled teaching manuals based on the oral lineage, in which he discussed his personal experiences leading up to the vision of the "enrichment of meditative experience."

After Gyalsé Zhenpen Tayé died, Jamgön Mipam Rinpoché continually praised Lungtok Tenpai Nyima, saying, "The one with the greatest understanding of the Nyingma school is Lungtok of Nyoshul." In later years, Lungtok wrote many essays answering questions about the Nyingtik teachings and *Timeless Awareness as the Guiding Principle.* At the monastery of Katok Dorjéden, he circumambulated the great shrine housing a hundred thousand statues. In a cave known as Jangsem Puk, which no one frequented except for wild animals and their hunters, he spent three years practicing the yoga of nonconceptual space. Although he experienced various upheavals, such as a hallucination in which he saw a tiger hiding in the kusha grass, [1.202b] all of these resolved themselves, and people were not even aware that a guru was staying there.

Lungtok Tenpai Nyima then went home once more to Shugushar, spending the next thirteen years engaged in spiritual practice based on *Engaging in the Conduct of a Bodhisattva* and *The Three Cycles of Being at Ease.* He carried out the requisite intensive retreats associated with the kama transmissions of the Nyingma school, and the indwelling confidence he gained through his practice of the stages of development and completion became fully evident; for example, the ritual dagger on his shrine would dance around by itself.

Following his guru's directives, he taught to countless fortunate students the entire range of the secret and profound Nyingtik teachings of utter lucidity. Whenever he taught the dharma, people found themselves settling quite naturally into states of meditative stability. He was invited to the encampment of Nyala Pema Duddul and there taught a host of accomplished, noble students. Foremost among them were his students, greatly accomplished adepts known as the "hundred or more named Dorjé," including Nyala Rang-rik Dorjé, Nyala Yeshé Dorjé, Nyala Özer Dorjé, Nyala Melong Dorjé, and Garab Dorjé. He stayed for nine years, turning the wheel of the dharma for many thousands—the students of Drupjé Pema Duddul who gathered there, as well as those in the surrounding areas of Peltsa, Kulung, Shinglung, and Drakar. [1.203a] He gave away everything he owned seven times.

He used to say, "A true Nyingma practitioner should follow the mainstream kama transmissions, adorning them with terma teachings." He gave extensive and profound teachings, such as the Nyingtik cycles of the Dzogchen approach, while focusing on the kama lineages of the Early Translation school.

In his sixtieth year, Lungtok Tenpai Nyima returned home, where he settled in a large encampment comprising hundreds of tents on the peak of Pema Rito in the region of Trom. There he turned the wheel of the secret Nyingtik teachings of the Dzogchen approach, emphasizing the writings of the Omniscient One Longchenpa and his spiritual heir, Jigmé Lingpa, and caring for countless fortunate students. Every corner of the region became part of a large tapestry of spiritual energy, to the point where there was not even one ordinary man or woman who did not know of the Three Jewels and the three phases—the preparation, main body, and conclusion—of spiritual practice. It was here that Lungtok Tenpai Nyima took Khenchen Ngawang Palzang, an emanation of Vimalamitra, under his care, entrusting to him all of the tantras, explanatory commentaries, and pith instructions of the secret Nyingtik teachings of the Dzogchen approach and investing him as his regent.

All of the fluids that Lungtok excreted from his body naturally crystallized, forming the "stones of Vajrasattva," [1.203b] and were renowned as the "crystalline fluids of Lungtok," some of which can still be seen today. No matter where he was, he never wavered from a daily schedule of four sessions of meditation practice. When people first arrived at his encampment, they would notice that their ordinary confused perceptions had come to a halt and would experience instead a natural state of meditative stability. Even the birds and wild animals were calm and elegantly graceful as they flitted and gamboled about. In front of the encampment flowed a large river called the Yilé. A couple of miles below the camp, the water flowed so gently that it made no sound. The local people said that even the water that came from Lungtok of Nyoshul's camp was meditating in silence.

The fifth Dzogchen Rinpoché, Tupten Chökyi Dorjé, told Lungtok Tenpai Nyima, "Since the passing of the lord of the dharma Paltrul, in all of eastern Tibet you are the only one who can demonstrate the key points of the Dzogchen approach without error, so please come to Dzogchen Monastery." Despite this honor, Lungtok never actually went, noting, "Paltrul Rinpoché told me to remain in a hermitage in my home region; [1.204a] there I would meet an emanation of the master Vimalamitra. Since this was my guru's wish, I will remain here."

He instituted the custom of giving courses on the Nyingtik teachings every summer and winter, attracting innumerable people with fortunate karma from all over eastern Tibet, as far away as Golok and Sertang to the north and Tsawa Rong to the south. Among these students were many tulkus and great beings of high social standing and lofty spiritual qualities, such pillars of the teachings as Sönam Chokdrup of Naktar and Khenchen Ngawang Palzang, who was an emanation of Vimalamitra, together with other lamas and masters, monastics, lay masters, and great meditators, as well as ordinary lay people. To all of them, Lungtok Tenpai Nyima gave teachings, which he varied according to each person's needs. Lungtok was noted for teaching without being too intellectual; nor did he engage in mere verbiage. Instead, he directly and without confusion brought his students to the key point in light of each one's immediate experience. Through personal experience and a thorough style of teaching, he imparted the living transmission of the great oral lineage of pith instructions. Thus all of his students gained an authentic degree of confidence in their own experiences and realization. People would often say, [1.204b] "There is no one who, having requested Dzogchen teachings from Lungtok of Nyoshul, does not experience a direct introduction to the true nature of mind." And this proved to be so.

The people of the region gave up rituals involving blood sacrifice, hunting wild animals, thieving and banditry, and all harmful actions involving the taking of life. They carved into stone the mantra *Om mani padme hum,* three popular discourses of the Buddha (including the sutras *The Fortunate Eon* and *The Holy Golden Light*), the sutra *The Urn,* which concerns Avalokiteshvara, and other texts. Many made the commitment to recite the six-syllable mantra *Om mani padme hum* and *Om ah hum vajra guru padma siddhi hum* a hundred million times. Every woman and man, even the humblest householders in the area, turned to the dharma, exerting a positive influence over the entire region. Wherever Lungtok Tenpai Nyima went, merely by focusing his attention on a situation, he could reverse and pacify harm caused by frost, hail, or epidemics among humans or livestock.

He lived thus until the age of seventy-two, a protector of all the teachings and all beings, manifesting unparalleled spiritual activities and, like a wish-fulfilling gem, masterfully meeting the needs of individual students. When he showed signs of illness, ceremonies for extending his life were performed. He commented, "These will not be of benefit, but I am prepared to transfer my consciousness into a pure corpse, if one can be found."[40] Under the circumstances, however, one was not found, [1.205a] and at daybreak on the seventeenth day of the fifth month,[41] he spoke the following words as a kind of testament:

> To be immersed in genuine, unfettered being is to be like the sun rising
> at dawn.
> This is the vision of dharmakaya—how marvelous!

Then, at a certain point, he allowed his enlightened intent to resolve back into the primordial state of inner basic space. He left no possessions behind except a small bag of roasted barley flour, proving that he had fully upheld the four standards of a simple way of life embraced by the Kadampa masters. When his remains were laid in state, the sky took on a lucency like molten aquamarine, with networks of rainbows shimmering against this background. A gentle rain, mingled with blossoms, fell over the whole region. Everyone present heard music and singing and other things that indicated the gods who support all that is positive were making offerings. Innumerable relics, impervious to the elements, appeared, so that all were moved to faith.

Lungtok Tenpai Nyima's immediate rebirth was Lungtrul Lodrö Shedrup Tenpai Nyima, recognized by Khenchen Ngawang Palzang; I and others were fortunate to have this teacher as the lord of our buddha family, [1.205b] the Vajradhara who resided at the monastic seat of Lungtok Tenpai Nyima.

Among the students of Lungtok Tenpai Nyima were two great tertöns, Lerab Lingpa and Tutop Lingpa, who were like the sun and moon. There were four great khenpos, who were like golden mountains: Khenchen Ngawang Palzang, Khenchen Dorjé Samdrup, Khenchen Gyaltsen Özer, and Khenchen Tenpel Zangpo. There were four sublime tulkus: Serdok Tulku, Naktar Tulku, Tulku Rang-rik Dorjé, and Tulku Tendzin Zangpo. There were other holy masters who upheld this lineage and who accomplished great things for the precious teachings of the Victorious One, including Lingda Norkho, the artisan Lhazo Rigdzin, Lama Pema Losel of Dokhok, and Pema Dorjé of Peltsa. Foremost among these students was Vajradhara Ngagi Wangpo, master of the ultimate lineage of inner realization and the emanation of Vimalamitra prophesied by Paltrul Rinpoché.

To enshrine his remains, Lungtok Tenpai Nyima's closest students built a memorial of earth and stone. On the auspicious occasion of its completion, the sky was filled with shimmering rainbows, and everyone saw nonhuman beings circumambulating it. In front of the memorial, Khen Lama Ngawang Palzang made the following supplication: [1.206a]

> Great and glorious Vajrakumara!
> I have been connected to you for thirteen lifetimes.
> You guide all of those connected to you, whether by positive or negative karma,
> to the palace of Pema Ö.

Each student with appropriate karma perceived many manifestations of Lungtok Tenpai Nyima's enlightened form and speech, so that those with a connection to him found that connection meaningful.

It was from this holy guru that Vajradhara Ngagi Wangpo received the tantras, explanatory commentaries, and pith instructions of the Dzogchen approach of utter lucidity.

Khenchen Ngawang Palzangpo (Khenpo Ngaga, Khenpo Ngakchung, Khenpo Ngagi Wangpo) (1879–1941)

The glorious protector, the holy guru Khenchen Ngawang Palzangpo, was born amid positive, marvelous omens in the "Intoxicating Year," the Female Earth Hare year, of the fifteenth sexagesimal cycle of the Tibetan calendar,[42] [1.206b] on the morning of the tenth day of the tenth month. Pematso, the village of his birth, was located on the banks of the Dri River, close to the ridge of Drida Zalmo Gang and near the mountain range of Shampo Rong in Katok—one of the twenty-five principal holy sites in eastern Tibet—on the slopes of Lingmok Pema Drakar, a place visited in the past by numerous great, holy people. He was born into a humble nomadic family known as Nyoshul, who were descendants of Lingtruk Atra, one of the "seven bandits of Lharu." This family line in turn hailed from the lesser of the three branches of the Ling clan (the other two being known as the greater and intermediate branches), who traced their origins to the Mukpodong clan. Ngawang Palzang's father was Namgyal, and his mother was Jupa of upper Dza.

For three days, the newborn sat in meditation posture, repeating the mantras of Vajrakila and other deities. He did not think or behave like other children his age, but instead clearly displayed the conduct of a siddha, recalling former lifetimes, making prophetic statements, and so forth, without concealing any of this information from others.

While being taught to read at the age of seven, Ngawang Palzang immediately learned the characters of the Tibetan alphabet without difficulty. With his excellent diction and clear understanding of all the subjects under discussion, [1.207a] he continually surpassed other children his age. The fifth Zhechen Rabjam, knowing the child to be a tulku associated with his own monastery, saw the need to ransom the boy from his home region[43] and gave him the name Tenpa Rabpel. Then the fifth Dzogchen ordained him, naming him Zhönnu Pema Lekdrup. Moreover, the eighteenth Dzipu Zhabdrung regent gave him the name Ngawang Palzang and foretold the extent of his spiritual development.

The boy then realized that he needed to rely on a qualified guru and to please that guru through the three kinds of service,[44] for he understood that one's pure realization of the three spiritual approaches of Buddhism depended entirely on a guru or spiritual mentor. With the sublime knowing acquired by listening to, contemplating, and meditating on the stainless mainstream traditions of sutra and tantra, he sought to gain spiritual realization for his own benefit, while teaching, writing texts, and debating in order to spread the teachings of the victorious ones without bias for the benefit of others. This, he felt, was the unsurpassable example that could be set by a holy being.

Ngawang Palzang's first mentor—Gyalsé Jangchub Dorjé, or Lungtok Tenpai Nyima Gyaltsen Palzangpo—was unrivaled throughout the three worlds. [1.207b] Among the constellations of students of Paltrul Rinpoché Jigmé Chökyi Wangpo, Lungtok Tenpai Nyima stood out like the majestic moon, endowed as he was with wisdom, love, and spiritual power. Fulfilling his guru's prophecy, Lungtok had come to Ngawang Palzang's region and established his principal monastic seat in this verdant valley. Earlier, when Lungtok was staying at the hermitage of Gyaduk, Ngawang Palzang's father had taken the lad, then five, to meet this master. Overjoyed, Lungtok took the boy under his care, making him his heart son.

When Ngawang Palzang turned fifteen, he took the vows of a novice monk in the presence of the requisite number of faithful monastics,[45] including the abbot, Khenchen Gyaltsen Özer; the preceptor, Khenpo Tsultrim Norbu of Kulung; the keeper of the records, Karma Damchö Özer; the helper, Tsewang Rigdzin; and the ritual assistant, Namdrol Gyatso, a Vajrayana master of Mindroling Monastery. Ngawang Palzang strictly observed all the points of moral discipline, without hypocrisy or pretension but with an attitude of certainty born of renunciation. [1.208a]

In particular, with Lungtok Rinpoché, his guru of unparalleled kindness, he studied the preliminary practices of the *The Heart Drop of Longchenpa,* up to and including the profound teachings on the main body of practice, supplemented by the oral lineage of instructions, receiving these like one vase being filled to the brim from another. Ngawang Palzang then put these teachings into practice, so that he directly experienced, just as they are described, the inner states of realization on the levels and paths. Such realization enabled him to prepare criticial editions of the excellent works of the Omniscient One Longchenpa and his spiritual heir, Jigmé Lingpa, as well as of tantras and other source works. He was cared for by the timeless awareness embodiment of the great Omniscient One and was graced with visions of him time and time again. His guru Lungtok would say, "Dear old Abu told me, 'An emanation of Vimalamitra is about to appear, and you will meet him.' It was this dear Ngawang he was referring to."

In short, for six years Lungtok conferred on Ngawang Palzang all of the tantras, explanatory commentaries, and pith instructions of the secret Nyingtik teachings of utter lucidity in their entirety, foremost among these the great *Seven Treasuries, The Four Higher Collections of the Heart Drop,* and the classes of tantras dealing with the definitive truth of the supreme secret. He transmitted these teachings to his student like one vase filling another to the brim. Ngawang Palzang became his guru's single inner heart son and a master of the ultimate lineage of realization. Without indulging in intellectual speculation about the true nature of phenomena, he put the teachings into practice and arrived at an ongoing experience of the enlightened intent of pervasive and extensive space, [1.208b] bringing the yoga of the four visions to consummation.

On the evening that Lungtok finished giving him the teachings concerning the main body of practice, he instructed Ngawang Palzang, "Pay attention to your dreams." That night, Ngawang Palzang dreamed that Yeshé Tsogyal gave him a volume of scripture, telling him that it was the treasury of the enlightened minds of the masters of awareness, the gurus of the three lineages. Later that night, he dreamed about an ancient monument, a stupa built by the Indian Buddhist king Ashoka, which crumbled from the spire downward and fell into the western ocean as though carried by a great flood, the ocean turning a murky red. From the sky, a voice said, "Millions of beings living in the ocean have seen the truth." This second dream seemed to have been an omen foretelling the destruction of the teachings in Tibet and their dissemination in the foreign lands of the Western Hemisphere.

When he reached the age of twenty, as his guru instructed, Ngawang Palzang took the full ordination of a monk from a group of ten ordained members of the sangha, including Khenpo Tupten Gyaltsen Özer. From then on, focusing on the ideals of having few desires and cultivating contentment, he conducted himself flawlessly according to the examples set by advanced spiritual practitioners. As a threefold vajra holder,[46] he was like a mountain of solid gold and firmly established the teachings of the Victorious One. [1.209a]

His precious root guru gave him the following advice: "The Victorious One's teachings will soon wane, so it is imperative that you pursue your studies unflaggingly. I have great hope that you will benefit others. You must go to Dzogchen Monastery to continue your studies without first waiting for me to die. Do not end up like me—an old monk who doesn't understand the texts, it thus being of no consequence if he becomes ill and dies." His guru was insistent, so on the twenty-ninth day of the ninth month of a Rat year,[47] Ngawang Palzang went to Dzogchen Monastery.

There he studied diligently under the tutelage of two figures: Khenzur Losel Tenkyong and Khen Sönam Chöpel of Letok, also known as Shedrup Chökyi Nangwa; Ngawang Palzang used to say that these two were his most important gurus. He also studied with such masters as Jamgön Mipam Rinpoché; Lama Rigdzin Dorjé of Minyak, a student of Jamgon Rinpoché's; Pema Dechen Zangpo of Mura; Khenpo Yeshé Gyatso; and Khenpo Apal of Minyak. He pleased numerous learned and accomplished mentors by rendering the three kinds of service and pursued his wide-ranging studies and contemplation with great energy, reaching the highest level of scholastic achievement. [1.209b]

In a Tiger year,[48] Ngawang Palzang had planned to return to his home region, but while he was at the plateau of Pemaitang, a messenger arrived from Chöying Rolpai Dorjé, the Druktrul Kuchen of Dzogchen Monastery. Ngawang Palzang immediately set off to seek an audience with this master, who told him, "*The Innermost Heart*

Drop of the Dakini is truly a cycle that gives the name of 'Dzogchen' to whoever holds it. Mingyur Namkhai Dorjé entrusted me with the maturing empowerments and liberating instructions for this cycle, and now the time has come for me to pass them on to you." He then joyfully bestowed the transmission on Ngawang Palzang, who received it as an expression of Chöying Rolpai Dorjé's aspirations.

Ngawang Palzang completed his study, contemplation, and meditation with innumerable learned and accomplished holy masters, such as Situ Rinpoché of Katok Monastery,[49] Katok Jé-ön, Khenpo Zhenga of Dzogchen Monastery, Khenpo Kunpel, and Khenpo Lhagyal. He thus became a master of the entire range of the Victorious One's teachings.

At Katok Monastery, he was appointed abbot, an office he held for thirteen years, acting as a mainstay of the teachings through his study and lectures. He was a source of learning and spiritual attainment, having trained thirty-seven great khenpos and presided over thirty thousand ordinations during his tenure. He founded shedras at Palyul and Dralak Monasteries, [1.210a] institutions that continue to uphold their traditions of teachings today. During his lifetime, Ngawang Palzang bestowed the maturing empowerments, liberating instructions, and supportive oral transmissions for *The Treasury of Precious Hidden Teachings* three times, the empowerments and oral transmissions for the termas of Longsel Dorjé Nyingpo three times, the transmission of the mother and child Nyingtik collections twenty-seven times, the teachings of *The Seven Treasuries* thirteen times, and the kama transmissions of the Early Translation school an unspecified number of times. In these and other ways, he drew from all of the spiritual teachings—those of the kama and terma lineages—of the Early Translation school without exception as the basis of his activities.

In his explanations, moreover, he did not use the empty words of someone focused on superficial points or a complex teaching style geared only to the sophisticated, nor was he bogged down by minutiae appealing to pedants. Rather, he insisted that his students apply the key points of his teachings to their own experience. This was especially true in the case of the principles underlying the oral transmission of the Dzogchen teachings. To teach the difference between ordinary mind and pure awareness in the approach of trekchö, he would introduce his students directly to their own true nature as timeless awareness in all its nakedness, the unity of awareness and emptiness. For the approach of tögal, he would impart the teachings specific to this unsurpassable path—the pith instructions concerning the so-called four lamps—in a very intimate way, relating them to the three phases of ground, path, and fruition in conjunction with the realization of the "precious enclosure of spontaneous presence." In such ways, his teachings were directly relevant to his students' own immediate experience; [1.210b] he thus irresistibly won the hearts of many leaders of the learned and spiritually adept. They would say, "Never before have such explanations of Dzogchen been heard!" and they would receive these teachings of Khenpo Ngakchung's oral lineage as often as possible. Such admiration was not limited to those of the Nyingma school; many scholars of other traditions accorded Ngawang Palzang the highest respect, regarding him as they would a jewel on the crown of their heads. In fact, during the later part of his life, he was famed as "Vimalamitra from Tromtal."

During this entire period, he continued to exert himself in the heart essence of spiritual practice and in the yogas of development and completion, so that he had visions of gurus and vast hosts of deities of the Three Roots. At times, his body seemed transparent, casting no shadow. The symbolic implements of the five buddha families would appear on his body, and the syllable *A* would spontaneously appear on the tip of his nose. On all holy days, such signs would be apparent to most who saw him. During his empowerments and teachings, people found themselves quite naturally resting in meditative stability.

Ngawang Palzang once had a vision of Guru Padmakara and his consort, who conferred on him the oral lineage of a major commentary on the practice of Vajrakila, *The Black Stupa*. He also journeyed to Oddiyana, the land of dakas and dakinis, where he received personal transmissions of such tantras as those of Guhyasamaja and Chakrasamvara. [1.211a] He went to the pinnacle pure realm of Akanishtha, where he received the empowerment for the secret cycle *The Heart Drop of the Dakini* and was given the name Ösel Rinchen Nyingpo Pema Ledrel Tsal.

He was guided in visions by Rigdzin Kumaradza, who conferred on him the pith instructions of the great Nyingtik teachings in their entirety and gave him the secret name Kunchen Longchen Rabjam Gangshar Rolpa Tsal. He was also graced with a vision of Her Majesty Kongjo, King Trisong Detsen's Chinese queen, from whom he received the complete transmission of all tantras, explanatory commentaries, and pith instructions for the various activity rituals associated with Tara. At Paro Taktsang in Bhutan, Ngawang Palzang had a pure vision of the glorious Dorjé Drolö and composed an important sadhana based on this deity. King Jah with fortunate karma, Panchen Vimalamitra, Longchenpa, Jigmé Lingpa, the lord Tsongkhapa, Nup Sanggyé Yeshé, the lord of the dharma Paltrul, Jamgön Kongtrul Lodrö Tayé—all these embodiments of timeless awareness, as well as those of countless other holy masters, guided and passed on to him the enlightened intent of the ultimate lineage.

When he presided over the practice to prepare medicine according to a cycle focusing on the Eight Commands, all of the medicine suddenly appeared in the form of the great and glorious principal deity, [1.211b] and many white flowers, a hand span or more in diameter, appeared to grow spontaneously on the surface of the mandala. The offering nectars of "medicine" and *rakta*[50] boiled, and the water in the vases turned into nectar.

Ngawang Palzang undertook intensive retreats on the deities of such cycles as *The United Intent of the Gurus,* those focusing on the Eight Commands on Sadhana Practice, the glorious Vajrakila, and the transcendent and accomplished conqueror

Yamantaka and had visions of these sublime deities. These and countless other amazing, pure visionary experiences are described in Ngawang Palzang's autobiography, *An Account of Marvels: Playful Dance in the Illusion.*

After thus serving as a protector of all the teachings and all beings for sixty-two years, he allowed his enlightened intent to resolve back into primordial inner basic space. Lungtrul Shedrup Tenpai Nyima, Choktrul Gyurmé Dorjé, and others cremated his remains, from which a stream of nectar flowed incessantly. People were moved to wonder and faith by the countless relics that appeared in all of the places where smoke from the pyre drifted. At weekly intervals thereafter, people heard rumbling noises, felt large earthquakes, and saw canopies of rainbow light shimmering in every direction. [1.212a] A small stupa was built on the cremation site, and for three years afterward, whenever people prayed to it, commensurate with their good fortune, relics issued forth uninterruptedly. The lord of my buddha family, Lungtrul Shedrup Tenpai Nyima, built a commemorative tomb decorated with gold and copper and inset with many precious stones. For three years, the outlines of various symbols—the eight auspicious emblems, the eight auspicious substances, and so on—spontaneously appeared in the water bowls in front of it.

Among the students guided by Ngawang Palzang's enlightened speech were Penor Tulku of Palyul Monastery, Chaktsa Tulku of Katok Monastery, Arik Tulku of Tromgé, and Lodrö Shedrup Tenpai Nyima, who was the tulku of Lungtok. These four were Ngawang Palzang's main heart sons, the "four great pillars." He also taught Choktrul Gyurmé Dorjé, who achieved high levels of erudition and spiritual attainment, lofty like the jeweled tip of a victory banner. In addition, his students included thirty-seven truly great scholars, such bulwarks of the teachings as Khenchen Gendun Gyatso of upper Nyarong, Khenchen Lekshé Jorden of Katok Monastery, Khenchen Gyaltsen Özer the Younger, Khenchen Dorjé of Polo, Khenchen Munsel of Golok, [1.212b] Khenchen Karma Tashi of Gonjo, and Khen Gönpo of Gyara. His students also included Choktrul Orgyen Chemchok (son of a tertön), Jadral Yoru Gyalpo, Jadral Drönma Tsering, Jadral Lama Orgyen Rigdzin, Chatral Sanjé Dorjé, Zhichen Bairo Rinpoché, Tokden Lama Yöndri, Lakar Tokden, and the dakinis Samten Drönma and Tsultrim Drönma. It is fair to say that during this time, throughout eastern Tibet, from Golok in the north to Tsawa Rong, Mesa-ngen, and Gonjo in the south, there was no one among all of the important lamas, teachers, and meditators, the venerable scholars, and the spiritual adepts who did not study at the feet of Ngawang Palzang. Through countless sublime individuals who maintained the vitality of the teachings under his tutelage, he caused the great oral transmission of pith instructions to spread throughout the ten directions. His heart sons—the "four great pillars," the "eight ridgepoles," the "twenty-one domes," the "twenty-eight rafters," the "thousand joists," and the "countless braces" [1.213a] —appeared just as he predicted. Among them, it was the lord of my buddha family, Lungtrul Shedrup Tenpai

Nyima, who was established on the golden throne of a spiritual ruler of the three realms and entrusted with Ngawang Palzang's principal monastic seat, serving as the regent of the guru's three secrets.

Thus this sublime being, Ngawang Palzang, was truly Vimalamitra returning in accordance with that master's promise to come back to Tibet once every century. During Ngawang Palzang's lifetime, he had three visions of the Omniscient King of the Dharma, Longchenpa, who passed to him the enlightened intent of the ultimate lineage—the realization of great perfection—so that he attained the most sublime siddhi. During his first vision, in an utterly lucid dream state, Ngawang Palzang beheld Longchenpa dressed in monastic robes, seated, holding a heart-shaped crystal and employing the dharmakaya gazing technique. Longchenpa bestowed on him the word empowerment for the three categories of Dzogchen. During a pure visionary experience of utter lucidity while practicing tögal, Ngawang Palzang beheld the Omniscient King of the Dharma for the second time; Longchenpa passed to him the enlightened awareness of the ultimate lineage. Given that he was resting in this enlightened intent in all its nakedness—the unity of awareness and emptiness, the infinite vision of the pure nature of phenomena— [1.213b] Ngawang Palzang did not describe the details of the vision, how the guru's face and hands appeared and so forth. The third time, he beheld Longchenpa directly with his ordinary senses, whereupon the guru granted him permission to write books of his own, saying, "If you compose treatises on the key tenets of the Dzogchen approach, you will benefit as many beings as there are atoms." Accordingly, he wrote such works as *A Commentary on the Enlightened Mind of Samantabhadra* and *The Innermost Record: A Detailed Exegesis of the Supremely Vast Expanse of Space*. During that third vision, with the timeless awareness embodiment of the Omniscient One Ngagi Wangpo as his witness, Ngawang Palzang composed *Bringing Meaning to All Who Have a Connection*, a prayer of aspiration concerning the definitive tantras of the supreme secret and the works of Longchenpa:

> How marvelous!
> Dharmakaya Samantabhadra, sambhogakaya Vajradhara,
> twelve teachers of the mind-to-mind transmission, perfectly awakened buddhas,
> Garab Dorjé and the rest of the five masters of awareness of the transmission through symbols,
> Tingdzin Zangpo, Dangma Lhungyal,
> and other masters of awareness—gurus of the oral transmission—heed me, I pray.
> Especially you, O victorious one, Longchen Rabjampa,
> my protector, hear this prayer of aspiration.

Henceforth and in all successive lifetimes, may I recall [1.214a]
the profound and extensive topics revealed
in the seventeen tantras—the innermost distillation of the heart essence of utter lucidity—
The Seven Treasuries, and the Yangtik cycles.
May the words and their underlying meaning arise in my mind through the power of complete recall.
May I, with immense self-confidence, open the doorway of the dharma for beings.
May my enlightened awareness, the true nature of phenomena, be uninterrupted.
O Vimalamitra! O Drimé Özer!
Directly guided by your timeless awareness embodiments,
may I receive the enlightened intent of realization, the ultimate lineage.
May I become like you, my omniscient gurus.

Once the teachings have waxed and waned in this universe,
the three sources that nurture them will rain down on the realm of Dzeden Köpa.
There may I study, contemplate, and meditate,
that I may uphold the teachings of the supreme secret
and bring beings to the threshold of that doorway.

Then, in the pure realm of Yangpa Kyöpa to the north,
in the presence of the buddha Utpala Metok Dzepa,
may I take rebirth as the first of that buddha's retinue.
May I rely correctly on that sugata,
fully imbibing the nectar of profound maturing empowerments and liberating instructions
and serving the buddhas' teachings. [1.214b]

Then the three sources that nurture the teachings will pass to the west,
raining down on the world known as Tsukpü Ying
that is guided by the buddha Krakuchanda,
where the teachings will endure for seven hundred thousand years.
Initially, may I be foremost among that buddha's spiritual children.
Subsequently, may I be that victorious one's regent.
Finally, may I alone bring to spiritual maturity and freedom all those remaining to be guided, without exception,
so that they journey to the sacred land of liberation.

In this and all successive lifetimes,
may I master with complete recall, intelligence, and self-confidence
the seventeen tantras of utter lucidity, the secret of all secrets.

Like a lord and his subjects convening, the heart essence of the tantras
comprises *Naturally Arising Awareness, The Natural Freedom of*
Awareness, and *The Tantra Without Words.*
May I hold these in my memory with unerring recall
and confidently send down a rain of spiritual teachings on beings.

The three quintessential tantras that clarify superbly
are *The Array of Inlaid Gems, The Mirror of Enlightened Mind*, and
Vajrasattva: Mirror of the Heart.
May I hold these in my memory with unerring recall
and confidently send down a rain of spiritual teachings on beings.

The three flowerings of the tantras
are *The Pearl Garland, The Perfect Dynamic Energy of the Lion*, and
Auspicious Beauty. [1.215a]
May I hold these in my memory with unerring recall
and confidently send down a rain of spiritual teachings on beings.

The single synopsis of the tantras is Naturally Occurring Perfection.
The perfection of the visions is *Adornment Through Direct Introduction.*
Timeless awareness is victorious in battle in the tantra *The Conjunction*
of Sun and Moon.
What is incomplete is supplemented in the two branches of the tantras,
The Heaped Jewels and *The Blazing Remains.*
May I hold these in my memory with unerring recall
and confidently send down a rain of spiritual teachings on beings.

The tantra The Blazing Lamp deals with total freedom.
The tantra *The Six Expanses* is similar to the heart.
The fundamental tantra *The Reverberation of Sound* is the secret source
text of this specific tradition.
The Wrathful Black Goddess is the tantra for crushing counterproductive
forces.
May I hold these in my memory with unerring recall
and confidently send down a rain of spiritual teachings on beings.

The great, secret Seven Treasuries present extensive demonstrations,
and the four mother and child collections of the Nyingtik teachings
constitute profound pith instructions.

From this lifetime on,
may I never be separate from the teachings of the vajra heart essence, the supreme secret.
May the oath-bound guardians and dakinis grant me this, [1.215b]
and may the Omniscient Guru actually impart these teachings.

May I gain the visionary intelligence of the six interpretations and four methods
that utterly reveal the profound meanings of the tantras and pith instructions.
May I discover the eye of pure sublime knowing that discerns in three ways
and so gain mastery over awareness endowed with threefold purity.
O Drimé Özer, may your view, enlightened intent,
meditative absorption, and conduct be mine,
and may I ensure benefit and happiness for beings!

These were the specific aspirations he made.

It was from such a holy guru as this that the lord of my buddha family, Lungtrul Shedrup Tenpai Nyima, heard the teachings. [1.216a]

Lungtrul Shedrup Tenpai Nyima (1920–?)

Lungtok Tenpai Nyima predicted that he would have thirteen incarnations named Nyima, who would guard the interests of those to be guided in this world. It was this master, Lungtrul, who proved to be the incarnation of his enlightened mind and who returned to his monastic seat.

In the jurisdiction of the great Buddhist ruler of Dergé in eastern Tibet, there was a clan known as Gyashö Nyalatsang. For seven generations, this family had produced seven successive chieftains who were like bloodthirsty demons in human form, engaging in warfare and banditry and inciting civil unrest, theft, robbery, and the use of force. Four tulkus were born into this family line. Through the generations, local people speculated that these sublime teachers had come to put a stop to the evil ways of the Nyalatsang clan.

As one of these tulkus, Lungtrul Shedrup Tenpai Nyima was born in an Iron Monkey year[51] amid limitless marvelous signs, the son of Yeshé Tendzin, a tertön in the region of Nyarong. When he reached the age of eight, his noble father, a great master of awareness, took him for an audience with the guru Khenchen Ngawang Palzang. The two men recognized the child as the tulku of their guru. They presented him with robes, gave him a name, and established him on a golden throne as a spiritual ruler of the three realms.

From then until the age of twenty-two, [1.216b] Lungtrul remained with Vajradhara Ngagi Wangpo. He studied the methods of the sutra and tantra approaches in general, and all of the tantras, explanatory commentaries, and pith instructions of the secret Nyingtik teachings in particular, especially the cycles of the oral lineage of pith instructions from great masters of the past, as well as the great *Seven Treasuries, The Four Higher Collections of the Heart Drop,* and the classes of definitive tantras concerning the supreme secret. He became his guru's single inner heart son and a master of the teachings who upheld the ultimate lineage of realization. Without indulging in intellectual speculation about the true nature of phenomena, he focused on spiritual practice and arrived at an ongoing experience of the enlightened intent of pervasive, extensive space, bringing the yoga of the four visions to consummation. He followed the discipline of a monastic vajra holder, having received the three-stage conferral of the vows of a fully ordained monk.[52]

With Choktrul Pema Gyurmé, Lungtrul studied many profound teachings, such as the glorious *Heart Essence of Secrets.* He received the bodhisattva vow in the traditions of profound view and of extensive conduct[53] from the lord of his buddha family, his guru, the great khenpo. From Lama Yönrin, he received teachings on *The Precious Treasury of Enlightened Qualities,* [1.217a] and from Lama Orgyen Rigdzin, the oral transmissions for the Kangyur. Lama Tashi Paljor taught Lungtrul Madhyamaka and Prajñaparamita, as well as fields of secular knowledge, such as Sanskrit grammar and poetics. Lungtrul thus studied and diligently practiced the teachings of the sutras, the tantras, and secular subjects.

Following the passing of his lord guru, Lungtrul saw to all the funeral arrangements, such as the construction of a great gilded tomb. In keeping with the wishes of his guru, the great khenpo, Lungtrul both explained and listened to teachings on subjects pertaining to the sutras, tantras, and other fields of knowledge and founded a shedra (constructing the building and installing its contents), ensuring that the needs of twenty-five to fifty inhabitants would be met. This institution was maintained through the tenure of six successive khenpos and produced many leading scholars, providing sustenance to the teachings in general. In such ways, Lungtrul's accomplishments embraced the three cycles of spiritual activity on a great scale. As regularly scheduled retreats, he instituted drupchens for such cycles as the glorious Vajrakila, the Eight Commands cycle *The Gathering of Sugatas, Mañjushri: The Lord of Longevity,* and the great ritual of *The Gathering of Secrets* performed on the tenth day of the lunar cycle, all according to the tradition of Mindroling Monastery. In addition, he commissioned the creation of the most elaborate dance costumes, choreography manuals, musical instruments, and so forth for these rituals. [1.217b]

Whenever the opportunity arose, he did intensive retreat involving the phases of approach and accomplishment, practicing such sadhanas as those of Vajrakila, the peaceful and wrathful forms of Mañjushri, and *The Gathering of Secrets,* a longevity practice. Indications of his successful completion of these practices were fully evident. He gained a consummate degree of indwelling confidence through his practice of the stages of development and completion. He had three visions of Vajradhara Ngagi Wangpo, inseparable from the Omniscient King of the Dharma, Longchenpa, and so was guided by this embodiment of timeless awareness. In fact, all of the lineage holders from Rigdzin Jigmé Lingpa down to Lungtrul attained the sublime siddhi through the guidance of the Omniscient King of the Dharma and their visions of him.

In surrounding regions, like Samé Gonjo, Lingshi, Minyak, and Dayul, Lungtrul established large encampments, turning the wheel of the dharma, basing his teachings concerning the preliminary and main practices primarily on the excellent works of the Omniscient One Longchenpa and his spiritual heir, Jigmé Lingpa. Over time, he brought more than a hundred thousand people to great states of omniscience and freedom. Whenever he taught, more than a hundred people would request teachings on the Dzogchen approach alone. Rather than merely imparting complex teachings for great minds or literal teachings for scholars, he helped everyone make a leap of understanding by conferring the experiential teachings of the Category of Direct Transmission, speaking from the perspective of his own direct experience. [1.218a] In this way, he irresistibly won the hearts of many leaders of the learned and spiritually accomplished, so that it was reported far and wide that Lungtok Tenpai Nyima had truly returned.

In encampments in which his audiences always numbered in the hundreds, Lungtrul ceaselessly turned the wheel of the dharma, teaching *The Seven Treasuries, The Four Higher Collections of the Heart Drop,* the root volumes of *The Heart Drop of Longchenpa,* and *Timeless Awareness as the Guiding Principle,* as well as instructions from the oral lineage of past masters on the approaches of trekchö and tögal. When he bestowed empowerments, there was almost never an occasion during which a sign visible to all did not manifest; nectar in the skull cup or offering bowl would boil, the vase water would increase in volume, and so on. Guardian deities such as Maheshvara and the yaksha spirit Tsiumar followed him around like servants.

He remarked, "We live in the final times of the spiritual teachings; it is said in *The Supreme System of Ati* that those who merely hear the term 'Dzogchen' will be guided by the dakini Palgyi Lodrö." Knowing that barbarians would someday do violence to the teachings and destroy centers of study and meditation practice, Lungtrul was quite free in dispensing the teachings, granting them to whoever asked.

Once he had completed his mission, [1.218b] beginning on the twenty-third day of the fifth Tibetan month, without any sign of illness whatsoever, Lungtrul Shedrup Tenpai Nyima went for three days without eating. On the twenty-fifth day, as the sun rose, he went out into the sunshine, saying, "We are so very happy today! This is the happiest we have been in our entire lives. We should celebrate!" His daily practice was that of Dechen Gyalmo, the feminine aspect of *The Heart Drop of Longchenpa*, and so he recited the ganachakra liturgies from memory, distributing the feast to all those present. In a state of rapture, he told them many stories, chatting at length. Then he imparted advice to each of them on the basis of their individual circumstances, covering such topics as faith, renunciation, and the conviction that one's actions have inevitable consequences.

Finally he said, "Now I must go indoors. The rest of you, stay here a while." Then he got up and went inside. His faithful students understood that he was about to pass from his body. They remained in meditation, praying and blending their minds with his. Inside, Lungtrul sat in a relaxed state of repose. Using the dharmakaya gazing technique, and all the while experiencing countless marvelous visions, [1.219a] he uttered "Phat!" several times in a low voice. At the appropriate moment, his enlightened intent resolved back into the expanse of the youthful vase body, the primordial state of supreme inner basic space. Those fortunate ones present were moved to wonder and faith.

Alas! Oh! Innately compassionate protector!
From primordial basic space, heed us with your innate compassion.
For the sake of all beings floundering in the ocean of conditioned existence,
I pray that you pull us out with the hook of your compassion.

O protector, although you dwell in the pinnacle pure realm of Akanishtha,
the scope of your timeless awareness is not limited by distance.
For the sake of all beings exhausted in the ocean of conditioned existence,
I pray that you lead us to the supremely blissful Isle of Liberation.

Great sun who illuminates self-knowing timeless awareness,
Glorious moon who dispels the darkness in the minds of beings,
great leader who guides us to the kingdom of dharmakaya,
O gracious guru, my only refuge, I carry you in my heart.

What is this? Has our source of hope faded from view?
Overwhelmed by unbearable yearning, day and night,
with one-pointed faith I call out to you, my protector.
O guru who points out the true nature of mind as dharmakaya, you know all.
Your kindness is beyond any repayment, O lord of the dharma. [1.219b]
Henceforth, until I reach the very essence of enlightenment,
stay with me inseparably, manifesting always on the lotus in the center of my heart.

Just as a vase of clay and one of gold are not the same,
but are equal in that the pure space within one is not better or worse than that in the other,
so too the spacious, open expanse of your unfettered enlightened mind
extends equally throughout samsara and nirvana—the "bad" and the "good"—without bias.
Our minds have merged inseparably, becoming one.
Grant your blessings that we may gain freedom in the youthful vase body,
the vast expanse of the enlightened intent of wholly positive dharmakaya.

Furthermore, for as long as space itself endures,
according to the capacities of all the countless beings to be guided, without exception,
may I satisfy their needs like a noble treasure vase,
a wish-fulfilling gem, a great wish-granting tree.
May I be capable, my protector, of nurturing those to be guided!

Lungtrul Shedrup Tenpai Nyima's principal heart sons and students were Chöjé Tulku of Dragyab, Karchung Tulku of Mukri, Jokhang Tulku Tupten Palzang of Palyul Monastery, Kala Tulku of Lingshi Monastery, the third Drupwang Pema Norbu, Khen Gyurmé Tsewang, Khen Trinlé Gyatso, and innumerable others who were excellent spiritual practitioners and who themselves nurtured the teachings of the heart essence. [1.220a] They effortlessly catalyzed the dissemination of the enlightened activity of Vajradhara Ngagi Wangpo to the furthest reaches of space. This accounts for the fact that, in more recent times, the mainstream transmission of the spiritual commands of this extensive lineage, the advice contained in the pith instructions of this oral lineage, has spread throughout eastern Tibet.

The Second Palyul Drupwang Pema Norbu, Rigdzin Palchen Düpa (1887–1932)

Another student of the guru Khenchen Ngawang Palzang was the second Drupwang of Palyul Monastery, Pema Norbu, also known as Palchen Düpa. He was the master of the victorious ones' teachings at Palyul Monastery. The leader of that monastic seat, Lord Chökyi Nyima,[54] once had a dream in which he was apparently sitting inside what resembled the tomb enshrining the remains of the Palyul masters. [1.220b] Someone, seemingly Dzongnang Lama, told him, "Pema Norbu is here," and he looked up to see the first Penor Rinpoché[55] with white hair, just as he remembered him. Chökyi Nyima arose and approached him, whereupon the latter turned into a young boy. This dream showed him the whereabouts of the Drupwang tulku. In addition, when the preceding incarnation, Penor Rinpoché, was preparing to pass from this life, he prophesied, "My incarnation will return to this monastic seat when the juniper tree growing outside my bedroom window bears fruit." A few years later, when the tree was laden with berries, the time seemed right, and indeed the master was found to have consciously taken rebirth. Lord Chökyi Nyima, Jamgön Kongtrul Lodrö Tayé, and other holy masters came to a collective decision, and at the age of seven, the tulku was established on the golden throne at his principal seat of Palyul.

Palchen Düpa pursued his studies, beginning with the basic skills of reading and writing, and at the age of nine had a vision of Guru Rinpoché, during which he attained siddhis by receiving the Guru's blessings. [1.221a] He was ordained as a monk by the lord Chökyi Nyima and received from him the core teachings of the monastic seat's tradition, including the terma teachings of Ratna Lingpa, the *Namchö* cycle, two traditions of the Eight Commands, and the cycles of Jatsön Nyingpo. He studied the lineages of *The Discourse on United Intent* from both eastern and central Tibet, as well as all the transmissions of the kama cycles of teachings. He received the oral transmissions for the precious Kangyur from Lama Tashi of Palyul Monastery. Khenchen Gyaltsen Özer bestowed on him *The Treasury of Precious Hidden Teachings,* and Situ Chökyi Gyatso of glorious Katok Monastery gave him many other profound teachings, including *The Treasury of Spiritual Instructions,* an entire range of rare transmissions of ancient terma teachings, and the profound teachings from the cycles of Longsel Dorjé Nyingpo. Jamgön Mipam Rinpoché bestowed on him the peaceful, wrathful, and longevity aspects of Mañjushri. After this, the master treated Palchen Düpa affectionately, training him in whatever studies he needed to undertake; furthermore, due to his prescience, Mipam Rinpoché made many prophecies about him. In these ways, he bestowed blessings on his student's mind. Palchen Düpa also met the great Jamgön Kongtrul Lodrö Tayé, who conferred on him the empowerment for the sadhana of enlightened mind discovered by Chokgyur Lingpa. He also gave Palchen Düpa a great deal of advice on how to maintain the teachings and train students and how to confer empowerments, oral transmissions, lectures, and so on.

In time, Palchen Düpa went to Norbui Lhunpo, [1.221b] the tantric college at the great monastic center of Katok Dorjéden, to study the sutras, tantras, and other fields of knowledge. He studied and contemplated the many treatises and commentaries from the Indian and Tibetan traditions of Buddhism, which together constitute the "one hundred scriptural sources of Katok"—in fact, more than one hundred texts of sutra and tantra. He learned these from two masters, Khenchen Kunzang Palden Chödrak and Khenchen Ngagi Wangpo, the inner lord of his buddha family and an emanation of Vimalamitra who had been his guru in many past lifetimes. In this way, he reached a consummate level of erudition and became a great scholar of the five fields of knowledge. Notably, Palchen Düpa took full monastic ordination from

Khenchen Ngawang Palzang, receiving the transmission of vows established in Tibet by Shantarakshita. He became a great monastic elder, upholding the discipline by maintaining qualities worthy of the arhat Kashyapa[56] himself. He was scrupulously ethical and never strayed from the guidelines of what was allowed or proscribed in the Vinaya codes of the sacred dharma.

One day during this time, his guru, Khenchen Ngawang Palzang, said to him, "Palyul Tulku, let us take a break and go to the site that is sacred to Mañjushri near this monastery." [1.222a]

"Very well, sir," Palchen Düpa replied. And they, master and student, went off hand in hand to visit the site.

The guru said, "Now let's sit here and relax."

Penor Rinpoché folded his shawl four times, offering it as a mat for his guru to sit on. Ngawang Palzang sat in meditation for a short while without saying a word. Then he noticed that his shoes had become caked with mud from the path and suddenly lost his temper, saying, "Now our shoes are all muddy!" With his left hand, he grabbed Palchen Düpa by the front of his shirt and, with his right, picked up a shoe and severely beat him with it. Penor Rinpoché was so frightened that he almost lost consciousness, but just as he was about to pass out, he felt as though he had awakened from a dull void state—the ground of all ordinary experience—and directly experienced the enlightened intent that is the true way of abiding, free of all intellectual speculation. In the wake of this realization, he experienced a dynamic awareness that could precisely discern phenomena and attained a state of total freedom: the eightfold treasure of unhindered confidence[57] concerning the entire range of teachings of the sutras and tantras. He became capable of expounding, debating, and writing about the teachings without hindrance. [1.222b] Thus the minds of master and student merged, becoming one.

"My son, that's all there is to it," Ngawang Palzang said and then instructed him in the personal tradition of Paltrul Rinpoché that he himself had received as the great oral lineage of pith instructions from Lungtok Tenpai Nyima. Palchen Düpa subsequently perfected his understanding of the sublime approach of the vajra heart essence, becoming one of his guru's heart sons and a true master of the teachings of natural great perfection.

Having finished his scholastic training, he returned to his home monastery of Palyul and founded a shedra where some fifty students could receive the teachings. He requested that his guru, the great khenpo, inaugurate it, and Ngawang Palzang came to do so. The shedra thus became a wellspring for the teachings of the Early Translation school. Palchen Düpa had many students, for he taught the great oral lineage in places such as the monasteries of the Gonjo region, turning the wheel of the dharma with great skill. He transmitted the great *Treasury of Precious Hidden Teachings* three times. In the later part of his life, Palchen Düpa became a wandering renunciant, planting the victory banner of spiritual practice. His powers of perception became truly extraordinary; he could see past, present, and future unhindered.

During his lifetime, all who upheld the teachings of the Early Translation school proclaimed [1.223a] that no one in the Dergé region could match either Zhechen Gyaltsap or this master. At his seat of Palyul, he was responsible for publishing the root volumes of *The Heart Drop of Longchenpa* and the collected works of Khenpo Ngawang Palzang. At the monastery, he instituted annual rituals associated with the kama lineages of teachings. He built temples and restored old ones and had *The Five Great Treasuries* published. He also founded many monasteries at which the entire cycle of *The Heart Drop of Longchenpa* was taught, such as Wanak Monastery in Gonjo and Samdrupzhung. In short, Penor Rinpoché Palchen Düpa spent his entire life pursuing the three cycles of spiritual activity on a vast scale.

At a certain point, the display of his emanated form resolved back into the palace of Pema Ö in the realm of Chamara. However, he has returned as a glorious protector for those of us to be guided, in the person of the third Penor, who is still living. The lord Palchen Düpa had many students, heart children who nurtured the teachings in general and specific ways, but foremost in the Palyul lineage was Dartang Choktrul Chökyi Dawa Rinpoché. [1.223b]

Dartang Choktrul Chökyi Dawa Rinpoché (1894–1959)

Choktrul Chökyi Dawa was born into the Zimgak clan of the rulers of the Gyalrong region in the easternmost part of Tibet. Fulfilling the prophecies of many holy masters, he was recognized at an early age as the rebirth of the previous Dartang Choktrul and was brought to the great monastic seat of Do-ngak Shedrup Ling, a community of more than a thousand monks on the plateau of Dartang in Golok. He was received with honors by a formal procession of the entire monastic community and by the local populace, a crowd numbering many thousands, and was established on the golden throne as a master of the teachings.

He had clear recollections of his former lifetimes and, upon cursory exposure, generally mastered all of the subjects he studied, such as reading and writing. [1.224a] He then studied with many gurus, tulkus, and mentors, listening to and contemplating a wide range of subjects, including Vinaya, Prajñaparamita, *The Heart Essence of Secrets,* and Madhyamaka. He abandoned the life of a householder and took the vows of a fully ordained monk. He was a true embodiment of the three qualities of stability, erudition, and venerability, untainted by the slightest flaw, living according to the standards of the exalted Upali.[58] Wherever he stayed, the fragrance of his discipline permeated the surrounding area. It was apparent to everyone that those who support the forces of good accompanied him. Choktrul Chökyi Dawa's conduct was entirely peaceful and restrained, and he rested unwaveringly in deep meditation. Unblemished by even the smallest fault of carelessness or indiscretion, he was so morally upright that the local people often likened him to a reflection of the Lord of Sages himself, always in a state of meditative equipoise. Aside from the fact that he would drink tea, he was so like a golden image that it was common for the people of Golok to refer to him as "the guru who is a golden image that drinks tea." [1.224b]

In time, Choktrul Chökyi Dawa came to study with the great gurus of the glorious Palyul Monastery, especially with Penor Rinpoché Rigdzin Düpa, from whom he received the profound teachings of the lineage passed from Rigdzin Kunzang Sherab. These included the Dzogchen teaching *Holding Buddhahood in One's Hand,* the terma cycles of Ratna Lingpa, the *Namchö* cycle, and *The United Intent of the Gurus.*

He also received transmissions of *The Treasury of Precious Hidden Teachings, The Treasury of Spiritual Instructions,* the teachings of the kama transmissions, *The Collected Tantras of the Nyingma School,* and the precious Kangyur. In particular, he studied the pith instructions that are like a wish-fulfilling gem: the profound instructions of the Dzogchen approach, such as those of trekchö and tögal. He also put these into practice in an extraordinary way, attaining the sublime siddhi by meditating diligently day and night. At one point, Chatsa Rinpoché of Katok Monastery said, "When we speak in these later times of a siddha of the Nyingma school of tantra—someone who has brought the four visions of great perfection to consummation—it is of someone like Dartang Choktrul." All holy masters were of one voice in lauding him, showering him with such praise.

Choktrul Rinpoché turned the wheel of the dharma at his own monastery of Dartang, as well as at its mother seat of Palyul and any other subsidiary institutions he visited. He became a leader of many thousands of the monastic sangha, [1.225a] and his personal estate and that of his monastery became very extensive. With all of his merit and influence, Choktrul Chökyi Dawa was as impressive and majestic as a mighty mountain, winning everyone's respect. He was truly a master of the teachings in these later times.

He instituted the traditional summer retreats and monthly purification ceremonies at which members of the monastic community renew their vows. He traveled to Lhasa in central Tibet, where he made abundant offerings of gold and pure water before statues such as those of the lord Buddha in the two main temples. At Dartang Monastery, he established drupchens, as well as rituals on the tenth day of the lunar cycle. He erected many temples, statues, and images; published numerous volumes of scriptures; and commissioned tangkas with gold highlights, as well as banners, canopies, and other articles. In such ways, he created innumerable representations of enlightenment.

To various groups of students in different areas, Choktrul Chökyi Dawa transmitted a wide range of teachings. These included the general teachings of both the kama lineages and the termas of the Early Translation school, as well as *The Treasury of Precious Hidden Teachings, Holding Buddhahood in One's Hand,* the earlier and later cycles of the Nyingtik teachings, and the profound instructions of Ratna Lingpa. He also ordained thousands of novices and monks. Thus, in recent times, he was a great representative of the lineage of teachings associated with the glorious center of Palyul and a unique adornment to the teachings of the supreme secret. He was truly a great master who appeared like the sun, with an effulgence that brought benefit and happiness. [1.225b]

Of his countless students and heart children, Dzongnang Rinpoché and Gonjo Khochim Rinpoché together founded Minling Ngedön Gatsal Ling in northern India[59] and, along with the excellent Bum-nyang Khenpo Rabgyé, other centers such as Palyul Chökhor Ling at the Dergé refugee settlement in Bir. Today, Minling Trichen Rinpoché,[60] a crown jewel of the teachings of the Early Translation school, continues to hold the main seat of Minling Ngedön Gatsal Ling, while Gonjo Khochim Tulku Rinpoché, Minling Khentrul Rinpoché, and others direct the shedra and retreat center. At Palyul Chökhor Ling, Ringu Tulku Rinpoché and others have constructed a new temple and look after communities of the sangha.

It was from both Choktrul Chökyi Dawa Rinpoché and Lungtrul Shedrup Tenpai Nyima [1.226a] that the third Drupwang Penor Rinpoché, Jigmé Tupten Shedrup Chökyi Drayang Pal Zangpo, received teachings on the tantras of the supreme secret.

The Third Palyul Drupwang Pema Norbu, Jigmé Tupten Shedrup Chökyi Drayang (Kyabjé Penor Rinpoché) (b. 1932)

The third Drupwang Pema Norbu was born in Powo, in the southern reaches of eastern Tibet. He was recognized as the indisputable tulku by the fifth Dzogchen tulku, Tupten Chökyi Dorjé, Khenchen Ngagi Wangpo, and other masters. He was established on the golden throne of the preceding Penor Rinpoché before an assembly of thousands of scholars and tulkus, headed by Choktrul Tupten Chökyi Dawa and Kuchen Rinpoché Karma Tekchok Nyingpo. [1.226b]

From Kuchen Rinpoché, he received such transmissions as the *Namchö* cycle, the termas revealed by Ratna Lingpa, the sadhanas and empowerments for the cycle focusing on the Eight Commands called *The Complete Secret,* the sadhanas and empowerments for *The United Intent of the Gurus,* the empowerment by Dodrak for *The Discourse on United Intent* entitled *The Ford for Crossing the Ocean of Mandalas,* the manuals written by Nyalwa Delekpa, and the tradition based on the empowerment for *The Discourse on United Intent* entitled *The Garland of Jewels.* From Khenchen Lekshé Jorden of Katok Monastery, Penor Rinpoché twice received the empowerment entitled *The Downpour of Honey,* the ritual known as the "eastern

Tibetan tradition" concerning *The Discourse on United Intent,* the empowerment for *The Discourse on United Intent* entitled *The Vajra Staircase,* the empowerments for the peaceful and wrathful deities of the tantra *The Web of Magical Display,* the empowerments and oral transmissions for *The Treasury of Spiritual Instructions,* the terma teachings of Ratna Lingpa, *The Gathering of the Gurus' Commands,* the *Hum* cycle of Nyingtik teachings, the Ngari tradition of the cycle focusing on the Eight Commands called *The Complete Gathering,* Lerab Lingpa's *Dispelling Flaws in Interdependence,* and other transmissions. Khenchen Jigmé Puntsok gave him the transmissions for *The Innermost Heart Drop of the Guru, Instruction on the Ultimate Meaning of the Vajra Heart Essence, A Detailed Commentary on the Seven-Line Supplication,* and other teachings. From Khenpo Nüden, Penor Rinpoché received teachings on the four volumes of the former's own newly written commentary on *The Discourse on United Intent,* Nup's commentary on this discourse entitled *Armor Against Darkness,* the overview written by Chöjé, [1.227a] Jigmé Lingpa's commentary on his own *Treasury of Enlightened Qualities,* Mipam's commentary on *The Ornament of the Middle Way* and his *Lamp of Certain Meaning,* as well as other explanatory teachings. Khenpo Pema Jigmé transmitted to him the nine volumes of Khyentsé's works, the thirteen "teachings on *A*" of Chakmé, the collected works of So Wangdrak Gyatso, as well as the Kangyur and Tengyur.

Later on, once he was in India, Penor Rinpoché received the extensive empowerments for both Kalachakra and Guhyasamaja from the Dalai Lama,[61] as well as other teachings. From Kyabjé Dilgo Khyentsé Rinpoché, he received the entire range of empowerments and oral transmissions of the kama lineages of the Early Translation school, explanations of the tantra *The Heart Essence of Secrets,* the root volumes of *The Heart Drop of Longchenpa,* the empowerments and oral transmissions for *The Four Higher Collections of the Heart Drop, The Seven Treasuries,* and *The Three Cycles of Being at Ease,* most of the collected works of Rongzom, the collected works of Mipam, and the collected works of Paltrul, among others. From Kyabjé Dudjom Rinpoché, Penor Rinpoché received a number of empowerments and oral transmissions, and in return offered Dudjom Rinpoché the oral transmissions for the Kangyur, as well as several rare transmissions. In all cases, Penor Rinpoché's mind merged with that of the master with whom he exchanged teachings. [1.227b]

Notably, the lord of his buddha family, the protector of his crown chakra, was Lungtrul Rinpoché Shedrup Tenpai Nyima, from whom Penor Rinpoché received the mind-to-mind transmission of the realization that is the lineage of enlightened intent. He has said, "When I requested from Lungtok Choktrul the oral transmission of pith instructions—transmissions such as the root volumes of *The Heart Drop of Longchenpa* and the text *Timeless Awareness as the Guiding Principle*—he twice bestowed on me the direct introduction to these teachings, section by section. For me the second occasion was like the sun rising at the break of day. From then on, I found that my realization was not subject to any transition or change. It would seem that this was an experience of timeless awareness, the unity of awareness and emptiness, in all its nakedness." In this regard, Kyabjé Penor Rinpoché has said that, although his primary source of transmissions such as the Palyul tradition of the *Namchö* oral lineage of enlightened mind was Dartang Choktrul Rinpoché, it was primarily from Nyoshul Lungtok Choktrul Shedrup Tenpai Nyima that he received the transmission of the great Nyingtik lineage. If any doubt this fact, they should consult the master himself, for Penor Rinpoché is still living.

From the lord of his buddha family, Choktrul Rinpoché Chökyi Dawa, [1.228a] Penor Rinpoché received the entire transmission for *The Treasury of Precious Hidden Teachings*, including those teachings that are under a seal of secrecy. As well, he received the *Namchö* cycle, the empowerments and oral transmissions for the termas revealed by Ratna Lingpa, the three empowerments (extensive, middle-length, and abridged) for Karma Lingpa's cycle of the mandalas of peaceful and wrathful deities,[62] and notably the individual sections of teachings from the Dzogchen text *Holding Buddhahood in One's Hand*. Like one vase being filled from another, he received the key transmissions of the tantras, explanatory commentaries, and pith instructions concerning natural great perfection—the oral lineage of pith instructions associated with his former incarnation.

He undertook a three-year retreat focusing on the Three Roots and emphasizing the main body of Dzogchen practice, the approaches of original purity, or trekchö, and spontaneous presence, or tögal, maintaining this practice continuously. He achieved great signs of success on the path and reached an advanced level of practice, as illustrated by the fact that he would spend an entire night in a single session of meditation.

Penor Rinpoché took his final monastic vows in the presence of ten members of the sangha, headed by the incomparably kind Choktrul Chökyi Dawa. Never sullied by the slightest fault or failing, he epitomizes the discipline that delights advanced spiritual practitioners. [1.228b] He has also ordained 2,300 fortunate individuals as novices and monks or nuns. His kindness in establishing and maintaining the monastic tradition is beyond imagination or expression.

After taking his vows, he traveled to central Tibet, through Lhasa, Drigung, Samyé, Dorjé Drak, Mindroling, and other areas, rendering great service and honor to the places he visited and the images therein, as well as to the lamas, tulkus, and communities of the sangha whom he met. He honored them with an enormous array of material offerings as well as offerings arising in his meditation. Penor Rinpoché eventually reached the holy country of India, where he founded Tekchok Namdrol Shedrup Dargyé Ling in Mysore State on the southern coast. It is a great center for the teachings of the Early Translation school, a place for the study and practice of Buddhism housing hundreds and sometimes thousands. Among the khenpos who expound the scriptures and theory of the teachings at the shedra are Khenchen Pema Sherab Rinpoché,

Khenchen Namdrol Rinpoché, Khenchen Tsewang Gyatso, Khenchen Rigdzin, Khen Wangchuk Sönam, Khen Katayana, Khen Tashi Tsering, Khen Jigmé Kalzang, Khen Tsering Dorjé, Khen Sang-gyé Rangjung, [1.229a] Khen Dorjé Palzang, Khen Orgyen, and Khen Dorjé. They ensure that the enlightened activities of explaining, debating, and composing teachings, both scriptural and experiential, continue to flourish in all directions. In addition, this shedra has provided khenpos and instructors for shedras throughout India, Nepal, Sikkim, Bhutan, and other countries.

When the dissemination of the Victorious One's teachings became possible once again in the Land of Snows, Penor Rinpoché journeyed there three times and contributed greatly to the restoration of whatever had been destroyed at his home monastery of Gyalwa Palyul. In particular, he spent 520,000 Indian rupees on the construction of a large new temple, Palri Pema Ö, which is impressive from the point of view of both the structure and the representations it contains. Moreover, he ensured the continuity of the transmissions of maturing empowerments and liberating instructions from both the kama and terma traditions. He also presided over the ordination of more than a thousand novices, monks, and nuns. His kindness in rekindling the embers of the Victorious One's teachings is beyond imagination or description.

Even before returning to revivify the teachings of the Victorious One in the Land of Snows, Penor Rinpoché bestowed the maturing empowerments and liberating instructions for the entire range of termas revealed by Namchö Mingyur Dorjé.[63] Later, at Palyul Monastery, [1.229b] he furthered his enlightened activities by passing on all of the teachings of the kama transmissions, the extensive empowerment and oral transmissions for the Eight Commands cycle *The Complete Secret,* and the sadhana and empowerment for *The United Intent of the Gurus.* At Namdrol Monastery in the holy land of India, he bestowed the empowerments and oral transmissions for the *Namchö* cycle and the teachings of Ratna Lingpa once each; the entire range of maturing empowerments and liberating instructions for the great *Treasury of Precious Hidden Teachings* once; the entire range of empowerments of the kama transmissions of the Early Translation school; the sadhana and empowerment for *The United Intent of the Gurus;* the empowerment and oral transmissions for the Eight Commands cycle *The Complete Secret;* the three empowerments—extensive, middle-length, and abridged—and oral transmissions for Karma Lingpa's cycle of the mandalas of peaceful and wrathful deities; the teachings concerning the four volumes of commentary on *The Discourse on United Intent;* the teachings on Jigmé Lingpa's commentary to his own work *The Treasury of Enlightened Qualities;* the oral transmissions for all of the collected works of the preceding Drupwang; the great commentary on the Dzogchen text *Holding Buddhahood in One's Hand;* and the oral transmissions for the exhaustive teachings on the supremely compassionate Avalokiteshvara. In such ways, he has extended his kindness over the years.

At the monastery of Shechen Tennyi Dargyeling in Nepal, fulfilling the wishes of

Kyabjé Dilgo Khyentsé Rinpoché, Penor Rinpoché bestowed the extensive empowerment for *The Discourse on United Intent* entitled *The Ford for Crossing the Ocean of Mandalas* and the extensive empowerment for the Karma Lingpa tradition of the mandala of peaceful and wrathful deities. [1.230a] At Puntsok Ling in Bhutan, he conferred the entire range of empowerments and oral transmissions for the *Namchö* cycle, while at Palyul Chökhor Ling in Bir, he gave all of the empowerments and oral transmissions for both the *Namchö* cycle and the teachings of Ratna Lingpa.

In the Western Hemisphere, Penor Rinpoché bestowed the empowerments and oral transmissions for the *Namchö* cycle, *The Innermost Heart Drop of the Guru*, the teachings of the kama transmissions, *The Treasury of Precious Hidden Teachings*, and other cycles in the United States; *The Innermost Heart Drop of Profundity* and the empowerments for the root volumes of *The Heart Drop of Longchenpa* in Canada; and the empowerments for *The Four Higher Collections of the Heart Drop* in England. With great kindness, by bringing his students to spiritual maturity and liberation without bias or prejudice, Penor Rinpoché has thus ensured through his enlightened activity that the precious teachings of the supreme secret will continue to spread and flourish throughout the nations of the world.

This concludes the description of the primary lineage of the secret Nyingtik teachings of utter lucidity passed on by the great bodhisattva Paltrul Rinpoché.

8

The Lineages of Jigmé Gyalwai Nyugu: Jamyang Khyentsei Wangpo

Jamyang Khyentsei Wangpo (1820–1892)

Now I shall discuss the lineage descending from Jigmé Gyalwai Nyugu's second heart son—one like the sun—Jamyang Khyentsei Wangpo. This great being was born on the fifth day of the sixth month of Chutö in the Iron Dragon year of the fourteenth sexagesimal cycle.[1] His father was Drungchen Rinchen Wangyal of the Nyö clan [1.230b], and his mother was Sokza Sönamtso. He was born amid many wondrous signs in Terchen Dilgo, a village near the cliff of Yaru Chungchen Drak in Dergé, eastern Tibet. From as early as he could remember, the six-armed protector of timeless awareness[2] and the guardian goddess of mantra Ekajati lovingly watched over him. He had random, sporadic memories of many of his past lives. In his childhood, his spiritual predisposition to follow the Mahayana approach was awakened, and his only wish was to be ordained as a monk. [1.231a] Endowed with incomparable intelligence and discernment, he learned to read and write without difficulty. Reading most books only once, he mastered both the words and their underlying meaning.

In his twenty-first year, Jamyang Khyentsei Wangpo requested the full ordination of a monk from Khenpo Rigdzin Zangpo of Orgyen Mindroling Monastery. He received both major traditions of the vow to arouse bodhichitta from Dorjé Rinchen of the Sakya school. He received empowerments for the practices of Chakrasamvara and Hevajra from Tartsé Khen Rinpoché and his brother. Trinlé Chödrön, the venerable female master of Mindroling Monastery, bestowed on him *The Four Higher Collections of the Heart Drop*. From the great throne holder Gyurmé Sang-gyé Kunga, Jamyang Khyentsei Wangpo received the So tradition of the deity Samyak Yangdak and *The Heart Drop of Masters of Awareness* and, from the great scholar Gyurmé Tutop Namgyal of Zhechen, empowerment for the mandala of peaceful and wrathful deities of *The Web of Magical Display*. These transmissions established the foundation of his vows in the tantric tradition.

Jamyang Khyentsei Wangpo underwent great hardship, completely eradicating any arrogance that may have arisen as a result of his status as a recognized tulku or his noble and wealthy ancestry. He relied on some 150 vajra holders, [1.231b] spiritual mentors, and scholars from central, southern, and eastern Tibet, all renowned in their respective fields of knowledge. He mastered the ten fields of knowledge—the arts, medicine, Sanskrit grammar, valid cognition, and so forth—as well as the scriptural sources of the dialectical approach, including Vinaya, Abhidharma, Madhyamaka, and Prajñaparamita. He received the entire range of maturing empowerments and liberating instructions of a number of ancient but thriving traditions, such as the kama and terma teachings of the Nyingma school; the earlier and later Kadampa; the three schools of Sakya, Ngor, and Tsarpa; the Kamtsang, Drigung, Taktsang, and Drukpa Kagyü; and the Jonang, Zhalu, and Bodong lineages. He received all of the available transmissions for the exegeses of such tantras and treatises as *The Heart Essence of Secrets* (also known as *The Web of Magical Display*) and the tantras of Kalachakra, Chakrasamvara, Hevajra, and Guhyasamaja, and actively sought out the extant lines of oral transmission for the precious Kangyur, *The Collected Tantras of the Nyingma School*, and those that were available for the Tengyur. In total, Jamyang Khyentsei Wangpo received oral transmissions for some seven hundred volumes that, taken together, cover all schools of Tibetan Buddhism without sectarian bias. In brief, he spent about thirteen years of his life entirely in study, learning most of the extensive traditions of the "ten great pillars upholding the lineages of exegesis."[3] [1.232a]

The extraordinary master of his buddha family, the guru with whom Jamyang Khyentsei Wangpo had been connected for lifetimes, was Jigmé Gyalwai Nyugu. He met this great being at the latter's encampment at Terlung in eastern Tibet. Due to the power of their previous connections, upon merely meeting one another, master and student felt boundless joy and love, like a father and son being reunited. Jigmé Gyalwai Nyugu then cared for Jamyang Khyentsei Wangpo with immeasurable compassion. Like one vase filling another, he bestowed on his student all the transmissions of a veritable ocean of spiritual methods—the tantras, explanatory commentaries, and pith instructions—from the first stages of the spiritual path (the preliminary practices) up to and including trekchö and tögal in the secret Nyingtik approach of utter lucidity. The enlightened intent of great perfection—the perception of awareness's naturally manifest appearances without bias—awakened in Jamyang Khyentsei Wangpo's heart. The yoga of the four visions became his living experience. Jigmé Gyalwai Nyugu invested him as his extraordinary heart son on the inner level, and with the aspiration that Jamyang Khyentsei Wangpo act as his regent in the ultimate sense, that of sharing his realization, he conferred on him the seal of entrustment. Thus the heart sons Paltrul and Khyentsé, the "paired sun and moon," were the lifelines who ensured the continuity of the teachings of the vajra heart essence of utter lucidity to the present day.

During this period, whenever Jigmé Gyalwai Nyugu conducted a course of instruction, [1.232b] from beginning to end everyone could see a bright aura of rainbow light enveloping his tent. The guru himself praised his student daily, saying things like, "The Dzogchen approach has not yet disappeared, for when I was explaining the preliminaries, someone already understood the main body of the teachings to which these preliminaries lead." The lord of the dharma Paltrul said, "He was referring to Jamyang Khyentsé." And my own holy guru[4] told me that this master Khyentsé exemplified someone who proceeds in quantum leaps, while Paltrul Rinpoché exemplified someone who proceeds developmentally.

The lord Jamyang Khyentsei Wangpo understood the ultimate meaning of a text simply upon first reading it; his incredible memory ensured that he never forgot anything. But to emulate those who never trivialize the dharma, he eschewed mere cursory study and thoroughly trained in and familiarized himself with all of his subjects. His spiritual vision was flawless, so that he understood precisely and without confusion the view and conduct of the various schools of philosophy and their respective key points, as well as what was or was not the uncontested tradition of any given extensive lineage. Today, there is no one of high or low standing who can rival such vision. Jamyang Khyentsei Wangpo passed on at least once all of the sutras, tantras, and treatises he studied; [1.233a] he passed on the maturing empowerments, liberating instructions, and supportive oral transmissions for a majority of these many times. His generosity in giving teachings was untainted by concern for material gain, and he did not withhold them on a single occasion. He fulfilled the hopes of the highest and most holy being down to the humblest beggar according to that individual's needs.

In addition, he never engaged in the ignoble activities of selling spiritual services or taking advantage of others while pretending to benefit those he was to guide. In fact, his qualities, manifesting in part as the "threefold blazing" and "threefold gathering,"[5] were so evident to others that material resources inevitably came to him. Wasting nothing on frivolity, Jamyang Khyentsei Wangpo used his resources to commission representations of enlightened form (some two thousand statues made entirely of gold and copper), enlightened speech (woodblocks for printing close to forty volumes of scripture and two thousand handwritten and printed volumes), and enlightened mind (more than a hundred stupas of gold and copper, foremost among them the great stupa of Lhundrup Teng). He also directed the construction of thirteen well-designed temples of various sizes to house these representations [1.233b] and later sponsored the daily offering ceremonies and regular commemorative rituals held therein. In his building projects, Jamyang Khyentsei Wangpo made few demands, for the circumstances were such that the construction of anything elaborate would have been difficult. But later in his life, owing to political unrest in both upper and lower Tibet, monasteries were damaged and he spent large sums of his own money to restore them in appropriate ways. He urged both Chinese and Tibetan officials, as well as the king and ministers of Dergé, to uphold their long-standing traditions of contributing to the restoration of old sites, building new monasteries, and ensuring that ceremonies were conducted regularly. In this way, his kindness was enormous, for he helped the teachings spread and flourish. Donating four thousand bricks of tea over the years, he sponsored annual ceremonies of mantra accumulation at spiritual centers, both great and small, all over the region.

Jamyang Khyentsei Wangpo's precious motivation of bodhichitta was unwavering; in particular, he had a pure view of and devotion for all spiritual systems, wishing only that these systems flourish. He never indulged in sectarian bias or cynicism and accepted countless students from all schools. His students included all of the most famous holders of the teachings—great masters of the Sakya, [1.234a] Kagyü, Nyingma, and Geluk schools—as well as mentors, retreatants, humble Buddhist practitioners, and even adherents of the indigenous Bön tradition of Tibet. Innumerable groups came to him daily, headed by many of the highest-ranking officials of China and Tibet, yet no one came away without having made some connection to this master (each according to his or her own interests), whether through teachings, empowerments, advice, blessings, or ceremonies for the removal of obstacles. Unfettered by the eight worldly concerns, Jamyang Khyentsei Wangpo truly lived as a king of renunciants. He had no concern for his own life and cut himself off from all complications dictated by worldly values; he treated everyone alike, regardless of status, without feeling the need to save face or indulging in hope and fear.

Altogether he spent about thirteen years meditating on the phases of approach and accomplishment for his many meditation deities from the Nyingma and Sarma tantras. He practiced each of the profound teachings he received, especially those found in *The One Hundred Teachings* of the venerable Kunga Drolchok. Jamyang Khyentsei Wangpo was exemplary and unrivaled in fulfilling the samaya commitments he made. [1.234b]

The foregoing is a concise outer biography of Jamyang Khyentsei Wangpo, describing his spheres of activity in spiritual practice, study, and spiritual projects.

Eight lineages are renowned throughout the Land of Snows as the "eight great lineages of accomplishment." These are the following:[6]

1. The Early Translation school, or Nyingmapa, deriving from the kindness of the abbot Shantarakshita, the master Padmakara, and the Buddhist king Trisong Detsen
2. The Kadam school, the tradition of the "venerable lord"—the glorious Atisha—which promulgates the "seven divine doctrines"[7]
3. The Lamdré cycle, the quintessence of the enlightened mind of the mahasiddha Virupa, imparted as advice through generations of masters of the glorious Sakya school

4. The four great and eight minor traditions of the Kagyü school, which were passed down from Marpa, Milarepa, and Dakpo Lhajé[8] and which constitute advice from the lineage of the "four spiritual commands"[9]
5. The glorious Shangpa Kagyü school, based on the "golden teachings"[10] of the learned and accomplished Chungpo
6. The Six Techniques of Union, emphasizing immersion in the vajra nature of genuine being—the stage of completion as found in the most majestic of all tantras, the glorious *Kalachakra Tantra*
7. The Sacred Teaching that is Zhijé, along with its auxiliary approach of Dükyi Chöyul, the tradition of the mahasiddha Padampa Sang-gyé
8. The Phases of Approach and Accomplishment in the Three Vajras, which the Vajra Queen[11] actually bestowed on Drupchen Orgyenpa [1.235a]

These ancient traditions have been maintained as unbroken lineages. Jamyang Khyentsei Wangpo had faith in all of them while respecting their individual integrity. Ignoring all hardship, he made a great effort to seek out tutors who held each of these authentic lineages and received from them all of the maturing empowerments and liberating instructions in their entirety and without error. He studied these teachings to cut through any intellectual speculation and meditated to gain personal experience. During this time, either in waking consciousness or in meditative visions, his body, speech, and mind were blessed by learned and accomplished Indian and Tibetan masters of the past, peaceful and wrathful meditation deities, and hosts of dakas and dakinis of the three levels.[12] He received advice from them all as direct lineages.[13] It is clear that he had pure visionary experiences in each and every moment, but because he referred to them only obliquely, never boasting about his visions or supernormal powers of perception, we know little of them. Jamyang Khyentsei Wangpo thoroughly mastered the two stages of meditation according to the foregoing eight lineages and so was unhindered in teaching, debating, and writing about them. Free of any taint of confusion, he was able to care for fortunate people.

This has been a mere fragment of his biography on the inner level. [1.235b]

Among the vajra prophecies of Drupchen Tangtong Gyalpo, we find the following:

A yogin who is none other than me, ༔
one endowed with five qualities, ༔
will appear some seven hundred years from now ༔
in eastern Tibet during a Dragon year. ༔
He will be the son of Gama, a master of awareness of the Nyö clan. ༔
His element will be metal, and he will bear the marks of a warrior. ༔
Blessed by Pema Gyalpo, ༔
he will be Do-ngak Lingpa, receiving seven modes of transmission. ༔

> Blessed by Vimalamitra, ༔
> he will be Ösel Trulpai Dorjé. ༔
> An emanation of Mañjushri, blessed by the sovereign, ༔[14]
> he will be called a mentor of the dharma, ༔
> one appearing like an illusion. ༔

Jamyang Khyentsei Wangpo proved to be one who mastered these seven modes of transmission, just as predicted in vajra prophecies like the foregoing and the clear reference found in *The Index of the Three Categories of the Great Perfection* and other sources.

When he was eight, Jamyang Khyentsei Wangpo fell seriously ill and was in great pain. He had a vision of Guru Rinpoché and Yeshé Tsogyal, who bestowed on him empowerments and blessings within the mandala of Vajrakila. [1.236a] They also counseled him, so that he was completely victorious in battling his obstacles.

In his fifteenth year, he had a pure vision in which he approached a nine-storied stupa in Bodh Gaya, India. He climbed it story by story and, on the eighth floor, met the great master Mañjushrimitra appearing as a scholar, with piles of books on either side of him. Jamyang Khyentsei Wangpo bowed and prayed with great devotion, whereupon Mañjushrimitra picked up a volume of scripture from a pile on his left and showed it to him. It was *The Compendium of the Perfection of Sublime Knowing* in Sanskrit. The guru placed it on the crown of Jamyang Khyentsei Wangpo's head and focused his attention on him while saying, "This is the complete oral transmission of all the teachings of the dialectical approach." He then took a volume from a pile on his right and showed it to Jamyang Khyentsei Wangpo. It was the Dzogchen tantra *Vajrasattva: Mirror of the Heart*. The master placed this, too, on the crown of Jamyang Khyentsei Wangpo's head and focused his attention on him, saying, "This holds all of the words, underlying meaning, and blessings of the secret mantra approach of the Vajrayana in general and of the three categories of Dzogchen in particular." [1.236b] After uttering some prophecies, Mañjushrimitra dissolved into light with great delight and merged with the lord Jamyang Khyentsei Wangpo. For a moment, the latter entered a nonconceptual state of meditative absorption. Rousing himself, he went outside, where he found a great fire burning in front of the door. He was drawn irresistibly into it, and his physical body was completely incinerated. He was transformed into a shimmering body of light and thought, "I am Vimalamitra."

On another occasion during the same period, the powerful lord of siddhas Tangtong Gyalpo came to Jamyang Khyentsei Wangpo in a dream and blessed him. Although he conferred on him much general and specific advice, Jamyang Khyentsei Wangpo recorded only the practice of a guru sadhana. Later, he relaxed the seal of secrecy concerning these teachings, which eventually appeared as *The Heart Drop of the Accomplished Masters* cycle, including *The Root Verses of the Six Stages of*

Completion, The Five Cycles of Sadhana Practice, and *The Gathering of the Sugata Herukas.*

In another vision, the lord of immortality, Amitayus, and his consort blessed Jamyang Khyentsei Wangpo, and from this came the extraordinary sadhana that enabled him to codify[15] the fundamental texts of *Chandali: Feminine Consort of Longevity.* Although he had countless such visions of the entire range of deities of the Three Roots, [1.237a] Jamyang Khyentsei Wangpo was deeply motivated to preserve their secrecy and so made no hint to others that they had taken place.

Although he had many opportunities to issue prophecies over the years, Jamyang Khyentsei Wangpo stated, "It is said, 'Unlike masters of the kama transmissions, tertöns are ruined by their prophecies.' Once a prophecy has been written down, it becomes necessary to follow the moral choices it dictates, but since no one actually puts these into practice, such prophecies never serve their purpose. Too much talk about them invites maras." Thus demonstrating a crucial point, he neither issued prophecies nor delighted in those made by others.

The Seven Modes of Transmission

THE KAMA TRANSMISSIONS When he was sixteen, Jamyang Khyentsei Wangpo had a pure vision at dawn on the tenth day of Saga, the fourth month,[16] in which he went to the palace of Pema Ö in the realm of Chamara. There, amid majestic cliffs, in a bank of especially white clouds, he beheld the Guru, Saroruhavajra, surrounded by a host of dakinis. The Guru blessed him with his enlightened intent, conferred empowerment on him through symbols, and greatly inspired him by predicting the seven modes of transmission he was to receive. Finally, the Guru looked at him one-pointedly and said:

> Unsullied by objectification,
> uncorrupted by concepts about self, [1.237b]
> the ongoing unity of awareness and emptiness, in all its nakedness—
> this is the enlightened intent of all buddhas.

Then the Guru and his retinue dissolved into the lord Jamyang Khyentsei Wangpo, who felt the Guru's enlightened mind blend inseparably with his own. From then on, he experienced the way of abiding, the state of original purity, with a natural sense of stability and, thus inspired, prayed one-pointedly to Guru Rinpoché. This enabled him to receive the most well known kama and terma instructions of the Nyingma and Sarma schools of the sutras and tantras—the maturing empowerments, liberating instructions, and supportive oral transmissions—and to effortlessly locate rare and dying lineages of transmission. Jamyang Khyentsei Wangpo rekindled their embers through his own practice as well as his propagation of these teachings.

This is the first mode of transmission.

THE EARTH TERMAS This mode of transmission comprises termas that were concealed in the earth. In his twentieth year, Jamyang Khyentsei Wangpo went to Drakmar Drinzang, where a dakini of timeless awareness offered him a casket of termas. From this he brought forth the cycle of teachings concerning Mahakarunika called *Being at Ease in the Nature of Mind* and the relics of twenty-one brahmins. At Damshö Nyingdrung, the local god Nyenchen Tangla revealed and offered to him the sadhana cycles for the four kayas of the Guru and relics that had issued from one of Guru Rinpoché's teeth. [1.238a] At the lake known as Singu Yutso, he received the cycle *The Three Roots: The Web of Magical Display* and, at Terlung Pemei Shelri, the cycle *The Gathering of All the Three Roots,* which was brought forth and offered to him through the magical power of dakinis. In many cases, although a terma was accessible, he revealed only some of the source texts and chose not to codify the entire cycle.

In addition, Jamyang Khyentsei Wangpo encouraged Chokgyur Lingpa to bring forth and codify *The Sadhana of Enlightened Mind: The Wish-Fulfilling Gem* and the "regent image" of Padmakara called Ngödrup Palbar,[17] which had been concealed at Tsiké Norbu Punsum. In general, there appear to have been many termas that this lord and Chokgyur Lingpa revealed together, such as *The Four Cycles of Guru Sadhana, The Heart Drop of Bairotsana,* and *The Three Categories of Great Perfection.*

THE RECONCEALED TERMAS This mode of transmission comprises termas (such as those in the preceding category) that, after having been revealed, were concealed again and rediscovered later.[18] In an Earth Sheep year[19] known as the "Accomplishment of Goals," Jamyang Khyentsei Wangpo had another pure vision. In it Guru Rinpoché appeared in the form of Terchen Sang-gyé Lingpa, gave him a volume of scripture, and blessed him. This extraordinary experience opened a doorway for him: he was able to clearly perceive the lives of the tertöns and all their teachings and was authorized to receive the transmission of all their spiritual commands. [1.238b] Thus dakinis of timeless awareness brought forth and offered to him the majority of yellow scrolls that had been reconcealed by tertöns in the past, and he deciphered them. He deciphered some when symbolic letters arose in his field of vision or when the teachings became naturally clear within the expanse of his enlightened intent. On such occasions, Guru Rinpoché appeared in person or in the forms of the respective tertöns and bestowed on Jamyang Khyentsei Wangpo the maturing empowerments and liberating instructions in a single, complete transmission.

Jamgön Lodrö Tayé felt that, above all else, preserving even one transmission of ancient termas was marvelous, so he fervently and repeatedly prayed to Jamyang Khyentsei Wangpo to reveal such teachings. Accordingly, the latter brought forth many direct lineages of reconcealed termas, which are found in *The Treasury of Precious Hidden Teachings.*

THE TERMAS OF ENLIGHTENED INTENT This mode of transmission comprises profound termas of enlightened intent. During an Earth Monkey year,[20] when he was twenty-nine and traveling to central Tibet, Jamyang Khyentsei Wangpo performed a ganachakra on the tenth day of the lunar cycle at Jangdrok Gegyé. Guru Rinpoché appeared to him and granted him blessings. [1.239a] When Jamyang Khyentsei Wangpo made offerings to the regent image of Saroruhavajra at Samyé Monastery, a statue that had been revealed by Nyang-ral Nyima Özer, the image actually turned into Saroruhavajra, who conferred blessings and spiritual advice on him. On the basis of this experience, Jamyang Khyentsei Wangpo brought forth the cycle of teachings called *The Heart Drop of the Lake-Born Vajra,* the secret practice for three cycles of guru sadhanas.

In his thirty-fifth year, that of a Wood Tiger, during the month of Gyal,[21] Jamyang Khyentsei Wangpo practiced the phases of approach and accomplishment for *The Wish-Granting Wheel of Immortality.* He had a vision of the exalted goddess Tara, chanting her ten-syllable mantra and blessing him. Later, he also received the blessings of the three masters who achieved immortality.[22] As a result of these experiences, the cycle of teachings entitled *The Heart Drop of the Exalted Goddess* came to him.

Another of these termas, the cycle *The Heart Drop of the Accomplished Masters,* has already been discussed. These are superb examples of termas of enlightened intent, for they constitute vajra verses beyond the comprehension of ordinary people and are indistinguishable from tantras.

THE RECOLLECTIONS This mode of transmission comprises Jamyang Khyentsei Wangpo's recollections.[23] Once, while he was traveling to central Tibet, he passed through the lower end of Uyuk Valley in the Tsang region. There he recalled precisely the place and time at which, in a former life as the great Chetsün, he had passed away into a body of light. On the basis of this, he codified *The Heart Drop of Chetsün.* His recollections of a former life as Langdro Könchok Jungné led him to reveal teachings that included the longevity sadhana *The Heart Drop of Bairotsana,* [1.239b] a practice for "extracting the vital essence"[24] based on the white form of Simhamukha.

THE DAKNANG TRANSMISSIONS This mode comprises the many transmissions Jamyang Khyentsei Wangpo received in pure visions. Notable examples are the cycle of spiritual instructions mentioned previously (*Chandali: Feminine Consort of Longevity* from *The Heart Drop of Immortality*) as well as his manual on the guru sadhana from *The Heart Drop of Longchenpa* entitled *Sealed with Bindu* and Chokgyur Lingpa's guru sadhana *The Gathering of the Families of the Three Kayas.* Although he received many such transmissions, these were the only ones he codified.

THE ORAL LINEAGES This mode of transmission comprises oral lineages.[25] While Jamyang Khyentsei Wangpo was staying at the important holy site of Deshek Düpa in Dzashö, he had a pure vision in which he journeyed to the stupa of Shankarakuta. In each of the eight cardinal and intermediate directions was one of the eight emanations of the Guru, with a ninth form, that of Guru Rinpoché as the union of them all, in the center. They bestowed on him, as oral lineages, the very essence of the maturing empowerments and liberating instructions for such cycles as those focusing on the Eight Commands on Sadhana Practice and the peaceful and wrathful deities of *The Web of Magical Display,* all of which he codified.

This has been a brief description of the essence of Jamyang Khyentsei Wangpo's life on the secret level.

Having completed such marvelous, wonderful deeds, he reached the age of seventy-three. On the morning of the twenty-first day (the second "Day of Joy" in the waning phase of the moon) of the second month of O in a Male Water Dragon year,[26] [1.240a] he scattered flowers and recited many prayers of auspicious benediction. Then he rested in meditative equipoise, whereupon his emanated form resolved back into basic space, the enlightened intent of the great master Vimalamitra.

The students nurtured by the nectar of his speech came to embody the seven modes of transmission he had received and, without sectarian bias, served as repositories of the precious teachings of the Victorious One. In the Land of Snows, among all of the learned and accomplished masters of the four schools—Sakya, Geluk, Kagyü, and Nyingma—as well as the indigenous Bön tradition, there was not one who did not bow at Jamyang Khyentsei Wangpo's feet. All were taken under his care and received his advice, which derived from the eight lineages of accomplishment. His students included Jamgön Lodrö Tayé; Adzom Drukpa Rinpoché Rigdzin Natsok Rangdrol; Tertön Lerab Lingpa; Gyurmé Ngedön Wangpo; the third Dodrupchen, Tenpai Nyima; Mipam Jampal Gyepai Dorjé; Situ Chökyi Gyatso of Katok Monastery; Gyaltsap Pema Namgyal of Zhechen Monastery; Jamyang Loter Wangpo of the Sakya school; Gatön Ngawang Lekpa; Dezhung Choktrul Lung-rik Tenpai Nyima; [1.240b] Jedrung Jampai Jungné; Khenchen Tashi Özer of Palpung Monastery; Tertön Rang-rik of Nyarong and his brother, Khenchen Dewai Nyima; Khenchen Rinchen Dargyé of the Karma Kagyü school; and Gyakor Tulku Kunzang Tekchok Tenpai Gyaltsen. These and the other sublime masters he taught all nobly upheld the fine activities of the threefold focus of spiritual endeavor, nurturing the precious teachings of the Victorious One. In this respect, Jamyang Khyentsei Wangpo was a second Buddha, ensuring the spread and flourishing of all the traditions of the eight lineages of accomplishment and the ten great pillars upholding the lineages of exegesis.

The principal source of this lord guru's ultimate lineage of the heart essence, the fundamental lineage of the Dzogchen teachings, was Jigmé Gyalwai Nyugu. But he held another lineage of the empowerments and oral transmissions of the Nyingtik teachings of utter lucidity. It had been passed down from Rigdzin Jigmé Lingpa to

Dodrup Jigmé Trinlé Özer, Chökyi Lodrö (also known as Dola Jigmé Kalzang), Gyalsé Zhenpen Tayé, and Khenpo Pema Badzra of Dzogchen Monastery, who passed it on to Jamyang Khyentsei Wangpo. He also held a lineage from the Mindroling tradition, [1.241a] passed down from Terdak Lingpa to Rinchen Namgyal, Mingyur Paldrön, Oddiyana, Trinlé Namgyal, and Trinlé Chödrön, who passed it on to Jamyang Khyentsei Wangpo. He in turn transmitted these lines to Gyakor Tulku Kunzang Tekchok Tenpai Gyaltsen; they were passed on to Khenchen Ngawang Palzang of Katok Monastery, then to the lord of my buddha family, Lungtrul Shedrup Tenpai Nyima, through whose kindness we received this transmission.

It was from this holy guru, Kunzik[27] Khyentsei Wangpo, that Pukhung Tulku Gyurmé Ngedön Wangpo of Dzapuk heard in their entirety the tantras, explanatory commentaries, and pith instructions of the secret Nyingtik teachings. [1.241b]

Dza Pukhung Gyurmé Ngedön Wangpo (19th–20th Centuries)

Gyurmé Ngedön Wangpo was born in eastern Tibet, in the region of Dergé, which was ruled by a great dharma king. He was enthroned as the senior of two tulkus associated with the administrative estate governing Khung Monastery in Dzapuk. He learned to read and write without difficulty. At six or seven, he went to the monastery of Zhechen Tennyi Dargyé Ling, where he studied with Mahapandita Öntrul Tutop Namgyal and other sublime beings, including tulkus and great, holy khenpos. He mastered all of the approaches of the sutras and tantras—Madhyamaka, Prajñaparamita, Vinaya, Abhidharma, and so forth—as well as fields of secular knowledge, and so reached the pinnacle of erudition. Today there are samples of his calligraphy in sixty-four different scripts at Khung Monastery in Dzapuk. He lived as a threefold vajra holder, a fully ordained monk upholding the Vajrayana teachings, and he became a true elder, standing out like a mountain of gold.

When he was fifteen, Gyurmé Ngedön Wangpo met the guru with whom he had been connected karmically for lifetimes, Jamyang Khyentsei Wangpo, Vimalamitra in human form. He remained with him for seven years, during which time he studied the entire range of methods of the sutras and tantras. In particular, like one vase being filled from another, he received without omission the tantras, explanatory commentaries, and pith instructions of the earlier and later cycles of the secret Nyingtik teachings of the Dzogchen approach of utter lucidity, [1.242a] lineages that descended from the Omniscient King of the Dharma, Longchenpa. Thus the ultimate enlightened intent of realization was born in his mind.

Gyurmé Ngedön Wangpo served his guru in various positions of responsibility—as shrine keeper, personal secretary, and so forth—rendering immeasurable service with his body and speech, relying on his guru while pleasing him in the three ways. He thus became an extraordinary heart son on an inner level. At times he acted as a substitute teacher of all subjects, both outer and inner.[28] He studied with other sublime masters who visited from time to time, such as Jamgön Kongtrul Lodrö Tayé, the lord of the dharma Mipam Rinpoché, and Khenchen Tashi Özer. From them he received an entire range of transmissions of profound source texts and pith instructions, foremost among these the great *Treasury of Precious Hidden Teachings* and *The Treasury of Spiritual Instructions.*

He also became quite proficient in such secular fields of knowledge as medicine and astrology. He once asked his guru, "Could it be that practicing medicine is nothing more than a distraction? Should I give it up for now?"

To this his guru replied, "Would you renounce your altruistic attitude of bodhichitta? Your practice of medicine will benefit many beings." [1.242b] And so he followed this advice and became a physician.

After this seven-year period with Jamyang Khyentsei Wangpo came to a close, the lord guru said to Gyurmé Ngedön Wangpo, "Now return to your home country and in time go to see Terchen Dudjom Lingpa. You have a karmic connection with him from past lifetimes, so meeting him will be enormously useful to the teachings and to beings." Gyurmé Ngedön Wangpo thus went back to his homeland, where he remained for a year. Then he bequeathed all of the horses and livestock and so forth, all of the property of the administrative estate, to the junior Pukhung Tulku. He said, "Please take good care of this monastic center. I am going to give up all activities, public and private, to practice the dharma to the greatest possible extent, and so shall be a wandering yogin with no fixed dwelling place."

Following his guru's prophecy, he traveled toward lower Ser to seek an audience with Dudjom Lingpa. Due to their karmic connection in previous lifetimes, their meeting was like a reunion of father and son; the guru was delighted to see Gyurmé Ngedön Wangpo, and spiritual father and son resided for a time at the same seat. The lord Dudjom Lingpa bestowed on Gyurmé Ngedön Wangpo all of the termas he himself had discovered, all of the profound tantras, explanatory commentaries, and pith instructions from such cycles as *The Treasury of the Spacious Expanse of the True Nature of Phenomena, The Profound Secret Heart Drop of the Dakini,* and *The Pure Vision: The Web of Timeless Awareness.* [1.243a] He empowered Gyurmé Ngedön Wangpo as the custodian of his teachings, as had been indicated in prophecies, and invested him as one of his heart sons on the inner level and a holder of the ultimate lineage of realization. Gyurmé Ngedön Wangpo composed numerous commentaries on Tersar[29] tantras and pith instructions such as *The Sharp Vajra of Awareness.* He stayed with Dudjom Lingpa, serving him in the three ways of pleasing a teacher, until the latter passed away. Finally, Gyurmé Ngedön Wangpo oversaw his memorial services, omitting nothing.

In accordance with the last testament and secret prophecies of Terchen Dudjom

Lingpa, he decided to go to that most majestic of hidden regions, the area of Pema Nampar Köpa, and so he set out in the direction of central Tibet. He journeyed in stages from lower Ser in the east, visiting all of the principal holy sites throughout Tibet that were powerful places of spiritual practice, such as glaciers, cliffs, mountains, and lakes. He formed a connection with these sites and practiced the sadhanas of a large number of his meditation deities. During this period, he also benefited many students without bias; among other things, he bestowed the empowerments and oral transmissions for the great *Treasury of Precious Hidden Teachings* five times. Thousands of people who forged a connection with Gyurmé Ngedön Wangpo through empowerments and teachings were thus brought closer to the level of omniscience and the enlightened state of supreme freedom. [1.243b] To all students regardless of status, he gave innumerable teachings on the preliminary practices, the main body of practice, and so forth, in regions such as Ser and in the northern solitudes of the nomads, bringing each person to spiritual maturity according to his or her own good fortune.

He eventually arrived in the sublime area of Pemakö, the most majestic of hidden regions, where he stayed for sixteen years. There he recognized Rigdzin Dudjom Dorjé as the sublime tulku of his lord guru and established him on the golden throne of the former Dudjom. It is evident that, through the illumination shed by this great being, Gyurmé Ngedön Wangpo, with his motivation and noble activity, we of the Early Translation school, as well as the protectors of this lineage, have been blessed. The splendor of this noble, effortless enlightened activity was later extended throughout the world by the sovereign lord of the hundred buddha families, Dudjom Drodul Lingpa,[30] who was a true emanation of the lord of victorious ones Padma.

During his entire time at Pemakö, Gyurmé Ngedön Wangpo had countless pure visions, including visions of the entire array of deities of the Three Roots, from whom he received prophecies. Through the secret path of natural great perfection, he directly experienced the enlightened intent of a master of awareness of the second degree.[31] [1.244a] He benefited innumerable beings who saw, heard, thought of, or touched him, and so completed his enlightened activities.

At a certain point, he directed his enlightened intent toward his final act to benefit others. Amid a great, boundless display of amazing signs—swirling pavilions of rainbow light and so on—his emanated form resolved back into the supreme inner illumination of primordial being. His students had his body cremated on a pyre, and the subtle essence of his remains—his heart, tongue, and eyes—blended together to form an image of the aspect of Padmakara known as Guru Dewachenpo. This image resides as the inner support of Mahakoti Monastery in Pemakö.

It was from this holy guru that Kyabjé Dudjom Jigdral Yeshé Dorjé heard all of the tantras, explanatory commentaries, and pith instructions of Dzogchen in their entirety.

Dudjom Rinpoché Jigdral Yeshé Dorjé (1904–1987)

This sovereign lord of the hundred buddha families, Kyabjé Dudjom Jigdral Yeshé Dorjé Gelek Nampar Gyalwai Dé, was a miraculous timeless awareness embodiment of those mentioned in a prayer of praise in his honor:

> In the past, you were the buddha Nüden Dorjé.
> In the future, you will be the sugata named Adhimukta. [1.244b]
> At present, you are the regent of Padma and the true presence of Drokben.[32]
> I pray to you, Jigdral Yeshé Dorjé.

In the account contained in a terma revealed by Orgyen Dechen Lingpa, we read the following:

> In the future, in the land of Tibet, to the east of nine snowy peaks,༔
> in the secret realm of the naturally occurring image of Varahi,༔
> from a noble line will appear an emanation of Drokben༔
> named Jñana, who will uphold the deportment of a tantric practitioner.༔
> Unpredictable in his appearance, childlike in his conduct, endowed with sublime knowing,༔
> he will reveal new termas and guard the teachings of older ones.༔ [1.245a]
> This guide will appear in order to lead those connected to him to Chamara.༔

In keeping with this prophecy, Kyabjé Dudjom Rinpoché was born amid innumerable marvelous signs in a Wood Dragon year.[33] He descended from the early Tibetan king Nyatri Tsenpo[34] and was of the Powo Kanam Gyalpo clan. His father, Norbu Tendzin, was a tulku of Katok Monastery, and his mother, Namgyal Drolma, was a descendant of Ratna Lingpa.

Earlier, the prescient Traktung Dudjom Lingpa had prophesied, "Now, in these final times of spiritual degeneration, I must go to the hidden region of Pemakö. All who place their hopes in me should go there as well. I, the old man, will be there before you youngsters arrive." Such pronouncements, which Dudjom Lingpa made at various times, proved that this great master, Dudjom Rinpoché, was the immediate rebirth of Dudjom Lingpa.

Dudjom Rinpoché clearly remembered his past lifetimes. As soon as he could talk, he spoke spontaneously about the deeds of his former incarnation, so that everyone proclaimed him to be the uncontestable tulku. Then, one by one, students from his preceding lifetime—Puktrul Gyurmé Ngedön Wangpo, Lama Tupten Chöjor of Ling, and others—made their way to him [1.245b] and performed the ceremonies of enthronement, offering him the robes and title of Traktung Dudjom Lingpa.

When the child began his formal studies in the usual subjects, such as reading and writing, the dynamic quality of his wisdom blazed like wildfire, and he mastered whatever was presented to him merely upon its being shown to him. He studied the commentaries on such mainstream works as *Ascertaining the Three Levels of Ordination* and *Engaging in the Conduct of a Bodhisattva.* Lama Könrap said that his capacity to reveal termas developed from the age of five. Dudjom Rinpoché relied for some sixteen years on the extraordinary master of his buddha family on the inner level, the master prophesied by his former incarnation, Dudjom Lingpa, to be the custodian of the lineage: Pukhung Tulku Gyurmé Ngedön Wangpo. From him Dudjom Rinpoché received, like one vase being filled from another, all of the tantras, explanatory commentaries, and pith instructions in their entirety for *The Heart Essence of Secrets*—the lineages that Gyurmé Ngedön Wangpo had received from the lord Khyentsei Wangpo, Jamgön Kongtrul Lodrö Tayé, the lord of the dharma Mipam, and other masters. He also received the complete transmission of the terma cycles revealed by Dudjom Lingpa.

The lord Dudjom Rinpoché himself said, "It was from two masters, Jedrung Jampai Jungné and Gyurmé Ngedön Wangpo, that I received some understanding and certainty concerning the Dzogchen approach." [1.246a] It was with these two masters that he studied all of the advice and instructions on this path, from the preliminaries up to the main body of practice. He studied the tantra *The Sharp Vajra of Awareness,* and the dynamic energy of his awareness welled up as the sublime knowing that discerns the true nature of phenomena. He easily and very naturally understood the difficult key points of the vast classes of tantras of the Vajrayana path. He said repeatedly, "Any understanding that I have is due to the kindness of the tantras."

Puktrul Rinpoché advised him, "*The Treasury of Precious Hidden Teachings* is an expression of the activity of the two masters who were emanations of the protector Mañjushri.[35] While I have given the transmission five times, you will give it ten. In your hands I have placed, like a mandala offering, the profound teachings of my lord, your former incarnation, returning this wealth to its rightful owner. I have fulfilled my root guru's command and have now finished everything I needed to accomplish. My advice is that you gain experience working with sublime masters and bring benefit to beings." Puktrul Gyurmé Ngedön Wangpo invested Dudjom Rinpoché as his regent on the ultimate level of realization, confirming him as a master of the secret mantra approach of the Nyingma teachings.

The lord Dudjom Rinpoché himself said, "From an early age, I had various unusual visionary experiences [1.246b] and my karmic predisposition for revealing profound termas was awakened." Accordingly, at the age of thirteen, he encountered Orgyen, king of the dharma, and his consort. He received his legacy from these extraordinary, naturally manifest teachers, and dakinis of timeless awareness offered him yellow scrolls. This was the first time he revealed profound termas. From then on, he had an enormous variety of pure visions and perceived without impediment all of the termas he was meant to discover, wherever they were concealed. He also received, from Tokden Tenpa Rabgyé, the great experiential transmission of pith instructions —the empowerments, oral transmissions, and so forth—for *The Four Higher Collections of the Heart Drop,* the lineage that originated with Nyoshul Lungtok Tenpai Nyima.

Dudjom Rinpoché then gradually made his way to central Tibet, where he studied at Kham Riwoché Monastery with Jedrung Trinlé Jampai Jungné, also known as Dudjom Namkhai Dorjé. From this master, he received the oral transmissions for the greater part of the precious Kangyur, *The Treasury of Spiritual Instructions,* and teachings concerning the great perfection of utter lucidity, such as the seventeen definitive tantras of the supreme secret and *The Four Higher Collections of the Heart Drop.* Jedrung Jampai Jungné made him one of his heart sons on the inner level. [1.247a]

Dudjom Rinpoché recounted, "When I was receiving the empowerment for Jamgön Kongtrul Lodrö Tayé's secret sadhana practice of Dorjé Drolö from Zilnön Namkhai Dorjé, the guru stared directly at me and forcefully uttered 'Phat!' My mind and body suddenly disappeared without a trace, and as I rested for a short while, the guru said, 'This is the timeless awareness that is the ultimate point of the empowerment; may it be stabilized in you! Tishtra vajra!'[36] Without having to concentrate, I experienced a spacious openness. That is the enlightened intent of the ultimate lineage."

Dudjom Rinpoché received many profound teachings, such as *The Collected Tantras of the Nyingma School,* from Gyakor Tulku Kunzang Tekchok Tenpai Gyaltsen of eastern Tibet. He received the oral transmissions for the entire Kangyur from two masters, Jangsem Lodrö Gyaltsen and Dungkar Ngédön Gyatso. He studied the cycles of teachings revealed by Terchen Pema Lingpa, *The Seven Treasuries* of the Omniscient One Longchenpa, and other teachings with Ngaktsün Gendün Gyatso. The vajra holder of Mindroling Monastery, Namdrol Gyatso, bestowed on Dudjom Rinpoché many profound teachings, among them the entire Mindroling tradition of Rigdzin Terdak Lingpa, including the ritual dances, mandala preparation, chants, and music [1.247b] for the innumerable classes of tantras of the supreme secret.

Jampal Dewai Nyima, also known as Pendai Özer, was a great khenpo from Nyarong in eastern Tibet and had been a student of the lord of the dharma Mipam. He passed on to Dudjom Rinpoché the kama transmissions of the Early Translation school, the extensive sadhana and empowerments for cycles focusing on the Eight Commands, *The United Intent of the Gurus* as revealed by Sang-gyé Lingpa, many commentaries on tantras (such as the Zur tradition of exegesis of the glorious *Heart Essence of Secrets* and his own commentary on that tantra), and cycles of the secret Nyingtik teachings of utter lucidity such as *The Four Higher Collections of the Heart*

Drop. Dudjom Rinpoché thus received from this master a veritable ocean of teachings, both profound and extensive. He said of Khenchen Jampal Dewai Nyima, "He was my second-kindest guru." It was from this master that Dudjom Rinpoché received most of the lineages he held concerning ordination: the vows of individual liberation, the bodhisattva vow, and the tantric vows.

Dudjom Rinpoché also received many profound teachings from Dilgo Khyentsé Rinpoché, including that master's own terma entitled *Padma's Heart Essence of Longevity,* and their minds blended, becoming one. He also studied with numerous masters, such as Chatral Sanjé Dorjé, Lama Orgyen Rigdzin, Katok Chaktsa Tulku, [1.248a] Choktrul Gyurmé Dorjé, and Pulung Sang-gyé Tulku; these were sublime, holy beings who had been students of the emanation of Vimalamitra, Nyoshul Khenchen Ngawang Palzang.

All of these masters encouraged him to focus on the very essence of spiritual practice, and this he did. He had visions of the entire range of his personal meditation deities. In particular, at the holy site of Puntsok Gatsal in the hidden region of Khenjong, Dudjom Rinpoché attained siddhis through the practice of the glorious Vajrakila and codified the cycle known as *Dudjom's Razor of Meteoric Iron,* a complete presentation of the graduated path according to the enlightened intent of the "fourfold penetration."[37] When he was practicing the sadhana of vajra longevity in the cave of Buddha Tsepuk, he witnessed signs of accomplishment; for example, the consecrated longevity alcohol began to boil, and he had a vision of the transcendent and accomplished conqueror Amitayus. When he was practicing the meditation on the glorious tamer of maras Dorjé Drolö, he received the terma of enlightened intent known as *Dudjom's Dorjé Drolö.* While he was pursuing the practice of Vajrakila at Paro Taktsang in Bhutan, there appeared within an expanse of pulsating rainbow light in the sky a scroll four inches wide and a foot and a half long, covered with symbolic dakini script; he thus received the entire cycle entitled *Kila: The Razor That Destroys at a Touch.* [1.248b] Dudjom Rinpoché also revealed a number of major termas—such cycles as the terma of enlightened mind called *The Heart Drop of the Lake-Born One* and that called *The Heart Drop of the Dakini*—concerning the deities of the Three Roots, the practice of guru yoga, Dzogchen, and the supremely compassionate Avalokiteshvara.

He codified the fundamental practices of each, but devoted himself primarily to preserving older traditions of termas rather than giving much effort to new revelations. He was aware of terma cycles of sadhana practice, of various lengths and focusing on Guru Rinpoché, hidden in the earth in such places as Gyala Sumdo in lower Kongpo, the Chimpu Uplands in Samyé, and Paro Taktsang in Bhutan. However, due to circumstances of time and place, he did not go to reveal them.

In brief, Dudjom Rinpoché spent days, months, and years meditating on a large number of his meditation deities at great holy sites, glacial wastelands, and caves. He gained mastery, attaining the sublime and more ordinary siddhis, while experiencing signs of having accomplished each practice.

To summarize the enlightened activities he undertook to benefit others: Dudjom Rinpoché fulfilled his guru's prophecy by bestowing the empowerments and oral transmissions for *The Treasury of Precious Hidden Teachings* ten times. He also passed on all of the empowerments and oral transmissions for the cycles of Pema Lingpa's teachings three times, the termas of his former incarnation on many occasions, the precious Kangyur, the oral transmissions for *The Collected Tantras of the Nyingma School,* [1.249a] the extensive sadhana and empowerments for cycles focusing on the Eight Commands, the background teachings for the cycle of peaceful and wrathful deities revealed by Karma Lingpa, the six volumes of Jatsön Nyingpo's termas, and the precious teachings of the kama transmissions of the Early Translation school. He thus turned the wheel of the vast and profound dharma on an enormous scale.

Dudjom Rinpoché's collected writings—his termas of enlightened intent as well as numerous treatises—fill about twenty-five volumes. They are indistinguishable from the works of Rigdzin Terdak Lingpa in both their style, which delights the erudite, and the pure, concise, and clear pith instructions they contain, which hit upon the key points of personal experience. He was also responsible for publishing a fifty-eight-volume edition of the background teachings of the precious kama transmissions of the Early Translation school.[38]

His construction projects included lodgings for both monastic and lay tantric communities and a temple in the hidden region of Pemakö, so that the Victorious One's teachings could flourish there. Dudjom Rinpoché had the foresight to have hundreds of texts brought out of Tibet to the holy country of India.[39] It is because of his inestimable kindness that both the oral transmissions and the empowerment lineages [1.249b] of the precious teachings of the kama tradition exist today. He restored the "border-taming" temple of Buchui Lhakhang in the region of Kongpo[40] and nearby erected the temple of Zangdok Palri,[41] including its interiors and statues. He founded the lay tantric retreat center Lama Ling,[42] which has produced many powerful masters of wisdom and realization. In India, Dudjom Rinpoché founded a retreat center at Tso Pema,[43] Tsechu Monastery in Darjeeling, the lay tantric center Duddul Rabten Ling in Orissa State, and the temple and meditation center of Zangdok Palri in Kalimpong. He also founded the centers Yeshe Nyingpo and Orgyen Chö Dzong in the United States, and Dorjé Nyingpo and Urgyen Samyé Chöling in France.[44] With such projects, which he personally oversaw, he firmly established the tradition of the teachings.

When Kyabjé Dudjom Rinpoché taught the dharma in India and Tibet, there was virtually no one among the great masters of our school today—the learned and accomplished gurus (both lay and ordained), teachers, meditators, and so forth—who did not receive teachings at his feet. They included the great throne holder of Mindroling Monastery; the two khenpo brothers;[45] Dodrak Rigdzin Chenmo; Taklung Tsetrul; Chatral Sanjé Dorjé; Zhadeu Trulzhik; Dudjom Rinpoché's sons Thinley Norbu Rinpoché and Shenpen Dawa Rinpoché; his grandsons Dzongsar Khyentsé Rinpoché, [1.250a] Tulku Garab Dorjé, and Tulku Jampal Dorjé; Choktrul Pema Wangyal; Sogyal Tulku; the sublime Bhutanese master Drupchen Sönam Zangpo;[46] Ngaktön[47] Tsewang Paljor; Ngaktön Pema Wangchen; Lama Pema Longdrol; Peling Sungtrul; Gangteng Tulku; Tuksé Tulku; Riché Ngaktön Tsewang Lhagyal; Ngaktön Dorjé Namgyal; Ngaktön Könchok Jungné; Soktsé Tulku; Tertön Namkha Drimé Rabjam; Ritrul Rigdzin Chögyal; Ngaktön Khetsun Sangpo; the Bhutanese master Ngaktön Kunzang Wangdü; Gelong Sang-gyé; Gelong Karpo; Gelong Namdrol Zangpo; Lama Chimé; Lama Jangchub; Lama Gönpo Tendzin; Bakha Tulku; Tsedrup Tarchin of Repkong; Dzatrul; Yomé Tulu of Spiti; Ngari Khen Yeshé Zangpo; and Khen Tupten Norbu. [1.250b] In addition, tens of thousands of students throughout the world—as far away as the United States—gathered around him out of faith, for the activities he undertook to benefit beings were as vast as the reaches of the sky. The fact that Jamgön Kongtrul Lodrö Tayé could uphold the ideals embodied in the lives of a hundred tertöns; that the sugata Adhimukta will care for as many who are to be guided as all the rest of the one thousand buddhas of this age;[48] and that the great master Dudjom Rinpoché was able to continue the activities of all of his former incarnations and to care for students—these were all the result of the forceful momentum of these masters' previous motivation and aspirations.

This master, then, sat firmly on the vajra throne as a glorious protector of all the teachings and all beings, his sublime form beautified by the major and minor marks of perfection that derive from a million aspects of his own merit. Of his students, the regents of his enlightened form, speech, and mind are his two sons, Dungsé Rinpoché Thinley Norbu and Shenpen Dawa Norbu, both of whom continue their father's work. An extraordinary heart son of both Kyabjé Terchen Dudjom Rinpoché and Dilgo Khyentsé Rinpoché [1.251a] is Choktrul Pema Wangyal Rinpoché, son of Kangyur Rinpoché Longchen Yeshé Dorjé. Pema Wangyal has carried out activities of great magnitude, such as founding monasteries, temples, shedras, and retreat centers, overseeing the publication of texts, and teaching at many gatherings.

Such a regent of Padma as this great, precious tertön Dudjom Rinpoché even saw gold where there was only dirt, establishing in the likes of fortunate ones such as I the potential to understand a vast ocean of profound and extensive teachings, including the two traditions of the Early Translation school, the kama and terma. Such kindness, the effects of which will last until my own enlightenment, is beyond measure. Let me conclude with Kyabjé Dudjom Rinpoché's own words:

How marvelous!

The essence of being is primordially unchanging, the unconditioned nature free of elaboration,
abiding as the youthful vase body, originally pure and profoundly lucid.
Dharmakaya guru, Yeshé Dorjé, you know all.
I beseech you, grant your blessings that I might attain the supreme, indwelling confidence of view. [1.251b]

The nature of being is unceasing primordial unity, the amassing of utter lucidity,
abiding as the display of spontaneous presence endowed with fivefold certainty.
Sambhogakaya guru, Dechen Dorjé, you know all.
I beseech you, grant your blessings that I might perfect the supreme dynamic energy of meditation.

The responsiveness of being, which does not fall into extremes, is timeless awareness free of limitations,
abiding as the naked essence, the all-pervasive unity of awareness and emptiness.
Nirmanakaya guru, Drodul Lingpa, you know all.
I beseech you, grant your blessings that I might train in conduct that greatly enhances my realization.

The primordial ground of being, self-knowing awareness, undergoes no transition or change.
As the dynamic energy of dharmakaya, whatever arises is neither good nor bad.
Since awareness in the ever-present moment abides as actual buddhahood,
in the center of my heart I have found the guru—spacious and carefree mind.
Once one realizes that this genuine mind is the guru's nature,
there is no need to whine with contrived prayers based on attachment.

The natural condition of uncontrived awareness is that of relaxation without restriction;
I experience the blessing of natural freedom: regardless of what arises, it has no fixed reference.
There is never any point at which buddhahood is accomplished on the basis of conditioned phenomena.

Speculation by ordinary consciousness is the seductive foe of meditation.
Now this eccentric lunatic, who has done away with all forms of attachment,
will spend this life in a state of bare repose, simply relating to events as they arise.

Whatever I do, I am joyful, a yogin of great perfection.
Whoever accompanies me, I am happy; this is the lineage of Padmakara's children.
There is no one to rival you as my protector—guru, great tertön.
There is nothing to compare to these teachings, the heart drop of the dakini. [1.252a]

With great ignorance, the darkness in my heart, cleared away in its natural place of rest,
the sun of utter lucidity shines constantly, never obscured.
I owe this good fortune to the kindness of the guru, the only father.
There is no way I can repay your kindness; my guru, my thoughts are only of you.
Henceforth, until I reach the very heart of enlightenment,
grant your blessings that I may never be separate from you.
Kind one, you know all!

Adzom Drukpa Rinpoché Drodul Pawo Dorjé (1842–1924)

Adzom Drukpa Rinpoché Drodul Pawo Dorjé held a lineage that he received from the lord Jamyang Khyentsei Wangpo. [1.252b] Born on the evening of the full moon during the sixth month of a Water Tiger year,[49] he was the son of Atra, a descendant of Tashi Bum, himself the son of a Mongolian named Dura Tau-ji. Tashi Bum had moved to the plateau of Gakyiltang in Litang six generations earlier, coming from Xining in the vicinity of the lake known as Kokonor.[50] Atra's son was recognized as the rebirth of Adzom Sang-gyé Tashi by the glorious second Katok Situ, Chökyi Dorjé, and the third Drimé Zhingkyong tulku of Katok Monastery. Because Druptop Gyalwa Jangchub of Trom praised the child as a tulku of Pema Karpo of the Drukpa Kagyü school, he became known as Adzom Drukpa. The preceding incarnation had lived for eighty-four years and on the point of death indicated that he would be reborn at a place from which the white cliffs of Dung-ra in Trom were visible; and so it happened.

An accomplished master of Chö, one Lama Chöpel, bestowed a longevity empowerment on the young Adzom Drukpa. The boy had dreamed that the sun was shining inside the family's felt tent, its radiance filling the entire region. Lama Chöpel gave Adzom Drukpa protection cords and other blessings, urging him to be scrupulously pure in conduct. Positive omens and indications, such as rainbows arching into the tent, were repeatedly observed.

Adzom Drukpa received the refuge vow from Zhechen Öntrul Gyurmé Tutop Namgyal, [1.253a] who gave him the name Pema Do-ngak Lhundrup Zangpo. In a dream, Gyurmé Tutop Namgyal had seen two conch shells, one larger than the other. When he blew the smaller one, its sound resonated all over Tibet, as far away as Lhasa. From this he concluded, "This boy is of a noble spiritual heritage."

When he was twelve, Adzom Drukpa accompanied his paternal uncle and brother to meet Chökyi Lodrö Tenpai Gyaltsen Palzangpo, the second Situ Rinpoché of Katok Monastery, who was giving the empowerments, oral transmissions, and teachings for the cycles of Longsel Dorjé Nyingpo. During the teachings on impermanence, Adzom Drukpa experienced profound uncertainty in the face of his own mortality and felt sad at heart; becoming pale and wan, he wept. During the last of his many audiences with Situ Rinpoché, the guru bestowed gifts on him, foremost among these some blessed representations of enlightened form, speech, and mind. Situ Rinpoché also impressed upon him more than once the necessity of passing on in turn the empowerments, oral transmissions, and teachings he had received.

From Gyatrul Do-ngak Tendzin of Palyul Monastery and Göntrul Rangdrol, Adzom Drukpa received empowerments and oral transmissions on a vast scale, including those for *Holding Buddhahood in One's Hand* from the *Namchö* cycle, the cycle of sadhanas of enlightened mind from Ratna Lingpa, the teachings on Simhamukha in the tradition of Mati, [1.253b] the cycle of the peaceful and wrathful deities entitled *The Natural Freedom of Enlightened Intent,* and teachings on the six bardo states.

The great Khedrup Drakpa Döndrup, a teacher of the Gelukpa school, came to Adzom Drukpa's hermitage at the white cliffs of Drakar and gave teachings on four chapters of *Engaging in the Conduct of a Bodhisattva.* He also gave empowerments and oral transmissions for the mandala of Guhyasamaja involving many deities, Ghantapada's tradition of Chakrasamvara, and the white and black forms of his protective deity. Delighted with Adzom Drukpa, the guru said, "Your spiritual heritage is that of a bodhisattva in his final incarnation, so train your mind in bodhichitta."

Later, Adzom Drukpa met the guru Nyala Pema Duddul (who eventually attained rainbow body). He served him, among other ways, by handing him the empowerment manuals during the great empowerment for *The Discourse on United Intent* that Pema Duddul bestowed at Serzhung in Trom. He fulfilled his tasks according to the guru's instructions. Pema Duddul told him, "You should let you hair grow long and become a householder wearing sambhogakaya ornaments and enjoying the pleasures of the five senses. If, while doing so, you explain and spread the teachings of the Dzogchen approach to everyone, high or low, commensurate with their individual fortunes, it will be for the teachings as though the sun has risen." However, from a young age, Adzom Drukpa had had his heart set on the humble way of life of a fully ordained monk, one who would eventually meet his death with no regrets. [1.254a] He therefore repeatedly requested his guru's permission not to take up the householder's path. Finally, Pema Duddul said, "The time will come when you will have no choice but to let your hair grow and so forth. This will eventually become clear to you."

Like one vase filling another, the guru bestowed on him the empowerments, teachings, and oral transmissions for the profound cycle *Natural Freedom Filling Space*. He prophesied that Adzom Drukpa would be the custodian of these teachings, in the introduction to which can be found the following verse:

> When the doorway to these profound and vast teachings opens, ༔
> an emanation of Druptop Matok Rinchen, ༔
> a master of profound termas, will appear in the region of Trom. ༔
> If they meet him, countless fortunate ones will find freedom. ༔

Despite this prophecy, the auspicious conditions did not arise for Adzom Drukpa to explain and spread these teachings or to codify the rituals for the practice.

When he went to the estate of the Ala Chushö family of upper Hor, he studied such texts as the annotated *Graduated Path to Enlightenment* by the lord Atisha and those on the graduated paths of Dzogchen and Mahamudra. He thus resolved any doubts and corrected any wrong opinions he had had about Jé Rinpoché Tsongkhapa, having discovered them to be groundless. With deep respect and devotion, he accumulated a hundred thousand repetitions of the Miktsema prayer of praise in Tsongkhapa's honor.[51] He thus adopted a pure outlook that embraced the Nyingma and Sarma schools of Buddhism as well as the Bönpo school, without sectarian bias.

Earlier, Situ Rinpoché had said to him, "Try to receive some extensive empowerments from Khyentsé, who is the protector Mañjushri himself. [1.254b] Today in eastern Tibet, he alone knows how to use the ritual vase properly." Accordingly, Adzom Drukpa sought out Jamyang Khyentsei Wangpo, the champion of the entire range of teachings in the Land of Snows. He met with him some twenty-seven times, delighting him and receiving a great many empowerments and oral transmissions.

In particular, Jamyang Khyentsei Wangpo bestowed on him, like one vase filling another, the mother and child cycles of the Nyingtik teachings and all of the tantras, explanatory commentaries, and pith instructions of the Nyingtik approach of utter lucidity without exception. He invested Adzom Drukpa as his inner heart son and recognized him as his regent in the ultimate sense of having gained the same realization. In addition, he gave him the transmissions for the Jangter, or Northern Terma,[52] cycle entitled *Unobstructed Enlightened Intent; The Sadhana of Enlightened Mind:*

The Treasury of Enlightened Qualities (the ultimate lineage for the cycle *Naturally Occurring and Naturally Arising Original Purity*); *The Accomplishment of Life Force by Masters of Awareness* revealed by Lhatsün Namkha Jigmé; the peaceful, wrathful, and lion-headed forms of Guru Rinpoché revealed by Jatsön Nyingpo; the Dzogchen teaching manual by Namkha Gyatso of Katok Monastery; the blessing ritual and teachings for the deity Naro Khechari; the extensive empowerment cycle *The Compendium of All Sadhanas;* the teachings of view, meditation, and conduct from *The Heart Drop of the Accomplished Masters; The Vajra Nectar* cycle; the full range of cycles from the oral lineage; *The Heart Drop of the Exalted Goddess of Immortality;* the sadhanas of enlightened mind entitled *Dispelling All Obstacles* and *Spontaneous Accomplishment of Wishes;* and *The Profound Heart Drop of Tara.* [1.255a]

Most notably, Jamyang Khyentsei Wangpo honored Adzom Drukpa as the custodian of the teachings of the cycle *The Gathering of All the Dakinis' Secrets* and bestowed on him the full range of primary and secondary empowerments and teachings. During the exorcising empowerment for the dakini of activity, as Adzom Drukpa put on the formal robes of a tantric master and cast out the ritual torma, Jamyang Khyentsei Wangpo had clear visions of the destruction of many cities of barbarians. When the empowerments and teachings ended, the guru offered a ganachakra and showed signs of delight, laughing heartily and often.

At Jamyang Khyentsei Wangpo's urging, Adzom Drukpa went to see Jamgön Kongtrul Rinpoché Lodrö Tayé, from whom he received the transmissions for the great *Treasury of Precious Hidden Teachings* and *The Treasury of Mantra of the Kagyü School.* Khenchen Pema Dorjé of Dzogchen Monastery granted him the extensive empowerments and teachings for the cycle *The Innermost Heart Drop of the Guru* and advised that he maintain the conduct of a yogin, like Lhatsün Namkha Jigmé.

Paltrul Chökyi Wangpo treated Adzom Drukpa with great affection, teaching him the preliminary practices from his work *The Oral Transmission of the Guru Samantabhadra* and giving him the maturing empowerments, liberating instructions, and physical exercises of advanced yogic practices for *The Heart Drop of Longchenpa;* the experiential teaching based on *Timeless Awareness as the Guiding Principle;* and a detailed teaching on *The Aspiration Prayer of Noble Conduct.* He also encouraged Adzom Drukpa to teach students of his own. [1.255b] From Önpo Jigmé of Nyukgya, Adzom Drukpa received the empowerments and teachings for the practice of Chö, as transmitted by Trulzhik Wangdrak Gyatso.

Adzom Drukpa studied extensively with the precious guru Nyoshul Lungtok, receiving teachings on *The Three Cycles of Being at Ease, The Seven Treasuries,* and *The Four Higher Collections of the Heart Drop* and twice receiving an explanation of *Engaging in the Conduct of a Bodhisattva.* Mipam Rinpoché, who was Mañjushri in person, taught Adzom Drukpa his own works, including explanations of the dohas of Saraha, *A Topical Survey of Buddha Nature,* a commentary on the sutra *The*

Compendium, The Lamp of Certain Knowledge, and the prayer known as the "Swift Accomplishment of Wishes." Tsamtrul Kunzang Dechen Dorjé, the tulku of Jigmé Gyalwai Nyugu, passed on to Adzom Drukpa the empowerments and oral transmissions for *The Heart Drop of the Dakini* and *The Oral Transmission of the Guru Samantabhadra.* Khenpo Norbu Tendzin of Minyak gave him the transmission for *The Compendium of All Sadhanas* in its entirety, as well as his own arrangements of empowerments and teachings for the combined practice of Mahakarunika and a longevity sadhana. Gyalsé Namgyal, who was the son of Do Khyentsé and a senior khenpo of Dorjé Drak Monastery, empowered Adzom Drukpa into the Northern Terma cycles. Situ Chökyi Gyatso of Katok Monastery bestowed on him the empowerments and oral transmissions for *The Three Roots: The Heart Drop of Utter Lucidity,* a terma of enlightened intent from Khyentsé Rinpoché. From Katok Jé-ön Pema Gyaltsen, Adzom Drukpa received the oral transmissions for the tantras of the Nyingma tradition [1.256a] and the collected works of Getsé Mahapandita. Sönam Gyaltsen, head abbot of the house of Khangsar in Ngor, bestowed on him three cycles focusing on Khechari, together with the exhaustive collections of instructions connected with them.

From Minyak Khenpo, Adzom Drukpa requested the oral transmissions for *The Precious Treasury of Enlightened Qualities*—Jigmé Lingpa's root verses as well as his own commentary—and *A Drop from the Ocean,* the commentary by Dodrupchen. Khenpo Tsultrim Gyatso of Lingtsang passed on to him the oral transmissions for the precious Kangyur, while Khenpo Kalzang Wangchuk of Katok Monastery gave him all of the existing lineages of oral transmissions for the Tengyur. In addition, he was recognized by Terchen Orgyen Rinchen Lingpa as the custodian of that master's revealed teachings; he received these in their entirety, so that his mind and that of the master blended, becoming one.

Adzom Drukpa made a firm commitment to practice only Dzogchen until he reached the furthest limit of the four visions. Although, over the years, numerous people approached him to urge that he oversee and direct monastic communities, he never accepted such positions. He did not fall into either extreme of having too many or too few material possessions, and he never amassed a personal fortune or administered a large estate. At thirty-two he was guided not only by his many gurus and meditation deities, but also by the timeless awareness embodiment of Kunchen Jigmé Lingpa; thus his realization deepened. [1.256b] Fulfilling the prophecy he had received, Adzom Drukpa took on the appearance of a lay tantric master, with long hair and a white felt hat, strings of agate and coral and a reliquary around his neck, full-sleeved robes, and the rest of what are known as the "attributes of royal ease." Although he had general indications and clear visions of profound termas, he revealed only a few treasures of enlightened intent, such as his accounts of Dorjé Drolö and Vajrapani.

Confirming the prophecies of many holy masters—principally Katok Situ Chökyi Lodrö, Kunzik Khyentsé Rinpoché, and Paltrul Rinpoché—Adzom Drukpa continually bestowed the empowerments, and the extremely detailed teachings that bring students to spiritual maturity, of the kama and terma traditions of the Dzogchen approach. Throughout his life, he taught numerous great masters, including many of the major and minor tulkus and gurus of the monasteries of Katok, Palpung, Zhechen, and Dzogchen; Gyalsé Namgyal; the Sikkimese master Tupten Chönyi; Tartsé Khenchen of Ngor; and Dezhung Tulku Jamyang Tendzin. He also taught many holders of the teachings of the pre-Buddhist tradition of Bön, including the two teachers Tingchen Dratrul and Möngyé Tulku. [1.257a]

Both the omniscient, all-seeing Katok Situ Pandita Chökyi Gyatso and Drupwang Dzogchen Rinpoché Tupten Chökyi Dorjé,[53] who was Vimalamitra in person, invited Adzom Drukpa to their respective seats. The former received from him the entire range of empowerments and teachings for *The Four Higher Collections of the Heart Drop,* while the latter received detailed developmental teachings on the preliminaries, the main body of practice, and the concluding phase of Dzogchen. Adzom Drukpa gave all of the gurus, tulkus, khenpos, and teachers residing at these monastic seats a great variety of appropriate empowerments and teachings, both extensive and abridged.

He attracted many students of all stations and from widely different language groups and regions, such as eastern, central, and southwestern Tibet, the northeastern region of Amdo, Khunu in northern India, China, the southern border region of Lhodrak, and Bhutan. Foremost among them were such masters as Yönten Gyatso of Gemang, Khenpo Kunzang Palden, Drupwang Lama Tayé, Lungtok Tenpai Nyima, and Terchen Sogyal, all of whom received empowerments, teachings, and advice from him. For everyone, from nobles such as the Buddhist king of Lingkar and his son the prince, King Jigdral Dorjé of Chakla and his daughter Princess Detsün Tsomo, down to the humblest subject, [1.257b] Adzom Drukpa carried out his enlightened activities fully, bringing purpose to all who were connected to him in many different ways through his profound and extensive empowerments and teachings. As the sun casting brilliant light on the teachings of the sublime Dzogchen approach, he thus completed his task.

To all of his students, Adzom Drukpa said, "It could have been my lot to reveal profound termas whose existence I received signs of. However, I have always focused solely on the Dzogchen approach of utter lucidity and have gained such confidence in it that I need not drool over other teachings, whether of the extensive kama lineages or the more direct terma lineages. You, too, should make Dzogchen your practice; I assure you, it will never let you down. I have never forgotten the aspiration I made as a child: that all those connected to me, even those who have only heard my name, but especially those who have made a connection by offering money or possessions, making aspirations, or receiving teachings, will take rebirth as part of my retinue in a pure buddha realm. Because I have not impaired my own or anyone else's samaya, I can be described as one who is 'delighted to pass away, yet happy to stay.' But now it would be better for me to pass away than to stay on as an old man, for the Guru prophesied that I am to lead some three hundred million beings to freedom in the bardo."

When he was about to pass away, he spoke briefly of his many visions—of the mandalas of hosts of peaceful and wrathful deities from *The Web of Magical Display* and of Vajrakila, [1.258a] of escorts of dakinis, and so forth. From midnight onward, many pea-sized spheres of light continuously issued from his nostrils, until at dawn his enlightened intent resolved into basic space. As his end approached, the brilliance of the sun's rays waned, deafening sounds were heard, and other portents were observed. His precious remains were kept in state for sixty days, while offerings and memorial rituals were carried out on a grand scale. On the tenth day of the second Tibetan month,[54] thirteen gurus, tulkus, khenpos, and teachers (including Palyul Yangsi)[55] presided over a corresponding number of mandala rituals during the cremation ceremony. On that occasion, the faithful had many visions. Adzom Drukpa's heart, tongue, and eyes were unharmed by the flames of the funeral pyre, and many relics appeared along with other amazing signs.

The precious lord guru's enlightened activity was carried on by the sublime children of his enlightened form, speech, and mind—his sons Gyurmé Dorjé and Pema Wangyal and his daughter Chimé—and by countless other students whose minds he had freed, having brought them to realization. His sublime tulku was born, [1.258b] fulfilling the prophecy of the fifth Drupwang Dzogchen Rinpoché, and is still alive.[56]

It was from this holy guru that Chökyi Lodrö, the tulku of Kunzik Jamyang Khyentsei Wangpo, heard the teachings.

Jamyang Khyentsé Chökyi Lodrö (1893–1959)

Jamyang Khyentsé Chökyi Lodrö was the activity emanation of Jamyang Khyentsei Wangpo. The great scholar Vimalamitra (the source of the Khyentsé emanations) had prophesied that, after Jamyang Khyentsei Wangpo's passing, five sublime tulkus—of his enlightened form, speech, mind, qualities, and activity—would appear to spread the teachings without sectarian bias. The form incarnation was recognized by the fifth Drupwang Dzogchen Rinpoché, Tupten Chökyi Dorjé, and lived at Dzogchen Monastery. The speech incarnation, born the son of the Beri chieftain of Hor, was recognized by Jamgön Kongtrul Lodrö Tayé [1.259a] and was associated with Palpung Monastery. The mind incarnation was Kyabjé Dilgo Khyentse Rinpoché Rabsel Dawa, who was recognized by

Gyaltsap Pema Namgyal of Zhechen Monastery. The incarnation of Vimalamitra's qualities took rebirth in the royal house of Puntsok Podrang in Sakya and was known as Ngawang Tutop Wangchuk. Jamyang Khyentsé Chökyi Lodrö was recognized as the activity incarnation by Jamgön Kongtrul Lodrö Tayé and lived at Dzongsar Tashi Lhatsé.

This master was born in the autumn of a Water Dragon year[57] of the fifteenth sexagesimal cycle in an area of eastern Tibet known as the Four Knots, specifically in Sa-ngen, the Knot of Earth. His father, a man of unparalleled wisdom and realization and an incarnation of Lochen Bairotsana, was Gyurmé Tsewang Gyalpo, and his mother was Tsultrim Tso. Gyurmé Tsewang Gyalpo was the son of Serpa Tergen, a master who had been responsible for maintaining the teachings of Terchen Duddul Dorjé[58] and had lived to the age of 180. The son of Gyurmé Tsewang Gyalpo was given the name Jamyang Chökyi Lodrö.

Kunzik Situ Rinpoché[59] insisted that Jamgön Kongtrul Rinpoché, [1.259b] with his visionary insight, make an unambiguous statement about the child's identity. Hence the latter proclaimed that, among the twenty-five principal holy sites in eastern Tibet, Katok Monastery was the primary site of enlightened activity that guides beings and that Khyentsé Rinpoché[60] had stated that an activity emanation of Langdro Lotsawa would appear. This was taken as a spontaneous indication—not the result of any deliberate plan—that the child belonged at the seat founded by Rigdzin Longsel Nyingpo, and so at the age of six, Jamyang Khyentsé Chökyi Lodrö was escorted to Katok Monastery. On the day he arrived, there was a great snowfall, which was seen as a very auspicious omen. Before the statue of the lord Buddha in Lhachen Palbar Hall, he received his preliminary monastic vows and the name Jamyang Lodrö Gyatso. He further took the vows of a novice monk from an assembly of five members of the ordained sangha, including the lord Situ himself and the boy's tutor, Khenpo Tupten Rigdzin Gyatso. On this occasion, he was also given the name Tsuklak Lungrik Nyima Mawai Seng-gé. Tartsé Zhapdrung Rinpoché bestowed on him the name Jamyang Chökyi Lodrö Rimé Tenpai Gyaltsen, and many other learned and accomplished masters gave him shorter names and titles, all containing "Lodrö,"[61] which he himself said later seemed significant. [1.260a]

Over time, Jamyang Khyentsé Chökyi Lodrö received extensive transmissions, including both traditions of the bodhisattva vow; the complete teachings from the kama transmissions of *The Discourse on United Intent, The Web of Magical Display*, and the mind teachings, as well as teachings on the deities Samyak and Vajrakila, and the cycle *Dredging the Pit of Cyclic Existence;* the extensive empowerment for the Eight Commands cycle *The Gathering of Sugatas; The Four Higher Collections of the Heart Drop;* Karma Lingpa's terma of the peaceful and wrathful deities; the empowerments for all of the cycles revealed by Longsel Nyingpo and Duddul Dorjé; the explanatory teachings concerning the major Indian and Tibetan commentaries on *The Heart Essence of Secrets* (also known as *The Web of Magical Display*); and the entire corpus of *The Collected Tantras of the Nyingma School.*

At about this time, the fearless Situ Panchen and his spiritual heir, Khenchen Kunpal, demonstrated real vision by founding a tantric college according to the directives of Jamgön Mipam Rinpoché. Jamyang Khyentsé Chökyi Lodrö enrolled in this institution and received a thorough education. He diligently and precisely studied such works as *Ascertaining the Three Levels of Ordination* (both the sources verses and commentary), *The Treasury of Enlightened Qualities, The Wish-Fulfilling Treasury, Entrance to the Ways of the Wise,* Abhidharma, the two "*Ornament*" and two "*Distinction*" texts of Maitreya,[62] *The Highest Continuum, The Fundamental Discourse of the Vinaya,* and *The Ornament of the Middle Way.* With his tutor, Rigdzin Gyatso, he studied calligraphy and reading, a work on orthography entitled *Lamp of Speech,* the basic works on Tibetan grammar, *Engaging in the Conduct of a Bodhisattva,* the *Sarasvata* commentary on Sanskrit grammar, [1.260b] the collected works of Getsé Mahapandita, teachings on the stage of development, the performance of rituals, and other subjects from both the Nyingma and Sarma traditions of Tibetan Buddhism.

During this period of study, another incarnation of Jamyang Khyentsei Wangpo had gone to Dzongsar Monastery and taken it as his seat; however, this responsibility proved to be an obstacle to his longevity. A nephew of Jamyang Khyentsei Wangpo presented Situ Rinpoché with a copy of his uncle's will, and on the basis of statements made in it, Jamyang Khyentsé Chökyi Lodrö came, in his fifteenth year, to live at Dzongsar Tashi Lhatsé. Situ Rinpoché conducted the formal ceremony of investiture and conferred Dzongsar Monastery on him as his seat.

Jamyang Khyentsé Chökyi Lodrö studied with Jamyang Loter Wangpo, a great holder of the teachings of the Mañjushri lords of Sakya, and received from him the extensive empowerments in *The Compendium of All Classes of Tantra,* the detailed teachings of the Lamdré cycle, explanations of *The Hevajra Tantra,* and the secondary empowerments in *The Compendium of All Classes of Tantra,* from that of the three families up to the section on Yogatantra. When he was being taught the causal aspect of tantra—the ground of all experience—from the Lamdré cycle, realization of the ultimate meaning underlying the empowerments arose in him.

His noble father, Rigdzin Gyurmé Tsewang Gyalpo, conferred on him *The Gathering of the Great Assembly* from the kama tradition and *The Treasury of Precious Hidden Teachings,* beginning with the empowerment for Khorwa Dongtruk, [1.261a] as well as the profound termas of Chokgyur Lingpa. Drakra Zhapdrung Rinpoché Tashi Gyatso passed on to him *The One Hundred Transmissions of Mitra,* the seven mandalas of the Ngor tradition of the Lamdré cycle according to Khenchen Ngawang Chödrak, and the extensive empowerments for the deity Vajrabhairava in the Ra and Tsar traditions.

Encouraged by Jamyang Loter Wangpo, Jamyang Khyentsé Chökyi Lodrö studied with Khenchen Samten Lodrö of Lhundrup Teng in Dergé, receiving from him all of the empowerments and oral transmissions in *The Compendium of All Sadhanas,* as well as detailed teachings on the deity Khechari, among others. Shar Lama Jamyang Chenrap Tayé of the great monastery of Dergé gave him the extensive empowerment for Kalachakra from the tradition of Butön, while Tartsé Zhapdrung Rinpoché Jampa Kunzang Tenpai Nyima completed the transmission of *The Compendium of All Classes of Tantra,* from the section on Yogatantra onward.

From Lama Tashi Chöpel, lord of the learned masters of Palpung Monastery, Jamyang Khyentsé Chökyi Lodrö received the extensive empowerments for Kalachakra according to the tradition of the lord Atisha, the extensive empowerment for the Khön family tradition of Vajrakila (a direct lineage from Jamyang Khyentsei Wangpo), as well as the entire cycle of teachings of the Shangpa Kagyü school. Gatön Ngawang Lekpa Rinpoché, a great holder of the teachings found in the oral lineages of the supreme secret, [1.261b] bestowed on him the extensive maturing empowerment from the detailed teachings of the Lamdré cycle, as well as the profound and extensive empowerments from the cycle of Khachö Jigmé Gönpo.

From the fifth Drupwang Dzogchen, he received such transmissions as *The Natural Freedom Underlying Reifying Concepts, The General Union of All That Is Rare and Sublime,* the empowerment into the dynamic energy of awareness from *Timeless Awareness as the Guiding Principle,* and *The Heart Essence of Profound Hidden Treasures* (the guru sadhana of Vimalamitra, a profound terma revealed by Jamyang Khyentsei Wangpo). Khedrup Tupten Gyaltsen Özer conferred on him many teachings from the kama transmissions; Pema Lingpa, a tertön from eastern Tibet, bestowed the Taksham cycle *The United Intent of the Meditation Deities,* the cycle of Yamantaka that he himself had revealed, and other teachings. Ratrul Tupten Shedrup transmitted to him the *Namchö* cycle and all of Ratna Lingpa's termas.

Khenchen Ngawang Palzang conferred on Jamyang Khyentsé Chökyi Lodrö the extensive empowerment for the Eight Commands cycle *The Complete Secret,* while Jamgön Kongtrul Lodrö Tayé transmitted to him the lineages that the former had received from Situ Panchen,[63] as well as the empowerment for *The Innermost Heart Drop of the Dakini.* From Zhechen Gyaltsap Rinpoché, he requested the empowerments, teachings, and oral transmissions for *The Treasury of Spiritual Instructions,* the direct lineage from Jamyang Khyentsei Wangpo for all of the Northern Terma cycles, three volumes of sealed teachings from *The Treasury of Precious Hidden Teachings,* and the entire range of termas of the Mindroling tradition. [1.262a] From Zhechen Kongtrul Rinpoché, he received the oral transmissions for the collected works of the second Rabjam of Zhechen Monastery, Gyurmé Kunzang Namgyal.[64] From the two tulkus of Chokgyur Lingpa associated with the monasteries of Neten and Tsiké, he received the empowerments and oral transmissions for two cycles of sadhanas of enlightened mind, *The Three Categories of Great Perfection, The Sadhana of Enlightened Mind: The Spontaneous Accomplishment of Wishes,* and *The Accomplishment of Life Force by Masters of Awareness.*

Adzom Drukpa conferred on Jamyang Khyentsé Chökyi Lodrö the empowerments, teachings, and oral transmissions for the Northern Terma cycle entitled *Unobstructed Enlightened Intent, The Innermost Heart Drop of the Guru,* and *The Heart Drop of Longchenpa.* He also passed on his own terma of enlightened intent and all the methods of the Nyingtik teachings of the Dzogchen approach that he had received from the lord Jamyang Khyentsei Wangpo, including the direct introduction of trekchö and the means of enriching meditative experience. Adzom Drukpa formally invested Jamyang Khyentsé Chökyi Lodrö as his supreme regent in the ultimate sense of realization and said that, when they first met, he had had a pure vision in which he actually encountered the latter's former incarnation, Jamyang Khyentsei Wangpo. He then offered his retinue of students to Jamyang Khyentsé Chökyi Lodrö.

From the third Dodrupchen, Kunchen Jigmé Tenpai Nyima, Jamyang Khyentsé Chökyi Lodrö received the maturing empowerments and instructions for *The Gathering of Masters of Awareness, The Most Secret Guru Sadhana,* and the empowerment into the dynamic energy of awareness from *Timeless Awareness as the Guiding Principle.* He also received this master's own explanations [1.262b] and overview of *The Heart Essence of Secrets* and the oral transmissions for his collected works, as well as the tantras, explanatory commentaries, and pith instructions of the Nyingtik teachings of the Dzogchen approach, which the third Dodrupchen himself had received in a lineage transmitted by his former incarnations. In offering these, he entrusted Jamyang Khyentsé Chökyi Lodrö with this lineage. In that Adzom Drukpa and Dodrup Jigmé Tenpai Nyima were foremost in transmitting the Dzogchen lineage to Jamyang Khyentsé Chökyi Lodrö, he considered them the extraordinary masters of his buddha family.

Terchen Lerab Lingpa conferred on him the cycle *The Heart Drop of Freedom: The Natural Freedom of Enlightened Intent,* as well as his own profound termas, including the cycle of Vajrakila, the three levels—outer, inner, and secret—of *Dispelling Flaws in Interdependence.* He also bestowed on him the empowerments and teachings for *The Heart Drop of Chetsün* and authorized him to pass on all of these termas.

From Tai Situ Rinpoché Pema Wangchok Gyalpo[65] of Palpung Monastery, he received the bodhisattva vow in the lineage of extensive conduct, the extensive empowerments for Hevajra and consort according to the tradition of Marpa, and the practice of White Tara according to the Karma Kagyü school. From the rebirth of the son of victorious ones Jamgön Kongtrul, Jamyang Khyentsé Chökyi Lodrö received Ratna Lingpa's cycle of Vajrakila and Jamgön Kongtrul's profound termas of the deities Samyak and Dorjé Drolö. And from Trungpa Rinpoché of Zurmang Monastery,[66] he received the empowerments, teachings, and oral transmissions for the dakinis' oral lineage of Chakrasamvara, *The Spacious Expanse of View of Dorjé Lingpa,* the Six Yogas of Naropa, and Mahamudra teachings. The fifth incarnation of Terchen Rolpai Dorjé [1.263a] bestowed on him the complete range of termas revealed by that tertön. The second Dabzang Tulku conferred on Jamyang Khyentsé Chökyi Lodrö the transmissions for the nine-deity mandala of Jinasagara, the Karma Kagyü tradition of Varahi, and the reconcealed terma of Jinasagara revealed by Jamyang Khyentsei Wangpo and originally revealed by Drimé Kunga. The ninth Sang-gyé Nyenpa[67] passed on to him the ultimate empowerment[68] for the deity Ayushpati revealed by Ratna Lingpa, as well as the Mahamudra text *The Ocean of Definitive Meaning* and other teachings. Tralek Choktrul bestowed on him *The Three Cycles of Light Rays* and other teachings, and Gyalwang Tupten Gyatso[69] gave him detailed teachings on the lord Atisha's *Lamp on the Path to Enlightenment* and *The Relaxed Encounter with the Golden Visage.* Finally, the lord of scholars Geshé Jampal Rolpai Lodrö conferred on Jamyang Khyentsé Chökyi Lodrö the extensive empowerments for the deities Guhyasamaja, Chakrasamvara, and Vajrabhairava.

In brief, Jamyang Khyentsé Chökyi Lodrö studied with more than eighty tutors —qualified mentors who were learned, venerable, noble, and accomplished, some of them quite renowned, others living in obscurity. With them he crossed to the far shore of a veritable ocean of study and learning, brooking no compromise in his quest for the dharma and the qualities of someone holy. He understood precisely, and without sectarian prejudice, the view, meditation, and conduct taught by all traditions [1.263b] and so was able to care for students according to their individual needs. As a matter of course, he served each of those traditions.

As for Jamyang Khyentsé Chökyi Lodrö's own spiritual practice, he did the requisite sadhanas and mantra repetitions for the following cycles: *The Guru, the Gathering of Secrets;* the Eight Commands cycle *The Gathering of Sugatas;* the black goddess Krodhi according to the Nyang tradition; the Mindroling tradition of Vajrasattva; the red form of Guru Drakpo; the preliminary practices of *The Heart Drop of Longchenpa;* the complete mandala of the peaceful and wrathful deities of the Three Roots; most of the terma cycles revealed by Jamyang Khyentsei Wangpo Rinpoché and Chokgyur Lingpa; the secret sadhana of Dorjé Drolö revealed by Jamgön Kongtrul; the secret longevity sadhana of the Ternying revealed by Ratna Lingpa; the Northern Terma cycle of Ayushpati and other practices of rejuvenation; and the profound cycles of teachings for averting obstacles from *The Heart Drop of Freedom.* He completed the main phase of approach through mantra repetition for the tradition of Hevajra according to Marpa and the practices of Vajrapani Bhutadamara, the goddess Khechari, and all of the meditation deities of *The Compendium of All Sadhanas* (especially those of the three buddha families), as well as the main phase of approach for the Sakya tradition of Vajrakila. He recited the heart essence mantra of the Pañjara form of Mahakala some eighty million times.

The extent to which Jamyang Khyentsé Chökyi Lodrö practiced the phases of approach and accomplishment for the entire array of his meditation deities defies imagination. He spent the earlier part of his life alternating between study and practice, [1.264a] but later spent most winters in strict retreat, during which he was cared for by his meditation deities and received signs of his splendid spiritual attainment. There were many marvelous accounts of how he reached advanced levels of attainment as a master of awareness; the following are a few examples that he himself recorded or spoke of.

Once when Jamyang Khyentsé Chökyi Lodrö was quite young, Drupchen Tangtong Gyalpo directly introduced him in a vision to a state of pure awareness using a crystal globe as a symbol; he later commissioned a new style of image to commemorate this vision. He was blessed in another vision by the elder Angaja of Buddhist India[70] and had recurring visions of Vimalamitra and the great Omniscient One. On one occasion, he prayed fervently to the Omniscient One Drimé Özer, invoking his enlightened mind. The Omniscient King of the Dharma came to him in a vision, appearing as a fully ordained monk and dressed as a Tibetan scholar, his mind resting in the enlightened intent of dharmakaya; his heart center was marked with an *A* syllable. Jamyang Khyentsé Chökyi Lodrö prayed to him:

> How wondrous! Omniscient lord of the dharma,
> universal form of the victorious ones of the three times,
> [1.264b]
> my sovereign lord and primordial protector:
> may you rest, if only once, in the center of my heart
> and bless my mind with your enlightened intent.

Having prayed in this way, he accepted empowerment from Longchenpa, after which the master dissolved into him, transferring to him the lineage of enlightened intent.

In dreams Jamyang Khyentsé Chökyi Lodrö met Ngorchen Dorjé Chang, Karmapa Rangjung Dorjé, and Karma Pakshi. Nupchen Sang-gyé Yeshé entrusted him with many tantric treatises, and the great lord Tsongkhapa himself passed on the direct lineage of the glorious Guhyasamaja. He had visions of Sachen Kunga Nyingpo and Sakya Pandita,[71] as well as many other gurus of the Lamdré cycle; and Lhatsün Namkha Jigmé encouraged him to adopt the uncontrived conduct of a tantric practitioner. He received a longevity empowerment from the lord Jamyang Khyentsei Wangpo, received the blessings of Nyoshul Lungtok Tenpai Nyima, and had three visions of Khenchen Ngawang Palzang, an emanation of Vimalamitra, who transferred to him the lineage of enlightened intent. From the great bodhisattva Paltrul Rinpoché,

Jamyang Khyentsé Chökyi Lodrö received instructions on the preliminary practices of *The Heart Drop of Longchenpa,* [1.265a] and when Dodrup Jigmé Tenpai Nyima conferred on him the empowerment for its most secret guru sadhana, he had a vision of the great Omniscient One Longchenpa. Once, in the presence of the Gyalwang Karmapa,[72] who was wearing his crown, Jamyang Khyentsé Chökyi Lodrö saw him as both Vimalamitra and the first Karmapa, Düsum Chenpa.[73] At Namgyal Monastery in Dzing, during ceremonies for propitiating the protective deity that banishes hindrances, Jamyang Khyentsé Chökyi Lodrö was focusing his attention on the statue of the protector, when it began to move; the shrine keeper saw this and ran away in terror. On another occasion, Jamyang Khyentsé Chökyi Lodrö passed his hand over some cracks in a jade teacup, causing them to vanish. He frequently manifested such signs of his spiritual attainment.

On yet another occasion, when he was conferring the permission blessing for the practice of the wealth deity Vaishravana from the Butön tradition, the deity appeared to him and caused gold dust and nuggets to rain down in the shrine hall, visible to all of the students there. Some, including Khenpo Chöpel of Dezhung, kept these for others to see in the future. The protectors Pañjaranatha and the four-faced Mahakala appeared to Jamyang Khyentsé Chökyi Lodrö and swore to carry out the enlightened activities with which he entrusted them.

Always self-effacing, he would say, "I have no indwelling confidence in my practice, for all I do is spend my time in idleness." [1.265b] But when he taught—whether the Lojong teachings; Madhyamaka; the view, meditation, and conduct of the Nyingma or Sarma schools; the practices of the stage of completion focusing on the subtle channels, energies, and bindu; or the Dzogchen approach—he would use vocabulary specific to that teaching, immediately hitting the key point, without contradiction or confusing one system with another. Thus he was no different from a master of any of those traditions. No one doubted that Jamyang Khyentsé Chökyi Lodrö was entirely trustworthy, one who had reached the furthest limit of the view and enlightened intent of the most sublime spiritual approach.

As for his spiritual projects, at the age of twenty-six, at Jematang in eastern Tibet he oversaw the building of the temple of Riksum Lhakhang and Shedrup Dargyé Ling, a shedra with residences for twenty-five people. From the outset, the shedra was directed by Zhenpen Chökyi Nangwa, the great khenpo of Dzogchen Monastery, and his regent, Öntö Khenpo Jamyang Chenrap (reputed to be an incarnation of Khedrup Ngawang Lekdrup of Dragang), and their lineage of students. It became an important center of learning in the lower region of eastern Tibet. At the meditation center of Dragang in the upper region, Jamyang Khyentsé Chökyi Lodrö founded an associated retreat site devoted primarily to the practice of the Lamdré cycle. This center was directed by Gatön Dorjé Chang Jamgön Lekpa Rinpoché, [1.266a] later succeeded by the great learned and venerable master Jamyang Gyaltsen.

Jamyang Khyentsé Chökyi Lodrö also restored the tantric college at glorious Katok Monastery, considered to be the Bodh Gaya of eastern Tibet. He instituted a new syllabus and completed the preceding Situ's[74] plan to erect a large statue of the Buddha Shakyamuni and a representation of Zangdok Palri. He oversaw the enthronement of the next Situ Rinpoché, Tupten Jamchen Chökyi Nyima,[75] and in such ways took responsibility for the administration of Katok Monastery.

He founded a center for the practice of the profound teachings of the eight lineages of accomplishment, especially the profound termas of Jamyang Khyentsei Wangpo, Jamgön Kongtrul, and Chokgyur Lingpa. In addition, Jamyang Khyentsé Chökyi Lodrö helped establish shedras and tantric retreat centers for all four schools of Tibetan Buddhism (especially the Sakya and Nyingma), as well as for the indigenous Tibetan tradition of Bön. He instituted ceremonies and drupchens, and in all regions directed ceremonies entailing the recitation of the mantra *Om mani padme hum* a hundred million times. He encouraged the promulgation of profound yet fragile lineages of empowerments and oral transmissions, the building of temples, and so forth. From eastern to central and southern Tibet, and as far away as Sikkim, no region was untouched by his enlightened activities. [1.266b]

This lord guru himself conferred all of the empowerments and oral transmissions for *The Collected Tantras of the Nyingma School* three times. He transmitted *The Heart Essence of Secrets* four times, *The Discourse on United Intent* and the explanation of the root tantra of Vajrakila five times each, *The Treasury of Precious Hidden Teachings* once, the Lamdré cycle (both the abridged and detailed versions) five times, *The Treasury of Spiritual Instructions* twice, *The Compendium of All Sadhanas* four times, and the empowerments for the seven mandalas of the Ngor tradition four times. He bestowed the empowerments for Chakrasamvara, Hevajra, Guhyasamaja, Vajrabhairava, and Khechari, as well as the extensive empowerment for Kalachakra, eight times each. He gave the explanatory teachings for *The Highest Continuum* and *The Two Chapters* according to the tradition of Marpa and Ngok five times, the explanatory teachings for the tantras *Pañjara* and *Samputa* three times each, the extensive empowerment for a cycle focusing on the Eight Commands three times, the extensive empowerment for *The United Intent of the Gurus* twice, and *The Four Higher Collections of the Heart Drop* five times. On many occasions, he transmitted *The Heart Drop of Longchenpa* and the oral lineage and profound terma teachings revealed by Jamyang Khyentsei Wangpo, Jamgön Kongtrul, and Chokgyur Lingpa. He conferred the oral transmissions for the collected works of the five early Sakya masters and of Ngorchen Kunga Zangpo once and for the collected works of Jamyang Khyentsei Wangpo twice. In that, throughout the spring, summer, and fall, he bestowed at least two or three empowerments or teachings daily without fail, it is clear that Jamyang Khyentsé Chökyi Lodrö spent all of his time expounding the dharma. [1.267a]

Foremost among his students were Situ Rinpoché, Moktsa Rinpoché, and Önpo Rinpoché, all from Katok Monastery; the sixth Dzogchen, Jigdral Jangchub Dorjé; Kuzhap Gemang Gyalsé Zhenpen Tayé; the sixth Rabjam and fourth Gyaltsap tulkus of Zhechen Monastery; Kongtrul Rinpoché; Dilgo Khyentsé Rinpoché; Sogyal Choktrul Rinpoché; and other sublime tulkus. He also taught ordained and lay khenpos, teachers, and meditators of the Nyingma school; all the vajra holders, gurus, khenpos, and teachers of such Sakya centers as Lhundrupteng in Dergé and Dzongsar Monastery. His students also included many gurus and tulkus of the Kagyü and Geluk schools. He guided the two khenpo brothers of Mindroling Monastery, the great master of awareness of Dorjé Drak Monastery, and the throne holders of both houses of Sakya and their heirs. The sixteenth Karmapa,[76] Tai Situ Pema Wangchok, the two tulkus, Tenga and Trungpa, of Zurmang Monastery, the Kongtrul tulku of Palpung Monastery, Litang Tselé Chöktrul, Geshé Namrol, and others all studied with Jamyang Khyentsé Chökyi Lodrö. In short, he taught the gurus, tulkus, and Buddhist practitioners of eastern and central Tibet and China; the rulers and ministers of Dergé, Lingtsang, [1.267b] and Nangchen; the members of the Tibetan National Cabinet and the generals of the Tibetan army; and great political figures, including some from China and India. The number of people who forged a connection with Jamyang Khyentsé Chökyi Lodrö, from these down to the humblest layperson, is inestimable.

At the age of sixty-three, fulfilling a secret prophecy, Jamyang Khyentsé Chökyi Lodrö journeyed from Nangchen in eastern Tibet through the central and southern regions of the country, visiting important holy sites, sponsoring ganachakras, and making offerings. During this time, the Chögyal, the ruler of Sikkim, formally requested that he perform purification rituals and consecration ceremonies in that great hidden kingdom, and he accepted the invitation. He also went on pilgrimages to holy places such as Drakar Tashi Ding in Sikkim, to the principal and secondary Buddhist holy sites of India, and to those in Nepal, making offerings, sponsoring ganachakras, and offering profound and extensive prayers of aspiration.

At sixty-six Jamyang Khyentsé Chökyi Lodrö passed away at twilight on the sixth day of the lunar cycle of the constellation Nron.[77] For three days, his remains stayed warm, while a continuous radiance dimmed even the electric light in the room. Earthquakes and other marvelous signs were evident to all present. [1.268a] Then the dance of his manifold incarnations manifested. Tsewang Dorjé, a relative of his, had a dream in which a single sun was fading as five great suns rose to illuminate the entire world. Thereafter, in accordance with this prophetic dream, Khyentsé Norbu, the grandson of Kyabjé Dudjom Rinpoché and son of Thinley Norbu, was recognized by Sakya Dakchen Rinpoché and Sakya Trizin Rinpoché[78] as Jamyang Khyentsé Chökyi Lodrö's primary incarnation and was thus enthroned. Two of his other incarnations are Khyentsé Gawai Lodrö (the son of Neten Chokling Rinpoché) and Jigmé Khyentsé Özer (the son of Kangyur Rinpoché, recognized by his own father). Thus Jamyang Khyentsé Chökyi Lodrö has continued to manifest as exemplary holy masters.

I myself had the good fortune to receive from this great master the empowerment and oral transmission for *The General Union of All That Is Rare and Sublime,* an empowerment for Vajrakila, and the oral transmission for the text *The Staircase Ascending to the Pinnacle Pure Realm* from *The Heart Drop of Longchenpa.* I offer heartfelt prayers to him, for I feel that this fortunate experience has given my human existence true meaning.

It was from this holy guru [1.268b] that the sublime Kyabjé Dilgo Khyentsé Rinpoché Rabsel Dawa, whose kindness cannot be repaid, heard the teachings.

Dilgo Khyentsé Rinpoché Rabsel Dawa (1910–1991)

The following is Kyabjé Dilgo Khyentsé Rinpoché's autobiographical account:

I was born in Denma, the name of which (Endowed) historically derives from poetic descriptions of the area as either "endowed with the splendor of gold" or "on the banks of the river endowed with gold." My birthplace was on the ridge of Drida Zalmo Gang in the region known as Four Rivers and Six Ridges[79] in the lowlands of the eastern part of greater Tibet. The area is protected by the facing peak of Jowo Gyokchen, one of the mountains of a great wilderness area called the Five Brothers. A great Buddhist scholar of India, a lord of siddhas named Shri Smritijñana, once visited this area and taught Abhidharma and other subjects. He stayed until the end of his life, [1.269a] and a stupa enshrining his remains still exists.

One of the temples erected to guard the frontiers is located here;[80] it houses the image known as Tara of Langtang. The Sakya master Drogön Chögyal Pakpa[81] passed through this area on his travels to and from Mongolia. Tsultrim Özer of Ngari, a student of the great Vajradhara of Ngor Monastery, founded Rabsam Monastery here as well. Also in the area are Drigung Kagyü monasteries such as Reralgön; Gelukpa monasteries such as Deng-gön, founded by the guru Tongpön Rasmidhvaja of Göntok, a student of Chöjé Rinpoché; and Kagyü monasteries such as Melong-gön, founded by Karmapa Chödrak Gyatso.[82]

Some sixteen holy masters were born here, including Drigung Kyobpa Jigten Sumgön,[83] Drupchen Sang-gyé Nyenpa, and Mingyur Namkhai Dorjé. It was home to my family, the Dilgo family, stewards of the government of Dergé and descended from the divine clan[84] of Nyo. In this household, on the fifteenth day of the third, or black, month of the year known as "Common" (an Iron Dog year) in the fifteenth sexagesimal cycle,[85] Mipam Rinpoché, Mañjushri in person, began giving a group of people an exegesis of the major commentary on that most majestic of tantras *The Concise Kalachakra Tantra*. [1.269b] I was born during this event, on the thirtieth day of the fourth month, when the new moon and the constellation Drozhin were conjunct. Before I first nursed at my mother's breast, the syllables *Hrih* and *Dhih* were traced on my tongue with melted butter, and I was given pills sacred to Mañjushri and Sarasvati.[86] About a month after my birth, I was taken into the august presence of Mipam Rinpoché, who performed on my behalf the purification rituals of the deities Ushnisha Vijaya and Bhurkumkuta, a ritual to ransom my life force, and a ritual for summoning the forces of longevity. He gave me the name Tashi Paljor.

Then, until he passed away on the twenty-ninth day of the fourth month of Saga in a Water Rat year,[87] Mipam Rinpoché frequently bestowed on me holy medicine and pills sacred to Mañjushri. From time to time, he also performed blessing ceremonies and injunction rituals on my behalf. Shortly before passing into nirvana, he granted me the blessings of the three vajras of form, speech, and mind, using an image of Mañjushri Jñanasattva, the focus for his own meditations. He promised that he would keep my entire family in his prayers until we all reached the heart of enlightenment. His kindness to us was truly incredible.

Around that time, I learned to read and write. When I was ten, [1.270a] I was burned by a fire and was very sick for about six months. The circumstances urged me in a positive direction, and I took the vows of a novice monk from Gyaltsap Pema Namgyal Rinpoché of Zhechen Monastery, who had been a student of the preceding Khyentsé. He gave me the name Gyurmé Lapsum Gyaltsen. He also bestowed the bodhisattva vows of both the Madhyamaka tradition and that of extensive conduct, giving me the name Gyalsé Chökyi Nyugu. From this master, I also received empowerments from the kama transmissions of the Early Translation school, including those for the peaceful and wrathful deities of *The Web of Magical Display*, *The Gathering of the Supreme Assembly*, Khorwa Dongtruk, and Samyak Heruka. He also conferred terma transmissions, such as the entire collection of *The Noble Vase Yielding All That Is Desired;* Vajrasattva according to the tradition of Mindroling Monastery; *The Crystal Cave of Padma* (the quintessential empowerment for the Eight Commands cycle *The Gathering of Sugatas* revealed by Nyang-ral Nyima Özer); *The Most Secret Razor* (the Vajrakila cycle revealed by Guru Chöwang); the longevity sadhana *The Gathering of Secrets* revealed by Ratna Lingpa; and *The Gathering of All*

Sugatas, an Avalokiteshvara cycle and terma of the Mindroling tradition. He also gave the empowerments, oral transmissions, and teachings for *The Four Higher Collections of the Heart Drop;* the oral transmissions for all of the collected works of the lord Mañjushri, Mipam Rinpoché; and *The Treasury of Precious Spiritual Instructions,* which contains the transmissions for the eight lineages of accomplishment. In conjunction with these transmissions, [1.270b] I was formally acknowledged as the emanation of the enlightened mind of Jamyang Khyentsei Wangpo by Gyaltsap Rinpoché, who also gave me the name Gyurmé Tekchok Tenpai Gyaltsen. He was an extraordinary guru of great kindness who influenced me on a deep level.

From Khen Rinpoché Pema Losel of Dzogchen Monastery, I received the empowerments, oral transmissions, and teachings for two volumes of the source texts of *The Heart Drop of Longchenpa,* as well as the teaching transmissions[88] for *The Three Cycles of Natural Freedom.* Pema Dechen Zangpo of Mura in Dza gave me the teachings on the six bardo states that are found in the section on the stage of completion in the cycle of peaceful and wrathful deities revealed by Karma Lingpa. With Adzom Drukpa Rinpoché Natsok Rangdrol, I studied the profound teachings on the preliminary practices of *The Heart Drop of Longchenpa.* With Tendzin Dorjé, a chant master of Palpung Monastery, I studied the basic works on Tibetan grammar (*Thirty Consonants* and *Case Endings*), spelling, and commentaries on Sanskrit grammar and poetics (the three chapters of *The Mirror of Poetics, Kapala's Discourse on Grammar,* and *Sarasvata's Discourse on Grammar*). With Khenchen Zhenga Rinpoché of Dzogchen Monastery, I studied the texts *Engaging in the Conduct of a Bodhisattva, The Entrance into the Middle Way, The Source Verses on Sublime Knowing,* and Nagarjuna's five other works on logical reasoning, as well as *The Four Hundred Verses.* It was he who gave me the name Rabsel Dawa.

With Khenpo Tupten Chöpel of Changma Batur, I studied *The Five Treatises of Maitreya.* In particular, he presented three times during a six-month period a very detailed treatment of *Dispelling Darkness in the Ten Directions,* [1.271a] Longchenpa's commentary on *The Heart Essence of Secrets* (also known as *The Web of Magical Display*). I studied other commentaries on this tantra, including *The Oral Transmission of the Lord of Secrets, The Ornament of Enlightened Intent,* the commentary by Rabjam Orgyen Chödrak, and the commentary entitled *The Rare and Sublime* by Rongzom Lotsawa, all with Khenpo Tekchok of Gemang. From Khenpo Rigdzin Özer, I received teachings on the source verses and commentary for *The Precious Treasury of Enlightened Qualities* and, from his elder brother, Sang-gyé Nyenpa, teachings on *Ascertaining the Three Levels of Ordination,* the annotated commentary on this by Khenpo Guna, and an exegesis of the commentary by Karma Ngedön of Litang on *The Treasury of Abhidharma.*

Khyentsé Rinpoché Jamyang Chökyi Lodrö of Dzongsar Monastery, the glorious and impartial protector of the teachings and beings, conferred on me the empowerments, oral transmissions, and teachings for the entire cycle of the kama transmissions of the Early Translation school; the empowerments, oral transmissions, and teachings for the great *Treasury of Precious Hidden Teachings;* the empowerments, oral transmissions, and teachings for *The Compendium of All Sadhanas;* all of the empowerments and teachings for the detailed, intimate transmission of the Lamdré cycle of the Sakya school; the extensive empowerments for the seven mandalas of the Ngor tradition; and the two extensive empowerments for Kalachakra deriving from the tradition of Zhalu Monastery and that of the lord Atisha. He presented several commentaries on *The Two Chapters,* such as that from the Ngok tradition, [1.271b] that by Ngok Zhedang Dorjé, *Rays of Sunlight* (the extensive commentary on *The Two Chapters* by Dakpo Tashi Namgyal), and the overview and commentary by Jamgön Kongtrul Rinpoché. He also gave me the detailed and extensive teachings on the commentaries and overviews from the Sakya tradition's three principal treatises on the tantras in general and *The Hevajra Tantra* in particular, as well as an explanatory teaching based on the source verses of *Encompassing the Knowable* by Kongtrul Rinpoché. He bestowed the transmissions for all the tantras, explanatory commentaries, and pith instructions of the major cycles of Nyingtik teachings of the Dzogchen approach, such as the entire transmission for *The Four Higher Collections of the Heart Drop* and the empowerments, oral transmissions, and teachings for two volumes of *The Heart Drop of Longchenpa.* I received as well the extensive empowerment for *The United Intent of the Gurus;* the extensive empowerment for the Eight Commands cycle *The Gathering of Sugatas;* the empowerments, oral transmissions, and teachings for all of the cycles of teachings revealed by Terchen Chokgyur Lingpa; the oral transmissions of the five-volume collected works of Tselé Natsok Rangdrol; and an explanatory teaching on *The Great Graduated Path* by Jé Rinpoché Tsongkhapa. Through the kindness of Jamyang Khyentsé Chökyi Lodrö, I received a veritable ocean of the profound and extensive methods of the dharma and had the good fortune to be invested as one upholding the ultimate lineage. In these and other ways, this guru was the extraordinary lord of my buddha family, the primary source of my lineage.

From my mentor Karma Lhundrup, [1.272a] I requested the oral transmissions for the entire collection of the Kangyur, the six volumes of Jatsön Nyingpo's termas, the thirteen volumes of the *Namchö* cycle, and the terma biographies of Guru Rinpoché and Yeshé Tsogyal revealed by Taksham Nüden Dorjé. From the sublime fifth Rolpai Dorjé, the tertön of Zurmang Monastery, I received the empowerments and oral transmissions for all of the termas revealed by the original Rolpai Dorjé, as well as all of the extensive empowerments for the dakini's oral lineage of Chakrasamvara. Tokden Tseten, also of Zurmang, bestowed on me the transmission for all of the collected works of Jetsün Taranatha of Jonang Monastery. From Norbu Tulku of Lalo, I requested all of the empowerments and oral transmissions for *The Treasury of Mantra of the Kagyü School.* Khenpo Zöpa Rapten of Benchen Monastery granted me the oral transmissions for all of the collected works of Paltrul Rinpoché, the important two-volume commentary on *The Precious Treasury of Enlightened Qualities* by Yönten Gyatso (a khenpo of Gemang), and other works. From the fifteenth Gyalwang Karmapa, I requested the empowerments and oral transmissions for the three volumes of *The Treasury of Mantra of the Kagyü School* and *The Treasury of Spiritual Instructions.* Khenpo Tendzin Dargyé of Zhechen Monastery bestowed on me the transmission of the nine volumes [1.272b] of Jigmé Lingpa's collected works. Kongtrul Rinpoché of Zhechen Monastery[89] gave me explanatory teachings on the thirteen volumes of the collected works of Minling Terchen Rinpoché and *The Wish-Fulfilling Frond,* a commentary on *Ascertaining the Three Levels of Ordination* by Minling Lochen Rinpoché. From Jamyang Losel of Zhechen Monastery, I received the oral transmissions for the thirteen volumes of the collected works of Zhechen Gyaltsap Rinpoché. Drung Namgyal Rinpoché bestowed the empowerments, teachings, and oral transmissions for the dakini's oral lineage of Chakrasamvara and the teaching transmission for *The Jewel Ornament of Liberation* by Gampopa. From the fourth Dodrupchen, Tupten Trinlé Palbar, I received all of the oral transmissions for the collected works of the third Dodrupchen, Jigmé Tenpai Nyima. Jamyang Drakpa Khargo conferred on me the oral transmissions for *The Seven Treasuries* and *The Three Cycles of Being at Ease* by Longchenpa. Kyabjé Dudjom Rinpoché bestowed on me many empowerments and oral transmissions from the Tersar cycles, such as the Vajrakila terma of enlightened intent. From Drupwang Kangyurwa Longchen Yeshé Dorjé, I received the empowerments and oral transmissions for *The United Intent of the Meditation Deities,* a cycle revealed by Taksham Nüden Dorjé, and *The Collected Tantras of the Nyingma School.* Khenchen Lozang Tendzin Gyaltsen of Nedo (in the lowlands of eastern Tibet) [1.273a] granted me the extensive empowerment for the most majestic tantra *Guhyasamaja*, as well as the teaching transmission for the *Four Combined Commentaries* based on this, and the extensive empowerment for Ghantapada's tradition of Chakrasamvara, with the teaching transmission of *Illuminating All Hidden Meanings,* Jé Rinpoché Tsongkhapa's commentary on this tradition.

As the foregoing illustrates, through the enormous kindness of many great, holy masters of the nonsectarian approach (more than seventy), I received the nectar of the dharma. In addition, from Khenchen Jamyang Yeshé Senggé of the Drukpa Kagyü school, I received the empowerments and oral transmissions for the teaching cycles of Dorjé Lingpa. This is merely a general account of the many transmissions I received.

In all, I spent at least twenty-two years practicing in solitary places, having started about the time I was eighteen. I made every possible effort, to the best of my ability, meditating and reciting mantras for such practices as those focusing on the Eight Commands, *The United Intent of the Gurus,* Vajrakila, the majority of termas from the Mindroling tradition, the general and specific practices of the Three Roots from *The Heart Drop of Longchenpa,* the most profound key practices from the teaching cycles of Jamyang Khyentsei Wangpo and Chokgyur Lingpa, and the peaceful and wrathful forms of Mañjushri from the works of Mipam Rinpoché. Signs and indications of successful practice for each of these were not lacking.

So as not to waste offerings that I accepted on behalf of people, living or deceased, I participated in numerous drupchens focusing on such rituals as the Mindroling tradition of Vajrasattva, [1.273b] *Vajrasattva's Realm of Manifest Joy: A Ceremony to Restore Tantric Samaya* revealed by Terchen Chokgyur Lingpa, the Eight Commands cycle *The Gathering of Sugatas, The Gathering of Commands: An Ocean of Spiritual Teachings,* the sadhana of the Guru entitled *The Sadhana of Enlightened Mind: Dispelling All Obstacles, The Seven Profound Aspects of Vajrakila,* and *The Gathering of the Great and Glorious Ones* from *The Heart Drop of Longchenpa.* I also sponsored the offering of a hundred thousand votive lamps on a number of occasions and any other activities appropriate for gathering the accumulations and purifying obscurations.

I transmitted *The Treasury of Precious Hidden Teachings* and *The Treasury of Spiritual Instructions* three times each; *The Treasury of Mantra of the Kagyü School* once; the precious Kangyur once; the collected works of Kongrul Rinpoché and Mipam Rinpoché twice each; the collected works of Paltrul once; the empowerments, oral transmissions, and teachings for *The Four Higher Collections of the Heart Drop* and *The Heart Drop of Longchenpa* more than ten times each; and *The Compendium of All Sadhanas* once.

This concludes my general account of the good works I accomplished before reaching my sixty-fourth year.

In addition to Khyentsé Rinpoché's own comments, I would like to quote some lines from one of his termas, *The Naturally Occurring Heart Drop of Padma,* [1.274a] which attests to the fact that he was a manifestation of both of the figures mentioned there:

> May immeasurable benefit for beings come from the meeting of this teaching
> with a sublime master of awareness,
> an emanation of the great Buddhist king
> and blessed by Vimalamitra.

As for his physical appearance, the mandala of his body was enormous. His nose was high-bridged, his head as large as the umbrella traditionally symbolic of majesty, and his upper torso like a lion's, with a broad, deep chest and wide shoulders. His eyes, shaped like crescent moons, sparkled brilliantly and never wavered from a gaze indicative of deep meditative absorption.

In all of his actions, words, and thoughts, Khyentsé Rinpoché exemplified someone the sutras describe as "preceded by timeless awareness and followed by timeless awareness." He never wavered from his true nature; his speech was mellifluous and resonant, his mind spacious and all-encompassing. He was tremendously compassionate, equal in his treatment of people regardless of their status. He was especially fond of those who were humble and never forsook anyone he had taken under his care. His mind was so expansive that, regardless of the great demands made on his time and energy, while engaged in activities for the sake of the teachings and beings, [1.274b] he maintained an air of natural relaxation and accomplished in months or years what would take an ordinary person a lifetime. We who were fortunate to be personally associated with Khyentsé Rinpoché over a long period witnessed his amazing, superb deportment firsthand.

In a similar vein, he traveled all over the globe, in the Eastern and Western Hemispheres, bestowing his blessings and transmitting the dharma in areas where even the name of these teachings had never been heard. Fulfilling the aspirations of Choktrul Pema Wangyal, the custodian of his teachings, Khyentsé Rinpoché established the retreat center of Tekchok Ösel Chöling in France. He also had a stupa built in Bodh Gaya, India.

In Nepal, near the Boudhanath stupa (which was constructed due to the aspirations of the abbot Shantarakshita, the master Padmakara, and the Buddhist king Trisong Detsen),[90] Dilgo Khyentsé Rinpoché built Shechen Tennyi Dargyeling, a major center dedicated to upholding his own tradition. The large, three-story temple is supported by eighty pillars and is surrounded by several hundred rooms for resident monks. The temple houses gilded images of the buddhas of the three times, all fashioned of precious substances, and on the interior walls are murals depicting the deities of the Three Roots according to the four major schools of Tibetan Buddhism—Sakya,

Geluk, Kagyü, and Nyingma— [1.275a] as well as extraordinary pure realms, visions experienced by great masters of the lineage, and other extraordinary themes. Behind the temple is the shrine hall dedicated to the Guru, which can accommodate a gathering of more than a hundred people. It houses an image of Guru Rinpoché one story tall, around which are gilded images of his intimate students, the king of Tibet and his subjects. Surrounding the whole complex are prayer wheels and the eight kinds of stupas. In short, this new center consists of an array of marvelous elements, both the supporting structures and the representations housed within.

In Bhutan, Khyentsé Rinpoché oversaw the construction of the new temples of Guru Lhakhang on the Kyichu River and Guru Lhakhang at Sisinang in lower Thimphu Valley. He erected a large statue of the Buddha at the great monastery of Dergé Gönchen in eastern Tibet. Khyentsé Rinpoché thus sponsored the three kinds of representations of enlightened form, speech, and mind on a vast scale.

As for representations of enlightened speech, he sponsored the offset printing of many thousands of volumes, including important scriptural texts such as *The Five Great Treasuries;* the collected works of Mipam, Zhechen Gyaltsap, Jigmé Lingpa, and other masters; and the precious *Collected Tantras of the Nyingma School.* With this achievement alone, [1.275b] Khyentsé Rinpoché's kindness in restoring the teachings was beyond measure.

Once the oppressive conditions imposed on Tibet by neighboring occupying forces[91] had abated somewhat, Khyentsé Rinpoché returned three times, and so was a key figure in restoring the Buddhist teachings in general and rebuilding, from the ground up, such monasteries as Zhechen, Dzogchen, Mindroling, and Samyé. There he gave empowerments, oral transmissions, and teachings (such as those of the great *Treasury of Precious Hidden Teachings*) and restored what was rare and valuable, ignoring any attempts by the occupying forces to interfere. Through this activity, Khyentsé Rinpoché ensured the extension of the life of the Victorious One's precious teachings. He bestowed innumerable cycles of empowerments, oral transmissions, and teachings: in Mysore, South India, the collected works of Jamgön Mipam, the Omniscient One Longchenpa, and other masters; in France, *The Three Roots: The Heart Drop of Utter Lucidity,* empowerments and teachings of the kama and terma traditions of the Dzogchen approach, as well as detailed teachings on the stages of development and completion and Dzogchen; in Bumthang, Bhutan, the kama transmissions of the Early Translation school; and at the monastery of the Khamtrul tulkus, *The Treasury of Spiritual Instructions.*

Over the years, Khyentsé Rinpoché directed hundreds of drupchens, focusing on such cycles as *The Gathering of the Great and Glorious Ones* (at Paro in Bhutan), [1.276a] *The Gathering of the Supreme Assembly* from the kama transmissions (at his own center in Nepal), and *The Great Sadhana of Nectar for the Consecration of Medicine.*

As for his own retreats, there does not seem to be one among the entire array of practices of the Three Roots, deriving from the kama tradition or the older or newer tradition of termas, for which Khyentsé Rinpoché did not complete the stages of development and completion. These included such practices as the wrathful deities of *The Gathering of the Great and Glorious Ones* and other practices of the Three Roots from *The Heartdrop of Longchenpa,* the peaceful and wrathful forms of Mañjushri, Vajrakila, cycles focusing on the Eight Commands, and the wrathful feminine mamo deities. During these retreats, Khyentsé Rinpoché was guided in visions by timeless awareness embodiments of the great Orgyen, Vimalamitra, Saraha, and many other siddhas of India and Tibet. In particular, at Paro Taktsang in Bhutan, he had a vision of Rigdzin Jigmé Lingpa, who empowered him as a master of the Nyingtik teachings. He also had visions of a vast array of his meditation deities, and so gained mastery through the sublime and more common siddhis. During his entire life, Khyentsé Rinpoché never let even a short period of time slip by, but taught without interruption, giving empowerments, oral transmissions, and teachings to all students regardless of status, [1.276b] according to each person's needs. This illustrates how he taught the dharma.

In brief, this great being exemplified what the scriptures describe as a great bodhisattva with spiritual mastery who can compress an eon into an instant or make an instant last for an eon. Khyentsé Rinpoché could clearly recall many of his previous lifetimes as various members of the Tibetan royal family, as Nyalo Chenpo, and others. He revealed many profound termas, including the oral lineage of Vajrakila from the tradition of Nyak Jñanakumara and the cycle called *The Naturally Occurring Heart Drop of Padma.* During a time of spiritual degeneration, seated firmly on the vajra throne, Khyentsé Rinpoché filled the entire world with his noble deeds in the three areas of practice, teaching, and spiritual projects, strengthening the foundation of the Victorious One's precious teachings.

One of the students he cared for, the present Dalai Lama, leader of the entire tradition of Buddhist teachings in Tibet, the Land of Snows, requested and received from Dilgo Khyentsé Rinpoché a veritable ocean of the profound dharma, including the cycles of Dzogchen teachings, the glorious *Heart Essence of Secrets, The Recitation of the Names of Mañjushri,* and *Timeless Awareness as the Guiding Principle,* and honored him as an extraordinary master of his buddha family.

The late king of Bhutan, the queen, and their son (the present king), the king of Sikkim, Namgyal Dorjé of Jagö, [1.277a] the king of Lingtsang in eastern Tibet, and many other nobles all regarded Kyabjé Dilgo Khyentsé Rinpoché as their spiritual adviser. Whenever he presided over a significant event, those present—many hundreds of thousands of teachers and meditators, ordained and lay practitioners, yogis and yoginis, and monks and nuns—were a mere fraction of the countless numbers who established a connection with Khyentsé Rinpoché in India, Nepal, Sikkim, Bhutan, central and eastern Tibet, and the Western Hemisphere as far away as the United

States. Among these students are such extraordinary lineage holders as Trulzhik Rinpoché of Zhadeu, the three Khyentsé tulkus (Dzongsar Khyentsé, Khyentsé Jigmé, and Khyentsé Yeshé), the two Kongtrul tulkus,[92] the tulku of Zhechen Rabjam, the tulku of Namkhai Nyingpo of Lhodrak, Choktrul Pema Wangyal, Tulku Rangdrol, Datong Tulku, the rebirth of Dartang Choktrul of the Palyul tradition, Yangtang Rinpoché of Domang, Gyatrul Rinpoché, Lhagong Tulku of Dzogchen Monastery, Choktrul Orgyen Tobgyal Rinpoché, and other holders of the teachings in Khyentsé Rinpoché's own school. Among the masters of the glorious Sakya school, his students included the Puntsok Podrang master and his consort[93] [1.277b] and Dezhung Choktrul Rinpoché.[94] Those from the Kagyü school included the buddha Karmapa,[95] Lama Kalu Rinpoché and Bokar Choktrul Rinpoché,[96] and others. Those who listened to Khyentsé Rinpoché and received the nectar of the dharma from him are truly innumerable.

Even a humble person like me experienced his kindness, beyond any scale of reckoning, which will sustain me until I reach the essence of enlightenment. Khyentsé Rinpoché bestowed on the very core of my being both the kama and terma teachings of the Nyingtik cycles, *The Treasury of Spiritual Instructions* containing the pith instructions of the eight lineages of accomplishment, and other transmissions of the nectar of the profound dharma, so rare in this world. I conclude with my own supplication to Khyentsé Rinpoché:

How marvelous!

You are the sovereign lord of both conditioned existence and the peace of nirvana—of naturally occurring, original buddhahood,
the state of utter lucidity, inexhaustible source of the kayas and enlightened qualities—
the teacher who is an embodiment of timeless awareness, permeating the basic space of phenomena.
O dharmakaya guru, Dorjé Tukchok Tsal, you know me.

You are a magician who performs incredible miracles of emanation and resolution
within the orderly display of an enormous variety of mandalas,
arising as the sphere of being that is simultaneously blissful and empty, without transition or change.
O sambhogakaya guru, Pema Wangchen Tsal, you know me. [1.278a]

Embodiment of the enlightened activity of all victorious ones and their spiritual heirs without exception,
arising as the glorious guru, the protector Mañjushri, with the major and minor marks of perfection,

you bring about positive conditions for the teachings and for beings,
without bias.
O nirmanakaya guru, Khyentsé Özer, you know me.

Guru of great kindness, whose grace is unequaled,
always remain inseparable from me, crowning the top of my head.
Illuminating sun of the profound blessings of the lineage of mind-to-mind
transmission,
swiftly enter my heart and grant me the empowerment of timeless
awareness.

Arouse bodhichitta in my experience by stirring my faith and
renunciation.
Through the path of the four levels of empowerment—bringing to
consummation the stages of development and completion—
grant your blessings that your mind and mine may merge,
that I may reach the primordial empire of dharmakaya at last.[97]

Yukhok Jadralwa Chöying Rangdrol (1872–1952)

Another who heard the instructions of the Dzogchen approach from Adzom Drukpa Rinpoché Drodul Pawo Dorjé was the itinerant master[98] Chöying Dorjé of Yukhok. He was born in an area known as Yukhok, a valley near the ridge of Drida Zalmo Gang in eastern Tibet. He said that from an early age, [1.278b] his conduct was inspired but erratic. Wild and undisciplined, he upset those whose impure minds perceived him erroneously. At about the age of fifteen, he abandoned his homeland to meet the guru Sang-gyé Palden at Gyangkhang Ritrö, the remote hermitage of Lhatsé Monastery in lower Ser. That guru's teachings emphasized the necessity of coming to the definitive understanding that all phenomena are empty. Chöying Rangdrol took this to heart just as his guru intended and thus realized the view of emptiness. For a long time after that, he wandered about the vicinity of Lhatsé Monastery, challenging the residents of the shedra to debates with questions like "What are you all meditating on? What do you mean by 'emptiness'?" [1.279a]

Then Sang-gyé Palden of Gyangkhang instructed Chöying Rangdrol to find Chagkong Terchen. He set out and eventually arrived at the latter's encampment. For some time, he was unable to obtain an audience with the guru, and he felt slightly discouraged. However, he finally succeeded in meeting with Terchen Rinpoché, who was sitting quietly on a lonely plateau.

"Where have you come from?" asked the guru. Chöying Rangdrol politely told him of his birthplace and personal history.

"So what do you understand?" came the question.

"I understand emptiness, sir."

"What is emptiness? Where is it?"

"All phenomena are emptiness," he replied.

The guru seized a knife and brandished it. "Get out of my sight!" he scolded. After reflecting briefly, he added, "Your guru from past lifetimes is Adzom Drukpa. Go to him!" As soon as Chöying Rangdrol heard Adzom Drukpa's name, his faith was such that the hair on his body stood on end and he felt boundless respect and devotion. [1.279b]

With a few provisions from Terchen Rinpoché, he immediately set out and, after a long, arduous journey, arrived at the encampment of Adzom Drukpa. As soon as he came into his guru's presence, boundless respect and devotion welled up in him. Meditative experiences and realization dawned in his mind, and he stayed at the encampment for a long time. On the basis of his own experience, Adzom Drukpa thoroughly imparted to him the transmissions for all the tantras, explanatory commentaries, and pith instructions of the secret Nyingtik teachings of natural great perfection, so that Chöying Rangdrol came to a definitive understanding of their specific key points. His guru introduced him directly to the enlightened intent of perceiving awareness's naturally manifest appearances without bias. For three years, according to his guru's instructions, he undertook the ultimate practice focusing on the essence of being, exerting himself on the path of pursuing only pure awareness, until he gained an authentic degree of confidence in his realization of natural great perfection. Extremely delighted, the guru gave him all of his instructions, like one vase filling another. Chöying Rangdrol was thus invested as a holder of the ultimate lineage of realization.

Then his guru told him to meditate in a remote place called Renang in lower Ser, to renounce all worldly concerns, and to plant the victory banner of practice. Obeying these injunctions, Chöying Rangdrol subsisted solely on nettles and water [1.280a] and undertook severe austerities reminiscent of those described in the life story of the venerable Milarepa. After meditating for three years, he directly experienced the unbiased enlightened intent of dharmakaya, natural great perfection. He returned to his guru and offered an account of his realization. Again overjoyed, Adzom Drukpa said to him, "The time has come for you to guide those you are meant to tame. Return to your homeland and take charge of the students who gather around you." So Chöying Rangdrol went to Yakyegar in lower Ser, near his home valley. Following the guru's instructions, he established an encampment, where he vowed to spend the rest of his life in spiritual practice.

Having heard of Dodrupchen Rinpoché's spiritual activities, Chöying Rangdrol urged Lerab Lingpa, the tertön of Nyarong, "Go study with Dodrup Tenpai Nyima and learn the difficult key points of the Category of Direct Transmission of the Nyingtik teachings, as well as the profound key points of the stages of development and completion. Then teach them to me." In this way, Chöying Rangdrol received in their entirety the oral teachings of Tenpai Nyima through the sublime tertön of Nyarong. He then turned the wheel of the teachings of natural great perfection, bestowing them on his students, who gathered from all regions of eastern Tibet, from Golok in the north to the Chinese border in the lowland regions. [1.280b] He brought countless fortunate students to spiritual maturity by teaching on the basis of their personal experience.

Both Khenchen Ngawang Palzang and this lord were widely considered to be emanations of the master Vimalamitra, and their enlightened activities as well as the benefit they brought to beings were enormous. Chöying Rangdrol could clearly recollect his former lifetime as Yudra Nyingpo. He had visions of his meditation deities and always maintained a pure view of the world. He introduced all of his students to their own true nature according to their individual capabilities, unfailingly arousing realization in each one's mind. By closing the mountains and valleys to hunting and fishing, and exhorting everyone to recite the mantra *Om mani padme hum* and to perform other kinds of virtuous actions, he made his influence felt throughout eastern Tibet.

He spent his entire life engaged in such enlightened activities, living into his eighties. His students—heart sons and daughters who were nourished by the nectar of his enlightened speech—included nobles, gurus, rulers, tulkus, scholars, siddhas, yogins, and others from all over eastern Tibet, so that virtually no one had not bowed at his feet. Among the holiest of his principal students who were lineage holders, two great yogins, Drimé Özer of Rakor [1.281a] and Chokden of Dowa, gained realization in a single leap. Purpa of upper Drong and many others dissolved into rainbow body; and there were other students, such as Khenpo Chönyi Seltong, Pema Dorjé, Dzigor Gongtsé, Lama Gardé, Gyarong Tsöndrü, Khenchen Chöchap, and Godzi Tertön. These students served on a vast scale the sublime teachings that focus on the essence of being. The extraordinary and holy master holding Chöying Rangdrol's lineage is the fourth Dodrupchen.

The foregoing account concerns one principal line of transmission from Jamyang Khyentsei Wangpo.

9

The Lineage of Rigdzin Jigmé Lingpa: The Dodrupchen Line of Incarnations

You are the vajra of all-pervasive space, timelessly unencumbered
by the elaborations of ordinary characteristics.
You are the perfection of youthfulness, resplendent with the major and
minor marks of ideal form, embodying spontaneously present timeless
awareness with its vast range of enlightened qualities.
With your vajra dance of myriad magical displays, you manifest
constantly for those to be guided.
O my guru, glorious protector, sovereign lord of the hundred buddha
families, protect me until enlightenment; never be separate from me![1]

Now [2.1b] I will describe the lineage held by the Dodrupchen incarnations, who have served as custodians of the teachings of Rigdzin Jigmé Lingpa.

The First Dodrupchen, Jigmé Trinlé Özer (1745–1821)

In a vajra prophecy of Kunchen Jigmé Lingpa, we read of "the incarnation of the prince who will open the doorway of the dharma." This is a reference to Dodrupchen Rinpoché as Jigmé Lingpa's prophesied heart son, the dramatic emanation of Prince Murub Tsepo of Tibet, Sang-gyé Lingpa, and other masters. In keeping with the clear prediction found in *The Sealed Prophecies* from *The United Intent of the Gurus,* revealed by Sang-gyé Lingpa, [2.2a] Jigmé Trinlé Özer's birthplace was in upper Do Valley, in the region of Nguldza Zalmo Gang, one of the six major ranges in the eastern part of greater Tibet. He was born in a Female Wood Ox year, the fifty-ninth year of the twelfth sexagesimal cycle.[2] As a child, he was given to acting in unusual ways, as if he were taming invisible gods. He received his refuge vow[3] from the second Rabjam of Zhechen Monastery, Gyurmé Kunzang Namgyal, who gave him the name [2.2b] Kunzang Zhenpen.

He devoted seven years to one-pointed spiritual practice at Dewachenpo, the upper hermitage on the glacier above Dzogchen Monastery, where he reached a high level of attainment. He journeyed to central Tibet four times during his lifetime. During the first two trips, he received many profound teachings at Dakla Gampo from masters such as Damchö Wangchuk and refined his meditative experiences and realization. In addition, in eastern Tibet, Jigmé Trinlé Özer studied and contemplated countless teachings (primarily those of the Early Translation school) with twenty holy guides, including Karma Tashi of Palyul Monastery, Gyurmé Kunzang Namgyal of Zhechen Monastery, Drimé Zhingkyong of Katok Monastery, Gyarong Jé-ön Pema Kundrol Namgyal of Dzogchen Monastery, and Ngedön Tendzin Zangpo, the third Pema Rigdzin of Dzogchen Rudam Monastery.

During his forty-first year (the Female Wood Serpent year of the thirteenth sexagesimal cycle),[4] Jigmé Trinlé Özer journeyed to central Tibet for the third time, specifically to meet Rigdzin Jigmé Lingpa, who recognized him as an incarnation of Prince Damdzin.[5] [2.3a] He cared for Jigmé Trinlé Özer with a father's great kindness, empowering him as the custodian of the Nyingtik teachings. It was Jigmé Lingpa who gave him the name Jigmé Trinlé Özer. When he returned for the fourth time, it was to study at the feet of the master Jigmé Lingpa, from whom he received all of the remaining teachings he needed.

Those were troubled times, with unrest stirring in upper Hor, and when Jigmé Trinlé Özer issued an injunction to Pehar at Kordzö Ling (the shrine to that protective god in Samyé Monastery), the statue bowed its head to him. He immediately performed a *lhasang* ceremony atop Hepo Hill.[6] Everyone present saw the smoke waft into the sky, taking the terrifying form of a garuda, which flew off in the direction of the impending threat and caused the invading army to turn back. Accorded many honors by the government and given the title of Dodrupchen,[7] Jigmé Trinlé Özer became highly renowned. He perfected the conduct characteristic of a siddha. He could make inanimate objects leap into the air by focusing on them and uttering "Phat!" He could also tame ghosts and reanimate corpses. He practiced at many holy lakes, glaciers, and cliffside caves, making, for example, a pilgrimage to Tsari Rongkor. [2.3b]

Then, fulfilling a prophecy found in a terma that he himself had revealed, Jigmé Trinlé Özer returned to eastern Tibet, where Tsewang Lhamo, queen regent of Dergé, and her son honored him as their spiritual adviser. They developed a close connection as patrons and teacher. When the fourth Dzogchen, Mingyur Namkhai Dorjé, came to Pemakö in Drakchen Yarlung, Jigmé Trinlé Özer bestowed on him an empowerment using the ritual offering of the "hero's potion" as the symbol.[8] The blessings of enlightened intent passed from the enlightened mind of Jigmé Trinlé Özer to Mingyur Namkhai Dorjé, who in his lifetime reached the level at which phenomena resolve into their true nature.

Jigmé Trinlé Özer recognized the tulku of Kunchen Jigmé Lingpa in the son of Sönam Pel, a lay teacher descended from the Buddhist ruler Akyong of Golok, and his wife Garza, whose clan was reputed to hail from tsen spirits. He conferred maturing empowerments and liberating instructions on the child, nurturing him in secular as well as spiritual ways and training him on outer, inner, and secret levels. This child was Do Khyentsé Yeshé Dorjé. In addition, Jigmé Trinlé Özer taught many great masters capable of upholding the teachings. These masters—the "four great roof beams" named Dorjé, the thirteen named Namkha, the hundred or more who upheld the mandala—included Gyalsé Rigpai Dorjé of Dzogchen Gemang, Mingyur Namkhai Dorjé, Chöying Tobden Dorjé, Repa Damtsik Dorjé, Lama Jigmé Ngotsar, Jigmé Losel, Gotsa Tulku, [2.4a] the third Zhechen Rabjam,[9] the third Dzogchen Pönlop,[10] Katok Situ,[11] Dola Jigmé Kalzang, Katok Getrul Mahapandita, and the lay vajra holder Palchen Namkha Jigmé from Repkong.

Jigmé Trinlé Özer turned the wheel of the dharma throughout his life, bestowing such teachings as the Nyingma tantras, the earlier and later cycles of the Nyingtik teachings, *The Seven Treasuries, The Accomplishment of Life Force by Masters of Awareness,* the cycle focusing on the Eight Commands entitled *Natural Arising* and others of the Northern Terma cycles, pure visions that bear the seal of secrecy, and *The Gathering of All Masters of Awareness.* He had numerous visions of Amitabha. Through the blessings of the great Orgyen, the Omniscient One Longchenpa and his spiritual heir Jigmé Lingpa, and Milarepa Zhepa Dorjé, he revealed termas of enlightened intent, complete cycles of maturing empowerments and liberating instructions. These included a sadhana cycle of outer, inner, and secret practices for Amitabha entitled *The Holy Teaching of the Sublime Path to Supreme Bliss; The Most Secret Aspect of Hayagriva,* a sadhana cycle focusing on the twelve Dzogchen teachers; a cycle uniting the four mainstream traditions of the Chö teachings, [2.4b] including a sadhana and empowerment focusing on Machik Lapdrön; and a cycle for the protective deity Mahadeva. Jigmé Trinlé Özer codified these teachings and disseminated them widely. He established two centers for upholding the extensive lineage of his teachings in the upper and lower regions of the watershed of the Dzachu River.

The following is taken from a prophecy found in a terma revealed by Dechen Lingpa:

> An emanation of the prince will appear, a courageous bodhisattva,
> a leader among teachers and meditators of the Ati approach of
> Dzogchen.
> He will establish three monastic centers in upper and lower Ser.

In keeping with this prophecy, Jigmé Trinlé Özer established the first of these centers, Drodön Lhundrup, at Shukchen in his birthplace of upper Do Valley. He founded the second, Pemakö Tsasum Khandroi Ling, at Drakchen Yarlung, where he remained for the rest of his life. Finally, he restored Arik Ragya Monastery, north of Pemakö, on the banks of the milky waters of the Ma River where it is said to bend clockwise. Due to inauspicious interdependence associated with the initial founding of Arik Ragya, about half of the monks had died while the rest had fled. When he arrived there, Jigmé Trinlé Özer established an encampment (which is still known as Garlung) and performed a fire ceremony related to the practice of Chö to exorcise the demon responsible for harming that great monastery. [2.5a] He then assured the surviving members of the community that they were no longer in danger and could return.

Behind the monastery, in a cave on a cliff called Anyé Chung-gön, Jigmé Trinlé Özer caused a spring to burst forth and spent a long time there practicing the phases of approach and accomplishment. This spring, a result of his spiritual attainment, still flows.

Moreover, Jigmé Trinlé Özer conferred maturing empowerments and liberating instructions in the area of Repkong, where his enlightened activity was particularly widespread and where Chöying Tobden Dorjé and his lineage of students—reputedly some 1,900 "bearers of the *kila* dagger"[12]—flourished. The Wang ruler of Mongolia honored Jigmé Trinlé Özer as his spiritual adviser and received from him a volume of prophecies that later was to become the most sacred possession of the monastic estate of Tashi Gomang.

Because of Jigmé Trinlé Özer's unimpeded psychic abilities and siddhis, people came from all over the upper and lower areas of eastern Tibet, as far away as Tachienlu[13] and other places in China and Mongolia, to study with him. As important people and patrons gathered around him like clouds, his secular and spiritual activities flourished greatly. Having concluded his activities, at the age of seventy-seven Jigmé Trinlé Özer passed away at midnight on the thirteenth day of the first month—a day commemorating the Buddha's miracles—in an Iron Serpent year.[14] [2.5b] Though he showed no signs of illness, after leaving extensive teachings as his testament he passed away into the supreme peace of the basic space of phenomena, amid many signs and miraculous occurrences visible to all. His heart children and intimate students cremated his remains and placed the mass of relics in a gilded stupa. Today, the stupa can still be found at his seat as a focus for the accumulation of merit by ordinary beings.

Jigmé Trinlé Özer's lineage has two aspects: that of his incarnations and that of the students who passed on his teachings. Let me begin by discussing the successive incarnations.

THE LINEAGE OF DODRUPCHEN'S INCARNATIONS

The Second Dodrupchen, Jigmé Puntsok Jungné (1824–1863)

The second Dodrupchen was Jigmé Puntsok Jungné. He was born into the Bochung clan amid countless marvelous signs. In keeping with prophetic statements by masters such as Do Khyentsé concerning his recognition, he was enthroned with great

ceremony. He encountered no difficulty in studying the necessary fields of knowledge, from reading and writing to spiritual practice and related activities. Although he revealed several profound termas, they subsequently vanished, with only a casket of agate remaining. He relied on such gurus as Do Khyentsé Yeshé Dorjé, [2.6a] Dzogchen Mingyur Namkhai Dorjé, and Paltrul Rinpoché. His realization grew, and he attained the sublime siddhi through the path of natural great perfection.

At that time, there was a wild, extremely malevolent demon known as Chakmo Senring of Golok, the rebirth of someone who had gone astray by performing the practices of wrathful deities while conceiving of them as real entities.[15] Jigmé Puntsok Jungné felt that there was only one master who could tame this being. He was called Chakmo Tulku and lived in Ngapai Shida, a town in the region of Amdo. A holy master who had five green locks of hair topped with the horse's head characteristic of the deity Hayagriva, [2.6b] he was a true emanation of Ngenlam Gyalwa Chokyang. This master became a particularly exalted and powerful siddha, one who had unimpeded psychic power to see what was hidden from others and who could liberate both Chakmo Senring and the violent king demon of Margu Dé from their evil ways. He had relied on Do Khyentsé Yeshé Dorjé as his guru, and his conduct in emulating him was uncontrived. Jigmé Puntsok Jungné knew that the spiritual attainment of these two sublime masters was unhindered and that, like the Indian siddha Saraha, they were capable of engaging in uncontrived tantric conduct just as it was intended. Nevertheless, negative circumstances prevented this demon from being tamed, and it became necessary for the second Dodrupchen to abandon this region as a site for his main seat and to move it elsewhere.

Accepting the invitation of the ruler of the Chakla region, Do Khyentsé Yeshé Dorjé and Jigmé Puntsok Jungné went to Tachienlu to serve as the king's spiritual advisers, staying there for a long time.

When Jigmé Puntsok Jungné was about thirty, a smallpox epidemic was devastating the local population. To avert it, [2.7a] he took the illness upon himself and died in bed. Do Khyentsé Yeshé Dorjé came to give him his final instructions. "Puntsok Jungné, are you dead?" he asked, and kicked the body three times, whereupon Jigmé Puntsok Jungné sat up suddenly in vajra posture and remained that way for a week without moving. During that time, countless marvelous signs, such as rainbow lights, moved all of his students to awe and faith.

The Third Dodrupchen, Jigmé Tenpai Nyima (1865–1926)

The third Dodrupchen was Jigmé Tenpai Nyima. His birth at Chak-khung had been referred to in a prophecy by Mingyur Namkhai Dorjé: "The handsome son fits the

noble mold of the iron cup."[16] There were equally clear indications that his father would be Dudjom Dorjé Drolö Tsal[17] and that his mother would be Sönam Tso, who came from a family of flesh-eating dakinis.[18] Jigmé Tenpai Nyima was born during the fourteenth sexagesimal cycle amid marvelous signs. Raised patterns of conch shells were clearly visible on the soles of his feet [2.7b] and remained even after his body matured. He was named Kunzang Jigmé Tenpai Nyima Trinlé Kunchap Palzangpo.

From an early age, he exhibited spiritual attributes and, at seven, learned to read and write after being instructed only once. He went to upper Dza specifically to meet with the heart son of Mañjushri, Paltrul Orgyen Chökyi Wangpo. While studying *Engaging in the Conduct of a Bodhisattva* with that master, Jigmé Tenpai Nyima became greatly frustrated [2.8a] because he could understand neither the words nor the sense of the text. Every night he would weep inconsolably, waking to find his face stuck to his pillow. Then one day he said to his teacher, "Last night I dreamed I was in a temple where three gurus dressed as herukas were sitting. The middle one held a text. I asked him, 'Who are you and what are you holding?' He replied, 'I am Do Khyentsé Jigmé Yeshé Dorjé, and this book helps those in this world who cannot learn their lessons.' I said, 'I beg you to give it to me,' and so he did. This made me very happy. It made me confident that I will understand something if I study today." From then on, Jigmé Tenpai Nyima was taken under the care of his meditation deity and blessed, so that the expanse of enlightened intent welled up in his mind. Within a few days, he no longer needed anyone to help him review his lessons, for the strength of sublime knowing had begun to unfold in him, and he could retain all of his guru's words and their underlying meaning as though they had been imprinted on his mind. [2.8b]

When Jigmé Tenpai Nyima was eight years old, he went to Dzagyal Monastery (founded by Dodrup Kunzang Zhenpen and Dza Trama Lama Jigmé Gyalwai Nyugu). After Paltrul Rinpoché made a mandala offering to request that he teach, the boy gave instructions on *Engaging in the Conduct of a Bodhisattva.* He inspired such faith in the students that tears sprang to their eyes. Paltrul Rinpoché was extremely delighted and showered praise on Jigmé Tenpai Nyima, saying, "Such teaching is not ordinary, but spiritual and given through the blessings of one's meditation deities. The fact that Dodrupchen, a child of eight, is capable of turning the wheel of the dharma like this means that the period during which the teachings will endure is not yet over."

Jigmé Tenpai Nyima studied with such masters as Paltrul Jigmé Chökyi Wangpo of Dzogchen Monastery, Mingyur Namkhai Dorjé, Namtrul Kunzang Tekchok Dorjé of Gyarong, Jamyang Khyentsei Wangpo, Khenchen Pema Damchö Özer (also known as Dzogchen Khen Pema Dorjé), Kongtrul Yönten Gyatso, Nyala Tertön Sögyal, [2.9a] Jamyang Mipam Namgyal, Gyurmé Tutop Namgyal of Zhechen Monastery, and Japa Alak Do-ngak. He was brought to spiritual maturity and liberated by a veritable ocean of teachings from the kama and terma traditions, all deriving from the four mainstream transmissions of the Early Translation school. He studied such teachings as the sources of the three yogas—*The Discourse on United Intent, The Web of Magical Display,* and the mind teachings; the three cycles (those focusing on the Eight Commands, *The United Intent of the Gurus,* and Vajrakila); and the earlier and later cycles of the Nyingtik teachings. He harbored no prejudice toward any of the valid systems of the Nyingma and Sarma schools of Tibetan Buddhism. He was never overconfident, arrogant, fainthearted, or smug when it came to studying, but learned all of the major traditions of teachings, principally Vinaya, Madhyamaka, valid cognition, and Prajñaparamita. At night he studied by the light of a lamp, absorbing all of the words and their underlying meaning, and thus acquired fame as a scholar.

At some point, it became difficult for him to continue as he had been doing, and when Pema Bum, a chieftain of Golok who ruled over eight clans, offered him a site called Tri in Do Valley, he saw this as an excellent opportunity. He moved to Do, where he founded a center called Sangchen Ngödrup Palbar Ling. [2.9b] Jamyang Khyentsei Wangpo prophesied that if Jigmé Tenpai Nyima went to central Tibet, he would not only ensure benefit for the teachings and for beings, but also dispel obstacles to his life. However, circumstances supportive of such a journey did not materialize; instead, things took a negative turn. In Nyikhok, south of his residence, lived an evil spirit, the rebirth of a sorcerer with perverse aspirations. One day, while Jigmé Tenpai Nyima was teaching, a violent windstorm came up suddenly, and from the moment he felt the first draft, he became ill. His health remained fragile for the rest of his life, and so he was unable to travel anywhere.

To one side of the monastery, on the heights of Dzé Tralep, stood a temple dedicated to the master Tangtong Gyalpo. Jigmé Tenpai Nyima lived in a hermitage there, practicing one-pointedly. He had visions of his meditation deities, from whom he received prophecies, and in other ways demonstrated his spiritual attainment.

He founded a library housing priceless statues and ritual implements, as well as many volumes of scripture, piled like veritable cliff faces; among these were the Kangyur and Tengyur, the tantras of the Nyingma school, the collected works of learned and accomplished masters from all schools of Tibetan Buddhism without sectarian bias (all the kama and terma teachings in the Land of Snows), [2.10a] and texts on all fields of secular knowledge. Three protective deities—Ekajati, Rahula, and Vajrasadhu—appeared miraculously to Jigmé Tenpai Nyima in the forms of mighty, forceful humans and offered many of these texts to him.

Four great khenpos, referred to in Jigmé Tenpai Nyima's sealed prophecies, equaled him in their view: Gar Khenpo Jigmé Ösel, Sershul Khenpo, Khenpo Damchö, and Lushul Khenpo. Due to their kindness and that of other masters, students from all regions gathered around Jigmé Tenpai Nyima like galaxies of stars. However, he considered this and other conventionally meritorious endeavors distractions from his spiritual practice and thus as obstacles to his enlightenment. He turned his back on the entanglements of life, such as trying to achieve political power and influence and striving for personal gain by acquiring retinues and students. Instead, he planted the victory banner of the teachings, devoting enormous energy to the three spheres of study, practice, and spiritual projects. At all times, he maintained the uncontrived conduct of a hidden practitioner, and so it was difficult for anyone to ascertain his secret qualities. But wherever he stayed was infused with the fragrance of his pure discipline. [2.10b]

He was childlike in his lack of arrogance, and others found his company delightful. Under certain circumstances, however, he would reveal his great charismatic qualities—the depth of his mind, the directness of his speech, and his command over the phenomena he perceived—so that everyone, even the most haughty, was humbled in his presence. From a distance, he miraculously consecrated the great stupa at Gogen Plain in Walshul Sertal, earning the admiration of his students. During breaks in his practice sessions, Jigmé Tenpai Nyima constantly pored over his books and otherwise trained in the methods of the dharma. His written works filled dozens of volumes and included such treatises as *A Key to the Treasury* (an overview of *The Heart Essence of Secrets*) and *A Detailed Commentary on the Power of Complete Recall,* collected prayers of praise and words of advice, dohas, and teachings on Dzogchen cycles.

Late in his life, he began a commentary on *Pith Instructions: The Garland of Views,* but at a certain point stopped writing and said, "This will suffice for now; I have come to the end of my present work. Wrap this manuscript up, and in the future someone who is held to be my incarnation will finish it." He then showed signs of illness, and when he was sixty-two years old, in the year known as "Completion," a Male Fire Tiger year, of the fifteenth sexagesimal cycle,[19] [2.11a] he passed out of his body.

Jigmé Tenpai Nyima had countless heart children. Foremost among them was the "second Khyentsé," Jamyang Chökyi Lodrö, whom Adzom Drukpa and the lord Jigmé Tenpai Nyima entrusted with the enlightened intent of their ultimate lineage. It is evident that their trust was well placed, for he ensured the flourishing of this precious lineage.

The Fourth Dodrupchen, Jigmé Trinlé Palbar (b. 1927)

Here is the life story of the fourth Dodrupchen, Jigmé Trinlé Palbar, in his own words:

To begin with, my birthplace was foretold by Tupten Chökyi Dorjé, [2.11b] the fifth Pema Rigdzin of Dzogchen Monastery, who said:

> The ground for the emanation of the vajra master, sovereign master of all buddha families,
> is Zangdok Palri in Chamara
> and the supreme central pure realm of the sambhogakaya,
> in which there are four emanations, those of form, speech, mind, and qualities.
> In particular, the dramatic emanation of enlightened activity
> will appear in a place close to his monastery, in the direction of the lord of the dead,
> near a cliff of precious stones and surrounded by forests.
> The union of the father of skillful means and the mother of sublime knowing,
> who will be called Ka and Da,
> will produce a child of spiritual heritage in a Fire Hare year[20]
> and there are positive signs that he will benefit the teachings and beings.
> Thus, in response to a request from those with faith,
> the fifth Dzogchen, Dharmavajra,
> has written down whatever came to his confused mind.
> May the vision of virtue and excellence cover the surface of the earth.

In fulfillment of this prophecy, I was born in upper Gyalrong, in a region where three main tributaries converge, specifically in the vicinity of the easternmost branch, which the local people traditionally referred to as the Serta Bokha Kalmar. South—the direction of the lord of the dead—of the monastery of the Dodrupchens in Serkhok, on the banks of the Ser River, is Tsai Drongpa. Behind it is a cliff face and in front are extensive groves [2.12a] of white willows. Here I was born into the community ruled by the Jekar Sholep chieftains. My father was Drala of the Jekar clan, and my mother was Kalikyi of the Kazhi clan, famed for its courageous and heroic people. My birth took place at dawn on a day in the year 1927 of the Western calendar, a Fire Hare year, the first of the sixteenth sexagesimal cycle. As I emerged from the womb, radiant light filled the entire house; my parents were afraid, thinking that this was the result of the machinations of gods and demons.

All kinds of indications attended my birth. The year I was conceived, a vague serpent-shaped light would often enter our house and move along the walls, and every night people from afar could see Rahula come to rest above the roof. From time to time, a bird known as Raven Yalo would fly into our village. Its beak was broken, and it was sacred to Dodrupchen Monastery. Furthermore, a flower grew on the roof of our house even though no seed had been planted.

The fifth Dzogchen sent the instruction, [2.12b] "Seek the tulku to the south of Dodrupchen Monastery, as far as Litsang." While many parties of lamas and monks searched accordingly, I was in Serkhok, studying secular and spiritual subjects with Yukhok Jadralwa, a yogin of the Dzogchen approach. One night I dreamed that the Dodrupchen had definitely been reborn. In another dream, I was riding a piebald horse and carrying a spear from which a red silk standard fluttered. I said, "Chöying Rangdrol, I have a mission to accomplish. Will I succeed?" He replied, "Follow this trail made by a dog's paw prints, and you will accomplish your goal." He added, "Strive to perform fulfillment and offering rituals for your protector Tsui Mar, and you will be rewarded."

Many other holy masters conferred and compiled a list of children born in the Fire Hare year.[21] They offered it to Dzogchen Rinpoché, who selected a name from it. He said, "This is the one, and his name [2.13a] will be Tupten Trinlé Palzangpo." He then returned to his own monastery. The renowned Khen Gangnam, Khenpo Kunga Lodrö, journeyed to Serkhok with his retinue and made arrangements for me to travel to Kyilkhor Tang. There I was enthroned amid great celebration. When I correctly identified the representations of enlightened form, speech, and mind that had belonged to the preceding Dodrupchen, all were convinced and tears came to their eyes. The khenpo became my tutor and personally took charge of my welfare.

When I was four, during the summer of a Male Iron Horse year,[22] I was escorted in three stages to my future home by parties from all of the various regions associated with Dodrupchen Monastery. They included monks and lay people from upper and lower Walshul Do; the three clans of Bochung in Walshul Sertal; the three clans of Golok; the eight clans under the chieftain Pema Bum of Golok; the inhabitants of the four valleys of Golok, Walshul Mewa, and upper and lower Dzirka; the eighteen clans of Gyalrong; the inhabitants of the region of Four Rivers and Six Ridges in Litsang; the chieftain and advisers of Walshul Chokhoma; and the people of the kingdoms of Mé and of Repkong in Shar Rongpo. [2.13b] I finally came to the monastery of Sangchen Ngödrup Palbar Ling, where I was again enthroned, given a ritual ablution, and invested with spiritual authority. I stood on my throne and recited the Seven-Line Supplication, the prayer for summoning the blessings that begins, "Arise, Padmakara...," and some aspirations in verse, amazing everyone. All of my escorts and companions were thanked profusely and with great delight.

When I went to the hall of the protective deities, from the texts of fulfillment and offering rituals, I selected a concise general offering to the feminine and masculine protectors composed by Dodrup Kunzang Zhenpen, which begins, "Guardian goddess of mantra Ekajati...." I had not previously studied this text, and I read it aloud, omitting one line of verse. Then I gave the text to my old father. Lushul Khenpo said in a commentary that the omission of that line of verse did not distort the meaning of the liturgy. Thus the activities surrounding my enthronement were brought to a successful conclusion.

It was during that year [2.14a] that I began speaking out spontaneously, saying things like, "Vajrakila told me this and that," but no more than a few instances were recorded, because they made my students uneasy. There is an extensive commentary by Khen Chöchok of Kyala on what they did manage to write down. Urged by Lushul Khenpo, my teacher Rang-rik bribed me with sweets and fruit to answer his questions: "Where did you come from?" I replied, "I came from Zangdok Palri." He asked, "Who lives there?" and I answered, "Someone called Guru Padmasambhava." "Who else lives there?" he asked. I said, "A brightly colored being with many mouths and many eyes. There are also lots of other strange people."

From the time I was quite young, I had numerous visions of gods and demons. From my fifth year (that of the Female Iron Sheep) until my sixth (the Male Water Monkey year),[23] I was cared for with kindness by my teacher, Bochung Rang-rik. I learned to read and write, and memorized such prayers as were appropriate for recitation. [2.14b]

In my seventh year (that of the Female Water Bird),[24] I began studying with Lushul Khenpo, one of the four great khenpos mentioned in the *Sealed Prophecies* from Sang-gyé Lingpa's *United Intent of the Gurus.* He first taught me the prayer of praise *The Noble Qualities of Glorious Timeless Awareness,* then *A Letter to a Friend* by the protector Nagarjuna, *Engaging in the Conduct of a Bodhisattva,* and *The Rain of Joy,* an explanation of *The Precious Treasury of Enlightened Qualities* (Kunchen Jigmé Lingpa's treatise on the graduated path of the sutras and tantras). Having requested these teachings, I studied them repeatedly.

During the summer of a Female Fire Ox year,[25] when I was eleven, I went to see Gegong Khenpo Kunzang Palden, known as Kunpal, in Dzachukha. This fulfilled a prophecy by the great emanated tertön[26] Orgyen Trinlé Lingpa (more widely known as Apang Tertön), who was the king of the dharma Orgyen in human form during these times of spiritual degeneration. From Khenpo Kunpal, I received the entire range of maturing empowerments and liberating instructions for the earlier and later cycles of Nyingtik teachings of Longchenpa. He said to me, "My lineage [2.15a] has authentic origins and is in fact a direct lineage with a store of blessings quite unlike any other. Now the father's legacy has been handed on to the son." He thus encouraged me, showing great delight. That winter I returned to my home monastery.

The winter I was fourteen (in a Male Iron Dragon year),[27] I fell extremely ill. I was taken to see the guru, the great Apang Tertön, who was staying on the slope of Drong-ri Mukpo in upper Ser. I undertook a monthlong retreat of intensive practice on Tachung Barwa, the wrathful aspect of the Guru from *The Heart Drop of Longchenpa,* to dispel obstacles; during this retreat, I went for an audience with the guru. He said to one of his personal attendants, "Serve the Rinpoché some beer." Taking his own bowl filled with beer, the tertön gave it to me. Although I was not a monk, I had been given the title "master of the teachings," and I feared that drinking might tarnish my image. I protested, saying, "But I don't drink beer." Then my body went numb and my senses reeled. I asked myself, "Have I possibly interfered with the circumstances under which the guru might have ensured my spiritual attainment?" [2.15b] I drank the beer without further hesitation, for although it was not my habit, I would make an exception for the sake of accepting the siddhi granted by my guru. For a short while, I experienced an indescribable, inconceivable, and ineffable state of awareness. Though I could respond to the guru, I was incapable of communicating with anyone else. When I emerged from this state, I went to the home of some of my spiritual companions. They asked me, "Are you sure you're not sick? You don't seem yourself." I went outside again, and as a cool breeze caressed my face, I knew with certainty that all of my perceptions were like a dream. Realization awakened in me, and I felt confident about my release from samsara, coupled with a mixture of joy and sadness impossible to articulate or even understand.

The following day, I spoke with my guru about my realization in a way that amounted to a child's babbling. He replied by prophesying what would befall me up to my twenty-fifth year, telling me that I was the custodian of Terchen Rinpoché's termas. As a means of establishing that interdependence, he ordered me to carve a seal with a design of the scorpion that is symbolic of Guru Drakpo. [2.16a] Later, he told me that I should rely on Yukhok Jadralwa as my teacher, since he had been my guru for lifetimes, and that in the short term, I should undertake a hundred-day retreat on the practice of the feminine deity, Yeshé Tsogyal, from *The Heart Drop of Longchenpa.* In the spring of my fifteenth year (a Female Iron Serpent year),[28] I returned to my own monastery, where I offered the entire range of empowerments and oral transmissions for *The Heart Drop of Longchenpa* to a large gathering.

In brief, from my tenth to my eighteenth year (that of the Male Wood Monkey),[29] I studied with Khenpo Gangnam of Chökor, Khenpo Chöchok of Kyala, Khenpo Shedrak of Shorbak, Khen Tuksung, and Gara Tulku Dorchok. I received explanations of valid cognition, Madhyamaka, Vinaya, commentaries on that most majestic of tantras *The Heart Essence of Secrets*, and the Lojong teachings. I trained in these repeatedly and completed more than three full sets of the "five hundred thousands,"[30] the preliminary practices for spiritual development and purification. I gained certainty by completing retreats on a vast array of mandalas, primarily those for the guru, meditation deity, and dakini practices from *The Heart Drop of Longchenpa*. I also performed supplementary recitations and fire offering ceremonies. [2.16b] Further, I trained in the activities befitting a vajra master, including ritual chanting, music, and mudras.

On the fifteenth day of the fifth month of a Female Wood Bird year[31] (when I was nineteen), I performed a lhasang ceremony on the front slope of Drong-ri Mukpo in Ser, then set off for central Tibet. From the upper part of Do Valley, we passed through Drimar Kadok and upper Ma, crossing the Drichu River at the Seven Fords of Chumar. We then went over the glacial waste known as Samten Gangzang and through the plain of Tashi Oma in Dam. Entering the central region from the north, we arrived at Radreng Gyalwai Ensa, the seat of Dromtön Gyalwai Jungné, where we viewed the important sites—the tombs containing the remains of the lord Jampai Dorjé, the guru Serlingpa, and the lord Dromtön—and the collection of thousands of volumes that constituted the monastery's representations of enlightened speech. We also saw the tomb housing the remains of Rongtön at Nalendra Monastery in Penpo. At the beginning of the tenth month, we sponsored three successive applications of gold leaf to the statue of Jowo Yizhin Norbu, the five naturally occurring images of the supremely compassionate Avalokiteshvara, the lord Mikyö Dorjé,[32] the lord Lokeshvara in Potala Palace, and others.

In my twentieth year (that of the Male Fire Dog),[33] we stayed in Lhasa during the New Year celebrations and attended the great Mönlam festival.[34] We visited each of the individual colleges at the three great universities of Sera, Drepung, and Ganden, [2.17a] making offerings and financial contributions and sponsoring meals for the students. We also made offerings at the great Tsé Palace. After this we continued on to Orgyen Mindroling Monastery, Tupten Dorjé Drak, and Gang-ri Tökar, where we made financial contributions and sponsored meals for the residents. While at Tsering Jong in upper Khar Valley in Dön, we visited the tomb of Kunchen Jigmé Lingpa and saw his personal effects, such as his bell and other musical instruments, as well as the private heirlooms of the Pushuk family of regional officials.

I spent about fifteen days in Jigmé Lingpa's personal chambers, carrying out my retreat on the practice of the feminine deity. To supplement this practice, I ended the retreat with a hundred thousand fire offerings. I offered to the community the empowerments for the Three Roots from *The Heart Drop of Longchenpa*, and we sponsored a thousand ganachakra offerings to the Three Roots.

We visited the site of the Red Crypt housing the tomb of King Songtsen Gampo at Chongyé, the monastery of Riwo Dechen, Takshen Bumpa, Yumbu Lagang Tengshö, the temple of Tsenden Yu, and the temple of Tradruk Tashi Jam in Yoru and made offerings at these places. We sponsored the application of gold leaf to the speaking statue of Tara, [2.17b] sponsored meals for the monastic communities, and made financial contributions. We also sponsored the gilding of the tomb of Orgyen Lingpa at Bentsang Monastery and of the face of the image of Guru Rinpoché that the Guru himself had called "Looks Like Me," at Sheldrak in Yarlung. There we also sponsored ganachakras and spent a week in strict retreat to foster our connection to it.

We crossed the Tsangpo River at Tsetang and made our way to Samyé Monastery. We toured that great center in its entirety and made offerings at Utsé Riksum as well as the temples known as the four "continents" and the "subcontinents." We saw all of the holy sites and objects, including the image called Guru Tsokyé Dorjé[35] revealed as a terma by Ngadak and the footprints that Guru Rinpoché left in the rock on the pass of Guntang when he was preparing to depart for the realm of bloodthirsty demons. We performed a lhasang ceremony on the summit of Hepo Hill. When we went to Kordzö Ling, the shrine of the Pehar oracle, the lightning of the yaksha spirits fell on the image of the king of the martial gods, which pleased the oracle enormously. He gave me a lasso belonging to the tsen spirits and in other ways showed me great favor, which inspired me. I spent a week of retreat in the cave of Drakmar Puk in the Chimpu Uplands of the Samyé region and saw the tomb housing the remains of the victorious one Longchenpa. We visited the tomb of Zur Khardo, as well as the lake sacred to Yeshé Tsogyal in lower Drak Valley, and I spent a week in retreat [2.18a] below the cave of Drubpuk at Yangdzong in Drak. Then, at the beginning of the fifth month of that Fire Dog year, we crossed into Go from the east and returned to our native region.

During the same year, when I was twenty, on the twenty-fifth day of the ninth month, I returned to my own monastery, escorted with great ceremony by those who lived around Dodrupchen Monastery. People of high and low status from both regions under the monastery's administration unanimously invested me as their spiritual and temporal leader, and for the next eleven years, until my thirtieth year (that of the Male Fire Monkey),[36] I bore this responsibility. I carried out all the duties of my position but kept my attention focused on my gurus and meditation deities. As my activities and functions proved more or less successful, I gained confidence in the cause-and-effect principle of karma. My policies were based on reports I had received of the activities of the populace, and I employed a firm but gentle touch—a silken knot, so to speak—in administering the discipline of the ten kinds of positive actions, curbing the ambitions of the mighty while protecting the interests of the lowly. In upholding the noble traditions of the past, in both the spiritual and secular realms, our region became famous throughout the nation; [2.18b] people flocked to live in such a pleasant area.

Because the endurance of the Victorious One's teachings depends on the study and practice of those teachings, I sponsored the construction of a hall for a shedra and provided the furnishings and decorations within it. I restored the retreat center, and my monastic estate arranged for the support of the residents of these places of study and practice. I was satisfied that our projects were even greater than they had been in the past.

However, I was certain—as sure as a stone thrown into a well—about the nature of my successes and failures in this life and, in fact, of all my moral choices. I concluded that spiritual practice focusing on the very essence was the only way to fully realize the potential of this human life and decided to prove worthy of the lineage of my gurus and their gurus before them. And so, in my twenty-fourth year (that of the Male Iron Tiger),[37] at the onset of the three winter months, I cut myself off from all worldly concerns and sat at the feet of Yukhok Jadralwa, also known as Chöying Rangdrol, who, according to prophecy, was an emanation of Vimalamitra. Putting aside all busyness and distraction, I diligently pursued my practice based on the maturing empowerments, liberating instructions, and advice concerning the entire Dzogchen approach of utter lucidity—the short path of trekchö [2.19a] and tögal—which this master imparted to me like one vase filling another. I gladdened my guru's heart with my offering of spiritual practice.

On the fifteenth day of the fifth Tibetan month in the Female Iron Hare year,[38] when I was twenty-five, motivated by my own experiences and the guru's prophecies, I set out for Dergé. I visited the following monasteries and centers: Dzogchen Rudam Orgyen Samten Chöling, Dzogchen Gyarong

Takten Drupdé retreat center, Zhechen Tennyi Dargyé Ling, and Dzongsar Tashi Lhatsé. In these places, I studied with the lord guru Jamyang Khyentsé Chökyi Lodrö; Namtrul Drodul Gargyi Dorjé of Gyarong; Kongtrul Pema Drimé Lekpai Lodrö of Zhechen Monastery; the sixth Dzogchen, Jigdral Jangchub Dorjé; Khenpo Tupten Nyendrak of Dzogchen Monastery; and my tutor, Khen Gönpo. They conferred on me many maturing empowerments and liberating instructions, including those of the kama transmissions of the Nyingma school, *The Treasury of Precious Hidden Teachings,* the three cycles (those focusing on the Eight Commands, *The United Intent of the Gurus,* and Vajrakila), the earlier and later cycles of the Nyingtik teachings, *The Drop of Freedom,* the terma cycles of Mindroling, the Northern Terma cycles, *The Treasury of Mantra of the Kagyü School,* [2.19b] the three deities (Guhyasamaja, Chakrasamvara, and Vajrabhairava), and the extensive empowerment for Kalachakra. In addition, I commissioned a life-sized statue of Guru Rinpoché, as well as statues, each a hand's span tall, of the entire lineage of gurus of the earlier and later Nyingtik cycles, all finished in gold and copper. I also commissioned the printing of texts for the tantra tradition of Vajrakila; the nine volumes of Jigmé Lingpa's collected works; the texts of the Kangyur; the sections of teachings found in the kama transmissions; the collected works of Gyalsé Zhenpen Tayé, of Rongzom Chökyi Zangpo, and of Dzogchen Paltrul; *The Five Great Treasuries* (including *The Treasury of Precious Hidden Teachings*); the collected works of Jamyang Khyentsei Wangpo; and other works.

During my twenty-ninth year (that of the Female Wood Sheep),[39] on the twenty-fifth day of the ninth month, I returned to my own monastery. There I commissioned my own center's set of woodblocks for Longchenpa's *Seven Treasuries.* To house the representations of enlightened form, speech, and mind that I had brought back, I commissioned a marvelous hall designed in the Chinese fashion, built by Chinese artisans. Within a very short time, [2.20a] I brought to bear all that I had learned on my spiritual projects, which took most of my time. Now and then, I was called on to fulfill the needs of the general monastic community; this also brought a greater sense of purpose to my life. These circumstances inspired me to offer the empowerments and oral transmissions for *The United Intent of the Gurus,* the thirteen sections of the kama transmissions, and the complete range of empowerments for *The Precious Treasury of Hidden Teachings* and to sponsor the concluding ganachakra. All of this ended on an excellent note on the tenth day of the Monkey month in the Fire Monkey year,[40] accompanied by excellent positive signs.

Around this time, the Chinese Communists began to foment unrest and discontent among all of the region's inhabitants, so that things were very unsettled. On the one hand, these negative circumstances encouraged me to pursue virtuous activities. I yearned to go once again on a pilgrimage to central and southern Tibet. Many tulkus, tertöns who had received prophecies from Guru Padma, warned of what the Guru foretold: "Hordes of Mongol border tribes[41] will soon encroach, so all of my students and patrons should leave behind everything they are attached to and flee to the southern reaches of Bhutan [2.20b] and the hidden valleys." I myself received several such prophecies, and though I wasn't sure if they had any significance or were just my hunches, I nevertheless decided to heed their warning. I put aside every thought of my country, my monastery, and my monks, knowing that it is in the nature of things that all coming together leads to parting.

In that same Male Fire Monkey year, I left Panchen Monastery in Mar under the cover of darkness. Traveling south, we crossed over passes and through valleys without following a road. At Kardzé in Hor, the local people gave us an automobile to use, and so, traveling through Chamdo in eastern Tibet, we were able to reach Lhasa. We made offerings at the three principal statues of the lord Buddha and other sites. Due to a collective lack of merit affecting the teachings and beings, my attendant, Kyala Khen Rinpoché, passed away, which caused me great sadness. To fulfill that holy being's intentions, I made offerings and prayers of aspiration in Lhasa and sponsored meals for those gathered at the large festival in the second month. With such acts of service, I attempted to add another drop to the ocean.

As relations between China and Tibet [2.21a] worsened daily, I traveled to the great center of Tashilhunpo in the region of Tsang and on through Pakri and Dromo Sahsi to Natö. On the nineteenth day of the eighth month in the Female Fire Bird year (Saturday, October 12, 1957), I arrived in Gangtok, Sikkim, at eleven o'clock in the morning. Later, during the winter of the Earth Pig year,[42] at the age of thirty-three, I went on a pilgrimage to holy sites, including Kalimpong, Calcutta, Bodh Gaya, Shitavana, Nairanjana, Vaishali, the stupa of Namdakdrung, Vulture Peak, Rajgir, Kashyapa Cave, Nalanda, Varanasi, the lotus lake at Rewalsar, Amritsar, Shravasti, Lumbini, and Kushinagar. I then proceeded to Kathmandu, the capital of Nepal, where I visited the stupas of Jarung Khashor, Sa-lhak Do-lhak, Takmo Lüjin, and Pakpa Shingkun,[43] as well as Lang-ri Lungten, Akhang Ukhung, the thousand buddha statues of Yerang, Bötang Gönpo, the speaking image of Tara, [2.21b] the birth water of Varahi, Yangleshö, and Asura Cave. I also saw the great, powerful lord of Gulang, the caves in which Tilopa and Naropa attained siddhis, the text of *The Perfection of Sublime Knowing in One Hundred Thousand Verses* that the exalted Nagarjuna brought back from the underworld of the nagas, the stupa housing the remains of Shariputra, Kadru Shambu, Sang-gyé Doda, the tomb of the buddha Kashyapa (who preceded Shakyamuni), the tomb of the master Vasubandhu, the thrones of the seven successors to the Buddha, the throne of Mañjushri, Vulture Peak, the É hall, and the stupa of King Ashoka. At all of these places, I offered prostrations, circumambulations, prayers, and aspirations. Then I completed the circuit by returning to Kalimpong.

The altruistic motivation of three figures of the past—the abbot Shantarakshita, the master Padmakara, and the Buddhist king Trisong Detsen—as well as that of the twenty-five intimate students of Guru Rinpoché (the king and his students), who were emanations, and the great tertön Rigdzin Gökyi Demtruchen, had great, far-reaching consequences. On the first day of the eleventh month in the Male Fire Dog year (the twentieth year of the eleventh sexagesimal cycle),[44] the victorious one Lhatsün Namkha Jigmé, Ngadak Sempa Chenpo, and the ruler, the Buddhist king Puntsok Namgyal, all gathered at the spacious site of Khachö Palmo [2.22a] in the hidden region of Sikkim (which lies at the very core of the pinnacle pure realm) to acknowledge this land as sacred. They performed a lhasang, a fire ceremony, a ritual ablution, and a ganachakra and bound the gods of the region to oaths. On that occasion, the master Padmakara, wreathed in rays of rainbow light, appeared to everyone gathered there.

In later times, at least some of Padmakara's blessings ripened according to his testament—that is, the aspirations he entrusted to the king and his subjects and to all who upheld his lineage. The altruistic motivation of King Tashi Namgyal, an emanation of a bodhisattva, and the great Buddhist king Palden Döndrup Namgyal has now found expression like a newly risen moon, bringing benefit to the teachings and to beings. In addition, their vision has provided opportunities for research into their country's spiritual history. I myself am as stupid and ignorant as an animal, without the slightest insight [2.22b] into either spiritual or secular matters. Although I lack the good fortune to serve the teachings or beings, the opportunity to establish auspicious interdependence nevertheless presented itself in a timely way. I received a command from the kings, which I could not under any circumstances refuse, and so in my thirty-fourth year—on the first day of the third month in the Male Iron Rat year of the sixteenth sexagesimal cycle (April 26, 1960)—I accepted the responsibility of acting as a nonsectarian leader and adviser of all students. I endeavored to meet the challenge of restoring the precious teachings of the Victorious One where they had waned and promulgating them where they had not. My work began with the Namgyal Institute of Tibetology, emphasizing research into a vast range of mandalas of the kama and terma teachings.

In addition, on four separate occasions, I gave to different groups the oral transmissions for *The Seven Treasuries,* which are treatises of pith instructions—termas of enlightened intent, [2.23a] flowing from the glorious throat of the noble Longchen Rabjam, that yogin of the sublime spiritual approach, in the form of vajra verses. I arranged for new offset editions of Longchenpa's *Three Cycles of Being at Ease* and *Three Cycles of Natural Freedom,* in addition to *The Seven Treasuries.* I was blessed by the timeless awareness embodiment of that powerful lord of victorious ones, and the supreme dynamic energy of his enlightened intent—the lineage of ultimate meaning—entered my heart. I was thus inspired, in these times of spiritual degeneration, to fan the embers of the teachings into flames. Twice I conferred the transmissions of the maturing empowerments and liberating instructions for *The Heart Drop of Longchenpa* (also entitled *The Spiritual Teachings from the Treasury of Space*); this terma of enlightened intent was revealed by Rigdzin Jigmé Lingpa, who was a second Garab Dorjé and was known as Dzogchenpa Rangjung Dorjé. I also published the volumes of this cycle. I conferred the empowerments and oral transmissions for the classes of tantras found in the kama transmissions, the Tromtruk cycle of the peaceful and wrathful deities, the peaceful and wrathful mandalas of that most majestic of tantras *The Heart Essence of Secrets, The Gathering of the Great Assembly,* and other cycles.

In brief, in that all of one's activities reflect the positive or negative aspects of one's motivation, I have tried to arouse in myself a sense of disenchantment with whatever has no true purpose, a sense of renunciation and a certainty of my release from samsara, compassion toward beings, [2.23b] and completely pure, altruistic motivation. Since there is no point in reinforcing self-centered attitudes, like the desire for greatness or personal aggrandizement, I have used every means at my disposal, through spiritual projects and activities conducted according to the principles of the dharma, to ensure continuous benefit and happiness for my students without sectarian bias and commensurate with their own good fortune. As I write this, in the Female Wood Hare year (1975), I am forty-nine and have spent the past fifteen years in exile, serving the teachings in as pleasing a way as I could. May everything be successful!

In the years since Dodrupchen Rinpoché Jigmé Trinlé Palbar wrote the foregoing personal account, he has founded a center in Sikkim housing some five hundred inhabitants; it includes a shedra and a retreat center. He has visited many countries in the Eastern and Western Hemispheres, including Bhutan, the United States, and Great Britain, where he has turned the wheel of the dharma, bestowing the kama transmissions, *The Treasury of Precious Hidden Teachings,* the cycles of Pema Lingpa's teachings, *The Seven Treasuries, The Four Higher Collections of the Heart Drop,* the six volumes of Jatsön Nyingpo's teachings, the source volumes of *The Heart Drop of Longchenpa,* and other teachings. He has also presided over drupchens focusing on such cycles as the "tantra tradition" of Vajrakila.[45] He still sits on his vajra throne, his form blazing with the splendor of the major and minor marks of perfection, [2.24a] and I pray that he lives for a hundred eons.

This concludes my discussion of the lineage of the Dodrupchen incarnations. If we consider the ultimate lineage of pith instructions from the standpoint of this lineage, the gurus of Dodrup Tenpai Nyima were Jamyang Khyentsei Wangpo and Paltrul Rinpoché. The gurus of the fourth incarnation were Jamyang Khyentsé Chökyi Lodrö, Yukhok Jadralwa, and Khenpo Kunzang Palden. And so this particular lineage derives from those of Paltrul Rinpoché and of Jamyang Khyentsei Wangpo.

THE LINEAGE OF THE FIRST DODRUPCHEN'S STUDENTS

As for the lineage of the first Dodrupchen's students, this can be considered to have two aspects: that of students who were also students of both Paltrul and Khyentsé and that of students specifically of the first Dodrupchen. [2.24b]

The Extraordinary Lineage of the First Dodrupchen

Let us first examine the lineage deriving from the first Dodrupchen, Jigmé Trinlé Özer. It was from this holy guru that Chögyal Ngagi Wangpo heard the teachings.

Chögyal Ngagi Wangpo (1736–1807)

Chögyal Ngagi Wangpo, also known as King Wam, was a mighty ruler of Urga in Mongolia. From an early age, he demonstrated the potential for attaining enlightenment and took delight in everything spiritual. He received numerous profound teachings from many gurus in his own region and trained his mind in many Gelukpa teachings, such as *The Great Graduated Path to Enlightenment.* It is said that although he remained on the throne, he was without arrogance or vanity and knew how to rely on mentors, for he followed the role model of Manibhadra.[46]

Having heard of the deeds of the renowned Dodrup Trinlé Özer, Chögyal Ngagi Wangpo realized that he had a karmic connection with that master. He accepted him as his main teacher, and his faith caused the hair on his body to stand on end. He received from him all of the tantras, explanatory commentaries, and pith instructions of the secret Nyingtik teachings of utter lucidity. He put these teachings into practice, and realization arose in him. He became a holder of the ultimate lineage and was renowned as Chögyal Ngagi Wangpoi Dé.

He cared for countless fortunate students, combining the graduated path of mental training from the Kadampa and Gelukpa schools [2.25a] with that of the tantric approach of the secret Nyingtik teachings. He founded a huge encampment with hundreds of residents and cared for his students in Mongolia proper.

Chögyal Ngagi Wangpo traveled to Lhasa in central Tibet, where he paid homage and made offerings to the three major monasteries and the statues of the lord Buddha. On his journey, he met with Dechen Gyalpo,[47] the great tertön from the southern region of Tsang. The tertön praised Chögyal Ngagi Wangpo as one who had been prophesied by Guru Rinpoché and conferred on him one of his own termas based on the sadhana of Hayagriva and Vajravarahi, *The Wish-Fulfilling Gem.* The tertön gave teachings on the graduated path found in the instructions of that terma and, in particular, imparted to Chögyal Ngagi Wangpo extensive and extraordinary teachings on the Dzogchen practices of trekchö and tögal. Chögyal Ngagi Wangpo practiced these in secrecy and developed countless qualities indicating success in his practice. In response to the request of Tsokdruk Rangdrol, he wrote *Dispelling the Darkness of Ignorance,* a manual for this sadhana. Guru Rinpoché had prophesied to Dechen Gyalpo that this lineage would be handed down to one student at a time for three generations, and it was this that Zhabkar Tsokdruk Rangdrol later promulgated.

Chögyal Ngagi Wangpo thus lived for a long time as a protector of the teachings and of beings. [2.25b] Finally, at a certain point, his emanated form resolved back into the palace of Pema Ö on Zangdok Palri.

It was from this great Buddhist king that Zhabkar Tsokdruk Rangdrol received the tantras of the sublime secret.

Zhabkar Tsokdruk Rangdrol (1781–1851)

Zhabkar Tsokdruk Rangdrol was born amid innumerable marvelous signs in a palace called Repkong Olka in Amdo, eastern Tibet. From an early age, faith and renunciation were part of his nature. His uncle and other relatives were lay tantric practitioners who encouraged him to take the householder life as his ideal, but he simply would not listen. Like a wild animal released from a trap, he rejected all ties to worldly life and took monastic ordination from faith-inspiring members of the sangha, [2.26a] including Arik Geshé Jampal Gelek Gyaltsen. Although he adopted the ways of a fully ordained monk, he continued to wear white robes and grow his hair long.

He relied on gurus such as Jamyang Gyatso, enrolling in the intermediate course of studies at Ladrang Tashichil.[48] There he received profound teachings from Rabjampa Chödar and many other mentors; he also decided to seek profound advice that would enable him to awaken to buddhahood in that very lifetime. Lama Gyal Khenchen of Tashichil told Zhabkar Tsokdruk Rangdrol of the teachings that Chögyal Ngagi Wangpo gave. Accordingly, Zhabkar journeyed to Urga in Mongolia to seek an audience with this great Buddhist king, who dwelled there with his court like the moon surrounded by a garland of stars. He begged the master to take him under his care. The master, greatly delighted, agreed to do so.

Chögyal Ngagi Wangpo said, "First you must train your mind," and he presented Zhabkar with a copy of Tsongkhapa's treatise *The Great Graduated Path to Enlightenment,* with which to undertake his training. [2.26b] Zhabkar applied this teaching to his experience just as his guru intended and received from him all the advice of the secret Nyingtik teachings of the Dzogchen approach, which Chögyal Ngagi Wangpo had received from Jigmé Trinlé Özer, beginning with the preliminary stages of the path. Zhabkar practiced according to the instructions on trekchö and tögal, and progressed in his meditative experiences and realization, becoming a master of the teachings. Chögyal Ngagi Wangpo also conferred on Zhabkar *The Wish-Fulfilling Gem,* the cycle of Hayagriva and Vajravarahi revealed by Terchen Dechen Gyalpo, which Chögyal Ngagi Wangpo held as a one-to-one transmission.[49] During the empowerment, Zhabkar's flower fell to the north, and he received the secret name Tsokdruk Rangdrol from his master, who prophesied that he would be the custodian of these teachings. Zhabkar then went to meet the seventh-generation descendant of Rigdzin Duddul Dorjé, from whom he received many empowerments and instructions of the secret mantra approach.

During this period, he generally had no fixed abode and few personal possessions and endured many privations. He returned to his home region in eastern Tibet in stages and then stayed for three years at Tsonying in the north, practicing Dzogchen. He frequented desolate places like the Anyé Machen range and Drakar Dzong, [2.27a] practicing in solitude. He remained alone, like a wild animal, a way of life described in the Dzogchen sources. He had countless meditative experiences and bound to oaths demons of broken samaya and other demons, beings who had taken such rebirth due to their extremely negative karma.[50]

About this time, Zhabkar's mother passed away, prompting him to return home, where he completed the funeral ceremonies of purifying and enshrining her bones. To fulfill her last wishes, he spent a long time in spiritual practice, delineating the gap between samsara and nirvana.[51] He directly experienced signs of success on the path, for he perceived that sensory appearances, and his own mind, lacked any true existence in their own right.

Zhabkar Tsokdruk Rangdrol then took as his inspiration the lives of past holy masters, coming to a firm decision to wander about with no fixed dwelling place. He journeyed to central Tibet, where he made offerings, prayers, and circumambulations at many holy sites, such as the statues of the lord Buddha in Lhasa. He also traveled to the most majestic places where Guru Rinpoché had attained siddhis, sites such as Sheldrak in Yarlung and Samyé, and continued on to the southern reaches. He planted the victory banner of his spiritual practice at lakes, cliffs, glaciers, and mountain ridges and at places like the ravines surrounding the important holy site of Tsari. [2.27b] He eschewed offerings made by the living or on behalf of the deceased and gave up all activity, so that he became renowned throughout the region as Jadral Tsokdruk Rangdrol. Then, in places where lord Milarepa had attained siddhis—Mount Kailash, Lake Manasarovar, the cave of Drakar Taso Puk—and other glaciers, cliffs, and lakes, he meditated and brought to completion his meditative experience and realization of the great perfection of utter lucidity. He composed numerous treatises that clearly set forth the key points of the Dzogchen approach, works such as *The Emanated Scripture of Marvels, The Emanated Scripture of Orgyen, The Emanated Scripture of Pure Visions,* the teaching manual *The Flight of the Garuda,* and his extensive autobiography.[52]

Turning the wheel of the dharma, Zhabkar Tsokdruk Rangdrol taught hundreds of thousands of students who gathered from all directions. Gradually he made his way through Purang and the three districts of the western Tibetan region of Ngari, through Kyirong and down into Nepal, where he offered prostrations and made extensive offerings at the three main stupas and contributed greatly to the restoration of Boudhanath. He then returned to the western regions in upper Tibet, where he stayed for many years, caring for his students. Finally, a party of many people from eastern Tibet approached Zhabkar [2.28a] and invited him there. For the sake of those to be guided in the eastern regions, he journeyed through central Tibet to Golok and other areas in the northern part of eastern Tibet, where he benefited an incalculable number of students. He turned the wheel of the dharma and conducted rituals, including those for the accumulation of a hundred million repetitions of the mantras *Om mani padme hum* and *Om ah hum vajra guru padma siddhi hum.* Zhabkar brought all who saw or heard him onto the path to liberation. He traveled with hundreds of students in his retinue, a veritable monastic tent city, eventually returning to his home region.

This lord had his heart set on pursuing spiritual practice entirely on his own. Simhamukha, the Lion-Headed Dakini of timeless awareness, prophesied to him that if he practiced in solitude, he would attain rainbow body, while if he guided students, he would ensure that the teachings flourished. He had only the altruistic intention to benefit others, and so he decided to care for his students. He traveled to such centers in eastern Tibet as Ladrang Tashichil and Repkong, guiding students and bringing many tens of thousands of people onto the path to liberation.

Among his countless students from all over Tibet, Pema Rangdrol from the lowlands of eastern Tibet and others were primarily responsible for guiding students in that eastern region. [2.28b] Kyabgön Pema Gyatso benefited beings in the three districts of Ngari in upper Tibet, as well as in the central regions. They all caused the teachings that focus on the heart essence to flourish. Zhabkar Tsokdruk Rangdrol having finished his mission, the mandala of his emanated form resolved back into the pure realm of Chamara.

It was from this holy guru that Kyabgön Pema Gyatso received the entire range of pith instructions concerning the sublime secret.

Kyabgön Pema Gyatso (19th Century)

Kyabgön Pema Gyatso reached the very pinnacle of both erudition and spiritual accomplishment. From an early age, he was moved by renunciation and followed the advice of numerous mentors [2.29a] from all over the upper and lower regions of Tibet. Having put their teachings into practice and trained his mind, Pema Gyatso thought, "Now I must seek a mentor who has realized the key points of the extraordinary Dzogchen approach." He had heard of the renowned lord Paltrul Rinpoché, but felt that eastern Tibet was too far away.

He had also heard of one named Zhabkar Tsokdruk Rangdrol, reputed to be a great yogin of Dzogchen in the lineage of the first Dodrupchen's students and foremost among itinerant masters, a great being comparable to the lord Milarepa. A karmic connection established in a former lifetime awakened in Pema Gyatso when he first heard of this master, and unshakable faith and devotion arose in him. He knew that he must meet him and so gradually made his way to his encampment. Upon meeting Zhabkar Tsokdruk Rangdrol, he received such profound blessings that he experienced true freedom.

For a long time thereafter, Pema Gyatso followed his guru wherever he went and was lovingly cared for. The master imparted to him experiential instructions, emphasizing the works of the Omniscient One Longchenpa and his spiritual heir, Jigmé Lingpa (such as the Dzogchen manual *Timeless Awareness as the Guiding Principle*). Pema Gyatso attained extraordinary realization and directly experienced the enlightened intent that is the true nature of phenomena, free of intellectual speculation. [2.29b] He studied innumerable spiritual methods, including those of *Hayagriva and Vajravarahi: The Wish-Fulfilling Gem* (a terma that had been recently revealed by Dechen Gyalpo, a tertön from Tsang), as well as Chögyal Ngagi Wangpo's work *Dispelling the Darkness of Ignorance* (the teaching manual for this cycle) and Tsokdruk Rangdrol's Dzogchen treatise, *The Flight of the Garuda*. Following his guru's intent and conduct, Pema Gyatso avoided formal avocations such as that of a monk.

Casting aside all concerns for this life as he would a mass of phlegm, he made a vow to spend his life as a renunciant uninvolved in ordinary activity. He applied himself to the very essence of spiritual practice, and his accomplishment was so impeccable that he became a student in the inner sense, one whom his guru held in his enlightened mind. Thus he became a lineage holder. The master appointed him head teacher of his encampment and, when he returned to eastern Tibet, left Pema Gyatso in charge of caring for his students.

After his guru had departed, Pema Gyatso led the encampment, consisting of hundreds of students, to all the places in upper Tibet where the lord Milarepa and his own guru had attained siddhis, including Mount Kailash, Lake Manasarovar, Kyirong, Ngari, Purang, Nupri, and other important holy sites, glaciers, and lakes. Maintaining his own uninterrupted daily schedule of four practice sessions, [2.30a] he bestowed the secret Nyingtik teachings and became renowned throughout the region as "Kyabgön Pema Gyatso, the regent of his lord guru." Countless fortunate students gathered around him. In that region of Ngari in upper Tibet, the enormous extent of his activities equaled that of his lord guru, and he became a master of the Nyingtik teachings.

Only in the later part of his life did Pema Gyatso journey to central Tibet to meet with Tekchok Tenpai Gyaltsen,[53] the rebirth of his guru, Zhabkar Rinpoché. While there, Pema Gyatso went on a pilgrimage to the principal holy sites of Lhasa and the central and southern regions and pursued spiritual practice in these places. He met with the precious tulku, with whom he exchanged many profound teachings. Pema Gyatso also exchanged profound teachings with the Chö master Dharma Seng-gé, whom he accompanied to holy sites and places of accomplishment, which they infused with blessings. During this time, Pema Gyatso cared for many students in central Tibet.

Finally, he entrusted his lineage to Rigdzin Chönyi Zangmo, foremost among all of his students. His work was thus completed, and Pema Gyatso's enlightened intent resolved back into primordial basic space, the supreme inner basic space of peace. His followers were moved to faith by the untold marvelous [2.30b] signs of his pure qualities that attended his passing, and his students saw to his funeral ceremonies and the construction of his tomb.

It was from this guru that the dakini Chönyi Zangmo heard the secret pith instructions without omission.

Dakki Chönyi Zangmo (Shuksep Jetsünma Mani Lochen) (1865–1953)

Chönyi Zangmo was born in the village of Manda, birthplace of the divine consort Mandarava, near the banks of Tso Pemachen (Rewalsar), a lake that is an important holy site in the region of Sahora in western India. Her birth took place at sunrise on the fifteenth day of the month, accompanied by the natural sound of the mantra *Om*

mani padme hum, a shower of blossoms, and a canopy of swirling rainbow light. At the same time, a servant girl named Pemakyi gave birth to a daughter, [2.31a] a ewe to a single lamb, and a bitch to a single puppy. Chönyi Zangmo's umbilical cord was wrapped around her body like a meditation belt. She moved her hands as though playing a bell and drum, sat with her legs half-crossed, and gazed into the sky without blinking her eyes. She uttered "A" and "Om mani padme hum," and her body was marked with white and red moles. The roof of her house was wreathed in swirling rainbow light. Many other such positive omens, too many to recount, marked her birth. Everyone in the encampment was amazed, and each person gave her a name. One called her Cho-ngamo, another Paldzommo, and her own father named her Sönam Drönma. She grew more in her first month than other babies did in their first year, and after a year she knew how to read and write without difficulty. She continually chanted the mantra *Om mani padme hum,* and any activity she engaged in was in keeping with the dharma. At times, she would sing of her experiences, but she seemed such a humble child that no one paid her any respect. [2.31b]

Her family was poor and barely able to make ends meet. When she was just over a year old, her father, a degenerate who drank to excess, decided to sell his wife for two rupees and his daughter for one in order to buy some alcohol. To prevent him from incurring the karma of such an act, the mother decided to flee into the forest at once, taking her daughter on her back. Eventually they came back to the man, and the family set off wandering. After about a year, however, Chönyi Zangmo's father again tried to sell her in order to pay for a large amount of alcohol he had drunk. Distraught and weeping, the mother once more took the child on her back and fled, this time in the direction of Piti in India. Along the way, they came to a great river, not far from which the mother found a sword lying in the road. Still carrying her daughter on her back, she cried out, "If my daughter is a dakini who can benefit the teachings and beings, let us be saved from the current; if not, let us die instantly!" Taking the sword in hand, she closed her eyes and leaped without hesitation into the middle of the river. As they were about to be swept along by the current, a woman appeared out of thin air, chanting "Ha Ri Ni Sa!" and grabbed the mother by the hand, pulling them both to safety. [2.32a] The woman then disappeared without a trace. Witnesses said that she vanished into the sky.

After some time had passed, they returned home once more. When Chönyi Zangmo was about five, the father beat his wife in a drunken fit, saying, "As we have no possessions to divide between us, we should divide our daughter. Let's cut her in half! You take one half, and I'll take the other." He pulled a knife out of its sheath, but his daughter overheard him and ran away in terror, jumping into the middle of a briar patch. Crouching there, she heard the pleasing sound of many people talking. She followed the voices and had the impression that she had arrived in a lovely pure realm. She spent some seven days in this visionary state.

When she regained her senses, she went home. Many of her playmates came to greet her, some setting up a throne, some preparing a seat, some pretending to play kanglings and gyalings. As they played, they chanted the mantra *Om mani padme hum*. Her parents were amazed by this, and tears came to their eyes, while the neighbors observed, "She truly is a dakini." [2.32b]

Upon hearing the news, hundreds, even thousands, came to see Chönyi Zangmo. A throne was built, and people begged her to lead them in chanting the *mani* mantra. Because she was still so small, however, not all of them could see her. She stood up and, taking a long staff in her hands, raised herself up even further. She chanted the *mani* mantra and encouraged them to practice virtue. Everyone was affected, some feeling a sense of renunciation, others regretting the conflicts they had had with their spouses, and others thinking of impermanence. Some grieved for their dead parents; others were so moved by the beauty of her voice that they wept, and faith caused the hair on their bodies to stand on end. It was rumored that a true dakini of timeless awareness had appeared. This inspired many people in the area, rulers and subjects, to practice the dharma.

Once, Chönyi Zangmo's father, still an incorrigible drunk, borrowed a handful of silver from a rich householder. To pay off his debt, he sold his young daughter to his creditor, obliging her to be a servant for six years. But her mother couldn't bear it and one night a few days later waited in hiding [2.33a] outside the rich man's house. When her daughter came out to give bones and food to the dogs, the mother quickly seized her by the hand, lifted her onto her back, and fled. On the road, they had no food, so in one village the mother sold the small piece of turquoise she wore around her neck and bought some chilies and peppers. They were forced to eat a stew made solely from bamboo shoots that they dug up and cooked, flavoring them with the spices and with oil they pressed from berries taken from the scat of bears.

They gradually made their way through the hill country, where Chönyi Zangmo encouraged many people, scattered among the hills like ants, to practice virtue and chant the *mani* mantra. They passed through Garzha, Puti, Nyungti, Khunu, and other areas, journeying toward Ladakh. In her sixth year, thousands of people gathered as Chönyi Zangmo chanted the *mani* mantra and spoke of practicing virtue and avoiding harmful actions. She sang to them:

> All of you fortunate men and women gathered here,
> pray to the deity, the exalted, sublime bodhisattva of supreme
>   compassion,
> and meditate with devotion again and again [2.33b]

on all forms as those of the bodhisattva of supreme compassion.
Think of all sounds as those of *Om mani padme hum.*
Know that all mental activity is the emptiness of awakened mind.
Rest without contrivance in unconditional love and compassion.
In conclusion, dedicate the virtue to all beings.
May there be the auspiciousness of the protector who is victorious
throughout the three times.
All of you faithful men and women gathered here,
I sing you this song with my pleasing voice
so that your minds will be inspired by a connection with the dharma.
Om mani padme hum!
All of you fortunate ones, this song that overwhelms the world of
appearances and possibilities
with its splendor was sung sweetly and melodiously.
In general, it was the melody sung by the great translator of yore.
In particular, it was the melody of Ratnabhadra.
Most particularly, it was the song sung by me, the beggar girl.
Since there is no impediment to enlightened speech,
I humbly ask that you chant these syllables clearly.

As she thus inspired them with the power of her small yet lovely form, her sweet voice, and her motivation of bodhichitta, Chönyi Zangmo gave these people great impetus to practice virtue. Many wept with faith, and some vowed to recite the mantra a hundred million times. [2.34a] A report of this incident reached a king named Ram in western India. He was amazed and moved to faith, and requested that the girl instruct him in reciting the *mani* mantra. Chönyi Zangmo inspired everyone in that area to engage in virtuous activities.

At about this time, a thief was killed in a large crowd, and the murderer was being sought. Chönyi Zangmo's father, who was drunk, confessed to the crime. Everyone then set upon him and tied him up with rope. According to local custom, the crime was punishable by "hog slaughtering": the father's arms and legs would be cut off, and he would be thrown alive into a charnel ground. Everyone agreed on his fate, convinced that punishment was unavoidable, but his noble daughter spent an entire night weeping and praying fervently to the deity Avalokiteshvara. People asked, "How could a daughter who is like a deity have a father who is like a demon? And how can we kill the father of a girl from whom we have received such teachings? Let him go free." And so Chönyi Zangmo's old father was released. [2.34b] She thus inspired many in that region—hundreds, thousands, tens of thousands—to be virtuous.

She then traveled in stages to Ladakh, where she met her first guru, Lama Tashi

Namgyal, the king's spiritual adviser. With him Chönyi Zangmo studied the biographies of several *deloks*, practitioners who had died and then returned from the realm of the dead:[54] Adruk of eastern Tibet, King Yulha, and Lekpai Döndrup. She sponsored the printing of texts, as well as portraits of these deloks. She was given the title "Mani Lochen," which in the local dialect signified "She Who Inspires Others to Chant the *Mani* Mantra," and became famous as such. She traveled through areas like Gar and Purang in the western region of Ngari in upper Tibet and throughout the upper and lower regions of the northern reaches of eastern Tibet, wandering while recounting the experiences of deloks and inspiring people to chant the *mani* mantra. Chönyi Zangmo then journeyed to central and southern Tibet, all the while establishing in tens of thousands of students, both human and nonhuman, virtuous habits that lead one along the path to liberation.

When she was thirteen, she went on a pilgrimage back to Tso Rewalsar in western India, bringing benefit to beings through the *mani* mantra. There Chönyi Zangmo met a nun named Lobzang, the niece of Pema Gyatso. Ani Lobzang related her uncle's life story, explaining that he had been [2.35a] a student of Zhabkar, his lord of refuge, and now resided at the cliff known as Okar Drak in the Kyirong area. Having heard all of these details, Chönyi Zangmo became convinced that Pema Gyatso had been her guru in past lifetimes. Simply hearing his name brought tears to her eyes, and her faith made the hair on her body stand on end. She thought, "I absolutely must meet him." Like a wild animal freed from a snare, she set out with her mother from Tso Rewalsar, traveling on foot through the hill country, over passes, through valleys, crossing mountains and rivers with difficulty, and arriving at last at Okar Drak in Kyirong. There the guru, dressed in rags, secretly lived, along with two other white-clad tantric practitioners who occupied caves on either side of his own. They dwelled in solitude surrounded by white prayer flags and bamboo groves inhabited by many species of monkeys and birds, on the very summit of Okar Drak as it touched the sky. Chönyi Zangmo was aware of the need to create the proper interdependent circumstances before approaching the guru, and so when she went to see Pema Gyatso she bore an offering of fruit and a vase filled with milk. Although he had foreknowledge of her visit, the master pretended not to know her, [2.35b] stared, and asked, "Who are you? Where are you going, and for what reason?"

As soon as Chönyi Zangmo heard Pema Gyatso's voice and saw his face, her ordinary perceptions ceased. She thought to herself, "Now I have met a true buddha. My life has real purpose." Feeling like a child who has found her father at last, she dropped to both knees and folded her hands. She sang to the master, "I have come from Rewalsar in India. I have come seeking a guru who is a buddha, for I wish to make this life truly meaningful by practicing the extensive teachings of natural great perfection. Please take me under your care." Having heard her request, the guru answered:

My girl, a noble name and lovely form
usher in both enemies and demons.
If you wish to practice the divine dharma with complete purity,
you must do so for a long time
with faith, renunciation, and disenchantment with the world.

He gave her much kind advice such as this, and from then on her former problems no longer troubled her. She had found the sacred dharma [2.36a] and encountered an authentic guru. She began to feel happy.

She then followed her precious guru wherever he went, and he taught her the path, from the preliminary stages up to the final instructions on trekchö and tögal. She requested many profound teachings difficult to find even if one were to fill the world with gold and offer it, such teachings as the Dzogchen manual *Timeless Awareness as the Guiding Principle, The Flight of the Garuda,* and the three texts entitled *The Emanated Scriptures.* Undergoing hardship, she practiced with intense courage, and innumerable qualities that arise on the spiritual path became evident in her. She grasped the very root of the lineage, experiencing direct realization of the true nature of phenomena based on the lineage of mind-to-mind transmission of natural great perfection. Chönyi Zangmo became a holder of the ultimate lineage.

With a specific purpose in mind, her guru would feign anger, scolding and beating this noble girl. One day he said, "To ransom my life force, go away to some border region, some hot place with deep ravines full of thorn bushes." Although he banished her to a site far away for three years and caused her much mental anguish, she trusted him, [2.36b] regarding him with faith as a real buddha, in the same way that Marpa, Milarepa, and the bodhisattva Manibhadra, as described in their life stories, had maintained their faith and trust in their gurus.

She was ordained as a nun by Ngawang Tenpai Nyima. She received the oral lineage of the teachings of the Taklung school from Matrul Rinpoché. Dzogchen Tupten Chökyi Dorjé conferred on her the extraordinary key points of the Nyingtik teachings, such as the empowerment into the dynamic energy of awareness from *Timeless Awareness as the Guiding Principle.* From Semnyi Tokden, she received the lineage of experiential teaching transmitted by Paltrul Rinpoché, including instructions on the practice of tögal in the Dzogchen approach. And Khenpo Rigdzin Zangpo taught her the explanatory commentary on *The Treasury of Enlightened Qualities,* along with the oral tradition of Paltrul Rinpoché.

From Chönyön Dharma Seng-gé, she received more than a hundred empowerments and extraordinary experiential teachings, profound instructions on Chö. Chönyi Zangmo frequented haunted places—a hundred springs, a hundred charnel grounds, and so forth—and said of herself, "I, the yogini who engages in the uncontrived conduct of fearlessness, moves in the measured tread of the dance that extends evenly throughout samsara and nirvana." She maintained the conduct of a siddha, instantly vanquishing the four maras with the supreme, uncontrived conduct of equal taste that is specific to the teachings on the profound Dükyi Chöyul, the extraordinary intent and conduct of Machik Lapdrön herself. [2.37a] She considered this lord Dharma Seng-gé and Pema Gyatso to be her two most extraordinary gurus.

She also received countless profound teachings from many other mentors. She did not stop at merely hearing these teachings or understanding them intellectually, but put them into practice one-pointedly, gaining realization and mastery of meditative experiences just as described in the tantras and other source texts. While Chönyi Zangmo was in retreat at Zang-ri Kharmar, the seat of Machik Lapdrön, she walked across a huge river without hindrance. While staying at Gang-ri Tökar, she traveled instantaneously to Lhasa, and her body passed right through solid cliff faces. During that time, Chönyi Zangmo also traveled instantaneously to the Karmapa's encampment in Tsurpu.[55] She constantly performed such miracles. While she was receiving tögal teachings from Longchen Özer, a guru from eastern Tibet, Chönyi Zangmo would stay in the retreat center by day, focusing on the visions of utter lucidity; by night, [2.37b] however, she would engage in uncontrived conduct in all the charnel grounds of the region, joining a host of a hundred thousand dakinis of timeless awareness. Her ordinary perceptions were cleared away so that she no longer had any fixed reference point, and she sang vajra songs like the following:

> My perceptions are spacious, without any fixed reference point.
> A beggar girl whose awareness is unobstructed,
> I dance in the courtyard of the purity of whatever arises,
> stamping out the measured tread of my dance
> on the heads of those who hold the eight worldly concerns to be supreme.
> I dance in the illusion of one taste.
> *Hum hum phat!*
> It is the concept of self that is to be cut through.
> It is the experience of the nonexistence of self, the freedom from conceit,
> that does the cutting.
> Dükyi Chöyul means cutting through the four maras.
> The result of Chö is the purity of subject, object, and their relationship.
> *Hum hum phat phat!*

She performed folk dances while singing such songs. On another occasion, she sang:

> I bow to the one named Padma,
> the sovereign lord of the hundred buddha families, the master of Chö,
> in whom all the lineages of the profound meaning of Dükyi Chöyul
> are united without exception.

Maintaining the uncontrived conduct of pure awareness, Chönyi Zangmo frequented the twenty-four holy gathering places[56] and Zangdok Palri. In waking consciousness, meditative experiences, lucid visions, and dreams, she journeyed to these realms without hindrance by various means of projecting and manipulating her perceptions. [2.38a] She passed through a vast array of pure realms, encountering all of the buddhas and bodhisattvas therein. At times, she had experiences comparable to those of deloks, going to impure realms such as the eighteen hells and drawing beings out of them. Or she miraculously journeyed to Sukhavati and countless other pure realms. She could transform her perceptions and conduct into a playful dance of illusion, bringing benefit as far-reaching as space itself to beings in pure and impure realms.

After the lord Pema Gyatso passed away, Chönyi Zangmo spent most of her time at Gang-ri Tökar, making it her main residence. There she founded the Shuksep Nunnery, an encampment of more than a thousand nuns, as well as innumerable lay and ordained practitioners, tulkus, khenpos, and teachers from all over eastern and central Tibet. For this gathering, she turned the wheel of the dharma, teaching the secret Nyingtik teachings of the Dzogchen approach developmentally, so that countless fortunate students attained sublime siddhis through the secret path of superb Atiyoga.

From Terchen Trulzhik Do-ngak Lingpa, Chönyi Zangmo received the transmissions of the teachings of the earlier and later incarnations of Trulzhik Dechen Lingpa [2.38b] and the experiential teaching of *Great Perfection: The Black Innermost Heart Drop* as revealed by Tertön Dungtso Repa. She practiced these and became a great holder of that lineage. It was she who passed on to Zhadeu Trulzhik Chenpo the lineage of the Nyingtik and Yangtik teachings of the Dzogchen approach, which still exist.

Chönyi Zangmo thus completed her tasks, and so her form resolved back into the ground from which her emanation had arisen, the expanse of Yeshé Tsogyal's enlightened mind, on Zangdok Palri in the realm of Chamara. Jigmé Dorjé Rinpoché, the rebirth of Semnyi Tokden, became the director of her seat at Shuksep.[57]

The Alternative Lineage of the First Dodrupchen

Trehorpa Kyabgön Yeshé Gyaltsen (18th–19th Centuries)

Another lineage of the first Dodrupchen was passed through Kyabgön Yeshé Gyaltsen of Trehor, who received teachings from Dodrupchen Rinpoché Trinlé Özer. Yeshé Gyaltsen was born near Kardzé in the Trehor area of eastern Tibet. In his youth, he was a householder, occupied with various worldly matters. Moreover, he was wild and a master merchant [2.39a] whom no one could best. One day, he assembled a caravan with a hundred pack animals loaded down with silk, tea, and more, and set

forth as the master merchant with many servants. Passing through a huge trading encampment in Golok, he and his party made their way through the northern reaches and down into China. They headed toward Xining, where they planned to conduct business, but on the road bandits overcame them, robbing them of everything, even their eating bowls, clothing, and bedrolls.

This left Yeshé Gyaltsen extremely disheartened by the things of this world. Setting his mind on the dharma, he went to see Dodrup Jigmé Trinlé Özer. [2.39b] In later years, he would say, "Those bandits were extremely kind; because of them, I found the dharma." He repeatedly said prayers of dedication on their behalf.

Over time, Dodrupchen Rinpoché bestowed on Yeshé Gyaltsen the cycles of the Dzogchen approach of the supreme secret in an experiential way, beginning with the preliminary practices and continuing through the stages of trekchö and tögal. His realization became fully evident. After lingering for a long time at his guru's encampment, Yeshé Gyaltsen obeyed the guru's instructions and returned to his home region, where he spent many years in solitary retreat at a remote site in the region of Hor. In time, he came to care for students and reached such a level of spiritual attainment that he became known as Kyabgön Yeshé Gyaltsen. He brought enormous benefit to the teachings and beings.

It was from this holy guru that Chönyön Dharma Seng-gé heard the tantras of the sublime secret.

Chönyön Dharma Seng-gé (19th Century)

Chönyön Dharma Seng-gé was born in a place close to Sertal in eastern Tibet. He enrolled in a number of monasteries in that region—Shukgang Monastery among others—and studied various teachings with numerous mentors. In particular, he received the profound instructions of the approach known as Dükyi Chöyul from a master called Gemang Chöpa, [2.40a] who had himself received the transmission of the Chö teachings.

He put these teachings into practice at more than a hundred springs and other holy sites, including charnel grounds. Dharma Seng-gé directly experienced the full measure of this tradition—the four ways in which one cuts directly through obstacles and so eliminates them—and he became a great holder of the Chö tradition, cutting through the four maras at their very root. He was renowned as Chönyön[58] Dharma Seng-gé.

His special guru, with whom he had had a karmic connection for lifetimes, was Kyabgön Yeshé Gyaltsen. Chönyön Dharma Seng-gé received from him the great experiential transmission of the secret Nyingtik teachings, reaching an advanced level of spiritual attainment. [2.40b] His guru directed him to benefit beings, and so he taught countless students. He traveled in stages to central Tibet, making his main seat Gang-ri Tökar, a place blessed by the fact that the Omniscient One Longchenpa had practiced there. There Chönyön Dharma Seng-gé cared for his students, conferring profound teachings—primarily the Chö and Nyingtik teachings—on innumerable students from eastern and central Tibet. He left many volumes of his works, and to this day specific lines of transmission, known as the "tradition of Dharma Seng-gé," including the Nyingtik teachings, Chö, the peaceful and wrathful deities, and other teachings, can be found throughout central Tibet and eastern Bhutan, as well as other regions. Chönyön Dharma Seng-gé was a key figure in the transmission of the Chö teachings, and so became widely renowned as the one primarily responsible for causing the teachings of the masters called the "three lions"[59] to flourish and spread in these later times.

It was from Chönyön Dharma Seng-gé that Lochen Rinpoché of Shuksep heard these teachings, so that several mainstream lineages merged into a single line of transmission.

Zhadeu Trulzhik Chenpo Ngawang Chökyi Lodrö (b. 1924)

Zhadeu Trulzhik Chenpo Ngawang Chökyi Lodrö is the only living master who received the pith instructions on the sublime secret from Shuksep Jetsün Rinpoché.[60] [2.41a] Many holy masters, with their psychic abilities, recognized him at an early age as the tulku of Terchen Trulzhik Dongak Lingpa, and he was enthroned. With many tutors and mentors, he undertook studies, beginning with grammar and continuing through Madhyamaka, Prajñaparamita, Vinaya, Abhidharma, and so forth. He trained in the sutras, tantras, and other fields of knowledge.

Ngawang Chökyi Lodrö received full monastic ordination, in the tradition of the great abbot Shantarakshita, from Gyurmé Chökyi Drakpa, the younger brother of the tulku of Mindroling Monastery. [2.41b] Pure in his moral conduct, he is in these later times a crown jewel for all those who uphold the monastic vows and the teachings associated with them. He received many teachings and transmissions of the Vajrayana, such as the commentaries on the tantra *The Heart Essence of Secrets,* which he received from the great khenpo of Mindroling Monastery. Kyabjé Dudjom Rinpoché conferred on him *The Treasury of Precious Hidden Teachings,* the kama transmissions of the Nyingma school, and other teachings, as well as profound termas, including Dudjom Rinpoché's own revelations, such as the Vajrakila cycle *The Razor That Destroys at a Touch.* Dudjom Rinpoché also prophesied, with words of praise, that Ngawang Chökyi Lodrö would be a custodian of these teachings. From Kyabjé Dilgo Khyentsé Rinpoché, Ngawang Chökyi Lodrö received the transmissions for the precious Kangyur, spiritual advice, and a veritable ocean of maturing empowerments and liberating instructions, including those for *The Treasury of Spiritual Instructions.* He practiced these until the minds of teacher and student merged, becoming one. Kyabjé Khyentsé Rinpoché praised Ngawang Chökyi Lodrö by honoring him as the custodian of Khyentsé Rinpoché's own terma *The Heart Drop of Padma.* In addition, Ngawang Chökyi Lodrö received the entire range of Khyentsé Rinpoché's other termas.

At Gang-ri Tökar, Ngawang Chökyi Lodrö studied with the dakini Dakki Chönyi Zangmo, whom he regarded as the extraordinary master of his buddha family. She transmitted to him the secret Nyingtik teachings of utter lucidity, *Great Perfection: The Black Innermost Heart Drop, The Flight of the Garuda,* and numerous other teachings concerning natural great perfection. [2.42a] He became a great holder of the ultimate lineage of realization.

In these later times of change, Zhadeu Trulzhik Chenpo Ngawang Chökyi Lodrö has founded a center in the hidden region of Solo Khumbhu in Nepal—Tupten Dongak Chöling—erecting the structures as well as the statues and other appointments contained within them. This is his main seat. He has turned the wheel of the dharma for many gatherings of the lay and ordained sangha, passing on the kama transmissions of the Early Translation school, the great *Treasury of Precious Hidden Teachings,* and other maturing empowerments and liberating instructions. Trulzhik Rinpoché has conferred the empowerments and teachings for the cycle *Great Perfection: The Black Innermost Heart Drop* and has bestowed monastic ordination in many countries—among them, India, Nepal, Sikkim, and Bhutan—serving as a principal guru for the teachings of the precious Vinaya. His writtten works to date include the empowerment manual, ritual liturgies, and teaching manual for *Great Perfection: The Black Innermost Heart Drop,* as well as many other manuals of pith instructions.

The foregoing accounts concern one of the mainstream lines of transmission among the many alternative lineages that have come down from Dodrupchen Rinpoché Jigmé Trinlé Özer. With these, I conclude my treatment of the primary Nyingtik lineage of the Dzogchen approach. [2.42b]

10

The Students of Longchen Rabjampa

Now I will give a summary of those who do not fall within the foregoing primary lineage—that is, some of the students of the sublime masters of the Nyingtik teachings and the successive incarnations of some of these masters. To begin with, my treatment of the students of the great Omniscient One Longchenpa includes the teaching lineage and the incarnation lineage.

THE LINEAGE OF LONGCHENPA'S TEACHINGS

As to the teaching lineage, Khenchen Chabdal Lhundrup was discussed earlier.[1]

Orgyen Chöjé of Drok Valley (14th Century)

Born in upper Uru, Orgyen Chöjé was ordained as a monk at the Drigung Kagyü center. He studied numerous profound teachings, among them arousing bodhichitta. In the Sangpu Uplands, he studied many of the source texts of the dialectical approach—Vinaya, Madhyamaka, Prajñaparamita, and so forth—becoming a highly accomplished scholar. From the khenpos and teachers of Densatel, he heard the entire range of profound teachings of Kyopa Jikten Gönpo and mastered them through contemplation and meditation. While he was practicing intensely in solitary retreat, the corrupt schemes of a Drigung partisan named Kunrik, who sought to gain regional control by force, disheartened him. Thus Orgyen Chöjé's predilection for the sacred teachings deepened.

Lama Orgyen Chöjé developed a strong interest in and attraction to the profound Dzogchen path [2.43a] and concluded that the great Omniscient One Longchenpa was without rival. With deep faith, he invited the Omniscient One to Drigung and received from him many empowerments and much spiritual advice. Orgyen Chöjé served and honored his guru devotedly—for example, by materially supporting Longchenpa's plan to restore the temple of Zhai Lhakhang and offering him Orgyen Monastery in the region of Drok. In so doing, Orgyen Chöjé came to discover the path to liberation. He heard all of the teachings that Longchenpa gave at various places, notably the Nyingtik teachings that the master transmitted at Gyamané and at Orgyen Monastery. Orgyen Chöjé pleased his guru with the three kinds of devoted service. By order of the great Omniscient King of the Dharma, Orgyen Chöjé was appointed director of the hermitage in Drok and conducted himself in a manner befitting a guru, pursuing meditation and spiritual practice while teaching the dharma.

The great Omniscient One then spent a long time ensuring benefit for beings in the southern land of Bhutan. When he returned to Tibet, Orgyen Chöjé journeyed to Yamdrok to greet him. Later on, Situ Shakya Zangpo of Drigung invited the great Omniscient One to Orgyen Monastery, and there Orgyen Chöjé served his guru according to the principles of the dharma. He listened to the whole range of teachings by Longchenpa, both public and private, foremost among these the Nyingtik teachings of the Dzogchen approach. [2.43b] He offered ganachakras and made other offerings that were pure in every respect.[2] Exceedingly delighted with Orgyen Chöjé, the guru took him under his care, conferring teachings on all of the tantras, explanatory commentaries, and pith instructions of Dzogchen in their entirety. He thus entrusted him with the responsibility of preserving the teachings in that region.

After the Omniscient One's passing, Orgyen Chöjé continued to conduct his activities on a vast scale. To Sang-ön Sherab Gyatso, the Omniscient One's nephew, he offered the wealth of empowerments and instructions of the Nyingtik teachings, as well as the practical techniques and means of carrying out activity. He dissuaded Sherab Gyatso from going to Mount Kailash in western Tibet to pursue spiritual practice, advising him instead to continue the work of the great Omniscient King of the Dharma in Drok. Thus Orgyen Chöjé was enormously helpful to this tradition of the dharma, for the centers of spiritual practice and lineages of teachings that Sherab Gyatso helped maintain lasted for a long time.

In the Omniscient One's works are references to the "site of the center of spontaneous presence," alluding to Orgyen Monastery in Drok, where, among other places, the guru Orgyen Chöjé continued to turn the wheel of the Dzogchen teachings. At a certain point, Drigung Paldzin (a master, also known as Uru Paldzin, associated with the monasteries of Tangkya and Ewam) [2.44a] felt he could not tolerate the large number of fortunate students who had gathered around Orgyen Chöjé. Disparaging the ancient Nyingma teachings, especially those of Dzogchen, he incurred a grievous karmic burden that only reinforced his obscurations. Sokdokpa Lodrö Gyaltsen and others published numerous rebuttals to his libelous allegations.[3]

Guru Ösel Rangdrol (14th Century)

Ösel Rangdrol was born in Yorpozhung amid marvelous signs. His father was called Palgön and his mother Semo. In his ninth year, he saw a wandering yogin wearing a dog's hide around his waist. The yogin said, "I am neither insane nor delirious," and prayed to his guru, fervently singing a song of yearning devotion. This encounter awakened Ösel Rangdrol's predilection for the sacred dharma. He pursued this guru and received from him advice on the practice of the supremely compassionate Avalokiteshvara. He soon directly experienced signs of success in this practice.

He received lay ordination from Lama Dampa Sönam Gyaltsen and, at the age of twenty-five, received full monastic ordination from Khenpo Zurpupa and the preceptor Shakdönpa, [2.44b] going on to train in Vinaya. Ösel Rangdrol heard a wide range of teachings of the dharma—Sakya, Nyingma, Dakpo Kagyü, Shangpa Kagyü, Zhijé, Chö, and so forth—from some thirteen mentors, including Lama Sherab. He integrated the essential principles he learned into his spiritual practice and received many signs of success. He practiced with exertion, undergoing great hardship to purify and train himself at Tsari and many other solitary retreat sites on mountains, near lakes, on glaciers, and in cliffside caves. He thus came to have excellent meditative experiences and realization.

To minimize distractions and pursue his practice one-pointedly, he left for Bhutan in the south with a few Tibetan companions. For a time, they shared a life of solitary retreat; however, his companions eventually wandered off, pulled by their desire to seek material gain in nearby villages. Ösel Rangdrol, committed to his practice, remained in strict retreat at Gyalekhar near the plateau of Bumthang. The local inhabitants were devoted to him and would say, "This master named 'guru' is a fine person"; thus he earned the title "Rinpoché Gurupa."

During that period, the Omniscient One reached Bumthang [2.45a] and Guru Ösel Rangdrol sought an audience with him. Encountering Longchenpa with his escort of western Bhutanese on their way to Ngen Valley, Guru Ösel Rangdrol bowed with unwavering devotion and entreated the master to take him under his care. He offered a ganachakra to Longchenpa, commemorating the holy tenth day of the lunar month, and in conjunction with this, thousands of the local people made offerings commensurate with their individual abilities. In this way, Ösel Rangdrol ensured that everyone connected to him benefited. He then became Longchenpa's attendant. In Lokkha, the area of Bhutan also known as Shar Kunzang Ling, he received from Longchenpa the complete transmission of the Nyingtik teachings. He was appointed director of Orgyen Ling by the King of the Dharma, and there he stayed for a time, having made it his monastic seat.

Guru Ösel Rangdrol accompanied Longchenpa back to Bumthang, officiating at rituals and serving as shrine keeper, instructor, and so forth. He thus delighted his master with all of his actions, words, and thoughts. He received a wealth of profound and extensive advice, and in particular received the comprehensive transmission of the Nyingtik teachings five times in all. He stayed with Longchenpa until the Omniscient One passed away into a state of peace. [2.45b]

Following Longchenpa's passing, the scope of Guru Ösel Rangdrol's activities on behalf of the dharma became vast. He oversaw the Omniscient One's memorial services and completed his unfinished teachings. Other spiritual sons of the Omniscient One, including Gyalsé Tulku Rinpoché Drakpa Özer, regarded Ösel Rangdrol as a guru.

Having renounced all distractions, he gave oral teachings to those striving for liberation. He remained at the principal holy site of the Chimpu Uplands, engaging solely in his spiritual practice. He entrusted the Omniscient One's nephew, Trulzhik Sang-gyé Önpo,[4] with Longchenpa's entire tradition of the secret Nyingtik and other teachings. When Tulku Drakpa Özer came from Bhutan to central Tibet, Ösel Rangdrol met him at Jamding in Dra and offered him much material wealth and many spiritual teachings. He served him with boundless faith and devotion, saying, "You are my guru's own flesh and blood." He heard many profound teachings of the dharma from Drakpa Özer, until their minds merged, becoming one.

After the passing of the Omniscient One, Ösel Rangdrol thus upheld his pledge to remain solely at the Chimpu Uplands, where Longchenpa had passed away, pursuing spiritual practice without any extraneous activities. He contributed all of the material wealth he came by to virtuous undertakings; [2.46a] for example, he funded the supplies for the ganachakras at all the monastic centers of the region, including Samyé Chökhor. In such ways, he served as a perfect example of a holy being whose conduct was like pure gold, until at last he passed away into a state of peace at the holy site of Chimpu amid countless marvelous, miraculous events.

The lineage deriving from these two sublime, holy masters, Orgyen Chöjé and Ösel Rangdrol, spread throughout central Tibet. Through it, the lineage of the Nyingtik teachings of Longchenpa, the Omniscient King of the Dharma, reached all of Tibet.

Tulku Paljor Gyaltsen (14th Century)

Tulku Paljor Gyaltsen was one of a group of four masters who were known as the "mentors through whom the teachings flourished."[5] He journeyed to Bhutan, where his activity was vast and ever-increasing. He built the temple of Tashi Tsemo in the Komo Gorge of eastern Bhutan, as well as the temples of Khewang Lhakhang and Damchen Lhakhang at Pojikha in Ngen Valley. In caring for his students, Paljor Gyaltsen made the entire southern Himalayan border region a stronghold for the teachings of the heart essence of utter lucidity. He fathered a son, Ngawang Drakpa, who also upheld these teachings. One can still see the enshrined remains of Tulku Paljor Gyaltsen at Khewang Lhakhang. [2.46b]

Dokhampa Dengom Chödrak Zangpo (14th Century)

Chödrak Zangpo was born in the region of Den, eastern Tibet. His innate tendencies born of training in previous lifetimes awakened, and he entered the path of the dharma, receiving monastic ordination. He studied widely with teachers throughout eastern Tibet. Upon reaching adulthood, he traveled to central Tibet to seek further teachings and stayed at Sangpu, the excellent shedra where the great Omniscient One studied and taught. Chödrak Zangpo became a consummate scholar, studying the most important sources of the dialectical approach of the Buddhist tradition, such as Madhyamaka, Prajñaparamita, Vinaya, Abhidharma, and valid cognition.

Chödrak Zangpo developed an unshakable faith in the great Omniscient One. When Longchenpa questioned him about ordinary mind as distinct from timeless awareness, his erudition—exemplified by Longchenpa's poem that begins, "You who shine with the bright light of the pure dharma's noble fame, this topic you are investigating is extremely difficult . . ."—earned the master's praise. Longchenpa in turn gave extensive answers to his student's questions about ordinary mind and timeless awareness and discussed the classification of ground, path, and fruition. With this, the uncontrived conviction that his guru was truly a buddha arose in Chödrak Zangpo, and he bowed at Longchenpa's feet, begging to be taken under his care. Longchenpa responded by bestowing on him the entire transmission of the tantras, explanatory commentaries, [2.47a] and pith instructions of the Nyingtik teachings of the Dzogchen approach, and under his care Chödrak Zangpo became an extraordinary student. He made the Omniscient One's tradition the core of his study and meditation, and innumerable qualities arose from his meditative experience and realization. By following the Dzogchen path, Chödrak Zangpo directly experienced the effortless enlightened intent of dharmakaya. Reaching a high level of spiritual attainment, he composed the following prayer of praise to the Omniscient King of the Dharma:

> Drimé Özer, you are like the effulgence of a thousand rays of light.
> You are like a king of empowerment into the secret Nyingtik teachings.
> You meet all wants and needs, making up for what is lacking in
> conditioned existence or in the peace of nirvana.
> When I beheld how Ngagi Wangpo explained the teachings,
> the methods of the "three brothers" seemed clumsy and halting.
> When I beheld the ordered reasoning of Longchen Rabjam,
> the teachings of Cha, Tsang, and Den seemed like nothing but squabbling.
> When I beheld the works composed by the great Omniscient One,
> the works of Butön, Dolpo, and Shakya Chokden seemed lackluster.
> When I beheld the view and enlightened intent of Natsok Rangdrol,
> the tenets of the "three great systems" seemed superficial.
> When I beheld the deeds and conduct of Penpa Zangpo,
> conduct that we usually consider to be great [2.47b] seemed trifling
> indeed.
> When I beheld the qualities of Pema Ledrel Tsal,
> those who bear the title of "realized ones" seemed very foolish indeed.

When I beheld the freedom from ordinary concerns of Guyang Lodé,
the conduct of supposedly noble people seemed distinctly inferior.
When I beheld the benefit that Drimé Özer brought to others,
those who thought of themselves as great seemed mere imitations of those
who truly benefit others.

These and other verses of praise arose from Chödrak Zangpo's overwhelming yearning. He also wrote the Omniscient One's biography. Frequenting holy sites throughout central Tibet, such as mountains, cliffside caves, glaciers, and lakes, he made Dzogchen the very essence of his own spiritual practice. By turning the wheel of the dharma and through other activities, he spread the Dzogchen teachings everywhere. From his students, like Ngamtön Nyima Özer and Dorjébum of Katok Monastery, came the "eastern Tibetan tradition," the "central Tibetan tradition," the "lineage of Lhalung," and other transmissions that were disseminated in all directions, flourishing in the upper, middle, and lower regions of the Land of Snow Mountains.

The Lineage of Both Khedrup Delek Gyatso and Takok Jadral Chöjé

Another very well known and long-lived lineage of the great Omniscient One's tradition [2.48a] comprises the teachings and transmissions passed down from Khedrup Delek Gyatso and Takok Jadral Chöjé.

Khedrup Delek Gyatso (14th Century)

Khedrup Delek Gyatso was born in Nara in the region of Uru and was ordained as a monk at a center in upper Tra Valley. He studied the sutras and tantras with Kyechok Dorjé of Gomo, Gyalsé Lekpa Rinpoché, and many other mentors, reaching a consummate level of erudition. Applying himself to spiritual practice in all of the hermitages and retreat sites in his region, he achieved numerous states of realization.

Certain that Dzogchen was the very essence of the dharma, he went in search of a fully accomplished mentor who could teach him that approach. He met the great Omniscient One, begged to be taken under his care, and was granted the transmissions for all of the tantras, explanatory commentaries, and pith instructions of the Nyingtik teachings of the Dzogchen approach in their entirety. Treating him as an extraordinary heart son, Longchenpa introduced Delek Gyatso directly to awareness as a naturally occurring state.

At Samten Ling in upper Zhok Valley, at the cave known as Garpuk, and at all the retreat sites and hermitages in the region, Delek Gyatso practiced assiduously, focusing on the very essence of being. He thus fulfilled his own purpose to the greatest extent, directly experiencing the enlightened intent that is the true nature of phenomena.

He then turned the wheel of the dharma, imparting the sutras and tantras in general [2.48b] and the excellent works of the great Omniscient One in particular. He gathered innumerable fortunate students around him, thereby bringing to spiritual maturity many who had the appropriate karma. In his later life, he established a great legacy that would continue to nurture the precious teachings (for example, refurbishing the practice center of Tarpa Samten Ling in Zhok) and carried out countless activities for the benefit of others. At the age of seventy-five, he passed away into a state of peace amid an abundance of marvelous signs.

Takok Jadral Chöjé Tashi Jungné (14th–15th Centuries)

Tashi Jungné, a nephew of Khedrup Delek Gyatso, was born into the Chungpo clan in Gön-nying, in Pen Valley. At the age of six, he was ordained by the Sakya master Lama Dampa Sönam Gyaltsen. He studied a wide range of teachings with such teachers as Chen-nga Jamchöpa, Joden Lodröpal, Lama Sang-gyé Ö, Gomopa of Pen Valley, and Guru Kunzhönpa. He also met the great Omniscient One and received much profound advice from him.

In particular, however, Tashi Jungné received full monastic ordination from Khedrup Delek Gyatso, [2.49a] who gave him the complete transmission of all the traditions of the Omniscient One, like one vase filling another to the brim. At many holy sites, glaciers, cliffside caves, and so forth, he practiced diligently—spending three years on the slopes of the peak known as Chukmo, for example—focusing on the very essence of being, and so directly experienced the enlightened intent of dharmakaya, natural great perfection.

Following his guru's passing, Tashi Jungné inherited the monastic seat, but after a period of time he delegated the responsibility to his lord guru's nephew. (In the accounts of certain lineages, there are references to "the nephew Sang-gyé," but these refer to Khedrup Delek Gyatso's nephew, who is not to be confused with Sang-gyé Önpo Sherab Gyatso, nephew of the Omniscient One.) Tashi Jungné went to live at the hermitage he had founded at Takgo in Penyul, where his activities benefited beings enormously. He guided many students, who later became lineage holders in their own right.

Guru Zhenpen (14th–15th Centuries)

Jadral Chöjé Tashi Jungné's student was Guru Zhenpen. The son of Sönam Sengé, he was born into the Mar clan; his older brother was a renowned teacher called Chöjé Dokuwa. Guru Zhenpen entered the doorway of the teachings at an early age. Vajrapani, the meditation deity of Chakdorpa of Lhodrak, had prophesied that eight students would receive transmission from Chakdorpa; Guru Zhenpen was one of the eight. After having pursued the practice of Vajrapani for six years, [2.49b] Guru Zhenpen had a vision of the deity and received the prophecy that his family would be blessed for seven generations.

He was instructed by many gurus, including Jadral Chöjé of central Tibet, who conferred on him the transmissions for *The Four Higher Collections of the Heart Drop*. He made the Dzogchen approach the very essence of his meditation, spiritual practice, teachings, and efforts to spread the teachings. He established the hermitage of Dung-gön in lower Gyal, where his widespread activities brought about the two kinds of benefit. Guru Zhenpen's son, Namkha Dorjé, received the teachings and transmissions from his father.

Namkha Dorjé (15th Century)

Namkha Dorjé was born in Dung-gön. He studied the dialectical approach at Tsetang and requested teachings on meditation at Tel. In particular, from his father he received the teachings of the Dzogchen approach. Namkha Dorjé meditated on these, so that experience and realization welled forth, and he became a master of realization of the great perfection.

Namkha Dorjé fervently practiced the sadhana of Vajrapani and had a vision of that fierce bodhisattva surrounded by a retinue of five garudas. He developed the ability to cure illnesses and pacify the malevolent influences that cause them—planetary forces, naga spirits, and so forth—merely by giving to whoever was sick a knotted protection cord or water blessed by his mantra repetition. In his practice of the secret Nyingtik teachings of the Dzogchen approach, by maintaining his father's seat and the center of Palding on Mount Trönteng, [2.50a] and in other ways, Namkha Dorjé worked only for the benefit of others. He passed the teachings and transmissions to his son, Ösel Longyang.

Ösel Longyang (15th–16th Centuries)

Ösel Longyang was born in Gyalmen Kyepuk and received monastic ordination at Chenyé. During his ninth and tenth years, he received and trained in his father's teachings. He was directly introduced to the way of abiding as his own true nature, and naturally manifest appearances arose for him as the mandala of peaceful and wrathful deities.

In many places over the years, Ösel Longyang studied with some fifty learned and accomplished gurus, including Drupchen Tangtong Gyalpo, Terchen Pema Lingpa, the lord Gyalwang of the Drukpa Kagyü school, Kunga Samten of Drakgo, Sönam Gyaltsen of Kunzangtsé, Dewa Rabjam of Telhün, the Dzogchen master Kunga Tashi, and Sang-gyé Namgyal of Jamding. He studied a vast range of spiritual instructions from the Nyingma and Sarma schools. He regarded his father and the lord Drukpa Gyalwang as his root gurus and studied, meditated on, explained, and spread their profound teachings. He attained siddhis through the paths of both Mahamudra and Dzogchen.

Ösel Longyang restored Gyemen Mikzhi, [2.50b] the main center of Namkha Dorjé (one of Rigdzin Kumaradza's gurus), which had fallen into disrepair over time. He founded the practice centers of Zangtso and Ösel Ling and instituted a program of meditation on Mahamudra and Dzogchen. He lived to be more than eighty years old, carrying out enlightened activities impartially and on a vast scale in central and southern Tibet and in the southwestern regions of Dakpo and Kongpo.

It was from Ösel Longyang that Dzogchenpa Sönam Rigdzin received the teachings.

Dzogchenpa Sönam Rigdzin (15th–16th Centuries)

Sönam Rigdzin was born in Nyalsekhun into the Chungpo clan. By the age of six, he was proficient at reading and writing. He was ordained as a monk by Sönam Lama of Katok Monastery. He received teachings such as *The Condensed Essence of the Great Perfection,* whereupon his predilection for the Dzogchen approach was awakened. Undergoing great hardship, he traveled to where the holders of these teachings lived and sought them out. He then focused on listening to, meditating upon, explaining, and spreading the Dzogchen teachings. He received the instructions and auxiliary transmissions for *The Four Higher Collections of the Heart Drop* from such teachers as the precious master Ösel Longyang, Drupchen Kunzang Dorjé, Terchen Pema Lingpa, Shakya Zangpo of Zap Valley, and Lodrö Gyaltsen of Mentsé. [2.51a]

Later in his life, Sönam Rigdzin retired into strict, solitary retreat in Gogu near the Brahmaputra River in the region of Kongpo, where he passed away in his sixty-eighth year. Until then, the environment had been harsh and so greatly disturbed by nonhuman beings that no one could go there. This lord master's spiritual practice, coupled with his cremation (according to his will) atop a four-sided boulder that was a place of spiritual power, tamed the spirits, and the area became peaceful by nature. Tsungmé Tendzin Dorjé founded a practice center in Gogu, and in this and other ways boundless benefit for the teachings and beings accrued in this area.

It was from Sönam Rigdzin that Kunchen Ngawang Pema heard the teachings.

Kunchen Ngawang Pema (16th Century)

Kunchen Ngawang Pema was the grandson of Palden Seng-gé, foremost of those prophesied to be the custodians of Sang-gyé Lingpa's termas. He was born in Kyenja Chung in Kongpo, the son of Palden Seng-gé's son, Tsa Palbar Wangchuk. In Kyenja Chung, one can still see distinct footprints that Ngawang Pema made when he was eight years old. From an early age, he clearly exhibited the predisposition of someone holy. He received instructions on and trained in many excellent techniques of both the sutra and tantra approaches, [2.51b] which he received from such mentors as his own father, as well as Dzogchenpa Sönam Rinchen[6] and many others.

He perfected his learning in and realization of the secret Nyingtik teachings and the termas of Sang-gyé Lingpa. Ngawang Pema also wrote many treatises on the principles expounded in these teachings. He was capable of producing and manipulating emanations, showing his students the forms of deities or, in solitary places, wild beasts such as tigers. He revealed several termas consisting of material objects. Ngawang Pema was a great mentor in the Kongpo region, and his knowledge and activity as a holder of the teachings of the Nyingma school were unparalleled.

It was from him that Dzogchenpa Sönam Wangpo heard the teachings.

Dzogchenpa Sönam Wangpo (1550?–1625)

Sönam Wangpo was born into the Kyura clan in Kyentsa Zhuk, Kongpo. As a young man, he was a householder, fathering a daughter who later became the spiritual consort of Gyalwang Tendzin of Jachung. At thirty-seven he was deeply moved by a strong sense of renunciation and disenchantment with what he perceived to be his karma in conditioned existence, so he and his wife entered the doorway of the dharma at Jachung Monastery. Sönam Wangpo received an extensive transmission of the Nyingtik teachings of Dzogchen and other cycles [2.52a] from Kunchen Ngawang Pema. Having begun his spiritual practice later in life, he had no great hope of making progress, but his guru foresaw the eventual outcome and thoroughly bestowed all of the instructions on him. Meditating steadfastly, Sönam Wangpo was directly introduced to his own true nature as the way of abiding. At such retreat sites as Tsari, Taktsang, Domtsang, Puri, and Zilchen, Sönam Wangpo pursued his spiritual practice one-pointedly while undergoing great hardship, bringing his meditative experience and realization to a consummate level.

Later, at the direction of Tsungmé Tendzin Dorjé, he stayed at the retreat center of Gogu near the Brahmaputra River, living in a meditation hut that he built out of bamboo. During that time, the great mentor Sokdokpa Lodrö Gyaltsen was at Samdruptsé in the southern region of Tsang. In the utter lucidity of a pure dream state, he became aware of Sönam Wangpo and praised him as an emanation of Gyalwa Drom, offering prayers to prolong his life.

Sokdokpa Lodrö Gyaltsen wrote verses of praise like the following:

> Many are skilled in the words that express the topics
> found in the 6,400,000 verses of Dzogchen,
> but who, if not you, is skilled in demonstrating the timeless awareness
> that is their ultimate point?

In this way, Sokdokpa opened the doorway for the enlightened activity of this lord master. [2.52b] Because of this, many requested teachings from Sönam Wangpo; he thus ensured benefit for beings by giving instructions on the profound and definitive meaning of the Nyingtik teachings of Dzogchen and other systems. He benefited many fortunate students, among them Tselé Tulku Pema Lekdrup, Lhatsün Kunzang Namgyal, and Bakha Tulku of Powo.

At the age of seventy-six, on the twenty-fifth day of the lunar month of the Pleiades in a Wood Ox year,[7] Sönam Wangpo passed away without illness at the Gogu retreat center. Many relics were found among his cremated remains, and a naturally occuring *A* was found on his skull.

It was from Dzogchenpa Sönam Wangpo that Lhatsün Namkha Jigmé, who was the natural manifestation of the innate compassion of both Panchen Vimalamitra and the Omniscient One Drimé Özer, received the teachings.

Lhatsün Namkha Jigmé (1597–1652)

Lhatsün Namkha Jigmé was born in the Female Fire Bird year of the tenth sexagesimal cycle,[8] in the region of Jar in the southern reaches of Tibet. His body bore numerous marvelous signs, such as a syllable *A* clearly visible at his midbrow, on his tongue, and on the tip of his nose. When he was eleven years old, [2.53a] he was ordained as a monk by Tulku Orgyen Paljor at the hermitage of Sung-nyen and was given the name Kunzang Namgyal.

He first studied and contemplated all of the appropriate subjects at the shedra of Tangdrok. Over time, he received the maturing empowerments and liberating instructions for many profound kama and terma teachings, such as the Eight Commands and *The Union of the Enlightened Intent of the Gurus,* from close to a hundred learned and accomplished gurus. He brought to completion the phases of approach and accomplishment for his personal meditation deities, and so attained siddhis and gained mastery over enlightened activity. In particular, he studied for seventeen years with Dzogchenpa Sönam Wangpo, from whom he received the entire range of Nyingtik teachings. He practiced these and gained the indwelling confidence born of realization.

As a means of enhancing this realization, Lhatsün Namkha Jigmé received all of the pith instructions on the "path of passion"[9] from the lord Ngawang Mikyö Dorjé. Training in the yogic methods that bring about the experience of timeless awareness as the unity of bliss and emptiness—methods focusing on one's own body as the source of skillful means and another's body as the consort—Lhatsün Namkha Jigmé felt any tendency to invest the four degrees of joy with solidity dissolving in its own place. He thus perceived all that was visible and audible to be an utterly lucid and innately joyful state of being.

He traveled to all of the principal holy regions of Tibet, [2.53b] such as the three southern areas of Jar, Dakpo, and Kongpo and the three central areas of Ü, Yoru, and Tsang, engaging in the uncontrived conduct of a tantric practitioner and thus reaching a high level of spiritual attainment. The blockages in the subtle channels in his throat center were released, so that everything he said was noble in both word and meaning. He journeyed to India, where he tamed a ruler who held extreme views and brought him to the Buddhist teachings. In Tibet, Lhatsün Namkha Jigmé mastered an incredible array of miraculous powers; for example, he invoked gods and demons as his allies in repairing damage done to Samyé, and at Tsari he focused his gaze and pointed with a threatening gesture to avert a great avalanche. While he was meditating at various important holy sites—including the valley of Zabbulung, Mikpoi Gatsal on the mountain of Rinchen Shelri, Pema Jaö Sheldzong, and Lhai Dingkhang on the mountain of Shelri in Yarlung—Lhatsün Namkha Jigmé was guided and blessed by the Omniscient One's embodiment of timeless awareness. Thus he had an incredible number of pure visionary experiences, on the basis of which the spacious treasury of enlightened intent welled up in him. This led to his revelation of such terma cycles as *The Innermost Heart Drop of All Treasure Troves, The Oral Lineage: Key Points of Purity,* [2.54a] and *Vajra Heart Essence: The Spontaneous Song of the Clouds,* which is renowned for bringing liberation upon sight, hearing, recollection, or touch.[10] He codified these cycles and conferred them on a few of his fortunate and extraordinary students.

Encouraged by such masters as Rigdzin Jatsön Nyingpo and Terchen Duddul Dorjé, in his fiftieth year—a Fire Dog year[11]—he went, for the universal welfare of Tibet, to Lhari Ösel Nyingpo in Sikkim and opened up that area as a sacred site.[12] In keeping with prophecies he had received, Lhatsün Namkha Jigmé founded a temple and retreat center. Following a prophecy given by the dakinis, he went to Drakar Tashiding; while staying there, he received in the form of a daknang transmission the cycle of teachings called *The Life Force of the Masters of Awareness,* extraordinary Nyingtik instructions of the unsurpassable Atiyoga approach. Having codified them, he conferred the nectar of these maturing empowerments and liberating instructions on his fortunate students.

Furthermore, because of Lhatsün Namkha Jigmé's extensive activities in teaching and promulgating the Dzogchen teachings, the renown of what came to be called the "extensive lineage of the Dzogchen master of Sikkim" spread far and wide. It is reputed that, in these later times, [2.54b] no siddha has appeared who has surpassed this master in the consummate mastery of uncontrived tantric conduct. The lines of transmission for *The Life Force of the Masters of Awareness* and *The Spontaneous Song of the Clouds*—the empowerments, oral transmissions, and pith instructions—have continued unimpaired to the present day, and the lineage of Lhatsün Namkha Jigmé has continued to flourish throughout most of the Tibetan region, especially in the hidden land of Sikkim.

Among Lhatsün Namkha Jigmé's students were Rigdzin Trinlé Lhundrup, Tulku Trinlé Namgyal, Drupchen Yeshé Puntsok, and other great masters who were in turn able to benefit beings. Many of his other students were men and women with great meditative experience and realization.

Lhatsün Namkha Jigmé had many contemporaries who maintained the teachings and study of Dzogchen, including Lochen Zhenpen Dorjé; the speech incarnation of the Omniscient One Longchenpa; Götsangwa of Kongpo; Rigdzin Nyingpo of the Nyingpu Uplands; Trinlé Lhundrup of Darding; and Rongpo Dzogchenpa. Nevertheless, Terchen Gyurmé Dorjé said, "This lord master Lhatsün Namkha is unrivaled in explaining and promulgating the Dzogchen approach."

Having thus completed his activities, Lhatsün Namkha Jigmé passed into a state of peace at the Sheldrak retreat center [2.55a] in a Male Water Dragon year,[13] when he was fifty-six. After Terdak Lingpa and his spiritual heirs received the transmission of Lhatsün Namkha Jigmé's teachings, this lineage and theirs converged. Lhatsün's autobiography clearly describes how his cycles of teachings originated from daknang transmissions and how his profound termas were revealed.

It was from Lhatsün Namkha Jigmé that Dzogchenpa Longdzok Tadral received the teachings.

Dzogchenpa Longdzok Tadral (17th Century)

Longdzok Tadral was Lhatsün Namkha Jigmé's nephew. From an early age, the development of his knowledge and realization was remarkable. Taught by many gurus, he studied and contemplated the teachings to a consummate degree. From the great Lhatsün, he received transmissions for countless spiritual methods and instructions, like one vase being filled from another. Foremost among these was *The Four Higher Collections of the Heart Drop,* focusing on the vajra heart essence of utter lucidity. In solitary retreats, Longdzok Tadral directly experienced the way of abiding as his own true nature. He perfected the dynamic potential of his meditative experience and realization, so that an expansive state of insight welled up.

Through the enlightened activities of explaining and spreading the teachings, primarily those of Dzogchen, he fulfilled his destiny to benefit beings. [2.55b] After the great Lhatsün's passing, he oversaw the funeral rites; he also ensured enormous benefit for the teachings and beings by continuing Lhatsün's activities.

Dzogchen Pema Rigdzin[14] of eastern Tibet received the transmission of the Dzogchen teachings from Longdzok Tadral. Pema Rigdzin then passed this so-called eastern Tibetan tradition to Guru Tashi, also known as Yangchen Gawai Lodrö. In the history of the "tradition of Nyima Drakpa,"[15] the accounts of the abbatial succession, and the records of the teaching methods from such monasteries as Zhechen and Dzogchen, there are no separate biographies for any holders of this lineage of ultimate meaning. This indicates that the lines of teachings converged from this point on, up to the present day, with the tradition of these monastic centers and their affiliates spreading throughout the world.

This concludes the discussion of students who transmitted the teachings of the great Omniscient King of the Dharma, Longchenpa.

THE LINEAGE OF LONGCHENPA'S INCARNATIONS

In the case of the second lineage, that of Longchenpa's incarnations, the first of these was Rigdzin Pema Lingpa, one of the "five kings" among tertöns,[16] a fact implicitly referred to in *Stainless Light*, Longchenpa's last will and testament.

Rigdzin Pema Lingpa (1450–1521)

Rigdzin Pema Lingpa was born in Chalpa Ridrang, in the central Bhutanese region of Bumthang, which is known as the "Wheel of Dharma." His father was Lama Döndrup Zangpo of the Nyö clan; his mother, Pema Drolma, hailed from a nomadic tribe. [2.56a] Their son was born amid a host of marvelous signs. As an incarnation of the Omniscient One Drimé Özer, he displayed at an early age the attributes of someone holy. He knew his letters and exhibited artistic talent without receiving any instruction.

On the tenth day of the first month of autumn in a Monkey Year,[17] Orgyen Rinpoché appeared to Pema Lingpa at the holy site of Yigé Drukma and blessed him. He also gave Pema Lingpa a record of 108 major terma caches[18] that he was to reveal. Accordingly, in his twenty-seventh year, Pema Lingpa revealed his first terma, the cycle *The Clear Expanse of the Great Perfection,* near the cliff of Naring Drak, retrieving it from the lake known as Mebartso, which looks like a complex knot of roiling water. Before a large crowd, Pema Lingpa walked straight into the lake, holding in his hand a lighted torch whose flame did not die. He retrieved a terma casket about the size of a large clay pot, tucked it under his arm, and returned to shore. Everyone was moved to faith and wonder, and word of this indisputable master spread over the face of the earth like the light of the sun and moon. At the Chimpu Uplands near Samyé, he similarly revealed the Dzogchen cycle [2.56b] *The All-Inclusive Intent of Samantabhadra.* He revealed many other termas from their places of concealment, such as the cycles *The Small Child: The Nondual Tantra of the Great Perfection; The Guru, Ocean of Gems; The Supremely Compassionate Avalokiteshvara: The Lamp That Dispels Darkness;* the Eight Commands cycle *The Mirror of Enlightened Mind; The Most Secret Practice of Vajrakila: The Razor of Life Force;* the "three medicinal practices" (the cycles of the Eight Commands, Vajrakila, and Vajra Amrita for creating spiritual medicine); *Vajrapani: Tamer of Arrogance* and *Vajrapani: Fierce Wrathful Deity* (extensive, intermediate, and condensed versions); *The Vajra Garland,* a teaching manual on longevity practice; *Carrying Gems on the Path,* a longevity practice; three cycles focusing on black deities; and cycles of minor activities.

In addition, he revealed an incredible number of the three kinds of representations as receptacles for sacred samaya substances, such as medicine that could liberate upon taste for seven generations; an image called Padma Guru, one of the so-called regents of Padmakara; and other objects. In particular, the temple of Kyerchu in the southern reaches, which resembles the temple of Paltsap Sumpai Lhakhang, had not been visible before Pema Lingpa unearthed it by clearing soil and rock from a ravine; it then became accessible to everyone. As for his wealth termas,[19] he revealed many especially exalted objects of wealth dating from the royal dynasties of the kings of Tibet, [2.57a] among them pieces of turquoise embodying the spirit of the kings (called Rinpoché Öbar and Gang-ri Khangmar), robes of the queens without any tears or flaws, and a spyglass.

Although the record of 108 major terma caches had been placed in his hands, Pema Lingpa was able to reveal only half of them. When this tertön was about to pass away, his son and spiritual heir, Dawa, asked whether he might reveal them. Pema Lingpa replied, "Although it might be difficult for you to reveal termas, if you maintain your samaya purely and pray to me, you may discover a few minor treasures." Accordingly, his heart son later brought forth several termas from concealment, thus enormously benefiting the teachings and beings.

The lineage of the successive incarnations of this master and his heart son has continued to the present day. Moreover, Pema Lingpa prophesied that in the future he would return as the buddha Dorjé Nyingpo in the pure realm of Pemakö and that those connected to him would be reborn in Pemakö as Dorjé Nyingpo's students.

Accepting a commission from the king of the region to turn the wheel of the dharma, Pema Lingpa erected the amazing temple of Lhundrup Chöling. [2.57b] Housed within it were a Vajrasattva statue that he had revealed; a set of three statues of Guru Padmakara and his retinue, their hollow interiors filled with special samaya substances such as yellow scrolls, the four kinds of relics, and so forth; images of the buddhas of the three times; and images of the eight manifestations of the Guru. Once the temple and its contents were complete, Rigdzin Pema Lingpa and Khenchen Tsultrim Paljor performed the full consecration ceremonies. Everyone felt that this sublime holy site would provide an opportunity for ordinary beings to gather merit.

With this, Pema Lingpa's work of guiding his students in that lifetime came to an end. Having lived to the age of seventy-two, he passed into a state of peace on the third day of the first Tibetan month in a Female Iron Serpent year.[20]

The Second Pema Lingpa, Tendzin Chökyi Drakpa (Yenpa Lodé) (1536–1597)

Strictly speaking, Rigdzin Pema Lingpa was actually the first incarnation of the Omniscient One, but he is traditionally referred to as the first Pema Lingpa,[21] followed by the second, and so on.[22] Thus the lord Tendzin Chökyi Drakpa was known as the second Pema Lingpa. He was born on Gen Pass leading into Ngen Valley in eastern Bhutan, the land of medicinal plants. His father, Tashi, was an emanation of Vajrapani; his mother was Samten Zangmo. He later said that the predilections established in his preceding lifetime as Terchen Pema Lingpa awakened clearly [2.58a] when he began to talk. When he was four, Rigdzin Pema Lingpa's spiritual successors invited him to Bumthang; they received him with honors as Pema Lingpa's tulku at their respective monastic seats.

At Pema Ling, where he received monastic ordination, Tendzin Chökyi Drakpa was appointed the successor to Könchok Zangpo, one of Pema Lingpa's spiritual heirs. He studied and trained in the empowerments, oral transmissions, sadhana practices, and activity rituals of Pema Lingpa's termas. Before long, the lord of the dharma Könchok Zangpo passed away, and Tendzin Chökyi Drakpa went to Dechen Ling, the seat of Dawa, son of the former Pema Lingpa, where he stayed for a time and received such teachings and instructions as were appropriate.

Then Tulku Natsok Rangdrol invited Tendzin Chökyi Drakpa, who was fourteen at the time, to Tibet. There, like one vase being filled to the brim from another, he received innumerable teachings of the sutras and tantras of the Nyingma and Sarma schools. In particular, he received the empowerments, teachings, oral transmissions, pith instructions, and practical methods of the cycles of Longchenpa, the great Omniscient King of the Dharma, and Tertön Pema Lingpa.

When he was twenty, Tendzin Chökyi Drakpa went to Lhodrak. All of the students and patrons of the former Pema Lingpa honored and venerated him, as illustrated by the fact that Tsoyul Drakarwa offered monasteries to him. [2.58b] He received certain empowerments and oral transmissions from a Lama Umdzepa, as well as training in ritual dance and chanting. From Gyalsé Dawa, he received empowerments for sadhana practices focusing on the Eight Commands and for teachings on longevity practice. Traveling throughout eastern and western Bhutan, Tendzin Chökyi Drakpa bestowed empowerments, teachings on sadhana practice, oral transmissions, and so forth on many beings according to their wishes.

He then returned to Tibet, where he studied numerous spiritual approaches with many tutors such as the great tulku Natsok Rangdrol (the master of Tendzin Chökyi Drakpa's buddha family); the great Sakya mantra holder, the venerable Jetsün Kunga Drolchok; and Nangtsé Rigdzin. Persevering in his practice of the profound path in places like the Chimpu Uplands, he realized the profound significance of the way of abiding. He had visions of myriad deities and received their prophecies.

Then the lord of the dharma Chöjé Natsok Rangdrol conferred on Tendzin Chökyi Drakpa his monastery, as well as the three kinds of representations it contained, authorizing him to take it as his seat. After Natsok Rangdrol passed into a state of peace, Tendzin Chökyi Drakpa continued his guru's enlightened activities. He cared for his students and patrons, as shown by the numerous rituals he conducted to commemorate his guru's passing, the monuments he built to enshrine the remains, and the empowerments for and teachings on sadhana practice that he bestowed in the summer and winter.

He ensured benefit according to the hopes of individual students from such areas as Rong and the southern Tibetan region of Tsang. People like Gyalsé Pema Chögyal [2.59a] and Jangdak Wangpoidé bowed to him with reverence. With both teachings and material support, Tendzin Chökyi Drakpa cared for Gyalsé Pema Trinlé, the son and spiritual heir of Pema Lingpa's son Dawa. Honoring Tendzin Chökyi Drakpa's request that his students found monasteries in their home regions, Gyalsé Pema Trinlé established the monastic center of Gangteng Sang-ngak Chöling in Bhutan, in the southern reaches. The successive tulkus of Pema Trinlé have caused the teachings concerning the heart essence of the supreme secret to spread and flourish in the southern land of Bhutan to the present day.

In central Tibet, the lord Natsok Rangdrol's incarnation, Do-ngak Tendzin, was invited to the monastic seat of Dargyé Chöding, where Tendzin Chökyi Drakpa bestowed on him all of the empowerments, oral transmissions, and pith instructions in their entirety. Before long, having thus invested Do-ngak Tendzin as a master of the teachings, Tendzin Chökyi Drakpa passed into nirvana in his sixty-second year, at the retreat center associated with Dargyé Chöding.

Khedrup Do-ngak Tendzin's spiritual heir was Sangdak Trinlé Lhundrup, [2.59b] whose son and heir was Rigdzin Terdak Lingpa, founder of the monastic seat of Orgyen Mindroling. Through this lineage, the teachings concerning the essence of the supreme secret spread throughout the three planes of existence down to the time of the present throne holder, the eleventh Kunzang Pema Wangyal. All of this, which led to the flourishing of Mindroling Monastery and its affiliates, was the result of the lord master Tendzin Chökyi Drakpa's strength of motivation and enlightened activities.

The Third Pema Lingpa, Kunchen Tsultrim Dorjé (1598–1669)

The third Pema Lingpa, Kunchen Tsultrim Dorjé, was the son of Tseten Döndrup of the Nup clan and his wife, Ramang Za Gyaga of the Chungpo clan. As soon as he could talk, he spoke of being Pema Lingpa's tulku. The omniscient master of Jonang[23] and a host of other great, holy beings—most notably the Sakya Dakchen—proclaimed Tsultrim Dorjé to be the embodiment of the magical display of both Pema Lingpa and the scholar Vinitadeva of Buddhist India. His life's direction was determined when he was recognized by Gyalsé Pema Trinlé, who then took responsibility for supporting and training him.

In his eleventh year, Tsultrim Dorjé visited Gyalsé Rinpoché at Ritra Sang-ngak Chöling in Tso, where he received all of the empowerments for and teachings on guru yoga, [2.60a] Dzogchen, the supremely compassionate Avalokiteshvara, the Eight Commands, and so forth. He received monastic ordination from the sixth Zhamar and was given the name Tsultrim Dorjé Gelek Palzangpo. Tsultrim Dorjé then accompanied Gyalsé Rinpoché to Gangteng Monastery in Ngen Valley, where he received empowerments, oral transmissions, teachings, and other pith instructions, like one vase being filled to the brim from another. He studied the entire range of teachings on the sutras, tantras, kama transmissions, and terma lineages with more than twenty mentors, such as Gung-ra Lochen, Norbu Wangyal, Karma Trinlé Gyatso, the great fifth Dalai Lama, Sönam Zangpo of the Sakya school, Rigdzin Nyingpo of Kongpo, Pema Lodrö of Katok Monastery, Tselé Götsangpa, and Pawo Tsuklak Gyatso.

He spent months and years in places like the Chimpu Uplands and the cliff of Tsokyé Drak in the valley known as Zablung, practicing the stages of development and completion for many meditation deities, and his realization became evident. Wandering through various regions, he bestowed empowerments, conducted drup-chens, and gave teachings, oral transmissions, and pith instructions. He mediated a conflict between Gelukpa and Drukpa factions,[24] [2.60b] ensuring a favorable outcome and granting each of those involved the gift of refuge from fear. Drukpa Rinpoché Tuchen Ngawang Namgyal was impressed by this lord master's qualities, and praised and honored him.

In brief, with enormous grace and kindness, Tsultrim Dorjé engaged in the three activities of the wise,[25] causing the teachings of the Victorious One in general, and the precious teachings of the Early Translation school of the Nyingma in particular, to flourish greatly. In his seventy-second year, Tsultrim Dorjé passed away at Rabkar Monastery into the vase body of utter lucidity.

The Fourth Pema Lingpa, Dorjé Mikyö Tsal (Ngawang Kunzang Rolpai Dorjé) (1680–1723)

The fourth Pema Lingpa, Dorjé Mikyö Tsal, was born in Dzabar, Lhodrak. His father was Yönten Tagyé of the Tsur clan, and his mother was Chöpal Drolma. Many holy masters, like Tuksé Rinpoché[26] and Minling Terchen, proclaimed him the undisputed tulku of Pema Lingpa. When the positive tendencies from his preceding lifetime awakened, his words moved everyone to belief and faith.

Dorjé Mikyö Tsal studied with many gurus, including Tuksé Tendzin Gyurmé Dorjé, a tulku of Gangteng Monastery named Tendzin Lekdön, Minling Terchen [2.61a] and his brother, and Tulku Bönlungpa. He received a vast range of the sutras and tantras, as well as empowerments, oral transmissions, pith instructions, and practical methods from the kama and terma teachings of both the Nyingma and Sarma schools. His education emphasized the teachings of the great Omniscient One and of Pema Lingpa. He also received the oral transmissions for all the volumes of the precious Nyingma tantras. Dorjé Mikyö Tsal was ordained as a novice monk by Khenchen Lotsawa Ngawang Chöpal Gyatso, with whom he also studied the mainstream teachings of the Indian Buddhist tradition.

He pursued the profound practices of the stages of development and completion in solitary retreats and had visions of his meditation deities and gurus, from whom he received prophecies. He frequently traveled throughout Bhutan and Tibet—to both the central region of Ü and the south central region of Tsang—and fulfilled the hopes of students he encountered. He built images and monuments in his home area and at Tashi Chöling in Lhonang. At many sites, he left hand- and footprints in solid rock. Dorjé Mikyö Tsal went to Gangteng Sang-ngak Chöling in Ngen Valley, where he met the lord master Tendzin Lekdön Rinpoché. The two journeyed to Kyitokha, where they bestowed profound teachings on one another. All of the lamas and rulers under the lord of the dharma in Bhutan bowed with respect to Dorjé Mikyö Tsal. [2.61b] Through countless teachings and instructions, such as *The Collected Tantras of the Nyingma School* (which concern the supreme secret), Ledrel Tsal's *Heart Drop of the Dakini,* the Minling Terchen termas, and especially Pema Lingpa's cycles, Dorjé Mikyö Tsal brought people with good fortune to the state of the four kayas. At the age of forty-four, he passed from his body amid numerous marvelous signs, such as the many earthquakes that shook the land both before and after his passing.

The Fifth Pema Lingpa, Kunzang Tsewang (Pema Tendzin Drupchok Dorjé) (1725–1762)

The fifth Pema Lingpa, Kunzang Tsewang, was born in the palace of Samdrup Dewa Chenpo. His father, the governor of Na Valley, was Sönam Dragyé, and his mother was Ngawang Palmo. The fifth Buksé, Gyurmé Chokdrup Palbar, had received a prophecy from a dakini about the incarnation, after which the Gyalwang Karmapa[27] and untold other holy masters recognized Kunzang Tsewang as the undisputed, sublime tulku of Pema Lingpa.

When he was four years old, Kunzang Tsewang assumed the throne of his former incarnations at Tekchok Rapgyé Ling in the valley known as Lhalung. Tuksé Rinpoché administered his initial monastic vows and named him Kunzang Tsewang Pema Tendzin Drubchok Dorjé. Under the direction of Tuksé Rinpoché, he assiduously studied and trained in the teachings [2.62a] of the dharma and fields of secular knowledge. At the age of eight, Kunzang Tsewang received many teachings of the kama and terma traditions from Rinchen Namgyal, Mindroling Monastery's throne holder.

The recognized rebirth of Tendzin Lekdön,[28] Pema Kunzang Trinlé Namgyal, was born at Sela in western Bhutan. He was invited to Tibet, where spiritual father and son reunited and paid one another honor. That tulku completed his study and contemplation and returned to his monastic seat of Gangteng, where he was enthroned.

At the age of twenty, Kunzang Tsewang went to Mindroling Monastery. From such teachers as the throne holder Rinchen Namgyal and Mingyur Paldrön, he received cycles of the Early Translation school, from both the kama tradition (such as the empowerment for *The Discourse on United Intent*) and the terma tradition (such as *The United Intent of the Gurus*). He studied and contemplated the teachings contained in *The Heart Essence of Secrets* (also known as *The Web of Magical Display*), *The Five Treatises of Maitreya,* and many other mainstream sources of the Indian Buddhist tradition with scholars such as Orgyen Kalzang, whose knowledge was encyclopedic. His fame as the "third Omniscient One"[29] spread far and wide.

He spent time in holy places like Taktsang in Paro, doing spiritual practice. [2.62b] He traveled throughout Bhutan, from west to east, caring for many students by bestowing empowerments and advice. He sealed himself off in strict retreat for three years in the hidden land of Khen Valley. At the age of thirty-eight, Kunzang Tsewang passed from his body at Kharchu, Lhodrak.

The Sixth Pema Lingpa, Kunzang Tenpai Gyaltsen Palzangpo (1763–1817)

The sixth Pema Lingpa, Kunzang Tenpai Gyaltsen Palzangpo, was the son of Karma Rapgyé of the Nyang clan; his mother was Tsering Lhadrön, a respected member of the Trengshar clan. The oracle at Samyé Monastery, as well as Lama Tangdrokpa, recognized the tulku and made predictions about him. As soon as he could speak, he clearly described the circumstances of his preceding lifetime, such as his situation at Drakar in the hidden land, his first activities, meditating, and giving empowerments.

At the age of six, Kunzang Tenpai Gyaltsen journeyed to Lhalung, where he was enthroned in the presence of the sixth lord Tuksé, Tendzin Chökyi Nyima. He studied both secular and spiritual fields of knowledge, including reading and writing, sadhana ceremonies and activity rituals, Indian and Chinese astrology, Sanskrit grammar, and poetry. He received all of the oral transmissions for the precious Nyingma tantras, as well as other empowerments and oral transmissions.

From Mindroling Monastery's throne holder, [2.63a] he received the empowerments and oral transmissions of the kama and terma traditions in their entirety, while from the monastery's great khenpo, he received empowerments for *The Gathering of the Sugatas* and other cycles, as well as monastic ordination. When he was twenty-one, Kunzang Tenpai Gyaltsen relied on Gyalsé Tendzin Sizhi Namgyal as the master of his buddha family and received the entire transmission of Pema Lingpa's cycles—empowerments, teachings, oral transmissions, and pith instructions—like one vase being filled to the brim from another. He also studied with many learned and accomplished masters of the Nyingma and Sarma schools, among them Rigdzin Khamsum Zilnön of Dorjé Drak Monastery and Lama Orgyen Puntsok of Tsamdrak. He received transmissions of innumerable approaches within the kama and terma traditions, completely absorbing the profound topics of the sutras and tantras without exception.

As a result of his perseverance in the practice of the development and completion stages, Kunzang Tenpai Gyaltsen came to perceive the true nature of phenomena, the way of abiding, just as it is. In his thirty-second year, he adopted the white robes and long hair of a lay practitioner. He retrieved secret termas from their places of concealment, such as the lake known as Namtso in northern Tibet. Traveling far and wide in the southern Tibetan regions of Dakpo and Kongpo, at sites such as Paro in western

Bhutan and other parts of that country, Kunzang Tenpai Gyaltsen gave empowerments, teachings, oral transmissions, and pith instructions impartially to the many students connected to him in the sacred dharma. In his fifty-fifth year, in Tsugna on the plateau of Mentang, [2.63b] he passed away to the palace of Pema Ö.

The Seventh Pema Lingpa, Pema Tendzin (Kunzang Ngawang Chökyi Lodrö) (1819–1842)

The seventh Pema Lingpa, Pema Tendzin, was born in Chumé on the plateau of Bumthang. His father was Sönam Tobgyal, an aristocrat of the Nyö clan, and his mother was Tsewang Lhamo. Numerous great masters of such monasteries as Dorjé Drak and Mindroling recognized the tulku, whose identity was confirmed by the oracle at Samyé Monastery. Therefore, at the age of five, Pema Tendzin journeyed to Lhalung to meet the seventh Tuksé, who enthroned him and named him Kunzang Ngawang Chökyi Lodrö. He easily mastered the traditional methods of religious rites, sadhana practices, activity rituals, and so forth. When he was six years old, Pema Tendzin went to Potala Palace in Lhasa, where he was ordained as a monk by the Dalai Lama.[30]

From Chöjé Orgyen Gelek Namgyal, Pema Tendzin received the empowerments and oral transmissions for this guru's own termas, as well as the oral transmissions for the entire canon of the Nyingma tantras. At sixteen he went to Mindroling Monastery, where he studied with the throne holder, Gyurmé Sang-gyé Kunga,[31] from whom he received the empowerments and oral transmissions for the profound teachings of the lord, the great Terdak Lingpa. Pema Tendzin received full monastic ordination in front of an assembly headed by his abbot, Gyurmé Sang-gyé Kunga, and his preceptor, the vajra holder Dordzin Gyurmé Tsewang Zangpo. [2.64a]

With Gyurmé Tsenor, Pema Tendzin thoroughly studied such things as the "five condensed subjects"[32] and the charts of the five major planets. He also received the nectar of maturing empowerments and liberating instructions of the entire range of the kama and terma traditions of the Nyingma and Sarma schools from many undisputed holy masters, including Paltrul Pema Wangyal. He did intensive retreats focusing on such practice formats as the Eight Commands and Vajrakila, receiving blessings heralded by auspicious signs. From Yöndo Choktrul, Pema Tendzin received empowerments for *The Gathering of All Masters of Awareness* and other teaching cycles, including Pema Lingpa's, and, from the vajra holder of Mindroling, the oral transmissions for the Kangyur. Having studied innumerable kama and terma cycles—empowerments, teachings, methods of exegesis, and so forth—Pema Tendzin cut through all imprecise speculation about them. He traveled throughout Bhutan, impartially conducting drupchens and giving empowerments, teachings, oral transmissions, and pith instructions commensurate with the individual fortunes of his students, causing the seedlings of supreme enlightenment to sprout in their minds. Thus he strove solely to serve the teachings and bring happiness to beings. In his twenty-fourth year, he passed into the supreme citadel of dharmakaya, the state of utter lucidity.

The Eighth Pema Lingpa, Kunzang Dechen Dorjé (Ngedön Tenpai Nyima Palzangpo) (1843–1891)

The eighth Pema Lingpa, Kunzang Dechen Dorjé, also known as Ngedön Tenpai Nyima Palzangpo, [2.64b] was the son of Chökyi Gyaltsen of the Nyö clan and his wife, Sang-gyé Pemo. There were marvelous omens at his birth and throughout his childhood. As soon as he could speak, he clearly recalled his former lifetimes, so that people were convinced that his identity as the tulku of Pema Lingpa was indisputable. At the age of four, he was invited to Lhalung and enthroned.

Relying on Pema Kunzang Rigdzin Dorjé, Pema Tendzin's son, as the master of his buddha family, he learned to read and write, memorized rituals, and studied chanting, music, and dance. He mastered these simply upon being shown them. Like one vase being filled from another, Kunzang Dechen Dorjé received empowerments, oral transmissions, pith instructions, and lineages of countless teachings from the kama and terma traditions, including the oral transmissions for the entire *Collected Tantras of the Nyingma School,* Longchenpa's *Seven Treasuries,* and all of Pema Lingpa's teaching cycles.

From Gyurmé Yizhin Wangyal[33] (Mindroling Monastery's throne holder), Dokham Dzogchenpa Zhenpen Tayé, and many other mentors, he received the empowerments, teachings, and oral transmissions for both early and more recent terma cycles, including those focusing on the Eight Commands, *The United Intent of the Gurus,* Vajrakila, and those of Terdak Lingpa. [2.65a] Kunzang Dechen Dorjé also received the oral transmissions for the Kangyur, all of the teachings from the kama transmissions of the Early Translation school, poetics and Tibetan grammar, and Indian and Chinese astrology. In addition, he studied drawing and the casting of deities' images, which included their traditional proportions; the science of medicine from texts such as *The Four Tantras;* and the explanatory traditions of Madhyamaka and other mainstream sources from the Indian Buddhist tradition. He studied subjects from various fields of knowledge and expertise, up to and including the thirteen major activities of a vajra master,[34] becoming a consummate scholar.

In such places as Samdrup, Guru Lhakhang, and the hidden land of Khenjong, he engaged in intensive retreats on the phases of approach and accomplishment for numerous meditation deities and experienced remarkable signs of successful practice, both inwardly and in the external world. Kunzang Dechen Dorjé's projects—building representations of the three aspects of enlightenment—were as limitless as his study and practice. He had a great many students who were later able to benefit both themselves and others; in addition, the students to whom he gave the preliminaries and main body of teachings, empowerments, instructions, oral transmissions, and so forth were truly beyond number. Kunzang Dechen Dorjé passed into nirvana in his forty-ninth year.

The Ninth Pema Lingpa, Tendzin Chökyi Gyaltsen (1894–1925)

The ninth Pema Lingpa, Tendzin Chökyi Gyaltsen, was the son of Chimé Dorjé of the Nyö clan (the lord of the dharma in Tamzhing) and his wife, Chödrön. [2.65b] Omens surrounded his birth, and signs of the circumstances of his preceding lifetime were evident when he was very young. He was recognized as the rebirth of the eighth lord master, and at the age of five, he was invited to Lhalung and enthroned.

With the vajra holder Pema Tsewang, he learned to read and write; he memorized rituals and trained in their traditional performance. His studies also included ritual dance, painting, and chanting. He received a number of empowerments and oral transmissions from Sherab Tendar, Mindroling Monastery's vajra holder, as well as the explanatory teachings on some of the major sources of the Indian Buddhist tradition. From Bakha Rigdzin Khamsum Yongdrol, he received the empowerments, oral transmissions, and pith instructions for a veritable ocean of profound termas, foremost among them the entire cycle of Pema Lingpa's teachings. When he was about twenty, at solitary sites such as Lhalung and Lagyap Drupdé, Tendzin Chökyi Gyaltsen began a series of intensive retreats on the phases of approach and accomplishment for the entire array of deities of the Three Roots.

Invited to Gangteng Monastery, he bestowed all of Pema Lingpa's teachings on Trinlé Dorjé (Pema Trinlé's eighth incarnation) and others. He established meaningful connections with many people, [2.66a] who came to have faith in him. He then returned to his monastic seat in Lhalung, where, as an indication that he had achieved independence from ordinary appearances and mind, he left hand- and footprints in solid rock as easily as if he were stamping them into clay. With his undistorted inner eye, he could clearly perceive and therefore describe phenomena otherwise hidden from ordinary view. Finally, at Rabkar Tashi Chöling, Kunchen Tsultrim Dorjé's monastic seat, the display of Tendzin Chökyi Gyalten's emanated form resolved back into the basic space of phenomena.

The Tenth Pema Lingpa, Pema Ösel Gyurmé Dorjé (Tupten Chökyi Dorjé) (1930–1955)

The tenth Pema Lingpa, Pema Ösel Gyurmé Dorjé, was born in Dekyi Khangsar in Pa Valley, Yamdrok. His father was Puntsok Gyalpo, renowned as a direct descendant of the tertön Samten Lingpa, and his mother was Jangchub Lamdrön. The thirteenth Dalai Lama, Tupten Gyatso, proclaimed him the unquestionable tulku of Pema Lingpa; at the age of five, he was invited to Lhalung and enthroned. His tutor was one Ngawang Chokden, with whom he initially learned to read and write. [2.66b] He then memorized rituals and ceremonies particular to his lineage, studying their traditional performance and how to put them into practice. He also studied ritual dance, painting, chanting, and other subjects, mastering all of them without difficulty.

When he was eleven, Pema Ösel Gyurmé Dorjé went on a pilgrimage to Lhasa and was ordained as a monk by the Ratreng regent.[35] He then invited Gyurmé Dechen Chödzin, Mindroling Monastery's vajra holder, to Lhalung. From him he received the empowerments, oral transmissions, and profound instructions for the entire cycle of Pema Lingpa's termas, Pema Lingpa's collected works, and those of his spiritual heirs, as well as the empowerments and oral transmissions of the Mindroling and Tersar traditions. The two then went to Samdrup Guru Lhakhang, where Pema Ösel Gyurmé Dorjé received all of the empowerments and oral transmissions for *The Noble Vase of Sadhanas Yielding All That Is Wished For* and the peaceful and wrathful deities of *The Web of Magical Display,* the major empowerment for *The Discourse on United Intent,* and the oral transmissions for the root volumes of *The Heart Drop of Longchenpa,* as well as the teaching transmissions for *The Seven Treasuries* and *The Three Cycles of Being at Ease.* He diligently studied the laying out and drawing of the mandalas associated with these transmissions, as well as related subjects.

In his fifteenth year, Pema Ösel Gyurmé Dorjé journeyed to Wangdü Chöling, where he had an audience with King Jigmé Wangchuk of Bhutan. When he returned to his monastic seat, he undertook intensive retreats on the phases of approach and accomplishment for many deities of the Three Roots. [2.67a] When he was nineteen, he went to Mindroling Monastery, where he received the empowerments and oral transmissions for *The Treasury of Precious Hidden Teachings* from the sixth Zhechen Rabjam.[36] He also received numerous empowerments and teachings from many holy masters, such as Khenchen Ngawang Khyentsé Norbu. At twenty-three Pema Ösel Gyurmé Dorjé received from Kyabjé Dudjom Rinpoché the entire range of empowerments and oral transmissions for the thirteen volumes of *The United Intent of the Gurus,* as well as the oral transmission for the main source text of the protective deity Ma-ning according to the tradition of Pema Lingpa. In response to a formal request by the lamas and monks of the Tarling and Nyimalung Monasteries, Pema Ösel Gyurmé Dorjé conferred the profound and extensive empowerments, teachings, and oral transmissions for all of Pema Lingpa's termas at Wangdü Chöling. Finally, at the age of twenty-six, he passed away into a state of peace.

The Eleventh Pema Lingpa, Kunzang Pema Rinchen Namgyal Ngedön Tenpai Nyima (b. 1968)

The eleventh Pema Lingpa was born at Pangtö Monastery in Chumé on the plateau of Bumthang amid extremely positive signs. His father was Trinlé Namgyal, a direct descendant of Druptop Chungtrul Pema Wangchen, and his mother was Rinchenmo. The proclamations of deities and gurus left no doubt that he was the rebirth of the former master and was in fact the embodiment of his enlightened speech. [2.67b] At the age of five, Kunzang Pema Rinchen donned the crown of the king of the dharma Pema Lingpa, and was enthroned and honored.

To increase his understanding of the dharma, he studied with a succession of tutors and mentors of recent times. In particular, he studied with the two greatest masters of the teachings of the Early Translation school: Kyabjé Dudjom Drodul Lingpa and Kyabjé Dilgo Khyentsé Rinpoché. From them he received the threefold transmission of empowerments, oral transmissions, and teachings, as well as the pith instructions and traditional methods, of the kama and terma traditions of the Early Translation school. He also received, without sectarian bias, empowerments, instructions, and oral transmissions of other schools. Today he continues to devotedly seek the boundless nectar of maturing empowerments and liberating instructions, his lotus feet standing firmly in the vajra realm.[37]

Rigdzin Pema Trinlé and the Family Lineages of the Pema Lingpa Tradition

As mentioned previously, the second figure in Pema Lingpa's family lineage was Rigdzin Pema Trinlé, the son of Pema Lingpa's son Dawa Gyaltsen (although certain accounts maintain that the second figure was actually the son of the lord Tendzin Chökyi Drakpa).[38] From an early age, this master of awareness was spiritually and materially cared for by the lord Tendzin Drakpa. The latter helped him perfect his study and contemplation of the lineage of the Omniscient King of the Dharma, as well as Pema Lingpa's termas and other cycles. [2.68a] Tendzin Drakpa was thus an extraordinary master, the lord of Rigdzin Pema Trinlé's buddha family.

Later, Rigdzin Pema Trinlé founded Gangteng Sang-ngak Chöling, a monastic center in Bhutan, following his guru's prophecy and directive. Since then, there have been successive form incarnations of Pema Trinlé,[39] down to the present Gangteng Choktrul Rinpoché;[40] he and Peling Dungsé Rinpoché Tuksé Dawa (who resides at Trakar Monastery in Bhutan) maintain these teachings. At Gangteng and Trakar, one can view tombs containing the embalmed remains of the former incarnations, as well as their personal effects, such as hand drums, bells, and malas.

The successive Tuksé incarnations have continued to take rebirth, down to the current Tuksé Rinpoché. The third Pema Lingpa, Lhalung Sungtrul Tsultrim Dorjé, was a greatly learned and accomplished master and a contemporary of the fifth Dalai Lama, who conferred on Tsultrim Dorjé the monastic seat of Lhalung in Lhodrak. It became the permanent seat of the successive incarnations, who henceforth were also called the Lhalung Sungtruls, down to the current Sungtrul Rinpoché.[41] As a result of the spiritual activity of the earlier and later incarnations, connections have developed between their respective monastic seats. Lhalung is considered the "mother" monastery, and the "children" include the monasteries of Tamshing (Pema Lingpa's seat), [2.68b] Tarpa Ling, and Samten Ling on the plateau of Bumthang; Trakar; and Gangteng. In order to pass on the profound teachings, the tulkus have alternated as each other's guru and student, the three incarnation lineages[42] having become renowned as those of the "triad of the father Pema Lingpa and his descendants." Together they guard the teachings in Bhutan, as well as throughout upper and lower Tibet. Their enlightened activity has ensured that the teachings of the very essence remain to this day in the kingdom of Bhutan and the southern reaches of the Himalayas.

Great lineage holders of the teachings of the very essence have been connected to these tulkus as either their gurus or students. These include Khedrup Bakha Tulku Khamsum Yongdrol, Dzogchenpa Sönam Rinchen, Ngawang Pema of Jachung, Dzogchenpa Drukdra Dorjé, Sokdokpa Lodrö Gyaltsen, Lochen Zhenpen Dorjé of Gong-ra, and Terchen Ngawang Zhikpo Lingpa. Through them the sunlike splendor of the teachings of the essence of utter lucidity has spread from the central, south central, and southern regions of Tibet to China, India, Mongolia, and beyond, to the entire world. [2.69a] All of this is proof of the superb motivation and enlightened activity of the victorious one Longchenpa, the Omniscient King of the Dharma.

This concludes my discussion of the incarnation lineage of the Omniscient One.

11

The Students of Rigdzin Terdak Lingpa

Rigdzin Terdak Lingpa is renowned in the Nyingtik lineage, for his gracious kindness and influence were instrumental in its development. The lineages of his students fall into two categories: that of students associated with his monastic seat and that of his other students.

THE LINEAGE OF RIGDZIN TERDAK LINGPA'S MAIN SEAT

As for the lineage associated with Terdak Lingpa's main seat, the role of Gyalsé Rinchen Namgyal was discussed in the context of the mainstream lineage.[1] However, this lineage was also passed from Terdak Lingpa to his daughter, Kunzang Mingyur Paldrön.

Kunzang Mingyur Paldrön (1699–1769)

The birth of Kunzang Mingyur Paldrön was prophesied in the fundamental tantra *The Reverberation of Sound,* which refers to the "dakini Paldzin." From an early age, she exhibited unparalleled wisdom and realization. Terchen Lama[2] praised her, saying, "The lineage of teachings in my family will be held not by a son, but by my daughter."

During a period of political upheaval brought on by an invasion of Mongol forces,[3] Kunzang Mingyur Paldrön went to Sikkim and so suffered no hardship. She remained there for a long time, benefiting her students enormously, pursuing her spiritual practice, and founding the Khachö Pema Yangtsé monastic center, [2.69b] where a lineage of teachings has been held and practiced to the present day in Sikkim.

She eventually returned to her main seat of Mindroling Monastery, where she stayed for an extended period at Khachö Dechen Ling,[4] continually bestowing the teachings of natural great perfection and gathering an enormous number of students—such was her great kindness in ensuring the continuity of the teachings. Kunzang Mingyur Paldrön could clearly recall her previous lifetimes as Yeshé Tsogyal and Azhé Nangsa Öbum.[5] She gained mastery over the energies in her subtle channels and realized the expanse of enlightened intent: the perception of awareness's naturally manifest appearances without bias. She wrote many commentaries, including a teaching manual based on the mother and child collections of the Nyingtik teachings. She came to have many fine students, among them Chung-ré Pema Longyang, the great throne holder Pema Tendzin, and Khenchen Oddiyana. She thus ensured consummate benefit for beings.

Khenchen Oddiyana (Orgyen Tendzin Dorjé) (1742–1789?)

Khenchen Oddiyana received the pith instructions of the supreme secret from both Rinchen Namgyal and Mingyur Paldrön. He was the son of the throne holder Rinchen Namgyal, and the younger brother of the throne holder Pema Tendzin. [2.70a] His habit patterns clearly indicated that he was an incarnation of Yudra Nyingpo. From an early age, he studied with both his lord father and Jetsün Mingyur Paldrön. He received an overview of the secret teachings (including the cycles of Pema Lingpa's teachings and of more recent Mindroling termas) and the secret Nyingtik teachings of the Dzogchen approach of utter lucidity (the three Yangtik cycles, *The Three Cycles of Being at Ease,* and so forth). Having received these profound instructions—maturing empowerments, liberating instructions, and supportive oral transmissions—in their entirety, Khenchen Oddiyana became a remarkable holder of the ultimate lineage.

He was fully ordained as a monk by Rabjam Gyurmé Chöden, becoming a great elder and holder of Vinaya. In the history of monks ordained at Mindroling Monastery, he is referred to as "the lord Orgyen Tendzin."

Khenchen Oddiyana memorized six major volumes of source texts on such subjects as Madhyamaka, valid cognition, Vinaya, Abhidharma, and Prajñaparamita, as well as *Ascertaining the Three Levels of Ordination* and *The Ornament of the Lord of Secrets' Enlightened Intent.* He perfected his training in these disciplines, following the methods of correct reasoning. The lotus of his wisdom blossomed fully in all topics of the sutras and tantras, as well as in fields of secular knowledge. [2.70b] Prolific in his activity, he encountered no impediment in the three spheres of explaining, debating, and writing about the teachings. His enormous kindness ensured the continuity of the teachings and benefit for beings to a consummate degree.

His successor as abbot was the vajra holder Rigdzin Zangpo of the Nyang clan in Lhodrak. From him the lineage of ordination was continued by such masters as Dokham Dzogchenpa Sengtruk Pema Tashi and Jamyang Khyentsei Wangpo. Khenchen Oddiyana was exceedingly gracious in ensuring the continuity, to the present day, of the teachings of the three bases of Vinaya[6]—the practical implementation of the lineage of monastic ordination handed down from the great Indian abbot Shantarakshita, which has flourished in all six of the great monastic centers of the Early Translation school that upholds the teachings of the supreme secret. He also transmitted the profound pith instructions of the supremely secret Vajrayana—most notably the extraordinary Dzogchen approach of the secret Nyingtik teachings—to the great throne holder Gyurmé Trinlé Namgyal. In these and other ways, Khenchen Oddiyana perfected his noble activities to ensure the spontaneous accomplishment of the two kinds of benefit.

It was from this holy guru that Trichen Gyurmé Trinlé Namgyal received the tantras, explanatory commentaries, and pith instructions concerning the sublime secret.

Trichen Gyurmé Trinlé Namgyal (1765–1812)

Gyurmé Trinlé Namgyal, an emanation of Vimalamitra, was born amid wondrous signs [2.71a] as the son of the great throne holder Gyurmé Pema Tendzin. From an early age, he studied and trained to a consummate degree with numerous mentors, including his lord father, the great master of awareness. He was then appointed to succeed his father as the holder of the great throne of Orgyen Mindroling Monastery.

He carried out activities on behalf of the teachings on a vast scale, ensuring the flourishing of all the traditions of his paternal ancestors. In particular, Gyurmé Trinlé Namgyal received all the transmissions of the tantras, explanatory commentaries, and pith instructions of the sublime secret from his paternal uncle, Oddiyana, like one vase being filled from another. He practiced these, gaining sublime accomplishment through the path of natural great perfection. Taken under the care of his meditation deities, he mastered the entire range of a vajra holder's activities and showed signs of having attained siddhis. He turned the wheel of the dharma for his students, primarily those who maintained the teachings at Mindroling, and was thus highly influential in ensuring that the teachings would flourish and the two kinds of benefit would be accomplished. Finally, he allowed his enlightened intent to resolve back into the basic space of a state of peace.

It was from this holy one that both Trichen Pema Wangyal—an emanation of the great, powerful Hayagriva—and [2.71b] the venerable Trinlé Chödrön received the tantras, explanatory commentaries, and pith instructions of the most sublime secret.

Jetsünma Trinlé Chödrön (18th–19th Centuries)

Marvelous positive signs heralded the birth of Jetsünma Trinlé Chödrön, daughter of the great throne holder Trinlé Namgyal. At an early age, she began her training with reading and writing and, having mastered all the subjects she studied, became a paragon of scholars. She pursued her studies of the methods of the sutras and tantras with her paternal relatives, as well as with the brilliant scholar Rabjampa Palgön. She received the cycles of the more recent Mindroling termas that were her father's legacy, as well as many other empowerments and teachings, such as *The Noble Vase of Sadhanas Yielding All That Is Wished For,* and those from Pema Lingpa's cycle.

She engaged in intensive retreats on the phases of approach and accomplishment for many deities of the Three Roots, and signs of having attained siddhis became fully evident. From her lord father, she received the cycles of the secret Nyingtik teachings of the Dzogchen approach and put them into practice. In so doing, Trinlé Chödrön directly experienced an authentic degree of confidence born of realization and reached the furthest limit of the four visions, becoming a lineage holder of natural great perfection.

To benefit others, she turned the wheel of the dharma on an incalculable scale, bestowing empowerments, spiritual instructions, and teachings. [2.72a] She had a multitude of students, whom she brought to spiritual maturity and liberation. Thus this venerable woman of Mindroling was the only one whose activities surpassed those of Mingyur Paldrön.

From three great teachers—Jetsünma Trinlé Chödrön, the throne holder Pema Wangyal, and his son, the throne holder Sang-gyé Kunga (an incarnation of the great Nupchen Sang-gyé Yeshé)—Jamyang Khyentsei Wangpo received a veritable ocean of spiritual methods. Foremost among these were the Nyingtik teachings of Dzogchen—the maturing empowerments, liberating instructions, entrusted advice, and so forth, of the Vajrayana approach of the supreme secret—transmitted through Mindroling.

It was Jamgön Kongtrul Lodrö Tayé's fortune to receive the transmissions of the direct lineages of the two lines of Nyingtik teachings, and in fact he received these transmissions from Jamyang Khyentsei Wangpo. He wrote teaching manuals on the mother and child cycles of the Nyingtik teachings and founded the important retreat center Tsadra Rinchen Drak.[7] Jamyang Khyentsei Wangpo, Gyalsé Zhenpen Tayé, and Jamgön Lodrö Tayé imparted to a succession of students the transmissions they had received from Mindroling and other traditions, thus ensuring that these teachings spread not only throughout Tibet but to every corner of the globe. [2.72b]

Although Jamyang Khyentsei Wangpo thus received transmissions from all three gurus of Mindroling, in the particular case of the Nyingtik teachings, the lineage he established came primarily from Trinlé Chödrön.

In the succession of Mindroling Monastery, there was an uninterrupted series of eight throne holders who were vajra masters of the Nyö clan, including Yizhin Wangyal (the son of Sang-gyé Kunga) and Dechen Chokdrup. Following that, the family line of Mindroling waned but was restored by an incarnation of Terdak Lingpa, the son of Nyarong Tertön Rang-rik Dorjé of eastern Tibet. This led to a renewed succession of three throne holders, the present-day holder, Kunzang Wangyal, being the eleventh. These masters constitute the lineage of throne holders who have served the teachings of the supreme quintessential secret, specifically the tradition of Orgyen Mindroling. More extensive accounts of their lives and activities can be found in *The Account of the Succession of Mindroling* and the records of its lineages.

OTHER STUDENTS OF RIGDZIN TERDAK LINGPA

Lotsawa Chöpal Gyatso (1654–1718)

Foremost among Terdak Lingpa's many students was his younger brother, Lotsawa Chöpal Gyatso. His birth was heralded in a prophecy, as follows:

> There will come one endowed with bodhichitta, faith, diligence, and courage— ༔ [2.73a]
> an intelligent one named Dharma,[8] an incarnation of Yudra Nyingpo. ༔

Chöpal Gyatso spent his entire life extensively explaining, debating, and writing about the teachings. He wrote explanatory commentaries on many fields of knowledge, a major commentary on *Ascertaining the Three Levels of Ordination,* and innumerable treatises concerning empowerments, sadhana practices, and permission blessings from the outer and inner cycles of the mantra approach. He composed four texts on *The Discourse on United Intent:* an overview; a mandala ritual, *Stainless Garlands of Light;* a lineage supplication for this ritual; and a text, *The Lamp of Approach, Accomplishment, Empowerment, and the Four Activities.* In addition, he wrote *The Ornament of the Lord of Secrets' Enlightened Intent,* a commentary on *The Heart Essence of Secrets,* and an overview entitled *The Oral Transmission of the Lord of Secrets.* He also taught the tantras during the summer and winter sessions at the shedra, continually nurturing students and bringing them to spiritual maturity.

In various places and at various times, Chöpal Gyatso carried out intensive retreats on the phases of approach and accomplishment for the entire range of his meditation deities, had visions of them, and showed signs of spiritual attainment. He directly experienced the enlightened intent of great perfection: the perception of awareness's naturally manifest appearances without bias. As one who illuminated the teachings in a unique way, [2.73b] he maintained the theory and practice of Terchen Lama.

He journeyed to Tsang, Chamdo, and other regions. He was honored and venerated by his numerous students, among them such great personages as the Sakya Dakchen Kunga Tashi, Gyalwa Pakpalha of Chamdo, and Chakra Tulku. In this way, Chöpal Gyatso engaged in enlightened activities on a vast scale for all beings regardless of their status.

Finally, during the period of hardship brought on by the Dzungar Mongol invasion, Chöpal Gyatso passed away at sixty-five on the twenty-fourth day of the first lunar month.[9] Using the profound technique of the transference of consciousness, he withdrew his enlightened intent to a pure realm. Having studied with both brothers, this master's students are described in Terdak Lingpa's biography.

Riksé Choktrul Pema Gyurmé Gyatso (1686–1718)

Riksé Choktrul Pema Gyurmé Gyatso was born amid marvelous signs to Terchen Lama and Yönten Drolma. His birth was prophesied in his father's termas:

A son of the family, an emanation of Hayagriva, ༔
will engage in Vajradhara's conduct to benefit beings. ༔

At an early age, like one vase being filled to the brim from another, Pema Gyurmé Gyatso began receiving a host of profound teachings from the "two holy masters."[10] [2.74a] When he was twenty years old, he was fully ordained as a monk by Lochen. With the lord of the dharma Zhenpen Wangpo, he trained in many fields of knowledge—Vinaya, Abhidharma, Prajñaparamita, and so forth—until he had completely mastered them. He invited the tutor Wangchukpa from Gongkar Monastery and under him became learned in teachings, such as *The Vajra Garland,* of the Sarma schools of the secret mantra approach. He also became proficient in Sanskrit grammar, valid cognition, and secular subjects.

When he turned thirty, Pema Gyurmé Gyatso succeeded his lord father, the king of the dharma, to the throne. He wrote many treatises, including a commentary on poetry and poetics, overviews of Prajñaparamita and the tantra *The Heart Essence of Secrets,* a supplication to the lineage of the three levels of ordination, and pith instructions crucial to the enactment rituals of the longevity deity Tsedak. His father honored him with the pronouncement, "The rain of dharma is greater from the son than from his father." Pema Gyurmé Gyatso thus carried out his spiritual activities, until he finally passed away during the time of the Mongol invasion, the mandala of his emanated form resolving back into the basic space of a state of peace. [2.74b]

The "brothers of Mindroling"[11] and those in their family line, as well as the successive throne holders, have been enormously beneficial to the teachings of the three cycles—*The Discourse on United Intent*, *The Web of Magical Display,* and the mind teachings—and have had a great impact on their development. It is significant that they are lauded as "wellsprings of the teachings of the supreme secret."

Minling Trichen Kunzang Pema Wangyal (b. 1931)

Kyabjé Kunzang Pema Wangyal, the present Minling Trichen, lives in India.[12] He was born amid countless amazing signs and events into the second generation of the line of Nyarong Tertön Rang-rik Dorjé, who revivified the family line of Mindroling. At an early age, Kunzang Wangyal awakened to his holy heritage, as patterns established in previous lifetimes began to assert themselves, so that he could read and write and learn other subjects without any difficulty. He began by memorizing the collected prayers of the Mindroling tradition, following which he gradually studied its styles of ritual, chanting, music, dance, sacred art, and so forth. He mastered these skills while receiving personal training, so that he understood them thoroughly, without interpolating in the slightest from other traditions.

Foremost among his gurus were his uncle, Rang-rik Dorjé; Kyabjé Minling Chung Rinpoché;[13] Khenchen Rinpoché; Jamyang Chökyi Lodrö; and Kyabjé Dudjom Rinpoché. From these and other masters, he received such transmissions as the kama teachings of the Early Translation school, *The Treasury of Precious Hidden Teachings,* [2.75a] *The Four Higher Collections of the Heart Drop,* and the source text of the tantra *The Heart Essence of Secrets* and its commentaries. In addition, he received the cycles of Mindroling's own termas, including *The Heart Essence of the Profound Meaning of Ati.* Having heard these teachings, Kunzang Wangyal contemplated them and put them into practice. At the retreat center of his main seat, he undertook intensive retreats focusing on a number of his personal meditation deities—Mañjushri Yamantaka, the Eight Commands cycle *The Gathering of Sugatas,* peaceful and wrathful forms of Guru Rinpoché, and others—and so gained mastery through his attainment of the extraordinary and more common siddhis associated with these deities. He received personal transmissions of such profound terma cycles as the red form of Avalokiteshvara and *The Means to Avert the Four Maras* (pith instructions associated with the Lord of Sages, the tamer of maras).

When the land of Tibet was threatened by barbarian hordes, Minling Trichen Kunzang Wangyal, due to his motivation and aspirations of former lifetimes, was able to travel through Bhutan to India without hindrance. There he attended a council of the masters of general and specific traditions of the Early Translation school, headed by Kyabjé Dudjom Rinpoché. In response to the wishes of those assembled and with the encouragement of Gongsa Kyabgön Chenpo,[14] Kunzang Wangyal was installed, in the tradition of the Trichen masters of the past, with great ceremony as a king of the dharma for the three realms on the golden throne of the Trichens.

He then resided for some time [2.75b] at the temple of Zangdok Palri in Kalimpong. Eventually, at the invitation of Dzonang Rinpoché of the Palyul tradition and Gonjo Khochim Choktrul Rinpoché, Minling Trichen Kunzang Wangyal traveled to Minling Ngedön Gatsal Ling in Dehra Dun, India, where he still lives. Joining his aspirations with those of Khochim Rinpoché, Minling Trichen has established such rituals as the celebration of the tenth day of the lunar calendar, the year-end protector practices, sadhanas focusing on the Eight Commands, *The Supreme Assembly,* Khorwa Dongtruk, and so forth, according to the traditions of the past. In the sacred presence of Gongsa Kyabgön Chenpo, Minling Trichen presided over a ceremony for that master's long life and their minds merged, becoming one.

Minling Trichen often seems to sleep for months at a time, resting constantly in the state of utter lucidity, day and night. He demonstrates the conduct of a siddha in many amazing ways. For example, when he performs a ritual injunction to banish demons and hindering forces, they are quelled; when he grants his blessings, obstacles are overcome; and he is aware of events hidden from ordinary perception.

Furthermore, in his "Prayer of Calling the Guru from Afar," written for his scribe, Nordzin, this lord has said of himself:

> Although you have reached an advanced age,
> you pay no attention to anyone's advice.

> You engage in the uncontrived conduct of a child.
> O Kunzang Wangyal, you know all! [2.76a]

This verse is the extraordinary autobiography of this sublime master, for it is a spontaneous song that expresses his genuine state of being, indicating that he is free of the chains of hope and fear that derive from the eight worldly concerns, that for him confusion has collapsed within basic space, and that he has severed the four maras, which foster arrogance, at the root. Minling Trichen continues to uphold the example set by the great throne holders of the past, serving as a noble protector of the teachings of the supreme secret.

Katokpa Gyalsé Rinpoché Sönam Detsen (1675–1723)

Another of the great Terdak Lingpa's students was Katokpa Sönam Detsen. His noble father was Terchen Longsel Nyingpo, and his mother was Geden Lhakyi. He was born amid innumerable marvelous signs. From an early age, he exhibited extraordinary signs of someone holy.[15] He received many profound teachings from his noble father (for example, the recently discovered terma *The Vajra Heart Essence*) and from Dzogchenpa Drupwang Pema Rigdzin (especially *The Heart Drop of the Dakini*), and so came to experience naturally indwelling timeless awareness, as the realization that constitutes the ultimate transmission arose in his mind.

He journeyed through Lhasa and Samyé to Orgyen Mindroling Monastery. There he met Rigdzin Terdak Lingpa, from whom he received many profound transmissions, including the great Nyingtik teachings of Dzogchen [2.76b] passed down from the Omniscient King of the Dharma, Longchenpa.

Through the path of natural great perfection, Sönam Detsen attained the most sublime siddhi, becoming the foremost among Terdak Lingpa's extraordinary students. In addition, he went to meet Rigdzin Chenpo of Dorjé Drak Monastery and many other masters, receiving from them a vast range of teachings of sutra and tantra, including the kama and terma transmissions, all of which he heard, contemplated, and practiced to a consummate degree. Eventually, he returned to eastern Tibet and his home monastery, Katok Dorjéden, where he undertook intensive personal retreats, which led to experiences that ordinary people cannot fathom, such as visions of his personal meditation deities and signs of siddhis. Sönam Detsen thus continued to uphold the teachings of the Katok tradition until his forty-ninth year, when, amid immeasurable amazing omens, his emanated form resolved back into the palace of Pema Ö in the realm of Chamara.

The lineage of Sönam Detsen's tulkus has continued to the present day with the successive Zhingkyong tulkus.[16] Another of Sönam Detsen's incarnations was Duddul Rolpa Tsal, whose next incarnation was Traktung Dudjom Lingpa; the latter's incarnation in turn was my sublime guide, Kyabjé Dudjom Drodul Lingpa Tsal.[17] I offer this observation to those uninformed people who from time to time have expressed their doubts as to whether Dudjom Rinpoché belonged to an incarnation lineage associated with one of the six majors centers of the Early Translation school. [2.77a]

The Second Dzogchen Rinpoché, Gyurmé Tekchok Tendzin (1699–1758)

When the first Dzogchen Rinpoché, Drupwang Pema Rigdzin, was preparing to direct his enlightened intent to another realm, the fortunate students gathered around him prayed fervently that he would take rebirth. Thus this second incarnation appeared as the illusory display of his immeasurable, innate compassion. Gyurmé Tekchok Tendzin was born in a grove lush with flowers along the Dachu River in the northern reaches of eastern Tibet. After a thorough examination, the governor of Dergé and the preceding incarnation's heart sons recognized him as the indisputable tulku of the former master. Moreover, once such monasteries as Dorjé Drak and Mindroling had completed their investigations, it became certain that this was, in fact, the rebirth of the first Dzogchen Rinpoché. All doubts having been resolved, the boy assumed his formal titles (Pema Tendzin Tekchok Gyatso from Dorjé Drak and Gyurmé Tekchok Tendzin from Mindroling) and was enthroned at his great monastic seat.

He received lay ordination from Dzogchen Pönlop Rinpoché Namkhai Ösel (who had become Dzogchen Monastery's regent after the passing of the first Dzogchen Rinpoché);[18] the first Rabjam, Tenpai Gyaltsen;[19] and others. They offered him a number of empowerments; he accepted these, then put the methods into practice. [2.77b] At the age of eleven, during a visit to central Tibet, Gyurmé Tekchok Tendzin received the majority of profound termas revealed by Terchen Nyidrak (foremost among the preceding incarnation's students) and his son. From Könchok Trinlé Palzang of the Drigung Kagyü school, he received the Yamantaka cycle entitled *Molten Metal*. In Lhasa he made extensive offerings at shrines housing sublime representations such as the two statues of the lord Shakyamuni.

He then made his way to Dorjé Drak and Mindroling. From the regent of Padma, the king of the dharma Terdak Lingpa, Gyurmé Tekchok Tendzin received the lay ordination consisting of the vow of taking refuge in the Three Jewels; the bodhisattva vow; and empowerments and oral transmissions of the secret mantra approach on a vast scale. He honored Terdak Lingpa as one who was extremely gracious to him. At Sha-uk Takgo, this great tertön had revealed the profound terma of Mahakarunika entitled *The Gathering of All Sugatas*. Its written history contains the statement, "From eastern Tibet will appear one adhering to yogic practice, an incarnation of Langdro named Pema Drakpo." Terdak Lingpa praised Gyurmé Tekchok Tendzin as the one Guru Padmakara had thus prophesied to be the custodian of this teaching and enthroned him as the holder of a veritable ocean of teachings from the kama and terma traditions of the Early Translation school. From then on, Gyurmé Tekchok Tendzin regarded this guru, the great tertön, as his root guru and someone of extraordinary grace and kindness. [2.78a] In addition, he was ordained as a novice monk by

Zhabdrung Pema Trinlé of Dorjé Drak. Subsequently, on a second visit to central Tibet, he received full monastic ordination from Gyaltsep Kalzang Pema Wangchuk.

Gyurmé Tekchok Tendzin studied extensively. His teachers included Lochen Chöpal Gyatso, Rinchen Namgyal, and the brother and sister Pema Gyurmé Gyatso and Kunzang Mingyur Paldrön. From them Gyurmé Tekchok Tendzin received the teachings of the kama tradition in three sections: *The Discourse on United Intent, The Web of Magical Display,* and the mind teachings. He also received a host of other teachings, principally the termas of the Mindroling tradition. From Pari Tulku Ngawang Kunzang Pema, he received the Eight Commands cycle *The Gathering of the Sugatas,* and from Ngawang Kunzang Dorjé, the fourth Pema Lingpa, numerous profound teachings, foremost among these the tantras of the Nyingma school.

Returning to eastern Tibet, Gyurmé Tekchok Tendzin received the experiential instructions for the profound and secret cycle *The Heart Drop of the Dakini* from the first Pönlop Rinpoché, Namkhai Ösel, the lord of his buddha family. He absorbed everything without alteration, including the slightest comment on or suggestion about traditional methods of application, and became a virtual repository of advice on this system. In addition, he studied with more than twenty tutors, including Lingter Pema Wangchuk and two successive Khamtrul incarnations, and received a vast range of teachings, foremost among these the Kangyur. [2.78b] He thus listened to and contemplated an enormous number of teachings.

For twelve years, he engaged in intensive retreat on the phases of approach and accomplishment and came to experience all of samsara and nirvana as a cosmic array of purity, a never-ending web of magical display. Leaving nothing incomplete, he practiced the phase of approach for numerous deities of the four classes of tantra, especially all of the kama and terma traditions of the Early Translation school, until definite signs of accomplishment arose. His ongoing practice included *The Confession of Failings,* Tara meditation, and the prayer "The Spontaneous Accomplishment of Wished-for Goals." He recited each hundreds of thousands of times and completed more than two hundred million repetitions of the six-syllable mantra *Om mani padme hum.* He practiced trekchö and tögal to the point of total immersion in the experience of his ordinary thoughts as the display of timeless awareness. In such ways, he applied himself to spiritual practice.

As for the sphere of his activity, Gyurmé Tekchok Tendzin drew and sculpted hundreds of images of buddhas and bodhisattvas. He published *The Collected Tantras of the Nyingma School* and several printings of Longchenpa's *Seven Treasuries.* In a Water Bird year,[20] he installed the three kinds of representations, finer than the previous ones, in the great shrine hall of Dzogchen Monastery. He erected the magnificent gilded tomb of the lord of his buddha family, Pönlop Rinpoché Namkhai Ösel, and arranged splendid offerings around it. [2.79a] In addition, he made extensive offerings at all of the principal and secondary holy sites throughout eastern, central, and south central Tibet. He paid his respects and made offerings at monastic seats and monasteries throughout Tibet, primarily to all the great masters of the four schools of the Tibetan tradition of the Victorious One's teachings. He donated provisions to and honored the practice centers of the Chimpu Uplands, as well as Pari, Katok, and others of the Nyingma tradition.

As for Gyurmé Tekchok Tendzin's teachings of the dharma, he gave the oral transmissions twice for the Kangyur and five or six times each for cycles focusing on the Eight Commands, *The United Intent of the Gurus, The Discourse on United Intent, The Perfection of Sublime Knowing in One Hundred Thousand Verses* and other cycles (including five transmissions of the Nyingma tantras). In addition to his countless transmissions of the dharma—maturing empowerments, liberating instructions, advice, and so forth—he left two volumes of his own writings.

Among his heart sons and students were innumerable sublime masters who held his lineage. They included Kalzang Pema Wangchuk of Dorjé Drak; Pari Tulku; Zurtrul Trinlé Loden Gyatso; the first Drimé Zhingkyong Gönpo of Katok; Nyitrul Pema Tekchok Gyaltsen; the second Dzogchen Pönlop, Sang-ngak Tendzin;[21] the second Zhechen Rabjam; two successive Khamtrul incarnations;[22] [2.79b] Nyidrak Gyalsé Orgyen Tendzin; and Jé-ön Pema Kundrol Namgyal.

Gyurmé Tekchok Tendzin thus engaged in the three spheres of activity, extending incomparable kindness to the monastery founded by Drupwang Dzogchen, as well as to its affiliates. Having ensured the spontaneous accomplishment of the two kinds of benefit, amid innumerable marvelous events that heralded his complete liberation—such as visions of an oceanic array of the Three Roots and oath-bound guardians—Gyurmé Tekchok Tendzin resolved his outwardly apparent manifestation into the supreme basic space of the youthful vase.

Barchung Lama Tashi Gyatso (18th Century)

Barchung Lama Tashi Gyatso was foremost among the lord master Gyurmé Tekchok Tendzin's heart sons. He was born in the northern reaches of eastern Tibet, along the banks of the Dzachu, into the Barchung clan. His birth took place on the fifteenth day of the twelfth lunar month of the Victor in a Horse year.[23] Dzogchen Rinpoché Gyurmé Tekchok Tendzin named him Pema Gyurmé Namdrol, declaring, "He is the rebirth of my own guru, Terdak Lingpa." Starting at the age of eight, Tashi Gyatso learned to read, write, and so forth; he easily understood everything and demonstrated a consummate degree of sublime knowing gained in previous lifetimes. At nineteen he was ordained as a monk by one Lama Karma Yeshé [2.80a] and was given the name Gyurmé Tashi Gyatso.

At twenty-two Tashi Gyatso went to Dzogchen Monastery in Rudam, where he studied under the second Dzogchen Rinpoché, Gyurmé Tekchok Tendzin, receiving the empowerments, oral transmissions, and teachings for *The Heart Drop of the Dakini* and many other transmissions of experiential instruction. He also received transmissions for the earlier and later cycles of the secret Nyingtik teachings of the Dzogchen approach, perfectly refining his experience of the true nature of mind. Not content with a mere intellectual evaluation of the nature of phenomena, Tashi Gyatso came to directly experience timeless awareness as the naked unity of awareness and emptiness. The minds of guru and student blended, becoming one, and Gyurmé Tekchok Tendzin conferred on Tashi Gyatso the seal of entrustment for these spiritual instructions, authorizing him to teach, for he had reached the level of a siddha.

When Khamtrul Rinpoché Ngawang Kunga Tendzin of the southern region came to Dza, Tashi Gyatso met him and took monastic ordination. From Kangtsa Lama Dargyé, he received the major empowerment for *The Discourse on United Intent,* together with the seal of entrustment. He received many profound transmissions, such as the recent Mindroling termas, the cycles of peaceful and wrathful deities, and *The Heart Drop of the Dakini.* At the age of twenty-three, he went on a pilgrimage to central Tibet and made offerings. He visited the two images of the lord Shakyamuni and other sites in Lhasa, where he met the seventh Dalai Lama, Kalzang Gyatso. [2.80b] He also met Gyalsé Rinchen Namgyal and other teachers, who conferred on him many tantras and pith instructions. Over a period of five months, Tashi Gyatso, along with Gyalsé Rinchen Namgyal and others, received from the Dratang regent, Khenpo Kunga Khyentsé Puntsok, the oral transmissions for the Kangyur in Kunga Podrang (the private chambers of Mindroling's throne holder). Later, Tashi Gyatso spread these transmissions widely throughout eastern Tibet, becoming known as "Kangyurpa Tashi Gyatso." Together with Rinchen Namgyal, he received the transmissions for the sealed pure visions of the fifth Dalai Lama, the new Mindroling termas, the kama teachings of the Nyingma school, and other teachings.

Having taken full monastic ordination from Dönyö Palzang of Mindroling, an incarnation of Lochen Kawa Paltsek, Tashi Gyatso gave up the life of a householder and became a "homeless one"[24] as well as a threefold vajra holder, standing like a mountain of gold. He then returned to eastern Tibet, where, throughout Kham—upper and lower Dza, Golok, and so forth—he turned the wheel of the dharma, giving such transmissions as those for the precious Kangyur and the Nyingtik teachings of the Dzogchen approach. He thus ensured for beings benefit equal to the sky and became an excellent holder of the lineage of the Drupwang Dzogchenpa in Dokham, eastern Tibet.

This master's tulku was Gyalsé Zhenpen Tayé, said to have been born with the ability to clearly recall the Kangyur due to habit patterns established by his former incarnation, Barchung Lama Tashi Gyatso. [2.81a] Tashi Gyatso's many students, and theirs in turn, have engaged to the present day in an enormous range of activities connected with the teachings concerning the essence of being, promulgating these teachings throughout the world.

This concludes my brief discussion of the groups of Rigdzin Terdak Lingpa's students.

12

The Students of Rigdzin Jigmé Lingpa and the First Dodrupchen, Jigmé Trinlé Özer

THE STUDENTS OF RIGDZIN JIGMÉ LINGPA

Rigdzin Jigmé Lingpa was an amazing, superb holder of these teachings, a mainstay of the Dzogchen approach, and renowned as the second Omniscient One. Foremost among his many students were the heart sons known as the "four named Jigmé." The first two, Jigmé Gyalwai Nyugu and Dodrup Jigmé Trinlé Özer, have already been discussed.[1]

Jigmé Kundrol Namgyal (18th–19th Centuries)

Jigmé Kundrol Namgyal was born in Dar Valley in the Thimphu Uplands of Bhutan. He was accepted into the ranks of the encampment of the Bhutanese spiritual ruler, the Drukpa Chöjé. Over time, he gained official recognition within the fortress of Chötsé.[2] During his tenure as an administrator, he became appalled and deeply saddened by the killing that his work involved,[3] and this awakened in him the latent attributes of someone holy. Abandoning the things of this life—pleasant talk, status, companionship, and so forth—as one would a drop of spittle, [2.81b] Jigmé Kundrol Namgyal turned to the sacred dharma.

Initially, he relied on mentors at Mindroling Monastery, listening to and contemplating teachings on the sutras, tantras, and other fields of knowledge. He then went to see the statue of the Buddha in Lhasa—Jowo Rinpoché—and visited important holy sites in central and south central Tibet. He gradually made his way to the Chimpu Uplands in Samyé, where he met the great master Kunchen Rigdzin Jigmé Lingpa. He relied on this mentor with strong devotion expressed in thought, word, and deed; in turn, Jigmé Lingpa cared for him, bestowing all of the tantras, explanatory commentaries, and pith instructions of the Dzogchen approach of utter lucidity. As he practiced, Jigmé Kundrol Namgyal achieved special states of meditative experience and realization. Jigmé Lingpa considered him an extraordinary heart son and gave him the name Jigmé Kundrol Namgyal.

After he had stayed for quite some time, his guru told him, "Go to your home country and pursue spiritual practice on the summit of a mountain shaped like the tip of Vajrakila's dagger; great benefit for the teachings and beings will result. You have the potential to establish the circumstances necessary to repel the hostile border tribes from Assam."[4] Obeying this instruction, Jigmé Kundrol Namgyal returned to Bhutan, where he undertook an intensive retreat on the phases of approach and accomplishment for Dechen Gyalmo, a practice focusing on the spiritual consort Yeshé Tsogyal, first at the cliff known as Tangtowa Drak on the plateau of Bumthang, [2.82a] then at Uruwang Monastery. During that time, he received prophecies from Yeshé Tsogyal in a vision and attained the sublime siddhi. (Today, his monastic seat still stands, fully preserved.)

Later, he went to a solitary place in eastern Bhutan called Dung Samyong Lekgön, one of the eight "spokes" of a wheel-shaped land formation. Nearby was a mountain, the blessings of which were no different from those of the great holy place called Tsari. On its summit, Jigmé Kundrol Namgyal founded a center whose community comprised both saffron-robed monks and white-robed, longhaired lay practitioners. There he maintained the unimpaired and extensive tradition of the essence of the supreme secret.

At one point, when Indian border forces threatened to invade, Jigmé Kundrol Namgyal hurled a wrathful torma toward them, whereupon serpents and tongues of flame issued from it, thoroughly defeating the enemy. It was as though the mahasiddha Virupa had actually returned.[5] From the Bhutanese capital came prayers of praise in his honor and official recognition of his status as a major spiritual teacher.

In more recent times, the great Bhutanese master Sönam Zangpo, a heart son of Tokden Shakya Shri, [2.82b] arranged for His Majesty the King of Bhutan to invite Kyabjé Dudjom Rinpoché to Jigmé Kundrol Namgyal's monastic seat. There he bestowed the empowerments and oral transmissions for the cycles of teachings revealed by Pegyal Lingpa[6] and presided over a drupchen focusing on Vajrakila practice. Later, Kyabjé Dodrupchen Rinpoché devoted great energy to refurbishing its supporting structures and the representations housed therein. By instituting an annual drupchen of Vajrakila practice, monthly rituals to commemorate the tenth day of the lunar month, and so forth, he ensured that worthy activities founded on theory and practice would continue to establish countless fortunate ones in states of liberation and omniscience.

Getsé Jigmé Ngotsar Tendzin (18th–19th Centuries)

Jigmé Ngotsar Tendzin was born, amid countless amazing omens attesting to the purity of his nature, into the Mukpo clan, on the banks of the Dzachu in Getsé, Dokham, the same area in the northern reaches of eastern Tibet in which Jigmé Gyalwai Nyugu was born. There he met and received empowerments and teachings from many gurus who had trained at Zhechen and Dzogchen Monasteries, as well as other lamas who traveled or lived in the upper and lower regions of Dza.

He thought, "Now that I have obtained a human existence as noble as this, endowed with freedom and opportunity, I must request some consummate advice on the Dzogchen approach of the sacred dharma." Having heard of the renowned Rigdzin Jigmé Lingpa, he journeyed to Lhasa. [2.83a] At the holy site of Jangchub Tsering Jong, he met his guru of many lifetimes and prayed to be taken under his care. Jigmé Lingpa cared for him with extraordinary affection, bestowing on him an abundance of the common and more remarkable pith instructions—his *Timeless Awareness as the Guiding Principle* and *Treasury of Enlightened Qualities,* among others—along with the seal of entrustment for this advice. He also gave him the name Jigmé Ngotsar. Through diligent practice, Jigmé Ngotsar Tendzin came to have meditative experiences and realization, boundless qualities arising within him.

Then his guru said, "Return to your home region. In a valley naturally resounding with the Vajrakila mantra is a cave in which the Omniscient One himself miraculously left footprints and other signs. If you establish your main seat there, you will greatly benefit the teachings and beings."

The support that the lord guru Jigmé Lingpa used for his own practice was a statue of the Omniscient One, one of many that had been cast in gold by Kunga Rinchen of Drigung Monastery. The great Omniscient One himself had consecrated these statues, which became renowned as "likenesses of the Omniscient One." Jigmé Lingpa gave his statue to Jigmé Ngotsar Tendzin, along with many other articles to be used as representations at his monastic seat. These included the original manuscripts of the tantra tradition of Vajrakila [2.83b] and *The Treasury of Enlightened Qualities,* handwritten by Jigmé Lingpa himself, as well as the texts *The Gathering of the Great and Glorious Ones, The Command of the Spiritual Consort,* a cycle focusing on the Eight Commands, the picture cards used in empowerments (each marked with Jigmé Lingpa's thumbprint), his ceremonial hat, his bell, and various teaching manuals.

Accepting these, Jigmé Ngotsar Tendzin returned to his home region, where he founded many monastic communities, the monastery of Dzaki Valley foremost among them. Due to the influence of his widespread activities undertaken to benefit the teachings and beings, this seat has endured to the present day. The lineages of Jigmé Ngotsar Tendzin's teachings and students have continued in conjunction with those of Jigmé Gyalwai Nyugu and Dodrup Jigmé Trinlé Özer. The "likeness of the Omniscient One" was later borrowed by Chung-rampa, general of the Tibetan government forces, and used to create the mold from which many replicas were cast in copper and gold. As well, Adzom Drukpa Rinpoché had at his encampment a "likeness" statue from the cave in which Longchenpa had slept at Gang-ri Tökar. He too commissioned replicas, so that each of his students could have a representation of enlightened form as a support for practice. One of these statues passed from [2.84a] Chöden, Jamyang Chökyi Lodrö's shrine keeper, to Kyabjé Dilgo Khyentsé Rinpoché, who in turn made this and earlier statues the basis for some one thousand replicas, cast in India, which he and others used as supports for gathering merit.

Other Students of Jigmé Lingpa

Jigmé Lingpa's students were beyond number, ranging from great gurus and powerful figures down to humble mendicants and venerable practitioners. They included such masters as Longchen Rolpa Tsal; the great throne holder of Sakya and his brother; the two sublime tulkus of the Drigung Kagyü school;[7] the Sungtrul and Tuksé incarnations of Lhodrak; the two abbots of Jangtsé and Shartsé colleges, who upheld the extensive tradition of the Gelukpa school; and Tsona Göntsé Tulku of Bhutan. Their enlightened activity, which promulgated the vision of the dharma from India in the south to China and Mongolia in the east, has not been equaled in these later times. The lord guru Jigmé Lingpa himself promised, "Because I spent seven years on a solitary mountain meditating on bodhichitta, the teachings will flourish and prosper in the future." [2.84b] True to this promise, to this day the secret Nyingtik teachings continue to spread throughout the world.

This concludes my abridged discussion of Jigmé Lingpa's students.

THE STUDENTS OF THE FIRST DODRUPCHEN, JIGMÉ TRINLÉ ÖZER

As for Dodrup Jigmé Trinlé Özer's students, the foundation or central pillar supporting the "four great vajra beams" was Do Khyentsé Yeshé Dorjé.

Do Khyentsé Yeshé Dorjé (Ngakchang Jalü Dorjé) (1800–1866)

Do Khyentsé Yeshé Dorjé, also known as Ngakchang Jalü Dorjé, was born in Golok, eastern Tibet. His father was Chökor Sönampel, and his mother was Tsewang Men. Their son was born in fulfillment of the prophecies of deities and gurus, amid extraordinary signs. At birth he sat in vajra posture and recited the Sanskrit vowels and consonants. Three days later, the infant was taken by dakinis to a pure realm, where they made prophecies about him and bathed him. He then journeyed to Zangdok Palri in the realm of Chamara, where he encountered Orgyen Rinpoché, the sole deity for these times of spiritual degeneration, and his retinue of heart children—the masters of awareness King Trisong Detsen and his subjects—celebrating an enormous ganachakra. Yeshé Dorjé joined the gathering of dakas and dakinis, and natural impulses of faith, devotion, and yearning welled up spontaneously within him, [2.85a] the hair on his body standing on end and tears falling from his eyes. During a profound pure vision, he received a direct lineage of all the tantras, explanatory commentaries, and pith instructions of the Vajrayana approach of the supreme secret. The assembly invested Yeshé Dorjé as a master of the teachings of the profound dharma, entrusted him with the seal of their enlightened intent, and paid him other honors.

Dzogchen Pönlop Sang-ngak Tendzin, Ngedön Tendzin Zangpo (the sublime tulku of Dzogchen Rinpoché Pema Rigdzin),[8] Dodrup Jigmé Trinlé Özer, and other masters acknowledged him as a tulku of Kunchen Rigdzin Jigmé Lingpa. The child immediately recognized people like Jigmé Losel Özer, his former incarnation's student who had served him flawlessly, as well as patrons and others. As soon as he could talk, exhorted by hosts of guardians of the teachings and dakinis, the young child clearly detailed his life as Kunchen Jigmé Lingpa. With that, the former master's faithful patrons and students were satisfied, certain that he was indeed the tulku. [2.85b]

He then went to Dergé, and at Lhundrup Gang the refuge lord of Dzogchen Monastery bestowed on him the maturing empowerments and liberating instructions for the excellent works of the Omniscient One and his spiritual heir, including *The Seven Treasuries* and *The Four Higher Collections of the Heart Drop.* During this time, Yeshé Dorjé saw the guru sometimes in the garb of a tertön, sometimes with the attributes of the great Orgyen, and beheld hosts of peaceful and wrathful deities daily. Thus he received the transmission that resulted in the realization embodied in the lineage of enlightened intent.

The queen mother of Dergé and her court, along with the great masters, tulkus, khenpos, and administrators of Katok, Zhechen, and Dzogchen Monasteries, requested that he identify the personal effects, the representations of enlightened form, speech, and mind, and so forth that had belonged to Jigmé Lingpa. In every case, his unfaltering accuracy brought tears to the eyes of those present, regardless of their status, and proved him worthy of their confidence. Led by the head of the Sakya school, the king of Dergé and the great masters of Tibet proclaimed him a tulku of Kunchen Jigmé Lingpa, using every means to establish auspicious interdependence. He was installed as the holder of the former master's precious golden throne and crowned as a king of the dharma with mastery over the three worlds.[9]

Then, urged by his aspirations and karmic predisposition from previous lifetimes and inspired by prophecies from deities and gurus, [2.86a] Yeshé Dorjé traveled to central Tibet, visiting Samyé, his former incarnation's seat of Tsering Jong, and other places. Due to habit patterns established during his life as Jigmé Lingpa, he spoke clearly of historical events and continued teachings that his former incarnation had left unfinished, evoking faith in his patrons and students. He was ordained as a novice monk by the Drigung Kyabgön and practiced such profound Drigung teachings as *The Two Systems of the Sacred Dharma* and *The Uniqueness of Enlightened Intent.* From Gyaltsap Rinpoché of Tsurpu Monastery in Tölung, Yeshé Dorjé received the oral transmissions for the collected works of former masters, foremost among them *The Heart Drop of Yutok,* the collected writings of the Karmapas, the empowerment and oral transmission for the protective deity Gönpo Trakshé, Gampopa's collected works, and the empowerment for the goddess Sarasvati. From Zhapdrung Rinpoché, Drigung Monastery's regent, he received the oral transmissions for the entire collection of the lord Ratna Lingpa's writings, the empowerments and oral transmissions for the entire cycle of the deity Yamantaka (including the sections on the aspect called Ayushpati: *Ironlike, Iron Scorpion, Molten Metal Face of Poison,* and so forth) and for all of the guardian deities of the Drigung teachings, the empowerment for White Mañjushri, and other transmissions. From the tulku of Tselé Natsok Rangdrol of Kongpo, [2.86b] Yeshé Dorjé received the empowerments and oral transmissions for a number of collections, including the tantra tradition of Vajrakila and the respective collected works of the first Tselé, Lhatsün Namkha Jigmé, and Jamyang Khyentsei Wangpo. From Longchen Rolpa Tsal, he received the entire cycle of empowerments and oral transmissions for *The Most Secret Heart Drop of the Three Roots,* as well as teaching transmissions for the Six Yogas of Naropa and the cycle *The Lord of Longevity* from the Mindroling tradition.

Yeshé Dorjé then returned to eastern Tibet. He studied with two masters, the great Katok Getrul Mahapandita and Zhingkyong Tulku, learning the physical exercises for the yogic practices of the subtle channels and energies. For six months, he studied the source tantra *The Heart Essence of Secrets* in great detail using Longchenpa's commentary *Dispelling Darkness in the Ten Directions.* In addition, he received many maturing empowerments and liberating instructions of the sutra and tantra traditions, such as those for the peaceful and wrathful deities of *The Web of Magical Display,* the cycle of the deity Samyak entitled *The Union of All Buddhas in Equalness,* Khorwa Dongtruk, and the Rong tradition of Vajrakila.

The lord protector of Yeshé Dorjé's crown chakra was Dodrupchen Rinpoché Jigmé Trinlé Özer, sovereign lord of all buddha families. In the presence of this master, Yeshé Dorjé studied the entire range of profound pith instructions of the supreme secret, great perfection, as well as the kama, terma, and daknang traditions. [2.87a] The minds of guru and student became indistinguishable. Yeshé Dorjé described how he reached the pinnacle of erudition and accomplishment:

> By the force of having accumulated great merit and deepened your experience of timeless awareness
> for immeasurable eons in the past,
> you are the second Buddha, the lord magically inhabiting a human form,
> completely noble and superbly kind in benefiting and bringing happiness to others.
> Ordinary mortals like me, subject to the external influences of delusion,
> spend our human lifetimes in laziness and indolence.
> Though I have not made the Victorious One's words—the sutras and tantras—my personal experience,

> that I am not without a path and have not fallen into the abyss is the grace of this lord.
> To understand the deep ocean of the Buddhist teachings, so difficult to fathom,
> I have not trained in the path of logicians,
> but through the blessings so thoroughly evoked by my threefold faith,
> I have been freed by receiving the intent of your enlightened mind.

Then the precious guru gave him instructions and prophecies for the near and distant future, saying, "You are a yogin who has realized the enlightened intent of great perfection. Thus you must henceforth live the life of a lay tantric practitioner whose conduct befits a siddha and ensure benefit for ordinary beings. [2.87b] Moreover, in my next lifetime, both of us will conduct ourselves as tantric masters." With this, Dodrupchen Rinpoché passed on to him the crown of spiritual command. Yeshé Dorjé then became a deer hunter. With the uncontrived conduct of one who could revive the animals he had killed, he ensured that samsara would end for all who saw, heard, remembered, or touched him; in this he was similar to such powerful lords among the Indian siddhas as Saraha and Shavaripa.

He spent some three years journeying throughout Tibet, China, Mongolia, and surrounding regions. When he visited great holy sites and met gurus, words and nectar would issue from representations of enlightened form, speech, and mind; rays of light would also emerge from them and dissolve into his heart center. He was able to move unhindered through rock, lakes, buildings, and so forth and had the power to tame unruly human and nonhuman beings. He could fly through the sky, accompanied by his horse and attendants, all surrounded by light. He could participate in ganachakras celebrated by dakas and dakinis in the twenty-four gathering places and other pure realms that can potentially be experienced in our human realm, and there engage in various kinds of liberating conduct befitting a siddha.

Yeshé Dorjé had visions of hosts of peaceful and wrathful deities of the four classes of tantra [2.88a] and of the timeless awareness embodiments of such scholars and siddhas of India and Tibet as the great masters Garab Dorjé, Guru Rinpoché, and Padampa Sang-gyé, as well as Drupchen Tangtong Gyalpo. In these visions, the deities and gurus took him under their care and issued prophecies about him. He could command guardian deities like servants, for hosts of dakinis, protective deities, and local spirits were always waiting to serve him.

In his usual waking state or in meditative experiences, Yeshé Dorjé journeyed to an array of pure realms in the ten directions, such as Zangdok Palri, and requested teachings from the victorious ones and their spiritual heirs. He also journeyed to impure realms such as the hells and other lower states of rebirth. In a pure vision in which awareness manifested quite naturally, he encountered Yama, lord of the dead, seeing him as his root guru. He then saw himself leading all beings without a single exception, equal to space in extent, to pure realms. In short, Yeshe Dorjé demonstrated his total liberation on the outer, inner, and secret levels in incredible ways that the rational mind cannot comprehend. More information can be found in his extensive autobiography. [10]

In addition, he bestowed maturing empowerments and liberating instructions on a vast and profound scale to those fortunate ones of royal birth whom he served as spiritual adviser, including the king of Chakla in Dartsedo, [2.88b] the king and queen of Dergé, and the ruler of Gyalrong. During the later part of his life, he lingered for a long time in Dartsedo, eastern Tibet, caring for his students, and came to be known as Do Khyentsé Yeshé Dorjé, a title resounding throughout a hundred million three-thousand-fold universes.

Although it had often been prophesied that Yeshé Dorjé would reveal many profound termas, most of these auspicious opportunities were lost due to the negative influences of places, companions, and the times. He did reveal some termas of enlightened intent—*The Object of Cutting Through: The Natural Freedom of Grasping Perceptions*, *Five Major Keystones of Spiritual Practice*, and others—numerous volumes of which still exist.

Having thus spontaneously accomplished his own and others' welfare, at a certain point the display of Yeshé Dorjé's emanated form resolved back into Zangdok Palri in Chamara. Of his countless students, his most intimate heart children for the most part also studied with both Paltrul and Khyentsé, as well as with Gyalsé Zhenpen Tayé. In addition, Yeshé Dorjé taught the king of Chakla, as well as Pema Rangdrol, Nyima Özer, and innumerable other sublime masters who upheld the Nyingma teachings. [2.89a] Moreover, Kunchen Rigdzin Jigmé Lingpa had said:

> . . . Following this, for the sake of those who revile and slander others,
> the display of the vajra of timeless awareness
> will emanate in various ways; I supplicate you.

In keeping with this supplication, from the infinite manifestation of Yeshé Dorjé's specific emanations in a hundred million human and other realms, the incarnation known as Doring Tulku[11] was born in Minyak in eastern Tibet. Traveling from places such as Dzogchen Monastery in eastern Tibet to as far afield as India and Bhutan in the south, this master benefited the teachings and beings on an enormous scale. In the far northeastern Tibetan region of Amdo, the incarnation known as Alak Zenkar Rinpoché[12] undertook extensive activities in order to serve the teachings concerning the essence of being. His tulku in turn, the second Zenkar, Alak Tupten, has lived to see the present-day revitalization of the teachings and continues to engage extensively in noble undertakings, such as the compilation of a major Tibetan–Chinese dictionary, thereby extending the vitality of the teachings and of beings.[13]

The Fourth Dzogchen Rinpoché, Mingyur Namkhai Dorjé (1793–1870)

Mingyur Namkhai Dorjé was born into an important clan called Rakho Pöntasang, [2.89b] whose members ruled the Den region. His birth was heralded by many amazing omens that manifested in his parents' dreams. Before long, the infant was repeatedly reciting, "Dzogchen, Dzogchen!" Later, he would beat a small drum while melodiously chanting the mantra *Om ah hum vajra guru padma siddhi hum* and would pretend to give empowerments and explain the dharma, for the attributes of someone holy had awakened in him.

When he was seven, amid an amazing, vast array of positive signs, the child, marked by the five aspects of excellence, assumed the lion throne of fearlessness at the great meeting hall of Orgyen Samten Chöling, the preceding incarnation's seat in Rudam. Then the great Khedrup Namkha Tsewang Chokdrup bestowed on him the initial vows and the name Jigmé Khyentsé Wangchuk Namgyal Dorjé. Under his mentor, Chödrak, he began his studies with reading and writing, and continued on to the sutras and tantras and the rest of the ten fields of knowledge, receiving the traditions of spiritual advice transmitted by the "ten pillars of exegesis" and the founders of the eight mainstream lineages of accomplishment.[14]

Mingyur Namkhai Dorjé was ordained as a novice monk by the third Zhechen Rabjam, [2.90a] Rigdzin Paljor Gyatso, and was given the monastic name Rigdzin Gyurmé Kunzang Tekchok Tendzin Palzangpo, along with investiture as the regent of the sublime teacher Shakya Seng-gé. He scrupulously observed the practical guidelines of Vinaya, such as abstaining from food after midday.

At the age of twenty, he journeyed specifically to meet Drupwang Jigmé Trinlé Özer. He received from that master the kama and terma traditions, daknang teachings, and treatises associated with the Omniscient One Longchenpa and his spiritual heir, Jigmé Lingpa, the oral lineage known as *The Vajra Bridge,* and other empowerments, oral transmissions, and teachings on a vast scale. In particular, the blessings of the ultimate lineage—the extraordinary enlightened intent of the Nyingtik teachings, the pith instructions of Dzogchen—were passed on to him. By the strength of this transmission, Mingyur Namkhai Dorjé directly experienced the realization of the path of seeing, the first level of a bodhisattva's realization: the true nature of phenomena as the unity of awareness and emptiness. He considered both the lord Namkha Tsewang Chokdrup and Dodrupchen to be his root gurus, regarding them with extraordinarily reverent faith and devotion.

He traveled to the central region, where he was acknowledged and highly honored by the ninth Dalai Lama, Lungtok Gyatso,[15] and his regent in Lhasa; he was also honored at the three centers of the dharma, as well as Dorjé Drak, Mindroling, and other places. Because the Dalai Lama and he were of the same clan and therefore related, Mingyur Namkhai Dorjé was treated with boundless affection and regard. [2.90b] In the presence of the regent, Demo Rinpoché, an incarnation of the great

Indian abbot Shantarakshita, he took full monastic ordination from a quorum of faithful members of the sangha. The great khenpos bestowed on him unparalleled honors and praise. Along with the Dalai Lama and his regent, he was invited to preside over the annual Mönlam festival and received great honors and recognition. The lord Mingyur Namkhai Dorjé delivered the explanatory discourse during the symbolic offering of the universe, captivating the hearts of all the saffron-robed sangha present. During this large gathering, he sponsored particularly noble activities, such as the distribution of food and tea to the multitudes, and the drumbeat of his fame resounded in all directions.

Mingyur Namkhai Dorjé's principal practices were such cycles as those focusing on the Eight Commands, *The Gathering of Great and Glorious Wrathful Ones,* and the terma of enlightened intent of Pema Gyalpo. He engaged in numerous intensive retreats on the phases of approach and accomplishment for guru and deity practices from authoritative cycles of the kama and terma traditions. He had visions of the entire array of his meditation deities. The lord of the dharma Paltrul Rinpoché offered a hundred thousand prostrations in his presence,[16] saying, "In these times of extreme spiritual degeneration, this sublime being has brought the four visions of the great perfection to consummation, having experienced phenomena resolving into their true nature, just as is intended." [2.91a]

Throughout his life, regardless of who supplicated him, Mingyur Namkhai Dorjé was delighted to bestow the empowerments, oral transmissions, and teachings of the kama and terma traditions of the Early Translation school on a vast and uninterrupted scale, thus increasing the vitality of these teachings. He erected symbolic representations, beginning with statues of the abbot Shantarakshita, the master Padmakara, and the Buddhist king Trisong Detsen, each fashioned from gold and copper and one story high. His activities, such as regularly commissioning tangkas and ritual implements for retreat centers, were beyond description and defy the imagination.

At a certain point, the lord Mingyur Namkhai Dorjé's monastic seat was destroyed in a large earthquake. He restored it without hindrance, using funds gathered from faithful donors, principally Damtsik Dorjé, the king of Dergé. Both he and Gyalsé Zhenpen Tayé rebuilt the monastery and temple, as well as the statues and other installations within, making everything much grander than before. Mingyur Namkhai Dorjé's enlightened activities were unimaginable in scale, exemplified by his unceasing kindness in overseeing incomparable restoration projects. In particular, he worked with Gyalsé Zhenpen Tayé to raise new buildings, such as Shri Simha Shedra, including the temple and its contents, as well as a hundred cells for monks and Gyalsé Zhenpen Tayé's private residence and estate. [2.91b]

Throughout the lower elevations of eastern Tibet, Mingyur Namkhai Dorjé ensured that Vinaya, the superb extensive tradition of the Lion of the Shakyas, was adhered to precisely. Consequently, instead of being consigned to memory, the traditional observance of the three bases, including the 101 ritual activities and other secondary activities, underwent such an unparalleled revival that people likened the region to a holy country. Mingyur Namkhai Dorjé also explained the sutra *Individual Liberation, The Fundamental Discourse of the Vinaya, The Source Verses for the Novice Monk, The Aspiration Prayer of Sutra and Tantra* (an excellent composition by Kunchen Prajñarasmi), two basic works on Tibetan grammar, and other texts. In so doing, he opened doorways to greater intelligence and freed a treasure trove of profound confidence.

Mingyur Namkhai Dorjé spread the tradition of expounding and studying the sutras and tantras, so that Shri Simha Shedra became like a second Shri Nalanda.[17] Condensing the essential elements of crucial mainstream sources, the syllabus included such works as the excellent treatises of both the father, the Omniscient King of the Dharma (*The Seven Treasuries, The Four Higher Collections of the Heart Drop, The Three Cycles of Being at Ease,* and *The Three Cycles of Natural Freedom*), and the son, Rigdzin Jigmé Lingpa (the source text *The Treasury of Enlightened Qualities* and its commentary); the source verses of and commentary on *Ascertaining the Three Levels of Ordination* by the one from Ngari; and tantras such as the glorious *Heart Essence of Secrets* (also known as *The Web of Magical Display*). Mingyur Namkhai Dorjé transmitted his oral explanations, entrusting them to Paltrul Jigmé Chökyi Wangpo [2.92a] and Khenchen Pema Dorjé, among others. These two transmitted them in turn to such masters as Jamgön Mipam Rinpoché, Ön Orgyen Tendzin Norbu, and Khenchen Zhenpen Chökyi Nangwa, passing on the lineages from mouth to ear and bestowing all of this spiritual advice without exception. Gyalsé Zhenpen Tayé and this great tulku, Mingyur Namkhai Dorjé, ensured that the superb tradition of the Early Translation school—this extensive legacy endowed with six superior qualities, this exegesis of sutras, tantras, and commentaries illuminating their enlightened intent—flourishes unimpaired today. The timely maturation of the enormously powerful motivation and deeds of these masters has caused the renown of the Nyingma tradition to spread over the entire surface of the earth.

As mentioned earlier, Mingyur Namkhai Dorjé's principal teachers were Khedrup Tsewang Chokdrup and Dodrup Jigmé Trinlé Özer—two vajra masters and most excellent gurus of unparalleled kindness. From Gyalsé Zhenpen Tayé, he received all the available lines of oral transmission for the Kangyur and Tengyur. [2.92b] In particular, he received extensive empowerments for and explanatory teachings on the Indian sources and commentaries, as well as the authentic instructions of Tibetan translators and Indian scholars, so prized by the Early Translation school.

In addition, he studied with such teachers as the second Dzogchen Pönlop Rinpoché, Pema Sang-ngak Tendzin; Lama Tsewang; the third Rabjam, Rigdzin Paljor; the third Nyitrul, Mingyur Pendé Gyatso; Tertön Pema Drodul of Ling; Gyutrul Dorjé of Kyayé in Yakzé; Boro Ön Orgyen Gyatso; Gyalsé Pema Namgyal of the Duddul clan; Terchen Pawo Lerab Tsal; Jigmé Gyalwai Nyugu; Khedrup Trinlé Dargyé; the second Zhingkyong Gönpo of Katok Monastery; the second Moktsa Rinpoché, Jigdral Chöying Dorjé; the two earlier and later Öntrul incarnations of Gyarong (both named Tenpai Nyima); the second Namtrul, Kunzang Tekchok Dorjé; the fourth Zhechen Rabjam, Mijé Zhingi Gönpo; Orgyen Rangjung Dorjé Chokdrup; the lord protector of Tibet, the Dalai Lama, Lungtok Gyatso; the Demo Hutoktu regent; the fifth Dokham, Drupgyü Nyima; Jampa Namkha Chimé, [2.93a] the Tartsé Khenchen of Ngor; Jampa Kunga Tendzin; the yogin Jampal Zangpo; Kunga Tenpai Lodrö, the khenpo of the house of Pendé; the teachers associated with Zhapdrung Tulku; and Zimok Choktrul Jampa Tendzin Nyendrak of Nalendra Monastery. He received a boundless range of teachings from these and other holy masters who upheld the teachings of the Sakya, Geluk, Kagyü, and Nyingma schools. The vast extent of these teachings is clearly reflected in the large volumes of his written works that list the teachings he received.

Mingyur Namkhai Dorjé explained and promulgated most of the teachings he had received many times. At the very least, it appears that he explained each one several times. He devoted his entire life to explaining and listening to teachings, meditating, and practicing on an impressive scale; as a result, his students were as innumerable as the stars in the sky. They included the third Pönlop, Namkha Chökyi Gyatso; three who became his major regents (the fourth Pönlop, Jigmé Chöying Ösel; and Nyidrak Könchok Jigmé Gyaltsen); five lineage holders who maintained the treasure troves of spiritual advice; [2.93b] three students who were emanated tertöns; a great, courageous bodhisattva; three lineage holders endowed with wisdom, love, and spiritual power; two great mendicants whose unrivaled wisdom made them lords among those with realization; ten great figures named Pema, who were khenpos of his own monastery; two foremost heart sons; four great upholders of the teachings of the kama and terma traditions; nine exemplary regents of traditional ritual activities; a sublime pair who upheld the practice lineages; ten great mentors; twenty-seven great figures who received personal transmissions for expounding the sutras and tantras; twenty-seven ascetics who upheld spiritual practice and directly experienced the enlightened intent of original purity and spontaneous presence; four prophesied holy beings who received the transmission of the Chö tradition; eight great lords of yogins who engaged in uncontrived tantric conduct; nine yogins who ensured benefit for beings impartially; two unparalleled heart sons who were like the sun and moon; ten great nonsectarian upholders of the teachings; ten great bodhisattvas who attained high levels of realization; five who received personal transmissions of termas; [2.94a] a pair who upheld the teachings concerning the essence of being; three spiritual guides who received the inspiration of Mingyur Namkhai Dorjé's vajra prophecies; four prophesied upholders of the teachings who were worthy of praise; three sublime tulkus exemplary at upholding and spreading the Victorious One's teachings; three great ones who received transmissions for the practices of wrathful mantras; fifty tulkus, administrators who spread Mindroling Monastery's influence in a hundred directions; sixteen mentors of the Nyingma and Sarma schools; and, throughout Tibet, more than a hundred lamas responsible for causing all that is positive and excellent to flourish for the teachings and for beings and whose names are mentioned in Mingyur Namkhai Dorjé's extensive biography. The number of Mingyur Namkhai Dorjé's students was truly incalculable.

To summarize, during that period in greater Tibet (primarily in the Dergé region), more than one hundred principal and one thousand secondary monasteries upheld the extensive tradition of the Early Translation school. All of the great masters of these monasteries, as well as the majority of holy ones of all schools, seem to have met this lord and made some connection with him. With such unrivaled, incredible, and far-reaching enlightened activity, Mingyur Namkhai Dorjé brought his life and his benefit for beings to consummation. He eventually passed away into a state of peace, within the basic space of primordial being. [2.94b]

Gemang Gyalsé Rigpai Dorjé (Gyalsé Zhenpen Tayé Özer) (1800–1869/70)

Gemang Gyalsé Rigpai Dorjé, also known as Gyalsé Zhenpen Tayé Özer, consciously took rebirth as the magical display of both the great Indian abbot Bodhisattva[18] and Lochen Bairotsana. At an early age, his innate attributes as a member of the Mahayana family awakened. He attained the pinnacle of erudition, having received teachings on the sutras, tantras, and other fields of knowledge from many mentors of the Nyingma and Sarma schools, such as Jigmé Gyalwai Nyugu, who was Avalokiteshvara in person. In particular, Zhenpen Tayé served Dodrup Jigmé Trinlé Özer in the three ways of delighting a teacher, and so received general teachings of the kama, terma, and daknang traditions and the pith instructions of Dzogchen, like one vase being filled to the brim from another. He thus became a crown jewel among a hundred learned and accomplished masters.

From that point on, from Mount Kailash in western Tibet to Langchen Riwo Gying-ri in the lower regions of Chinese territory, Zhenpen Tayé lived at important holy sites—on glaciers, in cliffside caves, near lakes—a wandering, hidden yogin of humble means who preferred solitary retreats. Seizing the victory banner of spiritual attainment, he engaged in, and cultivated real strength through, the stages of development and completion and the practices involving the subtle channels and energies. [2.95a] Through the path of great perfection—the very nature of phenomena—he reached an advanced level of spiritual attainment; for example, his body cast no shadow, and he was able to pass freely through the walls of buildings. Yet although his meditative experiences and realization were like those of the siddha Saraha, he was not indifferent to the laws of cause and effect. Rather, observing them most scrupulously, he awed the faithful with conduct as fine as flour. In these and other ways, he was a truly great, holy being with whom all connection was meaningful.

Once, when he was eight, an account of a profound terma—a teaching that could avert danger in the event that Samyé Monastery was threatened by fire—was placed in his hands. Unfortunately, he was unable to make the long journey to Samyé. Later, when he heard that it had indeed been damaged by fire, Zhenpen Tayé felt great regret. At another time, he had received a prophecy that floods would threaten Lhasa; he spoke of this to no one but secretly went to Lhasa, where he undertook a retreat on the form of Vajrapani called "Tamer of Arrogant Gods and Demons" and other practices within the time period prophesied. Although great floods arose, they did not cause any damage.

He thus manifested as one with the good fortune to be a great tertön, [2.95b] one who could carry out the enlightened activities of Padmakara, the lord of victorious ones. In his earlier life, he was a celibate lay practitioner of total purity, long-haired and clad in white robes. In later years, Paltrul Rinpoché and several other holy masters supplicated him to reveal profound termas through his conduct as a tantric master, saying that doing so would ensure him a long life and vast benefit for beings. They added that the enlightened activities associated with these profound termas would spread as far as China and Mongolia. He did not listen to them, however, but adopted the model established by the edicts of the great Buddhist king, observing the tradition of the Indian abbot in his conduct,[19] the tradition of Nagarjuna in his philosophical view, and the tradition of Padmakara and Vimalamitra, who became embodiments of timeless awareness, in his spiritual practice. He was motivated by the conviction that by doing so he would serve the teachings of the Victorious One in general and the extensive tradition of the Early Translation school in particular. Therefore, from Khenchen Sengtruk Pema Tashi, he received the lineage of monastic vows transmitted through Shantarakshita. Through the ritual of the four supplications,[20] he was fully ordained as a monk; it was as though the exalted Upali had returned to earth, unsullied as Zhenpen Tayé was by even the slightest fault or failing. Zhenpen Tayé thus maintained the kind of discipline that would delight exalted spiritual adepts, inspiring to states of liberation those who saw, heard, thought of, or touched him.

Fulfilling a prophecy by Dodrupchen Rinpoché, [2.96a] he went to Dzogchen Monastery in Rudam. The fourth Dzogchen, Mingyur Namkhai Dorjé—the perfect Buddha in person—viewed him with the unobscured eye of timeless awareness and expressed singular delight in and affection for this kindred spirit. He praised Zhenpen Tayé's great qualities of body, speech, and mind and insisted that he remain at the monastery. So it was that these two lords came to work together, experiencing the timely maturing of the results of pure motivation and aspiration shared for countless past eons, all the while pursuing the conduct of bodhisattvas.

When they went to view the site for a proposed monastic university, they beheld the timeless awareness embodiment of the learned and accomplished Indian master Shri Simha dwelling at the site and blessing it. The shedra was built, and they named it Dzogchen Shri Simha Shedra. It became a second Nalanda, a wellspring of learned and accomplished masters. At this institution, discipline was founded on the three bases of Vinaya; the curriculum was that of the extensive tradition of the abbot Shantarakshita, the master Padmakara, and the Buddhist king Trisong Detsen and incorporated the traditions transmitted by two victorious ones, Rongzom and Longchenpa, [2.96b] those of expounding and studying the sutras, tantras, and other fields of knowledge. The first abbot was Khenchen Sengtruk Pema Tashi, a great, holy being whose sense of purpose was reflected in his name.[21] When he was established on the golden throne of the institution, the presiding lord of the buddha families, Dzogchen Rinpoché Mingyur Namkhai Dorjé, said, "This name is an auspicious one ensuring that at this university khenpos who are wise, venerable, and spiritually accomplished will appear like lions, kings among beasts, unrivaled throughout the three planes of existence." Just as this flower of praise cast with his vajra speech indicated, the succession of masters has comprised incarnations of advanced spiritual practitioners who attained high levels of realization, resembling a continuous range of golden mountains.

To the present day, their influence has extended to the far corners of the earth. In addition, the lines of oral transmission for the Kangyur that flourished at Shri Simha Shedra have spread around the world. All of this has resulted from the motivation of the sublime, holy Zhenpen Tayé and the far-reaching activities combining the study and practice of the teachings to which he devoted his entire life. His innumerable students, foremost among the erudite of all directions and times, upheld and spread the Victorious One's teachings, [2.97a] like swans sporting in a pool of lotuses.

Having thus completed his activities for his students in that lifetime, Zhenpen Tayé passed away into the basic space of a state of peace. Although never formally enthroned, he was actually a sublime tulku whose immediate rebirth was the master of the dharma Khenchen Zhenpen Chökyi Nangwa.[22] The fact that, to the present day, those in his students' and their students' lineages have been as numerous as they are noble, spreading the teachings throughout this vast world, is evidence of his exceedingly great kindness.

Given that this great master and Khenchen Zhenpen Chökyi Nangwa were mainstays of the teachings of the Early Translation school, there should be more extensive biographies of both of them. Because of recent events, however, textual sources are not available to me; if they come to light in the future, I ask that people with spiritual insight insert such accounts at this point.

Chöying Tobden Dorjé (1785–1848)

Chöying Tobden Dorjé received permission to promulgate the vast ocean of wrathful Vajrayana practices, which employ powerful mantras like daggers of meteoric iron. He taught these in the northern reaches. He was born in Repkong in the northeastern region of Amdo. His began his studies by learning to read and write with some of the gurus, tulkus, and mentors of his home area; as his training progressed, he became quite learned. [2.97b] Entering the doorway of the dharma, he took the vows of individual liberation, the bodhisattva vow, and the tantric commitments and put these into practice.

He subsequently felt an intense desire to request the spiritual instructions that could bring freedom in a single lifetime. Setting forth to find a particularly exalted mentor, he arrived at the encampment of Dodrupchen Rinpoché Jigmé Trinlé Özer and stayed for a long time with that guru. From him he received and practiced an enormous range of general teachings on the development and completion stages of the secret mantra approach, as well as the tantra *The Heart Essence of Secrets, The Three Cycles of Being at Ease, Timeless Awareness as the Guiding Principle,* and other pith instructions of the Dzogchen approach. The enlightened intent of the true nature of phenomena thus arose in his heart.

As a result of this, the precious guru saw that Chöying Tobden Dorjé would become a glorious master of students in the future and that he had a karmic connection with certain deities. He conferred on him the profound key points of the "four penetrations" of the great and glorious Vajrakila, the cycles of Yamantaka (such as *The Four Wheels of Mañjushri*), *The Wrathful Imprecations of the Mamo Goddesses* to overturn negative omens, and so forth—that is, the profound wrathful mantra practices of the Early Translation school. Dodrupchen Rinpoché also bestowed on Chöying Tobden Dorjé much profound advice on fire rituals involving the three activities of suppression, incineration, and projection,[23] [2.98a] which enable a tantric practitioner to awaken to buddhahood. Chöying Tobden Dorjé practiced these, freeing himself through the realization that all dualistic thought patterns are the cosmic array of the mandalas of deity, mantra, and timeless awareness.

Then his guru said to him, "The time has come for you to free others through compassion, so return to your home region and care for groups of students. This will help the teachings and beings, bringing about ever-growing benefit." Accordingly, Chöying Tobden Dorjé returned to Repkong and cared for his students in that region, particularly with a vast array of activities involving wrathful mantras, and founded a settlement of lay tantric practitioners. The lineages of students of Chöying Tobden Dorjé and Palchen Namkha Jigmé founded Repkong Ngak-nakpa, a major center for the practice of the mantra path, renowned in every corner of Tibet as a site of unparalleled force and might in annihilating negative forces and hindrances. The residents of this practice center were renowned in oral accounts as the "1,900 bearers of ritual daggers in Repkong," and their lineage has continued to the present day. [2.98b] They had enormous power, the force to overthrow negative and demonic forces. There were many of them, and their amazing life stories illustrate their mastery of the activities of wrathful force—the ability to free others through compassion—and resemble the biographies of mahasiddhas of the past, such as Tumbu Gyazhangtrom and Nup Yönten Gyatso. The expressions of the power of wrathful mantras created a great wall shielding the teachings.

Among the many treatises the lord Chöying Tobden Dorjé is said to have written based on his oral teachings were treatments of the cycles for the practical application of wrathful mantras such as *Black Mount Meru: The Final Activity of Suppression*. His principal work was the major treatise *The Treasury of the Ocean of Sutras and Tantras*, which has survived to the present day.[24] His collected works were disseminated widely, and the lineage of his students spread throughout Repkong, Rongpo, and other northern regions for the sake of beings to be guided, so that he came to have students beyond number. Today, there are still many students of his lineage in those regions.

Choklung Repa Damtsik Dorjé (18th–19th Centuries)

Damtsik Dorjé received permission to promulgate the teachings on the subtle channels and energies and the cultivation of tummo. [2.99a] He was born in Choklung in Dergé, eastern Tibet. At an early age, he entered the doorway of the dharma through the Dzogchen approach taught by Nyidrak and studied various subjects. He also studied and trained under many gurus and tulkus of Dzogchen and Zhechen Monasteries and other places in Dergé and practiced on an immeasurable scale, becoming a holy yogin.

At a certain point, he became convinced that Dodrupchen Rinpoché had been his guru in many lifetimes. He journeyed to Dokhok to be in the guru's presence and received from him a complete transmission of the earlier and later Nyingtik cycles and the tantras, explanatory commentaries, and pith instructions of the Vajrayana. In particular, he studied the text *Timeless Awareness as the Guiding Principle* and its background literature and meditated on them, attaining the most sublime siddhi. The guru bestowed on him the practical instructions for the practices involving the subtle channels and energies, as well as the overview and extraordinary practice of tummo, from the Nyingtik teachings. Through these practices, Damtsik Dorjé awakened his latent karmic tendencies and achieved mastery of tummo.

Gaining control over subtle energy and mind, he exhibited signs of accomplishment, such as the ability to traverse large rivers and rush up the face of steep cliffs unhindered, like the wind. [2.99b] With the three phases of causing subtle energy to enter, remain, and dissolve within the central channel, Damtsik Dorjé perfected the experiences of the ten stages of "empty forms" in their own ground. He directly experienced timeless awareness marked by the four degrees of joy, blissful yet empty. Wearing only a thin cotton garment, he achieved such bliss and warmth that the biting winter cold posed no hardship. These and other signs were apparent to all who met him, and he became widely known as Repa Damtsik Dorjé. He lived for a long time at the hermitage of the cave known as Bapuk near the banks of the Kardzé River in Trehor, caring for his students. In addition, he spent a long time in Golok, caring for students in these northern reaches; he also founded a hermitage, which in later times Tertön Sögyal Rinpoché restored.

Although many volumes, large and small, of Damtsik Dorjé's collected works and songs existed at one time, these texts have become quite rare. The extraordinary instructions and advice on the practices involving the subtle channels and energies that were transmitted by this master were once found all over the northern reaches of eastern Tibet. Damtsik Dorjé spent his entire life solely engaged in benefiting others, bringing glory to the teachings and to all beings. [2.100a]

Thus through the manifestation of innumerable students—the four great "vajra ridgepoles," the thirteen bearing the name Namkha, and others—the lineages of teachings and of students have continued to the present day. They have come from both Paltrul and Khyentsé, with the transmission passing back and forth, so that they have blended together into a single mainstream transmission of the teachings of the sublime heart essence that has spread over this great earth. This concludes my overview of the lineage transmitted primarily by Jigmé Trinlé Özer to his students and, in turn, to their students.

13

The Students of Jamyang Khyentsei Wangpo

Now I shall discuss the groups of students associated with the two heart sons of Jigmé Gyalwai Nyugu—that is, Khyentsé and Paltrul.

The foremost of Jigmé Gyalwai Nyugu's students was Jamyang Khyentsei Wangpo, a universal monarch of all the teachings. Of his students, Jamyang Loter Wangpo and the teacher Ngawang Lekpa of Ga, among others, served the teachings of the Sakya school. Jamgön Lodrö Tayé, Khenchen Tashi Özer, Jedrung Jampa Jungné, and others focused on the Dakpo Kagyü tradition. Students such as [2.100b] Litang Geshé Jampa Puntsok ensured benefit for the teachings of the Riwo Ganden school. His principal students in the Nyingma school included Jamgön Mipam Rinpoché, Adzom Drukpa, Dodrup Tenpai Nyima, and Zhechen Gyaltsap, all of whom ensured the vitality of the teachings concerning the essence of being. Many sublime beings like Changlung Druptop,[1] Shardza Tashi Namgyal,[2] and others ensured benefit for beings through the teachings of Bön (the "tradition of the swastika").[3] Thus Khyentsei Wangpo's students became great nonsectarian models of the precious teachings of the Victorious One. Though their lives nearly defy description, I have already discussed two figures of the Nyingma school, Adzom Drukpa and Dodrupchen.[4]

Jamgön Kongtrul Yönten Gyatso Lodrö Tayé (1813–1900)

Jamgön Kongtrul Yönten Gyatso Lodrö Tayé was Lochen Bairotsana in person. His name and deeds were clearly prophesied by the glorious words of the Lord of Sages, the Buddha himself, in such discourses as *The Most Majestic Meditative Absorption* and *The Journey to Shri Lanka*. In addition, Orgyen, knower of the three times, praised him in numerous terma cycles, both ancient and more recent. Fulfilling these prophecies, he manifested as a succession of innumerable learned and accomplished masters of India and Tibet—among them Ananda, the Buddha's attendant, and Lochen Bairotsana, [2.101a] who was an emanation of the buddha Vairochana—and clarified the Victorious One's teachings. This magical emanation was born during the fourteenth sexagesimal cycle; his father was Tendzin Yungdrung of the Chung Gyaldrup clan, and his mother was the yogini Tashi Tso.

Kongtrul Lodrö Tayé began learning his letters when he was five, mastering everything upon merely being introduced to it. He had an effortless, unflagging devotion for Orgyen Rinpoché. At about the age of ten, spiritual inclinations from training in previous lifetimes awakened, and he developed a firm resolve to pursue the sacred dharma. He studied and mastered such subjects as art and medicine with ease, simply by looking at the texts. He studied the ten fields of knowledge and more with many learned and accomplished tutors, among them Gyurmé Tutop Namgyal of Zhechen Monastery, a scholar proficient in the five major fields of knowledge. With respect to the extraordinary inner field of knowledge, Kongtrul studied many texts of the Kangyur and Tengyur according to the dialectical approach, focusing primarily on Madhyamaka, Prajñaparamita, Vinaya, *The Treasury of Abhidharma,* and the treatises of Maitreya. As for the most extraordinary approach, he studied all of the available major classes of tantra [2.101b] of the Nyingma and Sarma schools, and the kama and terma traditions of the former. His wisdom became as vast as the vault of the sky, and he acquired significant status, earning the title Sarvajñana Mahapandita.[5]

He accepted Jamgön Tai Situ Pema Nyinjé Wangpo[6] as the lord of his buddha family; this is evident from the fact that he received the nectar of the three levels of ordination from Situ Rinpoché. He experienced the definitive secret—the consummate state of innate, supremely blissful timeless awareness—and became empowered as a regent of the ultimate lineage of the essence of being. Before more than fifty mentors of all lineages—principally Khyentsei Wangpo, who was Mañjushri in person—Kongtrul received, without sectarian bias, complete transmissions for a vast range of profound, vital teachings, the maturing empowerments and liberating instructions of all traditions of the eight lineages of accomplishment that existed in the Land of Snows. Evidence of his study, contemplation, and meditation can be found in the collections he wrote and compiled:

The Treasury of Knowledge, a compendium of the entire range of sutras and tantras, from the ordinary fields of knowledge up to and including Atiyoga, which is the consummation of the nine spiritual approaches of the extraordinary teachings [2.102a]

The Treasury of Spiritual Instructions, bringing together in a single collection the essential teachings of the eight lineages of accomplishment, including the most profound maturing empowerments and liberating instructions

The Treasury of Mantra of the Kagyü School, uniting three cycles of the kama tradition of the Early Translation school—Samyak, Vajrakila, and Yamantaka—with the maturing empowerments and liberating instructions associated with the sadhanas and mandalas of the tantras transmitted by Ngok of the Later Translation school of the Kagyü

The Treasury of Precious Hidden Teachings, distilling the quintessential elements of a veritable ocean of profound termas of the Early Translation school

The Treasury of Extraordinary Works, containing the special wealth of secrets from profound termas—the original yellow scrolls, revealed samaya substances, and so forth—and, in connection with this, *The Treasury of Extensive Instructions,* Kongtrul's collected works on a variety of subjects

Thus Kongtrul brought forth a new tradition in the form of these so-called five great treasuries, which had not previously existed in the human realm.

When we examine his legacy of some ninety volumes of original works—a marvelous nonsectarian contribution to the continuity of the teachings—it would seem as though he spent his life engaged solely in composition. When we reflect on his efforts to transmit the empowerments, teachings, pith instructions, and oral transmissions of the Nyingma and Sarma schools without sectarian bias, it would seem as though he devoted himself entirely to explaining and promulgating teachings. [2.102b] When we consider the ways in which he engaged in the profound stages of development and completion for an incredible range of practices, from the preliminaries to a vast array of mandalas, it would seem as though he spent his entire life sealed away in a retreat center. When we examine how he pursued the ten kinds of spiritual conduct, it would seem as though he spent his life wholly engaged in the pursuit of spiritual activities. He founded monastic centers such as that at Tsari Rinchen Drak, contributed to the restoration of older sites by erecting new representations of enlightened form, speech, and mind, organized more than 150 rituals for offering ganachakras, served the sublime Three Jewels, and so forth. He certainly exemplified the conduct of an advanced practitioner.

More specifically, let us consider how Kongtrul received transmissions of profound termas. When this lord was fifteen, he encountered Guru Rinpoché in a pure vision and received his blessings. On the basis of such visions, he revealed numerous classes of teachings. While he was in intensive retreat on the phases of approach and accomplishment for *The United Intent of the Gurus,* he received from Guru Rinpoché in a dream the blessings of the four levels of empowerment, as well as some mantras. This dispelled the obstacles to his longevity that had arisen that year. [2.103a] Guru Rinpoché said to him, "Several years from now, you will encounter me in person, and I will give you advice." These words were borne out in Kongtrul's fortieth year when he met Terchen Chokgyur Lingpa for the first time and their minds blended, becoming one. When the sacred place of Deshek Düpa at Dzongshö was being opened up, Kunzik Khyentsé Rinpoché and Chokgyur Lingpa together enthroned the lord Kongtrul Lodrö Tayé in the cave known as Tzitta Sangpuk. In conjunction with offerings they made on an enormous scale to establish auspicious interdependence, he received the title Chimé Tennyi Yungdrung Lingpa, which had earlier been conferred on him by Orgyen, knower of the three times, and his renown rang out like the peal of a great bell.

In his fifty-eighth year, Kongtrul revealed the cycle of teachings entitled *The United Intent of the Three Roots,* which had been concealed at Dechen Pemakö in Lamdo Burmo. From the cave of Dechen Puk in Kumchok, he brought forth the yellow scroll containing background teachings on *The United Intent of the Three Roots,* as well as the secret undergarment of Humkara and other treasures. In the cave of Jetsün Puk in the central mountain of the Pema Lhatsé range, [2.103b] he revealed the regent statue of the Guru known as Tashi Palbar,[7] as well as longevity pills that the Guru had rolled with his own hands at Maratika, garments of the great abbot Shantarakshita, a sash that had belonged to the Buddhist king Trisong Detsen, and other objects. From Tashi Terdzong in Marong Drugu, Kongtrul revealed the background teachings on the practices of the spiritual consort[8] from *The United Intent of the Three Roots,* the cycle of sadhana practice associated with the goddess Chandali, and other cycles. At Özong on the cliff of Rongkha Sheldrak, he revealed yellow scrolls on the cycles of sadhana practice of Amitayus and Hayagriva and longevity pills of Mandarava, among other objects. It was at Yeshé Tsogyal's cave in the cliff face at Tsari Rinchen Drak that Kongtrul revealed the yellow scrolls for the sadhana practices of the father and mother consorts[9] of the cycle *The Secret Heart Drop,* as well as longevity pills of some thirteen immortal masters of awareness. As part of each of these terma caches, he revealed an indescribable number of especially sacred samaya substances.

Furthermore, he once had a vivid meditative experience at dawn in which he found himself inside an elegantly appointed temple. He bowed with devotion to an indistinct figure who turned out to be the luminous unity of form and emptiness, manifesting in form as lord Khyentsé Rinpoché but in essence as Guru Rinpoché. Khyentsé Rinpoché had him repeat the refuge and bodhisattva vows and a seven-branch supplication, [2.104a] then visualized a deity and performed the ritual of summoning blessings. Taking a vase in hand, he placed it on the crown of Kongtrul's head. He bestowed on him the secret empowerment with the nectar of bodhichitta resulting from his union with a consort, and the empowerment of sublime knowing and timeless awareness by conferring a consort on him. From Khyentsé Rinpoché's heart center, a crystal emerged; holding it up for Kongtrul to look at, he said the following, directly introducing him to the true nature of mind:

> All phenomena are originally pure, profoundly clear like this orb of crystal.
> The dynamic radiance of spontaneous presence arises as anything and everything,
> like the radiance of the crystal's light shining outwardly.

With this, Khyentsé Rinpoché's form disappeared.

Later, during a ganachakra, Kongtrul received signs of blessings descending on him, such as a dramatic upwelling of bliss and warmth and exhilarating meditative experiences. On that occasion, he revealed *The Profound Path of the Seven Chapters*, and from the cave of Dagam Puk, he brought forth a sadhana based on the Seven-Line Supplication. He also codified the sadhana of the deity Dorjé Drolö that he had revealed in Taktsang at Rongmo Karmo.

Kongtrul Lodrö Tayé conferred the empowerments and oral transmissions for these termas on a wide range of fortunate people, principally sublime masters of the monasteries of Katok, Palyul, Zhechen, and Dzogchen, as well as masters of the Sakya, Geluk, Drigung Kagyü, Taktsang, and Karma Kamtsang[10] traditions. Through this kindness and the samaya substances he revealed, [2.104b] he ensured benefit for beings directly and indirectly, his enlightened activities spreading in all directions to open doorways of opportunity that brought meaning to all connected to him. At his empowerments, drupchens, ganachakras, and so forth, everyone present witnessed various marvelous portents, among them nectar offerings spontaneously boiling, rakta offerings overflowing, the fragrance of medicine offerings wafting over great distances, canopies of rainbow-colored clouds filling the sky, and blossoms showering down. In addition, Kongtrul could pass through solid buildings and houses and leave impressions of his hands and feet in stone.

Despite the prophetic account found in his profound termas, which clearly stated that his life span would be short, his practice of vajra yoga[11] and the methods involving the subtle channels and energies extended his life. He lived to be eighty-seven, yet his body remained youthful and his eyesight was restored, evidence of the superior inner qualities[12] that resulted from his spiritual attainment. With such deeds as the foregoing, he brought his activity in that lifetime to a conclusion, and the display of his emanated form resolved back into the expanse of the enlightened mind of the daka Töpai Tumbu Tsal in the western city called Shantapuri.[13]

Of the innumerable students this great being taught, [2.105a] the principal one was Jamyang Khyentsei Wangpo. The two alternated as each other's guru and student, so that their renown—these "two emanations of the protector Mañjushri, Khyentsé and Kongtrul"—spread over the face of the earth. In addition, Kongtrul Lodrö Tayé taught sublime masters of the Karma Kagyü and Drukpa Kagyü schools, such as the fourteenth and fifteenth Karmapas and the tenth[14] and eleventh Tai Situ Rinpochés; Jamyang Loter Wangpo, the lord of the dharma Kunga Jamyang, and others of the Sakya school and its branch, the Ngor; Mipam Jamyang Namgyal, Tertön Lerab Lingpa, the lord Gyurmé Ngedön Wangpo, Jedrung Trinlé Jampai Jungné, and others of the Early Translation school; and Chungtrul Pema Wangchen, Gyümé Khenpo Yeshé Gongpel, Dongtrul Tulku of Dragyab, Khechok Ngawang Gyatso, and others of the Riwo Ganden school. In brief, during that time, from the central regions of Ü and Tsang to eastern Tibet, in all of upper, middle, and lower Tibet, among all the scholars, realized meditators, [2.105b] and mentors regardless of stature, it seemed that there was no one who was not the student of Kongtrul Lodrö Tayé.[15]

Chungtrul Pema Wangchen (1870–?)

Among these students was Chungtrul Pema Wangchen. He went to central Tibet, where he conferred innumerable spiritual teachings, such as the empowerments and oral transmissions for *The Treasury of Precious Hidden Teachings*. In this way, he gathered around him countless students to be guided, who came like bees to collect nectar from a flower. By transmitting to them the teachings of the Dzogchen approach—the preliminary practices, the main body of teachings, and especially the great oral lineage of experiential transmission—he brought enormous benefit to beings, helping them to mature spiritually along the path and leading them toward the fruition according to their individual capabilities. He served as a master of the teachings of the supreme secret throughout the four regions of central Tibet. His legacy was incredible, for he caused the activities of the two emanations of Mañjushri to extend everywhere.

Among his students were Kharchen Rinpoché of Drak, Lama Trinlé (who was born in the region of Sakya in Tsang), and others who fled to India when the situation worsened in Tibet.[16] [2.106a] When Drak Kharchen Rinpoché passed away into a state of peace, there were amazing signs of his marvelous qualities, such as canopies of rainbow light and large and small spheres of five-colored light filling the sky. This aroused faith in countless students who had been guided by this master. His physical remains turned entirely into a mass of relics, including the five kinds of sharira. These relics are still enshrined in the vase of a stupa in Darjeeling, India. Following Kharchen Rinpoché's passing, the death of his steward (who was a hidden yogin) was also marked by numerous amazing signs. Such events help to make these signs more credible to people from other countries, who otherwise might not accept them.

The tulku of Chungtrul, recognized by Kyabjé Dilgo Khyentsé Rinpoché, lives in Nepal, where he is undergoing training.

Mipam Jamyang Namgyal Gyatso (1846–1912)

Mipam Jamyang Namgyal Gyatso, the great mainstay of the teachings of the Early Translation school, [2.106b] was born in the Fire Horse year of the fourteenth sexagesimal cycle.[17] His father was Gönpo Dargyé of the divine clan of Ju; his mother was Singchungma of the Dong branch of the Mukpo clan. He was born in Yachui Dingchung along the slowly flowing Dokham River. His paternal uncle, a hereditary lama[18] named Pema Dargyé, honored him with the name Mipam Gyatso. From an early age, he had the inborn attributes and strengths of someone of the Mahayana family, such as faith, renunciation, sublime knowing, and compassion. When he was six or seven years old, Mipam memorized the text *Ascertaining the Three Levels of Ordination* and studied the introductory teachings of Indian and Chinese astrology. At ten, with a firm command of reading and writing, he began composing essays on all kinds of topics. From the age of twelve, Mipam lived as an ordinary monk at Mehor Sang-ngak Chöling, a branch monastery in Ju affiliated with Zhechen Tennyi Dargyé Ling and transmitting the lineage of Orgyen Mindroling Monastery. Everyone praised him and called him the "learned little monk."

When he was fifteen, he spent several days studying an ancient manuscript of *The Arising of Vowels*. [2.107a] After praying to Mañjushri, he understood it in its entirety. For eighteen months, he undertook the practice of Vadisimha, a form of Mañjushri, at the hermitage in Junyung and performed the rituals for preparing pills, whereupon he had a vision of the deity. He received other special signs of success and was cared for by the timeless awareness embodiment of the deity. From then on, he easily understood any text he examined, be it on the sutra or tantra approach or some secular field of knowledge, so that he never had to study assiduously, but merely received oral teaching transmissions.

When he was seventeen, this lord accompanied a large number of nomads from the Dza region who were fleeing to Golok from the warfare in Nyarong.[19] From this period on, he became famous for his great skill in performing astrological calculations. At eighteen Mipam accompanied a nobleman named Gyurzang on a pilgrimage to Lhasa and stayed at the college of Ganden Monastery for about a month. Later, he traveled widely in the southern regions, going to Kharchu in Lhodrak, where all of his ordinary perceptions were transformed by his experience of the unity of bliss and emptiness. [2.107b] For several days, he thrived on these feelings of well-being and physical warmth. He remarked, "It would seem that this was due to the blessings of that site." On his journey back north, he had a pure vision in which a volume entitled *Crystal Mirror: The Great Arising of Vowels* was placed in his hands; a clear account of this vision is included as a colophon to that text. Continuing his travels, from the refuge lord of Lap, Wangchen Gyerab Dorjé, Mipam received the permission blessing of White Mañjushri according to the Mati tradition. During the empowerment itself and the associated activity rituals that he subsequently performed, he directly experienced signs of success, just as they are described in the source texts, and his wisdom blossomed like a lotus. For five days, Mipam studied the chapter on sublime knowing in *Engaging in the Conduct of a Bodhisattva* with Paltrul Rinpoché Orgyen Jigmé Chökyi Wangpo. He completely mastered the words of the entire text and their underlying meaning and later wrote works like his *Commentary on the Chapter on Sublime Knowing*.

In particular, he remained at the lotus feet of the lord of his buddha family, with whom he had been karmically connected for lifetimes—Pema Ösel Do-ngak Lingpa, Jamyang Khyentsei Wangpo—serving him in the three ways that delight a guru.

Khyentsé Rinpoché considered him a unique inner heart son and began caring for him by opening the doorway of the dharma, [2.108a] granting him the permission blessing of White Mañjushri according to the Mati tradition. From then on, Khyentsé Rinpoché, like one vase filling another to the brim, instructed Mipam Rinpoché in numerous fields, both secular and spiritual, and bestowed on him various special transmissions of source texts from the sutra and tantra traditions (which Khyentsé had received as direct lineages). He conferred a vast range of maturing empowerments, liberating instructions, supportive oral transmissions, pith instructions, traditional methods of practice, and detailed advice from all of the existent kama and terma traditions in the Vajrayana approach of the supreme secret.

In addition, at various times in his life, Mipam Rinpoché studied with Jamgön Kongtrul Lodrö Tayé, receiving instructions in such fields of knowledge as the Sanskrit grammar of Chandragomin and the process of refining mercury, as well as various extraordinary maturing empowerments and liberating instructions, such as the *Ironlike* and *Iron Scorpion* transmissions of the aspect of Mañjushri called Ayushpati. With Khenpo Pema Badzra of Dzogchen Monastery and numerous other mentors, he studied an unlimited range of cycles from the sutras, tantras, and other fields of knowledge. He would not leave it at simply hearing these teachings, but thoroughly put them into practice. As for the force of his positive qualities, the causal factor was his excellent training in and familiarization with spiritual practice over countless lifetimes. [2.108b] The conditioning factors were his gurus' compassion and their transmission of the blessings of their enlightened intent to him, so that his potential underwent a complete awakening. Without contradicting the four kinds of reliance,[20] Mipam Rinpoché used the four states of authentic discernment[21] to gain an inner mastery of the unlimited methods found in the profound and extensive teachings of the Sugata. He achieved a level of mastery whereby he experienced the visions of naturally occurring timeless awareness, which are equal in extent to space itself, gaining the freedom of the eight great treasures of inner confidence.

From the mentor Lama Jigmé Dorjé of the Ju clan, he received a simple oral transmission for the root verses of the sutra *The Compendium in Verse of the Perfection of Sublime Knowing* and then immediately proceeded to give explanatory teachings on the text for a month. While studying the text *The Entrance into the Middle Way* with Bumsar Geshé Ngawang Jungné, he requested an oral transmission with a brief explanation so as not to inconvenience his mentor. After bestowing the transmission, the teacher had him take an oral examination. Mipam Rinpoché then gave his teacher a discourse based on *The Entrance into the Middle Way* from beginning to end, causing the scholar to remark in front of his retinue, "Although I have myself received the title of geshé, I do not possess even a fraction of an intellect like this." [2.109a]

In addition, Mipam Rinpoché received teaching transmissions for *The Treasury of Understanding Valid Cognition* from Pönlop Loter Wangpo and for the treatises of

Maitreya and *The Levels of a Bodhisattva* from Loter Wangpo's attendant, Sölpön Pema. He then gave extensive explanations back to these teachers. This illustrates his innate comprehension of a boundless range of sutras, tantras, and commentaries on their intent. Unhindered and undaunted, he was like a fearless lion among those whose knowledge of scriptural sources was encyclopedic, as he proclaimed the teachings, gave discourses, and wrote commentaries on those sources. This was everyone's experience, and no one could deny the facts.

The lord Mipam himself said:

> When I was very young, although there were many fine mentors from both the Nyingma and Sarma schools—as though the Buddha were again turning the wheel of the dharma—I myself did not study widely. I did, however, listen to Paltrul Rinpoché's teachings on the chapter concerning sublime knowing in *Engaging in the Conduct of a Bodhisattva*. After that, due to the grace of my gurus and meditation deities, the key points in books that I had merely read [2.109b] became fully evident to me without any great difficulty.
>
> Furthermore, whenever I undertook new studies, I found the texts of the more modern schools quite easy to understand. Yet, although the scriptural sources of the Early Translation school were more difficult to grasp, except to acknowledge my own lack of comprehension, I never for an instant experienced any doubt. Rather, I thought, "Great and crucial points of understanding are to be gleaned from these scriptures of the lineage of masters of awareness." Consequently, sublime knowing completely matured in me. Thereafter, whenever I looked at texts, I recognized that all of the limitless, profound key points were to be found solely in the traditions passed down through the lineage of the precious masters of the Early Translation school. I was powerfully certain of this.
>
> At that point, my lord of refuge, Khyentsé Rinpoché, who was Vajradhara himself, said to me, "Compose teaching manuals for your own tradition." To fulfill my guru's command and enhance my own intellect, I wrote a few teaching manuals on sutras and the like, holding the precious teachings of the victorious ones in my heart. In so doing, I expounded a bit while emphasizing the positions held in my tradition. Unfortunately, others construed these as denunciations [2.110a] of their own professed philosophies, so that many polemical attacks from all sides followed.[22] In actuality, I had been motivated only to obey my guru's command. Today, the teachings of the Early Translation school are almost like a mere sketch of a burning lamp; most people just mimic the traditions of the principal scriptural sources. Rare are those who realize what constitute the key points of our own system of thought and address them in their works. Through my writing, I had hoped to improve this situation, if only slightly. Other than this, I have never

> for a moment, not even in my dreams, been motivated by a desire to defame other traditions or brag about my own. Were people with the eye of timeless awareness to scrutinize this statement, I would still have nothing to be ashamed of!
>
> As for what I have written in reply to these polemical attacks, without having achieved the perspective of someone spiritually advanced, how can I claim to have realized the limitless, profound range of all that it is possible to know? In deciding what is logical or not, my guiding lamp has been the flawless words of the Sugata and the commentaries on his enlightened intent—that is, the works of great masters of the mainstream traditions of India and Tibet. [2.110b] To a small extent, I have done some investigating of my own to determine which issues are reasonable or not. And if I have expressed my opinions, they may conceivably benefit someone slightly (although I have no idea who can, in fact, benefit whom). If, through my own lack of realization or wrong-headed thinking, I have corrupted the Buddha's profound words and the commentaries on his enlightened intent, then I have closed the doorway to liberation for myself and many other people. There is no greater or more serious way than this to ensure perpetual ruin! So, if those endowed with the vision of the dharma were to refute my position according to authentic scriptural sources and reasoning, I would rely on them as I would on a doctor (although no one should ever engage in refutation out of animosity or fanaticism). It is with a fair-minded attitude that I have engaged to some extent in debate.

In refuting wrong-headed thinking, truly advanced spiritual beings fulfill a great purpose, that of preserving the treasuries of the sacred dharma. In this vein, the sublimely learned Lobzang Rabsel and the lord Mipam exchanged fine gifts [2.111a] of excellent explanatory teachings; ultimately, their minds blended, becoming one, and each showered the other with praise. When Mipam Rinpoché read *The Detailed Commentary on Valid Cognition,* he dreamed of someone who was in essence Sakya Pandita, appearing as a scholar-siddha of India, his nose slightly hooked. This yogin asked him, "What do you not understand in *The Detailed Commentary on Valid Cognition?* It has two sections: one on refutations, the other on proofs." The yogin then divided a copy of the commentary into two parts and handed them to Mipam, saying, "Combine these two!" He did as he was told, and the two parts immediately turned into a sword; it then seemed to him that all knowable phenomena lay before him. Making a pass with the sword, he had the vivid experience of cutting through all of them with one stroke, unimpeded. Mipam Rinpoché later noted that, thereafter, he understood every single word of *The Detailed Commentary.* In addition, when he had first read *The Fundamental Discourse of the Vinaya,* a few points seemed difficult to understand. Later, however, he read the Kangyur once through, [2.111b] including all thirteen volumes dealing with Vinaya. He said that as a result of this study, there remained nothing in *The Fundamental Discourse* that he still did not comprehend. He also said that with respect to the extraordinary and profound key points distinguishing the Nyingma from the Sarma schools, he did not rely on books. Rather, while he was in intensive retreats on the phases of approach and accomplishment, the subtle channel of awareness opened for him. The blessings of his gurus and meditation deities allowed these key points to arise in his mind in a natural, effortless way. He said that it was imperative that he write of these things.

One auspicious day, the lord Khyentsé Rinpoché arranged on a shrine some volumes of sutras and tantras, as well as certain texts on fields of secular knowledge, specifically texts for which the transmissions were rare or the subject matter vitally important. He made extensive offerings to these texts and had the lord Mipam sit in front of them on a high seat covered with symbols of divination. He empowered him as a master of the dharma with the words, "As I am conferring the instructions of these texts on you, henceforth you must uphold them without impairment through the three means of explanation, debate, and writing. Ensure that the precious teachings of the Victorious One shine in this world for a long time." [2.112a] Khyentsé Rinpoché offered him valuable symbols of enlightened form, speech, and mind, including a tangka of White Tara and a handwritten manuscript of a prayer for Mipam Rinpoché's longevity that Khyentsé Rinpoché had composed based on Mipam's various names. As a sign of Mipam's authority, Khyentsé Rinpoché conferred on him a scholar's cap with long earflaps that he himself had worn, thus investing Mipam as his true regent, and praised him fervently. In later conversations with others, the lord Khyentsé would say, "These days, there is no one on the face of the earth more learned than Mipam Rinpoché. If I were to write about the succession of his previous incarnations and superior qualities, a volume the size of the sutra *The Perfection of Sublime Knowing* would not suffice, but this would not please him." (This, by the way, is from a reliable source.) Jamgön Kongtrul Yönten Gyatso referred to him as Mahapandita Mipam Gyatso and received from him the teaching transmissions for Mipam Rinpoché's own works, including *The Detailed Commentary on Valid Cognition* and *The Detailed Explanation of the Eight Commands.*

At a certain point, Japa Do-ngak, greatly learned in the Sarma schools, criticized what he felt were inconsistencies in the logic of Mipam Rinpoché's commentary on the chapter concerning sublime knowing in *Engaging in the Conduct of a Bodhisattva.* [2.112b] A debate of several days ensued between the two masters, and Paltrul Rinpoché, leader of the wise, venerable, and accomplished, was appointed witness. While it was taking place, ordinary people could not tell who was winning or losing, only whether what was being said was consistent with their own opinions. At one point, a Lama Rigchok asked Paltrul Rinpoché, "Who is winning?"

Paltrul Rinpoché replied, "I cannot decide or bring this to a conclusion. There is a proverb: 'A son is to be praised not by his father, but by his enemies; a daughter is to be praised not by her mother, but by her neighborhood.' Nevertheless, some of Do-ngak's monks told me that during the early stages of the debate, they clearly saw a ray of light connecting the heart center of the Mañjushri statue that is Lama Mipam Rinpoché's support for his spiritual practice to the lama's own heart center. This seems to sum up the outcome of the debate." On that occasion, Paltrul Rinpoché also instructed the debaters, "Japa Do-ngak has written a commentary on the quotation 'The great perfection is the universal matrix of timeless awareness.' It seems that some consider it to be refutable and others provable; [2.113a] so each of you, please present an argument bearing directly on this." After they had done so, the lord Mipam emerged victorious. He was then invested as a master of the teachings of the Early Translation school, receiving honors such as the permission to write commentaries elucidating the tantras, the explanatory texts based on these, and the pith instructions.

As an expression of this great being's motivation, Mipam Rinpoché collaborated with Katok Situ Rinpoché in founding Norbui Lhunpo Shedra. He said, "The conduct of the superb khenpo of Sahora and the view of the incomparable and glorious Nagarjuna are sealed together to form an integrated oral tradition," and "Not to be bought even by the gift of a field of gold studded with gems, the spiritual teachings, the heart treasure of the dakinis of basic space, are lovingly revealed only to the fortunate."[23] Accordingly, the splendid power of lord Mipam's superb motivation has ensured that the view and philosophical system of the two masters, the victorious ones Rongzom and Longchenpa, along with that of the lineage of the Early Translation school, have continued to the present day, promulgated by the masters of Katok Monastery, and that centers for the explanation and study of these teachings exist throughout the world. [2.113b]

Later in his life, Mipam Rinpoché spent thirteen years at that most majestic practice site, Karmo Taktsang, planting the victory banner of spiritual attainment. The particular deity on which this lord's flower had fallen was the wrathful aspect of Mañjushri, Yamantaka Ayushpati. Mipam Rinpoché said that when he was carrying out an intensive retreat on the phase of approach for this deity at Karmo Taktsang, there was not one sign of successful practice, as explained in the source texts, that he did not experience. He also said that in his many years of retreat, while reciting mantras he never once—not even during a single round of his mala—uttered them mechanically, let his eyes wander, or strayed from one-pointed immersion in the stages of development and completion as the source texts instruct.

Once, Khyentsé Rinpoché asked him, "When you are in retreat, what practice do you do?"

Mipam humbly replied, "In my studies, I take care to ensure that my investigation is thorough; during intensive retreat on the phase of approach for my meditation deity, I make certain that I am practicing the stage of development to the highest degree."

Khyentsé Rinpoché rejoined, "That is a difficult task. As the great Omniscient One said, [2.114a] 'One is to rest right where one is, without doing anything at all.' I have done so myself, and although by resting I have not seen anything with a white complexion and a reddish tinge that could be called the true face of mind, still, were I to die now, I would not have a trace of fright or anxiety." And he laughed. Mipam Rinpoché realized that this was the guru's advice to him.

By focusing on the key points of the subtle vajra body in practicing the stage of completion, Mipam Rinpoché largely purified the stirring of the subtle energy of karma by resolving it into the basic space of the central channel. He refined his personal experience of supremely blissful, innate timeless awareness—the genuine state of utter lucidity, both as a foretaste and as the ultimate experience—the unity of bliss and emptiness elicited by the four degrees of joy and the four degrees of emptiness.[24] Relying on the Dzogchen approach in particular—the intensive practices of trekchö to arrive at a state of original purity and of tögal to arrive at a state of spontaneous presence—Mipam Rinpoché brought his direct experience of the true nature of phenomena to full expression instead of being satisfied with intellectual speculation. Thus he gained mastery of the display of the kayas and timeless awareness within the sphere of his perception.

On the strength of the total purification of his subtle network of channels into a mandala of massing mantra syllables, sublime knowing born of meditation welled up in him. He composed his termas of enlightened intent as commentaries[25] spanning an enormous range of profound topics. [2.114b] His collected prayers of praise and biographical accounts encourage faith as the avenue to blessings. His collected works on fields of secular knowledge resolve doubts about the range of the knowable. Those on the profound and extensive inner knowledge of spiritual teachings provide an entranceway to the path of total freedom. And his collected prayers of dedication, aspiration, and auspicious benediction set up circumstances for the teachings to endure, as well as for fulfillment and excellence to be spontaneously accomplished always and everywhere. These four major divisions of his written works can be broken down into numerous subcategories, filling precious volumes equal in number to the thirty-two major marks of perfection. Together they serve as the very life force of the teachings of the victorious ones in general and those of the Early Translation school in particular.

Mipam Rinpoché spent the rest of his life mainly practicing the two stages of meditation, while in the breaks between sessions, he wrote all kinds of pith instructions and commentaries. He ended his retreat on the thirteenth day of the first month in a Water Rat year.[26] Around the eighteenth day, he became concerned about several negative premonitions, so that on the twenty-first, he suddenly wrote a poem that begins as follows:

Namo mañjushrisattvaya![27]

Having gained mastery over the vast range of conduct befitting children
of the victorious ones [2.115a]
in such pure realms as Abhirati,
I vow to hold, for as long as space endures,
a mind of supreme compassion for beings throughout space.
I, a proponent of spiritual teachings who is oppressed by karma in these
degenerate times,
have been afflicted with a virulent disease of the nerves for seventeen years,
suffering greatly without respite, and up to now
I have remained in this realm, relying on the cage of this illusory body.
Now, in anticipation of my death,
I have written down what will be my last words of advice.

Thus he composed his last testament and concealed it. During the second and third months of the year, he repeated the dharani mantra[28] of Akshobhya some two hundred thousand times, and he gave words of advice as needed to his attendant, Lama Ösel. On one occasion, he said:

> Today, if one tells the truth, generally no one listens, while if one tells a lie, it is taken as truth, so I have never spoken of these things before. I am not an ordinary mortal person; rather, I am a bodhisattva who has taken rebirth by the power of his aspirations. In this present existence, it has been necessary for me to greatly benefit the teachings and beings in general, [2.115b] and the teachings of the Early Translation school of the secret mantra approach in particular. Because of the Nyingmapas' lack of merit, they face many harmful obstacles, and due to certain critical circumstances, I too have had a severe illness. For these and other reasons, I do not feel that I have created as much benefit as I might have.
>
> Nonetheless, I have completed my commentaries and other works. I had intended to write a clear, extensive overview of Madhyamaka, but have not succeeded in doing so. However, it doesn't make much difference. Were I to complete my cycle *The Genuine Nature of Mind,* it would be a great nonsectarian contribution to the vitality of the teachings. I have wondered whether I can finish this cycle, but up to now have not been able to do so.
>
> In these final times, barbarians from border countries threaten the very existence of the teachings.[29] For this and other reasons, it would not be beneficial for me to take rebirth under any circumstances whatsoever. Were this the period in which the brothers of Mindroling lived, I might indeed benefit

> the teachings and beings to some degree, but in these times it would prove difficult. Therefore, I have no intention of ever taking rebirth again in an impure realm. [2.116a] It is my nature to dwell solely in pure realms, with the playful dance of my emanations guiding beings in whatever way is required through the power of my aspirations, without interruption, for as long as samsara continues.

These were the kinds of sentiments Mipam Rinpoché expressed. Around the twenty-second day of the month, he said, "Now that I have recovered from my nervous disorder and other ailments, I feel absolutely no pain. Every day and night, I experience only the visions of tögal arising as rays and spheres of rainbow light, enlightened forms, and pure realms."

He granted audiences to the faithful students and patrons who gathered around him from all directions and prayed on their behalf. People urged him to live longer, arguing that doing so would benefit the teachings and beings, but he replied, "I definitely will not remain, nor will I take rebirth. I intend to go to Shambhala in the north." At sixty-seven years of age, on the twenty-ninth day of the fourth month, Saga, in a Water Rat year,[30] Mipam Rinpoché sat with his legs crossed loosely in the posture of a bodhisattva and with his hands in the gestures of meditative equipoise and of giving spiritual teachings. His enlightened mind rested evenly in the basic space of inexhaustible primordial peace. His precious remains were placed on a funeral pyre, [2.116b] and all present beheld canopies of rainbow light and other such marvelous, positive omens. Lama Ösel ensured that the tasks following the passing of Mipam Rinpoché were completed in order to fulfill the guru's enlightened intentions.

Among the principal students of this lord were Dodrup Jigmé Tenpai Nyima (who studied with all three of the Mañjushri emanations); Tertön Sögyal; the fifth Dzogchen Rinpoché; Gemang Tulku; the fifth Rabjam and fourth Gyaltsap tulkus of Zhechen Monastery; the third Katok Situ Rinpoché; Gyatrul Tulku of Palyul Monastery; Adzom Drukpa; Drupwang Shakya Shri; and Pönlop Tulku of Ngor Monastery. In brief, from the great monasteries of Katok, Palyul, Zhechen, Dzogchen, Palpung, and Dergé, from as far away as Amdo and Repkong, his students included great, holy tulkus of the Sakya, Geluk, Kagyü, and Nyingma schools, as well as scholars who could expound on the entire range of the mainstream source texts of Buddhism, khenpos who upheld the three higher trainings, Vajrayana practitioners with confidence born of experience in the two stages of meditation, and mendicants who had cast off all concern for the things of this life. It was impossible to count those who became his spiritual heirs through his enlightened speech. The great, holy beings who were his heart children strove diligently [2.117a] to extend the range of their guru's enlightened activities.

Although this lord made no effort to reveal earth termas, in response to specific needs he left many pith instructions on the stages of development and completion, collections of activity rituals, and so forth, composing these as treatises, though they welled up in his awareness as termas of enlightened intent. In fact, Mipam Rinpoché was a king among tertöns, for he was sublimely accomplished, with mastery of the treasury of the vast expanse of profound enlightened intent, which is the most majestic of all such termas.

Khenchen Jampal Dewai Nyima (19th–20th Centuries)

Khenchen Jampal Dewai Nyima was lord Mipam's student. He was the brother of the tertön Lama Rang-rik Dorjé of Nyarong. He studied the mainstream traditions of Madhyamaka, Prajñaparamita, Vinaya, Abhidharma, valid cognition, and so forth, becoming a consummate scholar with untrammeled understanding of the five fields of knowledge. With such teachers as Nyoshul Lungtok, Lama Rang-rik, Jamgön Kongtrul, the lord Khyentsei Wangpo, and others, he studied and trained in the sutras and tantras in general, including the most majestic of tantras, *The Heart Essence of Secrets,* and the three sources of the Early Translation school: *The Discourse on United Intent, The Web of Magical Display,* and the mind teachings.

Jampal Dewai Nyima also received in their entirety the empowerments, oral transmissions, teachings, and so forth of the kama tradition, *The Treasury of Precious Hidden Teachings,* [2.117b] and the tradition of Mindroling Monastery. He thus became a repository of spiritual advice. He served the protector Mañjushri himself, Jamgön Mipam Rinpoché, the extraordinary lord of his buddha family, receiving the great cycles of the Nyingtik teachings of the Dzogchen approach.

He also trained in the tantras, explanatory commentaries, and pith instructions concerning the peaceful and wrathful aspects of Mañjushri. Mipam Rinpoché gave him the secret name Jampal Dewai Nyima within the mandala of empowerment and conferred on him the seal of entrustment to carry on the ultimate lineage. Through his spiritual practice on the sublime Mañjushri, Jampal Dewai Nyima was taken under the care of this deity's timeless awareness embodiment, so that he gained accomplishment through the deity's mantras of awareness.

Jampal Dewai Nyima lived mainly at Absé Lhumorap Monastery in his native region, where he wrote many treatises, such as a major commentary according to the Zur tradition on *The Heart Essence of Secrets.* He had hundreds of students throughout upper and lower Nyarong, as far away as Gojo to the south. Every day Jampal Dewai Nyima taught the mainstream Buddhist traditions, or the extraordinary cycles of Dzogchen pith instructions, or at the very least such subjects as medicine and astrology. Giving about ten lectures a day, he served the teachings on an enormous scale. At his monastic seat, he built a temple, its structure and contents reputed to be marvelous magical emanations. [2.118a] In addition, he commissioned countless representations of enlightened form, speech, and mind. He founded a shedra and in other ways engaged in a wide array of spiritual activity.

The holders of his lineage were Choktrul Chödor (a nephew of Jampal Dewai Nyima and the tulku of Rigdzin Longsel Nyingpo), his daughter Kunzang Chödrön, Choktrul Pema Namgyal, Tulku Angak Rinpoché, and others. These masters' nephews, grandnephews, and students—khenpos, masters, and sublime tulkus who covered the surface of the earth—came to Jampal Dewai Nyima's monastic seat at Lhumorap in eastern Tibet, and thus the teachings spread widely.

When Terdak Lingpa was on the point of passing away, he had said, "Now I must take seven steps toward the east," thus prophesying that after seven generations of throne holders had served the teachings, his family's spiritual lineage would be restored by someone from the east. In keeping with the implication of this prophecy, by the order of the thirteenth Dalai Lama, Tupten Gyatso, Terchen Rang-rik Rinpoché (Jampal Dewai Nyima's older brother) was invited to Mindroling Monastery to reestablish the family lineage there, and Jampal Dewai Nyima accompanied him. [2.118b] There he transmitted the general teachings of the kama and terma traditions, the empowerments and instructions of the Mindroling tradition, and the innumerable cycles of teachings deriving from the three emanations of the protector Mañjushri (the explanations of tantras, Dzogchen, and other teachings). He thus gathered countless students throughout the central, southern, and eastern regions of Tibet, and the vitality of the monastic seat of Mindroling thereby increased.

To that monastic seat came the two khenpo brothers who were Jampal Dewai Nyima's nephews, as well as Kyabjé Dudjom Rinpoché and others, making this a holy center of the teachings. Most of the transmissions of the lineages on three levels—those of individual liberation, the bodhisattva discipline, and the mantra approach—that Dudjom Rinpoché received were bestowed by Jampal Dewai Nyima, who Dudjom Rinpoché considered to be one of the three most important gurus with whom he studied.[31]

Eventually, Jampal Dewai Nyima returned to his native Nyarong, where, having spontaneously accomplished the two kinds of benefit, his emanated form resolved back into basic space, leaving physical remains that were only a cubit in length. Earthquakes, showers of blossoms, networks of rainbow light, and other signs manifested, inspiring faith in his students. In more recent times, Lodrö Gyaltsen was recognized as the sublime tulku of Jampal Dewai Nyima; he currently lives in India.[32] [2.119a] A student of the two khenpo brothers, he is known as Kyabjé Minling Trichen Kunzang Pema Wangyal,[33] one who nurtures the teachings of the supreme secret, his lotus feet standing firmly in the vajra realm.

The Fourth Zhechen Gyaltsap, Gyurmé Pema Namgyal (1871–1926)

The father of Gyurmé Pema Namgyal was Adro Sherab, and his mother was Namkha Drönma. He was recognized by both Dzogtrul Mingyur Namkhai Dorjé and Jamyang Khyentsei Wangpo as the tulku of Orgyen Rangjung Dorjé Tsewang Drupa

Tsal, the previous Zhechen Gyaltsap. The great hidden yogin Gyurmé Namgyal offered him his ink bottle, bamboo reed pen, walking staff, and other personal effects and told him, "This will provide the interdependence by which all of my renunciation and realization will be perfected in you." When Gyurmé Pema Namgyal was five years old, he was escorted to Zhechen Tennyi Dargyé Ling Monastery and enthroned. He studied and trained with numerous tutors and mentors, among them Jamgön Kongtrul Lodrö Tayé; [2.119b] the lord of the dharma Mipam Rinpoché; the fifth Zhechen Rabjam, Khenchen Pema Dorjé; Chungtrul Tupten Chöpel; Karma Chökyi Nyinjé, the precious Drungpa Tulku of Zurmang Monastery; Jetsün Gyurmé Dechen Chödrön; Gyatrul Tulku of Palyul Monastery; Rabjam Ön Tukjé Gyatso; Göntö Choktrul Orgyen Tsewang Rigdzin; Khenchen Kunzang Palden; and Choktrul Palden Chögyal. Gyurmé Pema Namgyal served these and many other learned and accomplished masters, attaining a definitive level of understanding by listening to, contemplating, and meditating on a vast array of teachings from the mainstream traditions of sutra and tantra.

From the extraordinary inner lord of his family, Jamyang Khyentsei Wangpo, he received untold maturing empowerments and liberating instructions, as well as a full range of profound advice on the pith instructions of the Dzogchen approach, like one vase being filled by another to the brim. With this, the realization of the ultimate lineage awakened in him. Gyurmé Pema Namgyal then took a vow to remain at the hermitage of Tashi Chöling and not to travel anywhere. He strictly observed a vow to pursue his spiritual practice until he passed into nirvana. Graced with numerous visions of many of his meditation deities, [2.120a] particularly the great and glorious Vajrakumara, he demonstrated signs of accomplishment defying imagination or description, such as leaving footprints in solid rock. Gyurmé Pema Namgyal maintained the deportment of a hidden yogin; he wore ragged clothing and took a low seat, saying, "I don't know or understand anything." So profound was his mind that no one could fathom the depths of his conduct, which was that of a siddha. Even evil individuals would turn away from samsara and develop renunciation simply upon meeting him. For the innumerable beings who saw, heard, thought of, or touched him, Gyurmé Pema Namgyal ensured that samsara would come to an end.

During his empowerments, the timeless awareness aspect of the deity would actually descend. While bestowing empowerments into the dynamic energy of awareness, Gyurmé Pema Namgyal would rest in a state of enlightened intent, his body especially resplendent and radiant, causing people's ordinary perceptions to be arrested as a matter of course. He manifested these and untold other signs of erudition, venerability, and spiritual attainment.

It is said, "The erudite will be known as such if they write elegant explanatory teachings." Since the three conditions for writing treatises were complete for him,[34] Gyurmé Pema Namgyal composed works with the power to captivate people's minds

—well-written treatises of excellent meaning, manifestations of the speech of a scholar with discriminating intelligence. [2.120b] He wrote many volumes of commentaries on the sutras, tantras, and pith instructions, such as *The Drumbeat of the Gods: Remarks on the Treasury of Precious Hidden Teachings* and *White Lotus Pond: A Religious History of the Eight Great Lineages of Accomplishment.* In particular, praying fervently to the great Omniscient One, Gyurmé Pema Namgyal had a vision of the timeless awareness embodiment of that guru and was taken under his care. He then composed the prayer of praise *The Chariot That Inspires Faith and Devotion.*

Although the lord Gyurmé Pema Namgyal devoted himself primarily to the very essence of spiritual practice, he still managed to continually bestow maturing empowerments and liberating instructions on his heart children. Among these were the sixth Zhechen Rabjam, Drungpa Rinpoché Karma Chökyi Nyinjé of Zurmang Monastery, Kyabjé Dilgo Khyentsé Rinpoché, Kongtrul Karma Palden Chöwang, Lodrö Drimé, Pema Drimé Lekpai Lodrö, Nyentrul Karma Shedrup Tenpai Nyima, Dzogchen Lingtrul, Khenchen Tsultrim Gyatso, Gemang Khenchen Yönten Gyatso, Khen Söchö of Dzogchen Monastery, Khen Lhagong, and Pukung Zhetrul. [2.121a] These masters exemplify the countless great scholars and holy tulkus who, as his students, were alike in reaching the pinnacle of renunciation and realization.

He thus brought the activities he undertook for the sake of the teachings and beings, and his life, to a close. As his final testament, he told one of his heart sons, the sixth Rabjam, "Pray to Guru Rinpoché!" As truly marvelous signs manifested, Gyurmé Pema Namgyal's emanated form resolved back into primordial basic space.

The Fifth Dzogchen Rinpoché, Tupten Chökyi Dorjé (1872–1935)

In the prophecies of the great and glorious Orgyen, we read statements like, "Vimalamitra will appear in the southern reaches of eastern Tibet in a Monkey year and will be named Dharmavajra.[35] He will serve the teachings of the heart essence in an excellent way." In keeping with these prophecies, Tupten Chökyi Dorjé was born in a Water Monkey year[36] amid myriad marvelous, amazing signs. Before very long, indications that he was the next Dzogchen Rinpoché came from deities and gurus, and he was enthroned in a ceremony attended by many thousands of people, including a number of patrons (the great king of Dergé foremost among them), the fourth Pönlop, Gyurmé Gyatso of Zhechen Monastery, Gyarong Choktrul Kunzang Tekchok Dorjé, [2.121b] and others of his own Dzogchen Monastery, along with gurus and tulkus from affiliated monasteries of the same lineage and many of the local inhabitants. They offered many prayers to him as a source of refuge and as a protector of human beings and gods.

Tupten Chökyi Dorjé clearly exhibited the intelligence that had characterized his previous incarnations, and he learned how to read and write simply upon being shown how to do so. He studied and trained in such mainstream subjects as Vinaya, Prajñaparamita, and Madhyamaka with many tutors and mentors. In particular, he studied Dzogchen with Jamyang Khyentsei Wangpo (whom he considered the extraordinary master of his buddha family), the great bodhisattva Paltrul Rinpoché, Khenchen Pema Badzra, Pönlop Chöying Ösel, and others. He received from these masters the three Yangtik cycles of the Dzogchen approach of utter lucidity, *The Three Cycles of Being at Ease,* the Dzogchen manual *Timeless Awareness as the Guiding Principle,* and so forth. In this way, he directly experienced the way of abiding that is the very essence of being, discovering the full measure of confidence born of realization. As signs of his spiritual attainment, Tupten Chökyi Dorjé left footprints in solid rock, [2.122a] the inner offering of nectar on his shrine would boil on its own, and the torma offering would dissolve into light. When he practiced, the sky was filled with light. These and a host of other signs manifested.

He became a great master of the teachings of the Early Translation school. In particular, the motivation that Tupten Chökyi Dorjé had aroused in previous lifetimes matured with time, so that he conferred innumerable sacred transmissions, both extensive and profound, of the supreme secret—with maturing empowerments and liberating instructions—on countless students from as far away as India and China. The white umbrella of his activity in turning the wheel of the dharma spanned the three planes of existence. He visited the monastic communities associated with the lineage of the Drupwang Dzogchen tulkus in Golok and in Xining in the northern reaches. He even traveled as far as the black-tent communities of Mongolia and Minyak in the east, visiting the thirteen monastic institutions of the eastern Tibetan lowlands, the twenty-five monasteries of the midlands, and so forth. There he bestowed the maturing empowerments, liberating instructions, and supportive oral transmissions of the Vajrayana, thus ensuring that these teachings spread and flourished. When he gave empowerments, he would place the vase in empty space with no physical support, and the nectar of the medicine and rakta offerings would boil. He could hang his robes on sunbeams [2.122b] and showed numerous other signs of spiritual attainment.

Tupten Chökyi Dorjé could see without hindrance throughout the three times. Just before he passed away, he summoned the geshé of Nera, saying, "Bring him to me!" The geshé was called from Dergé, and when he approached Tupten Chökyi Dorjé, the latter said to him, "Go tomorrow to the forest on the monastery's land and see whether there is enough timber to build a new temple." Although the geshé agreed to do this, he thought, "These are the words of a realized guru, and no one can predict what realized gurus mean by what they say.[37] However, there shouldn't be any need for the monastery's timber." The next day, he and his servant walked a short way, not looking far before turning back. When the geshé went to see Tupten Chökyi Dorjé, the guru asked, "Does there seem to be enough wood?" The geshé answered, "There will definitely be enough for your needs." Tupten Chökyi Dorjé exclaimed, "Well, that's wonderful! In the future, it will be entirely up to you to provide for the monastery." And he sent the geshé away, charging him with this great responsibility.

The guru passed away into a pure realm in the tenth month of that year. [2.123a] In the second month of the following year, that of the Fire Rat,[38] disaster struck: the entire monastery, including the temple and guru's estate, burned down. It was clear that the guru's words had been prophetic, and since the monastery had to be rebuilt, the geshé took up the task without being asked to do so, saying, "Last year, Rinpoché deliberately gave me this order." He was instrumental in rebuilding the monastery from the ground up, which greatly inspired him; he had such faith that he truly saw the guru as a buddha.

Over the years, this sublime master, Tupten Chökyi Dorjé, journeyed three times to Zangdok Palri in the realm of Chamara. The great system of ritual dances for Vajrakila maintained by Dzogchen Monastery was instituted on the basis of these pure visions.

Tupten Chökyi Dorjé also traveled to Lhasa in central Tibet, where he met with the thirteenth Dalai Lama and was treated with boundless kindness. In numerous ways, Tupten Chökyi Dorjé provided funds for continuous offerings and sponsored spiritual practices at all of the principal holy sites—gilding statues such as that of the lord Buddha in Lhasa and distributing offerings and sponsoring meals and tea for the monastic communities of Sera, Drepung, Ganden, Samyé, and others. [2.123b] When he arrived at Samyé, the protector of that region, Pehar, immediately vowed to do whatever Tupten Chökyi Dorjé required of him and offered the guru a very special set of cymbals. Known as the "cymbals that delight Pehar," they can be found among the inner representations of Dzogchen Monastery. In association with Khenchen Zhenga Rinpoché, Tupten Chökyi Dorjé sponsored the many residents at the great Dzogchen Shri Simha Shedra affiliated with his monastery. He extensively taught the thirteen basic source texts in the curriculum, ensuring benefit that far surpassed anything that had been achieved earlier and causing this system of education to spread everywhere. No one can compare with Tupten Chökyi Dorjé in his enormous activity, which also included founding the meditation center Purkhang Chenmo and conferring the maturing empowerments, liberating instructions, and supportive oral transmissions for the mandala of peaceful and wrathful deities as well as for the earlier and later cycles of the Nyingtik teachings.

Among his students were many masters associated with his own monastery, such as Pönlop Tulku, the tulku of Khenchen Pema Badzra, Purtsa Tulku, Tokden Tulku, [2.124a] Gotsa Tulku, Kunzang Tulku, Böpa Tulku, the two Doring tulkus (the elder and the younger), Barné Tulku, Khyentsé Tulku of Dzogchen Monastery, Kongtrul, two successive Gyapak tulkus, and Minyak Garwang Tulku. He also taught the great khenpos Tupnyen, Gönpo, Lhagyal, Chötsa, Chönyi, Amön, and others. In addition, tens of thousands—teachers, meditators, monks, nuns, lay tantric masters, and other lay people—forged a connection with Tupten Chökyi Dorjé. In such ways, he nurtured the precious teachings of the Victorious One through his noble activity in the three spheres of study, practice, and spiritual projects. His heart children, endowed with erudition, venerability, and nobility, made their influence felt throughout eastern Tibet, in both the highlands and lowlands.

In those days, Tupten Chökyi Dorjé was unsurpassed at recognizing tulkus and predicting events, [2.124b] both good and bad. Everyone regarded him as their source of refuge and their glorious and holy protector. He brought his students to spiritual maturity merely by his presence. When Tupten Chökyi Dorjé was about sixty years old, amid innumerable marvelous signs, the manifest mandala of his emanated form resolved back into the peaceful basic space of all phenomena. His sublime tulku was the sixth Dzogchen Rinpoché, Jangchub Dorjé; the latter in turn took rebirth as the seventh and present Dzogchen Rinpoché, who moved to India and still ensures great benefit for the teachings and for beings.[39] Likewise, the two tulkus of Gyalsé Zhenpen Tayé and Pönlop Namkha Ösel[40] live in the holy country of India, pursuing their studies.

Terchen Orgyen Chokgyur Lingpa (1829–1870)

Terchen Orgyen Chokgyur Lingpa was an incarnation of Murub Tsepo, one of King Trisong Detsen's sons. He was born in Nangchen, eastern Tibet, part of the so-called southern reaches. His father was a lay tantric master named Pema Wangchuk, and his mother was Tsering Yangtso. Their son was born amid wondrous portents [2.125a] on the tenth day of the month of Chutö in an Earth Ox year.[41] From an early age, the boy effortlessly exhibited the innate attributes of someone holy. He was named Norbu Tendzin.

Once, when he was thirteen, Norbu Tendzin was playing in an area known as Manikha. There he actually met Orgyen Rinpoché, who asked him about the place, his name, and so forth. The boy answered each question, whereupon Guru Rinpoché said, "My boy, the circumstances surrounding you are extremely auspicious. The fact that this place is called Manikha, that your name is Norbu Tendzin, and that this valley is called Arya Nang[42] means that you have come into this world as someone especially exalted." Having uttered these words, Guru Rinpoché faded from Chokgyur Lingpa's perception, like a rainbow fading in the sky. It was about this time that Chokgyur Lingpa received ordination as a novice monk from Matrul Rinpoché of the Taklung Kagyü school.

He received the extensive empowerment for *The United Intent of the Gurus* and other transmissions from the eighth Pawo, Tsuklak Chökyi Gyalpo, and his meditative experience and realization were awakened. This guru cared for him with great delight, entrusting him with the ultimate lineage of termas. Over time, Chokgyur

Lingpa also studied [2.125b] with the Gyalwang Karmapa,[43] the Kyabgön Drukchen of the Drukpa Kagyü school, and many other mentors, receiving maturing empowerments, liberating instructions, and supportive oral transmissions, as well as training in ritual dance, the layout of mandalas, chanting, and music. He learned all of these without error, applying himself diligently to his training.

At twenty-five, encouraged by Guru Rinpoché's words, Chokgyur Lingpa went to the monastic seat of Palpung in Dergé, eastern Tibet. There he met Tai Situ Pema Nyinjé Wangpo, to whom he offered terma objects such as the ritual kila dagger known as Wangchen Zhepa. Situ Rinpoché was very pleased, which established auspicious circumstances for the extension of his life. He privately told Chokgyur Lingpa that it was necessary for him to fulfill his destiny by unlocking the seals of secrecy and revealing termas.

Guru Rinpoché had prophesied that two masters, Jamyang Khyentsei Wangpo and Jamgön Kongtrul Lodrö Tayé, would be gurus for lifetimes and primary custodians of the teachings of Chokgyur Lingpa, the three having been connected to one another in a former life as the king of Tibet and his sons.[44] Chokgyur Lingpa went to see both of these masters, who cared for him with great delight and extraordinary loving kindness. He received a host of empowerments, teachings, and advice from them, [2.126a] and his mind and theirs blended, becoming one. Notably, from Khyentsé Rinpoché he received the empowerment, codified by the victorious one Longchenpa, for *The Innermost Heart Drop of the Guru,* whereupon he had a pure vision in which he actually encountered Vimalamitra and was introduced directly to natural great perfection, timeless awareness as the naked unity of awareness and emptiness. When the "conferral of life force" for the guardian deities was performed, he beheld the guardian Ekajati, who said to him, "In three years, I will grant you a supreme siddhi." (This is understood to have been a reference to *The Three Categories of Great Perfection,* a terma he revealed.)

When Chokgyur Lingpa was twenty-seven, he received the extensive empowerment into the nine-deity mandala of Samyak, during which his lord guru appeared to him in the form of the heruka and dissolved into the crown of his head. This opened blockages in the subtle channels of his heart center. From that point on, Chokgyur Lingpa could spontaneously sing vajra songs without impediment, and termas welled up in his enlightened mind. Previously, he had been unable to record the symbolic script of the sadhana of enlightened mind entitled *Dispelling All Obstacles;* now it all arose in his mind, freely and naturally. This terma and one revealed by Khyentsé (the sadhana of enlightened mind entitled *The Gathering of All Sugatas*) were not only identical in meaning, but virtually identical in their wording, [2.126b] connected like a mother and child. Together, the masters used both cycles to carry out the ceremonies ensuring the successful codification of these termas. Thus many auspicious circumstances arose; for example, they had countless pure visions, and records of numerous terma caches came into their possession. Because the minds of these two masters had blended, becoming one, some of the maturing empowerments and liberating instructions of Chokgyur Lingpa's Tersar teachings are said to have been revealed by the lord Khyentsé Rinpoché. These two became great tertöns of indisputable renown, like the sun and moon.

Then, fulfilling a prophecy he had received from Guru Rinpoché, Chokgyur Lingpa went to the Karmapa's seat and stayed there for three years with a strict commitment not to leave the area. He diligently pursued his spiritual practice and brought to consummation the stages of development and completion as well as the Dzogchen approach. Countless signs of success manifested, for he had reached a lofty level of spiritual mastery. It became fully evident that he had, for example, mastered the four kinds of enlightened activity. In Guru Rinpoché's prophecies, we find verses like the following:

> There are kama lineages of oral commands passed on from generation to generation. ༔
> There are profound termas that are physical objects and termas of enlightened intent. ༔
> There are reconcealed termas that are then revealed again and termas based on recollections. ༔
> There are daknang transmissions and oral transmissions. ༔ [2.127a]
> These are the seven modes of transmission, ༔
> which fall to this father and son as their share of good fortune. ༔

With this, Guru Rinpoché prophesied that each of the two great tertöns who had been King Trisong Detsen and his son would be a master of these seven modes of transmission (which are in turn variations of the three lines of the kama, terma, and daknang transmissions).

In keeping with this prophecy, when the lord Chokgyur Lingpa was thirteen, he brought forth from their place of concealment at Drakar Dzongchung a number of termas, including the twenty-four sadhanas that had formed the core of Prince Murub Tsepo's spiritual practice and the vajra, skull cup, and mirror that were the symbolic objects associated with *The United Intent of the Gurus.* At thirty-nine he retrieved innumerable termas, among them *The Seven Cycles of Gems of the Sacred Dharma,* a regent statue of Guru Rinpoché, and the ornaments of Seng-gé Dradrok, from the hills called Tseké Norbu Punsum; *The Seven Cycles of Profound Spiritual Practice,* from a place behind Ogmin Tsurpu, the Karmapa's seat; *The Sacred Dharma: The Three Categories of Great Perfection,* from the cave known as Pema Shelpuk in Dzongshö; and a cycle focusing on the Eight Commands and *Profound Great Perfection: Molten Gold,* from an area south of Yegyal. In each case, the terma cache yielded teachings, statues, sacred samaya substances, symbolic implements, and many other objects, amounting to an enormous number of treasures. [2.127b] Most of these revelations occurred before large crowds; thus no one could contest the authenticity of what everyone, regardless of status, had witnessed. In a similar way, just as the prophecy had stated, from more than a hundred sites Chokgyur Lingpa brought forth countless other termas of enlightened form, speech, mind, qualities, and activity, such treasures as the one hundred Nyingtik teachings and numerous samaya substances that bring liberation upon taste. In such ways, the activities he undertook in connection with each of the seven modes of transmission, and the benefit they brought, were beyond measure.

Chokgyur Lingpa had visions of the deities of the Three Roots and received prophecies from them. The guardian deities actually carried out enlightened activities that he requested of them. On many occasions, he journeyed to Zangdok Palri in the realm of Chamara. He had boundless marvelous experiences. In addition, he oversaw some thirty extensive rituals involving the four phases of approach and accomplishment.[45] He performed ceremonies to consecrate principal holy sites in central Tibet—such as Hepo Hill in Samyé and Chuwori—and in eastern Tibet—Karmo Taktsang in Rongmé, Deshek Düpa in Dzongshö, and others. He issued strict commands to the local spirits inhabiting many regions. [2.128a] With such activities, Chokgyur Lingpa averted border wars and other unrest, signs of the troubled times,[46] and ensured peace and prosperity in these regions. He accomplished just what Guru Rinpoché had referred to in his prophecies, so that the benefit Chokgyur Lingpa brought to beings was as vast as the sky.

His students and heart children were affiliated primarily with the branches of the Kagyü school (particularly the Karma, Drukpa, Drigung, and Taklung Kagyü) and those of the Nyingma school (Katok, Palyul, Zhechen, Dzogchen, and other monasteries). He also taught masters of the Sakya and other schools without sectarian bias, conferring on them many maturing empowerments and liberating instructions, such as his own termas. These teachings were disseminated among the communities of these gurus and tulkus. Chokgyur Lingpa's influence was also felt all over Tibet through the gifts he made of substances that liberate upon taste.

The primary lineage of his terma teachings was passed to ten principal custodians and, due to favorable circumstances, spread throughout Tibet, so that Chokgyur Lingpa ensured that all who saw, heard, touched, or remembered him were placed on the supreme path to omniscience and enlightenment. Thus he lived as the splendor of the teachings and of beings for some forty-two years. [2.128b] At a certain point, he departed for the pure realm of Chamara. On a full moon day in the year he died, the lord Khyentsé met the great tertön in a vision—appearing in the form of a bodhisattva named Pemai Nyugu in Pemay Khepar, a pure realm to the west—and received transmissions of sadhanas, empowerments, and spiritual advice from him. Khyentsé

Rinpoché kept this a strict secret for a month. He then codified the transmissions during a ganachakra on the tenth day of the twelfth month, Gyal, whereupon the region suddenly warmed, flowers blossomed, and countless other signs and omens manifested—for example, the frozen river melted and flowed again—indicating the abundance of very special blessings in these teachings.

The lord Chokgyur Lingpa's principal seats were at Karma Ri, the meeting point of three valleys at Tsiké Norbu Punsum, and the ridge of Neten Gang. At the latter two sites, he built temples and furnished these to accommodate large communities of the sangha, as well as centers for the study and practice of the sutras and tantras. His two sublime tulkus resided at these two seats, and thus became known as Tsiké Chokling [2.129a] and Negang Chokling; both benefited the teachings and beings enormously. Of their two incarnations, the second Tsiké tulku is the son of Urgyen Tulku Rinpoché and lives at his father's monastery in Nepal, while the other was Nakön Lama Rinpoché Samten Gyatso, who was the son of the first Chokling Terchen's daughter. The latter tulku was from the Tsangsar family and stayed at Latsap Monastery and the hermitage of Dzong-go; he lived a life of spiritual practice, becoming a great, holy being.

Urgyen Tulku Rinpoché (1920–1996)

Urgyen Tulku Rinpoché was Orgyen Chokgyur Lingpa's great-grandson and Nupchen Sang-gyé Yeshé's most recent incarnation. Urgyen Tulku held his uncle, Lama Rinpoché Samten Gyatso, to be the extraordinary master of his buddha family. He also relied on and trained under the buddha Karmapa,[47] Karsé Kongtrul Rinpoché, Dilgo Khyentsé Rinpoché, Khyentsé Chökyi Lodrö, Chungtrul Karma Gyatso, Khenchen Dorjé of Polu, and other masters, studying the sutras and tantras in general, [2.129b] and Terchen Chokgyur Lingpa's cycles in particular, as well as the oral tradition of Lungtok Tenpai Nyima's pith instructions and his cycle *The Heart Drop of Samantabhadra*. Urgyen Tulku practiced these teachings and spent his entire life pursuing their very essence, manifesting indications that he had traversed advanced levels and paths of spiritual development, such as signs of success in the stages of development and completion. Kyabjé Dilgo Khyentsé Rinpoché confirmed that Urgyen Tulku had attained the level known as "awareness reaching full measure."

This great master, who brought purpose to everyone connected to him, lived primarily at his own monastery, Ka-nying Shedrup Ling,[48] and at the hermitage of Nagi (both in Nepal); he also traveled throughout India and Nepal, as well as to the United States and other countries, East and West, turning the wheel of the dharma for his students. Among his students are his descendents, who are still living, including his sons, Chökyi Nyima Rinpoché, Chokling Rinpoché, Tsoknyi Rinpoché, and Yongey Rinpoché, as well as his grandson, Pakchok Tulku.[49]

Negang Chokling (1928–1973), Orgyen Tobgyal (b. 1951), and the Second Dzigar Kongtrul (b. 1964)

Negang Chokling relied on extraordinary masters, including Khyentsé Chökyi Lodrö. [2.130a] Due to the changing times, he went to India, where he established his monastic seat in Bir, the refugee center of which houses people from Dergé and Nangchen. He founded a place for the study and teaching of the sutras and tantras, and so ensured much benefit for the teachings and for beings. After he passed away into a state of peace, his tulku—Chokling Yangsi Rinpoché—was found in Bhutan and is still alive, pursuing his study and training.[50]

Negang Chokling's son, Orgyen Tobgyal Choktrul Rinpoché, has built a temple at his noble father's seat, instituted regular ceremonies on the tenth day of the lunar cycle, as well as annual drupchens and ceremonies to commemorate holy days, and refurbished the centers for study and meditation practice. He has thus continued his noble father's enlightened activity.

His relative, Dzigar Kongtrul, relied on Dilgo Khyentsé Rinpoché as his guru, from whom he received profound and extensive teachings; he also trained under Khen Rinchen[51] and other masters, studying various subjects, and now lives in the United States.[52]

The Third Katok Situ, Kunchen Orgyen Chökyi Gyatso (1880–1923?)

Fulfilling one of the unerring prophecies made by the victorious one Saroruhavajra, [2.130b] Orgyen Chökyi Gyatso was born in Dilgo, a valley filled with termas northeast of Katok Dorjéden Monastery. He received monastic ordination, along with his name and a prayer for his longevity, from two emanations of Mañjushri, Jamyang Khyentsei Wangpo and Jamgön Kongtrul Lodrö Tayé. When he was enthroned at Katok Monastery, Orgyen Chökyi Gyatso had a vision of Guru Rinpoché and recalled much about his previous incarnations.

From his tutor and mentor, Tupten Rigdzin Gyatso, he first learned how to read and write, then continued with the sutras, tantras, and other fields of knowledge, bringing his studies and training to consummation. He studied with more than eighty great, holy masters of all schools, including the two Mañjushri emanations (Khyentsé and Kongtrul), Kuzhap Yönten Gönpo, Chamtrul Jigdor, Jampal Dorjé (another emanation of Mañjushri), Mipam Choklé Namgyal, Dzatrul Kunzang Namgyal, Palyul Gyatrul Pema Do-ngak Tendzin, Khenchen Tashi Özer, Jamyang Loter Wangpo, Karmapa Khachap Dorjé, [2.131a] Adzom Drukpa, Dudjom Yeshé Rolpa Tsal, and the "beggar lama" Kunzang Gyurmé (a student of Tukchok Dorjé of Kyiling). All told, it seemed as though there was no transmission—maturing empowerment, liberating instruction, or supportive oral transmission—that Orgyen Chökyi Gyatso did not receive from these masters; they bestowed on him the transmissions for the

Kangyur and Tengyur in general, and for the eighteen schools of study and practice[53] in particular. Most notably, the lord Khyentsei Wangpo conferred on Orgyen Chökyi Gyatso his blessings and the entrustment of his enlightened intent, for the latter had attained the true realization of the ultimate lineage. In his extensive biography, one can read of the signs of success he received in his practice of the phases of approach and accomplishment for the entire array of his meditation deities.

Having perfected his skills in study, contemplation, and meditation, Orgyen Chökyi Gyatso brought purpose to all who were connected to him in any way, by having seen, heard, touched, or remembered him. To help his students, he traveled to the principal holy sites in Gyarong, Golok, Nyarong, Godrak, Jangyul, Riwo Jakang in China, and as far away as Khawa Karpo. [2.131b] On his journey to Lhasa, Orgyen Chökyi Gyatso stopped at all of the holy sites and shrines along the way and visited all of the blessed spiritual places and monasteries in central, southern, and southeastern Tibet, praying and making offerings on a vast scale. He had a private audience with the Dalai Lama, Tupten Gyatso, to whom he made a very large offering. In the main temple of the Jokhang in Lhasa, at Samyé and the Chimpu Uplands, and at other places, the statues manifested to him as the actual deities and uttered prophecies about the welfare of the land of Tibet. Thus, in direct and indirect ways, Orgyen Chökyi Gyatso's aspirations to accomplish his excellent goals were fulfilled.

He invited Jamgön Kongtrul and Terchen Chokgyur Lingpa to Katok Monastery, where they built the great temple of Purkhang and founded a center for meditation. Once, the lord Orgyen Chökyi Gyatso had a pure vision of an enormous lake, in the center of which were a sword and a volume of scripture at the heart of a lotus flower so large it covered the earth and filled the sky. In each of the four cardinal directions was a similar lotus. From all of these shone rays of light, on the tips of which were many swords and texts, filling space in all directions. [2.132a] Someone standing in front of the lake said to him, "This central lotus is an auspicious representation of the shedra you will found. The flowers in the four directions represent the shedras of your four principal students, while the light shining from them indicates that there will be a great flourishing of the teachings throughout Tibet, all as a result of your shedra." In keeping with this vision, in a Fire Horse year[54] Orgyen Chökyi Gyatso and Kunchen Mipam Rinpoché founded the shedra of Norbui Lhunpo, also known as Katok Gyüdei Shedra Zhung Gyama. It was a center for the study and practice of one hundred source texts, supporting the practice of the stainless extensive lineage of the king Trisong Detsen, the master Padmakara, and the abbot Shantarakshita, a lineage fully capable of standing on its own without drawing from any other. In addition, Orgyen Chökyi Gyatso was directly or indirectly responsible for founding twenty-five other institutions where these hundred and more sources of sutra and tantra were taught and studied. His legacy, which illuminated the Victorious One's teachings, is such that no one can dispute his renown.

Khenchen Ngawang Palzang, who was among the first to graduate from the main institution at Katok, [2.132b] founded a shedra in his home region of Jangchub Jöngpalung in Nyoshul. With Chaktsa Rinpoché of Katok Monastery, Orgyen Chökyi Gyatso founded Tralek Shedra in Getsé; inspired by the motivation of Penor Rinpoché, the sublime tulku of Palyul Monastery, he founded Palyul Shedra; and with Lingshi Choktrul, he founded the shedra of Jangkar Monastery. These are the five shedras for which Orgyen Chökyi Gyatso was primarily responsible. There were also affiliated institutions; these included the shedra of the encampment of Khampa Gar, founded by Khenchen Döndam Chöchok on the order of Kyabjé Khamtrul Rinpoché; the shedra at Neten Chokling Rinpoché's monastery, founded by Khenchen Tsultrim Nyima; the shedra at Kham Riwoché, founded by Khen Achi Pema Gyaltsen; the shedra of Zhichen Monastery in lower Ser, founded by Ngulkhar Khenchen; and most recently, the shedra of Tekchok Namdrol Shedrup Dargyé Ling, founded in Mysore, South India, under the superb direction of Kyabjé Penor Rinpoché. [2.133a] (Although neither the circumstances of my birth nor my training have afforded me any status, I, the devoted servant, had the opportunity to serve the latter institution; however, my teaching there was merely like a seed, intended to set in motion a process for the motivation and auspicious circumstances ensured by holy masters of the past to start coming to fruition.) Thus, in conjunction with those in charge of their respective monasteries, Orgyen Chökyi Gyatso was instrumental in founding some twenty-five shedras and their affiliates, all in fulfillment of the prophecy.

At the principal shedra at Katok Dorjéden, through the three activities of explaining, debating, and writing about the sutras, tantras, and other fields of knowledge, great khenpos illuminated both the theory and practice of the teachings. The first in the succession of abbots to hold the throne of Katok Shedra was Khenchen Kunzang Palden; the second was Khenchen Ngawang Palzang. This shedra also counted among its graduates Zhichen Khen Tenzang, Nyoshul Khenpo Dorjé Samdrup, Tupten Lekshé Dulwai Dé, Nüden Khyentsei Lodrö, Gulok Tulku Gyurmé Dorjé, Nyarong Khenpo Kalzang Wangchuk, [2.133b] Druktö Khen Agé, Khamgar Khenpo Tsedo, Nyarong Khenpo Jampal Gyatso (who went to Gulok), Nyarong Khenpo Sherab Gyatso, Shingtri Khenpo Kunga Tendzin, Haja Khenpo Döndrup, Gotsa Khenpo Pema Rabgyé, Khenpo Gyaltsen Özer of Horpo, Palyul Khenpo Pema, Nyarong Khenpo Sherab Rabsel, Biklu Khenpo Drimé Lodrö, Chungpo Khenpo Döndam Chöchok, Ngulkhar Khenpo Sherab, Nyarong Khenpo Gendün Pelgyé, and Tsangdo Khenpo Dorjé Lodrö. The excellent, illuminating explanations of many such renowned, fully qualified scholars caused the teachings specific to the Early Translation school to spread throughout the entire Land of Snows from west to east, and even as far as India and China.

In the Early Translation school, there developed two principal approaches to study; one was based on the Indian commentaries and the other on the Tibetan. [2.134a]

The first was a personal transmission of Khenchen Zhenpen Chökyi Nangwa, who formulated a way to explain the works of Indian Buddhist masters, such as the thirteen great source texts. The second was the transmission of Jamgön Mipam Rinpoché, who relied primarily on the works of two masters, Rongzom Chökyi Zangpo and Longchen Rabjampa, as well as other Tibetan commentaries, such as those by Ngari Panchen. Of these two approaches, it was the latter that the majority of those who trained at Katok Shedra followed.

Orgyen Chökyi Gyatso also instituted annual rituals focusing on the kama and terma traditions of the Early Translation school in general and three cycles in particular: the Eight Commands, *The United Intent of the Gurus,* and Vajrakila. The performance of these rituals provided a model for everyone. He restored the great Katok meeting hall and its statues, and commissioned its murals. He provided vessels for offerings and built a "golden temple,"[55] which housed more than a thousand statues of the deities of the classes of sutra and tantra. He commissioned more than three hundred tangkas, including an enormous brocade hanging depicting the Buddha Shakyamuni that was thirty arm spans across. Having actually been encouraged by the guardian deities to write treatises, Orgyen Chökyi Gyatso revealed a number of rare and ancient texts, [2.134b] even the titles of which—such as *Armor Against Darkness* (a commentary on *The Discourse on United Intent*) and *The Command of Chimpu: A Commentary on Secret Teachings*—were difficult to hear of. He wrote many original works and collected those of other masters, amassing more than seven thousand volumes that together constituted a huge nonsectarian library. Most notably, he constructed a five-story temple that was modeled on the pure realm of Zangdok Palri and incorporated artistic representations of the entire array of the pure realms of the three kayas.

Day and night, Orgyen Chökyi Gyatso taught his fortunate students, presenting a veritable ocean of teachings on the sutras and tantras in a nonsectarian way, nurturing them with explanations according to their own traditions and becoming revered by all in the Nyingma and Sarma schools. He had visions of many deities and gurus, including Orgyen Rinpoché, Avalokiteshvara, the Buddha Shakyamuni, the future buddha Maitreya, and Kunchen Dampa Deshek, and received many direct lineages of spiritual advice. He could communicate with the guardian deities of the tantras (such as the only mother Shridevi and Gönpo Lekden) as though he were conversing with ordinary people, [2.135a] and they did whatever he requested.

In a Wood Ox year,[56] Orgyen Chökyi Gyatso invited, without sectarian bias, many great masters of the Nyingma and Sarma schools, as well as a sangha of more than 3,700 members from all schools, and instituted the drupchen ritual for the preparation of "pills of the three kayas," deriving from the Longsel Dorjé Nyingpo tradition. In that same year, having paid the teachings such honor, Orgyen Chökyi Gyatso passed away, departing for another realm.

In that this great being had students all the way from the banks of the Ganges in India to Tashi Trigo in China, I could not possibly speak of each of them but will mention a few of the most important: Jamyang Chökyi Lodrö; the sublime Getsé tulku of Katok called Gyurmé Tenpa Namgyal; Katok Jé-ön Pema Gyaltsen; Moktsa Jigdral Choklang; Drupwang Jigmé Dechen Dorjé; the fourth Chaktsa, Pema Trinlé Gyatso; Gyakhol Tulku Kunzang; Drakmar Choktrul Pema Gyaltsen; Lhatsün Rinpoché of Sikkim; Jangkar Tulku Mingyur; [2.135b] Khenchen Kunzang Palden; Kunchen Ngagi Wangpo; Mewa Khenchen Sönam Chödrup; Khenchen Lekshé Jorden; Khen Kalzang Wangchuk; Tupten Chökyi Langpo (the second Penor Rinpoché and rebirth of Drupwang Pema Norbu); Palyul Choktrul Chökyi Dawa; Muksang Nejap Tulku; Jamyang Lodrö; and numerous others who became masters of erudition and spiritual attainment. In addition, Orgyen Chökyi Gyatso was both the guru and student of Zhechen Gyaltsap Pema Namgyal; the third Dodrupchen, Tenpai Nyima; Terchen Lerab Lingpa; the tertön of Go, Dudjom Yeshé Rolpa Tsal; the fifth Dzogchen, Chökyi Dorjé; Khenchen Atop Tupten Gyaltsen Özer; and Dechen Rongta Tobgyal Rinpoché. He also had many connections as a guru and a student in the Sakya, Kagyü, and Geluk schools.

Furthermore, Orgyen Chökyi Gyatso journeyed throughout central Tibet and neighboring regions, turning the wheel of the dharma, so that more than a hundred thousand people received empowerments and teachings from him, [2.136a] while thousands more received complete transmissions of instructions. Such was his contribution to the Victorious One's precious teachings. There exists a lengthy biography of this master, written by Muksang Negyap Tulku.

Gyakor Tulku Kunzang Tekchok Tenpai Gyaltsen (19th–20th Centuries)

Kunzang Tekchok Tenpai Gyaltsen, the tulku of Gyakor, was the son of the renowned Drupchen Drodul Sang-ngak Lingpa, also known as Tergöma of Gyarong. Kunzang Tekchok Tenpai Gyaltsen was born into the Gyakor family of Washul Tromtö and was Katok Situ Rinpoché's half-brother, sharing the same father.

Kunzang Tekchok Tenpai Gyaltsen's main gurus were the two emanations of the protector Mañjushri, Khyentsé and Kongtrul. He also studied extensively with nearly one hundred masters, including Mipam Rinpoché and Khenchen Kunzang Palden, of all schools. So vast, in fact, was his field of study that he became enormously learned and accomplished, and no one in the upper regions or the lowlands of eastern Tibet could compare to him.

His principal residence was Katok Monastery, where he pursued his own meditation and spiritual practice and explained the scriptural sources of the teachings as well as the experience based on them. [2.136b] Turning the wheel of the dharma for his students, he ensured the continuity of the theory and practice of the teachings. In addition, Kunzang Tekchok Tenpai Gyaltsen traveled to Bodh Gaya and other places in the holy country of India, and to the three stupas and other sites in Nepal, wandering as a mendicant yogin with a very simple way of life. At the Asura Cave in Parping,[57] he engaged in the practices and had visions of Vajrakila and Samyak; he had countless such pure visions. He also carved statues of Vajrakila and Samyak Heruka out of stone and placed them inside the cave, where they can be seen to this day.

Similarly, he applied himself to the very essence of spiritual practice in all of the principal places of accomplishment in Tibet, including Samyé, Lhasa, Sheldrak in Yarlung, and Zang-ri Kharmar. Taking the holy masters of the past as his model, he was so plain and simple in appearance that, aside from knowing he was a lama, people had no idea who he was. Through his practice of the stage of development, Kunzang Tekchok Tenpai Gyaltsen brought the "three objects of perception"[58] to consummation, while through the stage of completion he gained mastery of the four degrees of joy, the unity of bliss and emptiness. He also reached the furthest limit [2.137a] of the path of the four visions in the Dzogchen approach. In such ways, he attained great siddhis. He stayed for a long time at the holy place of Gang-ri Tökar, where the Omniscient One Longchenpa had practiced, then wandered throughout the land, randomly visiting holy sites. He maintained uncontrived tantric conduct equal to that of the Indian mahasiddhas of old. He was graced by visions of the Omniscient One, through which he gained deeper states of realization.

In addition, Kunzang Tekchok Tenpai Gyaltsen conferred transmissions for the Kangyur and Tengyur, *The Collected Tantras of the Nyingma School,* the three categories of Dzogchen, and the cycles of the Longsel teachings. Bestowing maturing empowerments and liberating instructions in monasteries, retreat centers, and other communities of the sangha in all directions, he thus came to have students throughout Tibet.

His own root gurus, from whom he received teachings, were Kyabjé Dudjom Rinpoché (who taught him texts such as *The Heart Essence of Secrets*) and Kangyur Rinpoché Longchen Yeshé Dorjé (from whom he received transmissions for *The Collected Tantras of the Nyingma School, The Heart Essence of Secrets,* and *The Treasury of Enlightened Qualities*). Kunzang Tekchok Tenpai Gyaltsen gathered rare volumes of texts that were difficult to obtain and received rare empowerments and oral transmissions; [2.137b] he offered these to his half-brother, Katok Situ; Dzatrul Dorjé Chang Kunzang Namgyal; and Khenchen Atop Rinpoché. He also restored a number of representations of the enlightened form, speech, and mind of holy masters of the past, which had become damaged or worn with age. In addition, he arranged for offerings to be made continuously at these restored sites. Kunzang Tekchok Tenpai Gyaltsen had the psychic ability to see events hidden from ordinary view; in many similar ways, he exhibited innumerable qualities through his marvelous deeds. He brought far-reaching benefit to beings; for example, he offered the lineage of the Kham tradition[59] of the Nyingtik teachings to Khenchen Ngawang Palzang, the vajra holder who was an emanation of Vimalamitra, thus becoming that master's root guru.

In the later part of his life, Kunzang Tekchok Tenpai Gyaltsen lived at Gang-ri Tökar. One day, without manifesting any illness whatsoever, he said, "My mission to benefit beings is over." As he rested in an unwavering state of meditative equipoise, the mandala of his emanated form resolved back into a state of supreme peace as myriad marvelous signs manifested, such as pavilions of rainbow light pulsating against a cloudless, royal blue sky. [2.138a] His students were, for the most part, also students of such masters as Katok Situ Rinpoché, Khenchen Ngawang Palzang, and Dzatrul Kunzang Namgyal.

Drugu Tokden Shakya Shri (1853–1919)

Shakya Shri was a student of Drugu Chögyal Rinpoché. He studied and trained thoroughly in the "three combined mainstreams" and the other teachings of the Drukpa Kagyü school, including Mahamudra and the Six Yogas of Naropa. Practicing these brought him realization, and he gained mastery over the energies in his subtle channels. At all times, summer and winter, he wore only a simple cotton garment and displayed other signs of his spiritual attainment, such as leaving footprints in rock and reading others' minds. With all of his asceticism and courageous undertakings, Shakya Shri's life was equal to the lord Milarepa's, and he became a great holder of the Drukpa Kagyü lineage. All the lineages of teaching and advice found today in the glorious Drukpa school derive from this lord.

Shakya Shri met many of the greatest masters of Dergé, [2.138b] including Jamgön Kongtrul, the lord Khyentsé, and Mipam Rinpoché, who helped resolve the doubts he had about his realization. In particular, he requested from Khyentsé Rinpoché the teachings that the latter had received as a personal transmission, *The Heart Drop of Chetsün*. Khyentsé Rinpoché replied, "That is a one-to-one lineage of advice, which I have already entrusted to Adzom Drukpa, so you should go to see him." Following this instruction, Shakya Shri went to Adzom Drukpa's encampment. Upon merely meeting, guru and student felt their minds merge, becoming one. The guru Drukpa Rinpoché, being a nomad from Washul Tromtar, said in the dialect of that region, "To experience the true nature of great perfection, just rest straight out, just rest. I don't suppose there's anything else but that." Shakya Shri understood what the guru was saying to him, that there was nothing to this enlightened intent other than resting naturally, without contrivance. Adzom Drukpa transferred to Shakya Shri the enlightened intent of dharmakaya, unbiased timeless awareness as the naked unity of awareness and emptiness. Distinguishing between his ordinary mind and pure awareness, [2.139a] Shakya Shri attained the realization of great perfection in a quantum leap, having been directly introduced to it in the immediacy of his own true nature. With great delight, he said, "My realization came from within like a wild yak being freed from its tether or like the sun rising." Thereafter, he thoroughly trained all of his own students, first in Mahamudra and then in Dzogchen, so that they came to a decisive experience of these. He thus instituted a tradition of combining the two approaches, which his entire lineage of students has continued to spread to this day.

Shakya Shri had numerous visions of and received prophecies from the glorious Orgyen, king of the dharma, the Indian siddha Saraha, and others. He received transmissions of profound termas—cycles of sadhanas of the Three Roots, techniques for the transference of consciousness at death, and yogic practices for developing tummo that bear a seal of secrecy—the lineages of which still exist. Notably, after Drupwang Shakya Shri's death, his eldest son, Pakchok Rinpoché, was cared for by the father's timeless awareness embodiment and thus received an oral lineage of the Dzogchen teachings. As for the groups of Shakya Shri's heart children and students, [2.139b] he taught his own two sons, as well as the throne holder of Ladakh, Pema Chögyal; Lopön Rinpoché Memé Sönam Zangpo of the Drukpa Kagyü school; and countless others. Shakya Shri's enlightened activities spread throughout Tibet—the western, central, and eastern regions—and into Bhutan in the south. An extensive biography of this master was written by the third Katok Situ.

Lopön Rinpoché Lama Sönam Zangpo (1892–1983)

Lopön Rinpoché Lama Sönam Zangpo was a powerful lord among masters accomplished in wisdom and realization. He was reputed to have consciously taken rebirth as an incarnation of Rechung Dorjé Drakpa, the heart son of the lord Milarepa Zhepa Dorjé (that crown jewel among hundreds of siddhas), who had attained the rainbow body of timeless awareness. Sönam Zangpo was born into a wealthy family of Kurtö Ruling; his mother was Sonam. Disenchanted with the world from an early age, the boy was moved to renunciation and entered the monastic community of Lhundrup Tsei Dzong. He thoroughly pursued a course of studies in works like the collection of prayers compiled by the glorious Chöjé Drukpa. At Tarpa Ling on the plateau of Bumthang, Sönam Zangpo undertook spiritual exercises, including the preliminary practices, which he pursued for a long time.

Finally, moved by karmic tendencies established in previous lifetimes, he traveled to eastern Tibet [2.140a] to meet Drupwang Shakya Shri. For more than twelve years, he trained under this guru and received the complete transmission of all the pith instructions in the tradition of the "three combined mainstreams" of the Drukpa Kagyü tradition, beginning with the preliminary practices and continuing on to the Six Yogas of Panchen Naropa, *The Equal Taste* cycle and *Auspicious Interdependence* teachings of Chöjé Tsangpa, and the Mahamudra transmission from Dakpo Gampopa.[60] The lord Milarepa said, "To bear the hardship of practicing the dharma, one needs an unlimited store of merit." In keeping with this statement, Sönam Zangpo's merit was such that he pursued his practice while enduring great hardship, and so his realization became fully evident. He attained siddhis through the path of the so-called mother tantras of the secret mantra approach; he could actually enjoy the bliss and warmth of the inner heat that comes about by the power of the energies in the subtle channels. He served his guru tirelessly, day and night, with his body, speech, and mind, becoming the most refined of Shakya Shri's heart children. In particular, when his guru, Drupwang Rinpoché, was restoring the great stupa in Nepal, Sönam Zangpo took responsibility for the work with such pure motivation [2.140b] that his efforts to fulfill his guru's intentions were unparalleled.

In addition, Sönam Zangpo received thorough instructions in natural great perfection—such teachings as *Timeless Awareness as the Guiding Principle, The Heart Drop of Chetsün,* and Longchenpa's *Seven Treasuries*—from many learned and accomplished mentors, including Terchen Dudjom Lingpa Jigdral Yeshé Dorjé, Katok Situ Chökyi Gyatso, Karmapa Khachap Dorjé, and Pakchok Rinpoché (the son of Shakya Shri). He directly experienced the enlightened intent born of realization, called "beyond meditation" in Mahamudra and "the perception of awareness's naturally manifest appearances without bias" in Dzogchen.[61]

Over time, he planted the victory banner of spiritual practice at all of the principal holy sites and places of accomplishment in Tibet and Bhutan—Tsari, the hidden valley of Khenjong, Taktsang in Bhutan, and so forth—never deviating from a schedule of four practice sessions daily. Sönam Zangpo did not spend a single day in the worldly atmosphere of towns and villages, but instead frequented mountainsides and isolated places, [2.141a] applying himself one-pointedly to spiritual practice focusing on the very essence. He was cared for by the timeless awareness embodiments of many gurus and by his personal meditation deities. He conferred on many fortunate students the advice and instructions of profound teachings such as the Six Yogas of Naropa and Dzogchen.

Moreover, Lopön Rinpoché Sönam Zangpo built temples, furnishing them with statues and other accoutrements, as places in which merit could be gathered for the benefit of the teachings and beings. Although it would be impossible to mention all of his activities, which defy imagination and description, a partial listing follows: He built a temple at the great Tibetan holy site of Tsari, placing within it a statue of the goddess Vajravarahi, surrounded by figures of the "golden garland" (the lineage of the Kagyü school) as well as a three-story statue of Guru Rinpoché. In the hidden valley of Khenpa Jong, he erected a temple modeled on the pure realm of Zangdok Palri, complete with a main statue of Guru Rinpoché in gold and copper as well as other furnishings. His temple in Kurtö housed statues of Guru Rinpoché and Avalokiteshvara in gold and copper. On the slopes of a great holy site—the mountain pass of Punying—he built the temple of Norbu Sergyi Dramtang Lhakhang. He commissioned murals of multitudes of deities to adorn the walls at Tashi Gangdzong and built a temple on the upper reaches of the mountain pass of Tashi Gonyön that was modeled on the Jokhang in Lhasa and contained a statue of the lord Buddha. [2.141b] He also built a temple on the plateau of Dewatang and the temple of Dungsam Kulikati. In collaboration with the master of Dungsam Yonglek Monastery, Sönam Zangpo made extensive renovations to that institution so that Kyabjé Dudjom Rinpoché could be invited there to participate in a drupchen and turn the wheel of the dharma by teaching the cycles of Pegyal Lingpa. In addition, he founded the Wangdzong Langpozé meditation center.

During the later part of his life, Lopön Rinpoché Sönam Zangpo established his seat at the temple and stupa he built at Do Rangtang Paljor Ling. He constructed the great stupa on Dochung Pass, founded a meditation center and built a stupa at Lhungtso, founded the Lhungtso Tashi Gang meditation center, and commissioned the carving of a marvelous image of Guru Rinpoché in the face of the cliff known as Samar Dzingkhai Drak in Thimphu. He installed the dharani mantras to bless the great stupa of Thimphu, which contains representations of the Eight Commands, *The United Intent of the Gurus,* and Vajrakila. Sönam Zangpo oversaw many other such projects. He founded the Pajoding meditation center, installed statues of the "golden garland" of the Kagyü lineage in the Tago meditation center, and erected a marvelous statue of Drupwang Shakya Shri that was imbued with great blessings. He had tangkas depicting all of the protective deities of the Kagyü school painted in gold [2.142a] and commissioned a statue of Dorjé Drolö at Paro Taktsang[62] and other statues. He adorned these statues with jewels and clothed them in fine garments. He installed banners and canopies, provided fuel for the continuous offering of votive lamps, and made many other offerings.

In the three spheres of study, meditation, and spiritual projects, Sönam Zangpo gave true meaning to his name.[63] Due to his mastery over subtle energy and mind, he lived to the age of ninety in Bhutan, the land of medicinal plants, serving as a model for his fortunate students.

Ritrul Rigdzin Chögyal (20th Century) and Namkha Drimé Rabjam (b. 1938)

Both Rigdzin Chögyal (the tulku of Ripa Monastery) and his brother, Terchen Namkha Drimé Rabjam, are from the lineage of Drupwang Shakya Shri's daughter and the bloodline of Taksham.[64] They received the entire cycle of the secret Nyingtik teachings of the Dzogchen approach from Chöjung Lingpa, who was a student of Adzom Drukpa. Namkha Drimé has brought great benefit to the teachings and to beings with his own termas—cycles of practice, such as *The Secret Sphere of the Three Families,* that focus on Gesar,[65] the Wish-Fulfilling Gem.

Jedrung Jampa Jungné (19th–20th Centuries)

Jampa Jungné was born in the Zhol Danak family of Kham Riwoché Monastery. [2.142b] Of the two lineages of the principal masters of the institution, who were known as "the pair Jé and Pak,"[66] he was one in the series of tulkus called the Jedrung. As he studied with Khenchen Lhagyal (a student of the lord Khyentsei Wangpo) and many other learned and accomplished masters, his tendencies from former lifetimes awakened, and he himself reached a consummate level of erudition.

As the extraordinary master of his buddha family, he relied on a truly amazing mahasiddha, Jo Rigdzin, who was accomplished in the Mahamudra and Dzogchen approaches and had attained the level known as "beyond meditation," the primordial empire of dharmakaya. For example, he received the oral transmissions for the extensive, intermediate, and concise versions of the sutra *The Perfection of Sublime Knowing* during a vision that lasted for just a single meditation session.[67]

Jampa Jungné also studied with Karmapa Khachap Dorjé, Jamgön Kongtrul, and other teachers, becoming a great master of the teachings deriving from the lineage of spiritual accomplishment. In particular, he received from the extraordinary lord Jamyang Khyentsei Wangpo the great transmission of the Nyingtik teachings of Dzogchen, as well as tantras, sadhanas, empowerments, oral transmissions, pith instructions, and advice from the Nyingma and Sarma schools. The minds and intent of master and student merged inseparably, and Jamyang Khyentsei Wangpo entrusted Jampa Jungné with his teachings, so that the latter became his inner heart son.

During the earlier part of his life, [2.143a] Jampa Jungné turned the wheel of the dharma for countless fortunate people at his own monastery of Kham Riwoché, as well as at centers such as Riwoché in the regions of Nangchen and Chamdo. He thus served as a mainstay of the teachings deriving from the lineage of spiritual accomplishment. In the later part of his life, he moved to Pemakö, a hidden region sacred to Guru Rinpoché, and opened the area up as a place of spiritual power. He then received a directive from the Dalai Lama, Tupten Gyatso, to move to central Tibet. Accordingly, he established his seat north of Lhasa at Taklung Monastery. There he served as a master of the teachings, conferring the sutras and tantras—*The Treasury of Spiritual Instructions,* the precious Kangyur, and more—to communities of many hundreds of people in Lhasa and throughout western, central, and eastern Tibet. (Jampa Jungné is one of the three principal gurus from whom Kyabjé Dudjom Rinpoché received his extraordinary lineage of Dzogchen teachings.)

In general, the lord Jampa Jungné had visions of and received guidance from a vast array of gurus and his personal meditation deities. In particular, his visions of Guru Padma [2.143b] awakened his spiritual tendencies from an earlier lifetime as Langdro Könchok Jungné, and he received a personal transmission of profound termas. Many of his termas, such as those with Yeshé Tsogyal as the feminine aspect and the longevity sadhana *The Secret Heart Drop of Padma,* still exist. Jampa Jungné revealed many caches of termas—such as *The Guru and Vajrakila: The Sphere of Enlightened Mind*—along with Kangyur Lama, who had been prophesied by Guru Rinpoché to be the custodian of his teachings. These termas and the thirteen volumes of Jampa Jungné's collected writings appeared like a great sun, illuminating the teachings of both the Kagyü and Nyingma schools.

Kangyur Rinpoché Longchen Yeshé Dorjé (1897–1975)

One of Jampa Jungné's students was Kangyur Rinpoché Longchen Yeshé Dorjé. He was born in a district known as Dukrima in the region of Riwoché in eastern Tibet. From an early age, he exhibited the attributes of someone holy and had clear recollections of his former lifetime as Khenchen Mitrukpa. His wisdom developed in past lifetimes enabled him to learn such skills as reading and writing merely upon being introduced to them. When Jamgön Mipam Rinpoché came to the hermitage of Kowo in Dzagyal, Longchen Yeshé Dorjé was one of many who sought an audience with him. Mipam Rinpoché conferred on him many extensive empowerments, as well as a support for his samaya, a sword of Mañjushri that can be seen to this day.

Longchen Yeshé Dorjé was ordained and entered the Nyingma monastic community of Riwoché. Exceedingly venerable, [2.144a] he eschewed all possessions but his three monastic robes and remained committed to his training. He received a host of teachings, both profound and extensive, from the many gurus, tulkus, khenpos, and teachers at the monastic seat. For many years, he was the chant master during group ceremonies. He became erudite, training in the sutras and tantras, and receiving, for example, the oral transmissions for *The Collected Tantras of the Nyingma School* from Gyakor Tekchok Tenpai Gyaltsen.

In particular, Longchen Yeshé Dorjé relied on Jedrung Jampa Jungné as the extraordinary master of his buddha family, receiving from him the complete transmission of all the tantras, explanatory commentaries, and pith instructions of the Dzogchen approach. As a result of his meditative experiences and realization, unfathomable enlightened qualities arose in him and he served as his master's holy heart son. He received a wide range of profound teachings and his lord guru's own termas in an intimate transmission. The guru gave Longchen Yeshé Dorjé advice and made prophecies, saying, "Stay at the Vajrakila retreat center and recite the mantra three hundred million times. Then go to Paro Taktsang in Bhutan; an opportunity for spiritual attainment awaits you there." Obeying his guru's instructions, Longchen Yeshé Dorjé remained at the Vajrakila center, [2.144b] recited the mantra of Vajrakila three hundred million times, and was taken under that deity's care.

He then journeyed to Lhasa, Jang Taklung, and Yardrok Taklung. Because he had given the oral transmissions for the precious Kangyur twenty-three times, he was known everywhere as "Kangyur Rinpoché," his title deriving from that of the texts. His marvelous deeds were boundless; for example, he was taken under the care of

Mañjushri, who granted him the ability to read aloud six times faster than usual, so that he could give the oral transmissions for six volumes of the Kangyur in a single day. Eventually, in keeping with his guru's prophecy, Longchen Yeshé Dorjé reached the cave of Paro Taktsang in Bhutan, where the local spirits appeared to him and escorted him inside. There he engaged in the phases of approach and accomplishment for the practice of Vajrakila and revealed termas such as *The Guru and Vajrakila: The Sphere of Enlightened Mind.*

Kangyur Rinpoché then went on a pilgrimage to India. At Bodh Gaya, he revealed a terma, a statue of Maitreya six inches high, which had been the focus for the exalted master Asanga's spiritual attainment through meditation on the coming buddha. [2.145a] Longchen Yeshé Dorjé continued on to the holy site of Tso Pema, where he revealed a terma of enlightened intent, an entire cycle of source texts and auxiliary practices entitled *The Heart Drop of Secrets.* A profound terma of extraordinary spiritual advice, it was originally given by Guru Rinpoché to his twenty-five intimate students, including the king of Tibet and Namkhai Nyingpo, at Samyé. Longchen Yeshé Dorjé codified the source of this cycle, entitled *A Shower of Blessings: A Guru Yoga Based on the Seven-Line Supplication,* and other texts. For the sake of the teachings and ensuring enormous benefit for beings, he recited prayers and made offerings, both extensive and profound, at all of the Buddhist holy sites in India.

He then returned to central Tibet by way of Mount Kailash. At the cliff of Drakmar in Rong, he revealed profound termas of practices for achieving longevity. He also revealed many profound termas focusing on the deities Vajrapani and Samyak. Fulfilling Guru Rinpoché's prophecies, Jangchö-la, an emanation of Vajravarahi, acted as his companion during these revelations, most of which took place in secret. Longchen Yeshé Dorjé had recollections of many previous lifetimes, [2.145b] including that as the monk Namkhai Nyingpo. He built a large stupa in Taklung and, when obstructive forces caused it to split in two, made it whole again with his miraculous powers. When one of his students was dying and asked to see him, Kangyur Rinpoché couldn't go in person, but cared for the man through his timeless awareness embodiment. He showed many other signs of attainment and performed many miracles. He repeatedly had visions of numerous learned and accomplished masters of India and Tibet, including Khyentsé Do-ngak Lingpa, Mipam Rinpoché, Do Khyentsé Yeshé Dorjé, and So Pema Wangyal. In a pure vision, Longchen Yeshé Dorjé went to Wu Tai Shan, the sacred five-peaked mountain in China, where he encountered Panchen Vimalamitra, who took him under his care. He journeyed to Zangdok Palri and beheld Guru Rinpoché, who blessed him. He had countless such visions.

When the Tibetan people were being menaced by barbarian hordes, Longchen Yeshé Dorjé, wishing to preserve the teachings, departed for India with many hundreds of volumes (especially the precious Kangyur), passing through the hidden valley of Pemakö and enduring much hardship. [2.146a] In India he met with such masters as Kyabjé Dudjom Rinpoché and Dilgo Khyentsé Rinpoché, and as they exchanged the nectar of the dharma, giving teachings to and receiving them from one another, their minds blended, becoming one. Kangyur Rinpoché bestowed many rare lineages of empowerments, instructions, and oral transmissions from the Early Translation school—such as *The United Intent of the Gurus,* a Hayagriva cycle revealed by Taksham—on gatherings of many hundreds of people, Kyabjé Khyentsé Rinpoché's and his own children foremost among them. He founded a monastery, Orgyen Kunzang Chökhor Ling, in Darjeeling, India, the site of Terchen Dorjé Lingpa's terma revelations. He bestowed spiritual instructions and advice on many students from as far away as the United States and France, teaching them according to their individual needs.

Finally, having completed such tasks, Kangyur Rinpoché Longchen Yeshé Dorjé reached the age of seventy-eight, and the display of his emanated form resolved for a time back into the palace of Pema Ö in the realm of Chamara. At dawn three days later, Kangyur Rinpoché's timeless awareness embodiment appeared to Kyabjé Khyentsé Rinpoché in a lucid dream, conferring on him the complete transmissions for a number of terma teachings [2.146b] and prophesying future events. In this and other ways, Longchen Yeshé Dorjé inspired wonder and faith in people. In these times of spiritual degeneration, he rendered enormous service to the teachings of the Early Translation school.

His three sons became lineage holders of his three secret aspects of form, speech, and mind. Of the three, Choktrul Pema Wangyal trained extensively under the guidance of his noble father and Terchen Dudjom Rinpoché and showed great resolve in serving the teachings of the Early Translation school, without relying on any other tradition. In keeping with the instructions and prophecies of the two great tertöns Dudjom Rinpoché and Dilgo Khyentsé Rinpoché, Pema Wangyal moved to France, where he founded a large retreat center, Tekchok Ösel Chöling, and has published many books. He has supported the restoration of most of the damaged Nyingma centers in Tibet and has founded centers himself. In France, Germany, and other countries, Pema Wangyal's activities have allowed the lineages of his noble father and of the two great tertöns to flourish. In such ways, he has served as an example of a noble, holy being. [2.147a] His brothers have trained in the same way.

This concludes the brief overview of the students of the lord Jamyang Khyentsei Wangpo.

14

The Students of Adzom Drukpa Rinpoché and Yukhok Jadralwa Chöying Rangdrol

THE STUDENTS OF ADZOM DRUKPA RINPOCHÉ

Generally speaking, the holy master Adzom Drukpa Rinpoché had an enormous number of students. Such masters as Dzogchen Rinpoché and Katok Situ invited Adzom Drukpa to their respective monasteries, where he turned the wheel of the dharma and so came to have countless students among the gurus, tulkus, khenpos, teachers, and others residing at those institutions. Foremost among Adzom Drukpa's heart sons who upheld his lineage were Khyentsé Chökyi Lodrö, Yukhok Jadralwa, Tsö Paltrul, Golok Lama Kunzang, and his own son, Gyurmé Dorjé.

Gyalsé Gyurmé Dorjé (1895–?)

Gyalsé Gyurmé Dorjé, a master who upheld the ultimate lineage, was born amid numerous marvelous signs as the guru Adzom Drukpa's own son. He was considered to be the most recent incarnation of Rigdzin Terdak Lingpa and was named Gyurmé Dorjé. He had clear recollections of his previous lifetimes as the victorious one Rongzom, [2.147b] Terchen Sherab Özer, Kunzang Sherab of Palyul Monastery, among others.

He was inseparable from his father and guru, who with great love transmitted to him the very essence of the pith instructions, the path of natural great perfection, from the preliminary practices to the advanced stages of trekchö and tögal. Adzom Drukpa conferred on Gyurmé Dorjé the entire secret treasury of spiritual advice, including the teachings of the secret Nyingtik, *The Heart Drop of Chetsün,* and his own profound termas, such as the daknang transmission entitled *The Oral Lineage: The Twenty-five Spheres.* Gyurmé Dorjé put them into practice, and realization arose in him. Adzom Drukpa entrusted his son as a master of the teachings of the ultimate lineage, installing him as his successor at their main seat.

Gyurmé Dorjé also trained under many other gurus, tulkus, and mentors, including Khenchen Düpa Gyatso of Dokhol Monastery in Trom, studying a wide range of subjects pertaining to the sutras, tantras, and other fields of knowledge. After his guru Adzom Drukpa had passed away, Gyurmé Dorjé followed his directive and turned the wheel of the dharma, including the very essence of the supreme secret. From Dzati Yukdung Jesa on the border of India and western Tibet [2.148a] to Gyamo Chudartak in China to the east, all the communities of his hundreds of thousands of students regarded Gyurmé Dorjé as indistinguishable from the precious lord guru Adzom Drukpa. Even the older students, overcoming their hesitation, bowed at his feet. Gyurmé Dorjé's activities and the benefit he ensured for beings spread to fill all of space. In these later times, he was a pivotal figure in transmitting the Dzogchen teachings. In carrying out the enlightened activities of the victorious one Padmakara, he was like the lofty pinnacle of a victory banner. Gyurmé Dorjé wrote many commentaries, including *A Commentary on the Great Graduated Path of Magical Display* and *A Commentary on "The Recollection of the Three Jewels."* Although Gyurmé Dorjé received the transmission of many caches of profound termas in his visions of Guru Rinpoché, he did not codify many of them, but focused instead on transmitting more ancient termas.

This sublime master's life is described on the ultimate level in the following supplication based on his successive tulkus:

> Though primordially enlightened within unchanging dharmakaya,
> through the inconceivable display of the vajra of timeless awareness
> you reveal the vast array of magical illusion [2.148b]
> of the victorious ones and their heirs in countless pure realms. To you
> I pray.
>
> In the past, in the pure realm Achintya,
> you were Nateshvara, one who had reached the state of suchness,
> and in the first of the twenty-five realms of Vairochana,
> you were the buddha Meghagarbha. To you I pray.
>
> In the city of Chamara in the realm of Namkö,
> you were born the son of the couple Lekjin and Chokjin,
> were named Manimala, and, in the presence of the victorious one Lekchö,
> studied the nectar of the vast and profound teachings. To you I pray.
>
> In Namkhai Nor in the land of Dewai Nyö,
> you, named Lekjin, were the son of Lokö Namnang Sem
> and heard the dharma from the victorious one Gewai Lodrö,
> awakening to buddhahood yourself as Norbui Pungpo. To you I pray.
>
> In the presence of Nangwa Dampa, teacher of manifest perfection,
> you were Gajé Wangchuk, child of the gods who codified the teachings,
> and in this world of sorrow, in the presence of Ö Mitrukpa,
> you were the youth who guided the dakinis. To you I pray.

In the presence of the teacher Jigpa Kyopa, who appeared in a mass of light, [2.149a]
you were the bodhisattva Chöpai Gyalpo,
and within the display of the supreme secret, in the presence of Pakmé Tobden,
you were the child of the victorious ones Tringyi Shuk. To you I pray.

At Bodh Gaya, in the presence of Ngöndzok Gyalpo,
as Vajrapani you codified all of the teachings concerning the definitive meaning,
and in the pinnacle pure realm of Akanishtha, in the presence of great Vajradhara,
you manifested as the Lord of Secrets. To you I pray.

In the holy places of the Three Roots, you emanated as Vajrasattva
and codified the Dzogchen teachings.
When the guides of this fortunate eon were giving rise to their initial motivation,
you among them were the child of the victorious ones Dharmasattva. To you I pray.

You were Denpak in the presence of Tupka Zhönnu,
and Ananda, the attendant of our sublime Teacher, the Lord of Sages.
You codified all of their vast and profound teachings
and so caused the teachings to flourish. To you I pray.

You became Rahula, the exalted one of the warrior class,
protecting the teachings until the advent of the fifth buddha of our age,
and Indrabhuti in the land of Oddiyana,
as well as the Buddhist king Chandrabhadra.[1] To you I pray. [2.149b]

You were Garab Dorjé, teacher of Dzogchen,
Shri Simha, who received the transmission of the three categories and nine expanses,
Gartong Tsen,[2] minister to kings and emanation of the protective deities in the Land of Snows,
and Lochen Namnang Sung.[3] To you I pray.

You were Palgyi Dorjé, who vanquished the hordes of Yisup,
Shakya Jungné, Rongzom Chökyi Zangpo,
and the moonlike heart son of Mila Zhepa Dorjé,
the truly exalted Rechungpa. To you I pray.

You were the Omniscient King of the Dharma, Longchenpa,
the powerful lord of siddhas Tangtong Gyalpo,
Prajñarasmi, Shantapuri,
and Terchen Drodul Lingpa. To you I pray.

You were Kunzang Sherab, who illuminated the Nyingma teachings,
and the guardian of the spiritual treasures of the glorious Sakya tradition,
the vajra holder Khöntön Wangdü Nyingpo,
and other great masters. To you I pray.

Spiritual mentors who teach the sutras and tantras
and other victorious ones are identical in the basic space of timeless awareness,
but are still immeasurable in their manifestations as one or many.
You have appeared as numerous such protectors of the teachings and beings. To you I pray. [2.150a]

In this present lifetime, you radiate the major and minor marks of perfection, the scion of a family line of siddhas.
You blossom with the holy qualities that are your very nature.
Since your youth, you have mounted the throne of the supreme spiritual approach
and upheld your role as a regent of siddhas. To you I pray.

With great renunciation, you have followed the Sage's teachings.
Your completely pure discipline has delighted advanced spiritual practitioners.
With great compassion, you have sounded the excellent drum of the dharma.
You are a great victory banner of the teachings. To you I pray.

The teachings and beings are now threatened by the spiritual degeneration of the times.
The teachings of the sublime approach are particularly on the wane.
O protector, think of us with love and compassion.
I pray that you live for a hundred eons, turning the wheel of the dharma.

Through the power of my own and others' one-pointed, heartfelt prayers,
may we purify ourselves with renunciation, maintain our vows and samaya purely,
uproot our fixations on the eight worldly concerns and on things as they appear,

refine our bodhichitta, and bring the stages of development and
completion to fruition.

May we take up the path with devotion, perfect our experience of the
timeless awareness of the four visions, [2.150b]
be cared for in all lifetimes, and, becoming enlightened as victorious ones
in the infinite display of the pure realm adorned with lotuses,
awaken to buddhahood in the uniform expanse of enlightened intent.

Such is the prayer composed by a monk named Yeshé.

Gyurmé Dorjé's countless heart children and students included Rago Choktrul, Kharlek Tulku, Tulku Losel, and Tulku Kunga of Dartang Monastery. Most notably, the rebirth of his lord father, Drukpa Rinpoché, was a great upholder of the ultimate lineage.

Having thus completed his mission for the sake of the teachings and of beings, Gyurmé Dorjé allowed his enlightened intent to resolve back into the supreme inner basic space of peace. Then, once again, an array manifested outwardly—that of his three sublime tulkus, including one who came in fulfillment of Gyurmé Dorjé's own testament: "I will return as the son of Kalzang on the plateau of Bumthang in Bhutan." These tulkus have continued to reside in centers of the Early Translation school in the holy country of India, where they study and train in the sutras and tantras.[4]

Druktrul Rinpoché (20th Century)

Druktrul Rinpoché, the rebirth of Adzom Drukpa Rinpoché, [2.151a] was a student of Gyalsé Gyurmé Dorjé, from whom he received the ultimate lineage. Despite the great calamities and upheavals in Tibet, due to aspirations made in his preceding lifetime and the merit and glory of his students, Druktrul Rinpoché appeared in modern times, during the later dissemination of the teachings. At his own seat, the encampment of Dungkar Adzom, he followed the example of his former incarnation, transmitting the dharma, including the Dzogchen approach of the supreme secret. He conferred the nectar of his advice on gatherings of innumerable Chinese and Tibetan students, using texts such as the Dzogchen manual *Timeless Awareness as the Guiding Principle*. Druktrul Rinpoché rebuilt, from the ground up, monasteries that had been reduced to ruins by the barbaric invading forces, making them better than they had been before their destruction. He thus carried out the three cycles of spiritual activities. He passed away recently, a glorious protector of the teachings and of beings, and I pray that his activity will flourish for a hundred eons.

Khen Rinpoché Karma Dorjé (b. 20th Century)

The sublime master Khen Rinpoché Karma Dorjé was born near Namgyal Monastery in the Dzing area of Dergé, eastern Tibet. At an early age, he enrolled in Podzong

Monastery of the noble Sakya school, [2.151b] where he trained in various fields and became quite erudite. He then went to Drasa Tsang-ngor Monastery, where he took full ordination as a monk. He engaged in the practices of the Sakya tradition and undertook an extensive retreat on the glorious deity Hevajra. Later, Karma Dorjé entered the shedra of Khamjé at Dzongsar Monastery. There he studied the thirteen major source texts—those of Madhyamaka, Prajñaparamita, Vinaya, Abhidharma, and so on—and became a renowned scholar.

Khen Rinpoché Karma Dorjé also relied on Jamyang Chökyi Lodrö and Adzom Gyalsé Gyurmé Dorjé as the extraordinary masters of his buddha family, training in the secret Nyingtik teachings of the Dzogchen approach, the yogic practices for harnessing the energies in his subtle channels, *Timeless Awareness as the Guiding Principle,* and more. Through this training, he realized the enlightened intent of the ultimate lineage and became a holder of the lineage of the very essence of being.

When hard times befell Tibet, Karma Dorjé was not harmed, despite the disruptive events. His previous aspirations enabled him to fulfill a prophecy he had received from Jamyang Tapké, the precious guru of Makgur, who could clearly see the three times. He told Karma Dorjé, "Although the teachings may have been destroyed, you are destined to restore the religious institutions." [2.152a] Indeed, Khen Rinpoché Karma Dorjé rebuilt Podzong Monastery, both the structure and all of its accoutrements. In such ways, he served the precious teachings.

In particular, he turned the wheel of the dharma, conferring the great Nyingtik cycles of the Dzogchen approach, the empowerments and instructions for harnessing the energies in the subtle channels, the preliminary practices, *Timeless Awareness as the Guiding Principle,* and so forth, as well as many of the source texts of the dialectical approach. He thus inspired countless students and others to pursue what is positive, bringing the minds of even the humblest lay people to the dharma and illuminating the teachings that focus on the ultimate heart essence at his seat of glorious Podzong Monastery.

Tarthang Tulku Kunga (b. 1935) and Zurmang Trungpa Rinpoché (1939–1987)

The sublime Tarthang Tulku Kunga[5] went to India during the times of trouble and served as a professor at Sanskrit University in Varanasi. After his tenure there, he moved to the United States, where he found students who spoke and wrote in a different language and for whom the vision of the dharma was in no way obvious. [2.152b] He and Trungpa Rinpoché,[6] a tulku from Zurmang Monastery, were two masters who introduced the great tradition of Buddhism in the United States and so enormously benefited the Dzogchen teachings. Tarthang Tulku built Odiyan,[7] a center with temples and stupas, and published Tibetan-language editions of the Kangyur and Tengyur, many Nyingma works, Longchenpa's *Seven Treasuries* and

Four Higher Collections of the Heart Drop, and other texts. A supreme master who illuminates the teachings, he has provided copies of the Tibetan texts of *The Seven Treasuries* and *The Four Higher Collections* to the majority of monasteries of his own school. Tarthang Tulku instituted the annual Mönlam Chenmo[8] at Bodh Gaya, India, and continues to sponsor it. He is still living, his lotus feet standing firmly, renowned throughout the world as one whose noble activities are a unique source of nourishment for the precious teachings.

Tsö Paltrul Rinpoché (20th Century)

Another of the sublime Adzom Drukpa Rinpoché's students was Paltrul Rinpoché of Tsö. His former incarnation, the lord of the dharma Paltrul Rinpoché, had said, "Alas, I must die. [2.153a] If I were truly a bodhisattva with control over death and rebirth, why wouldn't I be reborn in Tsöyul, the area in Amdo where the border tribes eat insects?" He had also said, "I sometimes hear that I, Abu, could be of benefit to beings east of here, but that's probably just a product of my confusion." The meaning behind such utterances led many great masters to recognize this boy as a tulku of the holy master Paltrul Rinpoché. He was in fact born near Repkong in Tsö and entered the doorway of the dharma. He trained in a vast range of subjects, beginning with reading and writing.

When Paltrul Rinpoché grew up, he set out, with no companions to guide him, for Dergé in eastern Tibet, following his awakening spiritual instincts and searching for teachings. He became intent on finding Adzom Drukpa Rinpoché and, on his long journey, encountered such hardships as frozen rivers, windstorms, and roads blocked by snow. He was without adequate provisions and endured hundreds of difficulties that endangered his life. Finally, he met a nun from Lang-nga named Gyatso Drönma, who showed him the way [2.153b] and brought him to the guru.

Paltrul Rinpoché stayed at the encampment of Adzom Drukpa for many years. In the company of that master, he studied all of the profound advice found in the secret Nyingtik teachings, as well as a host of profound teachings, such cycles as *The Heart Drop of Chetsün, The Twenty-five Spheres,* and *Unobstructed Enlightened Intent.* He also received many profound transmissions from Gyalsé Rinpoché Gyurmé Dorjé.

Gaining mastery over the energies in his subtle channels, Paltrul Rinpoché could survive the bitter cold of winter by practicing tummo. He gave rise to innumerable such powers, signifying his progress on the spiritual path. Through the approaches of trekchö and tögal, he attained the most sublime siddhi; his realization awakened and he became an extraordinary heart son of his guru.

His guru advised him, "Now that you have received all of these spiritual instructions, return to your home region and benefit beings there." So he went back to Tsö in Amdo, where he pursued practice focusing on the very essence of being. Fulfilling the aspirations of his preceding lifetime, Paltrul Rinpoché turned the wheel of the dharma, teaching the preliminary practices and other aspects of the earlier and later cycles of the Nyingtik teachings and gathering around him hundreds of thousands of students. He cared for even the humblest layperson, leading rituals for the accomplishment of a hundred million recitations of the mantras *Om mani padme hum* and *Om ah hum vajra guru padma siddhi hum,* [2.154a] fasting rituals,[9] prayers for rebirth in Sukhavati, and more. Because of him, the dharma's positive influence illuminated the entire region.

A contemporary of Paltrul Rinpoché, the sublime Alak Jetsün, also came to this region and benefited beings, so that the enlightened activities of the Nyingma school were widespread in Repkong and Gyarong. In more recent times, following the directive of Jamyang Chökyi Lodrö, Dilgo Khyentsé Rinpoché traveled to Tsö, where he benefited the teachings and beings greatly by bestowing such transmissions as *The Treasury of Precious Hidden Teachings* and the great Nyingtik cycles.

Sertar Rinpoché (20th Century)

Sertar Rinpoché, born in Sertar, was a master whose lineage was that of Katok Monastery. Convinced that Drukpa Rinpoché had been his guru for lifetimes, he went to study with him, becoming renowned as Sertar Rinpoché. At the encampment of Adzom Druktrul, he trained in the preliminary practices and studied such texts as *The Oral Transmission of the Guru Samantabhadra* and *The Lamp Illuminating the Path to Liberation.* Putting these into practice, he gave rise to qualities that reflected the progress he had made on the spiritual path.

His guru told him, "If I instruct you in the main body of practice of the Dzogchen approach, you must go to western Tibet and benefit beings there." He then conferred on Sertar Rinpoché such teachings as the Dzogchen manual *Timeless Awareness as the Guiding Principle, The Innermost Heart Drop of the Guru, The Heart Drop of Chetsün,* [2.154b] and his own daknang transmission, *The Twenty-five Spheres.*

"Now practice these," Adzom Druktrul told Sertar Rinpoché. "As is said, 'If one does not practice, how will one attain siddhis? Plant the victory banner of spiritual practice in your mind.' So now you must meditate in solitude." Accordingly, Sertar Rinpoché returned to Sertar, where he received from the first Dudjom[10] that master's profound terma revelations, such as the cycle of the wrathful goddess Krodhikali. He then visited more than a hundred springs and other isolated, haunted places, becoming a mendicant with no fixed abode. He also journeyed to the region of Ngari in western Tibet to practice in places like the glacial mountain Kailash.

Sertar Rinpoché met with Degyal Rinpoché, a heart son of Dudjom Lingpa residing at Namkha Chungdzong on Mount Kailash. Sharing the same birthplace and spiritual heritage, these two masters experienced the remarkable merging of their minds. From then on, Sertar Rinpoché relied on this guru as the extraordinary master of his buddha family and remained with him, guru and student together caring for those to be guided. Through the teachings on Krodhikali and the Nyingtik teachings, these two masters benefited beings enormously, so that the effects of their extensive activities were felt throughout [2.155a] the three areas of Ngari, as well as in Nepal and all of the foothills.

Sertar Rinpoché was renowned throughout that part of the world. He turned the wheel of the dharma and gathered hundreds of thousands of students from all over the region. So great were his wisdom, love, and spiritual power that no other such holder of the teachings was said to be found in western Tibet in those times. His psychic abilities gave him untrammeled awareness of the three times. He had visions of Guru Padma, the Indian siddha Saraha, and many others, all of whom cared for him through their timeless awareness embodiments, so that he received countless daknang transmissions. A number of Sertar Rinpoché's works exist, including his manual of instructions on the preliminary practices. Having lived into his eighties as a protector of the teachings and of beings, Sertar Rinpoché eventually moved to India, where at a certain point the display of his emanated form resolved back into the state of peace, supreme inner basic space.

Both Sertar Rinpoché's son, Choktrul Tsewang Rinpoché, and the rebirth of Degyal Rinpoché continue Sertar Rinpoché's work, benefiting beings in Nepal, Dzomnang, Karmo Rong, [2.155b] and the area around Mount Kailash in western Tibet with profound teachings such as the Chö cycle of Krodhikali.

Golok Lama Kunzang (20th Century)

Another of Drukpa Rinpoché's students was Lama Kunzang of Golok. After Drukpa Rinpoché had conferred his entire transmission of spiritual instructions and advice on him, Lama Kunzang returned to his native region. He practiced intensively for a long time, gaining true realization. Through his transmissions of extensive and profound teachings, he cared for those to be guided, including two successive Akyong incarnations of Golok. He brought consummate benefit to the teachings and beings through his widespread activities, promulgating the Dzogchen teachings throughout the entire northeastern region of Tibet.

Once, when a student asked Lama Kunzang to interpret a dream, the latter replied, "For twelve years, whenever I have slept, I have experienced an utterly lucid state of limpid awareness. Ordinary thoughts never arise in my sleep, so I do not become lost in a self-sustaining state of confusion, the way most people do when they dream."

Limitless amazing signs attended his death, and sharira and other relics were found in his physical remains. Pavilions and spheres of rainbow light filled the entire region [2.156a] as he passed away into a state of peace, the citadel of dharmakaya. This moved countless students who had been guided by his teachings to unshakable faith.

Thus the innumerable students of Adzom Drukpa Rinpoché and their students in turn continue to spread the teachings that focus on the sublime heart essence in China, Tibet, Mongolia, and in fact throughout the world. This concludes the brief overview of these students.

THE STUDENTS OF YUKHOK JADRALWA CHÖYING RANGDROL

The countless students taught by Yukhok Jadralwa Chöying Rangdrol included Rakor Khen Drimé Özer, Gyarong Tsöndrü, Khen Chöchap, the fourth Kyabjé Dodrupchen, and others. Dodrupchen Rinpoché has already been discussed.[11]

Rakor Khen Drimé Özer (19th–20th Centuries)

Rakor Khen Drimé Özer was born in Rakor Gongma, in an area known as Tongza Rakor, close to Getsé Dayul in the northern reaches of eastern Tibet. At an early age, he entered the path of the dharma, studying and training under many of the gurus and tulkus of that region, starting with reading and writing and continuing on to the completion of his studies. [2.156b] He then studied further with a succession of masters, including Nyoshul Khenpo Dorjé Samdrup, Ngaga Rinpoché, and Tokgö Lama Melong, receiving numerous profound teachings, such as the preliminary practices, *The Heart Essence of Secrets*, and *The Three Cycles of Being at Ease*. He completed the accumulations for the preliminary practices ten times.

Finally, Rakor Khenpo met Yukhok Chöying Rangdrol, who had been his guru in past lifetimes. He remained with him for many years, receiving all of his spiritual advice and gaining realization. The guru praised him, saying, "Drimé Özer of Rakor truly exemplifies someone who progresses in leaps and bounds." Chöying Rangdrol also recognized Rakor Khen as an incarnation of the Omniscient One Longchenpa.

Eventually Rakor Khen Drimé Özer returned to his home region and lived at Getsé Tralek Monastery, a center with more than a thousand monks, in Sang-ngak Podrang in Dayul. He collaborated with Chaktsa Rinpoché, originally of Katok Monastery, who also resided at Getsé Tralek Monastery, and the minds of the two masters merged, becoming one. They thus ensured that their enlightened activities—caring for their students, establishing an abbatial succession at the monastery, and so on—were vast in scope.

Adopting the life of a wandering mendicant, Rakor Khen journeyed to Lhasa, as well as to Gang-ri Tökar [2.157a] and all the other places where the Omniscient One had resided. He eschewed all material possessions and practiced in what the Dzogchen tantras refer to as the "style of a beggar." In such ways, he followed the example set by victorious ones of the past and lived up to the traditional saying, "A true son of the mountains wraps himself in mist and contents himself with the poorest of food, clothing, and conversation." Rakor Khen Drimé Özer spent the last part of his life at

Tralek Monastery, caring for students and rendering enormous service to the teachings of the most sublime spiritual approach, so that the benefit he brought to beings filled space.

Gyarong Tsöndrü (19th–20th Centuries)

Like Rakor Khen, Gyarong Tsöndrü encountered many gurus in his home region and practiced their profound teachings extensively, so that meditative experiences and realization arose in him. At a certain point, he began to have numerous incredible visions, including sudden encounters with the peaceful and wrathful deities, and became rather proud of what he felt was a result of having attained the level of "awareness reaching full measure." Many years passed thus, and he eventually became quite ill from an imbalance of subtle energy. Inspired by what he had heard of the renowned guru Yukhok, he went to that master's encampment.

When he described his experiences to the guru, [2.157b] the latter said nothing about whether they were good or bad but told him, "Go into retreat for a week, and recite and practice these," conferring on Gyarong Tsöndrü a sadhana of Guru Drakpo and a terma of enlightened intent revealed by Drukpa Rinpoché.

While following these instructions, Gyarong Tsöndrü had a disturbing experience. Unable to wait until the next morning, he went during his evening practice session to see the guru. Yukhok wrathfully rebuked him, saying, "I thought you had such great realization that you had attained the level of awareness reaching full measure! If you really want to impress me, take this kerchief that I use to wipe my nose, rub it all over your upper and lower body, go to sleep, and stay that way!" Gyarong Tsöndrü returned to his retreat hut and followed the guru's command, wiping the snotty rag all over his body and lying down to sleep. Thereupon the entire world of appearances and possibilities manifested for him in the forms of deities; he directly experienced all of the visions that he would have earlier had he truly attained the level of awareness reaching full measure. Finally, as though he were dissolving a visualization during the completion stage, the deities faded one by one, until a single wrathful deity remained. [2.158a] A short while later, that wrathful form turned upside down, seemingly embarrassed; with a hissing sound, it faded like a spark dying out, until nothing was left.

Gyarong Tsöndrü reported these events to his guru, who said, "Ha! Ha! You attained the level of awareness reaching full measure. Your central channel opened up, so that you could perceive the hosts of wrathful deities in your cranium and so forth; then why haven't you realized the state of great perfection?" And he laughed loudly, clapping his hands. He then bestowed step-by-step instructions and advice on Gyarong Tsöndrü, beginning with the preliminary practices and the examination of the three phases of thought (its initial occurrence, duration, and cessation), and the latter's realization became fully evident. Gyarong Tsöndrü applied himself to his spiritual practice, following his guru's instructions. He turned the wheel of the dharma in his home region and its surrounding areas, furthering his lord guru's enlightened activities in Gyalrong in the east and throughout the northern reaches. In these ways, he ensured that his own and others' benefit was brought to consummation.

Today, Yukhok Jadralwa's and Gyarong Tsöndrü's students live in northeastern Tibet, spreading the teachings of the sublime spiritual approach and carrying out indescribable activities, [2.158b] causing the tradition that focuses on the very essence of being to flourish widely.

The precious, sublime Chöying Chabdal Dorjé, also known as Khenpo Chöchap, was a special holder of the lineages of both the lord Yukhok Jadralwa and Bötrul, so his biography will follow that of Bötrul.[12]

15

The Students of Jamyang Khyentsé Chökyi Lodrö and Other Masters

THE STUDENTS OF JAMYANG KHYENTSÉ CHÖKYI LODRÖ

That glorious protector of the teachings and beings, Jamyang Khyentsé Chökyi Lodrö, gathered innumerable students from all schools of Tibetan Buddhism without sectarian bias, as recounted previously in his life story.[1] He taught Katok Situ, Katok Öntrul, Dilgo Khyentsé Rinpoché, Zhechen Rabjam, Dzogtrul Jigdral Jangchub Dorjé, and others of the Early Translation school, thus serving this school of the Vajrayana tradition. The life of Dilgo Khyentsé Rinpoché has already been discussed.[2]

Jamyang Chökyi Lodrö passed away for a while into a state of peace, due to the degeneration of the teachings and of beings in general, and to the waning fortunes of the Tibetan people in particular, as well as to the machinations of the invading barbarians. Nevertheless, once again the innate compassion of this victorious one has manifested as part of an uninterrupted succession. Because of ineluctable interdependence (like that accounting for the moon's reflection in water), [2.159a] his precious, sublime tulku[3] has been born and is studying and training in India, once again ensuring benefit for the teachings and for beings.

Those of the Sakya school who received profound teachings from Jamyang Chökyi Lodrö and so constitute a lineage of his students include the heads of the two royal houses,[4] the khenpos of the four houses of Ngor,[5] and others. They are still alive and teach from the throne worthy of a spiritual ruler of the three realms, promulgating the precious words of the Lamdré cycle as mainstays of that lineage.

Lakar Sogyal Choktrul Rinpoché (b. 1947)

On the Nyingma side, Sogyal Choktrul Rinpoché was born in Trehor into the Lakar family, which for more than five hundred years has unfailingly served as a patron to all four schools of Tibetan Buddhism; to the three great monasteries of Sera, Drepung, and Ganden; and to such masters as Dzogchen Tupten Chökyi Dorjé, Paltrul Rinpoché, and Mipam Rinpoché. Sogyal Rinpoché's mother, Tselu, was praised by

Khenchen Ngawang Palzang as an emanation of the feminine deity Ushnisha Vijaya,[6] [2.159b] while his father was related to Dilgo Khyentsé Rinpoché.

Khyentsé Chökyi Lodrö recognized Sogyal Rinpoché and took him under his care, treating him with enormous kindness. He instructed him personally, beginning with the most basic skills, including reading and writing. He also conferred countless empowerments, oral transmissions, and teachings on Sogyal Rinpoché, who has thus received the majority of empowerments and teachings found in the Nyingma and Sarma schools. Before he died, Jamyang Khyentsé Chökyi Lodrö left specific instructions, saying, "As my son is still young, I have not been able to complete his education; it will be up to Khenpo Appey and others to take up this task in the future." When he went to the cave known as Drubpuk at Kharchu in the region of Lhodrak, Jamyang Khyentsé Chökyi Lodrö said, "I need only this boy to come with me." He conferred on Sogyal Rinpoché the extraordinary Dzogchen empowerment into the dynamic energy of awareness and entrusted him with the blessings of the lineage. "In the future, this son of mine will benefit my teachings," he said with foresight.

Following the demise of his master, Sogyal Rinpoché continued to study in India with Kyabjé Dudjom Rinpoché, Kyabjé Dilgo Khyentsé Rinpoché, and other masters, [2.160a] and today lives and turns the wheel of the dharma in the United States and other countries throughout the world.

Sakya Khen Rinpoché Appey (b. 20th Century)

Khenpo Appey, the precious Sakya khenpo, reached India and, following the directives of Sakya Dakchen Rinpoché, founded Sakya College in Mussorie, as well as other institutions. He has visited Nepal and such Eastern countries as Taiwan, Hong Kong, and Singapore. He is still alive, turning the wheel of the dharma.[7]

Other Living Masters

Jamyang Khyentsé Chökyi Lodrö's students who live in the West include Gang-na Choktrul, Ngari Tulku, and the great scholar Dongthog Tulku. Namkhai Norbu Rinpoché, who lives in Italy, was a student of both Nyala Jangchub Dorjé and the lord Jamyang Khyentsé. [2.160b] Khenchen Kunga Wangchuk Rinpoché of the Sakya school is still alive and teaching within that tradition.[8]

In Tibet itself, in the midst of a revitalization of the teachings, students of this great master—such highly learned masters as Choktrul Tekchok Rinpoché, Mipam Tulku Rinpoché, and Pé Tulku Rinpoché, as well as Moktsa Rinpoché and Khenpo Jamyang Lekshé, both of Katok Monastery—can be found throughout the eastern and central regions. Tekchok Rinpoché restored his Seng-ri Monastery, the structure and its contents, while Moktsa Rinpoché serves the tradition of the victorious Katok Monastery[9] in the lowlands of eastern Tibet.

Katok Öntrul Rinpoché (20th Century)

Öntrul Rinpoché of Katok Monastery went to India during the times of trouble. At first, he served as a professor at the Tibetan Institute of Higher Studies in Varanasi. Later, he moved to the refugee settlement in Zheyul near Dehra Dun, where the people hold the Katok tradition. [2.161a] There he founded a monastery for the teachings of the Katok lineage and carried out other noble works until he passed away, to the loss of the teachings and of beings.

His sublime tulku was born at Tashi Gang in Bhutan and was recognized with the eye of timeless awareness by Kyabjé Dudjom Rinpoché, who also enthroned and bestowed his title on him. This Katok Öntrul Rinpoché studied at Ngedön Gatsal in Mindroling Monastery in India under the direction of Kyabjé Trichen Rinpoché, Khochim Rinpoché, Tektsé Tulku, Khenpo Könchok Özer, and other masters. It is my prayer that he will carry on the work of his illustrious former incarnation and complete the noble activities the latter undertook to nurture the teachings and beings.

This concludes the section concerning Jamyang Khyentsé Chökyi Lodrö's students, primarily those who are still living.

THE STUDENTS OF DUDJOM RINPOCHÉ, DILGO KHYENTSÉ RINPOCHÉ, AND OTHERS

The students of Kyabjé Dudjom Rinpoché include his sons, Dungsé Rinpoché Thinley Norbu and Shenpen Dawa Rinpoché, [2.161b] as well as many other sublime masters who are still living. In turn, Dungsé Thinley Norbu's students include his sons, Garab and Jampal Dorjé, and others. Kyabjé Dilgo Khyentsé Rinpoché's students include his extraordinary heart sons: Zhechen Rabjam Rinpoché,[10] Dzongsar Khyentsé Rinpoché, and three other Khyentsé tulkus, the two Kongtrul tulkus, the precious rebirth of Namkhai Nyingpo of Lhodrak, Orgyen Tobgyal (son of a tertön), the two Chokling tulkus, and many other sublime tulkus who are still in their prime, like a bed of young lotuses. Similarly, many of the students of Kyabjé Dodrupchen Rinpoché, Kyabjé Penor Rinpoché, Kyabjé Trulzhik Rinpoché, and Kyabjé Chatral Rinpoché are also still living. I have not included biographies of these students, but simply ask that the holders of their respective lineages record them in the future.

The abridged accounts in this and the preceding two chapters concern those who were students of Jamyang Khyentsei Wangpo, as well as their students in turn, [2.162a] beings appearing in such numbers as to cover the earth and ensuring that the extensive tradition of the secret Nyingtik teachings of the Dzogchen approach will not wane, but will spread to all countries throughout the world.

16

The Students of Paltrul Rinpoché

Of those taught by the great bodhisattva Paltrul Rinpoché, there were four principal students more learned than the guru himself.[1]

Tendzin Drakpa (19th Century)

The sublime scholar Tendzin Drakpa was more learned than Paltrul Rinpoché himself in logical reasoning. Although it would seem fitting to include a biography of this master, under the circumstances I have refrained from doing so, since it appears that there are some who, for whatever reason, do not hold this master in high regard.

The Second Katok Situ, Chökyi Lodrö (1820–1879?)

Situ Chökyi Lodrö of the glorious Katok tradition was born in the Dergé region of eastern Tibet. His birth was accompanied by countless amazing indications of his pure nature. He was recognized at an early age as the next Situ Rinpoché, the refuge lord of Katok Monastery. Accordingly, he was established on the golden throne of his former incarnation in the midst of many thousands of monks who had gathered at the monastery, an event that was confirmed by gods and humans.[2]

Over time, Situ Chökyi Lodrö studied with numerous highly qualified tutors and mentors, beginning with reading and writing [2.162b] and continuing with the five fields of knowledge. Due to training in his past lives, he demonstrated unparalleled intelligence. In particular, he heard teachings on and studied many major and minor source texts and scriptures, such as *The Perfection of Sublime Knowing in One Hundred Thousand Verses,* the treatises of Maitreya, Vinaya, and Abhidharma. He also studied the glorious *Heart Essence of Secrets* and other source texts for the teachings on *The Discourse on United Intent* and *The Web of Magical Display,* as well as for the mind teachings. Through such thorough study and related practices, he attained the heights of erudition and spiritual attainment.

After Situ Chökyi Lodrö had trained comprehensively at the feet of so many gurus, who taught him the more common and extraordinary fields of knowledge, Paltrul Rinpoché came to Katok Monastery. Upon meeting, master and student felt their minds merge, becoming one. Situ received from Paltrul general teachings on the more common graduated path of sutra and tantra (beginning with an explanation of *Engaging in the Conduct of a Bodhisattva*) and the complete transmission of the unerring key points of Paltrul's pith instructions on the Dzogchen approach. In this way, the lineage of ultimate, naturally occurring enlightened intent was transmitted to Situ's mind, so that the true nature of phenomena was no longer an object of intellectual speculation. He gained the ability to experience this intent as the panoramic and infinitely pervasive sweep of the basic space of phenomena.

After this, Situ Chökyi Lodrö relinquished all of his responsibilities as the director of the monastery and monastic community. Taking Paltrul Rinpoché's sublime way of life [2.163a] as his model, he lived like an animal in the wild, practicing in such areas as the glacial wastes of Shar Shing-go and Rongtsen Kawa Karpo. He thus attained the level of a spontaneously present master of awareness and so ensured consummate benefit for himself and others.

Minyak Kunzang Sönam (19th–20th Centuries)

Minyak Kunzang Sönam was the student of Paltrul who surpassed his guru in conduct. He was born in the region of Minyak, eastern Tibet. He entered a Gelukpa monastery and became a consummate scholar of a vast range of the mainstream traditions of teachings, receiving the title of geshé. Accounts of the renowned lord of the dharma Paltrul Rinpoché inspired Kunzang Sönam's faith in this master, whose qualities appealed to his wise mind. He set off for the Dza region and sat at the lotus feet of dear old Abu, Paltrul Rinpoché, studying the mainstream traditions of sutra and tantra. Most notably, he received the transmission for *Engaging in the Conduct of a Bodhisattva* some eighty times with his fellow student Nyoshul Lungtok. He also received the great transmission of the Nyingtik teachings of the Dzogchen approach. By putting these teachings into practice, he came to have meditative experiences and to gain realization.

Kunzang Sönam's spoken words revealed a mind that was completely suffused with the dharma; he said things like, "In the presence of the kind Paltrul, [2.163b] three indelible designs have been engraved on my spine."[3] Dear old Abu treated him with deep affection, and when Kunzang Sönam expressed his intention to spend his whole life as a mendicant, wandering with no fixed dwelling place, Paltrul told him, "There is no need for you to wander from place to place. You and Lungtok should return to your native regions and stay in retreat. This will ensure benefit for the teachings and for beings." As Kunzang Sönam was preparing to leave in compliance with this directive, dear old Abu Rinpoché made him presents of a brick of tea and his own copy of *Engaging in the Conduct of a Bodhisattva*.

Taking these gifts, Kunzang Sönam returned to his homeland of Minyak. There he pursued his spiritual practice in solitary places—on mountains, near lakes, on cliffs—

such as Bazhap Drakar and the hermitage of Belo. He turned the wheel of the dharma on a vast scale, giving the oral transmissions for the precious Kangyur and teaching *Engaging in the Conduct of a Bodhisattva,* Prajñaparamita, Vinaya, Abhidharma, and other subjects. His method was to combine the sutra traditions as taught in the Sarma schools with the treatment of tantra found in the Early Translation school. His activities were widespread in such areas of the eastern lowlands as Tau, Tongkor, and Drak-ok. [2.164a] Kunzang Sönam wrote commentaries on many source texts covering subjects such as Prajñaparamita. His most important work, in some seven hundred folios, was an extensive commentary on *Engaging in the Conduct of a Bodhisattva* according to the oral explanations of dear old Abu—a single work covering a hundred mainstream sources and of a quality seldom found in the past, in India or Tibet. This alone ensured that Kunzang Sönam would stand as a unique model for future generations.

Kunzang Sönam's faith and devotion were so heartfelt that he wrapped the tea brick given to him by dear old Abu in silk and placed it above his head wherever he stayed. He said, "When I set out for my homeland, with his own two hands my master gave me this tea and his copy of *Engaging in the Conduct of a Bodhisattva,* accompanying these gifts with his prayers and asking in his Dzachukha nomad dialect, 'Kunsö, do you understand that this will bring you long life?'" Whenever he laid eyes on the tea, Kunzang Sönam would fold his hands in prayer and shed tears, saying, "Kind Abu, you know all." Every New Year's Day, he would break off a piece of the brick and boil it on the hearth. He would then gather all of his students around him, and they would share the tea; Kunzang Sönam, [2.164b] in a mood of great devotion, would say, "This is the nectar of bodhichitta and blessings that dear old Abu gave to me."

Among his foremost students were many leading scholars from Minyak, Tau, Drak-ok, and other places to the east, who contributed greatly to the continuity of the teachings. One such scholar was Apal of Minyak, who was completely versed in the Abhidharma teachings and whom the fifth Dzogchen invited to teach at Dzogchen Shri Simha Shedra. In his outer deportment, Kunzang Sönam was always scrupulous about observing the minutest detail of the Vinaya. He was never careless, but rather served as a model for the faithful and a source of refuge for all beings, even the gods. He was the epitome of a spiritual elder, like a golden mountain, a holy being who had a positive influence on every region in which he lived and who gave purpose to all connected to him.

Dzogchen Khenchen Pema Dorjé (1867–1935)

Another of Paltrul's students was Khenchen Pema Dorjé. At an early age, he entered the doorway of the dharma and exhibited boundless wisdom deriving from his former lifetimes. He met many mentors at Dzogchen Monastery and throughout the Dza region. He considered Jigmé Gyalwai Nyugu, Dodrup Kunzang Zhenpen, Gyalsé

Zhenpen Tayé, [2.165a] and Paltrul Rinpoché to be the extraordinary masters of his buddha family. He studied the mainstream traditions of sutra and tantra, achieving the status of a learned and accomplished master. He was one of a succession of abbots at the monastery of the Drupwang Dzogchen tulkus. He wrote many detailed works, such as *The First Light of Dawn,* his response to criticism leveled against the Early Translation school by opponents with erroneous opinions.

Pema Dorjé was considered an incarnation of Deshek Zurpoché.[4] The glorious tantra *The Heart Essence of Secrets,* as well as the works of the Omniscient One and his spiritual heir, Jigmé Lingpa, were the very heart of his study and practice. He gave these teachings widely, gathering countless students and ensuring that the roots of the teachings would be nurtured.

Pema Dorjé studied with Jamyang Khyentsei Wangpo and many other great masters, receiving the precious teachings of the kama transmissions of the Early Translation school and many profound teachings (including the empowerment and instructions for *The Discourse on United Intent,* which focuses on the mandala of the Gathering of the Great Assembly).[5] Many lineages have been passed down through this master, Pema Dorjé. It was prophesied that he would be the custodian of *The Three Roots: The Web of Magical Display,* Khyentsé Rinpoché's terma. It is clear from his own record of the teachings he received that there was virtually no aspect of the pith instructions of the great Nyingtik teachings—the empowerments, advice, and oral transmissions—that he did not hold. [2.165b] Thus the holy master Pema Dorjé was single-handedly capable of passing on the traditions of the Early Translation school, and his enlightened activities were as extensive as space.

Pema Dorjé went with the lord of the dharma Paltrul Rinpoché to meet Drupchen Chöying Rangdrol, a great master who lived in the glacial wastes of Shang-go in eastern Tibet. This master, who eventually attained rainbow body, was Nyala Pema Duddul's guru. Pema Dorjé and Paltrul Rinpoché received from him the transmission of instructions from the very early line of Katok Monastery. Pema Dorjé thus served as a primary upholder of the traditions specific to the Early Translation school. For the most part, those he guided were also students of Mingyur Namkhai Dorjé, Paltrul Rinpoché, and other masters.

Golok Lang Lama Tupten Chökyi Jorpa (19th–20th Centuries)

Another student of Paltrul Rinpoché was Lang Lama Tupten Chökyi Jorpa. He was born into the Langtsang clan in the northeastern Tibetan region of Golok. With the mentors in his region, he studied Madhyamaka, *Engaging in the Conduct of a Bodhisattva, Ascertaining the Three Levels of Ordination,* the Lojong teachings, and many other subjects. In particular, he relied on Paltrul Rinpoché, Jamgön Mipam Rinpoché, and Traktung Dudjom Lingpa as his most extraordinary gurus. He studied and contemplated the Dzogchen manual *Timeless Awareness as the Guiding*

Principle, [2.166a] *The Seven Treasuries,* and the rest of the earlier and later cycles of Nyingtik teachings, as well as the Dudjom Tersar cycles. Tupten Chökyi Jorpa became both learned and accomplished in these fields.

He adopted the way of life of a monk, wearing the robes of his ordination. He was meticulously pure in his spiritual practice and deportment; he recited the tantra *The Stainless Confession* aloud some thirty thousand times. He had the ability to benefit his students enormously by turning the wheel of the dharma.

Finally, following Dudjom Lingpa's instructions, Tupten Chökyi Jorpa went to the holy place of Pemakö, the most majestic hidden valley, where he lived for the rest of his life, teaching profound and extensive subjects in innumerable ways. It was this lord who was primarily responsible for offering the oral lineage of the lord of the dharma Paltrul Rinpoché—the tantras, explanatory commentaries, and pith instructions—to Kyabjé Dudjom Rinpoché Jigdral Yeshé Dorjé, who in turn held Tupten Chökyi Jorpa in high esteem, referring to him as "Lang Lama, the master of my buddha family."

At last, Golok Lang Lama Tupten Chökyi Jorpa passed into a state of peace in the hidden realm of Pemakö amid marvelous signs, leaving relics behind. This guru was perhaps the most crucial link [2.166b] between Dza Paltrul Rinpoché and Kyabjé Dudjom Rinpoché.

KHENCHEN YÖNTEN GYATSO AND HIS STUDENTS

Khenchen Yönten Gyatso (19th–20th Centuries)

Khenchen Yönten Gyatso was another of Paltrul Rinpoché's students. He was born in Gemang (Gyalsé Zhenpen Tayé's birthplace) in the northern reaches of Tibet. Yönten Gyatso entered the doorway of the dharma at an early age and met many mentors at Zhechen and Dzogchen Monasteries and throughout the northern reaches. He studied Vinaya, Abhidharma, Madhyamaka, valid cognition, Prajñaparamita, and other subjects, reaching the heights of erudition in the whole range of mainstream teachings. He took monastic ordination and was scrupulous about upholding the Vinaya codes, taking as his example the lives of the exalted elders of the early Buddhist tradition and never committing even the slightest infraction of any of the three levels of ordination.

The special masters of his buddha family were dear old Abu (Paltrul Rinpoché) and Orgyen Tendzin Norbu, whom he served in the three ways for a long time and who conferred on him the key points of advice found in the tantras, explanatory commentaries, and pith instructions, like one vase filling another. He studied the sutras and tantras in general and, as the vast expanse of his wisdom unfolded, became especially learned in the tantras of the secret Nyingtik approach of utter lucidity. [2.167a] Yönten Gyatso became a unique source of benefit for future generations, composing works informed by the oral explanations of dear old Abu, such as his "Sun" and "Moon" commentaries on *The Treasury of Enlightened Qualities* and his commentary on *Ascertaining the Three Levels of Ordination.*

He made Gemang Monastery his main seat, where he directed many hundreds of monks in the Vinaya codes and the practice of the three bases of Vinaya. He also gave regular discourses on the mainstream teachings in general, as well as profound texts of sutra and tantra such as *The Treasury of Enlightened Qualities.* Yönten Gyatso thus became a great illuminator of the teachings.

He tried to institute an approach whereby students would memorize *Dispelling Darkness in the Ten Directions* and the explanations of the tantra *The Heart Essence of Secrets* according to Paltrul's oral tradition, but there were many obstacles. Mipam Rinpoché advised, "First give all of the teachings in ten days; then have tutors repeat the material in great detail." When Yönten Gyatso followed this advice, the obstacles were eliminated. It was this approach that accounted for the ability of such modern-day teachers as Khenchen Jigmé Puntsok Rinpoché in Golok, Kyabjé Dilgo Khyentsé Rinpoché in India and Nepal, and the six great khenpos of Gemang Monastery [2.167b] to explain *The Heart Essence of Secrets* from memory. Throughout the northern reaches of eastern Tibet, Dzachukha, and Dergé, the students of these masters and their students in turn have greatly expanded the memorization and explanation of *The Heart Essence of Secrets.* It is evident that, in these final times, the continued flourishing of the explanatory teachings concerning this tantra, like a hundred thousand suns shining, is due to the kindness of these teachers.

In addition, Yönten Gyatso encouraged the ordinary men and women of his region to practice, teaching them the preliminary practices, the *Om mani padme hum* mantra, and the practice focusing on the pure realm of Amitabha.[6] Thus, throughout Golok and the uplands and lowlands of the northern reaches of eastern Tibet, even all of the rough and wild people to be guided by his teachings were brought to the sacred dharma. Simply upon meeting him, evil people and nonhuman spirits felt their malevolent intentions fade away. The blessing cords and protection amulets he gave out—even small personal articles of his clothing or other possessions—ensured the removal of hindrances and obstacles, for he was a great bodhisattva whose mastery of spiritual power gave a sense of purpose to all connected to him. He owned nothing but his three monastic robes and enough for his immediate needs, [2.168a] adopting the way of life of a true monarch among mendicants and carrying out the four principles of the early Kadampa masters[7] to perfection.

Among his students were many who upheld the lineage of the teachings, masters such as the elder Sang-gyé Nyenpa tulku of Ga, Lushul Tulku, Changma Khen Rinpoché Tupten Chöpel, Khenchen Tsewang Rigdzin of Mewa, and Golok Khenpo Rigdzin Zangpo. They filled their hearts with the three higher trainings and attained the pinnacle of erudition and spiritual accomplishment. Thus the lineages of Yönten Gyatso's teachings and students spread throughout the northern reaches, and the benefit he brought to beings was equal to space itself.

Changma Khenchen Tupten Chöpel (1886–1956)

Khenchen Tupten Chöpel of Changma was a student of Khenchen Yönten Gyatso. He was born into the direct bloodline of the Mukpo clan in Getsé. His birthplace was a nomadic community in the Batur region of the Dalung river valley in the northern reaches of eastern Tibet. From an early age, Tupten Chöpel naturally exhibited the attributes of someone holy, such as faith, renunciation, a lack of interest in worldly matters, and compassion. At the age of eleven, he entered the monastic community of Puntsok Norling and, beginning with reading and writing, [2.168b] trained in all the usual fields of knowledge. He was ordained as a novice by Khenchen Yönten Gyatso. At twenty-four Tupten Chöpel requested additional vows and became a fully ordained monk.

Khenchen Yönten Gyatso was by then living at the hermitage of Lhundrup Dechen Ling, where he taught Tupten Chöpel grammar and other fields of secular knowledge, Indian and Chinese astrology, Sanskrit grammar, poetry, Madhyamaka, Prajñaparamita, Vinaya, Abhidharma, and the precious tantra classes of the secret mantra approach of the Vajrayana. With many other mentors (including those he referred to as the "three great khenpos whose kindness to me was unparalleled"), Tupten Chöpel studied myriad source texts and pith instructions of the Early Translation school, such as the teachings on *The Discourse on United Intent* and *The Web of Magical Display* and the mind teachings. In particular, from Khenchen Yönten Gyatso, the extraordinary master of his buddha family, Tupten Chöpel received the earlier and later cycles of the secret Nyingtik teachings of the Dzogchen approach, as well as teachings on the most majestic tantra, *The Heart Essence of Secrets,* and other cycles, receiving these as experiential transmissions based on the oral instructions of the lord of the dharma Paltrul Rinpoché. He put these teachings into practice and experienced the enlightened intent that is the ultimate lineage.

Following his guru's instructions, Tupten Chöpel applied himself to spiritual practice focusing on the very essence. [2.169a] He established a center called Samten Dargyé Ling at the hermitage of Changma, where the lord of the dharma Paltrul Rinpoché had spent a long time engaged in spiritual practice. There he turned the wheel of the dharma, attracting innumerable students from eastern, central, and southern Tibet and beyond. He liberated the minds of countless students, presenting things in a thorough and experiential way using pith instructions as he explained the teachings, from the most rudimentary Vinaya codes to the most majestic tantra, *The Heart Essence of Secrets*, and the pinnacle spiritual approach of the heart essence of utter lucidity (with texts like the Dzogchen manual *Timeless Awareness as the Guiding Principle*).

Tupten Chöpel ensured that the monastic tradition flourished; his monastery followed to the letter the full system of discipline found in the Vinaya, and the residents were untainted by any flaw or moral failing. He also inspired ordinary lay people by teaching them the practice for rebirth in Sukhavati and the mantras *Om mani padme hum* and *Om ah hum vajra guru padma siddhi hum*. He encouraged them to give up hunting and banditry and to adopt more virtuous ways. Thus he exerted a positive influence on the whole region.

During his entire life, Tupten Chöpel focused on the very heart of spiritual practice. He never once concerned himself with material possessions or accepted offerings to benefit people, living or dead, [2.169b] but took as his example the life of the lord of the dharma Paltrul Rinpoché. His lived as a true holy being—like a wish-fulfilling gem—so that he became renowned in the vernacular as Khenga Yizhin Norbu.[8]

Serving thus as a glorious protector of the teachings and of beings, Tupten Chöpel lived for seventy-one years. Finally, he lay down in the posture of a sleeping lion,[9] and the display of his emanated form resolved back into the basic space of phenomena. When his students performed the cremation ceremony, his skull flew into the air, canopies of rainbow light formed, and soft raindrops in the shape of blossoms fell throughout the region. Countless relics were found among his ashes, and other amazing signs manifested without limit. In these ways, Changma Khenchen Tupten Chöpel caused the vision of the Victorious One's precious teachings to spread in the ten directions.

Of his students, the foremost were Khenchen Trinlé Gyatso of Tromtar, Jigmé Lungtok Gyatso, Kyabjé Dilgo Khyentsé Rinpoché, and Khenchen Jigmé Puntsok of Sertar. [2.170a]

Washul Mewai Khenchen Tsewang Rigdzin (1883–1958)

Khenchen Tsewang Rigdzin of Washul Mewa was another of Khenchen Yönten Gyatso's students. He was someone in these modern times who everyone knows vanished into the state of rainbow body. Tsewang Rigdzin was born amid various marvelous signs in Washul Mewa, a region in Amdo in the northernmost part of eastern Tibet. At an early age, he entered the doorway of the dharma and devoted himself to his studies, beginning with reading and writing and continuing on to other fields of knowledge. His conduct was restrained and his mind sharp. His wisdom and other qualities were unequaled, and his elders used to say, "Look at the intelligence of this venerable little monk; he will surely turn out to be a scholar who is renowned as 'the great khenpo of Mewa.'"

When Tsewang Rigdzin was a little older, he went to Lak Drakdzong Monastery, where he studied under many mentors, including Khen Chödrup,[10] Kharpa Tulku Tenpai Nyima, and Khargya Tertön Rinpoché. He studied *Engaging in the Conduct of a Bodhisattva, Ascertaining the Three Levels of Ordination,* the sutra *Individual Liberation, The Source Verses for the Novice Monk,* orthography, poetics, and other subjects. [2.170b] He received many profound transmissions of empowerments, advice, and instructions and put these into practice.

Then he gradually underwent more hardship for the sake of the dharma, abandoning his home and journeying to Dergé in eastern Tibet and Dzachukha in the northern reaches in search of teachings. He encountered Nyoshul Khenchen Ngawang Palzang, Khen Dorjé Samdrup, Khen Kunzang Palden, Dzogchen Khenpo Losel Tenkyong, Drodul Pawo Dorjé, Dzogchen Tupten Chökyi Dorjé, and other masters. With them he studied *The Source Verses on Sublime Knowing* and Nagarjuna's other works on reasoning, *The Four Hundred Verses on the Middle Way, The Ornament of the Middle Way, The Two Levels of Truth in the Middle Way,* Prajñaparamita, the works of Maitreya (such as the two treatises *The Distinction Between Phenomena and Their True Nature* and *The Distinction Between Center and Limit*), the sources on valid cognition (such as *The Detailed Commentary*), and the earlier and later schools of Abhidharma. Tsewang Rigdzin trained in these mainstream systems, becoming a great scholar. In Dzachukha he met Jamgön Mipam Rinpoché, from whom he received the blessings of Mañjushri and cycles of empowerments, instructions, and advice.

The most extraordinary master of his buddha family was Khenchen Yönten Gyatso, from whom Tsewang Rigdzin received teachings such as the Dzogchen manual *Timeless Awareness as the Guiding Principle.* [2.171a] He put these into practice and directly perceived the enlightened intent of natural great perfection, the true nature of phenomena beyond intellectual speculation. He received a host of profound teachings, such as *Dispelling Darkness in the Ten Directions,* Longchenpa's commentary on *The Heart Essence of Secrets;* Mipam's overview of this tantra, entitled *The Heart Essence of Utter Lucidity; The Ornament of Enlightened Intent; The Oral Transmission of the Guru Samantabhadra;* and the Omniscient One's *Seven Treasuries, Four Higher Collections of the Heart Drop,* and *Three Cycles of Being at Ease.*

In addition, Tsewang Rigdzin studied and contemplated teachings with many mentors in Dergé, receiving transmissions for *The Treasury of Precious Hidden Teachings,* the kama transmissions of the Early Translation school, *The Treasury of Spiritual Instructions,* the oral transmissions for the precious Kangyur, the Tengyur, and more. In all of the breaks during these periods of study, he devoted himself to spiritual practice on many deities of the Three Roots, so that he directly experienced signs of accomplishment.

Tsewang Rigdzin then returned to his home region of Mewa and took up residence at his old monastery, Tri Dargyé, where he presided over a community of many hundreds of novices and monks. He instituted a curriculum of spiritual practice and strict observance of the monastic disciplines and rituals, following the methods outlined by Gyalsé Zhenpen Tayé. [2.171b] He founded a shedra whose syllabus was based largely on the works of Jamgön Mipam Rinpoché. Tsewang Rigdzin turned the wheel of the dharma, expounding the sutras, tantras, and other fields of knowledge and serving the teachings on an enormous scale by producing many fine scholars, including Khenchen Yeshé, Khen Jampal, Khen Norten, Alak Chaktreng Rinpoché, and Khen Sönam Wangyal. These khenpos of Mewa were renowned for their great erudition in Abhidharma. Tsewang Rigdzin brought great benefit to beings by teaching the local inhabitants and students from all regions using mainstream sources, giving spiritual advice, explaining the preliminary practices, and so forth.

With Alak Dzong-ngön, Tsewang Rigdzin went to Chözhi in Hor, where on the basis of a shared vision they founded a shedra whose syllabus emphasized the works of Mipam Rinpoché. This caused the teachings of the Early Translation school, which are endowed with four mainstream transmissions, to flourish in the eastern part of the northern reaches. As a result of the aspirations of the successive abbots of the shedra, as well as those of Gurong Tulku Rinpoché and others, the flawless system of the Early Translation school still endures in Amdo, Repkong, [2.172a] and other places as far away as the historical border with China.

At the same time that Tsewang Rigdzin finished such tasks, due to the degeneration of the teachings and of beings, barbarians brought great tragedy to Tibet. During the conflict, people of evil intent seized Tsewang Rigdzin and sentenced him to prison. As they escorted him there, he began chanting the mantra *Om ah hum vajra guru padma siddhi hum*. In a manner reminiscent of the learned Indian Buddhist master Shantideva,[11] Tsewang Rigdzin rose higher and higher into the air in plain view of everyone, finally dissolving into a mass of light, an event still remembered throughout eastern Tibet. This is reminiscent of the biographical accounts of the master Garab Dorjé, Pang Mipam Gönpo, and others, who attained the most sublime siddhi through the path of natural great perfection and faded into space in a mass of light.

Among Khenchen Tsewang Rigdzin's countless students, Alak Chaktreng Rinpoché, who was born in the Mé region, studied and trained with all the khenpos of Mewa in the Dzogchen lineage, [2.172b] in particular Tsewang Rigdzin himself, and received from them the entire transmission of the profound Dzogchen teachings. He was unharmed by the upheavals of recent times and still lives in Washul Mewa. There he has built a monastery that houses more than a thousand monks and has established a shedra and meditation center. He has commissioned the three kinds of spiritual representations, provided the requisite articles for the ceremonies celebrating the tenth day of the lunar month and other rituals, and guides his students with his teachings. In such ways, he continues to serve the teachings on a vast scale.

Khenchen Jigmé Puntsok (1933–2004)

Khenchen Jigmé Puntsok was a student of the aforementioned Changma Khen Tupten Chöpel, who was also known as Tupga of Batar. He was born in Seryul in the eastern Tibetan lowlands. His father was Pété of the Nup clan, and his mother was Yutso. Their son was born amid various marvelous signs, including a caul that draped over him like a formal monastic robe. As soon as he was born, the baby showed many signs that he was capable of extraordinary behavior; for example, he sat upright and recited the most majestic mantra of awareness, *Om a ra pa cha na dhih,*[12] seven times. [2.173a] At an early age, his predilection for the supreme spiritual approach of the Mahayana awoke in him. He prayed to Mañjushri, the Lion of Speech, and through the blessings of that deity, felt his wisdom unfold as unhindered realization in all fields of knowledge, beginning with reading and writing. At nine Jigmé Puntsok took monastic ordination from Sönam Chödrup, the khenpo of Drakdzong.

When he was eighteen, he went to Dzachukha and other areas in the northern reaches of the nomads in search of teachings. Over the next few years, he served his mentors, receiving teachings on the Dzogchen practice of trekchö and the six bardo states from Mani Lama Pema Siddhi; *The Innermost Heart Drop of the Guru* and the empowerment for the peaceful and wrathful deities from Paltrul Namkha Jigmé; *The Heart Drop of Chetsün* from Khenpo Yönten Gönpo of Dzogchen Monastery; *The Four Higher Collections of the Heart Drop* and the extensive empowerment for Kalachakra from Bötrul Rinpoché Do-ngak Tenpai Nyima; teachings on Madhyamaka from Khenpo Gyatso; oral explanations of *The Treasury of Abhidharma* and the oral transmissions for the precious Kangyur from Lama Tsulga; [2.173b] the commentary on the Vinaya entitled *Rays of Sunlight* from Khen Orgyen Gönpo; and teachings on Prajñaparamita, valid cognition, astrology, and other subjects from Lhatrul Rinpoché. Jigmé Puntsok studied with many others, including Lama Garchö, Khenpo Daö, and Gendün Dargyé, training in all subjects pertaining to the sutras and tantras and becoming a consummate scholar.

In particular, the extraordinary inner master of his buddha family was Tupga of Bartar, also known as Changma Khen Rinpoché Tupten Chöpel, the heart son of both Orgyen Tendzin Norbu and Khenchen Yönten Gyatso, who were students of dear old Abu. Jigmé Puntsok relied on this master as his crown jewel, initially taking the vows of a fully ordained monk with him. Over time, Jigmé Puntsok received from Changma Khen teachings concerning many of the principal commentaries on the most majestic tantra, *The Heart Essence of Secrets;* the works of the Omniscient One and his spiritual heir, Jigmé Lingpa (that is, the earlier and later cycles of the Nyingtik teachings); and trekchö and tögal. He received these like one vase being filled to overflowing from another, and countless enlightened qualities born of meditative experience and realization arose in him. He became a great holder of the ultimate lineage of realization in his own right.

Crossing to the far shore of the ocean of erudition, Jigmé Puntsok became a greatly learned and accomplished master, with an untrammeled understanding of every aspect of the vast range of the sutras and tantras; [2.174a] his explanations, debates, and writings about the Buddhist teachings are unparalleled. He traveled throughout eastern Tibet and to Wu Tai Shan in China, turning the wheel of the dharma, his enlightened activities extending to gatherings of innumerable students. His principal seat was at Lama Rong, near Ngala Taktsé in lower Ser. When Jigmé Puntsok went to the holy country of India, he served as a guru to all of the learned and accomplished masters there, including the present Dalai Lama and Kyabjé Drupwang Penor Rinpoché.

At various intervals, Jigmé Puntsok undertook intensive retreats on the phases of approach and accomplishment for a vast array of deities of the Three Roots. He was cared for by the timeless awareness embodiments of these deities as well as those of Jamgön Mipam Rinpoché and Mañjushri Jñanasattva. From his own point of view, the vast expanse of enlightened intent welled up as the full-blown experience of timeless awareness and sublime knowing of dharmakaya. He wrote many commentaries on the principles expounded in the sutras and tantras, drawing these works from the secret treasury—the expanse of his awareness unfolding as the dynamic energy of the naturally occurring lamp of sublime knowing. [2.174b] Jigmé Puntsok thus demonstrated greater and greater nobility in his study, practice, and spiritual projects, restoring the Victorious One's precious teachings. He was alive until recently, his lotus feet standing firmly in the vajra realm, dwelling in Ser Valley in the eastern Tibetan lowlands.[13]

Among the students who maintain his lineage are Tulku Lungtok of Shukchung, Tulku Chökyi Nyima of Wané, Khenchen Namdrol Rinpoché,[14] Tulku Tendzin Gyatso, Tulku Rigpai Dorjé of Wané, Khenpo Tsultrim Lodrö, Khenpo Guru of Minyak, Khenpo Kunzang of Golok, Khenpo Chimé Rigdzin of Mewa, and Khenpo Sherab Zangpo of Dergé. These and other living masters are still serving the teachings of the Victorious One.

The foregoing were students in the lineage of dear old Abu's student Khenchen Yönten Gyatso.

KHENCHEN KUNZANG PALDEN CHÖDRAK AND HIS STUDENTS

Khenchen Kunzang Palden Chödrak (1872–1943)

Another of Paltrul Rinpoché's students was Khenchen Kunzang Palden Chödrak. He was born in Dzachukha in the northern reaches of eastern Tibet, into a family related to Paltrul Rinpoché. His parents being poor and without resources to seek teachings, Kunzang Palden underwent countless hardships when he was young. [2.175a] He served the lord of the dharma Paltrul Rinpoché as the extraordinary master of his buddha family, pleasing him in all ways. Since he had no shoes, Kunzang Palden always arrived barefoot in the wind and snow to request teachings. Blood would ooze from the cracks in his weathered soles. When dear old Abu saw this, he praised him and gave him much kind advice, saying, "Kunpal, pursue your studies courageously, and nothing bad will happen to you."

Kunzang Palden had nothing to wear but a ragged old coat. But he bravely kept up with his studies, day and night. Because he had no oil to fuel a lamp at night, he would go out into the moonlight to keep studying. As the moon fell lower and lower behind a hill, he would climb higher to continue reading his texts, by dawn reaching the hill's summit. Some of his spiritual companions teased him, saying, "In this world, people and the sun go to the summit during the day to tend the herds; only Kunpal and the moon go to the summit at night to tend books." [2.175b]

One day, someone offered dear old Abu a mandala plate made of bell metal. Kunzang Palden asked him, "Abutsang,[15] would you be willing to give me this mandala plate so that I can begin my five hundred thousand repetitions of the preliminary practices?" Dear old Abu Rinpoché thought for a moment and then replied, "Of course, I would be more than willing to do so. It is said that in this world nothing is impossible, that in fact anything is possible. It is entirely possible that you will take my mandala plate and one day, instead of being someone with a ragged old coat as you are right now, you will be seated in the midst of thousands of ordained members of the sangha, reciting the liturgy of offering that begins, 'The ground is anointed with perfumed water. . . .' Ah! Take care! Take care and no harm will come to you."

Later in life, after Kunzang Palden had been appointed to sit on a khenpo's throne, he was bestowing the bodhisattva vow to an enormous gathering at Katok Monastery. As the assembly recited the mandala offering portion of the Seven-Branch Supplication, he remembered what his guru had told him. "That was truly a prophecy," he said. "My guru really was a buddha who could see the three times without hindrance! Even if I were to fill the three-thousand-fold universe with gold, I could not repay the smallest fraction of dear old Abu's compassionate kindness to me." [2.176a] He folded his hands in prayer and shed tears.

He always served his guru with extraordinary devotion, seeing him as a true buddha. This delighted dear old Abu, who conferred on Kunzang Palden the general mainstream teachings of the sutras and tantras, as well as teachings on *Engaging in the Conduct of a Bodhisattva, The Heart Essence of Secrets,* and many tantras, explanatory commentaries, and pith instructions of the Dzogchen approach of utter lucidity (including cycles that had never been written down, such as the oral lineage of the secret Nyingtik teachings of Dzogchen). Kunzang Palden did not treat these as mere words, but put them into practice, and boundless meditative experiences and realization arose in him.

He also studied and contemplated extensively, learning such subjects as Madhyamaka, Prajñaparamita, Vinaya, and Abhidharma from Jamyang Khyentsei Wangpo, Dodrup Tenpai Nyima, Jamgön Mipam Rinpoché, Önpo Tenga (also known as Orgyen Tendzin Norbu), Drupwang Dzogchen Rinpoché Tupten Chökyi Dorjé, and many other mentors. He applied himself to spiritual practice focusing on the very essence, staying at solitary hermitages, like Gegong and Changma, where dear old Abu had lived. [2.176b] He was filled with renunciation and bodhichitta and was extremely kind to those who were humble and poor. At the very core of his practice was a sincere and completely self-sufficient devotion, for he never wavered from the perception of his guru as a true buddha.

Whenever he taught the dharma, Kunzang Palden spoke at length on the motivation of bodhichitta and on proper deportment; he unfailingly recited extensive prayers before and after his teachings. He would say, "I studied my texts in the presence of dear old Abu, and I made a vow to him that when any opportunity to teach them arose, I would teach even a pillar if there were no one present to listen." He spent his life teaching at least once, but often dozens of times, a day without fail.

Following the wishes of Jamgön Mipam Rinpoché and at the invitation of Situ Chökyi Gyatso, the great master of Katok Monastery, Kunzang Palden went to the vajra seat of Katok. He was appointed the first abbot of the newly founded Shedrup Norbui Lhunpo, an excellent shedra for the study of the classes of tantra. It was Katok Situ Rinpoché's express wish that Kunzang Palden inaugurate the series of teachings known as the "hundred mainstream sources of Katok," a collection of more than a hundred commentaries on mainstream texts composed by the learned masters of India and Tibet, [2.177a] the explanation of which would take some five years. Kunzang Palden remained at this shedra for three years, in this way supporting and serving as a pillar of the teachings. To this seat came Khenchen Ngawang Palzang, an emanation of Vimalamitra; Khenchen Gyaltsen Özer; Khenchen Chödrup of Lak, also known as Jampal Chökyi Lodrö; and others in the golden garland of Katok Monastery's abbatial succession, who through their study, teaching, and activities caused this tradition to spread in all directions. Kunzang Palden's enlightened activity was as extensive as the sky itself in that he ensured that the oral traditions (based on commentaries and summaries of the mainstream scriptural sources) of the lord of the dharma Paltrul Rinpoché, Jamgön Mipam, Gyalsé Zhenpen Tayé, and other masters who defined the position of the Early Translation school would spread wherever the lineage of Katok Monastery flourished.

Kunzang Palden then returned to his home of Dzachukha, where he cared for countless students from all over Dza. His works, including his marvelous extensive commentary on *Engaging in the Conduct of a Bodhisattva* (arranged according to the pith instructions of dear old Abu) and his large collection of stories taken from the Vinaya, [2.177b] are still available to the generations that have followed him. Kunzang Palden kept whatever he taught within the guidelines of the pith instructions on bodhichitta, and he focused on the oral traditions of dear old Abu and Mipam Rinpoché, relating the teachings to the key points of inner meditative experience. He lived for a long time, bringing his activities for the benefit of beings to completion.

Among the students dear to his heart were Khen Jamdor of Troshul, Bötrul Do-ngak Tenpai Nyima, Batar Tupga (also known as Tupten Chöpel), Dodrup Jigmé Trinlé Palbar, Chagdud Choktrul,[16] and others. Kunzang Palden thus rendered enormous service to the Nyingma teachings.

Bötrul Do-ngak Tenpai Nyima (1900–1959)

Bötrul Do-ngak Tenpai Nyima was born in Dakpo, in the eastern part of central Tibet. When he was very young, his spiritual predisposition awakened and he entered the path of the dharma. At a certain point, he joined an eastern Tibetan merchant on a pilgrimage and journeyed to eastern Tibet in search of teachings. Because he was still so young and his homeland so far away, Do-ngak Tenpai Nyima had no provisions for supporting himself while receiving teachings [2.178a] and therefore endured many hardships, including a lack of adequate clothing, and adopted a way of life reminiscent of the lord Milarepa's.

He finally reached Dzogchen Monastery in eastern Tibet and studied with all of the gurus, tulkus, khenpos, and teachers residing there, investigating the thirteen great source texts and teachings from the sutras, tantras, and other fields of knowledge. He himself joined the ranks of the learned. From Dzogchen Tupten Chökyi Dorjé, he received many empowerments and oral transmissions for the practice of tantra. Dzogchen Rinpoché took responsibility for Do-ngak Tenpai Nyima and accorded him many honors. For example, he conferred the title of tulku on him, seated him during large gatherings on a throne that stood in the center at the back of the hall, and assigned several monks as his attendants when he traveled. Everyone honored him as Böpa Tulku.

It was about that time that Do-ngak Tenpai Nyima developed an avid interest in the teaching methods of Jamgön Mipam Rinpoché. He thought it imperative that he meet a mentor who held that tradition. Upon investigation, he found that Khenpo Kunpal Rinpoché of Gegong Monastery had been both Paltrul's and Mipam's student [2.178b] and was an extraordinary holder of their lineages. He went to meet that great khenpo and lived for a long time in the Dza region, becoming a consummate scholar in his own right in all the mainstream traditions of the sutras and tantras. He also met Batar Khen Tupga at the hermitage of Changma.

Do-ngak Tenpai Nyima attracted many students from all directions and upheld and fostered Mipam Rinpoché's teaching methods. Among his students were Khen Chöchap, Pema Tsewang Lhundrup, Khen Tupten of Mepa, Khen Tupten of Rahor, Khen Dazer, and many other learned masters. He wrote numerous extensive and more concise works, including *The Delineation of the Tenets of the View, An*

Overview of the Perfection of Sublime Knowing, and *A Word-by-Word Commentary on the Perfection of Sublime Knowing*. Do-ngak Tenpai Nyima stayed at the shedra of Zhechen Tennyi Dargyé Ling Monastery, where he turned the wheel of the dharma. Once his guru, Kunpal, had passed away, he carried out his activities on a much broader scale throughout the Dza region. Do-ngak Tenpai Nyima went to see Yukhok Jadralwa Chöying Rangdrol, who, delighted to meet him, treated him with immeasurable respect. Each felt his mind blending and becoming one with the other's. The guru Yukhok Jadralwa Chöying recognized Do-ngak Tenpai Nyima as one of the tulkus of the lord of the dharma Paltrul Rinpoché and spoke of his own memories of having been Dola Jigmé Kalzang.[17] [2.179a]

In the later part of his life, Do-ngak Tenpai Nyima went to Nyima Chang-ra Shedra at Drigung in the northern region of central Tibet. There he unstintingly gave many fortunate people the practice associated with the realm of Sukhavati and teachings on the sutras and tantras. The scope of his enlightened activities was truly enormous in these times of spiritual degeneration.

His student Khenchen Dazer taught the tradition specific to the Early Translation school at such institutions as the shedra of Palyul Monastery in Mysore in the holy country of India, the monastic shedra in Sikkim, and Baprön Tarpa Ling on the plateau of Bumthang in Bhutan. Khenchen Dazer then returned to his home in Tibet, the Land of Snows, where he upheld the teachings at places such as Shri Simha Shedra of Dzogchen Monastery.

Mewa Khenchen Tupten (20th Century)

Mewa Khenchen Tupten, one of Bötrul's own students, was born in the region of Mé in the lowlands of eastern Tibet; his family line included such masters as Khartrul Tenpai Nyima[18] and Khenchen Tsewang Rigdzin[19] (who attained rainbow body). Khenchen Tupten entered the path of the dharma at an early age. [2.179b] He heard teachings and studied at the feet of many mentors, beginning with reading and writing and continuing with the mainstream spiritual sources and other fields of knowledge. In particular, he met Böpa Tulku Do-ngak Tenpai Nyima at Dzachukha in the northern reaches of eastern Tibet. With him, Khenchen Tupten trained extensively, studying the mainstream traditions of sutra and tantra and other subjects.

When the times grew difficult in Tibet, Khenchen Tupten fled to India, where he received from Kyabjé Dudjom Rinpoché empowerments and oral transmissions of the kama and terma teachings of the Early Translation school. He studied the Dzogchen teachings as well, including numerous cycles he learned from Khunu Lama Tendzin Gyaltsen and the great oral transmission from Polu Khenchen Dorjé. Khenchen Tupten also studied any number of teachings with masters such as Kyabjé Dilgo Khyentsé Rinpoché.

He founded a retreat center, called Pang-gar Ritrö, in the region of Kullu in the western part of India, which is one of the twenty-four gathering places. He taught the dharma (principally the Dzogchen approach of the supreme secret) in the foothills of the Himalayas, in such regions as Garzha, Spiti, Khunu, and Ladakh, [2.180a] where he cared for the countless students to be guided who gathered around him with faith, among them lamas, tulkus, monks, nuns, lay people, and tantric practitioners. As well, Khenchen Tupten traveled to Sikkim, Dzogchen Monastery in South India, Bodh Gaya, Nepal, and other areas, teaching the preliminary practices, Vinaya, Abhidharma, Madhyamaka, Prajñaparamita, *The Heart Essence of Secrets, The Four Higher Collections of the Heart Drop,* and other subjects. In such ways, he carried out his enlightened activities to support the study and practice of the precious teachings of the Victorious One, the mandala of his form, adorned with the major and minor marks of perfection, seated on the vajra throne. He passed away recently.

Rahor Khenchen Tupten (20th Century)

Another of Bötrul's students was the sublime Khenchen Tupten of Rahor. In recent times, he traveled to North America and Europe, where he gave teachings and instructions according to the needs of those fortunate enough to be guided by this master. He also restored the monastery in his home region of Rahor, where he sponsored the installation of images and the provision of articles required for group rituals. He passed away recently, having thus nurtured the teachings and beings.

Khen Rinpoché Pema Tsewang Lhundrup (Khenpo Petsé) (1931–2002)

Khenpo Pema Tsewang Lhundrup, another of Bötrul's students, was born in Dzachukha in the Dergé region. He entered the doorway of the dharma at an early age and completed a course of study [2.180b] covering the whole range of subjects pertaining to the sutras, tantras, and other fields of knowledge. In particular, he studied with such masters as Gyalsé Gyurmé Dorjé, Kunchen Bötrul Do-ngak Tenpai Nyima, and Khenchen Tupten Chöpel, receiving the entire body of maturing empowerments and liberating instructions of the profound, secret approach of Dzogchen and putting them into practice. Pema Tsewang Lhundrup became a great mentor in his own right, combining the three qualities of erudition, moral purity, and nobility.

Pema Tsewang Lhundrup taught at Dzogchen Shri Simha Shedra and other institutions, bestowing the nectar of the dharma through his profound and extensive explanatory teachings and written works on the sutras, tantras, and other fields of knowledge. His enlightened activities had a wide impact, with hundreds of thousands of his followers and students supporting the teachings and helping beings throughout India and Tibet.

Khen Chöchap (1920–1997)

Another of Bötrul's students, Khen Chöchap, spent three years studying with Yukhok Jadralwa Chöying Rangdrol, training in the tantras, explanatory commentaries, and pith instructions of the Nyingtik teachings of the Dzogchen approach. As a result, the extraordinary enlightened intent of dharmakaya arose in his mind, so that he could clearly differentiate between ordinary mind and pure awareness. He therefore became known as Chöying Chapdal, or Khenpo Chöchap for short. Following his guru's instructions, [2.181a] Khen Chöchap stayed with Bötrul Do-ngak Tenpai Nyima for twelve years, studying subjects pertaining to the sutras and tantras. He thus reached advanced levels of both erudition and spiritual attainment.

Khen Chöchap's way of life was reminiscent of that of the lord of the dharma Paltrul Rinpoché in that he eschewed all material possessions, living as a true mendicant and renunciant. The attributes of someone holy were as naturally apparent in him as the luster of fine gold. An adornment of the approach of the vajra heart essence, he lived in lower Ser in eastern Tibet. He contributed to the recent revival of the teachings by transmitting the traditions of both the sutras and tantras, emphasizing the Dzogchen approach of utter lucidity.

The foregoing were students of Khenchen Kunpal Rinpoché.

Orgyen Tendzin Norbu (1827–1888)

Another of Paltrul Rinpoché's students—the one even greater than he in explaining the teachings—was Orgyen Tendzin Norbu. From an early age, he showed unparalleled compassion, renunciation, and disenchantment with the world, and so Gyalsé Zhenpen Tayé cared for the boy with great affection.[20] When he was thirteen, Orgyen Tendzin Norbu took ordination and considered his advanced training in the monastic discipline to be as dear to him as his eyes. [2.181b]

With his lord of refuge, Gyalsé Zhenpen Tayé, he studied *The Fifty Verses of a Novice* from the sutra tradition and received from him the entire range of empowerments and instructions for *The Heart Drop of Longchenpa*—both the preliminaries and the main body of practice—from the tantric tradition. He also requested numerous other profound teachings, such as the Six Yogas of Naropa. The fourth Dzogchen, Mingyur Namkhai Dorjé, conferred on him the oral transmissions for the kama tradition of the Early Translation school, as well as the entire range of empowerments and oral transmissions for the great Omniscient One's *Seven Treasuries* and *Four Higher Collections of the Heart Drop*. Orgyen Tendzin Norbu also received teachings based on the enlightened intent of the "four learned masters of India and Tibet," such as those focusing on the Eight Commands and the commentary on Vajrakila entitled *The Black Stupa*, as well as the termas revealed by such masters as Nyima Drakpa of the Mindroling tradition, Ngadak,[21] and the latter's spiritual heirs.

From two masters—Khenchen Pema Badzra and Lingla Tulku Tupten Gyaltsen Palzang—Orgyen Tendzin Norbu requested the oral transmissions for the precious Kangyur, the existing lines of oral transmission for the Tengyur, and the oral transmissions for *The Collected Tantras of the Nyingma School*. He also received the empowerments and oral transmissions for such cycles as *The United Intent of the Gurus* and the collected works of Rongzom Chökyi Zangpo. Terchen Chokgyur Lingpa bestowed on him the Dzogchen cycle *Refined Gold*. [2.182a] Kunzang Tekchok Dorjé taught him the preliminary practices of the Nyingtik cycles, and Drupchen Sönam Palgé thoroughly instructed him in the yogic practices of the Nyingtik teachings that are used to harness the subtle energies. One of his relatives, Jigmé Tapké, who was also known as "the Chö master of Gemang," transmitted to him the entire range of outer and inner pith instructions for the practice of trekchö, the holy guru Nyoshul Lungtok Tenpai Nyima explained the cycle *Being at Ease in the Nature of Mind*, and Geshé Jampa Puntsok taught him works such as *The Entrance into the Middle Way*.

In addition, Orgyen Tendzin Norbu studied with such consummate scholars as the lord of the dharma Mipam, Getsé Lharampa, Kunzang Sönam of Minyak, and Khenpo Lonam, and his discussions with them resolved his doubts. He reached the pinnacle of erudition and accomplishment by training in the presence of many holy masters, like someone refining gold by burning, cutting, and polishing it. It was a matter, as the saying goes, of "the learned adding to the renown of the learned and the learned proclaiming the qualities of the learned." Most notably, Orgyen Tendzin Norbu held discussions with the omniscient lord of the dharma Mipam, so that both might resolve their doubts. [2.182b] Mipam was thoroughly delighted with Orgyen Tendzin Norbu and showered him with praise.

As for his mentors, generally speaking Orgyen Tendzin Norbu served many accomplished masters of awareness; these included some twenty-five learned and accomplished gurus; thirteen gurus who were even kinder in granting him empowerments, instructions, and oral transmissions; two sons of the victorious ones who were as renowned as the sun and moon; one very exalted, unequaled master; and one who was, for Orgyen Tendzin Norbu, the great Vajradhara himself and whose kindness was sublime. Relying on these masters, he received all of their heart advice and became in his own right a master of the entire range of the Victorious One's teachings.

Orgyen Tendzin Norbu had a very special connection with Jamyang Khyentsei Wangpo, who truly was Mañjushri. He received from him the empowerments, oral transmissions, and instructions for *The Heart Drop of Longchenpa;* explanatory teachings on the two "*Chariots*,"[22] commentaries on *The Treasury of Enlightened Qualities*; the bodhisattva vows from the two traditions of the Madhyamaka and Chittamatra[23] schools of Buddhist philosophy; empowerments and oral transmissions for texts such as the Vajrakila commentary *The Black Stupa;* and the entire range of empowerments and oral transmissions for cycles such as *The Heart Drop of Garab*.

Even more important for Orgyen Tendzin Norbu [2.183a] was his connection with the master of his buddha family—the protector of his crown chakra—Paltrul Rinpoché Orgyen Jigmé Chökyi Wangpo, at whose lotus feet he sat from the age of seventeen until he was forty-seven. From him he received teachings on *Engaging in the Conduct of a Bodhisattva, A Compendium of Training,* the collected works of Nagarjuna concerning Madhyamaka, the sutra *The Wise and the Foolish, The Account of Punyabala,* some of the treatises of Maitreya (including *The Ornament of the Sutras, The Ornament of Higher Realization,* and *The Highest Continuum*), *The Treasury of Abhidharma,* Vinaya, and other Indian scriptural sources from the Kangyur and Tengyur. Orgyen Tendzin Norbu listened to and contemplated these teachings, resolving all of his remaining doubts. In addition, although the transmission was not complete, Orgyen Tendzin Norbu received from Paltrul Rinpoché teachings on most of the well-known treatises of the Indian Buddhist tradition, such as *The Classification of the Levels of Realization,* and resolved any doubts he had about these works. Similarly, he studied that most majestic of tantras, *The Heart Essence of Secrets,* and *The Kalachakra Tantra;* the treatise *A Treasury of Enlightened Qualities; The Aspiration Prayer of Sutra and Tantra;* and *Ascertaining the Three Levels of Ordination.*

It was due to his holy guru Paltrul that Orgyen Tendzin Norbu resolved his doubts about all of the theoretical and practical considerations in *The Seven Treasuries,* [2.183b] *The Four Higher Collections of the Heart Drop,* and the collected works of Jigmé Lingpa. Therefore, he would say, "From the point of view of their enlightened qualities, I make no distinctions among my gurus, for the vast majority of them are spiritually advanced beings who have attained high levels of realization. In terms of kindness to me, however, dear old Abu has absolutely been unsurpassed. For me there is no one like him in the three worlds." And he would fold his hands, tears flowing down his cheeks. He also said, "No matter which of the sources of the sutras or tantras I study, I know that all of them are nothing but a means of uniting my mind with that of my root guru, and I know how to unite them all in my cultivation of bodhichitta. That I know these things is due to the compassion of kind old Abu."

Orgyen Tendzin Norbu then pursued his spiritual practice, undertaking intensive retreats on the phases of approach and accomplishment for numerous deities associated with sublime knowing. His intelligence grew like a blazing fire. He had visions of Guru Rinpoché and a large number of his meditation deities. Taking compassion and bodhichitta as the foundation of his spiritual path, he practiced Dzogchen exclusively for twelve years, [2.184a] following in the wake of masters of the past, so that he directly experienced the realization that is the ultimate lineage. He reached the end of the path of trekchö and that of tögal, the path of the four visions. Once he had perfected the dynamic energy of the naturally occurring lamp of sublime knowing, a vast ocean of teachings of the sutras and tantras arose clearly in Orgyen Tendzin Norbu's mind.

Ethically, he was extremely pure, emphasizing the sacred teachings of Vinaya, so that people flocked to him like swans to a lake, and the entire region of Dza in the northern reaches of eastern Tibet became filled with those who had received their novice and full ordinations from him. Until he was fifty-eight, Orgyen Tendzin Norbu took care of his own needs, making his own tea, never requiring even a single monk to serve him. He took as his model the shravaka Mahakashyapa, who embodied the twelve qualities of training. In this and other ways, his conduct was incredible and indescribable—truly that of someone spiritually advanced—and he was foremost among those itinerant masters who have cast off the things of this life. For the benefit of others, he turned the wheel of the dharma during successive periods in his life, teaching as far away as the higher elevations of the central and southern regions of upper Tibet and the lowlands of China. He served those whose intelligence and motivation led them to seek teachings and whose desire to meditate led them to seek pith instructions. [2.184b] He taught at least five times daily on the mainstream sources of the sutras, tantras, and other fields of knowledge, sometimes not stopping even for a cup of tea.

Thus, over the years, he taught *Engaging in the Conduct of a Bodhisattva* more than two hundred times; *The Source Verses on Sublime Knowing* twenty-five times; *The Entrance into the Middle Way* nineteen times; from the treatises of Maitreya, *The Ornament of the Sutras* thirty-nine times, *The Ornament of the Perfection of Sublime Knowing* sixteen times, *The Highest Continuum* thirty-eight times, and the two "Distinction" texts seven or eight times each; *The Fundamental Discourse of the Vinaya* once; *Ascertaining the Three Levels of Ordination* thirty-eight times; *The Treasury of Abhidharma* five times; *The Treasury of Reasoning in Valid Cognition* once; *The Wish-Fulfilling Treasury* nine times; *Being at Ease in the Nature of Mind* thirteen times; *The Treasury of Philosophical Systems* once; *The Heart Essence of Secrets* (also known as *The Web of Magical Display*) twenty times; and *The Treasury of Enlightened Qualities* forty times. Orgyen Tendzin Norbu also taught many times *The Recollection of the Three Jewels, The Source Verses for the Novice Monk, The Twenty Vows, The Seventy Verses on Taking Refuge, The Prayer of Aspiration to Attain the Realm of Bliss* by Chakmé, various extensive explanations of philosophy, *The Six Topics for Gaining Wisdom, The Three Principles of the Spiritual Path, Parting from the Four Attachments,* [2.185a] *The Five Principles of Mahamudra, In Praise of the Vinaya, Verses Summarizing the Compendium of Sublime Knowing, A Letter to a Friend,* Sanskrit grammar, poetry, medicine, the proportions and construction of mandalas and stupas, Indian and Chinese astrology, works on Tibetan grammar, *The Seventy Aspirations,* and many other subjects. Also among the things he taught many times were the preliminaries and the excellent teaching manuals of *The Heart Drop of Longchenpa, The Sevenfold Training of the Mind,* the commentary on the stage of development entitled *The Stairway Ascending to the Pinnacle*

Pure Realm, the yogic practices for harnessing the subtle energies, the Dzogchen teaching manual *Timeless Awareness as the Guiding Principle,* all of the foundational material, *The All-Creating Monarch,* the six bardo states, and various aspects of the practice of Chö. Orgyen Tendzin Norbu thus ensured that the teachings of the lineage of spiritual practice shone like the sun.

Having carried out his enlightened intention to benefit the teachings and beings, with the coming of a Male Earth Rat year,[24] in which he turned sixty, Orgyen Tendzin Norbu gazed into space, making a threatening gesture with his right hand and holding his left hand in his lap in the gesture of meditative equipoise. His last words were his testament:

> I am Guru Padmakara of Orgyen, a buddha free of birth and death.
> Awakened mind is unbiased and free of the concepts of the four or eight extremes. [2.185b]

With these words, Orgyen Tendzin Norbu passed away into the pure realm endowed with twofold purity, Zangdok Palri in the realm of Chamara.

Some of his many students were ones he had in common with the lord of the dharma Paltrul Rinpoché, such as Khen Kunzang Palden, Khen Yönten Gyatso, and Tulku Pema Dechen Zangpo. In particular, his most extraordinary inner heart sons were Zhenpen Chökyi Nangwa, who was a king of the dharma throughout the three realms and who received Orgyen Tendzin Norbu's personal transmission of the explanatory teachings, and Lama Kunga Palden of Dergé, who received the guru's personal transmission of spiritual practice. I fold my hands with heartfelt veneration when I think of the kindness that Orgyen Tendzin Norbu demonstrated in serving the precious teachings.

17

The Students of Orgyen Tendzin Norbu

Orgyen Tendzin Norbu gave two of his students personal transmissions; on one, he bestowed the transmission for spiritual accomplishment and, on the other, that for explanatory teachings.

THE PERSONAL TRANSMISSION FOR SPIRITUAL ACCOMPLISHMENT

Dergé Lama Kunga Palden (19th–20th Centuries)

Orgyen Tendzin Norbu bestowed the transmission for spiritual accomplishment on Kunga Palden, a guru who had been born into a poor family in Galenteng in Dergé. From an early age, Kunga Palden's sole desire was to pursue spiritual practice that focused on the innate experience of the nature of mind. [2.186a] Accordingly, he undertook an intensive retreat on the deity Vajrapani Bhutadamara; during that time, he read the biography of the lord Milarepa, which inspired a deep sense of renunciation in him.

Kunga Palden met Paltrul Rinpoché and, most importantly, the master of his buddha family, Orgyen Tendzin Norbu. He said to them, "Please take me under your care, for I wish to spend my life in spiritual practice, doing intensive retreats on the phases of approach and accomplishment." Both masters saw that he had the appropriate karma and, to begin with, conferred on him many mainstream transmissions from the sutras and tantras. He studied these, after which he said to his precious guru, Orgyen Tendzin Norbu, "I intend to make my life and my spiritual practice one and the same." The guru first granted him teachings on *Being at Ease in the Nature of Mind* and told him, "Meditate for three years, and then we shall see." Consequently, Kunga Palden spent three years at a mountain hermitage focusing his practice on *The Three Cycles of Being at Ease.*

He then returned to his guru, to whom he offered an account of his meditative experiences and realization. Orgyen Tendzin Norbu bestowed on him the pith instructions of *The Innermost Heart Drop of the Guru* through experiential teaching. He said to Kunga Palden, "Spend the rest of your life in solitude in the mountains, focusing your spiritual practice on the very essence." He thus entrusted Kunga Palden with the teachings, granting him a personal transmission of spiritual practice. [2.186b] Kunga Palden practiced accordingly and eventually attained the sublime siddhi through the path of natural great perfection, spending the rest of his life at Ziltrom Nepu, near the glacial retreat area of Dzogchen Monastery. Eschewing even a pillow or a long bed, he sat with his body tied in meditation posture, making his life and his practice one and the same. His practice of trekchö and tögal brought him to the experience of enlightened intent—the perception of awareness's naturally manifest appearances without bias—the point at which phenomena resolve into their true nature. After completing those practices, he undertook a "dark retreat" and directly experienced the visions of utter lucidity, so that the world of appearances and possibilities arose as spheres and enlightened forms, a vast array of purity. Within a sphere of light barely the size of his fingernail, he could see, like magical apparitions, countless buddha realms, as well as pretas and beings in the rest of the six states of existence. This enriched his meditative experiences and realization enormously; Kunga Palden thus became a crown jewel among hundreds of siddhas.

Numerous great masters such as Dzogchen Rinpoché Tupten Chökyi Dorjé, the eleventh Kyabjé Tai Situ Rinpoché of Palpung Monastery, and Khyentsé Rinpoché of Dzongsar Monastery invited Kunga Palden to their respective seats. They received from him the transmission of the great experiential Dzogchen instructions, honoring him as the master of their buddha families. [2.187a] Similarly, he conferred these experiential instructions on the gurus, teachers, meditators, ordained nuns and monks, and lay people who lived in Zhechen, Dzogchen, Katok, Palyul, and other monasteries. His heart children and students included the aforementioned Dzogchen Rinpoché, Palpung Tai Situ Rinpoché, and Dzongsar Khyentsé Rinpoché,[1] as well as Dilgo Khyentsé Rinpoché, Khenchen Tsewang Rigdzin, Sönam Gönpo, Norbu Tendzin, Kardzé Choktrul Lozang Tendzin (a great master who presided over a seat of the Gelukpa school), Jigmé Lodrö, Könchok Zangpo, Chimé Yeshé, Pema Chöpal, and Khunu Lama Tendzin Gyaltsen. The majority of Kunga Palden's students were also students of Khenchen Zhenga Rinpoché. Khunu Lama Tendzin Gyaltsen and Dilgo Khyentsé Rinpoché later went to India and passed the transmission on to the fourteenth Dalai Lama. [2.187b] In such ways, the legacy of Kunga Palden's spiritual instructions continues to spread throughout the world.

Apang Terchen Orgyen Trinlé Lingpa (1895–1945)

Choktrul Lozang Tendzin of Trehor studied with the lord Kunga Palden and the Chö master Dharma Seng-gé, and Apang Terchen in turn studied with Lozang Tendzin. Apang Terchen, also known as Orgyen Trinlé Lingpa, was renowned as the rebirth of Rigdzin Gödem. He was reputed to have been conceived in the following way: Traktung Dudjom Lingpa focused his enlightened intent while resting in the basic space of timeless awareness, whereupon Apang Terchen's mother experienced an intense surge of delight. This caused all ordinary concepts based on confusion to be arrested in her mind for a short time, and it was then that Apang Terchen was conceived in her womb.[2] From that moment on, his mother constantly had dreams that were amazing omens. For example, she found herself among groups of dakinis enjoying the splendor of ganachakras, or being bathed by many dakas and dakinis, or dwelling in pavilions of light, illuminating the entire world with her radiance.

The child was born one morning at dawn, in the area of Serta in eastern Tibet, his mother having experienced no discomfort. Her dwelling was filled with [2.188a] and surrounded by light, as though the sun were shining brightly. There were also pavilions of light, and a fragrance pervaded the entire area, although no one could tell where it came from. Everyone saw numerous amazing signs on the child's body, such as a tuft of vulture feathers adorning the crown of his head.[3] The mother's brother, Sönam Dorjé, asked, "What will become of this boy who has no father? How shameful it would be if people saw these feathers!"[4] But although he cut the feather tuft off the child's head several times, it grew back on its own, just as before. This upset Sönam Dorjé even more, and he berated his sister angrily, saying on numerous occasions, "How could your child have no father? You must tell me who he is!" His sister retorted, "With the truth of karma as my witness, I swear I have never lain with a flesh-and-blood man of this world. This pregnancy might be a result of my own karma." She became so extremely depressed that her fellow villagers couldn't bear it and used various means to bring a halt to her brother's inappropriate behavior.

From an early age, this great master, Apang Terchen, felt an innate and unshakable faith in Guru Rinpoché and had a clear and natural knowledge [2.188b] of the *vajra guru* mantra and the Seven-Line Supplication. He learned how to read and write simply upon being shown the letters and exhibited incredible signs of his spiritual potential awakening. For example, his intelligence, which had been developed through training in former lifetimes, was such that no one could compete with him. As he grew up, he turned his attention toward seeking the quintessential meaning of life. He studied at the feet of many teachers and mentors, including the Nyingtik master Gyatsok Lama Damlo and Terchen Sögyal, studying many of the mainstream traditions of the sutras and tantras, especially those of the kama and terma.

The most extraordinary lord of his spiritual family was Trehor Drakar Tulku,[5] with whom he studied for a long time, receiving the complete range of empowerments, oral transmissions, and pith instructions of the secret Nyingtik cycles of utter lucidity. He went to solitary ravines throughout the region, making caves and overhangs on cliffs his dwelling places, taking birds and wild animals as his companions, and relying on the most ragged clothing and meager diet. He planted the victory banner of spiritual practice, meditating for a long period of time. He was graced by visions of an enormous array of his personal meditation deities, [2.189a] including Tara, Avalokiteshvara, Mañjushri, Sarasvati, and Amitayus. He was not content to leave the true nature of phenomena an object of intellectual speculation, and his realization progressed in leaps and bounds.

Apang Terchen bound the eight classes of gods and demons—including such spirits as Nyenchen Tanglha, Ma Pomra, and Sergyi Drong-ri Mukpo[6]—to his service. He communicated directly with Tsiu Marpo, the white form of Mahakala, Ganapati, and other protective deities, like one person conversing with another, and enjoined them to carry out his enlightened activities. So great was his might that he also bound these protective deities to his service, causing lightning to strike and so forth, so that those who had become his enemies were checked by very direct means, before years, months, or even days had passed.

Notably, he beheld the great master of Orgyen in a vision and was blessed as the regent of Guru Padmakara's three secret aspects. On the basis of a prophecy he received at that time, Apang Terchen journeyed to amazing holy sites, such as Draklha Gönpo in Gyalrong, Khandro Bumdzong in the lowlands of eastern Tibet, and Dorjé Treldzong in Drakar, where he revealed countless terma caches consisting of teachings, objects of wealth, and sacred substances. He revealed some of them in secret, others in the presence of large crowds. In these ways, he revealed a huge trove of profound termas. [2.189b] Those revealed publicly were brought forth in the presence of many fortunate people and in conjunction with truly incredible omens, which freed all present from the bonds of doubt and inspired unshakable faith in them. Apang Terchen's fame as an undisputed siddha and tertön resounded throughout the land, as though powerful enough to cause the earth to quake. His terma teachings are found in the numerous volumes of his collected works and include *The Hidden Treasure of Enlightened Mind: The Thirteen Red Deities*, practices focusing on the Three Roots, cycles concerning guardian deities and the principle of enlightened activity, and his large instruction manual on Dzogchen teachings.

Apang Terchen's students, from Dartsedo in the east, to Repkong in Amdo to the north, to the three regions of Golok and other areas, included mentors who nurtured the teachings and beings, masters such as those known as the "four great illuminators of the teachings," the "four vajra ridgepoles," the "four named Gyatso," the "great masters, the paired sun and moon," and Jangchub Dorjé (the custodian of Apang Terchen's termas).[7] He also taught important political figures who exerted great influence over the people of their areas, including the "four great chieftains of the region of Dza in the north," [2.190a] that is, Getsé Tsering Dorjé of Dza in the northern reaches of eastern Tibet, Gönlha of Akyong in Golok, Mewa Namlo of the Mé region of Golok, and the chieftain of Serta in Washul. Apang Terchen's students also included countless monks, nuns, villagers, and lay tantric practitioners. He transmitted his own termas and the great Nyingtik cycles of the Dzogchen teachings, and so numerous were those he guided that he truly embodied the enlightened activity of one who held sway over the three realms. In these times of spiritual degeneration, he alleviated problems caused by disease, famine, border wars, and civil unrest. In such ways, Apang Terchen rendered great service to the land of Tibet. His kindness to the Tibetan people as a whole was truly extraordinary, for he worked to ensure a glorious state of peace and well-being.

During a pilgrimage to Jowo Yizhin Norbu, the statue of the lord Shakyamuni in Lhasa, Apang Terchen paid respect to many tens of thousands of ordained members of the sangha, sponsoring ganachakras, making offerings, and offering meals, tea, and donations at such monastic centers as Sera, Drepung, and Ganden. He sponsored the gilding of statues in these centers and in such ways strove to reinforce his positive qualities. Everyone could see that no matter how many avenues he found to extend generosity, his resources of gold, silver, and other valuables [2.190b] continued to increase, as though he had access to a treasure mine.

Among his heart children and intimate students were his sons, Gyurmé Dorjé, Wangchen Nyima, and Dotrul Rinpoché; his daughter, Taré Lhamo; and the custodian of his termas, Jangchub Dorjé. Until recently, Taré Lhamo lived in eastern Tibet, maintaining the teachings.[8]

Thus did Apang Terchen benefit beings with his incredible compassion and activities. As his life was nearing an end, he remarked, "For the sake of the teachings and of beings, I must enter the bloodline of the glorious Sakya school." This fearless lion's roar proved to be his last testament, spoken with an unobscured awareness of past, present, and future. He then manifested incredible miracles and departed for the great palace of Pema Ö.

Jangchub Dorjé (20th Century)

The custodian of Apang Terchen's teachings was Jangchub Dorjé. He was clearly prophesied in *The Record of the Transmission of Varahi:*

> There will be a man of short stature, powerful and quick of mind, ༔
> short-tempered, speaking few words, ༔
> of serious demeanor, with diligence and renunciation, ༔
> marked with the sign of a rabbit[9] on his left breast ༔
> and a black mole on his shoulder. ༔ [2.191a]
> He will be the custodian of an entire body of profound termas. ༔
> He will be a child of the innermost heart essence of the lineage holders. ༔
> If none of the auspicious circumstances is interfered with, ༔
> this sun that benefits beings will shine in all directions ༔
> and will certainly dispel darkness throughout the four continents. ༔
> He will lead all those connected to him to Pema Ö. ༔

Born in the household of Gyakor of the Akyong clan of Golok, Jangchub Dorjé embraced the dharma at an early age. He was taken under the care of Terchen Lama,[10] from whom he received a complete transmission of profound teachings. He also studied with Kunzang Nyima (the speech incarnation of Dudjom Lingpa), Jamyang Chökyi Lodrö, Kyabjé Dudjom Rinpoché, and many other mentors.

Having completed his study and contemplation of the topics presented in the tantras, explanatory commentaries, and pith instructions, Jangchub Dorjé went to central Tibet, where he focused on his spiritual practice in all the holy places. Because of the changing times, he fled to Bhutan and India. He pursued his practice in Bhutan at such holy places as Kuretö and Seng-gé Dzong. He transmitted the lineage of Apang Terchen's termas [2.191b] to the latter's tulku, a great master of the glorious Sakya school,[11] and others and spent the rest of his life serving the needs of those to be guided.

The foregoing accounts concern the personal transmission for spiritual practice.

THE PERSONAL TRANSMISSION FOR THE EXPLANATORY TEACHINGS

Zhenga Dorjé Chang (Zhenpen Chökyi Nangwa) (1871–1927)

Orgyen Tendzin Norbu bestowed the second personal transmission, that for the explanatory teachings, on Zhenga Dorjé Chang. Zhenga was born into the wealthy Gyakor family in Dzachukha in the northern reaches of eastern Tibet. Until he was about twenty, he lived as an ordinary householder, engaged in various worldly pursuits.

Then, as the result of several circumstances, he developed a sense of renunciation, his mind turning toward the dharma. He told his household, "You all know what to do with my property. I have decided never to return to this house, even at the cost of my life." Thoroughly disenchanted with samsara, Zhenga resolved to pursue a life of spiritual practice. He went to a hermitage to meet his guru of past lifetimes, Orgyen Tendzin Norbu. There he endured hardships equal to those recorded in the biography of the lord Milarepa, for his home was far away and he had no provisions for his practice. Because his renunciation was so strong, he understood that all of the experiences of his present life [2.192a] were impure and without purpose, like a mass of phlegm to be coughed up. His deportment always respectful, Zhenga applied himself to his studies, beginning with reading and writing and gradually progressing.

He encountered many difficulties along the way. His resources were so meager that he would retrieve the old butter pouches the guru's attendants had discarded, scrape off the film of butter with his nails, and eat it to assuage a nervous condition. This condition forced Zhenga to walk bent over when he went to draw water. But his fortitude, that of someone holy, increased like a raging forest fire, and he redoubled his efforts to listen to and contemplate teachings. Several of his unruly fellow students would mock him, saying, "Here's this young scion of the Gyakor family, just like a little kid first learning his ABCs. We should call him the 'the old kid.'" Thus his way of life caused Zhenga much hardship.

Once as he hobbled to fetch water, his guru, Orgyen Tendzin Norbu, saw him and folded his hands to pray, tears falling from his eyes. He thought to himself, "This student truly has the appropriate karma," and decided that he should provide Zhenga with some means of support. [2.192b] But after reflecting further, he gripped his hands and said to himself, "Wait! Wait! Sit still! Don't interfere with Zhenga, who conducts himself like a bodhisattva in enduring such hardship for the sake of the dharma, just like the exalted masters of the past." And so he kept his peace and pretended not to see what was going on.

It was about this time that he said to Zhenga, "As an extension of your studies, you should undertake a retreat on the goddess Sarasvati." Zhenga did so and directly experienced signs of accomplishment. The goddess Sarasvati revealed herself to him in visions, and his intelligence blazed like a fire, awakening tendencies established during his training in previous lifetimes. He instantly mastered all the key points of whatever his guru taught him, gained confidence in debating and writing without impediment, and even composed a prayer of praise to Sarasvati. When he debated with many of his fellow students at the encampment, no one could best him. Occasionally, one of the older students would gain a point and try to circle Zhenga's head with his hand in the ritual gesture that indicates victory in a formal debate. But the guru Orgyen Tendzin Norbu would say, "Hey, don't do that! [2.193a] Don't do that! Don't put your hands over Zhenga's head! Just leave it alone!"

One day, an older student said to Orgyen Tendzin Norbu, "Precious guru, I thought you were above prejudice, but you're not. You always treat this new, talented student Zhenga with some deference. It seems inappropriate for a guru to show favoritism toward a student. Can you explain this?"

Orgyen Tendzin Norbu replied, "Well, it's not that I favor Zhenga; it's that all of you are so dense and have such impure perceptions. Zhenga is what the sutras refer to as a bodhisattva who has only one lifetime left before attaining enlightenment. Treating him with disrespect—stepping over him or touching him on the head—will harm the activities of such teachers as Kundri and Yöndri" (the nicknames for Kunpal and Yönga[12] in the nomad dialect of the Dza region) "and interfere with their ability to benefit beings as teachers of the dharma. So I am really showing favoritism toward you, my older students."

From then on, all the residents of the encampment treated the lord Zhenga as they did their guru. [2.193b] Orgyen Tendzin Norbu gradually conferred on him teachings from the oral traditions of Gyalsé Zhenpen Tayé, the lord of the dharma Paltrul, and other masters; these included *Engaging in the Conduct of a Bodhisattva, The*

Source Verses on Sublime Knowing, The Entrance into the Middle Way, The Ornament of the Sutras, Prajñaparamita, *The Highest Continuum,* the two treatises *The Distinction Between Phenomena and Their True Nature and The Distinction Between the Center and Limit, The Fundamental Discourse of the Vinaya, Ascertaining the Three Levels of Ordination, The Treasury of Abhidharma, The Treasury of Reasoning in Valid Cognition, Being at Ease in the Nature of Mind, The Twenty Vows, The Five Principles of Mahamudra, The Three Principles of the Spiritual Path, Parting from the Four Attachments,* Sanskrit grammar, poetics, *A Letter to a Friend,* medicine, and Indian and Chinese astrology. Zhenga went on to study the sutras, tantras, and other fields of knowledge.

Most notably, Orgyen Tendzin Norbu bestowed on Zhenga an extraordinary transmission of all the tantras, explanatory commentaries, and pith instructions of his own tradition of the Early Translation school. It consisted of everything from Vinaya and Abhidharma up to the pinnacle approach of the heart essence of utter lucidity and included *The Seven Treasuries,* commentaries on *The Heart Essence of Secrets, The Treasury of Enlightened Qualities, Timeless Awareness as the Guiding Principle,* the three Yangtik cycles, and other works by the Omniscient One and his spiritual heir, Jigmé Lingpa. Zhenga listened to and meditated on these teachings, and realization born of his meditation arose in him. His wisdom blossoming, he discovered a fearless confidence concerning the entire range of mainstream sources. [2.194a]

Unhindered in explaining, debating, and writing about the teachings, and having taken full monastic ordination, Zhenga took as his inspiration the lives of great elders of the Indian Buddhist tradition. A threefold vajra holder, he was like a mountain of gold, untainted by the slightest fault or failing. He thus attained the pinnacle of the three qualities of erudition, venerability, and nobility, and his guru came to consider him his single heart son on the inner level. He gave Zhenga his own copies of commentaries on the sutras and tantras, especially the so-called thirteen great source texts—commentaries on Madhyamaka, Prajñaparamita, Vinaya, Abhidharma, and so forth, written by Indian Buddhist scholars and included in the Tengyur. He told Zhenga, "Base your teachings primarily on these. The students who uphold your lineage will be like the constellations of stars in the sky, so that the precious teachings of the Victorious One will shine like the sun." With such prophecies, Orgyen Tendzin Norbu entrusted Zhenga with the teachings, investing him as a lineage holder with permission to explain them.

Zhenga conducted himself like someone who had received a personal transmission from the Buddha, and his mind blended inseparably with his guru's. For thirteen years, he served his guru in this way. [2.194b] He would say things that reflected his deep satisfaction, such as "Whether or not I rely on many other tutors and mentors, my guru is Orgyen Tendzin Norbu" and "I am not lacking in positive karma; in fact,

I am so very fortunate to have taken Orgyen Tendzin Norbu as the master of my buddha family."

From time to time, Zhenga engaged in intensive retreats on the deities of the Three Roots, and signs of his accomplishment of these practices were evident. He had countless visions of the deities. With unwavering faith and devotion, he prayed especially to the Omniscient King of the Dharma, Longchenpa, and had a vision in which he was cared for by Longchenpa's timeless awareness embodiment. Zhenga directly experienced the realization of the ultimate lineage and composed a prayer of praise to the great Omniscient One. In the aftermath of this vision, the dynamic energy of the naturally occurring lamp of sublime knowing unfolded for Zhenga, who mastered the entire range of mainstream sources. Regardless of what difficult point he was asked to clarify in the sutras and tantras, without looking at the text in question, whether from the Kangyur or the Tengyur, he could visualize the pertinent page and verse and explain it from memory without error. [2.195a] The guru Orgyen Tendzin Norbu would say to his students, "Whatever doubts you have or clarification you need, ask Zhenga. He is my equal."

After his guru passed away, Zhenga stayed at Orgyen Tendzin Norbu's seat to fulfill the guru's intentions. Acting as his regent, he taught students from all over, turning the wheel of the dharma many times, teaching such texts as *The Fundamental Discourse of the Vinaya; The Three Hundred Verses;* many treatises of the Indian Buddhist tradition, such as the commentaries on *The Immense Display, The Journey to Shri Lanka,* and the sutra *The Request of Akshayamati; The Treasury of Reasoning in Valid Cognition;* Madhyamaka texts (*The Source Verses on Sublime Knowing, Engaging in the Conduct of a Bodhisattva, The Four Hundred Verses,* and *The Entrance into the Middle Way*); *The Five Treatises of Maitreya; The Treasury of Enlightened Qualities; Ascertaining the Three Levels of Ordination; The Wish-Fulfilling Treasury; The Heart Essence of Secrets;* the basic works on Tibetan grammar; the commentary on Sanskrit grammar entitled *Illumination;* the treatise on metrics entitled *The Source of Jewels;* the four medical tantras; and *The Six Topics for Gaining Wisdom.* In addition, Zhenga continued to receive teachings from many of the gurus and tulkus of Zhechen, Dzogchen, and other monasteries, teachers such as Khenchen Pema Dorjé, Tsamtrul Kunzang Dechen Dorjé, and Mura Tulku.

Then, by the directive of Dzogchen Tupten Chökyi Dorjé, [2.195b] Zhenga was invited to Shri Simha Shedra at Dzogchen Monastery and appointed one of the successive khenpos of that institution. He wrote a great many works on the sutras, tantras, and other fields of knowledge. Among these were his annotated commentaries on the works of Indian Buddhist scholars, the thirteen great source texts foremost among them. These thirteen texts included Vinaya sources (the sutra *Individual Liberation* and *The Fundamental Discourse of the Vinaya*), Abhidharma sources (*The Treasury of Abhidharma* and *The Compendium of Abhidharma*), the sources of the "lineage of profound view" (*The Source Verses on Sublime Knowing, Engaging in the Conduct of a Bodhisattva, The Four Hundred Verses,* and *The Entrance into the Middle Way*), and the sources of the "lineage of vast conduct" (the five works known as *The Five Treatises of Maitreya*). He composed an annotated commentary on *The Heart Essence of Secrets,* a collection of popular essays, a collection of prayers of praise, dohas, pithy advice, and a biography of his own guru, Orgyen Tendzin Norbu.

Students from Dzogchen Monastery and its affiliates flocked to the shedra like geese to a lake in summer. Zhenga imparted to them general teachings from the oral traditions of Gyalsé Zhenpen Tayé and the lord of the dharma Paltrul, primarily the thirteen great source texts. More specifically, he extensively taught *The Heart Essence of Secrets, The Seven Treasuries,* and other works, emphasizing those of the Omniscient One and his spiritual heir, Jigmé Lingpa. [2.196a] As a result of his explanations of *The Seven Treasuries* and the fact that he was said to have memorized the thirteen great source texts and the precious Kangyur, he became renowned throughout that part of the world for his erudition. From upper Tibet and the Khunu region of India to the west, and from Bhutan to the south, to the lowlands of eastern Tibet and as far away as China and Mongolia, students flocked to him like constellations of stars in the sky, and his guru's prophecies concerning him were fulfilled.

When Zhenga taught, he did not confine himself merely to the literal sense of the words. He would present the profound view of the Prasangika school in keeping with the enlightened intent of the glorious Chandrakirti,[13] which involves applying the scriptures and reasoning of Madhyamaka to one's inner sense of self and the seeming reality of things. His students thus experienced all phenomena decisively according to the eight metaphors for illusion; they found, moreover, that their tendency to invest things (such as buildings) with reality was undermined and that they could perceive the world without obstruction. When Zhenga taught *Engaging in the Conduct of a Bodhisattva, The Entrance into the Middle Way,* and other such works, he would recite passages like the following: "Whenever the ordinary mind is free of concepts of what is or is not substantial, no other specific concern exists, and there is utter peace without any fixed frame of reference," and "Whenever there is unborn suchness, the mind is free of any question of origination." The guru would rest in meditation, and as he directed his enlightened intent, born of the realization of originally pure great perfection, many people were introduced to their own true nature. [2.196b] His amazing qualities were truly indescribable. Scholars unanimously praised Zhenga because of his definitive conclusions concerning the enlightened intent of the Prasangika school, saying, "A second Chandrakirti has come."

Indistinguishable as he was from the principal deity of the mandala, he became known as Zhenga Dorjé Chang.[14] He was known to impart the main body of Dzogchen teachings to those who had not completed the usual preliminary practices, for he felt that there was no greater way to refine away obscurations than to study the thirteen great source texts. He received all of the empowerments, instructions, and advice of the glorious Sakya school's Lamdré cycle from Jamyang Loter Wangpo. Once during that time, the deity as an expression of timeless awareness appeared to him; he also directly experienced other signs associated with this path. He thus accepted the lord Loter Wangpo as the master of his buddha family and composed a prayer of praise to him.

Zhenga was repeatedly praised as an emanation of Sakya Pandita by Gatön Ngawang Lekpa,[15] who said, "I dreamed that the lord Mañjushri, Sakya Panchen, returned to this world, [2.197a] and he is Zhenga." Jamgön Mipam Rinpoché showered praise on Zhenga, stating, "My commentaries on the mainstream sources are my legacy to the teachings of the Early Translation school; may they ensure for future generations that the precious teachings of the Victorious One endure. But the directive Zhenga Rinpoché received was that of spreading the theory and practice of the teachings in all directions, while holding to the enlightened intent of the glorious Chandrakirti, and of Rongzom and Longchenpa, as the life force of those teachings. Zhenga received this directive as a result of Gyalsé Zhenpen Tayé's aspirations and the fact that he is Gyalsé Zhenpen's rebirth."

As for his heart children, Zhenga's songs of realization make it clear that an incredible number of his students were great, spiritually advanced beings in human form. Not all of them can be listed, but to give some idea of those he taught, there were Chökyi Lodrö (who was Mañjushri in person), [2.197b] Tai Situ Rinpoché Pema Wangchok Gyalpo of Palpung Monastery, Kyabjé Dilgo Khyentsé Rinpoché, Tuksé Rahor Chödrak, Serkha Chödrak, Khenchen Öntö Jamyang Chenrap, Zurmang Khenchen Pema Namgyal, Khenchen Tupten Nyendrak, Khenchen Lhagong, Khenchen Yönten Gönpo, Khenchen Ngawang Norbu, Khenchen Pema Tsewang, Nyarong Guru Tulku, Bo Gangkar Tulku, Dzigar Kongtrul, Ayang Tupten (also known as Gelong Rinpoché), the sublime tulku of the Gelukpa school Tendzin Nyendrak, Khunu Tendzin Gyaltsen of India, Geshé Tenpa Rinchen of Bhutan, Geshé Rinchen Dorjé, Geshé Pema Tsering, Geshé Tsultrim Palzang, Geshé Namgyal Palzang, Drupgyü Rinpoché, Lukru Khenchen, Chapra Khenchen, and others. The gurus, tulkus, teachers, meditators, monks, lay masters, and nuns who were Zhenga's students and his students' students [2.198a] came from a vast area that encompassed the lowlands of China, Xining in the north, Mongolia, Dergé, India, and the Himalayan border regions of Nepal and Bhutan.

Zhenga was invited by Jamyang Chökyi Lodrö, Palpung Tai Situ Rinpoché Pema Wangchok Gyalpo, the Drigung Kyabgön, and other masters to found such institutions as Khamjé Shedra, Palpung Shedra, Nyima Chang-ra Shedra at Drigung, Kyekundo Shedra, and Menyak Shedra. Here the sutras, tantras, and other fields of knowledge were taught and studied, with special emphasis on the thirteen great source texts. Zhenga was responsible, directly or indirectly, for the founding of eighteen such shedras and, in this and other ways, supported the precious teachings of the Victorious One. He was also renowned as Sang-gyé Zhenpenpa,[16] for he was like a second Buddha in serving the teachings during these times of spiritual degeneration.

In the later part of his life, Zhenga lived like lord Zhepa Dorjé,[17] frequenting solitary mountain sites such as the glacial waste above Dzogchen Monastery and Gyawo Nenang. There he applied himself entirely to planting the victory banner of spiritual practice, [2.198b] practicing continuously day and night, immersed in what is genuine without deliberate design, natural great perfection. He lived as an itinerant master, foremost among renunciants.

Having completed his practice and fulfilled the purpose of his life, Zhenga attained the most sublime siddhi through the pinnacle approach, the path of the heart essence of utter lucidity. Without any signs of illness or discomfort, the outward manifestation of his emanated form resolved back into the inner basic space of original purity, the youthful vase body. His remains shrank to a cubit in height. Tai Situ Rinpoché Pema Wangchok, Khenchen Lhagyal, Dzogchen Rinpoché, Khenchen Gönpo, and others of his heart children and students performed the cremation ceremonies. The sky was a deep, dark blue, a pure field against which pavilions of rainbow lights played. Flower blossoms showered down, and a natural state of meditation arose in all present. As an indication that Zhenga had awakened to buddhahood within the basic space of the five kayas by following the path of the sublime spiritual approach, relics impervious to the elements, small and large relics of the five buddha families, were found (the large relics are called *shariram, churiram, nyariram, bariram,* and *seriram*). [2.199a] Zhenga passed away amid innumerable such amazing signs, inspiring faith in his fortunate students.

Among the teachings of the Victorious One,
by explaining, writing about, and promulgating the traditions of
Nagarjuna and Asanga
you caused them to spread throughout the three planes of existence.
Your deeds on behalf of the Lord of Sage's teachings were those of the
Sage himself.
You, Sang-gyé Zhenpenpa, are the buddha for these times of degeneration.

This great master thought only of the Victorious One's teachings, promoting the higher training in discipline everywhere—for that is the basis of the teachings—and implementing the practice of the monastic tradition. Zhenga founded shedras in these monastic communities, where he taught the sutras, tantras, and other fields of knowledge, thus ensuring that the very essence of the teachings would endure. His students and the lineages still flourish.

For a general idea of his activities, consider the following. After his tenure as the director of Dzogchen Shri Simha Shedra, Zhenga was accepted by both Jamgön Chökyi Lodrö and the eleventh Tai Situ Rinpoché of Palpung Monastery [2.199b] as the master of their buddha families. He founded shedras at their respective seats. The first of these was Kham Jema Ling at Dzongsar Monastery, where he was the first abbot to mount the golden throne. There, for students who came from all directions, he turned the wheel of the dharma, teaching the sutras, tantras, and other fields of knowledge and producing many leading scholars, including Khenchen Öntöpa Jamyang Chenrap and Khenchen Lama Jamyang Tapké. Khamjé became a second Nalanda University in eastern Tibet. Next in the abbatial succession was Chenrap Rinpoché, followed by Khangmar Khenchen Rinchen, Dezhung Khenchen Chöpel, Dragyab Khenchen Lodrö, Minyak Khenchen Damchö, Dotsul Khenchen Tupten, Khenchen Chenrap Seng-gé, and others. Zhenga founded many other shedras—branches of Khamjé—throughout eastern Tibet, at the monasteries of Trom Dokhol and Öntö, among other places.

He promulgated the transmission of the scholarly approach to the teachings, and such figures as Khenchen Appey of the Sakya tradition, [2.200a] Khen Rinchen, Öntö Khen Khedrup, Khen Kunga Wangchuk Rinpoché, and the lord of scholars Dongtrul Tenpai Gyaltsen represent this tradition in India to this day. There these masters have founded centers such as the Sakya College and Dzongsar College (in the Dergé refugee center). Through their activities of explaining, debating, and writing about the teachings, the tradition of teachers explaining and students listening to the teachings has spread to the Western Hemisphere, as far away as the United States.

Khenchen Jampal Zangpo also founded a Sakya shedra in the western Tibetan highlands and from that base founded an affiliate shedra at Ngor Monastery in the Tsang region. The tradition of giving and receiving teachings flourished throughout Tsang and greatly influenced the Sakyapa lineage's approach to the explanation of the major source texts.

According to a plan he developed in collaboration with Jamyang Loter Wangpo, Zhenga founded a shedra at the great monastery of the glorious Sakya tradition in Ga, called Kyekundo, and became its first abbot. There he turned the wheel of the dharma, training many great masters who became lineage holders in their own right in the regions of Ga and Denkhok. [2.200b] His principal student was Khenchen Jamyang Gyaltsen of Ga, who reached consummate levels of both erudition and spiritual attainment.

Zhenga's activities extended to all of the eastern Tibetan Sakya centers, where he gave teachings on a vast scale. He served as a great pillar of this tradition. Thus, for the Sakyapas, Zhenga Dorjé Chang was a second Jamgön Sakya Pandita. That his activities served the teachings is clearly evident to everyone.

The Students of Zhenga Dorjé Chang

Palpung Tai Situ Rinpoché Pema Wangchok Gyalpo (1886–1952)

Tai Situ Rinpoché Pema Wangchok Gyalpo of Palpung Monastery accepted Zhenga Dorjé Chang as the master of his buddha family. He received from him the great experiential teachings of the Dzogchen approach and the extraordinary profound empowerment for Dechen Gyalmo, the feminine aspect of *The Heart Drop of Longchenpa*. Thus Pema Wangchok Gyalpo directly experienced realization of the great perfection. He helped to found a shedra at his seat of Palpung Chökhor Lhunpo[18] and held a post as teacher there, a king of the dharma throughout the three realms. He turned the wheel of the dharma, teaching the sutras and tantras, and eventually had many learned and accomplished students, such as Khenchen Pema Namgyal, Lukru Khenchen, Chapra Khenchen, Bo Gangkar Tulku, and Dzigar Kongtrul. [2.201a] He also oversaw the abbatial succession at the main shedra and instituted a curriculum focusing on the great source texts. His enlightened activities increased, becoming as extensive as the sky itself.

Zurmang Khenchen Pema Namgyal (20th Century)

Khenchen Pema Namgyal, Mañjushri in person, founded the shedra at Zurmang Namgyaltsé Monastery.[19] There he turned the wheel of the dharma, benefiting beings enormously. Lineages of his students who upheld this mainstream tradition spread beyond Zurmang to all areas of Tibet: the western highlands, the central region, and the eastern lowlands. He wrote a practice associated with the pure realm of Sukhavati that inspired all those connected to him to aspire to rebirth in that pure realm.

Heeding his guru's instructions, Pema Namgyal composed many works that captivated the minds of fine scholars, such as teaching guides, structural analyses, and overviews of the great source texts; *The Timely Moon,* a collection of answers to his students' questions; and a commentary on *The Prayer of Aspiration to Attain the Realm of Bliss*. He thus rendered immeasurable service, nurturing the teachings and beings.

During the time that Pema Namgyal's emanated form finally resolved back into its ultimate nature, he sat for three days on the teaching throne, while canopies of rainbow light swirled and flower blossoms showered down. [2.201b] Large and small relics were found wherever the smoke from his funeral pyre billowed. This incarnation thus withdrew for a time to the blissful realm of Ö Migyurwa amid such amazing signs and events.

Among Pema Namgyal's students were Zurmang Tenga Tulku Rinpoché, Khenchok Losel, and Khen Chenrap Tarchin. Their students in turn included such figures as Nyima Lungtrul Lama and Geshé Pema of Bumthang in Bhutan, and the lineage of students has continued to the present day with masters like Lama Yeshé.

Zurmang Tenga Rinpoché (20th Century)

Tenga Rinpoché was invited by the sixteenth Gyalwa Karmapa to Tsurpu Monastery in the valley known as Tölung. With this monastery as his base, he taught the dharma throughout the western highlands of Tibet.[20]

The First Dzigar Kongtrul Rinpoché (1901?–1963?)

Dzigar Kongtrul Rinpoché moved to Kham Riwoché in eastern Tibet, where he founded and oversaw a shedra. Becoming a consummate scholar, he bestowed such transmissions as those for *The Treasury of Precious Hidden Teachings* and *The Treasury of Spiritual Instructions*. His many written works include extensive and concise commentaries on the great source texts, as well as collections of songs of realization. He carried out a vast range of activities in that region.

Bo Gangkar Rinpoché (Karma Shedrup Chökyi Seng-gé) (1892–1957)

Gangkar Rinpoché embodied a consummate degree of erudition, venerability, and nobility. He and Zurmang Pema Namgyal studied together [2.202a] with Zhenga Rinpoché at Shri Simha Shedra. Gangkar Rinpoché was extraordinarily intelligent and could memorize more than a hundred pages of the Kangyur daily. For a considerable time, he was the tutor of the sixteenth Gyalwa Karmapa. He then returned to his home region of Bokhok, where he studied and taught at the shedra. In time, he went to China, where he turned the wheel of the dharma extensively.

His students, who not only have faith in and devotion for, but also support, both the Kagyü and Nyingma schools, are to this day to be found in Hong Kong and Taiwan, as well as in mainland China. They have continued the transmission of the monastic discipline and the explanation of the teachings. Gangkar Rinpoché served as a true pillar of the teachings; his activities made him as important to the Dakpo Kagyü school as was the seventh Karmapa, Chödrak Gyatso.[21]

Nyarong Guru Tulku (20th Century)

Guru Tulku of Nyarong, a student of Zhenga Rinpoché, was invited by the Drigung Kyabgön to found the illustrious Nyima Chang-ra Shedra at Drigung in the northern part of central Tibet. [2.202b] There he bestowed a wealth of teachings, explaining the sutras and tantras (especially the thirteen great source texts) and conferring maturing empowerments and liberating instructions. His activities on behalf of the Victorious One's teachings were so superb that it was as though the Victorious One himself had returned. The victorious ones of the ten directions and their heirs showered him with praise.

The first abbot of that institution was Guru Tulku himself; the second, Khenchen Norbu Gyaltsen; the third, Namlang; the fourth, Tsenden Zangpo; and so on. Guru

Tulku's countless students included many learned and accomplished masters. Many of them, including Khenpo Ngedön of Takmo Lüjin, Nepal, are still living.

Drukpa Geshé Tenpa Rinchen (20th Century)

Geshé Tenpa Rinchen of Bhutan was another of Zhenga's students. This holy master founded a monastery and shedra in Tarpa Ling, which had been the seat of the Omniscient One when he was in Bhutan. There Tenpa Rinchen studied and taught the sutras, tantras, and other fields of knowledge on an enormous scale. [2.203a] Due to his kindness in promoting the theory and practice of the teachings, many of his students, including Geshé Pema Trinlé, Katok Lama Ngawang Trinlé, the lord Khenchen Yeshé Seng-gé, Lopön Norwang, and Lama Terchung, became lineage holders in their own right.

Geshé Pema Trinlé and Lama Terchung founded Tali Shedra. The two lord khenchens received teachings from Katok Lama. In these and other ways, a vast array of activities was accomplished for the sake of the teachings and beings.

Other Students

Another of Zhenga's students, Geshé Rinchen Dorjé, served for a long time as a guru at both Chödrak Monastery and Tarpa Ling, teaching at and restoring these monastic centers. He also initiated extensive projects to create new representations of enlightened form, speech, and mind—statues, texts, and stupas, respectively.

In a similar way, Geshé Pema Tsering traveled throughout eastern Bhutan, serving as a guru at all of the monasteries there. He promoted the teachings by turning the wheel of the dharma, explaining the sutras and tantras. Geshé Tsultrim Palzang taught at Kujé in Bumthang, the site sacred to Guru Rinpoché, explaining the source texts and conferring maturing empowerments and liberating instructions. Drupgyü Rinpoché of Golok [2.203b] went to Tarpa Ling, where he gave to his fortunate students many profound transmissions, both common and extraordinary, such as those for *Timeless Awareness as the Guiding Principle,* the Dzogchen teachings of *The Treasury of the Basic Space of Phenomena,* and the great experiential instruction lineage of the Nyingtik teachings.

As recorded in Zhenga Rinpoché's biography, an incredible number of learned and accomplished masters, like a range of golden mountains, came from his main seat of Shri Simha Shedra at Dzogchen Monastery. They included Khenchen Lhagyal (also known as Khenchen Lhagong), Khenchen Gönpo, and Khenchen Tupten Nyendrak. Their activities, which included studying and teaching at the Dzogchen shedras and affiliate monasteries throughout eastern Tibet, flourished everywhere, like grass growing in the summertime. This lineage has continued to the present day, extending from Tibet to India, Sikkim, Bhutan, and beyond to the rest of the world.

Lama Gyalwang Nyima and Khenchen Tsöndrü (both of whom were students of Khenchen Gönpo), Khenchen Tupten Nyendrak, Khenchen Lhagyal, and others moved to India. The government school of Semtok Kharik officially opened in Bhutan, and Kyabjé Dilgo Khyentsé Rinpoché [2.204a] and Khenchen Tsöndrü served as its head teachers for more than two years. After this, Lama Gyalwang Nyima served for two terms as headmaster. There he taught fortunate, intelligent students, training them in fields of secular knowledge and commenting on the source texts. He thus ensured benefit for beings throughout Bhutan.

Khenchen Tsöndrü (1920–1979)

Khenchen Tsöndrü was born in Akyong Gongma, Golok. He entered the path of the dharma at an early age and gradually made his way to the hermitage of Batar and to Dzogchen Monastery in eastern Tibet, where he relied on a number of teachers—Khenchen Tupten Chöpel, Khenchen Tupten Nyendrak, Khenchen Gönpo, Khenchen Lhagyal, and others—and accepted Kongtrul Rinpoché of Zhechen Monastery as the extraordinary master of his buddha family. He studied the sutras, tantras, and other fields of knowledge on an enormous scale. His nature was such that he became a wandering mendicant, and he studied, trained, and practiced diligently at random sites throughout the region.

He traveled to Lhasa in central Tibet, where he offered prostrations to and circumambulated the three statues of the Buddha; [2.204b] he also trained for a time at Sera Monastery. He gradually made his way to India, where he served Kyabjé Dudjom Rinpoché and Kyabjé Dilgo Khyentsé Rinpoché, receiving many profound teachings from them.

Khenchen Tsöndrü taught, debated, and wrote treatises at such institutions as Tekchok Namdrol Shedrup Dargyé Ling, the monastery of the Palyul lineage in Mysore, South India; Ngedön Gatsal Ling at Mindroling Monastery in Dehra Dun; the Tibetan Institute of Higher Studies in Varanasi; and the shedra in Sikkim. He thus promoted the teachings of the Victorious One. Several volumes of his written works have survived.

Two of his students, Khenpo Dazer and Khenpo Palden Sherab, live in the United States. He also taught Khen Pema Sherab, Khenpo Namdrol, Gyalsé Tulku, Dakpo Tulku, Khen Gyurmé Trinlé, Khen Dechen Dorjé, Khen Rigdzin, Ngari Khen Yeshé Zangpo, Khen Könchok Özer, Khen Norbu, and others. Thus Khenchen Tsöndrü's activities have flourished in the holy country of India and in many countries of the West. [2.205a]

In addition, students of Khen Lhagyal and Khen Gönpo, including Mewa Khenchen Jampal and Gulok Khenpo, have taught extensively in Mekhok (at the great center of the Early Translation school called Tri Darjé Monastery), the region of Golok to the north, and other areas, caring for students throughout the northern ranges of eastern Tibet.

Nyoshul Khenchen Ngawang Palzang Rinpoché (20th Century)

Khenchen Ngawang Palzang of Nyoshul was an emanation of Panchen Vimalamitra and studied under Zhenga Rinpoché, learning the sublime spiritual approach, the profound Madhyamaka view as found in the entire corpus of Nagarjuna's works on reasoning, especially *The Source Verses on Sublime Knowing*. He passed on these teachings at the shedra of glorious Katok Monastery to ensure that they flourished, and thus they spread throughout that region.

Tuksé Serkha Chödrak (19th–20th Centuries)

Serkha Chödrak, learned, venerable, and noble, was a heart son of Zhenga endowed with such profound bodhichitta that simply meeting him inspired faith in people. As part of his mission to benefit beings, he went to Minyak and other areas in eastern Tibet, [2.205b] where he founded monasteries and shedras within the extensive tradition of the Early Translation school. He invited Zhenga, the master of his buddha family (whom he regarded as an actual buddha), to these places, and spiritual father and son together carried out innumerable activities—the result of their collective noble aspirations—for the sake of the teachings and beings. They taught the mainstream source texts extensively, training a great many who became holders of the tradition of Dzogchen Monastery. In these and other ways, their activities spread to fill all of space. Tsara Chödrak and others continued to serve the teachings of the heart essence in these regions.

Rahor Palden Chökyi Drakpa (?–1901)

Rahor Palden Chökyi Drakpa, another heart son of Zhenga Rinpoché, lived at Rahor Monastery in his youth. At the age of twenty, he completed the preliminary practices of the Dzogchen approach, as well as personal retreats focusing on the deities of the Three Roots. He then made a vow to his guru, who presided over the monastery, to abandon everything related to this life. His guru accepted his vow and instructed Rahor Chödrak to go to Shri Simha Shedra at Dzogchen Monastery, where with Zhenga Rinpoché he studied the sutras, tantras and other fields of knowledge. With constant devotion and great diligence, Rahor Chödrak relied on his mentors [2.206a] for sixteen years, reaching the pinnacle of erudition and spiritual attainment.

Since everyone who attended Shri Simha Shedra was a scholar—there was no one who was not learned—it was difficult to acquire a reputation as someone erudite. However, among Zhenga's heart sons, the "two named Chödrak" did achieve this status, and people said, "Rahor Chödrak is most learned in the tantric approach."

While at the shedra, he had few provisions and endured many hardships for the sake of the teachings. At his full monastic ordination, he did not even have a formal robe, so his guru, Zhenga Rinpoché, lent him one. Zhenga would praise him to the skies, saying things like, "Chödrak is such a yogin, always absorbed in his practice; no one can rival him."

Chödrak then returned to his own monastery of Rahor, where he founded a shedra and turned the wheel of the dharma for more than three years, teaching many fortunate people the sutras, tantras, and other fields of knowledge. Many of his students became learned and accomplished masters in their own right.

Rahor Chödrak went back to Shri Simha, where he served with body, speech, and mind [2.206b] as his guru's personal attendant. During that time, he did not take so much as a cup of water from his guru, for as he said, "To misappropriate something belonging to one's guru is more serious than taking something from others." Never careless in even the smallest matter of karmic causality, Rahor Chödrak set an example that inspired awe in the faithful.

One day, Zhenga Rinpoché was invited to teach Chung-rampa, a general in the Tibetan army. The guru replied, "I cannot come, but will send Chödrak instead." He gave Rahor Chödrak a set of three monastic robes and a ceremonial hat and told him, "Go to Lhasa in central Tibet to serve as tutor to Chung-rampa. You have students to guide in Drigung to the north of Lhasa, my son; go there as well." Accordingly, Rahor Chödrak set out, planting the victory banner of practice while applying the teachings of the ultimate heart essence. He journeyed in stages through eastern, central, and southern Tibet, as well as to the southern borders and Bhutan, visiting all of the holy places. He finally took up residence at the hermitage in the valley known as Chölung, near Nyima Chang-ra Shedra at Drigung. There he dwelled like the lord Milarepa, a true king among renunciants and a crown jewel among a hundred siddhas. Day and night, he pursued his spiritual practice, [2.207a] living an incredible life and bringing all who saw, heard, thought of, or touched him to various levels of realization. He completed intensive retreats on numerous peaceful and wrathful deities—primarily those of the Three Roots—and experienced signs of success; in particular, he completed four hundred million repetitions of the mantra of the great and glorious Vajrakumara, in addition to the supplementary repetitions.

In the later part of his life, Rahor Chödrak continued to turn the wheel of the dharma, teaching the sutras and tantras. On two occasions, he bestowed the empowerment for the peaceful and wrathful deities of *The Web of Magical Display* and explained the tantra *The Heart Essence of Secrets*. He directed his students and patrons from the Drukpa Kagyü school to found a shedra, which was later renowned as Druk Monastery, located near the five stupas of Zung Khardo.[22]

Having thus completed his life and his mission, Rahor Chödrak passed away. From the thirtieth day of the twelfth month in an Iron Rat year until the nineteenth day of the first month in an Iron Ox year,[23] he sat upright in an utterly lucid state of meditation. Amid amazing signs, the display of his emanated form resolved back into basic space. When his remains were cremated, a rain of large and small relics fell, and the fortunate ones present were moved to faith. [2.207b]

Of his many students who upheld the transmission of the theory and practice of the teachings, his heart son Lama Tendzin Özer and Khen Sönam Döndrup together greatly benefited the teachings and beings by restoring the shedra and meditation center at Tarpa Ling, which had been the Omniscient One Longchenpa's seat, and by founding others. His heart son Pema Namgyal became the headmaster of the Semtok Kharik School; for many years, he gave teachings four or five times daily without fail on the source texts of fields of secular knowledge. Pema Namgyal was also responsible for printing new woodblock editions of both the thirteen great source texts and the commentaries on them, as well as tables of contents and secular treatises. With far-reaching vision, Rahor Chödrak founded Orgyen Shedrup Ling in Tsangkha, a shedra—complete with interior furnishings and appointments—for the study of the source texts, fields of secular knowledge, and astrology. He thus carried out boundless enlightened activities, contributing to an impeccable transmission of the theory and practice of the teachings.

Khunu Rinpoché Tendzin Gyaltsen (1884–1977)

For twelve years during the later part of Jamgön Zhenga Rinpoché's life, a great eclectic scholar and a true master of mendicants [2.208a] named Tendzin Gyaltsen from the Khunu region of western India lived in eastern Tibet. He studied with Jamyang Chökyi Lodrö, the third Katok Situ, Drigung Jamdrak, Khenchen Kunpal, Khenchen Jorden, Khenchen Ngawang Palzang, and other teachers. He received teachings on all of the thirteen great source texts, as well as the experiential Dzogchen teachings and dear old Abu's oral tradition of pith instructions on bodhichitta.

While Zhenga Rinpoché was staying in the Gyawo Uplands, Tendzin Gyaltsen met him and requested teachings. The guru initially replied, "It has been many years since I gave explanatory teachings. It is time to practice, for death is waiting; there will be no explanations of the dharma." Once Tendzin Gyaltsen had explained his situation in more detail, the guru said, "You have come from such a distance; moreover, it would be helpful if you benefited the teachings and beings in the future." He then conferred on Tendzin Gyaltsen all of the pith instructions in their entirety, emphasizing the thirteen great source texts. He entrusted Tendzin Gyaltsen with the ultimate transmission, even giving him his own copies of these thirteen texts.

Tendzin Gyaltsen then returned to his home region in India [2.208b] and applied himself to spiritual practice focusing on the very essence. Traveling widely, he planted the victory banner of his practice. He wrote many works, including *In Praise of Bodhicitta, the Awakening Attitude.*[24] He offered many scholars of the Sakya, Gelukpa,

Kagyü, and Nyingma schools teachings on the source texts, as well as instructions in fields of secular knowledge and so forth, fulfilling each person's wishes. In fact, the present Dalai Lama relied on Tendzin Gyaltsen as a master of his buddha family, receiving and practicing all the oral traditions of profound teachings; thus the transmission of the teachings was fostered within the Gelukpa school.

Tuksé Doring Choktrul Rinpoché (20th Century)

At an early age, Doring Choktrul entered the path of the dharma and studied with numerous spiritual mentors. In particular, the extraordinary masters of his buddha family were Zhenpen Chökyi Nangwa (Zhenga Dorjé Chang) and Nyarong Tulku, with whom he studied the sutras and tantras, particularly the thirteen great source texts, continuing through the great Nyingtik teachings of the Dzogchen approach; he practiced these and became his gurus' heart son.

Doring Choktrul went on a pilgrimage to Lhasa in central Tibet, planting the victory banner of spiritual practice in all the hermitages he visited, as well as turning the wheel of the dharma and caring for his students. [2.209a] He eventually arrived at Bumthang in Bhutan and, responding to an invitation from his patron, Chumé Drungpa Gönpo Dorjé, founded Shedrup Dargyé Ling Monastery in Nyima Valley. He stayed there for a long time, giving many explanatory teachings on the sutras and tantras, instructions in fields of secular knowledge, as well as maturing empowerments and liberating instructions. Doring Choktrul then returned to Tibet, where the display of his emanated form resolved back into its ultimate nature, as he rested in meditation for many days. When his remains were cremated, the amazing signs and the large and small relics that appeared inspired many faithful people to enter the path to liberation.

Among the heart children who were his students was the master Pema Tsewang of Bhutan.

The foregoing were the direct students of Orgyen Tendzin Norbu and their students.

18

The Students of Nyoshul Lungtok Tenpai Nyima

The following is a discussion of the students of Nyoshul Lungtok Tenpai Nyima, the student of Paltrul Rinpoché who was more learned than the guru himself with respect to the view. Khenchen Ngawang Palzang Rinpoché was discussed earlier in the context of the mainstream lineage.[1]

Khen Rinpoché Dorjé Dzinpa Tobden (Tupten Gyaltsen Özer) (19th–20th Centuries)

Khen Rinpoché Dorjé Dzinpa Tobden, [2.209b] also known as Tupten Gyaltsen Özer, was the son of Karma Tashi, a student of Drupchen Pema Duddul. Tupten Gyaltsen Özer received all of the teachings on the preliminary and main practices of the cycles of Longsel Dorjé Nyingpo. He studied the sutras and tantras in general, and in particular received countless empowerments and teachings from the kama and terma traditions of the Early Translation school of the Vajrayana. He trained under the guidance of numerous great masters who were both learned and accomplished, including Dzaka Choktrul Rinpoché, the two Jamgöns (Khyentsé and Kongtrul), and Nyoshul Lungtok. The extraordinary master of his buddha family on the inner level was Nyoshul Lungtok, from whom Tupten Gyaltsen Özer received the great oral transmission of the Nyingtik teachings according to the explanatory teachings of the lord of the dharma Paltrul Rinpoché. He put these teachings into practice and gained direct realization.

Tupten Gyaltsen Özer had visions of a vast array of deities of the Three Roots and completed intensive retreats on them. He resided at the hermitage of Draktong at Katok Monastery, where he regularly bestowed empowerments, oral transmissions, and instructions for many cycles of the kama and terma traditions, including the transmissions for the kama tradition of the Early Translation school and for *The Treasury of Precious Hidden Teachings* three times each.

He journeyed to Palyul, Gardzé, and other places, caring for many fortunate students. [2.210a] In particular, Tupten Gyaltsen Özer was a great holder of the Longsel Dorjé Nyingpo cycles and other oral lineages that have been passed down for generations in the Katok tradition. He ensured that the two kinds of benefit were spontaneously accomplished, for he spent his entire life helping beings.

Naktar Tulku Sönam Chokdrup (19th–20th Centuries)

Sönam Chokdrup was the director of Dokhol Monastery in Trom, a Sakya institution housing a thousand monks. Although he studied with and trained under many mentors, he was not satisfied, for he had not yet received teachings on bodhichitta or Dzogchen, which he considered to be the very essence of the dharma.

He knew that in his area of eastern Tibet, the guru who could teach him these key points was Dza Paltrul Rinpoché, so he went to meet him. By the time Sönam Chokdrup reached Dzachukha, however, the guru had passed away, so he trained under Paltrul's heart son Orgyen Tendzin Norbu, receiving from him teachings on *Engaging in the Conduct of a Bodhisattva,* Madhyamaka, and *The Five Treatises of Maitreya,* all according to the oral tradition of dear old Abu. When Sönam Chokdrup asked Orgyen Tendzin Norbu to teach him Dzogchen, the guru replied, "My dear old master used to praise Lungtok as the holder of his lineage of those instructions, so go to him. I will give you a letter of introduction." [2.210b]

Taking the letter, Sönam Chokdrup went to meet Lungtok at a place not far from where he himself had been born and remained there for three years. At first, Lungtok conferred on him teachings on *The Three Cycles of Being at Ease*—the Dzogchen cycle *Being at Ease in the Nature of Mind* and the other two—according to the oral tradition of dear old Abu. He had Sönam Chokdrup meditate on these as part of the process of experiential instruction.

Next Lungtok bestowed teachings on *The Heart Essence of Secrets, The Highest Continuum,* and other texts. Then he conferred the transmission of the Dzogchen manual *Timeless Awareness as the Guiding Principle* and the rest of the earlier and later cycles of the Nyingtik teachings, in particular a condensed version of the great oral transmission of pith instructions that he had received from Paltrul Rinpoché. In all of these instances, Sönam Chokdrup did not "leave the words on the page," but applied the key points of experience through meditation according to his guru's instructions, so that his realization was unrivaled.

His guru Lungtok said to him, "Following Önpo Rinpoché's directive, I have made you fit to carry on the teaching tradition. Now return to your home region and care for your students." Obeying his guru, Sönam Chokdrup went to Dokhol Monastery, as well as other institutions, such as Naktar Bachung and Khar Tama, where he gathered thousands of students. He imparted profound teachings to them according to each one's circumstances. [2.211a] His activities were extensive, for countless people came to him, including teachers, meditators, ordained and lay people, and yogins with profound meditative experience.

Sönam Chokdrup was a venerable master and, like a mountain of gold, maintained his monastic vows. Extremely diligent in his spiritual practice, he repeated each of the preliminary practices of the Nyingtik teachings three hundred times every day without fail in order to purify himself and develop his positive qualities. He lived to the age of seventy-two, and during his life he finished the hundred thousand repetitions of these five practices alone some fifty times. In addition, he practiced the two-day fasting ritual more than a thousand times, recited *The Aspiration Prayer of Noble Conduct* a hundred thousand times, freed beings destined for slaughter a hundred thousand times, and so on. Except when he was teaching the dharma, Sönam Chokdrup observed silence for most of his life. He carried out innumerable conventional acts of virtue, encouraging even simple peasants to carve sutras (such as *The Fortunate Eon, Liberation,* and *The Vajra Cutter*) and mantras (such as the hundred-syllable mantra and *Om ah hum vajra guru padma siddhi hum*) in stone; leading ceremonies for a hundred million repetitions of the mantra *Om mani padme hum;* and raising hundreds of thousands of prayer flags. His virtuous, auspicious activities extended to fill space; in all of the places where he stayed, diseases afflicting humans and livestock were cured, war and strife were pacified, and so on. [2.211b] He combined elements of the Sakya and Nyingma teachings, using the Sakya approach for the sutras and the Nyingma for the tantras.

Having thus ensured benefit for himself and others, Sönam Chokdrup passed away at Seng-gei Drakar in the region of Trom, allowing his enlightened intent to resolve back into the peaceful state of basic space amid countless amazing signs, such as large and small relics and pavilions of light.

Lhazang Lama Rigdzin (19th–20th Centuries)

Another of Lungtok's students was Lhazang Lama Rigdzin, a learned and accomplished master whose activities were widespread throughout upper Nyarong. His guru treated him with great affection, and because of his devotion he was the student who received the most complete transmission of the teachings. He practiced the entire cycle of the Nyingtik teachings of Dzogchen, leaving nothing out. In upper Nyarong, there is a woodblock edition of at least three volumes of his collected songs and other works.

Sa-ngen Lama Wangchen (19th–20th Centuries)

Lama Wangchen of Sa-ngen was born in the lower part of that region. From an early age and as his spiritual potential awakened, he was motivated by his faith and devotion to enter the doorway of the dharma. He went to Dergé in eastern Tibet, where he met many gurus, receiving all of their profound teachings.

In Dergé, Lama Wangchen met Lungtok Tenpai Nyima [2.212a] as the latter was about to begin teaching *Engaging in the Conduct of a Bodhisattva*, and so the auspicious circumstances were set in motion for Lama Wangchen to undertake a study retreat. He stayed with this guru for many years and received many thorough instructions, such as those of the earlier and later cycles of the Nyingtik teachings, the Dzogchen manual *Timeless Awareness as the Guiding Principle*, and other texts. His meditative experiences and realization were consummate, and he meditated with extraordinary diligence day and night. Having come such a long distance, he had meager provisions to support his studies, but while he bore much hardship, he applied himself to the very essence of spiritual practice without losing inspiration.

In the later part of his life, Lama Wangchen returned to his home region; he spread his guru's oral transmissions throughout Sa-ngen, Markham, and other places. In this way, he nurtured the teachings and benefited beings enormously.

Lama Ngakchen (Orgyen Tutop Lingpa) (1858–1914)

Of two great tertöns said to be like the sun and moon, one was Lama Ngakchen, who was also known as Orgyen Tutop Lingpa.[2] He was born amid marvelous signs into the influential Asang family of Nyoshul. He studied under Lama Tayé, who was also known as Chomden Dorjé and had been a student of Nyala Pema Duddul. From this master, Lama Tayé, Lama Ngakchen received the profound cycle of teachings entitled *Natural Freedom Permeating All of Space*. [2.212b]

In time, Lama Ngakchen went to Katok Dorjéden Monastery, where he received from the third Drimé Zhingkyong Gönpo many profound teachings, empowerments, and instructions, including a direct introduction to the true nature of mind. Finally, he returned to his home region, where he met with Lungtok Tenpai Nyima, whom he knew to be an excellent teacher of Dzogchen. He received from him the entire body of Nyingtik teachings of the Dzogchen approach. His meditative experiences and realization led him to a state of irrefutable decisiveness. His guru told him, "Do a hundred thousand repetitions of a guru yoga practice focusing on Nyala Drupchen."[3] Accordingly, Lama Ngakchen composed a guru sadhana to carry out this practice.

Once, when he was participating in a drupchen with many monks, meditating on the deity Khorwa Dongtruk, he beheld a vision of Nyala manifesting in a rainbow body as large as a mountain and received the enlightened intent of the ultimate lineage. He thought, "I must tell my guru Lungtok about this." During an audience with Lungtok, he found that the clairvoyant guru already knew about the event. Lungtok said to him, "Now you have become a 'glorious heruka.' I should escort you out and formally introduce you to others. There is an auspicious precedent to be set." And taking a stick of incense in his hand, Lungtok opened the flap of his tent and praised Lama Ngakchen at great length to those outside. [2.213a] Then he said, "The time has come for you to benefit beings. You will be given a share of Guru Padma's profound teachings."[4] Turning to the daughter of the Ayum family, he added, "Take this woman as your companion in revealing termas, for she is of a remarkable and sacred nature, her character is noble, and she bears all the signs of a spiritual consort." Lungtok then placed in the young woman's right hand an arrow beribboned with silk and in her left a vase containing nectar—substances that had been consecrated by some thirteen great tertöns. He told her, "Put these into Lama Ngakchen's hands without letting anyone else touch them. There is a reason for this; benefit for the teachings and for beings will result."

From then on, Lama Ngakchen was renowned as Terchen Orgyen Tutop Lingpa. He revealed many caches of termas, such as *The Profound Innermost Heart Drop,* through the seven modes of transmission, as well as substances that were termas, among them representations of enlightened form, speech, and mind, sacred samaya substances, and medicines.

Together with the holy master Lerab Lingpa, Terchen Drimé, and the three masters known as Jamgön—Khyentsé, Kongtrul, and Mipam—Orgyen Tutop Lingpa forestalled for sixty years the threat of invasion from Tibet's neighbors. [2.213b] When Terchen Orgyen Tutop Lingpa hurled the torma while performing rituals to avert warfare, people actually saw flames blazing from his long hair and forms of the demons of broken samaya being forced into the fire pit. They watched as he took on the form of Dorjé Drolö and his horse turned into a tigress.[5] Sparks flew from the guru's body, and some ill-intentioned monks from Dargyé Monastery who were bent on harming him were so frightened that they could not come near him. On occasion, he would sit cross-legged in the air or walk right through the walls of his room. He had "accomplished the power of truth" with respect to his speech, so that whatever he said came about. Thus his psychic and miraculous powers were beyond limit.

The activities he undertook to benefit beings were great; he turned the wheel of the dharma, teaching the earlier and later cycles of the Nyingtik teachings as well as his own terma cycles, and supported the residents of some twenty-five monastic communities. He directly experienced signs of his accomplishment, including visions of Guru Rinpoché in the pure realm of Zangdok Palri, Vajrapani in the pure realm of Alakavati, and many other learned and accomplished masters of India and Tibet, as well as the glorious deity Vajrakila, Guru Drakpo, and others. Orgyen Tutop Lingpa's psychic abilities enabled him to see the three times without obstruction; he would say things like, [2.214a] "When I sit at home during my practice sessions, all the thoughts in the minds of my students living in this encampment are as clear to me as if I were gazing at a reflection in a mirror."

Through his immeasurable activity, Orgyen Tutop Lingpa benefited all beings connected to him; for example, he made the following commitment, proclaiming it as a fearless lion's roar: "All who see, hear, remember, or touch me, or even hear my name, will have the good fortune to be guided by me to a pure realm."

The lineage of Orgyen Tutop Lingpa's students consisted of many learned and accomplished masters, such as Lama Tashi Dargyé of Tsarak in Sa-ngen. He had five sons, all of whom proved to be worthy recipients of their father's transmissions of tantric teachings, were endowed with spiritual powers and psychic abilities, and had opportunities to reveal termas without hindrance. Of the five brothers, it was Tulku Kunzang Norbu and the eldest son, Aka, who maintained their father-guru's activities on a vast scale. Aka's son, Orgyen Chemchok, is still living in Gojortso, in the southern reaches of eastern Tibet. Through father and son, the teachings of the heart essence have flourished throughout such eastern Tibetan regions [2.214b] as Gojo, Sa-ngen, Tsawa Rong, and Lankashi, to the point that the local people speak of "Ngak's sphere of influence and Druk's sphere of influence," meaning that the lineages of students of Adzom Drukpa, this lord, and Khenchen Ngawang Palzang blanket these areas of the southern reaches, all the way to China.

Terchen Lerab Lingpa (Tertön Sögyal) (1856–1926)

Lerab Lingpa was born into the Satö Zhiwatsang family, a clan of powerful chieftains, in the Nyarong region of eastern Tibet, where he met the lord Pema Duddul and his heart son Chomden Dorjé. In his early years, he was a worldly, exceedingly bold householder who had many enemies and devoted himself to things like war and banditry. However, once when he was hunting deer, he found he couldn't kill anything because the barrel of his rifle was blocked by syllables in the symbolic script of the dakinis. In this and other ways, his positive tendencies from past lifetimes arose spontaneously.

In time, Lerab Lingpa's full spiritual potential awakened, and he became disenchanted with samsara. His mind filled with renunciation, he left his house, property, possessions, and followers behind and, taking only a simple layman's garment, went first to the encampment of Lama Tayé, [2.215a] where he received training in the preliminary and main practices of the cycle *Natural Freedom Permeating All of Space.*

He then went to other encampments, such as that of Nyoshul Lungtok. Having abandoned samsara, Lerab Lingpa studied with this guru, enduring hardship with real courage, receiving the complete transmission of myriad profound teachings, especially the earlier and later cycles of the secret Nyingtik teachings. While training in establishing the gap between samsara and nirvana, he could shatter water pots with his mind, his perception in waking consciousness was unobstructed by physical objects, and so forth. In short, his tendency to invest things with reality was undermined, and he directly experienced the enlightened intent that is the true nature of phenomena, the great perfection. When he asked his guru about these things, Lungtok replied, "That's what happens when you do this practice. When Mingyur Namkhai Dorjé was training using the *Hum* syllable, none of the clay containers at Dzogchen Monastery held any water!"

Eventually, Lerab Lingpa's aspirations from former lifetimes to reveal profound termas awakened. He had visions of many of his meditation deities and received transmissions for such termas. He revealed innumerable other caches of termas, including *The Most Secret Wrath of Vajrakila, Dispelling Flaws in Interdependence*, and other teachings, as well as material objects and sacred samaya substances. [2.215b] He also became a greatly learned and accomplished master, receiving extensive teachings of the Nyingma and Sarma schools from such masters as Jamyang Khyentsei Wangpo, Jamgön Mipam Rinpoché, the lord Kongtrul, and Dodrup Tenpai Nyima. In the later part of his life, Lerab Lingpa served as guru to the thirteenth Dalai Lama, Tupten Gyatso, the supreme teacher of Tibet. In these and other ways, he exerted an influence that filled all of space, ensuring benefit for beings.

His lineage continued with his sons—Chöpel Gyatso (the tulku of Kalzang Monastery in Nyarong) and Adzin Peltsa Lodrö—as well as the latter's son, Tromgé Tulku Khachö Dechen Dorjé (who still lives at the Tromgé encampment in eastern Tibet).[6] At a certain point, Lerab Lingpa's enlightened intent resolved into the basic space of phenomena. One of his tulkus is Sogyal Rinpoché, who was born into the Lakar family of Trehor. Another was Khen Jigmé Puntsok, who lived until recently at Serta in eastern Tibet. A third incarnation was a great master named Geshé Drakpukpa Gendün Rinchen; [2.216a] as Terchen Lerab Lingpa had indicated in the last testament he gave to his student Dretsé Tulku, this tulku was a child born in a Tiger year[7] in a cave at Paro in Bhutan. These three tulkus have accomplished enormous benefit for the teachings and for beings.

Lerab Lingpa's students also included countless others, such as Choktrul Pema Gyaltsen (the activity incarnation of Kongtrul), Dretsé Tulku, and Sungtrul Kunzang Nyima (also known as Nüden Dorjé, the speech incarnation of Traktung Dudjom Lingpa).

Pema Gyaltsen (19th–20th Centuries)

Of these students, Lerab Lingpa's heart son, Pema Gyaltsen, embraced the dharma at an early age and possessed the innate qualities of someone destined to be a holy master. He studied and contemplated many of the mainstream traditions of sutra and tantra—including the treatises of Maitreya, *The Collections of Reasoning*, and *The Heart Essence of Secrets*—with numerous learned and accomplished tutors.

Notably, from Terchen Lerab Lingpa, he received the complete experiential transmission of pith instructions for the secret Nyingtik teachings of utter lucidity. Pema Gyaltsen then spent a long time in solitary places applying himself to his spiritual practice, and so gained true realization. In a pure vision, he actually journeyed to Zangdok Palri, [2.216b] where he received teachings from Guru Rinpoché and Yeshé Tsogyal. They conferred on him the seal of entrustment with their enlightened intent, so that he received personal transmissions of many profound termas. But he did not exert a great deal of effort transmitting these new termas, working instead to preserve older termas.

Pema Gyaltsen had countless students whom he guided in the southern reaches of Tibet, teaching the ordinary students the preliminary practices and the extraordinary ones the great oral lineage of the Dzogchen teachings. He bestowed the empowerments and oral transmissions for *The Treasury of Precious Hidden Teachings* three times, as well as those for *The Treasury of Spiritual Instructions*. In such ways, he ensured that students were brought to spiritual maturity and liberation commensurate with their individual capacities, so that his enlightened activities spread in all directions.

Dretsé Tulku (19th–20th Centuries)

Dretsé Tulku's home region was Trehor. He conferred the instructions and teachings of Dzogchen on countless students to be guided, in such areas as Nyarong, Trehor, Tongkor, and Dzagyü.

Sungtrul Kunzang Nyima (1904?–1958?)

Sungtrul Kunzang Nyima was born at the great holy site of Pemakö. He was the son of Khyentsé Tulku, who was himself the son of Traktung Dudjom Lingpa. When the boy was a little older, he was invited to Dudjom Lingpa's home region of Serta in the lowlands of eastern Tibet. [2.217a] There Kunzang Nyima embraced the dharma and studied at the feet of many tutors and mentors. He completed a thoroughgoing process of study and contemplation that focused on the whole range of mainstream traditions of the sutras, tantras, and other fields of knowledge. He thus attained a high degree of erudition and accomplishment.

In particular, Kunzang Nyima studied at the feet of Terchen Lerab Lingpa, the extraordinary lord of his buddha family, serving this master in the three ways. Kunzang Nyima received a complete transmission of the great Nyingtik teachings of Dzogchen, as well as Terchen's own profound termas, and realization—the ultimate state of enlightened intent—dawned in his mind. Terchen Lama prophesied to him, "If you strive at the phases of approach and accomplishment, you will be graced by visions of your meditation deities. You will receive personal transmissions of profound termas, and so benefit will ensue for countless students to be guided by you."

Kunzang Nyima applied himself to his spiritual practice and, fulfilling Terchen's prophecy, had visions of a vast array of deities of the Three Roots. Notably, he was actually taken under the care of an embodiment of timeless awareness, that of the glorious Orgyen, king of the dharma, who conferred empowerment on Kunzang Nyima and blessed him. This caused him to realize directly the great perfection, the state of enlightened intent that is the perception of awareness's naturally manifest appearances without bias. [2.217b] Kunzang Nyima thus became one whose realization made him a great regent, in the ultimate sense, of the secret Nyingtik teachings of utter lucidity. Through the personal transmissions of profound termas that he received, he brought forth countless termas of teachings, objects of wealth, and sacred substances, including cycles of practice focusing on deities of the Three Roots and practices such as those of the venerable Tara and Kurukulle.

He gathered around him innumerable students to be guided, who came from all the regions of eastern Tibet, including Repkong to the north, Golok, Serta, and Doyul. Transmitting the Dzogchen approach and other teachings, Kunzang Nyima brought benefit to the teachings and to beings, his enlightened activities equal in extent to space itself. His son, Tulku Tekchok Rinpoché, carried on his father's tradition of benefiting the teachings and beings in eastern Tibet.

This concludes the overview of the students of Nyoshul Lungtok.

19

The Students of Khenchen Ngawang Palzang

Next, I will discuss the students of Khenchen Ngawang Palzang. These students—the heart sons known as the "four great pillars," the "thirty-seven great khenpos capable of benefiting others," and so on—and their students were innumerable. The life of one of the foremost of these, the second Pema Norbu, Rigdzin Palchen Düpa, was discussed earlier in the context of the main Nyingtik lineage.[1]

Katok Chaktsa Rinpoché (19th–20th Centuries)

Chaktsa Rinpoché of Katok Monastery [2.218a] was perhaps the most renowned of Khenchen Ngawang Palzang's four heart sons who were called the "four pillars." An incarnation of Kunzang Ngedön Wangpo,[2] he was the fourth in the line of incarnations known as the Chaktsa tulkus. They were so named because the first, Kunzang Ngedön Wangpo (an incarnation of Tragowa Tsöndrü Gyatso, the custodian of Rigdzin Duddul Dorjé's termas), was born into the Chaktsa clan of local rulers. The fourth Chaktsa Rinpoché was born amid marvelous signs near Getsé Tralek in the Trang Nyikha region of Golok. He was recognized by Katok Situ Rinpoché and enthroned at Katok Dorjéden Monastery with elaborate ceremonies involving thousands of gurus, tulkus, and monks. He then went to Getsé Tralek Monastery, the seat of his former incarnation, where he succeeded to the throne of the prior Chaktsa Tulku, with authority over thousands of households of both high and low social standing, principally in the eighteen districts of Golok and Getsé Dayul.

It was at Getsé Tralek Monastery that Chaktsa Rinpoché began studying with many great masters, such as Deshul Lama and Tokgö Lama Melong. He started with reading and writing and continued on to train extensively in many subjects related to the sutras, tantras, and other fields of knowledge. Reaching his majority, [2.218b] he returned to Katok Dorjéden to further his studies. He enrolled at Norbui Lhunpo Shedra, where he studied under Khenchen Kunpal Rinpoché, Khen Gyaltsen Özer the elder, Khen Chödrup of Nyarong, Lekjor, Khenchen Ngaga, and a host of other teachers. From them he learned many mainstream traditions, including Madhyamaka, Vinaya, Prajñaparamita, and Abhidharma. On a more extraordinary level, from Katok Situ Rinpoché and Khenchen Ngawang Palzang, Chaktsa Rinpoché received the maturing empowerments and liberating instructions for such cycles as the kama transmissions of the Early Translation school, *The United Intent of the Gurus, The Heart Essence of Secrets,* and *The Treasury of Precious Hidden Teachings,* as well as the earlier and later cycles of the Nyingtik teachings, *Timeless Awareness as the Guiding Principle,* and Lungtok Tenpai Nyima's great oral lineage of Dzogchen teachings. Chaktsa Rinpoché studied and contemplated these teachings extensively. He put them into practice with constant devotion, attaining the sublime siddhi through the stages of development and completion.

Chaktsa Rinpoché then returned to his home monastery of Tralek, teaching there as well as throughout the northern reaches of eastern Tibet, at such places as Traling Monastery and Wangchen Töyul in Golok. [2.219a] He taught, among other cycles, *The Treasury of Precious Hidden Teachings, The Seven Treasuries, The Four Higher Collections of the Heart Drop,* the source volumes of *The Heart Drop of Longchenpa,* and Duddul Dorjé's and Longsel Dorjé Nyingpo's terma teachings. He continually imparted the nectar of the dharma to gatherings of countless students, principally in the northern reaches of eastern Tibet and as far away as Amdo. At his own monastery, he taught at the shedra and meditation center and presided over ceremonies on the tenth day of the lunar cycle, as well as at drupchens. He commissioned a two-story, copper-and-gold statue of the Lord of Sages, tangkas depicting buddhas and bodhisattvas painted with gold, and brocade raiment for hundreds of statues. Chaktsa Rinpoché saw to it that many thousands of volumes of scriptures were printed. In such ways, he was an invaluable source of support for the teachings.

He inspired the peasants of the region to recite the mantras *Om mani padme hum* and *Om ah hum vajra guru padma siddhi hum,* to practice the sadhana focusing on Sukhavati and the fasting ritual, and to hang hundreds of thousands of prayer flags. The region of Golok had been rife with warfare, banditry, and civil unrest. Throughout the land, ruthless thieves and bandits committed atrocities like beheading people, answering to no one. Chaktsa Rinpoché was able to pacify these wrongdoers and to resolve conflicts and grudges, [2.219b] providing the people with refuge from fear.

In brief, Chaktsa Rinpoché used a variety of skillful means to exert a positive influence over the entire region, lifting the darkness with the light of the extensive deeds he undertook to nurture the teachings in general and his school in particular. He engaged in the far-reaching activities of someone learned, venerable, and noble, and his wisdom, love, and spiritual energy were superb sources of benefit and happiness.

Finally, during the troubles of recent times, I and others served Chaktsa Rinpoché unhesitatingly with body, speech, and mind and invited him to Achen Gangchak in the northern reaches of eastern Tibet, near Chumar Rabdun on the banks of the upper Drichu River. There he stayed without showing any illness or pain.

His nephew, Pesang, asked him, "Trulga Rinpoché,[3] wouldn't it be better to go to a place where we can devote our lives to the dharma than to remain under the barbarians without it?"

Chaktsa Rinpoché replied, "Yes, indeed, it would. You go, and I will join you shortly." Thereupon his nephew sat in meditation with his hands in his lap, and in the time it takes to drink a cup of tea, he had passed away to a pure realm through the profound method of the transference of consciousness. [2.220a] At sunrise the next day, amid pavilions of radiant rainbow light, Chaktsa Rinpoché lay down in the posture of the sleeping lion and uttered "Phat!" several times. The display of his emanated form then resolved back into the vast expanse of the state of peace, the basic space of phenomena.

His precious, sublime tulku, Tsultrim Lodrö Chökyi Gyaltsen Palzangpo Rinpoché,[4] was born near the plateau of Dzotang in Golok. He relied on gurus like Khenchen Munsel Rinpoché as the masters of his buddha family and studied and trained in the Dzogchen approach. Until his demise, his sublime vajra form displayed the major and minor marks of perfection and brought liberation upon sight, for he was truly a leader of the teachings and beings at the seat of his former incarnation, Gétsé Tralek Monastery.

Tromgé Choktrul Arik Rinpoché (1905?–1988)

Arik Rinpoché was born into the eminent and spiritual Atsap Ladong family of Washul Trom, which was under the jurisdiction of Dergé in eastern Tibet. He was the nephew of Tromgé Jigmé Do-ngak Tendzin, a greatly learned and accomplished student of Dzatrul Kunzang Namgyal. [2.220b] From an early age, he was cared for by his uncle, Jigmé Do-ngak Tendzin. Arik Rinpoché was formally enthroned as the rebirth of Tromgé Yizhin.

He showed natural signs of someone holy and could read and write without difficulty. He received from his uncle the entire extraordinary lineage of the victorious Katok tradition, from the preliminaries to the main body of practices of the Longsel Dorjé Nyingpo cycles. He studied and contemplated the sutras, tantras, and other fields of knowledge extensively under such masters as Khenchen Düpa Gyatso of Dokhol Monastery in Trom and Khenchen Gendün Gyatso of Nyarong.

Arik Rinpoché went to Katok Monastery, where he received full monastic ordination from the third Katok Situ Rinpoché and Khenchen Ngawang Palzang, thus becoming a great regent of the Sage, the lord Buddha. He was exceedingly venerable, a personification of the twelve enlightened qualities that arise from training, modeling himself on the Indian Buddhist elder Mahakashyapa. Learned and noble, Arik Rinpoché was never stained by the slightest flaw or moral shortcoming. [2.221a] He said, "I attribute the fact that I am a pure monk to the aspirations of my former incarnation, Tromgé Yizhin." He ordained anyone who made the request, thus causing the monastic tradition to flourish.

In particular, his guru from past lifetimes was Khenchen Ngawang Palzang, Vimalamitra in person. Arik Rinpoché went to study at the guru's seat, Nyoshul Shugushar, also known as the hermitage of Jangchub Jönpalung. There he received from him the complete transmission of the tantras, explanatory commentaries, and pith instructions—the empowerments, instructions, and advice of the secret Nyingtik teachings—as well as the authorization to carry on the lineage. His guru, Khenchen, showered him with praise, saying, "Nowadays, those who are called tulkus are mere imitators who sit around and misappropriate offerings. But someone like Tromgé Arik is what is meant by a 'real tulku.'" He entrusted his teachings to Arik Rinpoché, who became his sublime, extraordinary heart son.

Arik Rinpoché remained at his home monastery for some years, where he and his uncle taught annually, and regularly gave advice and instructions, continually looking after students from all over. He could explain the words of scholars and the key points of meditation so that they were easy to understand and apply directly to one's own experience. [2.221b] All of his students, whether advanced or not, thus held him in the highest regard, saying, "He is no different from our lord, Tromgé Yizhin."

At about that time, several events aroused Arik Rinpoché's sense of renunciation, and he cast aside his monastery, country, and retinue as he would a drop of spittle, saying, "In these times of spiritual degeneration, it would be far more profitable for me to practice by applying the teachings to my experience than to be caught up in things that seem to be truly beneficial for others but actually are not." With that, he followed the example of our Teacher, who out of compassion renounced his kingdom. Taking Tokden Kalzang Nyima as his attendant, Arik Rinpoché set off like a wild animal leaving its lair, with neither clothing nor food, and wandered throughout western and central Tibet, including Lhasa. He applied himself to the very essence of spiritual practice, frequenting glaciers, cliffs, and other holy places such as Sheldrak in Yarlung and the Chimpu Uplands of Samyé. Having no food to put in his mouth or clothes to wear on his back, he was a "child of the mountains," eating the food of meditative absorption and asceticism, with only the birds and wild animals as his companions in these solitary places. As a result, he had visions of the entire array of deities of the Three Roots. [2.222a]

He then returned to eastern Tibet to see his guru, the great khenpo. The local inhabitants and the administrators of the monastic estate all felt that Arik Rinpoché should remain and occupy his monastic seat, but no matter how much they urged him, he would not break his vow to remain in retreat. As one whose way of life is referred to in the Dzogchen tantras as "like that of a wild animal," Arik Rinpoché frequented uninhabited places in the mountains and cliffs of the lowlands of eastern Tibet—Kaburné and other places where great masters had practiced—and lived as a humble mendicant, no one even aware that he was a lama. His attendant, Kalzang Nyima, related that during this period Arik Rinpoché was graced with visions of deities of the Three Roots and that, in particular, on countless occasions he had visions of the Omniscient One Longchenpa and received prophecies. But Arik Rinpoché himself was so private about such matters that he spoke of them to no one else.

From then on, Arik Rinpoché did not often teach, but spent the rest of his life engaged in spiritual practice. From the great Sakya lineage holder Dezhung Choktrul Ajam,[5] [2.222b] he received the entire transmission of the precious words of the great Lamdré cycle, including the oral tradition; Dezhung Choktrul had originally received this transmission from the first Khyentsé and Gatön Ngawang Lekpa. Arik Rinpoché practiced the entire cycle as well, and Dezhung Choktrul praised him, saying, "My dear Arik of Tromgé is someone we call a true lineage holder and a spiritually advanced being." He was able to see past, present, and future, as well as events hidden from view, all directly and without hindrance.

His principal heart sons, all fine lineage holders, included his uncle's rebirth, Choktrul Jigmé Namgyal; the tulku of Tromgé Kachö, Dechen Dorjé; Chagdud Tulku Padma Gargyi Wangchuk; and Tromtok Lama Khen Rinpoché Achuk. Wherever this master stayed, thievery, banditry, robbery, and hunting ceased. Arik Rinpoché inspired ordinary students to recite *Om mani padme hum* and *Om ah hum vajra guru padma siddhi hum*. By his presence alone, he pacified diseases among humans and livestock, averted frost, hail, blight, and drought, and even caused wild animals to be calm and to avoid harming one another as they naturally gathered around him.

Arik Rinpoché was a majestic wish-fulfilling gem, a treasure vase yielding all that is positive and auspicious. [2.223a] He lived to the age of eighty-four, a glorious and holy protector of the teachings and of beings, turning the wheel of the dharma for recent generations of Tibetans in Dergé, eastern Tibet, seated firmly on the vajra throne.

In this modern-day resurgence of the teachings, his student Chagdud Choktrul Padma Gargyi Wangchuk bestowed Dzogchen teachings in the United States, Brazil, and other countries of the Western Hemisphere,[6] while the two sublime tulkus[7] turned the wheel of the dharma at their own Tromgé Monastery in the lowlands of eastern Tibet.

Khen Lama Rinpoché Achuk (Drupwang Lungtok Gyatso) (b. 20th Century)

At an early age, Khen Lama Rinpoché Achuk, also known as Drupwang Lungtok Gyatso, who was a student of Arik Rinpoché, enrolled in the shedra of Dokhol Monastery, a great Sakya center in Trom. He received the Sakya teachings on the Lamdré cycle from the sublime Dezhung Ajam Kunga Gyaltsen. Lama Achuk trained extensively in the thirteen great source texts and the mainstream Sakya sources of the sutras and tantras, becoming a consummate scholar. [2.223b]

Eventually, he went to Tromgé Arik Rinpoché, whom he served for thirty-three years, relying on him as the extraordinary master of his buddha family. During the military occupation of Tibet, Lama Achuk served as his guru's attendant, enduring great hardship without regard for his own health or life, and so proved to be an ideal heart son. Arik Rinpoché conferred on him all of the advice and instructions of the Lamdré cycle and the Dzogchen approach, like one vase filling another to the brim. He empowered Lama Achuk as a holder of his lineage, urging him to teach in order to benefit beings.

Lama Achuk is still living in the lowlands of eastern Tibet, in the Yachen Khamdo district of Washul Tromtar. Following his guru's instructions, he has founded a monastery and is turning the wheel of the dharma, teaching the sutras and tantras, especially the great oral lineage of pith instructions, and serving the precious teachings of the Victorious One while caring for communities of countless fortunate students.[8]

Khen Rinpoché Lekshé Jorden (Khenchen Dulwai Dé) (20th Century)

The precious khenpo Lekshé Jorden, also known as Khenchen Dulwai Dé, was born close to Yönten Monastery, near the birthplace of Nyaké[9] of the Chagdud clan. [2.224a] From an early age, he showed signs of someone holy. Following the advice of the third Katok Situ Rinpoché, he went to Katok Monastery and enrolled in Norbui Lhunpo Shedra. There he completed his studies, developing the qualities of a scholar. Lekshé Jorden studied with such teachers as Jamyang Chökyi Lodrö, Katok Situ Rinpoché, Khenchen Kunzang Chödrak, Gyurmé Tenpa Namgyal of Getsé, and Khenchen Atop Rinpoché Gyaltsen Özer. From them he received, like one vase being filled to the brim from others, complete transmissions of empowerments, instructions, and advice from the kama and terma lineages of the Early Translation school, with emphasis on the traditions of his own school.

From Khenchen Ngawang Palzang in particular, he received a general range of profound teachings on the sutras and tantras, as well as the great oral lineage of Dzogchen teachings that Ngawang Palzang had himself received from Lungtok Tenpai Nyima. Lekshé Jorden put these teachings into practice, directly experiencing the realization of ultimate enlightened intent. Having become considerably erudite, he served for seven years as the khenpo of the tantric college at Katok Monastery.

His foremost students were some thirteen great khenpos, each of whom gained acclaim, such as Nüden Khyentsei Lodrö. He had clear recollections of his lifetimes as Khedrup Yeshé Gyaltsen [2.224b] and Chagdud Sherab Gyaltsen and was renowned as an incarnation of both these masters. After Katok Situ Rinpoché's passing, Lekshé Jorden—a victory banner of the theory and practice of the teachings—ceaselessly taught those who came to Katok Monastery from China, Tibet, and Mongolia. He conferred a veritable feast of maturing empowerments and liberating instructions on the khenpos, tulkus, and holy ones who held the lineages of Katok Monastery, as well as on countless monks.

Having completed his practice of the stages of development and completion, and especially the Dzogchen paths of trekchö and tögal, Lekshé Jorden truly realized the sublime level of the supreme mandala. His rebirth, Lodrö Tenpai Gyaltsen, was recognized by the lord Jamyang Chökyi Lodrö's flawless eye of timeless awareness. He was enthroned at Katok Monastery and studied with Khenchen Lama Gyaltsen Özer. He is still alive and actively promotes the theory and practice of the dharma.

Khenchen Nüden Khyentsei Lodrö (20th Century)

Khenchen Nüden Khyentsei Lodrö was born in Setar. Renowned as the tulku of Serlo Tönpa, a lord among wise scholars, he was an excellent, learned master blessed by the venerable lord Milarepa.[10] [2.225a] While in Lhasa on a pilgrimage, he met the third Katok Situ Rinpoché and immediately felt an upwelling of faith, seeing Situ Rinpoché as a true buddha. Heeding the guru's advice, Nüden Khyentsei Lodrö went to Katok Monastery, where he met Khenchen Lekshé Jorden, director of the shedra. Nüden Khyentsei Lodrö studied extensively with him, mastering all of the mainstream sources of the Indian and Tibetan Buddhist traditions. He also received many profound teachings of sutra and tantra from Katok Situ Rinpoché and Khenchen Kunpal. He served as the khenpo of the Katok shedra for three years.

Nüden Khyentsei Lodrö received an entire range of profound instructions and advice, especially the great oral lineage of Dzogchen teachings, from such teachers as Druptop Jampa Chödzin, Jamgön Chökyi Lodrö, and especially Khenchen Ngawang Palzang, the extraordinary inner master of his buddha family. Sublime knowing born of meditation welled up in him, and he composed such works as the important four-volume commentary on *The General Discourse on United Intent,* the commentaries on both this discourse and the Category of Mind (such as *Great Perfection: Supreme Space* and *Explaining the Treasury of Jewels*), and the commentaries on Mipam's works *The Entrance to the Ways of the Wise* [2.225b] and *The Lamp of Certain Meaning.* There are more than nine volumes of Nüden Khyentsei Lodrö's collected works, treatises in which profound and secret key points of view and philosophy illuminate the flawless extensive tradition of the Early Translation school.

Nüden Khyentsei Lodrö traveled to Katok, Palyul, Muksang, and other monasteries and hermitages at random, his teaching activities and spiritual practice increasing more and more to fill all of space, reaching China and India and beyond to the rest of the world.

Khenchen Yizhin Norbu Tupten Gyaltsen Özer (19th–20th Centuries)

Khenchen Yizhin Norbu Tupten Gyaltsen Özer manifested as a second Lord of Sages in these times of spiritual degeneration. He was born in Horpo, which was under the jurisdiction of Katok Monastery. Having enrolled at Norbui Lhunpo Shedra, he studied with Khenpo Lekshé Jorden, who taught from the commentaries of Indian and Tibetan Buddhist masters on the Buddhist source texts. Tupten Gyaltsen Özer applied himself to his studies thoroughly, learning the full range of mainstream traditions, including Vinaya, Abhidharma, Madhyamaka, valid cognition, and Prajñaparamita.

From an early age, he had the abundant qualities of someone holy, including a faith so stable that it never wavered, a great sense of moderation in his way of life, and a pure perception of his gurus and meditation deities. [2.226a] He studied and contemplated the entire range of the countless methods of the sutra and tantra traditions, both kama and terma—including those found in *The Heart Drop of Longchenpa* and *The Four Higher Collections of the Heart Drop*—which he received from such masters as Katok Situ Rinpoché, Kunchen Ngagi Wangpo, Gyurmé Tenpa Namgyal of Getsé, and Khenchen Lekshé Jorden. In particular, he trained with Khenchen Ngawang Palzang in the great oral lineage of Dzogchen teachings and in the works of the Omniscient One and his spiritual heir, Jigmé Lingpa (for example, *Timeless Awareness as the Guiding Principle*). Immeasurable meditative experiences and realization arose in him. He became his guru's foremost heart son and was entrusted with spreading the teachings. Tupten Gyaltsen Özer succeeded Khenpo Orgyen Tenpel as the director of tantric studies at Katok Monastery's shedra, Norbui Lhunpo, a post he held for five years.

Even during the recent times of upheaval, Tupten Gyaltsen Özer encountered no obstacles; instead, in keeping with his superb intention to revivify the Katok line, he built temples and commissioned the three kinds of representations. Whenever he traveled in his native region and elsewhere, [2.226b] he taught other gurus and tulkus, as well as lay people, restoring lineages on the point of disappearing by teaching the preliminary practices, explaining the source texts, and bestowing maturing empowerments and liberating instructions. These days, due to the harm caused by barbarian encroachment, the monastic tradition of the sacred dharma is like a lamp that has run out of oil. Tupten Gyaltsen Özer specifically propagated the traditions of the novice and full monastic ordination, so that once again those who don the victory banner of saffron robes populated the land. With such gracious and compassionate activities, Tupten Gyaltsen Özer was a lamp illuminating the teachings of the Victorious One in general and those of the victorious Katok tradition in particular. He was like the radiance of a thousand powerful suns shining together in the midst of banks of hundreds of thousands of marvelous, superb white clouds.[11]

Golok Khenchen Munsel (1916–1993)

Khenchen Munsel was born in the region of Golok in the northern reaches of eastern Tibet amid amazing signs. He was tutored at home, in Wangchen Tö, in reading, writing, and reciting prayers. When he reached his majority, he went to Katok Dorjéden and enrolled in the shedra. [2.227a] One day, Munsel joined the many monks escorting Gyurmé Tenpa Namgyal (Getsé Mahapandita's third incarnation) from Tromkhok back to his own monastery. At a certain point, the guru asked the party, "Monks, are you well?" At the mere sound of his voice, all the thoughts stirring in Munsel's mind vanished like evanescent clouds, and he rested for a short time in the uncontrived way of abiding. This experience convinced him that Gyurmé Tenpa Namgyal was his guru from past lifetimes.

He received a wealth of profound teachings from the many gurus and tulkus of Katok Monastery, including the fourth Drimé Zhingkyong Gönpo,[12] Katok Situ Chökyi Gyatso, Öntrul Pema Gyaltsen, and Khenpo Kunpal. In particular, he sat at the feet of Khenchen Ngawang Palzang, Vimalamitra in person and the extraordinary inner master of his buddha family. Having enrolled at the great tantric college of Katok, Munsel completed his study and contemplation of the sutras, tantras, and other fields of knowledge, including Madhyamaka, Prajñaparamita, Vinaya, Abhidharma, valid cognition, and the tantra *The Heart Essence of Secrets.* He became renowned as a scholar and known as Khenchen Munsel.[2.227b]

He then came to feel that all of his learning was like an outer shell. He thought to himself, "Having met such a guru as this great khenpo—Vajradhara in person—I should request some extraordinary advice that will enable me to awaken to buddhahood in this lifetime. It would be a pity if, having such freedom and opportunity and having encountered a guru who is a buddha, I were distracted by what only seems beneficial to others but is not truly so." With such thoughts, Munsel prayed to his guru, Khenchen. In response, Khenchen Ngawang Palzang granted him teachings on the Dzogchen manual *Timeless Awareness as the Guiding Principle,* the great oral lineage of pith instructions that Khenchen had received from Lungtok Tenpai Nyima, *The Four Higher Collections of the Heart Drop,* and all of the spiritual instructions found in the earlier and later cycles of the secret Nyingtik teachings.

With the noble vase of his heart filled with gems—the instructions of the Three Repositories—Khenchen Munsel returned to his home region, where he pursued his spiritual practice in places uninhabited by humans, in the manner of the lord Milarepa. He practiced the yoga of the four visions of spontaneous presence, and these unfolded for him. He lived up to the praise heaped on him by Chaktsa Rinpoché of Katok Monastery, who said, "These days, what the Dzogchen tantras mean by 'the unity of basic space and awareness emerging from the midbrow'[13] is found in someone like Khenpo Munsel." [2.228a]

At a certain point, the powerful karma of the general population of Tibet resulted in Khenpo Munsel's imprisonment by evil barbarians. While serving his sentence, he secretly and from memory taught thousands of fellow prisoners such texts as *Timeless Awareness as the Guiding Principle* and the Dzogchen commentary *The*

Treasury of the Basic Space of Phenomena. Many of them entered the spiritual path before they died and manifested signs of having died with real control, such as remaining in meditation posture after their passing. In particular, Khenpo Munsel trained many spiritual people who were capable of holding the lineage of the heart essence, among them Göngyal Tulku, Nangchen Adei Tulku, and Gyalpo.

More recently, as the sun of the dharma began to rise anew for the people of Tibet, Khenpo Munsel established a great encampment in Wangchen Tö, Golok, which served as his base while he taught throughout the upper and lower areas of the Dza region, Amdo, Golok Akyong, Washul Serta, Tromkhok, Nyarong, and other areas. He trained many spiritual beings who were capable of upholding the lineage of the heart essence, and his innumerable students have disseminated his teachings in India and China and the world beyond. [2.228b] Turning the wheel of the secret unsurpassable dharma while seated on the vajra throne, Khenpo Munsel was a mainstay of the Dzogchen teachings of utter lucidity.

Choktrul Garwang Nyima Rinpoché (b. 20th Century)

Choktrul Garwang Nyima Rinpoché of Dartang Monastery was a student of Khenchen Munsel Rinpoché of Golok. Studying at the feet of his guru, he was given instructions in the great oral lineage of Dzogchen teachings that had come down from Lungtok Tenpai Nyima and his spiritual son Khenchen Ngawang Palzang; he received this transmission with nothing omitted, like one vase being filled from another. Having studied these teachings, Garwang Nyima devoted himself to his spiritual practice.

He now lives at his home monastery. He has restored the monasteries of Dartang Tengön, which were completely destroyed by the barbarian forces, building these anew from their foundations, constructing temples, and commissioning the installation of statues. He has built shedras and retreat centers, which support the ordained sangha, and has provided articles for the ceremonies held on the tenth day of the lunar month (such as masks and robes for ritual dances). In addition, Garwang Nyima has contributed horns, drums, gyalings, cymbals, and other ritual instruments; he has also instituted annual drupchens and provided funds to support them. [2.229a] In such ways, he has ensured that the teachings are well established on the outer, inner, and secret levels, his actions indistinguishable from those of his former incarnation, the preceding Choktrul. In caring for members of the ordained sangha, numbering in the thousands, and enabling them to maintain their purity through the three higher trainings, Garwang Nyima has brought benefit to the teachings and to beings, covering the earth with groups of saffron-robed monastics. He still lives in the northern reaches of eastern Tibet, continuing this work.

Pema Tumpo (Orgyen Kusum Lingpa) (b. 1930?)

Lama Pema Tumpo of Golok is a student of Dodrup Rigdzin Jalü Dorjé, Ön Lozang Namdak, and other masters. He has built temples and installed images therein, and has founded shedras and meditation centers. He spreads the teachings, including the profound termas that are his personal destiny, and continues in such ways to maintain the secret teachings through his activities in the three spheres.

Golok Lama Garchö (20th Century)

Lama Garchö of Golok was a fellow student of Khenchen Munsel. He gained the sublime siddhi through the secret path of natural great perfection. He had unhindered powers of supernormal perception, so that he could read the minds of others. Having gained the alchemical power of extracting the essence, this remarkable and sublime master was able to live for twelve years without relying on coarse food. [2.229b] He lived in the northern reaches of eastern Tibet, rendering enormous service to the teachings of the sublime heart essence.

Choktrul Orgyen Chemchok (b. 1915?)

Choktrul Orgyen Chemchok is the son of a mahasiddha named Tulku Aka, who was himself the eldest son of Terchen Ngawang Tendzin (also known as Orgyen Tutop Lingpa). It was in fact Tulku Aka who recognized his son as his own father's rebirth. The boy was named Orgyen Chemchok. From an early age, he clearly showed tendencies that had carried over from his former lifetime as the great, precious tertön, and he manifested unmistakable signs of someone holy.

This tertön had told Khenchen Ngaga Rinpoché, "We have alternated as each other's guru and student for many lifetimes." Accordingly, Orgyen Chemchok studied with Khenchen himself, living at his encampment from a tender age and completing his studies and contemplation there. In particular, Khenchen Ngawang Palzang bestowed on him the entire oral lineage of the great experiential teachings of pith instructions that he had originally received from Lungtok Tenpai Nyima. He also conferred on Orgyen Chemchok the authorization to pass these teachings on. He treated the boy with great affection, [2.230a] saying, "You are truly the rebirth of my guru, Terchen Rinpoché."

In time, Orgyen Chemchok went to live in the southern reaches of eastern Tibet, in his mother's birthplace of Gojo and other areas. There he cared for his students, benefiting numerous fortunate people. During that time, the Land of Snows was enveloped in the darkness of the barbarian blight, and he spent twenty years in prison, enduring great hardship. Nevertheless, because of his holy nature, Orgyen Chemchok was never daunted; rather, even while incarcerated, he secretly taught many of his fellow prisoners according to their individual needs, imparting numerous extraordinary pith instructions of the Dzogchen approach. A large number of prisoners were thus directly introduced to the enlightened intent of dharmakaya dwelling within all beings. Specifically, Orgyen Chemchok trained a number of sublime heart sons capable of upholding his lineage, including his own son, Choktrul Jigmé Rinpoché, and Sang-ngak Tendzin, the tulku from Namchak Tsasum Lingpa's seat. With such noble deeds, amazing under the circumstances, Orgyen Chemchok was able to continue his teaching without being crushed by the oppression of the invading armies.

Due to his holy attributes [2.230b] (as natural to him as the properties of gold are natural to gold) and his fine character, Orgyen Chemchok was at peace with everyone, whether his fellow prisoners—ordinary men and women who knew nothing about the dharma—or his foreign jailers. Because he was free of dishonesty or hypocrisy toward anyone inside or outside the prison, all regarded him as an unbiased witness, and no one could silence his direct, honest speech. He was considered quite amazing, for everything he said with fearless confidence naturally inspired people's respect.

Since the recent revivification of the teachings resulting from the easing of the Tibetan people's oppression by the barbarian forces, Orgyen Chemchok has been living in his home area of Gojo, eastern Tibet, still serving as a glorious protector of the teachings and all beings. He is a true ornament of the teachings of the supreme secret, turning the wheel of the dharma for his students in the southern reaches of Gojo, Markham, Tsawa Rong, and other places.

Choktrul Sang-ngak Tendzin (Tulku Sang-ngak) (b. 1952)

Choktrul Sang-ngak Tendzin traveled to Nepal and India, and to France in the Western Hemisphere, where he served Kyabjé Dudjom Rinpoché, [2.231a] Kyabjé Dilgo Khyentsé Rinpoché, and other masters. He continues to benefit the teachings and beings.[14]

Trakya Lama Rinpoché Palden (1910?–1990?)

The excellent Trakya Lama Rinpoché Palden was born in Nyarong, eastern Tibet. From an early age, he felt a natural sense of renunciation and continually recited the mantra *Om mani padme hum*. Eventually, he entered a monastic institution in Nyarong and lived as an ordinary monk. There Trakya Palden met Lama Yeshe Dorjé, a student of Pema Duddul, the guru of Nyarong who attained rainbow body. He moved to his guru Yeshé Dorjé's encampment, known as Powakhuk, where he thoroughly trained in the graduated path according to the glorious Katok tradition, beginning with the preliminary practices from the cycles of Longsel Dorjé Nyingpo.

As Trakya Palden trained extensively in practices to harness the energies in his subtle channels, his subtle energy and mind became quite pliable. Even in the winter, he could get by with just a thin cotton garment and refused to wear anything made of leather or hide. Because of his command of the alchemical power of extracting the essence, he was able to absorb the vital essence of the elements. Although he was an ordained monk of pure discipline, he wore white cotton and wool, had hooped earrings of conch shell, [2.231b] and let his hair hang in long plaits.

Eventually, Trakya Palden met Khenchen Ngawang Palzang, from whom he received the Nyingtik cycles of the Dzogchen approach, including Lungtok Tenpai Nyima's oral lineage of pith instructions. All of his thought patterns faded into basic space as he directly experienced timeless awareness, the naked unity of awareness and emptiness. From then on, he conducted himself like the extraordinary guru that he was. His guru remarked, "When they say that one can gain freedom in this very lifetime, in this very body, through the Dzogchen approach, they are speaking of someone like Trakya Palden."

He was extremely meticulous in his spiritual practice. He would sit unmoving in his meditation hut with a lighted votive lamp on his head. He never loosened his meditation belt or lay on a bed, but practiced the "threefold unwavering stance,"[15] remaining walled up in his retreat places for many years. Trakya Palden frequented solitary places, such as glaciers, cliffs, mountain hermitages, forests, and river valleys.

On the glacial waste of Nangné situated on the snowy peak of Kabur in the eastern Tibetan lowlands, he practiced in a cave that was snowbound all year, except for about a fortnight during the fifth month. [2.232a] Once, for some reason, the passage through the snow never opened up, so that Trakya Palden was trapped for a whole year and no one could get any sustenance to him. The following year, several of his sponsors said to one another, "The yogin has been trapped in his snow cave for a year. We should recover his remains and perform funeral rites." That summer, when the path across the glacier opened up, they dug through a deep layer of snow at the mouth of the cave; when they looked inside, they saw the guru, completely unharmed and radiant, sitting in meditation.

"What are you doing, throwing all that snow around?" he asked them. "Through the compassion of the Three Jewels, I have not died. Ha! Ha!"

In fact, by practicing the path of natural great perfection, Trakya Palden had been completely absorbed for two years, day and night, in the nonconceptual yoga of space, an ongoing experience of utter lucidity. All deeply ingrained thought patterns had vanished into basic space, and he abided in the supreme state of the equal taste of everything. He later said, "During that period, for the most part I could see all things—outwardly and inwardly—without impediment, for I experienced them as naturally unobstructed visions of utter lucidity. [2.232b] I was immersed in a vast, spontaneously present array of purity in which the entire world appeared as enlightened forms and pure realms. Because of this, I had no ordinary need for food, clothing, or the like." All the people of the region came to have deep faith in Trakya Palden and urged him to teach. Eventually, he began to guide those whose personal circumstances were compatible with his own.

In the later part of his life, Trakya Palden lived at a hermitage called Seng-ri Monastery, a branch of Katok founded by Terchen Drimé and Choktrul Pema Gyaltsen (Kongtrul's activity incarnation). There he cared for his students, who came from all over—Washul Tromtar, Adzi, Nyarong, Gonjo, Lingshi, Katok, Rakchap, and other areas—to receive transmissions of the earlier and later cycles of the Nyingtik teachings and the cycles of Longsel Dorjé Nyingpo. He thus rendered great service to the teachings of the heart essence.

Finally, at the age of eighty, Trakya Palden passed into a state of peace as pavilions of rainbow light appeared. He left innumerable large and small relics, and all the signs of having awakened to perfect buddhahood through the path of the sublime spiritual approach were present. For his entire life, this guru had eschewed material possessions and personal ownership. When he passed away, he left nothing but a small bag of barley flour, [2.233a] taking as his model the example set by the lord of the dharma Paltrul Rinpoché.

His countless heart children included many gurus and tulkus from such monasteries as Katok and Rakchap, as well as gurus and tulkus from the hermitages he had frequented. In more recent times, with the renewed spread of the teachings, Trakya Palden's heart children have restored his hermitage, Seng-ri Monastery, and in other ways have continued his noble activities of study and practice, as well as his spiritual projects.

Polu Khen Rinpoché Dorjé (1897?–1970)

The excellent Khen Rinpoché Dorjé was born in the Polu Valley of Dergé; his father was Lhagyal of the Gangzhap family. At a certain age, he entered Polu Monastery, where he learned to read, write, memorize texts, and so forth, [2.233b] encountering no difficulties in his studies. He trained in many major and minor fields of knowledge, including grammar and astrology, under Gönchen Shar Lama Jamyang Chenrap, who had been one of Mipam's students. With numerous tutors at Palyul, Dzongsar, and other institutions, Polu Khenpo Dorjé studied a wide range of source texts, including those of Madhyamaka (such as *The Collections of Reasoning), The Five Treatises of Maitreya,* and the three inner classes of tantras of the Vajrayana. Through study and contemplation, he cut through his hesitation and reached a consummate level of erudition.

He was appointed to the abbot's throne of Polu Monastery and guided the community for a long time. From such masters as Drupwang Pema Norbu (the tulku of Palyul) and Kunzik Khyentsé Chökyi Lodrö, he received an amazing array of maturing empowerments, liberating instructions, explanations of the tantras, pith instructions, and practical methods for the entire range of the kama and terma traditions of the Vajrayana. He thus attained the rank of a precious vajra master. In particular, like one vase being filled to the brim from another, Polu Khenpo Dorjé received the oral lineage of natural great perfection—the tantras and pith instructions of profound meaning—from Khenchen Ngagi Wangpo of Katok Monastery, who was truly Vimalamitra in person. He was empowered as a holder of the ultimate lineage of realization. [2.234a]

When he went to Dokhol Monastery in Trom, Polu Khenpo Dorjé met a mahasiddha called Nyönpa Ngawang Chimé, who behaved like an inspired madman but whom no one recognized as such. This siddha introduced Polu Khenpo Dorjé to the nature of mind simply by nodding his head three times.[16] This enhanced Polu Khenpo's practice enormously, and he felt as though the sun had risen at daybreak.

In the later part of his life, Polu Khenpo Dorjé went to central Tibet and planted the victory banner of his spiritual practice at the principal holy sites of the central and southern regions of Ü, Tsang, Dakpo, and Kongpo, especially in the Chimpu Uplands of Samyé and in Kharchu, Lhodrak. He directly experienced all of the higher states of realization and siddhis that arise on the spiritual paths and levels. He met Panchen Vimalamitra in the form of an Indian sadhu, who used a symbolic gesture to introduce Polu Khenpo Dorjé directly to the true nature of his mind, so that the extraordinary realization that is the ultimate transmission awoke in him.

Later, when Tibet fell under the control of barbarians, Polu Khenpo Dorjé fled the country, going into exile in India, where he taught Bhutanese, Sikkimese, Nepalis, and Tibetans according to their individual circumstances, granting advice, instructions, teachings on major source texts and fields of secular knowledge, and so forth. [2.234b] He imparted these teachings generously and unstintingly. He went on a pilgrimage to the principal holy sites—places sacred to Guru Rinpoché—in Bhutan on Tibet's southern border, where he made offerings. On the plateau of Bumthang, he had a clear vision of the Omniscient One Longchenpa and received the transmission of a cache of termas of enlightened intent. He turned the wheel of the dharma at Tashi Gang and other centers throughout Bhutan. At the invitation of Bhutan's queen grandmother, the excellent Puntsok Chödrön, Polu Khenpo Dorjé went to live at the mountain hermitage of Dechen Chöling. There he rendered great service to the teachings of the heart essence, constantly guiding his faithful and devoted students according to each one's circumstances, by conferring profound teachings and pith instructions—the tradition of advice concerning Dzogchen from the Omniscient One and his spiritual heir, Jigmé Lingpa, including *The Seven Treasuries, The Four Higher Collections of the Heart Drop,* and *Timeless Awareness as the Guiding Principle.*

When Polu Khenpo Dorjé reached the age of seventy-four, he found himself less agile than he had once been and constantly gave appropriate advice about impermanence. On the eighteenth day of the ninth month in an Iron Dog year,[17] he suddenly experienced difficulty breathing, although he felt no illness or pain. [2.235a] He said to his attendant, Kunzang Wangdü, "Now I have no ordinary mind, for my awareness has dissolved into utter lucidity. I suppose that what they mean by 'death' is a bit like this." Sitting up straight, Polu Khenpo placed his hands palms down on his knees, the gesture known as that of "being at ease in the nature of mind," and with the dharmakaya gaze, looked into space. He then allowed his enlightened intent to resolve back into inner basic space.

His passing was accompanied by earthquakes and the sound of thunder, which were felt and heard by everyone. When Kyabjé Dudjom Rinpoché and Dzongsar Khyentsé Rinpoché committed his precious remains to the funeral pyre, a dome of bright rainbow light, about the size of a shield, rose to the center of a limpid sky. Relics of various colors were left; the skull in particular was not damaged by the flames but yielded the light yellow relics called shariram. Such signs inspired awe and faith in his students.

Among Polu Khenpo Dorjé's heart children were numerous holders of his lineages, including the great Bhutanese khenpo Kunga Lekpa, [2.235b] Taklung Tsetrul, the third Zhingkyong Choktrul, Soktsé Tulku, Gelong Karpo, and Lama Namdrol Zangpo.

Taklung Tsetrul Rinpoché (b. 1926)

Taklung Tsetrul Rinpoché, who received teachings from Khenpo Dorjé, was recognized as the rebirth of Tupten Chökyi Nyima by both the ninth Dodrak Rigdzin and Chuzang Khenchen Tenpai Nyima. At the age of five, he entered the path of the dharma at Taklung Tsé Monastery, and from Khenchen Tenpai Nyima he received his initial vows, the name Shedrup Nyinjé Trinlé Zangpo, and great honors. He also received a longevity empowerment and instructions on *Engaging in the Conduct of a Bodhisattva* from this holy master, and so undertook the process of receiving maturing empowerments and liberating instructions.

Taklung Tsetrul eventually went to sit at the feet of the guru Pawo Rinpoché of Dranang Gyaltsok, with whom he studied and contemplated some of the principal source texts. He received his novice ordination from the precious vajra holder of Mindroling Monastery and his final vows from its precious khenpo. Taklung Tsetrul became the epitome of stability, erudition, and venerability, [2.236a] a great holder of the teachings who maintained his vows with scrupulous discipline, widely bestowing the vows of the novice and full ordinations.

From Kunzang Tenpai Nyima, the sixth Rabjam of Zhechen Monastery, he received the entire transmission of the empowerments and oral transmissions for *The Treasury of Precious Hidden Teachings* and teachings on most of the collected works of Jigmé Lingpa. Sungtrul Rinpoché of Lhalung and the master of Tekchok Chöling bestowed on him the empowerments and oral transmissions for the entire corpus of Pema Lingpa's termas. From Tsewo Rinpoché of Golok, Taklung Tsetrul also received the oral transmissions for all of the Omniscient One's collected works.

At Dorjé Drak Monastery, he received from Gotsa Khenchen Tekchok Tendzin and Gotsa Choktrul Rinpoché all of the empowerments and oral transmissions for the Northern Terma cycles. Kangyur Rinpoché of Riwoché Monastery conferred on him the oral transmissions for the precious Kangyur, *The Collected Tantras of the Nyingma School, The Collected Teachings on the Mani Mantra,* the tantra tradition of Vajrakila composed by Jigmé Lingpa, and the works by that master known as the two "*Chariots.*"

From Kyabjé Dudjom Rinpoché, [2.236b] Taklung Tsetrul received the empowerments and oral transmissions for *The Treasury of Precious Hidden Teachings* and the kama tradition of the Nyingma school. The Gyalwa Karmapa, Rangjung Rigpai Dorjé, conferred on him the empowerments and oral transmissions for *The Treasury of Mantra of the Kagyü School* and *The Treasury of Spiritual Instructions.* From Trulzhik Rinpoché, he received the empowerments, instructions, and advice for *The Black Innermost Heart Drop* and other transmissions. Taklung Tsetrul studied extensively with Dilgo Khyentsé Rinpoché, from whom he received empowerments, oral transmissions, and instructions for such cycles as the collected works of Mipam, *The Four Higher Collections of the Heart Drop, The Treasury of Spiritual Instructions,* the six volumes of Jatsön Nyingpo's teachings, *The Heart Essence of Secrets,* and *The Treasury of Enlightened Qualities.* Polu Khen Rinpoché taught him the *Ketaka* (Mipam's commentary on the chapter concerning sublime knowing from *Engaging in the Conduct of a Bodhisattva*), *The Ornament of the Middle Way,* and the great experiential teachings of the Dzogchen approach, including instructions on original purity and spontaneous presence. In addition, Taklung Tsetrul studied with several great masters of the Rimé approach,[18] forging whatever connection was appropriate.

Taklung Tsetrul completed the preliminary practices of reinforcement and refinement[19] and undertook extensive retreats on the main practices. He served for five years as the presiding khenpo of Dorjé Drak, and when Tibet was lost, he went to India as a refugee. He rendered incalculable service to the teachings of the Northern Terma cycles [2.237a] at Draktok Monastery in Ladakh. He founded Dorjé Drak Monastery in Simla, building the structure and furnishing it, and established new monastic communities. Explaining, practicing, and working on behalf of the teachings, he is still living in the realm that epitomizes the seven vajra attributes, undaunted in his efforts to uphold, protect, and promote the precious teachings of the Victorious One.

Chatral Rinpoché Sanjé Dorjé (b. 1913)

The sublime Chatral Rinpoché Sanjé Dorjé, a holder of the transmission of the Dzogchen approach of utter lucidity, learned from numerous mentors in an eclectic way, studying and contemplating teachings without sectarian bias. In particular, for thirteen years, he served Pema Ledrel Tsal[20]—an emanation of the Omniscient Lord of Speech, Longchenpa—as a sponsor, an attendant, and a student. Sanjé Dorjé mastered a veritable ocean of teachings, especially those on the Dzogchen approach of utter lucidity.

Adopting a wandering mendicant's way of life, Sanjé Dorjé frequented places associated with spiritual attainment—isolated mountains and valleys—and applied himself one-pointedly to the ultimate significance of the heart essence of utter lucidity, developing to a consummate degree the enlightened qualities associated with the spiritual paths and levels.

When Sanjé Dorjé went to India, [2.237b] fulfilling an incontrovertible vajra prophecy, he founded several centers for the practice of the heart essence of utter lucidity, including one in Parping, Nepal, the sublime site where the great Orgyen undertook the practice of the great and glorious deity Vajrakumara and attained the siddhi of Mahamudra. Chatral Rinpoché Sanjé Dorjé is still alive, his lotus feet standing firmly in the vajra realm, and his kindness in nurturing the taproot of the teachings, the pith instructions of the Dzogchen approach, through his widespread activities is indescribable.

Among his students and heart children are many who are still living, including Katok Situ,[21] the rebirth of Kyabjé Dudjom Rinpoché,[22] Lama Ralo, Jigmé Tutop of Repkong, and Lama Sönam Tobgyé.

Tersé Chimé Rinpoché (20th Century)

Tersé Chimé Rinpoché was born in the southern part of eastern Tibet, on the border between Markham and Rongmo. His father, known as Serpa Terchen, belonged to a branch of the blood lineage of Rigdzin Duddul Dorjé and lived for more than 110 years. The father's family line was remarkable in that all of his sons—Nüden, Jamyang Chökyi Lodrö, [2.238a] and Tersé Chimé Rinpoché—were great exemplary masters in their own right.

From an early age, Tersé Chimé Rinpoché showed innate signs of spiritual attainment, such as supernormal powers of perception and a consummate degree of love and compassion. He even learned how to read and write quite naturally, without having to study. The guardian deities Zhingkyong Kunga Zhönnu and consort followed him like his shadow, serving as his allies. Chimé Rinpoché himself said, "It would seem that I am experiencing the effects of positive habit patterns from previous lifetimes, for even though I have not exerted myself much in this life, again and again I keep having clear visions of meditation deities of the Three Roots, and especially of Guru Rinpoché."

From his noble father, a great master of awareness, he received transmissions of the latter's own termas and those of Duddul Dorjé. In addition, Chimé Rinpoché studied at the feet of numerous other mentors, from whom he received countless profound teachings, including the great *Treasury of Precious Hidden Teachings* and the termas of Longsel Dorjé Nyingpo.

Especially, he studied again and again at the feet of the guru with whom he had shared karma for lifetimes, an emanation of Vimalamitra, Khenchen Ngawang Palzang. From him he received the complete transmission of the oral lineage that communicates the profound meaning of the great perfection of utter lucidity, [2.238b] a veritable river of spiritual advice, as well as thorough instructions on the practical application of these teachings. He also received the complete transmission of another "river," that of the wrathful mantras of the guardian deities of the teachings, including instructions for performing the sadhana practices and activity rituals.

Having come to consider all of his previous practice an outer shell, Tersé Chimé Rinpoché strove to attain siddhis. Like the sun rising at daybreak, there arose in him the experience of timeless awareness as the naked unity of awareness and emptiness: the way of abiding that is natural great perfection, the true nature of phenomena beyond intellectual speculation. His guru was enormously delighted with him, saying, "Now you have liberated your own mind through realization. Being of the blood line of Duddul, you must carry out enlightened activities to liberate others through compassion."[23] Accordingly, Chimé Rinpoché returned to his home region, where he bestowed countless profound teachings on those to be guided, including instructions on the preliminary and main practices, *The Treasury of Precious Hidden Teachings,* and the cycles of Longsel Dorjé Nyingpo and Duddul Dorjé. In ensuring benefit for beings without any personal bias, he exerted a positive influence over every region in the southern reaches of eastern Tibet, as far afield as Markham, Rongpo, Gonjo, Sa-ngen, Jedrok, and Bayul. [2.239a] He caused the teachings of natural great perfection to shed their light in all directions.

The people of Rongpo and Sa-ngen were thieves and bandits, engaged in warfare, strife, murder, blood sacrifice, as well as eating the flesh and drinking the blood of live animals. No one had been able to make any inroads in these areas, which were like realms of tsen spirits. The people made not even the slightest distinction between positive and harmful actions. Yet this lord was unhindered in his activities to annihilate evil and promote good in these regions. His skillful actions associated with the wrathful power of sorcery brought the people under his control and subdued them. On numerous occasions when Chimé Rinpoché performed a ritual focusing on wrathful activity, many of those present had visions of enemies of the teachings gathered in large crowds, blood pouring from their mouths.[24]

Meeting Tersé Chimé Rinpoché in person, one was impressed by his powerfully built body, his majestic locks of hair, his booming voice, compelling presence, and bloodshot eyes glaring like those of a wrathful deity. No one was able to budge in his presence. All gods and demons of the eight classes listened to his commands and carried out his enlightened activities. In such ways, Chimé Rinpoché's nature was such that he held mastery over the three realms [2.239b] and overwhelmed the three planes of existence with his charisma. He thus was a living example of what is meant by the expression "awakening to buddhahood out of the mouth of the fire pit."[25]

Chimé Rinpoché was cared for by Guru Padma's embodiment of timeless awareness. Although there were indications that he could have received many personal transmissions of profound termas, he did not make much effort to do so (other than in a few cases, in order to maintain his auspicious connection with these termas); rather, he focused his energy on the preservation of older termas. He would say, "If your wish is to ensure that the Early Translation school remains authentic, you must implement the saying, 'Take the kama teachings as your primary mainstay and adorn these secondarily with the terma teachings.'"

In these ways, Tersé Chimé Rinpoché ensured benefit for countless beings to be guided, both humans and formless gods and demons. Having brought all of his activities for his own and others' benefit to completion, he remarked, "Now these are very troubled times in China and Tibet. The blinding glare of spiritual degeneration has truly made itself known. Rather than stay here, I will go to Zangdok Palri for a while to remain at the feet of the lord Orgyen."

Without showing any sign of illness, Chimé Rinpoché adopted the gaze of the dharmakaya, and the display of his emanated form resolved back into the palace of Pema Ö in the realm of Chamara. Following his passing, his remains faded away into light, shrinking until only a sphere of light was left. [2.240a]

Bairo Rinpoché (b. 20th Century)

Bairo Rinpoché received complete transmissions of teachings from such masters as Chaktsa of Katok and Rakor Khen Drimé Özer of Getsé. He became a great holder of the lineage of the Katok tradition. In particular, he received *The Four Higher Collections of the Heart Drop* and other cycles of the secret Nyingtik teachings from Khenchen Ngawang Palzang. During the recent resurgence of the teachings in Tibet, Bairo Rinpoché has joined his efforts and aspirations with those of Zhichen Öntrul Rinpoché, a student of Shukchung Tulku Tsulo, who in turn was a student of Dodrup Tenpai Nyima. Bairo Rinpoché has restored his home monastery of Raktrom and others, founding shedras and meditation centers, and is still living, carrying out such enlightened activities.[26]

Lama Rinpoché Orgyen Rigdzin (1900–1960?)

The precious guru Orgyen Rigdzin was born in a nomadic encampment known as Rali, near Minyak in easternmost Tibet. He entered the monastery of his area at an early age. He was a wild young monk whom no one could control and so arrogant that he felt no hesitation about wanting to kill everyone he met. When he was around fifteen, Orgyen Rigdzin experienced an extraordinary awakening of his spiritual potential. He realized that nothing he might do in this world would be of great purpose. [2.240b] Looking through a copy of *Engaging in the Conduct of a Bodhisattva,* he had come across the following lines:

> What is accomplished by the insignificant things of this life,
> which are not rare and can be achieved even by animals?[27]
>
> . . . .
>
> If they do not understand the mind's secret,
>
> . . . .
>
> beings wander in meaningless misery.[28]

These words aroused a sense of renunciation in Orgyen Rigdzin. He thought to himself, "If I do not seek out extraordinary teachings and train myself, it will truly be as people say: 'One's human life is pointless, and one wanders in samsara pointlessly.'"

He joined a large group of people from his region on a pilgrimage and eventually arrived at Katok Dorjéden Monastery. There such masters as Khenchen Dulwai Dé and Nüden Khyentsé Özer taught him many of the mainstream sources, including *The Source Verses on Sublime Knowing, The Entrance into the Middle Way, The Fundamental Discourse of the Vinaya, The Illumination of the Middle Way, The Two Levels of Truth, The Ornament of the Middle Way, The Ornament of the Sutras* and the rest of the treatises of Maitreya, *The Detailed Commentary on Valid Cognition,* and works of poetry. Orgyen Rigdzin studied these texts for five years, day and night, even tying himself up in a sitting posture through the night.

Even this did not satisfy him, [2.241a] for he thought, "All of this is just the outer shell. Now I must seek the extraordinary advice of the Dzogchen approach." He went to upper Dza in the north to meet Khenchen Kunzang Palden Chödrak, who had been a student of both dear old Abu and Mipam Rinpoché, and begged to be taken under this master's care. This delighted Khenchen Kunpal, who gave Orgyen Rigdzin much advice and instruction from the Nyingtik teachings, including *Timeless Awareness as the Guiding Principle,* as well as a concise version of the oral lineage based on the tradition of Abu. Orgyen Rigdzin meditated on these for a long time, until realization dawned in his mind.

Then his guru prophesied, "These days, Nyoshul Khenchen Ngawang Palzang, renowned as an emanation of Vimalamitra, is transmitting the Dzogchen teachings in Washul Trom, east of Dergé. You will receive from him the great oral transmission of Dzogchen according to the tradition of Abu, my dear old master." Consequently, Orgyen Rigdzin set off for Washul Trom and met Khen Ngawang Palzang at the encampment of Nyoshul in Jangchub Jönpalung.

He remained associated with that monastery for the rest of his life. He trained in the extraordinary teachings found in the guru's works, among them *The Converging of the Streams of Lungtok Tenpai Nyima's Oral Lineage,* [2.241b] *The Vast Expanse of Space: A Further Commentary on Two Works,* and *A Commentary on the Enlightened Mind of Samantabhadra.* Orgyen Rigdzin frequented solitary places such as Dzong Karnak and Negyap. With great and ever-devoted diligence, he rejected all busyness, avoiding such conventional practices as accepting offerings, whether on behalf of the living or deceased, and amassing material possessions. Living alone like a wild animal, he meditated day and night until the realization that is the ultimate lineage awakened in his mind. He directly experienced the enlightened intent of natural great perfection, the true nature of phenomena beyond any intellectual speculation.

After Khen Rinpoché Ngawang Palzang passed away into a state of peace, Orgyen Rigdzin formed a close bond with Lungtrul Rinpoché (Lungtok Shedrup Tenpai Nyima), and they served as mentors to one another. It was Lungtrul who urged Orgyen Rigdzin to teach at various monasteries, where he gave many profound teachings on *Engaging in the Conduct of a Bodhisattva* and the preliminary practices, as well as the oral transmissions for the precious Kangyur. He offered the latter, along with many other profound teachings, to the precious rebirth of his guru, Khenchen Ngawang Palzang.

Finally, Orgyen Rigdzin returned to his home region, where he spent his remaining days on mountains, on cliff sides, and near lakes, places such as Bazhap Drakar, [2.242a] where Bairotsana and Pang Mipam had gained accomplishment in the past. Living alone, he maintained a schedule of four practice sessions spanning day and night. He once presided over a drupchen focusing on the deity Avalokiteshvara. As the participants began consecrating medicinal pills with the mantra *Om mani padme hum,* countless signs of successful practice manifested; the entire valley filled with rainbow light, a fine fragrance could be detected for miles, and the pills themselves multiplied. Orgyen Rigdzin inspired the local people to undertake virtuous actions, such as ceremonies for a hundred million repetitions of the mantra *Om ah hum vajra guru padma siddhi hum,* the fasting ritual, and the release of animals doomed to slaughter. Consequently, everyone throughout the region, down to the humblest peasant, was transformed by his positive influence. Everywhere Orgyen Rigdzin stayed, illness, epidemics, and obstacles were quelled, crops and livestock multiplied to abundance, and all that was virtuous and auspicious flourished. He was like a wish-fulfilling gem, a great being who brought purpose to all those connected to him.

Most of his students were also those of Lungtrul Rinpoché; in addition, he taught Karchung Tulku of Mukri, Tsultrim Chöpal of Rali, and many others, nurturing the precious teachings of the Victorious One through his noble deeds. [2.242b] His students' students, and theirs in turn, continue to ensure the dissemination and flourishing of the teachings of the vajra heart essence of utter lucidity throughout the world, East and West.

This concludes the discussion of the students of Khenchen Ngawang Palzang.

20

The Students of Lungtrul Shedrup Tenpai Nyima

Next I will discuss the students of my own holy guru, Lungtrul Shedrup Tenpai Nyima. Of the many who studied with him, I have already discussed the third Drupwang Penor, Shedrup Chökyi Drayang, in the context of the main Nyingtik lineage.[1]

Khen Ngawang Palzang Yangsi Rinpoché (Tekchok Tenpai Gyaltsen) (b. 1944/5)

Shedrup Tenpai Nyima's foremost heart son on the inner level, his holy regent in the ultimate sense, was the precious rebirth of Khen Ngawang Palzang. In his autobiography, *An Account of Marvels: Playful Dance in the Illusion,* the preceding Ngawang Palzang had written that he would be reborn seven times as a powerful tantric master, once at Dekyi Khangsar Tsang near the temple of Buchu Lhakhang in Kongpo. Yangsi Rinpoché was in fact born there in a Wood Monkey year.[2] He was recognized by such masters as Chaktsa Choktrul of Katok, Lama Orgyen Rigdzin, and Polu Khenchen Dorjé, all of whom visited him over a period of time. Permission for the tulku to move to eastern Tibet was obtained [2.243a] from the Ratreng regent of Tibet, who was also asked to name the boy and confirm his investiture. He was enthroned at both Katok Dorjéden and Khen Ngawang Palzang's homeland of Nyoshul Shugushar, also known as Jangchub Jönpalung. His enthronement was attended by the students of his former incarnation, as well as many thousands of local people and monks.

Lungtrul Rinpoché, the holy regent of the preceding Ngawang Palzang, and others took charge of Yangsi Rinpoché, giving him the name Tekchok Tenpai Gyaltsen and investing him as a king of the dharma throughout the three realms. Then, in time, a Lama Asang came to serve as his primary tutor, and Yangsi Rinpoché began to learn reading, writing, and so forth. With his former incarnation's students—the holy guru Orgyen Rigdzin, Chaktsa Rinpoché of Katok, and others—he studied and contemplated a variety of subjects, receiving profound teachings and the oral transmissions for the precious Kangyur, *The Treasury of Precious Hidden Teachings,* and so forth.

Specifically, the extraordinary masters of Yangsi Rinpoché's buddha family were Lungtrul Rinpoché Shedrup Tenpai Nyima, Tromgé Arik Rinpoché, Khenchen Munsel of Golok, and others. He served them and in return received general introductions to the secret Nyingtik teachings of Dzogchen, [2.243b] especially the great oral lineage of pith instructions from Lungtok Tenpai Nyima—teachings on trekchö, tögal, and so forth—which he studied and practiced. He had no interest in material gain, such as taking offerings on behalf of people, living or dead, and lived at the retreat hermitage of Jangchub Jönpalung as a truly great king of mendicants on the ultimate level.

During the barbarian occupation, he was imprisoned for a long time, but due to his own lofty motivation and the residual merit of the Tibetan people in these times, he was not seriously harmed. Upon his release, the same motivation led him back to his home monastery of Jangchub Jönpalung, which had meanwhile been devastated by the barbarians. Yangsi Rinpoché restored both the buildings and their contents to a condition finer than the original. He reinstituted the traditions of ritual dances on the tenth day of the lunar cycle, drupchens, ceremonies for consecrating medicine, and so forth.

Yangsi Rinpoché has bestowed the great *Treasury of Precious Hidden Teachings* three times, at Katok Dorjéden, Getsé Tralek Monastery, and his own monastery. He has also bestowed teachings on the preliminary practices, the pith instructions of the oral Dzogchen lineage, *Timeless Awareness as the Guiding Principle,* and other transmissions on many people, whatever their status, according to their circumstances.

In brief, Yangsi Rinpoché has followed the ideal example set by the noble Khen Ngawang Palzang [2.244a] and still resides at the hermitage of his home monastery, seated firmly on the vajra throne as he shines like the sun, adorned with the major and minor marks of perfection. His son, Lungtrul Do-ngak Shedrup Nyima, lives there as well, serving the teachings of the sublime secret. I pray that both of them live for incalculable eons!

Choktrul Nyima Gyaltsen Rinpoché (b. 1945?)

Choktrul Nyima Gyaltsen Rinpoché was born in a village called Kyidü Ruwa in upper Trom. He entered the shedra of Jangchub Jönpalung in Nyoshul at an early age and studied and contemplated a vast range of the mainstream sources of sutra and tantra under such masters as Khenchen Trinlé Gyatso, Khen Rinpoché Ayik, and Choktrul Pema Gyurmé. There are some who feel that Nyima Gyaltsen is the speech incarnation of Khenchen Ngawang Palzang.

Nyima Gyaltsen studied on a more profound level with Lungtrul Rinpoché Lodrö Shedrup Tenpai Nyima, Khen Rinpoché Munsel of Golok, Tromgé Arik Rinpoché, and others, receiving the earlier and later cycles of the Nyingtik teachings, [2.244b]

The Four Higher Collections of the Heart Drop, Timeless Awareness as the Guiding Principle, and two editions of the source texts for *The Heart Drop of Longchenpa.* He put these teachings into practice in the Trom region of eastern Tibet, focusing on the heart essence while setting an example of erudition, venerability, and nobility.

Nyima Gyaltsen, who is still living, is a teacher of such extraordinary capabilities that he can teach works like the thirteen great source texts and Mipam's *Entrance to the Ways of the Wise* from memory.

Dragyab Lama Chöden Rinpoché (b. 20th Century)

Lama Chöden Rinpoché was born in Dragyab, in the southern reaches of eastern Tibet. He embraced the dharma at an early age. Journeying to the region of Dergé in search of teachings, he heard of the fame of Khenchen Ngawang Palzang and his spiritual heir[3] and continued on to Nyoshul Monastery. He enrolled in the shedra there and spent many years studying and training in the mainstream traditions of the sutras (Madhyamaka, Prajñaparamita, Vinaya, Abhidharma, and so forth) and the tantras (*The Heart Essence of Secrets* and others), becoming quite learned.

In particular, he met Lungtrul Rinpoché and received from him a complete transmission of the entire oral lineage of experiential instructions of the Dzogchen approach, [2.245a] so that realization dawned in his mind. Following his guru's directive—"Exert yourself in practice!"—Chöden Rinpoché returned to his home region, where he practiced for many years in meditation huts that he built in solitary places like glacial wastes and cliff faces. Through the paths of trekchö and tögal, he gained the sublime siddhi.

During the changing times of the barbarian occupation, he was not harmed at all, and with the recent revivification of the teachings, he has transmitted those concerning natural great perfection throughout the southern reaches of eastern Tibet, including Dragyab, Markham, and Gonjo. In this way, still living and seated firmly on the vajra throne, he continues to spread the enlightened activities of his guru throughout space.

Jokhang Choktrul Rinpoché (b. 20th Century)

The excellent Jokhang Choktrul Rinpoché was born in eastern Tibet. At an early age, he succeeded his former incarnation as throne holder at the seat of the victorious Palyul lineage, having been invested as a master of the teachings under the guidance of many sublime teachers at that institution.

It was there that Jokhang Choktrul received oral transmissions for the precious Kangyur from many tutors and mentors. With Khen Pema Jigmé, [2.245b] Serta Khenchen Nüden Khyentsé Özer, and others, he studied the sutras and tantras in general and received from them countless profound teachings, including the empowerments, oral transmissions, instructions, and mainstream sources for the Nyingtik teachings, the *Namchö* cycle, and the termas of Ratna Lingpa.

In that all of Jokhang Choktrul's lineages are identical to those held by the third Drupwang Penor, Tupten Jigmé Shedrup Chökyi Drayang, these two masters became vajra brothers; their minds blended, becoming one, for they shared many of the same gurus, empowerments, teachings, and pith instructions.

The extraordinary masters of Jokhang Choktrul's buddha family were Dartang Choktrul Rinpoché and Shedrup Tenpai Nyima (the rebirth of Nyoshul Lungtok Rinpoché). He studied at their feet, receiving the great experiential transmission of the secret Nyingtik teachings of the Dzogchen approach. For many years, he studied and practiced the comprehensive pith instructions of the oral lineage of tögal and other cycles. He thus discovered the enlightened intent that is the ultimate lineage. His lord guru Shedrup Tenpai Nyima told him, "You are the one who was intended to receive from me all of these empowerments, oral transmissions, and instructions. [2.246a] Now I am content." He thus entrusted Jokhang Choktrul with the advice on ultimate reality, fulfilling a prophecy that had arisen from the guru's prescience.

At a certain point, during the great upheavals of the barbarian occupation, Jokhang Choktrul was sent to prison and encountered various other obstacles, but due to his superb motivation as a victorious one with unwavering compassion, he continued to direct his activities, never wasting any time. As a scripture states:

> The time for waves of the ocean, home to many creatures, may
> conceivably be past,
> but the time for buddhas to act on behalf of children to be guided
> is never over.[4]

In the spirit of this quotation, Jokhang Choktrul emerged victorious in his battle against obstacles.

In more recent times, there has been a renaissance of the Victorious One's precious teachings among the Tibetan people. For more than thirty years, Jokhang Choktrul has joined forces with Rigdzin Kunzang Sherab and many other excellent masters to rebuild the Palyul seat, which was completely destroyed. There is now a base for the teachings, with a temple and all its furnishings—statues, murals, robes for ritual dances, and shrine implements—as well as a shedra and meditation center. Ceremonies are held on the tenth day of the lunar month, drupchens take place annually, [2.246b] and training in ritual dance, painting, chanting, and music is provided. All of the traditions have been fully restored, and Jokhang Choktrul has accepted the responsibility of ensuring that the teachings will flourish even more than in the past.

This master was invited by Drupwang Penor Rinpoché to India, where he conferred the empowerments of his own tradition—the *Namchö* cycle, the termas of Ratna Lingpa, and the kama transmissions—as well as training in rituals and ceremonies, pith instructions, and other traditional methods. He has thus rendered great service to the precious teachings of the supreme secret of the Vajrayana and left an enormous legacy. Even now, shining like the sun and adorned with the major and minor marks of perfection, Jokhang Choktrul is continually engaged in spiritual projects, serving as a glorious protector of all the teachings and all beings. Living at his home monastery, the seat of the Palyul school, he bestows the teachings of the heart essence of utter lucidity, guiding his students, regardless of their status, according to their individual capabilities, instructing them in the preliminaries, the main body of practices, *The Commentary on the Enlightened Mind of Samantabhadra,* and so forth. In maintaining these activities to ensure benefit and well-being, Jokhang Choktrul continues to spread the enlightened activities of his holy and venerable guru throughout space.

As for the students of contemporary masters like Drupwang Penor Rinpoché, [2.247a] Jokhang Rinpoché of Palyul Monastery, Chatral Sanjé Dorjé, Drupwang Lungtok Gyatso, Adzom Druktrul Rinpoché, Khenchen Munsel Rinpoché, and Khenchen Jigmé Puntsok, I request that the respective lineage holders write accounts of their lives that are similar to the ones herein.

The accounts in this chapter, as well as Chapters 16–19, concern the lineage transmitted by the great bodhisattva Paltrul. It has been said:

> The students' students are better than the students themselves,
> and future generations of students will be as extensive as the sky.

Paltrul's students and their students in turn have appeared like constellations arrayed across the vault of the night sky, serving the teachings of the ultimate heart essence throughout the world in an excellent way.

21

A Summary of the Nyingtik Lineage

The accounts in Chapters 10–20 concern the hosts of students in the Nyingtik lineage, whose presence was like that of the powerful sun with its rays shining everywhere. With this I conclude my discussions of the students of great masters in this supreme lineage.

The biographies of the individual lineage masters clearly show that these holy beings treated the teachings with the highest respect, receiving them not once but many times and often from a variety of teachers. [2.247b] This accounts for the fact that authentic parallel lineages may consist of differing numbers of gurus, and some of the gurus may have had many students in common with other gurus. In the Nyingtik lineage, the lines of succession in monastic centers are interconnected, so that the biographies of some living masters precede accounts of masters of the past.

In this work, I have emphasized the mainstream transmissions of the ultimate lineage of the Dzogchen approach—the gurus from whom, and the students to whom, they were passed on. However, I have had to consider such cases as the following: Through one master, Paltrul, two lineages were transmitted, those of Jigmé Gyalwai Nyugu and Khyentsé Yeshé Dorjé. Jamyang Khyentsei Wangpo, who studied with more than a hundred gurus, transmitted lineages for each of these, most notably the two transmissions of Dzogchen teachings that he received: one from Trinlé Chödron of the Mindroling tradition and the other from Jigmé Gyalwai Nyugu.

There is some overlap between the lineage of the Dzogchen teachings and those of both Dzogchen and Katok Monasteries, since many of the gurus and students of these institutions were also students in the lord Khyentsé's lineage of the Dzogchen teachings, but I have chosen not to discuss the Dzogchen lineage strictly along the lines of succession at Katok or any other monastery. This should not be seen in any way as contentious on my part.

Likewise, in discussing what I refer to as the primary and secondary lineages, I have regarded as primary the particular lineage I myself have received, for, as is said, it is "the deity on whom my flower has fallen." [2.248a] It should be understood that it is on this basis alone, and not on the basis of any assumption of superiority or inferiority, that other lineages have been considered "secondary." Those who are small-minded or prejudiced might think that the distinction I have made between primary and secondary Dzogchen lineages is somehow fixed in stone. I humbly request that people respect my attempt to portray the realization that masters of awareness in the lineage have attained in the past due to their skillful practice in following the example of our Teacher, the Buddha. In the words of the Omniscient One Longchenpa:

> Thus, concerning this precious lineage of the unsurpassable secret, the ongoing flow of blessings that derive from empowerment has not been interrupted, and so the personal transmission of the profound teachings of the secret mantra approach has not been disrupted. This lineage of pure samaya is like a golden chain untarnished by broken commitments, and so whatever one hopes to accomplish can come to be, just as one wishes. The experience it entails comes from direct introduction to one's true nature, and so is unsullied by theoretical descriptions based on intellectual speculation. This lineage bears witness to the Buddha's words, the explanatory commentaries, and the pith instructions, and so can be taken as ultimately trustworthy. This lineage of those who gained siddhis remains uninterrupted and so is imbued with an enormous transmission of blessings. [2.248b] Therefore, one with the highest degree of diligence can awaken to buddhahood in this lifetime; one with average diligence can awaken in the bardo; at the very least, one can awaken to buddhahood in a naturally occurring nirmanakaya pure realm. Such is the profound path of natural great perfection, and the lineage of these teachings is referred to as "a garland of light, with precious wish-fulfilling gems strung one after another. . . ."
>
> . . . The sun that is the treasury of these teachings
> arose with the original victorious one's discovery of utter lucidity.
> It is for masters of awareness today to follow that example,
> so apply yourselves diligently to these words.

Let me close with my own verse:

> Masters of awareness are as numerous as the stars in the constellations
> shining across the vault of the vast nighttime sky—the pinnacle spiritual approach.
> Although my small mind cannot encompass the example they set with their lives,
> I have recorded a brief account for the sake of future generations.
> May the virtue of this endeavor ensure that the illumination of the Victorious One's precious teachings
> endures as the foundation of benefit and happiness.

May the sublime hosts of those who uphold these teachings live long,
their lotus feet standing firmly for incalculable eons. [2.249a]
May the sun of benefit and happiness shine in all directions,
spreading its light—the theory and practice of the teachings.

22

The Transmission of the Teachings of the Early Translation School

In addition, I will briefly discuss the transmission of the Early Translation school. This school, the Nyingma, is the ancestral spring or headwater of all the Victorious One's teachings found in the Land of Snows. The existence of Buddhism in Tibet was first recorded during the reign of King Lha Totori,[1] an emanation of the bodhisattva Samantabhadra. Later, the tradition itself was established by King Songtsen Gampo, an emanation of Avalokiteshvara. Finally, three figures (the abbot Shantarakshita, the master Padmakara, and the Buddhist king Trisong Detsen) along with King Ralpachen and others, convened the 108 Indian scholars and Tibetan translators and similar groups. These groups translated into Tibetan the sutras, tantras, and secular treatises—the words that constitute the excellent speech of the Victorious One and the commentaries written to explain them. Seven men were selected as the first to receive monastic ordination. As well, there were such masters as the twenty-five intimate students of Guru Rinpoché, the residents of the meditation communities of Chuwori, and the eighty mahasiddhas of Yerpa. As the basis for the teachings, temples, like the great hall at glorious Samyé, were built to represent enlightened form, scriptures were printed to represent enlightened speech, and chapters of the ordained sangha were established to represent enlightened mind. Under this positive influence, the Land of Snows became a spiritual country, and with the establishment of the tradition [2.249b] that has six distinguishing characteristics,[2] the teachings spread and flourished.

There are said to be three great mainstream lines of transmission of the Nyingma teachings. In upper, or western, Tibet, a lineage came from three kings among tantric masters: Nyak, Nup, and Zur; in central Tibet, from three great omniscient masters: Rong, Long, and Shak; and in lower, or eastern, Tibet, from three lords of the dharma of Katok Monastery: Dam, Tsang, and Jam. In addition, in more recent times, there were three masters bearing the title Jamgön, for they were emanations of the bodhisattva Mañjushri.

Of these, the first mainstream line came from Yeshé Zhönnu,[3] the great master of the Nyak clan, who promulgated the teachings and whose students included the "eight named Pal." It also came from Sang-gyé Yeshé Rinpoché of the Nup clan, who promulgated the teachings and had innumerable students. Among them were the "four sublime heart sons" and a fifth, the holiest of his sons, Yönten Gyatso of the valley known as Khulung. This first line also came from three generations of masters from the Zur clan. The students of Zurpoché Shakya Jungné included the "pinnacle students," the "eight lesser peaks," the "eight great meditators," and others. Zurchung Sherab Drakpa had countless students, such as the "four pillars," the "eight beams," the "sixteen joists," and the "thirty-two rafters." [2.250a] And Zur Shakya Seng-gé's students included the "four ancestors," the "four named Nakpo," the "four teachers," and the "thousand bearers of the parasol."

The second mainstream line of transmission came from the three masters Rong, Long, and Shak. Rongzom's students included the "seventeen translators who were his equals," the "thirty-five siddhas," the "180 yogins," and the "500 bearers of the parasol." The Omniscient One Longchenpa had a connection with innumerable people, among whom were the "three who gained fame for erudition," the "five heart sons," the "four mentors who spread the teachings," and the "four accomplished yogins." The students of Shakya Dorjé of Katok Monastery included the renowned "thousand bearers of the parasol." The students of these masters, and their students in turn, seemed to cover the surface of the earth, promulgating the teachings of the Early Translation school.

In the lower elevations of eastern Tibet, the third mainstream line of transmission came from the three lords of the dharma of Katok Monastery—Dampa Deshek, Tsangtönpa Dorjé Gyaltsen, and Jampa Bum—and their students, including the thirteen successive gurus and thirteen regents of that institution. Among these were a hundred thousand who attained rainbow body. The three masters with the title Jamgön had many students, including tens of thousands of mentors who spread the teachings.

Similarly, with respect to the terma tradition, [2.250b] the great lineage holders of the Early Translation school included three kings among the hundred tertöns—Nyang Nyima Özer, Guru Chöwang, and Rigdzin Gödem of the northern steppes—as well as Ngari Panchen Pema Wangyal, the great tertön of Trengpo named Sherab Özer, the great Rigdzin Pema Trinlé, the great tertön of Mindroling and his brother, and the second Omniscient One, Jigmé Lingpa. These masters, along with their students and their students' students, ensured that this lineage still flourishes and has spread to all corners of the earth. Notably, Guru Rinpoché said of these termas, "The final days of the teachings will be delayed by the termas," and there is no Tibetan Buddhist tradition or part of the world where their presence is not felt.

THE FOUNDING OF NYINGMA CENTERS

Let us now consider how the main religious centers of the Nyingma school and their lines of succession came into being. In ancient times, the main centers in the central regions were the three major temples of Lhasa, Tongtang Denkar, Doyi Lhakhang in Unchang, and others. In eastern Tibet, the centers included those at the cliffs known as Wa Seng-gé Drak and Korong Seng-gé Drak, as well as the temple of Oru Jamchen Tsuklak Khang [2.251a] and Kham Longtang Drönma. In all regions of Tibet, upper, central, and lower, innumerable Buddhist centers were founded to maintain the specific tradition of the abbot, the master, and the Buddhist king. Hundreds of thousands of people joined the ordained sangha, thus serving the precious teachings of the Victorious One. In those days, all of Tibet was influenced by the Early Translation school of the Nyingma, which spread and flourished enormously.

Later, during the time of the three generations of the Zur clan (the third source of the first mainstream line of transmission), there were major Buddhist centers in the valley known as Ukpalung in the region of Tsang, at Drak Gyawo, and at the temple of Palchen Lhakhang (in lower Shang Valley). In short, the teachings continued to spread and flourish in the western, central, and southern regions of Tibet. The monastic communities were very large, with tens of thousands of monks. Once, when a horseman rode up a valley, his horse shied at the sound of the monks opening the cases of their texts as they set them out for a teaching session.

Likewise, in lower Tibet, there were three masters of the monastic tradition: Mar, Yo, and Tsan. Within this region were Dentik Shelgyi Yangdzong (the residence of the great guru Gongpa Rabsel),[4] as well as the seats of Bairotsana's student Yudra Nyingpo, Aro Yeshé Jungné, [2.251b] and others—places like the temple of Kham Longtang Tsuklak Khang, Katok Dorjéden, and other religious centers where hundreds of thousands of monks were enrolled. During this period, the teachings of the Early Translation school spread throughout Tibet, while the Sakya, Gelukpa, and other schools had only a small presence.

Later, during the lifetimes of Terchen Duddul Dorjé, Longsel Nyingpo, Minling Terchen, and others, the custom arose of referring to the major centers of the Early Translation school in abbreviated forms: Dor (Dorjé Drak), Min (Mindroling), and Pal (Palri Tekchok Ling) in the higher regions; Ka (Katok), Pal (Palyul), and Dzog (Dzogchen) in the lower-lying areas. These primary monastic centers and their affiliates maintained the teachings of the Early Translation school in Tibet.

When Palri Tekchok Ling eventually closed down, the major centers of the Early Translation school were fixed at six: Dor (Dorjé Drak) and Min (Mindroling) in the upper regions, Zhe (Zhechen) and Dzog (Dzogchen) in the middle elevations, and Ka (Katok) and Pal (Palyul) in the lowlands. These centers, the so-called mother monasteries, and their affiliates have ensured that the precious teachings of the Early Translation school of the Nyingma are maintained throughout the world. The following is a brief account of the founding of these six major centers. [2.252a]

THE SIX MAJOR MONASTERIES

Tupten Dorjé Drak

Of the two centers in the upper elevations, Dorjé Drak and Mindroling, the first was Tupten Dorjé Drak. In the past, Ngari Panchen Pema Wangyal and his brother were masters of the teachings, both kama and terma, of the Early Translation school, especially those of the Northern Terma cycles. During the lifetime of the glorious Tashi Tobgyal, a large encampment, Ewam Chokgar, was devoted to the specific tradition of Guru Padma. During the time of Rigdzin Ngagi Wangpo, the spiritual center Tupten Dorjé Drak was founded.[5] Later, the successive tulkus of Rigdzin Gödem appeared, including Rigdzin Pema Trinlé, as did masters like Chuzang Rinpoché, as well as their students and their students' students, beyond number. The flawless tradition specific to Tupten Dorjé Drak spread throughout western, central, and eastern Tibet.

Today this tradition is maintained in Tibet and India, by Rigdzin Chenpo in Tibet, Taklung Tsetrul Rinpoché in India, and other masters. Accounts of this monastery and Mindroling can be found in *The Great Lines of Succession at the Monastic Seats of the Nyingma School,* [2.252b] a work written by the lord Khyentsei Wangpo.

Ogmin Orgyen Mindroling

Mindroling Monastery was founded in the Iron Dog year of the eleventh sexagesimal cycle[6] by the king of the dharma Terdak Lingpa. From the time of the great tertön himself and his brother, Lochen Chöpal Gyatso, the succession fell to his sons and daughter, and continues to the present day with the great throne holder Trichen Kunzang Pema Wang-gi Gyalpo. These successive masters have maintained an unparalleled transmission of the general teachings of the tantras and sadhana classes as found in the kama tradition of the Early Translation school, and in particular the traditions of profound termas, especially those of the Lhoter, or Southern Terma, cycle.[7]

Most remarkable are the teachings that have been preserved at Mindroling: the oral explanations and traditional methods associated with *The Discourse on United Intent* and *The Web of Magical Display* of the Early Translation school according to the system of the Zur masters and the transmission of the *Seven Treasuries,* works of the enlightened intent of Longchenpa, the Omniscient King of the Dharma.

Mindroling Monastery is renowned as the "headwater of the teachings of the supreme secret," because its tradition has, like the sun, illuminated the philosophical system unique to the Nyingma school. The Mindroling tradition is an inspiration to all who are associated with the Early Translation school, for it does not require support from any other source, but rather stands on its own. [2.253a] Its influence on both the kama and terma traditions in their entirety has been unparalleled in terms of the explanation and promulgation of maturing empowerments and liberating instructions and the passing on of traditional rituals and sadhanas.

From this mother monastery came affiliates throughout upper and lower Tibet. The two sublime tulkus Minling Trichen and Khenchung,[8] as well as Khochim Rinpoché[9] and other masters, live in the holy land of India, where they maintain these teachings. In addition, Samdrup Tulku Rinpoché (the son of Tokden Yeshé Nyingpo) lives in Thimphu, Bhutan, benefiting the teachings and beings with his projects, which include building temples, statues, and stupas and printing texts.

Palri Tekchok Ling

Palri Tekchok Ling Monastery[10] enjoyed a period of great flourishing during which its lineage was found in all regions of Tibet. Even Jigmé Lingpa traced his origins to this spiritual lineage,[11] and such circumstances account for its prominence in the expression "Dor, Min, and Pal." Later, however, with the changing times, Palri Tekchok Ling fell into ruins, until one could not tell at all what had once been there. [2.253b]

With the recent renaissance of the teachings in Tibet, the lay and ordained populations of the area have joined forces and are making a great effort to restore the monastery and the traditional seat of this lineage.

Dzogchen Rudam Orgyen Samten Chöling

Of the two major centers in the middle elevations, Zhechen and Dzogchen, the latter—the monastery of the Drupwang Dzogchen tulkus in eastern Tibet—was founded during the eleventh sexagesimal cycle[12] by the Dzogchen master Pema Rigdzin (an emanation of the buddha Ratnashikin) when he established the major Buddhist center Rudam Orgyen Samten Chöling.[13] This seat was held in the following generations by the successive tulkus of Pema Rigdzin and those of his foremost heart sons, such as Namkha Ösel.

Then the three masters called Choktrul, including the tulku of Gyalsé Zhenpen Tayé, a model of erudition, venerability, and nobility, served as the monastery's directors. This post was later held by successive tulkus of Dzogchen Khyentsé, Purtsa Choktrul, and Lingtrul, as well as Khenchen Pema Dorjé, Khenchen Zhenpen Chökyi Nangwa, and others, universal monarchs among the learned and accomplished. [2.254a]

The Omniscient One prophesied, "My cycle *The Innermost Heart Drop of the Dakini* has been established as a mainstay and will ensure that the precious teachings of the Victorious One will not vanish for another five hundred years." In keeping with this statement, the tradition of Dzogchen Monastery has emphasized the cycles *The Heart Drop of the Dakini* and *The Innermost Heart Drop of the Dakini,* as well as the termas of Rigdzin Nyima Drakpa, the transmissions specific to this line. Dzogchen Monastery has also served as a base for the teachings of the entire Nyingma school of the supreme secret, both the kama and terma traditions. As such, it is known throughout Tibet as the Drupwang Dzogchenpa tradition.

The primary masters of these teachings have been the three Choktruls (that is, the rebirths of Dzogchen Pema Rigdzin,[14] Dzogchen Pönlop,[15] and Gyalsé Zhenpen Tayé), who in modern times escaped to the holy country of India, studied and trained there, and continue the noble activities of their holy former incarnations in maintaining monastic communities and so forth. The sublime tulku of Khenchen Pema Dorjé, Choktrul Kalzang Rinpoché, [2.254b] Arik Khenchen Tsewang Lhundrup, and other masters still hold the original seat in eastern Tibet, maintaining the theory and practice of the teachings at the great centers of Dzogchen, that is, the monastery of Rudam Samten Chöling and the shedra of Dzogchen Shri Simha. The three Choktruls, masters of the teachings who fled to India, have shown themselves to be exemplary in their own right. Their noble deeds and the legacy they are creating are like refined gold. Those associated with this lineage pray from their hearts that these masters will continue their activities.

A more complete discussion can be found in *The Lines of Succession at the Seat of Dzogchen Monastery* by Lama Gyalwang Nyima Rinpoché.

Zhechen Tennyi Dargyé Ling

Rabjam Tenpai Gyaltsen, a heart son of Drupwang Dzogchenpa,[16] was an emanation of the buddha Ashoka. His rebirth, the second Rabjam, Kunzang Namgyal Losel Gyatsoi Dé, founded Zhechen Monastery in the Wood Hare year of the twelfth sexagesimal cycle,[17] [2.255a] establishing it as a major center for the theory and practice of the sutras and tantras. It became the mother monastery from which sprang all of the monasteries in the entire region.

Associated with Zhechen Monastery were the successive tulkus of the lord Rabjam, Gyaltsap Tendzin Chögyal, Kongtrul, Göntö, and Öntrul. Of particular note were Panchen Gyurmé Tutop Namgyal (a master of the five fields of knowledge) and the fourth Gyaltsap, Panchen Gyurmé Pema Namgyal. The incarnation lineages and students of these masters—an incredible number of learned and accomplished masters—have left a superb, unrivaled legacy of explaining and promulgating the teachings of the Early Translation school in general and those of the Mindroling tradition in particular. It is this legacy that is responsible for the fact that many hundreds of monasteries and centers associated with this tradition have endured and continue to raise high the victory banner of the Early Translation school's teachings concerning the supreme secret. The fact that Mipam Rinpoché, Mañjushri in person, traced his origins to this lineage is another testament to the great legacy of this line and the enormous kindness of its masters. [2.255b]

The current master of these teachings, Rabjam Rinpoché, is Dilgo Khyentsé Rinpoché's grandson. He lives and maintains the teachings at the newly established center of Shechen Tennyi Dargeling in Nepal. Zhechen Kongtrul Rinpoché was reborn as the son of Zurmang Trungpa Rinpoché and was recognized by Kyabjé Dilgo Khyentsé Rinpoché. In such ways, the teachings of the Zhechen line are flourishing in both India and Tibet.

Pal Katok Dorjéden

The "glorious vajra seat of Katok," another headwater of the teachings of the Early Translation school, was famed as a second Magadha[18] in the southern part of eastern Tibet. The seat of Pal Katok was established in the Female Earth Hare year of the third sexagesimal cycle[19] by Katokpa Dampa Deshek (also known as Lama Popa Tayé) in his thirty-eighth year. Dampa Deshek was a great being prophesied to be an emanation of such extraordinary Indian Buddhist masters as the elder Bharadhvaja and Shantideva and such Tibetan masters as Yeshé Tsogyal and the translator of the Nyak clan, Yeshé Zhönnu. Tens of thousands of students, from Karu Nakru in the Chungpo region of upper Tibet in the west to China and Mongolia in the east, gathered around him. [2.256a]

He established a tradition, based on the sutras, tantras, and other fields of knowledge, that emphasized the three main sources of the Early Translation school, that is, *The Discourse on United Intent, The Web of Magical Display,* and the mind teachings. His philosophical view was grounded in the tenets of these three sources. His teaching methods focused on three further subjects: Madhyamaka, Prajñaparamita, and Vinaya. His guardian deities were the "three black ones." He thus founded a lineage in ancient times, and the entire length and breadth of Tibet was influenced by the lineage holders of the glorious Katok tradition. Katok Monastery steadily grew, until some 180,000 monks were associated with it. When they met to renew their vows, the light reflected from their formal outer robes turned the sky yellow.

Foremost among the great Dampa Deshek's heart sons was his regent, Gyaltsap Tsangtön Dorjé Gyaltsen, whose regent in turn was the lord Jampa Bum. These are renowned as the "three masters, Dam, Tsang, and Jam, of Katok." They were followed by thirteen successive gurus (beginning with U-ö Yeshé Bumpa), thirteen successive administrators, thirteen successive khenpos, thirteen successive siddhas, the Drimé Zhingkyong tulkus (responsible for holding the monastic seat), and the generations of masters in the ultimate lineage of pith instructions. By the time of Situ Chökyi Gyatso of Katok Monastery,[20] [2.256b] there had been some eighty successive abbots of the monastic seat and 123 successive presiding lamas.

Like the glorious shining sun, the Katok line illuminated the theory and practice of the precious teachings of the Victorious One in general and those associated with the Early Translation school of the Vajrayana in particular. The students of this lineage have been as numerous as the stars in the nighttime sky. A hundred thousand of them attained rainbow body. Many mastered the four kinds of enlightened activity and attained the sublime siddhi, so that with their control over the four elements, they could pass through solid rock and so forth. The lineages of the learned and accomplished students of the line, and of their students in turn, spread to India, China, and Yunnan as well as throughout the eastern, central, and southern regions of Tibet.

The Katok tradition enjoyed widespread influence, for 108 principal and 1,002 secondary monasteries were said to uphold this lineage, making it a source of the teachings of the Early Translation school. The masters of the teachings at the main seat were the successive tulkus of Katok Drimé Zhingkyong, Moktsa, Chaktsa, [2.257a] Kunchen Katok Situ, Nyingön Jamyang, Getsé Mahapandita, and Önpo Tulku,[21] as well as the more recent incarnation lines of the great khenpos Ngawang Palzang and Lekshé Dulwai Dé. These and other masters maintained the tradition with their noble activities of studying, practicing, and engaging in spiritual projects.

With the changing times, the main seat was completely destroyed. However, the sublime, precious tulkus of Katok have restored it to more than its former glory, building a temple, a shedra, a meditation center, and more, so that the Katok teachings can illuminate this world as the sun does. Kunchen Katok Situ and Önpo Tulku have both been reborn in Bhutan, where they are studying and training. A more extensive discussion of the Katok tradition can be found in its own accounts of its history and the successive generations of its masters.

Palyul Namgyal Jangchub Chöling

The great master of awareness of Palyul, Kunzang Sherab, received his initial vows from Chökyong Gyatso of Ga, a holder of the oral lineage of the glorious Katok tradition. [2.257b] He then received the complete transmission of the ancient Katok line from such masters as Serlo Tönpa Gyaltsen, the prophesied master Chönyi Gyatso, and Ronpo Rinchen Dorjé. Rigdzin Longsel Nyingpo invested Kunzang Sherab as the custodian of his terma *The Most Secret Unsurpassable Cycle of the Dakini* and bestowed many empowerments and oral transmissions on him.

In particular, the extraordinary masters of Rigdzin Kunzang Sherab's buddha family were Namchö Mingyur Dorjé (the immediate rebirth of Katok Monastery's Trulzhik Wangdrak Gyatso) and Khedrup Karma Chakmé. He was cared for by both of these masters and received from them personal transmissions for the *Namchö* cycle and the termas of Ratna Lingpa. He perfected his positive qualities through study, contemplation, and meditation.

At the age of thirty-two, during the Wood Serpent year of the eleventh sexagesimal cycle, "Utterly Wrathful,"[22] Rigdzin Kunzang Sherab went to Namgyaltsé in Palyul. He founded a monastery there, following a directive he had received from the Buddhist king of Dergé, and turned the wheel of the dharma, emphasizing the ancient traditions of Katok Monastery, the oral lineage of the *Namchö* cycle, and the tradition of Ratna Lingpa. His personal influence grew greatly as a result of his studies, contemplation, and spiritual projects, and many thousands of students gathered around him. This center became the mother monastery of the entire lineage of the victorious Palyul tradition. [2.258a]

In the later part of his life, Rigdzin Kunzang Sherab lived at the hermitage on the ridge of Ösel Gang, bringing the four visions of spontaneous presence to consummation. He passed into nirvana at the age of sixty-three amid marvelous signs. This lord guru gave his nephew and spiritual heir, Pema Lhundrup Gyatso, his last testament, which begins, "It is necessary that the teachings of the Katok lineage of definitive truth be upheld by those who receive them as a personal transmission. . . ." With these words, Rigdzin Kunzang Sherab entrusted Pema Lhundrup Gyatso with the ultimate teachings and invested him as his lineage holder. The lineage passed from him to the first Drupwang Pema Norbu, then to Khedrup Karma Tashi, and so on.

This lineage of students has included the successive tulkus of Drupwang Pema Norbu Rinpoché, Karma Kuchen Rinpoché, Palyul Jokhang, Dzonang, Gyatrul, Lhatrul, and others, all of whom maintained the teachings. In particular, Gyatrul Rinpoché Pema Do-ngak Tendzin, the second Penor (Tupten Chökyi Langpo, also known as Drupwang Palchen Düpa) [2.258b], and other masters undertook the enormous responsibility of promulgating the theory and practice of the entire range of precious teachings, both kama and terma, deriving from the Early Translation school. Thus the banner of what came to be called the Drupwang Palyulpa tradition spread to the limits of existence, and this great lineage, with its mother monastery and many hundreds, even thousands, of affiliates, flourishes in both India and Tibet. A more extensive treatment can be found in *The Great Account of the Lines of Succession at the Seat of the Victorious Palyul Tradition*.

Thus the Early Translation school has six major centers and numerous branch monasteries that derive from them. From Katok Dorjéden and the other five main seats have come hundreds, even thousands, of branch monasteries and monastic communities. The students of the sublime masters discussed previously, and their students in turn, seemingly as numerous as the motes of dust on the earth's surface, visited and lived at these centers. For many hundreds of years—in fact, more than a thousand—they have maintained the precious teachings of the Early Translation school of the Vajrayana through the three spheres of activity: study, contemplation, and spiritual projects.

The historical and biographical records of these masters are too numerous for all of the details to be taken into account in this work. [2.259a] I suggest that the reader consult more detailed presentations by learned and accomplished masters whose spiritual eyes are wide open. For example, there are the *Records*, which contain biographies of Guru Rinpoché, his consort, and the powerful Buddhist king Trisong Detsen. The great Omniscient One Longchenpa wrote the most important accounts of the lines of transmission found in the collections of the Nyingtik teachings. Likewise, there are numerous accounts of individual lines of succession, histories, indices, and so forth, written by such masters as Sokdokpa Lodrö Gyaltsen, the tertön of Mindroling and his brother, Dodrak Pema Trinlé, Kunchen Jigmé Lingpa, Getsé Mahapandita, Gurtra Yangchen Gawai Lodrö, the three masters bearing the title Jamgön, Kyabjé Dudjom Rinpoché, Chatral Rinpoché Sanjé Dorjé, and Katok Khenchen Jamyang Lekshé Tenpai Gyaltsen.

The masters I have mentioned did not become embroiled in tedious issues of what was or was not, or what should or should not have been, included in a history such as this small effort of mine, but used their discerning intelligence in a spacious way to write many thousands of other texts, including empowerments, instructions, commentaries on source texts and tantras, and histories specific to the Early Translation school. [2.259b] I pray that they will inspire sublime beings in the future, generation after generation, to preserve the teachings of the Early Translation school until the end of the eon, raising high the victory banner that never falls.

This concludes the discussion of the origins of the great Nyingtik tradition of the Dzogchen approach, the general lines of transmission within the Early Translation school, and all the auxiliary topics.

PART II

The Instructions

23

The Tantras That Concern the Supreme Secret

My presentation of the instructions that derive from the Nyingtik lineage has two parts: the identification of the vajra sources—the definitive tantras that concern the supreme secret—and an explanation of the three phases of ground, path, and fruition.

First, I will identify the vajra sources, the definitive tantras that concern the supreme secret. These sources, the tantras spoken by the guide Samantabhadra—the inseparability of the three kayas—define what we mean by the term "Dzogchen." All such tantras, both those that are well known and those that are not, were codified by the siddha Garab Dorjé and dakinis of timeless awareness on the summit of Mount Nyima Nangjé in the northern part of Oddiyana. [2.260a] From their efforts emerged some 22,000 individually titled tantras that collectively consisted of 6,400,000 verses. These are classified into three sections: the Categories of Mind, Expanse, and Direct Transmission. In the following subsections, I list the texts within these categories that were translated in Tibet, the Land of Snows.

THE CATEGORY OF MIND (SEM DÉ)

Twenty-one texts fall into the Category of Mind: eighteen "major tantras" and three "general tantras." Five of the eighteen major tantras are known as the "earlier translations":

The Harbinger of Awareness
The Stirring of Supreme Dynamic Energy
The Soaring of the Great Garuda
Refining Gold from Ore
The Victory Banner That Never Falls

Thirteen are known as the "later translations":

The Pinnacle State Victorious Under All Circumstances
The Monarch of Space
The Blissful Array of Inset Jewels

The General Scope of Perfection
The Sphere of Awakened Mind
Immense Bliss
The Wheel of Life Force
The Six Spheres
A General Definition of Perfection
The Wish-Fulfilling Gem
All-Embracing Awareness
The Sacred and Venerable One
Meaningful Meditation

Together, these two groups constitute the eighteen "lower tantras" of the Category of Mind. To these are added *The All-Creating Monarch, The Superb Ruler,* and *The Ten Discourses,* giving a total of twenty-one texts. [2.260b]

THE CATEGORY OF EXPANSE (LONG DÉ)

The Category of Expanse has three divisions: the White Expanse, the Black Expanse, and the Multicolored Expanse. The White Expanse has three subdivisions: the Expanse of Space, the Expanse of the Ocean, and the Expanse of Precious Jewels. The Black Expanse has three subdivisions: the Black Expanse of Responsiveness, the Black Expanse of Enlightened Actions, and the Black Expanse of Emanations. The Multicolored Expanse has three subdivisions: the Multicolored Expanse Conforming to the Category of Mind in Positing Existence, the Multicolored Expanse Conforming to Its Own Key Point in Positing Nonexistence, and the Multicolored Expanse Conforming to the Category of Direct Transmission in Transcending Existence and Nonexistence. These teachings, then, fall within these "nine expanses."

The tantra entitled *The Vast Array of the Expanse* is not counted separately, for it serves as an overview that subsumes all of these divisions. The Omniscient One Longchenpa states that this category contains some three thousand individually titled tantras, including *Precious Secrets, Dredging the Pit of Cyclic Existence, Freedom from Concerted Effort,* and *The Sweeping Expanse of Space.*

THE CATEGORY OF DIRECT TRANSMISSION (MEN-NGAK DÉ)

The Category of Direct Transmission has four divisions: miscellaneous pith instructions, oral advice, methods for dispelling hindrances, and the pith instructions found in the tantras themselves. The fourth division includes four major cycles: the outer, inner, secret, and most secret unsurpassable [2.261a] (the last being referred to as the secret Nyingtik, or Heart Drop). Within each of these cycles, moreover, are many texts, including general and specific tantras.

The Outer Cycle

The outer cycle of teachings contains extensive explanations of such topics as the primordial way of abiding that is the ground of being and the way in which spontaneous presence arises as the manifest aspect of that ground. However, there is no detailed treatment of the following topics: the way in which the path becomes evident through symbols, in actual experience, and through signs of success; the way in which the four visions arise as indications of success on the paths of trekchö and tögal; the way in which the so-called lamps arise in the bardo; and the fruition, the way in which one awakens to buddhahood within the basic space of the youthful vase body—inner basic space as the secret embrace of precious spontaneous presence. And so *The Supreme System of Ati* states, "The outer cycle is similar to the body. It makes extensive use of conventional designations."

The Inner Cycle

Although the inner cycle of teachings contains a discussion of various elements of the path—symbolic, actual, and indicative—the ultimate significance of the ground and fruition is only implicit in the treatment. *The Supreme System of Ati* notes, "The inner cycle is similar to the eyes. It concerns a symbolic process of perception."

The Secret Cycle

The secret cycle includes an extensive discussion of the fruition, the way in which freedom takes place within the secret embrace of precious spontaneous presence. [2.261b] The two aspects of ground and path, however, are not dealt with at great length. The *Supreme System of Ati* states, "The secret cycle is similar to the heart. It concerns the process of recollection in one's consciousness."

The Most Secret Unsurpassable Cycle

The most secret unsurpassable cycle reveals, in their entirety, all the elements of the path by which a single individual awakens to buddhahood, with nothing left out. These include the primordial way of abiding that is the ground of being; the way in which the path becomes evident through symbols, in actual experience, and through signs of success; the way in which the four visions of spontaneous presence unfold; the way in which the fruition of freedom is gained within the secret embrace of precious spontaneous presence; and finally (should the yogin encounter hostile forces) the tantra of the secret heart essence, that of the black wrathful goddess Ekajati, the guardian deity who when incited to action is like a sharp sword drawn from its scabbard. Thus the source cited above states, "This cycle is like a whole person, with a complete body and faculties complete."

As for the number of tantras in the Category of Direct Transmission, there are seventeen that define the supreme secret and an eighteenth, that of the wrathful feminine guardian of the teachings. Of the seventeen, the first is the source tantra, *The Reverberation of Sound,* which, as the principal element, is like a body, for it serves as the ground from which sixty-four thousand tantras grow. The other tantras include the following:

Naturally Arising Awareness
The Natural Freedom of Awareness
Naturally Occurring Perfection
The Perfect Dynamic Energy of the Lion
Auspicious Beauty
The Array of Inlaid Gems [2.262a]
The Pearl Garland
The Tantra Without Words
Vajrasattva: Mirror of the Heart
The Mirror of Enlightened Mind
The Conjunction of Sun and Moon
Adornment Through Direct Introduction
The Blazing Remains
The Heaped Jewels
The Blazing Lamp
The Six Expanses

The eighteenth tantra is *The Secret Heart Tantra of the Wrathful Black Goddess.* These eighteen are the texts of the extensive transmission, the lineage of oral commands, transmitted by Vimalamitra. The majority of termas that constitute the tradition of Guru Padmakara are also based on a nineteenth text, *The Blazing Clear Expanse,* which in that tradition is considered the primary source for the texts listed above.

For the sake of analysis, the tantras are grouped into the three foregoing categories of Mind, Expanse, and Direct Transmission. The Category of Direct Transmission also includes the classes of General Yoga (which delineates all the key points of the pith instructions in a general way) and Innermost Yoga (which condenses these instructions into a single lineage of oral transmission). The tantras of these General and Innermost classes were received by Guru Rinpoché from Shri Simha and Garab Dorjé and in the very presence of Vajradhara at the supremely blissful place of Meri Barwa.

Within the Dzogchen approach, there exist a limitless number of tantras, both general and specific. The underlying intent of these source tantras is also found in such major caches of terma teachings as those of Longsel Dorjé Nyingpo; [2.262b] *Great Perfection: Unobstructed Enlightened Intent; Ati: The Heart Essence of Profound Meaning;* and *The Oral Lineage of the Namchö Cycle.* Together, these sources and teachings make up the principal tradition of Guru Rinpoché, referred to as the "direct lineage of successive revelations of termas." This does not exclude other teachings, however, for the profound terma teachings also include any number of termas that belong to the traditions of Vimalamitra and Bairotsana.

Generally speaking, the three categories of Dzogchen are virtually the same with respect to the way in which they define the primordial way of abiding, the originally pure ground of being. The distinction between them, of any one category being considered "higher" than the others, is made on the basis of how they define other factors. These range from the arising and subsiding of the eight avenues of spontaneous presence (the manifest aspect of the ground of being) to the ultimate fruition (the way in which freedom is gained within the state of inner lucidity—the youthful vase body, the embrace of precious spontaneous presence).

As for the commentaries on the principles expounded in these teachings, the master Garab Dorjé wrote an important text entitled *The Precious Golden Garland.* Mañjushrimitra composed *Refining Gold from Ore* (a commentary on the Category of Mind), *The Oral Transmission of Mañjushri,* and other works. Shri Simha composed *The Soaring of the Great Garuda,* [2.263a] *The Padlock of Profound Enlightened Mind,* and other works, and some also maintain that he was responsible for *The Supreme System.* These works are practically tantras by virtue of their subject matter. Vimalamitra wrote commentaries on the fundamental tantra (*The Reverberation of Sound*), *The Conjunction of Sun and Moon,* and *The Pearl Garland,* as well as *The Ninefold Lamps* and other works in the cycle *The Heart Drop of Vimalamitra.* Guru Padmakara wrote *Pith Instructions: The Garland of Views, The Graduated Path of Secret Mantra, Answers to Questions: The Golden Garland of Nectar,* and other texts in *The Heart Drop of the Dakini.* In addition, he was responsible for numerous tantras, commentaries, sadhanas, pith instructions, and other texts found in individual terma caches.

Longchenpa, the Omniscient King of the Dharma, treats the key points of all the kama and terma teachings at great length in his extensive scholarly cycles (*The Seven Treasuries*) and profound yogic cycles (the three Yangtik cycles, which include the pith instructions of *The Innermost Heart Drop of the Guru*). [2.263b] He deals unerringly with the entire path, both its extensive and profound aspects, in *The Great Chariot of Definitive Meaning, The Three Cycles of Being at Ease, The Three Cycles of Natural Freedom, The Three Cycles of Dispelling Darkness,* and other works.

There are also the great commentaries written by gurus of the Dzogchen lineage of masters of awareness—texts that draw on pith instructions to elaborate the meaning of the tantras—and all of the other existing collections of explanatory commentaries and pith instructions. To summarize, the key literature is subsumed under the three headings of tantras, explanatory commentaries, and pith instructions.

These works are associated with the Early Translation school, which is said to consist of four primary transmissions:

1. The transmission of traditional explanatory teachings based on standard sources, which includes commentaries and summaries
2. The transmission of the blessings of empowerment, which includes the means of conferring empowerment and techniques for directly introducing the nature of mind
3. The transmission of the oral lineage of instructions, which includes thorough, practical methods
4. The transmission of the guardians of the teachings and their wrathful mantras, which includes sadhanas and other traditional methods of practice

These four transmissions apply to the entire tradition of the Early Translation school.

In this book, I have focused on the Nyingtik teachings in a general way. Numerous alternative treatments can be found in individual texts of both the kama and terma teachings, each with its respective framework of classification and analysis. It should be understood that these differ merely in their emphasis.

Furthermore, this spiritual approach of the most sublime secret is distinguished by four kinds of superiority:

1. The superiority of the victorious ones' spiritual directives, the words of the teachers, which are the governing factor. These are the teachings bestowed by Vajradhara, the guiding principle that constitutes the inseparability of the three kayas: Samantabhadra in the context of dharmakaya, Mahavajradhara [2.264a] in the context of sambhogakaya, and Shakyamuni in the context of nirmanakaya.
2. The superiority of the definitive conclusions reached through reasoning and scriptural authority. Such great scholars as the learned Mañjushrimitra, Panchen Vimalamitra, the victorious one Longchen Rabjam, and others who excelled in the five fields of knowledge developed the teachings through the three kinds of correct reasoning, rendering them like gold that has been refined, hammered, and polished.
3. The superiority of the spiritual attainment that great lords among yogins attained through authentic experience. Rigdzin Shri Simha, the master Padmakara, Chetsün Seng-gé Wangchuk, and others put these teachings into practice and so discovered the sublime vajrakaya, the rainbow body that leaves no physical residue.

4. The superiority of the uninterrupted flow of definitive pith instructions from India and Tibet. From teachers who were perfectly enlightened buddhas, down to one's own guru, the protector of one's crown chakra, the lineage of masters of awareness spans successive generations like an unbroken range of golden mountains. [2.264b]

24

The Three Phases of Ground, Path, and Fruition

Here I will give an analysis of the three phases of ground, path and, fruition in the Dzogchen approach, which is characterized by the four kinds of superiority listed in the preceding chapter. One can understand these topics by studying the entire range of works by Longchenpa, the Omniscient King of the Dharma, and *The Precious Treasury of Enlightened Qualities* by Rigdzin Jigmé Lingpa.

GROUND

First, *The Precious Treasury of Enlightened Qualities* offers an extensive treatment of the nature of the ground of being.

> In the middle turning of the wheel, the Victorious One spoke of the three gateways to total liberation;
> the essence of what he revealed is one's individual self-knowing awareness.
> This is renowned as the great perfection, for it dwells naturally
> in ordinary beings as their buddha nature.
> Because the boundless sacred meaning of this vast, noble Dzogchen path
> simply entails refining the ordinary rational mind,
> the three levels of ordination, the six transcendent perfections, the stages of development and completion, and so forth
> are all but steps on that path.
> In this approach, it is understood that the phenomena of samsara and nirvana
> do not waver from or become anything other than basic space.
> Samsara and nirvana have never existed.
> The true nature of phenomena, which is the ground of being,
> is perfect in its three aspects of essence, nature, and responsiveness.
> Within this very context, the purity of buddhas [2.265a]

and the impurity of ordinary beings are the two sides of samsara and nirvana.
Like dreams that do not waver from the context of sleep,
they neither come from somewhere nor go anywhere.
In our current situation, these are the tenets concerning the way the ground of being is present.
Original purity and spontaneous presence are what define the indefinable.
This ground of being can be anything and can be posited in a variety of ways.
All seven interpretations of the ground that are variously posited
are merely specific aspects of the oneness that is the essence of original purity;
they are imputed by those who hold to their own scriptural sources
like the seven blind men trying to describe the appearance of an elephant
or discuss the color of a swan.
In this approach, the essence of being is originally pure,
yet enlightened qualities are spontaneously present, neither identical to nor separate from it.
Given freedom from the elaborations of substance or characteristics, there is original purity,
while given the unceasing quality of profound lucidity, there is spontaneous presence.
There is no contradiction between these within the single ground of being.
Just as one can fall asleep and still know one is sleeping,
one need not experience samsara, but rather its essence as original purity.
Still, the display of the dynamic energy of spontaneous presence manifests as anything whatsoever. [2.265b]
Just as the natural luster of a gemstone
is an indwelling clarity, not created by any other conditions and not shining outwardly,
so too original purity is the radiance of being, in which substance and characteristics are left behind.
The bounds of spontaneous presence are not breached; this is the "vase body."
Although it abides as the ground from which all appearances arise
(since it is empty in its very essence and unceasing by virtue of its glow),
awakened mind, which does not stray from this ground,
does not manifest outwardly with distinct characteristics.
This is neither the state of buddhahood nor that of an ordinary being.

It is neither a state of oneness nor a state of difference, neither extreme nor center,
neither a void nor something with substance.
Unconditioned, it is consistent with the three levels of perception.[1]
In suchness itself lies the epitome of awareness,
the heart essence of the five aspects of subtle energy that emerges due to awareness's radiance,
and so the bounds of inner lucidity, the youthful vase body, are breached,
and the manifest aspect of the ground of being arises without ever straying from that ground.
At that point, the radiance of awareness, its responsiveness,
arises as consciousness that distinguishes sense objects.
An aspect of the nonrecognition of awareness is reified,
so that within the limpid state of original purity, like a cloudless sky,
the stirring of spontaneous presence arises in eight ways. [2.266a]
This is to pass through the doorway that connects samsara and nirvana.
The mountain range of the pinnacle spiritual approach, Atiyoga—
its classes of tantras, its dazzling key pith instructions—
is illuminated solely by the manifold rays of Drimé Özer's stainless light.
In the instant the manifest aspect of the ground is perceived,
the original buddha, Samantabhadra,
does not allow appearances to evolve into confusion,
but is aware that they are awareness's own manifestations emerging from the completely neutral ground.
With the sublime knowing that allows the ground of being to ripen into the fruition state,
the distinction[2] instantly becomes perfectly clear.
In the immediacy of that distinction, sublime knowing itself ripens into the kayas,
abiding in its own place with no need to rely on other, incidental circumstances.
In an instant, there is awakening to buddhahood with its manifest qualities,
as the epitome of the vast range of the kayas and timeless awareness.
Then, without straying from the basic space of dharmakaya,
the avenue of spontaneous presence, which allows the qualities of total freedom to unfold,
manifests as sambhogakaya.
Its dynamic energy accounts for the development of this eon of great purity. [2.266b]

Through the avenue of natural nirmanakaya pure realms
and that of impure samsara,
unceasing enlightened activity empties samsara
by guiding beings according to their perceptions.
The supreme guide is perfect mastery
of the positive factors that result from recognizing one's own true, inexhaustible nature,
and the pure realms and actions of one with such mastery are equal in extent to the basic space of phenomena.
All of this is simply the vision of buddhahood itself.
Since it does not involve dualistic perception,
there is no concept of one to be guided or of one to guide,
but, like a sublime gem or a wish-granting tree,
an effortless responsiveness manifests in individuals' perceptions.
Even though there is no confusion within the original ground of being,
ordinary beings in the three realms, unaware of this,
fail to recognize that forms arise as the manifest aspect of that ground;
this adventitious circumstance is virtually identical to the ground of being itself.
It degenerates further into an almost innate nonrecognition of awareness
and then to an all-consuming state of ascribing names, meanings, and identity.
The four conditions of confusion evolve from these three levels of nonrecognition: [2.267a]
the ground itself is the causal condition, abiding like a dwelling place;
the arising of intellectual speculation about it is the governing condition;
the further sense of objects and a subject perceiving them is the contextual condition;
and the simultaneity of these three is the condition that provides cohesiveness.
With their coming together, confusion gradually gains strength,
so that negative emotions increase and the states of samsara come about.
Like the turning of a wheel, the twelve links of interdependence
cause the six classes of beings and the four modes of rebirth to manifest
as natural expressions of illusion, apparent yet ineffable.
Even as they manifest, they have never known existence, being empty forms from the outset,
but six aspects of conceptual mind are aroused to speculate about them, and the six avenues of consciousness arise.
The bondage that comes from investing concepts with their own identity

is extremely powerful, binding even the true nature of mind, which like
the vault of space has no finite essence.
The fixed idea that some identity exists goes on like the whirling of a
firebrand,
so that in conditioned existence some see light while others remain in
darkness,
some perceive nectar while others perceive water or fire.
These entirely contrary concepts
follow in the wake of habit patterns, and there is nothing definitive about
them.
Even so, perceived sense objects are not mind; [2.267b]
the reflection of one's face seems to be inside a mirror,
but this is simply due to a process of interdependence,
for face and mirror never blend.
Appearances manifest yet are ineffable, but the confused mind takes them
to be this or that,
like someone taking a striped rope to be a snake.
The first moment of consciousness is the perception of phenomena as
objects,
and in its wake is the perception of a subject that speculates about them.
If one were to say that the perception of what appears to be a snake
is in fact the consciousness of the subjective perceiver,
then, without one's making a distinction between a perceived object and
the perception of it,
the perceiver would be united with the appearance itself, which is not so.
In the absence of recognition of awareness, dualistic perception is still just
an adventitious circumstance.
If one can cut through the root of confusion, of what seems to exist but
does not,
in the gap between one "I" and another—the masters of conditioned
existence—
lies the all-creating monarch, naturally occurring and naturally in
repose.

PATH

Second, there is an extensive treatment of the nature of the spiritual path.

The supreme path, which draws one toward the state of primordial unity,
in which there is nothing more to learn, is that of the six transcendent
perfections,

and all of these enlightened qualities depend on the perfection of sublime knowing.
This path never serves as the cause of anything else.
Thus emptiness, the secret of all perfect buddhas, [2.268a]
does not abide in the realm of characteristics,
and there is no object to be reified in the center that is ultimately free of limitations.
Leaving behind any sense of finite essence ensures realization of the great perfection.
Sophists, who like to foment controversies,
apply their labels and play out their deductions,
but the realm of the ultimate is at odds with them.
An individual's self-knowing awareness is beyond the realm of description.
Those who posit the existence of things are sophists in the philosophical sense,
while those on a lower level of understanding are sophists in the everyday sense.
The timeless awareness of victorious ones, which is beyond intellectual speculation,
is primordially free; this is the path of the great perfection.
The true impact of emptiness is that objects of knowledge manifest but do not bind one.
Emptiness, by nature, is imbued with the heart essence of lucidity;
such are the realms of the kayas and timeless awareness that abide as awareness.
This is a unity beyond union and separation, like the orb of the sun.
There are three ways to evaluate it, according to one's mental development:
according to the Category of Mind, things arise as a dynamic display;
according to the Category of Expanse, they are an adornment, the ordering of naturally manifest appearances;
according to the Category of Direct Transmission, they are expressions of emptiness, apparent yet ineffable.
All of these have to do with awakened mind, which has no basis for being "freed."
For anyone who leaves the concept of freedom behind, the naturally lucid radiance of being [2.268b]
is clearly evident within the expanse that has no basis or foundation.
Since it is not created or contrived, it is timelessly free.

It is naturally free in itself, for it does not depend on any conditions.
Since it is free in the immediacy of being perceived, it is not dependent on any foundation.
It is free of limits imposed by considering it to be one or many.
Since it is free as awareness, a state of oneness, it has no characteristics.
Awareness beyond any sense of ordinary mind
is the special feature of natural great perfection.
For those with realization, there is freedom in awareness within the ground of being,
while ordinary beings who lack realization wander within that same state.
Making distinctions based on seeming differences is like distinguishing between water and the bubbles in it.
Ordinary mind and awareness resemble one another in nonconceptual states,
but awareness, ineffable by nature, is unobstructed,
whereas ordinary mind is deluded and goes around in circles like a whirlpool.
Awareness, in its profound lucidity, is like the new moon,
whereas ordinary mind, in its involvement with sense objects, is like the full moon.
The properties of awareness are its limpidity and lack of a specific object,
whereas the particular characteristic of ordinary mind is its complete entanglement in sense objects.
Similarly, awareness is sublime knowing that abides naturally,
meditative stability that relies on no method, yet is free of laxity and agitation.
The one-pointed focus of ordinary mind on an object of attention
is a kind of meditative absorption that relies on a support. [2.269a]
Although awareness experiences objects, it is not overwhelmed
by the allure of appearances, being like mercury spilled on the ground.
Ordinary mind, because it entails aspects of dualistic perception,
is caught up in what perpetuates concepts.
Although awareness is not divorced from the nature of mind,
ordinary mind and awareness cannot function simultaneously.
So ordinary mind flees, taking with it negative emotions,
which are united with it through a bond of shared objects and manifestation.
When it flees thus, one is definitely released from the prison of negative emotions;

this is the special feature of the Category of Direct Transmission.
Alternatively, negative emotional patterns are rejected by shravakas,
tamed with antidotes by bodhisattvas, made the path in the general tantric approach,
freed in the immediacy of their fundamentally unconditioned nature in the Category of Mind,
or purified within the single nature of phenomena in the Category of Expanse.
How amazing that anything has to be done away with in the expanse of awareness!
Similarly, although the basis of all ordinary experience and dharmakaya
are one in basic space, dharmakaya is like the ocean,
whereas consciousness as the basis of all ordinary experience obscures it;
like someone in a boat, that consciousness drifts about in samsara and nirvana.
Within the ground of being, confusion and freedom are, by nature,
like sleep and wakefulness. [2.269b]
Confusion is like deep sleep with the senses shut down,
whereas freedom is like one's state upon waking.
The spontaneous presence of the original, indefinable ground of being
and the immaculate, original purity of the final state of freedom are in fact one,
but it is crucial to understand the distinction
between what does and does not function as the basis of confusion.
Likewise, the originally pure state of freedom that is basic space
and the originally pure awareness experienced on the path in the moment
are equal in that they are not restricted or localized.
However, the state of freedom is the original purity of samsara and nirvana,
with the factors of subtle energy and ordinary mind completely refined away.
Awareness as it is experienced on the path is still accompanied by impure influences of subtle energy and mind,
leading to the distorted states of ordinary mind and mental events.
Because one's recognition of awareness is thus contaminated and burdened, one can truly rest in awareness only from time to time.
Similarly, the radiance of awareness in the first stage of the bardo
and the illusory body of the deity with which one's conceptual mind is familiar

are alike in being forms of deities, but there is a distinction between the lack of freedom in the latter state
and freedom in the immediacy of recognition when the phenomenal world arises as a pure realm.
In particular, those who are committed to this path [2.270a]
but do not reach the level of sambhogakaya
(which is perceptible only to those on the tenth level of realization)
can still perceive a reflection of it, for they swiftly reach natural nirmanakaya realms.
Therefore, this is the most sublime vajra path.
Originally pure awareness, primordially free,
is empty, without any finite essence, beyond imagination or description,
and removed from any conceptual characterization by the ordinary mind.
It is beyond intellectual speculation, and its qualities are perfect.
Awareness, moreover, does not abide in the ordinary realm of the knowable,
and so is free of the concepts of "I" and "mine."
It involves no meditation or anything to meditate on,
but if one rests in genuine being without contrivance, one sees it in all its nakedness.
If one does not deviate from the essence of one's being,
one cannot be led into conditioned existence by the machinations of nonrecognition.
External objects and one's fixations on their identity
are not made by some creator, but result from the entrenched concepts of ordinary mind.
Everything is born from what has no basis or foundation,
yet in merely seeming to be born, things are perfect in being unborn.
No realization other than that is necessary.
When one does away with the ordinary mind's endless philosophizing—
reading, memorizing, meditating, and contemplating treatises—that is buddhahood, in which there is no speculation. [2.270b]
Especially in the unsurpassable approach of tögal,
the radiance of awareness is beheld directly, so there is little chance of going astray.
This is the path on which the solidity of the outer elements—earth, rock, mountains, cliffs, all perceived sense objects—
is distilled into supremely and utterly lucid timeless awareness,
and they become the true elements, for distortions have fallen away.

While tögal makes this evident, the approach of trekchö can only distill the outer elements down to their atoms and no further.
With tögal, the inner elements ripen into the supreme transference to vajrakaya,
which benefits others until samsara is emptied.
Therefore, for those of our school, the pith instruction
is to delineate precisely what distinguishes this particular approach
from all view, meditation, conduct, and fruition based on intellectual speculation.
But while that is so, until the adventitious tendency to invest things with identity
has subsided within the pure expanse that is the basic space of phenomena,
beginners can be obstructed by thought patterns that derive from this tendency—
by the controlling influence of conditioned existence, which is ultimately self-perpetuating.
Therefore, there are two ways to instruct people in calm abiding and profound insight:
as essentially identical or as separate processes.
In the first case, one rests in a state free of extremes, [2.271a]
with no duality, only the unity of calm abiding and profound insight—
meditative stability as the aspect of abiding and sublime knowing as the aspect of clarity.
In the second case, there are two possibilities,
deriving either from sublime knowing or from spiritual instructions.
What derives from sublime knowing accords with the letter of the teachings:
one achieves a state of calmness by focusing one-pointedly on the meaning of teachings one has heard
and, from that, authentic insight into what has ultimate meaning.
What derives from pith instructions follows the spirit of the teachings:
there is calm abiding in the unwavering quality of mind
and profound insight in one's understanding of its nature.
In brief, for the best practitioners, even ignoble thoughts turn out to be dharmakaya;
if good and bad are equal, there is no need to rely on antidotes.
For average practitioners who are familiar with the path of integrating the nature of being and its radiance,

all concepts without limit, good or bad, resolve into basic space.
If lesser practitioners first seek calm abiding alone
and then, having gained stability in focusing on a given object,
become familiar with the discerning timeless awareness of profound insight,
they become like someone who cannot find any stones on the Isle of Gold.
Regardless of what the ordinary mind does, of what mental events or concepts occur, [2.271b]
sensory appearances and mind arise inseparably as the supremely free ground of being.
In the best case, regardless of what concepts arise,
they need not be blocked, nor is there anything to indulge in.
Without straying from the state in which one does not follow after them,
one achieves the unlimited qualities of refined faculties:
clairvoyance, higher states of perception, and psychic powers.
If one attaches concepts to sense objects, that is very ordinary.
But if sense objects manifest without impediment in limpid awareness,
like the planets and stars reflected vividly in a mirror,
and the ordinary mind does not taint these with its constructs,
the connection between perceived objects and a perceived subject is severed.
One has now reached the level of "timeless awareness as the guiding principle,"
one's individual, completely nonconceptual self-knowing awareness.
In brief, the path of basic space is that of the unique nature of phenomena;
the path of awareness is the special quality of sublime knowing;[3]
the path of utter lucidity is that of the two "lamps";[4]
the path of trekchö is that of thoughts arising and simultaneously being freed;
and the path of tögal is that of basic space and awareness.
Please understand that these are the five extraordinary paths
of natural great perfection. [2.272a]
Ignorant companions and the seductive machinations of confusion
have trapped you until now in the fearsome wasteland of endless samsara,
bound by the chains of karma, negative emotions, and concepts.
Please give rise to disenchantment with all that
and follow the sublime path that leads to nirvana
within the sacred citadel of peace.

FRUITION

Third, there is an extensive presentation of the nature of the fruition.

> Once one has thus thoroughly realized what constitutes the ground of being,
> the consummate fruition—the kayas and timeless awareness—does not come from anything else.
> The sediment that is the basis of all ordinary experience settles.
> Ordinary mind and mental events are pacified within the basic space of phenomena.
> No matter how the manifest aspect of the ground of being stirs from that ground,
> the habitual investing of things with identity leads to a reification of all objects of knowledge;
> the eight avenues of consciousness, thus perpetuated, are like clouds.
> Yet the sun of totally pure timeless awareness
> remains unobscured and utterly lucid by nature.
> All adventitious flaws having been cast off,
> it is the sublime actuality of awakened mind, endowed with twofold purity.
> Primordial buddhahood is basic space that entails no speculation.
> Just as the full moon that illuminates all outer elaborations [2.272b]
> resolves into space as it reaches its new phase,
> the true nature of phenomena, without transition or change, is completely nonconceptual.
> The permanence of basic space is unchanging vajrakaya,
> the basic space of peace, endowed with the most sublime of all qualities.
> The entire range of enlightened qualities, the strengths and so forth, that express themselves fully
> is the manifestation of distinct aspects—
> the kaya of manifest enlightenment, deriving from renunciation and realization.
> The reactions of ordinary consciousness to objects of knowledge are pacified.
> The relative level of reification by that knowing consciousness is left behind.
> One's individual self-knowing awareness does not fall into the extreme of affirmation or denial.
> Subtle timeless awareness, inwardly directed but not dull,

is the unceasing aspect of knowing that supports the kayas and timeless awareness.
It is experienced by those who rest in utter equipoise.
That state of peace is referred to as "dharmakaya."
It is the realm of victorious ones appreciated by one's individual self-knowing awareness.
Neither one thing nor many, it is beyond substance or the lack thereof
and, like space, is completely nonconceptual.
It is unsullied, for all elaborations have been stilled.
It is beyond the realm of space, subsumed within what is ultimately true.
It cannot be illustrated by concepts, speculation, conventional designations, or reasoning.
Because it is incompatible with ordinary consciousness, thought, or metaphor, [2.273a]
it is not the province of even powerful masters on the tenth level of realization.
It is the direct experience of enlightened guides.
Buddhas of the three times dwell forever
in the fine mansion of the youthful vase body, profound and peaceful,
although they do not perceive one another in any conventional sense.
They are a single expanse of enlightened intent within basic space, by nature free of elaboration.
Due to the natural radiance of the unceasing quality of knowing,
sambhogakaya is the clear outward expression of responsiveness.
Its environment, time frame, teacher, teachings, and retinue
are a fivefold certainty, for it is the epitome of enlightened forms,
pure realms, the major and minor marks of perfection, and the entire range of enlightened qualities.
The environment is the pinnacle pure realm of Ghanavyuha, spontaneous and perfect,
resplendent with the brilliant rays of the five aspects of timeless awareness,
like a rainbow arching across the vault of the sky.
On the soft, springy ground
stands the lovely immeasurable mansion, beautified by four gates with eight pediments,
walls of the five aspects of timeless awareness,
architraves, ornamented friezes, coping, parapets,
the surrounding plinth on which the wide-eyed goddesses of sense pleasures [2.273b]
bear a delightful feast of offerings that unite bliss and emptiness,

balconies, banners, parasols, victory banners with jeweled tips,
brocade canopies, and a vaulted dome.
Its extent is indeterminate, and wherever one looks
it cannot be quantified, but is like an environment of open space.
Within this mansion, the basis of support for the mandalas,
are five thrones and their seats as the primary focus of what is supported.
These are borne by lions, elephants, horses, peacocks, and *shang-shang.*[5]
On lotuses, sun disks, and moon disks
are the five teachers, perfect expressions, free of transition or change.
Their wholly positive time frame is that in which past, present, and future
  are complete within the ground of being.
These teachers are Vairochana, Akshobhya, Ratnasambhava,
Amitabha, and Amoghasiddhi.
Each is joined by the consort of that buddha family,
and they abide as the supreme epitome of the seven facets of integration.
Their retinues are masculine and feminine bodhisattvas, who are not
  different from them.
There are the four gatekeepers and their respective consorts as well.
The wheel of the dharma of natural great perfection
turns such that it is beyond terms and characteristics.
In this upper mansion—the environment that is the very essence of
  enlightenment— [2.274a]
are the forty-two peaceful deities who hold sway over that state,
among them the sacred masculine and feminine consorts,[6] the ground for
  the emanation of the rest.
They are dharmakaya, infinite in extent,
arising as the six sages of awareness,
who benefit beings in the six states of existence.
There are thirty-four deities within the naturally manifest realm of
  sambhogakaya:
ten principal deities, with twenty-four as their retinue.
These deities are pure analogues of the mind-body aggregates, sense fields,
  and other components of experience.
This is the supreme mandala of the three planes in their entirety.
In its total purity, it accords with all that *The Web of Magical Display*,
  The Union of All Buddhas in Equalness,
and the other unsurpassable tantras reveal
concerning the mandala inherent in one's body.
Below this is another mansion, the palace in which the great assembly
  gathers,

a blazing immeasurable mansion with nine outer and inner sections.
The gateways of the outermost section have the double pediments of cause and effect.
In the center of the innermost section of the palace
is a great plateau of vajras.
Above this is a thousand-petaled lotus,
on which rest the sun and moon disks of skillful means and sublime knowing.
On top of these are the twenty-one powerful gods and goddesses.
Above them stand the eight animals (the savage tiger,
the terrible lion, the cruel leopard,
the fierce bear, the powerful elephant, [2.274b]
the magnificent buffalo, the ravenous makara,[7]
and the wrathful serpent),
who seize and trample male and female arrogant gods and demons.
Above them is the universal glory of all samsara and nirvana: the transcendent, accomplished conqueror,
the supreme deity Mahottara, with the luster of a sapphire
and the radiance of a million suns, twenty-one faces,
eight feet, and forty-two hands
bearing the forty-two peaceful deities.
The sublime feminine consort, whose face is the sky, has nine heads and eighteen hands.
Her two primary hands hold a vajra and a skull cup of blood
and the rest bear the animal-headed mamo goddesses of the realms.
The masculine and feminine consorts, in this wrathful mode, are united in their equalness.
The entire realm of the phenomena of samsara and nirvana
is perfect by nature in these transcendent and accomplished conquerors,
from the thrones and seats beneath their feet
to the wheels that crown their heads.
Also present are the sublime, powerful deities and the nine glorious herukas.
On the four sides and in the four corners of the palace
are Gauri and the rest of the eight goddesses who are pure analogues of the eight avenues of consciousness.
On the first tier surrounding this mandala are the eight animal-headed goddesses,
on the second tier down are the eight edifying goddesses, [2.275a]
and on the third tier down are the twenty-eight powerful goddesses.

Each of these tiers has its own four gatekeeper deities,
a magnificent display of forms resplendent with the nine moods of the dance.
These three tiers constitute the naturally manifest mandala of sambhogakaya,
which is the pinnacle pure realm in the ultimate sense, the manifest aspect of the ground of being, spontaneously present.
On the fourth tier down are the thirty-two dakinis;
on the fifth are the four groups of seven mamo sisters;
on the sixth are the three groups of six *kingkara* warriors;
on the seventh are the sixty masculine and feminine wrathful deities;
on the eighth are the 240 messengers;
and on the ninth are the sixty mamo goddesses.
In order to guide those who lead astray and to attract beings by producing emanations,
these mamos appear in the perceptions of those to be guided as creators of hindrances and so on.
They therefore are not part of the naturally manifest mandala of the pinnacle pure realm.
The outwardly clear radiance of the timeless awareness of dharmakaya
is the environment of sambhogakaya, endowed with fivefold excellence.
The primary deities and their retinues are equal in status, with no hierarchy,
because they are the display that is subsumed within the experience of buddhahood alone,
having eliminated all of the limitless levels of obscuration. [2.275b]
The enlightened minds of all of them are nonconceptual,
their enlightened speech is beyond description, and their enlightened forms are perfect, adorned with the major and minor marks.
With their eyes, which purely perceive the natural manifestations of timeless awareness,
they see one another, for there is never any obscuration.
Because the range of experience for victorious ones of the three times
is unsurpassable, and because it is not subsumed within samsara or nirvana,
even the greatest of pure ordinary beings cannot see it,
for they have not yet eliminated the obscurations
that are incompatible with the timeless awareness of the victorious ones.
In the supreme pinnacle pure realm, which is beyond the predictable framework

of the three times of past, present, and future,
dwell the buddhas who epitomize this "fourth dimension of time."
They are the natural manifestations of the principal deities and their retinues, in essential harmony with one another.
Within that very context, in order to guide beings
there is an array of three kinds of teachers who guide:
natural emanations, emanations who guide beings,
and emanations in all their variety.
Of these, natural emanations are manifestations of the timeless awareness of victorious ones—
the manifest aspect of basic space, the pinnacle pure realm.
In the polished mirror of the sambhogakaya's symmetry
appear reflections that are "quasi-nirmanakaya" emanations within the environment of sambhogakaya. [2.276a]
In the center is Akanishtha, to the east Abhirati,
to the south Shrimat, to the west Padmakuta,
and to the north Sukarmasiddhi.
In these five realms are the five sublime teachers—the ruler of forms and so forth—
with their major and minor marks of perfection, epitomizing the vast range of enlightened qualities.
There are countless peaceful and wrathful expressions,
and each of these five aspects of timeless awareness
has a retinue of four, for a total of twenty-five.
Timeless awareness as the basic space of phenomena is unwavering,
beyond the limits of what can ordinarily be known, like the "form" of space.
Mirrorlike timeless awareness is free of the dust of dualistic perception;
while entailing no overt concepts, it serves as the ground for their evolution.
Timeless awareness as equalness has none of the characteristics of all ordinary phenomena,
but entails the basic space of peace in which samsara and nirvana are inseparable.
Discerning timeless awareness is forever untrammeled in knowing the true nature of phenomena,
while still knowing all objects of knowledge in their multiplicity.
Timeless awareness as spontaneous fulfillment entails altruistic activity that benefits others—

the spontaneous accomplishment of actions that have nothing to do with attachment or impediment.
The retinues are made up entirely of bodhisattvas on the tenth level of realization, [2.276b]
whose forms radiate the light that illuminates all phenomena.
Like people who clearly see their dirty faces in a mirror,
they see the difference that still exists between them and their teachers,
and so they refine away the deeply ingrained obstructions to enlightenment that are difficult to fathom
and reach the eleventh level, "total illumination."
The time frame extends to the point at which teacher and retinue are one in enlightened intent,
when these great, powerful masters on the tenth level of realization
merge with the basic space of the protectors of the world, which has no finite essence—
the continuum of inexhaustible adornment that is enlightened form, speech, and mind.
This continuum is "permanent," since it vanquishes the mara of death and is continuously involved in the world.
For the sake of those to be guided, the five forms of the five families manifest as teachers
and supreme pure realms in order to serve as antidotes to ignorance
and the rest of the five negative emotions.
As states of transformation, experiences of the five aspects of timeless awareness
begin with the path of seeing and are gradually perfected up to the tenth level of realization, the final stage of the process,
culminating in the very essence of enlightenment.
The realms that manifest only to bodhisattvas on the tenth level
are not within the range of others' experience. [2.277a]
By the same token, while the teachers are sambhogakaya manifestations,
those who make up the retinues are not awareness's own manifestations, but have their own individual experience.[8]
This is referred to in the great tantra *The Conjunction of Sun and Moon*
as the "natural nirmanakaya that is semimanifest."
Those who are empowered by a guru of sublime perception
into the approach of natural great perfection within the sacred mandala of timeless awareness's own manifestations,

and who do not impair their samaya,
by day experience utter lucidity directly as naturally manifest
and by night familiarize themselves with the radiance in the heart center.
Even if the nature of their realization is such that it has not reached consummation,
due to the truth of the nature of phenomena and the blessings of their gurus,
their lot is comparable to that of those on the various levels of realization,
and they attain nirmanakaya realms in the ten directions—the spontaneously present ground of being manifesting as appearances.
In particular, there are five aspects that deeply inspire them to attain total freedom.
Beginning in the east, there are, successively, immeasurable mansions of crystal, gold,
ruby, emerald, and sapphire.
These have gateways, courtyards, pediments, atriums,
and, on their four corners, pearl garlands, stupas, and bells.
They are festooned with chains of small chimes that tinkle as they stir in the breeze,
resounding with the song of the dharma proclaiming the three gateways to liberation.
In the four directions are four banners that fan clouds of incense. [2.277b]
Surrounding these mansions are pools of water with eight qualities,
on the banks of which are verdant palms strung with loops and chains of pearls.
There are pheasants, peacocks, *kartari* birds, and parrots
that speak the language of humans, as well as youthful swans,
sparrows, finches, warblers, *kangkari* birds,
divine birds with calls like bells, cuckoos,
kritipa birds with bodies like golden vajras—
flocks of birds of variegated colors
like turquoise, coral, sapphire, and that of conch shell.
The melody of their calls rings out sweetly in all directions.
The bodhisattvas who abide in these realms
are not afflicted by illness, for they have bathed
in the rivers that pacify the harmful effects of negative emotions.
Whatever they wish for comes to pass as soon as they think of it.
Their enjoyment is equal to that of the gods in the heaven of the Thirty-three.[9]
On the perimeters are porticoes made of the seven kinds of jewels.

In these sublime pure realms, the teachers of the four buddha families
proclaim the dharma without interruption throughout the fourth dimension of time.
Space in all directions is the pure realm of the herukas,
the great charnel ground of Meri Barwa,
in which the teacher, the transcendent and accomplished conqueror Zhönnu Pawo,
heroes like Vajrapani,
and dakas and dakinis gather like banks of clouds. [2.278a]
In the center of these realms, the teachers turn the wheel of the unsurpassable dharma on the level of fruition.
These victorious ones have countless heirs, all born from lotuses.
All are spiritually accomplished seers
in the form of youthful gods and goddesses.
Having no concepts, they are free of the three aspects of ordinary mind.
They experience none of the six avenues of ordinary consciousness, none of the six negative emotions.
They do not suffer from a nonrecognition of awareness, nor do they perpetuate ordinary circumstances.
No one compares to them.
Because by its very nature all of this is set in place
by the blessings of the guiding principle, Vajradhara,
these realms are proclaimed to the heirs of victorious ones to be "natural nirmanakaya pure realms."
In the secret path of natural great perfection,
they are described in the great tantra *Naturally Arising Awareness.*
In addition, realms renowned as Sukhavati, Khechara,
Bhuchara, and the like
are those of innately present dakas and dakinis, who have mastered the ultimate experience of utter lucidity,
or realm-born dakas and dakinis, who meet in the twenty-four gathering places,
or hosts of other heroes and yoginis.
Therein abide vajra gurus, masters of awareness, whose training on the path [2.278b]
has brought them into the assembly of those masters whose fortune is equal to that of these dakas and dakinis.
There they engage in the enormously powerful view and conduct of the tantric approach.
These realms are natural manifestations of positive potential

that appear to those who gain accomplishment in the secret mantra approach
by bringing the uncontrived conduct of the profound stages of development and completion to consummation.

Do not otherwise think of them as specific, separate places
to which one can go simply because one wishes to.
Within these realms, profuse light rays coming from clouds of mantra syllables
emanate from the sambhogakaya,
causing the sublime embodiments of "emanations who guide beings" in the world
to manifest within the six states of existence and in the perceptions of those to be guided.
They manifest, according to the significance of their respective names,
as the six sages, spiritual beings who guide others through awareness.
Emanating throughout the entire range of three-thousand-fold universes
in the infinite reaches of the ten directions,
they create inconceivable benefit through the four means of guiding beings.
The actions of enlightened form are the twelve great deeds,[10]
through which beings are guided by these emanations' enormous merit.
The actions of enlightened speech are the three spiritual approaches or the single one,[11]
which they proclaim with the intention that these will act as antidotes to the negative emotions
of beings whose attitudes are in some way consistent with these approaches. [2.279a]
Thus some eighty-four thousand avenues of teachings can be enumerated.
Although these teachings manifest as enlightened speech, they are not "things"
with self-defining words and expressions, but through blessings arise in the minds of beings
in ways that are congruent with their understanding.
Guiding through enlightened mind, these emanations perceive and understand the three times.
The time frame is unpredictable and not subject to rigid guidelines,
for the natural, primordial Samantabhadra
is aware of the minds of beings
and is also imbued with truly miraculous vision, hearing,

as well as the rest of the six sublime states of perception, and there is no point at which this ceases to be so.
Guiding beings through enlightened activity involves the inconceivable secrets of universal form,
universal pure realms, universal mind,
universal presence, and universal speech.
Enlightened form, speech, and mind bring only direct benefit,[12]
while enlightened activity benefits in all ways, directly and indirectly.
Thus these sublime embodiments who emanate from basic space
free the minds of those to be guided through timeless awareness that,
from the standpoint of the true nature of phenomena, knows how things are
and, from the standpoint of phenomena themselves, knows them in their multiplicity.
They teach beings precise spiritual methods that lead to utter peace.
The further emanations that derive from these emanations are truly indescribable. [2.279b]
In as many circumstances as are found among the six classes of beings,
Brahma, Indra, Narayana, and others manifest to guide gods,
and shravakas, pratyekabuddhas, bodhisattvas, and universal monarchs manifest to guide human beings.
In like fashion, Vemachitra manifests among demigods,
Rathi among birds,
the lordly lion Sududha among wild animals, and so forth.
In brief, these emanations manifest in every realm, even the hell and preta realms,
in forms that are appropriate to guide the beings there,
and never hesitate to benefit those beings.
This is a matter of teachers creating benefit
in ways consistent with the perceptions
specific to beings in the six states of the universe,
states that involve the positive and negative causes and effects of karma and habit patterns.
The teachings can vary, too, for they must be congruent with the thoughts of those to be guided.
The time frame also accords with the individual circumstances of the respective states.
Thus do these manifestations appear to beings in impure realms.
Those who see a buddha in a dream

may be given dreamlike teachings by that emanation,
but this experience has no true essence, has never existed with any independent nature,
and is to be understood to be without identity, empty, and hollow.
This is proclaimed in the classes of profound discourses given by the Buddha. [2.280a]
And so, although the buddhas that manifest in the dreamlike display of samsara and nirvana
are pure in their very essence,
because they manifest in ways appropriate for those to be guided
they are "impure" emanations, the display of responsiveness,
appearing ceaselessly in suitable ways within samsara until it is emptied.
In that context, there appear "emanations in all their variety."
They may be naturally present or they may come about by circumstances.
They may be sculptures, paintings, temples, halls, gardens,
cities that emanate magically in harsh deserts,
great fish that feed people during a famine,
noble creatures who help those afflicted with illness,
the wise horse Balaha in the land of bloodthirsty demons,
a golden insect in a filthy swamp, and so on.
Emanations in all their variety have no deliberate idea of serving others for the sake of their happiness,
yet they never stray from that function,
ever present and, due to the enormous benefit they bring, magnificent.
If it ever happened that there were no longer any context for guiding others, [2.280b]
the major and minor marks that adorn these guides would resolve into basic space,
just as if, were there no body of water to reflect the moon,
the moon's reflection could be said to dissolve back into the moon, which is the basis for the reflection.
Thus the emanations that manifest in the perceptions of those to be guided
would "dissolve" into the basic space of naturally manifest sambhogakaya.
This, however, would not be an instance of one new moon dissolving into another,
but of the outwardly directed radiance of being
resolving back into its inner basic space, which has no such elaboration.
In a similar way, the natural manifestation that is sambhogakaya

merges with the supreme timeless awareness that is dharmakaya.
Followers of Madhyamaka hold this resolution
to be the "sacred peaceful state of cessation within basic space,"
but in the Dzogchen approach it is one's individual self-knowing timeless awareness.
Subtle timeless awareness is inner lucidity, the basic space of phenomena.
Inwardly directed but not dull, it is the youthful vase body.
Even as its manifestations appear in any way to guide beings under any circumstances,
it serves as the ground for the emerging of timeless awareness as an unceasing responsiveness.
The true nature of phenomena, a state of resting in utter equipoise,
is the fruition of supreme spontaneous presence.

Thus the approach of natural and utterly lucid great perfection is the distillation of all pith instructions, [2.281a] the extracted essence of all classes of tantra, the profound direct transmission for realizing the true nature of phenomena through naked perception. The lineage of masters of awareness above us has not been disrupted. The oceanic nectar of medicine and rakta around us has not dried up. The warm, steamy breath of the mamos and dakinis beneath us has not faded. The Dzogchen approach has not been corrupted by the compromises of those who break samaya. The key points of personal experience have not been lost. The storehouse of siddhis has not toppled. The golden necklace of the precious lineage has not been tarnished by the stain of broken samaya. The elements of the spiritual path are integrated and all-encompassing; there is no need to rely on any other source. The training has not been debased by ordinary people.

This direct transmission is like a warm, beating heart placed in one's hands. It is the treasury of Samantabhadra's secrets, the quintessence of the enlightened minds of hundreds of thousands of dakinis, the enlightened intent of a hundred thousand masters who attained siddhis. Hearing these teachings banishes the darkness of ignorance; contemplating them brings realization of what has ultimate meaning, the way of abiding; meditating on them brings freedom within the expanse that is the true nature of phenomena. Explaining these teachings naturally causes one's sublime knowing to flourish; hearing them causes [2.281b] the lotus of one's intellect to bloom; studying them causes the flaws of negative emotions to vanish; examining them brings one to discovery of the path to liberation and enlightenment.

When a universal monarch takes the throne, all that is entailed—empire, subjects, and retinue—is ensured naturally and spontaneously. Likewise, within the natural place of rest that is dharmakaya, an effortless state of natural rest, there is release from the fetters of samsara and nirvana, with sensory appearances and mind arising as the free ground of being. At death, one's body dissolves into atoms, and one's mind into the true nature of phenomena. Without any further involvement in successive rebirths, one is led effortlessly and spontaneously to the level of fearless Samantabhadra, the supreme transference to rainbow body.

These teachings have great purpose yet entail little hardship, are highly effective yet easy to implement, and their profound key points can be summarized concisely. This approach is replete with positive qualities, just as Vairochana is permeated by the entire cosmos.[13] By transcending causality and concerted effort, all masters, from the primordial protector down to one's root guru, have reached a final decision about this profound path. They have discerned the implications of the naked, unobstructed state, in which nothing need be done. They have embraced its larger scope as a supreme state of equalness that is naturally ensured. In this way, these teachings have been transmitted for many hundreds, even thousands, of years without the key points being confounded. Like one vase filling another to the brim, [2.282a] a hundred thousand accomplished masters of awareness have handed on these teachings in the way that parents bequeath inheritances to their children. As the Omniscient Guru Longchenpa states:

> Although I, Drimé Özer, depart for the land of liberation,
> I have left the very essence of my heart in this text, withholding nothing.
> For you fortunate people, I have torn out my heart and actually entrusted it to you.
> Please use this text always, with perseverance!
> . . . .
> My fortunate followers in future generations,
> please follow this advice always, with perseverance!
> It will free you and others from the ocean of conditioned existence.
> Both kinds of benefit for beings will be spontaneously accomplished without doubt.

Since Longchenpa gave us this advice, I ask that these teachings be held in the highest respect by generation after generation, on into the future.

PART III

Conclusion

Prayers of Dedication, Aspiration, and Auspicious Wishes

The conclusion of this text has two parts. The first adorns the work with final prayers of dedication, aspiration, and auspicious wishes. The second is the colophon.

On the golden ground of all-seeing timeless awareness,
from the center of the ocean of the eighty-four thousand collections of the dharma,
rises the most majestic mountain—the sublime Dzogchen approach—
exalted in the three worlds because of its many superior qualities.
In this work, the excellent biographies of the learned and accomplished masters [2.282b]
who have illuminated the approach seem to vie with one another.
These accounts are major constellations in the vault of the nighttime sky filled with the lives of great beings.
See that they are not lost in these final times.
Those who are like leaders aware of the true value of a jewel,
who are of great acumen and are led by the lords of the dharma—
who among them would not take delight in entering this fine mansion of precious gold
and seek earnestly to do so?

While the darkness of these degenerating times spreads everywhere,
no matter how fiercely the winds of negative emotions blow,
the flame of the jeweled lamp of Samantabhadra's heart
only burns larger and brighter—thus the primordial protector proclaimed.
Having found my own faith and conviction
in these authentic teachings and teachers,
in order to inspire all my friends who share my goals
I have published this jeweled stairway to the spiritual approach of the sublime secret.

I have composed this collection of biographies, *A Marvelous Garland of Rare Gems,*
delineating the lineages of transmission—those passed from mind to mind, through symbols, and orally— [2.283a]
of the Dzogchen approach of utter lucidity,
the sublime secret that is the wellspring of the long-lasting teachings of the Victorious One.
May the white cloud banks of powerful virtue arising from this endeavor
fill the vault of the basic space of phenomena,
sending down a joyous rain of benefit and happiness
to soothe the tormented minds of beings.
May the warm nectar of pure timeless awareness—the mind-to-mind transmission—
arouse the fascinating scent of the lotus of intense faith,
so that the gardens of the fortunate are filled
with amazing, lovely thousand-petaled lotuses—the ultimate lineage of realization.
By the majesty and blessings of Mañjushri—the sword of sublime knowing, the dynamic energy of awareness—
who rejoices within the lotus of my heart,
may I never tire of explaining, debating, and writing about the teachings
with far-reaching songs of view, meditation, and conduct, vast and profound.
May all the valleys unpolluted by distractions and busyness
be filled with practitioners who have shattered the chains of the eight worldly concerns,
so that, through the profound key points of the four visions that unite basic space and awareness,
we may gain natural freedom in rainbow body, the body of light.
May our lovely bodies glow with renunciation,
may our gemlike eyes open wide with faith and compassion, [2.283b]
and may all excellent solitary places
be filled with students victorious in their battle with perceptions based on confusion.
May the roar of the lion of the sublime spiritual approach, which brings liberation upon being heard,
strike terror in the hearts of the jackals who speculate about it,
and may the golden-eyed lion of that approach, shaking its turquoise mane,
gaze into the sky of view, the true nature of phenomena.

The key points of the profound pith instructions of this most perfect, pinnacle approach
cannot be embraced by the minds of ignoble pedants;
may this meaningful speech drown out
the babbling prattle of those with wrongheaded concepts.
May I never be separate, in any lifetime, from the omniscient lord, my teacher,
or from Dzogchen, the noble dharma that is the victorious pinnacle approach.
As I bear these on my head as crown jewels,
I pray that the two kinds of benefit be accomplished as though by a wish-fulfilling gem.
The golden chain of this noble lineage
is unsullied by the base tarnish of broken samaya;
thus the resplendent radiance of its blessings
is the special feature of natural great perfection.
To fulfill the intentions of my venerable gurus [2.284a]
and to nurture the Nyingma teachings that they might long endure and their authentic origins be preserved,
I have filled the minds of future lineage holders, like noble jeweled vases,
with the precious treasure of these accounts of masters of the Nyingtik lineage.
The legacy of what earlier generations of siddhas realized in their lives
matures in the hearts of future generations as the fruit of faith and devotion.
May the elephant of their motivation thus gain strength,
and may they consummate their noble deeds of study, practice, and spiritual projects.
This *Marvelous Garland of Rare Gems*
is an ornament that graces the throat of one who can speak definitively about authentic scriptures,
which I offer as the sun and moon to illuminate with certainty
and as a support for diligence that is as steadfast as the most majestic mountain.
The turquoise gems of ground, path, and fruition are arrayed
on the golden mandala of this noble spiritual method.
I have written this history to encourage those who will serve as sublime lineage holders in the future
to turn the wheel of these teachings.
Since the awakening of the primordial protector to buddhahood,

how and when the sun, the treasury of the dharma, has shone in our times
has been influenced by the lineages of masters of awareness up to the present day, [2.284b]
so hold these accounts very dear to your heart.
May I, too, from now until the three planes of existence have come to an end,
gain mastery of *The Seven Treasuries, The Four Higher Collections of the Heart Drop,*
and all the other profound secrets of the enlightened speech
of the Omniscient Guru, the perfect buddha.
May I be capable of upholding and promulgating the precious teachings of the Victorious One.
With the armor of firm, unfailing courage,
though my flesh-and-blood body had to pass through thickets of thorns,
and even fire and forests of sharp razors,
still I would delight in experiencing the sublime heart essence of my mind.
Simply to hear its name rends the veil of existence asunder,
while to put it into practice ensures that one attains buddhahood in this single lifetime.
All of you fortunate ones, hold this teaching, so difficult to come by in this world,
as the very quintessence of your heart.
With these words, I, the bad monk, the vagabond Jamyang Dorjé—
who was born in Tibet, the Land of Snows,
but who, due to karma, now wanders throughout the world—
have set this down to ensure that the teachings of the heart essence endure.
In all the places where these teachings exist, [2.285a]
may the blessings of their powerful commands be palpable and may all that is auspicious gather.
May the illumination of these utterly positive, renowned, and noble teachings
spread in all directions and times.
Atop the heaped jewels of the tantras, explanatory commentaries, and pith instructions,
the victory banner of the theory and practice of the teachings rises to a majestic height.
I pray that the flow of activities of the Early Translation school of the supreme secret,

the headwater of the teachings, be ongoing and stable for incalculable
eons.
Within the spacious expanse of dharmakaya, naturally occurring and
infinitely extensive,
may the auspiciousness of the way of abiding become fully evident
as the genuine unconditioned state of supreme bliss underlying all
samsara and nirvana,
endowed with the splendid mastery of a million aspects of virtue and
excellence!

Colophon

This text is entitled *A Marvelous Garland of Rare Gems: Biographies of Masters of Awareness in the Dzogchen Lineage—A Spiritual History of the Teachings of Natural Great Perfection*. Since the time of Rigdzin Terdak Lingpa, more than three hundred years ago, works have emphasized the lines of succession at various monastic seats and the revelation of termas, but no one has written or compiled biographies related to the kama transmissions of the Nyingtik teachings, which make up the ancestral line of teachings of the Early Translation school as a whole. Nor has there ever been an extensive spiritual history [2.285b] of the Dzogchen approach in its own right. It occurred to me that leaving things as they stood would be, as the proverb says, like "losing the whole herd of horses in one fell swoop." That is, though people of future generations might accept that there had been Dzogchen lineage holders, they would rarely be exposed to even a definitive listing of what constitutes this ultimate lineage.

With this in mind, I consulted the works of holy masters of the past, including the Omniscient One Longchenpa's major accounts of the lines of transmission of the Nyingtik teachings, Terdak Lingpa's supplements of the accounts of gurus in the lineage, and the collected works of Jigmé Lingpa. Whenever a point was unclear or difficult to interpret, I sought the advice of Kyabjé Dudjom Rinpoché and Kyabjé Dilgo Khyentsé Rinpoché, two great, peerless crown jewels among a hundred tertöns. Moreover, they repeatedly urged me to compile this collection. In addition, I consulted many of the learned and accomplished contemporary masters whose spiritual vision is most extensive in the area of the Early Translation school. When biographies were available I used them, and when they were not I wrote brief summaries.

It is said that in the case of the lineage passed down from the master Vimalamitra, [2.286a] "the headwater of which is found at the glacier," it proved impossible for the enlightened intent of the victorious ones to be corrupted by obstinacy, hypocrisy, interpolation, omission, or seeming contradictions in their pith instructions. Rather, from the time of the completely and perfectly awakened buddha to the present day, the ultimate lineage has been passed from one master to another uncorrupted by verbosity. It is like a precious heirloom passed down from hand to hand or a treasure sealed in trust by a monarch's edict, for nothing has been added or taken away.

[2.286b] And so the lineage of blessings is still an uninterrupted legacy, the lineage of words is still an unbroken oral transmission, and the ultimate lineage is such that the key points of direct experience are not subject to intellectual speculation. Thus the line of transmission of the supreme secret is unbroken and has produced an undisrupted succession of sublime individuals.

It is further said that such matters are key points that will inspire faith in future generations. Accordingly, my intention is that in the future this work will inspire people's confidence in the authenticity of the teachings. I also believe that there might be some benefit for a few others whose lot at present is similar to my own. It has been my good fortune that the dust on the feet of many tutors and mentors—most important of all, the perfect buddha Lungtrul Rinpoché Lodrö Shedrup Tenpai Nyima, regent of the three secret aspects of Khenchen Ngawang Palzang (himself an emanation of Vimalamitra)—has touched the crown of my head. But since, whether due to birth or training, my abilities are lacking and my character bad, I am a misfit, like a dog trying to fit in among people or a person trying to fit in among dogs.

This work was written by me, the one called Nyunzhi Khenpo Jamyang Dorjé. [2.287a] The first draft was completed 2,942 years after the advent of our Teacher, the incomparable lion of the Shakya clan; 2,856 years after the birth of the second Buddha, Padmakara; 2,699 years after the coming of Garab Dorjé, who illuminated the teachings concerning the great perfection of utter lucidity; 673 years after the first appearance of the completely perfect buddha Drimé Özer, the glorious protector of those to be guided in this universe, [2.287b] who filled the three planes of existence with the lion's roar of the three categories of Dzogchen; and sixty-one years after the appearance of the master of my own buddha family, Lungtrul Tenpai Nyima, as the adornment of the very essence of this sublime approach. The first draft was completed in the Iron Monkey year of the sixteenth sexagesimal cycle,[1] on the tenth day of the waxing moon in the fifth month,[2] during an auspicious conjunction of the constellation Pushya and the planet Jupiter.

The text was composed in the spiritual kingdom of Bhutan on Tibet's southern border, at Ogmin Dechen Ling, where the topography is impressive, with land like a thousand-petaled lotus and a panoramic view of the sky. The site is adorned with gardens of multicolored flowers, beds of medicinal shrubs, sandalwood trees, and intertwined vines and creepers. It is a delightful, healing place with a natural sense of peace, having all the qualities of a solitary retreat site. I wrote this book in my meditation hut in this isolated place, which has enriched me with a thousand kinds of auspicious joy. Due to various circumstances, I then let the project drop for a long time. Later, my Bhutanese wife, Damchö Zangmo, repeatedly urged me to take it up again, for she felt that it would benefit future generations and contribute to the completion of my own activities. [2.288a] She also arranged the financing necessary to print the Tibetan text.

A number of people corrected and edited the manuscript, among them the excellent Tendzin Dorjé and Tarling Lama, headmasters of Semtokha, the Bhutanese higher institute of learning; the master Chöten Tsering; Yeshé Zangpo of Ngari (my own student, a khenpo of Dzogchen Monastery); and Tupten Trinlé Norbu. Thanks to their kindness, this work was finally completed at Ösel Chöling retreat center on the hill called Norbui Pungpo, on the slopes of Riwo Langchen Drak [2.288b] in eastern Bhutan, a very important place of spiritual attainment sacred to Guru Padma. It was finished on the day commemorating the passing into nirvana of the Omniscient Guru Longchenpa: the eighteenth day of the twelfth month, called "Victory," in a Water Monkey year.[3] This final version included my earlier draft on the primary lineage of the great Nyingtik teachings, as well as the accounts of the heart children and students, the supplementary material on the lines of transmission of the Early Translation school in general, and the definitive treatments of the ground, path, and fruition of the heart essence.

May the publication of this work ensure that the general tradition and specific lineages of the Victorious One's precious teachings spread and flourish as a source of benefit and happiness. May all of the sublime, holy beings who uphold these teachings, wherever they dwell, live for a long time, their lotus feet standing firmly in the vajra realm, turning the wheel of the dharma without interruption. May all of the countless illnesses, famines, wars, conflicts, and other problems in this world and in these times of spiritual degeneration be eliminated, and may all beings enjoy a banquet of wealth as though a new golden age had dawned. May all beings, so numerous as to equal space itself in their extent, and in particular my parents, my father Jashö Tashi and my mother Tsering Chökyi, [2.289a] whose kindness brought me into this body, awaken to buddhahood as one with the sacred gurus, masters of awareness, within the mandala of timeless awareness, the expanse of enlightened intent of the glorious Samantabhadra, the transcendent and accomplished conqueror, the supreme state of omniscience, enlightenment, and freedom!

Good fortune! Good fortune! Good fortune!

Afterword

In conclusion, I offer the following comments to those who have done me the honor of reading this spiritual history. Some of you may extol this work of mine and sing its praises. And why not? For it is an account of masters of awareness who have appeared in a long succession over many centuries and so deals with countless marvels. Nevertheless, for your acclaim, I offer my sincere thanks.

However, some of you may feel a bit disappointed, due to your opinions about such matters as my interpretation versus your own, or which lineage succession I deemed more or less important, or how long or short a given biography happens to be. You might even be flushed with irritation and view my work askance. Nevertheless, I thank you sincerely, for I, the author, am just an ordinary being, subject to the failings that that entails. Because I have countless flaws, such as the four kinds of limitations that affect one's speech, I apologize in full recognition of those faults; at the same time, I fold my hands and respectfully request that you, my excellent critics, compose hundreds of fine works that are devoid of such flaws.

Furthermore, some of you may feel indifferent toward my book, idly reading it without really caring what it is or isn't. Nevertheless, I once again offer my sincere thanks. This book contains nothing harmful—no accounts of how to make war, rob people, or cause unrest—and so reading it has for you been a pastime unlike getting drunk, watching movies, or playing cards or dice. On the contrary, it is a work that deals with things of great importance for this and all our future lives: the deeds of masters of awareness, siddhas, buddhas, and bodhisattvas. If reading it has caused a positive thought to arise in your minds for even a second, I, the author, pray that the effect will increase so that the blessings of the ultimate lineage transform your experience.

On this note, I ask that we all remember the advice of that lord of victorious ones, Longchen Rabjampa, who exhorts us as follows in *Being at Ease in the Nature of Mind:*

> If someone praises me,
> why should I feel displeasure at someone else's censure ?

And if someone censures me,
why should I feel joy at someone else's praise?
. . . .
The realm of reality for victorious ones is flawless, utter lucidity,
yet we wander in this state of conditioned existence, caught up in our
ignorance.
Finding ourselves exhausted in the vast desert of karma, negative
emotions, and sorrow,
let us now, today, find ease in the very nature of our minds!

EKAJATI

RAHULA

VAJRASADHU

GÖNPO MANING

SHENPA MARPO

SOKDRUPMA

TSIU MARPO

APPENDIX

Lineage Diagrams

KEY TO THE DIAGRAMS

These lineage diagrams represent the mainstream transmissions of Dzogchen teachings as outlined in this book. The diagrams do not depict all possible connections between these masters.

═══════════	Teacher-to-student lineage
‐ ‐ ‐ ‐ ‐ ‐ ‐ ‐	Incarnation lineage
▪▪▪▪▪▪▪▪▪▪	Familial relationship, although not necessarily consecutive generations; this is often a teacher-to-student lineage as well
Dudjom Yangsi† *(b. 1991)*	A dagger denotes that a given master appears in another location in the diagrams.

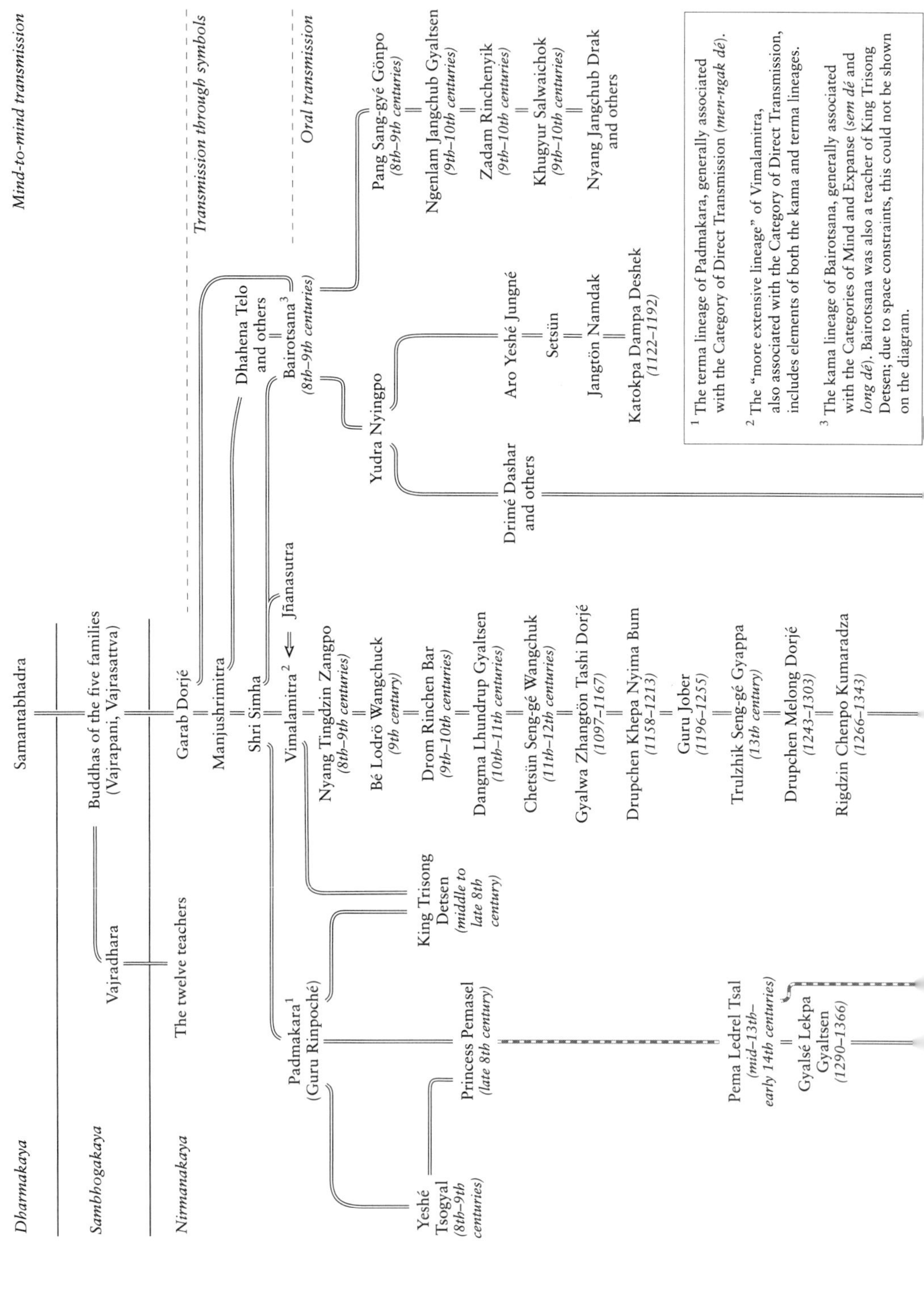

[1] The terma lineage of Padmakara, generally associated with the Category of Direct Transmission (*men-ngak dé*).

[2] The "more extensive lineage" of Vimalamitra, also associated with the Category of Direct Transmission, includes elements of both the kama and terma lineages.

[3] The kama lineage of Bairotsana, generally associated with the Categories of Mind and Expanse (*sem dé* and *long dé*). Bairotsana was also a teacher of King Trisong Detsen; due to space constraints, this could not be shown on the diagram.

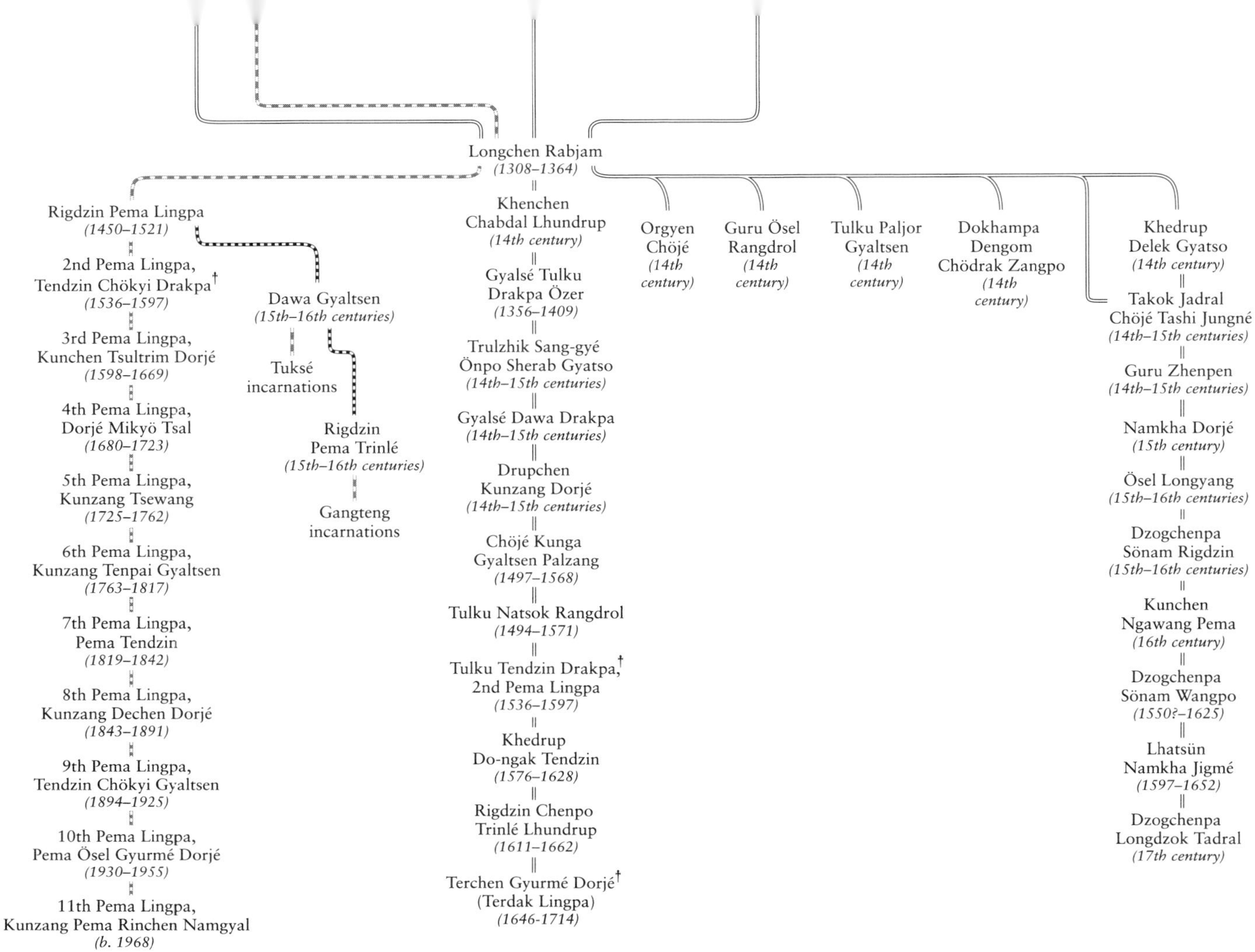
Longchen Rabjam
(1308–1364)
Rigdzin Pema Lingpa
(1450–1521)
2nd Pema Lingpa,
Tendzin Chökyi Drakpa†
(1536–1597)
3rd Pema Lingpa,
Kunchen Tsultrim Dorjé
(1598–1669)
4th Pema Lingpa,
Dorjé Mikyö Tsal
(1680–1723)
5th Pema Lingpa,
Kunzang Tsewang
(1725–1762)
6th Pema Lingpa,
Kunzang Tenpai Gyaltsen
(1763–1817)
7th Pema Lingpa,
Pema Tendzin
(1819–1842)
8th Pema Lingpa,
Kunzang Dechen Dorjé
(1843–1891)
9th Pema Lingpa,
Tendzin Chökyi Gyaltsen
(1894–1925)
10th Pema Lingpa,
Pema Ösel Gyurmé Dorjé
(1930–1955)
11th Pema Lingpa,
Kunzang Pema Rinchen Namgyal
(b. 1968)
Dawa Gyaltsen
(15th–16th centuries)
Tuksé
incarnations
Rigdzin
Pema Trinlé
(15th–16th centuries)
Gangteng
incarnations
Khenchen
Chabdal Lhundrup
(14th century)
Gyalsé Tulku
Drakpa Özer
(1356–1409)
Trulzhik Sang-gyé
Önpo Sherab Gyatso
(14th–15th centuries)
Gyalsé Dawa Drakpa
(14th–15th centuries)
Drupchen
Kunzang Dorjé
(14th–15th centuries)
Chöjé Kunga
Gyaltsen Palzang
(1497–1568)
Tulku Natsok Rangdrol
(1494–1571)
Tulku Tendzin Drakpa,†
2nd Pema Lingpa
(1536–1597)
Khedrup
Do-ngak Tendzin
(1576–1628)
Rigdzin Chenpo
Trinlé Lhundrup
(1611–1662)
Terchen Gyurmé Dorjé†
(Terdak Lingpa)
(1646-1714)
Orgyen
Chöjé
(14th
century)
Guru Ösel
Rangdrol
(14th
century)
Tulku Paljor
Gyaltsen
(14th
century)
Dokhampa
Dengom
Chödrak Zangpo
(14th
century)
Khedrup
Delek Gyatso
(14th century)
Takok Jadral
Chöjé Tashi Jungné
(14th–15th centuries)
Guru Zhenpen
(14th–15th centuries)
Namkha Dorjé
(15th century)
Ösel Longyang
(15th–16th centuries)
Dzogchenpa
Sönam Rigdzin
(15th–16th centuries)
Kunchen
Ngawang Pema
(16th century)
Dzogchenpa
Sönam Wangpo
(1550?–1625)
Lhatsün
Namkha Jigmé
(1597–1652)
Dzogchenpa
Longdzok Tadral
(17th century)

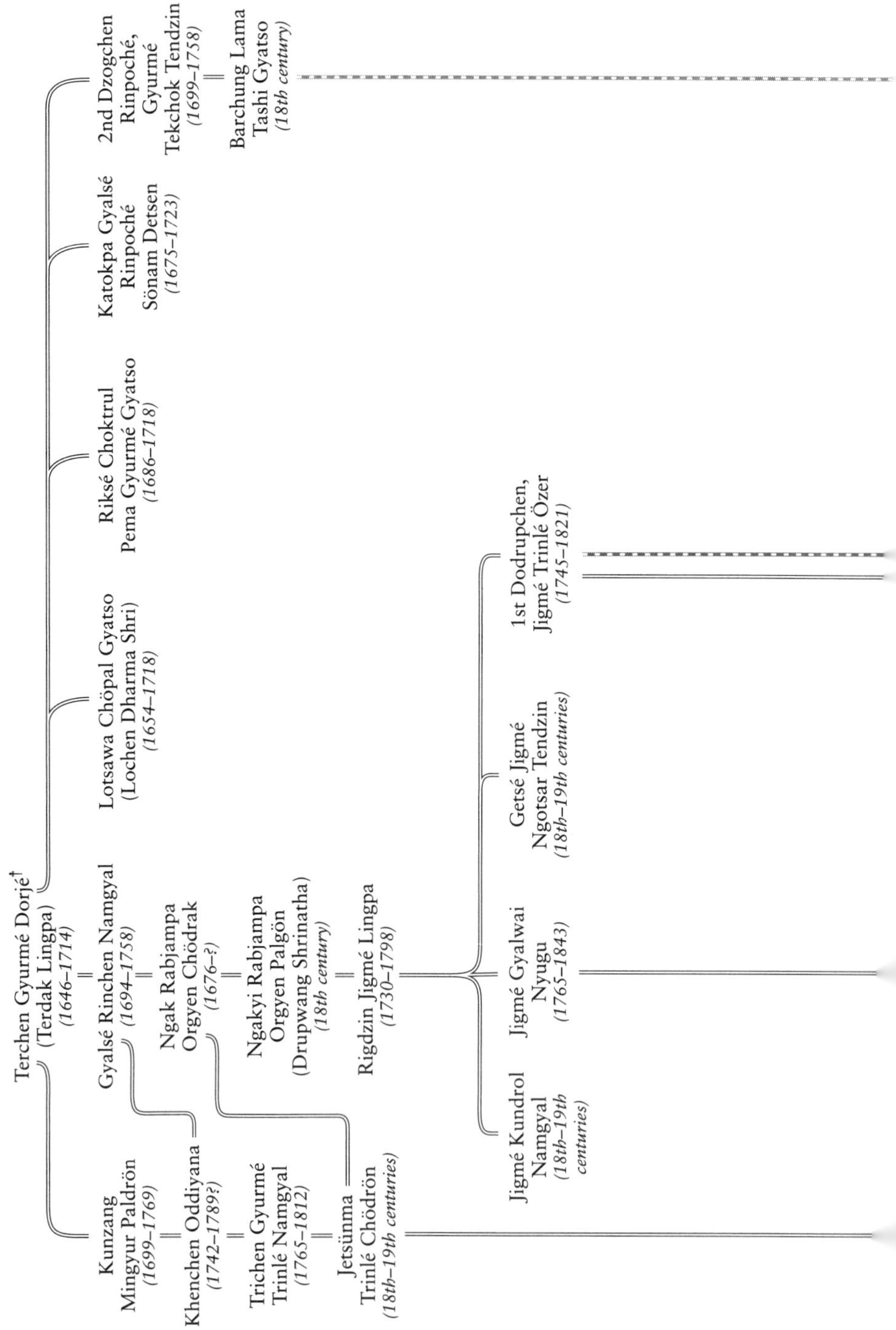

Terchen Gyurmé Dorjé†
(Terdak Lingpa)
(1646–1714)
Kunzang
Mingyur Paldrön
(1699–1769)
Khenchen Oddiyana
(1742–1789?)
Trichen Gyurmé
Trinlé Namgyal
(1765–1812)
Jetsünma
Trinlé Chödrön
(18th–19th centuries)
Gyalsé Rinchen Namgyal
(1694–1758)
Ngak Rabjampa
Orgyen Chödrak
(1676–?)
Ngakyi Rabjampa
Orgyen Palgön
(Drupwang Shrinatha)
(18th century)
Rigdzin Jigmé Lingpa
(1730–1798)
Jigmé Kundrol
Namgyal
(18th–19th
centuries)
Jigmé Gyalwai
Nyugu
(1765–1843)
Getsé Jigmé
Ngotsar Tendzin
(18th–19th centuries)
1st Dodrupchen,
Jigmé Trinlé Özer
(1745–1821)
Lotsawa Chöpal Gyatso
(Lochen Dharma Shri)
(1654–1718)
Riksé Choktrul
Pema Gyurmé Gyatso
(1686–1718)
Katokpa Gyalsé
Rinpoché
Sönam Detsen
(1675–1723)
2nd Dzogchen
Rinpoché,
Gyurmé
Tekchok Tendzin
(1699–1758)
Barchung Lama
Tashi Gyatso
(18th century)

Jamyang Khyentsei† Wangpo *(1820–1892)*

Paltrul Orgyen† Jigmé Chökyi Wangpo *(1808–1887)*

Chögyal Ngagi Wangpo *(1736–1807)*

Zhabkar Tsokdruk Rangdrol *(1781–1851)*

Kyabgön Pema Gyatso *(19th century)*

Dakki Chönyi Zangmo *(1865–1953)*

Zhadeu Trulzhik Chenpo Ngawang Chökyi Lodrö *(b. 1924)*

Trehorpa Kyabgön Yeshé Gyaltsen *(18th–19th centuries)*

Chönyön Dharma Seng-gé *(19th century)*

Do Khyentsé Yeshé Dorjé *(1800–1866)*

4th Dzogchen Rinpoché, Mingyur Namkhai Dorjé *(1793–1870)*

2nd Dodrupchen, Jigmé Puntsok Jungné *(1824–1863)*

3rd Dodrupchen, Jigmé Tenpai Nyima *(1865–1926)*

4th Dodrupchen,† Jigmé Trinlé Palbar *(b. 1927)*

Gemang Gyalsé Rigpai Dorjé (Gyalsé Zhenpen Tayé Özer) *(1800–1869/70)*

Chöying Tobden Dorjé *(1785–1848)*

Choklung Repa Damtsik Dorjé *(18th–19th centuries)*

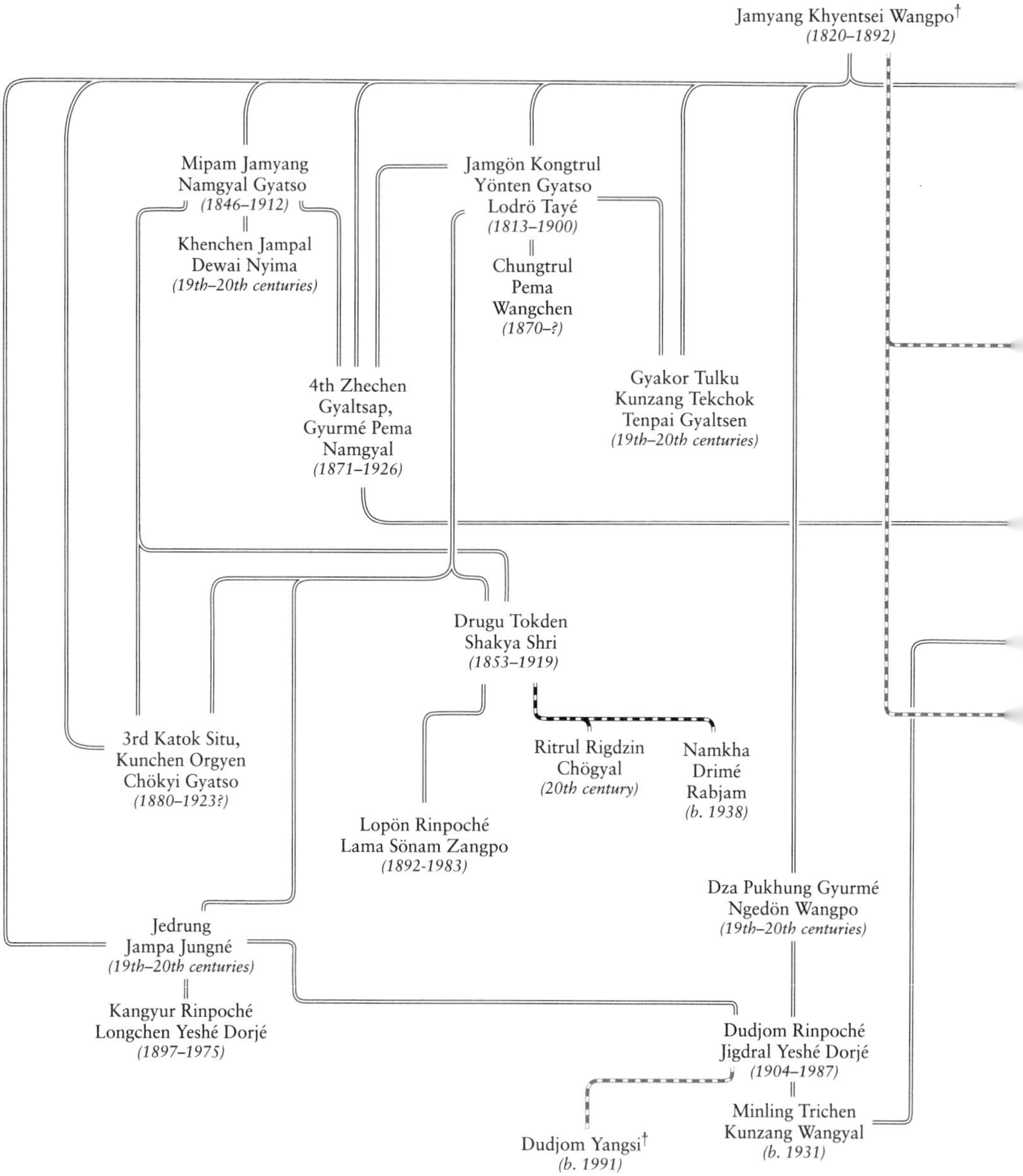
Jamyang Khyentsei Wangpo†
(1820–1892)
Mipam Jamyang Namgyal Gyatso
(1846–1912)
Khenchen Jampal Dewai Nyima
(19th–20th centuries)
Jamgön Kongtrul Yönten Gyatso Lodrö Tayé
(1813–1900)
Chungtrul Pema Wangchen
(1870–?)
4th Zhechen Gyaltsap, Gyurmé Pema Namgyal
(1871–1926)
Gyakor Tulku Kunzang Tekchok Tenpai Gyaltsen
(19th–20th centuries)
Drugu Tokden Shakya Shri
(1853–1919)
3rd Katok Situ, Kunchen Orgyen Chökyi Gyatso
(1880–1923?)
Ritrul Rigdzin Chögyal
(20th century)
Namkha Drimé Rabjam
(b. 1938)
Lopön Rinpoché Lama Sönam Zangpo
(1892-1983)
Dza Pukhung Gyurmé Ngedön Wangpo
(19th–20th centuries)
Jedrung Jampa Jungné
(19th–20th centuries)
Kangyur Rinpoché Longchen Yeshé Dorjé
(1897–1975)
Dudjom Rinpoché Jigdral Yeshé Dorjé
(1904–1987)
Minling Trichen Kunzang Wangyal
(b. 1931)
Dudjom Yangsi†
(b. 1991)

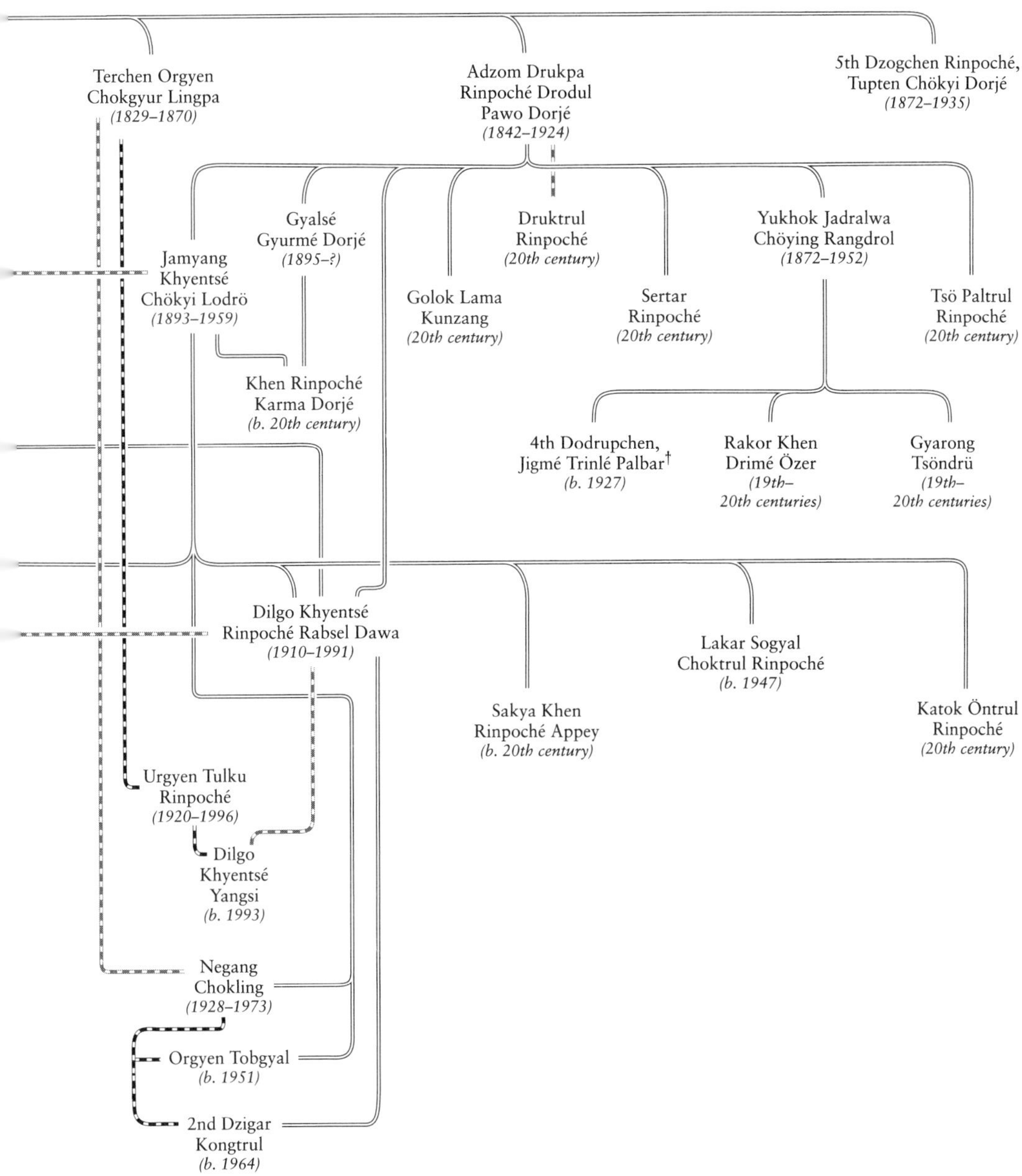
Terchen Orgyen Chokgyur Lingpa (1829–1870)
Adzom Drukpa Rinpoché Drodul Pawo Dorjé (1842–1924)
5th Dzogchen Rinpoché, Tupten Chökyi Dorjé (1872–1935)
Gyalsé Gyurmé Dorjé (1895–?)
Druktrul Rinpoché (20th century)
Yukhok Jadralwa Chöying Rangdrol (1872–1952)
Jamyang Khyentsé Chökyi Lodrö (1893–1959)
Golok Lama Kunzang (20th century)
Sertar Rinpoché (20th century)
Tsö Paltrul Rinpoché (20th century)
Khen Rinpoché Karma Dorjé (b. 20th century)
4th Dodrupchen, Jigmé Trinlé Palbar† (b. 1927)
Rakor Khen Drimé Özer (19th–20th centuries)
Gyarong Tsöndrü (19th–20th centuries)
Dilgo Khyentsé Rinpoché Rabsel Dawa (1910–1991)
Lakar Sogyal Choktrul Rinpoché (b. 1947)
Sakya Khen Rinpoché Appey (b. 20th century)
Katok Öntrul Rinpoché (20th century)
Urgyen Tulku Rinpoché (1920–1996)
Dilgo Khyentsé Yangsi (b. 1993)
Negang Chokling (1928–1973)
Orgyen Tobgyal (b. 1951)
2nd Dzigar Kongtrul (b. 1964)

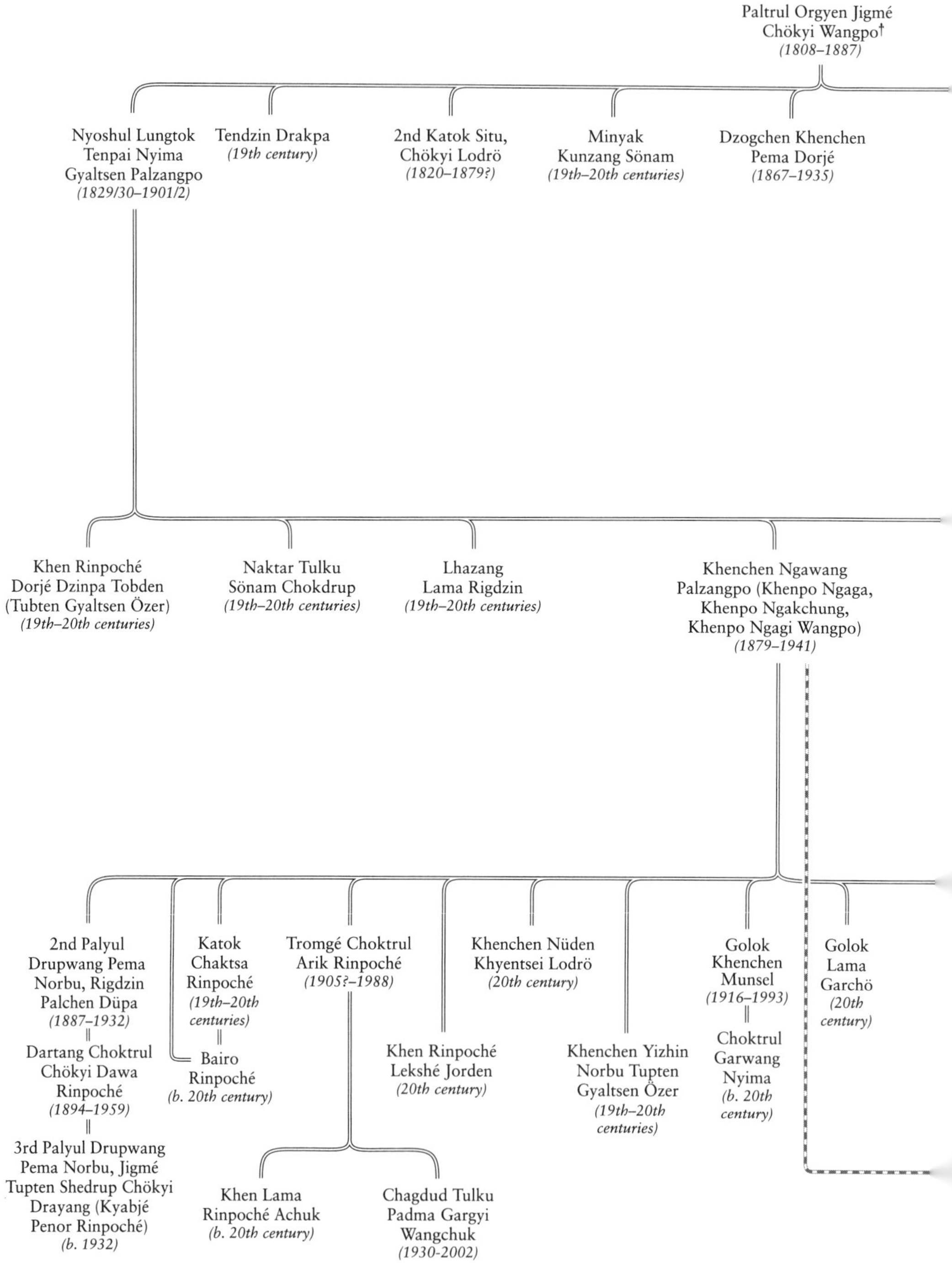
Paltrul Orgyen Jigmé Chökyi Wangpo† (1808–1887)
Nyoshul Lungtok Tenpai Nyima Gyaltsen Palzangpo (1829/30–1901/2)
Tendzin Drakpa (19th century)
2nd Katok Situ, Chökyi Lodrö (1820–1879?)
Minyak Kunzang Sönam (19th–20th centuries)
Dzogchen Khenchen Pema Dorjé (1867–1935)
Khen Rinpoché Dorjé Dzinpa Tobden (Tubten Gyaltsen Özer) (19th–20th centuries)
Naktar Tulku Sönam Chokdrup (19th–20th centuries)
Lhazang Lama Rigdzin (19th–20th centuries)
Khenchen Ngawang Palzangpo (Khenpo Ngaga, Khenpo Ngakchung, Khenpo Ngagi Wangpo) (1879–1941)
2nd Palyul Drupwang Pema Norbu, Rigdzin Palchen Düpa (1887–1932)
Dartang Choktrul Chökyi Dawa Rinpoché (1894–1959)
3rd Palyul Drupwang Pema Norbu, Jigmé Tupten Shedrup Chökyi Drayang (Kyabjé Penor Rinpoché) (b. 1932)
Katok Chaktsa Rinpoché (19th–20th centuries)
Bairo Rinpoché (b. 20th century)
Tromgé Choktrul Arik Rinpoché (1905?–1988)
Khen Lama Rinpoché Achuk (b. 20th century)
Chagdud Tulku Padma Gargyi Wangchuk (1930-2002)
Khen Rinpoché Lekshé Jorden (20th century)
Khenchen Nüden Khyentsei Lodrö (20th century)
Khenchen Yizhin Norbu Tupten Gyaltsen Özer (19th–20th centuries)
Golok Khenchen Munsel (1916–1993)
Choktrul Garwang Nyima (b. 20th century)
Golok Lama Garchö (20th century)

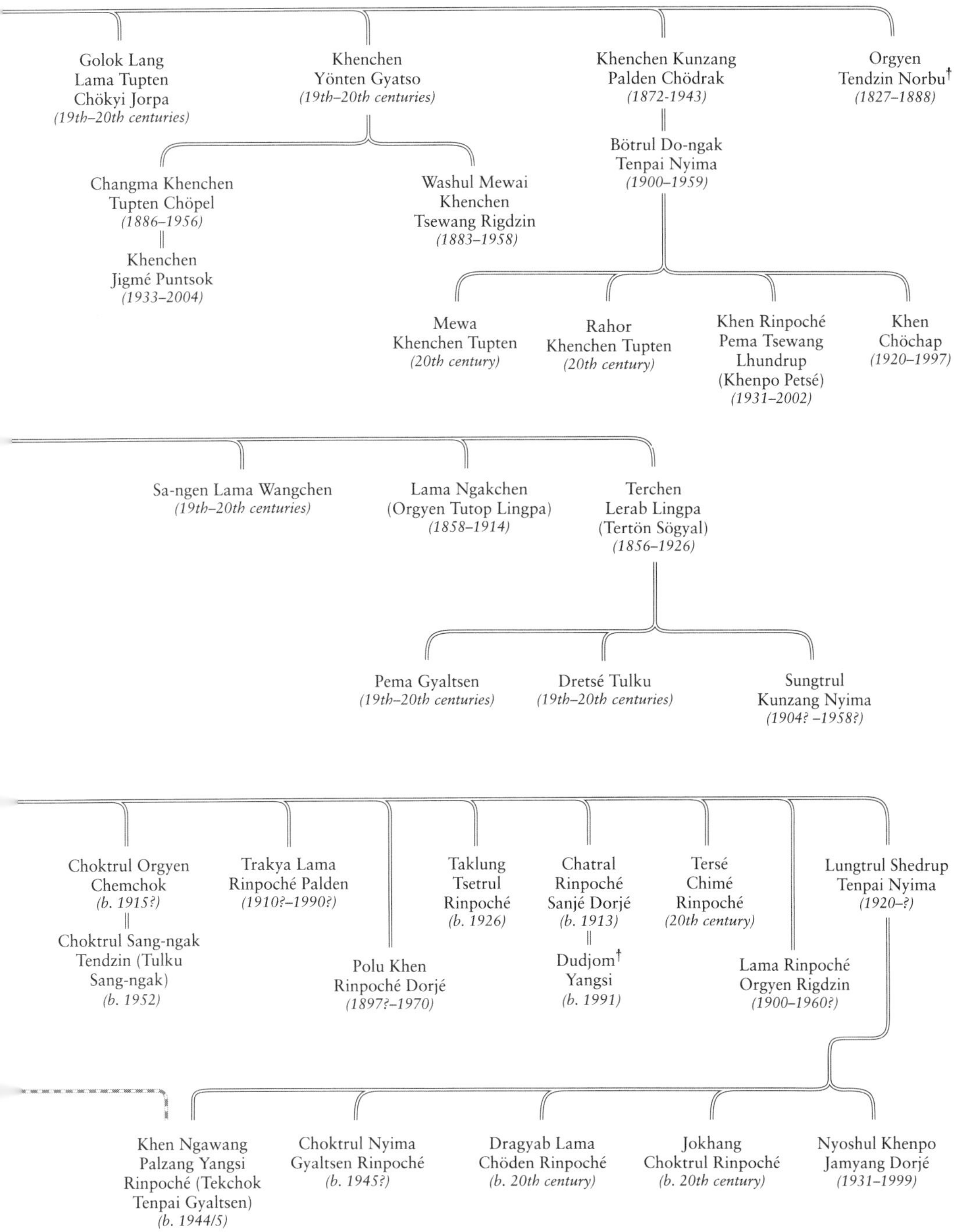
Golok Lang Lama Tupten Chökyi Jorpa
(19th–20th centuries)
Khenchen Yönten Gyatso
(19th–20th centuries)
Khenchen Kunzang Palden Chödrak
(1872-1943)
Orgyen Tendzin Norbu†
(1827–1888)
Changma Khenchen Tupten Chöpel
(1886–1956)
Khenchen Jigmé Puntsok
(1933–2004)
Washul Mewai Khenchen Tsewang Rigdzin
(1883–1958)
Bötrul Do-ngak Tenpai Nyima
(1900–1959)
Mewa Khenchen Tupten
(20th century)
Rahor Khenchen Tupten
(20th century)
Khen Rinpoché Pema Tsewang Lhundrup (Khenpo Petsé)
(1931–2002)
Khen Chöchap
(1920–1997)
Sa-ngen Lama Wangchen
(19th–20th centuries)
Lama Ngakchen (Orgyen Tutop Lingpa)
(1858–1914)
Terchen Lerab Lingpa (Tertön Sögyal)
(1856–1926)
Pema Gyaltsen
(19th–20th centuries)
Dretsé Tulku
(19th–20th centuries)
Sungtrul Kunzang Nyima
(1904? –1958?)
Choktrul Orgyen Chemchok
(b. 1915?)
Choktrul Sang-ngak Tendzin (Tulku Sang-ngak)
(b. 1952)
Trakya Lama Rinpoché Palden
(1910?–1990?)
Polu Khen Rinpoché Dorjé
(1897?–1970)
Taklung Tsetrul Rinpoché
(b. 1926)
Chatral Rinpoché Sanjé Dorjé
(b. 1913)
Dudjom† Yangsi
(b. 1991)
Tersé Chimé Rinpoché
(20th century)
Lama Rinpoché Orgyen Rigdzin
(1900–1960?)
Lungtrul Shedrup Tenpai Nyima
(1920–?)
Khen Ngawang Palzang Yangsi Rinpoché (Tekchok Tenpai Gyaltsen)
(b. 1944/5)
Choktrul Nyima Gyaltsen Rinpoché
(b. 1945?)
Dragyab Lama Chöden Rinpoché
(b. 20th century)
Jokhang Choktrul Rinpoché
(b. 20th century)
Nyoshul Khenpo Jamyang Dorjé
(1931–1999)

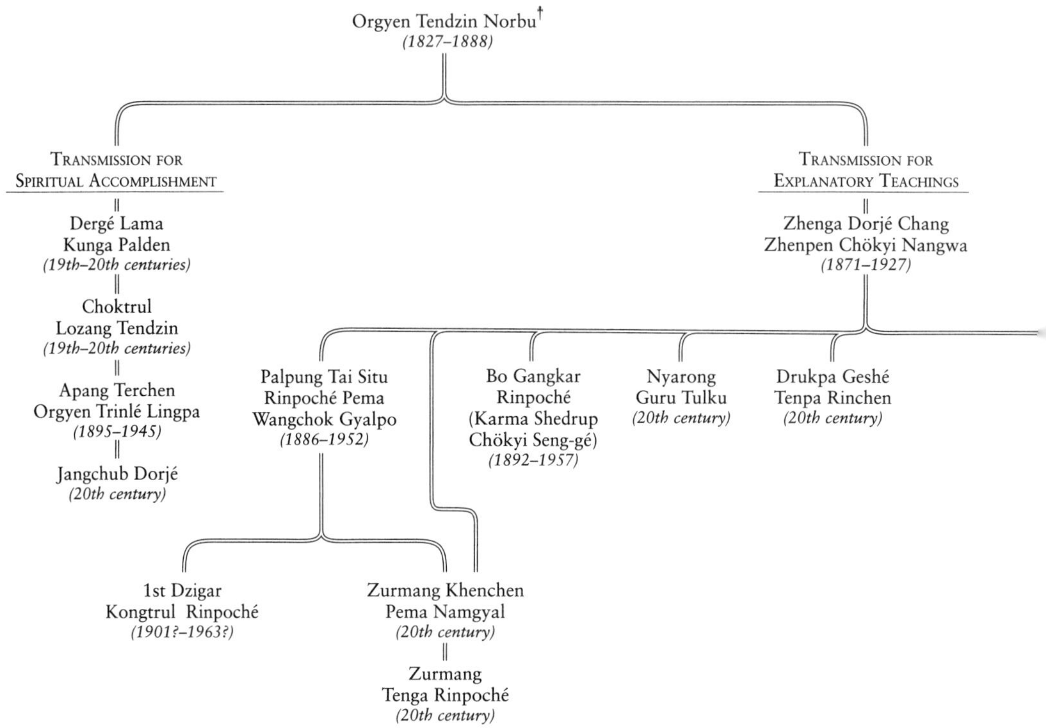
Orgyen Tendzin Norbu†
(1827–1888)
Transmission for Spiritual Accomplishment
Dergé Lama Kunga Palden
(19th–20th centuries)
Choktrul Lozang Tendzin
(19th–20th centuries)
Apang Terchen Orgyen Trinlé Lingpa
(1895–1945)
Jangchub Dorjé
(20th century)
Transmission for Explanatory Teachings
Zhenga Dorjé Chang Zhenpen Chökyi Nangwa
(1871–1927)
Palpung Tai Situ Rinpoché Pema Wangchok Gyalpo
(1886–1952)
Bo Gangkar Rinpoché (Karma Shedrup Chökyi Seng-gé)
(1892–1957)
Nyarong Guru Tulku
(20th century)
Drukpa Geshé Tenpa Rinchen
(20th century)
1st Dzigar Kongtrul Rinpoché
(1901?–1963?)
Zurmang Khenchen Pema Namgyal
(20th century)
Zurmang Tenga Rinpoché
(20th century)

Khenchen Gönpo
(1899-1959)

Khenchen
Tsöndrü
(1920–1979)

Nyoshul Khenchen
Ngawang Palzang
Rinpoché
(20th century)

Tuksé
Serkha
Chödrak
(19th–20th centuries)

Rahor Palden
Chökyi Drakpa
(?–1901)

Khunu Rinpoché
Tendzin Gyaltsen
(1884–1977)

Tuksé Doring
Choktrul Rinpoché
(20th century)

Notes

Unless otherwise indicated, all dates refer to the Common Era.

The Precious Lamp: Author's Introduction

1. The lineages of: mind-to-mind transmission by victorious ones; transmission through symbols by masters of awareness; and oral transmission by human individuals.
2. The Indian abbot Shantarakshita, the master Padmakara (or Guru Rinpoché), and the Buddhist king Trisong Detsen of Tibet.
3. King Trisong Detsen sponsored the training of Tibetan translators, invited Buddhist scholars from India, and supported their collaboration in the translation of Buddhist scriptures from India into the Tibetan language.
4. "Early Translation school" refers to the Nyingma school, the most ancient of the four major schools in the Tibetan Buddhist tradition, which was established in the eighth century by Guru Padmakara and others. More recent schools are collectively referred to as Sarma (New) or Later Translation schools.
5. The Tibetan term *kama* refers to teachings that have been passed on from generation to generation in an unbroken succession. *Terma* refers to teachings that were concealed by a great master such as Padmakara and later revealed under very specific conditions by a *tertön,* i.e., a recognized rebirth of the student who originally received the teaching when it was concealed and who is capable of revealing the teaching in an authentic way. Once a terma has been revealed, the lineage becomes one of transmission from generation to generation.
6. Minling Terchen is a name for Terchen Gyurmé Dorjé (1646–1714), also known as Terdak Lingpa. He produced the first standardized collection of the kama teachings, in thirteen volumes.
7. Longchen Rabjam. The title "Kunchen" (Omniscient One) is sometimes appended to the names of masters (e.g., Kunchen Jigmé Lingpa); used alone, however, it refers to Longchenpa.
8. Guru Rinpoché was active in Tibet during the eighth century; Sang-gyé Lama lived ca. 1000–1080.
9. The guru yoga has not been included in the present volume.
10. This section comprises three separate texts: the fulfillment ritual, in five folios; the concise ganachakra, in one folio; and the song for the ganachakra, in three folios. These have not been included in this volume.

11. These have not been included in this volume; selections can be found in Nyoshul Khen Rinpoché's *Natural Great Perfection,* trans. Lama Surya Das (Ithaca, NY: Snow Lion, 1995).
12. At this point in the original Tibetan text, Nyoshul Khen Rinpoché outlines the contents of the book; we have omitted the outline here, however, and incorporated it into a standard table of contents at the front of the book.
13. Longchen Rabjam, *The Precious Treasury of the Way of Abiding,* trans. Richard Barron (Junction City, CA: Padma Publishing, 1998), p. 267.
14. This is a reference to indications in the Buddhist teachings that we currently live in a cycle of degeneration and that, in the distant past, human beings' lives were much longer.
15. Approximately one hundred line drawings from the original Tibetan text have been reproduced in this volume.
16. A Tibetan title meaning "great scholar."
17. A Tibetan title meaning "lord of refuge."
18. A Tibetan title meaning "lord of siddhas" or "lord of accomplished masters."
19. This common Tibetan idiom refers to the point in a major empowerment when one casts a flower onto a depiction of the mandala of deities. Where the flower falls on the mandala signifies the karmic connection one has with that cycle.
20. The term "youthful vase (body)" is unique to the Dzogchen approach. It refers to the ultimate nature of being, "youthful" in that it is not subject to degeneration, comparable to a "vase" in that its integrity is inviolate, and a "body" in that it serves as the foundation for the qualities of enlightenment.

The Precious Mirror: Preliminary Remarks

1. Tib. Pema Jungné (Lotus Source). An epithet of Guru Rinpoché.
2. The Tibetan master Bairotsana was named after the sambhogakaya buddha Vairochana ("Bairotsana" being the Tibetan pronunciation). In this volume, we use the Tibetan rendering to distinguish between the master and the buddha.
3. The first Teacher in this instance was the primordial buddha, Samantabhadra.
4. Upper Tibet consists of the mountainous western region; middle Tibet, of the steppes, plateaus, and valleys of the central region; and lower Tibet, of the lowland valleys of the eastern region.
5. A Tibetan title meaning "learned and accomplished one."
6. The term "heart son (or daughter)" refers to a student who has received the most complete transmission (both scriptural and experiential) that a master has conferred in that lifetime.
7. "Tulku" (the Tibetan equivalent of the Sanskrit term *nirmanakaya*) indicates one who is recognized as the rebirth of a great master.
8. A Tibetan title meaning "master of awareness."
9. It is held that after a highly realized master passes away, the master's mind can manifest under certain circumstances in a form similar to that of the living master. This manifestation is perceptible to those who have great devotion for the master and a significant degree of realization.
10. Primarily *The Seven Treasuries* of Longchenpa.

11. *Kusulu* (or *kusali*) is a term of Sanskrit derivation for a spiritual practitioner whose way of life is very simple and whose approach to spiritual practice is direct and experience-based, with little emphasis on study of the scriptures.
12. Daknang, or pure visionary, transmissions are received by highly realized practitioners during visions of deities or past masters.
13. Nyak Jñanakumara (eighth century), Nup Sang-gyé Yeshé (ninth century), and Zurchen Shakya Jungné (1002–1062) were important figures in the early development of the Nyingma school.
14. Rongzom Chökyi Zangpo (eleventh century), also known as Rongzom Mahapandita or Rongzom Lotsawa, was one of the most important early writers in the kama tradition of the Nyingma school.
15. Ngari Panchen Pema Wangyal (1487–1542) was the author of *Ascertaining the Three Levels of Ordination,* an important Nyingma work on the relationship between the Hinayana vow of individual liberation, the bodhisattva vow of the Mahayana, and the samaya of the Vajrayana. An English translation of a commentary on this source text by Dudjom Rinpoché Jigdral Yeshé Dorjé has been published as Ngari Panchen, Pema Wangyi Namgyal, *Perfect Conduct: Ascertaining the Three Vows,* trans. Khenpo Gyurme Sandrub and Sangye Khandro (Boston: Wisdom, 1996).
16. Terchen Gyurmé Dorjé (Terdak Lingpa) and his younger brother, Lotsawa Chöpal Gyatso (Lochen Dharma Shri).
17. That is, Jamyang Khyentsei Wangpo. When it stands alone, the name "Khyentsé" does not take the case ending "-i."
18. See Chapter 23.
19. Based on the teachings of the Buddha, as interpreted by the Indian master Nagarjuna, Madhyamaka (the Middle Way) is the highest expression of philosophy according to the Buddhist sutra tradition.
20. *The All-Creating Monarch* is the primary source tantra for the Category of Mind; *The Entire Array of Space* is an important source for the Category of Expanse teachings.
21. "The changing times" is a euphemism often used by Tibetan authors for the Chinese Communist military occupation of Tibet.
22. A way of indicating how perverse certain customs or behavior patterns can be.
23. The term "equal taste" or "one taste" refers to a level of realization where dualistic frameworks have been transcended and everything is experienced as having the same ultimate nature—the "same taste.
24. Although the term "naturally occurring lamp of sublime knowing" often signifies one of the four or six so-called lamps in the practice of tögal (see Chapter 5, note 38), it is also a more general idiom for a state of realization in which knowledge flows effortlessly, without the need for training or study.
25. Located at the crown of one's head.

The Precious Lattice: A Synopsis of the Oral Lineage of Dzogchen

1. The two approaches in the teachings and practice of Dzogchen. Trekchö (cutting through seeming solidity) is said to be for those with lesser diligence and places emphasis on allowing the mind to rest in the authentic view of reality; tögal (surpassing the pin-

nacle) is for those with greater diligence and employs techniques intended to facilitate the arising of a series of "visions" that bring one to the consummate level of realization.
2. The tögal approach is referred to as the "path of the four visions," which are also termed the "four visions of spontaneous presence" or the "four visions of utter lucidity."
3. The two "mother" cycles are *The Heart Drop of the Dakini,* which was originally transmitted by Guru Padmakara, and *The Heart Drop of Vimalamitra,* from Vimalamitra. The three "child" cycles were compiled by Longchenpa: *The Innermost Heart Drop of the Dakini,* which is a refinement of *The Heart Drop of the Dakini; The Innermost Heart Drop of the Guru,* a refinement of *The Heart Drop of Vimalamitra;* and *The Innermost Heart Drop of Profundity,* a further refinement of the first two child cycles.
4. Longchenpa and Jigmé Lingpa.
5. A reference to those who are unsure of their situation. Before entering a dark cave, one throws a stone inside to determine how deep it might be and whether it holds any danger.
6. It is said that the milk of a snow lioness can be poured only into a vessel of pure gold; any other vessel will crack and the contents will spill out. The vessel is a metaphor for those receiving the Dzogchen teachings, who must be of the highest caliber if the teachings are not to be wasted on them.
7. A "custodian of the teachings" is responsible for preserving and propagating the terma teachings revealed by a tertön; the terma itself usually contains a prophecy indicating who the custodian will be.
8. A notation in the published Tibetan version states that this refers to Dudjom Drodul Lingpa, that is, Kyabjé Dudjom Rinpoché.

The Precious Garland: A Supplication to the Lineage of the Secret Nyingtik Teachings of Utter Lucidity

1. A title of Indian derivation meaning "great scholar."
2. Oddiyana is a naturally occurring nirmanakaya pure realm within our human realm, accessible only to those of advanced spiritual development.
3. A Tibetan title meaning "great translator."
4. A Tibetan title meaning "learned one."
5. A Tibetan title meaning "greatly accomplished master."
6. Paltrul Rinpoché.
7. The personal teachers of Nyoshul Khen Rinpoché. In the guru yoga liturgy he composed as an auxiliary practice to this history, he lists thirteen tulkus (including Dudjom Rinpoché Jigdral Yeshé Dorjé, Dilgo Khyentsé Rinpoché, and their consorts), seven khenpos, and five mentors.
8. Gang-ri Tökar, in the mountains of central Tibet south of Lhasa, was Longchenpa's favorite retreat site.
9. A practitioner who maintains an unassuming profile and whose qualities and realization are not obvious to others.

Introductory Verses

1. Numbers in brackets correspond to the volume and folio numbers of the original Tibetan text. Folio 1.1a is the title page.

2. The Sanskrit term *sugata* (literally, "one who has reached a state of bliss") refers to a buddha.
3. Longchenpa was considered to be an emanation of this buddha; see Jigmé Lingpa's prayer of praise to Longchenpa in Chapter 6.
4. An epithet of the Buddha Shakyamuni.
5. See Chapter 4, note 2.
6. Because Tibetan names have literal meaning, a common device in Tibetan poetry is to embed the components of an individual's name in the verses, so that these words carry their basic meaning as well as "spell out" the name. In such passages in this book, the phonetics of the Tibetan words that make up Longchenpa's names are given in parentheses.
7. Referring to Jigmé Lingpa as the second Omniscient One is a way of acknowledging his importance in the lineage and his intimate connection with Longchenpa (often referred to as "the Omniscient One"), from whom he received the cycle *The Heart Drop of Longchenpa* in a series of visions.
8. In Vajrayana contexts, "master of my buddha family" refers to one's primary guru. The mandalas of deities discussed in these teachings are arranged according to principles and archetypes termed "buddha families." A practitioner's "family" is the principle of transformation that is most suitable for that practitioner's psychological makeup.
9. On the basis of statements found in the sutras, various commentators expounded theories about the length of time the Buddhist teachings would endure in this world. According to the most common of these, the teachings will last for five thousand years, divided into ten periods of five hundred years each. Three of these periods constitute the "time of fruition," three the "time of scriptural transmission," three the "time of spiritual practice," and one the "time of holding to mere outer signs." Regardless of the actual chronology, it is customary to regard the period in which one lives as that of the "final times," in which spiritual degeneration is rampant.
10. A footnote in the original Tibetan text identifies these as "Kyabjé Dudjom and Kyabjé Dilgo Khyentsé."
11. The Buddhist teachings are both profound in their implications and extensive in their detailed treatment. In particular, the profound teachings are the so-called mind teachings of Mahamudra and Dzogchen.

1. *The Mind-to-Mind Transmission by Victorious Ones*

1. Samantabhadra (Tib. Kuntuzangpo) is the "primordial buddha," the personification of the innately enlightened state that is the true nature of all beings.
2. Known as the "three gifts of the Dzogchen teachings," these three kinds of emanations are naturally occurring manifestations of enlightened form, speech, and mind that are present in our world as long as the Dzogchen teachings endure. When the teachings die out in our realm, these manifestations will vanish and appear in other realms.
3. The six worlds are those of ordinary beings in samsara: hell beings, pretas, animals, humans, demigods, and gods.
4. The "seven successive buddhas" are part of a greater succession of buddhas who have appeared or will appear in this universe. The first three—Vipashyin, Shikin, and Vishvabhu—appeared in the preceding eon; the remaining four—Krakuchandra, Kanaka-

muni, Kashyapa, and Shakyamuni—have appeared in the present eon. Most Mahayana sources maintain that a total of 1,002 buddhas will have appeared by the time this eon comes to an end.

5. Among the many classes of tantra, the "father tantras" emphasize the development stage and the manifest aspect of experience, whereas the "mother tantras" emphasize the completion stage and the emptiness of all phenomena.
6. Vulture Peak was the site of the Buddha Shakyamuni's teachings on emptiness and Prajñaparamita.
7. "Vajra seat of Bodh Gaya" refers to the place where the Buddha Shakyamuni attained enlightenment.
8. The bodhisattvas Mañjushri, Avalokiteshvara, and Vajrapani, who are associated with the families of enlightened form, speech, and mind, respectively.
9. One of the Buddha Shakyamuni's principal lay students and patrons.
10. The four groups consisted of monks, nuns, laymen, and laywomen.
11. The buddha who will follow Shakyamuni, as the fifth in the succession of 1,002 buddhas to appear in this eon.

2. *The Transmission Through Symbols by Masters of Awareness*

1. In the Dzogchen tradition, Vajrasattva is the central buddha of the buddhas of the five families.
2. "Vajra of Perfect Joy."
3. The Three Repositories are the fundamental teachings of the sutra approach: Vinaya, or ethical codes; the Sutras, or discourses of the Buddha; and Abhidharma, or metaphysical teachings.
4. There are traditionally ten such fields: the arts, medicine, Sanskrit grammar, valid cognition, the Buddhist teachings, poetics, synonymy and etymology, prosody, drama, and astrology. The first five are usually considered major subjects; the latter five, minor.
5. Identified by some scholars as Kamarupa in Assam.
6. See the more extensive biography of Vimalamitra in Chapter 4.
7. The Sanskrit term *tathagata* (literally, "one who has reached the state of suchness") refers to a buddha.
8. The protector of Sukhavati is the buddha Amitabha.
9. To gain the merit necessary to father a son and heir.
10. Tib. Tsokyé Dorjé (Lake-Born Vajra), an epithet of Guru Rinpoché, or Padmakara.
11. In taking the life of the minister's son, Padmakara was able to liberate the youth's mind from samsara.
12. Marajita is a name for Simhamukha, the Lion-Headed Dakini.
13. Nagas are nonhuman beings who influence weather and sources of water; it is believed that, when provoked, they cause various skin diseases, such as leprosy, in humans.
14. See Chapter 3, note 45.
15. The Sanskrit term *siddhi* refers to specific powers and abilities, both physical and mental, that result from one's spiritual development.
16. According to the Nyingma school, there are four degrees of attainment as a master of

awareness: (1) A master of awareness still experiencing the consequences of karma is one who, in the context of the path of seeing (one of the "five paths"), has gained stability in the practice of the Vajrayana stage of development, so that the true nature of mind is experienced as manifest in the form of a deity, although the physical body (the "consequences of karma") has not yet been purified. (2) A master of awareness with power over longevity is one whose attainment on the path of seeing brings about a transformation of the physical body into a subtle "vajra form," while the mind experiences timeless awareness to its greatest extent, so that birth and death are overcome. (3) A master of mahamudra awareness is one who, in the context of the path of meditation (which still involves learning), experiences the body as an embodiment of timeless awareness. (4) A spontaneously present master of awareness is one who has attained the path of no more learning, the level of Vajradhara, where the five kayas of enlightened being are spontaneously present.

17. A cave in northwestern Nepal near the Tibetan border.
18. These are all mahasiddhas of the Vajrayana Buddhist tradition of ancient India.
19. Often grouped into eight classes, these "gods and demons," though imperceptible to ordinary beings, can exert both positive and negative influences on them.
20. Guardians are either deities (expressions of enlightened being) or, as in this case, worldly spirits whose function is to protect the Buddhist teachings and those who practice them purely.
21. These are: degeneration due to desire, which constitutes the negative emotions in the realm of desire; degeneration due to states of conditioned existence, which constitutes these emotions in the higher realms of samsara; and degeneration due to nonrecognition, which constitutes the nonrecognition of one's true nature, the underlying cause of the preceding two kinds of degeneration. A fourth, that of belief systems, is sometimes discussed; this constitutes the emotionally biased belief systems of beings in the three realms of desire, form, and formlessness.
22. The region of Zhang Zhung, in the far western reaches of Tibet, is the ancient source of the teachings of the pre-Buddhist Tibetan tradition of Bön, which maintains its own lineage of Dzogchen teachings.
23. A state of advanced spiritual attainment in which one's physical body scatters into particles of light at the moment of death.

3. *The Oral Transmission by Human Individuals*

1. According to most accounts, although Trisong Detsen was the son of King Mé Aktsom and his Chinese queen, Kimsheng Kongjo, one of the Tibetan queens, Nanamza of the Zhang clan, falsified records to claim the child was hers. There is some dispute concerning King Trisong Detsen's dates. According to many histories, including that of Butön (written in the fourteenth century), he was born in 730 and died in 845, but documents found in the Tun-huang caves fix the date of his birth at 742. According to most sources, he was born in 742 or 743 and ascended to the throne in 756 after the assassination of his father. However, Tulku Thondup, in *The Tantric Tradition of the Nyingmapa* (Marion, MA: Buddhayana, 1984), p. 150, gives his dates as 790–844. On the Tibetan Buddhist Research

Center website (tbrc.org), the dates given are 746–796, which are corroborated by accounts that Trisong Detsen's eldest son, Muné Tsenpo, succeeded him to the throne in 797.

2. Certain teachings, considered very secret, are placed under a seal of secrecy; they are normally conferred only under stringent circumstances and often only to a single student or small group of students at one time to guard against their misinterpretation.
3. Longchenpa discusses these divisions within the Category of Expanse in his *Treasury of Philosophical Systems;* a translation of this work is in preparation by Padma Publishing.
4. As discussed in Bairotsana's biography, these are: to utilize the instructions as one's eyes, in order to see all of samsara and nirvana clearly; to utilize them as one's heart, because they represent the quintessence of all spiritual approaches; and to utilize them as one's life force, because they lie at the very heart of what is spiritual. See Dudjom Rinpoche Jikdrel Yeshe Dorje, *The Nyingma School of Tibetan Buddhism: Its Fundamentals and History,* trans. Gyurme Dorje (Boston: Wisdom, 2002), vol. 2, p. 123.
5. The latter eight situations are also discussed in Bairotsana's biography. The instructions are imparted when a student is of good character, is trustworthy, is sincerely motivated, and is not cynical but devoted. They are not imparted when the student shows signs of poor character, has little faith, is not motivated to practice, and is selfishly motivated. Ibid., p. 125.
6. Presumably the timeless awareness embodiment of Garab Dorjé, although the text is not explicit.
7. According to Tulku Thondup in *The Tantric Tradition of the Nyingmapa,* p. 26, these five texts are: *The Harbinger of Awareness*, *The Stirring of Supreme Dynamic Energy*, *The Soaring of the Great Garuda*, *Refining Gold from Ore*, and *Supreme Space: The Victory Banner That Never Falls. Refining Gold from Ore* has been translated into English (see Mañjushrimitra, *Primordial Experience,* trans. Namkhai Norbu and Kennard Lipman [Boston: Shambhala, 2001]).
8. A region in southeastern Tibet, also known as Gyalmo Tsawa Rong, Gyalmo Rong, or simply Gyalrong. According to some accounts, Tsepongza, one of Trisong Detsen's wives, was infatuated with Bairotsana and arranged to have him exiled because he refused her advances. Queen Tsepongza is described in the ancient histories as an evil person. She is held to have had Prince Muné Tsenpo (her own son by King Trisong Detsen) and his wife assassinated after he succeeded his father to the throne; the reign of Muné Tsenpo was therefore very brief (ca. 797–799). See Yeshe De Project, *Ancient Tibet* (Berkeley: Dharma Publishing, 1986), p. 290.
9. Yudra Nyingpo, a prince of Gyalrong, studied with Bairotsana when the master was in exile. He later met Vimalamitra when the latter came to Tibet, and they collaborated with Nyak Jñanakumara on the "thirteen later translations" of tantras of the Category of Mind. According to Longchenpa's *Treasury of Philosophical Systems* (fol. 179.a.6–179.b.1), these texts are: *The Pinnacle State Victorious Under All Circumstances, The Monarch of Space, The Blissful Array of Inset Jewels, The General Scope of Perfection, The Sphere of Awakened Mind, Immense Bliss, The Wheel of Life Force, The Six Spheres, A General Definition of Perfection, The Wish-Fulfilling Gem, All-Embracing Awareness, The Sacred and Venerable One,* and *Meaningful Meditation.*

10. This took place during Bairotsana's return from exile, on his journey from Tsawa Rong back to central Tibet.
11. In *The Tantric Tradition of the Nyingmapa*, pp. 158 and 196 n. 189, Tulku Thondup (who gives the princess's name as She-rab Drol-ma) locates her homeland of "Li" in the Sinkiang (Xinjiang) region of far northwestern China.
12. It was Lhalung Palgyi Dorjé who assassinated King Langdarma of Tibet, a grandson of Trisong Detsen. During his brief reign (836?–841), Langdarma tried to eradicate Buddhism in Tibet and largely succeeded in the central regions. His death opened the way for a revival of the Buddhist teachings.
13. Nupchen Sang-gyé Yeshé was one of the twenty-five intimate students of Guru Padmakara. Nupchen is credited with having displayed such great spiritual power to King Langdarma that when the latter began persecuting Buddhist practitioners, he avoided lay tantric practitioners and focused his efforts on destroying the monastic communities.
14. In the region of Gyalrong.
15. Yarlung is a side valley branching to the south from the valley of the Tsangpo, the main east–west river in central Tibet. The Tsangpo becomes the Brahmaputra when it enters Indian territory in Arunachal Pradesh. Chongyé was the ancestral home of the earliest dynasty of Tibetan kings, some of whose tombs are still extant.
16. These three are the primary scriptural sources, respectively, for the teachings of Anuyoga, Mahayoga, and Atiyoga. The term "mind teachings" here refers not simply to the teachings of the Category of Mind in the Atiyoga approach, but to those of all three categories (Mind, Expanse, and Direct Transmission).
17. Prajñaparamita (the Perfection of Sublime Knowing) is a field of study based on a collection of the Buddha's teachings on emptiness and their interpretation by later masters.
18. Most likely a reference to the principal protective deities of the Dzogchen tradition: Ekajati, Rahula, and Vajrasadhu.
19. Tsangtön Dorjé Gyaltsen (1126–1216) was Katokpa Dampa Deshek's student and regent and the first in the succession of heads of Katok Monastery. The "three named Bumpa," those who followed Tsangtön as the second, third, and fourth in the succession of gurus of Katok, were: Jampa Bum (1197–1252), Chen-nga Mangpuwa Sönam Bumpa (1223–1283?), and U-ö Yeshé Bumpa (1254–?). According to Dudjom Rinpoche, *The Nyingma School of Tibetan Buddhism*, vol. 2, p. 171, there are several versions of this list of thirteen gurus. Jamyang Khyentsei Wangpo gives the following list of the regents who followed Ka Dampa Deshek (Lama Popa Tayé): Tsangtön Dorjé Gyaltsen, Jampa Bum, Chen-ngawa Sönam Bumpa, Ü-ö Yeshé Bumpa, Jangchub Pelwa, Sönam Zangpo, Kunga Bumpa, Lodrö Bumpa, Lodrö Seng-gé, Jangchub Lodrö, Jangchub Seng-gé, Jangchub Gyaltsen, and Khedrup Yeshé Gyaltsen.
20. According to Jamyang Gyaltsen's *History of Katok Monastery,* these thirteen regents were: Namkha Seng-gé (Tsöndrü Bumpa), Dorjé Lodrö, Khenpo Natsa Gendun Bum, Namkha Pal, Ardo Könchok Gyaltsen, Khenpo Bubor Tashi Gyatso, Lhazo Lama Hepa Chöjung, Orgyen Namgyal, Sang-ngak Tendzin, Takla Gyal, Rinchen Bummé, Sönam Bum, and Namkha Gyaltsen.
21. A khenpo is one who has completed a long course of study focusing on various subjects

in the Buddhist teachings. The degree implies a thorough knowledge of those subjects. Khenpos may specialize, e.g., in the sutra or tantra tradition.

22. According to Jamyang Gyaltsen's *History of Katok Monastery,* these thirteen khenpos, whose reigns were interspersed with those of the thirteen gurus, were: Horpo Shakya Dorjé, Nam Tengpa Dorjé, Palbarwa Namkha Dorjé, Yangtröpa Tönpa Gön Gyaltsen-bum, Meshöpa Sang-gyé Dorjé, Tsultrim Bumpa, Drao Chökyi Bumpa, Ngapa Chökyi Dorjé, Laptön Namkha Rinchen, Kusulu Rinchen Pal, Chokmé Jangsem Chöjé, Mön Katok Könchok Zangpo, and Moktön Dorjé Palzang.
23. According to Jamyang Gyaltsen's *History of Katok Monastery,* these thirteen, who were associated with the Katok affiliate monastery of Moktsa Gön and whose reigns were interspersed with those of the thirteen successive regents, were: Birtsön Awadhuti, Dunpa Chen, Chak Gyepa, Resham Mok Nakpa, Moknyön Tönpa, Orgyen Birwapa, Könchok Gön, Moktön Chökyi Drakpa, Roktön Chökyi Zangpo, Jinpa Gyatso, Orgyen Lupel, Trinlé Lhundrup, and Orgyen Sampel.
24. The Tibetan equivalent of the Sanskrit title "siddha," or "accomplished master."
25. Jang is on the far southwestern border of the Tibetan cultural region, located in the province of Yunnan in modern China.
26. See Dudjom Rinpoche, *The Nyingma School of Tibetan Buddhism,* vol. 1, pp. 542–543.
27. Three great masters of the Zur clan—Zurchen (or Zurpoché) Shakya Jungné (1002–1062); his nephew, Zurchung Sherab Drakpa (1014–1074); and the latter's son, Zur Dropukpa Shakya Seng-gé (1074–1134)—were important figures in the early transmission of Mahayoga, Anuyoga, and the mind teachings in Tibet.
28. An alternative line of transmission, based on the writings of the third Dodrupchen, Jigmé Tenpai Nyima, can be found in Tulku Thondup, *The Tantric Tradition of the Nyingmapa,* pp. 27–28.
29. For a listing of the nine expanses, see Chapter 23.
30. The first of these was Songtsen Gampo (ca. 569–650); his marriages to princesses from the Nepalese and Chinese courts led to the first real introduction of Buddhism to Tibet, for his consorts brought its influence with them. The second king was Trisong Detsen (ca. 742–797), the fifth-generation descendant of Songtsen Gampo. The third was Tri Ralpachen (ca. 806–836?), Trisong Detsen's grandson, who gave strong support to Buddhism during his reign; he was assassinated and succeeded by his brother Langdarma.
31. Three of the most important translators of the group that, during Trisong Detsen's reign, produced the first systematic translations of Indian Buddhist works into the Tibetan language.
32. The formal name of the main complex at Samyé Monastery.
33. Youths from the Tibetan aristocracy chosen by the abbot Shantarakshita to determine whether Tibetans were capable of observing monastic discipline.
34. The original Buddhist monks in India wore saffron-colored robes. Although the color was different in other Buddhist countries (including Tibet, where the robes are maroon), the idiom has been preserved out of respect for the origins of the monastic tradition.
35. This short offering prayer is recited in all schools of Tibetan Buddhism. The complete verse is as follows:

The earth is anointed with perfumed water
and adorned with the sun and the moon.
By my imagining it to be a buddha's realm,
may all beings enjoy a completely pure realm of experience.

36. King Trisong Detsen, his subject Bairotsana, and his queen Yeshé Tsogyal (who became Padmakara's consort).
37. Mingyur Lhungyi Druppai Tsuklak Khang at Samyé Monastery.
38. There is some variance in the historical records concerning King Trisong Detsen's heirs. Most state that he had three sons, although others, such as *The Red Annals* and *The Banquet for the Wise,* give the number as four. The eldest, Muné (or Mutri) Tsenpo, succeeded his father to the throne in 797 but was poisoned within two years by his own mother, Queen Tsepongza (one of Trisong Detsen's five wives). The second son was Murub Tsepo (also known as Muruk Tsenpo). He killed the son of Zhang, one of his father's cabinet ministers, after which he was banished to Tibet's northern border to command troops against Turkish and Chinese forces. Following the death of his elder brother, however, Murub Tsepo was recalled to the capital. Before he could assume the throne, Queen Nanamza, one of the wives of his grandfather, Mé Aktsom, conspired to have him killed. The third son, Mutik Tsenpo (also known as Desong), succeeded his elder brother to the throne in about 800 and, upon assuming power, was given the name Senalek. He was responsible for furthering his father's and elder brother's efforts to establish the Buddhist tradition in Tibet, inviting masters from India and Nepal and sponsoring the translation of texts into Tibetan. He bound his ministers and subjects to an oath that they would never renounce Buddhism. Trisong Detsen also had a daughter, Pemasel, by his queen Droza Jangchub Drön. All of the king's children were sources of important incarnation lineages during the succeeding centuries.
39. This prayer is found in the volumes of prayers of praise contained in Mipam Rinpoché's collected works.
40. An epithet of King Trisong Detsen.
41. A ritual for preparing and consecrating medicine made of various herbs; masters give such medicine as a blessing to their students.
42. The Sanskrit term for Tibet.
43. These sites are enumerated in Dudjom Rinpoche, *The Nyingma School of Tibetan Buddhism,* vol. 2, pp. 181–182.
44. With rare exceptions, tertöns must take a consort in order for the process of revelation to proceed. Failure to make contact with the prophesied consort can render the terma inaccessible, even though the tertön is qualified to reveal it.
45. Maras, a class of beings who cause harm, are often associated with the influences of certain heavenly bodies (and in fact personify these stars and planets). Rahula is an example of a worldly being bound to an oath to protect the Buddhist teachings and thus elevated to the status of a protective deity.
46. Vajrasadhu (Tib. Dorjé Lekpa), an important guardian of the Nyingma teachings in general and the Dzogchen teachings in particular, is a powerful worldly spirit who was tamed by Padmakara and bound to the service of the Buddhist tradition in Tibet.

47. Tsen are a class of nonhuman spirits renowned for their warlike and aggressive character.
48. The region that this clan inhabited, east of Lhasa, is called Drak.
49. Three English translations of *The Biography of Yeshé Tsogyal* have been published: *Mother of Knowledge,* trans. Tarthang Tulku and Jane Wilhelms (Berkeley: Dharma Publishing, 1983); *Sky Dancer: The Secret Life and Songs of the Lady Yeshe Tsogyel,* trans. Keith Dowman (Ithaca, NY: Snow Lion, 1996); and Gyalwa Changchub and Namkhai Nyingpo, *Lady of the Lotus Born,* trans. Padmakara Translation Group (Boston: Shambhala, 2002).
50. This prayer of praise, entitled *The Melody of the Hand Drum,* is found in Jamgön Kongtrul's collected works.
51. "Homage to the guru, the dakini of timeless awareness."
52. A famous retreat site associated with Guru Padmakara, located in the hills above Samyé Monastery.
53. A ritual feast performed by Vajrayana practitioners to renew their samaya commitments and to purify themselves of any breaches thereof, as well as to celebrate the successful completion of empowerments, teachings, and so forth.
54. Those of the shravaka, pratyekabuddha, and bodhisattva and the six levels of tantra (Kriya, Upa, Yoga, Mahayoga, Anuyoga, and Atiyoga).
55. The "hidden flaw" can be understood on two levels. In the relative sense, karmic causality is "flawed" because it reinforces one's confusion and leads to suffering. Ultimately, since the nature of everything is emptiness, nothing that takes place on the relative level exists as it seems to.
56. The dream state, the ordinary waking state, deep sleep, and sexual orgasm. These four states are the primary focus of transformation in the advanced yogic practices of Vajrayana Buddhism.
57. Successive stages of experience that mark the successful practice of methods involving the subtle channels and energies.
58. A fundamental practice of the stage of completion in Vajrayana Buddhism. The practice generates an intense experience of bliss and warmth that eclipses all ordinary emotions and thought patterns and leads directly to the awakening of a state of timeless awareness.
59. In Vajrayana iconography, the six bone ornaments are symbols of the six transcendent perfections of Mahayana Buddhism; wearing them indicates one's mastery of those perfections. The ornaments are a necklace, bracelets and anklets (counted as one ornament), earrings, a tiara, a ceremonial belt (consisting of two bands that hang from the shoulders and cross over the chest and back), and crematory bone ash smeared on the body.
60. An epithet of the Buddha Shakyamuni.
61. The sons of King Trisong Detsen, who were also students of Guru Rinpoché.
62. Tashi Cheu Dren and Kalasiddhi.
63. The palace in the pure realm associated with Guru Padmakara, to which he journeyed after leaving Tibet. Pema Ö (Lotus Light) is located on Zangdok Palri (Copper-Colored Mountain of Glory) in the realm of Chamara, which, according to traditional Buddhist cosmology, is a subcontinent located to the southwest of our human world. It is inhabited by bloodthirsty demons, who would invade our world were it not for the Guru's suppression of them.

64. The pure realm associated with dakinis, feminine embodiments of enlightenment.
65. Not a literal seal, but a metaphor for the decisiveness with which entrustment is conferred. Such a seal usually involves the formal investiture of a student by a master, conferring on the student the responsibility to serve as the next holder of the master's lineage.
66. Princess Pemasel had already died, at the age of eight, from a reaction to a bee sting, when Guru Padmakara summoned her consciousness back into her body in order to confer these transmissions on her. See Dudjom Rinpoche, *The Nyingma School of Tibetan Buddhism,* vol. 1, pp. 554–555, and Tulku Thondup, *The Tantric Tradition of the Nyingmapa,* p. 144. By conferring the empowerments and the seals of aspiration and entrustment on the princess, Guru Padmakara was acknowledging that her rebirth would be the tertön who would reveal the terma.
67. In Dudjom Rinpoche, *The Nyingma School of Tibetan Buddhism,* vol. 2, p. 427, Pema Ledrel Tsal's birth year is given as 1248. This corresponds to a Male Earth Monkey year in the Tibetan calendar; a Female Iron Hare year would correspond to the period from early 1231 to early 1232. Pema Ledrel Tsal's immediate rebirth was Longchenpa, who was born in 1308, placing Pema Ledrel Tsal's death sometime shortly before that.
68. An ancient Tibetan clan whose members included Nyang Ralpachen (or Nyang-ral) Nyima Özer, one of the "five kings" among tertöns. See Chapter 10, note 16.
69. Corresponding to the period from early 1253 to early 1254. Pema Ledrel Tsal would have been about twenty-three years old at this time.
70. A reference to the termas he would reveal.
71. An auspicious symbol of ancient India.
72. Terma teachings are often contained in a kind of casket, which can be opened only by the tertön destined to reveal the terma.
73. Rangjung Dorjé (1284–1339) was the third Gyalwang Karmapa, head of the Kagyü school of Tibetan Buddhism. He was credited with having combined the Mahamudra teachings of the newer schools and the Dzogchen teachings of the Nyingma school on the basis of a vision he had of Vimalamitra.
74. Although the Indian cultural reverence for members of the brahmin, or priestly, class is not a Buddhist tenet, the Tibetans inherited it to some degree and regarded the preserved flesh of a brahmin as a sacred substance.
75. Apparently a fairly minor tertön, not to be confused with Ratna (or Rinchen) Lingpa (1403–1479).
76. The death of a tulku does not take place in the usual way, according to the dictates of karma; the display of the nirmanakaya is described as resolving back into the basic space of emptiness that is its ultimate source. However, this honorific expression does not imply the attainment of rainbow body.
77. Orgyenpa Seng-gé Pal (or Rinchen Pal) (1229/30–1309) was a master of the Kagyü lineage of Mahamudra teachings, a student of the second Gyalwang Karmapa, Karma Pakshi (1204–1283), and a teacher of the third Karmapa, Rangjung Dorjé. From a dakini in the realm of Oddiyana, Orgyenpa received a transmission of teachings known as the Orgyen Nyendrup cycle, which he passed on to Rangjung Dorjé.
78. A Tibetan title meaning "realized one."

79. A cycle of teachings established in the early twelfth century by the Indian master known to Tibetans as Padampa Sang-gyé. Its practices are based on the sutras concerning the perfection of sublime knowing (Prajñaparamita), and its name (Zhijé means "Pacification") derives from the line in *The Heart Sutra* describing the mantra of Prajñaparamita as one that "pacifies all suffering."
80. Tropu Lotsawa Jampa Pal (1172–1225) was a translator who contributed to the codification of the Mahamudra teachings, especially those known as *The Five Principles of Mahamudra*. He invited several scholars to Tibet, including the Kashmiri scholar Khaché Panchen Shakya Shri Bhadra (1127–1225), and founded a tradition known as the Tropu Kagyü.
81. One of the eight minor branches of the Kagyü school. The others are the Drukpa, Tropu, Taklung, Martsang, Yerpa, Yazang, and Shukshep.
82. The mahasiddha Saraha was a major figure of the Indian Vajrayana tradition, whose teachings (often in the form of *dohas,* or spontaneous songs of spiritual realization) were an important source for the Tibetan tradition.
83. An idiom referring to the realization, gained through Dzogchen practice, that everything perceived is the expression of the pure awareness that is the true nature of mind and so is beyond the constraints of ordinary dualistic consciousness.
84. See note 63, this chapter.
85. The Female Wood Serpent year corresponds to the period from early 1365 to early 1366; since Gyalsé Lekpa Gyaltsen passed away toward the end of a Serpent year, his death would have been early in 1366.
86. See the more extensive biography of Longchenpa in Chapter 5.
87. Nyang-ral Nyima Özer (1136–1204), Guru Chöwang (1212–1270), and Rigdzin Gödem (1337–1409) were three of the most important early tertöns.
88. The tertön Longsel Dorjé Nyingpo (1625–1692), whose terma teachings are known by his name, was one of those responsible for restoring Katok Monastery, which, after four and a half centuries, had fallen into disrepair.
89. The eighth Khamtrul, who lived from 1930 to 1979.
90. Body, speech, and mind.
91. A reference to Dudjom Rinpoché's two-volume *The Nyingma School of Tibetan Buddhism.*

4. *The Lineage of Vimalamitra*

1. Throughout this section, the name is given as Indrabhuti, a common variant spelling of Indrabodhi, who is mentioned in Chapter 2.
2. This refers to an advanced level of spiritual accomplishment, also known as "rainbow body," in which an individual's physical body is transformed into one of light, although there is no change in outward appearance. Such a form can endure indefinitely, but it may be perceptible only to those with sufficient spiritual development. Both Padmakara and Vimalamitra attained this "form of transference." Vimalamitra had done so before he came to the court of King Indrabodhi the Younger. See Dudjom Rinpoche, *The Nyingma School of Tibetan Buddhism,* vol. 1, p. 501, and vol. 2, p. 39, n. 528.

3. A variant of the name Mingyur Lhungyi Druppai Tsuklak Khang.
4. The central temple in the monastic complex of Samyé.
5. The Tibetan idiom denotes someone considered to be an emanation, in human form, of a sambhogakaya manifestation. King Trisong Detsen was thought to be an emanation of the bodhisattva of wisdom, Mañjushri.
6. This small temple located within the Samyé monastic complex was established during King Trisong Detsen's reign to house the Indian scholars and Tibetan translators who collaborated on translations of Buddhist texts.
7. Also known as Muné Tsenpo; the eldest of Trisong Detsen's sons.
8. A retreat site used a generation later by the famous Kagyü master Milarepa.
9. A region north of the Tsangpo River in the central Tibetan region of Tsang.
10. A large tableland south of Lhasa, site of the confluence of the Tsangpo and Kyichu Rivers.
11. The Nyang River runs southeast of the Tsangpo River in the central Tibetan region of Tsang; its valley is more than 150 kilometers long.
12. "A Hundred Thousand Suns."
13. A number of great masters belonged to the Ngok clan, foremost among them Ngok Chöku Dorjé, one of the four principal students of Marpa Lotsawa Chökyi Lodrö, the founder of the Kagyü school.
14. Drakpa Gyaltsen (1147–1216), one of the "five elders" of the Sakya school of Tibetan Buddhism, was the second son of Sachen Kunga Nyingpo (1092–1158), the school's founder.
15. *The Three Continua* is one of two major sections of Lamdré (the Path and Fruition), a principal cycle of teachings transmitted by the Sakya school. Based on *The Hevajra Tantra, The Three Continua* is the Vajrayana section of the teachings; it discusses the principles of ground (the view of the inseparability of samsara and nirvana), path (the methods associated with the four levels of empowerment), and fruition (the enlightened qualities of the five kayas and five aspects of timeless awareness). The other section, *The Three Visions,* is a treatment of Hinayana and Mahayana themes; it discusses the impure vision, or perceptions, of ordinary beings, the relatively pure vision of spiritual practitioners, and the utterly pure vision of buddhas.
16. Chakrasamvara is one of the principal deities of the Sarma schools.
17. The Tsalpa Kagyü lineage, established by Zhang Yudrakpa Tsödrü Drakpa, is one of the four major branches of the Kagyü school (the others are the Kamtsang, Baram, and Pakmodrupa Kagyü); it is possible that Kyitön is another of the founder's titles.
18. When the remains of highly realized practitioners are cremated, such relics are often found in the ashes. Sharira are small, extremely hard spheres that may be white or of five colors: white, yellow, red, green, and blue.
19. A Sanskrit term denoting a spontaneous song of spiritual realization.
20. "Mahamudra,"a Sanskrit term meaning "Great Seal," is the name of a system of teachings focusing on the true nature of mind and all reality, the experience of which is a "seal that validates." These teachings, developed from the instructions of Indian mahasiddhas, are found in various forms in all schools of Tibetan Buddhism.
21. A statue of the Buddha, also known as Jowo Shakyamuni or Jowo Yizhin Norbu (the

Lord, the Wish-Fulfilling Gem), that was brought from China to Tibet in the seventh century by Kongjo, the Chinese queen of King Songtsen Gampo, as part of her dowry. The statue was originally housed in the temple of Ramoché, but was later relocated to the temple known as the Jokhang in the capital city, Lhasa, where it still resides.

22. The Female Wood Hare year (early 1255 to early 1256).
23. The Tibetan idiom refers to the emergence of patterns established in former lifetimes into conscious experience in this life. It primarily indicates a powerful urge to engage in spiritual practice.
24. Throughout Tibetan history, a major role was played by masters known as *nyönpa* (madmen), who expressed their realization through highly unconventional behavior. Although this behavior was not rebellious per se, or a deliberate attempt to shock people, it called into question social conventions and assumptions about spiritual practice. There are many popular stories of these madmen and the havoc they often wrought on the minds of those filled with preconceptions and smugness.
25. "Gyalpo demons" and "senmo demonesses" are generic Tibetan terms for male and female nonhuman spirits.
26. There were three masters named Seng-gé Gyappa, after the place where they lived; Trulzhik Seng-gé Gyappa, the third of these masters, received teachings from the second.
27. The Chö and Zhijé schools were related. The latter was founded by the Indian master Padampa Sang-gyé; the Chö lineage derives from his spiritual descendant, the Tibetan female master Machik Lapdrön.
28. Kharchu is an area in the Lha Valley of the southern Tibetan region of Lhodrak.
29. Sang-gyé Repa Rinchen Mönlam (1203–1280) was a master of the Zhijé teachings.
30. The Female Water Hare year (early 1303 to early 1304).
31. "Kumaradza" is a Tibetan rendering of the Sanskrit name Kumararaja; the Tibetan equivalent is Zhönnu Gyalpo.
32. There are several levels of Buddhist lay ordination. In addition to the fundamental commitment, which is the vow of refuge, five lay vows may be taken in any combination: not to kill, steal, lie, take intoxicants, or commit adultery. An alternative form of lay ordination involves celibacy. Before one reaches the age of eighteen or so, the ordination often consists simply of the vow of refuge, but Kumaradza received the full ordination of five vows at the age of nine.
33. A deity associated with wealth.
34. It was the custom of high lamas to issue injunctions against the taking of human or animal life in a particular region. Even ruthless bandits would respect such injunctions out of respect for the lamas (as well as guilt and fear of the lamas' powers).
35. Early 1343 to early 1344.
36. "The Omniscient Guru" refers to Longchenpa, who as Kumaradza's principal student would preside over the memorial ceremonies after his guru's death and take over Kumaradza's affairs.
37. A technique of the tögal practice of Dzogchen.
38. A reference to Tara.

5. Longchen Rabjampa Drimé Özer

1. Masters of the Indian Buddhist tradition who are models of erudition and realization

and who composed the authoritative source texts in their fields of expertise. Of the "six ornaments," Nagarjuna and Aryadeva were masters of Madhyamaka, Asanga and Vasubandhu were masters of Abhidharma, and Dignaga and Dharmakirti were masters of valid cognition. The "two sublime ones," Shakyaprabha and Gunaprabha, were masters of Vinaya.

2. A biography on the outer level is an account of a master's life in the world, and so corresponds most closely to what the English word "biography" conveys. A biography on the inner level describes the qualities that were not as obvious to the ordinary observer and lists the works the master composed. A biography on the secret, or ultimate, level records the master's profound spiritual experiences and realization, which were usually inaccessible to others and known only from the person's own accounts or through the insights of another, highly realized individual who knew the subject well.
3. Here "Teacher" is a reference to the Buddha Shakyamuni.
4. Early 1308 to early 1309.
5. Götsangpa Gönpo Dorjé founded the "upper lineage" of the Drukpa Kagyü, one of the eight minor branches of the Kagyü school.
6. Dharmakirti was the most influential logician of the Indian Buddhist tradition.
7. A shedra is a college, usually associated with a monastery, that offers courses involving the detailed study of various subjects in the Buddhist tradition, leading to the degree of khenpo.
8. "The One from Samyé Monastery Who Holds Many Scriptural Transmissions."
9. Ra Lotsawa Dorjé Drak was an eleventh-century Nyingma master who studied in Nepal with a master of the lineage that had been passed down from the Indian mahasiddha Naropa. Ra Lotsawa established a famous lineage of teachings concerning the wrathful deities Yamantaka and Vajrabhairava and produced superb Tibetan translations of these and other tantras.
10. This process was the basis of much of Tibetan metallurgy and alchemy.
11. Lama Dampa Sönam Gyaltsen lived from 1312 to 1375 and was Longchenpa's junior by four years.
12. A permission blessing is an abbreviated form of empowerment, usually associated with transmissions found in the lower classes of tantra.
13. "The Hundred Thousand Images of Early Tibetan Translators."
14. A popular style of composition consisting of a poem in thirty lines, each of which begins with a word that starts with a successive letter of the Tibetan alphabet.
15. The term *geshé,* used largely in the Gelukpa and Sakya schools, denotes someone who has reached a high level of scholastic achievement and has passed a series of formal examinations; the corresponding term in the Nyingma and Kagyü schools is *khenpo.*
16. A reference to advanced yogic practices that one does in total darkness, in strict retreat (called "dark retreat" or "retreat of the yoga of darkness"). The lack of visual stimulation facilitates the unfolding of the visions that are the basis of the Dzogchen practice of tögal.
17. A wrathful manifestation of Guru Rinpoché.
18. One of the twelve Tenma sisters, Tibetan spirits tamed by Guru Rinpoché in the eighth century and bound by oaths to serve the Buddhist teachings.
19. Local spirits who were tamed by Guru Rinpoché and bound by oaths to serve the Buddhist teachings; as part of their commitment, they took lay ordination as Buddhists from the Guru.

20. The Female Earth Hare year (early 1339 to early 1340).
21. A reference to the feathers traditionally placed in the mouth of a ritual vase during empowerment. The peacock, reputedly able to ingest and transmute poison in order to increase the beauty of its plumage, symbolizes the Vajrayana principle of transforming ordinary experiences into spiritual practice without having to renounce the world of the senses.
22. In the old style of Tibetan pronunciation, prefix and suffix letters were enunciated. This custom has fallen away in more recent times, resulting in many more homophones, which can lead to confusion in writing and speech. The word *rigs* signifies "family" or "class" and indicates one's personality type in Vajrayana contexts; the word *rig*(*-pa*) means "awareness."
23. The Female Water Sheep year (early 1343 to early 1344).
24. Tibetans attribute the death of a teacher to a lack of merit on the part of those the teacher benefits, so that the circumstances are no longer appropriate for the teacher to remain.
25. A reference to Longchenpa's rebirth as the tertön Pema Lingpa.
26. The termas that would be revealed by Pema Lingpa, which had been hidden in central Bhutan.
27. Guru Rinpoché, or Padmakara.
28. A reference to Longchenpa's guru, Kumaradza, who was an emanation of Vimalamitra.
29. Pang-gangpa Rinchen Dorjé (no connection to the master of the same name who asked the question) was one of Longchenpa's previous incarnations.
30. It is not that these teachings will completely disappear, but that they will no longer be practiced widely.
31. "Vajra songs" and "vajra verses" are uttered or written down as spontaneous expressions of profound insight and realization.
32. Trumpets made of human thighbones.
33. Here Longchenpa is referring to Pema Ledrel Tsal, his former incarnation and the revealer of *The Heart Drop of the Dakini*.
34. So sacred are the teachings that one who transmits them incurs a great karmic responsibility; sharing them too openly or casually could have serious repercussions.
35. The third level of empowerment in higher Vajrayana practices can be conferred through a ritual consort or simply through the use of symbols. The latter method is used almost exclusively, due to the risk of misinterpretation.
36. A reference to the termas associated with Princess Pemasel, the daughter of King Trisong Detsen.
37. Threads coated with chalk dust are used to lay out the grid for drawing a mandala. The threads are held just above the drawing surface and snapped to leave lines of dust that guide the application of colored sand.
38. In the practice of tögal, certain factors (figuratively termed "lamps") contribute to the unfolding of the four visions, which are the context in which the true nature of mind manifests in the practitioner's experience. The usual enumeration is of four such factors (the "four lamps"): the "naturally occurring lamp of sublime knowing" (Tib. *shes rab rang byung gi sgron ma*), the innate nature of mind that is the basis for the visions; the "water lamp of the far-reaching lasso" (Tib. *rgyangs zhags chu'i sgron ma*), which provides the avenue of perception and experience through which the visions can unfold; the "lamp of

totally pure basic space (Tib. *dbyings rnam dag gi sgron ma*), which is the context in which the visions manifest; and the "lamp of empty spheres" (Tib. *thig le stong pa'i sgron ma*), which is the specific configuration of the visions. Occasionally, there is reference to six lamps, two of which are factors associated with the water lamp of the far-reaching lasso: the "corporeal lamp of the heart" (Tib. *tsitta sha'i sgron ma*) and the "lamp of the subtle white channels" (Tib. *dkar 'jam rtsa'i sgron ma*). There is a more concise enumeration of two lamps, as is given here, i.e., the "lamp of totally pure basic space" and the "lamp of empty spheres."

39. The form of Vimalamitra associated with longevity practice.
40. The third of the four visions of tögal.
41. Dedication of the merit of one's spiritual practice in a state of nonduality, in which one does not conceive of the "three focal points" of subject, object, and the relationship between them.
42. A temple containing (or perhaps built of) stones on which the mantra *Om mani padme hum* is carved.
43. Longchenpa was exiled from central Tibet to Bhutan by the first Tai Situ hierarch of the ruling Pakmodrupa faction, Jangchub Gyaltsen (1302–1364), who viewed Longchenpa's affiliation with the Drigung branch of the Kagyü school with suspicion (due largely to political troubles that were thought to have been caused by Longchenpa's Drigung student, Gomchen Kunrin). Eventually, the two were reconciled, and Longchenpa was able to return to Tibet.
44. One of the authors of the biography of Longchenpa.
45. Presumably a reference to three masters of the early Kadampa school of Tibetan Buddhism, founded by the Tibetan students of the Indian master Atisha (ca. 980–1052). The "three brothers" were Potowa, Chen-ngawa, and Puchungwa; all were students of Atisha's principal student, Dromtön Gyalwai Jungné.
46. Presumably a reference to three early Kadampa scholars: Cha Chökyi Seng-gé, the sixth abbot of the shedra of Sangpu in central Tibet; his student Tsangnakpa Tsöndrü Seng-gé; and Denbakpa Mawai Seng-gé.
47. A reference to three early masters of the Kalachakra teachings: Butön Rinchen Drup, Dolpopa Sherab Gyaltsen, and Shakya Chokden.
48. One of Longchenpa's many names.
49. The Maha-madhyamaka (Great Middle Way), Mahamudra (Great Seal), and Mahasandhi, or Dzogchen (Great Perfection).
50. Founded in the seventh century by King Songtsen Gampo's Chinese consort, Princess Wengchen, Ramoché is located about a kilometer north of the Jokhang, the main temple in the center of Lhasa.
51. Situ Ön Shakya Zangpo (fourteenth to fifteenth centuries) was the nephew of Chökyi Gyaltsen (1377–1448), the first Tai Situ of the Karma Kagyü school.
52. A reference to the Buddha's passing into nirvana at Kushinagar in northern India.
53. The trainings in ethics, meditation, and sublime knowing.
54. The Buddhist spiritual path is described as a sequence of five paths or phases: those of accumulation, application, seeing, meditation, and no more learning (which corresponds to the fruition of buddhahood).

55. The Buddha Shakyamuni.
56. Probably a reference to Longchenpa's guru, Kumaradza.
57. Early 1363 to early 1364. Longchenpa died toward the end of the Hare year, in other words, in early 1364. In *Kindly Bent to Ease Us* (Emeryville, CA: Dharma Publishing, 1975), vol. 1, p. xv, Dr. H. V. Guenther fixes the date as Wednesday, January 24, 1364.
58. An "inner support" is a statue or other likeness housed within a structure, such as a stupa or temple, which is the "outer support." Alternatively, the tomb of a great master might include a building (the outer support) containing a stupa (the inner support) in which the remains were interred.
59. Traditionally, texts were read aloud; a treatise such as *The Illuminating Moon* would address the correct pronunciation of words.
60. In each of the following three titles, a play on words can be inferred: the idiom *khams 'dus pa* (saddened) could also be interpreted to mean "the faction from Kham (or eastern Tibet)," referring to the monks whose harrassment of Longchenpa during his stay at Sangpu precipitated his writing of these tracts.
61. Located on a high hilltop in Yarlung south of Samyé and the Tsangpo River, Yumbu Tsuklak Khang is the site of the oldest recorded building in Tibet, thought to be the palace of the first kings of Tibet, dating back to the third century.
62. Sublime knowing that derives from listening to teachings, contemplating, and meditating.
63. According to oral history, many of Longchenpa's original drafts of these texts were lost before they could be published when a pack animal stumbled while crossing a deep ravine in central Bhutan, sending the manuscripts into the abyss below.
64. "Homage to the Omniscient Guru."
65. That is, a very stupid person. Paltrul Rinpoché often used folk idioms and expressions in his written works.
66. An epithet of the Buddha Shakyamuni.
67. In the Buddhist tradition, faith has three qualities: a sense of awe or wonder, a desire to emulate the object of one's faith, and a conviction based on the trust that is born of one's understanding.
68. An epithet of the Buddha Shakyamuni.
69. An epithet of the Buddha Shakyamuni.
70. In the higher tantras, the fourth of the four levels of empowerment, sometimes called the "word empowerment," involves a direct introduction to the true nature of mind.
71. An empowerment in the Dzogchen approach whereby students are introduced to the practices of trekchö and tögal.
72. Longchen Rabjam, *A Treasure Trove of Scriptural Transmission: A Commentary on "The Precious Treasury of the Basic Space of Phenomena,"* trans. Richard Barron (Junction City, CA: Padma Publishing, 2001), pp. 215–216.

6. *The Combined Lineages from Longchenpa to Jigmé Gyalwai Nyugu*

1. The term "Densa" refers to a monastic center that is the principal seat of an important tulku or other master or the primary institution associated with a given lineage of teachings.
2. Lha Valley is in the southernmost part of central Tibet, near the Bhutanese border.

3. Khenchen Sönam Drakpa (1273–1345) was a holder of the main lineage of Lojong teachings (see note 5, this chapter). He is also referred to below by the title Jangsem (Bodhisattva).
4. A traditional simile comparing a great monastic figure to the first generation of Buddhist elders after the Buddha's passing into nirvana.
5. Lojong (mental training) comprises various systems of contemplative exercises intended to awaken love, compassion, altruism, and bodhichitta in the practitioner in a developmental way.
6. Gyalsé Tokmé Zangpo (1295–1369) was another student of Khenchen Sönam Drakpa and the author of several highly regarded commentaries on various aspects of the training involved in the bodhisattva path.
7. Normally, a master passes away before the next incarnation appears, but in some instances it has been accepted that the master's death did not precede the birth of the reincarnation.
8. Kyipala was a nun whom Longchenpa took as his consort while in Bhutan. Although their relationship would seem to have been a violation of their monastic vows, in fact it was an edification of their spiritual training, and the birth of a tulku was simply one of the things that justified the relationship.
9. An epithet of the deity Rahula.
10. The Female Earth Ox year (early 1409 to early 1410).
11. Presumably his parents took this life-threatening episode as a sign that they should allow their son to follow his own inclinations.
12. According to the concept of "contamination," someone's involvement or contact with others may have a negative effect, whether physical or emotional. It does not necessarily imply that the individual who is the source of the contamination is morally culpable. In this case, Drakpa Özer did not contract leprosy, but his exposure was thought to have impaired his studies.
13. These masters belonged to a number of traditions other than the Nyingma: Karmapa Rangjung Dorjé was the head of the Kagyü school. Butön Rinchen Drup (1290–1364) was a master of the Kalachakra teachings and was responsible for the first systematic editing of the Kangyur. Gyalsepa was a logician and principal student of Lama Dampa Sönam Gyaltsen, a master of the Sakya school who lived from 1312 to 1375. Chokgyalwa, or Choklé Namgyal (1306–1386), was the fifth Jonang Khenchen. "Khenchen Sönam Drakpa" may be a reference to Butön's teacher, Joden Khenpo Sönam Drakpa (thirteenth to fourteenth centuries).
14. Most likely the Female Iron Bird year (early 1381 to early 1382).
15. Located on the south bank of the Tsangpo River in central Tibet, Tsetang became the government seat of the ruling Pakmodrupa dynasty of Kagyü hierarchs in 1349. Several important monastic centers were established there in the later fourteenth century by Tai Situ Jangchub Gyaltsen, the Pakmodrupa ruler who exiled Longchenpa to Bhutan.
16. Probably Ewam Chokden Monastery in Ngor, founded in 1429 near Zhigatsé by Ngorchen Kunga Zangpo of the Sakya school; Evam Chokden was the center of the Ngorpa branch of that school.

17. Here a reference to *The Heart Drop of the Dakini* (transmitted by Padmakara) and *The Heart Drop of Vimalamitra* (transmitted by Vimalamitra).
18. Ratna Lingpa (1403–1479) revealed a large number of important termas, foremost among them his Vajrakila cycle.
19. Given the uncertainty of Gyalsé Dawa Drakpa's dates, this was most likely the Male Fire Rat year (early 1456 to early 1457) or the Male Earth Rat year (early 1468 to early 1469). A third possibility is the Male Water Rat year (early 1492 to early 1493).
20. *The Innermost Heart Drop of the Dakini, The Innermost Heart Drop of the Guru,* and *The Innermost Heart Drop of Profundity.*
21. That is, he received from Dawa Drakpa the most profound transmission possible, the direct experience of the true nature of mind.
22. Early 1497 to early 1498.
23. The Kangyur (Translated Words of the Buddha) is a collection, in approximately one hundred volumes, of the Tibetan translations of sutras, tantras, and other sources from the Indian Buddhist tradition that were considered authoritative records of the Buddha's words. Its companion collection, the Tengyur (Translated Treatises), in more than two hundred volumes, comprises the Tibetan translations of the most authoritative commentaries by Indian Buddhist masters. Together, the Kangyur and Tengyur constitute the canon of Indian works on which the Tibetan schools based their scholastic approach to the Buddhist teachings. The oral transmissions for these two large collections, which took months, were often conferred by masters on a large number of students.
24. Early 1568 to early 1569.
25. The Male Wood Tiger year (early 1494 to early 1495).
26. With the exception of the Nyingma school, all of the lineages mentioned are Sarma schools. Taken together, these lineages constitute the range of teachings available in Tibet, including those collectively known as the "eight lineages of spiritual accomplishment."
27. The title "Jé-ön" indicates that the bearer is a blood relative (usually a nephew) of a high-ranking tulku of a monastery.
28. These are being concerned with gain or loss, fame or notoriety, praise or blame, and pleasure or pain.
29. The Female Wood Sheep year (early 1535 to early 1536).
30. Könchok Bang (1525–1583), also known as Könchok Yenlak, was the fifth Zhamarpa of the Karma Kagyü school.
31. Zhikpo Lingpa Gargyi Wangchuk Tsal (1524–1583).
32. Important regions in central Tibet, south of Lhasa and the Tsangpo River.
33. The Male Iron Horse year (early 1570 to early 1571); the date mentioned would have fallen very early in 1571.
34. Located in Yarlung south of the Tsangpo River and Samyé, Tradruk is one of the temples erected by King Songtsen Gampo in the seventh century to define his kingdom's borders.
35. Also known as Yenpa Lodé; for his biography, see Chapter 10.
36. The Male Fire Monkey year (early 1536 to early 1537).
37. Statues, texts, and stupas and temples.
38. Early 1597 to early 1598.

39. A Tibetan title meaning "incarnation of speech." It is thought that a highly realized master can produce multiple incarnations, which are usually classified as incarnations of various facets of the master's total being; hence there can be incarnations of a master's form (Kutrul), speech (Sungtrul), mind (Tuktrul), and occasionally qualities and activity.
40. Ngawang Lozang Gyatso (1617–1682).
41. Early 1576 to early 1577.
42. The ninth Karmapa, Wangchuk Dorjé (1556–1603), author of several important works on Mahamudra, including *Pointing Out the Dharmakaya*, *Dispelling the Darkness of Ignorance*, and *The Ocean of the Definitive Meaning.*
43. The sixth Zhamar of the Karma Kagyü school, Chökyi Wangchuk (1584–1630).
44. The ordinations of the Hinayana (individual liberation), the Mahayana (the bodhisattva vow), and the Vajrayana (tantric samaya).
45. A drupchen (supreme accomplishment) is an intensive group ritual that takes place over a number of days and focuses on a specific sadhana practice. The format was introduced by Guru Padmakara in the eighth century and is particularly widely practiced in the Nyingma school.
46. Rigdzin Chenpo Trinlé Lhundrup, whose biography appears below; he was also known as Sangdak Chenpo.
47. Early 1628 to early 1629.
48. Early 1611 to early 1612.
49. Tsuklak Gyatso (1567/8–1633), the third Pawo incarnation of the Karma Kagyü school, was a student of the ninth Karmapa, Wangchuk Dorjé.
50. That is, Tsultrim Dorjé.
51. The ten elements of Vajrayana practice in which a trained master is proficient. Although there are numerous variations of this list, they generally include such topics as mandalas, meditation, mantras, mudras (symbolic hand gestures), protection and consecration rituals, fire rituals, and various stages of sadhana practice such as the invitation of the deities.
52. The practice known in Tibetan as *powa* is intended to facilitate the process of dying in order to ensure liberation or, at least, the most favorable rebirth possible. The training prepares one to apply the technique of transference at the point of one's own death, but accomplished practitioners are often summoned to help others on their deathbeds.
53. The Male Water Tiger year (early 1662 to early 1663).
54. The Male Fire Dog year (early 1646 to early 1647).
55. "Naturally Occurring Noble One of Kyirong," a statue of Avalokiteshvara, the bodhisattva of compassion, first discovered in the seventh century at Kyirong on the Nepal–Tibet border. According to legend, it was found, along with three other such images, inside a sandalwood tree by an emissary of King Songtsen Gampo. The image was brought to Lhasa, but taken back to Kyirong due to the political machinations of some of the king's ministers, who were opposed to the new Buddhist influence at court. The statue was not returned to Lhasa until 1656, the year of Gyurmé Dorjé's ordination.
56. Gyalwai Wangpo, a title of the Dalai Lamas.
57. Qualities traditionally assigned to the holy river Ganges in India: water that is sweet, cool, soft, light, transparent, pure, and soothing to the throat and stomach.

58. A "master of the ten powers" is a buddha, here a reference to Longchenpa.
59. An inspired and powerful seer of the Vedic period of India and the author of a number of hymns.
60. Also known as Ashvaghosha, Vira was a Hindu logician who converted to Buddhism and became one of the greatest poets of the Indian Buddhist tradition.
61. These "four great rivers" are: textual commentary, oral instructions, blessings and empowerments, and practical methods and rituals.
62. Hearing and contemplating the teachings.
63. The Female Water Hare year (early 1663 to early 1664).
64. The Male Fire Dragon year (early 1676 to early 1677).
65. The Male Iron Monkey year (early 1680 to early 1681).
66. Termas are classified according to the way in which they were originally concealed and revealed. For example, an "earth terma" is a text or some other physical object concealed in a place such as a rock face. A "terma of enlightened intent" is a transmission that was originally "sealed" within the mind of one of Guru Padmakara's intimate students during the master's stay in Tibet in the eighth century. The terma then remains "concealed" in the mind of the student through successive incarnations, until in some lifetime a rebirth of the student encounters circumstances that trigger the memory of having received the original transmission. "Terma of enlightened mind" is a generic term that does not necessarily signify a terma of enlightened intent. For more details on the terma tradition, see Tulku Thondup Rinpoche, *Hidden Teachings of Tibet* (London: Wisdom, 1986).
67. The Female Water Pig year (early 1683 to early 1684).
68. A euphemism for practices involving a consort.
69. There are several texts dealing with various aspects of Terdak Lingpa's life; these contain some autobiographical accounts, but are primarily the work of his younger brother, Lochen Dharma Shri.
70. Of study, meditation, and projects (such as building temples, erecting statues, and printing books).
71. The Male Wood Horse year (early 1714 to early 1715).
72. Reed horns played in Tibetan rituals, often to welcome the arrival of an honored master.
73. Desi Sang-gyé Gyatso (1653–1705) concealed the fifth Dalai Lama's death and ruled in his stead for a number of years before being forced to abdicate in 1702. See note 78, this chapter.
74. The sun and moon, symbols of widespread influence and fame, are often used metaphorically to refer either to a spiritual teacher and a patron (as in this case) or to two principal students of a single master (such as Jamyang Khyentsei Wangpo and Paltrul Rinpoché).
75. The Sanskrit for the Tibetan name Rinchen Namgyal.
76. The Male Wood Dog year (early 1694 to early 1695).
77. Pema Gyurmé Gyatso (1686–1718), one of Terdak Lingpa's sons, who served as the throne holder of Mindroling Monastery; for his biography, see Chapter 11.
78. The Mongols had exerted influence in Tibet since 1642, when Gushri Khan, leader of the Qøsot tribe, helped the fifth Dalai Lama defeat the rulers of central Tibet, who were based in the southern region of Tsang. Gushri Khan then installed the Dalai Lama as his

co-ruler of Tibet, conferring on him the title "Dalai," the Mongolian word for "ocean." (The four previous Dalai Lamas were accorded the title posthumously.) The fifth Dalai Lama died in 1682, but his regent, Desi Sang-gyé Gyatso, concealed the death for twelve years, after which the sixth Dalai Lama (Tsangyang Gyatso, 1683–1706) was enthroned. However, his unconventional behavior (he was fond of women and drinking parties, and was the author of some mildly erotic poetry) caused him to be deposed in 1705 by Lhazang Khan, a successor of Gushri Khan who attempted to foist his own son on the Tibetans as the "true" sixth Dalai Lama in order to consolidate his power as the ruler of Tibet. This provoked the Tibetan authorities to call on another Mongol tribe, the Dzungars, to restore order, and they invaded central Tibet in 1717. Although Lhazang Khan was killed, his false candidate deposed, and the seventh Dalai Lama, Kalzang Gyatso, installed, the Dzungars nevertheless plundered a number of holy sites, including the principal Nyingma monasteries of Mindroling and Dorjé Drak. Among those killed were Terdak Lingpa's younger brother Chöpal Gyatso (Lochen Dharma Shri) and Jangdak Pema Trinlé (the fourth Rigdzin of Dorjé Drak).

79. Kalzang Gyatso lived from 1708 to 1757.
80. Following the Dzungar Mongol invasion of 1717, the seventh Dalai Lama was enthroned in 1720 with the support of forces sent by the Manchu emperor of China. (Tibet's relations with the Manchus dated back to the reign of the great fifth Dalai Lama seventy years earlier.) Once Kalzang Gyatso was officially installed as the Dalai Lama, the Qing dynasty began a policy of suzerainty toward Tibet that lasted until the early twentieth century; nevertheless, the Dalai Lama was able to restore the policies of religious tolerance and ecumenism that had been lost under the Mongols. As part of this, he recalled Gyalsé Rinchen Namgyal from self-imposed exile and officially recognized him as the next throne holder of Mindroling. Kalzang Gyatso thus ensured the continuity of the lineages of the Mindroling tradition, which had been threatened when the monastery was sacked only a few years earlier.
81. A reference to the office of the supreme head, or "throne holder," of Mindroling Monastery.
82. Terchen Gyurmé Dorjé died in 1714, three years before the Dzungar Mongol invasion that devastated Mindroling.
83. During the Dzungar invasion.
84. Early 1758 to early 1759.
85. "Master of the Entire Range of Vajrayana."
86. Between 1790 and 1798, the royal family of Dergé in eastern Tibet sponsored the carving of the woodblocks used to print Jigmé Lingpa's collected works in nine volumes and *The Collected Tantras of the Nyingma School* in twenty-six volumes. Both collections were edited by Getsé Mahapandita Gyurmé Tsewang Chokdrup (1761–1829), a scholar of Katok Monastery who studied with Jigmé Lingpa's student, the first Dodrupchen, Jigmé Trinlé Özer.
87. Terdak Lingpa and Ngak Rabjampa Orgyen Chödrak.
88. A master of the Vajrayana teachings who is also a fully ordained monk.
89. The beginning of the eighteenth century.

90. A skirt, an everyday shawl, and a shawl worn on formal occasions.
91. A reference to the entire body of teachings that Jigmé Lingpa received from Longchenpa in these visions.
92. These are (in the order mentioned in the poem): the Buddhist teachings, Sanskrit grammar, logic, the arts, and medicine).
93. Dromtön Gyalwai Jungné, the eleventh-century Tibetan student of the Indian master Atisha, and Gyalwa Chokyang, one of Guru Padmakara's twenty-five intimate students.
94. Early 1308 to early 1309. Each year in the sixty-year cycle of the Tibetan calendar has a poetic epithet; the Male Earth Monkey year is known as the year of Jupiter. In *Kindly Bent to Ease Us,* vol. 1, p. xiii, Guenther fixes the date of Longchenpa's birth as Friday, March 1, 1308.
95. The main schools of grammar studied in Tibet.
96. These were the subject of certain classical works in the Indian tradition; a section of the Tengyur contains Tibetan translations of such works.
97. Yutok Yönten Gönpo, who reputedly lived from the mid-eighth to the mid-ninth century, was the one of the founders of the Tibetan medical tradition and physician to the court of King Trisong Detsen—hence the metaphor of Longchenpa as a physician.
98. A reference to the emptiness that is the ultimate nature of all phenomena.
99. *The Kalachakra Tantra* has three major areas of application: the outer dimension, focusing on the macrocosm and astrology; the inner dimension, pertaining to the microcosm of the practitioner's subtle body; and the transcendent dimension, concerning the practices associated with the deity Kalachakra.
100. In this verse, Longchenpa is compared to a garuda soaring majestically in space, an image frequently found in the Dzogchen teachings.
101. A reference to the Hindu god Brahma, whose four faces gaze in all directions, indicative of omniscience.
102. An epithet of the Buddha Shakyamuni.
103. Shambhu is an epithet of the Hindu god Shiva; many of the metaphors in this prayer of praise are traditional motifs found in classical Indian literature.
104. The eight extremes are conceptual frameworks concerning the ultimate nature of phenomena that limit one's view of reality; they are concepts about origination, cessation, naive realism, nihilistic denial, going, coming, identity, and separateness. The six special attributes define the process of gaining realization within the ground of being according to the Atiyoga teachings: awareness emerging from the ground of being, perceiving its own manifestation, distinguishing itself from any state of confusion, gaining freedom in that distinction, not relying on any external condition for its presence, and resting in its own natural lucidity.
105. The structural metaphors in this verse refer to a stupa. The four-sided base consists of steps above which sits the "vase" (the main section of the stupa), serving as a shrine that houses a statue of a buddha or deity and that is topped by a dome.
106. Activity can be either wrathful and direct, focusing on "annihilating" negativity, or peaceful and indirect, focusing on "nurturing" positive potentials or qualities.
107. *The Innermost Heart Drop of the Dakini, The Innermost Heart Drop of the Guru,* and *The Innermost Heart Drop of Profundity.*

108. This verse employs the legendary model of a universal monarch, whose victory is ensured by a thousand-spoked wheel of pure gold that flies in the sky before his armies, causing any foe to surrender before a battle becomes necessary.
109. The four divisions are the infantry and warriors fighting on elephants, horses, and chariots.
110. A universal monarch's victory is ensured merely by the force of karma from previous lifetimes maturing in the present; the monarch requires no other skills. Longchenpa achieved "victory" by positively influencing beings in the following four ways: being generous with material goods and spiritual teachings, speaking pleasantly, acting according to the wishes of those to be guided, and acting in ways that ensured they were guided spiritually.
111. The metaphor in this verse compares Longchenpa to the god Indra in his palace in the Trayastrimsha heaven of the desire realm; Indra's forces constantly defeat those of the demigods in battle.
112. There are three ways to validate a conclusion reached through reasoning: direct experience, inference based on evidence, and inference based on belief or common knowledge. Direct experience involves nonconceptual and undeluded awareness, such as the sensory perception of an object, the telepathic knowledge of someone else's mind, or the meditative equipoise of an advanced spiritual practitioner. Inference based on evidence involves direct awareness of something that provides irrefutable proof of a conclusion that might otherwise remain obscured, such as the knowledge that there is fire when one sees smoke rising from behind a hill. Inference based on belief involves knowledge of something that can be relied on to prove a conclusion that might otherwise remain highly obscured, such as knowledge based on authentic scriptural sources. Inference based on common knowledge permits conclusions such as the term "rabbit-marked" referring to the moon, given that the moon is commonly known to bear such a mark on its surface.
113. Perhaps a reference to the three schools of Kagyü, Sakya, and Nyingma or alternatively, within the Nyingma school itself, the three traditions of So, Zur, and Nup.
114. The level of twofold purity is the realization of dharmakaya, which is innately and timelessly pure in itself, as well as pure from the perspective of the individual practitioner in the immediacy of its discovery.
115. Sakya Pandita (1182–1251) was one of the greatest scholars in the history of Tibetan Buddhism.
116. Gandharvas are gods in the desire realm who are noted for their skill as musicians.
117. A reference to the "three ancestral kings"; see Chapter 3, note 30.
118. The Madhyamaka philosophy of Mahayana Buddhism.
119. The buddha Vairochana, the basis for the succession of emanations of which Longchenpa was one.
120. "Danun" is the Tibetan translation of the Sanskrit name Saraha, meaning "He Who Shot the Arrow."
121. This verse refers to the fact that Saraha of India and Bairotsana of Tibet were early figures in the succession of incarnations that included Longchenpa; despite the latter's similarity to Nagarjuna and Garab Dorjé, he is not held to be an incarnation of either master.

122. "Supreme expanse" is a play on Longchenpa's name.
123. An ancient Indian expression (found in the *Rig Veda*) for the sun, which derives from the image of the sun being drawn across the sky by seven horses representing the seven days of the week.
124. Not necessarily a specific deity, but a personification of basic space or emptiness, the feminine principle.
125. The period from early 1788 to early 1789, when Jigmé Lingpa was sixty years old by Tibetan reckoning.
126. The mantra associated with Guru Padmakara, *Om ah hum vajra guru padma siddhi hum.*
127. That is, in his written works.
128. *The Heart Drop of Longchenpa.*
129. A reference to the three principal Gelukpa monasteries in and around the capital of Lhasa: Sera, Drepung, and Ganden.
130. Located about forty-five kilometers east of Lhasa in central Tibet, Ganden was established in 1409 by Tsongkhapa Lozang Drakpa (1357–1419), founder of the Gelukpa school. It was the first Gelukpa monastery in Tibet and consisted of two teaching colleges, Shartsé and Jangtsé.
131. The extensive lineage is the kama tradition, the direct lineage is the terma tradition, and the pure visionary transmission is that of daknang.
132. See Chapter 9.
133. This river becomes the Yalung in central China.
134. A guardian spirit who is not enlightened but is bound by an oath to uphold the Buddhist teachings.
135. The life of Milarepa (1052–1135), who was one of the forerunners of the Kagyü school, is regarded as the ideal of dedication to spiritual practice and accomplishment.
136. Zangdok Palri, the pure realm of Guru Rinpoché, is described as containing the palace of Pema Ö, whose three stories, from lowest to highest, correspond to the nirmanakaya, sambhogakaya, and dharmakaya.
137. Here "Nyingtik cycle" refers to *The Heart Drop of Longchenpa.*
138. In this case, a reference not to Longchenpa, but to Jigmé Lingpa, who is often referred to as Kunchen (Omniscient) Jigmé Lingpa.
139. An English translation of this has been published as *Words of My Perfect Teacher,* rev. ed., trans. Padmakara Translation Group (Boston: Shambhala, 1998).
140. See Chapter 9.
141. The second Jigmé Gyalwai Nyugu was Kunzang Dechen Dorjé, also known as Pema Kunzang (ca. 1845–ca. 1925). See Tulku Thondup, *Masters of Meditation and Miracles: The Longchen Nyingthig Lineage of Tibetan Buddhism* (Boston: Shambhala, 1996), p. 172.
142. The white light and white shawl were symbols of lay tantric practitioners.

7. *The Lineages of Jigmé Gyalwai Nyugu: Paltrul Rinpoché*

1. Here the outer level refers to Paltrul as an incarnation of the Indian Buddhist master Shantideva (a somewhat public historical figure of the Mahayana tradition), the inner

level to Paltrul as an incarnation of Shavari (one of the eighty-four mahasiddhas of the Vajrayana tradition of ancient India, and thus a more mystic and enigmatic figure), and the secret level to Paltrul as an emanation of the sambhogakaya buddha Avalokiteshvara (the so-called basis of emanation for all three historical figures).

2. Of the many forms of Avalokiteshvara, the one called Duk-ngal Rangdrol (Natural Freedom That Underlies Suffering) is associated with *The Heart Drop of Longchenpa*. The guru yoga practices of this cycle are classified on four levels: outer, inner, secret, and most secret; the meditation on Duk-ngal Rangdrol constitutes the secret level.
3. The Male Iron Dragon year (early 1808 to early 1809).
4. The Mukpodong clan is one of the most ancient in Tibet, dating back to the beginning of recorded history in the seventh century.
5. For a short biography of Dola Jigmé Kalzang, see Tulku Thondup, *Masters of Meditation and Miracles*, pp. 173–174. His incarnation was Yukhok Jadralwa Chöying Rangdrol, whose biography can be found in Chapter 8.
6. Zhechen Öntrul Gyurmé Tutop Namgyal (1787–?). The title "Öntrul" refers to those in a line of incarnations of someone who was originally a relative of the principal tulku of a monastery, usually a nephew ("Ön" means "nephew") or perhaps a younger brother or cousin. For the most part, these incarnations were no longer related by blood to the original tulku.
7. Unconventional behavior demonstrated by someone authentically engaged in "uncontrived conduct" undermines the ordinary fixations and habit patterns of those who observe it and triggers in them higher states of realization. This does not imply license to act irresponsibly or immorally. Khyentsé Yeshé Dorjé was noted for his consumption of alcohol and often seemed intoxicated. When Paltrul met Yeshé Dorjé and smelled alcohol on his breath, he was inwardly critical of him. Although Paltrul said nothing, Yeshé Dorjé was aware of his reaction and berated him, beating him senseless. When Paltrul regained consciousness, he found that he was directly experiencing the true nature of his mind.
8. Due to the nomadic way of life of much of the Tibetan population, monasteries were often housed not in permanent structures, but in encampments, which, along with the lay community associated with them, would change locations seasonally.
9. So called because they lie in the northern part of the eastern Tibetan region of Kham.
10. The second Katok Situ (1820–1879?); for his biography, see Chapter 16. One of the students of Chökyi Jungné (1699/1700–1774), the eighth Tai Situ of the Karma Kagyü school, was a lama of the Nyingma monastery of Katok who instituted the recognition of a parallel line of Situ incarnations there. Thus the Palpung Tai Situs were Kagyü masters, whereas the Katok Situs were Nyingma. The first Katok Situ was Chökyi Seng-gé (1775?–1819?).
11. The Drimé Zhingkyong incarnations are an important line in the tradition of Katok Monastery. The tulku mentioned here was the third Drimé Zhingkyong, Jigmé Yönten Gönpo (?–1898).
12. Pema Tekchok Tenpai Gyaltsen (1864–1909).
13. "Kyabgön" is a Tibetan title meaning "protector who grants refuge."
14. A name for the Gelukpa school founded by Tsongkhapa.
15. Another name for the Gelukpa school; the name derives from Ganden Monastery. Gyaltsap Jé Darma Rinchen (1364–1431) was the elder of Tsongkhapa's two foremost students.

16. The earlier cycles of the Nyingtik teachings are those compiled or composed by Longchenpa in *The Four Higher Collections of the Heart Drop;* the later cycle is *The Heart Drop of Longchenpa*, revealed by Jigmé Lingpa.
17. Orgyen Tendzin Norbu was the nephew of Gyalsé Zhenpen Tayé, whose biography can be found in Chapter 12.
18. The Tibetan term *nyong-tri* (translated in this volume as "experiential teaching" or "experiential instruction") refers to a method whereby a teacher presents a stage of teaching and practice to a student, who then practices until a significant level of experience and insight develops. Only then does the teacher present the next stage of the training. Much of what constitutes such an experience-oriented transmission may not be written down in texts, but is dependent on the teacher's ability to work skillfully with individual students.
19. The Male Wood Monkey year (early 1884 to early 1885).
20. The Female Fire Pig year (early 1887 to early 1888).
21. This refers to a technique in which all the details of a visualization are called to mind instantaneously, rather than stage by stage.
22. These are yogic postures and breathing exercises that facilitate the harnessing of energy in the subtle body to bring about states of realization.
23. This visualization is a sign of mastery in this cycle of yogic practices. The "ten signs of empty forms" are progressive stages of experience and realization associated with tummo and other yogas involving the harnessing of subtle energies. As such, they are steps in a process of gaining an increasingly profound experience of emptiness as the true nature of all sensory appearances.
24. "Upheavals" are powerful experiences that may be caused by external factors or may be purely subjective states. They may be traumatic or extremely pleasant, but in either case, they have the potential to distract one from spiritual practice. "Machinations" refer to the actions of gods or demons who use their limited powers to interfere in people's affairs, particularly those of practitioners.
25. The four maras personify forces that keep one's mind entangled in samsara; they are termed "the mind-body aggregates," "the lord of death," "the negative emotions," and "the child of the gods." The second refers to the circumstances that contribute to one's mortality, the fourth to psychological impediments to the attainment of advanced states of meditation and realization.
26. "Homage to the Omniscient One!"
27. A more complete name for the system of teachings and practice known popularly as "Chö" (literally, "cutting through" or "severance"). It was established by the Tibetan female master Machik Lapdrön (1055–1149) and was unique in that it was the sole system of teachings that originally developed in Tibet and was taken back to India and practiced there.
28. Terdak Lingpa Gyurmé Dorjé.
29. In the dialect of Paltrul's home region of Dza, the nickname Palgé is an affectionate variant of Paltrul.
30. It is customary to "offer one's realization," i.e., to discuss one's spiritual insights and experiences with one's master, in order to ensure that one is making authentic progress in practice and not deceiving oneself or coming to false conclusions.

31. Also called *balu,* this root is noted for its medicinal properties; it is bitter and warming, useful in treating digestive disorders and other stomach ailments.
32. In the dialect of Dza, "Abu" is an affectionate term of address for an older male relative. Paltrul Rinpoché often signed his works with the nickname Abu Hrulpo (Ragged Old Guy) and is often referred to as Abu Rinpoché or simply Abu.
33. The strongest tea, in the morning, corresponds to the nirmanakaya, the most obvious manifestation of enlightened being; the somewhat weaker tea of midday, to the pure form manifestation of sambhogakaya; and the very weak tea of the evening, to the formless dharmakaya.
34. When making such a journey, a renunciant like Lungtok would ordinarily receive offerings of food and other supplies from people he met on the way. Accepting such gifts establishes a karmic connection with the donor. If the gifts were originally misappropriated by theft, swindling, or other unethical means, or if the recipient cannot meet the expectations of the donor, who may be offering the gifts for a particular reason (e.g., to request prayers for the higher rebirth of a deceased relative), they are considered morally contaminated or "tainted," and their acceptance can adversely affect the recipient and interfere with his or her spiritual development.
35. Palchen Dorjé, a companion of Lungtok's during this retreat, was engaging in a preliminary practice of the Dzogchen tradition. The nature of this practice, which breaks down habitual tendencies that contribute to rebirth in samsara, accounts for Palchen Dorjé's otherwise inexplicable behavior. Lungtok reacted to his companion by seeing through the seeming solidity of his habit patterns. The "practice with the syllable *Hum*" is another of the preliminary practices of Dzogchen, which is intended, in part, to undermine the mind's tendencies to reify and solidify what it perceives.
36. The merit of a significant spiritual achievement can be dedicated to the longevity of one's master or masters.
37. Kong-nyön Namkha Jigmé, also known as Lhatsün Namkha Jigmé; for his biography, see Chapter 10.
38. A seventeenth-century master who studied with Dzogchen Pema Rigdzin, the founder of Dzogchen Monastery.
39. The Sakya master Jamyang Loter Wangpo (1847–1914) was a principal student of Jamyang Khyentsei Wangpo.
40. A reference to the extremely rare practice of transferring one's consciousness into the corpse of a newly deceased person, before one's own death occurs or putrefaction of the corpse sets in.
41. In the Male Iron Rat year (early 1900 to early 1901).
42. Early 1879 to early 1880.
43. When a tulku was born in a region that was under a jurisdiction other than that of his home monastery, it was often necessary for the monastic administration to make large offerings (amounting to bribes) to the local authorities under whose control the tulku's family was living. This resulted in a release being granted, so that the monastic administration could legally move the tulku and his family to the region of the monastery, where he would eventually be enthroned and trained.

44. Through his practice, personal service, and financial support.
45. The ordination ceremonies for both novices and fully ordained monks or nuns require that a quorum of ordained persons (usually five) conducts the ceremony.
46. One who maintains monastic discipline on the outer, social level; the bodhisattva training on the inner level, that of personal motivation; and the samaya of a tantric practitioner on the secret level of profound spiritual experience and transformation.
47. The Male Iron Rat year (early 1900 to early 1901).
48. The Male Water Tiger year (early 1902 to early 1903).
49. The third Katok Situ, Chökyi Gyatso (1880–1923?); for his biography, see Chapter 13.
50. "Medicine" (also called the "inner offering") and rakta are symbolic offerings made in small skull cups placed on either side of the central torma offering in Vajrayana rituals.
51. The Male Iron Monkey year (early 1920 to early 1921).
52. The most complete form of monastic ordination, as distinct from the ordination of a novice monk.
53. The bodhisattva vow was transmitted, first in the Indian Buddhist tradition and later in Tibet, through two major lineages. The "lineage of profound view," also known as the Madhyamaka (Middle Way) lineage, originated with the bodhisattva of wisdom, Mañjushri, from whom it passed to the Indian Buddhist master Nagarjuna (ca. second century). The "lineage of extensive conduct," also known as the Chittamatra (Mind Only) lineage, originated with the bodhisattva Maitreya (who will become the next buddha); he transmitted this system of training to the Indian Buddhist master Asanga (ca. third to fourth centuries).
54. Do-ngak Chökyi Nyima (1854–1906) was the third Karma Kuchen incarnation of the Palyul tradition and the eighth throne holder of Palyul Monastery.
55. The first Penor Rinpoché, Palyul Drupwang Pema Norbu (1679–1757), studied with the tertön Namchö Mingyur Dorjé, from whom he received the *Namchö* cycle, which continues to be a major component of the Palyul tradition of the Nyingma school.
56. Not to be confused with the buddha of the same name, who appeared in this world before Shakyamuni, the arhat Kashyapa (or Mahakashyapa) was a student of the Buddha Shakyamuni who was renowned for the purity of his monastic discipline. The Buddha appointed Kashyapa to succeed him as the holder of the teachings.
57. This eightfold treasure is that of mindfulness, intelligence, realization, complete recall, self-confidence, spirituality, and enlightenment.
58. Upali, a student of the Buddha Shakyamuni, codified the teachings of the Vinaya and was regarded as a paragon of ethical discipline.
59. Near Dehra Dun in the state of Uttar Pradesh.
60. The title "Minling Trichen" signifies "Supreme Throne Holder of Mindroling."
61. The present, fourteenth Dalai Lama, Tenzin Gyatso (b. 1935).
62. Karma Lingpa lived in the fourteenth century. His teachings focusing on the peaceful and wrathful deities (*The Natural Freedom of Enlightened Intent*) are the primary terma source for the practices of this mandala of deities.
63. Namchö Mingyur Dorjé (1645–1667) took his name from the terma cycle he revealed, the *Namchö* (*Sky Teachings*), which were based on visions he had beginning in his early teens. He died in his early twenties, and much of the work of codifying the *Namchö* cycle fell to his student, the Kagyü master Karma Chakmé (1610?–1678).

8. *The Lineages of Jigmé Gyalwai Nyugu: Jamyang Khyentsei Wangpo*

1. The Male Iron Dragon year (early 1820 to early 1821).
2. The six-armed form of the protective deity Mahakala.
3. Ten great Tibetan masters who contributed to the founding of various scholastic traditions of Tibetan Buddhism: Tönmi Sambhota (who was a minister of the seventh-century Tibetan king Songtsen Gampo and journeyed to India, where he studied Sanskrit and is credited with having formulated a standardized written script for the Tibetan language); the Nyingma translators Bairotsana, Kawa Paltsek, Chokro Luyi Gyaltsen, Zhang Yeshé Dé (all active in the ninth century); the Sarma translators Rinchen Zangpo (958–1055, whose career is taken as the historical starting point for the Sarma schools of translation) and Ngok Lotsawa Lekpai Sherab (a tenth-century translator and student of both Atisha and Rinchen Zangpo); Dromtön Gyalwai Jungné (1004–1064, a student of Atisha and the first Tibetan master of the Kadampa school); Sakya Pandita (1182–1251); and Gö Khukpa Lhétsé (an eleventh-century translator and student of Atisha's).
4. Nyoshul Khen Rinpoché's guru, Lungtok Shedrup Tenpai Nyima.
5. The "threefold blazing" is that of bliss and warmth "blazing" in one's body, power and force being expressed in one's speech, and meditative experiences and realization awakening in one's mind. The "threefold gathering" is that of people being gathered—i.e., being attracted by one's spiritual energy—during the day, dakas and dakinis being gathered at night, and food and wealth being gathered in the morning and evening.
6. The first four lineages are the four major schools of the modern Tibetan Buddhist tradition: Nyingma, Geluk (sometimes called the "New Kadampa" tradition), Sakya, and Kagyü. The latter four, while still maintained as unbroken lineages, have been absorbed into these major schools.
7. The seven divine doctrines of the Kadampa school consist of the Three Repositories of the Buddha's teachings (the Sutras, Vinaya, and Abhidharma) and four meditations (focusing on the Buddha Shakyamuni and the deities Avalokiteshvara, Tara, and Achala).
8. One of the names of Gampopa Sönam Rinchen (1079–1153).
9. The Indian mahasiddha Tilopa (988–1069) was reputed to have received teachings directly from the dharmakaya buddha Vajradhara. When people refused to believe his claims, he studied various teachings with four masters from the north, south, east, and west of India. He then synthesized what he had learned in a single system, which he passed on to his student Naropa (1012–1100). It was through Naropa's student Marpa Chökyi Lodrö (1012–1097) that these teachings entered the Tibetan tradition. The name "Kagyü," which means "lineage of spiritual commands," refers to the lines of teachings that Tilopa received and synthesized.
10. The structure of the teachings of the Shangpa school, founded by the Tibetan master Chungpo Naljor (978–1127), is metaphorically compared to that of a tree: the roots are the Six Yogas of Niguma (comparable to the Six Yogas of Naropa in the Kagyü school); the trunk is the Mahamudra teaching called "Amulet Box"; the branches are the "three methods of integrating all one's experiences into one's spiritual practice"; the flowers are the meditations on red and white forms of Khechari; and the fruit consists of the technique known as "unerring immortality."
11. An epithet of the deity Vajrayogini.

12. "The three levels" can be interpreted as body, speech, and mind or the heavens, the surface of the earth, and the underworld. Given the context, the former sense is more likely.
13. Without anyone else acting as an intermediary.
14. A reference to King Trisong Detsen; Jamyang Khyentsei Wangpo was regarded as an incarnation of the king ("sovereign"), and both were emanations of the bodhisattva of wisdom, Mañjushri.
15. When a tertön reveals a terma, the original teaching (whether written down or received in a vision) is often so cryptic as to be unintelligible to the average person. It is the role of the tertön, often working with the prophesied custodian of that terma, to decipher the text and write it in a format accessible to others.
16. In the Female Wood Sheep year (early 1835 to early 1836).
17. Regent images are statues of Guru Padmakara that were made by his intimate students and blessed by the Guru himself during his stay in Tibet. Such images are especially holy and are said to function as Padmakara's "regents," in that they convey his blessings to those of future generations who come into contact with them. They were concealed as termas and later revealed by tertöns who were incarnations of the students who made them. Ngödrup Palbar means "Blazing Glory of Spiritual Attainment."
18. If the initial revelation of a terma took place at a time when circumstances did not permit its dissemination, the tertön would reconceal the terma so that it could be revealed in the future, when circumstances were more appropriate.
19. The Female Earth Sheep year (early 1859 to early 1860).
20. The Male Earth Monkey year (early 1848 to early 1849).
21. The twelfth month (Gyal) of the Male Wood Tiger year corresponds to early 1855.
22. Padmakara, Vimalamitra, and Bairotsana.
23. Transmissions that are recollections of transmissions received in a former lifetime.
24. A genre of practice that enables practitioners to sustain their lives by ingesting the subtle essence of flowers, minerals, and so forth.
25. Bodies of teachings that have been transmitted orally from one generation to the next. The teachings are not initially recorded, but are usually written out at a later time to offset the possibility of their being lost forever.
26. In the spring of 1892.
27. A Tibetan title meaning "all-seeing."
28. That is, fields of secular knowledge and Buddhist teachings, respectively.
29. Tersar (new termas) were revealed in relatively recent times, especially in the nineteenth and twentieth centuries. Ter-nying (old termas) were revealed up to the eighteenth century or so. The delineation between these periods is not precise, however.
30. The late Dudjom Rinpoché Jigdral Yeshé Dorjé.
31. See Chapter 2, note 16.
32. Drokben Cheu-chung Lotsawa was one of the twenty-five intimate students of Padmakara.
33. The Male Wood Dragon year (early 1904 to early 1905).
34. Nyatri Tsenpo (third century B.C.E.) was considered the first king of Tibet.
35. A reference to Jamgön Kongtrul Lodrö Tayé, who compiled *The Treasury of Precious Hidden Teachings,* and Jamyang Khyentsei Wangpo, who encouraged him to do so and

contributed numerous original works to the collection. The titles Jamgön and Jamyang are Tibetan names for Mañjushri, the bodhisattva of wisdom, and identify these masters as emanations of that bodhisattva.

36. A Sanskrit phrase, usually recited by the presiding master of an empowerment to stabilize one's sense of unity with the deity. Here Zilnön Namkhai Dorjé is stabilizing Dudjom Rinpoché's direct experience of the true nature of mind.
37. A reference to various stages of practice associated with the deity Vajrakila; in each case, the metaphor of a *kila*, or dagger, stabbing or penetrating conveys the sense of insightful awareness cutting through ignorance and confusion.
38. The original Nyingma kama collection, in 13 volumes, was codified by Rigdzin Terdak Lingpa Gyurmé Dorjé in the late seventeenth century. Dudjom Rinpoché expanded this collection to 58 volumes, which included a large number of commentaries, primarily those on *The Heart Essence of Secrets*, the main scriptural source for the tantras in the Nyingma school. An even larger collection, consisting of 108 volumes, has recently been prepared at Katok Monastery.
39. That is, when he fled before the Chinese Communist takeover in 1959.
40. Kongpo is in southeastern Tibet, near the border of the district of Arunachal Pradesh in northeastern India. The "border-taming" temple of Buchu was one of four built by King Songtsen Gampo in the seventh century to secure the borders of his kingdom.
41. So named because it was modeled on the three-story palace of Pema Ö in Padmakara's pure realm of Zangdok Palri.
42. Lama Ling grew up around the temple of Zangdok Palri. The original structure was destroyed in an earthquake in 1930, but the temple was restored by Dudjom Rinpoché and lasted until its destruction in the 1960s during the Cultural Revolution. In the late 1980s, the entire complex was rebuilt under the direction of Dudjom Rinpoché's daughter, Semo Dechen Yudrön, and her husband, Lama Chönyi Rinpoché.
43. Known to Indians as Rewalsar, this holy site in the district of Himachal Pradesh is associated with Guru Padmakara. The Guru and his Indian consort, Mandarava, were arrested by her father the king, who attempted to burn them alive. The Guru and Mandarava not only survived the flames, but transformed the blaze into a lake. Tso Pema (Lake of Lotuses) is held to be that lake. A small but thriving community of practitioners lives on the site under the direction of Lama Wangdor Rinpoché.
44. Yeshe Nyingpo, a network of centers in the United States and other countries, is under the direction of Dudjom Rinpoché's son Shenpen Dawa Rinpoché. In 1980 Orgyen Chö Dzong was established by Dudjom Rinpoché in Greenville, in the Catskill Mountains of upstate New York, as the international retreat center of Yeshe Nyingpo. Dorjé Nyingpo is in Paris, while Urgyen Samyé Chöling is in St. Leon-sûr-Vézère in the Dordogne region of southwestern France.
45. Khenpo Palden Sherab and his younger brother, Khenpo Tsewang Dongyal, live and teach in the United States, where they maintain the center Padma Samye Ling in Sidney Center, New York. Tibetans often refer to them as "the two khenpo brothers."
46. Sönam Zangpo lived from 1892 to 1983.
47. A Tibetan title meaning "tantric teacher" (usually a lay Vajrayana master).

48. Adhimukta's motivation during his training as a bodhisattva will prove to have been such that he alone will be able to care for as many beings as all the other previous buddhas combined.
49. The Male Water Tiger year (early 1842 to early 1843).
50. Now known as Quinghai Hu, in the former Tibetan region of Amdo.
51. A well-known prayer of praise to Tsongkhapa, also known as Lozang Drakpa. There are several versions, from four to nine lines in length. The nine-line version is as follows:

    You are Vajradhara, lord of sages and source of all siddhis.
    You are Avalokiteshvara, great treasury of compassion without fixation.
    You are Mañjushri, lord of flawless and sublime knowing.
    You are Vajrapani, who annihilates all the lords of maras.
    Lozang Drakpa, you are the crown jewel of sages in the Land of Snows.
    To you, my guru, a buddha embodying the three sources of refuge,
    I pray, showing respect with body, speech, and mind.
    Grant your blessings that I and others may mature and become liberated.
    Bestow the sublime and more common siddhis!

52. Based on the termas revealed by Rigdzin Gödem (1337–1409).
53. The fifth Dzogchen Rinpoché.
54. In the Male Wood Rat year (early 1924 to early 1925).
55. The recognized rebirths of certain high masters are referred to by the title "Yangsi."
56. The biography of Druktrul Rinpoché, the rebirth of Adzom Drukpa, can be found in Chapter 14.
57. The Female Water Dragon year (early 1893 to early 1894).
58. The tertön Duddul Dorjé lived from 1615 to 1672. With his student, Longsel Dorjé Nyingpo, he restored Katok Monastery.
59. The third Katok Situ, Chökyi Gyatso, who would have been about thirteen at the time.
60. Presumably Jamyang Khyentsei Wangpo, predicting his own rebirth as Jamyang Chökyi Lodrö.
61. "Intelligence."
62. The two "*Ornament*" texts are *The Ornament of the Sutras* and *The Ornament of Higher Realization*. The two "*Distinction*" texts are *The Distinction Between Phenomena and Their True Nature* and *The Distinction Between Center and Limit*. Together with *The Highest Continuum*, these constitute *The Five Treatises of Maitreya*.
63. The third Katok Situ, Chökyi Gyatso.
64. The second Zhechen Rabjam lived from 1713 to 1769.
65. The eleventh Tai Situ of the Karma Kagyü school, who lived from 1886 to 1952; for his biography, see Chapter 17.
66. The tenth Zurmang Trungpa, Chökyi Nyinjé.
67. The first master in the line of Sang-gyé Nyenpa tulkus of the Karma Kagyü school was Tashi Paljor (1445–1510); the ninth Sang-gyé Nyenpa, Karma Shedrup Tenpai Nyima (1897–1962), was the elder brother of Dilgo Khyentsé Rinpoché.
68. Usually a very abbreviated form of the empowerment ceremony, focusing on the realization of the true nature of mind that is the ultimate point of all empowerments.

69. The thirteenth Dalai Lama (1876–1933).
70. Angaja was directed by the Buddha Shakyamuni to teach in the Himalayan regions of northern India.
71. Sachen Kunga Nyingpo was the founder of the Sakya school, and his grandson Sakya Pandita was its greatest scholar.
72. The fifteenth Karmapa, Khachap Dorjé (1871–1922).
73. Düsum Chenpa lived from 1110 to 1193; the connection between Vimalamitra and the Karmapas dates from the vision the third Karmapa, Rangjung Dorjé, had of Vimalamitra.
74. The third Katok Situ, Chökyi Gyatso.
75. The fourth Katok Situ, who was born about 1926.
76. Rangjung Rigpai Dorjé (1924–1981).
77. In the later part of the fourth Tibetan month; the year was that of the Female Earth Pig (early 1959 to early 1960).
78. The Sakya school is headed alternately by the Sakya Dakchen and the Sakya Trizin; these two offices are hereditary, and the leadership also passes from generation to generation between the two families of the Khön clan of Sakya.
79. This traditional name refers to the eastern region of Tibet; in the 1950s and 1960s, it was used by the Tibetan guerrillas who tried to defend eastern Tibet against the invading Communist forces. The four rivers (which originate in Tibet but flow east or south into other Asian countries, where they are known by other names) are the Drichu (Yangtze), Machu (Huang-ho), Gyalmo Ngulchu (Salween), and Dachu (Mekong). The six ridges are Mardza Gang, Drida Zalmo Gang, Markham Gang, Tsawa Gang, Pobor Gang, and Minyak Rabgang.
80. These temples were erected by King Songtsen Gampo in the seventh century. The sites were chosen on the basis of the topography's resemblance to the form of a demoness lying on her back; the temples were built at places representing points on the form, effectively pinning it down and suppressing the negative forces it embodied.
81. The last of the "five founding fathers" of the Sakya school, Chögyal Pakpa Lodrö Gyaltsen (1235–1280) forged strong ties with the court of the Mongol emperor Kublai Khan, which did much to strengthen Sakya rule over central Tibet.
82. Chödrak Gyatso (1454–1506) was the seventh Gyalwang Karmapa.
83. Jigten Sumgön (1143–1217) was the founder of the Drigung Kagyü tradition.
84. Many Tibetan clans are believed to have descended from gods. In traditional Buddhist cosmology, once a universe forms, beings first appear in the gods' realms. Initially, they are able to visit the human realm and then return to their own, but a process of degeneration sets in, and eventually they are unable to leave the human realm. Thus they become the first humans.
85. The Male Iron Dog year (early 1910 to early 1911).
86. These are standard practices to ensure that a child will be highly intelligent.
87. The Male Water Rat year (early 1912 to early 1913).
88. An oral transmission usually consists of a rapid reading of the text, with no attempt to convey its meaning. A "teaching transmission" involves reading at a rate that allows listeners to follow the text and may include parenthetical comments by the reader.

89. Zhechen Kongtrul Pema Drimé (1901–1960).
90. The original construction of the stupa of Boudhanath in Kathmandu, Nepal, is believed to have been conceived by an old woman and carried out by her three sons; in future lifetimes, these brothers incarnated as Guru Padmakara, Shantarakshita, and King Trisong Detsen. The entire account is given in *The Legend of the Great Stupa,* trans. Keith Dowman (Berkeley: Dharma Publishing, 1973).
91. The Chinese Communist forces.
92. Palpung Kongtrul Karma Lodrö Chökyi Seng-gé (1954–1992) and Dzigar Kongtrul Jigmé Namgyal (b. 1964).
93. H.H. Jigdral Dakchen Sakya and Damo Kusho Jamyang Sakya.
94. Dezhung Lungrik Kunga Tenpai Nyima (1906–1987). His life story is told by David P. Jackson in *A Saint in Seattle: The Life of the Tibetan Mystic Dezhung Rinpoche* (Boston: Wisdom, 2003).
95. The sixteenth Karmapa, Rangjung Rigpai Dorjé.
96. Kalu Rinpoché Karma Rangjung Kunkhyab (1905–1989) was a Karma Kagyü master and the primary modern-day holder of the lineage of the Shangpa Kagyü school; his principal student was the second Bokar incarnation, Karma Ngedön Chökyi Seng-gé (1940–2004).
97. An impressive account of Dilgo Khyentsé's life, with numerous photographs by Matthieu Ricard (Dilgo Khyentsé Rinpoché's closest Western student), has been published as *Journey to Enlightenment: The Life and World of Khyentse Rinpoche, Spiritual Teacher from Tibet* (New York: Aperture, 1996).
98. The Tibetan term *jadralwa* (literally, "someone free of having anything to do") refers to someone with advanced realization who has adopted a simple, often itinerant way of life with few possessions and little concern for worldly matters.

9. The Lineage of Rigdzin Jigmé Lingpa: The Dodrupchen Line of Incarnations

1. These verses introduce the second volume of the original Tibetan text.
2. Early 1745 to early 1746.
3. Before a person is old enough to receive monastic ordination, he or she can be given an "ordination" consisting basically of the vow of refuge and can begin studying with the intention to request the actual vows of a monk or nun later in life.
4. Early 1785 to early 1786.
5. Damdzin Rolpa Yeshé Tsal was another name of Murub Tsepo, the second son of King Trisong Detsen.
6. Such smoke offering ceremonies are often performed on hilltops and other prominent places, both as religious rituals and as means to establish or restore harmony with the spirits of a region. Hepo Hill is located near Samyé Monastery.
7. "The mahasiddha of Do."
8. "Hero's potion" refers to consecrated alcohol, which often functions as a symbol of realization in empowerment ceremonies, during which it is imbibed by the participants.
9. Rigdzin Paljor Gyatso (1770–?).
10. Namkha Chökyi Gyatso (1806–1821).

11. The first Katok Situ, Chökyi Seng-gé.
12. A term indicating mastery of the practices associated with the deity Vajrakila. Repkong, an area in the Amdo region of far northeastern Tibet, was renowned as the home of large communities of such masters, who had great spiritual powers.
13. A large town, known in Tibetan as Dartsedo, on the border between Tibet and southwest China. It was an important trading center, particularly for the importation of Chinese tea into Tibet.
14. The Female Iron Serpent year (early 1821 to early 1822).
15. There are numerous accounts in Tibetan literature of those who engage in such wrathful practices without understanding the proper use of the imagery involved or cultivating compassion; instead, by becoming obsessed with the power inherent in the imagery, they go astray and are reborn as demons who wreak havoc on others.
16. The Tibetan for "iron cup" (*chak-kong*) echoes the name of the third Dodrupchen's birthplace, Chak-khung.
17. Dudjom Lingpa (1835–1904).
18. Although the term "dakini" usually refers to feminine deities who are embodiments of enlightenment, it can also refer to certain female beings who are of this world.
19. Early 1926 to early 1927.
20. The fourth Dodrupchen was born in the Female Fire Hare year (early 1927 to early 1928).
21. As part of the process of recognizing and enthroning a tulku, the names of several candidates (usually based on indications left by the preceding incarnation) were put forward, the final decision depending on a thorough investigation. In the case of the fourth Dodrupchen, two candidates were chosen and enthroned in the same ceremony. (In fact, it is not so uncommon for more than one tulku of a great master to be recognized.) The second tulku, Rigdzin Tenpai Gyaltsen, was born in 1927 (the same year as Jigmé Trinlé Palbar) and died in 1961. See Tulku Thondup, *Masters of Meditation and Miracles*, pp. 298–313.
22. Early 1930 to early 1931.
23. Early 1931 to early 1932 and early 1932 to early 1933, respectively.
24. Early 1933 to early 1934.
25. Early 1937 to early 1938.
26. Whereas many tertöns are an incarnation of one of Guru Padmakara's twenty-five intimate students, an "emanated tertön" is recognized specifically an emanation of the Guru himself.
27. Early 1940 to early 1941.
28. Early 1941 to early 1942.
29. Early 1944 to early 1945.
30. The term "five hundred thousands" refers to the five preliminary practices (*ngöndro*) of Vajrayana Buddhism, each of which is performed a hundred thousand times before one receives more advanced teachings.
31. Early 1945 to early 1946.
32. A statue of Buddha Shakyamuni commissioned by Bhrikuti, Trisong Detsen's Nepalese queen, which was installed in the temple of Ramoché in Lhasa to replace the Jowo statue.

33. Early 1946 to early 1947.
34. The "great Mönlam festival" was an annual religious gathering in Lhasa during the first month of the Tibetan year. The tradition was instituted by Tsongkhapa in 1409 and continued until 1438. It was reinstituted by the second Dalai Lama, Gendun Gyatso (1476–1542), and continued until the Chinese Communist military occupation in 1959. The Communist authorities allowed it to take place from 1985 to 1990, after which it was prohibited.
35. The form of Guru Rinpoché known in Sanskrit as Saroruhavajra (Lake-Born Vajra).
36. Early 1956 to early 1957.
37. Early 1950 to early 1951.
38. Early 1951 to early 1952.
39. Early 1955 to early 1956.
40. The Male Fire Monkey year (early 1956 to early 1957).
41. A historical idiom for the Chinese living north and east of Tibet.
42. The Female Earth Pig year (early 1959 to early 1960).
43. Jarung Khashor is the Tibetan name for the stupa of Boudhanath in the eastern quarter of Kathmandu. Sa-lhak Do-lhak (Leftover Earth and Stone) is a small stupa near Boudhanath, said to have been built with the materials left over from the construction of the former. Takmo Lüjin (Gift of the Body to the Tigress), known also as Namo Buddha, is a site on the outskirts of the Kathmandu Valley where the Buddha is believed to have sacrificed himself in a former lifetime in order to feed a starving tigress and her cubs with his own flesh and blood. Pakpa Shingkun is the Tibetan name for the stupa of Swayambhunath, located in the western quarter of Kathmandu.
44. Early 1646 to early 1647.
45. This lineage of Vajrakila was codified by Jigmé Lingpa.
46. Manibhadra, a figure in the sutras who had 108 gurus, is often cited as the epitome of someone skilled in serving a spiritual master.
47. Kunzang Dechen Gyalpo (1736–?).
48. Most shedras offered programs of varying length and detail to accommodate students' interests and capacities.
49. Lineages of teachings and practices are sometimes conferred on a single student. Often, the master who initiates such a lineage (e.g., on the basis of a daknang transmission or discovery of a terma) receives a prophecy indicating that this one-to-one transmission must be maintained for a certain number of generations. Secrecy helps to augment the "store of blessings" imbuing the transmission and so contributes to the length of time the lineage will remain viable.
50. Violating one's samaya as a Vajrayana practitioner can result in rebirth as a demonic being bent on causing harm to others.
51. A reference to the special preliminary practices of the Dzogchen approach.
52. The autobiography of Zhabkar Tsokdruk Rangdrol has been published as *The Life of Shabkar: The Autobiography of a Tibetan Yogin,* trans. Matthieu Ricard (Albany: State University of New York Press, 1994).
53. The second Zhabkar Rinpoché, Jigmé Tekchok Tenpai Gyaltsen, also known as Rongnyön Rigdzin Gyatso (1853–1914).

54. This was a relatively common occurrence among Tibetans. Deloks, usually young girls, would appear to die but later regain consciousness and record their experiences. The message of the delok accounts is generally one of moral instruction, to instill a respect for the workings of karma. For an account by a twentieth-century delok, Dawa Drolma, see *Delog: Journeys to Realms Beyond Death,* trans. Richard Barron (Junction City, CA: Padma Publishing, 1995).
55. This would have been the encampment of the fifteenth Karmapa, Khachap Dorjé.
56. Sites in ancient India considered sacred in the Vajrayana tradition and associated with points in the channels and chakras of the subtle body. Chönyi Zangmo would have experienced going to these places in visions.
57. The Shuksep Nunnery is now under the direction of Zhadeu Trulzhik Rinpoché.
58. Literally, "Madman of Chö."
59. The names of these three masters, including Chönyön Dharma Seng-gé, contained the word "Seng-ge" (Lion), and hence they were known as the "three lions." They were major figures in the transmission of the Chö teachings.
60. Dakki Chönyi Zangmo.

10. *The Students of Longchen Rabjampa*

1. See Chapter 6.
2. The Tibetan idiom refers to "threefold purity," signifying that Orgyen Chöjé made the offering in a nondualistic state of mind, without conceptualizing in ordinary terms of (1) himself as the one making the offering, (2) Longchenpa as the one receiving the offering, or (3) the object being offered. To undertake any positive action from such a perspective adds enormously to its spiritual efficacy.
3. Sokdokpa's rebuttal, *A Reply to the Spitefulness of Drigung Paldzin: One Who Rejects the Arguments of the Nyingma School of Mantra,* was published by Chatral Rinpoche, Sangje Dorje (New Delhi, 1975).
4. The previously mentioned Sang-ön Sherab Gyatso.
5. The others were Sang-gyé Kunga, Lodrö Zangpo, and Takok Jadral Chöjé Tashi Jungné; Tashi Jungné's biography appears later in this chapter.
6. Dzogchenpa Sönam Rigdzin and Dzogchenpa Sönam Rinchen were contemporary masters of the Nyingma school. It appears that Ngawang Pema studied with both, although it was the former from whom he received the Nyingtik teachings.
7. The Female Wood Ox year (early 1625 to early 1626).
8. Early 1597 to early 1598.
9. The "path of passion" consists of methods that lead to the taking of a consort; the term refers to the fact that sexual desire is transmuted and incorporated into one's practice as a means of spiritual development.
10. Termas may include components conveying blessings that contribute to one's liberation: texts of teachings, which are heard (in that they are taught orally); statues or other images, which are seen; and sacred substances, which are touched (such as amulets that are worn on the body) or tasted (medicines). Blessings are also conveyed when one recalls any of these.
11. The Male Fire Dog year (early 1646 to early 1647).

12. This refers to the process whereby a realized master recognizes a sacred site of spiritual power and, by consecrating it, makes it a place of pilgrimage and practice.
13. Early 1652 to early 1653.
14. The first Dzogchen Rinpoché, Pema Rigdzin (1625–1697), founded Dzogchen Monastery in 1684 or 1685 at the behest of the fifth Dalai Lama and with the patronage of Sang-gyé Tenpa, the ruler of Dergé in eastern Tibet.
15. Nyima Drakpa was a student of the first Dzogchen Rinpoché, Pema Rigdzin.
16. These "five kings"—Nyang-ral Nyima Özer, Guru Chöwang, Dorjé Lingpa, Rigdzin Pema Lingpa, and Jamyang Khyentsei Wangpo—were all emanations of King Trisong Detsen.
17. The Male Fire Monkey year (early 1476 to early 1477).
18. Generally speaking, a major terma cache contains teachings and practices concerning three topics: guru yoga, Dzogchen, and Avalokiteshvara; other termas are considered "minor," although this rubric is not pejorative.
19. Termas that focus on practices to promote wealth and prosperity, both material and spiritual.
20. Early 1521 to early 1522.
21. Because of Pema Lingpa's importance, he is referred to not as "the second Longchenpa," but as the first in his own series of incarnations.
22. These successive incarnations are referred to by the title "Peling Sungtrul" (incarnation of Pema Lingpa's enlightened speech).
23. An epithet of Taranatha (1575–1634), one of the major figures in the Jonangpa lineage of Tibet.
24. Because of the close relationship between the politics and religion of Tibet, there have been periods in its history during which sectarian members of different schools have quarreled; at times, this has led to open warfare, with both monks and laity making up the opposing forces.
25. Explaining, debating, and writing about the teachings.
26. The fourth Tuksé incarnation, Tendzin Gyurmé Dorjé (1641–?). The Tuksé incarnation line began with Dawa Gyaltsen, the son of Pema Lingpa. (The Tibetan term *tuksé* is honorific for both "heart son," i.e., spiritual heir, and someone's progeny.)
27. The twelfth Karmapa, Jangchub Dorjé (1703–1732).
28. The preceding Pema Lingpa's guru.
29. The first two were Longchenpa and Jigmé Lingpa.
30. The tenth Dalai Lama, Tsultrim Gyatso (1816–1837).
31. Gyurmé Sang-gyé Kunga was the seventh in the succession of throne holders of Mindroling Monastery, which began with Terdak Lingpa.
32. The study of astrology comprises five subjects: planetary positions, dates, constellations, conjunctions, and progressions.
33. The son of Gyurmé Sang-gyé Kunga.
34. Activities associated with Vajrayana rituals, such as the use of mantra and mudra and the laying out of mandalas for empowerments.
35. During the infancy of a Dalai Lama, a regent was appointed to rule the country in the child's stead, until he reached his majority. The fifth Hotuktu incarnation of Ratreng

Monastery, Tupten Jampal Yeshé Tenpai Gyaltsen (1912–1947), served as the regent ruler of Tibet from 1934 to 1941, during the minority of the present Dalai Lama.

36. Nangdzé Druppai Dorjé (1910–1959).
37. An honorific idiom referring to a living master; it conveys the aspiration that the master live a long and successful life as a teacher.
38. In this system of enumeration, the first figure in Pema Lingpa's blood lineage was his son, Dawa Gyaltsen, and the second was the latter's son, Rigdzin Pema Trinlé. According to the other accounts to which Nyoshul Khen refers, the blood lineage stems from the second Pema Lingpa incarnation, Tendzin Chökyi Drakpa, whose son was then the second figure in the lineage.
39. These are the Gangteng tulkus, considered the incarnations of Pema Trinlé's—and, by extension, Pema Lingpa's—enlightened form.
40. The ninth Gangteng tulku, who was born in Bhutan in 1955.
41. The eleventh Peling (or Lhalung) Sungtrul is Kunzang Pema Rinchen Namgyal (b. 1968).
42. Those of the Peling Sungtruls, the Tuksé tulkus, and the Gangteng tulkus.

11. *The Students of Rigdzin Terdak Lingpa*

1. For Gyalsé Rinchen Namgyal's biography, see Chapter 6.
2. A familiar title for Rigdzin Terdak Lingpa.
3. See Chapter 6, note 78.
4. A retreat center affiliated with Mindroling Monastery.
5. Azhé Nangsa Öbum was a semilegendary figure whose life serves as a model of devotion to the Buddhist teachings under adverse conditions. Her story is the basis of an opera much loved by Tibetans. See *Tales from Tibetan Opera,* trans. Wan Yao (Beijing: New World Press, 1986), pp. 160–190.
6. Ceremonies that regulate monastic life: the bimonthly renewal of vows, the three-month summer retreat, and ceremonies dealing with specific infractions or periodic changes in the monastic regimen.
7. This retreat center is located in eastern Tibet, in the hills above Palpung Monastery, the seat of the Tai Situ Rinpoché incarnations of the Kagyü school. An excellent study of its history and program of practice has been published as *Jamgon Kongtrul's Retreat Manual,* trans. Ngawang Zangpo (Ithaca, NY: Snow Lion, 1994).
8. Chöpal Gyatso usually signed his works "Dharma Shri," the Sanskrit equivalent of Chöpal.
9. He was assassinated by the Dzungar invaders during the destruction of Mindroling Monastery in the Male Earth Dog year (early 1718 to early 1719); see Chapter 6, note 78.
10. His father, Terdak Lingpa, and his uncle, Chöpal Gyatso.
11. Terdak Lingpa and Chöpal Gyatso.
12. Minling Trichen Rinpoché was appointed the head of the Nyingma school in 2003.
13. The Minling Chung Rinpoché line of incarnations derives from Yizhin Lekdrup, the younger brother (*chung*) of Terdak Lingpa's first son and heir, Pema Gyurmé Gyatso.
14. The present, fourteenth Dalai Lama, Tenzin Gyatso.

15. Sönam Detsen was considered the rebirth of Terchen Duddul Dorjé.
16. The first incarnation was born in 1724, the year following Sönam Detsen's death; the present incarnation is the fifth Drimé Zhingkyong, Jigmé Trinlé Gönpo, born about 1940.
17. Dudjom Rinpoché Jigdral Yeshé Dorjé.
18. Namkhai Ösel was the first Dzogchen Pönlop incarnation; he died in 1726.
19. Tenpai Gyaltsen lived from 1650 to ca. 1712.
20. The Female Water Bird year (early 1753 to early 1754).
21. Sang-ngak Tendzin lived from 1731 to 1805.
22. The third Khamtrul, Ngawang Kunga Tendzin (1680–1728), and the fourth, Tendzin Chökyi Nyima (1730–1779/80).
23. Given the dates of his teacher, the second Dzogchen Rinpoché, Tashi Gyatso was probably born in the Male Fire Horse year (early 1726 to early 1727). Another possibility is the Male Earth Horse year (early 1736 to early 1737).
24. A term for one who has given up the life of a householder to become a monk or nun.

12. *The Students of Rigdzin Jigmé Lingpa and the First Dodrupchen, Jigmé Trinlé Özer*

1. See Chapters 6 and 9, respectively.
2. A network of ancient fortresses served as civil administrative centers throughout Tibet.
3. Overseeing either the execution of criminals or the slaughter of animals.
4. The region of Assam in northwestern India, which borders Bhutan on its eastern side, has long been considered by Tibetans to be a land whose forests are inhabited by savage primitive tribes.
5. The Buddhist mahasiddha Virupa of ancient India was famed for such displays of magical power.
6. Drodul Pegyal Lingpa (1924–1988) revealed the terma cycle *The United Intent of the Three Kayas.*
7. The Drigung Chetsang and Drigung Chungtsang. Of these successive incarnations, the ones who were contemporaries of Jigmé Lingpa (1730–1798) were the third Chetsang, Könchok Tendzin Drodul (1724–1766); the fourth Chetsang, Tendzin Pemai Gyaltsen (1770–1826); the second Chungtsang, Döndrup Chögyal (1704–1754); and the third Chungtsang, Könchok Tendzin Chökyi Nyima (1755–1792).
8. Ngedön Tendzin Zangpo (1759–1792) was the third Dzogchen Rinpoché. Given that 1800 is generally accepted as the year of Do Khyentsé Yeshé Dorjé's birth, it is unclear how the third Dzogchen could have recognized him as a rebirth of Jigmé Lingpa.
9. An honorific idiom for the enthronement of a tulku.
10. Entitled *The Oral Transmission of the Dakinis,* this work was completed by Do Khyentsé's students Özer Tayé and Kalzang Döndrup.
11. For the biography of Tuksé Doring Choktrul Rinpoché, see Chapter 17.
12. Alak Zenkar Rinpoché, Pema Ngödrup Rolpai Dorjé, lived from 1881 to 1943. For a short biography, see Tulku Thondup, *Masters of Meditation and Miracles,* pp. 275–277.
13. The second Alak Zenkar, Tupten Nyima (Tudeng Nima; b. 1943), has been active in edit-

ing and publishing works from all schools of the Tibetan Buddhist tradition. An English translation of the three-volume dictionary prepared under his direction is in progress; the first volume is already in print (*An Encyclopaedic Tibetan–English Dictionary* [Beijing: Nationalities Publishing House; London: School of Oriental and African Studies, 2001]).

14. Eight Tibetan masters who founded systems of spiritual practice in Tibet: Bairotsana (Nyingma), Dromtön Gyalwai Jungné (Kadam), Chungpo Naljor (Shangpa), Drokmi Lotsawa (Sakya), Marpa Lotsawa Chökyi Lodrö (Kagyü), Padampa Sang-gyé (Zhijé), Kyijo Lotsawa (Jordruk), and Orgyenpa (Dorjé Sumgyi Nyendrup).
15. Lungtok Gyatso lived only a short time, from 1805 to 1815.
16. These prostrations would obviously have been performed over a period of time; the point is that Paltrul Rinpoché undertook them with the intention of dedicating the virtue to Mingyur Namkhai Dorjé's long life and success as a teacher.
17. A Buddhist university in central India, famed for the erudition of its scholars.
18. An epithet of Shantarakshita.
19. Although tertöns were traditionally lay masters with consorts, Zhenpen Tayé chose to take monastic ordination, modeling himself on the Indian abbot Shantarakshita, who was a fully ordained monk.
20. A reference to the structure of the ordination ceremony, during which an initial petition by the recipient is followed by the main ceremony, involving a threefold repetition of the ordination process. This methodical approach helped to discourage people from taking ordination hastily or impulsively.
21. Sengtruk means "Lion Cub." The cub of a snow lion is considered to surpass its parents.
22. That is, Zhenga Dorjé Chang; for his biography, see Chapter 17.
23. Such rituals are performed to suppress negative or demonic forces or energies, to burn them in a fire, or to avert them by casting effigies in the direction from which they are coming.
24. An English translation of this monumental collection is in preparation; the project is overseen by Tarchin Rinpoché of the Repkong lineage, who resides in California at the center Pema Ösel Ling.

13. *The Students of Jamyang Khyentsei Wangpo*

1. Possibly the Bön master also known as Changlung Tulku Yungorung Tenpai Gyaltsen.
2. Also known as Shardza Tashi Gyaltsen (1859–1935), one of the most influential writers of the Bön tradition in recent centuries.
3. The ancient symbol of the swastika became the symbol of the Bön tradition, just as the eight-spoked wheel became that of the Buddhist teachings.
4. See Chapters 8 and 9, respectively.
5. A Sanskrit title meaning "great omniscient scholar."
6. The ninth Tai Situ of the Karma Kagyü school, who lived from 1774 to 1853.
7. "Blazing Glory of Auspiciousness."
8. Yeshé Tsogyal.
9. Guru Padmakara and Yeshé Tsogyal.
10. Another name for the Karma Kagyü school.

11. An advanced yogic discipline in the Vajrayana tradition.
12. "Inner qualities" refer to one's experience of one's body, "outer qualities" to one's perceptions of the external world, and "secret qualities" to one's mental experiences.
13. Töpai Tumbu Tsal is one of twenty-four deities in the retinue of Chakrasamvara; Shantapuri is one of the twenty-four gathering places.
14. The tenth Tai Situ of the Karma Kagyü school was Padma Kunzang Chögyal (1854–1885).
15. For an autobiographical account of Jamgön Kongtrul Lodrö Tayé's life, see *The Autobiography of Jamgön Kongtrul: A Gem of Many Colors,* trans. Richard Barron (Ithaca, NY: Snow Lion, 2003). This volume also includes Kongtrul's recollections of his former lifetimes, as well as a description of his final days and the funeral ceremonies following his death, written by his student Nesar Karma Tashi Chöpel.
16. That is, when the Chinese Communist military occupation took place in the 1950s.
17. The Male Fire Horse year (early 1846 to early 1847).
18. A lama from a family in which there are spiritual teachers in each generation.
19. The region of Dzachukha (literally, "the banks of the Dzachu") is north of Dergé. By 1862 the Nyarong chieftain Gönpo Namgyal had conquered Dergé and was encroaching on territories to the north. So fearsome was his reputation that many fled further north into Golok. Gönpo Namgyal waged war over much of eastern Tibet, beginning in 1837 with skirmishes with neighboring tribes in Nyarong and culminating in 1862 in his conquest of Dergé, the most important population center of eastern Tibet. He was killed by the forces of the central Tibetan government in 1865. For a well-researched article on Gönpo Namgyal's military campaigns, see Tashi Tsering, "Ñag-ron mgon-po rnam-rgyal: A 19th Century Khams-pa Warrior," in *Soundings in Tibetan Civilization,* ed. Barbara Nimri Aziz and Matthew Kapstein (New Delhi: Manohar, 1985), pp. 196–214.
20. Reliance on: (1) the teachings, not the teacher; (2) the meaning, not the words; (3) the definitive, not the provisional, meaning; and (4) timeless awareness, not ordinary consciousness.
21. According to the Mahayana teachings, these are ways in which one can unerringly know the characteristics of phenomena. They are: (1) to understand the specific characteristics of phenomena in detail; (2) to understand the specific functions of phenomena; (3) to understand the speech and terms used by various kinds of beings, so that one understands the implications of any given word without confusion or conflation; and (4) to understand the teachings one receives so as to dispel one's doubts and be capable of teaching others confidently, without hesitation or imprecision, in order to dispel their doubts.
22. A number of Mipam's works provoked philosophical controversies throughout his life. Some of these works were refuted by other authors, which led Mipam to write further clarifications and refutations.
23. These are lines from Mipam Rinpoché's famous prayer, "The Oral Transmission That Delights the Dharma Kings."
24. Successive stages in one's experience of the emptiness that is the true nature of reality.
25. That is, his treatises were written and published in the way that commentaries usually are, but they are considered to have the same status as termas, even though Mipam never "revealed" them as such.

26. The Male Water Rat year (early 1912 to early 1913).
27. "Homage to the courageous one Mañjushri!"
28. Dharanis are a class of long mantras.
29. This seems to indicate that Mipam had foreknowledge of the Chinese Communist military occupation that took place four decades after his passing. He may have seen the political upheavals in China itself in the early years of the twentieth century as indications of greater troubles to come.
30. The Male Water Rat year (early 1912 to early 1913).
31. The other two gurus were Dza Pukhung Gyurmé Ngedön Wangpo and Jedrung Jampa Jungné; for their biographies, see Chapters 8 and 13, respectively.
32. Lodrö Gyaltsen (Lodi Gyari Rinpoché) lived in India at the time Nyoshul Khen Rinpoché began writing this history. He has since moved to the Washington, D.C., area, where he serves as Special Envoy to His Holiness the Dalai Lama and heads negotiations with the People's Republic of China over the future of Tibet.
33. For his biography, see Chapter 11.
34. According to the Buddhist tradition, in order for masters to write authoritative treatises, they should ideally have some realization of the true nature of reality; failing this, they should have received permission during visions of their meditation deities to compose these works; at the very least, they should be scholars learned in both the Buddhist teachings and the fields of secular knowledge associated with them.
35. "Dharmavajra" is the Sanskrit equivalent of the Tibetan name Chökyi Dorjé.
36. The Male Water Monkey year (early 1872 to early 1873).
37. Tibetans often take the comments of highly realized masters to be symbolic rather than literal.
38. The Male Fire Rat year (early 1936 to early 1937).
39. The sixth Dzogchen Rinpoché, Jigdral Jangchub Dorjé, lived for a very short time (1935–1959). The seventh incarnation, Jigmé Losel Wangpo, was born in 1964 and currently directs Dzogchen Monastery in southern India.
40. The seventh Dzogchen Pönlop Rinpoché, Karma Sungrap Ngedon Tenpa Gyaltsen (b. 1965), graduated in 1990 with an *acharya* degree (the equivalent of a master's degree in Buddhist studies) and now directs Nitartha International and centers around the world.
41. The Female Earth Ox year (early 1829 to early 1830).
42. Manikha means "Jeweled Gateway," Norbu Tendzin means "Gem Who Upholds the Teachings," and Arya Nang means "Inner Spiritual Superiority."
43. The fourteenth Karmapa, Tekchok Dorjé (1798–1868).
44. Jamyang Khyentsei Wangpo was regarded as an incarnation of King Trisong Detsen, and Jamgön Kongtrul and Chokgyur Lingpa as incarnations of two of the king's sons.
45. Personal sadhana practice involves the two phases of approach and accomplishment. A more elaborate format for group rituals often involves four phases: approach, intimate approach, accomplishment, and supreme accomplishment.
46. This may be a reference to Nyarong Gönpo Namgyal's campaigns in eastern Tibet. Tibetan Buddhist masters often played a mediating role in such disputes and wars.
47. The sixteenth Karmapa, Rangjung Rigpai Dorjé.

48. Located in Boudhanath, near Kathmandu, Nepal.
49. The eldest son of Tulku Urgyen, Chökyi Nyima Rinpoché (b. 1951), and the second son, Tsikey Chokling Rinpoché Lungtok Gyatso (b. 1953), are the spiritual directors of the Chokling Tersar Foundation. The third Drupwang Tsoknyi Rinpoché (b. 1966) heads the Pundarika Foundation. The youngest son, the seventh Yongey Mingyur Dorjé Rinpoché (b. 1976), founded the Yongey Mingyur Dorjé Foundation. The seventh Pakchok Rinpoché, Tendzin Jigmé Drakpa (b. 1981), and Dilgo Khyentsé Yangsi (the rebirth of Dilgo Khyentsé Rinpoché; b. 1993) are both sons of Tsikey Chokling Rinpoché.
50. The present incarnation, the fourth Negang (also known as Neten-gang or Neten) Chokling, was born in Bhutan in 1974.
51. Khen Rinchen trained at Doseb Monastery in Dergé, eastern Tibet, and then studied at the shedra of Dzongsar Monastery. He later fled to India.
52. Dzigar Kongtrul Rinpoché lives with his family in Crestone, Colorado.
53. Ten historical lineages of exegesis and eight lineages of accomplishment.
54. The Male Fire Horse year (early 1906 to early 1907).
55. A temple with a gilded roof.
56. The Female Wood Ox year (early 1925 to early 1926).
57. On the southern edge of the Kathmandu Valley in central Nepal.
58. These are the three levels of success in Vajrayana development stage practice: first one experiences oneself as the clear form of the deity in meditation, then one perceives this with one's senses in everyday waking consciousness, and finally others may perceive one as the deity due to the stability of one's visualization.
59. The lineage transmitted by masters from Kham, or eastern Tibet, who were principally associated with such monastic centers as Katok and Dzogchen.
60. These are systems of Vajrayana practice associated with branches of the Kagyü school.
61. "Beyond meditation" is the fourth of the so-called four yogas (i.e., the highest level of realization) in the Mahamudra approach; "the perception of awareness's naturally manifest appearances without bias" constitutes the equivalent level of realization in the Dzogchen approach.
62. It is held that Guru Padmakara manifested in the form of Dorjé Drolö when he first visited and consecrated the cliffside holy site of Taktsang in the Paro Valley of western Bhutan.
63. "Noble Merit."
64. Taksham Nüden Dorjé was a tertön who lived in the seventeenth to eighteenth centuries. Namkha Drimé Rabjam Rinpoché is the current lineage holder of the Taksham teachings, especially those concerning Gesar. His father, Jigmé Tsewang Chokdrup Dudlé Namgyal Palzangpo, was the third in the line of the gurus of Ripa. His mother was Palden Tsomo, the granddaughter of Drupwang Shakyi Shri.
65. Gesar was a semilegendary king of a region of eastern Tibet. Stories about his exploits are a major source of Tibetan cultural values.
66. Tibetan names are often shortened to familiar ones of affectionate respect. Here Jé and Pak are abbreviated forms of Jedrung and Pakchok.
67. Such a transmission would involve the reading of more than seventeen large volumes of scriptures.

14. *The Students of Adzom Drukpa Rinpoché and Yukhok Jadralwa Chöying Rangdrol*

1. Reputed to be the author of the first major commentary on *The Kalachakra Tantra.*
2. Gartong Tsen was a powerful minister of the seventh century, who served both the Tibetan king Songtsen Gampo and the latter's son and successor, Mangsong Mangtsen. He was instrumental in bringing the daughters of the Nepalese king and Chinese emperor to court to serve as consorts of Songtsen Gampo, which paved the way for the introduction of Buddhism to Tibet.
3. "Namnang" is the Tibetan translation of the Tibetan rendering of the Sanskrit Vairochana (Bairotsana).
4. The incarnation born in Bhutan, Gyalsé Tulku (b. 1980), now teaches at the shedra of Shechen Tennyi Dargeling Monastery in Kathmandu, Nepal.
5. Tarthang Tulku's full name is Kunga Gelek Yeshé Dorjé.
6. The eleventh Trungpa tulku of Zurmang Monastery, Chökyi Gyatso, better known in the West as Chögyam Trungpa. He went first to England, then to the United States, where he founded a network of spiritual centers. His life story has been recounted in his autobiography, *Born in Tibet* (Boston: Shambhala, 2004), and his biography, by Fabrice Midal, *Chögyam Trungpa: His Life and Vision,* trans. Ian Monk (Boston: Shambhala, 2004).
7. In Mendecino County, northern California.
8. A gathering of Nyingma lamas and practitioners that focuses on prayers for the flourishing of the Buddhist teachings, particularly those of the Nyingma school.
9. A two-day ritual, known in Tibetan as *nyung-nay,* that focuses on the deity Avalokiteshvara and involves visualization, mantra repetition, and the recitation of liturgies. A partial fast (after midday) is observed on the first day of the ritual and a total fast on the second day. The practice belongs to the introductory level of Vajrayana known as Kriyatantra, which emphasizes ritual purity, including hygiene and a vegetarian diet.
10. Dudjom Lingpa Dorjé Drolö Tsal. Dudjom Rinpoché Jigdral Yeshé Dorjé was the incarnation of Dudjom Lingpa and hence the "second Dudjom."
11. See Chapter 9.
12. See Chapter 16.

15. *The Students of Jamyang Khyentsé Chökyi Lodrö and Other Masters*

1. See Chapter 8.
2. See Chapter 8.
3. Dzongsar Khyentsé Rinpoché Jamyang Norbu (b. 1961).
4. The head of the house of Drolma Podrang is H.H. Sakya Trizin, Ngawang Kunga Thegchen Palbar Trinley Samphel Wanggi Gyalpo (b. 1945), the forty-first patriarch of the Sakya school, who now lives in Rajpur, northern India. The head of the house of Puntsok Podrang is H.H. Jigdral Dakchen Sakya (b. 1929); since 1960 he has resided with his family in Seattle, Washington, where he directs his center, Sakya Monastery.
5. The Ngor branch of the Sakya school was traditionally headed by one of four khenpos, who were associated with four aristocratic houses and assumed the office in a regular rotation. The present khenpos are: Luding Khen Rinpoché and Thartse Khen Rinpoché

(Ngor Monastery, Manduwala, northern India), Phende Khen Rinpoché (Ngor Evam Phende Ling, Normandy, France), and Khangsar Khen Rinpoché.

6. A deity of longevity. Sogyal Rinpoché's mother currently resides at his center, Lerab Ling, near Montpellier in southern France.
7. In 2001 Khenpo Appey Yöntan Zangpo founded the International Buddhist Institute in Kathmandu, Nepal.
8. Khenchen Kunga Wangchuk (b. 1921) founded a Dzongsar shedra at Chontara Bir in northern India.
9. Moktsa Rinpoché, Jigdral Choklé Namgyal, has overseen the restoration of Katok Monastery, which was destroyed during the Cultural Revolution, reinstituting the shedra and meditation centers as well.
10. Jigme Chökyi Senge, who was born in India in 1966, is the seventh Rabjam Rinpoché; he is the grandson of Dilgo Khyentsé Rinpoché.

16. *The Students of Paltrul Rinpoché*

1. Lungtok Tenpai Nyima's biography can be found in Chapter 7. The accounts of the other three students—Tendzin Drakpa, Minyak Kunzang Sönam, and Orgyen Tendzin Norbu—follow in this chapter.
2. An honorific idiom for the enthronement of a tulku.
3. A metaphorical reference to the thoroughgoing process of listening to, contemplating, and meditating on the teachings.
4. Zurchen Shakya Jungné.
5. The "Gathering of the Great Assembly" (Tib. Tsokchen Düpa) is the name of the principal mandala of Anuyoga.
6. Part of the approach in Chinese and Japanese Buddhism commonly referred to as "Pure Land."
7. These four principles are: spiritual practice as the foundation of one's goals, a life of poverty as the foundation of one's spiritual practice, death as the outcome of one's life of poverty, and an empty cave as the place where one will die.
8. "Our Dear Khenpo, the Wish-Fulfilling Gem."
9. The posture adopted by the Buddha Shakyamuni when he passed into nirvana, lying on his right side, his head resting on the palm of his right hand.
10. Khenchen Chödrup (1862–1944) was the speech incarnation of Dzogchen Pema Rigdzin.
11. Shantideva spontaneously composed his masterpiece, *Engaging in the Conduct of a Bodhisattva,* while seated on a throne before an assembly. As he spoke the lines of the ninth chapter, concerning sublime knowing, he began to rise into the air. His body rose until it vanished, but his voice could still be heard, reciting the final, tenth chapter.
12. The principal mantra of the orange form of Mañjushri, the bodhisattva who embodies the sublime knowing that is an innate quality of buddhahood.
13. Khenchen Jigmé Puntsok passed away on January 7, 2004, in Chengdu, China.
14. Born in 1953 in eastern Tibet, Khenchen Namdrol studied at Penor Rinpoché's Namdroling Monastery near Bylakuppe in Mysore State, India. He served there as an attendant to Nyoshul Khen Rinpoché and in 1978 cofounded the Ngagyur Nyingma Institute. He

returned to Tibet to study with Khenchen Jigmé Puntsok, whom he accompanied on his only tour of the West in 1993.

15. In the dialects of Golok and Dza, the suffix "-tsang" (family member, relation) is often added to someone's name or title to indicate one's affectionate regard.
16. The fifteenth Chagdud incarnation. The sixteenth was Padma Gargyi Wangchuk (1930–2002).
17. The relationship between teacher and student in the preceding lifetime (Dola Jigmé Kalzang and Paltrul Rinpoché) was thus continued in the next lifetime (Yukhok Jadralwa Chöying and Do-ngak Tenpai Nyima).
18. Khartrul Tenpai Nyima, a student of Paltrul Rinpoché and Gyalsé Zhenpen Tayé, was considered the activity incarnation of the first Dodrupchen, Jigmé Trinlé Özer.
19. Khenchen Tsewang Rigdzin (1883–1958) was a student of such masters as Jamyang Khyentsei Wangpo, Mipam Rinpoché, Lungtok Tenpai Nyima, and Khenchen Ngawang Palzang.
20. Gyalsé Zhenpen Tayé was related to Orgyen Tendzin Norbu on the latter's father's side.
21. Ngadak Nyang-ral Nyima Özer.
22. *The Chariot of the Two Levels of Truth* and *The Chariot to Omniscience* make up Jigmé Lingpa's two-volume commentary on his own work *The Treasury of Enlightened Qualities*.
23. Literally, "Mind Only." A school of Mahayana Buddhist philosophy that asserts that mind is all that truly exists.
24. Early 1888 to early 1889.

17. The Students of Orgyen Tendzin Norbu

1. The previous Dzongsar Khyentsé, Jamyang Khyentsé Chökyi Lodrö.
2. According to the late Chagdud Tulku Padma Gargyi Wangchuk, although Traktung Dudjom Lingpa had several sons that were conceived in the usual way, Apang Terchen was conceived miraculously when his mother, a nun, encountered Dudjom Lingpa in a field; he called her to him and stared at her intently for a few moments, after which he sent her on her way. She later discovered that she was pregnant.
3. This was an indication that Apang Terchen was a rebirth of Rigdzin Gödem, who had a similar tuft of feathers protruding from his head and is depicted in artwork as such.
4. Sönam Dorjé misinterpreted the feathers on the infant's head as a negative omen indicating that the child was a bastard. The fact that his sister was a nun added to his sense of the shame this brought on the family.
5. Trehor Choktrul Lozang Tendzin.
6. Powerful local gods or spirits associated with important holy places in eastern Tibet.
7. It was after Jangchub Dorjé went into exile in northern India that the late Chagdud Tulku Padma Gargyi Wangchuk received from him the transmission of Apang Terchen's teachings, including the Red Tara practice that Chagdud Rinpoché taught so widely in the West.
8. Taré Lhamo lived from 1938 to 2003.
9. Possibly a reference to the moon, in which Tibetans see the outline of a rabbit (much as Westerners see "the man in the moon").

10. Apang Terchen.
11. Apang Terchen's tulku is the Sakya Trizin, Ngawang Kunga Tegchen Palbar, the current head of the Sakya school. According to the Sakya Trizin's elder sister, Jetsun Kusho Chimé Luding, who is a fully trained master of the Sakya school, Jangchub Dorjé had been sent by Apang Terchen to Sakya, where he knew his next incarnation would be born. When Sakya Trizin was about five years old, he and Jetsun Kusho were playing on the roof of their ancestral home. She recalls that an old monk, whom neither of them had ever seen before, came up on the roof. Sakya Trizin seemed to recognize the monk and called out, "Come here!" addressing him with a nickname that had been Apang Terchen's name for Jangchub Dorjé. The monk, who proved to be Jangchub Dorjé, burst into tears, for this confirmed that he had found his master's tulku.
12. Kunzang Palden and Yönten Gyatso.
13. The Indian Buddhist master Chandrakirti (ca. sixth to seventh centuries) is considered by the vast majority of those in the Tibetan Buddhist tradition to have been the definitive commentator on the Prasangika interpretation of the Madhyamaka philosophy developed by Nagarjuna (ca. second to third centuries).
14. Dorjé Chang is the Tibetan equivalent of the Sanskrit Vajradhara, the name of the dharmakaya buddha of the sixth family.
15. Gatön Ngawang Lekpa (1867–1941) was a great master of the Lamdré cycle of the Sakya school.
16. "The Buddha Who Benefits Others."
17. The secret name that Milarepa received from his guru, Marpa.
18. Palpung Monastery, the most important Kagyü monastery in eastern Tibet, has been the seat of the Tai Situ incarnations of the Karma Kagyü lineage since the eighth Tai Situ, Chökyi Jungné, was granted this right by the ruler of Dergé, Denba Tsering (1678–1739).
19. The monastery under the direction of the Zurmang Trungpa tulkus.
20. The present Zurmang Tenga Rinpoché is a son of Chögyam Trungpa Rinpoché.
21. Karmapa Chödrak Gyatso was noted for his scholarship, prolific writing, and skill in forging positive political relationships within Tibet and with the neighboring countries of India and China.
22. This site is on the north bank of the Tsangpo River in central Tibet, west of Samyé Monastery. The stupas commemorate the occasion in the eighth century when King Trisong Detsen met Guru Padmakara, who had come to Tibet at the king's invitation.
23. That is, he sat for approximately three weeks in early 1901 (from the end of the Male Iron Rat year until early in the Female Iron Ox year).
24. This has been published as *Vast as the Heavens, Deep as the Sea: Verses in Praise of Bodhicitta,* trans. Gareth Sparham (Boston: Wisdom, 1999).

18. *The Students of Nyoshul Lungtok Tenpai Nyima*

1. See Chapter 7.
2. The other was Terchen Lerab Lingpa, whose biography follows.
3. An epithet of Nyala Pema Duddul.
4. An idiomatic way of indicating that Lama Ngakchen had the potential to reveal termas.

5. Dorjé Drolö, a wrathful aspect of Guru Padmakara, is depicted standing on the back of a tigress.
6. Now in his mid-seventies, Tromgé Dechen Rinpoché was a student of Arik Tulku and is the most senior of the Tromgé tulkus.
7. Lerab Lingpa died in 1926, a Male Fire Tiger year. Gendün Rinchen was born in the same year and died in 1997. He was the sixty-ninth successive holder of the title of Jé Khenpo, the supreme head of Buddhism in Bhutan, first held by Pekar Jungné (1604–1672).

19. *The Students of Khenchen Ngawang Palzang*

1. See Chapter 7.
2. Also known as Kunzang Pema Trinlé Gyatso.
3. "Dear Precious Tulku."
4. The fifth Chaktsa Rinpoché, also known as Tupten Lodrö Chökyi Gyaltsen.
5. Dezhung Ajam Kunga Tenpai Gyaltsen lived from 1885 to 1952.
6. Born in 1930, Chagdud Tulku Rinpoché passed away on November 17, 2002, having established numerous centers in both North and South America.
7. The tulku of Arik Rinpoché's uncle Jigmé Namgyal and the tulku of Tromgé Kachö.
8. Lama Achuk, one of Nyoshul Khen Rinpoché's fellow students, was recognized as someone who had truly attained the fruition of Dzogchen practice.
9. Gönpo Namgyal, the warlord of Nyarong who overran much of eastern Tibet from 1837 to 1865 (see Chapter 13, note 19).
10. That is, Nüden Khyentsei Lodrö was considered an emanation of Milarepa. He is sometimes referred to as Zhepa Dorjé, which was Milarepa's secret name.
11. Tupten Gyaltsen Özer passed away at least twenty years ago; his tulku is currently studying at the shedra of Katok Monastery.
12. Jigmé Dechen Dorjé (1899–1939?).
13. A reference to the development of the four visions of tögal.
14. Choktrul Sang-ngak Tendzin received much of his education from Orgyen Chemchok during his ten years of imprisonment under the Communist regime. He currently makes his home in the United States, where he directs the center of Evam, based near Missoula, Montana.
15. A term from the Dzogchen approach of trekchö. It refers to sitting meditation practice in which the body is unwavering in that it maintains a steady posture, the speech is unwavering in that one observes silence and breathes naturally, and the mind is unwavering in that it rests in the direct experience of its true nature as pure awareness.
16. A more extensive and moving account of this incident is described by Sogyal Rinpoché in the introduction to this volume.
17. The Male Iron Dog year (early 1970 to early 1971).
18. Though not a formal school or movement, the Rimé (nonsectarian) approach gained prominence in the nineteenth century, primarily in eastern Tibet. Championed by such masters as Jamyang Khyentsei Wangpo and Jamgön Kongtrul Lodrö Tayé, the approach was and is an attempt to break down sectarian biases and misconceptions among the schools of the Tibetan Buddhist tradition. It emphasizes tolerance and respect for other

traditions, while stressing the importance of one's commitment to one's chosen path. The truly great Rimé masters studied and practiced methods promulgated by all schools.

19. The preliminary practices both reinforce one's positive qualities (merit and the experience of timeless awareness) and refine away negative factors (obscurations and the effects of negative karma).
20. That is, Khenchen Ngawang Palzang, whose secret name was Pema Ledrel Tsal.
21. The fifth Katok Situ, who was born in recent times in Bhutan.
22. Born in eastern Tibet in 1991, Dudjom Yangsi was recognized by Chatral Rinpoché.
23. This statement echoes a well-known aphorism in the Buddhist teachings regarding the proper progression of one's spiritual development: "Liberate your own mind through realization, then liberate the minds of others through compassion."
24. This imagery symbolizes Chimé Rinpoché's ability to overwhelm the violence in others' minds with his spiritual powers.
25. A fire pit is the central focus of rituals connected with wrathful activity, which, if performed properly, is an effective path to enlightenment. Tibetan texts, however, are filled with cautionary references to the pitfalls and dangers of misinterpreting such practices and abusing them for selfish gain.
26. Bairo Rinpoché, Jamyang Tenpai Gyaltsen, the third Zhichen Bairotsana, is the father of the present Gyalwang Drukpa (the twelfth incarnation), Jigmé Pema Wangchen, who was born in 1963. The Gyalwang Drukpa tulkus are principal masters of the Drukpa Kagyü school of Buddhism.
27. *Engaging in the Conduct of a Bodhisattva,* chap. 8, verse 81a–b. The version cited by Nyoshul Khen Rinpoché differs slightly from the more common Tibetan translation, which reads, "For the sake of things that are insignificant in this life, / which are not rare and can even be accomplished by animals, . . ."
28. Ibid., chap. 5, verse 17b,d.

20. *The Students of Lungtrul Shedrup Tenpai Nyima*

1. See Chapter 7.
2. The Male Wood Monkey year (early 1944 to early 1945).
3. Lungtrul Shedrup Tenpai Nyima.
4. This somewhat cryptic verse emphasizes the commitment that bodhisattvas undertake for the sake of beings, one that never wavers and is never relinquished.

22. *The Transmission of the Teachings of the Early Translation School*

1. According to the Yeshe De Project, *Ancient Tibet,* p. 180, King Lha Totori lived from 374 to 493.
2. That is, the Nyingma teachings, which are distinguished by the teachings themselves, the patrons who sponsored their dissemination, the locations in which they were codified, their translators, the scholars who explained them, and the offerings made to request them.
3. Usually known by the Sanskrit form of his name, Jñanakumara.
4. Gongpa Rabsel (953–1035) was a key figure in the reintroduction of the Vinaya lineage of monastic ordination to central Tibet following the reign of King Langdharma in the mid-ninth century.

5. In 1632, according to Gyurme Dorje, *Tibet Handbook*, 2d ed. (Chicago: Passport Books, 1999), p. 162.
6. Early 1670 to early 1671.
7. Based on the termas of Pema Lingpa (1450–1521).
8. The present Khenchung Tulku is in his mid-thirties.
9. The principal director of Mindroling Monastery near Dehra Dun in northern India.
10. As mentioned previously, this monastery no longer exists and is not one of the six major Nyingma centers.
11. Palri was the birthplace of Jigmé Lingpa; see Dudjom Rinpoche, *The Nyingma School of Tibetan Buddhism*, vol. 1, pp. 205–206.
12. In the Male Wood Rat year (early 1684 to early 1685).
13. Pema Rigdzin founded Dzogchen Monastery at the urging of the fifth Dalai Lama, who was one of his teachers.
14. The seventh Dzogchen Rinpoché.
15. The seventh Dzogchen Pönlop Rinpoché.
16. The first Rabjam incarnation, Tenpai Gyaltsen (1650–1712?), was a student of the first Dzogchen Rinpoché.
17. The Female Wood Hare year (early 1735 to early 1736).
18. Magadha was a region in the central Ganges plain of ancient India, famed as a center of the Buddhist tradition even during the time of the Buddha.
19. Early 1159 to early 1160.
20. The late nineteenth century.
21. That is, the tulkus of Jé-ön Tashi Puntsok, nephew of Longsel Dorjé Nyingpo.
22. The Female Wood Serpent year (early 1665 to early 1666).

24. The Three Phases of Ground, Path, and Fruition

1. The perception of an ordinary being, an advanced spiritual practitioner, and a buddha.
2. Between enlightenment and ignorance.
3. A reference to the "naturally occurring lamp of sublime knowing," the innate nature of mind that underlies the path of trekchö and tögal.
4. The "lamp of totally pure basic space" and the "lamp of empty spheres," the basic elements of the path of the four visions.
5. Mythical beings depicted as men with wings.
6. Samantabhadra and Samantabhadr›.
7. A mythical sea monster.
8. Even on the tenth level of realization, there is a slight degree of dualism that results in the appearance of a teacher separate from the retinue, although this is not the case from the ultimate perspective.
9. One of the states of gods in the desire realm; the "Thirty-three" are the ancient Indian gods of the Vedas.
10. The deeds performed by a sublime nirmanakaya buddha such as Shakyamuni.
11. The three approaches are those of shravakas and pratyekabuddhas (together constituting the Hinayana) and that of bodhisattvas (the Mahayana). The single approach is "Buddhayana," the entire process by which any and all beings can awaken to enlightenment.

12. Benefit that can be directly sensed or perceived by the recipient.
13. In Mahayana cosmology, our universe is one of many held in the hands of a cosmic buddha, a form of Vairochana known as Gangchentso (Glacial Ocean).

Colophon

1. The Male Iron Monkey year (early 1980 to early 1981).
2. The early summer of 1980.
3. The Male Water Monkey year (early 1992 to early 1993). The actual date was early in 1993.

Index

NAMES

(Boldface numbers indicate the pages on which a master's biography appears.)

Abu, 240, 241, 242, 243, 248, 456, 466, 467, 469, 470, 475, 477, 478, 479, 484, 509, 537, 645 n. 32 (*see also* Paltrul Rinpoché)
Achuk, Khen Lama Rinpoché, 9, **521–2**, 667 n. 8 (*see also* Drupwang Lungtok Gyatso)
Adhimuktika, 36
Adzom Drukpa (Drodul Pawo Dorjé), 9, 84, 227, 279, **290–6**, 300, 308, 316, 317, 326, 394, 410, 424, 436, 442, 445, 450, 451, 454, 456, 458, 473, 513, 650 n. 56
Apang Terchen Orgyen Trinlé Lingpa (Apang Tertön), 329–30, **488-91**, 492, 665 nn. 2, 3, & 7, 666 nn. 10 & 11
Arik, Tromgé Choktrul, 9, 252, **519–21**, 521, 522, 540, 667 nn. 6 (ch. 18) &.7 (ch. 19)
Aro Yeshé Jungné, 52, 223, 549
Atisha, 273, 292, 299, 301, 309, 633 n. 45, 640 n. 93, 647 n. 3

Bairo Rinpoché, 252, **536**, 668 n. 26
Bairotsana, 11, **49–51**, 54, 57, 82, 188, 211, 297, 404, 410, 538, 549, 563, 616 n. 2, 622 nn. 4, 5, 8, & 9, 623 n. 10, 625 n. 36, 641 n. 121, 647 n. 3, 648 n. 22, 659 n. 14, 663 n. 3 (ch. 14)
Barchung Lama Tashi Gyatso, **390–1**
Bé Lodrö Wangchuk, **83–4**
Bo Gangkar Rinpoché, 497, 500, **501**
Bokar Choktrul (Karma Ngedön Chökyi Seng-gé), 315, 652 n. 96
Bötrul Do-ngak Tenpai Nyima, 9, 461, 475, **479–80**, 481, 482
Buddhaguhya, 43, 54, 79, 195
buddhas of the five families, **31–2**, 54, 81, 87, 203, 583, 620 n. 1

Chabdal Lhundrup, Khenchen, 11, 116, 117, 158, 161, **162–3**, 164, 354
Chagdud Tulku Pema Gargyi Wangchuk, 479, 521, 522, 665 n. 16 (ch. 16), 2 & 7 (ch. 17), 667 n.6
Chaktsa, fifth (Tupten Lodrö Chökyi Gyaltsen), 252, 525, 536, 539, 667 n. 4
Chaktsa, fourth (Pema Trinlé Gyatso), 286, 438, 440, 459, **517–19**
Chatral Sanjé Dorjé, 9, 76, 252, 286, 288, 464, **533–4**, 543, 556, 656 n. 3, 668 n. 22
Chetsün Seng-gé Wangchuk, **85–8**, 564
Cheu-chung Khading Tsal (form of Padmakara), 44
Cheu Nangwa (one of the twelve teachers), 33
Cheu Ö Mitrukpa (one of the twelve teachers), 33
Chöchap, Khenchen, 9, 318, 459, 461, 479, **482**
Chödrak Gyatso, 306, 501, 651 n. 82, 666 n. 21 (*see also* Karmapa, seventh Gyalwang)
Chögyal Ngagi Wangpo, **338–9**, 340, 342
Chöjé Kunga Gyaltsen Palzang, **171–2**, 172
Chokgyur Dechen Lingpa, Terchen, 13, 225, 226, 261, 277, 278, 298, 299, 301, 304, 309, 311, 412, **431–5**, 437, 483, 661 n. 44
Chokro Luyi Gyaltsen, 55, 78, 79, 82, 647 n. 3
Chökyi Dawa, **263–5**, 267, 440 (*see also* Dartang Choktrul)
Chökyi Gyatso, Orgyen, 261, 279, 294, 295, **436–40**, 444, 478, 525, 553, 646 n. 49, 650 nn. 59 & 63, 651 n. 74 (*see also* Katok Situ, third)
Chökyi Lodrö, 227, 291, 295, **465–6** (*see also* Katok Situ, second)
Chönyi Zangmo, **343–50**, 353, 655 nn. 56 & 60 (*see also* Mani Lochen; Shuksep Jetsünma)

Chönyön Dharma Seng-gé, 343, 348, 349, **351–2**, 488, 655 n. 59
Chöying Tobden Dorjé, 321, 322, **407–8**
Chungtrul Pema Wangchen, 378, 414, **415**

Dalai Lama, fifth (Ngawang Lozang Gyatso), 176, 182, 190, 194, 371, 378, 391, 637 n. 40, 638 nn. 73 & 78, 639 n. 80, 656 n. 14, 669 n. 13
Dalai Lama, fourteenth (Tenzin Gyatso), 266, 314, 476, 488, 507, 646 n. 61, 656 n. 35, 657 n. 14, 661 n. 32
Dalai Lama, ninth (Lungtok Gyatso), 400, 401, 403, 659 n. 15
Dalai Lama, second (Gendun Gyatso), 654 n. 34
Dalai Lama, seventh (Kalzang Gyatso), 192, 391, 639 nn. 78, 79, & 80
Dalai Lama, sixth (Tsangyang Gyatso), 639 n.78
Dalai Lama, tenth (Tsultrim Gyatso), 374, 656 n. 30
Dalai Lama, thirteenth (Tupten Gyatso), 301, 376, 426, 430, 437, 446, 514, 651 n. 69
Dampa Deshek, Katokpa, 13, **52–3**, 439, 548, 553, 623 n. 19
Damtsik Dorjé, 321, **408–9**
Dangma Lhundrup Gyaltsen, **84–5**, 253
Dartang Choktrul, 263, 264, 267, 315, 542 (*see also* Chökyi Dawa)
Dawa Drakpa, Gyalsé, 164, 165, **168–70**, 636 nn. 19 & 21
Dawa Gyaltsen (son of Pema Lingpa), 378, 656 n. 26, 657 n. 38
Dengom Chödrak Zangpo, 118, 158, **357–9**
Dharma Shri, Lochen, 190, 194, 617 n. 16, 638 n. 69, 639 n. 78, 657 n. 8 (*see also* Chöpal Gyatso)
Dilgo Khyentsé, 9, 76, 226, 266, 269, 286, 288, 296, 305, 306, **306–16**, 353, 378, 394, 415, 428, 435, 436, 449, 457, 463, 463, 464, 470, 472, 480, 488, 497, 503, 528, 533, 553, 598, 618 n. 7 (Supplication to the Lineage), 619 n. 10, 650 n. 67, 652 n. 97, 662 n. 49, 664 n. 10 (*see also* Rabsel Dawa; Tashi Paljor)
Do Khyentsé, 294, 321, 322, 323, 324, **395–9**, 448, 658 nn. 8 & 10 (*see also* Yeshé Dorjé)
Do-ngak Tendzin, Khedrup, **176–8**, 370
Dodrupchen, first, 216, 218, 220, 221, 223, 224, **319–22**, 338, 342, 350, 351, 353, 392, 393, 395, 397, 398, 400, 405, 407, 408, 640 n. 86, 659, 665 n. 18 (*see also* Jigmé Trinlé Özer)
Dodrupchen, fourth, 310, 318, **326–38**, 459, 464, 653 nn. 20 & 21 (*see also* Jigmé Trinlé Palbar; Tupten Trinlé Palzang)
Dodrupchen, second, **322–3** (*see also* Jigmé Puntsok Jungné)
Dodrupchen, third, 279, 300, 310, 317, **323–6**, 411, 440, 624 n. 28, 653 n. 16 (*see also* Jigmé Tenpai Nyima)
Dola Jigmé Kalzang, 223, 224, 280, 321, 480, 643 n. 5, 665 n. 17
Dombi Heruka, 44
Doring Choktrul, 399, 430, **507**, 658 n. 11
Dorjé Drakpo Tsal (form of Padmakara), 42
Dorjé Drolö, 60, 251, 324, 512, 663 n. 62, 667 n. 5
Dorjé Dzinpa Tobden, Khen, **508–9** (*see also* Tupten Gyaltsen Özer)
Dorjé Mikyö Tsal, **371–2** (*see also* Pema Lingpa, fourth)
Dorjé Ziji Tsal (Longchenpa's secret name), conferral by Yeshé Tsogyal, 112
Dragyab Lama Chöden, **541**
Drakpa Özer, Gyalsé Tulku (son of Longchenpa), **163–5**, 168, 196, 357, 635 n. 12
Drangsong Tröpai Gyalpo (one of the twelve teachers), 35
Dretsé Tulku, 514, **515**
Drimé Özer (Longchenpa's secret name), 75, 76, 104, 112, 116, 130, 198, 213, 254, 256, 302, 318, 358, 359, 364, 367, 568, 590, 599; conferral by Guru Padmakara, 112
Drimé Zhingkyong, first, 390
Drimé Zhingkyong, fourth, 525
Drimé Zhingkyong, second, 320, 397, 403
Drimé Zhingkyong, third, 227, 290, 511, 532, 643 n. 11
Drom Rinchen Bar, 83, **84**
Drukpa Geshé Tenpa Rinchen, **502**
Druktrul Rinpoché, **454**, 457, 543, 650 n. 56
Drupchen Khepa Nyima Bum, **88–9**
Drupwang Lungtok Gyatso, 9, **521–2** (*see also* Achuk, Khen Lama Rinpoché)
Drupwang Shrinatha, *see* Orgyen Palgön, Ngakyi Rabjampa
Dudjom (Drodul) Lingpa (Traktung Dudjom Lingpa, Dudjom Dorjé Drolö Tsal), 9, 229, 281, 282, 283, 284, 324, 387, 444, 457, 468, 469, 489, 492, 514, 515, 653 n. 17, 663 n. 10, 665 n. 2
Dudjom Rinpoché, Kyabjé (Dudjom Drodul Lingpa Tsal), 76, 266, 282, **283–90**, 305, 310, 352, 353, 377, 378, 385, 386, 387, 388, 393, 426, 441, 445, 446, 449, 463, 464, 469, 480, 492, 503, 528, 532, 533, 534, 556, 598, 617 n. 15, 618 nn. 8 (Synopsis) & 7 (Supplication to the Lineage), 619 n. 10, 622 n. 4, 623 n. 19, 624 n. 26, 625 n. 43, 627 nn. 66 & 67, 628 n. 91 (ch. 3), n. 2 (ch. 4), 648 n. 30, 649 nn.36 & 38, 650 nn. 42 & 44, 658 n. 17, 663 n. 10,

669 n. 11 (ch. 22) (*see also* Jigdral Yeshé Dorjé)
Dudjom Yangsi, 534, 668 n. 22
Dulwai Dé, 438, **522–3**, 537, 554 (*see also* Lekshé Jorden)
Düsum Chenpa, 303, 651 n. 73 (*see also* Karmapa, first Gyalwang)
Dzigar Kongtrul, first, 497, 500, **501**, 662
Dzigar Kongtrul, second, **436**, 652 n. 92, 662 n. 52
Dzogchen, fifth Drupwang, 227, 229, 244, 247, 265, 295, 296, 299, 323, 327, 328, 348, 424, **428–31**, 440, 450, 467, 498, 650 n. 53 (*see also* Tupten Chökyi Dorjé)
Dzogchen, first Drupwang, 388, 656 nn. 14 & 15 (*see also* Pema Rigdzin)
Dzogchen, fourth Drupwang, 221, 222, 224, 320, **400–4**, 405, 406 482 (*see also* Mingyur Namkhai Dorjé)
Dzogchen, second Drupwang, 190, 191, **388–90**, 402, 658 n. 23 (*see also* Gyurmé Tekchok Tendzin)
Dzogchen, seventh Drupwang, 431, 662 n. 39, 669 n. 14
Dzogchen, sixth Drupwang, 305, 334, 431, 661 n. 39 (*see also* Jigdral Jangchub Dorjé)
Dzogchen, third Drupwang, 320, 658 n. 8 (*see also* Ngedön Tendzin Zangpo)
Dzogchenpa Longdzok Tadral, **366**
Dzogchenpa Sönam Rigdzin, 362, **362**, 655 n. 6
Dzogchenpa Sönam Rinchen, 171, 172, 362, 379, 655 n. 6
Dzogchenpa Sönam Wangpo, **363–4**
Dzongsar Khyentsé, 288, 315, 464, 532, 663 n. 3 (ch. 15), 665 n. 1

Gampopa, 310, 396, 443, 647 n. 8
Garab Dorjé, 11, **37–8**, 50, 54, 211, 243, 253, 337, 398, 452, 474, 559, 562, 563, 599, 622 n. 6, 641 n. 121
Garchö, Lama, 475, **527**
Garwang Nyima, Choktrul, **526**
Gemang Gyalsé Rigpai Dorjé (Zhenpen Tayé), 305, **404–6** (*see also* Gyalsé Zhenpen Tayé)
Getsé Mahapandita, 215, 294, 298, 321, 397, 525, 554, 556, 640
Guru Chöwang, 76, 102, 307, 548, 628 n. 87, 656 n. 16
Guru Dewachenpo (form of Padmakara), 282
Guru Jober, **89–90**, 91
Guru Nangsi Zilnön (form of Padmakara), 222
Guru Rinpoché ("the Guru"), 2, 3, 12, 55, 56, 57, 60, 63, 64, 65, 66, 67, 68, 70, 72, 73, 74, 75, 76, 99, 105, 110, 112, 155, 175, 177, 178, 192, 199, 218, 219, 220, 261, 275, 276, 277, 278, 279, 286, 293, 296, 310, 313, 332, 334, 335, 336, 339, 341, 368, 386, 398, 412, 413, 428, 431, 432, 433, 434, 436, 444, 445, 446, 447, 448, 451, 484, 489, 502, 512, 514, 531, 534, 547, 548, 556, 562, 563, 615 nn. 2 & 8, 616 n. 1, 620 n. 10 (ch. 2), 626 n. 61, 631 nn. 17, 18, 19, & 27, 642 n. 136, 654 n. 35 (*see also* Padmakara)
Guru Zhenpen, **360–1**
Gyakor Tulku Kunzang Tekchok Tenpai Gyaltsen, 279, 280, 285, 343, **440–2**, 447
Gyalsé Dawa Drakpa, **168–70**, 636 n. 19
Gyalsé Gyurmé Dorjé, 9, **450–4**, 455, 481
Gyalsé Lekpa Gyaltsen, 71, 72, **73–5**, 628 n. 85
Gyalsé Rinchen Namgyal, 190, **191–4**, 195, 196, 280, 372, 380, 381, 389, 391, 639 n. 80, 657 n. 1
Gyalsé Zhenpen Tayé, 13, 215, 221, 224, 227, 239, 243, 280, 305, 334, 375, 383, 391, 399, 401, 402, **404–6**, 431, 467, 469, 474, 478, 482, 493, 496, 497, 551, 552, 644 n. 17, 659 n. 19, 665 nn. 18 & 20
Gyaltsap, fourth, 305, 424, 552
Gyaltsap, fourth Zhechen, 263, 299, 305, 307, 306, 310, 313, 410, 424, **426–8**, 440, 552 (*see also* Pema Namgyal)
Gyaltsap, third Zhechen, 227, 427 (*see also* Orgyen Rangjung Dorjé Tsewang Drupa Tsal)
Gyalwa Zhangtön Tashi Dorjé, **86–8**
Gyarong Tsöndrü, 318, 459, **460–1**
Gyurmé Ngedön Wangpo, 279, 280, 281, 282, 283, 284, **414**, 661 n. 31
Gyurmé Tekchok Tendzin, 190, 191, **388–90**, 391 (*see also* Dzogchen, second Drupwang)
Gyurmé Trinlé Namgyal, **382**
Gyurmé Tutop Namgyal, Zhechen Öntrul, 224, 270, 280, 291, 325, 411, 552, 643 n. 6

Indrabhuti, 78, 79, 452, 628 n. 1
Indrabodhi, 41, 42, 628 nn. 1 & 2

Jampa Bum, 13, 52, 53, 548, 553, 623 n. 19
Jampal Dewai Nyima, 285, 286, **425–6**
Jampal Jigpa Kyopa (one of the twelve teachers), 34
Jamyang Khyentsé Chökyi Lodrö (Jamyang Chökyi Lodrö, Jamgön Chökyi Lodrö), 9, 243, **296–306**, 309, 326, 334, 338, 385, 394, 435, 436, 440, 450, 455, 457, 462, 463, 464, 492, 497, 499, 506, 522, 523, 531, 534, 650 n. 60, 665 n. 1
Jamyang Khyentsei Wangpo, 215, 221, 224, 226, 228, 242, **270–80**, 281, 290, 292, 293, 296, 298, 299, 300, 301, 302, 304, 308, 311, 318,

324, 325, 334, 338, 381, 383, 397, 410, 414, 416, 426, 427, 429, 432, 436, 446, 449, 464, 468, 478, 483, 514, 544, 617 n. 17, 623 n. 19, 638 n. 74, 645 n. 39, 648 nn. 14 & 35, 650 n. 60, 656 n. 16, 661 n. 44, 665 n. 19, 667 n. 18
Jamyang Loter Wangpo, 242, 243, 279, 298, 299, 410, 414, 417, 418, 436, 497, 499, 645 n. 39
Jangchub Dorjé, 656 n. 27 (*see also* Karmapa, twelfth Gyalwang)
Jedrung Jampa Jungné, 410, **446–7**, 661 n. 31
Jigdral Jangchub Dorjé, 305, 334, 462, 661 n. 39 (*see also* Dzogchen, sixth Drupwang)
Jigdral Yeshé Dorjé, 76, 282, **283–90**, 444, 469, 617 n. 15, 618 n. 7 (Supplication to the Lineage), 648 n. 30, 658 n. 17, 663 n. 10 (*see also* Dudjom Rinpoché, Kyabjé)
Jigmé Gyalwai Nyugu, 12, **215–22**, 224, 225, 228, 270, 271, 272, 279, 294, 324, 392, 393, 394, 403, 404, 410, 467, 544, 642 n. 141
Jigmé Kundrol Namgyal, **392–3**
Jigmé Lingpa, 11, 12, 27, 158, 196, 197, **198–216**, 217, 218, 219, 220, 221, 222, 224, 238, 241, 242, 244, 248, 251, 258, 266, 268, 279, 294, 310, 313, 314, 319, 320, 321, 329, 332, 334, 337, 342, 392, 394, 395, 396, 399, 400, 402, 468, 475, 484, 494, 496, 524, 531, 532, 533, 548, 551, 556, 566, 598, 615 n. 7, 618 n. 4 (Synopsis), 619 nn. 3 & 7, 639 n. 86, 640 n. 91, 642 nn. 125 & 138, 644 n. 16, 654 n. 45, 656 n. 29, 658 nn. 7 & 8, 665 n. 22, 669 n. 11 (ch. 22)
Jigmé Ngotsar (Getsé Jigmé Ngotsar Tendzin), 215, 224, 321, **393–4**
Jigmé Puntsok, Khenchen (Khenchen Jigpun), 9, 226, 266, 470, 472, **475–6**, 514, 543, 664 n. 13
Jigmé Puntsok Jungné, **322–3** (*see also* Dodrupchen, second)
Jigmé Tenpai Nyima, 279, 300, 303, 310, 318, **323–6**, 411, 424, 440, 624 n. 28 (*see also* Dodrupchen, third)
Jigmé Trinlé Özer, 216, 220, 223, **319–22**, 338, 350, 353, 392, 395, 397, 400, 407, 639 n. 86, 665 n. 18 (*see also* Dodrupchen, first)
Jigmé Trinlé Palbar, **326–38** (*see also* Dodrupchen, fourth; Tupten Trinlé Palzang)
Jñanasutra, **40–1**
Jokhang Choktrul, 261, **541–3**

Kalasiddhi (Nepalese consort of Padmakara), 65, 626 n. 62
Kalu Rinpoché (Karma Rangjung Kunkhyab), 315, 652 n. 96
Kangyur Rinpoché Longchen Yeshé Dorjé, 288, 306, 310, 441, **447–9**, 533
Karma Dorjé, Khen Rinpoché, **454–5**
Karma Pakshi, 302, 627 n. 77 (*see also* Karmapa, second Gyalwang)
Karmapa, fifteenth Gyalwang, 303, 310, 349, 414, 436, 444, 446, 651 n. 72, 655 n. 55 (*see also* Khachap Dorjé)
Karmapa, first Gyalwang, 303 (*see also* Düsum Chenpa)
Karmapa, fourteenth Gyalwang, 414, 432, 433, 661 n. 43 (*see also* Tekchok Dorjé)
Karmapa, ninth Gyalwang, 177, 637 nn. 42 & 49 (*see also* Wangchuk Dorjé)
Karmapa, second Gyalwang, 627 n. 77 (*see also* Karma Pakshi)
Karmapa, seventh Gyalwang, 306, 501, 652 n. 82, 666 n. 21 (*see also* Chödrak Gyatso)
Karmapa, sixteenth Gyalwang, 305, 315, 435, 501, 533, 652 n. 95, 661 n. 47 (*see also* Rangjung Rigpai Dorjé)
Karmapa, third, Gyalwang 71, 72, 75, 94, 95, 101, 111, 166, 627 nn. 73 & 77, 635 n. 13, 651 n.73 (*see also* Rangjung Dorjé)
Karmapa, twelfth Gyalwang, 372, 656 n. 27 (*see also* Jangchub Dorjé)
Kashyapa the Elder (one of the twelve teachers), 35
Katok Situ, fifth, 663 n. 11
Katok Situ, first, 644, 653
Katok Situ, fourth, 651
Katok Situ, second, 290, **465–6**, 644 (*see also* Chökyi Lodrö)
Katok Situ, third, 424, **436–40**, 443, 506, 519, 522, 523, 646, 651 (*see also* Chökyi Gyatso, Orgyen)
Katokpa Gyalsé Rinpoché Sönam Detsen, 191, **387–8**, 657 n. 15, 658 nn. 15 & 16
Kawa Paltsek, Lochen, 55, 57, 78, 79, 82, 391, 647 n. 3
Khachap Dorjé, 436, 444, 446, 651 n. 72, 655 n. 55 (*see also* Karmapa, fifteenth Gyalwang)
Khugyur Salwaichok, **52**, 53
Khunu Rinpoché (Khunu Lama Tendzin Gyaltsen), 481, 488, 497, **506–7**
Kongtrul (Jamgön Kongtrul Yönten Gyatso Lodrö Tayé), 13, 61, 77, 251, 261, 277, 279, 281, 284, 285, 288, 293, 296, 297, 299, 300, 304, 305, 309, 310, 311, 315, 325, 383, **410–15**, 417, 420, 425, 427, 430, 432, 436, 437, 440, 442, 446, 508, 512, 514, 530, 552, 626 n. 50, 648 n. 35, 660 n. 15, 661 n. 44, 667 n. 18
Krishnacharin, 44, 46, 226
Kumaradza, Rigdzin, **93–7**, 102, 103, 104, 105, 107, 113, 155, 207, 251, 362, 630 nn. 31, 32, & 36, 632 n. 28, 634 n. 56
Kunga Gyaltsen Palzang, Chöjé, **171–2**

Kunzang Dechen Dorjé (tulku of Jigmé Gyalwai Nyugu), 222, 227, 294, 375, 376, 495, 642 n. 141
Kunzang Dorjé, Drupchen, **170–1**, 172, 362
Kunzang Mingyur Paldrön, Jetsünma, 190, 191, 193, 195, 280, 372, **380–1**, 383, 389
Kunzang Palden Chödrak (Kunpal), Gegong Khenchen, 9, 131, 227, 261, 295, 298, 329, 330, 338, 427, 438, 440, 473, **476–9**, 480, 486, 493, 506, 517, 523, 525, 537, 666 n. 12
Kunzang Pema Wangyal, 370, **385–7**, 426, 550 (*see also* Minling Trichen)
Kunzang Sherab, Rigdzin, 264, 450, 453, 554, 555
Kunzang Sönam (Kunsö), Minyak, 227, 240, **466–7**, 483, 664 n. 1
Kyabgön Pema Gyatso, **342–3**, 347, 349, 350

Lama Dampa Sönam Gyaltsen, 102, 117, 356, 360, 631 n. 11, 635 n. 13
Lama Ngakchen (Orgyen Tutop Lingpa), **511–12**, 513, 527, 666 n. 4
Lama Sönam Zangpo, Lopön Rinpoché, **443–5**
Lama Wangchen, Sa-ngen, **510–11**
Lekshé Jorden, Khen Rinpoché, 252, 265, 440, 522, 523, 524 (*see also* Dulwai Dé)
Lerab Lingpa, Terchen, (Tertön Sogyal), 239, 246, 266, 279, 295, 300, 318, 414, 440, 512, 513, 514, 515, 666 n. 2, 667 n. 7 (ch. 18)
Lhatsün Namkha Jigmé, 179, 293, 302, 336, **364–6**, 397, 645 n. 37
Lhazang Lama Rigdzin, **510**
Loden Choksé (form of Padmakara), 43
Longchenpa (Longchen Rabjam), 12, 13, 53, 54, 55, **75–6**, 83, 84, 97, **98–161**, 163, 164, 166, 167, 172, 173, 176, 179, 182, 183, 195, 198, 201, 202, 203, 204, 205, 206, 207, 208, 209, 210, 211, 213, 214, 215, 218, 226, 230, 241, 242, 244, 248, 251, 253, 258, 280, 285, 302, 303, 308, 310, 313, 321, 332, 334, 337, 342, 352, 354, 355, 356, 358, 359, 366, 367, 369, 375, 379, 387, 389, 394, 397, 400, 406, 421, 432, 439, 441, 444, 453, 455, 459, 473, 495, 497, 506, 521, 531, 533, 548, 550, 556, 563, 564, 566, 590, 598, 600, 601, 615 n. 7, 618 nn. 3 & 4 (Synopsis) and 8 (Supplication to the Lineage), 619 nn. 3, 6, & 7, 622 n. 3, 627 n. 67, 630 n. 36, 631 n. 11, 632 nn. 25, 28, 29, & 33, 633 nn. 43, 44, & 48, 634 nn. 56, 57, 60, & 63, 635 nn. 8 & 15, 638 n. 58, 640 n. 91, 94, 97, & 100, 641 nn. 111, 119, & 121, 642 nn. 122 & 138, 644 n. 16, 655 n. 2, 656 nn. 21 & 29 (*see also* Drimé Özer; Ngagi Wangpo; Omniscient Guru; Omniscient King of the Dharma; Omniscient One)
Longsel Dorjé Nyingpo (Longsel Nyingpo), Rigdzin, 76, 250, 261, 291, 297, 387, 426, 439, 508, 518, 519, 528, 530, 534, 535, 549, 554, 563, 628 n. 88, 650 n. 58, 669 n. 21
Lotsawa Chöpal Gyatso, 191, **384**, 389, 551, 617 n. 16, 639 n. 78, 657 nn. 8, 10, & 11 (*see also* Dharma Shri, Lochen)
Lungtok Shedrup Tenpai Nyima (Lungtrul Rinpoché), 9, 16, 27, 246, 252, **256–60**, 265, 266, 267, 280, 500, 538, 539, 540, 541, 542, 599, 647 n. 4, 669 n. 3 (ch. 20)
Lungtok Tenpai Nyima (Nyoshul Lungtok Tenpai Nyima Gyaltsen Palzangpo), 225, 227, 228, 229, 230, 238, **239–46**, 248, 249, 252, 256, 258, 262, 285, 293, 295, 302, 425, 435, 466, 483, 508, 509, 510, 511, 512, 513, 518, 522, 525, 526, 527, 529, 540, 542, 645 nn. 34 & 35, 665 n. 19

Machik Lapkyi Drönma, 100, 106, 321, 349, 630 n. 27, 644 n. 27
Maitreya (future buddha), 36, 78, 115, 439, 646 n. 53
Mandarava (Indian consort of Padmakara), 43, 67, 142, 343, 413, 649 n. 43
Mani Lochen, 343, 352 (*see also* Chönyi Zangmo; Shuksep Jetsünma)
Mani Rinchen, 53
Mañjushrimitra, **38–9**, 40, 54, 198, 199, 275, 563, 564
Marpa (Marpa Lotsawa Chökyi Lodrö), 51, 274, 300, 301, 304, 348, 629 n. 13, 648 n. 9, 659 n. 14, 666 n. 17
Melong Dorjé, **91–3**, 94
Milarepa, 217, 242, 274, 317, 321, 341, 342, 343, 348, 442, 443, 452, 479, 487, 492, 505, 523, 525, 629 n. 8, 642 n. 135, 666 n. 17, 667 n. 10 (*see also* Zhepa Dorjé)
Mingyur Namkhai Dorjé, 215, 221, 222, 224, 239, 242, 250, 306, 320, 321, 323, 324, **400–4**, 405, 406, 426, 468, 482, 513, 659 n. 16 (*see also* Dzogchen, fourth Drupwang)
Minling Terchen, 2, 310, 371, 372, 549, 615 n. 6 (*see also* Terdak Lingpa)
Minling Trichen, 265, **385–7**, 426, 551, 646 n. 60, 657 n. 12 (*see also* Kunzang Pema Wangyal)
Mipam Rinpoché (Jamgön Mipam Rinpoché; Mipam Jamyang Namgyal Gyatso; Mipam Jampal Gyepai Dorjé; Mipam Choklé Namgyal), 13, 51, 58, 227, 228, 243, 249, 261, 266, 279, 281, 284, 285, 293, 298, 307, 308, 311, 313, 325, 402, 410, 414, **415–5**, 427, 436, 437, 439, 440, 442, 447, 448, 462, 468, 470, 473, 474, 476, 478, 479, 483, 497, 512, 514,

523, 530, 533, 537, 541, 552, 625 n. 39, 660 nn. 22, 23, 25, 661, n. 29, 665 n. 19
Muné Tsenpo, 82, 622 nn. 1 & 8, 625 n. 38, 629 n. 7
Munsel, Golok Khenchen, 9, 252, 519, **524–6**, 527, 540, 543
Mutik Tsenpo, 57, 625 n. 38

Naktar Tulku, 245, 246, **509–10**
Namchö Mingyur Dorjé, 268, 554, 646 nn. 55 & 63
Namdrol, Khenchen, 476, 503, 664 n. 14
Namkha Dorjé, **361**, 362
Natsok Rangdrol, Tulku, **172–4**, 175, 176, 369, 370
Ngagi Wangpo, 118, 145, 183, 201, 358 (*see also* Longchenpa)
Ngagi Wangpo, Khenchen, 27, 239, 246, 247, 253, 257, 258, 260, 261, 265, 440, 524, 531 (*see also* Ngawang Palzang)
Ngari Panchen Pema Wangyal, 13, 439, 548, 550, 617 n. 15
Ngawang Palzang, Nyoshul Khenchen, 9, 16, 158, 244, 245, 246, **247–56**, 260, 262, 263, 280, 286, 299, 302, 318, 438, 442, 463, 473, 478, 506, 508, 513, 517, 518, 519, 520, 522, 523, 524, 525, 526, 527, 529, 535, 536, 537, 538, 539, 540, 541, 554, 599, 665 n. 19, 668 n. 20 (*see also* Pema Ledrel Tsal)
Ngawang Palzang Yangsi, **539–40**
Ngawang Pema, Kunchen, **362–3**, 655 n. 6
Ngedön Tendzin Zangpo, 215, 320, 396, 658 n. 8 (*see also* Dzogchen, third Drupwang)
Ngenlam Jangchub Gyaltsen, **51**
Ngöndzok Gyalpo (one of the twelve teachers), 35
Nüden Khyentsei Lodrö, Khenchen, 438, 522, **523**, 667 n. 10
Nupchen Sang-gyé Yeshé, 51, 53, 54, 251, 266, 302, 383, 435, 617 n. 13, 623 n. 13
Nyak Jñanakumara, 51, 57, 82, 314, 617 n. 13, 623 n. 9, 668 n. 3 (ch. 22)
Nyang Tingdzin Zangpo, 57, 78, **82–3**, 84, 202, 203
Nyang-ral Nyima Özer, 74, 76, 278, 307, 548, 627 n. 68, 628 n. 87, 656 n. 16, 665 n. 21
Nyarong Guru, 497, **501–2**
Nyima Gyaltsen, Choktrul, **540–1**
Nyima Özer (form of Padmakara), 44
Nyoshul Khenchen Ngawang Palzang, **504**

Oddiyana, Khenchen, 193, 280, **381–2**
Omniscient Guru, 96, 145, 146, 147, 148, 149, 151, 152, 155, 163, 201, 203, 212, 218, 230, 231, 232, 233, 234, 235, 237, 254, 258, 590, 596, 600, 630 n. 36, 634 n. 64 (*see also* Longchenpa)
Omniscient King of the Dharma, 54, 75, 98, 118, 145, 164, 167, 168, 170, 172, 173, 175, 176, 183, 201, 203, 230, 253, 258, 280, 302, 355, 357, 358, 366, 369, 378, 379, 387, 402, 453, 495, 550, 563, 566 (*see also* Longchenpa)
Omniscient One, 2, 3, 8, 12, 14, 19, 54, 83, 84, 105, 118, 152, 153, 154, 155, 161, 162, 163, 164, 165, 166, 167, 182, 183, 198, 201, 203, 211, 213, 214, 218, 226, 237, 238, 241, 242, 244, 248, 253, 258, 285, 302, 303, 313, 321, 342, 352, 354, 355, 356, 357, 358, 359, 360, 364, 365, 366, 367, 368, 371, 379, 394, 396, 400, 422, 428, 441, 459, 468, 473, 475, 482, 494, 495, 496, 502, 506, 521, 524, 531, 532, 545, 548, 551, 556, 560, 598, 615 n. 7, 619 n. 7, 644 n. 26 (*see also* Longchenpa)
Orgyen Chemchok, 252, 513, **527–8**, 667 n. 14
Orgyen Chödrak, 191, 192, **194–6**, 197, 308, 639 n. 87
Orgyen Chöjé, 158, **354–5**, 357, 655 n. 2
Orgyen Palgön, Ngakyi Rabjampa, **196–7**, 213
Orgyen Rangjung Dorjé Tsewang Drupa Tsal, 426 (see also Gyaltsap, third Zhechen)
Orgyen Rigdzin, Lama Rinpoché, 252, 257, 286, **536–8**, 539
Orgyen Rinpoché (name of Padmakara), 115, 367, 395, 411, 431, 439
Orgyen Tendzin Norbu, 227, 228, 402, 469, 475, 478, **482–6**, 487, 492, 493, 494, 495, 496, 509, 644 n. 17, 664 n. 1, 665 n. 20
Orgyenpa, Drupchen 73, 94, 274, 627 n. 77, 659 n. 14
Ösel Longyang, **361–2**
Ösel Rangdrol, Guru, 131, 158, 167, **355–7**

Padmakara, 11, **41–8**, 49, 52, 55, 56, 61, 62, 69, 70, 112, 188, 195, 208, 216, 222, 251, 273, 277, 282, 290, 312, 329, 367, 368, 388, 401, 405, 406, 437, 451, 486, 490, 547, 562, 563, 564, 599, 615 nn. 2, 4, & 5, 618 n. 3, 620 nn. 10 & 11 (ch. 2), 623 n. 13, 625 nn. 36 & 46, 626 nn. 52 & 63, 627 n. 66, 628 n. 2, 632 n. 27, 636 n. 17, 637 n. 45, 638 n. 66, 640 n. 93, 642 n. 126, 648 nn. 17, 22, & 32, 649 nn. 41 & 43, 652 n. 90, 653 n. 26, 659 n. 9, 662 n. 62, 666 n. 22, 667 n. 5 (ch. 18) (*see also* Guru Rinpoché)
Palchen Düpa, **260–3**, 517, 555 (*see also* Penor Rinpoché, second)
Paltrul Rinpoché (Dza Paltrul Orgyen Jigmé Chökyi Wangpo), 9, 12, 13, 145, 215, 220, 221, **223–38**, 239, 240, 241, 242, 244, 246,

248, 251, 262, 266, 271, 272, 293, 295, 302, 310, 311, 323, 324, 334, 338, 342, 348, 399, 401, 402, 405, 409, 410, 416, 418, 420, 421, 429, 462, 465, 466, 467, 468, 469, 470, 471, 472, 476, 478, 479, 480, 482, 484, 486, 487, 493, 496, 508, 509, 530, 543, 544, 618 n. 6 (Supplication to the Lineage), 634 n. 65, 638 n. 74, 642 n. 1, 643 n. 7, 644 nn. 29 & 32, 659 n. 16, 665 nn. 17 & 18

Pang Sang-gyé Gönpo (Pang Mipam Gönpo), **51**, 475, 538

Pawo Tsuklak Gyatso, 179, 371, 637 n. 49

Pema Dorjé (Pema Badzra), Khenchen 221, 227, 239, 246, 280, 293, 325, 402, 417, 427, 429, 430, **467–8**, 483, 495, 551, 552

Pema Gyalpo (form of Padmakara), 44, 113, 274

Pema Gyaltsen, Choktrul, **514–15**, 530

Pema Gyurmé Gyatso, Riksé Choktrul, 189, 190, **384–5**, 389, 639, 658

Pema Ledrel Tsal, **70–3**, 74, 129, 145, 204, 627 n. 67 & 69, 632 n. 33

Pema Ledrel Tsal (secret name of Khenchen Ngawang Palzang) 251, 533, 632, 668 n. 20 (*see also* Ngawang Palzang, Khenchen)

Pema Lingpa, Terchen (first Pema Lingpa), 173, 174, 175, 176, 285, 287, 338, 361, 362, **367–8**, 369, 370, 373, 374, 375, 376, 377–8, 379, 532, 632 nn. 25 & 26, 656 nn. 16, 21, 22, 26, 657 nn. 38, & 39, 669 n. 7 (ch. 22)

Pema Lingpa, eighth, **375–6**

Pema Lingpa, eleventh, **377–8**, 657 n. 41

Pema Lingpa, fifth, **372–3**

Pema Lingpa, fourth, **371–2**, 389

Pema Lingpa, ninth, **376**

Pema Lingpa, second, **368–70**, 657 (*see also* Tendzin Chökyi Drakpa; Tendzin Drakpa, Tulku)

Pema Lingpa, seventh, **374–5**

Pema Lingpa, sixth, **373–4**

Pema Lingpa, tenth, **376–7**

Pema Lingpa, third, **370–1**, 378 (*see also* Tsultrim Dorjé, Kunchen)

Pema Namgyal (Gyurmé Pema Namgyal), 279, 297, 307, **426–8**, 440, 552 (*see also* Gyaltsap, fourth Zhechen)

Pema Nyinjé Wangpo, 411, 432 (*see also* Tai Situ, ninth)

Pema Rigdzin, 366, 387, 388, 396, 551, 552, 645 n. 38, 656 nn. 14 & 15, 664 n. 10, 669 n. 13 (*see also* Dzogchen, first Drupwang)

Pema Tötreng Tsal (form of Padmakara), 43

Pema Trinlé (grandson of Pema Lingpa), 176, 371, 378, 549, 550, 657 nn. 38 & 39

Pema Tumpo (Orgyen Kusum Lingpa), **527**

Pema Wangchok Gyalpo, 300, 305, 497, 498, **500** (*see also* Tai Situ, eleventh)

Penor Rinpoché, first, 261, 646 n. 55

Penor Rinpoché, second, **261–3**, 264, 438, 440, 555

Penor Rinpoché, third, 9, **265–9**, 464, 476, 539, 542, 543, 664 n. 14

Polu Khenchen Dorjé, 435, 480, **530–2**, 533, 539

Pönlop Jigmé Chöying Ösel, fourth Dzogchen, 403, 429

Pönlop Karma Sungrap Ngedon Tenpa Gyaltsen, seventh Dzogchen, 661 n. 40

Pönlop Namkhai Ösel, first Dzogchen, 388, 389, 431, 658 n. 18

Pönlop Namkha Chökyi Gyatso, third Dzogchen, 321, 403

Pönlop Pema Sang-ngak Tendzin, second Dzogchen, 390, 396, 402

Prabhahasti, 43

Rabjam, fifth Zhechen, 227, 247, 424, 427

Rabjam, first Zhechen, 388, 552, 669 n. 16

Rabjam, fourth Zhechen, 403

Rabjam, second Zhechen, 299, 319, 390, 552, 650 n. 64

Rabjam, seventh Zhechen, 315, 464, 552, 664 n. 10 (ch. 15)

Rabjam, sixth Zhechen, 305, 377, 428, 462, 532

Rabjam, third Zhechen, 321, 400, 402

Rabsel Dawa, 76, 296, 306, 308 (*see also* Dilgo Khyentsé, Kyabjé; Tashi Paljor)

Rahor Khenpo Tupten, 479, **481**

Rahor Palden Chökyi Drakpa (Rahor Chödrak), 497, **504–6**

Rakor Khen Drimé Özer, **459–60**, 536

Rangjung Dorjé, 71, 75, 94, 95, 101, 166, 302, 627 nn. 73 & 77, 635 n. 13, 651 n. 73 (*see also* Karmapa, third, Gyalwang)

Rangjung Rigpai Dorjé, 533, 652 n. 95, 661 n. 47 (*see also* Karmapa, sixteenth Gyalwang)

Ratna Lingpa, 169, 171, 172, 225, 261, 264, 265, 266, 267, 268, 269, 283, 291, 299, 300, 301, 307, 397, 542, 554, 636 n. 18

Rigdzin Gödem, 76, 488, 548, 550, 628 n. 87, 650 n. 52, 665 n. 3

Rongzom Mahapandita Chökyi Zangpo, 13, 53, 54, 195, 266, 308, 334, 406, 421, 439, 450, 483, 497, 549, 617 n. 14

Sakya Pandita, 210, 302, 419, 497, 499, 641 n. 115, 647 n. 3, 651 n. 71

Saraha, 44, 74, 101, 211, 293, 314, 323, 398, 405, 443, 458, 628 n. 82, 641 n. 120

Seng-gé Dradrok (form of Padmakara), 44

Sengtruk Pema Tashi, 225, 381, 405, 406
Ser-ö Dampa (one of the twelve teachers), 35
Serkha Chödrak, Tuksé, 497, **504**
Shakyadevi (Nepalese consort of Padmakara), 44
Shakya Seng-gé (form of Padmakara), 43
Shakya Shri, Drupwang, 167, 393, 424, 442, 443, 444, 445
Shakyamuni, Buddha (one of the twelve teachers), 35, 78, 115, 139, 304, 336, 388, 391, 439, 491, 564
Shantarakshita (form of Padmakara), 42
Shantarakshita (Indian abbot), 55, 56, 239, 262, 273, 312, 336, 352, 381, 401, 405, 406, 413, 437, 547, 615 n. 2, 624 n. 33, 652 n. 90, 659 nn. 18 & 19
Shantideva, 101, 223, 227, 474, 553, 642 n. 1, 664 n. 11
Shenpen Dawa, 288, 464, 649 n. 44
Shri Simha, **39–40**, 41, 46, 47, 48, 49, 50, 61, 406, 452, 562, 563, 564
Shuksep Jetsünma, 343, 352 (*see also* Chönyi Zangmo; Mani Lochen)
Sogyal Rinpoché, 288, 305, **462–3**, 514, 664 n. 6, 667 n. 16
Sungtrul Kunzang Nyima, 492, 514, **515–16**

Tai Situ, eighth (Karma Kagyü), 643 n. 10, 666 n. 18
Tai Situ, eleventh (Karma Kagyü), 414, 488, 499, 650 n. 65 (*see also* Pema Wangchok Gyalpo)
Tai Situ, ninth (Pema Nyinjé Wangpo), 411, 442, 659 n. 6
Tai Situ, tenth (Karma Kagyü), 414, 660 n. 14
Tai Situ Jangchub Gyaltsen (Pakmodrupa ruler), 117, 118, 633 n. 43, 635 n. 15
Taklung Tsetrul, 288, **532–3**, 550
Takok Jadral Chöjé Tashi Jungné, 158, 359, **360–1**, 655 n. 5
Tangtong Gyalpo, 274, 275, 302, 325, 361, 398
Tashi Cheu Dren (Bhutanese consort of Padmakara), 65, 626 n. 62
Tashi Paljor, 307 (*see also* Dilgo Khyentsé, Kyabjé; Rabsel Dawa)
Tekchok Dorjé, 661 n. 43 (*see also* Karmapa, fourteenth Gyalwang)
Tendzin Chökyi Drakpa, **368–70**, 378, 657 n. 38 (*see also* Pema Lingpa, second; Tendzin Drakpa, Tulku)
Tendzin Drakpa, Tulku, **174–6**, 378 (*see also* Pema Lingpa, second; Tendzin Chökyi Drakpa)
Terdak Lingpa, 2, 11, 16, 158, **181–91**, 196, 280, 285, 287, 366, 370, 374, 375, 380, 383, 384, 387, 388, 390, 426, 450, 550, 598, 615 n. 6, 617 n. 16, 638 n. 69, 639 n. 87, 644 n. 28, 649 n. 38, 656 n. 31, 657 nn. 2, 10, & 11
Tersé Chimé, **534–6**
Thinley Norbu, 288, 305, 464
Trakya Lama Rinpoché Palden, **528–30**
Trehorpa Kyabgön Yeshé Gyaltsen, **350–1**, 352
Trinlé Chödrön, Jetsünma, 270, 280, **382–3**
Trinlé Lhundrup, Sangdak Rigdzin Chenpo, 177, **178–81**, 365, 366, 370, 637 n. 46
Trisong Detsen, 49, 55, 56, **57–61**, 70, 78, 191, 199, 251, 273, 312, 336, 395, 401, 406, 413, 431, 433, 437, 547, 556, 615 nn. 2 & 3, 621 n. 1, 622 n. 8, 623 n. 12, 624 nn. 30 & 31, 625 nn. 36, 38, & 40, 626 n. 61, 629 nn. 5, 6, & 7, 632 n. 36, 640 n. 97, 648 n. 14, 652 nn. 90 (ch. 8) & 5 (ch. 9), 653 n. 32, 656 n. 16, 661 n. 44, 666 n. 22
Tropu Lotsawa, 74, 89, 102, 628 n. 80
Trulzhik Seng-gé Gyappa, **90–1**, 92, 630 n. 26
Trulzhik Sang-gyé Önpo Sherab Gyatso, 158, **165–8**, 196, 355, 357, 360, 655 n. 4
Tsangtön Dorjé Gyaltsen, 548, 553, 623 n. 19
Tsewai Rolpai Lodrö (one of the twelve teachers), 35
Tsö Paltrul, 229, 450, **456–7**
Tsöndrü, Khenchen, **503**
Tsongkhapa, 251, 292, 302, 309, 310, 340, 642 n. 130, 643 nn. 14 & 15, 650 n. 51, 654 n. 34
Tsultrim Dorjé, (Sungtrul) Kunchen, 170, 179, **370–1**, 376, 378, 637 n. 50 (*see also* Pema Lingpa, third)
Tulku Paljor Gyaltsen, **357**
Tupten Chökyi Dorjé, 244, 265, 295, 296, 327, 348, **428–31**, 462, 473, 478, 479, 488, 495 (*see also* Dzogchen, fifth Drupwang)
Tupten Gyaltsen Özer, 249, 299, 440, **508–9** (*see also* Dorjé Dzinpa Tobden, Khen)
Tupten Gyaltsen Özer, Khenchen Yizhin Norbu, **523–4**, 667 n. 11
Tupten Trinlé Palzang, 310 (*see also* Dodrupchen, fourth; Jigmé Trinlé Palbar)
twelve teachers, **32–6**, 253, 321

Urgyen Tulku, **435**

Vairochana, 410, 616 n. 2, 641 n. 119
Vajradhara (one of the twelve teachers), 33, 34
Vajrapani, 33, 54
Vajrasattva, 33, 37, 38, 40
Vimalamitra, 11, **40–1**, 49, 55, 57, 74, **78–82**, 83, 85, 87, 92, 96, 103, 104, 107, 108, 109, 111, 113, 158, 188, 191, 242, 244, 245, 246, 248, 251, 253, 261, 275, 279, 280, 286, 295, 296, 297, 302, 303, 312, 314, 318, 333, 364, 382, 405, 428, 432, 442, 448, 478, 504, 520, 525, 531, 535, 537, 562, 563, 564, 598, 599, 618 n. 3 (Synopsis), 622 n. 9, 627 n. 73, 628 n. 2, 632 n. 28, 636 n. 17, 648 n. 22, 651 n. 73

Virupa, 44, 46, 273, 393, 658 n. 5

Wangchuk Dorjé, 637 nn. 42 & 49 (*see also* Karmapa, ninth Gyalwang)

Yeshé Dorjé, 215, 221, 224, 225, 230, 321, 323, 324, **395–9**, 448, 544, 643 n. 7, 658 n. 8 (*see also* Do Khyentsé)
Yeshé Tsogyal, 56, 57, **61–70**, 111, 112, 188, 249, 275, 310, 332, 350, 380, 393, 413, 446, 514, 553, 625 n. 36, 659 n. 8
Yönten Gyatso, Gemang Khenchen, 9, 226, 227, 295, 310, 428, **469–71**, 472, 473, 475, 476, 666 n. 12
Yudra Nyingpo, 50, 52, 54, 82, 318, 381, 384, 549, 622 n. 9
Yukhok Jadralwa, **316–18**, 328, 330, 333, 338, 450, 459, 461, 480, 482, 643 n. 5, 665 n. 17

Zadam Rinchenyik, **51–2**
Zhabkar Tsokdruk Rangdrol, 224, **339–42**, 343, 347, 654 n. 52
Zhadeu Trulzhik, 9, 288, 315, 350, **352–3**, 655 n. 57
Zhang Yeshé Dé, 55, 647 n. 3
Zhechen Kongtrul (Pema Drimé Lekpai Lodrö), 299, 334, 503, 553, 652 n. 89
Zhenga Dorjé Chang, Khenchen, 250, 308, 430, 488, **492–9**, 500, 501, 502, 504, 505, 506, 507, 659 n. 22 (*see also* Zhenpen Chökyi Nangwa)
Zhenpen Chökyi Nangwa, Khenchen, 13, 303, 402, 406, 439, 486, **492–9**, 507, 551 (*see also* Zhenga Dorjé Chang)
Zhepa Dorjé (Milarepa's secret name), 321, 443, 452, 498, 667 n. 10 (*see also* Milarepa)
Zhönnu Pawo Tobden Chenpo (one of the twelve teachers), 34
Zhönnu Rolpa Nampar Tsewa (one of the twelve teachers), 34
Zurchen Shakya Jungné, 13, 53, 548, 617 n. 13, 624 n. 27, 664 n. 4
Zurmang Khenchen Pema Namgyal, 497, **500**
Zurmang Tenga, 500, **501**
Zurmang Trungpa (Chögyam Trungpa), **455**, 553, 663 n. 6, 666 n. 20

TITLES

(Since many of the texts cited in this volume are familiar to Western readers by their short Sanskrit or Tibetan titles, the phoneticized versions of these titles have been included here.)

Accomplishment of Life Force by Masters of Awareness (Tib. *Rigdzin Sokdrup*), 293, 300, 321
Adornment Through Direct Introduction (Tib. *Ngotrö Traypa*) (one of seventeen tantras of the Category of Direct Transmission), 47, 255, 562
All-Creating Monarch (Tib. *Kunjé Gyalpo*) (one of three general tantras of the Category of Mind), 14, 54, 142, 155, 166, 486, 560, 570, 617 n. 20
All-Embracing Awareness (Tib. *Kundü Rigpa*) (one of the eighteen major tantras of the Category of Mind), 559, 622 n. 9
Amassing of the Rare and Sublime (Skt. *Ratnakuta*), 56
Application of Mindfulness (Tib. *Drenpa Nyerzhak*), 219
Array of Inlaid Gems (Tib. *Norbu Trakö*) (one of seventeen tantras of the Category of Direct Transmission), 47, 255, 562
Ascertaining the Three Levels of Ordination (Tib. *Dom-sum Nam-ngé*), 225, 284, 298, 308, 310, 381, 384, 402, 416, 468, 470, 473, 484, 485, 494, 495, 617 n. 15
Aspiration Prayer of Noble Conduct (Tib. *Zangchö Mönlam*), 293, 510
Aspiration Prayer of Sutra and Tantra (Tib. *Dongak Mönlam*), 402, 484
Auspicious Beauty (Tib. *Tashi Dzéden*) (one of seventeen tantras of the Category of Direct Transmission), 48, 255, 562

Being at Ease in Illusoriness (Tib. *Gyuma Ngalso*), 142, 240
Being at Ease in Meditative Stability (Tib. *Samten Ngalso*), 142
Being at Ease in the Nature of Mind (Tib. *Semnyi Ngalso*), 141, 179, 182, 228, 483, 485, 487, 494, 509, 532, 601
Biographies of One Hundred Tertöns (Tib. *Tertön Gyatsa*), 77
Black Innermost Heart Drop (Tib. *Yangti Nakpo*), 76, 350, 353, 533
Blazing Clear Expanse (Tib. *Longsel Barwa*), 28, 562
Blazing Lamp (Tib. *Drönma Barwa*) (one of seventeen tantras of the Category of Direct Transmission), 47, 255, 562
Blazing Remains (Tib. *Kudung Barwa*) (one of

seventeen tantras of the Category of Direct Transmission), 47, 255, 562
Blissful Array of Inset Jewels (Tib. *Dewa Trakö*) (one of the eighteen major tantras of the Category of Mind), 559, 622 n. 9
Buddha Skull Cup (Skt. *Buddha Kapala*), 101

Casket of Enlightened Mind: A Record of Key Points (Tib. *Nejang Tuk-kyi Drombu*) (prophecy concerning *The Heart Drop of Longchenpa*), 200
Chakrasamvara Tantra, 74, 251, 271
Classification of the Levels of Realization (Skt. *Yogacharya-bhumi*), 484
Collected Tantras of the Nyingma School (Tib. *Nyingma Gyübum*), 93, 101, 214, 215, 264, 271, 285, 287, 298, 304, 310, 313, 372, 375, 389, 441, 447, 483, 533, 639 n. 86
Collected Teachings on the Mani Mantra (Tib. *Mani Kanbum*), 225, 533
Compendium of Abhidharma (Skt. *Abhidharma-samuchaya*), 496
Compendium of All Classes of Tantra (Tib. *Gyüdé Kuntü*), 298, 299
Compendium of All Sadhanas (Tib. *Druptap Kuntü*), 293, 294, 299, 301, 304, 309, 311
Compendium (of the Perfection of Sublime Knowing) (Skt. *Prajñaparamita-sañchaya-gatha*), 81, 275, 294, 417, 484, 496
Compendium of Training (Skt. *Shiksha-samuchaya*), 101, 484
Compendium of Valid Cognition (Skt. *Pramana-samuchaya*), 100
Concise Kalachakra Tantra, 307
Conjunction of Sun and Moon (Tib. *Nyida Khajor*) (one of seventeen tantras of the Category of Direct Transmission), 28, 47, 255, 562, 563
Converging of the Streams of Lungtok Tenpai Nyima's Oral Lineage (Tib. *Lungtok Tenpai Nyimai Nyen-gyü Chuwo Chü-dü*), 537

Discourse on United Intent (Tib. *Düpa Do*) (primary source of Anuyoga), 52, 101, 182, 186, 188, 191, 214, 261, 265, 266, 268, 269, 291, 297, 304, 325, 372, 377, 384, 385, 389, 390, 391, 425, 439, 465, 468, 471, 523, 550, 553
Dispelling the Darkness of Ignorance (Tib. *Marik Munsel*), 137
Dispelling Darkness in the Mind (Tib. *Yichi Munsel*), 137
Dispelling Darkness in the Ten Directions (Tib. *Chokchui Munsel*), 136, 226, 308, 397, 470, 473
Dispelling Flaws in Interdependence (Tib. *Tendrel Nyesel*), 266, 300, 514
Distinction Between Center and Limit (Skt. *Madhyanta-vibhanga*), 473, 494, 650 n. 62
Distinction Between Phenomena and Their True Nature (Tib. *Dharma-dharmata-vibhanga*), 473, 494, 650 n. 62

Encompassing the Knowable (Tib. *Shéja Dzö*), 309
Engaging in the Conduct of a Bodhisattva (Skt. *Bodhicharyavatara*), 101, 168, 225, 227, 228, 240, 243, 284, 291, 293, 298, 308, 324, 329, 416, 418, 420, 466, 467, 468, 473, 477, 478, 484, 485, 493, 495, 496, 509, 511, 532, 533, 536, 538, 664 n. 11, 672 n. 27
Entrance into the Middle Way (Tib. *Madhayamakavatara*), 13, 308, 417, 483, 485, 494, 495, 496, 537
Entrance to the Ways of the Wise (Tib. *Khénjuk*), 298, 523, 541

Five Great Treasuries (Tib. *Dzöchen Nga*), 263, 313, 334, 412
Five Principles of Mahamudra (Tib. *Chakchen Ngaden*), 485, 494, 628 n. 80
Five Treatises of Maitreya (Tib. *Jamchö Dé-nga*), 100, 135, 308, 372, 495, 496, 509, 530, 650 n. 62
Flight of the Garuda (Tib. *Khading Shoklap*), 341, 342, 348, 353
Fortunate Eon (Skt. *Bhadrakalpika-sutra*; Tib. *Dodé Kalzang*), 245, 510
Four Higher Collections of the Heart Drop (Tib. *Nyingtik Yabzhi*), 2, 12, 14, 15, 173, 179, 213, 241, 242, 248, 257, 258, 266, 269, 270, 285, 293, 295, 297, 304, 308, 309, 311, 338, 361, 362, 366, 386, 396, 402, 456, 473, 475, 481, 482, 484, 518, 524, 525, 531, 533, 536, 541, 596, 644 n. 16
Four Hundred Verses (Skt. *Catuh-shataka*; Tib. *Zhi-gya-pa*), 308, 473, 495, 496
Four Means of Resting (Tib. *Zhaktap Zhipa*) (testament of Jñanasutra), 41
Fundamental Discourse of the Vinaya (Skt. *Vinaya-sutra*), 298, 402, 419, 420, 485, 494, 495, 537

Garland of Views (Tib. *Men-ngak Tatreng*), 56, 195, 326, 563
General Definition of Perfection (Tib. *Dzogpa Chi-chö*) (one of the eighteen major tantras of the Category of Mind), 560, 622 n. 9
General Scope of Perfection (Tib. *Dzogpa Chiching*) (one of the eighteen major tantras of the Category of Mind), 560, 622 n. 9

General Union of All That Is Rare and Sublime (Tib. *Könchok Chidü*), 299, 306
General Yoga (Tib. *chiti yoga*), 76, 562
Graduated Path of Secret Mantra (Tib. *Sang-ngak Lam-rim*), 56, 195, 563
Guhyasamaja Tantra, 74, 101, 251, 271, 310

Harbinger of Awareness (Tib. *Rigpa Khujuk*) (one of the eighteen major tantras of the Category of Mind), 559, 622 n. 7
Heaped Jewels (Tib. *Rinchen Pungpa*) (one of seventeen tantras of the Category of Direct Transmission), 47, 255, 562
Heart Drop of Bairotsana (Tib. *Bairo Nyingtik*), 50, 277, 278
Heart Drop of Chetsün (Tib. *Chetsün Nyingtik*), 226, 278, 300, 442, 444, 450, 456, 457, 475
Heart Drop of the Dakini (Tib. *Khandro Nyingtik*), 47, 69, 71, 72, 73, 74, 75, 106, 108, 113, 117, 130, 144, 155, 163, 169, 172, 204, 239, 249, 251, 281, 286, 290, 294, 299, 372, 387, 389, 390, 391, 551, 552, 563, 618 n. 3, 632 n. 33, 636 n. 17
Heart Drop of Longchenpa (Tib. *Longchen Nyingtik*), 12, 213, 220, 221, 224, 225, 228, 229, 248, 258, 259, 263, 266, 269, 278, 293, 300, 301, 303, 304, 306, 308, 309, 311, 330, 331, 332, 337, 338, 377, 482, 483, 485, 500, 518, 524, 541, 619 n. 7, 642 nn. 128 & 137, 643 n. 2, 644 n. 16
Heart Drop of Melong (Tib. *Melong Nyingtik*), 93
Heart Drop of Vimalamitra (Tib. *Bima Nyingtik*), 36, 41, 144, 563, 618 n. 3 (Synopsis), 636 n. 17
Heart Essence of Secrets (Skt. *Guhyagarbha Tantra;* Tib. *Gyü Sangwai Nyingpo*), 73, 137, 182, 191, 193, 195, 196, 197, 213, 224, 225, 226, 240, 241, 257, 263, 266, 271, 284, 285, 298, 300, 304, 308, 314, 326, 331, 337, 352, 372, 384, 385, 386, 397, 402, 407, 425, 441, 459, 465, 468, 470, 471, 473, 475, 477, 481, 484, 485, 494, 495, 496, 505, 509, 514, 518, 525, 533, 541, 649 n. 38 (*see also Web of Magical Display*)
Heart of Sublime Knowing (Skt. *Prajñaparamita Hridaya Sutra,* "Heart Sutra"), 101
Hevajra Tantra, 44, 45, 271, 298, 309, 629 n. 15 (*see also Two Chapters*)
Highest Continuum (Skt. *Uttaratantra;* Tib. *Gyü Lama*), 13, 179, 182, 225, 240, 298, 304, 484, 485, 494, 509, 630 n. 62
Holding Buddhahood in One's Hand (Tib. *Sanggyé Lakchang*) (from the *Namchö* cycle), 264, 265, 267, 268, 291
Holy Golden Light (Skt. *Suvarna-prabha-sutra*), 245

Immense Bliss (Tib. *Dewa Rabjam*) (one of the eighteen major tantras of the Category of Mind), 560, 622 n.9
Immense Display (Skt. *Lalitavistara*), 495
Individual Liberation (Skt. *Pratimoksha*), 402, 426, 473, 495
Innermost Heart Drop of the Dakini (Tib. *Khandro Yangtik*), 5, 113, 130, 144, 239, 249, 299, 551, 552, 618 n. 3 (Synopsis), 636 n. 20, 640 n. 107
Innermost Heart Drop (of the Guru): The Wish-Fulfilling Gem (Tib. *Lama [Yizhin Norbu] Yangtik*), 7, 130, 144, 228, 266, 269, 293, 300, 433, 457, 475, 487, 563, 618 n. 3 (Synopsis), 636 n. 20, 640 n. 107
Innermost Heart Drop of Profundity (Tib. *Zabmo Yangtik*), 144, 269, 618 n. 3 (Synopsis), 636 n. 20, 640 n. 107
Innermost Yoga (Tib. *yangti yoga*), 76, 562

Jewel Ornament of Liberation (Tib. *Dakpoi Tarjen*), 310
Journey to Shri Lanka (Skt. *Lankavatara Sutra*), 410, 495

Kalachakra Tantra, 75, 99, 101, 206, 271, 274, 484, 633 n. 47, 635 n. 13, 640 n. 99, 663 n. 1
Kangyur, 172, 178, 182, 189, 192, 239, 257, 261, 264, 266, 271, 285, 287, 288, 294, 306, 309, 311, 325, 334, 353, 374, 375, 389, 390, 391, 402, 406, 411, 419, 437, 441, 446, 447, 448, 455, 467, 473, 475, 483, 484, 495, 496, 501, 533, 538, 539, 541, 635 n. 13, 636 n. 23
Key to the Treasury (Tib. *Dzö-kyi Dé-mik*), 326

Lamp of Certain Meaning (Tib. *Ngéshé Drönmé*), 266, 523
Lamp on the Path to Enlightenment (Skt. *Bodhipatha-pradipa*), 301

Mahamaya Tantra, 101
Meaningful Meditation (Tib. *Gompa Döndrup*) (one of the eighteen major tantras of the Category of Mind), 560, 622 n. 9
Minute Scrutiny (Skt. *Vaidalya-sutra*) (one of Nagarjuna's *Six Collections of Reasoning*), 100
Mirror of Poetics (Skt. *Kavyadarsha*), 100, 308
Monarch of Space (*Namkhai Gyalpo*) (one of the eighteen major tantras of the Category of Mind), 559, 622 n. 9

Most Majestic State of Meditative Absorption (Skt. *Samadhi-raja-sutra*), 100

Namchö cycle, 76, 261, 264, 265, 267, 268, 269, 291, 299, 309, 542, 554, 555, 563, 646 nn. 55 & 63
Natural Freedom of Awareness (Tib. *Rigpa Rangdrol*) (one of seventeen tantras of the Category of Direct Transmission), 47, 255, 562
Natural Freedom of Equalness (Tib. *Nyamnyi Rangdrol*), 54, 142
Natural Freedom of the Nature of Mind (Tib. *Semnyi Rangdrol*), 54, 142
Natural Freedom of the Nature of Phenomena (Tib. *Chönyi Rangdrol*), 54, 142
Naturally Arising Awareness (Tib. *Rigpa Rangshar*) (one of seventeen tantras of the Category of Direct Transmission), 47, 255, 562, 585
Naturally Occurring Perfection (Tib. *Dzogpa Rangjung*) (one of seventeen tantras of the Category of Direct Transmission), 47, 255, 562
Northern Terma (Tib. *Jangter*), 292, 294, 299, 300, 301, 321, 334, 533, 550

Oral Transmission of the Guru Samantabhadra (Tib. *Kunzang Lamai Zhal-lung* [*The Words of My Perfect Teacher*]), 221, 293, 294, 457, 473
Oral Transmission of the Lord of Secrets (Tib. *Sangdak Zhal-lung*), 196, 308, 384
Ornament of Higher Realization (Skt. *Abhisamayalamkara*), 135, 225, 485, 650 n. 62
Ornament of the Middle Way (Skt. *Madhyamakalamkara*), 266, 298, 473, 533, 537
Ornament of the Sutras (Skt. *Mahayana-sutralamkara*), 225, 240, 484, 485, 494, 537, 650 n. 62

Parting from the Four Attachments (Tib. *Zhenpa Zhidral*), 485, 494
Pearl Garland (Tib. *Mutik Trengwa*) (one of seventeen tantras of the Category of Direct Transmission), 47, 255, 562, 563
Perfect Dynamic Energy of the Lion (Tib. *Seng-gé Tsal-dzok*) (one of seventeen tantras of the Category of Direct Transmission), 48, 255, 562
Perfection of Sublime Knowing in Eight Thousand Verses (Skt. *Ashta-sahasrika-prajñaparamita*), 91, 99
Perfection of Sublime Knowing in One Hundred Thousand Verses (Skt. *Shata-sahasrika-prajñaparamita*), 335, 390, 465
Perfection of Sublime Knowing in Ten Thousand Verses (Skt. *Dasha-sahasrika-prajñaparamita*), 101
Perfection of Sublime Knowing in Twenty Thousand Verses (Skt. *Pañcha-vimshati-sahasrika-prajñaparamita*), 99
Pinnacle State Victorious Under All Circumstances (Tib. *Tsemo Jungyal*) (one of the eighteen major tantras of the Category of Mind), 559, 622 n. 9
Praise of the Basic Space of Phenomena (Skt. *Dharma-dhatu-stotra*), 100

Refining Gold from Ore (Tib. *Dola Ser-zhun*) (one of the eighteen major tantras of the Category of Mind), 54, 559, 563, 622 n. 7
Refutation of Arguments (Skt. *Vigrahavya-vartani*), 100
Reverberation of Sound (Tib. *Dra Talgyur*) (one of seventeen tantras of the Category of Direct Transmission), 12, 33, 47, 88, 104, 204, 255, 380, 562, 563

Sacred and Venerable One (Tib. *Jetsün Dampa*) (one of the eighteen major tantras of the Category of Mind), 560, 622 n. 9
Samantabhadra: Mirror of Enlightened Mind (Tib. *Kuntu Zangpo Thuk-kyi Melong*) (one of seventeen tantras of the Category of Direct Transmission), 48, 255, 562
Seven-Line Supplication (Tib. *Tsikdun Soldep*), 266, 328, 414, 448, 489
Seven Linking Principles (Tib. *Zerbu Dunpa*) (testament of Shri Simha), 41
Seven Treasuries (Tib. *Dzö Dun*), 14, 15, 113, 147, 160, 173, 201, 208, 210, 213, 230, 241, 242, 248, 250, 254, 255, 257, 258, 266, 285, 293, 310, 321, 334, 337, 338, 375, 377, 389, 396, 402, 444, 455, 456, 469, 473, 482, 484, 494, 496, 518, 531, 550, 563, 596, 616 n. 10
Seven Treatises on Valid Cognition (Tib. *Tshema Dé-dun*), 100
Seventy Verses on Emptiness (Skt. *Shunyata-saptati*), 100
Six Collections of Reasoning (Tib. *Rik-tsok Druk*), 100, 514, 530
Six Expanses (Tib. *Long Drukpa*) (one of seventeen tantras of the Category of Direct Transmission), 48, 255, 562
Six Meditative Experiences (Tib. *Gom-nyam Druk-pa*) (testament of Mañjushrimitra), 40
Six Spheres (Tib. *Tiglé Drukpa*) (one of the eighteen major tantras of the Category of Mind), 560, 622 n. 9
Six Techniques of Union (Tib. *Jor-druk*), 75, 96, 101, 140, 168, 224, 229, 274

Six Yogas of Naropa (Tib. *Naro Chödruk*), 75, 93, 99, 101, 140, 301, 397, 442, 444, 482, 647 n. 10
Sixty Verses on Reasoning (Skt. *Yukti-shashtika*), 100
Soaring of the Great Garuda (Tib. *Khyungchen Dingwa*) (one of the eighteen major tantras of the Category of Mind), 559, 563, 622 n. 7
Source Verses on Sublime Knowing (Skt. *Mula-madhyamaka-karika*), 13, 100, 225, 308, 473, 485, 494, 495, 496, 504, 537
Sphere of Awakened Mind (Tib. *Jangchub Semtik*) (one of the eighteen major tantras of the Category of Mind), 560, 622 n. 9
Stirring of Supreme Dynamic Energy (Tib. *Tsalchen Trukpa*) (one of the eighteen major tantras of the Category of Mind), 559, 622 n. 7
Sun of the Clear Expanse of Samantabhadra (Tib. *Kun-zang Long-sal Nyi-ma*) (tantra of the Category of Direct Transmission), 48, 69
Superb Ruler (Tib. *Méjung Gyalpo*) (one of three general tantras of the Category of Mind), 560
Supreme System of Ati (Tib. *Ati Köpa Chenpo*), 12, 258, 561

Tantra of the Teachings: The Single Child (Tib. *Tenpa Bu-chik*), 32
Tantra Without Words (Tib. *Yigé Mépa*) (one of seventeen tantras of the Category of Direct Transmission), 47, 255, 562
Ten Discourses (Tib. *Do Chu*) (one of three general tantras of the Category of Mind), 560
Tengyur, 178, 266, 271, 294, 325, 402, 411, 437, 441, 455, 473, 483, 484, 494, 495, 636 n. 23, 640 n. 96
Three Continua (Tib. *Gyü Sum*), 88, 89, 102, 629 n. 15
Three Cycles of Being at Ease (Tib. *Ngalso Korsum*), 15, 142, 173, 208, 213, 240, 241, 243, 266, 293, 310, 337, 377, 381, 402, 407, 429, 459, 473, 487, 509, 563
Three Cycles of Dispelling Darkness (Tib. *Munsel Korsum*), 563
Three Cycles of Natural Freedom (Tib. *Rangdrol Korsum*), 54, 142, 308, 337, 402, 563
Three Verses Hitting upon the Key Points (Tib. *Tsiksum Nedek*) (testament of Garab Dorjé), 38
Three Visions (Tib. *Nang Sum*), 629 n. 15
Timeless Awareness as the Guiding Principle (Tib. *Yeshé Lama*), 15, 214, 219, 241, 242, 243, 258, 266, 293, 299, 300, 314, 342, 348, 394, 407, 408, 429, 444, 454, 455, 457, 468, 472, 473, 486, 494, 502, 509, 511, 518, 524, 525, 531, 537, 540, 541
Treasury of Abhidharma (Skt. *Abhidharma-kosha*), 195, 225, 309, 411, 475, 484, 485, 494, 495
Treasury of the Basic Space of Phenomena (Tib. *Chöying Dzö*), 55, 143, 156, 230, 232, 233, 241, 502, 526, 634 n. 72
Treasury of Enlightened Qualities (Tib. *Yönten Dzö*), 214, 225, 226, 257, 266, 268, 293, 294, 298, 308, 310, 329, 348, 394, 402, 441, 470, 483, 484, 485, 494, 495, 533, 566, 665 n. 22
Treasury of Extraordinary Works (Tib. *Thunmong Ma-yin-pai Dzö*), 411
Treasury of Knowledge (Tib. *Sheja Dzö*), 411
Treasury of Mantra of the Kagyü School (Tib. *Kagyü Ngak-dzö*), 293, 310, 311, 334, 411, 533
Treasury of Philosophical Systems (Tib. *Drupta Dzö*), 144, 231, 485, 618 n. 3, 622 n. 9
Treasury of Pith Instructions (Tib. *Men-ngak Dzö*), 4, 143, 231
Treasury of Precious Hidden Teachings (Tib. *Rinchen Terdzö*), 250, 261, 262, 264, 265, 267, 268, 269, 277, 281, 282, 284, 287, 293, 298, 299, 304, 309, 311, 313, 334, 337, 352, 353, 377, 386, 412, 415, 425, 428, 457, 473, 501, 508, 515, 518, 532, 533, 534, 535, 539, 540, 648 n. 35
Treasury of Spiritual Instructions (Tib. *Damngak Dzö*), 261, 264, 266, 281, 285, 299, 304, 310, 311, 313, 315, 353, 411, 446, 473, 501, 515, 533
Treasury of the Sublime Spiritual Approach (Tib. *Tekchok Dzö*), 36, 114, 144, 157
Treasury of the Way of Abiding (Tib. *Nayluk Dzö*), 3, 55, 143, 231, 616 n. 13
Treasury of Words and Their Underlying Meaning (Tib. *Tsik-dön Dzö*), 4, 144, 232
Two Chapters (Tib. *Tak Nyi*), 73, 93, 101, 304, 309 (*see also Hevajra Tantra*)

Unobstructed Enlightened Intent (Tib. *Gongpa Zangtal*) (Northern Terma cycle), 76, 292, 300, 456, 563
Urn (Skt. *Karanda-vyuha*), 245

Vajra Bridge (Tib. *Dorjé Zampa*), 14, 15, 53, 54, 57, 400
Vajra Cutter (Skt. *Vajra-chedika-sutra*, "Diamond Sutra"), 101, 510
Vajrasattva: Mirror of the Heart (Tib. *Dorjé Sempa Nying-gi Melong*) (one of seventeen tantras of the Category of Direct Transmission), 47, 255, 275, 562

Victory Banner That Never Falls (Tib. *Mi-nub-pai Gyaltsen*) (one of the eighteen major tantras of the Category of Mind), 55, 559, 622 n. 7

Web of Magical Display (Skt. Mayajala; Tib. *Gyu-trul Drawa*), 43, 52, 82, 101, 137, 182, 191, 195, 266, 270, 271, 279, 296, 297, 298, 307, 308, 325, 372, 377, 385, 389, 397, 402, 425, 465, 471, 485, 505, 550, 553, 579 (*see also Heart Essence of Secrets*)

Wheel of Life Force (Tib. *Sok-gi Khorlo*) (one of the eighteen major tantras of the Category of Mind), 560, 622 n. 9

Wish-Fulfilling Gem (Tib. *Yizhin Norbu*) (one of the eighteen major tantras of the Category of Mind), 560, 622 n. 9

Wrathful Black Goddess (Tib. *Tröma Nakmo*) (tantra of the Category of Direct Transmission), 255, 562

PLACES

Amdo, 224, 295, 323, 339, 399, 407, 424, 456, 472, 474, 490, 518, 526, 650 n. 50, 653 n. 12

Asura Cave, 335, 441

Bazhap Drakar, 467, 538

Bhutan, 60, 61, 68, 93, 105, 115, 116, 145, 161, 162, 163, 165, 166, 169, 170, 171, 173, 174, 175, 177, 181, 191, 214, 215, 217, 221, 251, 268, 269, 286, 295, 313, 314, 335, 337, 352, 353, 355, 356, 357, 368, 369, 370, 371, 372, 373, 374, 377, 378, 379, 386, 392, 393, 395, 399, 436, 443, 444, 445, 447, 448, 454, 464, 480, 492, 496, 497, 500, 502, 503, 505, 507, 514, 531, 551, 554, 599, 600, 632 n. 26, 633 n. 43, 634 n. 63, 635 nn. 2, 8, & 15, 657 n. 40, 658 n. 4, 662 nn. 50 & 62, 667 n. 7, 668 n. 21

Bodh Gaya, 35, 38, 39, 40, 42, 44, 275, 304, 312, 335, 441, 448, 452, 456, 481, 620 n. 7 (ch. 1)

Boudhanath (stupa), 199, 312, 341, 652 n. 90, 654 n. 43, 662 n. 48

Bumthang, 60, 108, 109, 115, 116, 145, 164, 165, 169, 171, 174, 175, 313, 356, 367, 369, 374, 377, 379, 393, 443, 454, 480, 500, 502, 507, 531

Chakla, 295, 323, 399

Chamdo, 190, 335, 384, 446

Chimpu Uplands, 105, 106, 112, 161, 166, 167, 175, 177, 198, 200, 208, 212, 217, 286, 332, 357, 367, 369, 371, 390, 392, 437, 520, 531

China, 40, 45, 56, 73, 82, 83, 85, 194, 221, 273, 295, 305, 322, 335, 351, 379, 395, 398, 405, 429, 437, 438, 440, 448, 451, 459, 474, 476, 485, 496, 497, 501, 513, 522, 523, 526, 536, 553, 554, 623 n. 11, 624 n. 25, 630 n. 21, 639 n. 80, 642 n. 133, 653 n. 13, 661 nn. 29 & 32, 664 n. 13, 666 n. 21

Chongyé, 52, 174, 177, 332, 623 n. 15

Chöten Drak, 72

Chuwori, 60, 434, 547

Dakpo, 70, 71, 96, 117, 188, 362, 364, 373, 479, 531

Dang Valley, 70, 92, 96

Dartang (monastery), 263, 264, 454, 526, 542

Dergé, 192, 215, 216, 221, 227, 239, 256, 263, 265, 270, 273, 280, 299, 305, 306, 313, 320, 333, 388, 396, 399, 401, 404, 408, 424, 428, 429, 432, 436, 442, 454, 456, 465, 470, 473, 476, 481, 486, 497, 499, 510, 519, 521, 530, 537, 541, 555, 639 n. 86, 656 n. 14, 660 n. 19, 662 n. 51, 666 n. 18

Deshek Düpa, 278, 412, 434

Dodrupchen (monastery), 328, 333

Dokham, 190, 216, 391, 393, 415

Dokhol (monastery), 450, 499, 509, 519, 521, 531

Dorjé Drak (monastery), 61, 267, 294, 305, 331, 373, 374, 387, 388, 389, 390, 400, 533, 549, 550, 639 n. 78

Drakar Taso (cave), 84, 341

Drakchen Yarlung, 320, 321

Drakmar, 82, 85, 192, 277, 332, 448

Drelkar Puk (cave), 218, 224

Drepung (monastery), 331, 430, 462, 491, 642 n. 129

Drigung (monastery), 114, 119, 164, 166, 267, 354, 355, 394, 397, 480, 497, 501, 505

Drintang, 70, 71, 72

Dza, 169, 220, 225, 238, 247, 308, 324, 391, 393, 416, 466, 467, 478, 479, 480, 485, 490, 493, 526, 537, 645 n. 32, 666 n. 15

Dzachu (river), 216, 220, 240, 321, 390, 393, 660 n. 19

Dzachukha, 225, 329, 467, 470, 473, 475, 476, 478, 480, 481, 492, 509, 660 n. 19

Dzagyal, 221, 225, 324, 447

Dzagyü, 218, 220, 224, 227, 515
Dzapuk (cave), 280
Dzogchen (monastery), 192, 224, 225, 226, 229, 239, 240, 241, 242, 244, 249, 250, 280, 293, 296, 303, 308, 315, 319, 320, 324, 327, 334, 388, 389, 390, 393, 396, 399, 405, 417, 428, 430, 467, 469, 475, 479, 480, 481, 488, 495, 496, 498, 502, 503, 504, 513, 552, 600, 645 n. 38, 656 n. 14, 661 n. 39, 662 n. 59, 669 n. 13
Dzogchen Shri Simha (shedra), 225, 401, 402, 406, 430, 467, 480, 481, 495, 499, 501, 502, 504, 552
Dzongsar (monastery), 297, 298, 305, 309, 333, 455, 488, 499, 612 n. 51, 664 n.8
Dzongshö, 412, 433, 434

Ewam Chokden (monastery), 632

Four Rivers and Six Ridges, 306, 328

Ganden (monastery), 33, 215, 227, 331, 416, 430, 462, 491, 642 nn. 129 & 130, 643 n. 15
Gang-ri Tökar, 25, 112, 135, 208, 331, 349, 350, 352, 353, 394, 441, 442, 459, 618 n. 8 (Supplication to the Lineage)
Gangteng Sang-ngak Chöling (monastery), 176, 370, 371, 372, 376, 378, 379
garden of Anathapindika, 35
Gegong (monastery), 71, 82, 85, 105, 329, 478, 479
Gemang (monastery), 226, 228, 295, 308, 321, 469, 470, 483
Getsé (monastery), 215, 223, 393, 438, 459, 471, 522, 524, 536
Getsé Tralek (monastery), 459, 517, 519, 540
Gojo Khochim (monastery), 191
Golok, 9, 225, 244, 252, 263, 264, 318, 320, 323, 325, 328, 341, 351, 391, 395, 409, 416, 429, 437, 458, 468, 470, 490, 492, 502, 503, 516, 517, 518, 519, 524, 526, 527, 532, 540, 660 n. 19, 665 n. 15
Gongkar (monastery), 117, 385
Gonjo, 252, 258, 262, 263, 530, 535, 541
Gyalrong, 50, 53, 263, 327, 328, 399, 461, 490, 622 nn. 8 & 9, 623 n. 14

Hepo (hill), 320, 332, 434, 652 n. 6
Hor, 52, 292, 296, 320, 335, 351, 474

Jamding (monastery), 164, 173, 357, 361
Jang, 53, 214, 447
Jangchub Jönpalung (monastery), 25, 520, 537, 539, 540
Jangtsé (college of Ganden), 215, 395, 642 n. 130
Jarung Khashor (stupa), 335, 654 n. 43

Ka-nying Shedrup Ling (monastery), 435
Kailash, 116, 167, 341, 343, 355, 404, 448, 457, 458
Kalimpong, 287, 335, 336, 386
Karmo Taktsang, 421, 434
Kashyapa Cave, 335
Kathmandu, 335, 652 n. 90, 654 n. 43, 662 nn. 48 & 57, 663 n. 4, 664 n. 7 (ch. 15)
Katok Dorjéden (monastery), 13, 52, 53, 190, 191, 215, 223, 227, 243, 247, 250, 252, 261, 264, 265, 279, 280, 283, 286, 290, 291, 293, 294, 295, 297, 304, 305, 320, 321, 359, 362, 371, 387, 390, 396, 397, 403, 414, 421, 424, 434, 436, 437, 438, 439, 440, 441, 442, 443, 444, 450, 457, 459, 462, 463, 464, 465, 468, 477, 478, 488, 502, 504, 506, 508, 509, 511, 517, 518, 519, 522, 523, 524, 525, 528, 530, 531, 534, 536, 537, 539, 540, 544, 547, 548, 549, 553, 554, 555, 556, 619, 620, 624, 636, 640, 642, 645, 647, 649, 662 n. 59, 664 n. 9 (ch. 15), 667 n. 11
Kham (eastern Tibet), 391, 441, 634 n. 60, 643 n. 9, 662 n. 59
Khamjé (shedra of Dzongsar Monastery), 455, 497, 499
Kham Riwoché (monastery), 285, 438, 446, 447, 501, 533
Kharchu, 67, 91, 92, 94, 95, 173, 177, 373, 416, 463, 531, 630 n. 28
Khotan, 51, 56, 106
Khunu, 295, 345, 480, 481, 488, 496, 497, 506
Kongpo, 75, 93, 95, 117, 174, 242, 286, 287, 362, 363, 364, 366, 371, 373, 397, 531, 539, 649 n. 40
Korong Seng-gé Drak, 549
Koro Drak, 70, 72
Kujédrak, 171
Kullu, 481
Kunzang Ling, 92, 116, 172, 356
Kushinagar, 120, 335, 633 n. 52
Kyirong, 341, 343, 347, 637 n. 55

Ladakh, 345, 346, 443, 481, 533
Lhalung (monastery), 116, 161, 165, 173, 176, 359, 372, 373, 374, 375, 376, 377, 378, 379, 532
Lharing Drak, 112, 113, 161
Lhasa, 71, 72, 83, 89, 106, 115, 118, 171, 178, 216, 264, 267, 291, 331, 335, 339, 341, 343, 349, 374, 377, 387, 388, 391, 392, 394, 400, 405, 416, 430, 437, 441, 445, 446, 447, 459,

491, 503, 505, 507, 520, 523, 549, 618 n. 8 (Supplication to the Lineage), 626 n. 48, 629 n. 10, 630 n. 21, 633 n. 50, 636 n. 32, 637 n. 55, 642 nn. 129 & 130, 653 n. 32
Lhodrak, 116, 161, 162, 163, 165, 167, 169, 172, 175, 176, 177, 178, 295, 315, 360, 369, 371, 373, 378, 381, 395, 416, 463, 464, 531, 630 n. 28
Lhundrup Chödé (monastery), 171, 172
Li, 51, 619
Lingshi, 258, 260, 530
Lumbini, 335

Magadha, 553, 666
Mahakoti, 282
Manasarovar (lake), 341, 343
Mé, 328, 474, 480, 490
Mehor Sang-ngak Chöling (monastery), 416
Meri Barwa, 34, 562, 585
Mindroling (monastery), 13, 183, 189, 192, 193, 194, 195, 196, 213, 248, 257, 267, 270, 285, 288, 305, 307, 313, 331, 352, 370, 372, 374, 375, 376, 377, 380, 381, 382, 383, 385, 387, 388, 391, 392, 400, 404, 416, 423, 425, 426, 464, 503, 532, 548, 549, 550, 556, 638 n. 77, 639 nn. 78, 80, 81, & 82, 646 n. 60, 656 n. 31, 657 nn. 4 & 9, 669 n. 9 (ch. 22)
Minyak, 227, 240, 249, 258, 294, 399, 429, 430, 466, 467, 476, 483, 499, 504, 536, 651 n. 79
Moktsa Gön (monastery), 624 n. 23

Nairanjana, 335
Nalanda, 335, 402, 406, 499
Nalendra, 331, 403
Namtso Chukmo (lake), 61
Nepal, 44, 51, 52, 63, 68, 199, 221, 268, 305, 312, 313, 314, 335, 341, 353, 415, 435, 441, 444, 458, 463, 470, 481, 497, 502, 528, 534, 553, 621 n. 17, 625 n. 38, 631 n. 9, 637 n. 55, 652 n. 90, 662 nn. 48 & 57, 663 n. 4, 664 n. 7
Nereng Seng-gé Dzong, 60
Ngari, 266, 306, 341, 342, 343, 347, 402, 457, 458, 600
Ngor (monastery), 271, 294, 295, 298, 304, 306, 309, 403, 414, 424, 462, 499, 635 n. 16
Norbui Lhunpo (shedra), 261, 421, 437, 478, 517, 522, 524
Nyang's caves, 202, 203
Nyarong, 192, 197, 252, 256, 279, 285, 318, 416, 425, 426, 437, 438, 501, 510, 513, 514, 515, 517, 519, 526, 528, 530, 660 n. 19, 667 n. 9
Nyoshul (monastery), 541

Oddiyana, 37, 42, 43, 45, 59, 64, 65, 109, 198, 208, 251, 452, 559, 618 n. 2 (Supplication to the Lineage), 627 n. 77
Orgyen Gön (monastery), 114, 130
Orgyen Kunzang Chökhor Ling (monastery), 449
Orgyen (monastery), 119, 354, 355
Oru Jamchen Tsuklak Khang, 549

Pakpa Shingkun (stupa), 335, 651
Palchen Lhakhang, 549
Palpung (monastery), 279, 295, 296, 299, 300, 305, 308, 424, 432, 488, 497, 499, 500, 657 n. 7, 666 n. 18
Palri Tekchok Ling (monastery), 198, 549, 551
Palyul (monastery), 250, 252, 260, 261, 262, 263, 264, 265, 267, 268, 269, 291, 315, 320, 386, 414, 424, 427, 434, 438, 450, 480, 488, 503, 508, 523, 530, 541, 542, 543, 549, 555, 646 n. 54
Paro, 61, 64, 116, 169, 171, 177, 251, 286, 313, 314, 373, 445, 447, 448, 514, 662 n. 62
Parping, 441, 534
Pemakö, 224, 282, 283, 287, 320, 321, 368, 413, 446, 448, 469, 515
Pema Ö, 68, 76, 215, 246, 263, 268, 276, 339, 374, 387, 416, 449, 491, 536, 627 n. 63, 642 n. 136, 649 n. 41
Penyul, 119, 167, 360
Podzong (monastery), 454, 455
Polu (monastery), 530
Puntsok Norbu Ling (monastery), 221
Purang, 94, 341, 343, 347

Rajgir, 35, 335
Repkong, 229, 288, 321, 322, 328, 339, 341, 407, 408, 424, 456, 457, 474, 490, 516, 534, 653 n. 12
Rewalsar, 335, 343, 347, 646

Sahora, 43, 343, 421
Sakya (monastery), 297, 298, 395, 415, 521
Samyé (monastery), 56, 57, 71, 78, 80, 99, 104, 130, 135, 145, 161, 165, 166, 171, 178, 182, 188, 197, 200, 201, 211, 214, 267, 278, 286, 287, 313, 320, 332, 341, 357, 365, 367, 373, 374, 387, 392, 396, 405, 430, 434, 437, 441, 448, 520, 531, 547, 624 n. 32, 625 n. 37, 626 n. 52, 629 nn. 4 & 6, 631 n. 8, 634 n. 61, 636 n. 34, 652 n. 6, 666 n. 22
Sangchen Ngödrup Palbar Ling (monastery), 325, 328
Seng-gé Drak, 51, 52, 549
Seng-gé Dzong, 60, 64, 92, 492

Sera (monastery), 331, 430, 462, 491, 503, 642 n. 129
Sertal, 224, 326, 328, 351
Sertar, 9, 457, 458, 472
Sha-uk Takgo, 91, 188, 388
Shartsé (college of Ganden), 215, 395, 642 n. 130
Shechen (monastery), 268, 312, 553, 663 n. 4
Shedrup Dargyé Ling (monastery), 267, 303, 438, 503, 507
Sheldrak, 60, 71, 173, 188, 216, 332, 341, 366, 413, 441, 520
Shinjé Drubpuk (cave), 225, 241
Shitavana, 38, 42, 48, 80, 130, 208, 335
Shravasti, 335
Shri Simha Shedra, *see* Dzogchen Shri Simha
Shuksep, 106, 115, 118, 161, 164, 169, 343, 350, 352, 655 n. 57
Sikkim, 177, 191, 268, 304, 305, 314, 335, 336, 337, 353, 365, 380, 440, 480, 481, 502, 503
Spiti, 288, 481

Taklung, 446, 447, 448
Takmo Lüjin, 335, 502, 651
Takshen Bumpa, 332
Taktsang, 64, 65, 171, 217, 251, 271, 286, 314, 363, 373, 414, 421, 434, 444, 447, 448, 662 n. 62
Tamshing, 379
Tarpa Ling (monastery), 116, 145, 164, 171, 379, 443, 480, 502, 506
Tidro, 63, 64, 69, 114, 115
Tradruk Tashi Jam, 332
Tralek (monastery), 438, 460, 518
Trama Valley, 220, 225, 228
Trehor, 350, 409, 462, 488, 514, 515
Trom, 244, 290, 291, 292, 450, 499, 509, 510, 519, 521, 531, 537, 540, 541
Tromgé (monastery), 521
Tsang, 51, 53, 60, 65, 83, 118, 168, 173, 175, 177, 218, 224, 278, 335, 339, 342, 358, 363, 364, 370, 371, 384, 414, 415, 499, 531, 539, 547, 549, 553, 629 nn. 9 & 11, 638 n. 78
Tsangpo (river), 332, 623 n. 15, 629 n. 9, 10, & 11, 634 n. 61, 635 n. 15, 636 nn. 32 & 34, 666 n. 22
Tsari, 95, 191, 217, 218, 320, 341, 356, 363, 365, 393, 412, 413, 444
Tsaritra, 116
Tsawa Rong, 50, 244, 252, 513, 528, 622 n. 8, 623 n. 10
Tsering Jong, 214, 216, 331, 394, 396
Tsetang, 166, 168, 332, 361, 632
Tso Pema (Rewalsar), 287, 343, 448, 646
Tsurpu (monastery), 92, 94, 95, 190, 349, 396, 433, 501
Tupten Do-ngak Chöling (monastery), 353

Ü, 173, 177, 364, 371, 414, 531
Uru, 51, 102, 110, 113, 167, 168, 354, 359

Vaishali, 335
Varanasi, 335, 455, 464, 503
Vulture Peak, 35, 106, 335, 336, 616

Walshul, 326, 328
Washul, 440, 442, 490, 519, 522, 526, 530, 537
Washul Mewa, 472, 474
Wa Seng-gé Drak, 51, 52, 549
Wu Tai Shan (mountain in China), 39, 82, 448, 476

Yangleshö, 44, 335
Yardrok, 86, 117, 165, 174, 447
Yarlung, 52, 63, 71, 94, 95, 115, 177, 188, 216, 224, 320, 321, 332, 341, 365, 441, 520, 619, 630, 633
Ya Glacier, 64
Yönten Kunjung, 25
Yönten (monastery), 522
Yumbu Lagang, 332

Zabbulung, 365
Zangdok Palri, 75, 188, 217, 220, 287, 304, 327, 329, 339, 350, 386, 395, 398, 399, 430, 434, 439, 444, 448, 486, 512, 514, 536, 626 n. 63, 642 n. 136, 649 n. 41
Zhai Lhakhang, 83, 84, 112, 113, 114, 130, 211, 354
Zhalu (monastery), 173, 271, 309
Zhang Zhung, 45, 56, 617
Zhechen (monastery), 224, 270, 279, 280, 295, 297, 299, 305, 307, 310, 313, 315, 319, 320, 325, 334, 366, 393, 396, 408, 411, 414, 424, 428, 434, 469, 480, 488, 495, 503, 532, 549, 551, 552, 553
Zurmang (monastery), 301, 305, 310, 427, 428, 455, 497, 500, 663 n. 6

N
C H I
T I B
NAMTSO
NYENCHEN · TANGLA
DRIGUNG · TIL
TSURPU
LHASA
DRIGUNG
GANDEN
DREPUNG
Ü
SANGPU
GANGRI · TÖKAR
CHIMPU
SAMYÉ
SHIGATSE
DORJE DRAK
NGOR
MINDROLING
CHONGYÉ
TSAR
T S A N G
HIMALAYA · RANGE
NERING · SENGE · DZONG
NEPAL
SENGE · DZONG
SIKKIM
BUMTHANG
THIMPHU
GANGTOK
B H U T A N